SECOND EDITION

ECONOMICS

ADDISON-WESLEY PUBLISHING COMPANY

Reading, Massachusetts · Menlo Park, California · New York

Don Mills, Ontario · Wokingham, England · Amsterdam · Bonn

Sydney · Singapore · Tokyo · Madrid · Bogotá · Santiago · San Juan

SECOND EDITION

ECONOMICS

ALLEN R. THOMPSON
UNIVERSITY OF NEW HAMPSHIRE

Sponsoring Editor:	Stephen Mautner
Developmental Editor:	Linda J. Bedell
Production Management:	Sherry Berg
Production Supervisor:	Nancy Behler
Copy Editor:	Jerrold A. Moore
Art Director:	Marshall Henrichs
Art Development:	Dick Morton; Meredith Nightingale
Text Design:	Margaret Ong Tsao
Layout Artist:	Lorraine Hodsdon
Illustrators:	Long Associates; George Nichols
Manufacturing Supervisor:	Roy Logan

Library of Congress Cataloging-in-Publication Data

Thompson, Allen R.

  Economics.

  Includes index.
  1. Economics.   I. Title.
HB171.5.T33 1988   330   87-912
ISBN 0-201-09682-X

ABCDEFGHIJ-RN-8987

P R E F A C E

Although only a few beginning students go on to become professional economists, everyone faces situations in which economic reasoning is very important. For example, economic reasoning can help you identify the benefits and costs of choosing between taking a job immediately after graduation or continuing your education. Businesses rely on economic reasoning in deciding whether to build a new plant or produce a new product. And, as citizens, we make political choices that are based in part on economic policies proposed by politicians. An understanding of economics can help you make more informed choices.

The aim of this textbook is to teach you economic reasoning. But even a casual reading of the newspapers reveals wide disagreements among professional economists. You may ask yourself, "How can I learn to use economic reasoning when economists themselves can't seem to agree on what is reasonable?" Despite the impression created by the media, economists do agree on many points. In particular, economists share some important and fundamental principles that constitute the economic way of thinking. These principles are the major focus of this book and the key to understanding a wide variety of economic issues.

As you approach your study of economics, try to focus on the practical applications of economic principles and economic reasoning. For example, when you encounter a new concept, ask yourself "How can I use this principle to answer economic questions in my own life?" Students who take this approach are not only the most successful students, but they come away from the course knowing how to apply what they have learned to their own lives.

Second, as you can see by flipping through the pages of this textbook, economic analysis relies heavily on graphs to clarify abstract concepts. I urge you to study the introduction to graphs in the appendix following Chapter 1. Since graphs are important both to learning and applying economic principles, I have carefully explained each new type of graph when it is introduced. (The *Workbook* that accompanies this text contains an introductory chapter devoted to graphs. In addition, the *Workbook* contains a special section on each new type of graph introduced in the text as well as considerable applications that allow you to practice reading and drawing graphs.)

Almost all graphs in this textbook have a numerical scale and all are color-coded: Demand-related curves are blue, while supply-related curves appear in red. In some exhibits the same information appears in both tabular and graphical form to facilitate understanding the graphs and the economic principles they illustrate. Be sure you understand how to read each type of graph and how to draw graphs yourself.

At first you may be perplexed by the new terms you encounter in introductory economics. However, this vocabulary was not developed to confuse you, but to enable economists and students to speak precisely. Learning this vocabulary is critical to learning economics. Each time a key economic term is introduced, it appears in bold print with a definition in the margin. For easy review, there is a glossary of key terms in the back of the textbook.

One final note: Economics may not be the easiest subject you ever tackle, but it is one of the most exciting and useful. In fact, I make a standing offer to my students. If they can find elements of my course that have no practical use, I promise to delete that material from the course and award them bonus points on their next exam. I can't offer the same bonus to you, but I will promise to delete material with no practical use from subsequent editions of this textbook. I don't, of course, expect that you will find any nonpractical concepts. But I believe that if you always look for the practical use of the concepts you encounter, your exam grades will be satisfactory even without those extra bonus points.

TO THE
INSTRUCTOR

The challenge in writing about or teaching principles of economics is to demonstrate the power of economics as a tool for understanding our world. I can think of no better way to convey that power than by proceeding with two parallel goals in mind. First, show the broad spectrum of problems that economics can help us solve, from increasing U.S. competitiveness to budget-balancing. At the same time, teach students economic analysis. Enable them to put this powerful tool to work for themselves.

My objective is not to prepare students for careers as professional economists but to teach them how to think like economists. One strategy for achieving this goal is to teach the basics very well, so that certain economic principles become more than ideas—they become actual perspectives on the world. In the text, I focus the students' attention on the most fundamental principles of economics and return to and extend these principles again and again. Concepts such as demand, supply, opportunity cost, rational choice, and the role of expectations are introduced early, explained carefully, and then constantly applied to new situations. Students quickly get into the habit of looking for opportunities to put economic analysis to work.

In preparing this revision, I drew on the advice and experience of many readers of the first edition of *Economics*. The book you are now reading benefitted not only from a thorough review of every draft of the manuscript, but also from a comprehensive evaluation by users of the previous edition. Many students and instructors who were using the first edition agreed to submit critiques on a regular basis, assessing the effectiveness of the presentation, the graphs, and the other pedagogical features. Their valuable input has allowed me to pinpoint features to retain and strengthen and others to add or revise.

Class-Tested Features

Several highly praised qualities of the first edition still distinguish this text. These features include careful step-by-step explanations of important concepts and the frequent *application* of these concepts, clear and readable graphs, abundant real-world examples to illustrate theory, built-in flexibility, and a distinctive, un-cluttered design.

A focus on core principles. As a teacher of economics, I have successfully used a unifying, step-by-step approach to help students grasp fundamental principles. Whenever I introduce a new concept, I carefully explain the logic behind it and its connection to previously learned material. For example, I present consumer choice, producer choice, and social choice as extensions of the principle of rational choice in different contexts rather than as discrete economic rules. And by carefully developing and then returning to basic themes like efficiency, price stability, and economic growth, the text enables students to see the common logic underlying apparently different economic decisions.

Graphs as analytical tools. A graph is the economist's shorthand for depicting an economic relationship. No single element in this textbook has received more attention than the treatment of the graphs. Several features in the text help students overcome the problems they commonly have with graphs. An appendix after Chapter 1 provides a simple introduction to the use of graphs. Throughout the book, the exhibits themselves are color-coded: Demand-related curves are blue, supply-related curves are red. This device helps students build on previously learned material. Almost all graphs contain background grids and display numbers on both axes. Students generally find such graphs more accessible than the type displaying only abstract symbols. Finally, any graph used to present a new economic concept is accompanied by a related table, enabling students to see that both the graph and table contain the same basic information.

The *Workbook,* available with *Economics, Second Edition,* also contains a chapter on graphs, a guide to each new type of graph introduced, and a host of exercises that ask the student to read, interpret, and utilize graphs to answer economic questions.

Applications and other pedagogy. I rely on applications and examples to illustrate how economic concepts help us understand the real world. Many are woven right into the text. We examine the effect of competition in a dynamic setting like the compact disc industry, or we take a look at the impact of the 1986 tax reform on saving and investment behavior.

We have two kinds of boxes in *Economics.* "Cases in Point," a feature retained from the first edition, are brief case studies that illustrate a specific economic concept. One case examines the fixed and variable costs of driving. Another looks at historical examples of expansionary gaps. The "Cases in Point" are always extensions, or clarifications through example, of topics covered in the text. Many new "Cases in Point" have been added to the second edition. An exciting new feature of the second edition is a series of brief articles called "Economic Encounters." These explore the economic aspects of trends and happenings in our world.

The textbook is full of useful pedagogical features. Chapters open with a series of "Questions to Consider" that alert students to the relevance of the material in the chapter. Definitions of new terms and recaps of important points are found in the margins. Figure captions fully explain each graph and diagram. The illustration program alone serves as a visual digest of the analytical content of each chapter. Coming at the end of the chapter are numbered summaries and a large variety of questions and problems designed to get students to apply the economic concepts presented in the text.

Flexibility. Since no two instructors teach the principles course in exactly the same way, I consider it important to maintain the text's great flexibility. My own preference in teaching economics is to build from the individual to the aggregate. So, as in the previous edition, microeconomics precedes macroeconomics. However, the book can as easily be used in a class in which macro is treated first. I have taken great care to make sure that no discussion in one half of the book depends upon material in the other half. Furthermore, while the text contains core chapters that are central to all principles courses, there are several optional chapters from which instructors can pick and choose.

Thirteen chapter-end appendixes offer the reader a more detailed look at topics covered in the main text. Indifference analysis, discounted present value, the algebra of the multiplier effect and joint equilibrium in goods and money markets are all covered in these optional sections, providing the instructor and student with additional means of approaching key economic principles. Boxes and end-of-chapter problems offer still other opportunities to explore economic topics in greater detail. This textbook was designed so that a variety of paths could be taken through it. Its flexibility allows it to suit many different course syllabi. Just as significant, however, is the capability of this textbook, through appendixes, boxes, and problems, to challenge the more motivated student.

What's New in This Edition

Economics, Second Edition offers several exciting new features, including a restructured treatment of macroeconomics, a new approach to economic policy issues, the addition of "Economic Encounters," and a special emphasis on international economics.

Presenting macroeconomics. To offer a contemporary and cohesive approach to macroeconomics at the principles level is a particular challenge. My objective in restructuring this half of the textbook was to simplify and condense the presentation while retaining full coverage of all important macroeconomic concepts. As a result, there are fewer chapters than in the previous edition. Yet there are more examples, both historical and current, of macroeconomics in action.

I have maintained a contemporary approach to macroeconomics, emphasizing the role of expectations and providing a full discussion of the aggregate demand and aggregate supply model. I introduce the AD/AS model early, actually in the first chapter of the macroeconomics section, but I fully develop it in a new, separate chapter only after all the elements of the model are fully explained. I then apply the AD/AS model to macroeconomic policies.

A new approach to economic policy issues.   *Economics, Second Edition* takes a major stride toward offering a more balanced and unified approach to economic policy than one typically finds in principles textbooks. Rather than devoting entire chapters to a very few individual policy issues such as agriculture or the federal budget deficit, or at the other extreme, touching on a wide variety of issues only briefly as examples in the text, I have developed two new chapters, one pertaining to microeconomics and one to macroeconomics, which contain several short essays on economic policies.

Each of these chapters begins with an introduction that explains how economists analyze policy issues and provides a general framework for policy analysis. The introduction is followed by a series of individual policy cases, averaging four to five pages each, that then apply that analytical framework. The microeconomics policy chapter includes issues like agricultural price supports and airline deregulation. On the macroeconomic side, I include sections on the budget deficit and international competitiveness, to name just two.

Naturally, the discussion of policy has not been confined to these chapters. The rationales and practical limits on government action, stabilization policy, public choice theory, market failure, and many examples of government policy in action are discussed throughout the text.

Economic Encounters.   We have added a series of short pieces to the textbook that further illustrate the economic content of the world around us. These two-page articles focus on economic aspects of our political, social, and commercial lives. They ask us to consider events at the gas station, on Wall Street, or in South Africa, always emphasizing that there are more sides to an economic story than might at first be apparent. Why does unemployment persist in a nation where almost any newspaper contains numerous help-wanted advertisements? What are the pros and cons of hostile corporate takeovers? What must it be like to live in a country experiencing hyperinflation? "Economic Encounters" bring us face to face with the economic forces that shape people's lives.

A spotlight on international economics.   International trade and finance is a crucial component of today's economy. It has been said that there are no closed economies in the world, only closed economists. If students are to leave the principles course with a proper understanding of the workings of the U.S. economy, then they must be aware that the United States is only one part of an increasingly interrelated world economy.

In this edition, international economics is not just a topic relegated to the back of the textbook; rather it is integrated throughout. I apply the principles of exchange to international trade in the introductory chapters. A simple circular-flow model in Chapter 6 shows both trade and capital flows. Examples drawn from the international economy abound. Throughout the text, students see that foreign firms compete with U.S. firms, that foreign individuals, businesses, and governments play a major role in U.S. financial markets and purchase U.S. goods and services, and that it is no longer possible to dissociate economic events in other countries from events in our own. Additionally, three chapters at the end of the book offer more in-depth discussions of international trade, finance, comparative economic systems, and economic development.

Supplements Available to Accompany This Textbook

Workbook. This supplement, written by Neil Niman of the University of New Hampshire and myself, is designed to enhance student comprehension. Like many study guides, it contains a list of learning objectives, fill-in questions covering key terms, and multiple-choice questions to test the student's understanding of the basic concepts in each chapter. A unique feature is a guide to each new graph encountered by the student, explaining what it shows and how to read and interpret the economic principles illustrated. Other features are "Avoid These Common Mistakes" and "Some Useful Tips." But the wealth of applications contained in this volume makes it more than a study guide. Students are given practice reading and drawing graphs, using data to make economic decisions, and solving numerical problems. The emphasis is not just on developing mechanical skills; students are asked to interpret data, make decisions, or otherwise show an understanding of the economic principles.

Instructor's Manual. Prepared by Richard Burdekin of the University of Miami and myself, this supplement contains answers to the Questions for Discussion, points of special emphasis, teaching hints and current applications, and other useful information.

Test Item File. A test item file containing over 2,000 multiple-choice questions has been prepared by Susan McHargue of Southern Methodist University, Kari Battaglia of North Texas State University, Teri Riley of Youngstown State University, and Jeffrey Wrase of Arizona State University. The file is available on hard copy and computer disk for ease of test preparation.

Transparencies. Approximately 200 color acetates developed from graphs in the text are available to adopters.

Graphecon II. An interactive computer tutorial written by Lee D. Olvey and James R. Golden of the U.S. Military Academy of West Point makes full use of computer graphics capabilities. This powerful program fully complements the text and offers students valuable practice in graphing and in putting economic concepts to work. Four instructional disks prompt the student to analyze problems in supply and demand, microeconomics, macroeconomics, and international trade. This enhanced version of *Graphecon* strongly reinforces correct answers and offers careful explanations in response to incorrect answers. Also, users have extensive control over the graphics on the screen, enabling them to see immediately the effect of new information on economic relationships.

ACKNOWLEDGMENTS

This book owes a great deal to other people. I would like to thank the students in my classes and my colleagues at the Whittemore School of Business and Economics—especially Manly Irwin, Neil Niman, Robert Puth, and Dwayne Wrightsman. I have learned much from each of them and they may well find some of their favorite examples included in the text. In addition, a former colleague, Michael Conti, along with the many reviewers of the first and second editions, provided many helpful suggestions.

I certainly owe a good deal to the professional assistance provided by the editorial and production staff at Addison-Wesley, including Debra Hunter and Steve Mautner who provided overall editorial direction; to Linda Bedell and Darlene Bordwell, whose development assistance was invaluable; to Dick Morton and Meredith Nightingale, who developed and produced the artwork; and to Sherry Berg, who skillfully guided the production of the manuscript. Working with such a professional and personable group was both a pleasure and an education.

Last, but certainly not least, I must acknowledge the contributions of my family—Dianne, Chris, Jen, and Lindsay. My wife Dianne not only assisted in word-processing, but read the manuscript in every phase, providing many useful suggestions. I cannot imagine completing this project without their support, encouragement, and patience.

REVIEWERS

CARLOS AGIULAR
El Paso County Community College

TED AMATO
University of North Carolina, Charlotte

KARI BATTAGLIA
North Texas State University

CARSON BAYS
East Carolina University

RONALD G. BRANDOLINI
Valencia Community College

NEIL BROWNE
Bowling Green State University

RICHARD BURDEKIN
University of Miami

RAYMOND L. COHN
Illinois State University

WILLIAM J. FIELD
DePauw University

DAVID GAY
University of Arkansas

JANET J. GLOCKER
Monroe Community College

TIMOTHY J. GRONBERG
Texas A&M University

RALPH L. GUNDERSON
University of Wisconsin, Oshkosh

CHRISTINE HAGER
University of Georgia

R. S. HANNA
Eastern Michigan University

ROBERT HORN
James Madison University

R. JACK INCH
Oakland Community College

E. JAMES JENNINGS
Purdue University, Calumet

ZIAD KEILANY
University of Tennessee, Chattanooga

ROBERT M. KENNEY
Miami-Dade C. C., South Campus

ARJO KLAMER
University of Iowa

SUSAN N. KOENIGSBERG
San Francisco State University

LEONARD LARDARO
University of Rhode Island

JULES LaROCQUE
Lawrence University

BOZENA LEVEN
Long Island University, C. W. Post

WADE E. MARTIN
University of Michigan, Flint

SUSAN MCHARGUE
Southern Methodist University

LEE R. MCPHETERS
Arizona State University

JOSEPH MESKEY
East Carolina University

DAVID J. MOLINA
North Texas State University

PANOS MOURDOUKOUTAS
Long Island University, C. W. Post

ARTHUR PETERSON
Middlesex County College

JOHN PETRAKIS
Long Island University, C. W. Post

JOHN PISCIOTTA
Baylor University

PHILIP ROBINS
University of Miami

REYBURN ROULSTON
Broward C. C., Central Campus

GEOFFREY P. RYAN
McHenry County College

JOHN SAPINSLEY
Rhode Island College

ROBERT F. SEVERSON
Central Michigan University

STEVE SHAPIRO
University of North Florida

STEVE SHEFFRIN
University of California, Davis

RONALD J. SKOCKI
Weber State College

GARY W. SORENSEN
Oregon State University

HELEN TAUCHEN
*University of North Carolina,
Chapel Hill*

JENNIFER L. WARLICK
University of Notre Dame

WALTER WESSELS
North Carolina State University

NANCY A. WILLIAMS
University of Alaska, Fairbanks

RICHARD WINKELMAN
Arizona State University

JEFFREY WRASE
Arizona State University

BRIEF CONTENTS

PART ONE   Introduction to Economics   1

   CHAPTER 1   The Economic Way of Thinking   3

   CHAPTER 2   Scarcity and Economic Choice   25

   CHAPTER 3   Laws of Demand and Supply   45

   CHAPTER 4   Elasticity of Demand and Supply   75

   CHAPTER 5   Market Economies and Resource Allocation   96

   CHAPTER 6   Overview of the U.S. Economy   120

PART TWO   Behind Demand and Supply   145

   CHAPTER 7   Consumer Choice and Demand   147

   CHAPTER 8   Producer Choice and Costs of Production   173

   CHAPTER 9   Producer Choice and Economic Decisions   206

PART THREE   Market Structure and Market Power   231

   CHAPTER 10   Competition and Efficiency   233

   CHAPTER 11   Monopoly and Economic Inefficiency   258

   CHAPTER 12   Imperfect Competition   286

PART FOUR   Resource Markets   311

   CHAPTER 13   Demand and Supply in Resource Markets   313

   CHAPTER 14   Capital Resources and Financial Markets   336

   CHAPTER 15   Labor Markets and Collective Bargaining   358

P A R T
FIVE   Microeconomic Role of Government   383

CHAPTER 16 Microeconomics of Public Finance   385
CHAPTER 17 Government Regulation and Economic Efficiency   411
CHAPTER 18 Income Distribution and Equity   441
CHAPTER 19 Microeconomic Issues and Government Policies   468

P A R T
SIX   Macroeconomic Measures and Models   497

CHAPTER 20 Introduction to Macroeconomics   499
CHAPTER 21 Gross National Product: Measuring Aggregate Output   532
CHAPTER 22 Aggregate Expenditures and Equilibrium Output   559
CHAPTER 23 Changes in Spending and the Multiplier Effect   591

P A R T
SEVEN   Money, Banking, and Economic Activity   615

CHAPTER 24 Money and the Banking System   617
CHAPTER 25 Money and Economic Activity   640
CHAPTER 26 Aggregate Demand and Aggregate Supply   660

P A R T
EIGHT   Macroeconomic Role of Government   687

CHAPTER 27 Macroeconomic Policy: Theory and Practice   689
CHAPTER 28 Unemployment: Some Microeconomic Foundations   719
CHAPTER 29 Inflation and Unemployment   738
CHAPTER 30 Economic Growth: Increasing Potential GNP   764
CHAPTER 31 Macroeconomic Issues and Government Policies   790

P A R T
NINE   International Economics   817

CHAPTER 32 International Trade   819
CHAPTER 33 International Finance   844
CHAPTER 34 Comparative Economic Systems and Economic Development   866

CONTENTS

P A R T
ONE   Introduction to Economics

CHAPTER 1   The Economic Way of Thinking   **3**
   WHAT IS ECONOMICS?   **4**
     Economics Is a Study of the Real World   5
     Economics Is a Study of Scarcity   5
     Economics Is a Study of Choices   6
     Economics Is a Study of Trade or Exchange   6
     Economics Is a Study of Organization   7
     Microeconomic and Macroeconomic Perspectives   8
   THE LANGUAGE OF ECONOMICS   **9**
     Resources   9
     Opportunity Cost   9
   METHODS OF ECONOMIC ANALYSIS   **10**
     Graphic Models   11
     Using Models to Predict Economic Outcomes   11
     Avoiding Logical Errors   13
     Maintaining Objectivity: Facts versus Opinion   14
   WHY DO ECONOMISTS DISAGREE?   **14**
     What Are the "Facts"?   15
     Which Theory Is Best?   15
     What Are the Benefits and Costs?   15
   CONCLUSION   **16**
   APPENDIX TO CHAPTER 1   USE OF GRAPHS   18

CHAPTER 2 Scarcity and Economic Choice   **25**
- **IMPLICATIONS OF SCARCITY**   **26**
  - Competition and Rationing   26
  - Economic Goals   27
  - Production Possibilities   29
- **ECONOMIC CHOICE**   **35**
  - Self-Interest   35
  - Minimizing Costs and Maximizing Benefits   36
  - Rational Expectations   36
  - Marginal Costs and Benefits   36
  - Economic Approach to Decision Making   37
  - Rational Public Choice   38
- **A Case in Point   How Many Prisons to Build?**   **39**
- **RATIONAL CHOICE IN ACTION**   **40**
- **CONCLUSION**   **41**

CHAPTER 3 Laws of Demand and Supply   **45**
- **DEMAND**   **47**
  - Law of Demand   48
  - Demand Schedules and Demand Curves   48
  - Changes in Demand and Quantity Demanded   50
  - Determinants of Product Demand   51
  - Demand and Quantity Demanded Reconsidered   54
  - Changes in Relative Prices   54
- **SUPPLY**   **55**
  - Law of Supply   55
  - Supply Schedules and Supply Curves   55
  - Changes in Supply and Quantity Supplied   57
  - Determinants of Supply   58
  - Supply and Quantity Supplied Reconsidered   59
- **MARKET EQUILIBRIUM**   **60**
  - Shortage   61
  - Surplus   62
  - Changes in Market Conditions and Equilibrium Prices   62
  - Changes in Equilibrium Reconsidered   65
- **GOVERNMENT PRICE-SETTING POLICIES**   **65**
  - Ceiling Prices   66
  - Support Prices   66
- **CONCLUSION**   **67**
- **A Case in Point   Effects of Price Ceilings and Price Supports**   **68**
- **APPENDIX TO CHAPTER 3   ALGEBRA OF MARKET EQUILIBRIUM   71**

CHAPTER 4 Elasticity of Demand and Supply   **75**
- **PRICE ELASTICITY OF DEMAND**   **76**
  - Price Elasticity as a Relative Concept   78
  - Price Elasticity of Demand and Total Revenue   82
  - Two Extreme Cases   84
  - Determinants of Price Elasticity of Demand   85

A Case in Point   Who Pays a Sales Tax?   86
    Price Elasticity of Demand in Action   88
OTHER TYPES OF ELASTICITY   89
    Price Elasticity of Supply   89
    Income Elasticity of Demand   90
    Cross Elasticity of Demand   91
    Supply and Income Elasticity in Action   92
CONCLUSION   93

CHAPTER 5   Market Economies and Resource Allocation   **96**
CIRCULAR FLOW OF ECONOMIC ACTIVITY   97
    Circular-Flow Model   98
    Role of Money   100
A Case in Point   The Economic Organization of a POW Camp   100
    Resource Markets and Product Markets   101
MARKETS: SELF-INTEREST AND RATIONAL CHOICE   102
    Self-Interest: The Invisible Hand   102
    Households and Rational Choice   103
    Businesses and Rational Choice   103
    Market Prices and Opportunity Costs   103
    Resource Allocation in Action   104
MARKETS, ECONOMIC QUESTIONS, AND GOALS   107
    What to Produce and the Goal of Allocative Efficiency   107
    How to Produce and the Goal of Technical Efficiency   108
    For Whom to Produce and the Goal of Equity   109
CAN THE INVISIBLE HAND FAIL?   110
    Private Property Rights   111
    Competition   111
    Information   112
    Resource Mobility   112
A Case in Point   The Ballpoint Pen Industry   113
    Macroeconomic Instability   113
    Different Economic Goals and Economic Views   114
CONCLUSION   114

ECONOMIC ENCOUNTERS   Labor Mismatch: Balancing Demand and Supply   118

CHAPTER 6   Overview of the U.S. Economy   **120**
THE PRIVATE SECTOR: BUSINESS   121
    Role of Business Firms   121
    Size of Business Organizations   123
    Types of Business Organizations   124
    Classification and Grouping of Businesses   126
    Business Finances   127
THE PRIVATE SECTOR: HOUSEHOLDS   129
    Size and Characteristics of the U.S. Population   129
    Sources of Personal Income   130
    Distribution of Personal Income   132

THE PUBLIC SECTOR 133
Role of Government 134
Government and Rational Choice 138
Size and Nature of the Public Sector 138
Size of Government: International Comparisons 140
THE FOREIGN SECTOR 140
Imports and Exports 141
International Trade and Capital Flows 141
CONCLUSION 143

P A R T
TWO Behind Demand and Supply

CHAPTER 7 Consumer Choice and Demand 147
RATIONAL CHOICE AND CONSUMER DECISIONS 148
A Case in Point   Economic Costs and Consumer Choice 149
MARGINAL UTILITY AND CONSUMER DEMAND 150
Total and Marginal Utility 150
Law of Diminishing Marginal Utility 150
Marginal Utility and Demand 152
Individual Demand and Market Demand 154
Equimarginal Principle and Consumer Choice 155
Criticisms of Marginal Utility Theory 159
Consumer Demand and Consumer Surplus 159
CONSUMER CHOICE AND THE LAW OF DEMAND 161
Income and Substitution Effects of a Price Change 161
CONCLUSION 162
APPENDIX TO CHAPTER 7   INDIFFERENCE THEORY AND CONSUMER
CHOICE   164

CHAPTER 8 Producer Choice and Costs of Production 173
RATIONAL CHOICE AND PRODUCER DECISIONS 174
Maximizing Profit 174
Opportunity Cost and Economic Profit 175
PRODUCTION AND COSTS IN THE SHORT RUN 176
Short-Run and Long-Run Decisions 177
Variable Resources and Short-Run Output 177
Increasing and Diminishing Marginal Returns 179
Productivity and Product Costs in the Short Run 181
Product Costs and Short-Run Cost Curves 183
A Case in Point   Average Total Cost and Tuition Scholarships 186
TECHNICAL EFFICIENCY AND OPTIMAL RESOURCE MIX 186
Cost Minimization and the Equimarginal Principle 188
COSTS AND ECONOMIES OF SCALE IN THE LONG RUN 188
A Case in Point   Economic Profit for Farmer Al Greene 189
Long-Run Costs 190
Economies and Diseconomies of Scale 191
CONCLUSION 195

APPENDIX TO CHAPTER 8   INDIFFERENCE ANALYSIS AND THE OPTIMAL MIX OF RESOURCES   198

ECONOMIC ENCOUNTERS   Changing Oil Prices: Who Wins?   204

CHAPTER 9   Producer Choice and Economic Decisions   **206**
RATIONAL CHOICE AND SHORT-RUN SUPPLY DECISIONS   **207**
   Assumptions   207
   Quantity to Supply in the Short Run   208
   Rational Choice and the Profit-Maximizing Rule for Supply   209
   Short-Run Profit Maximization: A Graphic View   211
OTHER ISSUES AND SHORT-RUN SUPPLY DECISIONS   **212**
   Minimizing Losses in the Short Run   212
A Case in Point   Do Special Orders Pay?   **214**
   Irrelevance of Sunk Costs   217
RATIONAL CHOICE AND LONG-RUN SUPPLY DECISIONS   **217**
   Normal Profits and Economic Profits   217
A Case in Point   Fixed and Variable Costs of Driving   **218**
   Quantity to Supply in the Long Run   220
   Additional Long-Run Options   223
CONCLUSION   **224**
APPENDIX TO CHAPTER 9   BREAK-EVEN ANALYSIS   227

P A R T
THREE   Market Structure and Market Power

CHAPTER 10   Competition and Efficiency   **233**
MARKETS AND MARKET STRUCTURE   **234**
COMPETITION AND COMPETITIVE MARKETS   **235**
   Competitive Behavior and the Model of Pure Competition   235
   Pure Competition and Price Takers   236
   Market Price and Demand for a Price-Taker's Product   236
SHORT-RUN SUPPLY IN PRICE-TAKER MARKETS   **238**
   Market Price and Marginal Revenue   238
LONG-RUN DECISIONS AND LONG-RUN EQUILIBRIUM   **241**
   Long-Run Adjustments to Economic Losses   241
   Long-Run Adjustments to Economic Profits   243
   Long-Run Equilibrium: Normal Profits and Optimal
      Plant Size   244
   Market Supply in the Long Run   245
   Competitive Markets and "Reasonable Prices"   248
COMPETITIVE MARKETS AND ECONOMIC GOALS   **248**
   Technical Efficiency and Pure Competition   248
A Case in Point   Efficiency of Competitive Markets   **249**
   Allocative Efficiency and Pure Competition   250
   Equity and Pure Competition   252
COMPETITION IN ACTION   **252**
CONCLUSION   **253**
APPENDIX TO CHAPTER 10   AN ALGEBRAIC LOOK AT COMPETITION   255

CHAPTER 11   Monopoly and Economic Inefficiency   **258**

MONOPOLY MARKETS AND MARKET POWER   **259**
  The Model of Pure Monopoly   260
  Barriers to Entry   261
  Absence of Close Substitutes   262

MONOPOLISTIC FIRMS AND ECONOMIC DECISIONS   **262**
  Price Searching versus Price Taking   263
  Price Searching: Demand and Marginal Revenue   264
  Price Searching: How Much to Charge?   265
  Price Searching: How Much to Supply?   267
  Market Power and Price Discrimination   269

MONOPOLY: MYTHS AND REALITIES   **270**
  Myth 1: A Monopolist Has Control Over Product Demand   270
  Myth 2: A Monopolist Is Unaffected by Increases in Costs   271
  Myth 3: A Monopolist Can Always Earn an Economic Profit   271

MONOPOLY AND INEFFICIENCY   **271**
  Monopoly Means Restricted Choice   273
  Monopoly Means Allocative Inefficiency   273

MONOPOLY IN ACTION   **275**
  A Case in Point   Inefficiency of Market Power   276
CONCLUSION   **277**
APPENDIX TO CHAPTER 11   AN ALGEBRAIC LOOK AT MONOPOLY   280

**ECONOMIC ENCOUNTERS   Corporate Takeovers:
The Raiders Strike**   **284**

CHAPTER 12   Imperfect Competition   **286**

MONOPOLISTIC COMPETITION   **287**
  Model of Monopolistic Competition   287
  Product Differentiation   288
  Short-Run Pricing Decisions   289
  Long-Run Equilibrium   290
  Nonprice Competition   292
  Monopolistic Competition and Efficiency   293

MONOPOLISTIC COMPETITION IN ACTION   **295**
OLIGOPOLY   **296**
  Model of Oligopoly   296
  Pricing Policies   297
  Pricing Decisions: A Game-Theory Approach   299
  Cartels: A Formal Agreement on Prices   299
  Price Leadership: A Tacit Understanding   301
  Nonprice Competition in Oligopolistic Industries   302
  Oligopoly and Inefficiency   303

OLIGOPOLY IN ACTION   **304**
  Breakfast-Cereal Industry   304
  Steel Industry   306

CONTESTABLE MARKETS AND LONG-RUN ECONOMIC EFFICIENCY   **307**
CONCLUSION   **308**

P A R T
FOUR Resource Markets

CHAPTER 13 Demand and Supply in Resource Markets **313**
    RATIONAL CHOICE AND BUYING RESOURCES **314**
        Optimal Choice of Resources   315
        Marginal Revenue Product and Resource Demand   317
    COMPETITIVE RESOURCE MARKETS **318**
        Model of Competitive Resource Market   318
        Demand and Supply: Market and Individual
        Firm Perspectives   319
    DETERMINANTS OF DEMAND AND SUPPLY **320**
        Supply of Resources   320
        Demand for Resources   320
        Relative Efficiency of Resources   321
        Elasticity of Demand for Resources   323
    EFFICIENCY AND INEFFICIENCY IN RESOURCE MARKETS **325**
        Competitive Resource Markets and Allocative Efficiency   325
        Imperfect Competition in the Product Market   326
        Imperfect Competition in the Resource Market   327
        Graphic Representation of Market Power and Efficiency   329
        Imperfect Information and Resource Immobilities   329
    CONCLUSION **331**
    APPENDIX TO CHAPTER 13   AN ALGEBRAIC LOOK AT RESOURCE MARKETS   333

CHAPTER 14 Capital Resources and Financial Markets **336**
    DEMAND FOR CAPITAL RESOURCES **337**
        Investment in Capital Resources   338
        Costs and Benefits of Capital Resources   338
        Investment Projects and Demand for Financing   339
    MARKET FOR LOANABLE FUNDS AND MARKET RATES OF INTEREST **340**
        Market for Loanable Funds   340
        Time Value of Money   342
        Interest Rates and Allocative Efficiency   343
    **A Case in Point   To Buy or Not to Buy a
    Photocopying Machine   344**
        Real Rate of Interest   344
        Usury Laws and Interest Rate Ceilings   345
    PROFIT: RISK, RENT, AND REWARD **347**
        Risk and the Opportunity Cost of Capital   347
        Economic Rent and Economic Profit   347
        Profits and Rewards   348
    CONCLUSION **350**
    APPENDIX TO CHAPTER 14   DISCOUNTED PRESENT VALUE   352

    ECONOMIC ENCOUNTERS   New Strategies on Wall Street **356**

CHAPTER 15 Labor Markets and Collective Bargaining **358**
    LABOR MARKETS AND RATIONAL CHOICE **359**
    LABOR MARKETS: DEMAND AND SUPPLY **360**
        Demand for Labor   361
        Supply of Labor   361
        Demand and Supply: Forces Behind Labor-Market Trends   363
    WAGE DETERMINATION: WHY WAGES DIFFER **365**
        Equalizing Tendencies of Markets   365
        Compensating Wage Differentials   366
        Productivity and Wage Differentials   367
        Human Capital: Investment in Human Resources   367
        Barriers to Entry and Wage Differentials   368
    UNIONS AND COLLECTIVE BARGAINING **368**
        Brief History of Unions in America   369
        Legal Status of Unions   370
        Labor-Relations Environment and Collective Bargaining   373
    ECONOMIC IMPACT OF UNIONS **375**
        Impact on Wages and Allocative Efficiency   375
        Impact on Inflation   378
        Impact on Technical Efficiency   378
        Impact on Equity   379
    CONCLUSION **379**

P A R T
FIVE Microeconomic Role of Government

CHAPTER 16 Microeconomics of Public Finance **385**
    GOVERNMENT IN THE MICROECONOMY **386**
        Government and the Circular Flow of Economic Activity   386
    FUNCTIONS OF GOVERNMENT **388**
        Facilitating Market Activity   388
        Correcting for Market Failures   388
        Income Redistribution and Economic Opportunity   389
    RATIONAL CHOICE AND GOVERNMENT POLICIES **389**
    EXTERNAL BENEFITS AND PUBLIC GOODS **391**
        External Benefits and Allocative Efficiency   391
        Low Transaction Costs and a Private Market for
           External Benefits   392
        Public Goods and Allocative Efficiency   393
    TAXES AND THE GOALS OF EQUITY AND EFFICIENCY **395**
        What Are the Alternatives to Taxes?   395
        Efficiency and Incentive Effects of Taxes   396
        What Is a "Good" Tax?   398
        Equity Effects of the Tax Burden   399
        Distribution of the Tax Burden   400
        U.S. Tax Systems   402
        Goals of U.S. Tax Systems   405
    CONCLUSION **406**

CHAPTER 17 Government Regulation and Economic Efficiency   **411**

ANTITRUST POLICY: LIMITING MARKET POWER   **412**

   Antitrust Laws   413
   Monopolization   415
   Collusion   417

A Case in Point   Electrical Machinery Conspiracy Case   **418**

   Mergers: Size or Market Power?   418
   Government Regulations that Reduce Competition   420
   Current Antitrust Issues   420

A Case in Point   Merger Guidelines:
Measuring Market Concentration   **421**

RATE REGULATION AND PUBLIC ENTERPRISES   **423**

   Mechanisms for Establishing Rates   423
   Regulation and Deregulation of Potentially
      Competitive Industries   425
   Issues in Rate Regulation   426
   Public Enterprises: Another Option   428

SOCIAL REGULATION   **428**

   External Costs and Allocative Inefficiency   429
   Imperfect Information and Market Failure   432
   Social Regulation: Issues for the Future   433

GOVERNMENT FAILURE: WHY REGULATION IS IMPERFECT   **434**

   Difficulty of Measuring Social Benefits and Costs   435
   Rational Ignorance   435
   Special-Interest Effect   435
   Short-Sighted Effect   436
   Lack of Incentives for Efficiency   436

CONCLUSION   **436**

CHAPTER 18 Income Distribution and Equity   **441**

RATIONAL CHOICE: EFFICIENCY AND EQUITY   **442**

DISTRIBUTION OF INCOME: THE FACTS   **443**

   Sources of Personal Income   443
   Inequality of Income   444

POVERTY: DEFINITION AND FACTS   **447**

   Two Approaches: Absolute versus Relative Poverty   447
   Official Definition of Poverty   448

CAUSES OF POVERTY AND INEQUALITY   **452**

   Inadequate Income from Labor   452
   Inadequate Demand for Labor   452
   Poverty and Human-Capital Deficiencies   453

POVERTY AND DISCRIMINATION   **454**

   What Is Economic Discrimination?   454
   Institutional Discrimination   455
   Differences versus Discrimination   456

ANTIPOVERTY AND ANTIDISCRIMINATION POLICIES   **456**

   Antipoverty Policies: The Range of Options   456
   Transfer Policies: Efforts and Results   457
   Transfer Programs: Problems and Issues   459

Negative Income Tax   460

Labor-Market Programs that Aid the Poor   462

CONCLUSION   **463**

**ECONOMIC ENCOUNTERS   South Africa: A National Policy
of Discrimination**   **466**

CHAPTER 19   Microeconomic Issues and Government Policies   **468**

Applying the Principles of Rational Choice to Policy Analysis   469

Why Economists Disagree About Government Involvement   471

Conclusion   471

19.1 THE FARM "PROBLEM" AND AGRICULTURAL PRICE SUPPORTS   **472**

Why Is Government Involved in U.S. Agriculture?   472

What Are the Benefits and Costs of Farm Programs?   474

Are There Superior Alternatives to Current Farm Policies?   478

Conclusion   480

19.2 DEREGULATION OF THE AIRLINE INDUSTRY   **481**

Why Did Government Become Involved in
Airline Regulation?   481

What Were the Benefits and Costs of Regulating the
Airline Industry?   481

Has Deregulation Been a Better Approach?   483

Conclusion   484

19.3 DRUG SAFETY AND THE FOOD AND DRUG ADMINISTRATION   **484**

Why Is Government Involved in the Drug Industry?   485

What Are the Benefits and Costs of FDA Regulation?   486

Are There Superior Alternatives to Current Drug Policies?   488

Conclusion   488

19.4 IMPACT OF MINIMUM WAGE LAWS   **489**

Why Has Government Set a Minimum Wage?   490

What Are the Benefits and Costs of a Minimum Wage?   490

Are There Superior Alternatives to a Minimum Wage?   491

Conclusion   492

19.5 ECONOMIC REGULATION IN THE OIL MARKET   **493**

Why Is Government Involved in the Oil Market?   493

What Are the Benefits and Costs of U.S. Oil Policies?   494

Are There Superior Oil-Policy Options?   495

Conclusion   496

P A R T
SIX   Macroeconomic Measures and Models

CHAPTER 20   Introduction to Macroeconomics   **499**

MACROECONOMIC CONCEPTS AND GOALS   **500**

Microeconomics versus Macroeconomics   501

FULL EMPLOYMENT, UNEMPLOYMENT, AND ECONOMIC GOALS   502
    Official Definition of Unemployment   502
    Types of Unemployment and Economic Goals   505
    Natural, or "Full-Employment," Unemployment Rate   508
    Full Employment and Potential GNP   509
PRICE STABILITY, INFLATION, AND ECONOMIC GOALS   509
    Measuring the General Price Level   509
    Economic Facts and Changes in the General Price Level   511
A Case in Point   Using Price Indexes   512
    Inflation and the Standard of Living   514
    Inflation and Equity   514
    Inflation and Efficiency   515
    Price Stability: What Should Be the Goal?   516
MACROECONOMIC PERFORMANCE: THE U.S. ECONOMY   516
    Economic Stability and Economic Growth   517
    Full Employment   517
    Price Stability   520
    Two Periods in Recent Macroeconomic History   520
A PREVIEW OF AGGREGATE DEMAND AND AGGREGATE SUPPLY   522
    Graphic Representation   522
    Interactions   524
CONCLUSION   524
APPENDIX TO CHAPTER 20   MEASURING PRICE LEVELS   528

CHAPTER 21   Gross National Product: Measuring Aggregate Output   **532**
DEFINING AND MEASURING AGGREGATE OUTPUT   533
    GNP Measures Market Values   533
    GNP Measures Output of Final Goods and Services   534
    GNP Measures Goods and Services Produced in the
       Current Period   535
    Measuring GNP: Real versus Nominal GNP   535
    First and Second Accounting Identities   537
    Two Ways to Measure GNP   538
    GNP: Does It Measure Social Value?   539
CIRCULAR FLOW OF INCOME AND OUTPUT:
A PRIVATE-SECTOR ECONOMY   541
    A Simple Private-Sector Economy   541
    A More Realistic Private-Sector Economy   542
    Financial Markets: The Link between Saving and Investment   545
    Stocks and Flows: Totals and Changes   547
CIRCULAR FLOW: GOVERNMENT AND FOREIGN SECTORS   547
    Government and the Circular Flow   547
    Foreign Trade and the Circular Flow   549
A Case in Point   Additional Accounting Identities   553
NATIONAL INCOME ACCOUNTING   554
    National, Personal, and Disposable Income   555
CONCLUSION   556

CHAPTER 22 Aggregate Expenditures and Equilibrium Output **559**

TWO VIEWS ON MACROECONOMIC EQUILIBRIUM **560**
Classical View: Full-Employment Equilibrium 560
Keynesian View: Equilibrium below Full Employment 564

CONSUMPTION AND SAVING: THE HOUSEHOLD SECTOR **565**
Consumption, Saving, and Disposable Income 566
Saving Schedules and the Marginal Propensity to Save 568
Consumption and Saving: A Graphic View 568
Other Determinants of Consumption Expenditures 570
Movement along Consumption Curve versus Shifts
in Consumption 572
Long-Run and Short-Run Views of Consumption 574

INVESTMENT AND THE BUSINESS SECTOR **576**
Autonomous Nature of Investment Decisions 576
Determinants of Investment Expenditures 577

EQUILIBRIUM OUTPUT IN THE KEYNESIAN MODEL **578**
Macroeconomic Equilibrium 579
Keynesian Equilibrium 579

EQUILIBRIUM OUTPUT AND FULL EMPLOYMENT **581**
**A Case in Point   Equilibrium—Planned Leakages
and Injections   582**
GNP Gaps and Cyclical Unemployment 583
Equilibrium Adjustments: Keynes and the
Classical Economists 584

CONCLUSION **584**
APPENDIX TO CHAPTER 22   ALGEBRA OF KEYNESIAN EQUILIBRIUM   588

CHAPTER 23 Changes in Spending and the Multiplier Effect **591**

MULTIPLIER EFFECT **592**
Multiplier Effect of a Change in Investment 592
Saving and the Paradox of Thrift 596
A Case in Point   Keynesian Analysis of the Great Depression   597

GOVERNMENT FISCAL POLICIES AND EQUILIBRIUM **599**
Government and the Circular Flow 599
Government Purchases and Equilibrium Output 599
Taxes, Consumption, and Aggregate Expenditures 602
Fiscal Policy and a Contractionary Gap 604
A Case in Point   The 1964 Tax Cut   607
Fiscal Policy and Timing of the Multiplier Effect 608

EQUILIBRIUM IN AN OPEN ECONOMY **608**
CONCLUSION **609**
APPENDIX TO CHAPTER 23   ALGEBRA OF THE MULTIPLIER EFFECT   612

PART SEVEN Money, Banking, and Economic Activity

CHAPTER 24 Money and the Banking System **617**
    WHAT IS MONEY? **618**
        Commodity Money 618
        Goldsmiths and the First Bank Money 619
        Creating Money in a Fractional Reserve System 621
        Checking Deposits: Modern Bank Money 622
    A Case in Point   Financial Innovation and the Supply of Bank Money 623
    THE FEDERAL RESERVE SYSTEM **625**
        Structure of the Fed 625
        Functions of the Fed 625
    MONETARY POLICY AND THE MONEY SUPPLY **627**
        Factors Determining the Quantity of Checking Deposits 627
        Monetary-Policy Tools of the Fed 627
        Creating Money in the Banking System by Open-Market Operations 628
        Multiplier Effect on Deposit Expansion 630
        Multiplier Effect on Deposit Contraction 632
        Other Monetary-Policy Tools 633
        Some Real-World Complications 633
    CONCLUSION **634**

    ECONOMIC ENCOUNTERS   Inside the Underground Economy **638**

CHAPTER 25 Money and Economic Activity **640**
    RATIONAL CHOICE AND DEMAND FOR MONEY **641**
        Benefits of Holding Money 641
        Costs of Holding Money 643
    EQUILIBRIUM IN THE MARKET FOR MONEY **644**
        Supply of Money 644
        What Is the Money Market? 644
        Adjusting to a Surplus of Money by Increasing Spending 646
        Adjusting to a Surplus of Money by Increasing Lending 647
        Comparison of Spending and Lending Responses 648
    MONEY AND ECONOMIC ACTIVITY: CLASSICAL AND MODERN VIEWS **650**
        Equation of Exchange 650
        Classical Quantity Theory 651
        Modern Monetary Theories 652
    CONCLUSION **655**
    APPENDIX TO CHAPTER 25   ALGEBRA OF JOINT EQUILIBRIUM IN THE FINAL GOODS AND MONEY MARKETS   657

CHAPTER 26 Aggregate Demand and Aggregate Supply   **660**
     AGGREGATE DEMAND   **661**
         Connecting Aggregate Expenditures and Aggregate Demand   661
         Negative Slope of the Aggregate Demand Curve   663
         Factors that Shift the Aggregate Demand Curve   665
         Changes in Aggregate Demand: The Multiplier Effect   666
     LONG-RUN AGGREGATE SUPPLY AND EQUILIBRIUM   **667**
         Factors that Change Potential GNP   668
         Long-Run Aggregate Supply and Potential GNP   669
     SHORT-RUN AGGREGATE SUPPLY AND EQUILIBRIUM   **670**
         Factors that Shift the Short-Run Aggregate Supply Curve   671
         Slope of the Short-Run Aggregate Supply Curve   672
         Short-Run Equilibrium   673
     ADJUSTMENTS TO GNP GAPS   **675**
         Adjustments to an Expansionary Gap   675
         Adjustments to a Contractionary Gap   677
         Automatic Adjustments: Fast or Slow?   679
     A Case in Point   Expansionary Gaps: A Historic Example   **679**
     A Case in Point   Aggregate Demand and Supply in Action   **682**
         Supply Shocks: Double Whammy   683
     CONCLUSION   **684**

P A R T
EIGHT   Macroeconomic Role of Government

CHAPTER 27 Macroeconomic Policy: Theory and Practice   **689**
     GOVERNMENT AND MACROECONOMIC POLICY   **690**
         Government and the Circular Flow   691
         Government Budget Deficits and Surpluses   691
         Government Stabilization Policies   693
     A Case in Point   Closing a Contractionary Gap: The 1964
     Tax Cut   695
     MACROECONOMIC POLICY: SOME COMPLICATIONS   **697**
         Budget Deficits and the Business Cycle   697
     A Case in Point   Response to a Budget Deficit: The 1932
     Budget Changes   699
         Crowding-Out Effect   700
         Rational Expectations: Are Fiscal and Monetary
           Policies Ineffective?   702
     MACROECONOMIC POLICY: ACTIVISM VERSUS NONACTIVISM   **703**
         Are Discretionary Policies Necesssary?   704
         How Fast Does the Automatic Adjustment Mechanism Work?   704
         What Is the Historical Evidence?   705
         What Information Is Required for Discretionary Policy Action?   706
         How Significant and Uncertain Are Policy Lags?   706
         Nonactivists' Case for Fixed Rules   708
         Activists' Case for Discretionary Policies   710

DEFICITS AND DEBT: ISSUES AND OPTIONS   **711**
    Myths and Realities about the National Debt   711
    Current Situation: What Are the Options?   714
CONCLUSION   **716**

CHAPTER 28   Unemployment: Some Microeconomic Foundations   **719**
LABOR MARKETS: A CLOSER LOOK AT THE UNEMPLOYMENT RATE   **720**
    Flows into and out of Labor Markets   721
    Reasons for Leaving and Entering Labor Markets   722
    Duration of Unemployment   723
EXPLAINING UNEMPLOYMENT: JOB-SEARCH AND
CONTRACTS THEORIES   **725**
    Job-Search Theory and Unemployment   725
    Contracts Theory and Unemployment   729
    Job-Search and Contracts Theories Compared   731
INCREASES IN THE NATURAL RATE OF UNEMPLOYMENT   **732**
    Unemployment: Official and Natural Rates   732
    Factors that Increase the Natural Rate of Unemployment   733
    Policies to Lower the Natural Rate of Unemployment   734
CONCLUSION   **735**

CHAPTER 29   Inflation and Unemployment   **738**
INFLATION   **739**
    Measuring Inflation   739
    Increases in the General Price Level: A Short-Run View   740
    Inflation: What Does *Not* Cause It   742
    Inflation: What *Does* Cause It   745
    Lingering Effects of Demand and Supply Shocks   746
A Case in Point   Money Supply versus Inflation: A Look at
International Conditions   **747**
    History of Factors that Influence Inflation   748
UNEMPLOYMENT AND INFLATION: IS THERE A TRADE-OFF?   **748**
A Case in Point   History of Inflation and Disinflation   **749**
    Unemployment and Prices: A Short-Run View   749
    Phillips Curves: Promise and Failure   750
    The Phillips Curve and Expectations:
    The Accelerationist Argument   752
    Rational Expectations and the New Classical Macroeconomists   756
A Case in Point   Effect of Expectations on Inflation and
Unemployment Policies   **757**
AGGREGATE DEMAND POLICIES: FIGHTING INFLATION   **758**
    The Expectations View and the "Cold Turkey" Approach   758
    The "Sticky-Price" View and the Gradual Approach   759
    The Historical Record   759
    Supply Shocks and Aggregate Demand Policies   760
    Popularity of Inflationary Policies   761
CONCLUSION   **761**

CHAPTER 30 Economic Growth: Increasing Potential GNP **764**

ECONOMIC GROWTH: DEFINITION AND CAUSES **765**
Growth: Increased Real GNP per capita 766
Change in Real GNP—Short-Run and Long-Run Views 767

FACTORS IN ECONOMIC GROWTH **771**
Classical Assumptions and Doomsday Predictions 771
Modern Assumptions and Expectations of Economic Growth 772
Changes in Natural Resources 773
Changes in the Labor Supply 773
Changes in Capital Resources 774
Changes in Technology 775
Reallocation of Resources 776

ACCOUNTING FOR ECONOMIC GROWTH **776**
Sources of U.S. Economic Growth, 1929–1973 777
Slowdown in Economic Growth Since 1973 778
A Case in Point   Sources of Growth:
An International Comparison 779

IMPROVING ECONOMIC GROWTH: POLICY OPTIONS **781**
A Case in Point   Supply-Side Effects of Tax Cuts 782
Raising Saving and Investment 782
Increasing Technological Change 783
Industrial Policy 784
Stabilization Policies and Economic Growth 785

CONCLUSION **785**

ECONOMIC ENCOUNTERS   Living With and Curing Hyperinflation **788**

CHAPTER 31 Macroeconomic Issues and Government Policies **790**
Applying the Principles of Rational Choice to Policy Analysis 791
Are There Superior Alternative Policies? 793
Why Economists Disagree about Government Involvement 793
Conclusion 793

31.1 DEREGULATION OF BANKING: IS THE SYSTEM SAFE? **794**
Why and How Had the Banking System Been Regulated? 794
Why and How Was Banking Partially Deregulated in the
Early 1980s? 795
What Are the Benefits and Costs of Deregulation? 796
Are There Superior Alternatives to Further Deregulation? 796
Conclusion 797

31.2 POLICY RESPONSES TO A SUPPLY SHOCK **798**
Why and How Might Government Respond to a Supply Shock? 798
What Are the Benefits and Costs of Taking Policy Action? 800
Would No Action Be a Better Policy? 802
Why Do Economists Disagree about Appropriate
Policy Actions? 802
Conclusion 803

31.3 REDUCING THE FEDERAL BUDGET DEFICIT **804**
Why and How Should the Deficit Be Reduced? 804
What Are the Benefits and Costs of Taking Policy Action? 805

Would No Action Be a Better Policy? 806
Why Do Economists Disagree about the Appropriate
  Policy Response? 807
Conclusion 807

31.4 INCOMES POLICIES: A CURE FOR INFLATION? 808
Why and How Might Government Impose Incomes Policies? 808
What Are the Benefits and Costs of Incomes Policies? 809
Is There a Better Alternative? 810
Why Do Economists Disagree about Incomes Policies? 811
Conclusion 811

31.5 THE TRADE DEFICIT AND GLOBAL COMPETITIVENESS 812
Why and How Might Government Policies
  Improve Competitiveness? 812
What Are the Benefits and Costs of Trade Deficit Policies? 814
Would No Action Be a Better Policy? 815
Why Do Economists Disagree about Trade Deficit Policies? 816
Conclusion 816

P A R T
NINE International Economics

CHAPTER 32 International Trade **819**
INTERNATIONAL TRADE AND THE UNITED STATES **820**
Volume of U.S. International Trade 821
Changing Pattern of U.S. International Trade 823

GAINS FROM INTERNATIONAL TRADE **824**
Differences in Resources 824
Differences in Preferences 824
Differences in Productivity: Absolute Advantage 824
Differences in Opportunity Cost: Comparative Advantage 826
Terms of Trade 828
Demand and Supply: International Equilibrium 829

INTERNATIONAL TRADE: GAINS AND LOSSES **832**
Higher Prices for Exported Goods 832
Decreased Demand in Import-Competing Industries 832
Lower Prices for Imports and Greater Demand for Exports 833
Distributional Effects of Trade 833

TRADE RESTRICTIONS AND ALTERNATIVE TRADE POLICIES **834**
Import Tariffs 834
Import Quotas 836
Other Nontariff Barriers 837
Arguments for Trade Restrictions 837
Alternatives to Trade Restrictions 839
Reasons for the Popularity of Trade Restrictions 840
U.S. Trade Policy 840

CONCLUSION **841**

CHAPTER 33 International Finance **844**

EXCHANGE RATES AND INTERNATIONAL TRADE **845**

FOREIGN-EXCHANGE MARKETS **847**

International Exchanges and the Flow of Dollars   847
Demand for and Supply of Foreign Exchange   849
Balance of Payments Accounting   853

FIXED EXCHANGE-RATE SYSTEMS **855**

Fixed Rates under the Gold Standard   855
The Gold Standard in Practice   858
Fixed Exchange Rates under the Bretton Woods System   858
The Current International Monetary System   860

CONCLUSION **861**

**ECONOMIC ENCOUNTERS   Third-World Debt: Can it Ever
Be Repaid?** **864**

CHAPTER 34 Comparative Economic Systems and
Economic Development **866**

MARKET CAPITALISM VERSUS PLANNED SOCIALISM **867**

Market Capitalism and Planned Socialism: A Comparison   868
How Well Do the Two Systems Work?   870

ECONOMY OF THE SOVIET UNION **871**

Early History of the Soviet Economy   872
Developing the Economic Plan   872
Implementing the Plan   874
The "Second Economy"   875
Success and Failure   876

ECONOMIC DEVELOPMENT AND THE THIRD WORLD **878**

Dimensions of Poverty   878

A Case in Point   The Dragons Are Coming!   880

Economic Growth versus Economic Development   880
Dimensions of Economic Development   881
Conditions for Economic Development   883
Strategies for Economic Development   884
What Will the Future Bring?   886

CONCLUSION **887**

Appendix   A-1

Glossary   G-1

Index   I-1

PART ONE

Introduction to Economics

The Economic Way
of Thinking

QUESTIONS TO CONSIDER

☐ Why is the study of economics important to an understanding of our world?

☐ What is the basis of all economic activity?

☐ In what ways do the economic meanings of resources and costs differ from their everyday meanings?

☐ How do economists study economic activity?

☐ Why do economists sometimes disagree about solutions to economic problems?

As you begin to study economics, you may be curious about what we will be discussing. Ask yourself the following questions: What determines the price of automobiles, TV sets, food, and other items you buy? What determines whether the economy next year will grow and prosper or experience problems such as unemployment and inflation? What determines the amount of income you can earn and the total income earned by all individuals in the economy? Should you spend your time tomorrow studying economics or in another way?

These and similar questions are what economics and this textbook are all about. Of course, to be able to answer them, you will have to learn something about the principles of economics and how to think like an economist. Economics has been jokingly described as "what economists do," which, although true, is not very revealing. In this chapter we will expand this definition and you will learn a great deal about what economists do and how they do it. You will also learn how the study of economics can be of value to you even if you do not plan to become a professional economist. But keep in mind that economics is, above all, a subject devoted to understanding how the economy works. For that reason, you should find economics interesting and exciting.

WHAT IS ECONOMICS?

No simple definition of economics can fully explain all that economists do. However, we can say that economists study how the economy works and why—as evidenced by such problems as poverty, unemployment, and inflation—it sometimes works poorly. In fact, economics can be characterized by the questions it seeks to answer.

Economics is also a way of thinking. Economists approach the study of real-world problems from the standpoint of certain basic economic principles. They assume that individuals choose those options that best help them achieve their goals. Economists also believe that a business seeks to maximize profits and that it will produce more goods when it can earn greater profits.

Economics may also be viewed as a collection of concepts about and perspectives on some of the problems societies face. These concepts and perspectives are derived from the economic way of thinking. In later chapters, you will learn many principles to help you understand and predict economic events. First, however, we need to look at what economists study and to see how these studies have led to some basic economic principles and ways of thinking.

Economics Is a Study of the Real World

First and foremost the study of economics is motivated by a desire to understand the real world. Although economists sometimes find it useful to consider how the economy might operate under hypothetical situations, they do so in order to help them understand how an economy in the real world operates. In the final analysis, *economics is a study of the real world*.

In this textbook our principal focus is on the economy of the United States— the individuals who work, manage businesses and households, and run the government. We want to understand why they engage in economic activities such as working, producing, saving, investing, and consuming. We want to know how they react to changes in economic circumstances that have occurred or might occur. For example, in the 1970s, certain events caused a significant rise in the world price of oil. Economists studied this unprecedented change and what happened as a result. And, when Congress was debating the tax reform measures passed in 1986, economists helped by predicting the results of various proposals.

When economists study real-world problems, they ask—and try to answer— many questions. Why is the unemployment rate so high and what, if anything, can be done to lower it? What causes inflation and what can be done to minimize it? What are the causes and consequences of the large federal budget deficit? Why does the United States have a large trade imbalance? What caused the Great Depression in the 1930s and the recession in the early 1980s? Should a business build a new plant, or produce a new product? What are the economic advantages and costs of buying a new house, or attending college? Without an understanding of economic principles you cannot answer such questions.

Economics Is a Study of Scarcity

One of the economic facts of life is that each of us has wants: food to eat, clothing to wear, cars to drive, and, of course, a college degree. Economists recognize, however, that individuals and societies must face the fundamental problem of **scarcity**: Although individual and collective wants are unlimited, the resources available to satisfy those wants are limited. Scarcity is one of the most important economic concepts, and you should understand what it means at the outset.

Economists agree that the individual and collective wants of society are unlimited. No matter how much we have, we always seem to want something else. Of course, we might have enough of some specific thing at some particular time— all the turkey we want during Thanksgiving dinner, for example. But history suggests that no matter how hard we work and how prosperous we become, we are unlikely to be able to satisfy *all* our wants.

Scarcity. The fundamental conflict between unlimited human desires and limited availability of resources.

At the same time the ability to satisfy wants is limited. Scarcity is most evident to each of us as the limited income we have and the limited amount of time in each day and week. We must decide how to spend our income and time. Society's ability to satisfy wants is also limited. At any one time, only so many natural resources, only so many factories, and only so many workers are available. Scarcity—the inability to have all that we want—is a fundamental fact of life. *Economics is a study of how society addresses the fundamental problem of scarcity*. We consider what economics has to say about the meaning and implications of scarcity in Chapter 2.

Economics Is a Study of Choices

Scarcity is important because it requires individuals and society to make choices. But how do individuals decide what to buy, how do businesses decide what to produce, and how does government decide what activities to undertake? Economists are very much interested in these questions, and many of the principles of economics that you will encounter are ideas about how choices are made and the factors that influence choices. All choices are related to the implications of scarcity. Since we cannot satisfy all wants no matter how hard we try, we have to choose among them. *Economics is a study of how individuals and society choose which wants to satisfy and how to satisfy them*. We begin to look at economic choices in Chapter 2.

Economics Is a Study of Trade or Exchange

Although scarcity means that we cannot have *everything* we want, we can obtain some of the things we want through trade or exchange. Trade or exchange between individuals and economies is an extremely important economic activity. Trade occurs in all types of societies and in all kinds of ways. Individuals in positions of authority may trade favors: "Help me with this, and I'll put in a good word for you" or "You vote for my bill and I'll vote for yours." Trade occurs between individuals, individuals and businesses, businesses and businesses, and economies. *Economics is a study of how trade or exchange is carried on.*

One very important economic principle is that trade can benefit both parties; that is, both parties to a trade may be better off as a result. For example, you want to eat at a nice restaurant this weekend but are short of funds. Your roommate has $20 and is in danger of flunking the upcoming economics quiz. By trading your tutoring services for the $20, you both gain: Your roommate passes the economics quiz, and you enjoy a nice meal.

Trade results from different preferences, different resources, and different capabilities. In each case, trade can lead to mutual gains. For example, you and I may have different musical preferences. I love opera but consider rock music to be noise. Your musical tastes are the opposite. If I trade you three tapes of rock music my teenaged children bought me for my birthday for three tapes of opera your parents bought you to improve your musical tastes, we will both be better off. Different preferences make trade desirable.

Countries often trade because they possess different resources. Saudi Arabia, for example, has a lot of oil but little land suitable for growing wheat. The United States, on the other hand, uses more oil than it produces but has a lot of land suitable for growing wheat. By trading wheat for oil, both countries can get more of what they want. Differences in resources make it possible for both parties to gain from trade.

Finally, trade allows individuals and countries to specialize, that is, to concentrate their efforts and resources, supplying goods that they can produce most efficiently. For example, suppose that we are neighbors, each with two jobs to do this week: paint our houses and build sheds in our backyards. I am a good carpenter but a lousy painter; your skills are just the reverse. If I build both sheds and you concentrate on painting both houses, we can both finish sooner and have more free time. Specialization offers many advantages to individuals, businesses, and countries. The increased efficiency of specialization offers the possibility of mutual gain from trade.

In the United States and similar economic systems, most exchanges take place in *markets*. A market is the economist's way of referring to the arrangements that bring together the buyers and sellers of some particular resource, good, or service. Because of their importance in the United States, we will devote a significant amount of time to understanding how markets work.

Economics Is a Study of Organization

In the United States, trade occurs most often between different components of the economy, which we can generally class as households (and the individuals within them), businesses, and government. These components interact in a variety of ways. Individuals work for businesses and government. Businesses produce goods and services for households, government, and other businesses. Government taxes households and businesses and provides roads, national defense, and laws regulating economic and noneconomic behavior. Viewed as a whole, economic interactions constitute an **economic system**, or the way society is organized to address the economic problem of scarcity. *Economics is a study of how different economic systems address the fundamental problem of scarcity*.

There are many types of economic systems. The economic system of the United States, for example, is known as **market capitalism**. It has two principal characteristics: (1) most resources are owned by private individuals; and (2) most economic interactions occur in markets, where resources, goods, and services are bought and sold. But there are other types of economic systems. The system in the Soviet Union is **planned socialism**. In this type of system most resources are owned and their use is controlled by the government. While both the United States and the Soviet Union face the problem of scarcity, their economic systems—how they address scarcity—are very different. *Economics is a study of the implications of different forms of economic organization*.

In this textbook we consider primarily market capitalism, the system used by the United States, Canada, Japan, and the countries of Western Europe. However, within the basic framework of market capitalism, alternatives and choices affect how each economic system operates. In the United States, for example, we constantly face the question of whether more or less of the basic economic choices should be made or controlled by government. While economists do not always agree about whether more or less government is better, they do agree that it is important to study how a change may affect the economy.

Economic system. The institutions and mechanisms used to determine what and how to produce and who will receive the goods and services produced.

Market capitalism. An economic system in which most resources are privately owned by individuals and most economic interactions occur in markets.

Planned socialism. An economic system in which most resources are owned by government and their use is controlled by a government plan.

Microeconomics. That level of economic analysis concerned with the activity of individual units of the economy and their interrelationships.

Macroeconomics. That level of economic analysis concerned with the activity of the entire economy and the interactions between large sectors of it.

Economics. The study of how individuals and societies, faced with the problem of scarcity, choose how to produce, exchange, and consume goods and services.

Regardless of the type of economic system, certain economic principles always apply. For example, trade or exchange plays a role in every society. In addition, all societies face the problem of scarcity; thus all are forced to make choices. And regardless of how a society is organized, all decisions are ultimately made by individuals. In the United States, where private ownership prevails, individuals decide how to use the resources and goods they own. In the Soviet Union, with its system of public ownership and centralized control, more decisions are made by individuals in government agencies. You can better understand either system by learning more about how choices are made.

Microeconomic and Macroeconomic Perspectives

Economic interactions take place on many levels: from trading clothes with your roommate to complex trade agreements among dozens of nations. Thus economists have to study economic activity from both the microeconomic and macroeconomic perspectives.

Microeconomics focuses on the activities of individual units within the economy. For example, at the microeconomic level an economist might explore how U.S. automakers have responded to the increased competition from Japanese and other foreign automobile producers, or how U.S. consumers are likely to react if automobile prices fall by 10 percent.

Macroeconomics, on the other hand, concentrates on the activities of the entire economy and the interactions among its major sectors—households, businesses, and government, both domestic and foreign. For example, at the macroeconomic level an economist might study why the average price of all goods in the United States increased by more than 10 percent per year from 1979 to 1981, or why 1.5 million more people were unemployed in 1980 than in 1979.

Consider how economists might study the impact of a proposed cut in income taxes. A microeconomic analysis would ask questions such as: "How will a tax cut affect house prices?" "How will it affect the behavior of producers of personal computers?" A macroeconomic analysis of the same policy would ask: "How will a tax cut affect the total amount spent by all households in the economy?" "What effects will it have on the general price level and unemployment?"

Although we make a distinction between them here (and generally throughout this textbook), a complete economic analysis of a government policy must consider both macro and micro implications. That is, the effects on individual units of the economy (the microeconomic level) *and* on the economy as a whole (the macroeconomic level) should be considered. In fact, a significant amount of research in economics over the past decade has been aimed at improving our understanding of the microeconomic foundations of macroeconomics, that is, to merging the two branches of the economic discipline.

In this brief overview we have identified what economists do. The broad range of topics mentioned may help you understand why it is difficult to give a simple yet comprehensive definition of economics. At the risk of oversimplification, however, we may define **economics** as the study of how individuals and societies, faced with the problem of scarcity, choose how to produce, exchange, and consume goods and services.

RECAP

Economics is concerned with scarcity and how individuals and society choose to use the limited resources at their disposal.

Economic trade takes place among different sectors in the economy in both market-based and planned economies.

Microeconomics is concerned with the actions and interactions of individual units of the economy (such as the households and businesses buying and selling a single good or service).

Macroeconomics is concerned with the whole economy and the interactions of major sectors of the economy (all households, all businesses, or government as a whole).

THE LANGUAGE OF ECONOMICS

Economists seek to understand how the real world operates and to address real-world problems such as unemployment, inflation, and scarcity. In order to describe the economic world and possible solutions to its problems, economists have developed an economics vocabulary. At times, the terms used in economics may seem like a foreign language. Worse, economists often have special meanings for common words. You may be tempted to ask, "Why don't economists just use plain, ordinary language?" Unfortunately, ordinary language is imprecise. For example, consider the word "competition." In everyday use the word is used to mean rivalry, as between two athletic teams. But the economic concept of competition has a special and technical meaning: the presence of sufficient numbers of buyers and sellers so that no one of them can influence the market price.

For now, you do not have to worry about remembering the special meaning of competition. But the technical precision of economic terms means that you must carefully note the *economic* meaning of terms like competition, demand, costs, unemployment, and inflation when we introduce them. To help you in your mastery of economic terms, such words appear in bold type in the text when first explained, and their definitions appear in the margin. A glossary of all these terms appears at the end of the book. To illustrate this method and how economic terms are a part of the economic way of thinking, let's consider how economists define and use the concepts of resources and opportunity cost.

Resources

A major part of economic activity is devoted to producing goods and services that satisfy wants. To provide goods and services businesses combine **resources**. You probably think you know what resources are, but the economic meaning of this term is somewhat broader than its common, everyday meaning.

Economists identify three types of resources that can be used to produce goods and services. Minerals, water, air, and land are **natural resources**. Buildings, factories, schools, machinery, computers, ships, railroads, and trucks—long-lasting goods—are **capital resources**.

As important as natural and capital resources are, they cannot produce goods and services by themselves. Society also relies on **human resources**—the skills, talents, and time of individuals. Human resources are required to operate machinery, extract minerals from the ground, make and assemble products, and provide services. Human resources are also required to organize, plan, and direct the use of resources. And human resources are used to develop improved machinery, better methods of organizing production, and new products.

Resources are one of the economy's fundamental building blocks. They enable goods to be produced and wants to be satisfied. By increasing the quantity and quality of resources or the efficiency of their use, society can satisfy more wants. The study of economics is largely the study of resources and resource use.

Opportunity Cost

Any business interested in earning a profit must consider the cost of the resources used to produce its product or service. But what is the cost? In everyday language, the cost of resources is the price businesses pay to acquire them. If

Resources. The human, capital, and natural resources that can be used to produce goods and services.

Natural resources. The land, water, minerals, climate, and other products of nature that can be used to produce goods and services.

Capital resources. The buildings, machinery, roads, transportation equipment, and other long-lasting items that can be used to produce goods and services. Also called *capital goods*.

Human resources. The strength, skills, training, and talents of society's population that can be used to produce goods and services.

Opportunity cost. The value of the next best option that must be sacrificed when a choice is made.

Economic model. A simplified verbal, tabular, graphic, or mathematical representation of a real economy that is used to analyze and predict how the economy would work under the specified conditions.

workers are hired for $10 per hour, a product requiring three hours of labor has a labor cost of $30 per hour.

But in the economic way of thinking, **opportunity cost** is a more precise measure of the cost. Because of the fundamental economic problem of scarcity, every time a resource is used in one way, it cannot be used to produce other goods. For example, if a business uses materials to produce blue suede sneakers, it cannot use those same materials to produce other types of shoes. If you faithfully attend your economics class, the hours you spend in that way cannot be used for another purpose. If the government chooses to spend tax dollars to provide subsidized housing, those same tax dollars are not available for other government expenditures or for private individuals to spend as they please.

Economists use the concept of opportunity cost to measure the sacrifice involved in a given choice. In particular, the opportunity cost is the value of the next best option. For example, if you choose to attend your economics class at eight o'clock in the morning, the opportunity cost of that decision might be the value to you of sleeping late (although some individuals have demonstrated an ability to combine these two activities). For a business, the opportunity cost of producing one product may be best measured by the profit it could have earned if it had produced a different product. For government expenditures, the opportunity cost is the value of other government expenditures that could have been made or the value to taxpayers of goods and services they otherwise could have consumed.

Because we live in a world characterized by scarcity, we face a sacrifice or opportunity cost for every choice we make. We explore choice and opportunity cost in Chapter 2. For now, though, you should note that thinking in economic terms requires an explicit recognition of sacrifice—that is, the opportunity cost—involved with every choice we make.

METHODS OF ECONOMIC ANALYSIS

In addition to defining terms precisely, economists construct models or theories of economic behavior. An **economic model** or theory is a simplified representation of how the economy, or parts of the economy, behave under particular conditions. In building a model, economists do not try to explain every detail of the real world. Rather, they focus on the most important influences on behavior because the real world is so complex.

For example, consider an economic model of consumer behavior, which seeks to understand what causes individuals to buy more or less of some particular product. This model focuses on only a few of the many possible influences, such as the benefits that consumers receive from the product, the income of consumers, the price of the product, and prices of other products. Economists assume that other factors—the smile of a salesclerk, the weather, and the whims of particular buyers—are irrelevant. By simplifying, the economist is able to concentrate on the most important variables and predict the behavior of consumers as a group.

You might ask, "Why don't economists just stick to the facts?" Facts are descriptions of the past, but economists are primarily interested in predicting the future. Facts are very important, however, in helping economists understand the past and present. Economists use facts in developing and testing their economic models and theories. Those that do not explain the facts of the past accurately or predict reasonably well what will occur in the future are worthless.

RECAP

Economic concepts such as resources and opportunity cost have special meanings in economics.

Opportunity cost is a measure of the sacrifice involved with any particular choice and, in particular, the value of the next best option.

Economic models or theories are descriptions of economic behavior under specific conditions.

Economic models can be used to predict the outcome of economic events or changes in government policy.

Economic models may be expressed as verbal descriptions, tabular data, graphs, or mathematical equations.

In addition, facts do not always tell a clear, unambiguous story. For example, suppose that you were given facts showing prices and quantities sold of a given product over a period of time. You might find that sometimes prices rose and quantities sold fell. But you will no doubt find that at other times both prices and quantities sold rose. What do these facts tell you? They appear to tell two different stories, not allowing you to easily predict prices and quantities. Economists combine a model of consumer behavior with a model of seller behavior to explain such apparently confusing facts. You will encounter this model of demand and supply in Chapter 3.

Many beginning students in economics (and other disciplines) ask, "Are we going to learn something practical and useful or just a bunch of theories?" Economics does offer a number of theories and models describing how the economy operates (and you will no doubt be asked to recall them on exams). Some people believe that theory belongs only in the classroom and is useless in the real world—definitely a false impression.

There is no major gap between well-developed theories and models and the real world. A good theory helps us to understand the real world. Moreover, a model allows us to predict the effects of a possible or proposed event, such as increased tuition at the state university, decreased federal income taxes, or improved production methods. That is, we can predict what is likely to happen, who is likely to benefit, and what policies to use to increase or lessen the event's effects.

Well-constructed models are not guesses or wishful thinking. Economists subject their models to a stern test: How well do they explain the past and predict future real-world events? Models or theories that do not pass this test are discarded or revised—an ongoing process in economics.

Graphic Models

Economic models are sometimes presented as verbal descriptions but more often as tables, mathematical equations, or graphs. The graph in Exhibit 1.1, for example, is a model that describes the relationship between the amount of household income and spending each year. The model indicates that if its income is $20,000 per year, the household will spend $20,000; if its income is $60,000, it will spend $40,000. To be useful, of course, the model must accurately reflect how the household's decisions are influenced by its income. Because graphs are so much a part of economics, we included a special appendix at the end of this chapter to explain more about how to construct and read graphs. In addition, the study guide that accompanies this textbook has an entire chapter on the use of graphs, including exercises to let you practice using the types of graphs you will encounter later in the text.

Using Models to Predict Economic Outcomes

Whatever their form, economic models are useful because they can help economists make predictions of economic outcomes. Using models, economists can consider the relationship between two economic variables. For example, when

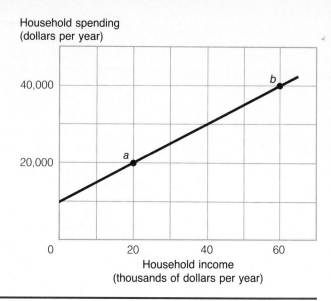

Exhibit 1.1
A Model of Houshold Spending
This graph shows a model that relates household spending to household income. The model indicates that the household will spend $20,000 per year, if its annual income is $20,000 (point *a*). If annual income is $60,000 per year, the household will spend $40,000 per year (point *b*).

studying the U.S. economy we are interested in the relationship between the price of a product and the quantity that consumers seek to buy. As you will see in Chapter 3, focusing on these two variables allows us to make the following statements: (1) if the price of a product falls, consumers will buy more; and (2) if the price rises, consumers will buy less.

A series of "if A, then B" propositions and assumptions about behavior comprise a model of how two economic variables—price and the quantity consumers seek to buy—are related. Using this model we can predict the economic outcome of a price change. For example, if producers lower prices, we can expect consumers to buy more. Of course, the outcome predicted reflects both the model used and the prediction of how prices will change. Economists who use the same model but expect different changes in price will predict different amounts of consumer purchases.

Models can also help economists understand the effects of a proposed government policy. Suppose that Congress is considering a law requiring foreign producers to raise their prices (thus making goods produced in this country relatively less expensive). The model of consumer behavior predicts that the law will cause consumers to buy fewer foreign goods. By helping economists forecast the results of a change in economic conditions or government policies, such models provide an important and useful tool for those who have to make far-reaching decisions.

Building, testing, and using economic models is an important part of the economic way of thinking. The objective of economics and economic models is to help you and others understand the real world. Without theories, economics would be neither useful nor practical. In fact, a good way to learn economics is to ask yourself continually what questions a given theory can help you answer. This method will not only test your understanding of the theory but also will help you put economic theory to work for you.

Avoiding Logical Errors

Because models are so important to our understanding of the economic world, they must be as accurate as possible. Thus in building and using models, economists must be aware of certain logical errors, most notably errors of causation and correlation, the fallacy of composition, and the fallacy of division. An understanding of these possible errors will help you detect the mistakes of others and avoid them yourself.

Causation and correlation. A model describes the relationships among the various factors selected as important to a particular economic activity. However, in building a model we must be careful not to confuse correlation with causation.

Correlation is a statistical term that measures the degree to which two variables tend to move together. For example, if the number of tickets sold to a football game increases each time the price of tickets rises, ticket sales are *positively* correlated with ticket prices. If unemployment in the U.S. economy decreases whenever the number of kangaroos born in Australia falls, unemployment is *negatively* correlated with the birthrate of kangaroos.

Serious mistakes can be made in model building if economists who find a high degree of positive or negative correlation between two factors assume that one factor *causes* the other. There may be no justification to assume **causation** and no proof of its validity. Correlation is a measure of a statistical relationship, *not* proof of cause and effect.

While correlation may suggest a relationship between two variables, a result may actually be caused by a factor not included in the analysis. For example, the positive correlation between ticket prices and ticket sales may be explained by the fact that ticket prices rise only when a team is highly successful. Correlation may even be merely a coincidence, such as the correlation between unemployment in the United States and the birthrate of Australian kangaroos.

Economic history is littered with stories of errors in causation and correlation. W. S. Jevons, a nineteenth-century economist, observed a correlation between sunspot activity and economic prosperity. From this correlation he derived a theory of how the economy operated. Later analysis found other economic factors that better explained the variations in economic activity and discredited the sunspot theory. Remember: Causation cannot be proved from correlation; it must be demonstrated in more direct and different ways.

Fallacy of composition. Another form of model-building error can arise as economists examine the facts of the real world and attempt to sort them into meaningful patterns. For example, some economists study how businesses that produce automobiles react to and are affected by increases in the price of their products. Economists may observe that profits rise when prices rise and that automakers produce more cars when prices increase. But can we conclude that businesses will be affected in the same way if *all* prices in the economy rise? No, and as a matter of fact that would not be true. Higher prices for automobiles are good for automakers when they rise relative to other prices. But if all prices in the economy increase, the cost of producing cars also rises, and automakers will not earn more profits or produce more cars.

Correlation. The statistical relationship between two factors and the extent to which changes in one factor are accompanied by changes in the other.

Causation. The presumption that a change in one factor causes a change in another factor with which it is statistically correlated.

Fallacy of composition. Incorrectly concluding that what is true of the part is also true of the whole.

Fallacy of division. Incorrectly concluding that what is true of the whole is also true of every part.

Positive statement. A statement limited to a factual description of what is or what will be.

Normative statement. A statement involving value judgments of what ought to be.

The preceding example illustrates the **fallacy of composition**. A change that affects only one individual or one business may not have the same effect if all individuals or businesses in an economy are affected. When economists try to predict what will happen to large groups of individuals and businesses, or the economy as a whole, they must be careful to avoid the fallacy of composition.

Fallacy of division. Another common mistake may occur when economists try to predict the effect on an individual from a prediction of an effect on a group. For example, when the economy goes into a recession, sales of goods and services in total, and the income of consumers as a group, will fall. However, this decline does not mean that sales by all firms will decline or that incomes of all individuals will be lower. The **fallacy of division** states that what is true for the economy as a whole is not always true of each part.

Maintaining Objectivity: Facts versus Opinion

One of the most important elements in model building is maintaining an objective attitude toward the subject being studied and the conclusions that emerge. Economists have feelings, beliefs, and opinions, just like everyone else. But in applying the tools of economics, they must make a distinction between facts and opinions and remain emotionally neutral.

Because their models can help predict what will happen, economists are often asked to give advice on the effects of proposed governmental policies. They may give one of two types of response. They may supply a factual answer, a projection of what they believe *will* happen if the policy is enacted. They might, for example, predict that a government policy will cause an increase in the price of some particular product or service. A statement of facts or a projection of what is likely to happen is a **positive statement**. Sometimes, however, economists may give an opinion on what the government *ought* to do about a problem. If this opinion is influenced by the values of the individual, it is called a **normative statement**.

It is difficult but necessary to distinguish facts from value judgments. But as some economists note, it is almost impossible to make a purely objective statement of fact, especially to a question such as "Is it in the best interest of the country to implement this policy?" The choice of models and the weighing of evidence are often influenced by personal biases. Still, to apply the economic way of thinking, we must distinguish between statements of objective fact (positive statements) and statements influenced by political and philosophical biases (normative statements).

RECAP

Economists must be careful not to confuse correlation and causation and must learn to avoid common fallacies such as those of composition and division.

Economists must try to maintain objectivity and not confuse fact and opinion.

Economists make a distinction between positive statements—factual descriptions or predictions of what is likely to happen—and normative statements—personal opinions of what should be done.

WHY DO ECONOMISTS DISAGREE?

If models have been checked for logic errors and philosophical bias, then why are they not perfect? Why do economists seem—at least in the news media—to disagree so much about what effects a given action will have and what economic policies should be followed? First, as we noted earlier, models are an attempt to simplify a complex world. Economists have yet to devise a model that explains or even attempts to account for *all* aspects of economic interaction in the real world. Sometimes economists disagree about the facts and what economic models are most appropriate. Moreover, value judgments are often required to choose the "best" solution to economic problems. Thus economic disagreements occur because economists have differing personal values.

What Are the "Facts"?

Even if they use the same models, economists may reach different conclusions if they cannot agree on the facts. It is difficult to measure economic activities precisely and accurately. Economists therefore must sometimes rely on imperfect and incomplete information when making predictions or policy suggestions. Naturally, interpretations of imperfect information may differ.

Economists also disagree about some fundamental aspects of the economy. Do individuals have the ability to make choices on their own, or are they dominated by powerful organizations? Are individuals able to acquire the goods and services they demand by their own efforts, or is government needed to provide many of the goods and services required in a modern economy? Strong arguments have been made for each position. Although many of the arguments are based more on philosophy than facts, it is not always easy to know which "fact" is the more accurate description of reality.

Which Theory Is Best?

Economists also disagree about how the economy will react to various changes in conditions. Because they are unable to conduct controlled experiments, economists sometimes cannot agree on the precise theoretical model that best describes the outcomes of economic policies. Thus at any one time, there are often several different, competing theories about how the economy operates and which policies will yield the desired results.

What Are the Benefits and Costs?

Even if economists could agree on the facts and on the best theory, they might still disagree on which policy is best. With the same theory and the same facts, economists would, of course, be able to agree on the predicted outcomes. But they may give very different opinions about whether such outcomes are desirable. The degree to which these differences are related to unclear aspects of *positive* economic factors and to *normative* economic factors is very hard to determine.

For example, economists strongly disagree about whether the government should intervene in economic activity. Part of the disagreement is over the relative importance of economic goals. Some economists emphasize the importance of maintaining individual freedom of choice. Others believe that government must occasionally step in to offset uncontrolled attempts by large organizations to alter individual behavior. Thus those who are concerned about freedom of choice may view advertising primarily as a means of providing information for individuals to use in making decisions. But those concerned about the power of large organizations may view advertising more as an attempt to manipulate the individual's decision-making process, thereby reducing the individual's autonomy.

Economists disagree about the relative benefits and costs of inflation and unemployment. Some believe that the effects of inflation are so damaging that it is preferable to accept high rates of unemployment for short periods, if doing so would eliminate inflation. Other economists suggest that a reduction in unemployment is worth some cost to the economy in terms of inflation. Behind this controversy are major disagreements over the relative costs of unemployment and inflation and over how much unemployment must fall to reduce significantly the rate of inflation.

Some economists believe that our major national goal should be maximum production. Others place more emphasis on a more equitable distribution of whatever is produced; some of these economists would accept a smaller economic pie in return for a fairer distribution of its pieces. This difference, of course, reflects opinions, not facts.

As you can see, individual economists are not likely to reach identical conclusions about what the future holds or about the effects of different economic policies. As individuals, they have different values and sometimes observe economic events in different ways. Although there are differences, there is also clearly an "economic way of thinking." It represents a common basis for economic analysis and a way of testing the validity of economic ideas. In this textbook we focus on the areas of agreement but point out where and why important differences exist.

CONCLUSION

In later chapters you will learn much more about what economists do and how they do it. Those chapters build on the foundation we laid in this chapter. Economics is a way of thinking that uses certain concepts (scarcity and opportunity cost, for example) to build models (like the model of consumer behavior). In all cases, the purpose of economic analysis is to learn to understand and predict real-world outcomes. Thus you should try to apply the concepts and models you learn. Remember: The test of economic theories—and your understanding of them—is how well they answer real-world questions.

SUMMARY

1. In this chapter we introduced you to the study of economics, what economists do, and the methods economists use.

2. Economics is the study of interactions in the real world that are related to the concept of scarcity: limited resources but unlimited human wants. Scarcity forces individuals and societies to make choices. Economics is also a study of how choices are made. Many choices involve trade among different sectors of an economy or among economies. And economics is a study of the implications of different forms of economic organization.

3. Economic activity can be studied on two levels: macro and micro. Microeconomics involves studies of the activities of individual units within the economy, such as the market for a single product. Macroeconomics covers studies of the activities of the economy as a whole or major sectors of the economy. Sound economic analysis requires consideration of both.

4. Economists use a special language, and economic concepts enable economists to communicate their ideas clearly. Resources are the minerals, land, buildings, machinery, and human talents used to produce goods and services. Opportunity cost is a measure of the sacrifice involved with any specific choice and, in particular, is the value of the next best option.

5. In order to describe economic behavior, economists build theories and models. Economic models are simplifications of the real world but can help the economist to predict the outcome of real-world economic events

or changes in government policy. Economic models may be expressed as verbal descriptions, tabular data, graphs, or mathematical equations.

6. Builders of economic models must be careful not to confuse correlation and causation and must learn to avoid common fallacies, such as those of composition and division. They must try to maintain an objective attitude toward the subject being studied and the conclusions reached. Economists distinguish between positive statements—those limited to factual descriptions or predictions of what is likely to happen—and normative statements—those involving personal opinions and values or suggestions of what should be done.

7. Economists share many common principles and theories, but they also disagree from time to time. Disagreements exist because unambiguous facts are not always available, because it is not always clear which model is best, and because economists have different values and stress different goals.

KEY TERMS

Scarcity, 5
Economic system, 7
Market capitalism, 7
Planned socialism, 7
Microeconomics, 8
Macroeconomics, 8
Economics, 8
Resources, 9
Natural resources, 9
Capital resources, 9
Human resources, 9
Opportunity cost, 10
Economic model, 10
Correlation, 13
Causation, 13
Fallacy of composition, 14
Fallacy of division, 14
Positive statement, 14
Normative statement, 14

QUESTIONS FOR REVIEW AND DISCUSSION

1. What facts of life underlie the study of economics?
2. What are the basic objectives of economic study?
3. Why do economists, applying the principles of econom-

ics, sometimes reach different conclusions? Can you always prove one group of economists to be wrong? If so, how?

4. What implication does scarcity have for a society? What implication does it have for a society if a resource becomes more scarce? Less scarce?

5. What do you believe is the appropriate role of economists in formulating economic policy? Can you think of situations in which there is no "correct" economic policy? What is the appropriate role of politicians in formulating policies to deal with economic problems?

6. The government is considering whether to raise or lower income taxes. What kinds of questions would you raise from a microeconomic perspective? From a macroeconomic focus?

7. Which of the following are *positive* statements and which are *normative* statements?
   a) "An increase in prices will reduce the quantity purchased."
   b) "The government shouldn't raise taxes because some groups in the economy will be worse off."
   c) "Businesses will produce more of their products when they expect to sell more."
   d) "Businesses should be more careful not to spoil the environment."

8. What is the purpose of theory? What kinds of questions do economists hope to answer by developing theories and models? Can you explain what causes inflation without a theory? If you were developing a theory of inflation, explain why it would be important to (a) identify which economic factors were related to inflation (and which were unrelated); (b) know whether the identified factor was directly or indirectly related to inflation; (c) test your theory against historical facts; (d) not let your philosophical ideas influence the choice of variables to include.

9. Explain why each of the following conclusions is incorrect.
   a) "Whenever there's a large snowfall, sales of snow shovels increase. Therefore, if we want it to snow, everyone has to buy more snow shovels."
   b) "The government reported today that the income of households in the United States increased by 6 percent last year. This implies that everyone in the nation is better off this year than last."
   c) "If a farmer can earn a greater income by producing a larger crop, the income of all farmers will increase when they're able to increase production."

10. Use the appendix to this chapter and the graph on the following page to answer questions (a)–(f).

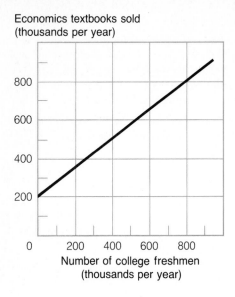

Economics textbooks sold
(thousands per year)

Number of college freshmen
(thousands per year)

a) Are the two variables shown in the graph—number of economics textbooks sold and number of college freshmen—directly or indirectly related?

b) Is the slope of the line shown in the graph positive or negative?

c) According to the graph, how many copies of economics textbooks will be sold next year if there are 400,000 college freshmen? If 800,000 copies of economics textbooks were sold last year, how many college freshmen were there?

d) What is the slope of the line? What is the intercept of the line?

e) According to the slope, how many more economics textbooks will be sold if the number of college freshmen increases by 100,000?

f) Write an algebraic expression to show the relationship between textbooks sold (T) and the number of college freshmen (F). Let textbooks sold be the dependent variable and college freshmen be the independent variable.

Appendix to Chapter 1

Use of Graphs

In Chapter 1 we noted that economists use graphs and mathematical models to depict economic data or to describe economic relationships. Because you will encounter graphs frequently in this textbook and in economic analyses, the ability to read a graph is an important skill for you to develop. The purpose of this appendix is to explain how to read a graph and how either real or hypothetical data can be plotted to form a graph. Data can be displayed in graphic form in many different ways. In this appendix we concentrate on only one: the simple arithmetic line graph. This form of graph is the one we use most often in this textbook and is a good one with which to begin.

In everyday experience, we often observe that one thing depends on another. For example, the time it takes to read a chapter of this textbook will depend on the number of pages in the chapter. Mathematicians speak of such dependencies as "functional relationships." How well you perform on your first economics exam will depend on—is a function of—the number of hours you have spent studying. In a dependent relationship, one variable (in this case, your exam grade) is said to be the **dependent variable**, whereas the other—the one that is free to fluctuate

Dependent variable. In any given relationship, an element that is affected by a change in the value of an independent variable.

Independent variable. In any given relationship, an element that is subject to independent change. A change in the value of an independent variable affects the value of the dependent variable.

Origin. The point on a graph representing a zero value for both variables; the intersection of the horizontal and vertical axes, generally the lower left corner of a graph.

or that can be directly controlled (in this case the number of hours you study)— is called the **independent variable**.

Much of what you study in economics can be expressed in terms of such dependent relationships. In fact, much of the work of economists consists of learning how, and to what extent, some variables, such as unemployment or product prices, depend on others. When we have only two variables, we can show their relationship on a two-dimensional graph. In mathematical terms, a graph is a pictorial display of the relationship that exists between two (or more) variables.

PLOTTING A GRAPH

To illustrate how a graph is plotted, we will use the hypothetical data in Exhibit 1A.1, which shows the relationship between the prices charged by Paulo's Pizza Parlor and the number of pizzas that people in Collegetown will buy from Paulo's in a given week. As the data in the table indicate, the number of pizzas Paulo can sell *increases* as the price charged *decreases*. Because the two variables move in opposite directions, they are said to be *inversely* related. (When two variables move in the same direction, they are said to be *directly* related.)

The graph accompanying the data indicates how a simple line graph is plotted. This particular graph shows the number of pizzas sold per week (the dependent variable) on the *horizontal axis* (along the bottom of the graph) and the price charged (the independent variable) on the *vertical axis*. At the bottom left, where the two axes intersect, is the **origin**.

Exhibit 1A.1
Paulo's Pizza Parlor: Prices Charged and Quantities Sold

(a)

Price (dollars per pizza)	Quantity sold (pizzas per week)
8.00	25
7.50	50
7.00	100
6.50	175

(b)

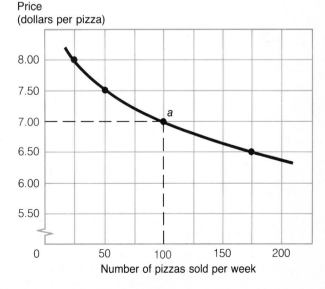

Moving to the right along the horizontal axis corresponds to an increase in the number of pizzas people will buy. The interval between each vertical grid line represents 25 additional pizzas. Moving up from the origin along the vertical axis represents an increase in price. The interval between horizontal grid lines represents $0.50. Note, however, that the first price shown is $5.50. The jagged line that interrupts the vertical axis between the origin and this price simply indicates that some of the dollar amounts have not been labeled.

Each point on the graph represents a combination of price and quantity (a price and the quantity that will be bought at that price). To plot a point, locate a price on the vertical axis and a quantity on the horizontal axis. Extend a line to the right from the price axis and up from the quantity axis. The point where the two lines intersect is the price and quantity combination for the two values you selected. (You should test your understanding of the connection between the data in the table and the points on the graph. Try your hand at plotting points on the graph.)

For example, the table shows that Paulo's customers will buy 100 pizzas each week if Paulo charges $7.00 per pizza; the corresponding point on the graph has been labeled *a*. (Be sure that you can see how point *a* represents this combination. Note that by following the dashed line down, you arrive at a quantity of 100; by following the other dashed line to the left, you arrive at a price of $7.00.) Typically,

Exhibit 1A.2
Unemployment Rate in the United States, 1960–1986

(a)

Year	Unemployment rate	Year	Unemployment rate
1960	5.4%	1975	8.3%
1961	6.5	1976	7.6
1962	5.4	1977	6.9
1963	5.5	1978	6.0
1964	5.0	1979	5.8
1965	4.4	1980	7.0
1966	3.7	1981	7.5
1967	3.7	1982	9.5
1968	3.5	1983	9.5
1969	3.4	1984	7.4
1970	4.8	1985	7.1
1971	5.8	1986	6.9
1972	5.5		
1973	4.8		
1974	5.5		

Source: Economic Report of the President, 1987, Table B-31.

when known points are plotted, a smooth line is drawn between them. In drawing the line, we assume that any intermediate point is both possible and a realistic approximation of the relationship.

On a two-dimensional graph we can show the relationship between two—and only two—variables. If we listed the variables that would influence the purchase of pizzas in this example, we would include the number of college students in Collegetown and the number of other places to eat and the prices they charge, among others. It is important to recognize that for any two-dimensional graph, the values of all variables other than the two that we are considering are held constant. In this case we see only the influence of price on the number of pizzas sold.

READING A GRAPH

Reading a graph is simply the reverse of plotting a graph. Consider the graph and table in Exhibit 1A.2, which shows the unemployment rate in the United States for the years 1960–1986. The two variables are the rate of unemployment (the dependent variable) and time (the independent variable).

To read the graph, first choose a year, say, 1980. Locate the year on the horizontal axis, then move vertically up from the horizontal axis to the line of the

(b)

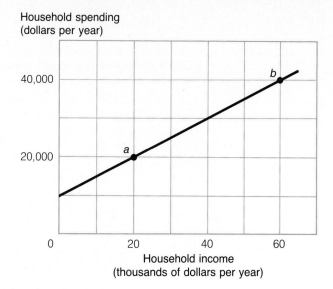

Household spending
(dollars per year)

**Exhibit 1A.3
A Model of Household Spending**

graph. At that point, move horizontally across to the vertical axis. You should find that in 1980 the unemployment rate was 7.0 percent.

Unlike Exhibit 1A.1, this is a graph of real data. The source of the data is given so that you can see where these numbers came from. The data on which the graph was based are also given, so you can practice reading the graph. Many of the graphs that you will encounter in this textbook are accompanied by data, but some are not. You must become thoroughly familiar with graphs and be able to read them if you are to understand many of the economic concepts presented. (Check your understanding by reading other points on the graph and verifying them against the data in the table. Some points lie between grid lines, so you will have to approximate some unemployment rates.)

SLOPE OF A LINE

A simple line graph shows how two variables are related. In Exhibit 1A.3 the graph shows that household spending is directly related to household income. When studying this relationship, economists will want to know how fast household spending increases when income increases. The answer to this important question is indicated by the **slope** of the line. The slope is the ratio of the change in the vertical direction to the change in the horizontal direction between two points on a straight line. For example, we can measure the slope of the line in Exhibit 1A.3 between points *a* and *b* by dividing the change in household spending—the change in the vertical direction—by the change in household income—the change

Slope. The ratio of the change in the vertical direction to the change in the horizontal direction between two points along a graph of a straight line.

in the horizontal direction. Thus

$$\text{Slope} = \frac{\text{Vertical change}}{\text{Horizontal change}}$$

$$= \frac{\text{Change in household spending (point } b - \text{ point } a)}{\text{Change in household income (point } b - \text{ point } a)}$$

$$= \frac{(\$40{,}000 - \$20{,}000)}{(\$60{,}000 - \$20{,}000)} = \frac{\$20{,}000}{\$40{,}000} = 0.50$$

The numerical value of the slope of a line is significant. A *positive slope* (as in this case) indicates that the two variables are directly related. On a graph, a positive slope is shown by a line that slopes upward and to the right (as in Exhibit 1A.3). A *negative slope* indicates that the two variables are inversely related and is shown on a graph as a line that slopes downward and to the right (as in Exhibit 1A.1).

The magnitude of the slope—a measure of the rate of change—also has economic significance. In this example, the slope measures how fast household spending increases as income increases. The value ($+0.50$) indicates the direct relationship between the two variables (more income results in more spending) and the magnitude of the relationship ($100 of additional income increases household spending by $50).

INTERCEPT OF A LINE

In a graph the point at which the line touches one of the axes is called the **intercept**. Often the intercept has economic significance. In Exhibit 1A.3 you can see that the intercept on the vertical axis shows that when household income is zero, household spending is predicted to be $10,000.

MATHEMATICAL MODELS

In addition to graphs, economists also use mathematical models to depict economic relationships. For example, an economist might describe the relationship between household spending and household income shown in Exhibit 1A.3 by the following equation.

$$C = 10 + 0.50Y$$

where the symbol C stands for household spending (in $000s) and Y for household income. In fact, this equation describes the relationship depicted in the graph. The constant term (10) is the amount of household spending when income is zero. This term represents the intercept (where the spending line touches the vertical axis). The coefficient of Y (income) is the slope of the household spending line; it says that spending increases by $0.50 for each $1 increase in income. Using the equation we predict that household spending will be $40,000 when household income is $60,000. That is,

Intercept. The point at which a line on a graph touches one of the axes.

$$C = 10 + 0.50(60) = 10 + 30 = 40 \quad \text{or} \quad \$40{,}000$$

Although the use of mathematical models in this textbook is limited to the mathematical appendices, you may find it useful to learn to use mathematical as well as graphic models in studying economics. To test your understanding of this equation and its relationship to the graph, determine (a) the level of household spending when income is $30,000 and (b) the level of income when household spending is $35,000. (The answers, which you can find from both the equation and the graph, should be (a) $25,000 of spending and (b) $50,000 of income.)

CONCLUSION

The ability to read and interpret graphs is essential to learning economics. You will have many occasions to use graphic skills. However, economics is not about graphs (or mathematical models) but about the economic relationships depicted by graphs. In addition to learning how to read graphs—and determining the value of the slope of a line—pay close attention to the economic significance of the relationships. Graphs (and mathematical models) are only tools for learning and expressing economic ideas.

KEY TERMS

Dependent variable, 18　　　　**Slope, 22**
Independent variable, 19　　　 **Intercept, 23**
Origin, 19

Scarcity and
Economic Choice

QUESTIONS TO CONSIDER

☐ What are the economic goals of every society and how are they interrelated?

☐ Why can we achieve allocative efficiency but not eliminate scarcity?

☐ What does the production possibilities curve mean to our goal of economic growth?

☐ What underlying principles do economists assume govern all economic decisions?

☐ Why do economists care more about marginal costs and benefits than absolute costs and benefits?

In Chapter 1 you learned that economics is, in part, a study of scarcity. In this chapter we take a closer look at the meaning and implications of scarcity. All societies face scarcity and, as a result, are forced to address certain basic economic questions. As we noted in Chapter 1, an important implication of scarcity is that individuals and societies are forced to make choices. In this chapter, we will look at what economists assume about how choices are made.

IMPLICATIONS OF SCARCITY

Scarcity exists because human wants are unlimited and economic resources are limited. Consequently, the individual and collective wants of a society exceed its capacity to produce goods and services. Since we can't have everything we want, we must make choices. Which wants will we satisfy and how will we use our resources?

Competition and Rationing

The limits imposed by scarcity mean that there will always be competition and rationing. Because society cannot produce all the new housing that individuals want, they have to compete for the new houses that are built. Because the amount of oil that can be produced in a specific period of time is limited, distributors and retailers must compete for the amounts that they receive. Such competition exists in every society. We are familiar with competition in market economies like that of the United States. But competition for scarce resources and products also exists in planned socialist economies like that of the Soviet Union. *Competition is inevitable and exists in all societies because of scarcity*.

Scarcity also means rationing. Rationing is the determination of how resources will be used—to produce education or new cars or national defense—and how goods and services will be distributed. But society needs criteria and mechanisms to determine how to ration resources. Scarce seats in medical schools may be rationed on the basis of college grades by an admissions committee. Distribution of new cars is rationed in the market by who will pay the highest price. Congress and the president ration the amount of national defense produced. Tickets to rock concerts are rationed partly by price, but also by a first-come, first-served process. There are many options, but *society must have some criteria and mechanism to ration every scarce resource and product.*

A study of scarcity is, in large part, a study of how competition operates and how rationing is performed. But we also want to be able to evaluate how well any rationing process operates. Economists approach the study of scarcity by assuming that a society would seek to do the best it can with its available resources. But just what is best?

In order to decide what is "best," every society must answer three questions: (1) What goods and services should be produced and in what quantities? (2) How should the goods and services be produced? (3) To whom will the goods and services be distributed? Obviously, these *fundamental economic questions* (as we shall refer to them) have many possible answers. Moreover, obtaining answers from individuals about what is best for them would be relatively easy. (You probably have a ready answer to the first and third questions, for example.) What is best from a society's perspective, however, depends on collective as well as individual values and requires recognition of certain goals.

Economic Goals

Each fundamental economic question is related to an economic goal that defines what is generally meant by the "best" answer. These goals are allocative efficiency, technical efficiency, and equity.

Allocative efficiency.   Let's begin with the question of what goods and services will be produced, or put another way: Which wants will society decide to satisfy? In seeking to answer this question in the best way, society must be careful not to waste resources on one product when another would better meet its wants. For example, we must choose between cleaner air and more autos and between more autos and more missiles. Economists define the "best" social choice by the term **allocative efficiency**. Allocative efficiency results when no other mix of goods and services that could be produced with the available resources would better satisfy society's wants. Thus the best answer to the question "What goods and services should be produced?" is the allocatively efficient mix of goods.

Defining allocative efficiency in terms of a society's wants means that different societies may choose to use their resources differently. In studying the U.S. economy, we generally define society's economic goals in terms of the wants and satisfactions of individuals. Thus allocative efficiency is achieved when no other mix of goods and services would give individuals greater total satisfaction. The economic goals of the Soviet Union, however, appear to be quite different. The concerns of Soviet leaders appear to be maximum growth of output and military strength. This choice leads to a different allocation of resources and a different mix of goods and services.

In addition, societies may use very different mechanisms for determining the goods and services to be produced. Under the U.S. economic system (market capitalism), markets are the primary mechanism for deciding what to produce. As a result, individual consumer wants greatly influence what is produced. Under the Soviet economic system (planned socialism), government officials decide what

Allocative efficiency. Producing the combination of goods and services that satisfies society's wants to the greatest degree.

Technical efficiency. Producing goods and services for the least possible cost while maintaining full utilization of resources.

Equity. Distributing goods and services in a manner considered by society to be fair.

will be produced. However, no real-world economic system is completely capitalistic or socialistic; all economies are mixed. Markets guide production of some goods and services in the Soviet Union and other socialist countries. Government determines the quantity of national defense, public education, and other public goods and services in the United States and other countries that have market economies.

Technical efficiency. A society must also decide how to produce the goods and services it wants. Because scarcity limits what can be produced, the full and effective use of available resources is important. To produce in any other way involves waste. Economists define this goal as **technical efficiency**. When a society is technically efficient, it is not possible to increase the total output of the economy for a given quantity of resources and technology. To be technically efficient, a society must produce each good and service at the lowest possible cost and maintain full utilization of resources. Technical inefficiency results when more resources than necessary are used to produce a product, when highly skilled workers perform tasks that fail to utilize their skills fully, and when resources—workers and/or machines—are allowed to remain idle.

Equity. In addition to deciding what to produce and how to produce, society must determine how goods and services are to be distributed. Since scarcity means that every want cannot be satisfied, a society must determine which wants (and whose wants) will be satisfied and which will not be satisfied. The question of distribution can also be expressed as society's desire for **equity**, that is, finding a fair or just way to distribute goods and services among its members.

Of course, deciding what is "fair" or "just" is not easy. In fact, the manner of distribution—and by implication the definition of equity—is fundamentally different in different types of economic systems. In market-oriented systems, such as the U.S. economy, equity is often associated with individual effort and productivity: The more productive you are, the greater your income will be and the more goods and services you can buy. Note that equity is not the same as equality (although a society can choose to distribute goods equally). In fact, in the United States, equality is clearly not the rule. Karl Marx defined equity as "to each according to his need," believing that the distribution system in market-oriented economies was unjust. However, productivity is still an important basis for the distribution of goods in the Soviet Union.

More so than the other questions of what and how to produce, the question of distribution is a normative one. Determining what is "fair" and "just" always involves value judgments. Positive economic theories and models can predict how goods and services are likely to be distributed, given certain economic events and government policies. But economic theories cannot decide whether the distribution is equitable. They cannot help us make those normative judgments about which manner of distribution is best.

Interrelatedness of economic goals. As with most economic choices, we often make trade-offs among economic goals. Achieving all three economic goals simultaneously can be difficult or even impossible.

Let's consider a single economic resource: soft coal. This resource has the following characteristics: (1) when mined and burned, it causes some damage to the environment; (2) in many industries it is less expensive to use than alternative

RECAP

Every society must answer three questions: (1) What goods and services should be produced and in what quantities? (2) How should the goods and services be produced? (3) To whom will the goods and services be distributed?

Allocative efficiency is achieved when no other combination of goods and services that can be produced would result in greater satisfaction of society's wants.

Technical efficiency is achieved when each good and service is produced with a minimal sacrifice of resources and when all resources are fully utilized.

Equity is achieved by distributing the goods and services produced in a manner considered by society to be fair.

fuels; and (3) it is a major, inexpensive source of heat for a large number of people.

Because clean air, clean water, and beautiful scenery are among the wants of society, the first characteristic of coal—causing environmental damage—creates a dilemma. The more soft coal we use, the fewer environmental wants we can satisfy. In seeking allocative efficiency we must ask whether our society will be better off enjoying more clean air or using more soft coal. At the same time, soft coal is less expensive for some industrial purposes than other fuels. Thus if we use less soft coal, technical efficiency will tend to decrease and our society will have to sacrifice the production of other goods. Finally, if we reduce the use of soft coal, some families will face increased heating costs and consequently a lower standard of living. Should those individuals be penalized in order to protect the environment? Is this type of trade-off equitable?

This example is typical of most economic choices facing our society and clearly shows how we are forced to make difficult trade-offs. Technical efficiency, and perhaps equity, may be improved when soft coal is used. But the costs associated with the resulting environmental damage may mean that the economy is worse off from the perspective of allocative efficiency. We can illustrate other trade-offs by examining the limits imposed on production.

Production Possibilities

We can express the limits faced by a society as a **production possibilities curve**. The economic model represented by this curve shows the various combinations of goods that an economy *can* produce during some period of time if it is technically efficient. This curve also reflects the fact that even if a nation succeeds in achieving technical efficiency, what it can produce is still limited by available resources and technology.

As with all economic models, the production possibilities curve is based on several assumptions. First, we assume that regardless of what goods society chooses to produce, it will always utilize its resources at maximum technical efficiency. Second, we assume that the supply of all resources is fixed—both in quantity and in quality—and that technology also remains constant. Finally, in order to easily depict the production possibilities, we assume that the economy produces only two goods. Like all models, the production possibilities curve cannot accurately represent a real-world economy. Economies produce more than two goods and do not always produce efficiently. However, despite these assumptions, we can use this model to illustrate some fundamental economic principles.

For the sake of discussion, let's consider the production possibilities for a hypothetical economy that produces only TV sets and ice cream. The table in Exhibit 2.1 summarizes the various combinations of TV sets and gallons of ice cream that can be produced in a year with the resources and technology available. For example, the society could produce 3 million TV sets and 15 million gallons of ice cream (combination D), or 4 million TV sets and 11 million gallons of ice cream (combination E). By transferring these data to a graph, we can illustrate the production possibilities model. We can let the horizontal axis represent the output of TV sets and the vertical axis the output of ice cream. By plotting each combination (A–G) and connecting the points with a smooth line, we get the production possibilities curve shown in Exhibit 2.1. Each point on the curve is a possible option for society; that is, it can be obtained if production is technically efficient.

Production possibilities curve. A curve showing the various combinations of output that an economy can produce with its existing resources when operating at maximum technical efficiency.

(a) Production possibilities schedule

(b) Production possibilities curve (PPC)

Possible combination	TV sets produced (millions)	Ice cream produced (millions of gallons)
A	0	21
B	1	20
C	2	18
D	3	15
E	4	11
F	5	6
G	6	0

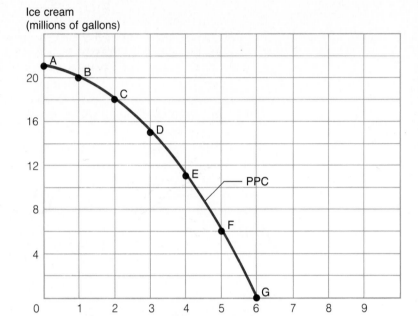

Exhibit 2.1
Production Possibilities Curve for TV Sets and Ice Cream
Each point on the production possibilities curve represents a possible combination of TV sets and ice cream that could be produced, with current resources and technology. However, these points can be reached only if the economy operates at maximum technical efficiency. The curve indicates only possibilities. It does not show what combination is best from the standpoint of allocative efficiency.

Note that the curve does not indicate which of the possible points is best. The answer to that question relates to allocative efficiency and depends on the relative values society places on the two goods. The production possibilities curve merely indicates the *possible* choices.*

Production possibilities and opportunity cost. The production possibilities curve illustrates the relationship between scarcity and opportunity cost. The curve itself reflects the limits of scarcity. For any point on the curve, we cannot produce more of one good (say, TV sets) without having to sacrifice producing some of the other good (ice cream). The magnitude of the sacrifice is the opportunity cost.

Suppose, for example, that the economy is currently producing 3 million TV sets and 15 million gallons of ice cream (combination D). What is the opportunity

---

* As you can tell by flipping through the pages of this textbook, we use many numerical examples like this one. If you are having difficulty with the graph used in this example, you should review the appendix to Chapter 1. The study guide that accompanies this textbook also contains helpful information and practice exercises on how to read and use graphs.

cost of increasing the production of TV sets to 4 million? If we move to combination E, in which 4 million TV sets are produced, the production of ice cream declines to 11 million gallons, a reduction of 4 million. In other words, to produce the extra 1 million TV sets the society must sacrifice the opportunity to have 4 million more gallons of ice cream. Thus the curve illustrates the following economic principle: *To increase the quantity of one product requires a sacrifice, or opportunity cost.*

Opportunity cost is a natural result of scarcity. Recall that for any one production possibilities curve, we assume that technology and the quantity of resources available remain unchanged. Thus by choosing to produce more of one good, the society also chooses to produce less of another. To test your understanding, calculate the opportunity cost of producing the third million TV sets, moving from point C to D. (The answer is an opportunity cost of 3 million gallons of ice cream.)

Increasing costs.   The production possibilities relationship we are using as an example also illustrates another economic principle: *The more the quantity of one product increases, the greater is the opportunity cost involved.* Exhibit 2.1 indicates that the opportunity cost of producing the first million TV sets (moving from point A to point B) is 1 million gallons of ice-cream. The opportunity cost rises as more and more TV sets are produced. In moving from point D to point E, for example, the opportunity cost of 1 million more TV sets is 4 million gallons of ice cream.

Why do opportunity costs increase? First, most workers, either by nature or by training, are better at one job than another. For example, a person trained to assemble TV sets is not likely to be as skilled an ice-cream maker as one with training in that field. In order to expand the production of TV sets, the society must (at full employment) move some workers (and other resources) from making ice cream to making TV sets. Workers better suited to assembling TV sets will be moved first. But continued expansion of TV-set production will mean moving workers who are less skilled in making TV sets and more skilled in making ice cream, resulting in higher costs. The cost of TV sets will rise both because more workers will be needed to make another 1 million TV sets and because the last workers switched to making TV sets could have produced more ice cream than the first workers moved. The same reasoning applies to other resources. Machines used to make ice cream cannot be used to manufacture TV sets, for example. As you will find, increasing cost characterizes many economic activities.

Technical inefficiency.   Although we have focused only on those combinations that lie on the production possibilities curve, every combination of TV sets and gallons of ice cream in the shaded area of Exhibit 2.2 (the area inside—to the left of—the production possibilities curve) can be produced. The combinations on the curve are *maximum* production levels that can be reached only if the society achieves technical efficiency. Whenever production is technically inefficient, the society will find that it cannot reach these limits.

For example, suppose that the actual output of the society is 11 million gallons of ice cream and 2 million TV sets (shown in Exhibit 2.2 as point U). This combination means that the society is not producing all its potential output. In fact, the economy could produce more TV sets and the same amount of ice cream (that is, a move to point E) or more ice cream and the same number of TV sets (a move to point C). It is even possible to produce more of both items (point D).

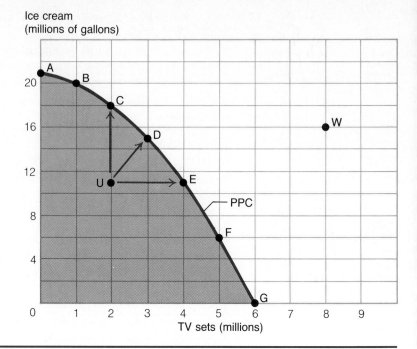

Exhibit 2.2
Production Possibilities and Inefficiency
The production possibilities curve (PPC) represents the maximum limits of production, assuming maximum technical efficiency. If society is inefficient, less than the maximum will be produced (point U). Society can produce more TV sets or ice cream or both, if technical efficiency is increased. Points outside the curve (point W) are beyond society's production possibilities for the current state of technology and the current supply of resources.

In short, the society is not achieving technical efficiency (the maximum output attainable from a given quantity of resources) whenever actual production is within the limits of the production possibilities curve (in the shaded area of the graph).

Technical inefficiency can occur if some workers are unemployed or if production of one or both goods unnecessarily wastes resources. By eliminating inefficiency, a society can increase its output of one or both of the goods.

Production possibilities and economic growth. For any particular production possibilities curve, production is limited because we assume that the society has a fixed supply of resources and a certain level of technology. This means that at any one time, points beyond the production possibilities curve (points to the right of the curve) cannot be obtained. For example, point W in Exhibit 2.2, representing 8 million TV sets and 16 million gallons of ice cream, is currently unattainable. This is not to say that the society can never achieve that level of production, but rather that it cannot do so currently, owing to the constraints of existing technology and resources.

What happens, however, if the quantity of resources increases, the quality of resources improves, or technology progresses? For example, what happens if the number of workers in the society increases, the current workers receive additional training, or someone discovers a more efficient way to make TV sets or ice cream? As illustrated in Exhibit 2.3, these changes would expand the production possibilities of the society and result in an outward (to the right) shift in the production possibilities curve (from PPC_1 to PPC_2). If the society had been producing at point E_1 on the original curve (4 million TV sets and 11 million gallons of ice cream), it would now be possible to expand ice-cream production to 20 million gallons without reducing the quantity of TV sets produced (point C_2), or to expand

Exhibit 2.3
Production Possibilities and Economic Growth
Any production possibilities curve (PPC) is based on the assumption that the level of technology and the supply of resources are fixed. When either technology improves or the supply of resources increases, society can produce more. This change is illustrated as an outward shift in the production possibilities curve (from PPC$_1$ to PPC$_2$). When economic growth occurs, society can produce more of one product without sacrificing any amount of the other product, or it can have more of both products.

production to 8 million TV sets while producing the same quantity of ice cream (point E$_2$). Either of these combinations—or any other combination on the new production possibilities curve—is a possible option. The changes in technology or availability of resources results in **economic growth**. Economic growth increases society's production possibilities, that is, the ability to satisfy more of society's wants.

Economic growth: Capital resources versus consumer products.
Economic growth may result from obtaining more natural resources, more highly skilled labor, or better technology. In addition, economic growth may result if a society produces more capital resources in the form of factories and equipment. An increase in the quantity of capital resources increases the capacity to produce. By investing more in capital resources today, society can produce more consumer goods and services in the future.

However, as with all economic choices, this trade-off means sacrifice. We cannot produce more capital resources without sacrificing some **consumer products**—food, cars, movies, and health care, for example—that are produced to satisfy society's current wants. Scarcity forces a trade-off between satisfying wants now or in the future. We can have more consumer products tomorrow if we produce more capital resources today. The effect of today's choice on tomorrow's production possibilities is illustrated in Exhibit 2.4.

The possibilities shown on this graph are consumer products (on the vertical axis) and capital resources (on the horizontal axis). The current production possibilities curve is labeled PPC$_1$. Two current options for the economy are labeled A and B on PPC$_1$. If society chooses option A, it will produce more consumer products and fewer capital resources than if it chooses option B. The results of

Economic growth. An increase in society's production possibilities.

Consumer products. Goods such as autos, food, appliances, and movies, and services such as health care that directly satisfy consumer wants.

Quantity of consumer products

PPC₁ PPC_A PPC_B

A

B

Quantity of capital resources

Exhibit 2.4
Capital Resources and Economic Growth
The economy's current production possibility is shown as PPC₁. Today, society must choose between two options: producing more consumer products (option A) or more capital resources (option B). The selection of either option will determine future production possibilities, shown as PPC_A or PPC_B. For example, society will experience greater economic growth if it chooses to produce more capital resources. But there is a price: The opportunity cost of more growth is less production of consumer products today.

this choice are shown as PPC_A, or the future production possibilities of the economy. However, if society chooses option B, it can further increase its production possibilities (to PPC_B) in the future; it will have produced more capital resources and thus increased its production potential.

Is society better off choosing option B? Not necessarily. Society must sacrifice consumer goods and services today in order to achieve greater production potential tomorrow. We can say only that the economy will be better off in the future but worse off today if option B is selected. Producing more capital resources today requires a willingness to sacrifice temporarily the production of some quantity of consumer products that would increase satisfaction today. The current wants that could have been satisfied represent the opportunity cost associated with the decision to increase capital spending.

All societies face this dilemma: To increase society's capital resources requires a sacrifice; to be able to produce more goods next year, we must consume less today. But all societies do not make the same choices. Production of capital resources accounts for about 16 percent of all output in the United States but about 35 percent in the Soviet Union. The higher output of capital resources in the Soviet Union has helped the Soviet economy achieve a relatively high rate of growth. This growth has come at the expense of satisfaction of individual wants because the production of consumer products is relatively low in the Soviet Union.

A production possibilities curve indicates the various combinations of goods that can be produced with the available resources and technology, assuming that society operates at maximum technical efficiency.

Points inside the curve (to the left) represent technical inefficiency. Points outside the curve (to the right) cannot be obtained with the resources and technology available.

The opportunity cost of increasing output of one good or service is measured as the amount of the other good or service that must be sacrificed.

Economic growth results from increasing the quantity or quality of resources, the production of capital resources, and development of better technology. Economic growth causes the production possibilities curve to shift outward (to the right).

If we assume that these differences reflect the preferences of the two societies, it would seem that growth has a higher priority in the Soviet Union and satisfying current consumer wants has a higher priority in the United States.

Production possibilities: To work or not to work?   At any one time society's production possibilities reflect levels of technology and resources. One of the important resources is labor—the skills, talents, physical effort, and time of individuals. We could increase the total output of the economy if everyone were willing to devote 10 percent more time to producing goods and services. In Japan, for example, the typical employee works 2250 hours per year compared to only 1900 hours in the United States. Increasing the number of hours worked would involve a cost: We would have to sacrifice other uses of our time. This sacrifice might include leisure activities, such as going to the beach, skiing, or reading a book for pleasure. It might also affect other activities—gardening, studying economics, or painting your house—that are not exactly leisure but clearly have value. Should we spend more time working? Would the extra benefits from the increase in output be worth the sacrifice? We cannot easily answer such questions but should be alert for economic events that may affect such personal decisions. Some economists, for example, believe that very high tax rates, such as those in Sweden and Great Britain, reduce the amount people work and thus affect not only current output but also future economic growth.

ECONOMIC CHOICE

Because production possibilities are limited, individuals and society must make choices. Economists want to understand how choices are made so they can predict the economy's response to economic events. Economists believe that decision making can be best understood and predicted by assuming that individuals apply the principles of **rational choice**, as discussed in this section.

Self-Interest

As we mentioned earlier, all decisions are ultimately made by individuals. Individual consumers decide what goods and services to buy. Individual business managers decide what goods and services to produce and how to produce them. Individual government officials decide what government goods and services to provide and what laws and regulations will govern economic and noneconomic actions. Economists believe that individual choices can be best understood by assuming that *individuals act in their own self-interest to gain what they see as the maximum advantage from the resources they control.*

It is easy to misunderstand what economists mean by rational choice. Some people wrongly interpret it as the economist's belief that individuals are selfish and greedy. No doubt some are, but self-interest does not exclude actions by individuals to make gifts or serve the "public interest." Even in those activities, economists see self-interest at work. Individuals give gifts because they get satisfaction from doing so. They may volunteer time and money to worthy causes because of the emotional benefits they receive. The idea of self-interest is important in developing a model of choice because it helps us to understand how individuals react to changes in economic conditions.

Rational choice. Selecting among economic alternatives by comparing extra benefits expected to be received with extra costs expected to be incurred; an economic model used to explain the choices made by individuals, businesses, and government.

Minimizing Costs and Maximizing Benefits

In assuming that individuals make rational choices, economists mean that decision makers choose deliberately, intending to "economize." That is, *people seek to minimize the costs of attaining any objective and to maximize the benefits of any expenditure*.

If individuals act rationally in their own self-interest, we can predict how they will react to changes in economic conditions. An increase in benefits or a decrease in costs will result in more activity; a decrease in benefits or an increase in costs will mean less activity. Thus rational choice theory allows economists to understand economic behavior and to predict the effect of changes in economic circumstances, including government policies.

For example, we predict that more individuals will attend college when expected salaries of college graduates increase. We expect members of Congress to be more likely to vote in favor of a particular bill if it is changed to increase their chances of reelection. We expect a business to produce more computers when the profits they expect to earn are greater.

At the same time, we can expect predictable responses to changes in costs. If your instructor announces a major exam for the next class period, the cost of skipping class will rise, and we can predict fewer absences. A decrease in personal computer prices will spur a major growth in sales. Government imposition of a new tax on imported automobiles will cause consumers to buy fewer foreign cars.

Rational Expectations

Because we live in an uncertain world, individuals cannot always know exactly what benefits and costs are associated with a choice. Thus *decisions are made on the basis of expectations*.

When you decide to pay $5 to see a new movie, economists say that you expect to receive at least $5 of benefits. Of course, you can be disappointed and believe after you saw the movie that it wasn't worth $5, but like most decisions, this one was made based on expectations. Similarly, when a business decides to produce a new product, it does so because it expects consumers to buy enough of the product at a high enough price to earn the firm a reasonable profit. A firm cannot be sure that it will earn a profit. Future prices and costs are uncertain. But a decision to produce is based on *expected* benefits and *expected* costs. You will find many occasions to note the effect of expectations on economic choices.

Marginal Costs and Benefits

Economists suggest that individuals making rational choices select those options for which the expected *extra* benefits outweigh the expected *extra* costs. Economists use the term **marginal** (meaning extra) because they recognize that few decisions require an all-or-nothing choice. You do not have to choose between eating 10 pizzas or none, for example. You can choose to eat 1, 2, or more. Moreover, you can choose incrementally, that is, you can eat one pizza before ordering a second one. When deciding whether to buy a second pizza, you would, following the principles of rational choice, consider how much additional satisfaction the second pizza would provide.

Marginal. A term used by economists to denote *extra* or *additional*.

The principles of rational choice also imply that economic choice involves considering only those factors that are likely to change as a result of a particular decision. For example, in deciding whether to attend your next economics class, the tuition payment you made at the beginning of the term is irrelevant because it will not change. In deciding whether to come to class, you would weigh the extra benefits of attending against the extra costs, and would not be concerned with anything not affected by the decision.

Economic Approach to Decision Making

Economists use this model of rational choice in two ways. First, by assuming that decision makers use this model, economists can derive other economic principles. In Chapter 5 we show how this model implies that smoothly functioning markets tend to result in allocative efficiency, for example. But the model of rational choice can also be used by individuals, business managers, and government officials to improve their economic choices.

The economic approach to decision making recognizes that each decision involves at least two possible options. The first step in making a rational choice is to list and evaluate the available options. For example, if you are hungry you may satisfy your hunger in several ways. Before deciding which is the best way, you consider your options.

Economists also recognize that options are mutually exclusive. That is, if one option is chosen, another one is precluded. If you choose to spend $5 on a movie, you cannot spend that same $5 to buy a book. In other words, each option chosen has an associated opportunity cost—an option that must be sacrificed. Thus the value of any one option must be compared to that of other options. Most importantly, considering opportunity cost reminds us that we cannot simply have cleaner air or more national defense or more clothes or more vacations. Every time we choose to have more of any one item, we have to accept less of another. Most of the time, those who argue that "there's no substitute for …" fail to recognize opportunity cost and fail to apply the principles of rational choice.

Economists also assume that decision makers have a particular goal or goals in mind. For example, economists most often assume that businesses seek to earn maximum profits. The goal of profits helps the business manager to determine how to value benefits and costs.

Finally, the model of rational choice suggests that decision makers collect information on the expected extra benefits and the expected extra costs of each option. This notion implies that they focus on those benefits and costs that *change* as a result of the decision they make. That is, the costs that remain constant are irrelevant. If a business uses the same machines and the same building regardless of the product made, there are no relevant costs for the building or machines. If we calculate marginal costs and compare them with marginal benefits, we can determine what information is relevant to a decision. Those who argue that "we can't forget what we've already spent on this project …" fail to focus on expected extra benefits and costs and, as a result, may make serious errors.

When collecting information, we must apply the same basic principles, weighing both benefits and costs. Typically, the potential benefits of collecting information are greater when there is more uncertainty initially. For example, we spend more time collecting information on the price and availability of new cars than we do for a newspaper. Acquiring information can also be expensive. For example, how much time and money would you have to spend to personally obtain information on the safety of a new prescription drug? In some cases, we consult individuals—such as stock brokers—who specialize in information. In other cases—such as finding the best buy in a new car—we tend to rely on our own efforts. The important point is that information is expensive. We collect only as much information as we can justify on the basis of extra benefits and extra costs.

In summary, the following steps represent an economic model of decision making.

1. Identify the several alternatives, or possible choices.

2. For each alternative, estimate the expected extra benefits and the expected extra costs, remembering to use the concept of opportunity cost and applying benefit–cost judgment to the collection of information.

3. Whenever the extra benefits of an alternative are expected to outweigh the extra costs—and this difference exceeds that for other options—that alternative has an advantage over the other options and should be accepted.

As you study economics, you will come across many applications of rational choice principles. Economists apply these principles in describing consumer choice, producer choice, and public choice. Although the circumstances differ, the principles remain a constant guide for making choices. Of course, when developing this model of rational choice, economists had to depart from reality to some extent. The model cannot predict the behavior of an individual consumer, who may act on whim and who is probably unable to obtain all the information available about all possible options. However, the model of rational choice does a good job of predicting behavior of consumers as a group. The purpose of any model is to predict, and evidence indicates that this model—and others based on rational choice principles—are good predictors. The use of rational choice principles is illustrated in A Case in Point: How Many Prisons to Build?

Rational Public Choice

Consumers and businesses and are not the only ones faced with economic choices. Even in the United States, where most economic decisions are made by individuals acting in their own private interests, political decisions have important effects on the economy. The federal, state, and local governments purchase about 20 percent of the nation's goods and services and employ about 25 percent of the labor force. Government laws and regulation limit many individual choices. We must understand public choice, as well as private choice, if we are to understand how our economy operates.

From the perspective of the economy as a whole, a socially desirable law or government decision would increase society's benefits more than its costs. But economists recognize that such decisions are made by individuals—politicians and government officials. In fact, a whole body of theory called **public choice theory** relates to how decisions are made in the public (government) sector. Public choice theory assumes that all individuals act in their own self-interest and uses this assumption to predict the behavior of voters and the choices of government officials.

Public choice theory. An economic theory based on rational choice principles that attempts to explain how choices are made in the public (government) sector.

A Case in Point
How Many Prisons to Build?

To illustrate the application of the principles of rational choice, consider the following situation. A state is considering building one or two additional prisons and has collected accurate information on the total benefits and costs to society. The cost of building one prison is $50 million; the cost of two, $120 million. This information is presented in the table below. Stop reading for a minute, consider the information and the options available, and decide what you think the state should do. Refer if necessary to the discussion on rational choice.

Benefits and Costs of Building More Prisons in the State

Number of new prisons	Total social benefits	Total social costs
0	—	—
1	$100 million	$ 50 million
2	150 million	120 million

How many prisons do you think the state should build? If you understood the principles of rational choice and are beginning to think like an economist, you decided that the state should build only one additional prison. Let's examine each option separately, weighing the extra benefits and extra costs.

Consider first the choice of building one additional prison. When the first new prison is built, the social benefits increase by $100 million, whereas the social costs rise by only $50 million. (Note that there are neither costs nor benefits if no new prisons are built.) By building the first prison, society gains $50 million, or $100 million of extra benefits less $50 million of extra costs. (Note that this conclusion is based on the fact that *all* costs and benefits have been included in the table.)

If two prisons were built, total benefits are still greater than total costs. But focusing on *extra* benefits and costs, you can see why it does not make economic sense to build the second prison. The extra benefits of the second prison are only $50 million (total benefits increase from $100 million to $150 million). However, society has to incur an extra cost of $70 million ($120 million for two prisons versus $50 million for one). Thus the second prison adds $50 million in extra benefits but $70 million in extra costs. Seen in this light, the second prison is clearly not a good idea. This example, although simple, is very important. The principles of rational choice that it illustrates are central to the study of economics.

Public choice theory suggests that the public choices made are not always those that are best for society as a whole. For example, a special interest group, such as the owners of a local sports team, will benefit greatly if the city builds a new sports arena with public funds. Individual taxpayers bear the costs, but no single taxpayer pays much more. Public choice theory predicts the owners (who will gain a lot) will lobby strongly. Taxpayers (who each lose a little) have less incentive to make their opinions known. The result, according to public choice theory, is predictable—there are many such public facilities.

Ultimately, politicians—elected officials, not professional economists—determine economic policy. As we have already stated, economic analysis often does not lead to a single conclusion. In Chapter 1 we noted some of the reasons why economists disagree on policy issues. The tendency of economists to note both benefits and costs led President Harry Truman to wish for a one-armed economist because he got tired of hearing economists say "on the one hand . . ., but on the other, ..." Even if economists agreed on the facts and used the same economic models, the normative, equity issues of any policy choice always raise issues of benefits and costs that cannot be decided by economic theory. Under our form of

RECAP

Economic behavior can be explained and predicted by the model of rational choice.

The model is based on the assumption that individuals act in their own self-interest and weigh expected extra benefits against expected extra costs.

To make a rational decision, options should be listed and evaluated in terms of expected extra benefits and costs. Cost must be defined as opportunity cost.

government, decisions about which segments of society to favor are left to the political process.

For example, in 1986 Congress passed a tax "reform" bill, seeking to raise the same total amount of tax revenues in a simpler, "fairer" manner. But in order to raise the same total amount of funds, it was necessary for every decrease in taxes paid by one group to be balanced by an increase in taxes paid by another group. If the poor were to pay less, other groups would have to pay more. Economic models were used to predict the effects of various policy changes. That is, the models enabled economists to make some positive statements about the "facts." But decisions about the normative aspects of the legislation—whether such changes were "good"—were necessarily political judgments.

Unfortunately, the political decision-making process adds a new set of goals and potential conflicts. These conflicts sometimes cause politicians and government officials to make choices that meet their personal objectives but not society's economic goals. Policies that make good economic sense may not meet political objectives such as attempting to ensure reelection, rewarding political friends, or penalizing political opponents. One of the most important aspects of this economics course is to enable you to understand the differences between economic theory and political reality. Politicians will be more willing to implement sound economic policy if they believe that the voters understand and accept economic realities.

Although economists cannot always determine which policies are best, sound application of economic principles can be a useful guide to policy making. If politicians focus on the expected extra benefits and costs of policies they are considering, they can avoid many mistakes. Economic reasoning tells politicians not to ignore the costs of policies (although some critics of government argue that this occurs frequently). Economic analysis can be used to predict whether a policy is likely to have the desired effects. Clearly, a policy that fails to achieve its purpose is undesirable. In addition, economic models can be used to forecast the results of several policy options, helping politicians find the one that achieves their objective at minimum cost and thus helping society achieve allocative efficiency.

RATIONAL CHOICE IN ACTION

As you have seen, rational choice requires recognition of scarcity and opportunity cost. In the following examples, we note the presence of scarcity, some of the options that may be considered, and the opportunity cost involved.

Example 1: A personal decision.   When you plan the expenditures you will make during the next month, you personally face the problem of scarcity. Your expenditures are limited by your income and by any savings you have. (We should add, of course, that the possibility of borrowing may exist, but for this example, we assume that the bank will consider you to be a poor credit risk.) You would very much like to have a stereo system that costs $450. Obviously obtaining the stereo will require a sacrifice.

While considering this option, you will, of course, want to consider how much it will cost. "That's easy," you say, "because I know the price is $450." But is $450 the *real* cost? An economist would recognize it as the monetary cost but suggest that you also think of the cost in terms of the satisfaction you might gain from spending the money in another way (on a skiing trip during winter vacation, for example). That is, the real sacrifice, or opportunity cost involved in buying the stereo is the value of the next best opportunity, or the most important alternative use of the scarce resources you have. Be careful not to confuse monetary cost with opportunity cost. Although these costs are sometimes related, they are not the same. Rational choice requires that you examine the opportunity cost.

Example 2: A public decision.   A second example of the concepts of scarcity and opportunity cost is the dilemma faced by Congress when trying to decide whether to spend an additional $3 billion on a particular public-works program. Consider, for example, the arguments of Senator Porkbarrel, a distinguished (but economically illiterate) member of Congress: "We must go ahead with this project, there *are* no substitutes. We've sunk too much money in the program to quit now. The benefits of the project to this great nation are incalculable."

In his statement, Senator Porkbarrel violated the principles of rational choice in three ways. First, his argument that there are no options ignores the fact that there are alternative ways to meet the objectives of virtually any program. Moreover, the Senator is acting as though scarcity is not a problem. Whether Congress explicitly recognizes it or not, scarcity means that the resources used by this program cannot be used for another public program or by the private sector.

Second, in his zeal to have Congress approve the project, the Senator wants his colleagues to consider the money already spent. The money already spent, however, cannot be recovered and used for another purpose. The Senate should focus its attention on the expected *extra* benefits and costs, according to the principles of rational choice. Because the money spent in the past cannot be recovered, it is neither an extra benefit nor an extra cost associated with the program.

Finally, Senator Porkbarrel engages in an old trick. Because he favors the program, he emphasizes the benefits of the program but ignores the costs. Rational decision makers must learn to be skeptical of such one-sided statements. Before making any decision the Senate needs to know both the expected extra benefits *and* the expected extra costs. Every expenditure has an opportunity cost.

In measuring the cost of this program, an economist would not really be interested in the monetary cost, the $3 billion. Instead, an economist would ask: "What will be sacrificed?" If Congress spends the additional $3 billion on this project, what other government projects may have to be delayed or scrapped? What is the value to individuals of the goods and services they could obtain with lower taxes? Because of scarcity, Congress should think of the sacrifice required to make any particular choice, that is, in terms of its opportunity cost.

CONCLUSION

In later chapters, we continue the discussion of the principles of rational choice in analyzing how economic systems function, because the choices made by consumers, business managers, and government officials are the driving forces of the economy. By better understanding how rational choices are made, we can better determine the effects on the economy of changes in economic conditions. Scarcity, we have seen, forces society to make choices. If society is to achieve the economic goals of allocative efficiency, technical efficiency, and equity, it must have some mechanism for determining wants and the relative scarcity of resources and for ensuring efficient production. One such mechanism, the use of markets, is the primary choice of the United States and most Western European nations, although there are other options. We devote the next three chapters principally to discussing how markets work.

SUMMARY

1. In this chapter we discussed the implications of scarcity and introduced the principles of rational choice.

2. Because of scarcity, three fundamental economic questions face all societies: (a) what goods and services to produce, (b) how to produce them, and (c) to whom they should be distributed. Related to these questions are the goals of allocative efficiency, technical efficiency, and equity.

3. Allocative efficiency is achieved when society obtains the greatest possible satisfaction from the available resources. Technical efficiency requires that each product be produced with the least sacrifice of resources and that all resources be fully utilized. Equity requires that goods and services be distributed fairly and justly but not necessarily equally. Achieving all three goals simultaneously may be difficult or even impossible.

4. A production possibilities curve shows the limits imposed by scarcity as the maximum combination of goods and services that can be produced with a particular quantity and quality of resources and the best technology available. Each point on the curve shows the economy operating at maximum technical efficiency.

5. The production possibilities model indicates that even if society achieves technical efficiency, all wants cannot be satisfied; that increased production of one good or service requires a sacrifice or opportunity cost of less production of another good or service; that failure to achieve technical efficiency imposes costs; and that economic growth—attainable by increasing the quantity or quality of resources, producing capital resources instead of consumer products, or developing new technology—can ease but not eliminate the problem of scarcity.

6. Economists believe that economic behavior can be best understood by assuming that individuals apply the principles of rational choice. According to this model, individuals act in their own self-interest. They respond predictably to changes in benefits and costs: Increases in benefits and/or reductions in costs will cause indi-

viduals to undertake more of any activity. The model is also based on the assumption that individuals react to expected benefits and costs. They make one-time or incremental decisions by focusing on these extra, or marginal, benefits and costs.

7. In order to make a rational economic choice, a decision maker must consider the most important alternative. For each option, the expected extra (marginal) benefits and expected extra (marginal) costs must be calculated and compared. Cost must be defined as opportunity cost. An option should be selected only when marginal benefits exceed marginal costs.

8. Economic analysis cannot always indicate which government policy is best because equity issues are normative and not subject to objective theorizing. Thus government officials—both elected and appointed—make many decisions about national economic policy. In keeping with the principles of rational choice, we can expect politicians to act in their self-interest in making public choices. Rational economic analysis can help guide public decision making by indicating the effects of current and proposed policies and by helping public decision makers avoid mistakes, such as failing to consider only extra costs or ignoring either benefits or costs.

KEY TERMS

Allocative efficiency, 27
Technical efficiency, 28
Equity, 28
Production possibilities curve, 29
Economic growth, 33
Consumer products, 33
Rational choice, 35
Marginal, 36
Public choice theory, 38

QUESTIONS FOR REVIEW AND DISCUSSION

1. Economists assume that economic resources are limited and that human wants are unlimited. Explain how the following statements indicate a misunderstanding of these assumptions.
   a) The development of technology offers a solution to the problem of scarcity.
   b) Economists are wrong to assume that wants are unlimited, because I have all the food I want to eat at each meal.
   c) Not all resources are scarce; consider the unlimited nature of the universe.

2. How do the three economic goals discussed in this chapter provide ideal answers to the three fundamental economic questions?

3. If all producers have achieved maximum technical efficiency, does allocative efficiency exist? If society has attained both allocative efficiency and technical efficiency, has the goal of equity also been reached?

4. Consider the statement: "The best things in life are free—air, a beautiful sunset, libraries, free speech. Moreover, other things ought to be free—such as medical care."
   a) Some goods are available at a zero price (you do not have to give anyone money to obtain them). Does this mean that the goods are free? Why or why not?
   b) What are the costs of libraries, free speech, and air? Who pays these costs?
   c) Can the government make medical care available at no cost to the user? Can the government make medical care free to society? Explain the difference between these two questions.

5. Consider the oportunity costs of going to college. What are some of the important expenditures you must make? What are some of the other costs involved? (Be sure to carefully note where and why the list of opportunity costs and the list of expenditures differ.)

6. If economists can so easily define the goals of a society, why is it so difficult to achieve them? If you and I agree that allocative efficiency is a desirable social goal, do we necessarily agree on what mix of goods and services should be produced?

7. In which (if any) of the following situations would you say that resources are not fully employed?
   a) A college student chooses to study full time rather than combine school and work.
   b) A parent of a preschool-age child chooses to work only at home.
   c) A 70-year-old couple retires from a lifetime of work in order to enjoy leisure.
   d) A worker trades an opportunity to work overtime on Saturday for a chance to go on a family camping trip.

8. Based on the following data, draw a production possibilities curve. Label the horizontal axis "guns" and the vertical axis "butter." Using the curve, answer the following questions.

Butter (millions of pounds)	Guns (millions)
0	30
1	25
2	15
3	0

   a) Can the economy produce 35 million guns? Can it produce 4 million pounds of butter? Can it produce 25 million guns and 1 million pounds of butter?
   b) What is the opportunity cost of producing 3 million pounds of butter instead of 2 million? Of producing 25 million guns instead of 15 million?
   c) How does the cost of butter change as more is produced?
   d) Which, if any, of the points on the curve are "best" for society? (Consider the question from the perspective of each of the three economic goals presented in this chapter.)
   e) Label the point on the graph where society is producing 1 million pounds of butter and 10 million guns as U. What does this point tell you about technical efficiency?
   f) How would the production possibilities curve change if new technology increased the productive potential of the economy? (Draw a new curve on the graph to indicate this new possibilities curve.) What other factors could cause this shift?

9. For each of the following social choices, note how two (or more) economic goals are in conflict.
   a) A choice between spending more for national defense or social welfare programs.
   b) A choice between protecting fishing grounds in New England and the Gulf of Mexico and developing offshore oil wells to provide more energy.
   c) A choice between higher taxes to build highways and bridges and lower taxes. (*Note:* Lower taxes mean that households would have additional income.)
   d) In what way(s) are such conflicts resolved?

10. Explain how, if at all, each of the following will affect a society's production possibilities. Also, indicate some of the opportunity costs involved, if any.
    a) Owing to increased exploration efforts, new supplies of natural resources are discovered.
    b) Society devotes more production to capital goods.
    c) Businesses devote fewer resources to research and development.
    d) The federal government increases expenditures on education and training.
    e) The economy fails to maintain full employment.

11. Applying the principles of rational choice to each of the following situations, what extra benefits and extra costs would need to be measured and compared?
    a) Whether to increase taxes in order to increase financial support for the state university.
    b) Whether (from a firm's perspective) to produce and sell a new product.
    c) Whether (from a family's perspective) to spend $500 for a vacation this year or to put that money in the bank to help pay for the future college education of two of its members.

12. Based on the following data and the principles of rational choice, how many miles of highway should the state build next year? (Assume that the data accurately measure *all* social costs and benefits.)

Number of miles	Total social costs	Total social benefits
1000	$100,000,000	$500,000,000
2000	250,000,000	700,000,000
3000	450,000,000	850,000,000

13. Explain how each of the following statements fails to apply the principles of rational choice correctly. (*Hint:* Rational choice requires a comparison of extra benefits *and* extra costs.)
    a) The more capital goods we have, the more goods we can produce in the future; therefore we should devote most of our current production to capital goods.
    b) We shouldn't build the proposed dam because there'll be some environmental costs.
    c) The city council mustn't cut the budgets of the police and fire departments. Those services are absolutely essential.

14. When discussing rational choice, we noted that individuals respond in predictable ways to changes in benefits and costs. Try using this simple proposition to analyze the actions that you would expect to occur if the price of oil is expected to rise significantly in the near future.
    a) What actions would you take? Would you expect other individuals to take similar actions?
    b) What actions would you expect businesses to take? (Consider the actions of oil producers separately from those of other businesses.)
    c) Why would economists say that all these actions are the results of efforts to "economize"? What does this word mean to you?

3

Laws of Demand
and Supply

QUESTIONS TO CONSIDER

☐ How does demand differ from wants?

☐ What factors affect quantity demanded? Demand?

☐ What factors affect quantity supplied? Supply?

☐ Why is equilibrium important in a market economy?

☐ How do government price ceilings and supports affect equilibrium price and quantity supplied?

Because we live in a world of scarcity, we must choose among alternative uses of scarce resources. We must decide how best to use our own resources to meet our individual goals. Society must decide what to produce, how to produce it, and to whom to distribute the goods and services produced. But how are these decisions made? In the United States and many other nations, households and businesses make most of the production, consumption, and resource allocation decisions by exchanging—or trading—in a **market**.

Markets do not always work perfectly. Nor is a **market economy** the only mechanism for answering economic questions. The economic systems of the Soviet Union and China, for example, rely heavily on central economic planning. Government authorities fix wages and prices, establish production levels, and ration products. Moreover, even in the United States, government is involved to some extent in setting prices and determining quantities produced. Nevertheless, we stress the operation of a market system in this textbook because a knowledge of markets is basic to understanding how our economy functions.

Trading, the core of any market economy, is a fundamental economic activity. You may agree to trade an hour of your time to help a friend with mathematics in exchange for an hour of help in studying for your economics exam. You may give the local grocery store $20 in exchange for a small bag of groceries. In any economy, millions and millions of such trades occur each day.

When trading, the parties involved must agree on a **price**, which is the amount of one item that an individual is willing to sacrifice to obtain another item. For example, if you are willing to sacrifice one hour of your time in exchange for one hour of help with your economics studies, the price of the exchange is one hour. An item has a price attached to its use because of scarcity; that is, an item such as time is not unlimited, so some sacrifice must be made if the item is used. The price reflects the *opportunity cost* of the sacrifice being made.

Of course, many exchanges take place in markets larger than two persons. Indeed, people often think of geographical places when they think of markets— the local grocery market, a flea market, or the stock market. Economists use the concept of a market to represent the trading that occurs between potential buyers and sellers. There are markets for resources—such as materials, labor time, and machinery—and for products—such as autos, haircuts, and restaurant meals. The markets for many products—autos, video cassette recorders, and wheat, for example—are international in scope. They represent trading between buyers and sellers in many countries.

Market. The interaction of buyers (market demand) and sellers (market supply) which determines a price and quantity exchanged.

Market economy. An economy in which households and businesses interact in markets to determine prices and thus answer the fundamental economic questions of what and how much to produce, how to produce it, and to whom to distribute goods and services.

Price. The amount of one item that an individual will sacrifice in order to obtain another item and often stated in terms of the quantity of money that must be sacrificed.

46

When describing a market, economists use the concept of demand to represent the behavior of buyers and the concept of supply to represent the behavior of sellers. Each participant in the market seeks to gain from exchange. Buyers, of course, want the lowest price possible; sellers, the highest price. The interaction of buyers and sellers in markets establishes a market price, generally stated in terms of a unit of money—dollars and cents in the United States. Markets also determine how much of each product is produced.

Consider a few economic questions. Why have prices of computers and video recorders fallen in the past few years? Why do hotels and airlines raise their prices during peak travel seasons? How do rent controls affect the quantity and quality of rental housing available? To answer these questions you must understand the concepts of demand and supply and how they interact to determine market prices.

DEMAND

Like other economic terms, demand has a specific and technical meaning. To an economist, **demand** means *the quantities* of a product that buyers are both *willing and able to buy* at *every possible price* during a *specified period of time*, with *all other things unchanged*. Each phrase in this definition is important to understanding how economists define and use the concept of demand.

Noneconomists often use the term *demand* to refer to a specific quantity. A sales representative, for example, may say that local customers demand 300 new cars per month. To an economist, demand is not a single, specific quantity but a *series* of price and quantity combinations. Can you say how many new automobiles you will buy next year or how many all U.S. consumers will buy without knowing the price? Would you expect different answers if the average price of a new car were $50,000 rather than $5000?

Economists recognize that the number of new cars bought during a specific period of time depends on price. In fact, because economists are especially interested in how quantity purchased changes with price, they define demand as a relationship between price and quantity. Thus the term **quantity demanded** refers to a particular quantity that consumers will buy at a particular price during a particular time. The distinction between demand and quantity demanded is important, and we explain it further later in this section.

It is also important to recognize that in the definition of demand we refer to quantities that buyers are "willing and able to buy." Consumers buy products to satisfy some want, but wanting is not the same as demanding. To demand a product, a buyer must not only want it, but must be willing and able to make the necessary sacrifice to obtain the product. For example, it matters little that you want a private yacht or an expensive automobile if you are unable or unwilling to make the sacrifice necessary to buy it. Economists stress the importance of distinguishing between demand and wants. (So do economics professors in making up exam questions, a fact that might increase your willingness to make the sacrifice necessary to learn the difference.)

Automakers in the United States discovered the difference between wants and demand the hard way. In the 1970s, while U.S. buyers were purchasing large numbers of small foreign cars, U.S. automakers were publicly stating, "Americans want large cars, and we're going to give them what they want." Although it may

Demand. All the quantities of a product that individuals are both willing and able to buy at every possible price during a specified period of time.

Quantity demanded. The amount of a product that consumers are both willing and able to buy at a specified price.

have been true that Americans still *wanted* large cars, they were no longer *buying* many of them. If automakers had been willing to *give* cars away (and that is the literal meaning of their words), it would have been appropriate to find out what consumers wanted. However, since the automakers wanted to *sell* cars, it was more important to focus on demand, or the willingness and ability of consumers to buy at various prices.

In addition, it is important to keep in mind that our definition of demand applies to quantities demanded within a certain period of time. Obviously, we would expect people to demand more cars in a year than in a month.

Law of Demand

The nature of demand has led economists to formulate the **law of demand**: When prices of products decrease, the quantities that buyers are willing and able to purchase increase; when prices rise, the quantity demanded falls. That is, there is an *inverse* relationship between price and quantities that consumers will buy. You can see this relationship at work in everyday life. We all tend to buy more when products are offered at a special price and to buy less when prices rise relative to those of similar products.

The law of demand follows directly from the principles of rational choice introduced in Chapter 2. An increase in price raises the extra cost to the buyer. Thus we would expect the willingness and ability to consume to diminish. Note that higher prices do *not* make consumers want fewer goods. You might get as much satisfaction from going to a movie if the ticket costs $10 or $5. But you will probably go to fewer movies each month if ticket prices are higher. Again, wants and demand should not be confused. Higher prices reduce quantity demanded, but not quantity wanted.

Demand Schedules and Demand Curves

Economists most often present information about demand either as a demand schedule or as a demand curve, both of which are illustrated in Exhibit 3.1. The table in Exhibit 3.1(a) is an example of a **demand schedule**. It shows quantities of doughnuts that consumers are willing and able to buy per week at different prices. You can see that consumers will buy 400 dozen doughnuts per week if the price is $3.00 per dozen. If the price is $3.50, quantity demanded drops to 350 dozen per week. This demand schedule supports the law of demand: Higher prices reduce quantity demanded.

The same information is shown by the graph in Exhibit 3.1(b), which is an example of a **demand curve**. We obtain a demand curve by plotting each combination of price and quantity demanded from a demand schedule and connecting the points with a smooth curve. Any one point on the graph shows a particular quantity demanded at a particular price. Point *a*, for example, indicates that at a price of $3.00 per dozen, consumers will buy 400 dozen per week.

Like a demand schedule, a demand curve shows a *relationship* between price and quantity demanded, that is, a *series* of price and quantity combinations. By convention, economists put price on the vertical axis and quantity on the horizontal

Law of demand. The principle that as the price of any product decreases (increases), the quantity of the product demanded will increase (decrease).

Demand schedule. A table showing quantities of a product that consumers are willing and able to buy at various prices during a specified period of time.

Demand curve. A graphic representation of the demand schedule; the demand curve always slopes downward and to the right.

(a) Demand schedule

Price (dollars per dozen)	Quantity demanded (dozens per week)
4.00	325
3.50	350
3.00	400
2.50	475
2.00	575

(b) Demand curve

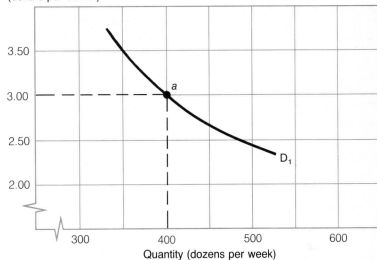

Exhibit 3.1
Demand for Doughnuts
The demand curve slopes downward and to the right, showing an inverse relationship between price and quantity demanded. Lower prices cause an increase in quantity demanded. Thus the demand curve reflects the law of demand. For any particular demand relationship, the all-other-things-unchanged assumption holds. That is, we observe the response of consumers to a change in the product's price. All other influences are assumed to remain constant.

axis. A demand curve thus slopes downward and to the right, reflecting the inverse relationship between price and quantity demanded, or the law of demand.*

We can read a demand curve in either of two ways. For a specific price, demand indicates the *maximum quantity* that buyers are willing and able to purchase at that price. For a specific quantity, demand indicates the *maximum price* that sellers could charge and sell that quantity. However, a demand curve (or a demand schedule) cannot tell us the "best" price or predict the actual price. Demand simply shows a range of possible outcomes for the relationship between price and quantity. At each price level, buyers acting rationally will compare the extra benefits of consuming additional units of the product with the extra costs they will have to pay.

The "all-other-things-unchanged" assumption.   Price is not the only factor determining the quantities that buyers will purchase. In constructing demand curves and schedules, however, economists make the **"all-other-things-unchanged" assumption**. That is, they isolate the effect of price on quantity

"All-other-things-unchanged" assumption. The assumption commonly made in demand-and-supply analysis that all determinants of quantity demanded and quantity supplied, except price, are held constant.

* As noted in Chapter 1, graphs are a convenient and often used economic tool. If you are still having some difficulty with graphs, reread the appendix to Chapter 1. Although economics is not about graphs, economic analysis is often presented in graphic form.

from the effects of all other factors that influence buying decisions. Why? Because price is the major source of information about the relative scarcity of resources, changes in wants, and other important economic events in a market economy.

Because of the all-other-things-unchanged assumption, along any given demand curve all influences other than the price of the product are assumed to remain constant. If, as quite often happens, one of the other factors changes, the demand curve will shift. A new demand curve is then required to describe the new relationship between price and quantity.

Changes in Demand and Quantity Demanded

When some factor other than price causes us to construct a new demand curve, we say that that demand curve has *shifted*, reflecting a *change in demand*. Noneconomists often fail to distinguish between changes in demand and changes in quantity demanded, but it is an important difference.

Exhibit 3.2 illustrates this difference for our doughnut example. In part (a), curve D_1 represents the original demand relationship shown in Exhibit 3.1. If the price of doughnuts falls from $3.50 to $3.00 per dozen, buyers will increase quantity demanded (purchased) from 350 to 400 dozen doughnuts per week. This change shows up as a movement along D_1 from point *a* to point *b*. Along any demand curve, quantity demanded changes in response to a change in the product's price, assuming that all other factors affecting demand remain unchanged.

Contrast this response to what might happen if scientists discovered that doughnuts prevent cancer. We would expect consumers to buy more doughnuts than before *at the current price*. In Exhibit 3.2(b), this change in demand for doughnuts is represented by a shift in the demand curve from D_1 to D_2. Note that along D_2, consumers are willing to buy 425 dozen doughnuts per week at a price of $3.50 per dozen, or 75 dozen more than when D_1 represented demand. (Compare point *a* on D_1 with point *c* on D_2.)

Any change in a nonprice factor will lead to a new demand relationship between price and quantity demanded. In this example, unless new evidence emerges or some other factor affecting demand changes, D_2 describes demand for doughnuts. Of course, if scientists reported instead that doughnuts *cause* cancer, demand would decrease, moving in the opposite direction. This change in demand is shown in Exhibit 3.2(b) as a shift from D_1 to D_0. *An increase in demand shifts the demand curve to the right; a decrease in demand shifts the demand curve to the left.*

Note that in describing a change in demand, we said nothing about a change in the price of doughnuts, as we did when discussing a change in quantity demanded. When a product's price falls, buyers will increase *quantity demanded* at the *new price*. On the other hand, a change in a factor such as a preference for doughnuts creates an entirely new demand relationship, not just a new quantity demanded. When demand increases, buyers will be willing to purchase more at each price or to pay more for any quantity bought.

If buyers purchase more only because the price of the product has fallen, economists say that there has been an increase in quantity demanded. If buyers purchase more at every possible price, economists say that there has been an increase in demand.

(a) Change in quantity demanded

Price
(dollars per dozen)

Quantity (dozens per week)

(b) Change in demand

Price
(dollars per dozen)

Quantity (dozens per week)

Exhibit 3.2
Changes in Demand and Quantity Demanded
In part (a) the curve D_1, representing demand, indicates that a decrease in price from $3.50 to $3.00 per dozen will cause an increase in the quantity demanded from 350 to 400 dozen per week (compare point *a* with point *b* on D_1). Buyers are responding only to a change in the product's price. If one of the other factors changes, as in part (b), a change in demand occurs and the entire demand curve shifts. For example, an increase in demand is shown by the shift to the right in the demand curve from D_1 to D_2. When there is an increase in demand, buyers will purchase a larger quantity at the same price (compare point *a* on D_1 with point *c* on D_2). A decrease in demand is shown as the shift to the left from D_1 to D_0 (compare point *a* on D_1 with point *d* on D_0).

Determinants of Product Demand

What other factors influence demand? Economists have identified five factors, or determinants of product demand: preferences, income, complements and substitutes, expectations, and number of buyers. Whenever one of these factors changes, demand shifts, creating a new relationship between price and quantity demanded. Be sure that you know the way in which each factor changes demand because later you will have to know whether a particular event will increase or decrease demand.

Tastes and preferences.   In choosing which products to buy, consumers consider the satisfaction they expect to receive. The value to you (and thus the price you are willing to pay) to attend a concert will depend on your preference in music. You may especially like classical music and be willing to pay $10 to hear the Collegetown Symphony Orchestra; if you like hard rock music less, you may be willing to pay only $3 to see Rocky Stone and the Rockettes. Economists refer to this influence as *tastes and preferences.*

Tastes and preferences are influenced by improvements in the quality of a product, successful advertising and marketing campaigns, fads, or the introduction of new products. We noted previously, for example, that the preference for doughnuts might increase because of evidence that doughnuts prevent cancer. *Whenever the taste or preference for a product increases, demand for the product will increase; a decline in taste or preference brings a decrease in demand.*

Using the principles of rational choice we can say that an increased taste for doughnuts increases the extra benefits consumers receive. As a result, consumers are willing to pay more for the same quantity than before, an indication that demand has increased. The increase in demand also means that consumers are willing to purchase more doughnuts at any given price.

Income.   Because consumers must be able to pay in order to demand products, it is not surprising to find that income is a determinant of demand. An increase in income will usually—although not always—cause consumers to buy more of most products. This effect is the reason for suggesting an income tax cut as a way to stimulate the economy. Lower taxes give consumers more spendable income; more income means greater demand for products. (Note that this simplified analysis ignores other economic variables. A complete analysis would consider both microeconomic and macroeconomic changes.)

Changes in income are also important in determining international trade. Consumers in the United States, for example, will buy more foreign imports if their incomes rise. Consumers in Europe or South America will buy fewer U.S. exports if their incomes fall.

Normal goods. Goods for which demand varies directly with income, rising as income rises and decreasing as income decreases—for example, steak.

Inferior goods. Goods for which demand varies inversely with income, decreasing as income rises and increasing as income falls—for example, margarine.

Substitutes. Goods that satisfy similar desires and therefore compete for the consumer's dollar. When two goods are substitutes, an increase in the price of one leads to an increase in demand for the other.

Complements. Goods that can be used with other goods, such as hot dogs and hot-dog rolls. When two goods are complements, an increase in the price of one leads to a decrease in demand for the other.

Finally, changes in income cause people to change the *types* of goods they buy. Economists recognize two types of goods based on the response of demand to a change in income. For **normal goods** demand varies directly with income; that is, an increase in income increases demand and vice versa. For **inferior goods** demand varies inversely with income; that is, demand decreases when income increases. Margarine is an inferior good; when incomes rise, less margarine is demanded. Steak, on the other hand, is a normal good; more is demanded when incomes rise. One study indicated that skiing in New England is an inferior good. When the economy is booming and incomes are rising, more East Coast skiers go to Europe or Colorado. When the economy is slumping and incomes are falling, demand for New England skiing rises.

Prices of substitutes and complements.   In making rational choices, consumers recognize that some goods are related to others. Hot dogs and hamburgers, for example, are **substitutes**. They can be used in place of each other; consumers can satisfy a desire for food by purchasing either of them. Hot dogs and hot-dog rolls are **complements**. They are used together, and consumers who buy one will typically buy the other as well.

For example, suppose that you go to the local grocery store planning to buy hamburger for dinner. A sign in the meat department indicates that hot dogs are on sale at 20 percent below the regular price. Confronted with an unexpected change in price you may revise the dinner menu: Hamburgers are out; hot dogs will be served instead. The change in the price of hot dogs caused a change in the *quantity* of hot dogs demanded. (Demand for hot dogs does not change; the response is due solely to a change in the product's price.) That is, you buy more hot dogs only because the price is lower.

The change in the price of hot dogs has two other effects. First, it causes you to demand less hamburger. Even though the price of hamburger has not changed in absolute terms, hamburger is relatively more expensive than hot dogs because the price of hot dogs has dropped. Demand for hamburger decreases because one of the factors affecting demand has changed. The price of hot dogs, a substitute product, has fallen.

In addition, you will probably buy hot dog rolls to go with the hot dogs. Because you will buy more rolls even though their price has not changed, demand for them has increased. You demand more hot-dog rolls because a nonprice factor affecting demand has changed. The price of hot dogs, a complement, has fallen.

A change in the price of a good directly affects demand for its substitutes. If a good's price increases, demand for its substitutes will increase. For complements, price and demand are inversely related. When a good's price increases, demand for its complements will decrease.

At this point, you should be aware of a good technique to use when studying economics. You have just read how changes in the price of one good affect demand for substitutes and complements—two of many relationships you will be asked to learn in this course. You may be tempted to try to memorize these relationships. If you are able to do so, fine. But if your memory has a way of fading at the most inopportune time—as in the middle of an exam—it is best to remember a simple example. You can then use the example—such as hamburgers, hot dogs, and hot-dog rolls—to reason out the relationships.

To illustrate this point let's suppose that you were asked how demand for good A is affected by an increase in the price of substitute good B. Hamburgers and hot dogs are substitutes and you can reason out how demand for hot dogs is affected by a change in the price of hamburgers: Higher prices for hamburgers will increase demand for hot dogs. In this way, you can rely on your reasoning and not just your memory. Using this technique not only will help you make better grades on exams, you will also be more likely to remember the useful tools of economic analysis after completing your economics course.

Expectations of buyers. Buyers are also influenced by expectations, especially anticipated changes in income and prices. For example, individuals tend to increase their spending immediately when they anticipate higher incomes in the near future. (How many college graduates wait until they receive their first paycheck to begin to spend their increased income?) In this way, *expectations* of higher incomes and actual increases in income have the same result: They increase demand for normal goods and decrease demand for inferior goods.

The converse is also true. When people fear that incomes will drop and unemployment will spread, they become less willing to buy those items that can easily be postponed, such as a new car. This reaction is why President Reagan was upset in 1982 when Wall Street analysts predicted that his economic program would not solve the nation's problems. His plans to increase demand by cutting taxes could not succeed if people expected that economic conditions would not improve, an expectation that decreases demand.

Expected price changes also affect consumer demand. Purchasing a product now or purchasing it in the future are alternative (substitute) choices. Therefore, if consumers expect a product's price to be higher in the future, they tend to increase their current demand for it. If they expect lower prices, they decrease current demand.

Similarly, expectations of a shortage can, by changing demand, actually create a shortage. In the early 1970s, rumors spread that toilet paper would become scarce. Consumers increased their demand for toilet paper in response, causing a toilet-paper shortage.

Number of consumers. The final factor affecting product demand is the number of consumers. Economists are mostly interested in market demand for products because it (together with market supply) determines the relative price of products. Market demand represents the sum of individual consumer demand. In other words, if you are willing to buy 10 rolls of film and your friend is willing to buy 15 at a price of $5, the market demand curve would reflect the fact that together you will buy 25 rolls at that price. Because market demand represents the sum of individual consumer demands, *an increase in the number of consumers will tend to increase demand, and a decrease in the number of consumers will tend to decrease demand*.

Thus an increase or decrease in population—whether because of births and deaths or migration—affects demand. Shifts in the age distribution of the population are also important for particular products. For example, a nationwide decline in the number of school-aged children will decrease demand for schools and teachers. The growing elderly population in the United States has increased demand for nursing-home care.

Demand and Quantity Demanded Reconsidered

The five determinants of product demand are the ones to which the all-other-things-unchanged assumption refers. For any demand curve, we assume that these factors remain unchanged and focus on the influence of price on quantity demanded. When any of these factors changes, we have a new demand relationship—an increase or decrease in demand—which is reflected by a shift in the demand curve.

In economic terms, a change in a product's price does not alter the demand relationship. However, a change in one of the other factors results in a new demand relationship, or a shift in demand. Thus an economist would not say, "Demand for cars rose this month because car prices fell," but rather, "Quantity of cars demanded increased as a result of the fall in car prices." This phrasing identifies the effect of a change in quantity demanded caused by a change in product price. It is not a change in demand, which results only from a change in some other factor affecting demand. This distinction is central to understanding demand.

Changes in Relative Prices

When the price of a good increases, quantity demanded falls. When the price of a substitute good increases or the price of a complement good falls, demand increases. In each case, however, we are talking about a change in **relative price**, that is, the price of one good in comparison to the prices of other goods.

Relative price. The price of one good in comparison to the prices of other goods.

In the real world, the prices of many goods rise or fall at the same time. Thus we must ask whether the price of a good has increased faster (increased relatively) or slower (decreased relatively) than other goods. For example, from 1974 to 1978, gasoline prices rose an average of 5.2 percent per year. However, because the average price of all goods rose an average of 7.3 percent per year, the *relative* price of gasoline decreased. The fall in the relative price of gasoline helps to explain why gasoline consumption increased during that period.

Price changes must also be considered in relation to income. Higher prices reduce quantity demanded if income is unchanged. However, in the real world prices and income often rise at the same time. Thus we must ask whether price increases more than income (which should decrease demand) or less than income (which should increase demand). For example, if the price of new cars increases by 5 percent while income increases by 10 percent, we might expect increased demand for new cars. On the other hand, if the price of new cars decreases by 5 percent while income decreases by 10 percent, we might expect decreased demand for new cars. In such a case, price has actually increased *relative to* income.

These examples show that changes in relative prices—not in absolute prices—cause changes in demand and economic decisions. Relative prices determine what consumers will buy, what producers will sell, and where individuals will choose to work.

SUPPLY

Buyers are not the only ones who must make choices. Sellers must decide how much to produce. **Supply** means the quantities of a product that sellers are both willing and able to offer for sale at every possible price during a specified period of time, with all other things unchanged. Economists use the concept of supply, like the concept of demand, in a precise and technical way. Like demand, supply refers to a *relationship* between price and quantity. And just as economists distinguish demand from quantity demanded, they also distinguish supply from **quantity supplied**.

Law of Supply

Supply. All the quantities of a product that suppliers are both willing and able to offer for sale at every possible price during a specified period of time.

Quantity supplied. The quantity of a product that suppliers are both willing and able to offer for sale at a specified price.

Law of supply. The principle that as the selling price of any product increases (decreases), the quantity of the product supplied also increases (decreases).

Supply schedule. A table showing quantities of a product that suppliers are willing and able to offer for sale at various prices during a specified period of time.

The nature of supply led economists to formulate the **law of supply**: Sellers will offer a larger quantity for sale when price rises. That is, there is a *direct* relationship between quantity supplied and price. The law of supply follows directly from the principles of rational choice. To a supplier, the extra benefit gained from supplying a product is the price received. The extra costs are the costs of supplying more of a product. Thus we can relate price and extra costs in the case of supply in the same way we related price and extra satisfaction in the case of demand. This result is helpful in understanding how supply is affected by various changes and how a market economy operates.

Supply Schedules and Supply Curves

Exhibit 3.3 shows the supply side of our doughnut example. Note that supply, like demand, refers to a quantity for a specified period of time, or in this case, doughnuts per week. We can express the supply relationship as a **supply schedule**, as we did for demand. The supply schedule supports the law of supply: As

(a) Supply schedule

Price (dollars per dozen)	Quantity supplied (dozens per week)
4.00	475
3.50	450
3.00	400
2.50	325
2.00	225

(b) Supply curve

Exhibit 3.3
The Supply of Doughnuts
The supply curve slopes upward and to the right, showing a direct relationship between price and quantity supplied. Higher prices cause sellers to offer greater quantities of their product. Lower prices reduce quantity supplied. Thus the supply curve reflects the law of supply. For any particular supply relationship, the all-other-things-equal assumption holds. That is, we observe the response of sellers to a change in the price of the product. All other influences are assumed to remain constant.

Supply curve. A graphic representation of the supply schedule; the typical supply curve slopes upward and to the right.

RECAP

Supply refers to the quantities of a product that sellers are willing and able to offer for sale at every possible price during a specified period of time.

The law of supply states that prices and quantities supplied are directly related.

Supply indicates how sellers balance the extra costs of producing additional quantities of a product against the extra benefits of selling as reflected by the market price.

price increases, so do quantities offered for sale. In this case, the quantity of doughnuts offered for sale increases from 400 to 450 dozen per week as price increases from $3.00 to $3.50 per dozen.

We can also plot this information graphically as a **supply curve**, as we did for demand. We put price on the vertical axis and quantity on the horizontal axis. The positive slope (upward and to the right) of the supply curve reflects the direct relationship between price and quantity (following the law of supply) and the relationship between extra cost and price. In Chapter 2 we noted that production is subject to increasing costs. That is, the extra cost of producing additional quantities rises as quantities produced increase. Supply expresses a direct relationship between price and quantity because extra costs rise as quantity increases. Sellers must receive higher prices for the product to cover higher extra costs.

We can read the supply curve in either of two ways. For a specific price, supply indicates the *maximum quantity* that sellers are willing and able to sell at that price. For a specific quantity, supply shows the *minimum price* that sellers will accept for that quantity. (We can assume that they would gladly take a higher price.)

Finally, as we did for demand, we make an all-other-things-equal assumption when referring to a supply relationship. That is, along a particular supply curve all factors except the price of the product are assumed to remain constant. When any of these factors changes, a new supply relationship occurs.

Changes in Supply and Quantity Supplied

As for demand, economists distinguish between a change in quantity sup-plied—which causes movement along a supply curve—and a change in supply—which causes a shift in the supply curve. Exhibit 3.4 illustrates this difference, again using our doughnut example. The original supply curve is labeled S_1. If price decreases from $3.50 to $3.00 per dozen, the sellers will reduce quantity supplied from 450 to 400 dozen per week. In part (a), this change shows up as a movement along S_1 from point a to point b. Since only the price has changed, this change represents a decrease in quantity supplied.

Suppose, however, that the cost of flour increases. This change raises the cost of making doughnuts. Because it costs more to produce each dozen, doughnut sellers will charge higher prices for each quantity they offer for sale. This change in the relationship between price and quantity supplied represents a decrease in

Exhibit 3.4
Changes in Supply and in Quantity Supplied
In part (a) where supply is S_1, a decrease in price from $3.50 to $3.00 per dozen results in a decrease in quantity supplied from 450 to 400 dozen per week (compare point a to point b on S_1). Sellers are responding only to a change in the product's price. If a factor other than price changes, as in part (b), a change in supply occurs. On the graph, a decrease in supply is shown by the shift to the left in the supply curve from S_1 to S_0. A decrease in supply results in sellers offering less for sale at each price (compare point a on S_1 with point c on S_0). An increase in supply is shown as the shift to the right from S_1 to S_2 (compare point a on S_1 with point d on S_2).

(a) Change in quantity supplied

(b) Change in supply

supply (from S_1 to S_0 in Exhibit 3.4b). This change also reflects the principles of rational choice, as sellers balance price (representing extra benefits to them) with the extra costs required to produce the product. A decrease in supply also means that sellers offer less for sale at each price. For example, at a price of $3.50, sellers now offer only 375 dozen doughnuts per week (point c on S_0) instead of 450 dozen (point a on S_1).

An increase in supply has the opposite effect. If supply increases from S_1 to S_2 in Exhibit 3.4(b), sellers will supply 525 dozen doughnuts per week (point d on S_2) at a price of $3.50 compared with 450 dozen (point a on S_1) before. *An increase in supply shifts the supply curve to the right; a decrease in supply shifts the supply curve to the left.*

Note that in describing a change in supply, we said nothing about a change in the price of doughnuts, as we did when discussing a change in quantity supplied. When a product's price falls, sellers will reduce *quantity supplied* at the *new price*. On the other hand, a change in a factor such as the ingredients used in doughnuts creates an entirely new supply relationship, not just a new quantity supplied. When supply decreases, sellers will sell less at each price or charge more for any quantity supplied.

If sellers offer more only because the price of the product has risen, economists say that there has been an increase in quantity supplied. If sellers offer more at every possible price, economists say that there has been an increase in supply.

Determinants of Supply

What other factors influence supply? Economists have identified five major factors, or determinants, of product supply: prices of resources, available technology, prices of alternative goods, expectations, and number of sellers. Whenever one of these factors changes, supply shifts, creating a new relationship between price and quantity supplied.

Prices of resources. Before a product can be offered for sale, it must be produced from various resources. Steel, labor, and rubber are some of the resources used to make a car, for example. To supply medical services requires the labor time of the doctor and support staff, rent on the office building, supplies, malpractice insurance, and other resources. Resource prices affect the cost of a product and hence are a determinant of supply. *An increase in the price of resources increases costs and decreases supply; lower resource prices decrease cost and increase supply.*

Available technology. Technology generally refers to the process by which a product or products are made. An improvement in technology implies that the product can be produced more efficiently, that is, at a lower cost. Thus *an improvement in technology lowers the cost of the product and results in an increase in supply.*

Prices of alternative goods. Like all rational decision makers, sellers consider alternatives when making a supply decision. A farmer may choose between planting corn or soybeans or between raising a crop or livestock. Makers of TV sets must choose between producing color or black-and-white models and between consoles or portables. Both the farmer and the maker of TV sets could produce some of each, but the capacity to produce is limited at any one time. If more of one good is produced, fewer alternative goods can be made. Thus one cost of producing color TV sets is the opportunity cost of not producing (and not selling) black-and-white models.

When the price of color TV sets rises relative to the price of black-and-white TV sets, the opportunity cost of producing black-and-white models increases. Sellers will produce the same quantity of black-and-white sets only if their price increases. But setting higher prices for each quantity supplied is a decrease in supply. Thus *supply of a good will decrease when prices of alternative goods that sellers could offer for sale rise. Supply will increase when prices of alternative goods fall.* Note, however, that a rise in *relative* prices is what causes seller decisions to change.

Expectations of sellers. You have seen how buyers take anticipated events into account in making demand decisions; sellers do the same when making supply decisions. For example, suppose that shoemakers expect demand for shoes to rise in the near future. They may react by increasing current shoe production so that they will have more shoes available to meet the higher sales expected.

More production by itself does not mean an increase in supply, however. Supply increases only if sellers are willing to offer more goods for sale at each price or to accept a lower price for each quantity offered for sale. We would not expect shoemakers to sell for a lower price today if they can sell for a higher price next week. An expected increase in prices raises the opportunity cost of selling today instead of next week. Like any other increase in costs, the higher opportunity cost decreases supply. Thus *when prices are expected to increase, current supply will tend to decrease; if prices are expected to decrease, current supply will tend to increase.*

Number of sellers. So far, we have discussed factors that relate supply to changes in direct costs (resource prices and available technology) or indirect or opportunity costs (expectations and prices of alternatives). Each of these changes affects the supply decisions of individual producers. Economists are mostly interested in the market supply, that is, in the total quantities supplied by all sellers in the market at each price. An increase in the number of sellers means that more goods will be offered for sale at each price. Thus, *an increase in the number of sellers increases market supply; a decrease in the number of sellers decreases market supply.*

Supply and Quantity Supplied Reconsidered

To derive a specific supply curve we make an all-other-things-unchanged assumption, holding constant the five determinants of product supply. When we consider the response of sellers to a change in the product's price, we move along the supply curve and observe only a change in quantity supplied. When one of the five other determinants of supply changes, however, sellers' responses will change, a new supply relationship will result, and the supply curve will shift.

RECAP

A change in the price of a product results in a movement along a relationship, that is, a change in quantity supplied.

A change in any factor other than the product's price results in a new supply relationship, that is, a change in supply.

Nonprice determinants of supply include prices of resources, available technology, prices of alternative goods, expectations of sellers, and the number of sellers.

Price
(dollars per dozen)

Exhibit 3.5
Market for Doughnuts
For demand D_1 and supply S_1 in this market, the equilibrium price is $3.00 per dozen and the equilibrium quantity is 400 dozen, located at the intersection of the two curves. If the price were $3.50 per dozen, a surplus of 100 dozen would result (the difference between 450 dozen offered for sale and 350 dozen bought). If the price were $2.50 per dozen, a shortage of 150 dozen would result (the difference between 475 dozen demanded and 325 dozen offered for sale).

MARKET EQUILIBRIUM

At the beginning of this chapter, we noted that decisions in a market economy are made through the interaction of buyers and sellers. Thus far we have discussed demand and supply—the actions of buyers and sellers—separately. To see how a market works to determine prices, we need to put the two together.

In examining this interaction, we return to the principles of rational choice. That is, we assume that buyers and sellers make decisions by comparing extra benefits and extra costs. Each strives to get more (in terms of extra benefits) for less (in terms of extra costs) out of the exchange. Thus, in a fundamental sense, the interests of buyers and sellers clash. Sellers would like to receive the highest possible price; buyers want to pay the lowest possible price.

Given the conflicting interests of buyers and sellers, how is market price determined? The market's solution is what economists refer to as the **equilibrium price**—a price at which quantity demanded and quantity supplied are equal. Exhibit 3.5 shows the market for doughnuts by combining the demand curve from Exhibit 3.1 and the supply curve from Exhibit 3.3. The demand and supply curves intersect at a price of $3.00 per dozen, where both quantity demanded and quantity supplied are 400 dozen doughnuts per week. Thus $3.00 per dozen is the equilibrium price in this particular market as represented by its demand and supply conditions.

The equilibrium price is a compromise between the interests of sellers and buyers and thus is not necessarily ideal for either. Equilibrium means that all of

Equilibrium price. The price at which quantity supplied equals quantity demanded; graphically, the point of intersection of the demand and supply curves.

Market equilibrium. A state in which neither buyers nor sellers have any reason to change quantity demanded or supplied; the market in balance, with quantity demanded equal to quantity supplied at the existing market price.

Shortage. A situation in which quantity demanded exceeds quantity supplied at the existing market price; excess demand.

a product that sellers offer for sale is purchased and that all of a product that buyers will buy is supplied. Because there are many buyers and sellers acting independently, no individual buyer or seller has the ability to influence the market price.

Market equilibrium is similar to physical equilibrium, meaning at rest or in balance. When a market reaches equilibrium price, the forces of demand and supply are in balance. Moreover, markets tend automatically to adjust to equilibrium whenever the forces of demand and supply are out of balance.

Shortage

Let's look at how markets achieve equilibrium by considering what happens if the market is unbalanced. Suppose, for example, that doughnuts sell for $2.50 per dozen, or below the equilibrium price. The demand curve in Exhibit 3.5 indicates that consumers are willing and able to buy 475 dozen per week at $2.50. The supply curve, however, shows that sellers will offer only 325 dozen for sale. That is, quantity demanded exceeds quantity supplied by 150 dozen per week at $2.50. Economists call excess quantity demanded a **shortage**. *Whenever the current market price is below the equilibrium price, quantity demanded will exceed quantity supplied, creating a shortage.*

When a shortage exists, we can predict market prices will rise to the equilibrium price. For example, some people who cannot buy as many doughnuts as they want at the current price are willing to pay more. Moreover, a shortage allows sellers to sell more at higher prices. Pressures from both sellers and buyers thus force prices up. As price rises, quantity supplied increases (a movement along the supply curve). At the same time, quantity demanded falls (a movement along the demand curve). These two changes reduce the size of the shortage. As long as the market price is less than $3.00 per dozen (the equilibrium price) the shortage will continue to put upward pressure on price. But once the price reaches $3.00 per dozen, the market is balanced: Quantity demanded equals quantity supplied at the equilibrium price; there is no shortage and no pressure on the market price.

Scarcity versus shortage. As we have mentioned, economists use some words in technical and precise ways to avoid confusion. Two such words are *scarcity* and *shortage*. Consider the following statement: "Scarcity is an unavoidable feature of the human condition, but shortages can be easily eliminated." This assertion may sound like nonsense to a noneconomist, but it makes perfect sense in economics.

As we noted in Chapter 2, scarcity reflects the fact that resources are limited, while wants are unlimited. It is true therefore that "scarcity is an unavoidable feature of the human condition." But a shortage is a market condition in which, at the prevailing market price, quantity demanded exceeds quantity supplied. Shortages can always be eliminated by allowing market prices to rise to equilibrium levels. When you mean that all wants of society are not being met, use the term "scarcity." When you mean that the current market price is too low (that is, below the equilibrium price) and thus quantity demanded exceeds quantity supplied, use the term "shortage."

Surplus

What if the current market price is too high, that is, above the equilibrium price? Exhibit 3.5 shows that at $3.50 per dozen, sellers will offer 450 dozen doughnuts for sale but buyers will purchase only 350 dozen. Once again, the market is out of balance: Quantity demanded is less than quantity supplied at the current price. Economists call excess quantity supplied a **surplus**. In our doughnut example, a surplus of 100 dozen per week occurs when the price is $3.50. *Whenever the current market price is above the equilibrium price, quantity supplied will exceed quantity demanded, creating a surplus.*

A surplus usually causes market prices to fall to the equilibrium price. Faced with a surplus, doughnut sellers have two choices: to eat the leftover doughnuts, or to cut prices to increase sales. A surplus also allows consumers to buy more at a lower price. Thus pressures from both the demand and supply sides of the market push market prices lower. The decline in prices decreases quantity supplied (a movement along the supply curve) and increases quantity demanded (a movement along the demand curve). Downward pressure on prices continues until the price reaches $3.00 per dozen. At this equilibrium price, the market is balanced: Sellers offer and buyers purchase 400 dozen doughnuts per week; there is no surplus and no remaining pressure on prices.

Changes in Market Conditions and Equilibrium Prices

The market's tendency to move to equilibrium allows us to predict how markets will respond to changes in demand or supply. We can expect prices to adjust to eliminate any shortage or surplus that may be created initially.

Changes in demand. Exhibit 3.6 provides an example of the market's response to changes in demand. As before, when D_1 represents demand and S_1 represents supply, the market is in equilibrium at $3.00 per dozen and 400 dozen doughnuts per week bought and sold (point *a*). What if some factor other than price changes? For example, what if income increases and doughnuts are a normal good? What if the price of blueberry muffins (a substitute for doughnuts) increases? In either case, the all-other-things-unchanged assumption is no longer valid. Demand for doughnuts would increase, and buyers would demand more doughnuts at each possible price.

As shown in Exhibit 3.6(b), an increase in demand causes the demand curve to shift to the right—from D_1 to D_2. Consumers will now buy 500 dozen (instead of 400 dozen) doughnuts per week at the old equilibrium price of $3.00. However, suppliers will continue to supply only 400 dozen, so the increase in demand creates a shortage of 100 dozen doughnuts per week at the old equilibrium price. Because a shortage puts upward pressure on the market price, the shortage is eliminated and upward pressure disappears when the market price rises to a new equilibrium level. The new equilibrium price lies where the new demand (D_2) and old supply (S_1) intersect—at $3.50 per dozen. The market price rises to $3.50, and the quantity demanded and supplied is 450 dozen per week (point *b*).

Surplus. A situation in which quantity supplied exceeds quantity demanded at the existing market price; excess supply.

(a) Demand schedules

Price (dollars per dozen)	Quantity demanded (dozens per week)		
	D_0	D_1	D_2
4.00	175	325	425
3.50	200	350	450
3.00	250	400	500
2.50	325	475	575
2.00	425	575	675

(b) Demand curves

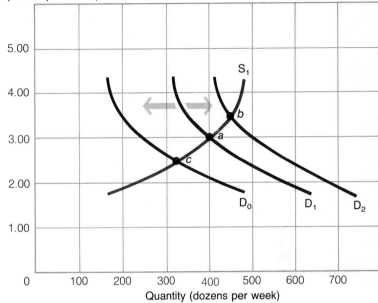

Exhibit 3.6
Changes in Demand for Doughnuts
An increase in demand results in a shift of the demand curve to the right from D_1 to D_2. It causes the equilibrium price to rise from $3.00 to $3.50 per dozen and the equilibrium output to rise from 400 to 450 dozen per week. A decrease in demand results in a shift to the left from D_1 to D_0. As a result, the equilibrium price drops to $2.50 per dozen and the equilibrium output falls to 325 dozen per week.

Conversely, an increase in the price of coffee (a complement to doughnuts) or a decline in income will cause demand for doughnuts to decrease. This effect is shown in the graph in Exhibit 3.6 as a shift to the left in the demand curve (from D_1 to D_0). Demand will fall from 400 dozen doughnuts at the old equilibrium price of $3.00 per dozen to only 250 dozen, creating a surplus of 150 dozen doughnuts per week. A surplus puts downward pressure on the market price until a new equilibrium price is reached—at the intersection of the new demand (D_0) and old supply (S_1). Thus when the price falls to $2.50 per dozen, 325 dozen doughnuts per week will be both bought and sold (point c), and the market will once again be in equilibrium.

In both cases, the final results reflect the market's automatic response. An increase in demand causes a shortage to develop, which automatically raises prices. A decrease in demand causes a surplus to develop, which automatically decreases prices. As long as the market is allowed to adjust, we can predict its response. *An increase in demand causes both market price and quantity sold to increase. A decrease in demand causes a decrease in both market price and quantity sold.*

(a) Supply schedules

Price (dollars per dozen)	Quantity supplied (dozens per week)		
	S_0	S_1	S_2
4.00	375	475	625
3.50	350	450	600
3.00	300	400	550
2.50	225	325	475
2.00	125	225	375

(b) Supply curves

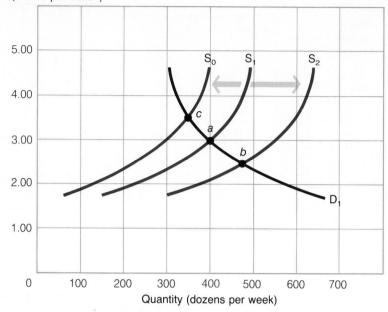

Exhibit 3.7
Changes in the Supply of Doughnuts
An increase in supply results in a shift of the supply curve to the right from S_1 to S_2. It causes the equilibrium price to fall from $3.00 to $2.50 per dozen and the equilibrium output to rise from 400 to 475 per week. A decrease in supply results in a shift to the left from S_1 to S_0. As a result, the equilibrium price rises to $3.50 per dozen and the equilibrium output falls to 350 dozen per week.

Changes in supply. Changes in supply also affect equilibrium. We expect a change in supply when any determinant of supply other than the price of the product changes. For example, the cost of flour (a resource) might fall; a more efficient machine for producing doughnuts (available technology) may be invented; or the price of blueberry muffins (which doughnut producers can make instead) may fall. In each case, the supply of doughnuts will increase and sellers will offer a larger quantity for sale at each possible price.

Exhibit 3.7 shows the effects of changes in supply. An increase in supply appears as a shift of the supply curve to the right (from S_1 to S_2). At the old equilibrium price of $3.00, sellers now offer 550 dozen doughnuts per week instead of 400 dozen. That is, an increase in supply means that a particular quantity will be offered for sale at a lower price. For example, sellers required a price of $4.00 per dozen to justify selling 475 dozen doughnuts per week before (on S_1). After the supply increases, they will sell 475 dozen per week for only $2.50 per dozen.

The increase in supply causes a temporary surplus of 150 dozen doughnuts at the old price, and the surplus creates downward pressure on price. The new equilibrium price is $2.50 per dozen, and the new quantity demanded and supplied is 475 dozen per week (the intersection of S_2 and D_1, or point b).

In contrast, a decrease in supply causes the supply curve to shift to the left (from S_1 to S_0 in this case), reflecting a shortage at the old price (sellers will offer less for sale). But the shortage also creates upward pressure on price. The new equilibrium occurs at a price of $3.50 per dozen and production of 350 dozen per week (the intersection of S_0 and D_1, or point c).

Supply adjustments are automatic responses to market conditions. An increase in supply creates a surplus and exerts pressure on prices to fall. A decrease in supply creates a shortage and exerts pressure on prices to rise. As long as the market is allowed to adjust, we can predict its response. *An increase in supply causes price to fall and quantity sold to increase. A decrease in supply causes price to rise and quantity sold to decrease.*

Changes in Equilibrium Reconsidered

While studying economics and trying to understand economic events in the real world, you should become comfortable with the mechanics of demand and supply analysis. You should practice drawing various shifts in demand and supply until you can draw the graphs easily. If you learn to draw increases and decreases in demand and supply on a graph, you need not memorize the effects that particular changes have on equilibrium conditions: A graph will show exactly how price and quantity adjust.

In addition, you should practice using the concepts of demand and supply to analyze economic changes taking place nationally or locally. Try to visualize these changes as demand and/or supply shifts in order to predict changes in price and quantity sold. As you will see throughout this textbook, economists use demand and supply analysis whenever they want to explain changes in relative prices. For example, if the price of ice cream rises relative to the price of other goods, economists will try to find out why demand might have increased or supply might have decreased (or perhaps both). Either of these changes can cause prices to rise and are the most likely reasons for an increase in relative prices. In a free market economy, a change in price can result only from a change in demand or supply.

GOVERNMENT PRICE-SETTING POLICIES

Demand and supply are the only influences on price in a totally free market. In the United States, as we noted at the beginning of this chapter, the market is subject to some types of government intervention. Sometimes prices set by the government exceed or fall below equilibrium prices. For example, economists generally agree that the federal minimum wage (minimum labor price) has often

RECAP ▰▰▰▰▰

Markets achieve equilibrium when, at current market prices, quantity demanded equals quantity supplied. Graphically, this point occurs where the demand and supply curves intersect.

An increase in demand—shown graphically as a shift to the right—causes both equilibrium price and quantity to increase (as the market moves along the supply curve).

A decrease in demand—shown graphically as a shift to the left—causes both equilbrium price and quantity to decrease.

An increase in supply—graphically, a shift to the right—causes equilibrium quantity to increase and equilibrium price to fall (as the market moves along the demand curve).

A decrease in supply—graphically, a shift to the left—causes equilibrium price to rise and equilibrium quantity to decrease.

exceeded the probable market equilibrium price for unskilled workers. Conversely, local rent control rates (maximum prices for rental housing) often fall below probable market equilibrium prices.

Why does government set such rates if, in some ways at least, the equilibrium price is ideal? Supporters of government intervention argue that the market price of rental housing is "too high" and that of minimum wages is "too low." Government actions often seek to stimulate production, to raise incomes, to prevent consumers from being exploited, or to compensate for some shortcomings of the market system. Such government policies usually involve trade-offs between efficiency and equity, and—like all economic activity—involve both benefits and costs.

Ceiling Prices

Government has often intervened to keep prices of some commodities low (or lower than they would be under market equilibrium). For example, during World War II, U.S. factories produced many defense goods but few civilian goods. One result was a severe shortage of consumer goods, such as appliances and cars. To prevent prices from rising too much in response to the shortages, the government instituted **ceiling prices**, that is, maximum legal prices. These prices were considerably below market equilibrium levels.

While these prices kept consumer prices low, they increased shortages; sellers were unwilling to produce and sell as many consumer goods. Some sellers chose to sell their products at illegally high prices in so-called *black markets*. Such markets thrive under price controls because shortages mean that unsatisfied buyers will pay higher prices for products. Black markets represent an illegal way in which buyers and sellers search for market equilibrium.

Support Prices

Some government regulations, such as minimum wage laws, create minimum prices. Such legal minimums are called **support prices** or floor prices. Support prices are common in U.S. agriculture. Farm prices vary tremendously from year to year, causing dramatic swings in farm income. Those who favor support prices claim that such intervention helps to stabilize farm income and ensure an adequate supply of essential food commodities. Similarly, they argue that without minimum wage laws, some workers would receive wages that are inequitably low. Clearly, price supports have both equity and efficiency benefits. However, price supports also involve costs that must be considered. These costs arise when a support price higher than the market price creates a surplus.

In the case of a minimum wage law, the costs include a labor surplus: unemployment. At the higher wage, firms will not hire some workers, especially the youngest and least experienced. As a result of minimum wage laws, some workers receive higher incomes, but others—especially teenagers and college students seeking summer jobs—have difficulty finding work.

In the case of farm products, the costs include the tendency for price supports to drive farm prices down, actually lowering farm incomes. The government has

Ceiling price. A legal maximum price established by government for a specific market.

Support price. A legal minimum price established by government for a specific market.

used a variety of means, including direct purchase of farm products, in attempts to prevent surpluses from pushing farm prices down.[*]

Economists are generally skeptical about imposing ceiling and support prices because of two major problems. First, by sending out false price signals, such policies distort the allocation of resources. If the price falls because of a ceiling price, sellers receive a signal identical to that caused by a decrease in demand. The signal suggests they are producing too much; they respond by reducing the quantity supplied. The signal to buyers is identical to that caused by a fall in product cost. They respond by increasing the quantity demanded. The result of this false signal is a shortage, meaning that too little is produced relative to allocative efficiency. A support price is also a false signal to buyers and sellers. In this case a surplus is created, meaning that too much is produced relative to allocative efficiency.

Second, in most cases ceiling and support prices do not achieve their stated objectives. A ceiling price benefits some consumers, but quantity supplied decreases, so fewer consumer demands can be met. Some consumers gain and others lose, but because the results are allocatively inefficient, society as a whole stands to lose. In addition, other policy options may address a problem more directly (see A Case in Point: Effects of Price Ceilings and Price Supports). Most economists do not claim that ceiling and price supports are never justified; however, they do suggest that such policies are very often inferior solutions to economic problems.

CONCLUSION

In this chapter we laid the foundation for the study of markets and the operation of a market economy. The true test of your understanding of demand and supply will come as you use these concepts to understand, describe, and predict the effects of economic changes on relative prices. As you do so, you should first identify whether the economic change affects demand or supply. Although in the real world many changes often occur at the same time, you will find it helpful to consider them separately, recognizing that the final result depends on putting them all together. Next, determine whether the identified change will increase or decrease demand or supply. Finally, graph the market effect as a shift in demand or supply, so that you can predict the effect on equilibrium price and quantity.

In this chapter we explained the factors that change demand and supply. But *how much* do demand and supply change in response to changing expectations, for example? The degree of change that we can expect is the topic of Chapter 4. Although we have described the individual market—a market for one particular product—we still need to consider how a market economy as a whole operates. In Chapter 5 we will look at how a system of markets interrelates to provide answers to the fundamental economic questions of what, how, and for whom to produce.

---

[*]The first issue in Chapter 19 is a study of agricultural price supports in the United States, which presents an in-depth description of price supports in action.

A Case in Point
Effects of Price Ceilings and Price Supports

The mayor of Collegetown has been presented with a petition from students at State University urging the mayor to do something about the lack of affordable local housing. Currently, the housing market is in equilibrium. All 800 apartments available are rented at an average price of $500 a month.

The students propose a ceiling price of $400 per month, a price most of them can afford. But the mayor explains that a ceiling price below the equilibrium price will not solve the problem, but will instead cause a shortage of apartments. As shown in the graph below, at $400 per month, quantity demanded (1200 units) exceeds quantity supplied (400 units). At the lower price, local landlords will rent fewer apartments to students. Students who succeeded in locating apartments would benefit from the lower price, but many students would have no place to live.

The head of the city council suggests a support price of $600 per month to encourage local builders to construct more apartments. The mayor noted that this policy will create a surplus. The graph at right shows that a support price would increase the number of apartments supplied to 1000 per month. But the number demanded would fall to 600 units because many students could not afford the $600 rent. The result would be a surplus of 400 apartments.

As this example illustrates, neither a support price nor a ceiling price will give students more housing at lower prices. In fact, each policy creates a new problem: what to do with the surplus in the case of the support price and what to do about the shortage in the case of the ceiling price. If the objective is to increase the quantity of apartments offered and rented, regulated prices will not help.

Two other options—an increase in supply and an increase in demand—offer some potential benefits. Lowering property taxes on apartments would increase the supply *and* lower the price of apartments. Alternatively, increasing the incomes of students who cannot afford existing housing would increase demand. Student income could be increased indirectly through training or employment programs, or directly through financial aid (loans and/or grants). Both solutions have costs, but unlike price ceilings and price supports they would at least address the problem of scarce, affordable housing.

What should the mayor do? Most economists would advise the mayor to reject regulated prices because they do not solve the problem. Other policies have both benefits and costs so a trade-off will have to be made. Ultimately, the decision will depend on whether the mayor feels that the extra benefits (more satisfied students) outweigh the extra costs (lost property taxes, for example).

SUMMARY

1. In this chapter we discussed the operation of a market, that is, how the forces of demand and supply, representing the interactions of buyers and sellers, determine market price.

2. Demand represents the quantities of a particular product that buyers are willing and able to purchase at every possible price during a specified period of time. Consumer wants and their desire to buy products do not represent demand if they are not willing and able to pay.

3. The law of demand states that price and quantity demanded are inversely related: A higher price will reduce the quantity consumers will demand; a lower price will raise the quantity they will buy. Demand shows how consumers balance the extra satisfaction received from a product against its extra cost (reflected by price).

4. For any particular demand relationship, economists assume that factors other than the price of the product are held constant; this is the *all-other-things-unchanged* assumption. A change in any factor other than price results in a new demand relationship, that is, a change in demand and a shift in the demand curve. A change in the product's price results in movement along a demand curve, representing only a change in quantity demanded.

5. Nonprice determinants of demand include tastes and preferences, income, prices of substitutes and complements, expectations of buyers, and the number of consumers. Demand for normal goods varies directly with income; demand for inferior goods varies indirectly with income. Substitutes can be used in place of each other, whereas complements are used together. When the price of a product rises, demand for its substitutes increases and demand for its complements decreases.

6. Supply represents to the quantities of a particular product that sellers are willing and able to offer for sale at every possible price during a specified period of time. The law of supply states that price and quantity supplied are directly related. Supply shows how sellers balance the extra costs of making a product against the extra benefits of selling it (reflected by price).

7. A change in the price of a product results in movement along a supply curve, representing only a change in quantity supplied. A change in any nonprice factor results in a new supply relationship, that is, a change in supply and a shift in the supply curve. Nonprice determinants of supply include prices of resources, available technology, prices of alternative goods, expectations, and the number of sellers.

8. A market is in equilibrium when at the current (equilibrium) price, quantity demanded equals quantity supplied. If the market price is below the equilibrium price, quantity demanded exceeds quantity supplied, resulting in a shortage. If the market price is above the equilibrium price, quantity supplied exceeds quantity demanded, resulting in a surplus. Market forces work to eliminate shortages and surpluses by causing the market price to adjust to the equilibrium price.

9. Changes in demand and supply affect equilibrium prices and output. An increase in demand shifts the demand curve to the right, resulting in higher prices and output. A decrease in demand shifts the demand curve to the left, resulting in lower prices and output. An increase in supply shifts the supply curve to the right, resulting in lower prices but higher output. A decrease in supply shifts the supply curve to the left, resulting in higher prices but lower output.

10. Government may intervene to establish a controlled price that is different from the equilibrium price. A ceiling price below equilibrium causes a shortage; a support price above equilibrium causes a surplus. Controlled prices may sometimes be justified, but can also cause inefficiency. They send false price signals to the market.

KEY TERMS

Market, 46
Market economy, 46
Price, 46
Demand, 47
Quantity demanded, 47
Law of demand, 48
Demand schedule, 48
Demand curve, 48
"All-other-things-unchanged" assumption, 49
Normal goods, 52
Inferior goods, 52
Substitutes, 52
Complements, 52
Relative price, 54
Supply, 55
Quantity supplied, 55
Law of supply, 55
Supply schedule, 55
Supply curve, 56

Equilibrium price, 60

Market equilibrium, 61

Shortage, 61

Surplus, 62

Ceiling prices, 66

Support prices, 66

QUESTIONS FOR REVIEW AND DISCUSSION

1. Recalling the definition of demand, comment on the statement: "Most people would prefer a Rolls Royce to a Toyota, but more people buy Toyotas. This choice indicates that people are irrational."

2. If the price of ice cream rises 5 percent while prices of all other goods rise 10 percent, in what sense has the price of ice cream actually fallen? How might this price change be expected to influence the market for ice cream?

3. Recognizing the difference between changes in demand and changes in quantity demanded, comment on the statement: "Increasing the tax on gasoline may cause the price of gasoline to fall because consumers will respond by reducing demand, and when demand falls prices tend to fall."

4. An appliance store owner scoffs at the law of demand: "Economists say that price and quantity sold are inversely related, but I raised my prices this year and I'm selling more." Explain how price and quantity sold can both increase.

5. Recalling the difference between scarcity and shortage, comment on the statement: "If the price of feed grains goes up again this year, there'll be a shortage of Thanksgiving turkeys, and everyone who wants one won't be able to buy one."

6. Comment on the following: "A shortage is simply another way of indicating that the current price is too low; a surplus just means that the current price is too high."

7. If you were the manager of a small retail store, how would you know which items were priced too high and which ones too low? Could you tell the difference if you were a customer?

8. There are two parties to a market exchange: buyer and seller. Do both parties to the exchange necessarily gain? Will they gain equally?

9. Markets for some items are seasonal. Explain why the price of fresh strawberries falls during their peak season, whereas the price of Christmas cards rises during their peak season.

10. When the price of beef goes up, the price of chicken also tends to rise. Give two reasons for this reaction, considering both demand and supply. Can you think of other products that react similarly?

11. What change in demand and/or supply best explains the following statements? (Be sure to note which specific factors cause the change in demand and/or supply.)
    a) Prices of personal computers have fallen in recent years, while quantities sold have increased.
    b) Airlines sell more tickets during the peak travel season at higher prices than at other times.

12. Use demand and supply analysis to explain the effect of each of the following changes on equilibrium price and quantity exchanged in the market for college textbooks (consider each case independently).
    a) An increase in the price of paper.
    b) An increase in tuition and other fees.
    c) An increase in the expected income of individuals with college degrees.

13. Over time the prices of some goods (such as home appliances) are fairly steady, but those of other goods (such as farm products) change constantly. How do you account for these differences? Can you think of other examples in each category?

14. Suppose that the Collegeville city council decides to help hold down the cost of rental housing for college students and passes an ordinance limiting the rent that can be charged (a ceiling price). Explain its effect on:
    a) The quantity of rental property available.
    b) The quantity and/or quality of new rental property being constructed in Collegeville.
    c) The welfare of the student population as a whole (or of subgroups that may gain or lose).
    Can you think of other effects (such as demand for bus service from neighboring communities and the amount of property taxes collected by the city)?

15. Use the appendix to this chapter and the following equations relating demand and supply in a market to answer questions (a) and (b).

$$Qd = 300 - 3P$$

and

$$Qs = 50 + 2P$$

    a) What are the equilibrium price and quantity in the market?
    b) If a support price of 60 is established by the government, how big will the resulting surplus or shortage be?

Appendix to Chapter 3

Algebra of Market Equilibrium

In this chapter, you saw how demand and supply interact to achieve an equilibrium price and quantity, how a market responds to a change in demand and/or supply, and how a market reacts when the government imposes a ceiling price or support price. The same concepts can be examined using algebraic expressions for demand and supply relationships.

EQUATIONS FOR DEMAND AND SUPPLY

We can use the following equation to represent the original market demand for a hypothetical product:

$$Qd_1 = 100 - 2P$$

where Qd_1 = quantity demanded and P = market price. The equation is a **demand function**, that is, an algebraic expression for the relationship between quantity demanded and market price. This equation reflects the all-other-things-unchanged assumption, as indicated by the single variable—the product's price—on the right-hand side. The influence of other factors is represented by the constant term, 100. This equation supports the law of demand: the higher the price, the smaller the quantity demanded. To be sure that you understand why this is true, find quantity demanded at a price of 5 and at a price of 10. (Your answers should be 90 and 80.)

Likewise, we can express the original market supply for a hypothetical product as

$$Qs_1 = 10 + 4P$$

Demand function. An algebraic expression showing how quantity demanded is affected by market price and other factors influencing demand.

Supply function. An algebraic expression showing how quantity supplied is affected by market price and other factors influencing supply.

where Qs_1 = quantity supplied and P = market price. This equation is a **supply function**, that is, an algebraic expression for the relationship between quantity supplied and market price. As we did for demand, we make the all-other-things-unchanged assumption, with market price being the only variable affecting quantity supplied. The influence of other factors is represented by the constant term, 10. This equation supports the law of supply: Market price and quantity supplied are directly related. Test this statement by calculating quantity supplied at a price of 5 and at a price of 10. (Your answers should be 30 and 50.)

DETERMINATION OF EQUILIBRIUM

Using the equations for demand and supply, we can determine the equilibrium price by finding the price at which quantity demanded (Qd) equals quantity supplied (Qs). For the expressions given in the preceding section,

$$Qd_1 = Qs_1$$
$$100 - 2P = 10 + 4P$$
$$6P = 90$$
$$P = 15$$

Thus the equilibrium price in this example is 15, a price at which quantity demanded equals quantity supplied. To find quantity sold, therefore, we need only to find how much will be supplied (or demanded) at a price of 15. Using the equation for quantity supplied, we get

$$Qs_1 = 10 + 4P$$
$$= 10 + 4(15)$$
$$= 10 + 60 \quad \text{or} \quad 70$$

Because the price of 15 is the equilibrium price, we know that quantity supplied equals quantity demanded equals quantity sold. To verify this statement, substitute the price of 15 into the demand equation. (You should obtain a quantity demanded of 70.) Thus in this example, the market will reach equilibrium at a price of 15, at which the quantity exchanged equals 70.

AN INCREASE IN DEMAND

So far we have considered only changes in quantity demanded and supplied. In contrast, an increase in market demand means that quantity demanded will be greater at each possible price. We can express an increase in demand using a new demand function for our hypothetical product:

$$Qd_2 = 130 - 2P$$

You can verify that this equation represents an increase in demand by examining quantity demanded at a market price of 15; that is,

$$Qd_2 = 130 - 2P$$
$$= 130 - 2(15) \quad \text{or} \quad 100$$

Note that the constant term (130) in this new demand function is greater than the constant term (100) in the original demand function. Thus at each price buyers will demand 30 units more than before. You can verify this answer by determining quantity demanded at a price of 15 under the new demand conditions. Instead of the 70 units demanded before, 100 units will be demanded now, indicating an increase in demand. (You should also prove to yourself that this result holds at other prices by calculating quantity demanded under both demand functions at a price of 10.)

To examine the effect of an increase in demand, we can determine the equilibrium price and quantity exchanged for the new demand function and the original supply function. To do so, we equate quantity demanded and quantity supplied as follows:

$$Qd_2 = Qs_1$$
$$30 - 2P = 10 + 4P$$
$$6P = 120$$
$$P = 20$$

To find quantity exchanged, we substitute the equilibrium price into the demand function.

$$Qd_2 = 130 - 2P$$
$$= 130 - 2(20) \quad \text{or} \quad 90$$

As you saw in the graphs in this chapter, the increase in demand increased both the equilibrium price and quantity sold. To check your understanding of this point, find the equilibrium price and quantity under the following demand and supply conditions:

$$Qd_1 = 100 - 2P \quad \text{and} \quad Qs_2 = 40 + 4P$$

You might first ask whether the new supply function represents an increase or a decrease in supply compared to the original relationship. (Your answer should be "an increase" because the constant term 40 is greater than the constant term 10.) Then you should ask whether the equilibrium price and quantity sold would be higher or lower. (Your answers should be $P = 10$, or "lower," and $Qs_2 = 80$, or "higher.")

EFFECTS OF A CEILING PRICE

What would happen if, under the original demand and supply functions (Qd_1 and Qs_1) the government imposed a ceiling price of 12, which is lower than the equilibrium price of 15? To answer this question, you have to substitute the ceiling price into both the demand and supply functions to find quantities demanded and supplied. Thus

$$Qd_1 = 100 - 2P \qquad Qs_1 = 10 + 4P$$
$$= 100 - 2(12) \quad \text{or} \quad 76 \qquad = 10 + 4(12) \quad \text{or} \quad 58$$

As noted in this chapter, a ceiling price below the equilibrium price results in a shortage. A price of 12 causes a shortage of 18, or the difference between quantity demanded (76) and quantity supplied (58). This shortage would normally cause prices to rise, but government imposition of a maximum price of 12 means the shortage will continue.

To test your understanding of the operation of ceiling and support prices, try to answer the following questions (assuming the original conditions for demand and supply): (1) What surplus would be created if the government established a support price of 18? (2) What would be the effect on the market if the government imposes a ceiling price of 18? [Your answers should be (1) a surplus of 18; and (2) equilibrium at $P = 15$ and $Q = 70$, because a ceiling price above equilibrium would not keep the market from reaching equilibrium.]

CONCLUSION

When you have identified demand and supply functions that indicate the algebraic relationships among quantity demanded, quantity supplied, and market price, determining equilibrium algebraically is a two-step process. First, find the equilibrium price from Qd = Qs; that is, find the one price that will equate quantity demanded and quantity supplied. Second, calculate quantity exchanged by substituting the equilibrium price into either the demand function or the supply function.

In both economic theory and real-world economics, algebraic representation of demand and supply—and other economic concepts—is extremely useful. Therefore, throughout this textbook, you will find a series of appendixes designed to give you a better mathematical understanding of economics.

KEY TERMS

Demand function, 71
Supply function, 71

Elasticity of Demand
and Supply

QUESTIONS TO CONSIDER

☐ Why is the concept of elasticity important in analyzing economic activity?

☐ How do goods with price-elastic demands differ from goods with price-inelastic demands?

☐ What factors determine the price elasticity of demand? The price elasticity of supply?

☐ Why is income elasticity an important factor in business decisions?

☐ When would you use the formula for cross elasticity of demand?

We discussed the laws of demand and supply in Chapter 3, and how demand and supply together determine an equilibrium price and quantity. We showed that a decrease in supply will cause an increase in price and a decrease in quantity. But our analysis did not tell us *how much* price and quantity would change. This chapter expands on the concepts of demand and supply and introduces the concept of *elasticity*.

The concept of elasticity allows us to predict how much price and quantity respond to changes in demand and supply. It also helps us answer a number of economic questions. For example, why do wheat farmers generally earn less when the weather has been exceptionally good than when poor weather wipes out part of the wheat crop? Why is New York State better off taxing tobacco products than wines produced in the state? Why does a rapid population increase in an already crowded metropolitan area often cause a relatively large increase in housing prices in a short period of time? Why does a general increase in income lead to a greater increase in the profits of motel owners than in those of farmers?

PRICE ELASTICITY OF DEMAND

We can use the concept of price elasticity of demand to help Mr. H. B. O'Neil, owner of the Showcase Theater. Showcase's ticket prices are currently $5 per person. On average, 1000 people attend movies at the Showcase each week, earning Mr. O'Neil $5000 per week from ticket sales. To finance his son's tuba lessons, Mr. O'Neil is considering raising ticket prices to $6. But will this change increase his income?

The law of demand tells us that if ticket prices are raised, fewer people will come to the Showcase Theater, but each person attending will pay more. (Conversely, attendance would increase if the price were lowered, but each customer would pay less.) We cannot predict whether increasing (or decreasing) ticket prices will increase Mr. O'Neil's income unless we know *how responsive* attendance will be to a price change.

To answer questions such as this, economists use one of several elasticity concepts. In this case, we want to apply the concept of **price elasticity of**

Price elasticity of demand. A measure of the response of buyers to a change in price, usually expressed as the percentage change in quantity demanded divided by the percentage change in price.

Price elastic. A situation in which the percentage change in quantity is larger than the percentage change in price, giving an elasticity coefficient greater than 1 (ignoring the sign).

Price inelastic. A situation in which the percentage change in quantity is smaller than the percentage change in price, giving an elasticity coefficient less than 1 (ignoring the sign).

demand, that is, the responsiveness of quantity demanded to changes in the product's price. If consumers are very responsive to changes in the product's price, we say that demand is **price elastic**; if they are not very responsive, we say that demand is **price inelastic**.

Exhibit 4.1 shows two possible demand relationships. In the first case (D_1), a $1 change in ticket price will gain (or lose) Showcase Theater 100 customers per week. In the second case (D_2), the change in ticket sales is much larger: 400 customers per week. Because quantity demanded responds more to price changes in the second case than in the first, economists say that demand is more price elastic in the second case and more price inelastic in the first.

Why does Mr. O'Neil care whether demand for more tickets is price elastic or price inelastic? The cost of showing a movie for 10 or 200 people is about the same. Thus Mr. O'Neil's profit depends largely on ticket sales. Suppose that he raises the ticket price from $5 to $6. If he loses only 100 customers, he will earn $5400 ($6 per ticket × 900 tickets), or $400 more than he currently earns. But if he loses 400 customers, he will earn only $3600 ($6 per ticket × 600 tickets), or $1400 less than he currently earns. In other words, he gains from an increase in ticket price if his customers are not very responsive to price (if demand is price

Exhibit 4.1
Two Possible Demand Relationships for Showcase Theater
The demand curve (D_1) in part (a) is price inelastic because consumers are relatively unresponsive to a change in price. The demand curve (D_2), in part (b) is price elastic because consumers are relatively responsive to a change in price. Along D_1, only 100 fewer tickets will be sold when the ticket price increases from $5 to $6 each. As a result, the increase in price will increase total revenue from $5000 to $5400 per week. Along D_2, 400 fewer tickets will be sold if ticket prices are raised from $5 to $6. In this case, total revenue will fall from $5000 to $3600 per week.

(a) Price-inelastic demand

(b) Price-elastic demand

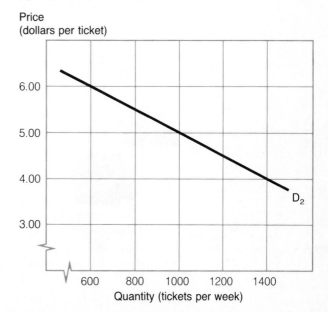

inelastic), but loses if they are quite responsive (if demand is price elastic). In fact, if demand is price elastic, Mr. O'Neil would earn more by *lowering* the ticket price to $4. (To check your understanding, verify this statement by calculating total receipts for both cases.)

This example clearly indicates the importance of price elasticity of demand. To apply this concept, however, you must learn how to recognize the circumstances under which demand is likely to be price elastic or inelastic and how to measure elasticity.

Price Elasticity as a Relative Concept

In the preceding example, a change of 400 in ticket sales was clearly larger than a change of 100. However, absolute changes in quantity sold are not always a good measure of response to price changes. If customers will buy 2000 more units of a product when its price is lowered, is that a small or a large response? We cannot answer that question unless we know how large current sales are. In the wheat market, where millions of bushels are exchanged each year, an increase of 2000 bushels per year is insignificant. But for a small-town shoe store, the sale of 2000 more pairs of shoes per month would be a very significant increase.

Percentage changes in quantity and price.   We can tell whether demand is price elastic or not if we know the *relative* size of a change in quantity. For this reason, economists measure elasticity as a percentage change. To calculate the percentage change in quantity we divide the difference in quantities demanded $(Q_2 - Q_1)$ by the *average* of the two quantities:

$$\text{Percentage change in quantity} = \frac{\text{Difference in quantities}}{\text{Average of quantities}} \times 100$$

$$= \frac{(Q_2 - Q_1)}{(Q_2 + Q_1)/2} \times 100$$

As we have mentioned before, memorizing formulas is not easy. To help you remember the principles involved, let's consider an example. Exhibit 4.2 shows the demand for tennis rackets at C&J Sports Center. If the price decreases from $90 to $80 per racket, the quantity of tennis rackets demanded increases from 1200 to 1300 per year. Substituting into the formula for percentage change in quantity, we find that

$$\text{Percentage change in quantity} = \frac{(1300 - 1200)}{(1300 + 1200)/2} \times 100$$

$$= \frac{100}{1250} \times 100$$

$$= 0.08 \times 100 \quad \text{or} \quad 8\%$$

You may be wondering why in the formula we divide by the average of the two quantities. If we did not use the average, we would have to divide by either the original quantity or the new quantity. As a result, we could get two different answers. In our example, if we divided by Q_1 (1200), we would get an answer of 8.3 percent. But if we divided by Q_2 (1300), we would get an answer of 7.7 percent.

Price (dollars per racket)	Quantity demanded (rackets per year)	Price elasticity of demand coefficient[a]
140	700 — — —	
		1.80
130	800 — — —	
		1.47
120	900 — — —	
		1.21
110	1000 — — —	
		1.00
100	1100 — — —	
		0.83
90	1200 — — —	
		0.68
80	1300 — — —	
		0.56
70	1400 — — —	

[a]The price elasticity of demand coefficient shown is the absolute value of the number obtained using the elasticity formula. Price elasticity is always negative; economists are interested in its magnitude, not the sign.

Exhibit 4.2
The Demand for Tennis Rackets at C&J Sports Center

By averaging the quantities, we get a divisor of 1250, and a constant answer of 8 percent change. This difference may seem trivial, but it can be significant. To prove this point to yourself, calculate the percentage change for quantities of 50 and 100, dividing by 50, 100, and 75 (the average of the quantities). (You should get answers of 100, 50, and 66.7 percent.)

We also measure the size of price changes in relative terms. Using a similar formula, we divide the differences in price ($P_2 - P_1$) by the average of the two prices. That is,

$$\text{Percentage change in price} = \frac{\text{Difference in prices}}{\text{Average of prices}} \times 100$$

$$= \frac{(P_2 - P_1)}{(P_2 + P_1)/2} \times 100$$

Substituting the prices $90 and $80 from Exhibit 4.2, we obtain

$$\text{Percentage change in price} = \frac{(\$80 - \$90)}{(\$80 + \$90)/2} \times 100$$

$$= \frac{-\$10}{\$85} \times 100$$

$$= -0.117 \times 100 \quad \text{or} \quad -11.7\%$$

Formula for price elasticity of demand.   Elasticity is a relative concept in a second sense as well. We want to measure the size of the consumer response *relative to* the size of the price change. We cannot tell whether a 10 percent change in quantity demanded is large or small unless we know whether price changed by 5 percent or 50 percent. To measure price elasticity of demand (the responsiveness of quantity demanded relative to changes in price) we combine the formulas for percentage changes in quantity and price as follows:

$$\text{Price elasticity of demand} = \frac{\text{Percentage change in quantity demanded}}{\text{Percentage change in price}}$$

$$= \frac{\text{Difference in quantities/Average of quantities}}{\text{Difference in prices/Average of prices}}$$

$$= \frac{(Q_2 - Q_1)}{(Q_2 + Q_1)/2} \div \frac{(P_2 - P_1)}{(P_2 + P_1)/2}$$

Again using the data from Exhibit 4.2, we can calculate elasticity of demand for a price change from $80 to $90:

$$\text{Price elasticity of demand} = \frac{(1300 - 1200)}{(1300 + 1200)/2} \div \frac{(\$80 - \$90)}{(\$80 + \$90)/2}$$

$$= \frac{100}{2500/2} \div \frac{-\$10}{170/2}$$

$$= \frac{0.08}{-0.117}$$

$$= -0.68$$

Mathematically, price elasticity of demand is *always* negative because price and quantity demanded are inversely related. For convenience, therefore, *economists generally ignore the sign* and express price elasticity of demand in *absolute-value* terms—in this case a value of 0.68. (Note that all the elasticity figures in Exhibit 4.2 are shown as positive values.)

Elasticity coefficients.   The value obtained from the formula (0.68 in this case) is what economists call a **price-elasticity coefficient**. If the price-elasticity coefficient is greater than 1, demand is price elastic; if the coefficient is less than 1, demand is price inelastic. In our example the elasticity coefficient was 0.68, meaning that the demand for tennis rackets at C&J Sports Center is—for this particular price change—*price inelastic*.

Why does this method of expressing elasticity work? Recall that price elasticity compares the percentage change in quantity to the percentage change in price. If the percentage change in quantity is smaller than the percentage change in price, buyers are not responding strongly to a price change. If the relative change in quantity is less than the relative change in price, the elasticity coefficient will always be less than one. Conversely, if the percentage change in quantity is larger than the percentage change in price, buyers are responding strongly to price changes. And when the relative change in quantity is greater than the relative change in price, the elasticity coefficient will always be greater than 1. Finally, in some cases, the percentage change in quantity is the same as the percentage change in price, making the elasticity coefficient equal to 1.

Price-elasticity coefficient. The number obtained by using the price elasticity formula. When its absolute value (ignoring the sign) is greater than 1, the demand (or supply) is price elastic; when it is less than 1, the demand (or supply) is price inelastic; when it equals 1, the demand (or supply) has unitary elasticity.

Unitary price elasticity. A situation in which the percentage change in quantity demanded (or supplied) equals the percentage change in price; the absolute value of the elasticity coefficient is 1.

Exhibit 4.2 indicates that price elasticity of demand is not constant. For a price change from $120 to $130 per racket, the coefficient is 1.47. Thus for this price range, demand for tennis rackets is *price elastic*. When the price of tennis rackets changes from $100 to $110, the coefficient equals 1. In this case, the price and quantity changes are identical in percentage terms. Economists use the term **unitary price elasticity** to refer to this type of situation. (As you will no doubt be asked to calculate price elasticities soon, you should use the price elasticity formula to verify some of the coefficients shown in Exhibit 4.2.)

Because price elasticity of demand is an important concept, the characteristics of the elasticity formula and the steps involved in its use are worth repeating. First, we obtain the percentage changes in quantity and price. Second, we calculate the percentage changes in quantity relative to the percentage changes in price. Third, we ignore all signs and express the price elasticity coefficient as a positive number. And finally, we compare the coefficient to 1 to determine whether demand is elastic, inelastic, or has unitary elasticity for a given price range.

Slope of demand curve versus price elasticity. Exhibit 4.3 shows the demand curve for tennis rackets. As you can see, at the upper end of the price range, demand is price elastic ($E_D > 1$), and at the lower end, it is price inelastic

---

Exhibit 4.3
Price Elasticity of Demand for Tennis Rackets
The price elasticity of demand for tennis rackets varies along the demand curve. The demand is price elastic at the higher range of prices ($E_D > 1$) and price inelastic at the lower range of prices ($E_D < 1$). Between $100 and $110, the demand has unitary elasticity ($E_D = 1$).

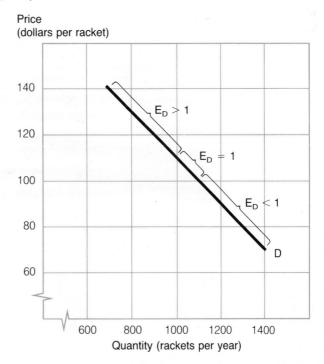

($E_D < 1$). This pattern is characteristic of price elasticity of demand because a small change in quantity represents a much larger percentage change when the original quantity demanded is small than when it is large. For example, a 10-unit change in quantity is a 100 percent change if the original quantity demanded was 10 units, but only a 1 percent change if the original quantity demanded was 1000 units.

Be careful not to confuse elasticity with the slope of the demand curve. The demand curve for tennis rackets in Exhibit 4.3 is a straight line and thus has a constant slope, but elasticity is not constant. Slope is the ratio of *absolute* changes in quantity and price between two points on the curve. Elasticity is the ratio of *percentage* changes in quantity and price. In Exhibit 4.3, for example, each $10 drop in price raises the quantity of tennis rackets demanded by 100. But the percentage change in price represented by a $10 drop in price and the percentage change in quantity demanded represented by an increase of 100 rackets are not the same. Thus elasticity changes as we move along the curve.

Price Elasticity of Demand and Total Revenue

Earlier we indicated that Mr. O'Neil would want to know price elasticity of demand before deciding whether to raise or lower ticket prices at his theater. We showed that if his customers were very responsive to a price change, he would lose money by raising the price of tickets; if they were relatively unresponsive, he would gain. In other words, the best price change in terms of total revenue for Mr. O'Neil's theater depends on the price elasticity of demand.

In fact, there is a general relationship between price elasticity and **total revenue (TR)**. Total revenue is simply the product of price (P) and quantity (Q) sold, or TR = P × Q. Exhibit 4.4 shows the relationship between total revenue and price elasticity of demand for C&J Sports Center. Note that as the price of tennis rackets falls from $130 to $120 each, total revenue rises from $104,000 to $108,000 per year. In this price range, the price-elasticity coefficient is greater than 1; that is, demand is price elastic. This relationship is true: *When demand is price elastic, a decrease in price will increase total revenue.*

The change in total revenue reflects two changes that occur when price is lowered. First, C&J can sell 100 more rackets at the new price of $120, a gain of $12,000. However, each of the 800 rackets it could have sold for $130 now sells for $10 less, a loss of $8000. Because the gain from increasing sales (reflecting the response of quantity) is more important than the loss from lowering the price, C&J has a net gain of $4000. Intuitively, this result also makes sense, because when demand is price elastic, the quantity response affects total revenue more than the price change does. In other words, the increased number of customers outweighs the fact that each customer pays a lower price.

In the lower price ranges, demand is price inelastic (the elasticity coefficient is less than 1). Thus a decrease in price from $100 to $90 will decrease revenue from $110,000 to $108,000. This relationship between elasticity and revenue is also true: *When demand is price inelastic, a price decrease will decrease total revenues.* Again, the net result reflects two changes. When the price is lowered, C&J sells 100 more rackets, a gain of $9000. But each of the 1100 rackets it could have sold at $100 now sells for $10 less, a loss of $11,000. The net effect—a loss of $2000—indicates that the increase in quantity sold is less important than the fact that each racket is sold for less. This is the expected result when demand is

Total revenue (TR). The total number of dollars received from sales, calculated as the product of price and quantity sold, or TR = P × Q.

Price (dollars per racket)	Quantity demanded (rackets per year)	Total revenues (dollars per year)	Change in total revenue (dollars per year)	Price elasticity of demand coefficient[a]
140	700	98,000		
			+6,000	1.80
130	800	104,000		
			+4,000	1.47
120	900	108,000		
			+2,000	1.21
110	1000	110,000		
			0	1.00
100	1100	110,000		
			−2,000	0.83
90	1200	108,000		
			−4,000	0.68
80	1300	104,000		
			−6,000	0.56
70	1400	98,000		

Exhibit 4.4
Demand for Tennis Rackets: Elasticity and Total Revenue

[a]The price elasticity of demand coefficient shown is the absolute value of the number obtained using the elasticity formula. Price elasticity is always negative; economists are interested in its magnitude, not the sign.

price inelastic; the effect of the quantity response is small, and the effect of the price change is large.

Note that the price-elasticity coefficient is 1 for a price change from $100 to $110. This relationship is also true: *When demand has unitary price elasticity, a change in price has no effect on total revenues*. In this case, the price and quantity changes, in percentage terms, are equal. Thus the effect on total revenue of having fewer customers as the price is increased is exactly balanced by the effect of each paying a higher price.

So far we have assumed that changes in price are relatively small. However, if price were doubled, we could move from a price-inelastic portion of the demand curve to a price-elastic portion of the curve. However, measurements of price elasticity tend to be meaningful only for relatively small price changes. Even so, elasticity is a useful concept in the real world. When trying to decide whether to raise prices, most business managers consider the effect of relatively small increases, not a doubling of prices overnight.

To remember the important relationship between percentage changes in quantity and price, focus on the law of demand, the meaning of price elasticity of demand, and the calculation of total revenue. The law of demand means that a price increase causes the quantity demanded to fall. The increase in price will tend to raise total revenue; the fall in quantity will tend to reduce total revenue.

To determine the net effect on total revenue, we must know by *how much* quantity demanded falls. If demand is price elastic and price increases, the percentage drop in the quantity demanded will exceed the percentage increase in price; hence a price increase will reduce total revenue. Try the other possibilities, using the law of demand to determine the *direction* of change in price and quantity, and price elasticity to indicate *how much* quantity demanded changes relative to price. See if you can verify that the following statement is true: *A price increase will result in higher total revenue if demand is price inelastic; total revenue will fall, however, if demand is price elastic.* See A Case in Point: Who Pays a Sales Tax? for another example of the relationship between revenue and price elasticity of demand.

Two Extreme Cases

Thus far we have assumed that the usual demand relationship and curve exist: an inverse relationship between market price and quantity demanded, and a curve that slopes downward and to the right. In two extreme cases, however, demand does not fit the usual pattern. Exhibit 4.5(a) shows a perfectly price-elastic demand curve, and Exhibit 4.5(b) shows a perfectly price-inelastic demand curve.

The perfectly price-elastic demand curve, shown in Exhibit 4.5(a), suggests that consumers are willing to buy an infinite amount of the product at or below a price of $3. Demand is said to be perfectly price elastic because if price increases by even a small amount above P_1, quantity demanded falls to zero—an infinitely large response. You may think that such a demand relationship could not exist. It is unusual, but not unheard of. Most often, this type of relationship exists when each individual seller is a very small part of a market. A common example is the wheat farmer who sells thousands of bushels of wheat in a market in which millions of bushels are exchanged. Individual farmers can sell all they want at the going price, but nothing at a higher price. Of course, a single farmer cannot really sell an infinite amount. By expanding sales enough (say, to 1 million bushels), the farmer would become a significant part of the market and could influence market price. Thus demand for the farmer's wheat is perfectly price elastic only over a rather small range of quantity.

The second extreme, shown in Exhibit 4.5(b), is perfectly price-inelastic demand. In this case, the vertical demand curve means that quantity purchased does not vary with price. Regardless of price or how much of their income it would take to buy a small quantity, buyers will purchase a total of 1500 units per week. Situations in which demand is completely insensitive to price are rare, and in most cases apply only to a reasonably small range of prices. Medicines are the most common example. Many diabetics must take a certain amount of insulin each day; taking more or less than the necessary dose can prove fatal. Because medical insurance and government health programs cover the insulin expenses of many diabetics, demand for insulin is probably perfectly price inelastic, at least across the usual range of prices. Even so, at some point price would become too high and quantity demanded would decrease.

Market demand for most products is far from being either perfectly price elastic or perfectly price inelastic and usually follows the law of demand. As a beginning student in economics, you should be careful to distinguish between price-inelastic demand and perfectly price-inelastic demand. When demand is price inelastic, the quantity response to a price change is small; when demand is perfectly price inelastic, the quantity response is zero.

(a) Perfectly price-elastic demand (E_D = ∞)

(b) Perfectly price-inelastic demand (E_D = 0)

Exhibit 4.5
Elasticity Extremes
Part (a) shows a perfectly price-elastic demand curve. Consumers will buy infinite amounts of this product, if the price is $3 or less. If price were to rise above $3, quantity demanded would fall to zero. Consumers make an infinite response in terms of quantity demanded (reducing purchases from an infinite amount to zero) to a price increase. Part (b) shows a perfectly price-inelastic demand curve. Consumers will buy the same quantity of this product, 1500 units per month, no matter how high or low the price is.

Determinants of Price Elasticity of Demand

Although price elasticity of demand is important, in the real world, data defining the demand relationship usually are not available. Without such data, we cannot apply the price elasticity of demand formula. How, then, can Mr. O'Neil and C&J Sports Center set their prices? By applying economic logic, they can identify some factors affecting price elasticity of demand and make an educated guess about whether demand is price elastic or price inelastic.

Availability of good substitutes. Consumers are usually more responsive to price changes when they have a number of options from which to choose. When good substitutes for a product exist, consumers can get much the same satisfaction from any of them. Thus we expect a significant response when the price of one of these products changes. For example, if you walk into the local supermarket and find that the price of one brand of cereal has risen, you have only to check the shelves to find many close substitutes. You can make a significant response to the price change if you stop buying one brand and switch to another. *Demand becomes more price elastic as the number of close substitutes increases.*

Note that we are talking about *good* substitutes, where there is little difference in the satisfaction received. Using the telephone to call your mother who lives 1500 miles away and driving over to her house for a quick chat are substitutes,

A Case in Point
Who Pays a Sales Tax?

State and local governments often use sales taxes to raise revenue. We can use the concept of elasticity to help determine how much revenue a sales tax will raise and who pays the sales tax.

The city council of Collegetown is considering placing a $1.50 tax on a six-pack of beer and a $1.50 tax on SuperSub sandwiches. To explore the importance of elasticity, let's assume that demand for beer is price inelastic and demand for SuperSub sandwiches is price elastic. The two graphs in Exhibit 4C.1 show the current market conditions and the changes that would occur with the sales tax. For ease of comparison, we assume that in both cases the market price without a tax is $3.00 and that the quantity sold of each product is 400 per week.

What is the impact of a sales tax? As the two graphs indicate, the sales tax shifts the supply curve (from the perspective of the buyer) up by the amount of the tax. Note that at each quantity, the price paid by the consumer will be $1.50 more. Because the tax raises the price paid by the consumer, we can expect quantity demanded to fall. In both graphs, the new equilibrium (where D intersects S_1 + tax) shows a higher price and lower quantity sold.

We are now ready to estimate revenue and identify who pays the tax. First, how much revenue will the sales tax raise? Because we have assumed the same supply relationship for each product, the answer depends on the price elasticity of demand. The tax to be paid in each case is the amount of tax ($1.50 per unit) times quantity sold. For beer, the tax revenue would be $525 per week, or 350 six-packs sold at $1.50 tax per six-pack. For SuperSubs, the city would receive $450 per week, or 300 sandwiches at $1.50 tax per sandwich. (On the graphs in Exhibit 4C.1, the shaded areas identify total taxes to be paid.)

The tax revenue from the sale of beer would be more than that from the sale of sandwiches because demand for beer is more price inelastic. (The absolute value of the price-elasticity coefficients for the change in price is 0.47 for beer and a 1.86 for sandwiches.) Because they are less responsive to the price increase, buyers of beer reduce quantity demanded less, but the city still collects more from the tax on beer.

You may think that the question of who pays the sales tax is silly. Perhaps you assumed that buyers pay the entire amount of the sales taxes. However, the taxes actually are paid partly by the buyer and partly by the seller. The buyer pays more because of the tax but the seller earns less. For beer the price (including tax) is $1.00 more than it was before. But the seller receives only $2.50 per six-pack instead of $3.00, given market demand. Of the total $1.50 per unit tax, two-thirds ($1.00) is paid by the buyer and one-third ($0.50) is paid by the seller. For sandwiches, the burden shifts. The seller pays two-thirds of the tax (receiving $1.00 less per sandwich); the buyer pays one-third ($0.50 more per sandwich).

too. Either choice allows you to talk with your mother, but they are hardly good substitutes. The availability of an alternative (driving 1500 miles) does not make the demand for telephone service price elastic. Only when good substitutes are available will consumers make a significant response to a relatively small price change.

This distinction is especially important to sellers. When a firm produces a product that is a good substitute for those of its competitors, demand for its product is always more price elastic than the market demand for all such products. For example, demand for gasoline (over a short period of time) is price inelastic, but demand for gas at Fred's Friendly Filling Station is likely to be quite price elastic if Fred is one of four stations in a two-block area. Price elasticity of demand also changes when new competitors enter the market. For example, in the 1970s demand for automobiles made in the United States became much more price elastic because of new competition from Japanese and Western European firms.

Who pays the sales tax depends on the price elasticity of demand. When demand is price inelastic (as for beer), buyers pay more of the tax because they are less sensitive to price changes. But when demand is price elastic (as for sandwiches), suppliers pay more of the tax.

(a) Demand for SuperSubs
(demand is price elastic)

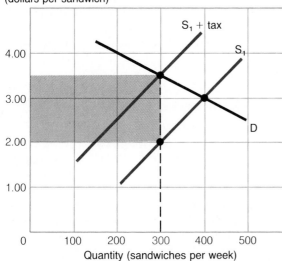

(b) Demand for beer
(demand is price inelastic)

Exhibit 4C.1

Product price relative to income. When a product has a price that represents a large share of the consumer's income, demand is often quite price elastic. For example, a 10 percent increase in the price of cars gets a greater consumer response than a 10 percent increase in the price of toothpaste. However, to a child with a $0.50 weekly allowance (income), a $0.05 increase in the price of a $0.40 candy bar *is* significant. In general, we say that *demand is more price elastic when a product's price is a large portion of the consumer's income; demand is more price inelastic when the price is a small portion of income.*

The relevant time period. The relevant time period for the demand relationship also affects elasticity. As we noted in Chapter 3, a demand or supply schedule refers to a specific time period—the number of tennis rackets demanded per year or the number of movie tickets sold per week. Given a longer time period in which to respond, consumers can find more alternatives. Thus, in general, *when the relevant time period is short, demand is price inelastic; when the relevant time period is long, demand is price elastic.*

For example, demand for oil tends to be quite price inelastic over a short period of time. Individuals who heat their homes with oil and drive their cars to work have few easy options and tend to make only small adjustments in quantity demanded. However, as the response of U.S. consumers to the sharp price increases in the 1970s indicated, demand for oil is price elastic over a long period of time. Better insulation for homes, smaller and more fuel efficient automobiles, and car pooling may take time to develop, but they permit significant changes in consumption.

Consider the following situation. It is an extremely hot day; you have been outside working up a thirst. You walk into the only grocery store in a small town (the next town is 20 miles away). You go to the cooler for a cold drink, only to discover that prices at this store are unusually high. What is your response? Under the conditions outlined, you probably pay the price, grumbling all the time. Your demand at the moment is price inelastic because you are thirsty, and a drink 30 minutes from now is not a good substitute for one right now.

Necessity or luxury?   Some believe that price elasticity depends on whether a product is viewed by consumers as a necessity or a luxury. They define necessities to include not only goods essential to physical survival (such as food and medical care) but also goods perceived as minimum requirements for a decent standard of living. As you might expect, they predict that demand for necessities will be price inelastic and demand for luxuries will be price elastic.

Be aware, however, that this distinction is not always clear-cut and is not always an accurate predictor of price elasticity. For example, demand for the best seats for a symphony orchestra concert is often rather price inelastic, although it is hardly a necessity. Moreover, many necessities have a number of relatively close substitutes and therefore have price elastic demand. Demand for food in general is certainly price inelastic, but no one eats "food in general"; we eat steak or chicken or spinach. Demand for some specific food items is price elastic. (Interestingly, the elasticity coefficient for beer is estimated to be 0.80, making demand price inelastic. Whether this condition makes beer a necessity depends on your point of view.)

Price Elasticity of Demand in Action

Now that you know something about price elasticity of demand, you should be able to answer some of the questions posed at the beginning of this chapter. For example, why are wheat farmers as a group likely to profit from a generally poor crop? Demand for wheat, like many agricultural products, is price inelastic. (How much more bread would you buy if the price of a loaf drops even by as much as 25 percent?) A poor crop decreases the supply of wheat, raising the market price. Since demand is price inelastic, quantity response will be relatively small and price response relatively large. Thus a poor crop means considerably higher prices and, consequently, higher farm incomes. (Recall that a price increase raises total revenue when demand is price inelastic.)

Why would New York State raise more tax revenue by taxing tobacco products instead of wines produced in the state? Consider the determinants of price elas-

Price elasticity of demand reflects the responsiveness of quantity demanded to a change in the price of a product. It is measured by the elasticity coefficient, calculated as the percentage change in quantity demanded divided by the percentage change in price.

When the elasticity coefficient is less than 1, demand is price inelastic; when the coefficient is greater than 1, demand is price elastic; when the coefficient equals 1, demand has unitary price elasticity.

Determinants of price elasticity of demand include the availability of close substitutes, the product's price relative to the consumer's income, and the length of the relevant time period.

ticity. To those who smoke (and chew) there are few good substitutes for tobacco products, so demand for tobacco is price inelastic. A tax on tobacco therefore would tend to raise a considerable amount of revenue for the state. Smokers would pay the higher price for nearly the same quantity demanded. Wines produced in New York State, on the other hand, have many good substitutes—wines produced in California or imported from other countries, for example. As a result, demand is price elastic, and consumers could easily avoid the tax by buying substitute products. Thus the tax would reduce the quantity of New York wines sold more than it would raise money for the state government.

OTHER TYPES OF ELASTICITY

We can also use the concept of elasticity to describe other responses that buyers and sellers will make to various changes. In this section, we discuss three other types of elasticity commonly used in economic studies: price elasticity of supply, income elasticity of demand, and cross elasticity of demand. Each has much in common with price elasticity of demand. In particular, we use variations of the formula for price elasticity of demand to calculate elasticity coefficients. And each type of elasticity refers to the responsiveness of quantity. The similarities should help you remember what these types of elasticity mean and, more importantly, how to use them.

Price Elasticity of Supply

Price elasticity of demand is the response of buyers to a price change; **price elasticity of supply** is the response of sellers to a price change. If sellers respond strongly to a price change, we say that supply is *price elastic*. If sellers do not respond much, we say that supply is *price inelastic*.

To measure the price elasticity of supply, we use a formula similar to that for price elasticity of demand. Here, however, the change in quantity refers to the change in quantity *supplied*.

$$\text{Price elasticity of supply} = \frac{\text{Percentage change in quantity supplied}}{\text{Percentage change in price}}$$

$$= \frac{(Q_2 - Q_1)}{(Q_2 + Q_1)/2} \div \frac{(P_2 - P_1)}{(P_2 + P_1)/2}$$

This formula expresses responsiveness of quantity supplied *relative* to a change in price (that is, in percentage terms), as does the formula used to measure price elasticity of demand.

Like that for the price elasticity of demand, this formula produces a coefficient, and again we ignore the sign. As with the demand coefficient, we compare the price elasticity of supply coefficient to 1 to determine whether supply is price elastic or price inelastic, or has unitary price elasticity. When the coefficient is greater than 1, supply is price elastic, since the percentage change in quantity supplied is greater than the percentage change in price, indicating sellers are very responsive to a change in price. When the coefficient is less than 1, supply is price inelastic, since the percentage change in quantity is less than the percentage change

Price elasticity of supply. A measure of the response of sellers to a change in price, usually expressed as the percentage change in quantity supplied divided by the percentage change in price.

in price. And when the supply elasticity coefficient equals 1, the percentage change in quantity equals the percentage change in price, and supply has unitary price elasticity.

Price elasticity of supply depends on the willingness and ability of sellers to respond to a change in price. Several factors affect seller responsiveness and thus how price elastic supply will be.

Cost and economic feasibility of storage. Some products are quite durable and can be easily and inexpensively stored. Oil producers, for example, can respond to a price drop by storing the oil they have on hand (or in the ground), while waiting for a better price. The ability to respond to a price change in this way makes supply price elastic. Other products—fresh vegetables, for example—are perishable or expensive to store. Sellers cannot pull large quantities of such goods off the market and store them economically. Supply of these products thus is often price inelastic. *The lower the cost of storage and the more practical storage is, the more price elastic the supply will be.*

Flexibility of the production process. For some goods, the production process does not allow a quick and easy response to price changes. For example, the high retooling and setup costs involved in making new car models limit the sellers' ability to make easy or quick responses. Similarly, construction of high-rise buildings cannot be changed much, once begun. For some chemical products, however, switching from one product mix to another is relatively easy. *When sellers can make quick and inexpensive responses to relatively small price changes, supply is usually very price elastic.*

The supply of by-products, such as kerosene, which is produced whenever gasoline is refined from oil, or sawdust produced by sawmills is typically price inelastic. Supply of these by-products depends primarily on demand for the primary product; seller response just to the price of kerosene or sawdust is not economically practical.

Cost and availability of resources. As we noted in Chapter 3, supply reflects the extra cost of producing an additional unit. Whenever this extra cost is high and rises quickly, supply tends to be price inelastic. If extra units can be produced for nearly the same cost as previous units, supply tends to be price elastic. *When increasing production requires the purchase of increasingly expensive resources, supply tends to be price inelastic.*

Relevant time period. As with demand, each supply curve measures quantity supplied over some specified period of time—a day, a month, a year. Given more time, sellers have greater flexibility and more options for supply. *The longer the time period, the greater the response suppliers can make to a change in price, and hence the more price elastic supply will be.*

Income Elasticity of Demand

In Chapter 3 we also noted that demand and supply, unlike quantity demanded and supplied, are affected by factors other than the price of the product. In discussing the effect of income on demand, we explained how demand for normal goods varies directly with income, and demand for inferior goods varies inversely with demand. That is, for normal goods increased income means increased demand. For inferior goods increased income means decreased demand. **Income elasticity of demand** measures responsiveness of demand to changes in income and is expressed as

$$\text{Income elasticity of demand} = \frac{\text{Percentage change in quantity demanded}}{\text{Percentage change in income}}$$

$$= \frac{(Q_2 - Q_1)}{(Q_2 + Q_1)/2} \div \frac{(Y_2 - Y_1)}{(Y_2 + Y_1)/2}$$

where Y represents income.

Price elasticity of demand and supply expresses the response of the quantity demanded and supplied to a change in price *along a particular demand or supply curve*. However, income elasticity of demand expresses the extent to which a change in income causes a change in the quantity demanded at the *current* price, or the extent to which the demand curve shifts. This difference is reflected in the way we treat the coefficient for income elasticity of demand. Recall that we ignore the sign of the coefficients for price elasticity of demand and supply because we assume that demand follows the law of demand and that supply follows the law of supply. The sign of the coefficient for income elasticity, however, has special significance. *A positive income-elasticity coefficient means that income and demand are directly related; thus the product is a normal good. A negative sign means that income and demand are inversely related; thus the product is an inferior good.*

Because the sign of the income-elasticity coefficient is so important, you must pay careful attention to the order of the quantity and income data when using the formula. If you do not associate Q_1 with Y_1 and Q_2 with Y_2, you will get the wrong sign and confuse normal goods with inferior goods. However, you still ignore the sign of the coefficient when comparing it to 1 to determine elasticity or inelasticity. When the percentage change in quantity is greater than the percentage change in income, the income-elasticity coefficient is greater than 1, and the demand is income elastic. An income-elasticity coefficient less than 1 indicates income-inelastic demand.

Income elasticity is a particularly important concept for business planning. The more income elastic the demand, the more sales will fluctuate with changes in national economic conditions. For example, income elasticity of demand for automobiles is estimated to be 4.0. Thus a recession causing a 10 percent drop in national income will cause auto sales to drop 40 percent (unless automakers respond by lowering price). On the other hand, brewers are less affected by changes in general economic conditions. Income elasticity of beer is estimated to be 0.4.

Cross Elasticity of Demand

The response of demand to changes in the prices of substitutes (such as hamburgers and hot dogs) and complements (such as hot dogs and rolls) can also be measured. When the price of a product rises, consumers increase their demand for substitutes. The demand for a product increases, however, when the price of a complement falls. The **cross elasticity of demand** measures responsiveness of consumer demand for product A to a change in the price of related

Income elasticity of demand. A measure of responsiveness of quantity demanded to a change in income; usually expressed as percentage change in quantity demanded divided by percentage change in income.

Cross elasticity of demand. A measure of the responsiveness of quantity demanded for one product to a change in the price of another product, usually expressed as the percentage change in quantity demanded for one product divided by the percentage change in the price of another product.

product B. The formula is

$$\text{Cross elasticity of demand} = \frac{\text{Percentage change in quantity demanded of product A}}{\text{Percentage change in price of product B}}$$

$$= \frac{(Q_2 - Q_1)_A}{(Q_2 + Q_1)_A/2} \div \frac{(P_2 - P_1)_B}{(P_2 + P_1)_B/2}$$

For example, you might use this formula to measure the change in quantity of large gas-guzzling automobiles demanded in response to a change in price of gasoline (a complement).

The sign of the cross-elasticity coefficient also is significant. A positive coefficient means that buyers will purchase more of one product when the price of a related product increases. A negative sign indicates that buyers will purchase more of one product when the price of a related product falls. Thus *a positive cross-elasticity coefficient means that the two products are substitutes; a negative cross elasticity of demand coefficient means that the two products are complements.*

As with the income-elasticity formula, be careful how you enter data into the cross-elasticity formula. If you are not consistent—matching initial and final values of both price and quantity—you will get the wrong sign and confuse substitutes and complements.

Again, the size of the coefficient, regardless of its sign, indicates the degree of responsiveness. When the cross-elasticity coefficient is greater than 1, the two products are closely related; thus a change in the price of one will greatly affect demand for the other. When the coefficient is less than 1, the two products are not closely related; thus a change in the price of one will have only a small effect on demand for the other. A coefficient of zero indicates that the products are unrelated (as we would expect to find, for example, if we asked how a change in the price of telephone service affects demand for pecans).

Supply and Income Elasticity in Action

Now that you are familiar with supply and income elasticity, you should be able to answer some of the other questions posed at the beginning of this chapter. For example, why would a rapid increase in the population of an already crowded metropolitan area cause a large increase in housing prices over a short period of time? The key here is to recognize that the supply of housing is price inelastic in the short run. That is, it is both difficult and expensive to expand the housing supply in a short period of time. An increase in demand, caused by a rapid population increase, will have a relatively greater effect on the price of housing than on the quantity of housing supplied. Of course, over a longer period of time, the construction industry will respond, and supply will become more price elastic.

This difference between short-run and long-run responses is also evident when government imposes rent controls that establish a ceiling price lower than the equilibrium price, as in New York City, for example. When controls are first implemented (or when the ceiling price is lowered), landlords have few reasonable options. Thus in the short run, supply does not respond much to the change in price. Over time, however, builders find it unattractive to construct new rental housing, and many landlords find it uneconomical to maintain existing structures. If permitted by law, some existing buildings will be converted to other uses—

RECAP ▉▉▉▉▉▉

Price elasticity of supply refers to responsiveness of quantity supplied to a change in price. Determinants of price elasticity of supply include cost and economic feasibility of storage, method of production, cost and availability of resources, and length of the relevant time period.

Income elasticity of demand refers to the responsiveness of demand to a change in income. Normal goods have a positive income-elasticity coefficient; inferior goods have a negative coefficient. The greater the absolute value of the coefficient, the more demand will change when income changes.

Cross elasticity of demand refers to the responsiveness of demand for one product to changes in the price of another product. Substitutes have a positive cross-elasticity coefficient; complements have a negative coefficient. The larger the absolute value of the coefficient, the closer the relationship between the two products.

condominiums, for example—not subject to rent controls. Thus in the long run, supply can become price elastic.

Finally, why does a general increase in consumer income lead to a greater increase in the profits of motel owners than in those of farmers? The key is income elasticity. Demand for food in general is income inelastic, while demand for vacation travel is income elastic. This pattern makes sense if you recognize that the quantity of food you eat is unlikely to increase substantially if your income rises (although the type of food you eat may change). On the other hand, if your income falls, you may cut back on vacation travel expenses, even to the point of eliminating them. Therefore, taking the nation as a whole, increased income will tend to result in a relatively greater increase in demand for vacation travel than for food. Consequently, incomes of motel owners are affected more than incomes of farmers.

CONCLUSION

The concept of elasticity is essential to the study of economics and extends our discussion of demand and supply presented in Chapter 3. Knowing the determinants of demand and supply, we can predict shifts in relationships and determine whether price and quantity exchanged will rise or fall. Knowing about elasticity, however, we can go on to predict *how much* quantity will rise or fall and whether a demand or supply shift will have a greater effect on price or on quantity. We can also predict *how much* demand will shift in response to changes in the price of other goods (cross elasticity) or income (income elasticity).

Thus far, however, our discussion has focused on the operation of a single market. In Chapter 5 you will learn how individual markets are interrelated in a market economy. Changing conditions in many markets are linked by price. In seeking to understand how a market economy may help to achieve the fundamental economic goals, we will use most of the tools discussed so far. Indeed, demand and supply analysis and the concept of elasticity are used continuously from here on to illustrate the effects of changing economic circumstances.

SUMMARY

1. In this chapter we discussed the meaning and implications of elasticity, a concept that measures responsiveness of buyers' and sellers' decisions to various changes in economic conditions. The more elasticity there is, the larger the quantity response will be; the more inelasticity there is, the smaller the quantity response will be.

2. Price elasticity of demand measures buyer response to a change in price. If buyers are very responsive to a price change, demand is price elastic; if buyers are not very responsive, demand is price inelastic.

3. The coefficient for the price elasticity of demand is the percentage change in quantity demanded divided by the percentage change in price. In calculating this coefficient, economists divide the change in quantity and price by the average quantity and price and ignore the sign.

4. When the coefficient is less than 1, demand is price inelastic (the percentage change in quantity demanded is less than the percentage change in price). When the coefficient is greater than 1, demand is price elastic. When the coefficient equals 1, the percentage changes in price and quantity are identical, and unitary price elasticity exists.

5. Total revenue is the product of quantity sold and price. A decrease in price will increase total revenue when demand is price elastic. A decrease in price will decrease total revenue when the demand is price inelastic. Total revenue is unaffected when demand has unitary price elasticity.

6. In extreme cases, a demand may be perfectly price elastic—shown graphically as a horizontal demand curve—or perfectly price inelastic—shown graphically as a vertical demand curve. When demand is perfectly

price elastic, consumers respond to any increase in price by reducing quantity purchased to zero. When demand is perfectly price inelastic, consumers buy the same quantity regardless of price.

7. Demand is more price elastic when many close substitutes exist, when product price is a large portion of the consumer's income, and when a long period of time is allowed for response.

8. Price elasticity of supply measures seller response to a change in price. If sellers are not very responsive to price, supply is price inelastic. If sellers are very responsive to price, supply is price elastic.

9. The coefficient for price elasticity of supply is the percentage change in quantity supplied divided by the percentage change in price. Supply is price elastic when the elasticity coefficient is greater than 1, price inelastic when it is less than 1, and has unitary elasticity when it equals 1.

10. Supply is more price elastic when storage of a product is easy and inexpensive, when the production process allows for quick responses to price changes, when there is little or no change in the extra cost for additional units, and when suppliers have a long period of time to respond to a price change.

11. Income elasticity of demand measures responsiveness of demand to income and is expressed as the percentage change in quantity demanded divided by the percentage change in income. If demand shifts only a little when income changes, it is income inelastic and the elasticity coefficient (ignoring the sign) will be less than 1. If demand shifts a great deal, it is income elastic and the coefficient (ignoring the sign) will be greater than 1. For normal goods the income-elasticity coefficient is positive; for inferior goods, it is negative.

12. Cross elasticity of demand indicates responsiveness of demand for one product to changes in the price of a related product. It is the percentage change in quantity demanded for one product divided by the percentage change in price of another product. The larger the coefficient (ignoring the sign), the more closely the two goods are related. Substitutes have a positive cross elasticity coefficient; complements, a negative coefficient.

KEY TERMS

Price elasticity of demand, 76
Price elastic, 77
Price inelastic, 77
Price-elasticity coefficient, 80
Unitary price elasticity, 81
Total revenue (TR), 82
Price elasticity of supply, 89
Income elasticity of demand, 91
Cross elasticity of demand, 91

QUESTIONS FOR REVIEW AND DISCUSSION

1. Why is the concept of elasticity important to the study of economics? Why would business managers want to know the price elasticity of demand for their product? The income elasticity of demand?

2. For which of the following products would you expect demand to be price elastic? Price inelastic? Why?
   a) A microwave oven.
   b) A degree from a private college.
   c) A piece of sculpture.
   d) Postage stamps used to mail letters.
   e) Cigarettes.
   f) Record albums.

3. A company currently sells 3200 candlesticks each month at a price of $8 each. The sales manager estimates that a $2 per candlestick increase in price would cause sales to drop by 400 candlesticks per month. What is the price elasticity of demand if the sales manager is correct?

4. Which of the following statements is true? False? Why?
   a) When demand is price elastic, total revenue will fall if price is decreased.
   b) The more price inelastic the demand for a good, the greater is the price increase caused by a decrease in supply.
   c) When demand is price inelastic, it's unlikely to shift, but if it does, the shift is likely to be smaller than it would be if demand were price elastic.
   d) If an increase in market supply causes a decrease in total revenue, demand is price inelastic.
   e) If a normal good has an income-elastic demand, there will be only a small decrease in demand if the economy goes into a recession and income falls.
   f) If a seller of a product having many substitutes raises the product's price, total revenue will increase.
   g) When demand is price inelastic, a price change will not affect quantity demanded because buyers have no choice but to pay the higher price.

5. Evidence shows that both the demand for and the supply of agricultural products are quite price inelastic. Moreover, records indicate that supply is subject to relatively large shifts from year to year. Given these facts, explain why the income of farmers often changes dramatically from year to year.

6. A state university facing a budgetary crisis is considering a tuition increase. Use the concepts in this chapter to answer questions (a) and (b).
   a) What will happen to tuition revenue if demand for education at the state university is price elastic?

b) Suppose that the price-elasticity coefficient is 1.50, current enrollment is 10,000 students, and the trustees are considering a $500 increase in the current tuition of $2000, or a 25 percent increase. By approximately how much would total tuition payments change as a result? (*Hint:* calculate the expected percentage change in enrollment, apply this percentage to the current number of students, and note the change in total tuition.)

7. Explain whether the following is true, false, or uncertain: "Over the past 3 years both the market price and total revenue have increased. This proves demand is price inelastic."

8. A nineteenth-century statistician, Ernst Engel, observed that households spend a smaller percentage of their income on food as their income increases, a result known as Engel's law. Does Engel's law suggest that demand for farm products in the United States would grow rapidly or slowly over time? Does it help explain why the number of farmers has declined?

9. Information on three related goods is shown in the following table. Is either X or Y a substitute for Z? A complement? Are the sales of Z greatly affected by a change in the price of X? By a change in the price of Y?

Quantity of Z demanded	Price of Y	Price of X
9,500	$1.45	$5.50
10,500	1.50	4.50

10. The following table shows price elasticity of demand for three products. (*Note:* Following convention, the signs of the coefficients have been eliminated.) For which products is demand price elastic? Price inelastic? Why?

Product	Price elasticity of demand
Furniture	3.04
Restaurant food	1.50
Beef	0.50

11. Answer questions (a)–(c), assuming that the price elasticity of demand for bicycles is 2.0.
a) If sellers raised bicycle prices by 5 percent, what percentage change in quantity demanded would you predict?
b) Would you expect sales at Tony's Bike Shop, one of many in town, to respond by the same percentage change if Tony were the only seller to raise prices? Why or why not?
c) How would your answer to (a) be affected if, during the same time period, all prices rose by 4 percent? (No numerical answer is required here.)

12. If sales of goldfish rise from 12,000 to 20,000 fish per month when per capita consumer income increases from $4000 to $5000 per year, what is the income elasticity of demand? Are goldfish a normal or an inferior good? Will sales by goldfish suppliers be greatly affected if the economy slumps and incomes fall?

Market Economies and Resource Allocation

QUESTIONS TO CONSIDER

☐ What are the conditions that allow a market economy to function smoothly?

☐ How does the circular-flow model depict the interaction of households and businesses in resource and product markets?

☐ How are allocative and technical efficiency encouraged in a market system when individuals act in their own self-interest?

☐ How does a market economy decide what to produce, how to produce, and for whom to produce?

☐ What types of market failures cause allocative inefficiency? Technical inefficiency?

E very society faces the fundamental problem of scarcity—unlimited wants but limited resources—and the fundamental question of how best to use those resources. This question is not easy to answer because each individual has different wants and each resource has different uses.

Gathering the information necessary to decide what to produce, how to produce, and for whom to produce is an enormous and complex task. To organize, coordinate, and direct the use of its limited resources, society must have some basic mechanism or economic system. As you saw in Chapter 1, various societies use considerably different mechanisms in making choices about resource allocation.

Different economic systems reflect different answers to key questions. For example, which decisions should be made by markets and which by government planners? To what extent should property be privately owned and publicly owned? To what extent should goods and services be produced by private industry operating for profits, by private industry on a not-for-profit basis, and by government?

In this textbook, we focus primarily on how market economies answer these questions. (Nearly all market economies are capitalistic—Yugoslavia is a rare exception—so for simplicity, we use the term market economy rather than market capitalist economy.) In market economies the economic role of government is generally limited. Government assists the market economy by issuing money and protecting private property rights through its legal system. But government regulation or planning is typically considered a second choice—something to be used if a market fails for some reason.

CIRCULAR FLOW OF ECONOMIC ACTIVITY

We have much more to say about the role of government in this and following chapters. But first we want to see how a pure market system would operate. In previous chapters, we have discussed the operation of individual markets. Now we want to consider how a system of markets can work to meet economic goals.

You may wonder what keeps the economy moving if individuals in it are free to do as they please. Certainly the U.S. economy does not always work smoothly. However, in order to look at a purer form, we can make some simplifying assumptions. In doing so we want to ensure that demand and supply—the market mechanisms—will work smoothly in moving the economy toward the goals of allocative and technical efficiency. These assumptions are as follows:

1. All resources are owned by private individuals, and private property rights are well-defined.

2. In every market, there are enough buyers and sellers to keep any single buyer or seller from influencing the market.

3. There are no restrictions on the mobility of resources.

4. Buyers and sellers have adequate information about the price and quality of products and resources they can buy and sell.

5. The basic economic activities—buying and selling—are carried out by households and businesses. Government plays no active role in deciding how resources will be used and neither produces nor buys goods. Nor is there any exchange with foreign nations.

Although these assumptions allow us to examine the basic forces underlying a market economy, they do not describe a real-world economy. Having seen the market system's best side, however, we can later examine the consequences when these conditions are not met.

In exploring the operation of this simple economy, we want to answer several questions. First, why and how do individual market exchanges occur? Second, how are markets connected into a system that responds to changes in tastes or scarcity of resources? And finally, how does a market economy answer the fundamental questions of what and how to produce and who receives the goods that are produced? That is, how can it achieve the goals of allocative and technical efficiency and equity?

Circular-Flow Model

In order to understand how a simple market economy works, you must understand something about its two elements—households and businesses—and how they interact. We refer here to households and businesses in an economic sense. No doubt you are familiar with the operation of at least one household, your own, though you may not think of it as an economic unit. When economists look at a household, they focus on its economic rather than its social activities. For this reason, the **household** in economic analysis is not necessarily the same as a family group. It is defined as any person or group of people living together and functioning as a single economic unit.

Similarly, from an economic standpoint, a **business firm** is an organization that produces goods and services for sale. The major function of business firms is to organize production, taking into account both household demand and the relative scarcity of resources.

Exhibit 5.1 shows the interaction of households and businesses in a pure market economy as a **circular-flow model**. In it, households own all economic resources and businesses produce all goods and services; that is, households are

Household. Any person or group of people living together and functioning as a single economic unit.

Business firm. An organization that produces goods and services for sale.

Circular-flow model. A model of a market economy that shows the interaction of households and businesses in product and resource markets.

Exhibit 5.1
Circular-Flow Model of Economic Activity
The circular-flow model shows two flows of economic activity. The inner loop is a real flow—the movement of resources from households to businesses, and the movement of goods and services from businesses to households. The outer loop is a money flow—the movement of money from households to businesses in payment for goods and services received, and the movement of money from businesses to households as payment for resources received. The exchange of goods and services for dollars takes place in product markets; the exchange of resources for money takes place in resource markets.

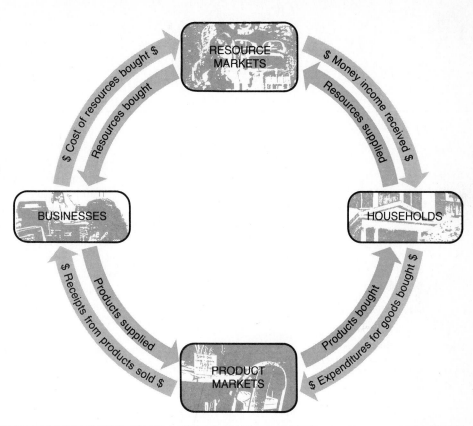

The two most common economic systems are the planned socialist economy and the market capitalist economy. While there are no pure types in the real world, the Soviet Union is primarily a planned socialist economy, and the United States is primarily a market capitalist economy.

In a market economy, households and businesses are connected by two circular flows—the real flow and the money flow—that move in opposite directions.

In the real flow, resources move from households to businesses and economic goods and services flow from businesses to households. In the money flow, money moves from households to businesses and back to households.

the only consumers and businesses are the only producers of goods and services. (For simplicity, we ignore goods and services that households produce for themselves and those bought by businesses because they do not affect the basic principles involved.) Individuals in both groups continually make economic choices and engage in market exchanges. As shown in Exhibit 5.1, there are actually two circular flows. The inner (red) loop is the flow of resources and goods and services. The outer (blue) loop is the flow of money.

Starting with the box representing households and the inner loop, we see that resources—land, labor, and capital—flow from households to businesses. Businesses use the resources to make products—such as automobiles, medical care, and food—that then flow to households. Thus the inner loop shows that households indirectly exchange what they have—resources—for what they want—products. Economists distinguish flows of resources and products—*real* flows—from *money* flows.

In contrast the outer loop shows that the money households spend to purchase goods returns to them when businesses spend the money they receive to buy resources. Money flows in the opposite direction from goods and resources. Together the two flows represent the fact that every market exchange involves the trade of something real—labor time or a haircut—for money.

Role of Money

What is **money** and what is its purpose in a market economy? We implied the existence of money in Chapter 3 when we defined market prices in monetary terms. When we say that the price of fancy sunglasses is $10, we mean that the seller is willing to exchange the sunglasses for $10 of money. All economies have some form of money. You probably know money as coins and paper bills. But the funds in your checking account are also accepted in market exchanges and thus are money. Many items have served the functions of money—cattle, gold, whiskey, beads, woodpecker scalps and, as discussed in A Case in Point: The Economic Organization of a POW Camp, cigarettes. In most modern economies only the government has the power to issue and regulate money.

Money is useful in a market economy because it increases the number and efficiency of exchanges. Without money, we would have to **barter** for everything. In fact, we barter for many items. You might ask a friend to help you study biology and offer, in exchange, to help him study economics. But barter can occur only if two parties can find a mutually satisfactory set of items to exchange. Imagine the difficulty of finding products or services to exchange with the local grocery or clothing store for every purchase you wanted to make. Every exchange involves a **transaction cost**, but the time and effort required to arrange barters can be excessive.

Money allows us to avoid some of the complications and transaction costs of bartering. Money allows each of us to specialize in producing what we can make best. In exchange for our services, we receive something everyone else in the economy will accept in trade: money. By reducing the time and effort it takes to trade, money can increase society's production possibilities.

Money. Items such as coins, paper bills, and checking account deposits that are widely accepted in market exchanges.

Barter. An exchange of one product or service for another; an exchange not involving money.

Transaction cost. The time, effort, and other costs of arranging and negotiating an exchange.

A Case in Point
The Economic Organization of a POW Camp

This case, which illustrates many of the basic features of a market economy discussed in this chapter, is based on the experiences of R. A. Radford,[*] who spent several years during World War II as a prisoner of war (POW). As he observed, the prisoners rather quickly developed economic organizations paralleling those in the outside world.

In the camps, each prisoner was provided with Red Cross food packets containing various foods, including margarine, jam, canned meat, chocolate, cheese, and cigarettes. "Very soon after capture people realized that it was both undesirable and unnecessary, in view of the limited size and the equality of supplies, to give away or to accept gifts of cigarettes or food. Goodwill devel-

oped into trading as a more equitable means of maximizing individual satisfaction." As trading became involved and more sophisticated, cigarettes took on the characteristics of money, and prices of various items were quoted in terms of cigarettes. Markets spontaneously developed, with prices determined by the forces of demand and supply.

The markets were better organized in some POW camps than in others. In nearly every new camp, as well as the "transit camps," individual desires and hence the equilibrium prices of commodities were not well known. In one new camp, Radford relates, "stories circulated of a padre who started off round the camp with a tin of cheese and five cigarettes and returned to his bed with a complete [Red Cross] parcel in addition to his original cheese and cigarettes; the market was not yet perfect." As the economic organization progressed, however, relative values of commodities in terms of cigarettes be-

[*]R. A. Radford, "The Economic Organization of a P.O.W. Camp," *Economica*, XII (November 1945), pp. 189–201.

Resource Markets and Product Markets

Money is exchanged in markets, and the circular-flow model in Exhibit 5.1 shows households and businesses connected by exchanges that occur in two types of economic markets: resource markets and product markets. It also indicates how these markets are connected.

Resource markets are markets in which households sell and businesses buy resources—such as labor and raw materials. Businesses enter resource markets on the demand side. They make monetary payments to households in exchange for resources. They use the resources to produce goods and services, which they sell in product markets. Households supply the resources they own in return for monetary payments that represent wages, rent, and other forms of income. *The forces of demand and supply in resource markets determine what resources are bought by which businesses and for what price.*

Product markets are markets in which businesses sell and households buy products—such as automobiles and medical care. As you can see in the circular-flow model, households enter product markets on the demand side. They make monetary payments to businesses in exchange for goods and services that they use to satisfy their wants. Businesses supply goods in exchange for monetary payments that represent revenue. These exchanges show as two flows: a real flow of economic goods from businesses to households and a money flow from households to business. *The forces of demand and supply in product markets determine what goods and services are bought and sold and at what prices.*

The circular-flow model clearly shows the connection between exchanges in resource markets and product markets. As we pointed out in Chapter 3, in order

Resource markets. Markets in which households sell and businesses buy resources used to produce goods and services.

Product markets. Markets in which businesses sell and households buy goods and services.

came well established, and were posted at convenient locations.

Prisoners were segregated by nationality, so that free trade between various segments of the camp was difficult. However, with appropriate bribes, some British and U.S. prisoners were able to visit other sectors. As a result, "the people who first visited the highly organized French trading center, with its stalls and known prices, found coffee extract—relatively cheap among the tea-drinking English—commanding a fancy price in biscuits or cigarettes, and some enterprising people made small fortunes that way."

Radford also observed how relative prices changed: "Changes in the supply of a commodity, in the German ration scale or in the makeup of Red Cross parcels, would raise the price of one commodity relative to others. Tins of oatmeal, once a rare and much sought after luxury in the parcels, became commonplace in

1943, and the price fell. In hot weather the demand for cocoa fell, and that for soap rose. A new recipe would be reflected in the price level: the discovery that raisins and sugar could be turned into an alcoholic liquor of remarkable potency reacted permanently on the dried fruit market."

Public opinion on trading "was vocal if confused and changeable. A tiny minority held that all trading was undesirable as it engendered an unsavory atmosphere; occasional frauds and sharp practices were cited as proof. Certain forms of trading were more generally condemned; trade with the Germans was criticized by many. Red Cross toilet articles, which were in short supply and only issued in cases of actual need, were excluded from trade by law and opinion working in unshakable harmony. But while certain activities were condemned as antisocial, trade itself was practiced, and its utility appreciated, by almost everyone in the camp."

to demand products, households must have the means to purchase those products. The circular-flow model shows that households obtain money—wages, salaries, and other forms of income—from exchanges they make in resource markets. The more money any household receives, the greater is its ability to demand and the greater is the quantity of goods and services it can consume. *Thus a household receives more goods when the resources it owns and sells are more valuable to businesses.*

Similarly, we know that businesses must have money if they are to demand resources. The monetary flow indicates that businesses obtain money by selling the goods and services they produce to households. The more successful a business is in meeting the demands of households, the more money it receives and the more resources it can demand. *Thus resources tend to flow to those businesses that supply the products households value most.*

The circular-flow model confirms that connections between demand and resource markets can help a market system decide what to produce, how to produce, and for whom the goods and services are produced. But within both product and resource markets, households and businesses must make many individual decisions. In the next section, we consider how they make these decisions and how their decision making helps markets direct the flow of products and resources.

MARKETS: SELF-INTEREST AND RATIONAL CHOICE

In a pure market system, no one tells households what products to buy or where to work. No one tells businesses how to produce or what products to supply. Households and businesses are free to make those choices. This description may sound like a recipe for chaos. If individuals do what they want, how will anything ever get done? More to the point, how can such an economy ever hope to achieve allocative or technical efficiency?

Self-Interest: The Invisible Hand

In fact, when markets function smoothly, we can show that self-interest can help the economy achieve its basic economic goals. Adam Smith first mentioned this tendency in his book *The Wealth of Nations*, describing the mechanism as an "invisible hand"; that is, an individual who acts to maximize personal gain

> Neither intends to promote the public interest, nor knows how much he is promoting it.... [H]e intends only his own gain, and he is in this, as in many other cases, led by an invisible hand to promote an end which was no part of his intention.... By pursuing his own interest he frequently promotes that of society more effectually than when he really intends to promote it.[*]

To understand how a market economy works, we must understand how households and businesses act to maximize personal gain.

---

[*] Adam Smith, *An Inquiry into the Nature and Causes of the Wealth of Nations*. New York: Random House, 1937, p. 423. Smith's book was originally published in 1776.

Households and Rational Choice

To predict behavior, economists typically assume that households seek to maximize satisfaction and that they apply the principles of rational choice discussed in Chapter 2. To satisfy wants, households make two kinds of market exchanges. They exchange resources they own for money, and they exchange money for goods and services. If they act rationally they will choose options that increase their satisfaction.

When choosing what to buy—another car this year or a vacation, for example—a household will compare the extra satisfaction from a new car with the extra satisfaction of a vacation trip. As we stated in Chapter 3, these decisions determine product demand. Products that give households the greatest satisfaction—within the limits of scarcity—are those in greatest demand. Thus if the economy responds to the demands of households, it will produce the goods and services that give households the greatest total satisfaction.

Households also have to decide what resources to sell and which businesses to sell them to. Generally, when individuals work outside the home, they choose to work where they earn the highest possible income. More income enables households to buy more goods and thus to satisfy more material wants. Thus *acting out of self-interest, households sell their resources to those businesses that pay the highest prices.*

However, obtaining maximum satisfaction is not necessarily the same as earning maximum income. Individuals may rationally take lower-paying jobs when they find the work especially desirable. In addition, in deciding how many hours to work, if any, members of the household have to trade the benefits of greater income for the opportunity cost of time. A household may decide it is more important for a teenager in the household to finish college than to seek employment. You may rationally choose to sacrifice the income you could earn from working on Saturdays for the value of the leisure time you can enjoy instead. By assuming rational behavior, economic theory concludes that such decisions contribute to maximum satisfaction in terms of the household's limited resources.

Businesses and Rational Choice

To predict the decisions of firms, economists typically assume that business managers seek to earn maximum profits. **Profits** equal total revenues less total costs. Following the principles of rational choice, firms will produce those goods and services that add more revenue than cost. Thus if revenues increase more than costs, profits will increase. If firms can buy resources for less or produce more efficiently, they can lower their costs. If firms produce the products most in demand, they can increase their revenues. Thus, *acting out of self-interest, firms will purchase resources at the least cost and will efficiently produce those goods and services that most satisfy households' demand.*

Market Prices and Opportunity Costs

Profits. The difference between the total of all revenues received from the sales of goods and the total of all costs of producing those goods.

We know that households and businesses are guided by market prices. Households use relative prices when they determine what to buy and where to sell their resources. Businesses consider relative prices when they decide what to sell and which resources to use in production. Market prices are a major source of information in a market economy. Indeed, in a smoothly functioning market system equilibrium prices are signals reflecting opportunity costs.

Suppose, for example, that lobsters are selling for $4.00 per pound. If this is an equilibrium price, lobsters are worth no less than $4.00 per pound. In fact, this price would be a good measure of value to the last buyer, who would buy a lobster at $4.00 a pound but not at a higher price. Equilibrium price also means that other products that could have been purchased are worth no more than the value of the lobster. Thus the price reflects the opportunity cost to the last buyer. In addition, equilibrium price reflects the lobsterman's opportunity cost. If the price were lower, the last lobster sold would have remained in the ocean. The price reflects the opportunity cost of the resources—time, boat, traps, and other resources—used to find and bring lobsters to market.

Prices also adjust as opportunity costs change. If demand for U.S. automobiles increases, U.S. automakers will demand more steel. As a result, steel prices will rise. Building construction costs will also rise, reflecting the increased opportunity cost of using steel in buildings instead of in automobiles.

Resource Allocation in Action

Price changes are market signals of changes in demand and supply; self-interest is the "invisible hand" that guides the decisions of businesses and households. As the following examples show, businesses and households are not forced to respond to price signals. They respond because it is in their best interest to do so. And as you will see, their self-interested responses to price changes help the economy achieve its goals of allocative and technical efficiency.

Response to increased scarcity. How would we want households and businesses to react if some economic resource became more scarce? From society's perspective, both should recognize this change and try to use less of the resource. That is, they should switch to other resources, eliminating the least valuable uses of the resource. In fact, this is the exact response they make by acting in their own best interest.

In 1972, a worldwide shortage of anchovies occurred when the anchovies failed to run off the coast of South America. Although few people were aware of it, nearly everyone responded to this economic event. Anchovies, in addition to being a topping for pizza, are a rich source of protein. Therefore they are often used in animal feed as a protein supplement.

The poor harvest of anchovies caused supply to decrease. As a consequence, anchovy prices increased. This price increase was the market's signal that anchovies were more scarce. Anchovy buyers, especially those producing animal feed, responded to higher prices by using fewer anchovies (that is, reduced quantity demanded). In place of anchovies, they substituted soybeans as a protein supplement. Although soybeans had previously been more expensive than anchovies, after the price change they were relatively less expensive. This change in relative prices caused increased demand for soybeans as shown in Exhibit 5.2.

Despite the switch to soybeans, the cost of animal feed increased, which in turn raised the cost to cattle ranchers and caused a reduction in the beef supply. The fall in the supply of beef caused higher beef prices in supermarkets and butcher shops. It was at this point that most households felt the effect of the

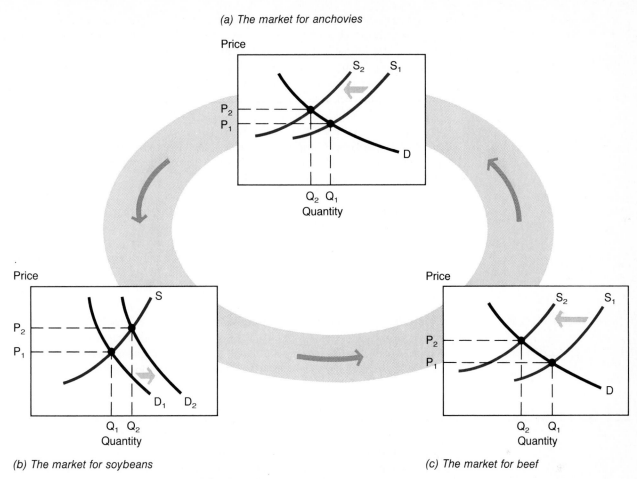

(a) The market for anchovies

(b) The market for soybeans

(c) The market for beef

Exhibit 5.2
Increased Scarcity of Anchovies: Effects on the Soybean and Beef Markets
As shown in part (a), increased scarcity of anchovies caused decreased supply (from
S_1 to S_2), and thus higher prices and reduced quantities exchanged. Higher prices for
anchovies caused increased demand for soybeans (a substitute), resulting in higher
prices and increased quantities of soybeans exchanged [part (b)]. Higher prices of
anchovies (and soybeans) increased the cost of producing beef, resulting in decreased supply, higher prices, and lower quantities exchanged [part (c)]. Increased
use of soybeans and decreased consumption of beef were the market's response to
increased scarcity of anchovies.

scarcity of anchovies. Acting in their own best interests, households responded by
buying less beef. In effect, although they may well have been unaware of the
cause, households helped the economy conserve on the use of anchovies. In
Exhibit 5.2, you can see that the response of households resulted in decreased
demand for beef.

Businesses and households responded to the increased scarcity of anchovies,
but not because they read about it in the newspapers or heard about it on TV, or
because the government informed them. As is typical of a market economy, their

source of information was a change in relative prices. This information worked its way through the economy—through the market for anchovies, the market for animal feed, the market for beef, and finally the local supermarket.

Changes in relative prices give households and businesses an incentive to make appropriate responses. It was in the profit-seeking interest of feed manufacturers to substitute soybeans, helping to conserve anchovies. It was in the profit-seeking interest of cattle ranchers to use fewer protein supplements and thus conserve anchovies. And it was in the satisfaction-seeking interest of households to cut back on beef consumption—indirectly reducing the use of anchovies. To be sure that you understand this example, trace the effect of the increased scarcity of anchovies on the markets for soybeans and beef in Exhibit 5.2.

Response to change in demand. In contrast, how would we want the economy to react if households increased demand for some product? From society's standpoint, businesses should offer more of that product for sale, using more resources for that product and fewer for products that are now less valuable. As you learned in Chapter 3, an increase in demand raises price. As businesses and households react to this price signal, we can expect a shift in resources that will help the economy meet the change in demand.

Suppose, for example, that households become more health conscious and, as a result, increase their demand for aerobics classes while reducing the demand for bowling. Exhibit 5.3 shows the effects of these changes as higher prices for aerobics classes and lower prices for bowling. We would expect businesses to

Exhibit 5.3
Change in Preferences: The Market Response
A change in preference from bowling to aerobics classes will increase demand and price for aerobics classes and decrease demand and price for bowling, as shown. Bowling alley owners respond by closing some businesses. Fitness clubs respond with increased aerobics classes. In a smoothly functioning economy, resources will move from production of bowling alleys, where they are no longer demanded, to production of aerobics classes.

(a) The market for aerobics classes

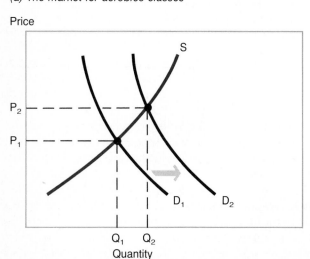

(b) The market for bowling

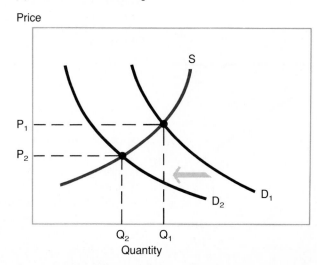

respond by increasing the number of aerobics classes offered (an increase in quantity supplied along the supply curve) and decreasing the number of bowling alleys operated.

Since changes in product demand also affect resource markets, demand for resources used by bowling alleys falls. Some resources formerly used in bowling are released to the economy. At the same time, demand for resources used by aerobics classes rises. As a result of changes in resource demand, some bowling alleys may be converted into fitness centers offering aerobics classes. Firms that made bowling shirts and shoes may now make exercise shoes and clothing. Individuals who used to work in bowling alleys may find jobs in fitness centers.

As in the anchovy example, all these changes happen automatically. No one has to survey households to discover that tastes have changed. Bowling alleys will notice the falloff in demand when fewer bowlers sign up for league play. Fitness centers will observe the increase in demand when more people sign up for aerobics.

These signals—together with the expected change in prices—will cause the market system to respond. Profit-seeking businesses will be happy to increase the number of aerobics classes because higher prices enable them to earn greater profits. Resources will begin to move so that the economy can adjust to the shift in demand. (Of course, not all these adjustments happen at once or without cost. But the direction of change is correct and more or less automatic.)

MARKETS, ECONOMIC QUESTIONS, AND GOALS

So far, we have only hinted at how market prices and the self-interested actions of households and businesses help the economy achieve its goals of allocative and technical efficiency. In this section we look more closely at why smoothly functioning markets are efficient. We also consider how a market system determines distribution of income and output. With a better understanding of these basic operations, we can find out whether a market economy can achieve not only allocative and technical efficiency, but also equitable distribution of goods and services.

What to Produce and the Goal of Allocative Efficiency

Who determines what goods and services will be produced in a market system? Noneconomists often assume that businesses make these decisions. Economists believe that in a more fundamental sense, households—the buyers of goods and services—determine what is to be produced. Product demand reflects the relative value of goods and services to households. Businesses seeking profits find it in their best interest to respond to changes in demand. Of course, what is produced also depends on supplies of resources and technology, that is, the limits of society's production possibilities.

This pattern suggests that household demand determines what is produced. But is this outcome the "best" product mix, that is, the mix consistent with the goal of allocative efficiency? In Chapter 2 we said that an economy achieves allocative efficiency by producing the mix of goods and services that best meets society's wants. To meet this goal, we must determine what society demands. In most market economies, satisfying the demands of individuals is considered a major economic goal. Thus allocative efficiency produces the mix of goods and services that best meets the demands of individuals.

In this and previous chapters, you have seen how market demand—the guiding force in a market economy—reflects the demands of individuals in a society. That is, it reflects individual decisions about how to spend the income received from selling resources. Demand indicates the relative value to households of different goods and services that could be produced. The limits of scarcity and the relative wants of households cause a smoothly functioning market economy to produce a mix of goods and services that is allocatively efficient.

Note, however, that achieving allocative efficiency does not mean overcoming scarcity. To eliminate scarcity, resources would have to be virtually unlimited, and wants would have to be limited. In contrast, the goal of allocative efficiency requires learning to live with scarcity and making the best use of available resources.

How to Produce and the Goal of Technical Efficiency

The dynamics of markets—the competitive forces of demand and supply—also work to answer the second basic economic question: how to produce. Society seeks technical efficiency, that is, the full employment of resources and production of goods and services at minimum cost. In other words, we want the economy to operate along its production possibilities curve, since points inside the curve represent wasted resources, or technical inefficiency.

How does a market economy provide incentives for households and businesses to be technically efficient? In our simple model of the economy, households own all resources and must decide whether or not to put them to work. The major objective of the household is to satisfy its wants. The quantity of wants that it can satisfy, however, depends on the income it earns from the sale of resources. This connection between employment of resources and satisfaction of wants gives households an incentive to fully employ resources. The more fully resources are employed, the greater the household's income and the more wants it can satisfy.

Although households own all resources, the circular-flow model indicates that businesses purchase resources from households and must then decide how to use these resources. These choices are guided by resource prices and the firms' desire to earn maximum profits. Maximum profits result when businesses fully utilize the resources they control. Idle resources earn no profits.

Businesses also decide which resources to buy and what technology to use to produce goods and services. For example, a firm may have to choose between skilled and unskilled labor to produce its products. It will weigh the extra benefits of skilled labor (more output per unit of time and less waste, for example) against the extra cost (higher wages). The technology that uses the least amount of material may not be the most efficient if it uses the greatest amount of labor. The relative price of resources helps businesses to select the mix of resources and the technology that allows them to minimize cost. This choice is not only best for the firm (maximum profits) but also for society, since it is the technically efficient choice.

Technical efficiency is particularly important in an economy that changes constantly, as ours tends to do. Resource prices and technology change frequently, putting constant pressure on businesses to be technically efficient. Because firms in a pure market economy compete for household dollars, standards of technical efficiency are usually high and businesses are quick to adjust to changes in produce demand and resource supplies.

We cannot conclude that the economy will achieve both allocative and technical efficiency all the time. However, we do know that a market system provides strong incentives for firms to be efficient. Businesses that are not allocatively or technically efficient will not survive. They will be pushed out of the marketplace by more efficient competitors, as in the following example.

Business instability: A sign of success or failure? Each year thousands of businesses fail, and thousands of new ones spring up. One result is considerable economic instability. Is this instability a sign of failure, an indication that a market system has problems? Why do some businesses fail, and why are there so many new businesses? By relating the answers to these questions to the goals of allocative and technical efficiency, we can assess whether the number of firms entering and leaving the market indicate success or failure of the market system.

New businesses spring up in response to either new or unmet demand. Thus the development of new firms is allocatively efficient. In some cases, new firms succeed because they introduce or can take advantage of technological improvements. In such situations, the development of new firms is technically efficient.

If new or existing firms do not respond to household demand—that is, if they do not produce the products households want at prices households will pay— they will fail. In weeding out these failures, the market system improves allocative efficiency. Businesses also fail when their costs are higher than those of their competitors. Unless they use the best technology and the best mix of resources, price will not cover the opportunity cost of producing other goods. Indeed, *to survive in a market economy, a firm must respond to household demand in both an allocatively and technically efficient manner.*

Firms can survive, however, only if they earn adequate profits. Profits are the difference between revenues generated by sales and opportunity costs of production. Inadequate profits and business failures thus result for two basic reasons: Revenues are too low and/or costs are too high. In terms of the economic goals, this indicates either technical or allocative inefficiency. Thus business failures often are a sign of success in meeting the economic goals.

For Whom to Produce and the Goal of Equity

Clearly, market prices guide the economy toward its goals of allocative and technical efficiency. But does the market system also work to achieve equity—the distribution of goods produced in a manner society considers fair? Before we can ask whether distribution in a market economy is equitable, we must know how distribution is determined.

In a pure market economy, no single individual or government agency determines how goods are distributed. Like other decisions, distribution is determined in markets. The exchanges that occur in product markets determine which households receive which goods. Every good is produced for and distributed to any household that is willing and able to pay the equilibrium price.

Because ability to pay is important to market demand, the total market value of goods and services received by a household depends on the income it earns

RECAP

A market economy improves allocative efficiency by producing those goods and services having the greatest market demand. In a smoothly functioning market, demand and supply reflect the relative scarcity of resources and the opportunity costs of producing alternative products.

A market economy improves technical efficiency in two ways. The link between household demand and income obtained from the sale of resources provides an incentive to maintain full employment. Competition forces businesses to maintain low-cost production.

A pure market economy does not directly address equity. Distribution of goods and services depends solely on income, with households that own and sell more valuable resources able to demand more goods. Attempts to change distribution to improve equity often involve sacrificing some efficiency.

by selling its resources. Households with higher incomes can buy more in product markets. Thus the distribution of products, therefore, depends heavily on the distribution of income. However, in a pure market economy, income is not really "distributed." It is determined by the forces of demand and supply. You can increase your income by working more, by acquiring more valuable skills, and by working for employers who will pay you the highest wage. The more resources you supply, the larger your income; the greater the demand for the resources you own, the greater will be your income.

But is the distribution determined by market forces fair or equitable? As we noted in Chapter 2, answers to equity issues depend on personal values, that is, on normative judgments. Whether any distribution is equitable is a subject of much debate. Although a pure market system automatically weeds out allocative and technical inefficiency, it does not directly address the goal of equity. No automatic adjustment mechanism exists to change an unfair distribution to one that is more equitable.

Distribution of income is an emotional issue, but we can identify some important economic issues involved. First, changing income distribution means changing product distribution. If society is operating on its production possibilities curve, it cannot produce more. If more is given to one group, less will be received by another; there will be both winners and losers. Only by growing—increasing the production possibilities—can society increase total output and improve the standard of living of all individuals.

Second, in a market system, income and efficiency are connected. Because income results from selling resources, households have strong incentives to fully utilize their resources. Moreover, the possibility of earning higher wages encourages individuals to increase their skills.

A distribution mechanism that is not connected to employment may create inefficiency as it tries to improve equity. For example, consider the effects of a welfare system. In order to provide income to those deserving of support (equity), society has to accept a potential weakening of the work incentive (efficiency).

We continue to raise the issue of equity because it is one of society's goals. However, as we noted before, economists have no scientific way to determine whether any decision improves equity. Debates over equity occur because individuals have different values and different perceptions of how well the economy is functioning. As you will see in the next section, when individual hardships result from problems in a market, concerns over the equity of income distribution often surface.

CAN THE INVISIBLE HAND FAIL?

Market failure. A condition that causes a market to fail to reach allocative or technical efficiency; for example, poorly defined property rights or lack of competition.

In discussing how a market system operates, we have assumed that markets function smoothly. In fact, we deliberately made certain assumptions that show the market system in the best possible light. These assumptions were critical to our finding that markets generate allocative and technical efficiency. In this section we examine these assumptions and consider what happens when they do not accurately describe the real world. That is, we will consider the effects of **market failure**.

Private Property Rights

When you sell something, the presumption is that you have a legal right to the property in question. Markets work on the basis of an exchange of property rights. For example, if you agree to sell your labor services to an employer, you obtain a property right to a paycheck. The business obtains a property right to determine (within limits) how you spend part of your time. If a business sells you a product, you obtain a property right to use that product as you see fit. The business obtains part of your income, which it can use to obtain property rights to additional resources.

Property rights help markets to function efficiently. When you sell something to which you have a property right, you will insist on receiving a payment equal to its opportunity cost. For example, would an oil company spend time and effort to discover new supplies of oil if it were required to give the oil to anyone who asked for it? Would you be willing to sacrifice your income to buy an automobile if you had to lend it to anyone who asked? When property rights are difficult or impossible to establish, exchange becomes difficult and markets do not work effectively.

You probably think of property rights as a legal mechanism, enforced by police and the legal system. But resources also exist for which property rights are difficult, if not impossible, to establish. Clean air, for example, is an economic good because we generally prefer more than less of it and because we must sacrifice to keep it free of pollution. However, there is no market for clean air. Where do you go to buy more of it? Moreover, air is owned by everyone in common. No one has any clear property right to it. Thus we can use this scarce resource without making any payment to its owners. Air has opportunity costs but a zero market price. With a zero price, no individual or business has an incentive to use air in an efficient way.

Property rights are important because otherwise we cannot be sure that market prices reflect opportunity costs. When market prices do not accurately reflect opportunity costs, the market fails, and society suffers. One of the interesting questions economists are currently exploring is whether property rights to such goods as clean air and clean water can be established. If such rights can be established, it may be possible to rely on the market system to determine how clean our air and water should be.

Throughout this textbook and in the real world, you will encounter other areas in which property rights are poorly defined or impossible to establish. As you will see, the tendency for markets not to work efficiently in such cases has often led to government intervention.

Competition

We have also assumed that there are sufficient buyers and sellers in each market to prevent any one of them from having a significant influence on the market. This situation, which economists call *competition*, is important because it prevents any buyer or seller from establishing a market price that favors one or the other. Competition also helps to ensure that market price reflects opportunity cost. In a competitive market, a seller has many opportunities to sell. As a result, no buyer can expect to pay less than the equilibrium price. Likewise, no seller can sell at a price above equilibrium, because buyers would turn to other sellers.

Competition pressures markets to quickly respond to market signals, as we see in A Case in Point: The Ballpoint Pen Industry. It forces businesses to utilize the best mix of resources and the best technology, that is, to be technically efficient. Otherwise, their competitors can sell for less. Competition also requires businesses to respond to the demands of households, that is, to be allocatively efficient. If they do not respond, they will not earn even the minimum profit necessary to survive.

In the real world, few markets are perfectly competitive. Many large industries—oil, steel, and soap, for example—are dominated by a small number of large firms. In such cases, the market may not operate smoothly. When firms have some control over market prices, these prices may not reflect opportunity costs, and allocative efficiency may suffer. Moreover, there is less pressure on these firms to adjust quickly to changes in tastes or relative resource scarcity, thus jeopardizing technical efficiency.

Information

Decisions made by households and businesses reflect the information they have about the prices of alternative products and resources, about the opportunity costs associated with alternative uses of resources, and so on. As you have seen, in a pure market economy each household or business need not gather information about all possible alternatives. Changes in market prices generally provide sufficient information about changes in resource supply and household demand.

However, information can be inadequate or incorrect. For example, even in a pure market economy, households might not automatically get sufficient information about workplace safety or dangers of new medicines. Moreover, while much information is available from market prices, demand and supply schedules sometimes inaccurately reflect relative scarcity of resources and relative wants. In such cases, the market system may not achieve allocative or technical efficiency.

In the real world, then, we are confronted with the possibility of imperfect or inadequate information. But since information, like any other product, is scarce, the cost to any decision maker for gathering all possible information is prohibitive. The market system does address the demand for information to some degree through businesses that specialize in selling information. Such businesses include employment agencies, real-estate brokers, and the publishers of *Consumer Reports*. These "middlemen" help markets achieve efficiency by supplying information at a price reflecting the value of that information. Nevertheless, beyond a certain point, the extra cost of acquiring more information exceeds any extra benefit.

Resource Mobility

If the economy is to operate efficiently, resources must be mobile. A change in household demand also means a change in demand for resources. To respond to the new demand, resources must move out of industries where demand is falling and into industries where demand is increasing. These adjustments take time and have costs. During the adjustment process, some resources will be underutilized or unutilized. Adjusting to a long-run change in demand may cause some firms to go out of business and others to enter business; it may require retraining and relocating workers. When resources are very mobile, the economy can adjust quickly, smoothly, and at low cost. If resources cannot adjust, or if the costs of adjusting are large, resources will not be fully utilized.

A Case in Point
The Ballpoint Pen Industry

The dynamics of competition can be illustrated by a short history of the ballpoint pen industry. The year 1945 marked the production of the first ballpoint pen in the United States. Its manufacturer, Milton Reynolds, sold it for $12.50, although it cost only $0.80 to produce. Still, the seemingly high price did not deter buyers, who responded eagerly to the new product, and Reynolds profited greatly. The high profits, however, attracted the attention of other firms, who saw an opportunity to profit themselves. As a result of the competition for ballpoint pen sales, by 1948 prices had fallen to $0.39 and production costs to only $0.10 per pen.

The results demonstrate how competition can help achieve economic goals. Households expressed a desire for the new product by their willingness and ability to pay a high price for it. Guided by buyer demand, businesses shifted resources to alter the mix of products in order to satisfy the new tastes of society—thereby moving toward allocative efficiency.

Prices in the industry fell as a result of competition. Reynolds could not continue to charge his original high price, because competitors were willing to sell the product for less. The desire for profits and the intensity of competition led manufacturers to outdo themselves in lowering costs. They developed new technologies and technical efficiency was stimulated. Although forces other than competition—such as a willingness to accept less profit on Reynolds's part—might also have led to lower costs, in this case competition clearly worked to further society's goals.

Resource mobility is important because it increases the economy's flexibility and lowers the costs of adjustment. Resources are seldom perfectly mobile in the real world, especially over a very short period of time. But the greater the mobility, the better is the economy's overall performance. Indeed, rapid adjustment and movement of resources are a sign of a successful economy.

Some resources are not very mobile, however. For example, specialized machinery that is useful in one industry may be worthless—or at least worth much less—to another industry. Human resources may not be mobile, either because the skills of individual workers are not easily transferable or because individuals are unwilling to make changes. This situation is particularly true for highly trained or skilled personnel.

For example, a fall in demand for textiles and a rise in demand for computers would cause demand for textile workers to decline and demand for computer technicians to increase. To become computer technicians, however, unemployed textile workers would have to receive significant new training. And if unemployed textile workers live in North Carolina and computer technician jobs are in California, relocation costs would be significant—if, in fact, the workers were willing to move.

In the case of human resources, the loss to society is not limited to the loss of production or to efficiency. Because unemployment means less income, households affected by unemployment are also likely to suffer personal loss, a matter that raises questions of inequity as well as inefficiency.

Macroeconomic Instability

An important, though controversial issue, is whether a market system can avoid major problems of macroeconomic instability. That is, can the market system avoid serious fluctuations in the overall level of employment, output, and prices? The U.S. economy has gone through periods of macroeconomic instability. Since 1970, for example, total output actually decreased on four occasions; rapid and erratic increases in overall prices occurred in the 1970s and early 1980s. Macroeconomic instability makes it difficult for the economy to achieve efficiency and equity. The causes and consequences of macroeconomic instability are a major topic in the macroeconomic portion of this book.

Different Economic Goals and Economic Views

Thus far we have implied that a smoothly functioning market economy is highly desirable from the standpoint of allocative and technical efficiency. But not everyone agrees. Critics of the market system believe that the invisible hand fails because the economic goals are wrong or because the market mechanisms— private property and competition—have undesirable consequences.

For example, in discussing market systems we defined allocative efficiency as the production of the mix of goods and services that best satisfies individual demand. However, not all economists agree that the goal of an economy should be to produce to meet individual wants. Some critics argue that social wants should take precedence. Others believe that market systems tend to divide the population into haves and havenots; to stress material wants instead of human values.

Another feature of the market economy that contributes to efficiency—the link between income and ability to buy goods and services—has also drawn fire. Critics argue that because of this link, market economies often overproduce luxury goods and services for the rich while underproducing essential goods and services for the poor.

Certainly, in the real world, market systems are not the perfect solution to all economic problems. We noted, for example, that the goal of equity is not directly addressed by a market economy. Also, some economists suggest that insufficient competition and information will always cause problems in market systems. But in the United States and other market economies there is a widespread belief that market systems provide the best way to organize most economic activities. At the same time, most economists believe that there are situations in which government activity may improve an economy's performance.

CONCLUSION

In this chapter we considered how a simple, smoothly functioning market economy addresses the questions of what to produce, how to produce, and to whom to distribute the goods and services produced. You learned how market forces provide strong incentives for households and businesses to act in a manner consistent with allocative and technical efficiency.

Achieving efficiency requires smoothly functioning markets. In the real world, not all markets have the conditions necessary, and maximum efficiency is not achieved. The important questions, however, are these: Are conditions in the real world close enough to the ideal world of smoothly functioning markets for us to conclude that efficiency is achieved? If there are market problems, what is the best approach to their solution? What, if anything, do we want to do about the distribution of income from the market system?

In the rest of this textbook, we focus on how the U.S. economy has answered these questions and how the answers have changed over time. As you will see, when real-world markets are perceived to be imperfect or to have failed to meet society's goal of equity, government has often intervened. In the course of your lifetime, you can certainly expect to see economic situations in which government action is proposed. Decisions about government's role in the economy are heavily influenced by political considerations. But by learning the principles of economics, and studying the strengths and weaknesses of our economy and past policies, you will be able to intelligently consider the issues as they arise in the future.

SUMMARY

1. In this chapter we discussed the operation of a market system and considered how it can help a society meet the economic goals of allocative and technical efficiency and equity.

2. All economies must have some means of organizing economic activity. In planned socialist economies, resources are owned collectively and allocated according to government plans. In market capitalist economies, most economic resources are privately owned and markets are the principal mechanism determining what, how, and for whom to produce. No real-world system is pure, however.

3. In a pure market economy (a) all resources are privately owned and property rights are well-defined; (b) all markets have enough buyers and sellers to prevent anyone from influencing the market; (c) resources are highly mobile; (d) buyers and sellers have adequate information on which to base decisions; and (e) households and businesses are the only buyers and sellers.

4. There are two circular flows in a simplified economy: one of money and one of products and resources. Money flows from households to businesses in exchange for products and returns to households as businesses exchange money for resources. Money is useful in a market economy because it makes exchange and specialization easier.

5. There are two types of markets: (a) resource markets, in which households sell to businesses the resources used to produce economic goods; and (b) product markets, in which businesses sell to households the goods and services used to satisfy wants.

6. Economists assume that households and businesses are guided by self-interest. Households seek maximum satisfaction, so they will sell their resources to the business offering the highest price and buy those products having the highest value per dollar of sacrifice. Businesses seek maximum profits, so they will choose to produce those goods and services that offer the greatest increase of revenue over cost.

7. In a pure market system, market price reflects opportunity cost. Market demand reflects the opportunity cost to households of other goods they could buy. Market supply reflects the opportunity cost to businesses of resources they must buy and other goods they could produce.

8. A change in market price is a signal that changes in resource use are desirable. If a resource becomes relatively scarce, its supply decreases and its price rises, motivating households and businesses to conserve. Shifts in relative demand cause demand for resources and market prices to change, motivating businesses and households to shift resources to meet changing tastes.

9. Within the limits of scarcity, market demand—the willingness and ability of households to buy—determines what is produced. Profit-seeking businesses must respond to changes in household demand if they are to survive. Thus a market economy encourages allocative efficiency.

10. A market economy encourages technical efficiency in two ways: (a) by linking household demand to income (thus providing an incentive to maintain full employment); and (b) by requiring businesses to keep resources fully employed and to produce at minimum cost (in order to earn sufficient profits to survive).

11. In a market economy the distribution of goods depends on the distribution of income. Equity, a normative issue, is not directly addressed by the market system, and the tie between income and distribution creates potential trade-offs between equity and efficiency.

12. A market system may fail to achieve efficiency when property rights are poorly defined, if competition is insufficient, if information is poor, or if resources are not sufficiently mobile. Macroeconomic instability is also a potential problem for a market system.

KEY TERMS

Household, 98
Business firm, 98
Circular-flow model, 98
Money, 100
Barter, 100
Transaction cost, 100
Resource markets, 101
Product markets, 101
Profits, 103
Market failure, 110

QUESTIONS FOR REVIEW AND DISCUSSION

1. What is the circular-flow model, and what connections between resource and product markets does it illustrate?

2. Economists typically assume that a business firm seeks maximum profits. In fact, some economists have said that the most socially responsible businesses are those that diligently do so. Do you agree or disagree with this statement? (Before answering, consider what the economists are saying, focusing especially on efficiency.)

3. What are the basic economic activities of households? In what ways do household decisions affect allocative and technical efficiency? (Consider how changes in the choices households make as consumers and resource owners affect the economy.)

4. Assuming a smoothly functioning market economy, answer questions (a) and (b).
   a) Drought wipes out a large portion of the wheat crop in the Soviet Union. How would the price of bread and the income of U.S. wheat farmers be affected?
   b) How did the increased popularity of video games affect the profits of firms specializing in pinball games and the price of rubber flippers used in pinball machines?

5. Steel is a resource that can be put to many uses. In a market economy, what factors would determine which firms producing which products would get the greatest quantity of steel? In what way is your answer to this question related to the relative values households place on various products?

6. What assumptions are associated with smoothly functioning markets? How does the absence of any of these assumptions show that market prices may not reflect opportunity costs? In achieving the goals of allocative and technical efficiency, why is it important for market

prices to reflect opportunity costs? (Give examples in each case.)

7. In a pure market economy, how is the relative scarcity of two resources reflected in market prices? How is the opportunity cost of not producing a certain product reflected in the market for another, unrelated product?

8. Adam Smith's doctrine of the "invisible hand" suggests that if individuals act so as to maximize their own welfare, the welfare of society is also maximized. Explain how this is true and what conditions are required to make it true.

9. Comment on the statement: "A reasonable price for a gallon of gasoline is what the average person can afford." In what sense are equilibrium prices always reasonable in a smoothly functioning market? If some of the conditions required for a smoothly functioning market were not present, would you still conclude that the price is reasonable?

10. Consider the statement: "Prices for eyeglasses are lower in states that allow advertising because those states tend to attract cheap, low-quality businesses." What other explanation can you give for lower prices if the market is smoothly functioning?

11. Recall the principles of rational choice explained in Chapter 2 and discuss the statement: "Because more information will help me make a better decision, I should postpone making a decision until I've gathered all relevant information." (*Hint:* Consider the difference in the amount of information you would typically gather before buying a new car and the amount you gather before buying a new pencil.)

12. Consider the statement: "If a product or resource is exchanged at other than its true value, one party to the exchange loses, and the other gains."
   a) Using the concepts of this chapter, what do you think a product's "true value" is?
   b) What arguments could you use to equate equilibrium price in a smoothly functioning market with a product's "true value"?
   c) Does market price reflect "true value" if the market is not smoothly functioning? Why or why not?
   d) In what way do government price supports or ceilings disturb the market's ability to signal a product's "true value"?
   e) What does an increase in a firm's profits signal about the "true value" of its products?
   f) Suppose that a firm enlists the government's help to make it the sole manufacturer of a product. It can then successfully raise the price and increase its profits. How does the firm gain and how do buyers lose?

g) In a pure market economy, does an increase in price mean that households lose and businesses gain? Does a decrease in price mean that households gain and businesses lose?

13. Changes in market prices not only imply shifts in resource use but also changes in income distribution. What groups would tend to be better off and which worse off as a result of the following?
    a) Foreign oil producers successfully raise the price of oil.
    b) U.S. textile mills get Congress to impose a tariff (a tax) on imported fabrics.
    c) Households decide to eat more fish and chicken and less beef and pork.

14. Consider the statement: "Information's nice, but it's certainly never worth paying for."
    a) Does information have any value?
    b) What does a real-estate broker sell? Do you think that sellers of houses would be better off if they did not use the services of real-estate brokers? Would buyers of houses?
    c) Why are individuals often willing to pay more for a used car they buy from a reputable car dealer than the same make and model of car from an individual who runs a newspaper ad?

Economic Encounters
Labor Mismatch: Balancing Demand and Supply

As we explained in the first few chapters of this textbook, for a market system to operate efficiently, resources such as machinery, raw materials, and people must be mobile. The mid-1980s saw dramatic shifts in U.S. labor markets, leading experts to ask, "How do we retrain workers, decrease unemployment, and make the economy run more efficiently?"

Baby Bust Blues After World War II, the population of the United States boomed because of, among other things, a healthy economy and medical advances. The teenage "baby boomers" found jobs quite easily in the blossoming economy of the 1960s. However, baby boomers decided to have fewer children, or to have children later in life, than did their parents.

The resulting "baby bust" of the decade spanning 1965 to 1975 caused a sudden drop in youth labor in the 1980s, a trend that experts predict will continue into the 1990s. In fact, the Bureau of Labor Statistics claims that by 1995 the United States will have 3.8 million fewer workers in the 16–24 age bracket (the traditional source of entry-level employees) than there are today.

To compound the problem, the U.S. economy began to grow vigorously during the 1980s. As business ac-

> **Shifting demand and supply created labor market imbalances in the mid-1980s.**

tivity increased, demand for labor increased. The result was a labor shortage, particularly in entry-level positions in the service sector. Assuming moderate growth, the Bureau of Labor Statistics projects that between 1984 and 1990, the creation of new jobs will outnumber new entrants in the work force by a million.

The Right People for the Right Jobs Finding the right people to fill the right jobs became a severe dilemma in the 1980s. In the early part of the decade, experts detected a shift in hiring demands. Demand increased for skilled employees in high-tech industries, such as electrical engineering and computers. At the same time, decreasing demand for labor in slumping industries such as farming and automaking drove workers with specialized skills into unemployment lines. Even more importantly, low-wage jobs in service industries, such as restaurants, increased dramatically.

Unfortunately, most blue-collar workers were reluctant or unable to make the transition to white-collar or service jobs. Take the story of Doris, mother of four living in a depressed area of Detroit, who lost her job as an autoworker due to layoffs. Unable to find work that put her skills to use, she faced a dilemma: Should she remain in Detroit, join the unemployment rolls, and possibly go on welfare? Should she accept a job as a waitress or clerk at a fraction of her former salary, just to keep her family at subsistence level? Or should she uproot her family, moving them across the country to search for retraining and employment as a computer programmer in Boston or Atlanta?

In the 1980s, auto workers found themselves on the unemployment lines, often unable to apply their skills to other types of jobs. (Donald Dietz/Stock, Boston)

Frank's story was similar. Born on a farm in Iowa, Frank inherited his father's property—and career—in turn grooming his three kids to take over when they reached adulthood. In the 1970s Frank's farm began to fail; he took out more bank loans for equipment and supplies, but couldn't make the payments when his crops were ruined by drought. He mortgaged his home, getting deeper into debt; his sons and wife took part-time jobs to help out, but eventually the family faced the inevitable. After bank foreclosures on their property, Frank and his family watched their possessions go up on the auction block. Left bankrupt, with few skills to apply to the modern world, Frank was a poor candidate for most jobs he applied for. Job retraining was too expensive for Frank; he finally took a job as a janitor in a local high school.

Labor mismatch (a situation in which workers like Doris and Frank are in the wrong place with the wrong skills and unable to meet the increased demand for skilled labor in other industries) was a common scenario all around the country. Certain industries, such as computer technology, suffered severe setbacks because of those labor shortages, and some businesses failed altogether.

> **When dealing with people as a resource, experts must recognize that human emotions come into play.**

Often the people searching for jobs and the jobs that were available were incompatible. Businesses in affluent areas outside cities lacked a worker pool from which to hire word processing specialists and computer programmers. On the other hand, many inner-city youths, living in neighborhoods where the unemployment rate sometimes hit 50 percent, were unable to find work, turning instead to drugs and street gangs. Some businesses tried to tap the concentrated youth

To compensate for the lack of young people looking for entry-level jobs in the 1980s, McDonalds began hiring older, semiretired workers who needed extra money or who found staying at home too dull. (Darlene Bordwell)

population by setting up training programs in inner-city communities. However, the cost of maintaining such programs proved more than many businesses were willing, or able, to bear.

Service with a Smile? Rapid increases in demand coupled with falling supplies of teenage workers forced service industry employers to try innovative ways of luring new workers. For example, fast-food franchises like McDonalds and Burger King had long provided summer jobs for high school students before they moved on to college or other careers. However, the baby bust of the late 1960s left the fast-food eateries in a labor crunch in the 1980s. In an unusual move, Burger King—employer of more than 160,000 people nationwide—advertised for management trainees on MTV, the cable rock channel, offering educational grants to crew members to attend college or vocational school. Faced with the same youth shortage, McDonalds launched a program aimed at hiring older or semiretired workers (called "McMasters") in positions previously held by teenagers.

Other service industries expanded day-care facilities in hopes of attracting young mothers back into the work force. Increasing salaries, another incentive, caused some restaurant owners to stretch the $3.35-an-hour minimum wage to as much as $8 an hour. Experts predict that a growing number of employers will turn to immigrants to fill jobs previously held by teenagers or young adults.

Learning New Skills The quality of public education was questioned as labor experts explored the problem of labor mismatch. One report revealed that 40 percent of 17-year-olds cannot adequately understand written material, while almost 70 percent cannot solve two- or three-step math problems. With American youth poorly prepared for entering the labor markets, employers faced the choice of lowering their hiring standards or spending more time and money in their search for capable employees. Poor career preparation also meant that there were a disproportionate number of employees available for lower-skilled service jobs than in more challenging positions.

For many businesses, job retraining has become a major goal. Because training and education are expensive, some labor experts called for reinstatement of government training programs such as those slashed by the Reagan Administration in the early 1980s. Other experts pointed to the public education system as a potential source of retraining for jobless workers.

As in any other market, the labor market possesses mechanisms to adjust supply to demand. But for many workers, this adjustment means lower incomes. Moreover, it is not as easy to pack up and move people as it is to transport coal or fruit to areas where demand is greater. When dealing with people as a resource, experts must recognize that human emotions, preferences, attitudes, and abilities come into play. In the service-oriented economy of the 1980s and 1990s, balancing supply and demand in the labor market will not be an easy task.

Overview of the U.S. Economy

QUESTIONS TO CONSIDER

☐ Why are business firms useful to the economy?

☐ What are the advantages and disadvantages of the three legal forms of business?

☐ Which sources of household income are the most important?

☐ In what ways can government potentially improve the economy's performance?

☐ How does the foreign sector affect the domestic economy?

R ecall that in Chapter 5 we presented a simple model of a market economy consisting of only two groups: households and businesses, which comprise the **private sector**. In the real world, of course, economic systems are more complex. To complete an overview of the domestic economy, we must also examine the **public sector**, that is, federal, state, and local government. And finally, we must consider the **foreign sector**, or the foreign individuals, governments, and businesses that participate in a nation's product, resource, and financial markets. We discuss how these sectors affect and are affected by the economy in later chapters. In this chapter, however, we lay the groundwork for that discussion by presenting some basic facts about the sectors of the U.S. economy.

THE PRIVATE SECTOR: BUSINESS

In primitive economies, households produce a large portion of the economic goods they consume. But in all modern economies business firms produce the vast majority of goods and services. This rule holds true regardless of the economic system. The difference is that in market economies businesses are privately owned, whereas in planned socialist economies firms are government owned.

The simple circular-flow model in Chapter 5 shows that business firms are the only producers of goods and services. In the real world, government also provides goods and services, such as roads, schools, and national defense. Moreover, the United States gets an increasingly large proportion of goods and resources from the foreign sector. Nevertheless, the business portion of the private sector, which consists of all U.S. firms, is extremely important.

Private sector. The part of a nation's economy made up of households and businesses.

Public sector. The part of a nation's economy made up of federal, state, and local governments.

Foreign sector. The part of a nation's economy made up of foreign individuals, businesses, and governments that participate in the nation's product, resource, and financial markets.

Role of Business Firms

To understand how the economy operates, you must understand the role played by businesses and why it is useful. Economists stress that businesses exist because they offer four advantages to society: (1) organizing and monitoring team production; (2) reducing the number and costs of market exchanges; (3) lowering costs through economies of scale; and (4) accepting risks. Economists also generally agree that businesses enable a society to be technically efficient.

Organizing and monitoring team production. Economists have long recognized that two or more individuals working together can produce more efficiently than if they worked alone. For example, a single individual could build an entire house working alone, but a team of carpenters can build the same house in fewer total hours of work. Another example of teamwork is the assembly line. Henry Ford used the assembly line to great advantage in producing automobiles. Before introduction of this method of production in 1914, one worker could produce a car in 728 minutes; the assembly line reduced the time required to 93 minutes.

Teamwork requires organizing and monitoring individual performance. Someone must spend time deciding what tasks need to be done, who is to perform them, how each task contributes to total output, and how well each individual performs the tasks assigned. The business firm performs these functions, and society gains the advantages of team production.

Reducing the number and costs of market exchanges. In Chapter 5 we described the advantages of market exchanges and noted that transaction costs are associated with exchanges. These costs include, for example, the time required to search for information and the costs of negotiating contracts.

A large corporation is in business on a long-term basis and can therefore offer jobs on a long-term basis. This allows the firm to avoid the costs of locating and hiring suitable employees every time it wants another task performed. Having a long-term relationship also enables the firm to acquire better and less costly information about employee skills and performance.

Similarly, a textile firm can manufacture many or all of the items it uses to make a finished product. The firm can dye its own thread, weave its own cloth, make its own patterns, cut the cloth, and stitch the final product. Using internal coordination, it can save the cost of negotiating contracts with other firms to do some of those tasks. Of course, substituting managerial for market coordination has costs as well. But when the savings outweigh the costs, technical efficiency increases.

Taking advantage of economies of large-scale production. Economists also recognize that production on a large scale can be more efficient. For example, the publisher of a large daily newspaper can use larger, more efficient presses that would not be economical for a local weekly newspaper. Large-scale production allows specialization of labor, which also offers significant cost advantages. Ford's assembly line, for example, enabled individual workers to concentrate on only a few tasks, at which they became proficient. Because of their size, large firms can afford more specialized machinery, production workers, and managers. Increased size does not always make a firm more efficient, but small firms are often at a competitive disadvantage.

Accepting risks. A final role of businesses is that of accepting risk. Many risks are associated with producing goods and services. If demand drops, for example, a firm may be stuck with products it cannot profitably sell. Firms invest large sums in plant and equipment, accepting the risk that these investments will enable them to produce profitably in the future. The owners of the firm enjoy the benefits of success (profits) but also suffer the costs of failure (losses).

Not all individuals view risks in the same way. Some are willing to accept the high risks of ownership. Others prefer the lower risks of being an employee.

Workers have to bear some risks—the possibility of losing a job, for example—but they generally agree to work for a specified wage or salary. They receive their pay as long as the business continues and regardless of profit levels. By pooling the resources of those willing to accept high risks, the firm can offer the advantages of lower risks to others.

Size of Business Organizations

Business firms vary in size from the small corner drugstore—owned and operated by a single individual—to the huge corporation—owned by thousands of shareholders and operated by thousands of employees. The largest corporations are indeed mammoth in size, as Exhibit 6.1 indicates. Sales by General Motors, for example, are larger than the total value of goods produced in Sweden. Sales by the five largest U.S. corporations exceed Canada's total output. The combined sales of the top 25 U.S. coporations represent 22 percent of the total output of goods in the United States.

Despite the advantages of size, we must recognize that costs become more important as the size of the business increases. First, as the business grows, its

**Exhibit 6.1
The 25 Largest U.S.
Industrial Corporations—
Ranked by Sales**

Rank	Name	Sales (millions)	Assets (millions)	Net income (millions)	Employees (number)
1	General Motors	$ 96,371.7	$ 63,832.8	$ 3,999.0	811,000
2	Exxon	86,673.0	69,160.0	4,870.0	146,000
3	Mobil	55,960.0	41,752.0	1,040.0	163,600
4	Ford Motor Company	52,774.4	31,603.6	2,515.4	369,300
5	IBM	50,056.0	52,634.0	6,555.0	405,535
6	Texaco	46,297.0	37,703.0	1,233.0	54,481
7	Chevron	41,741.9	38,899.5	1,547.4	60,845
8	AT&T	34,909.5	40,462.5	1,556.8	337,600
9	E. I. du Pont de Nemours	29,483.0	25,140.0	1,118.0	146,017
10	General Electric	28,285.0	26,432.0	2,336.0	304,000
11	Amoco	27,215.0	25,198.0	1,953.0	49,545
12	Atlantic Richfield	22,357.0	20,279.0	−202.0	31,300
13	Chrysler	21,255.5	12,605.3	1,635.2	107,850
14	Shell Oil	20,309.0	26,528.0	1,650.0	35,167
15	U.S. Steel	18,429.0	18,446.0	409.0	79,649
16	United Technologies	15,748.7	10,528.1	312.7	184,800
17	Phillips Petroleum	15,676.0	14,045.0	418.0	25,300
18	Tenneco	15,400.0	20,437.0	172.0	111,000
19	Occidental Petroleum	14,534.4	11,585.9	696.0	42,353
20	Sun Oil	13,769.0	12,923.0	527.0	37,818
21	Boeing	13,636.0	9,246.0	566.0	104,000
22	Procter & Gamble	13,552.0	9,683.0	635.0	62,200
23	R. J. Reynolds	13,533.0	16,930.0	1,001.0	147,513
24	Standard Oil	13,002.0	18,330.0	308.0	42,100
25	ITT	12,714.3	14,272.5	293.5	232,000
	Top 25	$773,682.4	$668,656.2	$37,145.0	4,090,973
	Top 10	549,766.5	452,817.4	28,723.6	2,847,923

Source: Fortune, April 28, 1986, pp. 182–183.

management costs grow. Beyond some point, there may be few additional advantages in relying on internal managerial coordination. Second, advantages of economies of scale are also limited. When a firm is large enough to take advantage of the best technology and the best level of specialization, becoming even larger will not lower its costs.

Finally, some economists fear that very large businesses may have too much economic and political power. A gain in economic power means a decline in competition, which (as we said in Chapter 5) is extremely important to society. A gain in political power may enable a firm to obtain political favors not in society's best interests. Whether current firms are too large and have too much power is a subject of much debate but little general agreement.

Types of Business Organizations

In Chapter 5 we defined the goal of businesses in a market economy as earning maximum profits. However, in the real world, some business firms—hospitals and educational institutions, for example—are classified as not-for-profit institutions. Although such firms do not seek profits, they are still interested in responding to consumer preferences and reducing costs. By being more efficient, they can provide more and better services to their customers. Recent research, however, suggests that such organizations do not always operate in an efficient manner. To some extent this result may reflect the absence of the incentives provided by profits. Although the not-for-profit portion of the private sector is growing in importance in the U.S. economy, we will generally assume as we develop economic principles that business firms operate with a profit motive.

Even though all business firms have similar goals, they can have one of three legal forms in the United States: proprietorship, partnership, or corporation. The legal structure is important because it determines who receives the profits, who has control, and who bears the risks.

Proprietorship. The simplest legal form of business is the **proprietorship**. A proprietor is the sole owner of the business, or the individual who receives all the profits and bears all the risks of the business. Many small retailers—clothing and hardware stores, service stations—and professionals—doctors, lawyers, dentists—operate their businesses as proprietorships.

Proprietorships are easy to form, requiring no extensive legal arrangements and, except for licenses in some cases, no government permission. In addition, the proprietor does not have to share decision-making authority with anyone else. A proprietor may hire employees and delegate some responsibility to a hired manager. But the proprietor is ultimately responsible for decisions and for the success or failure of the business.

Proprietorship. A firm in which one person owns all the productive property, receives all the profits, and is personally responsible for all the liabilities.

Proprietorships also have disadvantages. The financial resources of the firm are the savings of the proprietor, the proprietor's ability to borrow is often quite limited and, as a result, most proprietorships are small. A small firm may not be able to take advantage of economies of scale in buying equipment or hiring specialized workers. This drawback helps to explain the lack of proprietorships in the automotive and steel industries. In addition, small firms often cannot offer the job security that many workers desire. Finally, a proprietor has unlimited liability for the firm's debts. This characteristic is not a problem if the business is a success, but if it fails, the owner must personally cover the debts, if necessary selling personal property to pay off creditors.

Type of enterprise	Number of businesses		Sales		Net income	
	(thousands)	(%)	(billions)	(%)	(billions)	(%)
Proprietorship	11,262	70.1	$ 516.0	6.1	$ 70.8	24.4
Partnership	1,644	10.2	375.2	4.4	−3.5	−1.2
Corporation	3,171	19.7	7604.2	89.5	223.0	76.8
Total	16,077	100.0	$8495.4	100.0	$290.3	100.0

Exhibit 6.2
Distribution of Business Firms, Sales, and Profits by Type of Enterprise, 1984

Source: U.S. Department of the Treasury, Internal Revenue Service, *Statistics of Income Bulletin* (Winter, 1986–1987).

Partnership. A business firm with two or more co-owners who share the control and profits of the firm is called a **partnership**. Like a proprietorship, a partnership is relatively easy to form, although the partners must agree on the contributions each will make and how they will share profits and control. Partnerships are the least common form of business organization, accounting for only 5 percent of the total number of firms in the United States. They are most commonly found in firms of lawyers, doctors, and accountants.

Partnerships can have an advantage over proprietorships because they pool the talents and financial resources of more than one person. They offer a greater potential to take advantage of specialization and other economies of scale. On the other hand, decision making can be complicated because the partners share control. Partnerships can also be unstable because, legally, a partnership is dissolved when any one of the partners withdraws or dies. Moreover, each partner is personally liable for all the debts of the business if it fails, even if those debts and the failure resulted from the poor decisions of only one of the partners.

Corporation. By most measures the **corporation** is the major legal form of business organization in the U.S. economy. Exhibit 6.2 shows the sales and profits of the three forms of business. As you can see, less than 20 percent of all businesses are organized as corporations, but they accounted for almost 90 percent of all sales and three-fourths of all business profits in 1984. Corporations dominate the manufacturing, transportation, public utilities, and finance industries and account for slightly more than one-half of all business in the trade and construction industries. Some economists suggest that encouragement of the corporate form of business was an important factor in the growth and development of the U.S. economy.

In order to understand the advantages of the corporation, we can consider how one is formed and operates. First, a group of investors decides to form a corporation. To do so, they must obtain a charter from a state government. The charter establishes the corporation, in the eyes of the law, as a "legal person" separate and apart from the owners. After receiving a charter, the investors contribute to the firm's financial resources in return for shares of **stock**. Shares of stock are ownership claims entitling the holder to a share of the firm's assets and income. Usually, these shares also give the holders some control over the business's operations. In fact, however, large corporations often have thousands or even millions of individual shareholders. Thus most shareholders (owners) do not personally work in the business. The shareholders elect a board of directors

Partnership. A form of business organization in which two or more individuals share the ownership, profits, and liabilities of the firm.

Corporation. A firm created as a legal entity separate from the persons who established it. It is usually owned by many individuals, whose liability is limited to their investment in the firm.

Stock. Shares of ownership in a corporation.

to represent their interests. The board of directors hires managers, who actually make the business decisions under the board's control.

The most important legal characteristic of the corporation is that of *limited liability*. The owners (shareholders) are not personally liable for any debts of the corporation. If the business fails, they may lose whatever they have invested, but no more. Limited liability makes it easier for a corporation to raise funds by selling additional shares of stock, drawing on the resources of a large number of individuals. This would not be practical if all the investors had to be partners and were responsible for the corporation's total debts. (Would you risk investing in IBM if it meant that you were personally liable for all the firm's debts?)

The ability to attract funds is very important. It allows the corporation to grow large enough to take advantages of economies of large-scale production and specialization. The corporation can spend more for research and development and can hire professional managers and experts to help it produce more efficiently and respond more quickly to consumer demands.

The corporation also has a "permanent" life. That is, it continues as long as the business is solvent, regardless of what happens to individual shareholders. This permanency also enables shareholders to sell their stock to other individuals, generally without having any effect on the business.

However, corporations also have disadvantages. First, the separation of ownership and management may create conflict. Managers may be more interested in preserving their jobs than in seeking maximum profits. In Chapter 5 we described the importance of profit-seeking to allocative and technical efficiency. If managers do not seek to increase profits, corporations may not produce desirable results for society.

Second, corporations can grow quite large, as shown in Exhibit 6.1. If their size gives them too much economic or political power, we would have reason to be concerned. Before reaching any final conclusion about the desirability of corporations we must weigh their benefits against their possible costs to society.

Classification and Grouping of Businesses

All businesses, of course, are not alike. Economists find it useful to classify firms by **industry**, that is, a group of firms producing the same or similar products, such as the automotive industry. Using this definition, we can associate industries with product markets. In the automotive industry, for example, U.S. automakers compete both with each other and with foreign automakers. Often, a business firm is involved in more than one industry. For example, Ford Motor Company is also in the home appliance and television industries.

Economists also group industries into broader categories, as shown in Exhibit 6.3. Note that agriculture (including farms, fishing, and forestry) employs a relatively small percentage of the work force. In terms of total employment, the most important industries are manufacturing, financial services, and other services. Other services include hotels, education, health care, auto repair, and entertainment and employ the largest and fastest growing proportion of the private-sector work force. Employment in services increased by 80 percent from 1969 to 1984, compared with a less than 33 percent gain for all private-sector employment. Services and retail trade together accounted for over 70 percent of the new jobs

Industry. A group of firms producing the same or similar products.

Industry	Percentage of total employment		
	1969	*1984*	*1995*
Agriculture	4.4	3.1	2.5
Mining	0.6	0.6	0.5
Construction	5.4	5.5	5.4
Manufacturing	25.1	18.5	17.2
Transportation, utilities	5.7	5.1	5.1
Trade	20.5	22.7	23.0
Financial services	4.7	5.9	6.0
Other services	18.6	23.6	26.2
Federal government	3.4	2.6	2.3
State and local government	11.6	12.3	11.7
Total	100.0	100.0	100.0
Total employment (thousands)	81,508	106,841	122,760

**Exhibit 6.3
Employment by Industry,
1969 to 1995**

Source: Monthly Labor Review, November, 1985, p. 28.

created during this period and almost 80 percent of the expected increase between 1984 and 1995. Although manufacturing accounts for a declining proportion of all jobs, employment in manufacturing is expected to remain virtually constant.

Business Finances

You will be able to understand business activities better, if you know something about business finances. Consider Exhibit 6.4, which shows two reports for a fictitious firm, Longview Binoculars Corporation (LBC). The *income statement* shows that the firm sold $3 million worth of goods and that its net income after all costs and taxes was $240,000. Like most manufacturers, LBC's major production expenses were for the resources it bought from other firms (such as leather for straps and binocular cases) and for labor resources (wages of production workers and salaries of management). The firm also had a small amount of interest expense on loans it took out to finance its operations and to purchase machinery. In addition, the firm had to pay sales, property, and income taxes.

One expense, **depreciation**, requires further explanation. Most other expenses represent actual costs of resources—such as materials and labor—purchased and used during the year. Depreciation, however, is an estimate of that part of the original cost of plant (factory buildings) and equipment that has been used up or worn out during the year. For example, LBC bought a machine last year for $50,000. This machine is expected to be useful to LBC for 5 years. Thus LBC estimated $10,000 (one-fifth of the original cost) as the fraction of the machine used up in each of the 5 years. This $10,000, along with similar figures for other plant and equipment, represent the $500,000 of depreciation shown on the income statement. In effect, depreciation represents the amount of profit the firm would have to earn to be able to replace capital resources as they wear out or become obsolete.

Depreciation. An estimate of that part of the original cost of capital goods, such as machinery and buildings, that has been used up or worn out during a specific period of time.

Income Statement

Total revenues		$3,000,000
Less: Expenses		
Materials	$750,000	
Wages and salaries	950,000	
Interest	200,000	
Sales and property taxes	50,000	
Rent	150,000	
Depreciation, plant and equipment	500,000	
Total expenses		2,600,000
Net income before income taxes		$ 400,000
Less: Income taxes		160,000
Net income after income taxes		$ 240,000
Distribution of net income		
Dividends paid to shareholders	$ 40,000	
Retained earnings	200,000	
	$240,000	

Balance Sheet

Assets		
Inventory	$300,000	
Plant and equipment	900,000	
Other assets	400,000	
Total Assets		$1,600,000
Liabilities		
Bank loans	$200,000	
Bonds	400,000	
Other liabilities	100,000	
Total Liabilities		$ 700,000
Equity		
Common stock	$300,000	
Retained earnings	600,000	
Total Equity		900,000
		$1,600,000

Exhibit 6.4
Income Statement and Balance Sheet for the Longview Binocular Corporation for the Year Ending December 31, 1987

Depreciation is special in another way. The costs of other resources were amounts LBC had to pay its suppliers. But depreciated goods have already been paid for. Rather than being a cost to the firm, depreciation can actually add to the funds LBC can spend, since it reduces the firm's tax obligation. For example, LBC had to pay $160,000 in income taxes last year, or 40 percent of its income before taxes. Without depreciation, its pre-tax earnings would have been $900,000 and its tax bill $360,000 (40 percent of $900,000). Thus depreciation added $200,000 to LBC's available funds. However, in 1986 Congress decreased the rate at which

Dividends. The portion of a corporation's profits paid out to its shareholders.

Retained earnings. The portion of a corporation's profits not paid out to its shareholders but retained by the corporation to finance future production.

Bonds. IOUs of a business or government representing a promise to pay a specified sum of interest at regular intervals (usually every four or six months) for a specified period of time. At the end of the loan period, the borrower is obligated to repay the original amount loaned.

Transfer payments. Payments, usually made by government, to individuals for the purpose of redistributing income.

firms could charge depreciation expenses against income, forcing firms to borrow more money to have the same amount of available funds.

The lower part of the income statement shows what LBC did with its income from last year. First, it paid out a total of $40,000 as **dividends** to its shareholders. The remaining $200,000, shown as **retained earnings**, represents the portion of its income that LBC reinvested in the business.

Exhibit 6.4 also contains a second statement, called a *balance sheet*. This statement is called a balance sheet because it always shows the total value of assets as exactly equal to the total value of liabilities and equities. *Assets* are items of value, including a firm's inventory (resource materials on hand and goods ready for sale) and its capital resources (plant and equipment). As of December 31, 1987, LBC's assets were $1.6 million. In contrast, *liabilities* represent future payments the firm must make to nonowners, usually for money it has borrowed. The financial contributions made by owners are called *equities*.

The balance sheet also reflects the fact that every dollar spent by the firm to acquire assets has been obtained from one or more sources of financing. Bank loans and **bonds** are forms of liability financing. Both obligate the firm to make regular and specified interest payments and, at a specified time, to return the funds borrowed. There are two principal sources of equity financing. By selling new shares of stock, the firm acquires new owners and new financing. The firm also obtains funds from shareholders indirectly, by retaining a portion of its net income. In fact, about 75 percent of the funds firms use to buy new capital resources and expand operations are obtained from retained earnings and the tax savings from depreciation.

THE PRIVATE SECTOR: HOUSEHOLDS

As we discussed in Chapter 5, the household is a major decision-making unit in a market economy. Households own economic resources and household demand heavily influences the production of goods and services.

Size and Characteristics of the U.S. Population

Exhibit 6.5 presents some basic facts about the U.S. population. As you can see, the population is expected to increase from nearly 240 million individuals in 1985 to a projected 260 million in 1995. Some 117 million, just less than half of the population, are officially classified as members of the labor force—either working or looking for work. Most of the rest depend on income earned by other household members, accumulated wealth or savings, or government **transfer payments**. Among those not in the labor force are many of the 26 percent of the population under the age of 18 and the 12 percent over the age of 65. Many of these not officially part of the labor force—homemakers, for example—perform valuable economic services, although they are not paid wages.

Recent population statistics show several trends that have important economic implications. First, both the number and the proportion of the population over the age of 65 are growing rapidly. Although some of these individuals continue to work, a large number are retired. Many of those who are retired obtain a significant

RECAP

The roles of business firms are to organize and monitor team performance, to reduce the costs and number of market exchanges, to take advantage of economies of scale, and to accept risks. If they grow too large, however, costs of managing may rise and economic power may become too concentrated.

The three principal legal forms of business organization are the proprietorship, the partnership, and the corporation. Most goods and services are produced by corporations.

Business income is the difference between revenues (dollar sales) and costs (including materials, wages and salaries, rent, interest, and taxes). Income can be distributed as dividends to shareholders or reinvested in the firm as retained earnings.

All business assets—inventory and plant and equipment, for example—must be financed. Liabilities are funds borrowed by a business from nonowners such as banks; equity represents funds invested by owners.

	1965	*1975*	*1985*	*1995*[a]
Population (millions)	194.3	216.0	238.8	259.6
Under 18 years of age (percent)	35.9	31.1	26.3	25.9
Ages 65 and over (percent)	9.5	10.5	12.0	13.1
Labor force (millions)	76.4	95.5	117.2	129.2
Women (percent)	35.2	40.0	44.2	46.4
Teenagers (percent)	7.9	9.5	6.8	5.5

Exhibit 6.5
Selected Characteristics of the U.S. Population and Labor Force, 1965 to 1995

[a]Data for 1995 are projections.

Sources: U.S. Department of Commerce, Bureau of the Census, *Projections of the Population of the United States by Age, Sex, and Race: 1983 to 2080*, Current Population Reports, Series P-25, No. 952; U.S. Department of Labor, *Monthly Labor Review,* November 1985.

proportion of their income from government transfer payments, such as Social Security. Medicare, another government program, pays a substantial portion of the large medical bills of this group.

However, many people over the age of 65 have accumulated wealth in the form of land, buildings (especially homes), savings accounts, corporate stocks, and bonds. Should they be required to sell some of these assets instead of receiving government transfer payments? Should society support this growing group with transfer payments or encourage more employment and reliance on private means? As the older population expands, these policy issues will become increasingly important.

A second trend is the increasing proportion of women who work outside the home. In 1965 only one-third of all women were in the labor force. By 1985 over one-half of all women worked and by 1995 the proportion is projected to be almost 60 percent. This trend, in part, is caused by economic factors. Families are increasingly relying on the income of more than one person to satisfy household demands for goods and services. In many cases, the income of two working adults is necessary to keep the family income above the poverty level. In addition, the growing proportion of single-parent families (most headed by women) has further increased the percentage of women who work. The number of women entering the labor force has increased demand for many goods and services, especially child care.

Sources of Personal Income

When discussing the circular-flow model in Chapter 5, we noted that households receive income from the sale of economic resources they possess. **Personal income** represents the total income received by all households in the economy from all sources. There are six basic sources of personal income: wages, proprietor income, rent, corporate dividends, interest, and transfer payments. Exhibit 6.6 shows the absolute and relative sizes of these sources.

Personal income. The total amount of income, before taxes, received by all households from all sources.

Labor income. The largest single source of income for U.S. households is the wages and salaries paid by producers in exchange for labor. In fact, labor is the only resource that most households have to offer for sale. In 1986, wages and salaries made up about two-thirds of total personal income, a proportion that has changed very little over the years.

An additional 8 percent of total personal income was derived from proprietor income. This figure includes the businesses of professionals (doctors and lawyers, for example), beauticians, farmers, and the owners of small retail stores—any proprietorship. Proprietor income once accounted for a much larger share of total personal income—19 percent in 1947, for example. Some of that change reflects the choice by many former proprietors to incorporate essentially owner-operated business in order to reduce their personal liability.

Part of proprietor income represents returns on owners' investments in land, buildings, and equipment and on accumulated wealth. But in most nonfarm proprietorships, the owner's labor is the firm's principal resource; therefore most proprietor income is really a payment for labor. If we add proprietor income to wages and salaries, we find that almost three-fourths of all personal income derives from the sale of labor resources.

Income from other sources.   Although labor is the chief resource of households, it is not the only one. Money saved or inherited may be used to buy stocks and bonds or maintain a savings account from which households receive interest income. In 1986, households received $475 billion in interest income, representing 14 percent of total personal income; transfer payments accounted for $353 billion of household income, or some 10 percent of total personal income. Although a relatively small part of total personal income, transfer payments are a very important source of income for the elderly and for the poorest households.

In addition, some households receive dividends on corporate stock that they own. However, stock dividends presently account for only 2 percent of total personal income. Finally, a few households own land, capital resources (such as buildings), and natural resources that they rent or sell, but rental income accounted for less than 1 percent of total personal income in 1986.

Exhibit 6.6
Sources of Personal Income, 1986

| | *Amount* | |
Source	(billions)	(%)
Wages and salaries	$2282.6	65.5
Proprietor income	278.9	8.0
Rental income	15.6	0.5
Dividend income	81.2	2.3
Interest income	475.4	13.6
Total	$3133.7	89.9
Plus transfers[a]	353.3	10.1
Total personal income	$3487.0	100.0

[a] Total transfers less personal contributions to social insurance.
Source: U.S. Department of Commerce, *Survey of Current Business,* January 1987, Table 2.1.

Percent of total personal income received

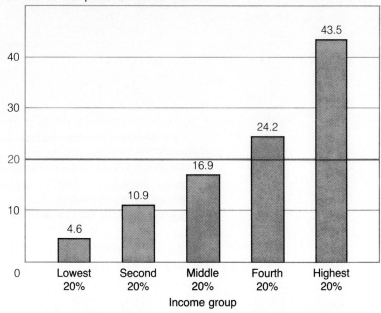

Exhibit 6.7
Income Distribution for U.S. Families, 1985

Source: U.S. Bureau of the Census, *Money Income and Poverty Status of Families and Persons in the United States: 1985,* Current Population Reports, Series 60, No. 154.

Distribution of Personal Income

These facts about personal income reveal nothing about the distribution of that income. Because income is required to demand goods and services in a market economy, the distribution of income largely dictates their distribution.

If families are grouped by income, as in Exhibit 6.7, we can see that income is unequally distributed. The data indicate that the poorest 20 percent of families received less than 5 percent of the total income, or only one-fourth of what this group would have received if income were equally distributed. By contrast, the richest 20 percent of families received more than twice their proportionate share.

Note, however, that the income proportions shown include cash transfer payments received but not taxes paid or value of medical care, housing, food stamp, and other public services provided to the poor. Although this definition of income closely matches the definition of personal income, it does make the income distribution appear somewhat more unequal than it actually is.

A household's income in a market economy depends on the value of its resources. Thus you might think that unequal resource distribution would explain the unequal distribution of income. In fact, however, relatively few households own any significant amount of land or capital resources; most depend largely on wages and salaries for income. Thus when studying income inequality, we must consider how labor markets operate. This topic is covered in detail in Chapter 15. While the data suggest that income is unequally distributed, they do not indicate whether the distribution is fair or equitable. That depends, of course, on personal values. But you should bear in mind that most economists do not associate equity with an equal distribution of income.

RECAP

Households and businesses together make up the private sector of the economy. Households own most resources and household demand significantly influences what is produced.

Personal (household) income includes wages, rent, interest, proprietor income, stock dividends, and transfer payments.

Income in the United States is distributed unequally. Most economists, however, do not associate equity with an equal distribution of income.

THE PUBLIC SECTOR

Our original simplified model of a market economy included only the two parts of the private sector: businesses and households. There is, however, another important part: the public sector, or government. Government plays an important role in all economic systems. The nature of this role depends on the type of economic system. In planned socialist economies, like that of the Soviet Union, government owns or directly controls the use of most economic resources. Government enterprises produce most goods and services. In market capitalist economies, like that of the United States, the public sector owns few economic resources. Nevertheless, it is a major influence in the economy.

Exhibit 6.8 shows a circular-flow model that includes the public sector. Government enters the real flow by purchasing from the private sector resources, goods, and services such as labor and missiles and provides goods and services such as education and national defense. Government also affects the circular flow by collecting taxes and making transfer payments.

In 1986, the public sector in the United States—federal, state, and local government—spent $1.5 trillion dollars and purchased some 20 percent of the

Exhibit 6.8
The Circular Flow of Government Activity
The government enters the circular flow to purchase goods (computers and police cars) and resources (labor and paper) from the private sector. Matching this real flow is a money flow of government payments. Government also provides goods and services (national defense and education) to the private sector. In return, the private sector provides monetary payments in the form of taxes and other charges (license fees and parking fines).

economy's total output. Many goods and services are produced by and for the public sector. National defense is a government service, although most weapons systems are produced by private firms. An agency of the federal government, the U.S. Postal Service, provides mail service. State governments provide college education and highways; local governments provide schools, libraries, and police and fire protection.

In addition, government regulations and taxes have far-ranging effects on the economic decisions of businesses and households. For example, the Environmental Protection Agency regulates air and water pollution. Taxes raise the prices of gasoline, entertainment, and other goods. Government tariffs and quotas restrict purchases of goods and services from other countries. Price supports encourage agricultural production. Government loans encourage more young people to attend college. Tax deductions for interest paid on mortgages increase demand for single-family housing.

Role of Government

Economists typically define the proper role of government as helping society achieve the economic goals of allocative efficiency, technical efficiency, equity, price stability, full employment, and growth. Most economists agree that the private sector sometimes fails to produce results consistent with those overall economic goals. These failures suggest that the performance of the economy *might* be improved through government action. (The stress on the word might is a reminder that government's role is controversial.)

Most economists agree that government can play an important economic role by: (1) facilitating market activity; (2) correcting for market failures; (3) redistributing income and economic opportunity; and (4) fostering economic stability and growth. In this section, we want to see *why* government is involved, *what* economists agree government should do, and *how* government should determine the limits of its activities with respect to the economy.

Facilitating market activity. You saw in Chapter 5 the importance of property rights to a market economy and how market transactions can be viewed as exchanges of property rights. Well-defined property rights promote allocative efficiency because they provide a strong incentive for resource owners to sell those resources to the highest bidder. For this reason, government often acts to establish, protect, and regulate property rights. Examples include laws protecting and defending ownership claims and making sure that individuals and businesses uphold contractual agreements involving the exchange of property rights. Indeed, most economists believe that government's help in establishing property rights is essential in a market system.

Protecting buyers and sellers promotes equity. For instance, the law states that sellers must deliver the merchandise selected by buyers. Sellers cannot substitute less valuable goods at the same price. Likewise, buyers must pay the full price agreed on with sellers. Buyers cannot pay for purchases in counterfeit bills, shoplift, ride an airplane without buying a ticket, or leave town without paying the landlord.

In addition, government facilitates market activity by establishing and protecting the integrity of money. As we noted in Chapter 5, money helps to simplify the exchange process by allowing individuals to sell resources—labor, for example—in one market and use the income they receive to buy goods and services in other markets. If many individuals or businesses in an economy question the value of the nation's money, exchanges become much more complex.

Correcting for market failures.
Facilitating market activity is important but does not account for much of the economic activity of government, especially on state and federal levels. A more common role for government is correcting for market failures that cause allocative and technical inefficiency. Why do markets fail? What, if anything, can government policy do to correct failures? What does our analysis suggest about desirable and undesirable policy solutions?

Failures due to lack of competition. We noted in Chapter 5 that competition is essential in a market economy. Government helps to maintain competition in a variety of ways. Federal and state laws prohibit many anticompetitive practices, such as collusion among firms to restrict supply and raise prices. When the technically efficient number of firms in an industry is very small—for example, electric power companies in the utilities industry—government regulations substitute for competition.

Failures due to public goods and services. A market system is geared to respond primarily to the household demand for **private goods**. Private goods include all the products and services that people buy from businesses, such as milk, clothing, and cars. Only those who are willing and able to pay the market price receive the benefits of a private good. Movies shown in theaters are private goods because only those who pay the price of admission are able to enjoy them; those who are unwilling or unable to pay are excluded. Because market demand reflects the value of private goods to households, allocative efficiency results as businesses seek to produce the mix of goods and services that best matches demand.

In contrast, markets fail to reflect demand for **public goods** like national defense and clean air. Public goods are collectively consumed. Generally, there is no practical way to exclude anyone from using public goods, even if they are unwilling to pay for them. Consider, for example, national defense. When a certain defense capability is established, you and your neighbors are equally protected. It is not practical to provide more national defense for you and less for your neighbor, regardless of how much you as an individual want or how much you as a taxpayer contribute to pay for the protection.

The characteristics of public goods make establishing a market for them difficult or impossible. If you know that others will pay for their production, there is little incentive for you to pay. Thus, private producers find it difficult to supply public goods profitably. Some public goods could be produced and sold in markets, but market demand always understates the value of public goods and services to society. Thus too little would be produced from the perspective of allocative efficiency.

To correct for this market failure, government provides many public goods and services by acting either as a collective producer or, more often, as a collective purchasing agent. The major problem is to find a substitute for markets that answers the questions of how much to provide and how to pay for what is

Private goods. Goods and services that benefit only those people who purchase them. People who are unwilling or unable to pay for them can be prevented from receiving their benefits.

Public goods. Goods and services that cannot benefit one person without benefiting all. People who cannot or will not pay for them cannot be prevented from receiving their benefits.

Externalities. Benefits and costs from any product that affect individuals other than those who demand and supply the product.

Social benefits. Benefits measured from the perspective of society; include both private benefits and external benefits.

Social costs. Costs measured from the perspective of society; include both private costs and external costs.

External costs. Costs of a product that are borne by individuals other than those who demand and supply it.

External benefits. Benefits from a product received by individuals other than those who demand and supply it.

provided. Typically, government uses a political decision-making process. But there are questions about whether this process functions well enough to meet the goals of efficiency and equity.

Failures due to external costs and benefits. For a market to function efficiently, market price must reflect not only demand for a product but also the value of the resource used to produce it. Some products, however, involve **externalities** that either increase the true cost of producing the product or the product's true benefit to society.

For example, when mills produce steel, they also create air pollution. When your neighbors play loud music while you are trying to study for your economics exam, they create study problems for you. When some families in your community get inoculations against a communicable disease, they also reduce your chances of getting the disease.

But who pays for the air pollution, your lost concentration, your decreased chance of illness? Not the automaker who buys the steel, or the party-goers who enjoy the music, or you, who paid for no medicine. Rather, residents of the area around the steel mill pay in terms of a reduced quality of life. You pay with a C on the exam. Families pay with the pain and cost of inoculation. Hence those who cause externalities are not charged for the costs they impose on others, and they do not receive compensation for any external benefits they create.

The market fails because of the difference between goods and services that involve externalities and those that do not. In making rational economic decisions, consumers and producers always weigh the extra *private* benefits and extra *private* costs. This behavior results in allocative efficiency when externalities do not exist, since producers pay for every resource they use and consumers pay for every product they receive. Firms will stop producing and consumers will stop buying when the next unit adds more to the costs than to benefits. But making rational social choices also requires weighing extra **social benefits** and extra **social costs**. If externalities do not exist, private benefits equal social benefits and private costs equal social costs. Thus consumer and producer decisions that balance private costs and benefits also balance social costs and benefits. When externalities exist, however, a balance of private costs and benefits does not yield a balance of social costs and benefits.

Externalities can arise when property rights are nonexistent or poorly defined. For example, the steel mill that produces pollution uses up one of society's scarce resources—clean air. However, because no one in particular owns the air, the mill pays nothing for the use of the resource. The clean air used up has real social costs, but they are **external costs** to steel producers because the clean air costs them nothing. When there are external costs, the social costs—the costs of all the resources used—exceed the private costs reflected in supply. Because supply does not reflect the full social costs, the output produced is not allocatively efficient. The market provides too much steel and too little clean air.

When there are **external benefits**, as in the case of public health services, some individuals receive benefits for which they pay nothing. The social benefits—the benefits to all members of society—exceed the private benefits to those who decide to buy inoculations. In such cases, market demand tends to undervalue the goods and services, and too little will be bought and sold.

In some cases, allocative efficiency may be achieved through private transactions despite external costs and benefits. If you have an apple orchard that benefits from the bees I keep next door, we might agree that you will pay me to keep more beehives. If your smoking in the dorm room or office we share is offensive to me, I may be able to bribe you to quit, compensating you for the benefits you lose.

But in most cases—public health services and the air pollution created by a steel mill, for example—too many people are involved and the transaction costs of negotiating an agreement are too high to make private arrangements practical. In such cases, the government may act to correct for the market failure and restore the balance between social benefits and social costs. For example, federal and state laws restrict the quantity of air pollution that steel mills can create. Communities regulate the amount of noise you and your neighbors can make. Government provision of public health services increases their use. Although government actions may lead to an improvement in conditions, the principles of rational choice remind us that we must also consider the costs of government action when deciding whether it is appropriate.

Failures due to imperfect information. Market failure also occurs when information available to private decision makers is imperfect. For example, if the potentially harmful effects of a new prescription drug are not known to buyers, those who buy it may be subject to unrecognized risks. Government may help the market to achieve efficiency by providing information that might not otherwise exist about potential benefits and costs. Warning labels on pesticides, studies of potential hazards of drugs, and listings of job opportunities are all examples of information provided by government in an effort to assist the market system.

Redistributing income and economic opportunities. In addition to outcomes that are allocatively and technically efficient, society wants outcomes that are equitable, that is, determined by rules that it believes are fair and just. We noted earlier in this chapter that income in the United States is unequally distributed: The richest 5 percent of U.S. families receive more than three times their proportionate share of income, whereas the poorest 20 percent receive less than one-fourth of their proportionate share. Equity, especially in a market economy, is not, however, generally defined to require equal incomes.

Economists and politicians agree that income is unequally distributed. However, they disagree strongly about the causes of this inequality. Some argue that inequities in the system—racial, sex, or age discrimination, for example—are responsible. Others believe that unequal incomes merely reflect individual choices about how much to work and how much education to obtain. But when the goal of equity is not being met by the market system, many economists believe the government should seek to improve equity by redistributing income and economic opportunity.

In the United States, transfer payments such as welfare and Social Security are the primary means by which government redistributes income. In addition, government laws and policies against discrimination and programs such as student loans seek to promote equal opportunity. Defining equity, however, requires personal value judgments. Moreover, it is difficult to determine the exact causes of inequalities. Because of these difficulties, government programs that seek to improve equity are controversial.

Fostering economic stability and growth. We also hope that the economy can grow and avoid major swings in economic activity that can lead to high unemployment and/or rapid inflation. By altering its levels of spending and taxation and by regulating credit, the government can affect the level and stability of total economic activity. Government can also affect the rate at which the economy grows over time.

Although most economists agree that government *can* affect the economy's stability and growth, not all agree that government can do so effectively. In the 1970s, in particular, the U.S. government was not very successful in maintaining price stability and avoiding high unemployment. The role of government in such activities is both complex and controversial and is a major topic in the macro-economics portion of this textbook.

Government and Rational Choice

Economists generally agree that the government roles discussed above are appropriate *in theory*. But many disagree with particular government actions *in practice*. One point on which there is a strong consensus, however, is that when government makes economic decisions, it should do so using economic analysis and the principles of rational choice. That is, it should weigh the costs and benefits of potential actions and act only when the extra social benefits outweigh the extra social costs.

Size and Nature of the Public Sector

The preceding discussion indicated some of the reasons why government is involved in the economy. Let's now consider the degree to which government is involved by looking at the size and distribution of government expenditures. As Exhibit 6.9(a) illustrates, the size of the public sector has increased greatly. In absolute terms, public sector—federal, state, and local government—expenditures increased from $13.4 billion in 1935 to $98.5 billion in 1955 to $1.5 trillion in 1986. Absolute increases, however, are potentially misleading because the size of the economy has also grown. However, government expenditures have also increased in relative terms as well, from 18 percent of total output in 1935 to 24 percent in 1955 and 35 percent in 1986.

Exhibit 6.9(b) divides government expenditures into purchases of goods and services and transfer payments. Government purchases—national defense, public education, roads, and the judicial system, for example—represent a transfer of resources from private sector to public sector use. After rising from 14 percent of total output in 1935 to almost 19 percent in 1955, government purchases have remained a fairly constant 20 percent of total economic output.

Unlike government purchases, transfer payments do not represent a reduction in the quantity of private goods and services consumed. (Although, as we point out in Chapter 18, transfer payments may slightly decrease work effort and hence output.) Instead, they represent a transfer of income from one part of the private sector to another and a substitution of public for private decision making. The growth of transfer payments is the major cause of public sector growth. For

(a) As a percent of total output

Percent
of GNP

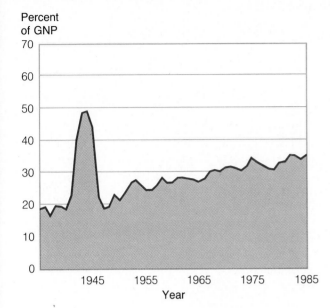

(b) By type

Percent
of GNP

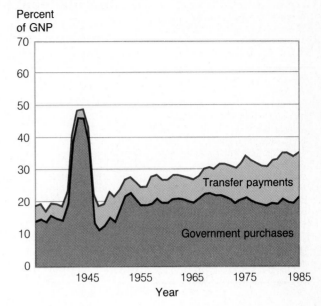

Exhibit 6.9
Government Expenditures
The graph in part (a) shows that government expenditures have steadily climbed from about 20 percent of GNP after World War II to over 30 percent in recent years. The graph in part (b) shows the distribution of expenditures. The lower area of the graph shows that government purchases of goods and services as a percent of GNP has remained relatively constant at about 20 percent of total output since 1955. The upper area of the graph shows transfer payment expenditures. It indicates that the growth in transfer payments accounts for the increased size of government spending, especially since the mid-1960s.

example, transfer payments grew from 4 percent of total output in 1935 to 6 percent in 1955 and 12 percent in 1986. Transfer payments in 1986 represented 34 percent of total expenditures and almost 40 percent of expenditures by the federal government.

Government purchases, however, are only one part of the economic impact of government because they do not include the costs of laws and regulations. The costs to businesses and individuals of complying with government laws are a cost of government, even though they are not government expenditures. For example, government regulations on air pollution force businesses to purchase, install, and operate pollution control devices. Tax laws encourage individuals to spend for health insurance, education, and home ownership, while discouraging other activities. Indeed, whether you receive Medicare or a tax deduction for health costs, you are in effect receiving a government subsidy. Such indirect government expenditures accounted for an estimated $388.4 billion in 1984. If they had been counted with direct expenditures, federal spending as a percentage of total output would have been 34, not 24, percent.[*]

---

[*]See Joseph Stiglitz, *Economics of the Public Sector*, New York: W. W. Norton, 1986, p. 30.

Size of Government: International Comparisons

As Exhibit 6.10 shows, government plays a larger role in other market-oriented economies than in that of the United States. Government expenditures account for over two-thirds of total output in Sweden, and one-half of total output in Italy, France, West Germany, and the United Kingdom. By contrast, government represents only a bit over one-third of the total economy in the United States and Japan. In addition, the government's share of the economy grew more rapidly in other countries between 1960 and 1982, almost doubling in Sweden, Italy, and Japan. Exhibit 6.10 does not include countries such as the Soviet Union, Hungary, or China because in planned socialist economies, virtually all economic activity is controlled by government.

Although such comparisons do not suggest that government in the United States is too small (or too large), they do show that government activity is greater in other countries. Nevertheless, government has a major impact on the U.S. economy, both in aiding the market system and in attempting to correct for market failures. In later chapters we will consider further the impact of government and whether its future role should be different.

THE FOREIGN SECTOR

Imports. The value of goods and services produced in foreign economies bought by U.S. individuals, businesses, and governments.

Exports. The value of U.S. resources, goods and services bought by foreign individuals, businesses, and governments.

To complete our overview of the U.S. economy, we must recognize the impact of foreign individuals, businesses, and governments—collectively known as the foreign sector. International trade between the United States and foreign economies is certainly important. **Imports**—including platinum, oil, industrial diamonds, coffee, bananas, automobiles, video cassette recorders, and textiles—account for a sizeable portion of the resources used and goods consumed in the United States. At the same time, **exports**—such as wheat, coal, beef, and computers—provide jobs and profits to many individuals and businesses in the United States. Our lives

Exhibit 6.10
International Comparisons of the Size of Government

Country	Expenditures as a percent of total output	
	1960	1982
Sweden	31.1	67.3
Italy	30.1	53.7
France	34.6	50.7
West Germany	32.5	49.4
United Kingdom	32.6	47.4
Canada	28.9	45.8
United States	27.6	37.6
Japan	18.3	34.2

Source: OECD "The Role of the Public Sector," *Economic Studies,* Spring 1985, p. 29.

Category	Exports (billions)	Imports (billions)	Net exports (billions)
Foods and feeds	$ 22.6	$ 24.0	$ −1.4
Industrial supplies	63.4	103.1	−39.7
Energy products	8.2	38.1	−29.9
Capital goods	79.2	75.7	3.5
Automobiles	23.9	78.1	−54.2
Consumer goods	14.5	78.0	−63.5
Other goods	18.2	10.6	7.6
Total merchandise trade	221.8	369.5	−147.7
Services	148.9	126.6	22.3
Trade of goods and services	$370.7	$496.1	$ −125.4

Exhibit 6.11
U.S. International Trade by Category, 1986

Source: U.S. Department of Commerce, *Survey of Current Business,* March 1987, Tables 2 and 3.

would certainly be different, in some cases difficult, without this international trade. In this section we examine some of the basic features of the foreign sector, reserving a full discussion of international economics to later chapters.

Imports and Exports

Exhibit 6.11 shows some of the major items imported into or exported from the United States in 1986. Agricultural products, industrial supplies, and capital goods were the major items exported. However, except for agricultural products and capital goods, more goods and services in each category were imported than exported.

In 1986, U.S. exports to the rest of the world totalled $371 billion, but imports totalled $496 billion of foreign goods and services. We discuss the complex causes and consequences of these flows in later chapters.

International Trade and Capital Flows

We can show how the U.S. economy relates to the economies in the rest of the world using a circular-flow model as in Exhibit 6.12. The foreign sector participates in both resource and product markets in the United States. The top half of Exhibit 6.12 shows these international trade flows. Like the circular-flow model in Chapter 5, dollars move in the direction opposite the real flow of goods and services.

In addition to trade flows, there are substantial international financial flows. The bottom half of Exhibit 6.12 shows these international financial, or capital, flows as the exchange of money for investments. Residents of the United States, for example, exchange money for foreign physical assets, such as factories, or financial assets, such as shares of stock in foreign companies or bonds of foreign companies and governments.

International capital flows have a major impact on an economy. In 1986, U.S. residents invested a total of $100 billion in foreign economies, while foreigners

Exhibit 6.12
The Flows of International Exchange
The exhibit shows the international exchanges between the U.S. economy and the rest of the world. The top of the exhibit shows trade flows; exports and imports of goods and services are matched by an equal but opposite flow of dollars. The bottom part shows international financial or capital flows representing financial investments in foreign assets by U.S. residents and financial investments by foreigners in U.S. assets.

invested $213 billion in the U.S. economy. In fact, because interest rates in the United States have been relatively high in recent years, foreigners have supplied large amounts of funds to U.S. financial markets, much of which helped to finance the large U.S. government budget deficits.

As you can see, the foreign sector is an increasingly important part of the U.S. economy. Foreign businesses have increased the level of competition in many U.S. product and resource markets. Foreign products have added much to the variety and quality of products offered for sale in this country. Foreign investment has helped fuel recent growth in the U.S. economy. Although we do not discuss details of the foreign sector's activities until the last chapters, we mention the foreign sector throughout the text, as appropriate.

CONCLUSION

In this chapter we focused specifically on the U.S. economy, although the features discussed—such as the role of the public sector—are characteristic of most market economies. This material completes your introduction to the study of economics. At this point you will go on to study the economy from one of two perspectives: microeconomics or macroeconomics. In the study of *microeconomics*, the focus is on activities of individual economic units and markets. In the study of *macroeconomics*, the focus is on activity of the economy as a whole or on major sectors of the economy. In either case you will have to draw on the principles you have learned so far to further understand how the economy operates.

SUMMARY

1. In this chapter we examined the roles of businesses and households (the private sector), of federal, state, and local government (the public sector), and of foreign individuals, businesses, and governments (the foreign sector) as economic units in a market economy.

2. The role of business firms in a market economy is to organize and monitor team performance, to reduce the costs and number of market exchanges, to take advantage of economies of scale, and to accept risks. If businesses grow too large, however, management costs rise and economic power may become too concentrated.

3. The three principal legal forms of business organization are the proprietorship, the partnership, and the corporation. Proprietorships are the simplest and most common form of business organization; partnerships are the least common. Corporations are the most important form of business organization because they produce most of the goods and services, employ most of the labor and other economic resources, and receive most of the profits.

4. Among the advantages of the corporate form of business organization are that (a) it limits the liability of its owners to their original investment; (b) it can raise more funds than can a proprietorship or partnership; (c) it is a more stable form of organization than the other kinds of business enterprise, which contributes to greater long-range certainty; and (d) it can expand to take advantage of the benefits of size.

5. Firms can either distribute profits to their shareholders in the form of dividends or reinvest them. Business assets—inventory and plant and equipment, for example—must be financed. Liabilities are the funds that a business borrows from nonowners, such as banks; equity represents the funds invested by owners, including the undistributed profits or retained earnings.

6. Households own most of the productive resources (land, labor, and capital), and their demand is significant in determining what is produced. Total personal income is derived from six basic sources: wages and salaries (the most significant source of income for most households), rent, interest, proprietor income, dividends, and transfer payments.

7. Economists define the economic role of government as helping the economy to achieve allocative efficiency, technical efficiency, equity, price stability, full employment, and growth. Specific economic activities of government include: (a) facilitating market activity; (b) correcting market failures; (c) redistributing income and opportunity; and (d) fostering economic stability and growth. The exact role government should play is controversial, and every government action involves both benefits and costs.

8. The size of the public sector has increased in the last 30 years. Government expenditures as a percent of total output increased from 24 percent in 1955 to 35 percent in 1986. Most of the increase represents growth in government transfer payments. The size of the public sector in the United States is smaller than in many European countries, but not as small as in Japan.

9. Foreign individuals, businesses, and governments—the foreign sector—have a growing influence on the U.S. economy. International trade—imports and exports—provides resources, goods and services, jobs, and income to residents of the United States. International capital flows—foreign investment in the United States and U.S. investment in foreign countries—are sizeable. The impact of foreign competition for U.S. businesses is growing. In important ways, the United States is but one part of the world economy.

KEY TERMS

Private sector, 121
Public sector, 121
Foreign sector, 121
Proprietorship, 124

Partnership, 125
Corporation, 125
Stock, 125
Industry, 126
Depreciation, 127
Dividends, 129
Retained earnings, 129
Bonds, 129
Transfer payments, 129
Personal income, 130
Private goods, 135
Public goods, 135
Externalities, 136
Social benefits, 136
Social costs, 136
External costs, 136
External benefits, 136
Imports, 140
Exports, 140

QUESTIONS FOR REVIEW AND DISCUSSION

1. The structure of U.S. business has changed in recent years. Manufacturing accounts for a declining percentage of employment and income, whereas service industries have expanded. What reasons can you give for this change?

2. A corporation is owned by shareholders, controlled by a board of directors, and operated by management. What keeps managers interested in making profits for shareholders? Why might the interests of management and shareholders conflict? What are the consequences of such conflicts for the goals of allocative and technical efficiency?

3. In this chapter we noted that households receive most of their income from wages and salaries. Explain the following statement in light of the link between income and the distribution of goods and services: "Society's distribution system will continue to keep most individuals interested in working, even if productivity gains greatly increase society's production possibilities."

4. How would you define the proper role of government in a market economy? How do economists tend to evaluate government? What criteria for evaluating government can you see in the principles of rational choice? Since economists believe that government should apply the principles of rational choice, why do

they sometimes disagree about whether government should undertake a particular project?

5. Evaluate the following statements using economic principles. (*Note:* Avoid the temptation to simply give your opinion. Give an economic critique of the statements; that is, are they logical?)
   a) Increases in taxes clearly make households and businesses worse off since they have less to spend.
   b) Public goods should be produced by the government even if their benefits are lower than their costs because they will tend to be ignored or underproduced by the private sector.

6. Consider the statement: "Government must assume the responsibility for goods and services that are too vital to be left to the whim of the marketplace. Thus government must provide for national defense, libraries, education, food, clothing, public health, and clean air and water." Which of these, if any, are what economists call public goods? Which of these, if any, involve externalities? Why do economists believe markets can be trusted to provide many vital goods, such as clothing? What economic criteria would determine whether government action will improve allocative efficiency?

7. How does the federal government intervene to correct inequities resulting from the market system? Is this an appropriate area for government action? Why do you suppose this is an extremely controversial area?

8. In evaluating government policies, economists are concerned with the effects on allocative and technical efficiency and on equity. Explain the possible effects each of the following policies might have on each of the three goals. (For equity, consider which groups will gain and which will lose.)
   a) A policy to increase the incomes of farmers that will also raise and maintain farm prices above market equilibrium levels.
   b) A policy that requires all soft drinks and beer to be sold in returnable bottles or cans.

9. If, as is true of almost all government policies, some groups will gain and others will lose, how can an issue be settled? How does your answer to this question help you to understand that what economists believe government *should* do is often different from what government *actually* does?

10. What are some of the benefits and costs from international trade? Do you think the U.S. economy would be better off if international trade were restricted? Why do you suppose that some industries—such as automobile, steel, shoes, and textiles—have asked for and received protection from foreign competition? Is it generally desirable for an economy to restrict trade?

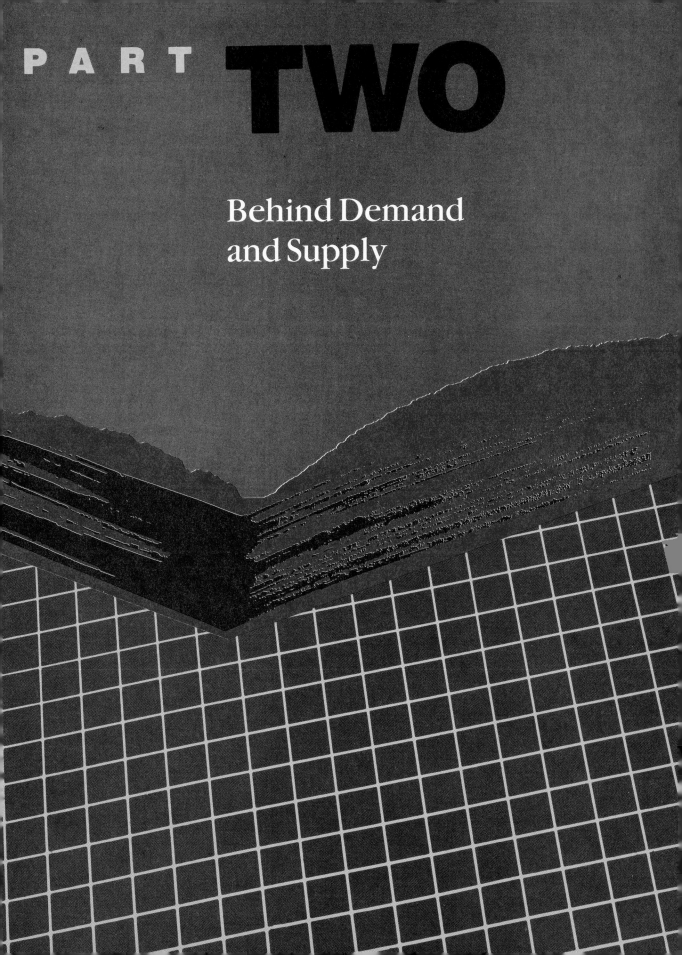

PART **TWO**

Behind Demand
and Supply

Consumer Choice
and Demand

QUESTIONS TO CONSIDER

☐ How do economists measure consumer satisfaction?

☐ Why is marginal utility more important than total utility in determining what consumers will buy?

☐ What does the equimarginal principle predict about consumer choice?

☐ Do all consumers receive a consumer surplus when they purchase a product?

☐ What two effects does a change in the price of a product have on quantity demanded?

Y ou can improve your grade in economics by studying more, so why don't you study 40 hours per week? If you get great satisfaction from owning an expensive new sweater, why don't you buy 20 of them? Why is the price of water—so essential to life—low and the price of diamonds—with no practical use—high? Why do retirees take longer vacation trips than people who work full time?

The answers to these questions depend on individual demand for products. In Chapter 3 you learned that demand represents individual choices about what to buy and that those choices depend on four factors: tastes and preferences, prices of related products, income, and expectations. (Market demand, the sum of individuals' demand, also depends on the number of buyers.) We also said that individual households apply the principles of rational choice in making their decisions.

In this chapter we explore the ways in which the principles of rational choice affect household decision making. In doing so, we take a closer look at demand and the reasoning behind the law of demand, or the tendency for quantity demanded to fall when price increases.

RATIONAL CHOICE AND CONSUMER DECISIONS

Economists and businesses want to know why people make the choices they do—choices that result in individual demand for products. In order to understand and predict consumer behavior, economists developed a theory of consumer choice. Applying this theory enables households to make good choices. The theory also enables businesses to plan ahead to meet consumer demand promptly and efficiently. And it enables us to answer the questions posed at the beginning of this chapter.

The theory of consumer choice is basically an application of the principles of rational choice, which we introduced in Chapter 2. Recall that every decision maker faces the limits of scarcity. In making decisions about what to buy, you and every other individual or household have only a limited amount of money to spend. Your personal limit depends on your past savings, your current income, and your ability to borrow. Although personal limits vary widely, everyone has some limit. Within this limit, you and other buyers must decide how best to use your funds.

Economists believe that rational consumers will not buy a product if the expected extra benefits they receive are outweighed by the expected extra costs. But what exactly are the benefits and how do economists measure the extra costs? We generally buy goods and services because they satisfy wants. We buy clothes to keep warm (and sometimes to impress others). We buy tickets to movies or basketball games to be entertained. We pay college tuition to acquire knowledge and, perhaps, better jobs in the future. In each case, the benefits are the satisfaction received.

But we do not buy everything that gives us satisfaction or even those products that give the greatest satisfaction. You may get more satisfaction from owning a yacht than a canoe, and yet rationally buy a canoe. The reason is simple: Like everyone else, you have only limited funds. Recall that when you decide to buy one item, you are automatically choosing not to buy something else; that is, every choice you make has an opportunity cost. (For more on costs, see: A Case in Point: Economic Costs and Consumer Choice.)

For example, you might choose to spend $10 to buy the latest record album by your favorite musical group instead of taking your nephew to see the latest movie. In economic terms, the cost of the album is not really the $10 you spent. Rather, it is the opportunity cost, the satisfaction you would have received from going to the movie with your nephew. Rational consumer choice means balancing the extra satisfaction received from one product against the extra satisfaction that could be received by purchasing another product. In applying this rule, individuals and households seek the combination of goods and services that gives the greatest total satisfaction within the limitations of their income.

A Case in Point
Economic Costs and Consumer Choice

In this chapter we focus mostly on the benefit side of consumer choice. But, as this example illustrates, to be rational consumers must also consider opportunity cost.

On Friday you buy a used car from R. O. "Ripoff" Riley. You pay him $600 cash and drive the car home. On Monday morning the car will not start. The lowest estimate for the repairs necessary to get it running again is $250. Jerry the Junkman will give you $50 for the car as is; fixed, its market value would be $450, according to Susan the Mechanic (who you should have let check out the car before you bought it). The question is, should you have the car repaired or junk it?

The economic approach to this problem involves the following considerations: First, disregard the money you paid Riley; he did not give you a warranty, so you cannot recover a penny from him. Second, in its current condition, the car is worth $50 to the market, the amount

Jerry will give you. Unless some fool will give you more, you should consider it the car's current value and the opportunity cost you forgo if you decide to keep it. If you are willing to spend an extra $250 on the car, however, its value will increase to $450. You stand to gain $150 by having Susan fix the car: The extra benefit of $400 ($450 − $50) is greater than the extra cost of $250. Thus, repairing the car is a better choice than junking it.

Rational economic choice then requires forgetting about money already spent. Learn from the past (do not buy from Riley), but do not let such costs influence your decisions. Then determine the best economic choice by comparing the extra benefits and extra costs of the best options available to you. In this case, comparing the car's current value with the increased value and extra costs after it is repaired, indicates that you should have the car fixed.

MARGINAL UTILITY AND CONSUMER DEMAND

In analyzing consumer choice, economists use the term **utility** to indicate the amount of satisfaction an individual or household receives from consuming a particular product. Be careful not to confuse the economic meaning of utility with a product's *usefulness*, as used in everyday speech. You may get the same amount of satisfaction (economic utility) from buying a diamond ring or putting extra insulation in your house. The insulation might be more useful in a practical sense, but usefulness is only one aspect of satisfaction.

Utility is a broader concept than usefulness. You can derive satisfaction, or utility—including ego gratification, status, and security—from a product's beauty, quality, comfort, durability, prestige, service, convenience, or function, even though the product may not be very useful. This distinction is important to businesses. Adding any feature to a product that increases utility can increase quantity sold. When economists say that consumer choice is influenced by utility, they mean that choice depends on the satisfaction individuals expect to get from a product they buy.

Our objective in this chapter is to understand consumer demand: the trade-off between price and the quantity that an individual will purchase. Putting the concept of rational consumer choice in utility terms, we can say: (1) the goal of a household is to maximize the **total utility**, or *total* benefits it receives by spending its funds; and (2) in order to determine what to buy, individuals compare the **marginal utility (MU)**, or extra satisfaction, from one product with that they could receive from some other purchase.

Total and Marginal Utility

It is important to distinguish between total and marginal utility and to remember that marginal, not total utility, determines consumer choice. For example, let's assume that you own several valuable diamonds. Compare the total utility you receive from the water you use in a week to the total utility of the diamonds you own. Unless you are very unusual, we can safely conclude that you would give up all the diamonds if you had to choose between them and water. By making that choice, you would indicate that the total value, or total utility, of the water is greater than the total utility of your diamonds.

But you do not have to choose between having no water and the amount you currently use. You can buy a few more gallons or a few less, as you can with any product. If you follow the principles of rational choice, you will buy an additional gallon of water only if you expect the extra benefits (marginal utility) to be greater than or equal to the extra costs. Like any rational buyer, you will pay no more than the value of the marginal utility of the last gallon purchased. *Consumers seek to maximize total utility, but they do so by carefully weighing marginal utility against extra costs*.

Law of Diminishing Marginal Utility

As a general rule—and with all other factors unchanged—economists believe that the marginal utility of the last unit will get smaller and smaller as more of a product is consumed. This tendency is known as the **law of diminishing marginal utility.** Like the law of demand, to which it is closely related, this law reflects a general observation about consumer behavior.

Utility. A measure of the satisfaction obtained from consuming a good or service.

Total utility. The total amount of satisfaction obtained from all units of a good or service consumed.

Marginal utility (MU). The additional satisfaction derived from consuming one additional unit of a good or service; the increase in total utility associated with a one-unit increase in quantity.

Law of diminishing marginal utility. The principle that beyond a certain point, the marginal utility of the last unit declines as more is consumed.

Exhibit 7.1
Total and Marginal Utility Schedules for Jim Harris
The total utility schedule indicates the total satisfaction (measured in units of utility) that Jim receives for each hamburger he consumes per week. If he consumes 2 hamburgers, for example, his total satisfaction is 110 units of utility. But Jim, as a rational consumer, bases his decisions on extra benefits, measured here as marginal utility. Jim's marginal utility schedule follows the law of diminishing marginal utility: Each additional hamburger consumed each week adds less to his total satisfaction. For example, the fourth hamburger gives Jim only 30 extra units of utility, in contrast to the first hamburger, which gives him 60 extra units of utility.

Number of hamburgers (per week)	Total utility (units of utility)	Marginal utility (units of utility)
0	0	
		60
1	60	
		50
2	110	
		40
3	150	
		30
4	180	
		20
5	200	

Exhibit 7.1 shows the total and marginal utility that Jim Harris, a student at State University, receives from consuming hamburgers in the downtown cafe. According to the table in Exhibit 7.1, Jim receives 60 units of satisfaction from the first hamburger he buys each week. If he buys 2, his total utility is 110 units.

Each additional hamburger adds to Jim's total utility, or total satisfaction. But the marginal utility schedule shown in the table indicates that each additional hamburger consumed adds less and less to his total utility. We calculate the marginal utility as the change in total utility divided by the change in quantity, or

$$\text{Marginal utility} = \frac{\text{Change in total utility}}{\text{Change in units consumed}}$$

Thus

$$\text{Marginal utility of second hamburger} = \frac{(110 - 60)}{(2 - 1)} \quad \text{or} \quad 50 \text{ units}$$

However, in real life, we cannot actually measure utility; that is, we have no satisfaction meter that registers the increase in Jim's total utility as he eats another hamburger. The imaginary units of utility shown in Exhibit 7.1 merely illustrate how the law of diminishing marginal utility operates.

Note that diminishing marginal utility does not mean that additional units of a product always have no value or a negative value. As long as marginal utility is positive, the buyer's total utility will increase as additional units are consumed. But diminishing marginal utility does mean that the increase in total utility is less and less as each additional unit is consumed.

Diminishing utility and rational choice. The concept of diminishing marginal utility also helps answer some of the questions posed at the beginnning of this chapter. You do not study economics for 40 hours per week, in part, because the extra benefits from the last few hours of study are not as large as those from the first few hours. Moreover, those last few hours probably have a relatively high opportunity cost. (Just think of all the things you could do if you did not

(a) Marginal utility in dollars

Number of hamburgers (per week)	Marginal utility (in dollars)
1	3.00
2	2.50
3	2.00
4	1.50
5	1.00

(b) Marginal utility and demand

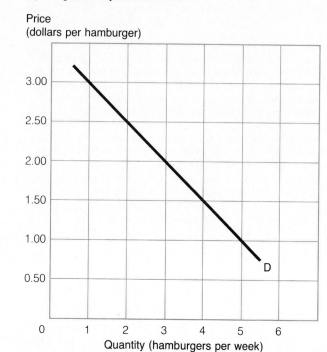

Exhibit 7.2
Marginal Utility and Demand
Jim's marginal utility schedule shows how much utility (satisfaction) he receives from each hamburger he eats. In this exhibit Jim's marginal utility is expressed in terms of dollars. We see how much he would be willing to pay for each additional hamburger (given his income, tastes, prices of related goods, and expectations). This marginal utility schedule is, in fact, Jim's demand for hamburgers. If hamburgers cost $2.00, Jim will be willing to buy 3 hamburgers because the first, second, and third hamburgers are each worth at least $2.00 to him. The graph in part (b) shows the marginal utility schedule plotted as a demand curve.

study economics for 40 hours per week.) Acting rationally, you will probably decide that the benefits are not worth the costs for the last few hours (maybe the last 30).

Similarly, the benefits you receive from owning an expensive sweater may be quite large. You may also receive fairly large benefits from owning a second one. But the law of diminishing marginal utility tells us that the extra benefits from each additional sweater will be less and less. And because your income is limited, you will likely encounter a larger and larger opportunity cost. How many sweaters you buy will depend on a comparison of marginal utility and extra cost.

Marginal Utility and Demand

In order to relate utility to the quantity of a product people will buy, we must measure utility in real, not imaginary, units. As you learned in Chapter 3, quantity demanded is a relationship between quantity and price. Thus economists generally use the amount of money that an individual is willing to sacrifice to obtain an additional unit of a product as a measure of the product's marginal utility.

We are now ready to see how Jim Harris will answer the basic question of consumer choice: How many hamburgers will he eat each week? Jim, like all rational buyers, wants to get the greatest total satisfaction from his limited funds. Exhibit 7.2 shows how much money Jim is willing to sacrifice to obtain each additional hamburger. Note that every hamburger he eats (at least up to 5 per week) adds to his total utility.

Since the hamburgers are not free and Jim has to pay for them, he will also have to sacrifice other purchases. By asking Jim how much he is willing to pay for each additional hamburger, we have, in effect, asked him how much he is willing to sacrifice to obtain the extra hamburger. Although his answers are given in terms of dollars, they really represent his opportunity cost—the satisfaction he could obtain from spending those dollars in another way.

The amount of money that Jim has to sacrifice depends on the price of hamburgers. The higher the price the more he will have to give up for another hamburger. To maximize his total utility, Jim will follow the principles of rational choice. That is, he will buy another hamburger if the marginal utility (measured in dollar terms) equals or exceeds the price. Beyond that point (that is, where price exceeds marginal utility), he will buy no more. If hamburgers sell for $2.00 each, we can expect Jim to buy 3 hamburgers per week, based on the data in Exhibit 7.2. Stated in more general terms, we can expect that *consumers will continue to buy up to the point where the marginal utility (MU) from the last unit bought is equal to the price (P), that is, up to MU = P.*

Thus you can now recognize that Exhibit 7.2 is not only a schedule of marginal utility, but also a demand schedule. As such, it links quantity demanded to price, assuming that all other factors remain unchanged. Jim has said he is willing to pay $3.00 for the first hamburger and $2.50 for a second one. If the price were $2.50, he would buy two hamburgers per week. If the price fell to $2.00, he would buy three hamburgers per week. The demand schedule was plotted on the graph in Exhibit 7.2 and labeled as demand.

Jim's demand for hamburgers is directly related to their marginal utility. Jim is willing to pay less and less for additional hamburgers because the marginal utility decreases. Thus the law of diminishing marginal utility supports the law of demand. Because additional units consumed add less and less marginal utility, individuals are willing to buy more of a product only if the sacrifice required (price) also is lower.

For example, if the price of hamburgers falls from $3.00 to $2.00, Jim will buy three hamburgers each week instead of only one. He will do so not because he likes hamburgers any more (his marginal utility schedule has not changed). Rather, at the lower price both the second and third hamburgers add enough satisfaction to be worth the sacrifice required. Note that *when consumers buy a product up to the point where price equals marginal cost, market price reflects the marginal utility (in dollar terms) of the last unit purchased.*

Solving the diamond puzzle. The relationship between diminishing marginal utility and price also answers a question that puzzled Adam Smith, author of *The Wealth of Nations* (published in 1776). Why do diamonds, a mere ornament without practical value, cost more than water, a commodity with almost infinite value, since water is vital to life?

We stated earlier that buyers weigh the value of each additional gallon of water against its cost. The first gallon of water used is extremely valuable for drinking and thus sustaining life. Not all uses of water are equally valuable, however. Additional uses of water (and gallons purchased) will depend on the perceived benefits (marginal utility) and the costs (price) of additional gallons.

Where water supplies are abundant and price is low, water will be used for many purposes besides drinking. Where water is scarce and price high, extra costs may quickly exceed marginal utility. For example, if you live in a desert, you may

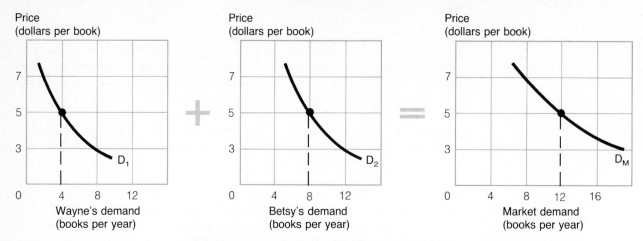

Exhibit 7.3
From Individual Demand to Market Demand
Market demand for a product reflects the demands of several individual consumers. The market in this exhibit has two consumers. At a price of $5, Wayne buys 4 books and Betsy 8. Since these are the only two consumers in this market, market demand is 12 books at a price of $5. Other points on the market demand curve are the total quantity demanded by both consumers at various prices.

find the cost of water to wash your car (high price, possible legal bans on such use) far greater than the marginal benefits (the car will be dusty again in an hour). Whether you live in a desert or a tropical rain forest, however, at some point the cost of water will exceed the marginal utility of a particular use and you will choose not to use it.

On the other hand, diamonds are nearly always less abundant than water, so their price is nearly always higher. Yet few people have so many diamonds that additional ones yield little marginal utility. Given the amounts of water and diamonds most of us possess, diamonds have a much higher marginal utility than water. Thus the price that consumers are willing to pay for the last diamond they buy will be higher than that for water.

Individual Demand and Market Demand

Thus far we have focused on demand of individual consumers. This focus is useful in understanding the forces underlying demand. But we are often more interested in the response of consumers as a group—market demand. Exhibit 7.3 illustrates a simple relationship between individual demand and market demand. Both the table and the graphs show the quantity of paperback books that Wayne and Betsy will buy each year at three different prices. When the price is $5 per book, Wayne will buy 4 per year and Betsy 8.

Market demand is the total quantity of books demanded by all buyers. If Wayne and Betsy are the only buyers in this market, the total demand is 12 books per year at a price of $5 per book. This combination of price and quantity is one point on the market demand curve. *Market demand shows the sum of quantity demanded by all buyers in the market at each price.*

Market demand reflects the marginal utility of each buyer in the market. The principles of rational choice imply that buyers, both individually and collectively, will increase quantity demanded to the point where marginal utility (in dollar terms) equals the product price. Up to that point, each unit purchased adds more to total benefits than to total costs. Purchases beyond that point would not be rational, since extra costs then exceed marginal utility. That is, buyers would be paying more for the last units purchased than the units are worth.

Equimarginal Principle and Consumer Choice

So far we have considered only the demand for a single product. But in the real world, buyers have many options, and rational choice requires that buyers consider the relative merits of each. How do buyers balance the extra benefits and extra costs of these options?

Choosing between two alternatives. Consider the case of Jane Ross who budgets $70 each month for entertainment and must decide how to divide this sum between movies and restaurant meals. Exhibit 7.4 shows the total and marginal utility Jane derives from restaurant meals and movies. (Again these units of utility are imaginary but indicate how much satisfaction Jane receives.) Jane gets more satisfaction from her first restaurant meal (1000 units of utility) each month than from going to the first movie (475 units of utility). In fact, the marginal utility of each of the first seven meals exceeds that of the first movie.

But marginal utility tells us only the extra benefits received. We cannot predict *how* Jane will spend her entertainment budget unless we also consider the sacrifice involved in each choice. If a restaurant meal and a movie had the same price, we could tell from marginal utility alone. However, each trip to the movies costs $5, whereas each restaurant meal costs $10.

Knowing price and marginal utility of both alternatives, we can apply the principles of rational choice and compare extra benefits and extra costs. Marginal utility measures extra benefits; price measures extra costs in dollars. Consider first the choice between 1 movie and 1 meal. The first meal has more than twice the marginal utility (1000 versus 475) and requires only twice the sacrifice ($10 versus $5). If Jane has only $10, she would be better off having 1 restaurant meal. The first restaurant meal gives her 1000 units of utility; seeing 2 movies, only 900 (475 for the first plus 425 for the second).

We can recognize both the benefits and costs by calculating the marginal utility per dollar of sacrifice for each movie and each meal, as shown in Exhibit 7.4. We divide marginal utility by price so that, for example, the marginal utility per dollar for Jane's first movie of the month is

$$\text{Marginal utility per dollar} = \frac{\text{Marginal utility}}{\text{Price}}$$

$$= \frac{475 \text{ units of utility}}{\$5 \text{ per movie}} \quad \text{or} \quad 95 \text{ units of utility per dollar}$$

If she wants to maximize her utility, Jane will spend each dollar of her entertainment budget on the option that adds the most utility per dollar. For example, the first restaurant meal has a marginal utility per dollar rating of 100; the first movie, 95. Taking both costs and benefits into consideration, the first

Movies

Quantity (movies per month)	Total utility (units)	Marginal utility (units)	Marginal utility (per dollar)
0	0		
		475	95
1	475		
		425	85
2	900		
		385	77
3	1285		
		360	72
4	1645		
		340	68
5	1985		
		325	65
6	2310		
		310	62
7	2620		
		300	60
8	2920		
		290	58
9	3210		
		280	56
10	3490		

Restaurant meals

Quantity (meals per month)	Total utility (units)	Marginal utility (units)	Marginal utility (per dollar)
0	0		
		1000	100
1	1000		
		850	85
2	1850		
		700	70
3	2550		
		650	65
4	3200		
		600	60
5	3800		
		550	55
6	4350		
		500	50
7	4850		
		400	40
8	5250		
		300	30
9	5550		
		150	15
10	5700		

Note: Price of movie = $5; price of restaurant meal = $10.

Exhibit 7.4
Marginal Utility and Rational Choice: Jane Ross's Monthly Entertainment Decision

meal is a better deal than the first movie: Jane gets 100 units of utility for each dollar spent on the meal but only 95 units for each dollar spent on the movie.

We can now predict how Jane will spend her entertainment budget for the month. The first choice—the one with the greatest marginal utility per dollar—is a restaurant meal. The next best option is a movie (95 units of marginal utility per dollar versus 85 for the second meal). Continuing in this manner, we can calculate that Jane will spend her $70 on 4 restaurant meals and 6 movies, given the marginal utilities and prices of the options we used. Test your understanding by checking this result. You might also calculate the total utility from other combinations to help you see that this is indeed the maximum total utility possible, for those prices and Jane's tastes and budget.

Equimarginal principle. The principle that for equilibrium to exist, the ratio of extra benefits to extra costs for each product (or resource) must be equal. For consumer choice it means that for each product consumed, buyers will receive the same marginal utility per dollar.

Equimarginal principle defined. The preceding example illustrates the **equimarginal principle**, which states that decision makers seek the largest extra, or marginal, benefit per dollar of sacrifice. In the case of consumer choice, rational buyers want the greatest marginal utility per dollar of cost. In equation form, we can express the equimarginal principle as applied to consumer choice for movies and restaurant meals as

$$\frac{\text{Marginal utility of movies}}{\text{Price of movies}} = \frac{\text{Marginal utility of restaurant meals}}{\text{Price of restaurant meals}}$$

The equimarginal principle states that two products (movies and restaurant meals) should be purchased in such a way that the marginal utility per dollar will be the same for both (or approximately the same). If it is not the same for both, buyers can increase total satisfaction by changing the mix of goods and services consumed.*

For example, Jane could spend $70 by seeing 10 movies and eating 2 restaurant meals. But that mix violates the equimarginal principle; the marginal utility per dollar for the third restaurant meal (70) exceeds that for the tenth movie (56). Instead, by eating 4 restaurant meals, Jane increases her total utility by 1350 units, or the marginal utilities for the third and fourth meal. She will have to see only 6 movies instead of 10, sacrificing the 1180 units of utility represented by the seventh to the tenth movies. But the increase in utility from the additional meals outweighs the utility sacrificed from seeing fewer movies. As a result, Jane's total utility is increased. *The equimarginal principle represents equilibrium for consumer choice. No other combination of products that can be purchased for the same price provides greater satisfaction.*

Effects of changes in relative price.   Applying the equimarginal principle under the conditions shown in Exhibit 7.4, we have obtained one point on Jane's demand curve for movies. At a price of $5 per movie, she will attend six movies per month. We can derive another point by observing how she responds when the price of movies drops to $4. Exhibit 7.5 shows that a fall in price increases the marginal utility per dollar for movies.

At the new price, Jane finds that the marginal utility per dollar for the sixth movie (81.25) exceeds that for the fourth restaurant meal (65). The equimarginal principle suggests that Jane can increase her satisfaction by decreasing the number of restaurant meals and increasing the number of movies she sees. Under these new conditions, Jane's best option is to eat 3 restaurant meals and to see 10 movies.

This example illustrates several other important points. First, a lower movie price causes less demand for restaurant meals (fewer meals consumed at the same price). This response is exactly what we would expect because the two products are substitutes. In addition, the lower movie price enables Jane to obtain greater total satisfaction from the same entertainment budget. At the original price, her total utility from entertainment was 5510 units, that is, 3200 from 4 meals and 2310 from 6 movies. For the lower movie price, her total utility rises to 6040 units, or 2550 from 3 meals and 3490 from 10 movies.

---

* We can also express the equimarginal principle in another way by rearranging the terms in the equation:

$$\frac{\text{Marginal utility of movies}}{\text{Marginal utility of restaurant meals}} = \frac{\text{Price of movies}}{\text{Price of restaurant meals}}$$

That is, the rule states that purchases will be in equilibrium when the relative values of the two products (the ratio of their marginal utilities) are equal to the relative costs (the ratio of prices).

Movies				Restaurant meals			
Quantity (movies per month)	Total utility (units)	Marginal utility (units)	Marginal utility (per dollar)	Quantity (meals per month)	Total utility (units)	Marginal utility (units)	Marginal utility (per dollar)
0	0			0	0		
		475	118.75			1000	100
1	475			1	1000		
		425	106.25			850	85
2	900			2	1850		
		385	96.25			700	70
3	1285			3	2550		
		360	90.00			650	65
4	1645			4	3200		
		340	85.00			600	60
5	1985			5	3800		
		325	81.25			550	55
6	2310			6	4350		
		310	77.50			500	50
7	2620			7	4850		
		300	75.00			400	40
8	2920			8	5250		
		290	72.50			300	30
9	3210			9	5550		
		280	70.00			150	15
10	3490			10	5700		

Note: Price of movie = $4; price of restaurant meal = $10.

Exhibit 7.5
Price Change and Rational Choice: Change in Jane Ross's Monthly Entertainment Decision

This result illustrates that a lower price increases buyer purchasing power. For a lower price, a buyer can obtain greater total satisfaction, or utility, from the same income. Of course, an increase in Jane's income would also increase her purchases of both products—and her total satisfaction. To test your understanding, determine what Jane would buy at the original prices if she added $20 to her budget. (Your answer should be 2 more movies and 1 more meal.)

Why retirees travel more. Thus far we have used product price as a measure of cost in finding equilibrium for consumer choice. As a general rule, price is probably an accurate estimate of cost, but not in all cases. Let's turn to the final question we asked at the beginning of this chapter: Why do retired individuals take longer vacation trips than those who work full time?

One reason, certainly, is different opportunity costs of time. If you work full time at a salary of $500 per week, you will lose that much income if you take an extra week off from work (that is, more than your allotted paid-vacation time).

You must add this cost to the other costs of the vacation trip. Retired individuals also have an opportunity cost of time, but it generally does not require an additional monetary sacrifice. To be entirely correct therefore, we should add the opportunity cost of time to the product price.

The opportunity cost of time is especially important when time is required to consume goods and services. The opportunity cost of time also helps to explain why individuals with higher incomes buy more time-saving gadgets, are more likely to fly than to take a train or bus, and demand more services such as laundry and housecleaning. In addition to their other benefits, these products and services reduce the opportunity cost of time.

Criticisms of Marginal Utility Theory

Not all economists accept marginal utility theory. Critics argue that people do not actually sit down and analyze various choices. It is true that few of us ever take the time to develop a schedule of marginal utility or to compare marginal utility per dollar, as required by the equimarginal principle. On the other hand, few of us are willing pay $5 for an item worth only $3. (If you are one of these persons, please write the author in care of the publisher; he has a deal for you.)

Buyers do have some notion of the relative values of different goods and services. And buyers generally seem to follow the principles of rational choice. An approach that measures only whether buyer satisfaction increases or decreases is covered in the appendix to this chapter. The conclusions reached by both approaches are the same, though. Bear in mind that the object of marginal utility theory is to predict and explain consumer behavior. Thus it is not important whether buyers actually calculate marginal utility or carefully weigh marginal utility and price. It *is* important that the responses predicted using the theory agree with actual consumer responses.

All buyers do not act rationally all the time, but their behavior as a group seems consistent with the principles of rational choice. For example, buyers react to changes in relative prices just as marginal utility theory predicts: They purchase more of a product that is relatively less expensive and less of one that is relatively more expensive. Of course, consumer decisions are more complicated than our simple illustrations suggest. We consider some of these complications in A Case in Point: Economic Costs and Consumer Choice.

Consumer Demand and Consumer Surplus[*]

Regardless of their attitude toward marginal utility theory, economists agree that actual quantity purchased by a household depends on product price. Consumers continue to buy until the marginal utility of the last unit equals its price. Thus market price reflects the value of the last unit sold. But buyers generally pay the same price for all units of a product purchased at any one time. In effect, they receive a bonus on all except the last unit purchased because all units but the last are worth more than buyers have to pay.

---

[*] This section contains more difficult, optional material.

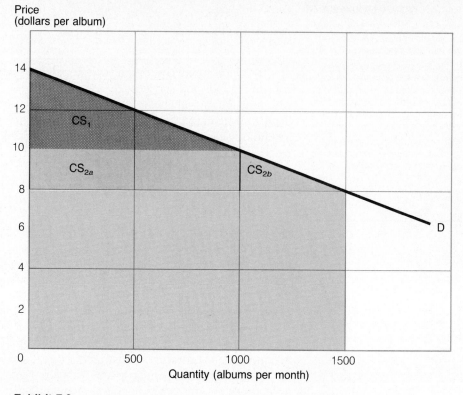

Exhibit 7.6
Consumer Surplus and Market Demand for Record Albums
The height of the market demand curve at any particular quantity shows the extra satisfaction (utility) of the last unit purchased. If market price is $10, then 1000 record albums will be bought. The person who bought the thousandth album obtained $10 worth of satisfaction from it. But each of the 999 other units are worth more than $10. For example, the five-hundredth album is worth $12. Buying an album worth $12 for $10 gives that consumer a surplus value of $2. Triangle CS_1 shows the consumer surplus obtained when price is $10. If price drops to $8, there are two additions to consumer surplus: (1) consumers of the first 999 receive additional surplus (measured by the rectangle CS_{2a}); and (2) consumers of units 1000 to 1499 also receive a surplus (measured by the triangle CS_{2b}). Total consumer surplus at a price of $8 is the total of areas CS_1, CS_{2a}, and CS_{2b}.

Consumer surplus. The difference between the total benefits buyers receive and the total expenditures they make for all units of a product they consume.

We can illustrate this point using demand for and marginal utility of record albums, as shown in Exhibit 7.6. If the price of records is $10, 1000 albums are demanded. At that point, price equals marginal utility. The price paid for the thousandth record equals its value to the buyer. But the five-hundredth record is worth $12, or $2 more than the buyer has to pay. Economists call this excess of total benefits over total costs a **consumer surplus**.

The size of a consumer surplus depends on price. If price falls to $8.00, buyers will spend $12,000 to buy 1500 records. Since they receive $16,500 in benefits (the sum of marginal utilities for all quantities up to 1500), a consumer surplus of $4500 results. In Exhibit 7.6, the area below the demand curve represents total utility. But the cost to buyers if records are $8 each is represented by the red-shaded rectangle. The entire blue-shaded triangle (CS_1, CS_{2a}, and CS_{2b}) thus represents the positive difference between total benefits and total costs to buyers—that is, the consumer surplus.[*]

Consumer surplus is a useful concept because it indicates how much buyers gain (or lose) from a price change. For example, at $10 per album, the consumer surplus is $2000; at $8 per album it is $4500. Exhibit 7.6 indicates that the increase in the consumer surplus is partly the result of an increased surplus for the 1000 albums previously purchased at $10 each (that part of the light-blue–shaded area labeled CS_{2a}). Another part of the consumer surplus results from the difference between marginal utility and price for all but the last of the additional albums purchased (that part of the light-blue–shaded area labeled CS_{2b}).

CONSUMER CHOICE AND THE LAW OF DEMAND

So far you have seen how consumer choice can be explained in terms of marginal utility and the principles of rational choice. You have also seen how marginal utility is connected to demand. In this section you will see the two effects of a price change: the income effect and the substitution effect. These effects explain why, in all but unusual cases, demand curves slope downward.

Income and Substitution Effects of a Price Change

The law of demand says that when price falls, buyers will demand a larger quantity. The equimarginal principle supports that conclusion: A decrease in price increases marginal utility per dollar and thus quantity demanded. Other reasons for the change in quantity demanded provide further support. For example, a lower price increases buyer purchasing power, as we saw in the movie ticket example earlier. Economists also refer to the amount of total utility you can purchase with the money you receive as income as *real income*. The increase in purchases caused by an increase in real income is known as the **income effect**.

Another reason for the change in quantity demanded also relates to a point we made earlier: When the relative price of a product rises, individuals will buy more relatively lower priced substitutes. For example, we would expect a rise in the price of video rentals to increase movie attendance. The change in purchases caused by a change in relative prices, holding real income constant, is called the **substitution effect**.

In the case of Jane Ross, both the substitution and income effects cause her to buy more movie tickets each month when the price falls. This is exactly the response we expect from the law of demand. But how much of Jane's response reflects the income effect and how much the substitution effect? At this point we cannot say. If movies are a normal good, however, we can say that Jane's response reflects a combination of both effects. In part she goes to the movies more often

Income effect. The change in quantity demanded resulting from a change in real income caused by a change in price.

Substitution effect. The change in quantity demanded resulting from a change in the price of a product relative to the price of substitute products.

---

[*] The surplus equals the area of the triangle, or one-half its length multiplied by its height. In this case, the length of the triangle is the quantity sold, or 1500. The height is the difference between the market price of $8 and the intercept of $14, or $6. Thus the consumer surplus is $4500 per month, or 0.5(1500 albums per month)($6 per album).

because their price has fallen relative to the price of other types of entertainment—the substitution effect. But her response also reflects the income effect—a lower price raises her real income and causes her to buy more movie tickets.

The substitution effect is always negative. A higher price for one good causes a decrease in quantity demanded as buyers turn to relatively cheaper substitutes. The income effect, however, can be either positive or negative. For normal goods the income effect is negative; a higher price reduces real income and the quantity demanded. But for inferior goods the income effect is positive; a higher price lowers real income but increases the quantity demanded.

Whether quantity demanded of inferior goods increases or decreases when price falls depends on whether the substitution effect or the income effect is stronger. Evidence from the real world suggests that in all but the most exceptional cases, the substitution effect outweighs the income effect. Thus for virtually all goods the law of demand correctly predicts consumer response.

CONCLUSION

The theory of consumer choice is based on the principles of rational choice. As we noted in this chapter, economists use this theory because it helps them to understand and predict consumer behavior. We can draw several important conclusions from our analysis. First, product demand is closely related to marginal utility. Thus we can interpret the demand curve as the marginal benefits received by individuals from the last unit purchased. This relationship is crucial in later chapters, when we attempt to assess market results in terms of allocative efficiency.

In the next two chapters we turn our attention to the supply side of a market economy. We look at what the principles of rational choice can tell us about the behavior of businesses. With a theory of producer choice and a theory of consumer choice, we can predict the response of both groups to economic change.

SUMMARY

1. In this chapter we used the principles of rational choice to develop a theory of consumer behavior and to show how that behavior is reflected in market demand.

2. Utility refers to the satisfaction that individuals receive from products they consume. In applying the principles of rational choice, economists assume that buyers seek to obtain the maximum possible total satisfaction (total utility) from their limited incomes. Thus for every choice, buyers compare extra (marginal) benefits to extra (marginal) costs.

3. Marginal utility represents the extra benefits or satisfaction that buyers gain from the last unit of a product consumed. In general, the law of diminishing marginal returns states that marginal utility of any product declines as more is consumed (holding all other factors constant). Because additional units have lower marginal utility, a consumer will buy more only if the price is lower. Thus the law of diminishing marginal utility sup-

ports the law of demand: Lower prices mean greater quantity consumed, and higher prices mean less quantity consumed.

4. Rational buyers will increase quantity demanded up to the point where marginal utility (expressed in dollar terms) equals product price. It would not be rational to buy more at that price, since diminishing marginal utility implies that the extra benefits will be less than the extra costs. It would not be rational to buy less, since each additional unit purchased will add more to benefits than to costs.

5. The equimarginal principle, as applied to consumer choice, states that buyers achieve maximum possible satisfaction when the marginal utility per dollar is the same for all goods consumed. Mathematically,

$$\frac{\text{Marginal utility of good A}}{\text{Price of good A}} = \frac{\text{Marginal utility of good B}}{\text{Price of good B}}$$

6. Market price reflects the marginal utility of the last unit purchased because consumers buy to the point where price equals marginal utility. Although each unit purchased costs the same, not all have the same value. Under the law of diminishing marginal utility, the first units consumed are worth more to buyers than the last unit. When total benefits received (total utility) exceed total price paid, the result is a consumer surplus. Consumer surplus increases when price falls and decreases when price rises.

7. A change in the price of a product has two effects on quantity demanded. The substitution effect measures the increase in quantity demanded caused by the change in relative price, holding real income constant. A decline in product price causes buyers to substitute that product for other, relatively more expensive products. The substitution effect supports the inverse relationship between product price and quantity consumed.

8. For normal goods the income effect supports the law of demand; a fall in price raises real income and hence quantity demanded. For inferior goods, however, the income effect is positive; a fall in price raises real income and hence decreases quantity demanded. In all but the most unusual cases, the law of demand remains valid.

KEY TERMS

Utility, 150
Total utility, 150
Marginal utility (MU), 150
Law of diminishing marginal utility, 150
Equimarginal principle, 156
Consumer surplus, 160
Income effect, 161
Substitution effect, 161

QUESTIONS FOR REVIEW AND DISCUSSION

1. Consider the statement: "'The more the merrier' contradicts the law of diminishing marginal utility." Do you agree? Why or why not?

2. Most people would prefer a Rolls Royce to a Toyota, but more Toyotas are sold. Use the equimarginal principle to explain why this preference does not mean that buyers are irrational.

3. Assume that the price of artichokes is $2 each and the price of broccoli is $3 per bunch.
   a) Chris is currently buying both artichokes and broccoli. The marginal utility he receives from the last artichoke purchased is 80; from the bunch of broccoli, 150. Is Chris maximizing his total satisfaction? What adjustment, if any, should he make?
   b) Sarah is currently buying 5 artichokes and 3 bunches of broccoli. If we assume that she has maximized her satisfaction, what can you infer about the ratio of the marginal utilities of the two goods?

4. Using the mathematical equation expressing the equimarginal principle, indicate why, if preference for compact discs increases, more discs will be consumed at each possible price. Why does an increase in the price of compact discs mean that less will be consumed? Describe the changes that occur as buyers adjust to a new equilibrium in each case.

5. Why do economists assume that buyers use the principles of rational economic choice when making purchases? For the assumption to be true, must buyers actually apply marginal utility theory in making their choices?

6. Each of the following statements is false; that is, the statement is not consistent with the principles of rational consumer choice. Explain why.
   a) As long as we continue to receive additional satisfaction from additional quantities of a product (that is, so long as marginal utility is positive), we should continue to buy more.
   b) As long as the total utility we receive from a product exceeds its total cost, buying another unit is a rational choice.
   c) If you see fewer movies each year, the extra benefits you receive from the last movie you see will be greater. Therefore you will be better off if you see fewer movies.

7. One of your friends buys a ticket to a rock-music concert. On the day of the concert, she is not feeling well but decides to go anyway, explaining that she must go because otherwise she would get nothing for her money. Refer to A Case in Point: Economic Costs and Consumer Choice to help you answer questions (a) and (b).
   a) On the day of the concert, how relevant is the price paid for the ticket to any choice she may make?
   b) She also says, "I might as well go; it won't cost me anything because I already have a ticket." Do you agree with her statement? How would you determine what, if anything, it will cost her to go?

8. In terms of the principles of rational choice and the concept of marginal utility, explain the meaning of each of the following statements.
   a) I'd really like to have a video cassette recorder, but I can't afford one.
   b) I don't understand why oil prices have fallen in recent years; oil is still as valuable as ever.
   c) I'd be willing to pay more for a ticket to a rock-music concert on the night after final exams are over than in the middle of final exams.

9. The marginal utility (in dollar terms) that Jay Samuels receives from tennis shirts is given below. Use this information to answer questions (a)–(c).

Quantity purchased (number of shirts)	Marginal utility (dollars of benefit)
1	25.00
2	20.00
3	15.00
4	10.00

a) If Jay is a rational consumer, how many shirts will he buy if the price per shirt is $15.00?
b) In this case what is the amount of consumer surplus he receives?

c) But suppose that the price is $25.00 per shirt or 3 shirts for $60.00. Having these two options, will Jay be better off with one or three shirts? How much consumer surplus will he receive? [Where did the consumer surplus Jay received in part (a) go? Why?]

10. The very poorest residents of Panne, a mythical country, subsist largely on bread. But when the price of bread rose last year, the poor Pannish actually bought more bread than before. Can you explain this unusual response? What does it say about the relative strength of income and substitution effects? (According to nineteenth-century English economist Alfred Marshall, this response actually happened in England. Others disagree, but all agree that such a response would be most unusual.)

Appendix to Chapter 7

Indifference Theory and Consumer Choice

As we noted in this chapter, critics of marginal utility argue that in real life, few (if any) people can or do measure the extra units of satisfaction they receive from additional units of a product. But nearly everyone could (and does, to some extent) rank choices in order to show preference, that is, indicate which of two choices they would prefer. In this appendix, we present a theory of consumer choice and demand using this alternative assumption.

Exhibit 7A.1 shows the combinations of food and clothing that would give Jennifer Lindsay identical amounts of satisfaction. That is, Jennifer would be as happy with 8 units of clothing and 28 units of food (combination A) as she would with 18 units of clothing and 9 units of food (combination D). Note that we are not saying that these combinations provide her with the maximum satisfaction she can buy with her current income, but only that Jennifer finds each combination equally satisfactory.

INDIFFERENCE SETS AND CURVES

Faced with having to choose among the various combinations shown in Exhibit 7A.1, Jennifer would be indifferent because each combination gives her the same level of satisfaction, or total utility. For this reason, economists call the data in Exhibit 7A.1(a) an **indifference set**, indicating that Jennifer has no particular preference. The plot of these data, shown in Exhibit 7A.1(b), is called an **indifference curve**. Any point along indifference curve I_1, for example, represents an identical level of total utility to Jennifer.

We can learn more about Jennifer's relative preferences for food and clothing and about indifference curves in general by examining the data more closely. In looking at the different combinations, you can see that Jennifer is willing to sacrifice some clothing to obtain more food, and some food to obtain more clothing. In fact, she must do without some food in order to buy more clothing, if her total satisfaction remains constant. Thus *the slope of an indifference curve is always negative* (assuming that the buyer prefers more to less of each good).

Jennifer's preferences also follow the law of diminishing marginal utility: The amount of food that she is willing to sacrifice for clothing declines as the quantity of clothing already obtained increases. For example, moving from combination A

Indifference set. A table showing several combinations of goods and services that would give a buyer the same total utility.

Indifference curve. A graphic representation of the indifference set.

Exhibit 7A.1
Jennifer Lindsay's Choices for Food and Clothing
The indifference curve I_1 is a plot of the data presented in part (a). Since every point on the curve gives Jennifer exactly the same amount of satisfaction, she is indifferent about which combination to choose.

(a) Indifference set for food and clothing

Combination	Food	Clothing	Marginal rate of substitution[a]
A	28	8	
			10/1 = 10.0
B	18	9	
			3/1 = 3.0
C	15	10	
			6/8 = 0.75
D	9	18	
			1/6 = 0.17
E	8	24	

[a] Marginal rate of substitution is the units of food sacrificed in order to obtain 1 more unit of clothing.

(b) Indifference curve for food and clothing

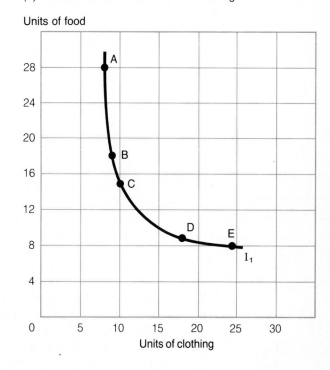

Marginal rate of substitution. The quantity of one product that may be sacrificed to obtain one unit of another product for the same total utility; the slope of an indifference curve, or mathematically,

Marginal utility of product A
Marginal utility of product B

Indifference map. A graph displaying several indifference curves representing different levels of satisfaction, or total utility.

to combination B, she is willing to give up 10 units of food to obtain 1 more unit of clothing. But moving from B to C, she is willing to give up only 3 units of food. Thus the marginal utility of clothing and food declines as she acquires more and more. Graphically, *the law of diminishing marginal utility causes the indifference curve to flatten out as it approaches each axis.*

We also noted in this chapter that the choice between two products depends on the relative value that a buyer places on additional quantities of each. To measure this relative value, economists use a concept known as the **marginal rate of substitution**. It is measured as the quantity of one good (for example, food) that a buyer is willing to sacrifice to obtain an additional unit of another good (for example, clothing), holding total utility constant. Mathematically, we express it as.

$$\text{Marginal rate of substitution} = \frac{\text{Change in quantity of product A}}{\text{Change in quantity of product B}}$$

Exhibit 7A.1 shows that between combinations A and B, Jennifer's marginal rate of substitution is 10 units of food for 1 unit of clothing. That is,

$$\frac{\text{Change in quantity of food}}{\text{Change in quantity of clothing}} = \frac{10}{1} = 10$$

Between combinations D and E, the marginal rate of substitution is 6 units of clothing for 1 unit of food, or

$$\frac{\text{Change in quantity of food}}{\text{Change in quantity of clothing}} = \frac{1}{6} = 0.17$$

We can also equate marginal rate of substitution with the ratio of the marginal utilities of the two products. For example, Jennifer is willing to sacrifice 3 units of food to get 1 more unit of clothing in moving from B to C. She is indifferent to the two combinations which suggests the value (marginal utility) of clothing is 3 times that of food. On the graph, *the absolute value of the slope of the indifference curve at any point measures the marginal rate of substitution or the ratio of the marginal utilities of the two goods.*

INDIFFERENCE MAPS

The combinations represented by an indifference curve all yield the same level of total utility. We can, of course, draw other indifference curves representing different levels of utility. A series of such curves drawn on the same graph is called an **indifference map**. Thus each of the four curves in the indifference map in Exhibit 7A.2 represents a different level of satisfaction. Since we assume that Jennifer would prefer more of either or both goods to less, her total utility is greater on indifference curve I_2 than on curve I_1. At point c_1 (on I_1) Jennifer has 15 units of food and 10 units of clothing. At c_2 (on I_2) she has 16 units of food and 12 units of clothing. Because she has more of both goods, we can conclude that her total utility is greater on I_2 than on I_1. In general, *indifference curves that lie farther away from the origin represent higher levels of total utility.*

We can also conclude that *indifference curves of a rational buyer cannot intersect, or cross.* Every combination of goods is represented by a point on a curve, and a point of intersection would have to be on two indifference curves.

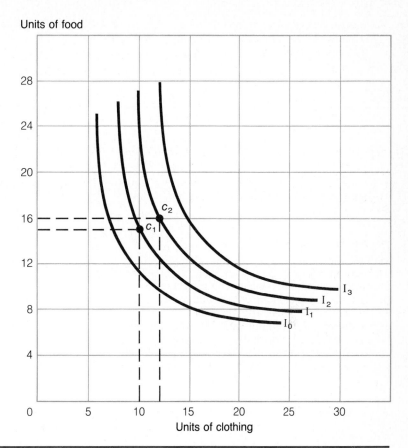

Units of food

Exhibit 7A.2
Jennifer Lindsay's Indifference Map for Food and Clothing
The indifference map shows a series of indifference curves. Curves lying farther away from the origin represent higher levels of satisfaction. That is, I_1 represents greater satisfaction than I_0, and so forth. Jennifer would prefer any combination on I_2 to any combination on I_1. Once on I_2, she is indifferent to any exchange of food for clothing that leaves her on I_2.

But since each curve represents a different level of total utility; intersection is impossible. No point (combination) can represent two different levels of total utility.

BUDGET CONSTRAINTS

Knowing Jennifer's preferences is not enough to tell us how much food and clothing Jennifer will choose to buy. We must also recognize that she cannot have everything she wants. Her choices are limited by two factors: her income and the prices of food and clothing. We want to see how, within these limits, she will decide what to buy.

Exhibit 7A.3 shows Jennifer's **budget constraint**. She can purchase alternative combinations of food and clothing on her income of $60 a week and at prices of $2 a unit for food and $3 a unit for clothing. If she spent all her income on food, she could buy 30 units of food but no clothing. She could also buy 20 units of clothing and no food. Or she could choose various combinations between the extremes. Like the production possibilities curve that we discussed in Chapter 2, the budget constraint line shows possible combinations but not which combination is best. Moreover, Jennifer can purchase more food only if she sacrifices some

Budget constraint. In indifference-curve analysis, a line indicating the combinations of two goods that a buyer can purchase, given the price of each good and the buyer's income.

(a) Possible combinations of food and clothing based on Jennifer's income and prices[a]

Food	Clothing
30	0
21	6
15	10
12	12
0	20

[a] Income = $60; price of food = $2; price of clothing = $3.

Exhibit 7A.3
Budget Constraint
The budget constraint line BC_1 shows combinations of food and clothing that Jennifer can purchase, based on her income and the prices of food and clothing. With an income of $60 per week and prices of $2 for food and $3 for clothing, she can purchase 30 units of food (and no clothing), 20 units of clothing (and no food), or any combination lying along BC_1. The budget constraint places an upper limit on her purchases. No combinations outside (to the right of) the constraint line are possible.

(b) Budget constraint

clothing. That is, she cannot attain any combination to the right of the budget constraint line. Note that *the absolute value of the slope of the budget constraint line measures the ratio of the two prices.*

EQUILIBRIUM CHOICE

If Jennifer is a rational consumer, she wants to get the most possible satisfaction given her preferences (shown in the indifference map) and her limitations (budget constraint). Exhibit 7A.4 shows three options, all of which are possible because they lie along the budget constraint line. She could buy 21 units of food and 6 units of clothing (point *a*), 15 units of food and 10 units of clothing (point *b*), or 9 units of food and 14 units of clothing (point *c*). Of the three, the combination at *b* represents Jennifer's best option because it lies on the highest indifference curve. Moving in either direction along the budget constraint, she gets less satisfaction than from being on I_1. Thus the combination at *b* is the equilibrium choice, or the point of maximum total utility.

This equilibrium choice is an application of the equimarginal principle we used in this chapter. Note that at point *b* the slope of the budget constraint line equals the slope of the indifference curve. The slope of the indifference curve is also the ratio of the marginal utilities, and the slope of the budget constraint is also the ratio of the two prices. Thus in equilibrium,

Slope of the indifference curve = Slope of the budget constraint

or

$$\frac{\text{Marginal utility of food}}{\text{Marginal utility of clothing}} = \frac{\text{Price of food}}{\text{Price of clothing}}$$

Rearranging terms, we have the equimarginal principle. That is,

$$\frac{\text{Marginal utility of food}}{\text{Price of food}} = \frac{\text{Marginal utility of clothing}}{\text{Price of clothing}}$$

Exhibit 7A.4
Equilibrium Combination of Food and Clothing: Indifference Curves and Budget Constraint for Jennifer Lindsay
The budget constraint line shows the maximum purchases possible. With this constraint, the highest indifference curve that Jennifer can reach is I_1, and she will choose to buy 15 units of food and 10 units of clothing. If she moves in either direction along the budget constraint line, she will not obtain satisfaction as great as I_1. Thus this combination represents the maximum satisfaction possible for her preferences and constraints.

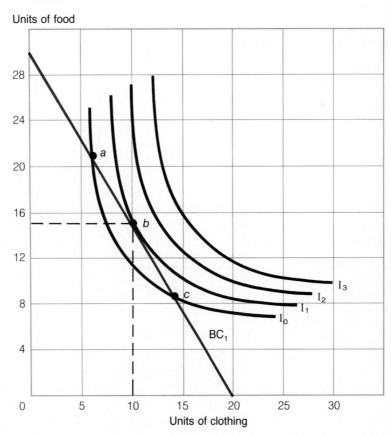

PRICE CHANGE AND DEMAND

We can also use indifference curves to show how an increase in clothing price from $3 to $4 per unit affects Jennifer's choices. We would expect her to buy fewer clothes and more food (unless she buys so much additional food that she can't wear her old clothing). The indifference analysis in Exhibit 7A.5 confirms this prediction.

The change in clothing price affects Jennifer's budget constraint. With her income fixed (in dollar terms) she can buy no more than 15 units of clothing, not 20 units as before. (Note that the new budget constraint BC_2 intersects the clothing axis at 15 units, whereas BC_1 does so at 20 units.) Similarly, if she continued to buy 10 units of clothing as before, she could buy only 10 units of food, not 15. Using the new budget constraint, Jennifer will again seek to reach the highest level of utility, that is, the indifference curve farthest from the origin. She will only be able to reach indifference curve I_0, however, and will buy 8 units of clothing and 14 units of food (point b_2).

As predicted, Jennifer buys less clothing when the price of clothing rises. As we noted in this chapter, the decrease reflects both the substitution effect—because of the change in relative prices—and the income effect—because of the reduction

---

Exhibit 7A.5
Effects of Price Change on Jennifer's Purchases of Food and Clothing
An increase in the price of clothing from $3 to $4 results in a change in Jennifer's budget constraint. Now Jennifer can buy only 15 units of clothing if she devotes all of her income to that one item. The maximum amount of food that she can buy is not affected, so the budget constraint simply pivots to the left, as shown. Under the new constraint, she reaches an equilibrium combination on indifference curve I_0, which represents a lower level of satisfaction, at point b_2. The new equilibrium combination is 8 units of clothing and 14 units of food. The price increase has forced her to a lower indifference curve, indicating that her total utility has been reduced.

Exhibit 7A.6
Jennifer's Demand for Clothing
This demand curve is derived from Exhibit 7A.5. It shows that at a price of $3, Jennifer will buy 10 units of clothing (b_1), whereas at $4, she will buy only 8 units (b_2).

in real income. The higher price of clothing reduced Jennifer's real income. Thus she will cut back on purchases of all normal goods, not just those that increased in price. Note also that her total utility is lower after the price increase.

We now know two points on the curve representing Jennifer Lindsay's demand for clothing. When the price of clothing is $3, she will buy 10 units. This decision is represented by point b_1 in both Exhibit 7A.5 and the demand curve in Exhibit 7A.6. When clothing price increases to $4, she will buy only 8 units, shown as point b_2 in both exhibits. By changing prices and locating the best possible combinations on the indifference map, we can find other points on the demand curve.

CONCLUSION

Indifference analysis yields two important results: (1) a demand curve that corresponds to the law of demand; and (2) a demand curve that is clearly connected to utility. First of all, higher price reduces quantity demanded, except in rare cases where the income effect for an inferior good is greater than the substitution effect. This conclusion is supported in part by the law of diminishing marginal utility; as marginal utility falls, we expect consumers to buy more only if price falls. The slope also reflects the budget constraint; to obtain more of any one good, buyers must sacrifice other goods. However, as price falls, the consumer buys more. This increase in consumption is also a shift to a higher indifference curve. In other words, the buyer's total utility increases.

KEY TERMS

Indifference set, 165
Indifference curve, 165
Marginal rate of substitution, 166

Indifference map, 166
Budget constraint, 167

Producer Choice and Costs of Production

QUESTIONS TO CONSIDER

☐ Why are economic profits a better basis for decision making than accounting profits?

☐ How does the short run differ from the long run? How do fixed costs differ from variable costs?

☐ What does the law of diminishing marginal returns imply about producer costs?

☐ How do product costs affect technical efficiency?

☐ In what ways do economies and diseconomies of scale affect producer costs?

In Chapter 7 we considered the theory of consumer choice and how those choices lead to market demand. In this chapter and Chapter 9, we consider the theory of producer choice and how those choices lead to market supply. As noted in Chapter 5, the basic role of business firms in a market economy is to buy resources and to supply goods and services to households. Thus firms make decisions that can affect society's goals of allocative and technical efficiency.

For example, business decisions about what to produce affect allocative efficiency. What mix of products should be produced? How much of each product should be produced? How much of each product should be offered for sale at various prices? How businesses answer these questions determines whether society's resources are being used to achieve maximum satisfaction.

Similarly, business decisions about how to produce affect technical efficiency. How many workers should be hired? What technology should be used? What combination of resources is best? What size plant should be built? How businesses answer these questions determines whether goods and services are produced at minimum cost.

The questions of what and how to produce are the basic questions of supply. In this chapter we begin to consider how businesses answer these questions in a market economy by applying the principles of rational choice.

RATIONAL CHOICE AND PRODUCER DECISIONS

Economists assume that the behavior of businesses, like households, can be best understood by assuming they apply the principles of rational choice in making decisions. Indeed, much of microeconomics explores the effects of rational choice on business decisions. Before proceeding, therefore, you should understand how a business that applies these principles decides what and how to produce.

Maximizing Profit

As we said in Chapter 5, economists assume that businesses act to maximize profits. Economists use the term *profit* in a special way, which we will discuss shortly. For now, we will consider profit to be the difference between total revenue and total cost. A firm may also seek to increase sales or build a reputation for quality. But if it does not earn a profit, it cannot survive very long in a market economy.

Rational choice always requires selecting only those options for which extra benefits are greater than extra costs. In order *to maximize profits, firms will choose those options that increase profit, that is, options for which extra revenue is greater than extra cost*. Thus the important question to ask for any decision is how profit changes. In mathematical terms,

Change in profit = Change in total revenue − Change in total cost

This formula seems simple enough, but to understand it and to see how it is applied, you must remember that cost—to an economist—is measured in only one way: as an opportunity cost.

Opportunity Cost and Economic Profit

Probably no term has as many definitions and is misused in so many ways as *cost*. But if businesses want to maximize profits, they must use the following principle: *all opportunity costs, but only opportunity costs, should affect decisions*. But what exactly is the opportunity cost of a producer decision? What is the significance of opportunity cost for measuring economic profits?

Explicit and implicit costs. In economic terms, *opportunity cost is a sacrifice that must be made in order to attain some result*. Opportunity cost, or sacrifice, is easy to identify in some cases. For example, when the manager of a hardware store stocks another 100 dozen flashlights to sell, the opportunity cost (or sacrifice) is the total amount it must pay its supplier. If a firm that makes electronic calculators hires another 10 workers, the opportunity cost is the total wages and other benefits—such as vacation time and health insurance—it must pay. Economists call opportunity costs representing additional expenditures that must be made **explicit costs**.

In other cases opportunity cost, or sacrifice, represents benefits not received. For example, suppose that Mr. Diamond owns the building he uses for his jewelry store. Although he pays no one rent for using the building, he still has an opportunity cost. For example, he might be able to rent the building to someone else for $1000 per month. If so, the $1000 per month he sacrifices by using the building instead of renting it is an opportunity cost. Economists call opportunity costs representing benefits not received from the next best option **implicit costs**.

Accounting versus economic profit. Now that you know a bit more about cost and its special economic meaning, we can redefine profit to reflect special economic meaning. Economists distinguish between accounting profit and economic profit. You are probably familiar with **accounting profit**. The profit that businesses report to the government (for tax purposes) and to their owners is accounting profit. So are the profits reported in the business sections of newspapers for large corporations such as IBM and General Motors. Accounting profit is a record of how well a firm performed in an *absolute* sense; it is the revenues a firm received from sales minus the explicit costs of resources used, or

Accounting profit = Total revenues − Explicit costs

Explicit costs. Costs involving direct payment for resources used by a firm. The only costs considered in calculating accounting profit.

Implicit costs. Opportunity costs for resources that a firm owns and uses; benefits not received from the next best use of the resource. Costs considered in calculating economic profit but not in calculating accounting profit.

Accounting profit. The difference between revenues and explicit costs, ignoring implicit costs.

	1986	1987
Total revenues	$250,000	$ 200,000
Less: Explicit costs	175,000	150,000
Accounting profit	$ 75,000	$ 50,000
Less: Implicit costs	60,000	60,000
Economic profit	$ 15,000	$ −10,000

Exhibit 8.1
Mr. Diamond's Profits

However, you probably have never heard of **economic profit**. Economic profit is the difference between revenues and *all* opportunity costs, that is, both explicit and implicit costs. Thus

$$\text{Economic profit} = \text{Total revenues} - \text{Explicit costs} - \text{Implicit costs}$$

$$= \text{Accounting profit} - \text{Implicit costs}$$

Because it includes all opportunity costs, economic profit measures a firm's *relative* performance—how well it is doing relative to its next best opportunity. Economic profit, therefore, is important to rational decision making. Since accounting profit ignores implicit costs, it is not a reliable guide to decision making. A firm that earns an accounting profit might be doing very well, or the owner might be better off in another business or out of business altogether.

For example, consider Mr. Diamond's revenues and costs, as shown in Exhibit 8.1. In 1986, his total revenues were $250,000, and his total explicit costs were $175,000. In 1987, his total revenues dropped to $200,000, while his explicit costs were $150,000. In both years he made an accounting profit. But his implicit costs—the costs of not renting his building and working at some other job—were $60,000 in both years. Thus he had an economic profit in 1986 but an economic loss in 1987. If he expects the future to look more like 1987 than 1986, he should get out of the jewelry business because earnings will not cover all opportunity costs.

Economic profit is a reliable guide to decision making because it represents earnings over and above all opportunity costs. Moreover, opportunity costs measure the value of the next best option. This means that a firm earning an economic profit has no better option. In the rest of this textbook, we use the term *profit* to refer to economic profit, unless we clearly state otherwise. But don't forget that the profits you read about in the newspapers are accounting profits.

PRODUCTION AND COSTS IN THE SHORT RUN

In Chapter 7 we related rational consumer choice to product demand. In this chapter we want to relate rational producer choice to product supply. We stated in Chapter 3 that supply is related to cost. A firm will not offer an additional unit for sale unless the market price is at least enough to cover the extra costs (opportunity costs) involved. We also noted that supply depends on the period of

RECAP

Profit is measured as the difference between revenues and costs. The principles of rational choice imply that firms will accept any option that increases profits—that adds more to revenues than to costs.

Accounting profit is the difference between revenues and explicit costs—payments a firm must make for resources it purchases for use.

Economic profit is the difference between revenues and all opportunity costs—both explicit and implicit. Implicit costs represent benefits not received from the next best use of resources.

time allowed for producers to respond to changes in demand. Thus in order to understand market supply, you must understand the relationship between opportunity costs and output and between time and ability to change resources and output.

Short-Run and Long-Run Decisions

To make a product, firms must utilize various resources (materials, labor, utilities, machinery, buildings). To respond to a change in demand, firms must change the amount and/or type of resources used, and to change resources, they must have time. Economists define two time periods—the short run and the long run—to reflect the time required to change resources.

In the **short run** a firm is unable to change all the resources it uses. For example, if a firm is deciding how much to offer for sale next week it will be unable to change the size of its factory and the number of machines it is using in time to affect quantity supplied. But with sufficient time, the firm could buy additional machines (or sell some) and build a larger or smaller factory. Thus in the **long run**, a firm has enough time to change all the resources it uses. How long is the long run? The answer depends on the industry involved. A new gasoline service station can be opened in only a few months, but a new plant to generate electricity takes years to build.

Variable Resources and Short-Run Output

In the next few sections we want to see how costs and output are related in the short run. For short-run decisions we must recognize that the firm will have some **fixed resources** which it cannot change. Machinery and buildings are typically among the firm's fixed resources. To change the output it produces, a firm must use more or less of its **variable resources**. Materials and labor can generally be considered variable resources which can be changed in a relatively short period of time.

To see how the distinction between fixed and variable resources affects cost and output in the short run, we consider the case of the M.T.R. Brush Company, a producer of hairbrushes. The company's fixed resources are one building and five brush-making machines. For simplicity, let's assume that M.T.R. has only one variable resource: labor. The company can hire more workers, but they must use the existing building and machines. (Of course, M.T.R. would have other variable resources—plastic for brush handles and electricity for the machines, for example. Ignoring such costs, however, does not change the conclusions of our analysis.)

Exhibit 8.2 shows the relationship between the variable resource—labor—and output—hairbrushes produced by M.T.R. This relationship, known as a **production function**, indicates the maximum output obtainable from a specific mix of resources, assuming the best available technology is used. Exhibit 8.2 also includes three new terms: total product, marginal product, and average product.

Total product. The total quantity of goods produced with a given quantity of resources in a specific period of time is called the **total product (TP or Q)**. Exhibit 8.2(a) shows the total number of hairbrushes that M.T.R. can produce in a

Short run. A period of time in which a firm cannot alter all its resources. In the short run, a firm can change only variable, not fixed, resources.

Long run. A period of time in which a firm can alter all its resources. In the long run, a firm can change all resources.

Fixed resources. Resources that in the short run do not vary directly with output; that is, output can be increased (within limits) without using more fixed resources. Typical examples are buildings and machinery.

Variable resources. Resources that vary directly with output; that is, any increase in output; requires greater use of variable resources. Typical examples are labor and raw materials.

Production function. The relationship between the quantity of resources used and the quantity of goods produced; the maximum amount of goods that can be produced using various combinations of resources and the best available technology.

Total product (TP or Q). The total quantity of goods that can be produced with a given quantity of resources in a specific period of time.

(a) Production data

Number of workers	Average product (AP) (brushes per worker)	Total product (TP = Q) (brushes per week)	Marginal product (MP) (brushes per worker)
0	—	0	
			50
1	50	50	
			170
2	110	220	
			260
3	160	480	
			320
4	200	800	
			355
5	231	1155	
			345
6	250	1500	
			320
7	260	1820	
			260
8	260	2080	
			170
9	250	2250	

(b) Total product curve

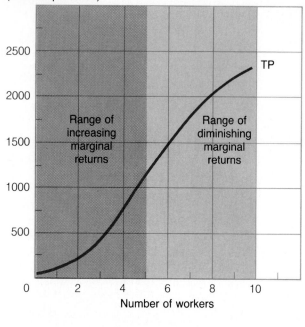

(c) Marginal and average product curves

Exhibit 8.2
Total, Average, and Marginal Product for the M.T.R. Brush Company
The table and graph of marginal product show the range of increasing marginal returns—from 1 to 5 workers—and of diminishing marginal returns—from 6 to 9 workers. Total product increases most rapidly in the range of increasing marginal returns and continues to increase through the range of diminishing marginal returns, but at a slower rate. Between the seventh and eighth workers, marginal product and average product are equal. This intersection occurs at the peak of the average product curve.

Marginal product (MP). The extra quantity of goods produced (change in total product) per unit of variable resource added. Mathematically, MP = Change in Q ÷ Change in variable resources.

Average product (AP). The ratio of total quantity produced (total product) to units of variable resources used to produce those goods. Mathematically, AP = Q ÷ Units of variable resources.

Increasing marginal returns. A situation in which each additional unit of a variable resource has a greater marginal product than the previous unit; total product increases at an increasing rate.

week with different quantities of labor (the variable resource). For example, with 3 workers total product is 480 hairbrushes per week; with 4 workers, 800 brushes per week. Exhibit 8.2(b) is the graph obtained by plotting the total-product data.

Marginal product. The extra units of output obtained by adding an extra unit of a variable resource are called the **marginal product (MP)**. In our example, marginal product is the additional number of hairbrushes produced when one more worker is employed. Marginal product is calculated as the change in total product (the number of extra units produced) divided by the change in the quantity of variable resources. Mathematically,

$$\text{Marginal product} = \frac{\text{Change in total product}}{\text{Change in variable resources}}$$

In Exhibit 8.2(a), you can see that adding the fifth worker increases total product from 800 to 1155 hairbrushes. Thus the marginal product of the fifth worker is 355 extra hairbrushes. Remember, *marginal* simply means extra; in this case, it means the extra hairbrushes produced when one additional worker is hired.

Average product. The quantity of goods produced per unit of variable resource is called the **average product (AP)**. (You will be pleased to know that *average* has the same meaning for economists as it does for other people.) In equation form,

$$\text{Average product} = \frac{\text{Total product}}{\text{Units of variable resource}}$$

In our example total product is the total quantity of hairbrushes produced per week, and units of variable resource are the number of workers employed that week. Thus average product is 250 hairbrushes per worker per week when 6 workers are employed (1500/6 = 250). To be sure you understand the terms marginal product and average product, try to verify some of the other values shown in Exhibit 8.2(a).

Increasing and Diminishing Marginal Returns

As Exhibit 8.2(a) shows, marginal product is not constant. Hiring the first worker increases total product by 50 hairbrushes per week. Hiring a second causes an increase of 170 brushes. Indeed, marginal product continues to increase until a sixth worker is hired. Economists would say that with one to five workers, the company is operating in the range of **increasing marginal returns**. That is, each additional worker (unit of variable resource) has a higher marginal product than the previous one. This pattern causes total product to increase at an increasing rate, as shown in Exhibit 8.2(b). As the term suggests, marginal product also rises in the range of increasing marginal returns, as shown in Exhibit 8.2(c).

However, the marginal product of the sixth worker is less than that of the fifth worker. Total product increases by only 345 hairbrushes per week, compared to the increase of 355 brushes per week when the fifth worker was hired. The seventh has a lower marginal product than the sixth: 320 compared to 345. From

Diminishing marginal returns. A situation in which each additional unit of a variable resource has a smaller marginal product than the previous unit; total product increases, but at a decreasing rate.

Law of diminishing marginal returns. The principle that beyond a certain point, additional variable resources added to a constant quantity of fixed resources will result in smaller and smaller increases in total product.

there, marginal product keeps declining as additional workers are hired. Economists would say that with 6 to 9 workers, the M.T.R. Brush Company is operating in the range of **diminishing marginal returns**. That is, each additional worker hired adds less to total product than the previous worker hired, but total product continues to increase, as shown in Exhibit 8.2(b). In this range, marginal product, although declining, is still positive, as shown in Exhibit 8.2(c). Each worker adds something to total product, but not as much as previous workers.

The graph in Exhibit 8.2(c) also illustrates the relationship between average and marginal product. Note that average product increases for a while and then falls. In fact, the graph shows that average product reaches its peak at the point where the average and marginal product curves intersect. This result is neither an accident nor a quirk of this particular example. It illustrates a fundamental relationship: As long as marginal product is greater than average product, average product will rise. When marginal product is less than average product, average product will fall. For example, consider your average in economics. Perhaps you started slowly and received only a 70 on your first exam. If your next mark is above 70 (that is, if your marginal score is above your average), your average will rise, and so on. (Let's not talk about the opposite situation, but you can imagine the result when the marginal is less than the average.)

Law of diminishing marginal returns. Why does the sixth worker add less to total product than the fifth worker? Is the sixth worker not as skilled or just lazy? Perhaps, but economists expect diminishing marginal returns to exist even if each worker hired is equally skilled and industrious. Diminishing marginal returns occur in this short-run situation because we are holding M.T.R.'s resources—except the number of workers—constant.

In this example, M.T.R. has five machines and one building. It seems reasonable to assume that each of the first five workers hired was assigned to operate one machine. There is no additional machine for the sixth worker (assuming one shift per day). But if that worker helps the others by taking part of their shift, all would be able to take rest breaks; rested, the workers might be more productive, increasing total product.

The seventh and subsequent workers might bring materials to each machine, saving some time spent on gathering materials. They might also take finished products to the warehouse. By doing these tasks, the extra workers add to total product; that is, their marginal product is positive. But hiring the sixth through the ninth workers will probably not add as much to total product as did hiring the first five workers.

In this example, hairbrush production is limited because we held the number of machines—a fixed resource—constant. With only five machines available, the marginal product of the sixth and subsequent workers hired declines. As you will see later in this chapter, however, removing this restriction and allowing all resources to change, permits total product to increase at a constant or an increasing rate over a wider range.

Nevertheless, beyond some point, adding variable resources to a constant quantity of fixed resources will add less and less to total product. This result is called the **law of diminishing marginal returns**. As economists sometimes note, if the law of diminishing marginal returns did not hold, the world supply of food could be grown in a flowerpot: Just add enough seed, fertilizer, sun, and so on.

Productivity and Product Costs in the Short Run

Average and marginal product reflect a resource's productivity. **Productivity** is the relationship between the quantity of goods or services produced (in this case, hairbrushes) and the quantity of a variable resource used (in this case, labor). If the same amount of labor produces more hairbrushes than before, we can say that labor productivity has increased. Productivity data are useful, but M.T.R. must also determine its product costs.

Productivity and cost are directly related because firms must pay for the resources they use. Earlier we classified resources as either fixed or variable. We can classify costs similarly. Costs of variable resources (such as labor) are **variable costs**. Costs of fixed resources (such as buildings and machines) are **fixed costs**. In order to translate productivity data into product costs, we have to know what a firm pays for resources.

Productivity. The relationship between the quantity of goods or services produced and the quantity of a variable resource used.

Variable costs. Costs associated with variable resources; they increase directly with total product in the short run. Examples include costs of labor and materials.

Fixed costs. Costs associated with fixed resources; they are constant in the short run. Examples include rental payments on buildings, interest paid on debt, and property taxes.

Total fixed costs (TFC). The sum of all costs associated with a particular quantity of fixed resources; they are typically constant over a given range of total product in the short run.

Total variable costs (TVC). The sum of all costs for the quantity of variable resources used; they increase as total product increases.

Total costs (TC). The sum of total variable costs and total fixed costs. Mathematically,

TC = TVC + TFC

Marginal cost (MC). The additional cost associated with producing one additional unit of output; calculated as change in total costs divided by change in quantity of goods or services produced (change in total product). Mathematically, MC = Change in TC ÷ Change in Q.

Total costs. Exhibit 8.3 shows that M.T.R. has **total fixed costs (TFC)** of $2400 per week, representing the costs of its building and machinery. Total fixed costs are constant, regardless of output, because in the short run a firm cannot change the quantity of its fixed resources. The M.T.R. Brush Company has the same costs for its one building and five machines whether it produces 50 or 5000 hairbrushes.

In contrast, **total variable costs (TVC)** are not constant because the amount of variable resources increases as total product increases. Total variable costs equal the quantity used times the unit cost of the variable resource. As shown in the table in Exhibit 8.3, M.T.R. will have to hire—and pay for—more workers if it wants to produce more hairbrushes. Assuming that labor is the only variable resource and that each worker is paid the same wage—$400 per week—total variable costs equal the number of workers employed times $400.

The fourth column of Exhibit 8.3 shows **total costs (TC)**, which are the sum of total variable and total fixed costs. For example, total costs of producing 800 hairbrushes are $4000, or $1600 (variable costs) plus $2400 (fixed costs). Total costs represent one of the basic relationships used in analyzing product costs and are expressed mathematically as

$$\text{Total costs} = \text{Total variable costs} + \text{Total fixed costs} \qquad \text{TC} = \text{TVC} + \text{TFC}$$

Marginal costs. The fifth column in Exhibit 8.3 shows **marginal cost (MC)**, which we define as the extra cost per unit associated with an increase in the quantity of goods or services produced (total product). Because marginal cost represents the extra cost of an extra unit, it is an essential factor in decision making. As the principles of rational choice indicate, firms make decisions by comparing extra revenues with extra costs.

For example, if M.T.R. hires a fourth worker, total product rises from 480 to 800 hairbrushes, an increase (marginal product) of 320 brushes per week. To obtain this increase in total product, M.T.R. had to increase total costs by $400, from $3600 to $4000 per week. The marginal cost—extra cost per additional

Number of workers (workers per week)	Total variable costs (TVC) (dollars per week)	Total fixed costs (TFC) (dollars per week)	Total costs (TC) (dollars per week)	Marginal cost (MC) (dollars per brush)	Marginal product (MP) (brushes per worker)	Total product (TP = Q) (brushes per week)
0	0	2400	2400			0
				8.00	50	
1	400	2400	2800			50
				2.35	170	
2	800	2400	3200			220
				1.54	260	
3	1200	2400	3600			480
				1.25	320	
4	1600	2400	4000			800
				1.13	355	
5	2000	2400	4400			1155
				1.16	345	
6	2400	2400	4800			1500
				1.25	320	
7	2800	2400	5200			1820
				1.54	260	
8	3200	2400	5600			2080
				2.35	170	
9	3600	2400	6000			2250

Exhibit 8.3
Total and Marginal Cost for the M.T.R. Brush Company
The M.T.R. Brush Company has total fixed costs of $2400 per week. Total costs are the sum of fixed and variable costs. Total variable costs equal the number of workers multiplied by $400 (one worker's weekly wage). Marginal cost equals changes in total cost divided by changes in total product (quantity produced). In the range of increasing marginal returns—from 1 to 5 workers—marginal cost falls; in the range of diminishing marginal returns—from 6 to 9 workers—marginal cost rises.

unit—is $1.25 per extra hairbrush. Mathematically,

$$\text{Marginal cost} = \frac{\text{Change in total costs}}{\text{Change in total product}}$$

$$= \frac{(\$4000 - \$3600)}{(800 - 480)}$$

$$= \frac{\$400 \text{ per week}}{320 \text{ extra units per week}} \quad \text{or} \quad \$1.25 \text{ per extra hairbrush}$$

We can also calculate marginal cost by using the change in total variable costs, since in the short-run, fixed costs do not change. That is, the change in total variable costs ($1600 − $1200 = $400) is the same as the change in total costs. The denominator does not change, and so the marginal cost is the same, or $1.25 per extra hairbrush.

Diminishing marginal returns and increasing marginal cost. Using the data in Exhibit 8.3 we can illustrate an important connection between marginal product and marginal cost. We noted earlier in our example that marginal product increases as the first five workers are hired. At the same time, marginal cost falls—to a low of $1.13 per hairbrush. In the range of increasing marginal returns—the first through the fifth worker—M.T.R. pays the same extra costs for each worker ($400 per week) but receives a greater increase in total hairbrushes produced.

Conversely, in the range of diminishing marginal returns—the sixth through the ninth worker—marginal cost rises. This change occurs because M.T.R. receives a smaller increase in total product by hiring each additional worker, but pays the same extra cost. We can also make this connection using the equation for marginal cost; that is,

$$\text{Marginal cost} = \frac{\text{Change in total costs}}{\text{Change in total product}} \quad \text{or} \quad \frac{\text{Change in TC}}{\text{Change in Q}}$$

$$= \frac{\text{Cost of additional worker}}{\text{Increase in total product}} \quad \text{or} \quad \frac{\$400 \text{ per week}}{\text{Marginal product}}$$

The change in total product associated with hiring another worker is just another way of expressing marginal product. Because the cost of an additional worker is constant, marginal cost is inversely related to marginal product.

Actually, we could call the law of diminishing marginal returns the law of increasing marginal cost. In the range of diminishing marginal returns, as marginal product falls, marginal cost rises. Similarly, when marginal product rises, marginal cost falls.

Product Costs and Short-Run Cost Curves

The relationship between cost and output is important for decision making. We can express this relationship in one of three ways: total cost, average cost, or marginal cost. Each can help us understand how firms answer the supply question: How many units do we offer for sale at a certain price?

The relationship between costs and the number of flags produced per week by the Yankee Doodle Company is shown in Exhibit 8.4. Since fixed costs are constant in the short run, the graph in Exhibit 8.4(b) shows total fixed costs (TFC) as a horizontal line at $1200. In contrast, both total variable costs and total costs increase as more flags are produced. Thus at each level of output, total costs are $1200 more than total variable costs, reflecting constant total fixed costs.

Average costs. We often express cost on a per-unit or average basis. Thus when Yankee Doodle makes 600 flags per week, **average total cost (ATC)** is $6.00 per flag; that is,

$$\text{Average total cost} = \frac{\text{Total costs}}{\text{Total product}} \quad \text{or} \quad \frac{\text{TC}}{\text{Q}}$$

$$= \frac{\$3600 \text{ per week}}{600 \text{ flags per week}} \quad \text{or} \quad \$6.00 \text{ per flag}$$

Similarly, we calculate **average variable cost (AVC)** as total variable costs divided by total product (quantity). **Average fixed cost (AFC)** is total fixed costs divided

Average total cost (ATC). Also called *unit cost*; calculated as total costs divided by the quantity of goods or services produced (total product). Mathematically, ATC = TC ÷ Q or ATC = AVC + AFC.

Average variable cost (AVC). Also called *unit variable cost*; calculated as total variable costs divided by the quantity of goods or services produced (total product). Mathematically, AVC = TVC ÷ Q.

Average fixed cost (AFC). Total fixed costs divided by the quantity of goods or services produced (total product). Mathematically, AFC = TFC ÷ Q.

(a) Production data

Total product (TP = Q) (units per week)	Average fixed cost (AFC) (dollars per flag)	Total fixed costs (TFC) (dollars per week)	Average variable cost (AVC) (dollars per flag)	Total variable costs (TVC) (dollars per week)	Average total cost (ATC) (dollars per flag)	Total costs (TC) (dollars per week)	Marginal cost (MC) (dollars per flag)
0	—	1200	—	0	—	1200	
							7
200	6.0	1200	7	1400	13.0	2600	
							3
400	3.0	1200	5	2000	8.0	3200	
							2
600	2.0	1200	4	2400	6.0	3600	
							4
800	1.5	1200	4	3200	5.5	4400	
							9
1000	1.2	1200	5	5000	6.2	6200	
							17
1200	1.0	1200	7	8400	8.0	9600	

(b) Total costs

(c) Marginal and average costs

Exhibit 8.4
Total, Average, and Marginal Costs for Yankee Doodle Company
Total fixed costs for Yankee Doodle Company are constant at $1200 per week, shown in part (b) as a horizontal line (TFC). Total variable costs and total costs increase as more flags are made. Total costs are always $1200 higher than total variable costs. Note in part (c) that both the AVC and ATC curves are U-shaped. The MC curve intersects both at their minimum points.

by total product. Thus if Yankee Doodle produces 600 flags, average variable cost is $4.00 per flag, and average fixed cost is $2.00 per flag, calculated as follows:

$$\text{Average variable cost} = \frac{\text{Total variable costs}}{\text{Total product}} \quad \text{or} \quad \frac{\text{TVC}}{\text{Q}}$$

$$= \frac{\$2400 \text{ per week}}{600 \text{ flags per week}} \quad \text{or} \quad \$4.00 \text{ per flag}$$

and

$$\text{Average fixed cost} = \frac{\text{Total fixed costs}}{\text{Total product}} \quad \text{or} \quad \frac{\text{TFC}}{\text{Q}}$$

$$= \frac{\$1200 \text{ per week}}{600 \text{ flags per week}} \quad \text{or} \quad \$2.00 \text{ per flag}$$

Since we can express total costs as the sum of total fixed and total variable costs, we can also express average total cost as the sum of the average variable and average fixed costs. That is, when 600 flags are produced,

$$\text{ATC} = \text{AVC} + \text{AFC}$$
$$= \$4.00 + \$2.00 \quad \text{or} \quad \$6.00 \text{ per flag}$$

Firms sometimes consider average total cost as their product cost. But average total cost can be very misleading because it includes both fixed and variable costs. Moreover, average total cost represents cost at a particular level of output. When total product changes, average total cost also changes. A Case in Point: Average Total Cost and Tuition Scholarships illustrates some mistakes that result from a failure to recognize that average total cost includes both average fixed cost and average variable cost. To test your understanding of these cost relationships try calculating some of the other marginal and average costs shown in Exhibit 8.4.

Shape of short-run cost curves. Average and marginal costs are plotted in Exhibit 8.4(c). With the cost of each additional worker held constant at $200 per week, marginal cost (MC) reflects changes in marginal product. Thus marginal cost decreases at first, as the firm experiences increasing marginal returns. However, because Yankee Doodle has some fixed costs, the law of diminishing marginal returns eventually applies. As marginal product declines, marginal cost steadily rises.

The graph indicates that the average variable cost curve is U-shaped. The initial drop in average variable cost reflects declining marginal cost. But average variable cost continues to decline even after the firm has reached the range of diminishing returns. In fact, as long as marginal cost is less than average cost, the average must be decreasing; each unit produced adds less than average to total variable costs. Eventually, as marginal cost equals and then exceeds average variable cost, the AVC curve turns upward.

The average total cost curve is also U-shaped. The initial decrease in average total cost reflects changes both in marginal cost and (importantly) in average fixed cost. Because Yankee Doodle has constant total fixed costs, average fixed cost declines as total product expands. (A firm with $1 million in total fixed costs has an average fixed cost of $10,000 if it produces only 100 units but only $1 if it

A Case in Point
Average Total Cost and Tuition Scholarships

A newspaper reporter quoted an economics professor at a financially troubled college as suggesting that the college offer partial tuition scholarships to attract more students and thus ease a projected budget deficit. The story also noted that the current tuition is $4000 per year but that the average cost per student is almost $7000. Does it make sense for the college to lower the tuition when the college is already losing $3000 per student?

In order to answer this question, you have to recognize the kind of information given and the kind of information required for a rational economic decision. The average cost per student of $7000 is clearly an average total cost and includes both fixed and variable costs. But if the college is considering enrolling only a few more students, what are the extra benefits and extra costs of that decision?

As long as the college continues to operate, most of its costs are fixed: costs of dormitory and classroom buildings, administrators' salaries, specialized equipment, and the like. Thus revenue from tuition must cover only marginal (extra variable) costs: costs of registering students, recording their progress, and so on.

Compared to fixed costs, these marginal costs are quite small. If it has additional space, the college can reduce its budget deficit if the extra tuition payments more than offset the extra costs for the additional students. Thus partial tuition scholarships—if they attract extra students who otherwise would not attend—are a good idea.

Whenever you encounter average total cost, be careful in using it to make decisions. Average total cost usually includes some fixed costs; fixed costs are constant and hence are irrelevant for short-run decisions. It is the extra costs—the costs that change—that matter in the short run.

produces 1 million units.) The upward slope of a portion of the average total cost curve is caused by the law of diminishing marginal returns.

The marginal cost curve intersects both the average variable cost curve and the average total cost curve at their minimum points, further illustrating the principle demonstrated by the marginal and average product curves. Whenever marginal cost exceeds average cost, average cost must be rising. Each unit then adds more than average to total costs. You can see these relationships in Exhibit 8.4. As long as Yankee Doodle produces less than 800 flags per week, marginal cost is less than average total cost, and average total cost decreases. When Yankee Doodle produces more than 800 flags per week, marginal cost exceeds average cost, and average cost increases.

RECAP

The following formulas summarize the important cost–output relationships.

$$TC = TVC + TFC$$

$$MC = \frac{\text{Change in TC}}{\text{Change in Q}}$$

$$ATC = TC \div Q \quad \text{or}$$
$$AVC + AFC$$

$$AVC = TVC \div Q$$

$$AFC = TFC \div Q$$

TECHNICAL EFFICIENCY AND OPTIMAL RESOURCE MIX

In addition to deciding how much to produce for sale at any given price, all firms must answer questions that relate to technical efficiency. What is the best way for us to produce? What technology should we use? What combination of resources should we use to obtain the lowest possible costs?

Technological considerations alone cannot determine a unique solution to these questions. Exhibit 8.5 shows two possible technologies that Southwestern Manufacturing Company could use to produce 100 pairs of sunglasses. Technology A uses more labor and less capital than technology B. But the important question for Southwestern is which technology is best.

Southwestern wants to maximize profits by minimizing production costs, so it will want to use the more technically efficient technology. How can the company tell which technology is more technically efficient? It can do so by combining information about resource productivity (marginal product) with information about the relative prices of the two resources used. That is, the company must determine whether it is less expensive to use 20 units of labor and 3 units of capital or 10 units of labor and 5 units of capital.

In the first case shown in Exhibit 8.5, the price of labor is $40 per day, and the price of capital is $150 per day. The total costs of producing 100 pairs of sunglasses are calculated for each of the two technologies. At these prices, technology B is more efficient: The total costs of 100 units are $1150, or $100 less than the $1250 for technology A. Technology B uses more capital—the more expensive of the two resources—but its higher total costs are more than offset by the lower total costs of labor. For those prices, technology B is less expensive (more technically efficient) for Southwestern to use.

Exhibit 8.5
Relative Productivity and Cost for Two Alternative Technologies

	Quantity required to produce 100 units per day	
Resource	Technology A	Technology B
Units of labor	20	10
Units of capital	3	5

Cost of 100 units if price of labor = $40 and price of capital = $150		
Technology A		
20 units of labor	× $40 per day	= $ 800
3 units of capital	× $150 per day	= 450
Total cost using A		= $1250
Technology B		
10 units of labor	× $40 per day	= $ 400
5 units of capital	× $150 per day	= 750
Total cost using B		= $1150

Cost of 100 units if price of labor = $40 and price of capital = $250		
Technology A		
20 units of labor	× $40 per day	= $ 800
3 units of capital	× $250 per day	= 750
Total cost using A		= $1550
Technology B		
10 units of labor	× $40 per day	= $ 400
5 units of capital	× $250 per day	= 1250
Total cost using B		= $1650

What if the price of capital were $250, not $150? The higher relative price of capital makes total costs for each technology greater than before. But technology A is now more efficient than technology B; the increased price of capital has a greater effect on the total costs of technology B because it uses more capital.

Technical efficiency—producing at minimum cost—always depends on two factors: (1) relative productivity of resources; and (2) relative prices of resources. Thus a change in either relative productivity or relative prices can cause a firm to choose a different technology.

Cost Minimization and the Equimarginal Principle

In the real world, firms usually have options similar to that of Southwestern Manufacturing. For example, they may use skilled or semiskilled labor, or they may substitute machinery for labor. In order to minimize costs, they must choose the best combination of resources. The principles of rational choice require firms to balance extra benefits (marginal product) against extra costs (price of the resource). Thus we can state that *a firm should combine resources so that the marginal product per dollar of cost is the same for each resource.* Mathematically, this means for resources A and B that the firm should seek to have

$$\frac{\text{Marginal product for A}}{\text{Price of A}} = \frac{\text{Marginal product for B}}{\text{Price of B}}$$

or

$$\frac{\text{MP}_A}{\text{P}_A} = \frac{\text{MP}_B}{\text{P}_B}$$

By following this approach, a firm can identify the combination of resources that will result in the lowest unit cost, or technical efficiency. If the marginal product per dollar of cost for resource A (MP_A/P_A) is greater than that for resource B, the firm can lower its costs by using less of B and more of A. (We apply this rule to the resource mix question in the appendix to this chapter.)

We return to the question of technical efficiency in Chapter 13 on resource markets. For the moment, however, let's focus on other kinds of producer decisions. In so doing, we assume that producers strive to be technically efficient and make appropriate choices about resource use.

COSTS AND ECONOMIES OF SCALE IN THE LONG RUN

So far we have considered only short-run cost–output relationships. We have assumed that the time period is too short for a firm to change any of its fixed resources. That is, in the short run a firm has to decide how best to use its existing fixed resources.

But given enough time, a firm can change any or all of its resources. Thus in the long run, a firm must decide whether to build a new plant, produce a new product, buy new machines, and so on. It must ultimately decide whether to stay in the same business, go into a new industry, or get out of business entirely. In this section and in A Case in Point: Economic Profit for Farmer Al Greene, we look at such long-run cost–output relationships and decisions.

A Case in Point
Economic Profit for Farmer Al Greene

Al Greene bought a 300-acre farm a few years ago for $1000 per acre. The farm now has a market value of $3000 per acre. His average operating costs are $450 per acre, including costs of fertilizer, seed, gasoline for his tractor, and so on. Al operates the farm by himself, using no hired labor. When he started the farm, Al bought tractors and other equipment for $75,000; they can be sold today for $40,000. Al can put his money in a local bank, where it will earn 10 percent per year in interest. He has a standing job offer at the local feed store that would pay him $15,000 per year. Should Al continue to farm or should he sell out and take the feed-store job? This relative comparison of long-run options is exactly what economic profit measures.

The accompanying table shows each of the resources Al uses in farming: fertilizer, seed, and other materials having variable costs; land; equipment; and Al's labor. We examine each one separately and—using opportunity cost analysis—show how to measure the real costs (economic costs) of Al's farm.

Resources used	Opportunity costs	
Fertilizer, seeds, etc.	($450/acre × 300 acres)	$135,000
Labor		15,000
Equipment	($40,000 × 10% per year)	4,000
Land	($900,000 × 10% per year)	90,000
Total opportunity cost per year		$244,000

The opportunity costs of the fertilizer, seed, and other resources Al uses in farming are the prices he must pay to buy them in the marketplace (that is, the explicit costs). They amount to $450 per acre, and assuming that Al farms all 300 acres, he will have an opportunity cost of $135,000 per year for those items.

Since Al himself provides all the labor, there are no explicit costs for labor. But there are implicit costs, measured as the $15,000 per year Al could earn working at the local feed store. If he continues to farm, he sacrifices the income from this other job, the next best opportunity for his labor. We consider this cost fixed, since Al either farms or does not farm. If he farms, he must turn down the other job and sacrifice $15,000.

The opportunity costs of the next two items—land and equipment—are a bit more complex. The land orig-

inally cost $300,000 ($1000 per acre for 300 acres) and the equipment $75,000. But Al is a profit maximizer and will not sell the farm for what it cost him if he can sell it for more. Al had his land and equipment appraised: The land's current market value is $3000 per acre, and the equipment's current value is $40,000.

Thus if Al sells for appraised values, he will receive $940,000 in cash that he did not have before. He will not be wealthier but will merely have exchanged $940,000 worth of land and equipment for $940,000 in cash. Thus to measure the opportunity costs of the land and equipment, we must consider Al's other options, that is, the other things he can do with the money. Since Al can put the money he receives from the sale in the local bank at 10 percent interest per year, the opportunity cost of having $940,000 in the form of land and equipment is the sacrifice of not earning $94,000 per year in interest from the bank.

This brings total opportunity costs of all the resources used to $244,000 per year. Al's crops produce annual revenues of $850 per acre, so his total revenues are $255,000, or ($850 per acre) × (300 acres). Thus we can calculate Al's economic profits from farming as

$$\text{Economic profit} = \text{Total revenues} - \text{Total costs}$$

$$= \$255,000 - \$244,000 \quad \text{or}$$

$$\$11,000 \text{ per year}$$

We can also express Al's options in terms of their relative values. The first option (to continue farming) has a value to Al of $120,000 per year, calculated as ($850 per acre of sales − $450 per acre of explicit costs) × (300 acres). His next best option (to sell the farm and go to work at the feed store) is worth $109,000 per year, calculated as $15,000 in salary + $94,000 in interest earnings. Thus Al's farming option is worth $11,000 per year more than his next best option.

Either method of analysis shows that Al can make an economic profit of $11,000 more each year by continuing to farm than he could if he sold his farm, banked the proceeds, and went to work at the feed store (his next best options for all his resources). Thus farming is the option that maximizes Al's income. Will he stay in farming? As always, the answer is "it depends." In this case, the answer depends on many noneconomic factors, including Al's age, his desire for leisure time, his family's desire to move into town, and so on. We can say, however, that for now farming is Al's most financially profitable option.

(a) Unit production costs

Units produced	Factory A (smaller)		Factory B (larger)	
	AVC	ATC	AVC	ATC
3,000	$ 2.25	$ 5.25	$5.00	$11.00
6,000	2.00	3.50	3.25	6.25
9,000	3.00	4.00	2.00	4.00
12,000	5.25	6.00	1.25	2.75
15,000	8.75	9.35	1.00	2.20
18,000	13.50	14.00	1.25	2.25

(b) Average cost curves

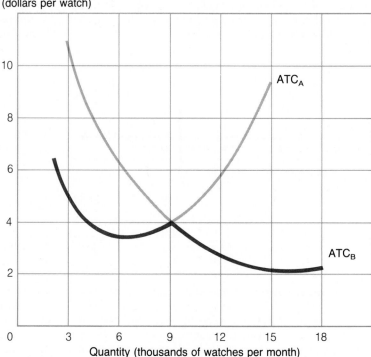

Exhibit 8.6
Choice of Plant Size for Timeout Watch Company
Timeout Watch Company can build one of two plant sizes. Factory A is smaller and has monthly fixed costs of $9000 compared with $18,000 for Factory B. However, variable costs are higher for Factory A. The graph in part (b) shows that the most technically efficient plant size depends on the expected level of production. If Timeout expects to make fewer than 9000 watches each month, Factory A is better because it has lower average costs. But if production is expected to exceed 9000 watches, Factory B is better. The darker sections of the two curves combine to yield the long-run average cost curve for Timeout. It shows how average costs change over the long run when the firm can vary all resources.

Long-Run Costs

A typical long-run question for a firm is whether it should build a small or large plant. Exhibit 8.6 shows average variable cost, average fixed cost, and average total costs for two factories that the Timeout Watch Company can build to make stopwatches. Factory A is smaller than factory B. As a result, factory A has smaller total fixed costs: $9000 per month compared to $18,000 per month for factory B.

Why do we show fixed costs for a long-run decision? In the long run the company can vary the quantity of every resource it uses. But when it makes a decision about factory size, it also chooses the level at which other resources—such as the number of machines it uses—become fixed. What you see in Exhibit 8.6, then, are short-run cost curves for the two factory sizes. This is still a long-run decision, however, since the firm can change the quantity of all resources it uses.

Which factory should Timeout build? Again, the answer to this question is "it depends." In particular, it depends on the quantity of watches that Timeout expects to produce each month. As Exhibit 8.6 shows, if Timeout plans to make fewer than 9000 watches per month, the average cost per watch will be less if it builds factory A. For example, the cost of making 3000 watches would average $5.25 per watch with factory A, but $11.00 per watch with factory B. However, if Timeout produces more than 9000 watches per month, factory B is the better choice. For example, the average total cost of producing 12,000 watches with factory B would be $2.75 per watch; with factory A, $6.00 per watch.

Like all economic decisions, the choice of factory size focuses on extra benefits and extra costs. The advantage of a larger factory is its lower average variable cost; the disadvantage is its higher fixed costs. When a large plant produces relatively few units, it is relatively inefficient (much of its capacity is idle). Thus for smaller volumes of output, a smaller plant may have a lower average cost.

You can now see how Timeout's average cost changes with total product in the long run. For its expected level of output, the firm will choose the plant size that allows it to produce for the lowest average cost. Thus Timeout would build factory A if it expects to produce fewer than 9000 watches per month but factory B if it expects to produce more than 9000 watches per month. The lowest average cost that the company can attain by varying all its resources is shown as the darker parts of the two curves in Exhibit 8.6(b). They contain points from the short-run cost curve for factory A for volumes of up to 9000 watches and points from the short-run cost curve for factory B for volumes of more than 9000 watches per month. This curve shows Timeout's **long-run average cost (LRAC)**, assuming in this case that there are only two relevant plant sizes.

Economies and Diseconomies of Scale

In real life, firms are not limited to choosing between two or even three different plant sizes. As shown for the Alsize Shirt Company in Exhibit 8.7, firms can choose among many different plant sizes (represented by the ATC curves). Again, the darker line along the bottom of the short-run curves represents long-run average cost, that is, combinations of resources that would produce goods at the lowest average cost.

The long-run average cost curve has the same shape as the typical short-run curves presented in this chapter. But the factors affecting the shape of the long-run curve are not the same as those affecting the shapes of the short-run curves. In Exhibit 8.7, the long-run average cost curve decreases until production reaches 8000 shirts per month. In effect, if Alsize expands the size, or scale, of its operation to this amount, it can reduce its average cost by taking advantage of **economies of scale**.

Economies of scale most often result from either specialization or technology. As a firm grows, it can divide work into many separate tasks. Each worker in a large organization may specialize in relatively few tasks. As a result, workers may

Long-run average cost (LRAC). The minimum average total cost for each level of output when a firm can change all its resources.

Economies of scale. A situation in which long-run average cost decreases as a firm increases the size (or scale) of its plant and output; implies that larger plants are more technically efficient than small plants if large quantities of goods are produced.

Exhibit 8.7
Long-Run Average Cost for Alsize Shirt Company
The long-run average cost curve (LRAC) for the Alsize Shirt Company represents the lowest average cost for each level of ouput when the firm can vary all its resources. For each quantity of output, there is a best plant size, as shown by the ATC curves. For example, plant 6 is best if Alsize wants to produce 12,000 shirts per month. Up to 8000 shirts per month, the LRAC declines, showing the effects of economies of scale. Between 8000 and 16,000 shirts per month the LRAC is flat, showing a range of constant returns to scale. Beyond 16,000 shirts per month the LRAC rises, indicating diseconomies of scale.

become more proficient in those tasks than do workers in smaller plants who are required to perform many different tasks. Managers in large firms can also specialize. With such tasks as inventory and production control, personnel, research, and planning performed by specialists, a large firm may be able to produce goods and services at lower costs than can a small firm.

Moreover, in some industries the lowest cost technology requires substantial investment in specialized machinery. Although plants with such machinery have relatively high fixed costs, they often have a substantially lower average variable cost. In industries where economies of scale are possible, firms that use small plants to produce small volumes have substantially higher costs than firms that use larger plants to produce larger volumes. Steel plants and automobile plants are typical examples of technology creating economies of scale.

Constant returns to scale. A situation in which long-run average cost is constant; implies that large and small plants have equal technical efficiency.

Diseconomies of scale. A situation in which long-run average cost increases as a firm increases the size (or scale) of its plant and output; implies that larger plants are less technically efficient than smaller plants.

But economies of scale have limits. In Exhibit 8.7, long-run average cost is constant as total product expands from 8000 to 16,000 shirts per month. This flat area reflects **constant returns to scale**. In this range, Alsize will achieve the same average cost ($2.00 per unit) producing 12,000 shirts per month with plant 6 or 14,000 shirts per month with plant 7.

Beyond 16,000 shirts per month, however, the long-run average cost curve in Exhibit 8.7 turns up, reflecting **diseconomies of scale**. In effect, the plant has grown too large: Communications between managers and workers and between top-level and bottom-level managers may be difficult. Employees may feel isolated and unimportant; mistakes that occur may not be easily discovered or quickly fixed.

Economies of scale and industry composition.

Some industries are made up of a large number of relatively small firms; others consist of only a few, relatively large firms; still other industries include firms of varying size. The existence (or absence) of economies of scale is important in determining costs and, in turn, industry characteristics.

Exhibit 8.8 shows three possibilities—representing different industry types—for the long-run average cost curve. In Exhibit 8.8(a), the long-run average cost curve ($LRAC_1$) reaches its minimum at 10,000 units of output. This means that the most efficiently sized plant would produce 10,000 units per week, or the minimum point on the long-run average cost curve. In this case there are few economies of scale, so that even a relatively small firm would be large enough to be efficient. Larger plants would actually suffer significant diseconomies of scale. Industries with this type of long-run average cost curve are likely to be characterized by a large number of small-sized plants or outlets. Examples include machine-tool shops and gasoline service stations.

In Exhibit 8.8(b), the long-run average cost curve ($LRAC_2$) is relatively flat, indicating constant returns to scale. Thus plants of very different sizes can be equally efficient. The most efficiently sized plant would be one capable of producing anywhere between 10,000 and 35,000 units per month. This situation is typical of agriculture. Although very small farms have higher average costs, most average-sized farms have the advantages of size. Moreover, evidence indicates that larger farms (although they may generate higher total income) have little, if any, cost advantages. This wide range of constant returns helps to explain the relatively large range of farm size.

In Exhibit 8.8(c), the long-run average cost curve ($LRAC_3$) declines sharply until it reaches 14,000 units per week, indicating significant economies of scale. Because the most technically efficient plant is relatively large, we would expect to find only a few, large-sized plants in this type of industry. Examples include manufacturing of large-scale equipment and automobiles. Although economies of scale are important in many industries, you should not automatically equate larger size with greater efficiency.

Economies of scale and diminishing returns.

In the first section of this chapter we defined the law of diminishing marginal returns: Beyond a certain point, marginal cost increases as total product increases. But economies of scale imply that costs fall as total product increases. Although these two concepts seem to be contradictory, they refer to entirely different situations. The law of diminishing marginal returns is a short-run phenomenon, holding only when some re-

(a) Few economies of scale

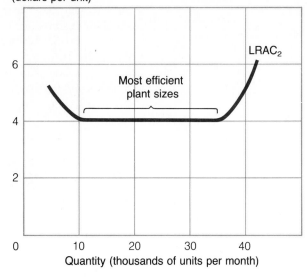

(b) Constant returns to scale

(c) Significant economies of scale

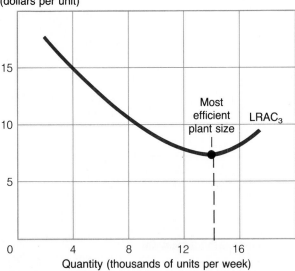

Exhibit 8.8
Economies of Scale and Long-Run Average Cost
The graphs in this exhibit show three possible long-run average cost curves. In (a), the most efficient plant is one capable of producing 10,000 units per week (the lowest point on $LRAC_1$). Beyond 10,000 units, the curve rises sharply, indicating significant diseconomies of scale. In (b), $LRAC_2$ is flat over a wide range of output, so there is no one best plant size. Average cost is the same for plants as small as 10,000 units per month and as large as 35,000 units per month. A variety of plant sizes occur in such industries. In (c), $LRAC_3$ shows significant economies of scale. Only relatively large plants can achieve maximum efficiency. A few large firms would dominate such industries.

sources remain constant. Economies of scale, however, are long-run phenomena, reflecting changes in all of a firm's resources.

However, even in businesses that benefit from economies of scale, the law of diminishing marginal returns holds once a firm fixes the quantity of some of its resources. For example, look at Exhibit 8.7 again: Once Alsize builds plant 6, it will have fixed costs in the short run. As long as it operates that plant, its marginal cost will indeed rise as total product increases.

Short-run and long-run costs and economic decisions. We have developed two different sets of economic costs in this chapter. You should understand why and how they differ. First, rational choice means focusing only on extra costs, that is, those that change for any decision. We developed two sets of cost curves to represent two decision-making conditions. Short-run cost curves indicate how costs and output are related, *assuming that a firm has a specific plant size*. In the short run, a firm has some fixed resources and costs (generally referred to as the firm's capacity costs). Since they are constant, they have no effect on short-run decisions. Thus for short-run decision making, only variable costs are relevant.

In contrast, long-run cost curves indicate how costs and output are related, *assuming that a firm is considering possible changes in plant size and other fixed resources*. In the long run, the firm can change the quantity and/or type of all its resources. Thus for long-run decision making, the cost of all resources is relevant.

Finally, because economic costs include opportunity costs, we must focus on economic costs and economic profits in making rational decisions. Translating accounting terms to economic terms requires—among other things—a focus on the future. For an economic decision, we want to know the likely future costs of available options.

CONCLUSION

In this chapter, we explored costs and how to get the optimal mix of resources. In Chapter 9, you will see how costs influence both short-run and long-run supply decisions. In that chapter—and in the remainder of the microeconomics section of this textbook—we use the cost concepts developed in this chapter. Costs are only half the story (benefits being the other half). But rational decision making requires that you understand and correctly apply the concepts of economic costs.

SUMMARY

1. In this chapter we discussed how firms determine product costs in both the short run—when they cannot change at least some of their resources—and in the long run—when they can change any or all of their resources.

2. To make rational decisions, we must consider all opportunity costs. Accounting profits consider only explicit costs, that is, payments a firm must make for resources it uses. Economic profits consider both explicit and implicit costs, that is, sacrifices of benefits not received from the next best options. Economic profit, not accounting profit, is the guide to rational decisions.

3. Producers make both short-run and long-run decisions. In the short run, a firm has some fixed resources—such as building and equipment—that it cannot change within a relevant period of time. To increase output in the short run, a firm adds additional quantities of variable resources—such as materials and labor—that it can change. In the long run, a firm can change the quantity and/or type of all its resources.

4. In studying the short-run relationship between variable resources and costs, economists observe how output (total product) changes as added variable resources are used. Marginal product measures the change in total product when one additional unit of a variable resource is used.

5. Marginal product increases during the stage of increasing marginal returns. But, following the law of diminishing marginal returns, at some point marginal product will start to decrease. In the stage of diminishing marginal returns, total product continues to increase, but at a decreasing rate.

6. In the short run, economists classify costs as either fixed or variable. In the short run, variable costs (costs of variable resources) change directly with total product. Fixed costs (costs of fixed resources) are constant in the short run. Total costs are the sum of total variable and total fixed costs (TC = TVC + TFC). Average total cost is the sum of average variable and average fixed costs (ATC = AVC + AFC).

7. Marginal cost measures the extra cost for an extra unit of output. When the price of variable resources is constant, marginal cost is inversely related to marginal product. Marginal cost falls in the range of increasing marginal returns and rises in the range of diminishing marginal returns. The law of diminishing marginal returns can also be called the law of increasing marginal cost.

8. Average cost initially declines because both marginal cost and average fixed cost fall when more goods or services are produced. But the average cost curve turns up because of the law of diminishing marginal returns. As long as marginal cost is less than average cost, average cost will decline. However, once marginal cost exceeds average cost, average cost will rise. The marginal cost curve intersects the average variable cost and the average total cost curves at their minimum points.

9. In order to produce each unit at the lowest possible cost, producers strive for technical efficiency. To choose the best combination of resources for any quantity of goods or services produced, firms weigh extra benefits (marginal product) against extra costs (resource prices). The equimarginal principle, applied to the choice of resources, states that resources A and B should be used so that $MP_A/P_A = MP_B/P_B$. This rule results in lower unit costs and thus ensures technical efficiency.

10. The long-run average cost curve (LRAC) shows the lowest possible average total cost for each level of output when a firm changes any or all of its resources. Long-run average cost declines as total product expands when there are economies of scale; firms with large plants will have a lower average cost when they produce large quantities. Long-run average cost rises when there are diseconomies of scale, reflecting perhaps the less efficient control and communications of large organizations. The curve is flat when there are constant returns to scale, since firms of varying size can be equally efficient and cost competitive.

KEY TERMS

Explicit costs, 175
Implicit costs, 175
Accounting profit, 175
Economic profit, 176
Short run, 177
Long run, 177
Fixed resources, 177
Variable resources, 177

Production function, 177
Total product (TP), 177
Marginal product (MP), 179
Average product (AP), 179
Increasing marginal returns, 179
Diminishing marginal returns, 180
Law of diminishing marginal returns, 180
Productivity, 181
Variable costs, 181
Fixed costs, 181
Total fixed costs (TFC), 181
Total variable costs (TVC), 181
Total costs (TC), 181
Marginal cost (MC), 181
Average total cost (ATC), 183
Average variable cost (AVC), 183
Average fixed cost (AFC), 183
Long-run average cost (LRAC), 191
Economies of scale, 191
Constant returns to scale, 193
Diseconomies of scale, 193

QUESTIONS FOR REVIEW AND DISCUSSION

1. Can a firm increase total product in the short run without adding variable resources? Can it increase total product in the short run with the same quantity of fixed resources? Explain your answers.

2. Analyze the statement: "Because overhead costs are fixed, costs fall as total product expands. So the more a firm produces, the lower its costs and hence the more efficient it will be." Be sure to note the kinds of costs (average, variable, marginal, and so on) being considered (or ignored).

3. Tom can produce 18 units per hour, but Jerry can produce only 12. Jerry will work for $5 per hour; Tom demands $10 per hour. Who is more productive? Who is more efficient? Which concept, productivity or efficiency, determines your hiring decision?

4. The Wilderness Manufacturing Company currently produces 10,000 tents each year at an average cost of $8 per tent. It is considering expanding production to 12,000 tents and estimates that each tent will then cost an average of $10.
   a) Calculate total costs for each level of output and marginal cost for the extra 2000 tents to be produced.

b) What is the minimum price that Wilderness must receive on each of the extra 2000 tents in order to cover its production costs (assuming that it sold the first 10,000 at a profit)?

5. If firms regard average total cost as the cost of their product, does this viewpoint help or hinder them in making good decisions? Consider what you know about the behavior of costs in the short run and provide examples to illustrate your answer.

6. Consider each of the following statements. Based on the concepts discussed in this chapter, decide whether each is true or false.
   a) A fall in the price of any resource tends to increase its efficiency even if marginal product doesn't change.
   b) Marginal cost isn't affected by any change in total fixed costs.
   c) In the short run, when fixed costs are constant, average total cost falls as total product rises, as long as average cost is higher than marginal cost.
   d) In the long run, the law of diminishing marginal returns eventually causes the long-run average cost curve to turn upward.

7. A farmer is trying to decide how much fertilizer to use on a field. The following data indicate the yield in bushels per acre for each 100 pounds of fertilizer per acre added. If the price of fertilizer is $35 per 100 pounds and the crop can be sold for $5 per bushel, how much fertilizer should the farmer use? (*Hint*: Think of the process by which we decided how many prisons to build in Chapter 2.)

Fertilizer (100 pounds per acre)	Yield (total bushels per acre)
0	100
1	110
2	116
3	120
4	122

8. Think about costs in the airline industry. List some examples of relevant costs (that is, extra costs) and some examples of irrelevant costs (that is, costs which are unchanged) for each of the following decisions.
   a) Flying an extra 300 miles.
   b) Lowering fares to increase the number of passengers on a particular flight.
   c) Adding one new route.
   d) Adding a significant number of new routes.

9. In each of the following cases, fill in the blanks using the three basic cost relationships: (1) TC = TVC + TFC; (2) AC = TC ÷ Q (used for both average total cost, and average variable cost); and (3) MC = Change in TC ÷ Change in Q.

a)

Q	TC	TVC	TFC
0	$600	$__	$__
10	700	__	__
20	__	250	__

b)

Q	TC	ATC	TVC	AVC	TFC
200	$800	$__	$__	$2.50	$__
400	__	3.00	900	__	__
600	__	__	__	2.75	__

c)

Q	TC	MC
5	$40 —	
		>$__
6	48 — <	
		> 12
7	__ —	

10. How do firms decide what combination of resources to use and what technology to use? How might a firm decide which of two technologies is more efficient? Is technology that uses more capital and less labor necessarily more efficient than one that is more labor intensive? Explain.

11. The Durham Manufacturing Company can produce 100 calculators using either of the resource combinations shown below. Can you tell from this information which combination is more efficient? Why not? Calculate the average cost per calculator if labor costs are $8 per hour and machinery costs are $50 per hour. Which technology is more efficient? Recalculate the average cost if machinery costs increase to $75 per hour. Which technology is more efficient now? Explain why a change in resource price affects the choice of technology.

Resource	Combination X	Combination Y
Labor	30 hours	15 hours
Machinery	3 hours	5 hours

Appendix to Chapter 8

Indifference Analysis and the Optimal Mix of Resources

In the appendix to Chapter 7, you learned how indifference analysis can be applied to choices of consumers seeking the mix of products that maximizes their satisfaction. In this appendix we apply a similar analysis to choices of producers seeking the mix of resources that minimizes their costs.

TECHNICAL POSSIBILITIES AND ISOQUANTS

In this chapter we noted that producers can make their goods using varying combinations of resources. For example, in Exhibit 8A.1 the TP_5 curve shows several combinations of labor and materials that Seymour Corporation can use to produce 5 telescopes. For example, Seymour may decide to use 8 pounds of materials and 4 hours of labor (combination C), or 4 pounds of materials and 8 hours of labor (combination B). In fact, the firm can choose any combination shown because each combination represents one possible technology for producing 5 telescopes.

Seymour Corporation is indifferent to the various combinations of resources in the sense that each option yields an identical number of telescopes. Thus we could call this curve a production indifference curve, just as we referred to consumer indifference curves in the appendix to Chapter 7. Economists, however, generally refer to it as an **isoquant**.[*]

Producers are not really indifferent to all choices on a given isoquant. Since each point on an isoquant has a different cost, producers prefer the point of lowest cost. In our example, we expect Seymour to choose the combination having the lowest cost for producing the 5 telescopes.

The cost of any technology depends on the costs of resources (labor and materials). Moving downward along the isoquant, the quantity of materials used increases, and the quantity of labor decreases while total product stays the same. Exhibit 8A.1 shows that as Seymour moves from combination B to C, it will use 4 fewer hours of labor and 4 more pounds of materials. The rate at which labor and materials can be substituted is known as the **marginal rate of technical substitution**. It is the ratio of the marginal products of the two resources; that is,

Isoquant. A curve showing combinations of two resources that will produce the same level of output.

Marginal rate of technical substitution. The ratio of marginal products of two substitute resources; the slope of an isoquant measures the marginal rate of technical substitution.

$$\text{Marginal rate of technical substitution} = \frac{\text{Marginal product of labor}}{\text{Marginal product of materials}} = \frac{MP_l}{MP_m}$$

---

[*] The term *isoquant* is derived from *iso*, which means the same, and *quant*, which stands for quantity. Thus isoquant means *the same quantity*, referring to the fact that all combinations on the curve represent the same quantity of goods or services produced.

(a) Four possible combinations

Combination	Materials (pounds)	Labor (hours)
A	2	16
B	4	8
C	8	4
D	14	3

(b) Isoquant

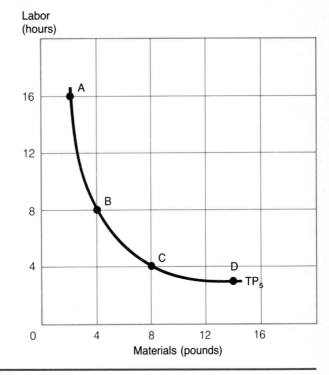

Exhibit 8A.1
Resource Combinations for Seymour Corporation

In Chapter 7, we measured the slope of the indifference curve for consumers as the marginal rate of substitution of one product for another. Here, *the absolute value of the slope of an isoquant measures the marginal rate of technical substitution.*

Characteristics of Isoquants

The shape and position of isoquants are determined by their characteristics.

1. *Isoquants have a negative slope.* Isoquants slope downward and to the right. Why? Because if a firm uses less of one resource (for example, materials) it must use more of the other resource (labor) to produce the same quantity of goods or services. Otherwise the points on the isoquant would not represent efficient technology options.

2. *Isoquants bend toward the origin.* Like consumer indifference curves, isoquants bend toward the origin. Why? Because as the firm substitutes labor for materials, it must add increasingly larger amounts of labor in order to achieve the same level of output (law of diminishing marginal returns).

3. *Isoquants farther from the origin represent higher levels of output.* Although Exhibit 8A.1 shows only one isoquant, we could draw others, as we did with multiple consumer indifference curves. Each isoquant represents a single level of output (as its name indicates). If we want to represent a higher level of

Isocost. A curve showing combinations of two resources that result in the same total costs; the slope of an isocost is the ratio of the prices of the two resources.

output (for example, 8 telescopes), we would draw an isoquant to the right of the existing curve. Why? Because an isoquant farther from the origin represents larger quantities of both resources, which generally yield higher levels of output.

ISOCOSTS

Isoquants provide only part of the information that Seymour Corporation requires to decide how to produce telescopes. Since it wants to produce at the lowest cost, Seymour must know the relative costs of its resources. To represent these costs, we use an **isocost**, which is a line representing a single level of total costs. Recall that we used a budget line in consumer analysis to indicate a single level of income.

We can construct an isocost if we know the costs of the resources. Suppose that the materials Seymour uses cost $8 per pound, and labor costs $4 per hour. Then, for a total cost of $64, Seymour can buy 8 pounds of materials, 16 hours of labor, or any combination of the two that lies along the isocost (labeled TC_1) shown in Exhibit 8A.2.

Exhibit 8A.2
Isocost Line for Seymour Corporation

(a) Resource combinations

Materials (pounds)	Labor (hours)
8	0
6	4
4	8
0	16

(b) Isocost

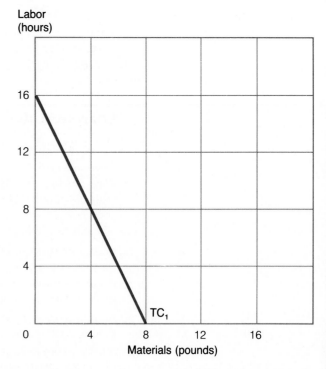

Characteristics of Isocosts

As for isoquants, the shape and position of an isocost is determined by its characteristics.

1. *The slope of any isocost equals the ratio of the prices of the two resources.* Why? Because the ratio of the resource prices reflects trade-offs that a firm can make and hold total costs constant. For example, in Exhibit 8A.2 the slope is 2.0—the ratio of the price of materials to the price of labor. That is, for the same total costs Seymour can trade two hours of labor for a pound of materials, moving along the isocost.

2. *Isocosts representing higher levels of total costs lie farther away from the origin.* Although Exhibit 8A.2 shows only a single isocost line, we could draw others representing different levels of total costs. Any isocost representing a greater expenditure would lie to the right of the one shown. Why? Because points to the right represent greater quantities of resources, which mean higher costs.

OPTIMAL COMBINATION OF RESOURCES

The optimal combination of resources along an isoquant is the combination with the lowest total costs. Thus Seymour Corporation will seek the isocost closest to the origin that will still enable it to produce 5 telescopes. We can find the optimal combination by using the isoquant of Exhibit 8A.1 and the isocost of Exhibit 8A.2.

As shown in Exhibit 8A.3, the isocost TC_1 representing $64 of total expenditures just touches (is tangent to) the isoquant TP_5 at combination B. This combination of 8 hours of labor and 4 pounds of materials is the most inexpensive way of producing 5 telescopes, given the prices of labor and materials. Moreover, 5 telescopes is the most that can be produced for a total cost of $64. Using an isocost closer to the origin (representing lower total costs), Seymour could not produce 5 telescopes. For an isocost farther from the origin, Seymour's total costs would be higher. You can verify that combination B is better by calculating the total cost of the other combinations shown in Exhibit 8A.1.

The choice of best technology is another example of the equimarginal principle. Note that at point B, the slope of the isoquant equals the slope of the isocost. We know that the slope of the isoquant is the ratio of the marginal products of the two resources and that the slope of the isocost is the ratio of the prices of the two resources. Thus the optimal combination occurs when the slope of the isoquant equals the slope of the isocost; that is, when

$$\frac{\text{Marginal product of labor}}{\text{Marginal product of materials}} = \frac{\text{Price of labor}}{\text{Price of materials}}$$

or

$$\frac{MP_l}{MP_m} = \frac{P_l}{P_m}$$

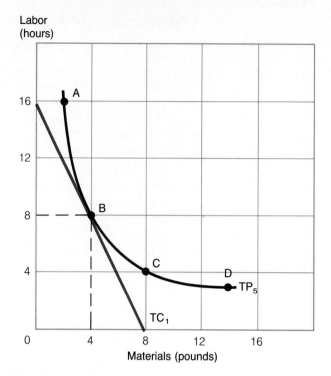

Exhibit 8A.3
Optimal Combination of Resources for Seymour Corporation

Rearranging terms, we have the equimarginal principle; that is,

$$\frac{\text{Marginal product of labor}}{\text{Price of labor}} = \frac{\text{Marginal price of materials}}{\text{Price of materials}} \quad \text{or} \quad \frac{MP_l}{P_l} = \frac{MP_m}{P_m}$$

CHANGES IN RESOURCE AND PRICE MIXES

A change in resource prices will cause the firm to adjust its resource mix. For example, if the price of labor rises from $4 to $10 per hour and the price of materials falls from $8 to $5 per pound, Seymour probably would utilize less labor and more materials to produce the 5 telescopes.

Exhibit 8A.4 shows the same isoquant as before (TP_5), but a new isocost (TC_2). The slope of the new isocost is 0.50, or the ratio of the new prices. Seymour will now choose to produce the 5 telescopes using 8 pounds of materials and 4 hours of labor. This optimal combination occurs at point C, where the new isocost and the isoquant touch. To determine the total costs represented by the new isocost, we multiply resource quantities by resource prices and add. Seymour will now have to spend $80 to produce 5 telescopes, calculated as ($5 per lb)(8 lb) + ($10 per hr)(4 hr).

Although the cost of producing telescopes is greater than before, this new combination of resources is the best possible one. It is technically efficient because

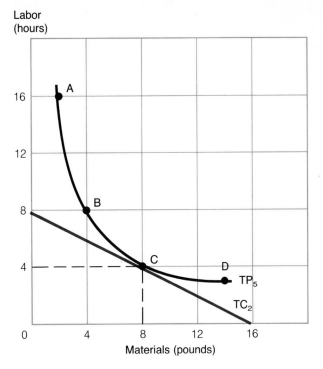

Exhibit 8A.4
Changes in Price and Resource Mix

no other combination of resources at the new prices will produce 5 telescopes more cheaply. Only changes in technology, productivity, or resource prices can lower total product costs.

CONCLUSION

The optimal combination of resources depends on two basic factors: relative productivities of resources (their marginal products) and relative prices of resources. Changes either in productivity—because labor skills increase, for example—or in resource prices will cause a firm to choose a different mix of resources. A change in the prices or productivity of resources also affects a firm's production costs. An increase in resource prices will increase a firm's total costs. Similarly, improvements in resource productivity will—by shifting the isoquant for any given level of output closer to the origin—lower a firm's total costs.

KEY TERMS

Isoquant, 198
Marginal rate of technical substitution, 198
Isocost, 200

Economic Encounters
Changing Oil Prices: Who Wins?

Some of our strongest images from the 1970s are of the 1974 oil crisis: endless lines of cars at gas stations; thermostats kept at a steady 68° or less; the spectre of OPEC in the form of a hooded Arabian sheik. In the 1980s, just the opposite: an oil glut, plunging petroleum prices; OPEC in disarray. From a 1980 high of $39 a barrel, the price of oil fell to below $10 in mid-1986. As with most economic changes, cheaper oil brings both good and bad news.

Cheap-Oil Winners The winners in the oil-price plunge—consumers in petroleum-needy areas such as the midwest, northwest, and New England in the United States, Europe, and parts of Asia—were jubilant over cheaper oil. For them, it meant lower fuel bills, cheaper petroleum-based products (such as plastics), and more driving miles per dollar. In contrast to the 1970s, a party atmosphere reigned at gas stations across the United States. In one instance, during the "gas wars" of the spring of 1986, drivers lined up at a Chevron station in Concord, California for gas selling at 0.1 cent per gallon.

Cheap oil gives European and Asian countries much-needed opportunities to reduce budget deficits and make fundamental economic improvements. In fact, many economists predict an era of overall economic growth based on bargain-priced oil—an era that could extend into the 1990s. Dollars saved on energy, they say, will be invested or spent elsewhere in the economy. For Americans not in the oil business, cheap oil has the effect of a huge tax break: Consumers have more money to spend on items that they otherwise might not have been able to afford in the early 1980s. One market research firm estimated that the average wage earner had $330 more to spend in 1986 than in 1985, thanks to cheap oil.

Cheap oil also offered relief to transportation companies, particularly the airlines. For instance, in 1986 People Express airlines cut its fuel bill by $16 million, or 30 percent. However, cheap jet-fuel prices weren't passed on to the consumer in terms of lower airfares, since ticket prices had already been slashed to the bone by discount wars and heavy competition. But cheap fuel *did* stabilize ticket prices. In addition, the U.S. trucking industry, responsible for moving about 75 percent of the nation's goods, predicted that lower fuel costs saved truckers $7.7 billion in 1986.

The financially strapped farmer also got a break from cheap oil; it was less expensive to run diesel-powered and gas-powered machinery and to buy petroleum-based pesticides and fertilizers. As a result, farmers could produce food and livestock at lower cost.

Dollars saved on energy will be invested or spent elsewhere in the economy.

In addition, homeowners, landlords, and builders came out winners. For example, in 1986 developers saved up to a dollar in energy costs per square foot constructed.

"Gas wars" forced pump prices downward—a boon for motorists and transportation industries. (Phil Huber/Black Star)

Failing Texas oil producers auction drilling equipment for $0.20 on the dollar. (Shelley Katz/Black Star)

Lost Jobs and Budget Deficits However, plunging oil prices had a negative effect on oil-related industries and their employees during the 1980s. Oil producers in the American southwest were hit especially hard. In Texas, a state that depends heavily on income from oil, exploration and production came to a virtual standstill. Large oil companies cut back their work forces, while small, independent firms went under altogether. The state could not fall back on beef production, its traditional moneymaker, because that industry had also been in trouble for more than a decade. Ranchers who supplemented their dwindling farm incomes by leasing land to oil companies for drilling saw their royalty checks evaporate.

In Dallas and Houston, new skyscrapers stood nearly empty, real estate loans went bad, and hotel occupancy plummeted. Texas state services, such as welfare, were cut by 13 percent or more, so the already poor suffered even greater hardships. It was estimated that every time the price of oil dropped by one dollar, 25,000 Texans lost their jobs.

The negative effects of cheap oil rippled through the entire economy: Unemployment rose to nearly 13 percent in Louisiana and Oklahoma, both major oil-producing states; shoplifting at local stores shot up, while sales of basic goods nosedived; jobs in banks and oil-related businesses disappeared; financial institutions failed. Because Texas, Oklahoma, and Louisiana account for the production of 10 percent of total U.S. goods and services, the economic woes of these three states became a drag on the entire economy.

The rapid and unexpected drop in oil prices also caught the American auto industry by surprise. Since automakers traditionally design cars three years ahead, accurate market predictions are essential to success. General Motors, erroneously foreseeing a late-1980s rise in oil and gas prices, unveiled its 1986 scaled-down luxury models that were intended to appeal to energy-conscious buyers. The plan backfired when oil prices abruptly fell; luxury car buyers again clamored for full-size gas guzzlers, and GM took a heavy loss. Although most U.S. car manufacturers now produce clones of small, fuel-efficient Japanese cars, they may find it difficult to accurately plan for new car models if oil prices continue to fluctuate dramatically.

Of course, the United States wasn't the only country affected by the drop in oil prices. Mexico's already suffering economy, which depends on oil for 70 percent of its income, took a severe blow in 1986. Unless oil prices rebound significantly, Mexico will find it virtually impossible to repay its $97 billion debt to foreign lenders. Oil-producing Iran and Iraq—in the midst of financing a costly war against each other—also faced serious financial trouble when oil prices dropped. In Africa, the price drop was especially bad news to Egypt, Nigeria, and Libya, countries with large deficits and no other high-profit export industries.

Even Saudi Arabia, the country that helped start the oil-price war, began to cut spending when oil resources brought in less revenue. Although Saudi Arabia was producing 4 million barrels of oil per day, the glut that production created caused all oil prices to plummet. In 1986, the kingdom's budget deficit ballooned by about $1 billion per month, slowing construction projects, leading to bank failures, and causing foreign workers to leave in droves.

> **For oil-rich areas like Texas, Louisiana, Oklahoma, and Alaska, the boom times of the 1960s and 1970s are over.**

For oil-rich areas like Louisiana, Oklahoma, and Alaska, the boom times of the 1960s and 1970s are over. Cheap oil has changed the way business is conducted; jobs are scarce and unemployment is high. States that have depended heavily on oil will have to diversify their local economies (if they can) or face long-term economic decline. But in areas where oil is essential for industrial production and heating homes and businesses, lower oil prices are good news.

Producer Choice and Economic Decisions

QUESTIONS TO CONSIDER

☐ How would firms apply the principles of rational choice to determine how much to supply?

☐ What decisions must firms make in the short run and what criteria would they use to make rational short-run decisions?

☐ Why are sunk costs irrelevant?

☐ How do normal profits reflect opportunity costs?

☐ What decisions must firms make in the long run and what criteria would they use to make rational long-run decisions?

Recall that in Chapter 8 we decribed how businesses identify the best combination of resources in both the short run and the long run. Resource decisions determine a firm's costs. In this chapter we consider how a firm's costs influence its decisions about how much to supply in both the short run and the long run. While discussing producer choice and supply decisions, we continue to assume that firms seek maximum profits. Using the principles of rational choice, we can derive rules that firms can use to maximize profits.

RATIONAL CHOICE AND SHORT-RUN SUPPLY DECISIONS

In Chapter 8 we said that rational firms choose options that increase their economic profits. That is, they accept options that add more to revenues than to costs. To see the results in terms of short-run supply decisions, let's consider the case of Maxpro Sports Company, a producer of top-quality tennis rackets.

Assumptions

In order to explore Maxpro's decisions about how much of its product to supply, we must make certain assumptions. First, we assume that the market is functioning smoothly. Second, we assume that Maxpro wants to maximize profits. These two assumptions allow us to use the principles of rational choice and give us a way to define extra benefits and extra costs. Third, we assume that Maxpro produces every unit at minimum cost; that is, the company is technically efficient. This assumption means that the firm has no other practical options for lowering its production costs. And finally, we assume that demand for Maxpro's product is given. This assumption means that the firm has no economically attractive options for increasing product demand.

Of course, in the real world firms make choices that influence each of these assumptions. In our example, we simply assume that Maxpro has already made the best decisions it can with respect to demand and costs. Its only remaining decision is how much to supply.

(a) Revenue and cost data

Total product (TP = Q) (rackets per day)	Total costs (TC) (dollars per day)	Total revenues (TR = P × Q) (dollars per day)	Economic profits (= TR − TC) (dollars per day)
0	525	0	−525
1	645	395	−250
2	725	790	65
3	795	1185	390
4	885	1580	695
5	1025	1975	950
6	1245	2370	1125
7	1575	2765	1190
8	2045	3160	1115
9	2685	3555	870
10	3525	3950	425

(b) Total revenues versus total costs

Exhibit 9.1
Maximum Profits for Maxpro Sports in the Short Run
Economic profits are the difference between total revenues (TR) and total costs (TC). The table in part (a) shows that maximum profits occur when 7 units are produced. Both total revenues and total costs are graphed in part (b). The vertical distance between the two curves represents the level of economic profits. For 0 rackets and 1 racket per day, total costs are higher than total revenues, resulting in a loss (the red-shaded area). When 2 or more rackets are sold, total revenues are more than total costs, resulting in an economic profit (the blue-shaded area). The vertical distance between TR and TC is greatest when 7 rackets are produced and represents maximum economic profits.

Quantity to Supply in the Short Run

To keep our example simple, we assume that Maxpro Sports Company makes only one product: tennis rackets. We further assume that Maxpro can sell as many as 10 tennis rackets per day at $395 per racket. Exhibit 9.1(a) shows total revenues, total costs, and economic profits based on those assumptions. How many rackets should Maxpro sell to maximize its profits? (Since we are considering a short-run situation, total fixed costs are constant, regardless of quantity produced.)

Total revenues versus total costs. Maxpro will choose to supply the quantity that yields the greatest profits. (As we noted in Chapter 8, profits mean economic profits, including all opportunity costs.) As Exhibit 9.1(a) shows, Maxpro's profits increase until it produces 7 rackets per day, after which profits decline. Thus Maxpro will earn *maximum* profits—$1190 per day—by producing and selling 7 rackets per day.

Exhibit 9.1(b) is a graph of the relationship between total revenues and total costs. When total revenues exceed total costs—for more than 2 rackets per day—Maxpro earns economic profits (the blue-shaded area). When total costs exceed total revenues—for 2 or less rackets per day—Maxpro has negative profits, or a loss (the red-shaded area).

Profits (or losses) at any quantity are measured as the vertical distance between the total revenue and total cost curves at that quantity. For example, at 7 rackets per day, Maxpro's total costs are approximately $1600 per day (or precisely $1575 in Exhibit 9.1a). Total revenues are approximately $2800 per day (precisely $2765). Thus Maxpro's economic profits are approximately $1200 per day (precisely $1190 per day in Exhibit 9.1a). The point of maximum profits is the quantity at which the total revenue curve is farthest above the total cost curve, or in this case, at 7 rackets per day.

Rational Choice and the Profit-Maximizing Rule for Supply

We can also approach the supply decision by applying the principles of rational choice. Because Maxpro wants to earn maximum profits, it will sell an additional racket only if its profits increase. To determine whether producing and selling another racket adds to profits, Maxpro can calculate the change in profits. That is, it can compare changes in total revenues with changes in total costs. Mathematically,

$$\text{Change in economic profits} = \text{Change in total revenues} - \text{Change in total costs}$$

$$= \text{Change in TR} - \text{Change in TC}$$

In Chapter 8, we noted that *marginal cost* measures the change in total costs for producing one additional unit. Similarly, the extra revenue that Maxpro earns from selling another racket is **marginal revenue (MR)**. We calculate marginal revenue as the change in total revenues divided by the change in quantity of goods produced (total product). That is,

$$\text{Marginal revenue} = \frac{\text{Change in total revenues}}{\text{Change in total product}} \quad \text{or} \quad \text{MR} = \frac{\text{Change in TR}}{\text{Change in Q}}$$

We assumed that Maxpro can sell each tennis racket it produces for $395. Since Maxpro's price is constant, marginal revenue equals price and is also a constant $395 each, as Exhibit 9.2(a) shows. By comparing marginal revenue and marginal cost, we can determine the quantity of tennis rackets that will maximize profits. For example, if Maxpro produces only 5 rackets per day, it will earn profits of $950, or total revenues of $1975 less total costs of $1025. But marginal revenue for the sixth racket ($395) exceeds marginal cost ($220). That is, if Maxpro increases total product to 6 rackets, its profits will increase. The difference between marginal revenue and marginal cost ($395 − $220 = $175) measures the *increase*

Marginal revenue (MR). The extra revenue obtained from the sale of one extra unit, calculated as

$$\text{MR} = \frac{\text{Change in total revenue}}{\text{Change in total product}}$$

(a) Revenue and cost data

Total product (TP = Q) (rackets per day)	Total costs (TC) (dollars per day)	Marginal cost (MC) (dollars per racket)	Marginal revenue (MR) (dollars per racket)	Total revenues (TR = P × Q) (dollars per racket)	Economic profits (= TR − TC) (dollars per day)
0	525			0	−525
		120	395		
1	645			395	−250
		80	395		
2	725			790	65
		70	395		
3	795			1185	390
		90	395		
4	885			1580	695
		140	395		
5	1025			1975	950
		220	395		
6	1245			2370	1125
		330	395		
7	1575			2765	1190
		470	395		
8	2045			3160	1115
		640	395		
9	2685			3555	870
		840	395		
10	3525			3950	425

(b) Marginal revenue versus marginal cost

Exhibit 9.2
Rational Choice and the Short-Run Supply Decision for Maxpro Sports
As long as the marginal revenue from an extra unit is greater than the marginal cost of producing it, selling it will increase profits. In the table in part (a), we look for the last unit for which marginal revenue is greater than or equal to marginal cost—in this case the seventh racket. In the graph in part (b), we look for the intersection of the MR and MC curves, where MR = MC—again, the seventh racket. If the firm makes and sells more than 7 rackets per day, MR is less than MC. The red-shaded area indicates how much profits will fall if 9 rackets are sold. If the firm makes and sells fewer than 7 rackets per day, MR is greater than MC. The blue-shaded area shows how much more profit the firm can earn by selling 7 instead of 5 rackets.

Price and cost
(dollars per racket)

in profits. Maxpro still earns $950 from selling the first 5 rackets. But selling the sixth racket increases profits by $175 to $1125.

Exhibit 9.2(a) shows that marginal revenue is greater than marginal cost for the seventh racket as well. Again, the difference between marginal revenue and marginal cost ($395 − $330 = $65) is the increase in profits. Maxpro will raise total product to 7 rackets per day because its profits will increase by $65. Note that *increases in total product raise profits whenever marginal revenue exceeds marginal cost.*

Marginal revenue is greater than marginal cost for all rackets up to the seventh one. But note what happens when Maxpro increases total product from 7 to 8 rackets. The eighth racket adds more to costs (MC = $470) than to revenues (MR = $395). If it sells the eighth racket, Maxpro's profits will fall by $75 ($395 − $470). Thus *increases in total product lower profits whenever marginal revenue is less than marginal cost.*

We can summarize these results and state a profit-maximizing rule for the supply decision: *To maximize profits, a firm should offer for sale all units for which marginal revenue exceeds marginal cost but no units for which marginal cost exceeds marginal revenue.* To test your understanding of this rule, assume that Maxpro can sell its rackets for $550 each. Find the new profit-maximizing quantity and profits. (Your answers should be a quantity of 8 rackets and profits of $2355 per day.)

Short-Run Profit Maximization: A Graphic View

We can also illustrate this profit-maximizing rule graphically. Exhibit 9.2(b) shows marginal revenue and marginal cost for Maxpro Sports. In general, *a firm should supply the quantity for which marginal revenue equals marginal cost (MR = MC).* For Maxpro, the marginal revenue curve intersects the marginal cost curve at a quantity of 7 rackets per day, or point *a* in Exhibit 9.2(b). However, in the real world and in tabular data there is often no point at which MR = MC exactly. Thus a firm should produce all units for which marginal revenue exceeds marginal cost but none for which marginal cost exceeds marginal revenue. Returning to Exhibit 9.2(b), let's see why the quantity of 7 rackets per day—no more and no less—provides maximum profits.

Marginal revenue less than marginal cost. Note what happens when Maxpro increases sales beyond 7 rackets per day. As we move to the right from point *a*, the marginal cost curve rises above the marginal revenue line. Under these conditions, Maxpro would be selling rackets for less than they cost to produce. The area between the marginal revenue line and the marginal cost curve (shaded red) indicates the amount by which profits will fall if total product increases from 7 to 9 rackets.

Marginal revenue greater than marginal cost. Compare this result with that for sales of less than 7 rackets per day. As we move to the left from point *a*, the marginal cost curve falls below the marginal revenue line. When marginal revenue is above marginal cost, the firm has an opportunity to increase its profits by selling more. Producing less than 7 rackets thus means a sacrifice of profits that could be earned. The area between marginal revenue and marginal cost (shaded blue) indicates how much profits will rise if total product increases from 5 to 7 rackets.

The difference between marginal revenue and marginal cost shows how much profits *increase* (or decrease) when an additional racket per day is sold. Maxpro receives the profits on the first 4 rackets plus the extra profit from the fifth, sixth, and seventh rackets. If it wants to maximize profits, Maxpro will produce no less than 7 rackets. Thus Maxpro will earn maximum profits by producing and selling 7 rackets per day, or the quantity for which marginal revenue equals marginal cost. There is no better short-run option, if the firm decides to produce.

OTHER ISSUES AND SHORT-RUN SUPPLY DECISIONS

So far, we have assumed that there is always a quantity at which a firm makes an economic profit. But as A Case in Point: Do Special Orders Pay? demonstrates, the most profitable quantity is not always obvious. You may have assumed that a firm that cannot earn an economic profit will choose not to produce at all. However, as you will see in this section, a firm may rationally decide to produce and sell its product in the short run even though its total profit is negative.

Minimizing Losses in the Short Run

Consider what Maxpro would do if the selling price were to fall to $175 per racket. Exhibit 9.3(a) shows costs and revenues for Maxpro at the new price. Unlike the earlier ones, Exhibit 9.3 shows only variable costs. We derive total variable costs by subtracting total fixed costs (a constant $525 per day) from each level of total costs shown in Exhibits 9.1 and 9.2. Then we divide total variable costs by total product (quantity produced) to find average variable cost.

How do we know the amount of total fixed costs? Recall that we define fixed costs as costs that are unaffected by changes in total product in the short run. Looking back at Exhibit 9.2(a), you can see that Maxpro has costs of $525 even if it produces no rackets. Hence $525 is the daily cost of Maxpro's fixed resources (factory and machinery, perhaps). By definition, Maxpro cannot change its fixed resources—and fixed costs—in the short run. Check your understanding of this point by calculating some of the total variable costs and average variable costs shown in Exhibit 9.3(a). Using that information, we can determine Maxpro's best short-run supply decision by using a two-step process.

Step 1: Find the best quantity to produce. The first step in any supply decision is to apply the profit-maximizing rule for supply: *Offer for sale all units for which marginal revenue exceeds marginal cost but no units for which marginal cost exceeds marginal revenue*. In other words, find the quantity for which marginal revenue equals marginal cost. The result of applying this rule is that Maxpro's best option—if it decides to produce—is 5 tennis rackets per day. You should verify this result by using both the table and the graph in Exhibit 9.3.

The phrase "if it decides to produce" is very significant here, for Maxpro is not obligated to produce or supply any rackets. It has two options to consider: (1) *produce* and supply 5 rackets for sale or (2) *shut down* (produce and supply

(a) Revenue and cost data

Total product (TP = Q) (rackets per day)	Average variable cost (AVC = TVC/Q) (dollars per racket)	Total variable costs (TVC) (dollars per day)	Marginal cost (MC) (dollars per racket)	Marginal revenue (MR) (dollars per racket)	Total revenues (TR = P × Q) (dollars per day)	Economic profits (= TR − TVC − TFC) (dollars per day)
0	—	0			0	−525
			120	175		
1	120	120			175	−470
			80	175		
2	100	200			350	−375
			70	175		
3	90	270			525	−270
			90	175		
4	90	360			700	−185
			140	175		
5	100	500			875	−150
			220	175		
6	120	720			1050	−195
			330	175		
7	150	1050			1225	−350

Exhibit 9.3
Minimizing Losses at Maxpro Sports in the Short Run
At a price of $175 per racket, in the short run the best quantity for Maxpro to produce is 5 rackets per day (where MR intersects MC). In the table in part (a), MC exceeds MR if 6 rackets are made. If it produces 5 rackets, Maxpro will incur a loss of $150, but producing that quantity is its best choice because it cannot change its fixed costs in the short run. If Maxpro produces nothing, it will lose $525 per day, or its total fixed costs. The area of the blue-shaded rectangle equals the dollar advantage gained by producing. The height of the rectangle is the difference between price ($175) and average variable cost ($100); the length is the number of rackets (5) per day; the area is $375 per day (length multiplied by height, or 5 rackets per day times $75 per racket).

(b) Price versus average variable cost

Price and cost
(dollars per racket)

A Case in Point
Do Special Orders Pay?

Helfmir Corporation, producer of stepstools, has been approached by a company seeking to buy 300 stools at a price of $10 each. Helfmir's managers have determined that accepting the special order will not affect regular sales and, because of unutilized capacity, they are strongly considering accepting the special order. However, the company's accountant notes that average total cost is $12.50 per stool. Would Helfmir therefore be better off rejecting the special order?

If they apply the principles of rational choice, Helfmir's managers will weigh the extra benefits and extra costs of this decision. They will then realize that average total cost is not the correct measure of extra costs. Why not? Recall that average total cost includes both variable and fixed costs. But in the short run, fixed costs do not change. The correct measure of extra costs is marginal cost, that is, the extra costs involved in producing additional stools.

Suppose that marginal cost is only $8.00 for each of the extra 300 stools. If Helfmir accepts the special order, it will increase its profits (or reduce its losses) by $2 per unit, or $600 in total. The correct decision (assuming that the firm has no better offers) would be to accept the special order. Although Helfmir would be selling the 300 stools below its average total cost, it would be earning more than its variable costs.

Thus the decision to sell is a good one. By accepting the special order, Helfmir will increase its profits (or reduce its loss). In the short run fixed costs cannot change, so a firm should focus only on its variable costs. There are no *extra* fixed costs in the short run.

---

no rackets). The profit-maximizing rule of supply we used in step 1 only indicates that 5 rackets per day is better than any other quantity. It does not tell Maxpro whether producing 5 rackets is better than producing none.

Step 2: Determine whether to produce or shut down. As you can see in Exhibit 9.3, Maxpro cannot avoid a loss if the price of tennis rackets is $175 each. Total costs exceed total revenues at each quantity shown. Because this is a short-run decision, it cannot eliminate its fixed costs. Maxpro has only two short-run options: produce or shut down.

How can Maxpro determine which option minimizes its losses? It can compare the profits (or losses) from producing with those from producing nothing (shutting down). In step 1 we found that Maxpro has no better quantity to produce than 5 rackets per day. The table in Exhibit 9.3 shows that Maxpro loses $150 per day if it produces 5 rackets. However, by shutting down, it will lose $525 per day. Producing nothing means Maxpro has no revenues and no variable costs, but it will still have fixed costs of $525 per day. In other words, producing nothing in the short run means a loss equal to the firm's total fixed costs.

In Chapter 7, we said that fixed costs are irrelevant to short-run decisions, and they still are. For example, compare Maxpro's losses for its two options if total fixed costs were $875 instead of $525 per day. Maxpro would then lose $875 if it shut down, compared with $500 from producing 5 rackets. It loses more because it has more fixed costs, but the *difference* between the two options does not change. In both cases, Maxpro is $375 per day better off if it produces 5 rackets.

Maxpro can make its decision by applying the principles of rational choice, that is, by comparing extra benefits with extra costs. For the short-run supply decision total fixed costs are constant. Because there are no extra fixed costs, fixed costs are irrelevant. The important question, then, is whether revenues exceed variable costs. In Exhibit 9.3(a) you can see that when Maxpro sells 5 rackets per day, total revenues are $375 greater than total variable costs. This amount, although not sufficient to cover total fixed costs, can pay at least some of the fixed costs. Indeed, a second short-run supply rule states that a firm should *produce the quantity at which marginal revenue equals marginal cost only if revenues are greater than or equal to variable costs.*

You can also see the same results in Exhibit 9.3(b). Maxpro's best option—if it produces—is 5 rackets (point *b* where the marginal revenue curve intersects the marginal cost curve). At that quantity, the firm's revenues are $175 per racket. With an average variable cost of $100, each of the 5 rackets sells for $75 more than its average variable cost. The blue-shaded rectangle indicates the advantage to Maxpro from producing 5 rackets. The height of the rectangle is $75 (the difference between price and average variable cost). The length of the rectangle is 5 rackets per day. The area (length times height) is the difference between total revenues and total variable costs, a $375 per day contribution to the company's fixed costs of $525.

Going out of business: Not a short-run option. You may wonder why Maxpro (or any other profit-seeking firm) would not just go out of business instead of operating at a loss. Remember, we are dealing with the short run—a time period too short for Maxpro to change all its resources. In the short run, a firm does not have the option of going out of business because some of its costs are fixed. Only in the long run can the firm change all its resources. Thus only for a long-run decision are economic profits—which include opportunity costs of options other than staying in the business—relevant. In the short run, Maxpro is stuck with its fixed costs. If the price is too low for it to earn a profit, Maxpro's best option is to find the quantity that minimizes its losses. When the price is $175 per racket, Maxpro's best choice is to produce 5 rackets per day.

Shut-down option. It is not always better to produce in the short run. In some cases, a company's best choice is to produce nothing, or in economic terms, to shut down. Note that a shutdown is not the same as going out of business. A firm that decides to shut down is making a short-run decision; it still must pay its fixed costs. As we discuss later in this chapter, going out of business is a long-run decision, which involves no fixed costs.

What should Maxpro do if the price for its rackets falls even further—to $75? We can answer this question by applying the short-run decision rules to the data in Exhibit 9.4(a). First, we find the best quantity to produce, if the firm decides to produce (step 1 of the short-run decision-making process). In this case, that quantity is 3 rackets per day, or point *c*, where marginal revenue equals marginal cost. Second, we find out whether it is better to produce this quantity or shut down (step 2 of the short-run decision-making process). In this case average variable cost is greater than price (marginal revenue) at every quantity shown, and Maxpro should shut down.

Whenever each unit sold would increase its loss, a firm will minimize its losses by producing nothing. That is, *if price is less than average variable cost at the quantity where marginal revenue equals marginal cost, the firm is better off shutting down in the short run.*

(a) Revenue and cost data

Total product (TP = Q) (rackets per day)	Average variable cost (AVC = TVC/Q) (dollars per racket)	Total variable costs (TVC) (dollars per day)	Marginal cost (MC) (dollars per racket)	Marginal revenue (MR) (dollars per racket)	Total revenues (TR = P × Q) (dollars per day)	Economic profits (= TR − TVC − TFC) (dollars per day)
0	—	0			0	−525
			120	75		
1	120	120			75	−570
			80	75		
2	100	200			150	−575
			70	75		
3	90	270			225	−570
			90	75		
4	90	360			300	−585
			140	75		
5	100	500			375	−650

(b) Price versus average variable cost

Exhibit 9.4
Shut-Down Case for Maxpro Sports in the Short Run
The minimum price justifying production by Maxpro in the short run is $88.75, the minimum value of average variable cost. If the price falls to $75 per racket, Maxpro would do better to produce nothing. If it does produce, the best quantity is 3 rackets per day (where MR = MC). But at that quantity, average variable cost is greater than price. The area of the red-shaded rectangle equals the amount that Maxpro loses by producing. The height of the rectangle is the difference between average variable cost ($90) and price ($75); the length is the number of rackets (3) per day; the area is $45 per day (length multiplied by height, or 3 rackets per day times $15 per racket).

Price and cost
(dollars per racket)

Whenever price exceeds average variable cost, the firm generates enough revenues to pay for all variable resources *plus* all or part of the fixed costs. Because the fixed costs must be paid regardless, they are of no concern for the short-run decision. To verify this important point, reconsider the decision of how much to produce when price is $375, $175, and $75 if Maxpro's total fixed costs are $875 and if TFC falls to $275. (You will find that the supply decisions are unchanged in each case.)

Sunk cost. Cost incurred as a result of a past decision; historical cost that cannot be recovered and that is irrelevant to economic decisions.

Exhibit 9.4(b) indicates that the minimum price justifying production by Maxpro in the short run is $88.75 per racket. This price occurs between 3 and 4 rackets per day at the bottom of the average variable cost curve. Because this amount is the minimum value for average variable cost, Maxpro would be better off producing nothing than to produce at any lower price. To justify producing in the short run, the firm must receive a price that at least covers its variable costs.

Irrelevance of Sunk Costs

Whether a firm is trying to decide how much to produce or whether to produce, the focus of economic decisions is on opportunity costs, that is, the extra costs associated with the decision. It is important to recognize that historical costs are irrelevant to economic decisions.

Let's consider the case of The Unlimited, a retail clothing store specializing in high-fashion merchandise. Last year the store purchased 10 copies of a dress by Bazar Fashions at $150 each and marked them up to sell for $300 each. Unfortunately, when the season ended, 5 of these dresses remained unsold. Knowing that her customers will not buy last year's fashions at any price, the manager is pondering an offer from a second-hand store for $25 per dress. Should she accept the offer? Would it be profitable to sell below cost?

The answer to both these questions is *yes*. The key point is that the price The Unlimited paid for the dresses is a **sunk cost**. Sunk costs cannot be recovered. Economic decisions and opportunity costs are based on *expected future benefits and costs*. If The Unlimited's only other options are to throw the dresses away or sell them for still less, $25 per dress is the store's best option. But in any case, the manager should ignore the original price of the dresses. Similarly, if you are trying to decide whether to sell your textbooks (not your economics text, of course), you must ignore the amount you paid for it (your sunk cost). You must consider only whether it is worth more to you to hang onto those books or to accept what another student will offer for them.

RATIONAL CHOICE AND LONG-RUN SUPPLY DECISIONS

So far we have been considering how a firm makes short-run decisions based on fixed resources and fixed costs. But a firm must also make long-run decisions—decisions that can involve changing any or all its resources. Should it build a larger plant? Should it sell off some or all of its capacity? Should it diversify? As you might expect, the answers to these questions hinge on the amount of a firm's profits. Thus in order to understand long-run decisions, you must first know how much profit is "normal."

Normal Profits and Economic Profits

Suppose that a friend of yours has an idea for a business: He wants to have T-shirts printed up with the motto of the business school—"Study business in the boonies." He asks you to join this venture, saying that he expects to return your

Normal profit. Opportunity cost of owner investment, the minimum level of profit necessary to justify a decision to produce in the long run, or an economic profit of zero; considered an implicit cost when calculating economic profit but ignored when calculating accounting profit.

$1000 investment plus a profit of $20 at the end of one year. Would you be willing to invest your savings for an expected profit of $20? If you actually received $1020 at the end of a year would you have made a profit?

Recall from Chapter 8 that economic profits are the difference between revenues and *all* opportunity costs, both explicit and implicit. In considering your friend's offer, you must therefore consider both your explicit costs—the $1000— and your implicit costs—what else you could do with that money. For example, if a local bank pays 6 percent interest on savings accounts, your implicit cost might be the $60 you could earn by putting your money in the bank. Comparing the potential interest earnings to the expected return from the T-shirt business, you would suffer a $40 economic loss by investing in T-shirts, even if your friend's projections are right.

In economic terms, the $60 return you could make on your next best investment is called a **normal profit**. In making long-run decisions, firms consider normal profit just as they do any other opportunity cost. To attract investors, a business venture must not only cover its explicit costs (in this case, T-shirts and ink), but also pay its investors (you) at least a normal profit (the return you could earn elsewhere). In fact, business investors generally require greater returns than they can earn by banking their money in order to compensate them for the risks they run. Thus a normal profit includes payment for risks, too.

Because economists use profits as a guide for and predictor of decisions, they subtract normal profits—the implicit costs of owner investment—when calculating economic profits. Thus economic profits are a *relative* measure of the firm's performance, that is, how well it is doing relative to all opportunity costs.

A Case in Point
Fixed and Variable Costs of Driving

While analysis of producer decisions may sound very abstract, in fact it has many applications in real life. Consider, for example, what it costs you to drive a car. The following table shows these costs as fixed and variable costs. Variable costs include tires, gasoline, repairs, and maintenance. Fixed costs include insurance, registration, and ownership costs. Costs shown are for a medium-priced, intermediate-sized sedan. Ownership costs are calculated as the average decrease in market price per year over a 12-year life.

Suppose that the data accurately represent the costs for your car, which you expect to drive about 10,000 miles each year. You apply for a new job, and are told that you will be required to drive your car an additional 10,000 miles a year for business purposes. The company will pay you $0.20 per mile for your business travel. Will this amount cover your costs? To answer this question, you should apply the principles of rational choice, remembering to focus on extra costs, that is, those that will change as a result of a particular decision.

The 10,000 miles of business driving will mean extra costs for gasoline, tires, and maintenance, because they change with the number of miles driven. Your fixed costs are unlikely to be affected much (if at all) by your decision. The vehicle registration cost does not change, and most of the ownership costs change with time, not

Average variable cost (dollars per mile)		Total fixed costs (dollars per year)	
Gasoline and oil	0.0735	License and registration	53
Repairs and maintenance	0.0503	Ownership cost	634
Tires, parking, tolls	0.0129	Insurance	333
	0.1367		1020

Source: U.S. Department of Transportation, *Cost of Owning and Operating Automobiles and Vans, 1982.* Washington, D.C., 1983.

With this in mind, what exactly do economists mean when they say that a firm is earning an economic profit? They mean that the firm is earning a return over and above *all* costs, including the opportunity costs of not being in some other business. Economic profit measures how much better a firm is doing than it could do under its next best option. For example, suppose that after you graduate from college you take a job paying $20,000 and turn down one paying $18,000. Your economic profit is $2000, or the amount by which you are better off, compared with your next best option. When a firm is making an economic profit, it has no better options to consider.

Similarly, an economic loss means that a firm was unable to cover all its opportunity costs. Its owners would be better off if the firm did something else or returned the owners' investment so they could invest in a profitable firm. A firm may be able to accept operating at a loss in the short run (because it cannot change the quantity of its fixed resources), but not in the long run. As A Case in Point: Fixed and Variable Costs of Driving shows, the distinction between long-run and short-run options also applies to personal decisions. In the long run, a firm that experiences an economic loss will, in fact, pursue other options. If it has no options that enable it to earn at least a normal profit, however, the firm will be forced to go out of business.

The minimum acceptable economic profit for the long run is zero. Zero economic profit does not mean that the owners receive no return. On the contrary, it means that they receive a normal profit, or the minimum return necessary to cover their opportunity costs. The firm has no incentive to do anything else. The value of its next best option (normal profit) has been recognized in the calculation

number of miles driven. If you ignore the possible rise in the cost of insurance, the costs listed as fixed are constant, will already be paid, and thus are irrelevant. Therefore you will have extra costs of only $0.1367 per mile. Since you will receive $0.20 per mile, you will be more than adequately compensated for your expenses. That is, the compensation more than covers your extra costs.

Let's change the problem slightly. What if you live in an urban area and do not own a car, relying instead on the excellent mass transit system for personal travel? You apply for the same job and are told that you will have to buy a car and drive it 10,000 miles for business purposes. Again, the company will pay you $0.20 per mile. Are you adequately compensated under these circumstances?

You should begin by comparing this and the previous situation. In the first case, you already owned a car. The costs of ownership, insurance, and so on were fixed and thus irrelevant, because you would have paid them anyway. Only the variable costs were relevant.

In the second situation, you do not own a car and have no personal use for one. If you buy a car and drive it for business, you will have to pay not only those costs that vary per mile driven but also all of the costs of insurance, ownership, and so on. If you decide to take the job, all the costs listed in the table are extra costs. The relevant total costs for driving 10,000 miles per year in that case would be $2387 per year, or $1020 in fixed costs plus $1367 in variable costs. Dividing this total cost by 10,000 miles gives an average total cost of $0.2387 per mile, all of which in this case is extra. Because the company will pay you only $0.20 per mile, you would not be adequately compensated. That is, the compensation of $2000 per year would not cover the $2387 in extra costs you would incur.

To test your understanding of cost behavior and relevant costs, answer the following question: In the second situation if you drive a total of 20,000 miles per year, would $0.20 per mile be adequate reimbursement? (Your answer should be that it would. In fact, you would be paid $246 per year more than your total costs.)

(a) Cost data

Total product (TP = Q) (rackets per day)	Average total cost (ATC = TC/Q) (dollars per racket	Total costs (TC) (dollars per day)	Marginal cost (MC) (dollars per racket)
0	—	525	
			120
1	$645.00	645	
			80
2	362.50	725	
			70
3	265.00	795	
			90
4	221.25	885	
			140
5	205.00	1025	
			220
6	207.50	1245	
			330
7	225.00	1575	
			470
8	255.63	2045	

(b) Maxpro earns an economic profit

Exhibit 9.5
Long-Run Supply Decision for Maxpro Sports Corporation
If price is $395 per racket, Maxpro's best quantity is 7 rackets (where MR = MC). The company will earn a profit, as indicated by the blue-shaded rectangle in part (b), since price ($395) is greater than average total cost ($225). The graph in part (c) shows that if price is $175, Maxpro's best quantity is 5 rackets. However, the company experiences an economic loss (indicated by the red-shaded rectangle), because

of economic profit. Thus we can state a rule for making long-run supply decisions: *A firm must expect to receive in the long run at least a normal profit; that is, economic profit must be greater than or equal to zero.* We demonstrate the implications of this rule in the following sections.

Quantity to Supply in the Long Run

We can now consider the best long-run option for the Maxpro Sports Company. With its particular costs and demand, should Maxpro produce tennis rackets or go out of business? As with the short-run supply decision, making the best long-run supply decision involves two steps.

(c) Maxpro experiences an economic loss

(d) Maxpro earns a normal profit

price ($175) is less than average total cost ($205). If price is $200, Maxpro can produce 5.5 rackets and earn a normal profit, since both price and average total cost are $200, as shown in part (d). In the long run Maxpro must earn at least a normal profit to justify staying in business; that is, it must sell each tennis racket at a price of at least $200.

Step 1: Find the best quantity to produce. The first step in making the long-run decision is the same as for the short-run decision: Apply the profit-maximizing rule for supply. That is, determine the point at which marginal revenue equals marginal cost.

Exhibit 9.5(a) shows Maxpro's costs. Recall our initial assumption that Maxpro can sell as many tennis rackets as it wants at $395 each; that is, marginal revenue is $395 per racket. And comparing marginal revenue and marginal cost, we found that Maxpro would want to offer 7 tennis rackets per day for sale. Be sure that you can locate this quantity in both the table (Exhibit 9.5a) and the graph (Exhibit 9.5b). Just as in the short-run situation, selling more than 7 units per day would add more to costs than to revenues. Selling fewer units would mean passing up the chance to add more to revenues than to costs.

Step 2: Determine whether to produce or go out of business. The best quantity to produce is 7 rackets per day. But are the profits from 7 rackets per day enough to justify Maxpro staying in business? Because this is a long-run decision, Maxpro can change the quantity and/or type of all its resources. In other words, the company can continue producing tennis rackets, go into another business, or get out of business altogether. Whether its current business is the best option depends on the amount of economic profits it can earn by producing *at the best quantity.*

Economic profits and the decision to stay in business. Exhibit 9.5(a) shows that Maxpro's total costs for producing 7 rackets per day—the best quantity, as identified in step 1—will be $1575. If each racket sells for $395, total revenues are $2765 ($395 per racket × 7 rackets) and economic profits are $1190 per day ($2765 − $1575).

You can see this same result in Exhibit 9.5(b). Marginal revenue equals marginal cost at 7 rackets per day. At this quantity, average total cost is $225 per racket (the height of the ATC curve at 7 rackets). The vertical distance between the ATC curve and the price line (marginal revenue) shows that Maxpro earns an average profit of $170 per racket on each of the 7 rackets it sells. The economic profit of $1190 per day is shown as the blue-shaded rectangle.

Since Maxpro is able to earn an economic profit of $1190 per day, it should remain in this business. Recall that the returns its owners could make on their next best option (normal profit) is included as one of Maxpro's costs. The economic profit indicates that Maxpro earns $1190 per day more than it would if the owners were to get out of this business and pursue their next best option.

Economic losses and the decision to go out of business. By contrast, if the price (marginal revenue) per racket falls to $175, Maxpro will suffer an economic loss. Exhibit 9.5(c) shows that marginal cost equals marginal revenue at 5 rackets per day. For the firm's costs and demand, the best quantity to produce is 5 rackets per day. But while Maxpro's revenues are only $875 per day ($175 × 5 rackets), its total costs are $1025 per day—an economic loss of $150 per day ($875 − $1025).

On the graph, the loss is shown as a red rectangle. The height of the rectangle is $30 per racket, or the difference between price and average total cost. The length of the rectangle is 5 rackets per day. Thus the area of the rectangle—length times height—shows the loss of $150 per day. Note that price is below the average total cost curve at each and every quantity. Maxpro cannot earn a normal profit at *any* quantity of production.

Under the circumstances Maxpro's owners should get out of the tennis racket business and pursue their next best option. Going out of business may seem like a rather drastic step, yet thousands of businesses make this long-run decision each year. However, large firms that make many products may not go out of business completely. Faced with long-run losses, they may choose to drop a particular product and to use existing machinery and buildings to produce another product.

Having an economic loss does not mean that Maxpro would necessarily report a loss to its shareholders or to the Internal Revenue Service. Recall that accounting profit is calculated on the basis of explicit costs. But economic profit is a *relative* concept; it includes all opportunity costs, that is, both explicit and implicit costs. As we noted earlier, a normal profit—the return that owners could make from other investments—is an implicit cost. Maxpro's loss of $150 per day simply means that its owners could do better in a different business.

Normal (zero economic) profits: To stay in or go out of business?

Finally, let's consider the situation shown in Exhibit 9.5(d). Here Maxpro is faced with a selling price of $200 per racket. As the graph indicates, marginal revenue equals marginal cost at 5.5 rackets per day. At that quantity, average total cost is identical to price (marginal revenue), giving the firm zero economic profit, or a normal profit.

You might assume that Maxpro's owners *want* to earn an economic profit and so will get out of this business. Even though all firms *want* to earn economic profits, they will settle for less. To make its long-run decision, Maxpro will compare its current accounting profit with a *realistic* estimate of what it could do otherwise.

An economic profit of zero means that a business has no better opportunity. Thus its owners have no incentive to go out of business because they have no better options. A normal profit is just high enough to justify a decision to remain in business. Thus in our example a price of $200 is the *minimum price* that will justify Maxpro's continuing to produce tennis rackets. (On the graph the marginal revenue line at $200 just touches the minimum point on the average total cost curve.) At any lower price the firm will not be able to cover all its costs, including the opportunity costs of doing something else.

Additional Long-Run Options

So far, we have assumed that a firm's long-run options are limited to producing or getting out of business by selling all its resources. This is one long-run option, but as noted in Chapter 8, a firm can also choose to increase or decrease plant size.

For example, we found that Maxpro suffers an economic loss of $150 per day if the price of tennis rackets is $175 each. Faced with a choice between producing at current capacity or selling out, Maxpro's owners would be better off selling out. But what if the firm were to sell some of its equipment and rent out part of its building, reducing its fixed costs by $200? In that case, it could earn an economic profit of $50 per day, or enough to cover all opportunity costs and justify a decision to stay in business.

In fact, if a firm can reduce fixed costs enough, it may be able to turn economic losses into economic profits (or at least normal profits) in the long run. This long-run option corresponds to building a smaller plant. As we noted in Chapter 8, a large plant may be less efficient when small quantities of goods are being produced. However, if there is no plant size or level of fixed costs that can yield at least a normal profit, the firm should get out of the business entirely.

In some cases, it may be to a firm's advantage in the long run to increase its fixed resources and fixed costs: to build a bigger plant, buy more and/or better machines, or expand into new products and new markets. For example, a larger plant may enable a firm to achieve economies of scale. If so, a lower average cost may enable it to earn at least a normal profit. As with other decisions, a firm must

RECAP

The long-run rules for the supply decision are

Step 1: Find the best quantity. The best quantity to produce, if a firm decides to produce, is the point at which marginal revenue equals marginal cost.

Step 2: Determine whether to produce or go out of business. The long-run decision is made by calculating economic profit (total revenues minus total costs) at the best quantity. If the firm makes at least a normal profit (total revenues greater than or equal to total costs), it should continue its present activities; if not, it should go out of business, that is, pursue its next best, and superior, opportunity.

weigh the extra benefits and extra costs of increased capacity. Because it is a long-run decision, a firm should choose the plant size that enables it to earn the maximum profit.

CONCLUSION

In this chapter we explored a range of producer choices, including both short-run and long-run decisions. In each case, we stated some rules for decision making based on the principles of rational choice. These rules are useful for various producer decisions, whether the firm must compete with many other firms for consumers' dollars or is the only firm of its kind.

In Chapters 10–12 we apply the rules we developed in this chapter to producers in both competitive and noncompetitive market situations. We look at how the degree of competition affects producer decisions. In all cases, economic theory predicts that producers will make those decisions that best achieve their goal of maximum profits. As you will see, competitive and noncompetitive producers apply these same rules. But the competitive characteristics of the market have important implications for allocative and technical efficiency.

SUMMARY

1. In this chapter you saw how the principles of rational choice can be used to understand and predict short-run and long-run producer decisions about how much to supply and whether to supply.

2. Economists assume that producers will choose to offer for sale the quantity of goods or services that maximizes profits. Following the principles of rational choice, producers will offer for sale all units for which the extra benefits (extra revenues) outweigh the extra costs.

3. Two steps are involved in making a short-run supply decision. In step 1 a firm determines the best quantity to produce, which is all units for which marginal revenue is greater than or equal to marginal cost but no units for which marginal cost exceeds marginal revenue. On a graph the best quantity is at the intersection of the MR and MC curves, that is, where MR = MC.

4. In step 2 of the short-run decision a firm decides whether to produce the best quantity or shut down. Producing is better only when total revenues are equal to or greater than total variable costs (or price is equal to or greater than average variable cost). Because fixed costs are constant, they are irrelevant to short-run decisions and should be ignored.

5. Economic profits measure the difference between revenues and all opportunity costs, including normal profits to the owners on their investment. Because they include the opportunity costs of a firm's next best option, economic profits measure how much better (or worse) the firm is doing in its current line of business relative to its next best option.

6. When making a long-run supply decision, a firm also follows a two-step approach. Step 1 is the same as the first step for the short-run decision: Find the best quantity, that is, the point at which marginal revenue equals marginal cost. In step 2 a firm decides whether to produce or to go out of business by comparing total revenues to total costs.

7. If total revenues exceed total costs, a firm makes an economic profit. If total costs exceed total revenues, a firm incurs an economic loss. If total revenues equal total costs, a firm makes a normal profit.

8. An economic profit signifies that a firm is doing better than it could do by choosing its next best option. An economic loss indicates that a firm has better options and should get out of its current business. A normal profit means that the firm has no better options; it is the minimum profit that justifies a long-run decision to continue to produce.

KEY TERMS

Marginal revenue (MR), 209
Sunk cost, 217
Normal profit, 218

QUESTIONS FOR REVIEW AND DISCUSSION

1. Analyze the following "rules." Are they consistent with the principles of rational choice? In what circumstances may firms that follow these rules end up with less than maximum profits?

   a) The owner of a local appliance store says, "Because I want to make profits, I refuse to sell any item in my store for less than what I paid for it plus a normal profit." (Does this rule also explain why some of the items in this store have been there for a long time?)

   b) A local lampmaker abides by this rule: "We always produce 300 lamps per week because that's the quantity at which average total cost is at a minimum. With lower costs, we have higher profits."

   c) A national gear manufacturer says, "We always refuse a special order unless the buyer is willing to pay a price that's more than our average total cost."

2. Kiddi Kars, Inc., produces toy trains at a minimum average total cost of $8 and a minimum average variable cost of $5. What will Kiddi Kars do in the short run if the market price is $10? $7? $4? What will the company do in the long run if the market price is $10? $8? $6?

3. Nick Nickelson owns and operates a craft-supplies shop known as Nick's Nacks. Why would the following statement prepared by Nick's accountant last year not necessarily mean that Nick should remain in business?

Revenues		$150,000
Less costs:		
Cost of supplies sold	$75,000	
Wages	35,000	
Taxes and insurance	10,000	
Other expenses	10,000	
Total costs		130,000
Accounting profit		$ 20,000

4. Continuing with Question 3, suppose that you agree to help Nick Nickelson figure out his economic profit for last year. Explain how each of the following facts would be used to translate the accounting profit statement into a statement showing economic profit.

   a) Nick draws $20,000 in salary from the business, which is included in the wages shown in the statement. If he went out of business, he could take a job paying $15,000.

   b) Nick owns the building used for the store. A local merchant has offered to rent the building for $5000 per month. If he takes this offer, Nick will still have to pay the taxes and insurance shown in the statement.

   c) A local merchant will buy Nick's inventory and fixtures for $100,000. Any money Nick has can be invested to earn 10 percent interest per year.

5. Consider each of the following statements about the Victoria Regina Company (VRC), producer of brass-plated rulers. Based on the concepts discussed in this chapter, is each one true or false in terms of the short run? The long run?

   a) If the price at which the rulers can be sold is less than average total cost at every quantity, VRC should not produce rulers.

   b) If marginal revenue is less than marginal cost, VRC can do better by increasing the number of rulers it makes and sells.

   c) If VRC cannot make an economic profit from rulers, it should produce something else.

6. Use the following cost information for Therles, makers of vacuum bottles, to answer (a)–(c).

Quantity	Total costs	Total variable costs	Marginal cost
0	$15	$ 0	
			$2
1	17	2	
			1
2	18	3	
			2
3	20	5	
			4
4	24	9	
			6
5	30	15	
			9
6	39	24	

   a) If Therles can sell all the bottles it wants to at a price of $5, what is its best short-run option? Its best long-run option?

   b) If the price is $7 per bottle, what is the firm's best short-run option? Its best long-run option?

   c) What are the firm's total fixed costs? How, if at all, would your answers to (a) and (b) change if total fixed costs increased by $8?

7. Analyze the following statement from both a short-run and a long-run perspective: "A decrease in average variable cost will increase the quantity that a firm will offer for sale at a given price. A decrease in fixed costs will have no effect."

8. HealthGlo has developed a new vitamin. The company believes that it can sell the product for $17 per bottle. Based on the following information, how many bottles should HealthGlo offer for sale? (*Hint:* First calculate total costs, then marginal cost.)

Quantity (bottles)	Average total cost	Total costs	Marginal cost
100	$11.00	$_____	
			$_____
200	11.00	_____	
			_____
300	12.50	_____	
			_____
400	15.25	_____	

9. Trade Winds is considering introducing a new fruit drink, Samoan Slap. A test survey indicated that it could probably sell 20,000 gallons at a price of $2.00 per gallon. The plant manager estimates that the firm must sell 25,000 gallons at $2.50 each in order to make a normal profit. What do you recommend that the company president do about Samoan Slap?

10. Your boss argues, "If we don't make our mortgage payment on the factory building, we'll lose it. Therefore the mortgage payment has got to be considered one of our costs."
    a) For a short-run decision, what do you think of your boss's argument? If you are trying to decide whether to use the building to produce typewriters or adding machines (both products cannot be produced in the same space), what is the relevant measure of the cost of the factory?
    b) For a long-run decision, what do you think of your boss's argument? Which do you think better measures the economic costs of the factory: the mortgage payment or the return the firm could make by selling the building and investing the money in something else?

11. Plastchic is considering producing styrofoam earmuffs that will require it to build a new plant. It has two choices:

	Plant A	Plant B
Average variable cost	$0.25/unit	$0.20/unit
Total fixed costs	$25,000/year	$40,000/year

    a) If the firm anticipates selling 400,000 units per year at a price of $0.35 per unit, which plant should it build?
    b) If sales are expected to be 150,000 units per year at a price of $0.40 per unit, which plant would have lower annual total costs? Which plant should be built?

12. Consider further the Case in Point on page 218 about the costs of driving a car. Assume that you own a car and are asked to drive for the company. How would the adequacy of compensation be affected by (a) a change in the price of gasoline? (b) a change in the price of insurance? Would the effects be the same if you did not own a car and had to buy one?

13. Use the information regarding break-even analysis in the appendix to this chapter and the following data to answer (a)–(c). The Broderick Company sells two-way radios for $125 each. Its average variable cost is $75 per unit, and its total fixed costs are $20,000 per month.
    a) If Broderick produces and sells 600 radios next month, what profit can it expect to earn? If sales fall to 250 radios?
    b) How many radios must Broderick sell each month to break even?
    c) How many radios must Broderick sell each month to earn a profit of $5000?

Appendix to Chapter 9

Break-Even Analysis

In making short-run decisions, business firms often use what is known as *break-even analysis*. The analysis consists of determining a quantity at which a firm will earn a certain level of profit.

Break-even analysis requires some assumptions about the way revenues and costs change as quantities produced and sold change. The most common of these assumptions are: (1) price (P) is constant, and the firm can sell all it wants to (Q) at that price; (2) average variable cost (AVC) is constant and marginal cost (MC) is constant; and (3) total fixed costs (TFC) are constant. Using these assumptions, we can express the firm's accounting profits[*] as follows:

$$\text{Profit} = \text{Total revenues} - \text{Total variable costs} - \text{Total fixed costs}$$

$$= \quad \text{TR} \quad - \quad \text{TVC} \quad - \quad \text{TFC}$$

$$= \quad (\text{P} \times \text{Q}) \quad - \quad (\text{AVC} \times \text{Q}) \quad - \quad \text{TFC}$$

If we know the values of price, average variable cost, and total fixed costs—and select a desired level of profit—we can calculate the quantity that would enable the firm to earn that amount of profit.

Consider, for example, the Evans Brake Company, which sells brakes for $20 each. Its average variable cost is $10 per brake and its total fixed costs are $50,000 per month. How many brakes must Evans sell in order to break even, that is, earn a profit of zero? Using the known price and cost values and zero profit, we solve the profit equation for quantity:

$$\text{Profit} = (\text{P} \times \text{Q}) - (\text{AVC} \times \text{Q}) - \text{TFC}$$

$$0 = 20Q - 10Q - 50,000$$

$$10Q = 50,000$$

$$Q = 5000 \text{ brakes per month}$$

You might wonder why a firm would want to know its break-even quantity. After all, no firm really wants to break even, at least not in the sense of earning zero accounting profit. Sometimes firms compare break-even quantities with expected sales to see whether a product will generate a profit. Break-even analysis is also helpful in determining how much profits will change if sales change. At other times firms use the same type of analysis to see what quantity is necessary to earn a particular target profit.

---

[*] We could also perform break-even analysis using economic profits by including the firm's normal profit as an additional cost.

Exhibit 9A.1
Break-Even Chart for the Evans Brake Company
Assuming price and average variable cost are constant, both the total revenue (TR) and total cost (TC) curves are straight lines. The slope of TR is the price; the slope of TC is the average variable cost. The intercept of the TC line indicates the firm's fixed costs ($50,000 per month). The profit earned for any quantity produced equals the vertical difference between the TR and TC lines. For example, at 15,000 brakes per month, profit is $100,000. The break-even quantity—where TR and TC are equal—is 5000 brakes per month.

Suppose, for example, that Evans Brake Company believes that it must earn $100,000 in accounting profits in order to justify producing brakes. Again, we solve for quantity using the data and the profit equation:

$$\text{Profit} = (P \times Q) - (AVC \times Q) - TFC$$

$$100,000 = 20Q - 10Q - 50,000$$

$$10Q = 150,000$$

$$Q = 15,000 \text{ brakes per month}$$

Thus 15,000 brakes and $100,000 represent normal profit, that is, the amount the firm believes that it must earn to justify staying in business.

We can also perform break-even analysis graphically as shown in Exhibit 9A.1. Because we have assumed that price is constant, the total revenue curve is a straight line (with a slope equal to the price). And because we have assumed that average variable cost is constant, the total cost curve is also a straight line. The slope of the total cost curve is the average variable cost and the intercept is the level of fixed costs.

The break-even quantity—zero profit—occurs when 5000 units are produced. (Note that the total revenue curve and total cost curve intersect at the break-even point, indicating that total revenue equals total cost.) Below that quantity, Evans will incur a loss. To earn a target profit of $100,000 per month, Evans must find the quantity at which the total revenue curve is $100,000 above the total cost curve. As shown in Exhibit 9A.1, this point occurs at a quantity of 15,000 units per month.

CONCLUSION

Although break-even analysis can be useful, it does have limitations. First, it is based on the assumption that price is constant, which is true only when a firm has many competitors. And even though average variable cost is fairly constant over a small range of output, the law of diminishing marginal returns tells us that it will not be constant over all ranges of output.

In applying break-even analysis, you must be aware that when actual revenues and costs do not conform to your assumptions, the results obtained may not reflect reality. Nevertheless, when used with caution, break-even analysis is a useful tool. It can help us to forecast expected profits from a change in total product and to know the minimum volume of sales necessary to achieve an acceptable profit.

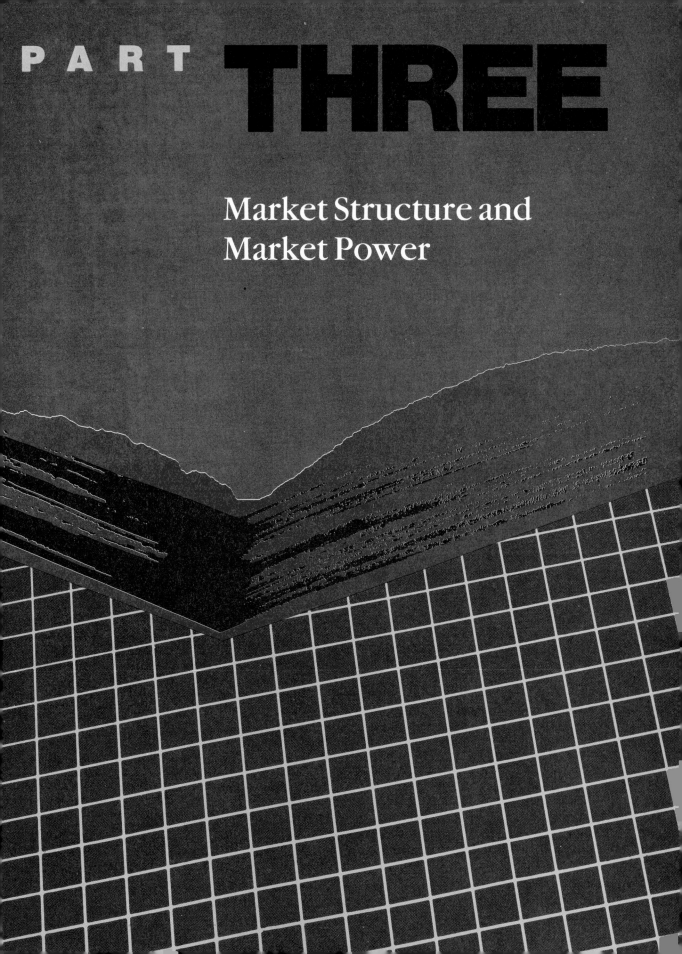

PART THREE

Market Structure and Market Power

CHAPTER 10

Competition and Efficiency

QUESTIONS TO CONSIDER

☐ What conditions comprise the model of pure competition and why is this model useful in economic analysis?

☐ Why are firms in competitive markets called price takers?

☐ How do firms in competitive markets make short-run and long-run decisions?

☐ How do short-run and long-run equilibrium differ in competitive markets?

☐ In what ways do competitive markets foster allocative and technical efficiency?

A s its title indicates, this chapter is about competition and, in particular, competition among business firms in a market economy. There are many examples of competition in the real world. Local grocery stores advertise special prices as they compete to sell groceries. When IBM announces a new type of computer, it hopes to gain an advantage over its competitors (such as Digital Equipment Corporation and Apple Computers). The opening of a new restaurant and the marketing of a new car produced in South Korea are both competitive moves. In a market economy businesses are constantly engaged in a competitive struggle for profits.

In Chapter 5 we observed that competition among firms is essential to the smooth functioning of a market economy. In this chapter we explore how firms behave under conditions of competition and why competition leads to allocative and technical efficiency.

MARKETS AND MARKET STRUCTURE

In a market economy there are a large number and many different types of markets. In many markets—wheat and retail clothing, for example—there are many firms. In a few markets—local telephone service and distribution of electricity—there is only one producer. In some markets—national television networks, soft drinks, and breakfast cereals—there are only a few large firms. Firms in some markets—wheat, oil, or steel—produce virtually identical products. In other markets—education, clothing, restaurants—products come in many varieties. In fact, real-world markets are far more numerous and complex than we can possibly describe in detail in this textbook.

Almost every market has some unique element. However, for analytical purposes, economists generally classify an industry's **market structure** as one of the following: (1) pure competition; (2) monopoly; (3) monopolistic competition; or (4) oligopoly. When classifying an industry, economists ask three questions about its fundamental characteristics. How many firms are in the industry? How much alike are their products? How easy is it for firms to enter and exit the industry? Exhibit 10.1 shows the differences in the four basic market types in terms of these characteristics.

Market structure. The characteristics of an industry, including number of buyers and sellers, uniqueness of goods and services produced, and ease of entry and exit.

Market structure	Number of firms	Nature of products	Entry and exit
Pure competition	Large number; each relatively small	Products identical or close substitutes	Easy
Monopolistic competition	Large number; each relatively small	Products some-what different	Easy
Oligopoly	Small number; each relatively large	Products either identical or different	Restricted
Monopoly	Single seller	Product with no close substitute	Restricted

**Exhibit 10.1
A Summary of Market
Structure Characteristics**

As you will learn in this chapter and Chapters 11 and 12, market structure affects the behavior of firms. By analyzing the characteristics of markets, economists can answer the following questions: Why did prices of video recorders and compact discs drop rapidly in recent years? Why did oil prices rise in the 1970s and fall in the 1980s? Why do airlines charge different customers widely varying prices?

COMPETITION AND COMPETITIVE MARKETS

Consider the statement: "There are only three firms in my industry, and believe me, competition's fierce." Implicit in this statement is the idea of competition as rivalry, or what we call *competitive behavior*. Competitive behavior can take a number of forms—such as advertising, technological innovation, and price cutting—any of which may give a firm a competitive edge over its rivals. Nearly every firm engages in some competitive behavior.

Competitive Behavior and the Model of Pure Competition

Economists also use the term *competition* in a narrower sense to refer to the **pure competition** model—a market with the following characteristics:

1. A large number of producers and consumers, each acting independently, and each too small to have any noticeable influence on supply and demand.
2. All the firms in the industry produce virtually identical goods or services.
3. Both consumers and producers are well informed about available alternatives and prices.
4. Entry and exit into the industry are unrestricted.

Note that these conditions are the same ones that we identified in Chapter 5 for a smoothly functioning market. These conditions force firms to respond to changes in market demand and in the relative scarcity of resources and thus foster allocative and technical efficiency.

In the real world, however, only a few markets—the stock market and the markets for wheat and certain other agricultural commodities, for example—actually have these characteristics. Why, then, did economists come up with a model of pure competition? Keep in mind that an economic model is not neces-

Pure competition. A model of a market with a very large number of firms, each producing virtually identical products. Perfect information exists and entry and exit are unrestricted.

sarily an accurate description of a real-world situation. Rather, it is a way of predicting economic behavior. And, as you will see, the model of pure competition can be used to predict behavior of firms in industries that do not have *all* the characteristics of that model.

In this chapter and Chapters 11 and 12, we consider several different models of markets. We begin with the model of pure competition because it is simple. It excludes most real-world complications and thus is easier to study than more complicated models. Moreover, the results predicted by the model of pure competition provide a standard against which to compare real-world industries. If the purely competitive model is, in some important sense, ideal, then the closer a real-world market compares, the better it is.

Pure Competition and Price Takers

To give you an intuitive feeling for the purely competitive market, let's suppose that you want to sell 100 shares of Generous Electric stock on the New York Stock Exchange. You had hoped to sell these shares for $40 each, but your broker informs you that the stock is currently selling for $25 per share. No buyer will pay you $40, or anything more than the current market price of $25. As one of a very large number of relatively small sellers, your choices are quite limited: You may sell at the going market price or not at all.

This example illustrates a basic point about behavior in a purely competitive market: No individual seller (or buyer) has any **market power**, that is, influence on the market price. Because a firm in a competitive market lacks market power, it is called a **price taker**. Unless the government imposes a ceiling or support price (see Chapter 3), the firm is theoretically free to charge any price for its product. But realistically, a firm selling in a purely competitive market can sell all it wants to at the going market price or below, but nothing above the market price. Like an individual selling stock, the price taker has two options with respect to price: Take it or leave it.

Market Price and Demand for a Price-Taker's Product

Consider the case of the Smallfellow Company, one of many firms manufacturing paper tablets. (We assume that the paper products industry meets the conditions of pure competition and that Smallfellow is a price taker.) Exhibit 10.2 shows the relationship of the Smallfellow Company to the entire market. Recall that market demand is the price that buyers will pay for any total quantity supplied by all firms in the market. Market supply is the total quantity offered for sale at each price by all price takers.

The interaction of market demand and supply determines the market price, as you learned in Chapter 3. If the current price is not at the intersection of the demand and supply curves, adjustments occur that push the price back to equilibrium. In Exhibit 10.2(a), for market demand of D_1 and market supply of S_1, the equilibrium price (P_1) is $1.75 per dozen tablets. If market demand increases to D_2, equilibrium price increases to $2.50 per dozen ($P_2$).

Exhibit 10.2(b) shows demand from the perspective of the Smallfellow Company. As a price taker, Smallfellow's demand curve is a horizontal line at the current market price ($d_1 = P_1$). (Note that we distinguish demand for an individual

Market power. The ability to influence market price.

Price taker. A firm in a purely competitive market; a firm facing a horizontal (perfectly price elastic) demand curve; a firm that can sell all it wants to at the market price but nothing at any higher price. A price taker has zero market power.

(a) The market

Price
(dollars per dozen)

Quantity (thousands of dozens per week)

(b) The price taker: Smallfellow Company

Price and cost
(dollars per dozen)

Quantity (dozens per week)

Exhibit 10.2
Market Price and the Price-Taker's Demand Curve
The graph in part (a) shows conditions in the competitive market for paper tablets. Market demand and market supply determine market price. The Smallfellow Company is one of many firms selling paper tablets and is too small to influence market price. Smallfellow sells all it wants to at the market price but nothing at any higher price. Its demand curve is a horizontal line at the prevailing market price. If market demand is D_1, market price is \$1.75 per dozen, and demand for Smallfellow's tablets is d_1. If market demand increases to D_2, market price rises to \$2.50 per dozen, and demand for Smallfellow's tablets increases to d_2.

firm's product from market demand by using a lowercase "d" for the firm's product and a capital "D" for market demand.) The horizontal demand curve at the market price of \$1.75 per dozen tablets indicates that Smallfellow's customers will pay no more than that. However, they will buy all the tablets the firm offers at that price.

The demand curve for Smallfellow—or any purely competitive firm—is horizontal because the firm is only one of many, each selling a product that is virtually identical. Smallfellow, like any price taker, is *relatively* small; that is, the firm supplies only a small share of the total market output. Therefore in this example we express demand for Smallfellow's tablets in dozens of tablets per week and market demand in thousands of dozens per week.

Because consumers view the paper tablets of all suppliers as identical, no buyer will pay more for Smallfellow's tablets than other suppliers are charging. Thus if market price increases to \$2.50 (because market demand increases to D_2), Smallfellow's demand curve also increases to \$2.50 per dozen ($d_2 = P_2$). Buyers will now buy all that Smallfellow will sell at this price (but none at any higher price). Under the conditions of pure competition, then, price takers face a perfectly price-elastic demand curve.

Note that the market as a whole is virtually unaffected by Smallfellow's supply decision. If Smallfellow were to produce a few dozen tablets more or less, the shift in market supply would not be noticed. Moreover, because of its small size, a price taker like Smallfellow does not gain if another firm fails. Price takers struggle to earn profits, but under the conditions of competition, no one firm has a long-run advantage over other firms. To see why, you must understand how price takers make decisions.

SHORT-RUN SUPPLY IN PRICE-TAKER MARKETS

In the short run, a price taker must decide how much to offer for sale at any particular price—the supply decision. Applying the principles of rational choice, the firm will determine the quantity that maximizes its profits (or minimizes its losses). That is, by following the decision rules discussed in Chapter 9, the firm first finds the best quantity by equating marginal revenue and cost; then it decides whether to produce that quantity or shut down by comparing revenues and variable costs.

Market Price and Marginal Revenue

Because price is constant at all levels of output for the firm, marginal revenue—the extra revenue the firm receives if it sells one more unit—equals market price. The initial demand curve for Smallfellow in Exhibit 10.3(b) has three labels: The first, d_1, identifies it as the firm's demand; the second, P_1, shows that the firm's demand is constant at the current market price; and the third, MR_1, says that Smallfellow's marginal revenue equals price. Because price is $1.75 per dozen for each dozen tablets sold, marginal revenue is also $1.75 per dozen tablets. In fact, *price always equals marginal revenue for a price taker*.

Exhibit 10.3(b) shows that Smallfellow's best quantity when market price is $1.75 is 175 dozen tablets per week, that is, the point at which $MR_1 = MC$. Because price exceeds average variable cost in this case, Smallfellow will choose to produce 175 dozen tablets per week, rather than shutting down in the short run. This decision gives us one point on Smallfellow's short-run supply curve: 175 dozen tablets at $1.75 per dozen.

However, Smallfellow's supply decision will change whenever market price changes. In Exhibit 10.3(b), an increase in market demand to D_2 raises market price to $2.50 per dozen and thus raises Smallfellow's demand curve. The new price and marginal revenue change Smallfellow's short-run supply decision. It can now maximize profits by selling 200 dozen tablets per week. This result gives us a second point on Smallfellow's short-run supply curve: 200 dozen tablets at $2.50 per dozen. (The increased quantity supplied by Smallfellow and the other price takers appears in Exhibit 10.3 as a movement along the market supply curve S_1.)

Marginal cost and supply. By observing how much Smallfellow offers for sale at various prices, we can find other points on its short-run supply curve. We always find the best quantity where marginal revenue equals marginal cost. Thus every point on the marginal cost curve is also a point on the firm's short-run supply curve. For each change in price we can read the quantity offered for sale from the marginal cost curve.

(a) The market

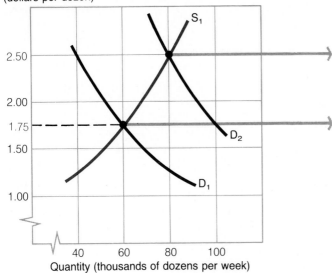

(b) The price taker: Smallfellow Company

Exhibit 10.3
Market Price and Short-Run Supply for a Price Taker
To maximize profits, Smallfellow will produce the quantity for which marginal revenue equals marginal cost (where MR = MC). As a price taker, its marginal revenue is equal to price. At a market price of $1.75 per dozen, Smallfellow will choose to sell 175 dozen tablets per week (where MR_1 = MC). If market price increases to $2.50 per dozen, the firm will choose to sell 200 dozen (where MR_2 = MC). However, if price drops below $1.25 per dozen, Smallfellow will supply no tablets because price is less than average variable cost. Thus this price taker's supply curve is the portion of its marginal cost curve that lies above average variable cost.

We must qualify the preceding statement, however, in light of the second decision rule. If the price falls below the minimum point of its average variable cost curve (in this case, a price of $1.25 per dozen), Smallfellow will choose to offer nothing for sale. When price is less than average variable cost, the firm will minimize losses by producing nothing, that is, by shutting down. Thus we can say that *the short-run supply curve for a price taker is the portion of its marginal cost curve that lies above its average variable cost curve.*

Market supply: From the firm to the market. Every price taker determines how much to supply at any price in the same way. Exhibit 10.4 shows the relationship between marginal cost and market supply in a market with only two price takers. The graphs indicate that at a price of $1, Cutting Edge Company supplies 3 hand-held can openers per hour, and Razor Sharp, Inc., supplies 2. The sum of these two quantities gives us a point on the market supply curve: 5 openers per hour at a price of $1. Similarly, at a price of $1.50 Cutting Edge supplies 4 openers and Razor Sharp supplies 3, for a total market supply of 7 openers per hour. What is true for this simple case involving only two firms is also true for

Exhibit 10.4
From Price-Taker Supply to Market Supply
Market supply in a competitive industry is the quantity that all the price takers together offer for sale at any particular price. If market price is $1.00 per opener, Cutting Edge will offer 3 openers per hour, and Razor Sharp will offer 2 openers per hour (where MR = MC). With these being the only two firms, the market will supply a total of 5 openers at a price of $1.00. If price is $1.50, the market will supply 7 openers—4 by Cutting Edge and 3 by Razor Sharp. In a competitive market, supply is the sum of the marginal cost curves of the individual price takers.

markets with many price takers. *Market supply in a price-taker market is the horizontal sum of the marginal cost curves of the individual firms in the market.*

This relationship between marginal cost and market supply indicates that any change in marginal cost will also affect market supply. Thus an increase in the price of variable resources (such as the metal that Cutting Edge and Razor Sharp use to produce openers) increases marginal cost. (Recall that fixed costs do not affect marginal cost in the short run.) An increase in marginal cost shifts the supply curve to the left, since at each quantity marginal cost is greater. Faced with such an increase, price takers will supply less at each price than before. This response causes market supply to decrease and market price to increase.

Short-run equilibrium in a price-taker market. In the short run we can expect Smallfellow and other price takers to respond to signals they receive from the market. For example, if market demand increases, market price will rise. In response to this signal, price takers will increase the quantity supplied (within the limits of their fixed resources).

We can also predict that a price-taker market will adjust to eliminate any shortage or surplus. In Chapter 3 you saw the automatic and powerful forces exerted on a market that is not in equilibrium. If there is a shortage at the current market price, buyers will offer higher prices and suppliers will raise their prices and increase the quantity supplied. These changes move the market to equilibrium. Similar adjustments can be expected for any change in market demand or supply. Thus we can predict the short-run effect of a change on market price and quantity bought and sold.

RECAP

Because price takers face a constant price, marginal revenue, market price, and demand are all the same (d = P = MR).

Price takers will operate where MR = MC, provided that P is greater than AVC at that point. Thus the short-run supply for the price taker is that portion of its marginal cost curve lying above the average variable cost curve.

Short-run market supply is the sum of all the marginal cost curves of the individual price takers.

Short-run equilibrium in a competitive market is reached when the market has adjusted to demand and supply so as to eliminate any shortages or surpluses.

LONG-RUN DECISIONS AND LONG-RUN EQUILIBRIUM

Knowing that markets adjust to equilibrium enables us to predict market responses to changes in demand and in resource supplies in the short run. But in the short run a firm's ability to maximize profits is limited by its fixed resources. In the long run a firm can change the quantity and/or type of its resources and thus may enter or leave an industry. Entering and leaving an industry are important adjustment mechanisms in a market economy. In the model of pure competition, we assume that entry and exit is easy. But how does a firm decide which industry to enter or whether to leave an industry?

Firms respond in the short run to signals of market demand and resource scarcity and in the long run to signals of economic profit and loss. An economic profit signals that the value of the products supplied exceeds their opportunity costs and that more should be produced. By the same logic, an economic loss signals that less should be produced and that resources could be more profitably used in some other way. As you will see in the following sections, when entry and exit are easy, we expect firms to leave industries where they incur economic losses and enter industries where they can make economic profits. Like the market's short-run adjustment to eliminate shortages and surpluses, this long-run adjustment eliminates economic profits and losses.

Long-Run Adjustments to Economic Losses

Let's consider these long-run adjustments by looking at the Rainbow Company, a manufacturer of paint and a price taker. The initial price of paint, P_1 in Exhibit 10.5(a), is $4 per gallon, or the point at which D_1 and S_1 intersect. At this price, Rainbow will produce and sell 8000 gallons of paint per month, that is, where $MR_1 = MC$ in Exhibit 10.5(b). (We assume that Rainbow's average variable costs are less than $4 per gallon. Otherwise, it would shut down.)

Although 8000 gallons is the best quantity to sell under existing market conditions, Rainbow incurs an economic loss at the $4 per gallon price. We can calculate the size of its loss by first locating the average total cost at current output on the ATC curve. Exhibit 10.5(b) indicates that Rainbow's average total cost is $7 per gallon, or $3 more than the market price of $4 per gallon. Thus it is losing $3 per gallon on each of the 8000 gallons it produces, for a total loss of $24,000 per month. More formally, we calculate

$$\text{Economic profit} = \text{Total revenues} - \text{Total costs}$$
$$= \quad P \times Q \quad - \quad ATC \times Q$$
$$= \$4(8000) - \$7(8000)$$
$$= \$32,000 - \$56,000 \quad \text{or} \quad -\$24,000 \text{ per month}$$

The minus sign in the result indicates an economic loss, as does the red rectangle on the graph. The height of the rectangle is $3 per gallon—the difference between the average total cost of $7 and the price of $4. The length of the rectangle is the quantity: 8000 gallons per month. Thus the area (height times length) measures the economic loss.

Although Rainbow can do no better than this in the short run, it will not be satisfied over the long run with an economic loss. An economic loss, however,

(a) The market

Price
(dollars per gallon)

Quantity (millions of gallons per month)

(b) Rainbow Company

Price and cost
(dollars per gallon)

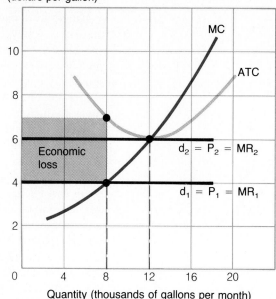

Quantity (thousands of gallons per month)

Exhibit 10.5
Long-Run Adjustment to Economic Loss
The initial price in this market is $4 per gallon (where S_1 intersects D_1). At this price, Rainbow will produce and sell 8000 gallons per month (where MR_1 = MC). But when it produces 8000 gallons per month, average total cost is $7 per gallon. Thus Rainbow incurs an economic loss of $3 per gallon, or $24,000 per month (the red-shaded area on the graph). Under these conditions, some price takers will leave this industry over the long run. With fewer firms, market supply will fall and market price will rise. Firms will continue to exit until market price is $6 per gallon. At that price Rainbow and other price takers earn only normal profits, or enough to justify staying in business because all opportunity costs are covered.

means that the owners could earn more if they invested in some other business. If Rainbow expects its economic losses to continue in the future, it will leave the industry. Indeed, unless a firm can expect to earn at least a normal profit over the long run, we would expect it to leave the industry.

If Rainbow's costs are typical, other price takers will also have long-run economic losses and will begin to leave the paint industry. An individual price taker is too small to have a significant effect on the market, but if many firms leave, market supply will decrease. (Recall that the number of firms is a factor in market supply.)

Decreased market supply causes market price to increase. Exhibit 10.5(a) shows that price rises to $6 per gallon as market supply falls to S_2. At this new price, Rainbow's marginal revenue equals its marginal cost at 12,000 gallons. At this quantity, average total cost is also $6 per gallon.* Thus Rainbow has an

---
* As we discussed in Chapter 8, marginal cost will equal average total cost when ATC is at its minimum. Remember this when you draw these curves. It is especially important for the long-run equilibrium picture where MR = MC = ATC.

economic (not an accounting) profit of zero, that is, a normal profit. (Recall that economists include the opportunity cost of the owners' investment—normal profit—as one of the firm's costs.)

Firms generally continue to leave an industry as long as price is too low for them to earn a normal profit. In this case, we expect firms to exit until the market price reaches $6 per gallon, the minimum price necessary to keep firms in this industry. In general, we predict that *price takers will leave an industry if there are economic losses. The exit of firms decreases market supply and increases market price. This adjustment continues until the remaining firms earn a normal profit.*

Long-Run Adjustments to Economic Profits

What about the opposite case—short-run economic profits? Exhibit 10.6 shows that at a market price of $9 per gallon (where D_1 and S_1 intersect), Rainbow Paint earns an economic profit. It will produce and sell 16,000 gallons of paint each month (where $MR_1 = MC$). At that quantity, average total cost is $7 (from the ATC curve). Rainbow earns a profit of $2 per gallon or $32,000 per month. Again, more formally, we calculate

$$
\begin{aligned}
\text{Economic profit} &= \text{Total revenues} - \text{Total costs} \\
&= \quad P \times Q \qquad - \quad ATC \times Q \\
&= \$9(16,000) - \$7(16,000) \\
&= 144,000 - 112,000 \quad \text{or} \quad \$32,000 \text{ per month}
\end{aligned}
$$

Economic profit is shown on the graph as a blue-shaded rectangle. The rectangle's height is $2 per gallon—the difference between the price of $9 and the average total cost of $7. The rectangle's length is the quantity: 16,000 gallons per month. Thus the area of the rectangle (height times length) measures the economic profit.

When Rainbow and the other price takers earn an economic profit, they have no reason to make long-run adjustments. However, economic profits in the paint industry signal other suppliers that resources can earn more than their opportunity costs if used to produce paint. Thus economic profits in the paint industry will attract new firms to that industry. The entry of one or two firms would have no noticeable effect. But if economic profits attract enough new firms, market supply will increase and market price will fall. Exhibit 10.6(a) shows these effects as a shift in market supply to S_2 and a decline in market price to $6 per gallon.

We would expect firms to continue to enter the paint industry until market price drops to $6 per gallon. At this price, Rainbow and the other price takers will earn only normal profits—enough to keep them in the paint industry but not enough to attract new firms. As this example illustrates, we can predict that *if price takers are currently earning economic profits, new firms will enter. Their entry will increase market supply and lower market price. This adjustment continues until the firms are able to earn only a normal profit.*

As you saw for economic loss, the long-run adjustment process ends when normal profits are being earned. At this point, the market has stabilized, or reached equilibrium. The assumption that we are making—that entry and exit is easy—is very important to our conclusion that only normal profits are earned. In industries where entry is not easy, this adjustment will not occur, or at least not as readily.

RECAP

Long-run adjustment to economic losses in a price-taker industry:

Economic losses
cause
some firms to leave the market
which causes
market supply to decrease
which causes
price to increase
which causes
profits to rise to normal levels.

(a) The market

(b) Rainbow Company

Exhibit 10.6
Long-Run Adjustment to Economic Profits
The initial market price is $9 per gallon (where S_1 intersects D_1). At this price Rainbow will sell 16,000 gallons per month. When it produces 16,000 gallons per month, its average total cost is $7 per gallon. Thus Rainbow will earn an economic profit of $2 per gallon, or $32,000 per month (the blue-shaded area on the graph). Economic profits will attract new competition in the long run. As new firms enter, market supply will increase and market price will fall. Entry will continue until market price falls to $6 per gallon. At that price Rainbow and other price takers earn only normal profits, or enough to justify staying in business—but not enough to attract new firms.

RECAP ▌

Long-run adjustment to economic profits in a price-taker industry:

Economic profits
cause
new firms to enter the market
which causes
market supply to increase
which causes
price to decrease
which causes
profits to fall to normal levels.

Long-run equilibrium in a competitive market is reached when individual firms earn only normal profits and have built plants of optimal size, which allow them to produce at the minimum of the long-run average cost curve.

It may sound strange that all price takers earn only a normal profit. Wouldn't a firm that is better managed have higher than average profits? Don't forget that economists conclude that price takers earn zero *economic* profit, not zero *accounting* profit. Economic profits recognize the opportunity cost of all resources used. Thus the owner of a small business who has superior management skills may earn more accounting profit than a competitor. But the owner's management talents are a resource with higher than average opportunity costs. Because she could earn a larger salary working for someone else, the higher accounting profits she earns may represent zero economic profits.

Long-Run Equilibrium: Normal Profits and Optimal Plant Size

In Exhibit 10.7 we see the Rainbow Paint Company, a price taker, in long-run equilibrium. The firm is producing 12,000 gallons of paint per week, the profit-maximizing quanity given the market price of $6 per gallon. There is no better

Long-run supply curve (LRS). The long-run relationship between price and quantity supplied by all firms.

Constant-cost industry. An industry in which entry and exit of firms has no effect on product costs; characterized by a horizontal long-run supply curve.

quantity to offer for sale. Rainbow, and other price takers, are earning only a normal profit. There is no reason for any firm to enter or leave the industry. The firm has built the optimal size plant, enabling it to produce at the minimum point on its long-run average cost curve. Costs are as low as technology and resource prices permit. At the market level, the quantity demanded equals the quantity supplied; there is no shortage or surplus. The firm and the market have fully adjusted to existing demand and cost conditions.

Market Supply in the Long Run

As we have noted, in the model of pure competition, market supply curves reflect the marginal costs of individual firms. But the supply curves we have been discussing since Chapter 3 are really short-run curves that indicate how the market responds to changes in demand in the short run. To get a **long-run supply curve (LRS)**, we must look at long-run market response to a change in demand.

Long-run supply in a constant-cost industry. How a market responds to a change in demand depends on how the entry or exit of firms affects costs in that market. In a **constant-cost industry** the entry or exit of firms has no effect on cost. Constant-cost industries must be relatively small, so as not to affect

Exhibit 10.7
Long-Run Equilibrium in a Price-Taker Market
The graph shows Rainbow, a price taker, in long-run equilibrium. The firm has built a plant of optimal size that allows it to produce at maximum technical efficiency—the minimum point on its long-run average cost curve (LRAC). Market price will be $6 per gallon and Rainbow will produce 12,000 gallons per month. Because average cost is also $6 per gallon, the firm will earn only a normal profit, which is consistent with allocative efficiency. For this market demand and costs, the economy is producing all that it can justify.

(a) The market

(b) Rainbow Company

Exhibit 10.8
Long-Run Supply in a Constant-Cost Industry
Under initial conditions (D_1 and S_1), market price is $6 per gallon. At this price the Rainbow Company, shown in long-run equilibrium in part (b), earns a normal profit. Thus a price of $6 and a market quantity of 200 million gallons per month (point *a*, where D_1 and S_1 intersect) is on the long-run supply curve (LRS). If market demand increases to D_2, market price will rise in the short run to $9 per gallon (point *b*). The price taker will earn an economic profit, attracting new firms until the supply shifts to S_2. In a constant-cost industry the entry of new firms does not affect the costs of the price taker. Thus the second point on the long-run supply curve is a price of $6 and a quantity of 400 million gallons (point *c*, where D_2 and S_2 intersect). With constant costs, the long-run supply curve is horizontal.

resource costs. The entry of new firms into the paint industry, for example, raises demand for chemicals. But if increased demand by the paint industry is small relative to total demand for chemicals, the cost of chemicals will not change. Similarly, we would expect the entry of new firms into the pencil industry to have an insignificant effect on the demand for wood.

Exhibit 10.8 shows the paint industry as a constant-cost industry. The initial market price of $6 per gallon (point *a*, where D_1 intersects S_1) will cause the Rainbow Company to produce 12,000 gallons per month (where $MR_1 = MC$). Since price equals average total cost at this quantity, Rainbow will earn only a normal profit.

If market demand increases to D_2 because more new houses are being built, in the short run quantity will increase and price will rise to $9 per gallon (a movement along curve S_1 to point *b*). But this new price is not consistent with

Increasing-cost industry. An industry in which entry of new firms raises the price of resources and product costs; characterized by an upward sloping long-run supply curve.

long-run equilibrium. Firms will earn economic profits of $2 per gallon (price of $9 minus average total cost of $7). New firms will enter the industry, raising market supply to S_2. Because this is a constant-cost industry, the entry of new firms has no effect on a firm's costs. Thus supply will increase until market price falls to $6 (point c, where S_2 intersects D_2). All points of long-run equilibrium in this constant-cost industry lie on the horizontal long-run supply curve (LRS) shown in Exhibit 10.8(a). That is, long-run supply is perfectly price elastic in this—and all other—constant-cost industries.

Long-run supply in an increasing-cost industry. Not all industries, however, are small enough to have insignificant effects on resource demand. For example, the entry of new producers in the auto industry would raise demand for steel significantly and, in turn, raise steel prices. As a result, both new and old automakers would have higher resource costs. Exhibit 10.9 shows that the long-run supply curve for an **increasing-cost industry** slopes upward and to the

Exhibit 10.9
Long-Run Supply in an Increasing-Cost Industry
The entry of new firms into an industry may raise costs for each price taker. If so, market price will have to rise to allow each firm to earn a normal profit. Thus, as shown on the graph, the long-run supply curve will slope upward and to the right.

The long-run market supply curve shows how price and quantity supplied are related when firms have time to build plants of optimal size and to enter and leave industries.

In a constant-cost industry, entry and exit of firms has no effect on cost. The long-run market supply curve for such an industry is horizontal at the market price that gives the typical firm only a normal profit.

In an increasing-cost industry, entry of new firms increases demand for resources and resource costs. The long-run market supply curve for such an industry slopes upward and to the right, reflecting the higher price required because of higher costs.

right. The upward slope reflects the increase in costs and thus in the market price that allows firms to earn a normal profit.[*]

Competitive Markets and "Reasonable Prices"

Let's consider equilibrium in competitive markets further in terms of the statement: "The price of gasoline is unreasonable. A reasonable price is one that the average person can afford to pay." All consumers find prices more attractive when they are lower. But there are two sides to the market. From the demand side, consumers think of *reasonable* as meaning not too high. On the supply side, however, producers think of *reasonable* as meaning not too low.

Considering both sides of the market, can we reconcile long-run competitive equilibrium and the notion of a reasonable price? Although producers would prefer higher prices, the equilibrium price is reasonable because it is high enough to cover all opportunity costs and thus to justify production. Although consumers would prefer lower prices, the equilibrium price is reasonable because producers only cover their opportunity costs. Finally, as you will see in the next section, the equilibrium price is reasonable because it fosters allocative and technical efficiency.

COMPETITIVE MARKETS AND ECONOMIC GOALS

Economists are interested in whether a market structure provides and produces at minimum cost the mix of goods and services that consumers demand. That is, how well does a market structure meet the economic goals of allocative and technical efficiency? Under certain conditions, we can show that markets resembling the model of pure competition will achieve efficiency. One way of judging the efficiency of competition is presented in A Case in Point: Efficiency of Competitive Markets.

Technical Efficiency and Pure Competition

Under conditions of pure competition, price takers tend to produce with maximum technical efficiency. As you learned earlier in this chapter, competition forces firms to build plants of optimal size and to operate at the lowest possible cost. Any firm interested in profits is also interested in technical efficiency because one way to increase profits is to cut costs.

Moreover, we noted that in the long run market price falls to a point where price takers can expect to earn only a normal profit. Thus firms that cannot produce efficiently cannot survive. And while normal profits are the rule over the long run,

---

[*] There is yet another possibility: a decreasing-cost industry. The expansion of an industry might, for example, allow firms supplying resources to take advantage of economies of scale. The lower cost might occur because the expansion makes it economical to improve transportation systems, as happens in the early stages of economic development. But decreasing-cost industries are certainly rarer than constant-cost and increasing-cost industries.

A Case in Point
Efficiency of Competitive Markets

One way to demonstrate the efficiency of markets in a model of pure competition is to use the concepts of consumer and producer surplus. Recall from Chapter 7 that a consumer surplus is the gain consumers receive when they can buy a product for less than its value to them. Similarly, a producer surplus is the extra gain to producers when they can sell a product for more than it cost them.

The graph below shows a purely competitive market for flashlights. Equilibrium occurs at a price of $8 and a quantity of 2000 flashlights per week. The demand curve shows marginal value, that is, the maximum price consumers will pay for the last flashlight consumed. Flashlight number 2000 is associated with market equilibrium and is worth only $8 to the person who bought it.

But flashlight number 1000 is associated with a price of $10, indicating that the consumer who bought

it would have paid as much as $10 for it. Since every unit sold for $8, the consumer who bought flashlight number 1000 obtained something worth $10 for only $8. That is, the person who bought that flashlight gained an economic surplus of $2. The area below the demand curve but above the market price is labeled "consumer surplus," indicating the value that consumers as a group receive over the price that they must pay.

We know that in the model of pure competition supply equals marginal cost, or the extra cost of the resources used to produce extra units. The graph indicates that flashlight number 2000 had an extra cost of $8, which was equal to the price. The producer who sold that flashlight gained no surplus. However, flashlight number 1000 had a marginal cost of only $6. The firm that produced it would have been willing to sell it for $6. Thus that producer gained a producer surplus of $2. The area below the market price but above the supply curve is labeled "producer surplus," indicating the value that producers as a group receive over all costs of production.

In this competitive market, producers will sell additional flashlights up to the point where they no longer gain any producer surplus. That is, they will supply up to the point where the price received for the last flashlight equals the opportunity cost of producing it. Consumers will buy additional units up to the point where they no longer gain any consumer surplus. That is, they will demand up to the point where the price paid for the last flashlight equals the extra benefit from consuming it.

In other words, free exchange under pure competition means that firms produce all units of a good or service that add more to social benefits than to social costs. That is, they produce a good or service up to the point where its marginal benefits to consumers (shown as the demand curve) equal opportunity costs to producers (shown as the supply curve). Because opportunity costs reflect the value of resources when used in other ways, the result is allocative efficiency. If we add the consumer and producer surpluses (the two shaded triangles) we get the gains to society from the free exchange of flashlights. Competitive markets ensure that this gain is maximized.

Price
(dollars per flashlight)

Consumer surplus

Producer surplus

Quantity (flashlights per week)

firms that develop more efficient means of production earn higher profits in the short run. We cannot conclude that the absence of competition necessarily means that firms will be inefficient. But we can conclude that competitive pressures lead to technical efficiency.

Allocative Efficiency and Pure Competition

In Chapter 2 we stated that allocative efficiency is achieved when the mix of goods and services provided best satisfies society's demands. In effect, allocative efficiency requires that firms produce as much of each product as they can justify, given current resource supplies and product demands.

Allocative efficiency in the short run. As we have noted, short-run equilibrium in price-taker markets means that quantity demanded equals quantity supplied. If we consider the meaning of market demand and supply under competitive conditions, we can see why economists view competitive markets as allocatively efficient.

We can interpret market demand as showing what consumers believe the marginal unit to be worth. (In Chapter 7 we noted that market demand reflects the marginal utility, or satisfaction, that the consumer of an additional unit receives from a product when compared with alternatives.) If we are willing to equate benefits received by individual consumers with benefits to society, we can say that market demand curves show **marginal social benefit (MSB)**. That is, demand shows what the last unit produced is worth to society, or D = MSB.

We also noted that in price-taker industries market supply is the marginal cost of producing the marginal unit. Marginal cost also reflects the opportunity cost to society of not using those resources to produce some other good or service. We can therefore conclude that market supply curves show **marginal social cost (MSC)**. That is, supply shows what the last unit costs society, or S = MSC.

Using the principles of rational choice, we can argue that society wants firms to produce the quantity where marginal social benefit equals marginal social cost. Producing more would not be desirable because each additional unit would cost more than it would be worth. Nor would producing less be desirable. By producing at the point where MSB = MSC, society obtains all units that add more to benefits than to costs. Exhibit 10.10(a) shows this conclusion; market demand is labeled MSB and market supply, MSC. Thus market equilibrium in a price-taker market meets one of the conditions for allocative efficiency: MSB = MSC.

Actually, to connect market demand and supply to marginal social benefit and cost, we must also make several other assumptions.

Marginal social benefit (MSB). The extra benefit society receives from one additional unit of some good.

Assumptions about supply	Assumptions about demand
1. Resource markets are purely competitive.	1. Product markets are purely competitive.
2. No external costs exist.	2. No external benefits exist.

Marginal social cost (MSC). The extra cost to society of producing one more unit of some good.

If all of these assumptions hold, we can expect market outcomes to be allocatively efficient.

(a) The market

Price
(dollars per gallon)

Quantity (millions of gallons per month)

(b) The price taker

Price and cost
(dollars per gallon)

Quantity (thousands of gallons per month)

Exhibit 10.10
Long-Run Equilibrium and Allocative Efficiency
In a price-taker industry, if there are no external benefits, market demand (the extra benefit to consumers of each additional unit) reflects marginal social benefit (D = MSB). Similarly, if there are no external costs, market supply (the marginal cost to producers of each additional unit) reflects marginal social cost (S = MSC). Thus market equilibrium is associated with allocative efficiency (MSB = MSC). All units produced add more to benefits than to costs. When an industry is in long-run equilibrium, each firm earns only a normal profit, or enough to justify staying in business—but not enough to attract new firms. Long-run equilibrium also signifies allocative efficiency because no additional resources can be employed profitably in this industry.

Allocative efficiency in the long run. In the short run, market response to changes in demand and supply is limited because some resources are fixed. In the long run all resources can be adjusted, and we expect price takers to earn normal profits. This condition is also necessary for allocative efficiency, as we can see by interpreting the signals of economic profits and losses.

Economic losses signal overproduction. Since revenues do not cover the full opportunity costs of all resources used, some of those resources could be better employed in other ways. Economic profits signal underproduction. An increase in output is desirable as long as the extra benefits outweigh the extra costs.

The easy entry and exit of firms in purely competitive markets mean that firms will respond rationally. Economic losses cause firms to exit an industry and output to fall. Economic profits cause new firms to enter an industry and output to increase. In long-run equilibrium, the firm earns only a normal profit (see Exhibit 10.10b), indicating that the quantity produced is all that can be justified under current conditions.

Equity and Pure Competition

In discussing the circular flow of goods and services in Chapter 5, we noted that consumers can express their wants only by demanding products, by spending their income. They earn income, by selling their resources. Thus the distribution of income depends on the distribution and relative values of resources.

In concluding that pure competition is efficient, we have taken income distribution as a given. In other words, the results of competition that we have presented so far say nothing about equity. We examine some issues of equity when we discuss resource markets, poverty, and discrimination in later chapters. Although we cannot draw any conclusions about the equity of market outcomes, our conclusions about efficiency are very important.

COMPETITION IN ACTION

We noted at the start of this chapter that markets having the characteristics of pure competition are rare in the real world. However, agricultural markets come very close to meeting those criteria. Literally thousands of farmers raise nearly every agricultural product, and their products are almost identical. The industry has been quick to absorb new technology and has an enviable record of improved productivity. Moreover, farming has no major barriers to entry and exit; thousands of farmers enter and leave the industry each year. As a result, individual farmers are powerless. They can offer more or less for sale at any price, decide what to grow, or enter and leave farming altogether. But they cannot exert any influence on market prices.

Nevertheless, agricultural markets in the United States (and elsewhere) do not behave exactly as the competitive model predicts. Their behavior is affected by government policies in general and price supports in particular. (In fact, as Chapter 19 shows, we can use the competitive model to show how government policies affect agricultural markets.)

Although other markets do not have all the traits of pure competition, we can best understand some of them by using that model. The competitive model can help us predict long-run changes in real-world markets when entry and exit are relatively easy. For example, in 1983 some 30,000 compact disc players were sold for about $1000 each ($750 at discount prices). Firms already in the industry earned economic profits. Entry and exit, however, were relatively easy, so a number of new firms were attracted to the industry. By the end of 1985, price had dropped to only $140, and some analysts were predicting a further drop to below $100. Production costs fell and firms improved their products, offering newer models with more features and higher quality than the original models. The compact disc player market does not meet all criteria of pure competition (for example, it still has only a few firms), but its behavior is what we would predict using the model of pure competition.

CONCLUSION

In this chapter we explored the characteristics and benefits of pure competition. But the type of competition involving a price taker is quite different from that among airlines or fast-food chains, for example. In those cases, firms know and carefully watch their major competitors. They may take strong action—building a "better burger" or offering discount fares—hoping to gain at least a temporary advantage in the hamburger or airline wars. By contrast, a price taker's activity seems quite passive. Smallfellow and other price takers simply react to the signals provided by the market. Nevertheless, as you have seen, the model of pure competition is useful both as an ideal standard and as a predictor of business behavior in many situations.

But is competition always the best solution? Or can a single producer sometimes offer greater benefits? In Chapter 11 we turn to the exactly opposite type of market structure and examine the implications of monopoly and market power. In this chapter we noted the connections between competition—the absence of market power—and allocative and technical efficiency. In Chapter 11 we discuss how monopoly and market power suggest inefficiency.

SUMMARY

1. In this chapter we looked at the short-run and long-run operation of firms in purely competitive markets and why purely competitive markets promote allocative and technical efficiency.

2. Economists define a purely competitive market as having four characteristics: (1) a very large number of relatively small producers and consumers; (2) producers and consumers who are well informed about alternatives and prices; (3) products that are virtually identical from firm to firm; and (4) a lack of significant barriers to entry or exit of firms.

3. A firm in a purely competitive market is a price taker; it has no market power. Its demand curve is a horizontal line at the existing market price and marginal revenue equals price. It can sell all it wants to at that price, but nothing at a higher price. Thus demand for the price-taker's product is perfectly price elastic; price takers will respond to changes in market conditions that change market price.

4. Price takers find the best quantity to offer for sale by equating marginal cost with marginal revenue (which equals market price). The short-run supply curve is the part of a price-taker's marginal cost that lies above average variable cost. (If price falls below that level, price takers will shut down rather than produce.) Market supply is the horizontal sum of price-takers' individual marginal cost curves. Short-run equilibrium occurs when quantity demanded equals quantity supplied.

5. In the long run each firm requires at least a normal profit to justify supplying a product. Economic losses signal firms to leave an industry. Economic profits signal firms to enter an industry. Thus long-run equilibrium is reached only when firms earn a normal profit. Long-run equilibrium also means that price takers have built the optimal plant size—the size associated with minimum long-run average cost.

6. The long-run supply curve relates price and quantity in the long run. In constant-cost industries, the number of firms entering or leaving has little effect on resource costs. Thus the price that yields normal profits is unchanged, and the long-run supply curve is horizontal. In increasing-cost industries, the entry of new firms significantly affects resource costs. Thus the long-run supply curve slopes upward.

7. Pure competition fosters allocative and technical efficiency. Price takers strive to produce with maximum technical efficiency by building the best plant size and operating at the lowest point on the long-run average cost curve.

8. Equating consumer marginal benefit with marginal social benefit and producer marginal cost with marginal social cost makes market equilibrium ($Q_d = Q_s$) the same as short-run allocative efficiency (MSB = MSC). Responses to economic profits and losses cause firms to enter and leave industries only until normal profits—and hence allocative efficiency—are achieved.

KEY TERMS

Market structure, 234
Pure competition, 235
Market power, 236
Price taker, 236
Long-run supply curve (LRS), 245
Constant-cost industry, 245
Increasing-cost industry, 247
Marginal social benefit (MSB), 250
Marginal social cost (MSC), 250

QUESTIONS FOR REVIEW AND DISCUSSION

1. "Economists say that individual firms in competitive markets consider price to be constant, but in many competitive markets, prices often change significantly." Can you reconcile economic principles with the apparent contradiction in that statement?

2. For cases (a) and (b) answer these questions about the best short-run decision for a competitive firm: Is the firm maximizing its profits? What adjustment, if any, should it make in its output?
   a) Current output is 5000 units; market price is $2.00 per unit; fixed costs are $2000 per month; total variable costs are $2500; marginal cost is $2.50 per unit and rising.
   b) Market price is $15 per unit; average total cost is at a minimum at $12 per unit; and output is 200 units. (*Hint:* Consider the relationship between marginal cost and average total cost.)

3. Farmers often complain that increasing resource prices cause their profits to be too low. Assuming that the farming industry is competitive, does it follow that farmers' profits would be higher if resource prices (price of fertilizer, for example) fell? Explain both the long-run and short-run responses of an individual farmer and the entire market in your answer.

4. Based on the concepts presented in this chapter, is each of the following statements true or false? (Consider each from both the short-run and the long-run perspective in a competitive market.)
   a) If market demand increases or variable costs fall, individual firms will supply more in the short run, and the industry will contain more firms in the long run.
   b) An increase in either fixed or variable costs will cause firms to supply less in the short run.
   c) Since an individual firm has no effect on price, market price will remain the same even if all firms decrease output by 5 percent.
   d) If market demand is price inelastic, competitive firms will earn long-run economic profits because consumers make few adjustments to price changes.

5. Suppose that a new type of machine will significantly lower production costs in a competitive industry. The manager of one of the firms in this industry says: "We can't afford to buy the new machine. We just bought machinery two years ago that was supposed to last for ten years." Can the firm afford *not* to buy the machine? If it cannot afford to buy it, what is its best long-run option if all the other firms in that industry buy the machine?

6. Consider the following cost information for a price taker.

Quantity	Total cost	Marginal cost
0	30	
		20
1	50	
		30
2	80	
		40
3	120	
		50
4	170	
		60
5	230	

   a) What is the firm's best short-run option if market price is $55? $35? How many units will it produce? (*Note:* When using tables, you may not be able to exactly match MR and MC. A profit-seeking firm will produce up to the point where an additional unit adds more to MC than to MR.)
   b) For each price, what is likely to happen to the number of firms, market supply, price, and profits in this industry in the long run?
   c) What price will prevail in the long run? Why?
   d) What are the total fixed costs for this firm? How, if at all, would your answers to (a), (b), and (c) change if total fixed costs were to increase by $30?

7. For cases (a), (b), and (c) assume that the industry is in long-run equilibrium before the indicated change and answer the following questions: What, in the short run, will happen to market price and to the profits and output of a typical competitive firm? What, in the long run, will happen to the number of firms?
   a) The price of a complementary product falls.
   b) The price of an important variable resource increases.
   c) The price of a major fixed resource decreases.

8. Which attributes of competitive industries are desirable in terms of meeting economic goals? Would you want to own a business in a competitive industry? Why? Why not? (Consider the characteristics that would make

being an owner desirable or undesirable.) If owners of firms in competitive industries can earn only normal profits, why don't they do something else?

9. Ernie's Sand and Gravel Company specializes in hauling sand to construction sites. The costs per cubic yard of sand are shown in the following graph. Use this infor-

Price and cost
(dollars per yard)

mation to answer the questions in (a)–(c), assuming that Ernie is a price taker.

a) How much will Ernie supply in the short run and what will his profits be if the market price is $6 per cubic yard? $4 per cubic yard? $3 per cubic yard (assuming that average variable cost is only $1.50 per cubic yard)?

b) What will happen to market price in the long run if it is currently $6 per cubic yard? $3 per cubic yard? $4 per cubic yard?

c) What price is consistent with long-run equilibrium in this market, assuming a constant-cost industry? Why?

10. Use the information in the appendix to this chapter to help you answer the questions in (a)–(c). Ace Business Consultants sell their services in a price-taker market for $55 per hour. Their costs are

$$MC = \$5 + \$0.1Q \qquad AVC = \$5 + \$0.05Q$$

$$TFC = \$7500 \text{ per week}$$

a) How many hours will Ace supply per week in the short run?

b) Will market price increase or decrease in the long run? Why?

c) Suppose that market conditions are

$$Qd = 4500 - 50P \quad \text{and} \quad Qs = 2050 + 20P$$

How many hours will Ace supply in the short run? What would happen to price in the long run?

Appendix to Chapter 10

An Algebraic Look at Competition

In this chapter, you have learned how competitive markets operate and how price takers choose the level of output that maximizes profits. In this appendix, we consider the short-run decision and the long-run adjustment process using an algebraic representation of a price-taker's costs.

EQUATIONS FOR MARGINAL AND TOTAL COSTS

Consider the case of Drillmaster, Inc., a price taker with production costs of

$$TC = 4000 + 2Q + 0.1Q^2 \quad \text{and} \quad MC = 2 + 0.2Q$$

where Q is quantity produced (drills per week), TC is total cost (dollars per week), and MC is marginal cost (dollars per extra drill). Remembering the definitions, we can divide the expression for total cost into fixed and variable costs. The term 4000 (dollars per week) represents total fixed costs (TFC), which are constant in the short run. The expression $2Q + 0.1Q^2$ represents total variable costs (TVC), which increase directly with output in the short run. We can also calculate the expression for average variable costs (AVC) by dividing the expression for total variable cost by quantity; that is, $AVC = 2 + 0.1Q$. With these cost relationships, we want to see how Drillmaster makes its short-run choices.

DETERMINING THE BEST SHORT-RUN OUTPUT

Like any price taker, Drillmaster must decide how much to offer for sale, based on its current capacity and costs. To maximize profits in the short run, Drillmaster will produce and sell the number of drills for which marginal revenue equals marginal costs (MR = MC). As we noted in this chapter, for a price taker marginal revenue is constant at the existing market price, or P = MR, and in this case is $40 per drill. Following step 1 of the short-run decision procedure, Drillmaster's best level of output is

$$\textbf{MR = MC}$$
$$40 = 2 + 0.2Q$$
$$0.2Q = 38$$
$$Q = 190 \text{ drills per week}$$

Thus if this price taker is to produce at a price of $40 per drill, it can do no better than to produce and sell 190 drills per week.

But should Drillmaster produce 190 drills or shut down? Drillmaster will maximize its profits (or minimize its losses) by producing and selling 190 drills at $40 each only if total revenues exceed total variable costs (or if price is greater than average variable cost). To see whether this condition has been met, we calculate total revenues and total variable costs:

Total revenues	**Total variable costs**
$TR = P \times Q$	$TVC = 2Q + 0.1Q^2$
$= \$40(190)$	$= 2(190) + 0.1(190)^2$
$= \$7600 \text{ per week}$	$= \$3990 \text{ per week}$

In this case, total revenues exceed total variable costs. Thus in the short run, Drillmaster will be better off producing 190 units. To test your understanding, find the best output for the firm in the short run if market price is $30. (Your answer should be 140 drills.)

DETERMINING PROFITS AND THE BEST LONG-RUN CHOICE

Knowing the market price, Drillmaster's best level of output, and total costs, we can determine the firm's profits:

$$\text{Profits} = \text{Total revenue} - \text{Total cost}$$

$$= (P \times Q) - (4000 + 2Q + 0.1Q^2)$$

$$= \$40(190) - 4000 - 2(190) - 0.1(190)^2$$

$$= \$7600 - 4000 - 380 - 3610$$

$$= \$7600 - 7990 \quad \text{or} \quad -\$390 \text{ per week}$$

Although Drillmaster is better off operating in the short run, the economic loss indicates that its best long-run decision is to get out of the business (assuming it already has the optimal plant size and cannot lower its costs). To test your understanding, find the firm's best level of output in the short run if the market price is $50, and make a prediction about market supply and market price in the long run. (Your answer should be 240 drills and that market supply will increase and market price will fall in the long run.)

CONCLUSION

To determine the best short-run choice for a price taker, first, find the level of output that equates marginal revenue (market price to a price taker) and marginal cost. Then at that level of output, compare total revenues with total variable costs (or price against average variable cost). As long as total revenues exceed total variable costs, the firm will maximize its profits (or minimize losses) by producing.

To determine the best long-run choice, first equate marginal revenue and marginal costs to find the best level of output for the firm. Then at that level of output, compare total revenues with total costs (including the cost of a normal profit). If total revenues equal total costs, the firm is earning a normal profit. If total revenues are less than total costs, the firm incurs an economic loss. If total revenues exceed total costs, the firm earns economic profits. Firms that earn normal profits and economic profits tend to remain in the same business because they have no better options. Firms with losses tend to leave an industry. The entry and exit of firms in response to economic profits and losses cause market supply and price to change until long-run equilibrium—normal profits—is reached.

Monopoly and
Economic Inefficiency

QUESTIONS TO CONSIDER

☐ What conditions comprise the model of pure monopoly and why is this model useful in economic analysis?

☐ Why are monopolists called price searchers?

☐ How does market power enable a monopoly to increase revenues through price discrimination?

☐ What forces prevent a monopoly from charging any price it wants to and earning guaranteed economic profits?

☐ In what ways do monopoly markets create allocative inefficiency?

Recall that in Chapter 10 we discussed the behavior of firms in competitive industries. The key characteristic of competitive markets is the inability of any price taker to influence the market. Moreover, a price taker is unable to protect its position in the market from the entry of new firms. We concluded that competition—Adam Smith's "invisible hand"—causes profit-seeking firms to produce what consumers demand at minimum cost—that is, to achieve allocative and technical efficiency.

But all firms are not price takers. Some firms clearly have an effect on the markets in which they sell. What would happen if IBM doubled the number of computers it offered for sale? If AT&T quit supplying long-distance telephone service? If General Motors developed a 100-mile-per-gallon version of the Buick? If your local public utility tripled the price of electricity? These firms have what price takers do not have: an ability to influence market price.

MONOPOLY MARKETS AND MARKET POWER

Imperfect competition. Any market structure that does not have the characteristics of pure competition; monopoly, oligopoly, and monopolistic competition are imperfect competition market structures.

Any market structure that does not meet the conditions of pure competition is an example of **imperfect competition**. In this chapter and Chapter 12, we will explore how firms operate under conditions of imperfect competition. We begin by considering the model of pure monopoly, in which there is only a single seller. We want to see how such firms differ from price takers and how the two types are alike. We know, for example, that price takers respond to market signals. They produce more when demand increases and less when variable costs increase. Do monopolists ignore such signals? How does a monopolist's response differ from that of a price taker? Why do economists tend to prefer price takers to monopolists? To answer these questions you must understand the nature and strength of market power.

	Structure	
Characteristic	*Competition*	*Monopoly*
Number of firms	Many small firms	Single seller
Related products	Each firm's product is a very close substitute	Firm's product has no close substitute
Entry and exit	No barriers limiting entry or exit of firms	Barriers prevent entry and exit of firms

Exhibit 11.1
Comparison of Competitive and Monopolistic Market Structures

The Model of Pure Monopoly

To study the impact of market power at its strongest, economists use the model of **pure monopoly**. As they do for pure competition, economists define pure monopoly in terms of its characteristics:

1. There is a single seller in the market.

2. The monopolist produces a product with no close substitutes.

3. Entry into and exit from the industry are very restricted.

These characteristics have two important implications. First, because a monopolist is the only seller of a product that has no close substitutes, the firm does not have to fear being undercut in price and losing customers. Second, because entry is restricted, the monopolist can make decisions without being concerned that other firms will enter the market, even in the long run. In effect, the monopolist does not feel the pressures of competition. The characteristics of pure competition and pure monopoly are contrasted in Exhibit 11.1.

As with the model of pure competition, few, if any real-world industries perfectly match all the characteristics of a pure monopoly. Even the local power and telephone companies have some competition. (You would probably use gas lighting if electricity became outrageously expensive.) However, the model of pure monopoly can help us to predict the behavior of many firms and industries that are not monopolies but that have significant market power. Examples include IBM in the early days of the computer industry, General Motors in its heyday, and the collective market power of OPEC.

Before you can understand how monopolies operate, you must learn more about their characteristics. What causes entry to be restricted? What divides close and not-so-close substitutes? Does a monopolist's unique product allow it to earn economic profits? These issues are of more than academic interest. We demonstrate what you already suspect: Monopolies that can exercise substantial market power create problems for a market economy. These problems have led to legal efforts to control monopolies. But to address these issues in the real world requires practical measures of barriers to entry and substitutes. As you might expect, government efforts to control market power create great controversy.

Pure monopoly. A market structure in which a single firm produces a product for which there are no close substitutes; entry and exit are very restricted; model used to predict behavior of a firm with significant market power.

Barriers to Entry

By definition, the monopolist is the only producer and/or seller of some product. The first producer of any new product is temporarily a monopolist. Thus Milton Reynolds, producer of the first ballpoint pen, and Sony, which introduced both the VCR and compact disc player, were initially the only sellers of those products. But these firms quickly found themselves in highly competitive markets because they could not keep other firms out. Thus for a monopoly to continue, **barriers to entry** must make it impossible or very difficult for new firms to enter a market. Economists have identified control of raw materials, economies of scale, patents, and government franchises as potential barriers to entry.

Control of raw materials.   A monopoly that controls the supply of essential raw materials can keep new firms from entering a market. For example, from the late nineteenth century to the 1940s, the Aluminum Company of America (ALCOA) controlled virtually the entire supply of bauxite, the principal source of aluminum. As a result, for many years ALCOA produced as much as 90 percent of the aluminum sold in the United States.

Economies of scale.   As you learned in Chapter 9, economies of scale may offer significant cost advantages. The necessity to be very large in order to be cost-competitive limits the entry of new firms into a market. Moreover, when economies of scale are very important, a single firm operating the most technically efficient plant may be able to satisfy the entire market demand. This situation, known as a **natural monopoly**, is often true of local public utilities. The natural monopoly presents a difficult choice between the benefits of competition and the cost advantages of monopoly. We discuss this issue of public choice in Chapter 17.

Patents.   In the United States and many other nations, firms developing new products or special processes may apply for a **patent**. A patent gives a firm the legal right to use or sell its discovery exclusively for a period of 17 years. The initial monopoly position of Bell Telephone Company, IBM, and Xerox all resulted from patents. Firms that violate these barriers can be sued by the patent holder. For example, in 1986 the courts held that Eastman Kodak had infringed on patents held by Polaroid and forced Eastman Kodak to leave the instant photography market. Patents grant market power, but their defenders argue that they provide research and development incentives, lead to new and better products, and increase productivity.

Government franchises.   Government also erects barriers to market entry in the form of required licenses or franchises. Entry into literally hundreds of occupations, including doctors, plumbers, and barbers, is controlled by state laws and examining boards. Government regulations also restrict entry and competition in the trucking, television and radio broadcasting, and other industries. Although these occupational licenses and government regulations do not always create market power, they effectively limit competition. Such regulations are sometimes imposed at the instigation of those already in the occupation or industry who want to gain market power by limiting competition.

Barriers to entry. Legal, technological, or economic factors that make it impossible or very difficult for a new firm to enter a particular market; examples include control of key resources, economies of scale, and government patents or licenses.

Natural monopoly. An industry in which a single producer, operating the most technically efficient plant, can supply the entire market demand; a result of economies of scale.

Patent. The legal right to produce a specified product or to use a specified process exclusively; granted for 17 years in the United States.

Government franchises can also create true monopolies. For example, local electrical utility and telephone companies are government-created monopolies. If the advantages of competition that we listed in Chapter 10 are real, why does government sometimes sponsor monopolies? Some are natural monopolies, but government franchises for anticompetitive behavior are based on a wide range of rationales. We will discuss their pros and cons in Chapter 17.

Barriers versus normal difficulties. Not every difficulty of entering an industry, however, should be classified as a barrier to entry. Firms normally have to invest in plant and equipment, acquire technical skills and experience, and accept a certain amount of risk. The greater these difficulties, the fewer will be the potential entrants. But it is necessary to a monopolist's continuing power that such entry be more than merely difficult or expensive or risky: Entry of new firms must be highly unlikely. Barriers to entry hardly ever prohibit *all* forms of entry or competition. However, we will assume that entry is prohibited when discussing pure monopoly in order to show the implications of that assumption.

Absence of Close Substitutes

The monopolist is also by definition the maker of a product that has no close substitutes. This characteristic permits a monopoly to ignore competition. Almost every firm is somewhat unique. For example, you can't buy a Wendy's hamburger at Burger King. But it would be silly to say that Wendy's hamburger has no close substitutes and can ignore its competition when setting price. If we want to reserve the term *monopoly* for a firm that makes a product having no close substitutes, we would not classify Wendy's as a monopoly. Unless we use *monopoly* to refer to situations in which consumer choice is restricted, the concept has little meaning.

Which is the appropriate definition of an industry? Because they have been given some responsibility for controlling monopolies, courts have had to wrestle with the concept of close substitutes. A famous example occurred in 1956. E. I. du Pont de Nemours was charged with monopolizing the production of cellophane. It produced 75 percent of all the cellophane sold in the United States (and received royalties on the remaining 25 percent). Lawyers for du Pont argued that cellophane had many close substitutes, including waxed paper, aluminum foil, and other "flexible wrapping materials." If all such products were included, du Pont accounted for only 20 percent of the total market. The court accepted du Pont's definition, dismissing the charges and ruling that the firm did not have a monopoly.

We return to the issue of what a monopoly is (and is not) later in the chapter. But first we want to show what the characteristics of pure monopoly imply about choosing a quantity of product to supply.

MONOPOLISTIC FIRMS AND ECONOMIC DECISIONS

In the model of pure monopoly, economists assume that monopolists seek maximum profits and follow the same short-run decision rules that price takers do. (See Chapters 9 and 10.) But a monopolist, unlike a price taker, has some market power; that is, a monopolist's decisions affect market price. This difference gives a monopolist options not available to price takers.

RECAP

Imperfect competition refers to any market in which firms are not price takers.

The model of pure monopoly is a market structure in which only one firm produces a product having no close substitutes and entry by new firms is very restricted.

Barriers to entry may result from control over essential materials, economies of scale, patents, or government franchises.

Almost every firm is unique in some way, but the monopoly model applies only when there are no close substitutes for the firm's product.

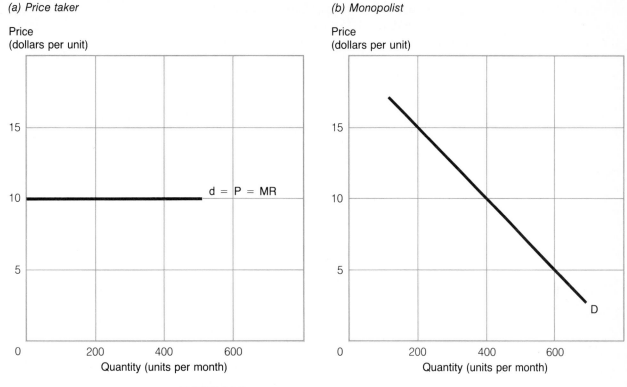

Exhibit 11.2
Demand for Price Taker and Monopolist
The graph in part (a) shows the demand curve for a price taker. Because the firm is one of many competitors, it has no influence on market price. Its demand curve is a horizontal line at the prevailing market price. A monopolist, however, is the only firm in its industry. Its demand curve, shown in part (b), slopes downward like any market demand curve. A monopolist is a price searcher. As such, it must search for the best price to charge, while recognizing that higher prices will result in fewer units sold.

Price Searching versus Price Taking

An implication of monopoly is that firm and market are essentially identical. Thus the demand curve for a monopolist's product looks like the market demand curves we have been using since Chapter 3. It slopes downward and to the right, as shown in Exhibit 11.2(b). In contrast and as we pointed out in Chapter 10, a price taker can sell all it wants to at the existing market price, but nothing at any higher price. Thus the price taker's demand curve is a horizontal line, as shown in Exhibit 11.2(a).

Price searcher. Any firm that is not a price taker; a firm that can influence price and must search for the price that maximizes profits.

Unlike a price taker, who has no pricing decisions to make, a monopolist can choose a price. With the shape of its demand curve, a monopolist knows that it will sell less as it raises price and will sell more as it lowers price. In fact, a monopolist is called a **price searcher** because it must search for the best price.

Price Searching: Demand and Marginal Revenue

The shape of a monopolist's demand curve has an important implication for its price-searching activities. If a monopolist wants to increase quantity sold, it must lower price. As a result, *the marginal revenue that a monopolist receives from selling an additional unit will be less than the price charged*. Why? Consider Exhibit 11.3, which shows demand and marginal revenue for the Mammoth Corporation, the only seller of giant robots.

The first two columns show demand for Mammoth's robots, that is, the quantity it can expect to sell each month at various prices. The third column reflects total revenues received at various prices. The fourth column shows marginal revenue as the change in total revenues per extra robot sold. Mammoth can sell only one robot per month if it charges $200,000. If it lowers its price to $180,000, however, it can sell two robots per month. Note that the marginal revenue associated with the second robot is $160,000, or the amount by which total revenues increased.

Why is marginal revenue less than price? Consider the two effects on revenues when Mammoth lowers its price to sell another robot. First, sale of the second robot causes revenues to increase by an amount equal to the price charged for the second robot ($180,000). Second, the price of the first robot falls from $200,000 to $180,000, a decrease of $20,000. The net effect on revenues is $160,000 ($180,000 for the second robot minus the $20,000 decrease in revenue for the first).

Because a monopolist must lower price to sell more, we expect marginal revenue to be less than price at each quantity. To test your understanding, calculate the changes that produce marginal revenue of $80,000 when price drops from $160,000 to $140,000 to sell the fourth robot.

Exhibit 11.3
Demand and Marginal Revenue for a Monopolist

Total product (TP = Q) (robots per month)	Price (P) ($000 per robot)	Total revenue (TR = P × Q) ($000 per month)	Marginal revenue (MR) ($000 per extra robot)
0	—	0	
			200
1	200	200	
			160
2	180	360	
			120
3	160	480	
			80
4	140	560	
			40
5	120	600	
			0
6	100	600	
			−40
7	80	560	

As Exhibit 11.3 demonstrates, the downward slope of a monopolist's demand curve means that marginal revenue could become zero or even negative. Of course, a monopolist would never willingly lower price if marginal revenue were negative. Thus Mammoth would not consider any price below $120,000, a prediction that we can link to our understanding of price elasticity. Since total revenues fall when price is lowered from $100,000 to $80,000, demand in this range is price inelastic. Thus we can conclude that a monopolist would not produce in a price-inelastic portion of its demand curve.

This relationship between price and marginal revenue is not a quirk of these particular data. It is true for all monopolists because of demand curves that slope downward. Price takers can sell more units at the same price, but price searchers must lower price to sell more units. Because each unit is sold at a lower price, marginal revenue (the extra revenue per extra unit) is less than price (the average revenue on all units sold).

Price Searching: How Much to Charge?

We noted earlier that monopolists follow the same decision-making steps as price takers. That is, first a monopolist must decide how much to produce, if it produces at all, by finding the quantity for which marginal revenue equals marginal cost. Then, at that quantity, a monopolist must check to see whether producing or shutting down is better. If revenues exceed variable costs, the firm will be better off producing. If revenue is less than variable costs, shutting down is better.

We can illustrate this point using the graph in Exhibit 11.4, which shows the situation facing the Cowes Corporation. Cowes holds a patent on a special design for a computer chip and must decide the quantity to produce and the price to charge. In keeping with the principles of rational choice, Cowes will maximize its profits by producing and selling 600 chips per week, the quantity for which MR = MC.

The best price to charge is determined from the firm's demand curve at the best quantity. In this case, Cowes should sell its chips for $50 each, the maximum price at which it can sell the best quantity or all 600 chips. Since the average total cost of producing 600 chips per week is $35 per chip, Cowes can earn a weekly economic profit of $9000 on its chips. Shown on the graph as the blue-shaded rectangle, economic profit is calculated as follows:

$$
\begin{aligned}
\text{Economic profit} &= \text{Total revenue} - \text{Total cost} \\
&= \quad \text{P} \times \text{Q} \quad - \text{ATC} \times \text{Q} \\
&= \$50(600) - \$35(600) \\
&= \$30,000 - \$21,000 \quad \text{or} \quad \$9000 \text{ per week}
\end{aligned}
$$

Following the profit-maximizing rules, Cowes should then compare price with average variable cost to decide whether to produce 600 chips or shut down. In this case, because Cowes earns an economic profit, producing is better than shutting down.

Price searching versus price making. But if Cowes has market power, what prevents it from raising its price above $50 per chip? Why isn't Cowes a price *maker*? Unless constrained by law, any firm—monopolist or price taker—can set its own price. But as we saw in discussing pure competition, the ability to set a price and the ability to sell a given quantity at that price are quite different. All firms are limited by demand for their product.

Suppose that Cowes decides to exercise its market power and raise the price of its chips to $60 each. The graph in Exhibit 11.4 indicates that sales will fall to 400 chips per week and average total cost will increase to $50 per chip. Under these conditions, the firm's profits will fall to $4000 per week, or $5000 less than if it charges $50 per chip. We calculate the new economic profit as follows:

$$
\begin{aligned}
\text{Economic profit} &= \text{Total revenue} - \text{Total cost} \\
&= \quad P \times Q \quad - \text{ATC} \times Q \\
&= \$60(400) - \$50(400) \\
&= \$24{,}000 - \$20{,}000 \quad \text{or} \quad \$4000 \text{ per week}
\end{aligned}
$$

Exhibit 11.4
Price Searching by a Monopolist
To maximize profits, the Cowes Corporation (a monopolist) will sell 600 chips per week, the quantity for which marginal revenue equals marginal cost (MR = MC). The best price, $50 per chip, is determined from the demand curve at the best quantity. Because the average cost is $35 per chip, Cowes will earn $15 per chip, or $9000 per week. The blue-shaded area on the graph represents the amount of economic profit. There is no better price to charge and no better quantity to sell.

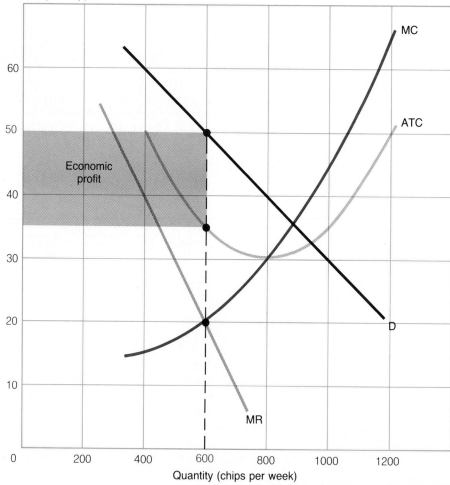

Price and cost (dollars per chip)

RECAP ▰▰▰▰▰▰▰▰▰

In a pure monopoly model, market demand and product demand are the same. The monopoly firm thus faces a demand curve that slopes downward and to the right. This give the monopolist market power and makes it a price searcher.

Because demand for the firm's product slopes downward, the monopolist must lower price to sell more. This relationship causes marginal revenue to be less than price and the marginal revenue curve to lie below the demand curve on a graph.

A monopolist follows the same profit-maximizing rules as a price taker. The best quantity to produce is found where MR = MC. The best price is the maximum that buyers will pay, which is found on the demand curve at the best quantity.

There is only one quantity (where MR = MC) and one price (from demand at best quantity) at which the monopolist maximizes profits. Raising or lowering price will cause profits to fall.

In fact, although a monopolist can set any price it wants, only one price (in this case, $50) is consistent with maximum profits. And a monopolist is called a price searcher because as a rational firm, it searches for the best price, the one that maximizes profits.

Exhibit 11.4 confirms this price is best. At a price of $60 per chip, marginal revenue is $40, which is much higher than the marginal cost of $15. This indicates that Cowes is not selling all the chips that add more to revenue than to cost. As a result, it is not maximizing profits. Similarly, Cowes will not do better by lowering price. (Check your understanding of this point by verifying that profits fall to $8000 per week if price drops to $40.)

Price Searching: How Much to Supply?

Determining both the best price and the best quantity to supply are really the same decision. The price searcher's demand curve relates price to quantity sold. Once a monopolist has chosen its best quantity, the best price is simply the highest price it can charge for that quantity. Thus there is no market supply curve for a monopolist but only a single quantity supplied for any demand and cost relationship.

Nevertheless, changes in costs affect price and quantity offered for sale just as they do in the model of pure competition. Such changes may result from changes in the prices of resources, technology, prices of other products, and expectations. For example, what would happen if Cowes's variable costs, such as wages paid to its workers or the price of electricity, increase? We would expect Cowes to raise its prices and lower the number of computer chips it offers for sale. Conversely, if variable costs fall, we would expect Cowes to lower prices and raise the number of chips.

Response to a change in variable costs. The conclusion that a monopolist will respond to changes in variable costs is important and worth a closer look. Exhibit 11.5 shows demand and cost conditions for the Reading Company, the only licensed producer of Humalong china figurines. Exhibit 11.5(a) shows the firm's initial cost conditions. As a rational firm, Reading wants to maximize its profits. Thus it will produce and sell 6 figurines per week.* (Note that marginal revenue for the seventh figurine is less than marginal cost.)

What will Reading do if variable costs fall by $10 per figurine, owing perhaps to a reduction in the price of porcelain? Will it be better off keeping the same price or lowering price? Exhibit 11.5(b) shows that both total variable costs and marginal cost fall as a result. (Note that marginal cost is $10 per figurine less at each quantity.)

To maximize its profits, Reading will respond by increasing output to seven figurines per day—a move that requires it to lower its price. Exhibit 11.5 confirms that Reading's profits will be higher if it passes a portion of the variable cost savings along to its customers. Thus we can conclude that *a monopolist will lower price and increase quantity sold when variable costs fall; it will raise price and*

---

* When using tables of data, you may not be able to match marginal revenue and marginal cost exactly. A profit-seeking firm will produce up to the point where an additional unit adds more to cost than to revenue.

decrease quantity sold when variable costs increase. This result is exactly the change predicted by the model of pure competition. To check your understanding, calculate the effect if Reading's variable costs *rise* by $20 per figurine. (You should find that Reading will maximize profits by selling five figures.)

Lack of response to a change in fixed costs. What short-run response would the Reading Company make to a change in its fixed costs? For example, what if Reading gives its managers raises to reward them for producing high

Exhibit 11.5
A Monopolist Responds to Changes in Variable and Fixed Costs

Total product (TP = Q) (units per week)	Price (P) (dollars per unit)	Total revenues (TR = P × Q) (dollars per week)	Marginal revenue (MR) (dollars per unit)	Marginal cost (MC) (dollars per unit)	Total costs (TC = TVC + TFC) (dollars per week)	Profit (Profit = TR − TC) (dollars per week)
(a) Initial cost conditions						
4	135	540			300	240
			110	75		
5	130	650			375	275
			100	85		
6	125	750			460	290
			90	95		
7	120	840			555	285
			80	105		
8	115	920			660	260
(b) Costs after a $10 per unit decline in variable costs						
4	135	540			260	280
			110	65		
5	130	650			325	325
			100	75		
6	125	750			400	350
			90	85		
7	120	840			485	355
			80	95		
8	115	920			580	340
(c) Costs after a $50 increase in total fixed costs						
4	135	540			350	190
			110	75		
5	130	650			425	225
			100	85		
6	125	750			510	240
			90	95		
7	120	840			605	235
			80	105		
8	115	920			710	210

Price discrimination. Selling identical goods and services at different prices to different groups of buyers.

profits? Exhibit 11.5(c) shows the effects of a $50 per week increase in fixed costs. Total costs rise and profits fall by $50 per week at each level of output, but marginal costs are unaffected. (Although total costs are higher, the *difference* between total costs for any two quantities is the same.)

Reading can still maximize its profits by producing and selling 6 figurines per week at $125 each. Its profits are lower (because of the $50 increase in fixed costs), but no price or quantity change will improve profits. Thus we can conclude that *a monopolist faced with an increase in fixed costs will face lower profits but will be unable to do anything about it. Raising price will just make the situation worse.*

We have, of course, been considering the firm's short-run supply decision. But the conclusion is the same for the long run. A monopolist's best price and best quantity are determined by marginal revenue and marginal cost. A change in demand (and therefore in marginal revenue) or in variable costs (and therefore in marginal cost), will cause a change in price. A change in fixed costs will affect the monopolist only if it causes an economic loss and thus forces the monopolist out of business.

Market Power and Price Discrimination

Thus far we have assumed that a monopolist will charge all its customers the same price. Price takers have no other option. If a price taker tried to charge one customer more than the market price, the customer would simply buy from another seller. But firms with market power may be able to increase their profits by charging some customers more and others less. Economists call this practice **price discrimination**.

Price discrimination is common and is not limited to monopolies. Movie theaters charge more for adults than for children and senior citizens. Electric utilities charge businesses less than households. State universities charge out-of-state students more than state residents. Airlines have a broad range of prices covering a wide variety of travel options.

Conditions necessary for price discrimination. For price discrimination to be effective, three conditions must be met. First, the seller must have some market power, that is, some ability to control price. Second, the seller must be able to easily and cheaply distinguish customers with more price-inelastic demand from customers with more price-elastic demand. Third, the seller must be able to prevent resale of the product by one buyer to another.

Preventing the resale of services—movies, education, and medical care, for example—is often easy. But preventing resale is more difficult with goods such as cars or groceries. If a firm cannot limit resale, it cannot practice price discrimination. Preventing all resales is not necessary to make price discrimination work, but when resale is easy, it will not work.

Why price discrimination is profitable. Price discrimination usually increases a firm's profits. To see how, consider the case of airline tickets. We can classify airline customers broadly as either business travelers or vacationers. Demand by these two groups differs in an important way. Business travelers are typically less concerned about price. Time is money, and alternatives to air travel are expensive in terms of time. The vacationer, however, has more options. Price can be a factor in whether vacationers will fly or where they will fly.

These preferences tell us something about the price elasticity of demand by these two groups. Demand by business travelers is more price inelastic (less sensitive to price) than demand by vacationers. As we noted in Chapter 4, when demand is price inelastic, revenues can be increased by raising price; when demand is price elastic, revenues can be increased by lowering price. Higher airline fares for business travelers will have only a small impact on the number of business trips but can increase airline profits. At the same time, lower fares for vacationers will increase the volume of such traffic and more than make up for lower revenues per ticket.

Economic theory cannot tell us whether price discrimination is good or bad from the standpoint of equity. Buyers are not asked to pay more than the product is worth to them. Firms that use price discrimination do gain at the expense of some consumers, and customers with price-elastic demand gain more than those with price-inelastic demand. We should and do condemn price discrimination when it is used to eliminate rival firms and increase market power. But this is not the typical motive or effect of most uses of price discrimination.

MONOPOLY: MYTHS AND REALITIES

There are reasons to be concerned about monopolies, at least those with significant market power. But there are also a number of common myths about monopolies—ideas that are often accepted by noneconomists but consistently rejected by economists.

Myth 1: A Monopolist Has Control Over Product Demand

We have noted that a monopolist has some market power and can decide what price to charge. Many people mistakenly assume that market power gives the monopolist absolute control in its market. Consider the statement: "A monopolist can charge whatever it wants to, and people will still buy its product because they have no choice." But in a voluntary exchange, no one is forced to buy any particular product. The quantity that a monopolist can sell at any particular price depends on the amount that buyers are willing and able to pay—that is, on demand. If demand for a monopolist's product falls, its profits will also fall. A monopolist can set any price, but the quantity that it can sell depends on demand.

Moreover, we know that demand for a product depends on the existence of close substitutes. Thus high prices set by a monopoly can boomerang. The Organization of Petroleum Exporting Countries (OPEC) learned this lesson the hard way. In the 1970s, a number of countries banded together and formally agreed to coordinate pricing and production decisions. In the short run, they succeeded in boosting oil prices and their profits. But in the long run, high oil prices stimulated more exploration and development of more substitutes: solar energy, wood stoves, car pooling, and the like. Thus the price increase created new substitutes for oil and weakened OPEC's market power.

Myth 2: A Monopolist Is Unaffected by Increases in Costs

Some people mistakenly believe that a monopolist can simply pass along any cost increase to its customers. As you saw earlier in the Reading Company example, this statement is false. A monopolist can, of course, raise its price when variable costs increase, and its customers will bear part of the increase in costs. However, a monopolist cannot avoid a reduction in profits (unless it is selling to the government on a cost-plus basis).

Myth 3: A Monopolist Can Always Earn an Economic Profit

Another common myth is that market power and the ability to keep rival firms out of its market guarantees that a monopolist will earn economic profits. In fact, the level of profits that a monopoly earns depends both on its costs and on product demand. (Actually it is fairly easy to become a monopolist. Thousands of individuals and firms do it every year by getting a patent from the government. However, only a few patents are worth very much.)

Exhibit 11.6 shows three possibilities for a monopolist. Exhibit 11.6(a) shows Alpha Corporation earning an economic profit. Note that the demand curve lies above average total cost at the quantity at which marginal revenue equals marginal cost. (The blue-shaded rectangle represents economic profit—that is, the difference between price and average cost multiplied by quantity sold.) Exhibit 11.6(b) shows Beta, Inc., earning only a normal profit. At the best quantity (where MR = MC), price and average total cost are equal. Exhibit 11.6(c) shows Gamma Enterprises incurring an economic loss. At the best quantity, the price is less than average total cost. At every quantity on the graph, demand is less than average total cost. For these levels of demand and cost, this is one monopoly not worth having.

MONOPOLY AND INEFFICIENCY

The myths about monopoly indicate that no firm is immune to pressures. Every firm has some incentive to respond to market signals provided by changes in demand and resource supplies. But the responses of monopolies are not as likely to satisfy society's economic goals.

In Chapter 10 you saw that the pressures of competitive markets force price takers to produce with both technical and allocative efficiency. This result depends on the individual firm's lack of market power in a competitive market and the absence of barriers to entry and exit. A monopoly, however, does not face the pressure of competition. A monopoly has market power and is protected by substantial barriers to entry and exit. The lack of competition imposes certain costs on society.

(a) Alpha Corporation earns an economic profit

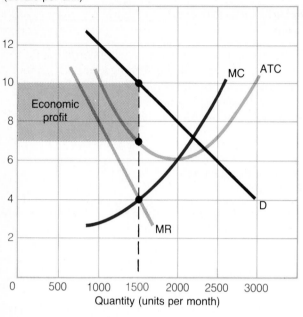

(b) Beta, Inc., earns a normal profit

(c) Gamma Enterprises has an economic loss

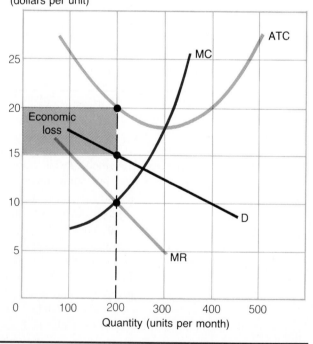

Exhibit 11.6
Monopolies and Economic Profit
These three graphs show how monopolies may earn
economic profits or normal profits, or incur losses, depending on the relationship between demand and costs.
In part (a), the Alpha Corporation will choose to sell
1500 units a month at a price of $10 each (where
MR = MC). Average cost is $7 per unit, giving Alpha an
economic profit of $3 per unit or $4500 per month (represented by the area of the blue-shaded rectangle). In
part (b), Beta, Inc., is able to earn only a normal profit.
At its best quantity (40 units per month), both average
cost and price are $250 per unit. For demand and costs
shown in part (c), Gamma Enterprises' best short-run
decision is to produce 200 units per month (where
MR = MC). However, average cost is $20 per unit, and
price is only $15. Thus it will lose $5 per unit, or $1000
per month.

Monopoly Means Restricted Choice

One of the desirable aspects of competition is the fact that it gives the consumer a wide range of choices. For example, competition is vigorous in the retail clothing industry. If you do not like the styles or selection of clothes at one store, you can easily go to another. The availability of options means greater choice for you and makes clothing stores more anxious to stock merchandise that consumers want to buy. By contrast, what are your options when you dislike the service you receive from the local electric utility? You can complain, of course, but there are no alternative sellers.

Entry barriers also reduce options. In Chapter 10 you saw how new firms entered the compact disc player market, driving down prices and offering improved quality. If this product had been introduced by a firm that could have kept competitors out, the changes that we noted might not have taken place, at least not with the same speed.

Monopolists can earn greater profits if they can increase demand for their products. They do have incentives to improve product quality and service. Missing is the pressure to do so that competition implies.

Monopoly Means Allocative Inefficiency

Recall that allocative efficiency means that the economy produces the best mix of goods. The best mix, in turn, means that each good or service is produced up to the point where the extra cost of an additional unit exceeds the extra benefit it provides. We have also identified two requirements for allocative efficiency: (1) the market must operate where marginal social benefit equals marginal social cost (MSB = MSC); and (2) firms must earn no more than a normal profit in the long run (economic profits = 0). When monopolies are allowed to exercise their economic power, these conditions will typically not be met.

Market power and allocative inefficiency. As we noted in Chapter 10, we can equate demand and the marginal benefit that consumers receive from the last unit produced. Similarly, we can equate marginal cost and the opportunity costs of additional resources used to produce a good or service. But what happens in a monopoly? Consider the case of Shurbet, Ltd., which holds a patent on production of Panacea, a new "miracle drug." In Exhibit 11.7, Shurbet's demand curve is also labeled marginal social benefits (MSB) and its marginal cost curve is also labeled marginal social costs (MSC). We assume that all other product markets are competitive and, as in Chapter 10, that there are no external costs or benefits and that resource markets are competitive. By making these assumptions, we can focus on the implication of this single market imperfection: market power.

Following the principles of rational choice, Shurbet will choose to maximize its profits by producing only 400 bottles of Panacea per week (where MR = MC). Although this quantity is best for Shurbet, it does not satisfy the conditions for allocative efficiency. Note that at 400 bottles, marginal social benefit is greater than marginal social cost. This result suggests that producing additional bottles of Panacea would add more to society's benefits than to its costs. Allocative efficiency requires producing every bottle that adds more to benefits than to costs. In this case, allocative efficiency requires producing 600 bottles (where MSB = MSC).

Exhibit 11.7

Monopolies and Allocative Inefficiency

In the absence of external benefits, market demand also measures marginal social benefits (D = MSB). In the absence of external costs, marginal social costs can be measures of marginal cost (MC = MSC). Shurbet, Ltd., will maximize profits by producing 400 bottles per week (where MR = MC). But allocative efficiency requires producing 600 bottles per week (where MSB = MSC). The red-shaded triangle shows the loss to society from the monopolist's market power. Each bottle produced from 400 to 600 per week would add more to social benefits than to social cost.

As a rational decision maker, Shurbet will maximize its profits by producing less than the allocatively efficient quantity. It does so because marginal revenue, not demand, determines the firm's extra benefit from producing an additional bottle. Because Shurbet's demand curve slopes downward, however, marginal revenue lies below the demand curve. Thus the extra benefits to society of additional bottles of Panacea are greater than those Shurbet receives. As a result, Shurbet, like any monopolist, underproduces.

In Exhibit 11.7, the loss to society is represented by the area of the red-shaded triangle. The vertical distance between the marginal cost curve and the demand curve indicates the net gain society receives from each additional bottle produced. The red-shaded area, then, represents the benefits that society would receive if production were increased to 600 bottles per week. Because Shurbet does not produce these extra units, the red-shaded area also is the magnitude of an opportunity cost (benefits not received). This opportunity cost measures the inefficiency associated with market power.

We can summarize this in the following way: *A monopolist maximizes profits by producing less than the allocatively efficient quantity. Marginal social benefit will exceed marginal social cost at the monopoly's profit-maximizing level of output, indicating that society would prefer a larger quantity.* However, because the monopolist operates where marginal revenue equals marginal cost, any greater output would lower the firm's profits. For an alternative way of measuring allocative efficiency under monopoly, see A Case in Point: Inefficiency of Market Power.

Barriers to entry and allocative inefficiency. The economic power of a monopoly in the long run is secured by barriers to entry. There is no guarantee, of course, that a monopoly firm will earn an economic profit. However, we do know that barriers will reduce the possibility of new firms entering the monopolist's market and reducing its profits. Entry barriers are good for Shurbet, which can charge $40 per bottle without fear of competition. But entry barriers can cause the market not to fully respond to the signal of economic profits. Fewer firms and less output in the long run will jeopardize allocative efficiency.

MONOPOLY IN ACTION

The monopoly model is obviously ideal for studying the behavior of local telephone, electric, gas and other utility companies, which have many of its characteristics. We can see how such companies could exercise their market power to raise prices substantially above the level that a competitive market would charge. The undesirable effects of market power led society to substitute the visible hand of government (see Chapter 17) for the missing "invisible hand" of competition in some markets.

Monopolies also exist outside the utility industry. As we mentioned earlier in this chapter, the U.S. aluminum industry was dominated from its beginnings in the late 1800s to the 1940s by a single company: The Aluminum Company of America (ALCOA). ALCOA's original monopoly position resulted from some patents it held. To protect itself after the patents expired, it also made agreements with foreign producers to stay out of the U.S. market. ALCOA bought up much of the world's bauxite deposits, guaranteeing itself control of the raw material from which aluminum is produced. It secured other supplies with long-term contracts that barred the suppliers from selling to any ALCOA competitor.

The anticompetition contracts were voided by the courts in 1912. Nevertheless, for many years ALCOA maintained its position largely by increasing its capacity to meet increases in demand and by an aggressive pricing strategy. The company defended its pricing strategy as one that did not seek to maximize short-run profits but rather passed on to buyers the benefits of economies of scale and advances in technology.

The courts ultimately rejected this argument, ruling that ALCOA was a monopoly and had violated the antitrust laws. By the time the case was settled, however, ALCOA had two competitors—Kaiser and Reynolds—that had entered

RECAP

Monopoly means restricted choice for buyers. The pressure to respond quickly to consumer demand is absent.

Market power means that extra benefits to a monopolist (MR) are less than for society (D = MSB). As a result, the quantity that maximizes the monopolist's profits (where MR = MC) is less than the quantity that is allocatively efficient (where MSB = MSC).

Barriers to entry mean that monopolies may earn economic profits over a relatively long period of time. Barriers prevent new firms from responding to the market signal of economic profits and therefore mean allocative inefficiency.

A Case in Point
Inefficiency of Market Power

One way to demonstrate the inefficiency of markets in a model of pure monopoly is to use the concepts of consumer and producer surplus, as we did for pure competition in the Chapter 10 Case in Point: Efficiency of Competitive Markets.

Consider the graph below. It shows a market for a new herbicide that will kill kudzu but leave other plant life intact. (Kudzu, a climbing vine, has threatened to take over parts of the southeastern United States.) If this were a competitive market, 1500 barrels of this herbicide would be produced (where demand intersects supply) at a price of $6 per barrel. But Greenpowder,

Inc., has an exclusive right to produce this herbicide, which it developed and calls "Gonzu." Assuming that Greenpowder has no cost advantages from economies of scale, it will maximize profits by selling 1000 barrels of Gonzu per week (where MR = MC) for a price of $8 each.

Greenpowder's market power has three effects. First, because output is restricted, consumers lose the surplus they would have received from buying the extra 500 barrels of Gonzu (from 1000 to 1500 per week) at a price of $6. This result shows as the top part of the red area on the graph (above the price of $6 and below the demand curve).

Second, Greenpowder can raise its price and thus transfer value from consumer surplus to producer surplus. That is, under competitive conditions, the area shaded blue (above the competitive price but below demand) would be a part of consumer surplus. It would represent value consumers received but did not pay for. When Greenpowder raises its price, however, this area becomes part of the area of producer surplus and represents the gain the monopolist makes from possessing market power. Third, in restricting output, producer surplus is reduced by the amount of the other part of the red triangle (below the price of $6 but above the supply curve).

These effects can be summarized as follows. Market power causes a reduction in total welfare. The value represented by the red triangle on the graph is consumer and producer surplus that simply disappears. This lost value is a measure of the cost to society—the amount of allocative inefficiency—resulting from Greenpowder's market power. In addition, by restricting output, Greenpowder causes resources to be used in other industries where their oppportunity costs are represented by the value consumers would have paid to have them produce this product. Finally, consumers lose because market power causes a transfer of value from consumer to monopoly owner.

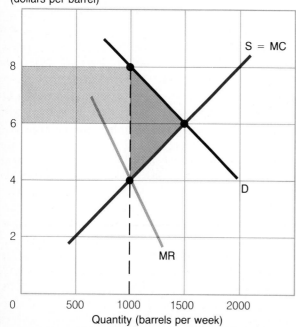

the industry by buying government plants established during World War II. In this example, we see a monopoly responding, as the model predicts, to changes in demand and costs, but in ways that protected its long-run position. In Chapter 12 you will see how the monopoly model predicts the behavior of certain nonmonopolies, particularly groups of firms that band together to set prices.

To be successful, a monopoly must erect effective barriers to entry. In some cases this is done with the help of government. Government patents, for example, made Xerox synonomous with photocopying and enabled it to earn substantial profits. Bell Telephone gained its initial monopoly power by winning a legal battle for patent rights. Patents are especially important in the prescription drug industry. Hoffman-LaRoche's patent on Valium, for example, enabled the firm to earn large profits. Because the legal system protects patent holders from potential competition, patents are often a very effective barrier to entry. By enforcing Polaroid's patent rights, the courts forced Eastman Kodak, a successful new entrant, out of the instant photography market and restored Polaroid's monopoly position.

Although legal fees may be substantial, firms do not purchase government patents. In theory, the social costs of patent monopolies are supposed to be balanced by the social benefits from increased innovation. Cable-TV companies, however, must pay for their legal monopoly. In return for an exclusive government franchise, a company pays the city a franchise fee, generally a percentage of gross revenues. In effect, the fee transfers some of the monopoly profits from the cable-TV company to the city government.

CONCLUSION

In this chapter and Chapter 10, we explored the two extremes of market structure: pure competition and pure monopoly. Both price takers in competitive markets and price searchers in monopoly markets can be expected to follow the same rules for maximizing profits. The outcomes, however, are quite different from the social perspective. With competition we expect to find allocative efficiency, both in the short run (MSB = MSC) and the long run (normal profits). Market power and barriers to entry, however, mean that the monopolist will not fully respond to market signals.

Most real-world market structures fall somewhere between these two extremes. We consider those markets in Chapter 12. However, we do not abandon the two models that we have used so far. In fact, we use these models to understand and predict behavior for a wide range of real-world situations. When a market is characterized by significant competition, we can apply the model of pure competition. When market power is substantial and barriers to entry exist, we can apply the model of pure monopoly. The real world, of course, is more complex than these simple models. But the models help us to focus on underlying forces instead of the details that can obscure these forces.

SUMMARY

1. In this chapter we explored the economic meaning of monopoly and the significance of this market structure for the social goal of allocative efficiency.

2. A monopoly market consists of a single firm producing a product for which there are no close substitutes. The typical monopoly market has significant barriers to en-

try. These barriers may be the control of raw materials, economies of scale, patents, or government franchises. When economies of scale are so great that the most efficiently sized plant can supply an entire market, the industry is called a "natural monopoly."

3. Because a monopolistic firm has market power, it must

decide the best price to charge for its product. Monopolists are thus known as price searchers. Because a monopolist faces a demand curve that slopes downward, it must lower price to sell more units. Thus its marginal revenue curve lies below the demand curve.

4. A monopolistic firm makes short-run decisions according to the same rules as competitive firms: selling the quantity at which marginal revenue equals marginal cost, as long as revenues are no less than variable costs. A monopoly prices its products according to the price for that quantity on the demand curve.

5. A monopoly will not make a short-run adjustment to a change in fixed costs, even though higher fixed costs reduce its profits. The firm does respond in the short run to changes in variable costs, since these changes affect marginal costs. The firm will raise its price if variable costs rise, although it cannot fully protect its profits against higher variable costs. It will lower its price if variable costs fall, sharing cost savings with its customers.

6. Price discrimination is the practice of selling the identical good or service to different groups of consumers for different prices. In this way a firm can increase its profits by charging a higher price to customers with more price-inelastic demand and a lower price to customers with more price-elastic demand. This policy is profitable only when the firm has some market power, when it can distinguish between groups of consumers with different price elasticities of demand, and when it can prevent the resale of its product.

7. Myths about monopolies include the notion that they can control demand for their products, are unaffected by increases in costs, and always earn economic profits.

8. Allocative efficiency requires that marginal social benefits equal marginal social costs. But in monopoly markets, market demand equals marginal social benefits, and the monopolist's marginal cost curve equals marginal social costs. However, marginal revenue is less than demand; that is, the extra benefits to the firm are less than the extra benefits to society. The firm thus chooses to operate where marginal revenue equals marginal cost, at which point marginal social benefit exceeds marginal social cost.

9. Allocative inefficiency also results from the presence of barriers to entry and exit. Barriers prevent new firms from entering and increasing output when economic profits arise.

KEY TERMS

Imperfect competition, 259
Pure monopoly, 260

Barriers to entry, 261
Natural monopoly, 261
Patent, 261
Price searcher, 263
Price discrimination, 269

QUESTIONS FOR REVIEW AND DISCUSSION

1. Analyze the statement: "If the rules in the text are followed, even a monopoly firm may fail to earn normal profits. But many firms don't follow those rules. They determine the price by adding a profit margin to their average total cost. If this rule is followed, a firm will always earn profits." Why does the addition of a profit margin not guarantee profits? Under most circumstances, this rule is inferior to the one economists suggest. Why?

2. Statements (a) and (b) are false. For each situation explain what action a monopoly should take to maximize its profits and how price and output would be affected. (If necessary, distinguish between long-run and short-run responses.)
   a) An increase in market demand will increase output in a competitive industry, but a monopoly would be better off if it simply raised the price charged for the current volume of output.
   b) If a monopoly is unable to earn a normal profit where marginal revenue equals marginal cost, it can exercise its market power and raise prices rather than go out of business, as a price taker must do.

3. Consider the statement: "As a monopolist, I'm unconcerned about cost increases. I just pass them along to my customers." For each case (a)–(c) answer the following questions. What adjustment in price (if any) will a profit-maximizing monopolist make? What effect will the change have on the firm's profits? How do the rational choices that economists would predict for each situation agree or disagree with the statement?
   a) The prices of variable resources increase.
   b) The prices of fixed resources rise.
   c) The firm develops a new cost-saving technology.

4. Which of the following statements is true? (Consider each question from both the short-run and long-run perspectives, assuming that each refers to a monopoly.)
   a) If entry is relatively easy, only normal profits will be earned over the long run, even if the industry currently contains only one firm.
   b) If a monopoly is currently operating where marginal revenue exceeds marginal cost, it can increase profits by lowering price.

c) When a monopoly produces to maximize profits, marginal social benefit exceeds marginal social cost, indicating that too little is being produced in terms of allocative efficiency.

d) Because the exercise of market power leads to inefficiency, all efforts to restrict market power will increase efficiency.

5. Because monopolies are often quite large, they are able to make many of the product components they use and thus increase their profits. If a monopoly firm can either buy a component in a competitive market for $5 per unit or make it for $3, will the monopoly firm increase the profits it earns on its current products by making the component? Can it justify lowering the price of its product because costs are lower? Why or why not? (Be sure to consider the real opportunity cost to the firm for each unit of the component it uses.)

6. The following data show the demand for the product of Titanic Inc., a monopolistic company.

Quantity	Price	Total revenue	Marginal revenue
0	—	$_____	
			> $_____
1	$100	_____	
			> _____
2	95	_____	
			> _____
3	90	_____	
			> _____
4	85	_____	
			> _____
5	80	_____	
			> _____
6	75	_____	
			> _____
7	70	_____	
			> _____
8	65	_____	

a) Determine total revenues and marginal revenues for Titanic.

b) Assuming that all the units produced in this range have an average variable cost of $75, what is Titanic's best short-run decision? (Note that marginal cost equals average variable cost since AVC is constant.)

c) What is the maximum profit Titanic can earn if total fixed costs are $15? What happens to the firm's profits if fixed costs rise to $25? Should the firm raise its price to try to recover its profits? (Calculate profits if the firm raises prices by $5.)

d) What is the best short-run decision for Titanic if variable costs fall by $10, that is, if AVC = MC = $65? Compare price, output, and profits for the new and old costs, assuming that TFC = $15. Why does Titanic lower its price? Calculate the profit it would earn if it did not change price and quantity.

7. Consider the statement: "In some industries, society is better off with a monopoly than with a relatively large number of relatively small firms." In what sense is this true for the "natural monopoly" case? In what sense might we question the social desirability of a natural monopoly?

8. Adam Smith, author of *The Wealth of Nations*, wrote: "The price of monopoly is upon every occasion the highest which can be got, the highest which can be squeezed out of the buyers, or which, it is supposed, they will consent to give."

a) Consistent with the principles of rational choice, what does "the highest" price mean?

b) One meaning (which is inconsistent with those principles) would be the highest price that anyone will pay. At what level of output would the monopolist receive the highest price?

c) Why might a monopolist not charge a price that would maximize its profits in the short run? Under what circumstances would a rational monopolist (one interested in the greatest profits over the long run) not charge the highest price?

9. Electric utility companies often charge different prices to different customers; for example, customers with "all electric" homes pay lower residential rates and all residential users pay higher rates than industrial users. Can you justify this price discrimination from an economic perspective? Do you think it contributes to efficiency? If so, how? Is it, in your opinion, equitable? If so, why?

10. Use the information presented in the appendix to this chapter and the following information to help you answer the questions in (a)–(e). Demand for and costs of the product of Singleton Manufacturing, a monopoly, are as follows:

$$P = 65 - 0.05Q \qquad MC = 5 + 0.10Q \qquad TFC = 7500$$
$$MR = 65 - 0.10Q \qquad AVC = 5 + 0.05Q$$

a) What quantity will Singleton supply in the short run to maximize profits?

b) What price will Singleton charge?

c) How does an increase in fixed costs to $10,000 affect your answers to (a) and (b)? What decision would Singleton make if it expected these conditions to last?

d) Suppose that Singleton's variable costs increase by $2. How much profit would the company earn if it raised price by $2 above the prices you found in (b)? (Assume that TFC = 7500.) Find the maximum profit Singleton could earn. (*Hint:* When variable costs change, both MC and AVC change.)

e) What quantity is consistent with allocative efficiency (MSB = MSC)?

Appendix to Chapter 11

An Algebraic Look at Monopoly

In this chapter we showed how a monopolist chooses the level of output that maximizes its profits. In this appendix, we analyze the supply decision of a monopolistic firm using an algebraic representation of the firm's costs and market demand.

EQUATIONS FOR MARGINAL COST AND MARGINAL REVENUE

Consider Monolith, Inc., a monopoly producer of patented printing equipment. Its costs of production are

$$TC = 1500 + 2Q + 0.1Q^2 \quad \text{and} \quad MC = 2 + 0.2Q$$

where TC is total costs, Q is quantity of machines produced, and MC is marginal cost.

Monolith must search for the best price (P) along its demand curve. Suppose that its demand and marginal revenue curves are

$$\text{Demand:} \quad P = 50 - 0.1Q$$

$$\text{Marginal revenue:} \quad MR = 50 - 0.2Q$$

Using the information on both demand and cost, Monolith can determine its best level of output and best price to charge, that is, the quantity and price that maximize profits.

DETERMINING THE BEST SHORT-RUN OUTPUT

The first step in price searching is to locate the quantity for which marginal revenue equals marginal cost. Using the preceding equations, that quantity is

$$\textbf{MR} \quad = \quad \textbf{MC}$$
$$50 - 0.2Q = 2 + 0.2Q$$
$$0.4Q = 48$$
$$Q = 120 \text{ machines}$$

Thus Monolith can maximize its profits by producing and selling 120 machines. In order to determine whether to produce or shut down, Monolith must find the best price to charge and compare price with average variable cost (or total revenues with total variable costs). The best price is the highest price at which it can sell the best quantity (120 machines), or from the demand relationship

$$P = \$50 - 0.1Q$$
$$= \$50 - 0.1(120) \quad \text{or} \quad \$38 \text{ per machine}$$

So a price of $38 and a quantity of 120 is the best choice for Monolith.

CHECKING REVENUES AND VARIABLE COSTS

Before deciding whether to produce in the short run, Monolith must check revenues and variable costs as follows:

Total revenues	**Total variable costs**
$TR = P \times Q$	$TVC = 2Q + 0.1Q^2$
$= \$38(120)$	$= 2(120) + 0.1(120)^2$
$= \$4560$	$= \$1680$

Note that total variable costs equal total costs minus fixed costs. Because revenues exceed variable costs, Monolith will be better off in the short run producing 120 machines, which it can sell for $38 each.

PRICE SEARCHING AND MAXIMUM PROFITS

With current fixed costs of $1500, Monolith can make an economic profit of $1380 by producing and selling 120 machines for $38 each; that is,

$$\text{Economic profit} = \text{Total revenue} - \text{Total cost}$$
$$= \text{TR} - (\text{TVC} + \text{TFC})$$
$$= \$4560 - (\$1680 + \$1500)$$
$$= \$4560 - \$3180 \quad \text{or} \quad \$1380$$

What happens, however, if fixed costs rise to $3000? In that case, Monolith will incur a loss of $120. To prove to yourself that Monolith cannot raise its price to cover its loss without increasing that loss, calculate the profit or loss for a price of $40 per machine and the quantity demanded at that price. (You should find the loss is $200.) Thus there is no better price under current conditions, and unless demand or costs change, Monolith will leave this industry in the long run.

MARKET POWER AND ALLOCATIVE INEFFICIENCY

Because a monopoly has market power, the quantity at which it maximizes its profits (where MR = MC) is less than the allocatively efficient quantity (where MSB = MSC). Equating demand with marginal social benefits (D = MSB) and marginal cost with marginal social costs (MC = MSC), we can identify the allocatively efficient quantity.

First, to verify that allocative inefficiency results, we measure marginal social benefits and marginal social costs at Monolith's optimal level of output of 120 machines.

$$
\begin{aligned}
\text{MSB} &= \text{D} & \text{MSC} &= \text{MC} \\
&= 50 - 0.1Q & &= 2 + 0.2Q \\
&= 50 - 0.1(120) \quad \text{or} \quad 38 & &= 2 + 0.2(120) \quad \text{or} \quad 26
\end{aligned}
$$

We see that marginal social benefit exceeds marginal social cost. Society wants more than Monolith is willing to offer for sale.

Next we find the allocatively efficient quantity where marginal social benefit (MSB = D) equals marginal social cost (MSC = MC); that is,

$$
\begin{aligned}
\textbf{MSB} \quad &= \quad \textbf{MSC} \\
50 - 0.1Q &= 2 + 0.2Q \\
0.3Q &= 48 \\
Q &= 160 \text{ machines}
\end{aligned}
$$

A monopolist maximizes profits at a smaller quantity than is allocatively efficient. Why? Because marginal revenue measures the extra benefit that a monopolist gets from producing an additional unit. But the demand curve measures the extra benefit to society. Since marginal revenue is below demand, the optimal quantity from society's perspective will always be greater than the quantity that maximizes monopolist's profits.

CONCLUSION

A monopolist is a price searcher, but the rules for determining its best short-run choice are virtually identical to those for a price taker. First, the firm locates the quantity for which marginal revenue equals marginal cost. Second, the best price is located from the demand curve at the best quantity. In the short run, a monopolist must compare total revenues and total variable costs (or price and average variable costs) to decide whether to produce or shut down. In the long run, it must compare total revenues and total costs. If the firm cannot earn at least a normal profit, it should go out of business.

We also found that a change in fixed costs has no bearing on either the best price to charge or whether the firm should operate or shut down in the short run. The demand relationship is always a limiting factor. And finally, we saw that market power (which means marginal revenue below demand) implies allocative inefficiency. The quantity that maximizes profits for a monopoly firm is less than the quantity at which allocative efficiency is achieved.

Economic Encounters
Corporate Takeovers:
The Raiders Strike

The mid-1980s witnessed a massive restructuring of corporate America, the likes of which hadn't been seen since 1901, when J. P. Morgan merged three industrial empires to form the world's first billion-dollar corporation. Restructuring 1980s-style meant mergers: big corporations swallowing smaller corporations or corporate *raiders* engineering multimillion-dollar takeover deals. Between 1983 and 1987, more than 12,000 companies and corporate divisions, representing $490 *billion* in assets, changed hands. As with most economic trends, corporate merger mania carried both good and bad news.

among economists in the 1980s: Was corporate America going to be healthier and stronger after the dust of merger mania settled? Or would long-term effects be far more destructive than anyone realized?

Raiders as Heroes Supporters of merger mania claim that corporate wheeling and dealing stimulates the economy. In their view, U.S. business became stagnant during the first three-quarters of this century. Conglomerates got fat, top-heavy, and sluggish. Their inefficient operations failed to compete with market attacks from the more

> **Supporters of merger mania claim that corporate wheeling and dealing stimulates the economy.**

What Is a Takeover? In a friendly merger, two companies negotiate to cooperatively join their enterprises, hoping that by combining operations they will become more efficient and profitable. By contrast, a takeover usually begins with an offer by a corporation to purchase a large block of shares of stock in a target firm. The corporation (or perhaps an individual raider like Carl Icahn) has one goal in mind: to acquire enough voting shares of the target firm to wrest control from its current management.

The target firm has several options in fighting a takeover attempt. One approach, called *greenmail,* involves the target firm buying back, at a premium, the shares purchased by the raider. In return the raider agrees to halt the takeover attempt. As a result of this expense, the target firm's stock price often falls; however, the corporation remains intact (although with fewer resources).

Other approaches include selling off the company's "crown jewels" (the choicest, most profitable divisions) or taking on heavy debt to make the firm unattractive to raiders. Management might even restructure the company to gain greater efficiency, or design "poi-

son pills" (complex financial mazes) to elude raiders. Often managers write themselves lucrative job contracts or severance pay—so-called "golden parachutes"—to protect them in the event of a takeover. A firm may even buy back stock from shareholders, further adding to the firm's debt.

The positive and negative effects of these actions sparked great debate

Carl Icahn stirred up corporate America in the 1980s by raiding such huge corporations as TWA, Goodrich, and Gulf & Western. (Larry Burns/Gamma-Liaison)

streamlined companies of other nations, notably Japan. International competitive pressures make restructuring inevitable, supporters say; if raiders don't make this change in American corporate life, the Japanese will do it for us by driving our companies out of business.

Merger supporters believe that takeovers goad into action those corporate managers who have let their companies stagnate. In fact, the most likely victim of a takeover is a big company weakened by layers of inefficient bureaucrats. These companies often operate in mature industries that generate a high cash flow. However, they use that cash to diversify into other, possibly unstable industries, rather than pay it out as dividends to stockholders or investing in new plants or technology. All that changes with merg-

Sir James Goldsmith, successful corporate raider, lounges on his yacht off the coast of Italy. (J. Donoso/Sygma)

ers, or the threat of mergers, supporters say.

Supporters point to the continuing bull market in stocks as evidence that merger mania has helped the U.S. economy. In the late 1980s, the stock market assigned higher values to the assets of U.S. corporations because of the widely held belief that restructuring would lead to more profitable companies. As a result, shareholder optimism and confidence in the economy's future rose. In addition, shareholders of companies targeted for takeover frequently came out winners. To avoid takeover, the target companies often bought back shares at prices as much as 40 percent over the stock's market value. Such stock buybacks handed $75 billion to shareholders in 1984 and 1985.

Raiders as Bad Guys   Critics of merger mania are as vocal as its supporters. They say that managers and blue-collar workers alike are hit hard by restructuring and are not likely to be as committed if they survive within the new corporation. According to skeptics, businesses need the stimulation of innovation and new markets; takeover threats prevent companies from developing long-range, innovative strategies. They also argue that success depends heavily on a committed work force that does not have to fear layoffs or forced early retirement.

Furthermore, when confronted by raiders, management may react by digging in its heels and taking defensive actions—issuing large amounts of debt, for example—that may damage the company's financial future. Restructuring, skeptics fear, leads to widespread employee cynicism and less concentration on future growth.

Some economists predict that mergers could have an extremely negative impact on the economy by allowing a few companies to monopolize the resources of an entire industry. With stronger positions in the marketplace, these companies could charge consumers higher prices for goods and services. However, some sources indicate that only some 5 percent of all mergers occur between companies that are head-on competitors. These mergers are called *horizontal mergers*.

Skeptics also point to the loss of financial stability caused by fighting off raiders. Target companies must often sell important divisions or subsidiaries in order to raise cash or to buy back shares of stock at inflated prices. These actions can saddle a company with years of debt and make its financial base less stable. A serious recession, merger critics insist, could threaten the cash flow corporations need to keep ahead of mounting debt.

Critics also worry that the stock market may be overestimating the value of restructured companies. They point out that future growth may actually be harmed rather than helped. If corporate cash flow isn't adequate to cover interest on debt, where will companies get the money to invest in research and development or other productive activities? To such skeptics, the only long-term winners in a hostile takeover are the raiders themselves, who pocket huge profits after breaking up and selling the companies they acquired.

> **Change, especially change as drastic as that caused by merger mania, always causes a degree of anxiety.**

An Uncertain Future   Change, especially change as drastic as that caused by merger mania, always causes a degree of anxiety. Skeptics worry that the drastic restructuring of U.S. corporations is happening too fast and may result in permanent damage to the economy. Supporters of merger mania respond by pointing to a healthier stock market and to trimmed-down, productive corporations as evidence that this change is good. The 1990s will reveal the true winners and losers to emerge from the dramatic alterations in the structure of corporate America.

Imperfect Competition

QUESTIONS TO CONSIDER

☐ What does the model of monopolistic competition have in common with the models of pure competition and pure monopoly?

☐ How does monopolistic competition affect efficiency?

☐ What does the model of oligopoly have in common with the models of pure competition and pure monopoly?

☐ How does oligopoly affect efficiency?

☐ What is the significance of barriers to entry?

The economic models of pure competition and pure monopoly were examined in Chapters 10 and 11. You saw how these models can help us to understand the benefits of competition and the costs of market power. In addition, we can better understand and predict the behavior of real-world industries when they resemble one or the other of these models.

Not many real-world industries fit all the characteristics of either pure competition or pure monopoly; most fall somewhere between the two extremes. In order to understand and predict behavior more generally, you must learn to analyze industries that exhibit some characteristics of both models. For example, local restaurants, grocery stores, and various other retail stores compete vigorously but offer very different products. In contrast, the companies that produce breakfast cereal and steel offer similar products within their respective markets. However, those and similar industries are dominated by a few large companies.

In Chapter 11 we looked at monopoly, one type of imperfect competition. In this chapter, we focus on two additional types: monopolistic competition and oligopoly. We will observe how firms in these industries compete by offering new product designs, improved service, advertising, and in other nonprice ways. We will see how these firms make decisions, and what effect those decisions have on allocative and technical efficiency.

MONOPOLISTIC COMPETITION

Think about the retail clothing stores in your community. There probably are a large number of such stores, which means that a significant amount of competition exists. At the same time, each store has certain unique characteristics: its location, the styles it carries, the services it offers, and, of course, the price range of its merchandise. These elements give each firm a small amount of market power.

Model of Monopolistic Competition

Like hotels, barber shops, plumbers, stockbrokers, and movie theaters, among others, most retail stores seem to fit the model of **monopolistic competition**.

Monopolistic competition. A market structure in which a relatively large number of relatively small firms each produces a somewhat distinctive or differentiated product. Barriers to entry and exit usually are small. The distinctive nature of the products gives each firm a small amount of market power.

287

Characteristic	Pure competition	Monopolistic competition	Pure monopoly
Number of firms	Many small firms	Many small firms	Single seller
Related products	Each firm's product is a very close substitute; almost identical products	Each firm's product is differentiated, but is also a relatively close substitute for competitors' products	Firm's product has no close substitute
Barriers to entry and exit	No barriers to entry or exit	Low barriers to entry and exit	High barriers prevent entry and exit

Exhibit 12.1
Comparison of Pure Competition, Monopolistic Competition, and Pure Monopoly

Its characteristics are:

1. There are a large number of relatively small firms.

2. Each firm's product, although a good substitute for those of its competitors, is also differentiated, or distinctive.

3. There are no significant barriers to entry or exit.

Except for the second characteristic—differentiated products—the characteristics of monopolistic competition are identical to those of pure competition, as you can see in Exhibit 12.1. However, that characteristic is very important: It enables this type of firm to influence price.

Product Differentiation

The restaurant industry in an urban area is another good example of monopolistic competition. Each restaurant is unique in that its products and services differ in some respect from those of its competitors. All restaurants provide food. But consumers obviously prefer different types of food, combinations of food and service, and price ranges, as the wide variety of successful restaurants shows. Being different, though, does not guarantee a restaurant even a normal profit. For a restaurant to succeed, consumers must be willing to pay for the difference it offers.

Because the products of monopolistically competitive firms differ, we would not expect to find one market price, as we did under competition. Depending on how much difference consumers perceive and are willing to pay for, the price range can be small or large. For example, in the market for toothpaste, both brand and price differences are slight. In the restaurant industry, however, the enormous differences in the types of food and service offered result in widely varying prices.

In fact, it is difficult to specify an *industry* demand or supply relationship except by referring to some average product and average price. Graphic analysis is usually confined to an *individual* firm's perspective. Graphic analysis may also be used to describe the direction of change in price and output in response to a change in overall demand or costs affecting most firms in the industry.

Product differentiation. The strategy of making a product appear to be different from similar products, regardless of whether it actually is. It may be achieved by varying product design, features, and service, or through advertising.

Many firms in monopolistically competitive industries do compete on the basis of price. Grocery stores constantly advertise specials, and many types of retail stores have season-ending sales. But an even more important form of competition is **product differentiation**, which can be achieved, for example, through advertising, product design, and service after the sale. Firms seek to make their products distinctive in order to attract and maintain a steady supply of customers. Thus a restaurant may develop a reputation for quality that not only makes reservations hard to get, but allows it to charge a premium price.

On the one hand, the wide variety of goods and services offered enables consumers to select goods that match their wants and preferences. On the other hand, both consumers and producers face product differentiation costs. Does the money spent to differentiate Wendy's hamburgers from MacDonald's really make consumers better off? Such questions cause much disagreement among economists. Nevertheless, product differentiation is an economic fact of life in our society.

Short-Run Pricing Decisions

In pure competition the individual firm is a price taker. With many other firms selling an identical product, the firm has no market power and faces a perfectly price-elastic (horizontal) demand curve. The distinctive feature of monopolistic competition, however, is that each firm's product is somewhat different. If consumers value these differences, firms may be able to raise their prices without losing all their customers. In other words, the model of monopolistic competition includes an assumption that a firm has some degree of market power and faces a demand curve that slopes downward. These characteristics make the firm a price searcher, just like a monopolist.

But every other firm in a monopolistically competitive market produces a relatively good substitute. As a result, the market power of any one firm is quite limited. Its demand also is usually very sensitive to price changes (that is, quite price elastic), since consumers will not buy from any firm charging a price that they feel is unreasonable. This price elasticity of demand is a competitive element in the industry.

Exhibit 12.2(a) illustrates the short-run price and output decision for R&R Bleak's Bookkeeping Service, a monopolistically competitive firm. As a rational firm, Bleak follows the basic rules for short-run decision making. The firm finds that the best quantity to supply is 250 hours of bookkeeping service per week, where $MR_1 = MC$. The best price is $40 per hour, which they find on the demand curve at the best quantity. Under these demand and cost conditions, Bleak will earn an economic profit of $2500 per week. The blue-shaded rectangle on the graph shows the area corresponding to the economic profit: $10 per hour for 250 hours per week.

However, even though Bleak has some market power, there is no guarantee that it—or any other monopolistically competitive firm—will earn an economic profit. Under different cost or demand conditions, it might not even earn a normal profit. (Test your understanding of this point by drawing a graph in which Bleak has an economic loss. This would be the case when demand always appears below the average total cost curve.)

In reaching these conclusions, we made an important assumption. Because it is one of a relatively large number of firms, we assumed that Bleak's Bookkeeping

(a) Short-run equilibrium

Exhibit 12.2
Monopolistic Competition—
Short-Run and Long-Run Equilibrium
As a monopolistically competitive firm,
R&R Bleak faces a demand curve that
slopes downward. In the short run the
firm will maximize profits by supplying
250 hours of bookkeeping service per
week at a price of $40 per hour. With an
average cost of $30 per hour, Bleak will
earn an economic profit of $10 per hour,
or $2500 per week. As new firms enter
the industry to compete for economic
profits, the demand for Bleak's services
in the long run will decline. Entry will
continue until Bleak and its competitors
earn only normal profits. In part (b) you
can see that the best operating position
for Bleak is 400 hours of service per
week.

makes its short-run decisions without considering whether other firms will react
to its decision. It considers the general range of prices charged for similar services.
But it can (within limits) raise and lower its price without having much, if any,
effect on competitors because of its relatively small size. Thus independent decision making is an important feature of monopolistic competition. Firms cannot
get together and agree on one price, so they do not have collective market power.
Limited market power adds to the competitive nature of the industry.

Long-Run Equilibrium

The long-run equilibrium position of a monopolistically competitive firm can
be predicted from the most important long-run characteristic of the market: Entry
and exit are relatively unrestricted. This lack of barriers is also characteristic of
pure competition and thus another competitive feature of monopolistic competition.

When entry and exit are easy, we expect a long-run response to economic
profits and losses. Economic profits will attract new firms. Exhibit 12.2(b) shows
the effects of entry on Bleak Bookkeeping: Demand for Bleak's services has
decreased and become more price elastic [compare D_1 in (a) with D_2 in (b)]. This
result makes sense when we realize that the entry of new firms means that Bleak

(b) Long-run equilibrium

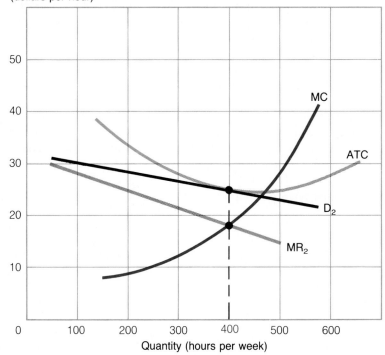

Price
(dollars per hour)

will have a smaller share of total market demand. Moreover, with new firms offering competitive services, demand will be more price elastic. With the new demand, Bleak's best quantity (where MR_2 = MC) is now 400 hours per week and its best price is $25 per hour. Because average total cost is also $25 per hour at this point, Bleak earns only a normal profit.

But there is a difference between monopolistic competition and pure competition. Because demand is not *perfectly* price elastic (horizontal), Bleak is not operating at the minimum point on its average total cost curve, as it would under pure competition. We consider the implications of this condition later, when we describe how monopolistic competition affects technical efficiency.

Because of the large number of relatively close substitutes and the ease of entry and exit, the level of profits in most monopolistically competitive industries is generally quite low. In fact, many firms incur economic losses. Low profits and a high risk of failure help to explain why so many monopolistically competitive firms, like restaurants and retail stores, go out of business each year.

Economic profit and opportunity cost. Studies of monopolistically competitive markets show that some firms in such industries barely survive and many fold, while others are able to earn significant profits over the long run. How can we reconcile this fact with the prediction that monopolistically competitive

Nonprice competition. Competing with other firms using approaches such as advertising and product differentiation instead of changing price.

firms will earn only normal profits over the long run? The answer lies, in part, in the difference between economic profits and accounting profits.

Let's consider two fast-food restaurants. One has an ideal location just off a busy highway, next to a large shopping center. As a result, it earns more money (and thus makes larger accounting profits) than a similar restaurant located in an out-of-the-way spot. But both firms may really earn only normal profits when we consider the *opportunity costs* of all the resources each uses.

The two restaurants do not use the same resources and do not have the same opportunity costs. The restaurant with the ideal location has a higher opportunity cost, because its location can be rented or sold for a higher price than can the poorer location. Thus the higher accounting profits of the restaurant with the better location still leave it with only a normal profit from the economic standpoint. (Note that the higher accounting profit reflects the higher value of the location, not the restaurant.)

Nonprice Competition

Sometimes monopolistically competitive firms may earn true economic profits. This ability depends, in part, on whether they can create relatively permanent and marketable product differences through **nonprice competition**. Because price depends on demand, the purpose of nonprice competition is to both increase demand and decrease price elasticity of demand.

In some cases, firms can earn economic profits by convincing consumers that their products are far superior to any substitutes. For example, a trial lawyer with a reputation for winning big cases may be able to charge higher fees and earn more than her competitors. Bayer aspirin consistently sells for more than other brands, even though all brands of aspirin have the same ingredients. Note that nonprice differences do not have to be real, only that consumers *believe* them to be and are willing to pay for the difference.

Advertising and other forms of product promotion are also forms of nonprice competition. They stress product differences and attempt to persuade consumers that one product is in some ways more desirable than another. For example, Frank Perdue has successfully used advertising to persuade shoppers that his chickens are better than those of other producers.

Does advertising help or hurt efficiency in a market economy? Advertising has come under fire from some economists who charge that some ads are misleading at best. They also fear that advertising has allowed large firms to grow at the expense of small firms that cannot afford advertising. Advertising raises producer—and thus potentially consumer—costs.

But other economists see benefits to advertising. It provides information to consumers and improves technical efficiency by fostering company growth. Those economists cite studies showing that advertising reduces the price consumers pay for goods and services. For example, one study concluded that eyeglass prices were 25 to 30 percent higher in states that restricted advertising.[*] A similar study found lower prescription drug prices in states that allowed advertising.[†] And nearly all economists agree that insofar as advertising is a form of competition, restricting it may cause allocative inefficiency.

[*] Lee Benham, "The Effect of Advertising on the Price of Eyeglasses," *Journal of Law and Economics*, October 1972, pp. 337–352.
[†] John F. Cady, "An Estimate of the Price Effects of Restrictions on Drug Price Advertising," *Economic Inquiry*, December 1976, pp. 493–510.

Like all rational decisions, the decision to engage in nonprice competition forces firms to weigh the potential benefits and costs. Thus a firm will advertise if it expects to increase revenues more than costs by doing so. But, of course, there is no guarantee that advertising will raise revenues. Monopolistically competitive firms are limited in their ability to influence the market. Without this limitation, a firm could always recover from an economic loss by spending more for advertising or by altering its product. Unfortunately for the firm (but fortunately for society), it cannot.

Earlier we discussed the short-run and long-run equilibrium positions for a monopolistically competitive firm. In that example, we ignored nonprice competition. We assumed that Bleak Bookkeeping had already made its best decision with respect to advertising and other forms of nonprice competition and thus its demand was given. Without that assumption, determining a final equilibrium position would require analysis of the market *after* changes in promotional and other nonprice policies.

When nonprice competition is profitable, maximizing profits can be complex. A firm in a purely competitive market has only one basic decision to make: how much to sell at the existing market price. Because other firms sell virtually identical products, price takers have virtually no opportunities for nonprice competition. A monopolistically competitive firm (and, as we describe later, an oligopolistic firm) must not only choose the best price but also select and develop the best product. It must also determine how much to spend on advertising and other forms of promotion. Because nonprice policies affect both costs and demand, the combination of policies that maximizes profits cannot be easily determined or modeled. The broader range of possible outcomes complicates the strategy for maximizing profits.

Monopolistic Competition and Efficiency

Economists are also interested in whether an imperfect market structure produces results that are imperfect from society's perspective. Will firms in monopolistically competitive industries provide consumers with the best mix of products? Will they produce at minimum cost?

The two basic questions we ask about the mix of products (allocative efficiency) are: (1) Does marginal social benefit equal marginal social cost when the firm reaches short-run equilibrium? and (2) Does the typical firm earn a normal profit in the long run? Under monopolistic competition, the answer to both questions is "almost, but not quite." But in such markets firms have relatively little market power, and entry and exit are relatively unrestricted. Thus a monopolistically competitive industry comes very close to reaching optimal allocative efficiency.

Exhibit 12.3 shows demand and marginal costs for haircuts at the Clip Joint, a monopolistically competitive firm. We assume that other conditions for a perfect market—no external costs or benefits, for example—are met. Thus demand represents the extra benefit consumers receive from the last haircut demanded, or the marginal social benefit (D = MSB). We can also equate marginal cost with marginal social cost (MC = MSC). To achieve allocative efficiency, haircuts must be produced up to the point where an additional haircut would cost society more than it is worth. Thus 105 haircuts per week (where MSB = MSC) would be the best quantity from society's perspective.

Price and cost
(dollars per haircut)

Exhibit 12.3
Monopolistic Competition and Efficiency
This graph shows the long-run equilibrium position for the Clip Joint, a monopolistically competitive firm. With no externalities, demand equals marginal social benefits (D = MSB), and marginal cost equals marginal social cost (MC = MSC). To maximize profits, the Clip Joint will supply only 100 haircuts per week (where MR = MC), or less than the 105 haircuts that achieve allocative efficiency (where MSB = MSC). The red-shaded triangular area represents the magnitude of allocative inefficiency. However, because of easy entry the Clip Joint cannot earn more than a normal profit in the long run. With a demand curve that slopes downward, the firm will not produce at the minimum point on its average cost curve. Thus to a small degree, the Clip Joint is technically inefficient.

But the Clip Joint, like any rational firm, will maximize profits by producing only 100 haircuts per week (where MR = MC), or less than the allocatively efficient quantity. Like a monopolist, a monopolistically competitive firm produces too little from society's perspective. Each additional haircut from 100 to 105 per week adds more to social benefits than to social costs. The opportunity cost to society—the cost of allocative efficiency—is measured by the red-shaded triangle.

The reason for this inefficiency is the same as for the monopolist: a demand curve that slopes downward. Because the firm has some market power, marginal revenue (the extra benefit to the firm) is less than demand (the extra benefit to society). However, market power under monopolistic competition is severely limited by the relatively large number of firms in an industry. As a result, the amount of allocative inefficiency is typically quite small.

The firm in a monopolistically competitive market not only has limited short-run market power, but virtually no long-run market power because of relatively easy entry. Thus profits of firms in monopolistically competitive industries tend to reach the normal level over the long run. Exhibit 12.3 shows the Clip Joint in long-run equilibrium. At its profit-maximizing output, price and average cost are the same, so the Clip Joint earns only a normal profit.

RECAP ▬▬▬▬▬▬▬

Monopolistic competition is a market structure with a relatively large number of relatively small firms. Barriers to entry are quite small. Products are distinctive or differentiated through nonprice competition, such as advertising. Thus each firm has a small amount of market power.

The demand curve for an individual firm's product slopes downward. Because many competitors produce similar products, however, demand is quite price elastic, giving the firm very little market power and creating only slight allocative inefficiency.

Because barriers to entry are small, a firm may not expect to earn much more than a normal profit in the long run.

Finally, Exhibit 12.3 illustrates another potential concern about monopolistic competition. The Clip Joint does not produce at the minimum point on its average cost curve, so some technical inefficiency results. Some economists believe that there are too many firms in a monopolistically competitive industry when this result occurs. If there were fewer firms, each could produce more, and average cost would be lower. The large number of gasoline service stations and fast-food restaurants are real-world evidence of this effect.

Considering all factors, are monopolistically competitive firms good for society? On the negative side, a small degree of allocative inefficiency results from a small amount of market power. There are also potential technical inefficiency and the costs associated with product differentiation and advertising.

On the positive side, competition in such industries is clearly vigorous. Because firms have very limited market power, in the long run they can expect to earn only normal profits. Thus they are forced to respond to changes in consumer demand and in resource supplies. In addition, consumers may select from a wide variety of products. On balance, most economists emphasize the competitive nature of this market structure and deemphasize its monopolistic element.

MONOPOLISTIC COMPETITION IN ACTION

The restaurant industry closely fits the model of monopolistic competition. There are many sellers: Some 500,000 establishments employed more than 8 million workers and generated more than $125 billion in sales in 1981.[*] However, most restaurants are small, both in absolute terms (such as annual sales) and relative to the total market.

Product differentiation is also evident. Restaurants range from short-order cafes to gourmet dining establishments and offer low-priced hamburgers to high-priced continental cuisine. A major competitive practice is the use of nonprice competition. Small restaurants are always looking for some special feature that will make customers want to come back and bring their friends. Advertising is heavily used by the fast-food portion of the industry. Those firms spend millions of dollars annually to persuade consumers that the Whopper beats the Big Mac or that Wendy's has the beef.

Finally, entry and exit are relatively easy. An entrant can begin with a small restaurant, requiring only a moderate investment, and test the market. Ease of entry means that even large, successful establishments still face competition and may not be able to exercise market power. And each year, many restaurants fold—some because they were not distinctive enough, others because they could not afford to advertise. (Of course, some restaurants fail because of poor management or poor food or poor service, but such failures indicate that the market is working to provide technical efficiency.) An industry rule of thumb is that almost half of all restaurants fail to survive their first year of business, and only 20 percent last as long as five years.[†]

---

[*] Data from "Restaurant Industry Operations Report '81," National Restaurant Association.
[†] Douglas C. Keister, *Food and Beverage Control.* Englewood Cliffs, N.J.: Prentice-Hall, 1977, p. 5.

OLIGOPOLY

Not all markets resemble the models that we have developed so far. For example, the soft-drink industry is dominated by two giant firms: Coca-Cola and PepsiCo. Similarly, the five largest firms in the beer industry—Anheuser-Busch, Miller, Stroh, Heileman, and Coors—accounted for almost 90 percent of all beer sales in the United States in 1984.[*] What can we say about industries that have only a few dominant firms? Do those firms compete? Is competition sufficient to ensure satisfaction of consumer demand and production at minimum cost?

Model of Oligopoly

The soft-drink, beer, automobile, computer, compact disc player, steel, and oil refining industries are all examples of the model of **oligopoly**. The characteristics of an oligopolistic market are:

1. A small number of relatively large firms.
2. The presence of significant barriers to entry.

This definition does not describe the products produced because there are two types of oligopolies. In one type—steel and oil refining, for example—products are relatively uniform. In the other type—automobiles, computers, and breakfast cereals, for example—products are highly differentiated.

The most important characteristic of an oligopolistic market is that it contains only a few competitors. When there are large numbers of firms—as in pure competition or monopolistic competition—no single firm can influence the market. Each firm can decide how much to supply—and, in the case of monopolistic competition, how much to advertise—without worrying about the reaction of other firms in its industry. A monopolist has no competitors, so it can also ignore other firms when it makes price decisions. The differences between the models of oligopoly, competition, and monopoly are summarized in Exhibit 12.4.

Because there are only a few firms in an oligopolistic market, firms are *mutually interdependent*. That is, when one firm makes a strategic decision—pricing, advertising, or product differentiation, for example—demand for competitors' products is affected. Successful advertising by IBM will increase sales of IBM computers and, at the same time, reduce sales of Apple and other brands of computers.

Moreover, oligopolistic firms must forecast the probable reactions of competitors and plan their strategies accordingly. Let's say that General Motors decides to announce a price reduction. It knows ahead of time that demand for Ford and Toyota automobiles will be affected and that the ultimate effect of its price change will depend on how they react. If Ford and Toyota ignore the price decrease, GM can sell many more cars (and its rivals many fewer). But the increase in GM sales will be much smaller if the other firms match the price reduction.

The broad range of possible behavior in oligopolistic industries is also a challenge to economists. No one simple model can be used to describe oligopolies. There are no simple answers to the questions posed in the introduction to this section. We discuss several possible models later in this section.

Oligopoly. A market structure in which a relatively small number of relatively large firms each produces goods or services that are close substitutes or are somewhat differentiated. Barriers to entry are typically high. Firms must consider the actions and reactions of competitors when making decisions.

---

[*] An interesting description of the beer industry (and the data cited in this paragraph) can be found in Kenneth G. Elzinga, "The Beer Industry." In Walter Adams (Ed.), *The Structure of American Industry*, 7th ed. New York: Macmillan, 1986, pp. 203–238.

Characteristic	Pure competition	Oligopoly	Pure monopoly
Number of firms	Many small firms	Few large firms	Single seller
Related products	Each firm's product is a very close substitute; almost identical products	Products may be differentiated or may be very close substitutes	Firm's product has no close substitute
Barriers to entry and exit	No barriers to entry or exit	Significant barriers to entry and exit	High barriers prevent entry and exit

Exhibit 12.4
Comparison of Pure Competition, Oligopoly, and Pure Monopoly

The second characteristic—barriers to entry—is the reason why there are only a few firms in an oligopoly. As we noted in the discussion of monopoly, there are several types of barriers: (1) control of essential raw materials; (2) economies of scale; and (3) legal constraints on entry, such as patents or licenses. In some cases (especially with government franchises), the barriers cause a monopoly to exist. In other cases, a few firms can hurdle the barriers and create an oligopoly.

Pricing Policies

As for all market structures, we assume that each firm in an oligopoly acts rationally to maximize profits. However, the mutual interdependence of firms in oligopolies makes all decision making more complex. Decision making is much like a game of chess. In order to discover the best move, you have to size up your current strengths (and weaknesses) and also consider what moves your opponents might make.

Impact of a price increase. Suppose that you are the manager of the Fun Valley Ski Lodge and are trying to decide what price to charge next season for lift tickets. Last season the price was $25 per day. If you and all the other nearby ski areas maintain this price, you can expect to sell 4000 tickets per week (point e in Exhibit 12.5). However, you are considering raising the price to $30 per day. Whether this increase will be profitable depends in large part on how the managers of three other nearby ski areas respond.

If you raise the price of lift tickets at Fun Valley and the other ski areas keep their prices at $25 per day, you can expect a large drop in skiing at Fun Valley. In Exhibit 12.5, this result shows as a movement along D_1, the demand for Fun Valley tickets assuming that other areas do not change their prices. Curve D_1 shows that you can expect only 2000 die-hard fans of Fun Valley to ski each week if you increase price to $30 per day (point a). Total revenues will fall from $100,000, or ($25 per ticket)(4000 tickets), to $60,000, or ($30 per ticket)(2000 tickets), per week. Thus if one or more areas keep last season's price, Fun Valley and the other ski areas will be forced to return to the old price.

In fact, this same pattern occurs frequently in the automobile and steel industries. One firm will announce a price increase and wait to see what other firms do. If, as sometimes happens, other firms announce smaller increases or no

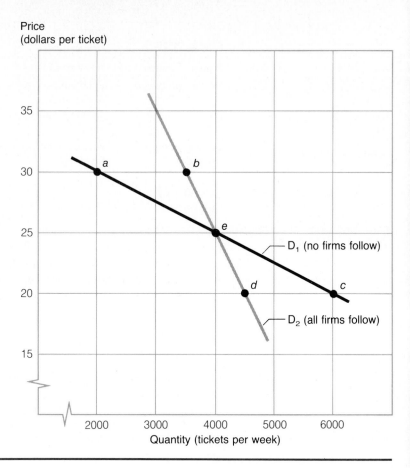

Exhibit 12.5
Demand Under Conditions
of Oligopoly
This graph shows the demand for ski lift
tickets at Fun Valley Lodge. At the current price of $25 per ticket, the lodge
sells 4000 tickets per week. If Fun Valley
increases the price to $30, the number of
tickets it sells depends on the reaction of
the other ski areas. If none of them
raises its price, Fun Valley can expect to
sell only 2000 tickets per week (point a
on D_1). If other areas also raise their
prices, sales will fall to only 3500 (point b
on D_2). If Fun Valley lowers its price to
$20 and the other areas do not lower
their prices, it can expect 6000 skiers
(point c on D_1). If the other areas also
lower their prices, Fun Valley can expect
only 4500 skiers (point d on D_2). Like
any oligopolist, Fun Valley must predict
the reactions of its competitors when deciding whether to change its price.

increases, the first firm will announce that it has reevaluated the situation. It will
reduce its price, often implying that it is doing so in the interest of its customers.
Competing on the basis of price is a risky business in oligopolistic situations. It is
hard to justify a price increase if the other firms do not follow.

Returning to our skiing example, if all the ski areas decide to charge $30 per
day, we use D_2—the demand if all ski areas change price—to see the effects. At
the higher price fewer skiers will ski at all the areas. But in this case, *relative*
prices at the four ski areas do not change. Fun Valley therefore will not experience
as large a drop in ticket sales as it did when it had the highest prices in the area.
Exhibit 12.5 shows that if all ski areas raise their prices, Fun Valley will sell 3500
tickets per week (point b). Under these conditions, you can justify raising price.
Total revenues will increase from $100,000 to $105,000, or ($30 per ticket) ($3500
tickets), per week.

Impact of a price decrease.   Predicting the response of other firms is
also important when considering a price decrease. In Exhibit 12.5, you can see
that a price decrease at Fun Valley makes more sense when other firms do not
follow than when they do. If you cut the price at Fun Valley to $20 per day and
none of the other firms follow, you can expect to sell 6000 tickets per week (a
movement along D_1 to point c). This move would increase your revenues to

RECAP

Oligopoly is a market structure dominated by a few relatively large firms. Barriers to entry are typically large, isolating existing firms somewhat from external competitors.

Because each firm can have a significant impact on other firms, the actions and reactions of competitors must be considered when making decisions.

A price increase by one firm will be an unprofitable decision if other firms do not match the increase. A price decrease by one firm will be less desirable when other firms match the decrease.

$120,000, or ($20 per ticket)(6000 tickets), per week, largely at the expense of the other ski areas. But if the others also lower their prices, you can expect to sell only 4500 tickets per week (a movement along D_2 to point d), bringing in only $90,000 in revenue.

This analysis illustrates the complexity of pricing decisions, but it does not tell us what the best decision is or what the outcome will be. However, we can draw three conclusions from it: (1) the best decision depends on the response of competitors; (2) all the firms can improve their revenues (and profits) if they all agree to raise prices; and (3) if the firms engage in a price war, all will end up with lower profits. Because price competition lowers profits, oligopolistic firms have an incentive to avoid price competition.

Of course, such firms do sometimes engage in price competition. The airline industry in the mid-1980s is a good case in point. But price competition usually will not increase a firm's market share, especially if all firms face similar cost conditions. Individual firms have little to gain by engaging in price competition. Other firms are forced to respond in kind to protect their markets. Although price-cutting wars benefit consumers, they usually result in lower profits for virtually all producers and sometimes drive weaker firms out of the industry altogether.

Pricing Decisions: A Game-Theory Approach

We noted earlier that decision making in an oligopolistic market is much like a chess game. In fact, economists have found it useful to model oligopolies using an approach known as *game theory*. We can use our skiing example to illustrate this approach and to arrive at some important conclusions about behavior in oligopolistic markets.

Knowing the likely outcomes of price changes in the local skiing market, you might be tempted to call the managers of the other ski areas and make the following proposition: "Why don't we all agree to charge $30 per ticket?" If everyone agrees—and sticks to the agreement—each of you can increase your total revenues. In fact, the temptation to agree *not to compete* is strong in all oligopolies. But your maximum payoff occurs if you can drop your price to $20 per ticket while the other areas keep theirs at $25. By cheating on the agreement, you can increase your profits to $120,000 per week—largely at the expense of your rivals, of course. This temptation to cheat on agreements is also strong.

Cartels: A Formal Agreement on Prices

Although game theory does not indicate what firms will do, it does suggest that benefits can be gained from cooperative, instead of competitive, behavior. One way to cooperate is to enter into a formal agreement to fix prices and/or to share markets. Such an arrangement is called a **cartel**. As long as everyone continues to cooperate, a cartel can maximize the collective profits of its members. However, cartels face major practical problems.

Cartel. A form of oligopoly in which firms formally agree to establish a common price, in effect acting as a monopoly.

Maximizing collective profits. In theory, a cartel acts like a monopolist. That is, it compares marginal revenue (derived from the industry demand curve) and marginal cost (the sum of individual producers' marginal costs) to find the best quantity to sell. It then finds the best price from the industry demand curve.

Each firm would, by agreement, charge this profit-maximizing price. But to maximize collective profits, the cartel must restrict supply. If the same amount is offered for sale at a higher price, a surplus will result, putting downward pressure on price.

Three conditions must be met for a cartel to succeed. First, the industry's product must have a fairly price-inelastic demand. That is, there must be few close substitutes for a cartel's product. Otherwise, total revenues will fall if a cartel raises price. Second, a cartel must organize the major producers in an industry. Otherwise, nonmembers will compete with the cartel, and it cannot sustain a high price. And finally, for long-run success, barriers to entry must exist. Otherwise, higher profits will attract new entrants, threatening a cartel's control.

Practical difficulties faced by cartels. In practice, the three conditions are seldom met. A cartel can maximize collective profits only by restricting supply. But the need to restrict supply creates two problems. First, *members often disagree about cartel price and production policies* because of different costs or objectives. Second, even if all agree on policy matters, *individual members have a strong incentive to cheat the cartel.* It is in the collective interest of cartel members to restrict total output. But it is in the individual interest of each firm to produce and sell as much as possible at or even below the cartel price. Thus a successful cartel must have some way to detect cheating and to discipline individual members. Establishing and enforcing production controls on members—each of which has an incentive to want a larger share—is a major obstacle to cartel success.

Despite these problems, a cartel may be in the best interests of an industry as a whole. But it is clearly not in the best interests of society, for the same reasons a monopoly is undesirable. Most cartels are unlawful in the United States, as are informal arrangements to fix prices. However, the federal government has sanctioned cartels in several industries, including until 1978, the airline industry. (We discuss the rationale offered for allowing such legalized cartels in Chapter 17, the specific case of the airline industry in Chapter 19.) Cartels are not uncommon internationally. The best known current example is the Organization of Petroleum Exporting Countries (OPEC).

OPEC: A cartel in action. The story of OPEC illustrates the requirements for a successful cartel, the benefits of collective price setting, and the difficulties of maintaining a cartel. The market for oil is a likely candidate for a cartel. There are few good short-run substitutes for oil, making short-run demand relatively price inelastic. Thus an oil cartel could raise market price significantly and receive more total revenues for selling less. In fact, from 1973 to 1980, OPEC—aided by some good fortune—raised oil prices from less than $3 to more than $30 per barrel.

OPEC was formed in 1960, and at the time, the event attracted little notice. Initially cartel members could not reach agreement on supply limits and the cartel had little market power. By the early 1970s, however, the governments of the Middle East oil-producing nations had wrested control of oil resources away from the major international oil companies. For the first time, control of these oil resources came into the hands of cartel members. Although OPEC–member nations accounted for only 40 percent of world oil production, they accounted for 90 percent of world exports, giving the cartel the *potential* for significant market power.

Most people first heard of OPEC in 1973–1974, when partly as a result of cartel actions, the world market price of oil quadrupled. In addition to the nationalization of Middle East oil production, several events combined to give OPEC the opening it needed. First, oil production in the United States peaked in 1970, but demand for oil continued to rise. Second, U.S. limits on oil imports imposed in the 1950s and 1960s were eliminated in 1973, while price limits were placed on domestic oil. The overall result was a large shift in U.S. demand to imported oil. The boost in demand provided an opportunity for OPEC to exercise significant market power.

In October 1973, the seven Arab members of OPEC announced a cutback in production and the first of a series of price increases that brought the world market price from less than $3 to more than $12 a barrel. At least part of the short-run success of OPEC can be attributed to the role played by its most powerful member, Saudi Arabia. Recall that in order to succeed, a cartel must lower supply enough to cause a price increase. During the 1970s, Saudi Arabia, with one-third of the cartel's productive reserves, allowed other members to sell as much as they wanted to produce at the going cartel price. The Saudis reduced their own production to prevent a surplus. This self-sacrifice, together with continued growth in demand in the 1970s, enabled OPEC to avoid production controls at the time. Events in the 1970s strongly favored the cartel, and by the end of the decade oil prices had increased to more than $30 a barrel.

Since that time, decreased demand and increased supply have combined to limit OPEC's market power and reduce prices. The short-run demand for oil is rather price inelastic, but long-run demand is considerably more price elastic. Higher prices stimulated efforts to develop substitutes and to conserve. As a result, demand for oil decreased: In 1984, worldwide oil consumption was 39 million barrels per day compared with 47 million in 1973.

On the supply side, the discovery of additional oil reserves in the North Sea, the North Slope of Alaska, and Mexico greatly increased the supply of oil by non–OPEC members. In addition, several oil-producing nations, including Iran, Nigeria, and Mexico, have increased their oil production in efforts to solve internal economic problems. Indeed, the recent failures of OPEC to agree on production controls have led some observers to question whether OPEC ever operated as a cartel. The world price for oil fell to $12 a barrel in the spring of 1986, but had rebounded to about $18 a barrel by early in 1987. However, some observers predict that the price is ultimately headed for $6 to $8 a barrel, which they view as the long-run competitive equilibrium price. The cartel's internal problems and the current conditions in the oil market make it unlikely that OPEC will be able to force price up by any significant amount.

Price Leadership: A Tacit Understanding

In the absence of a formal agreement to fix prices, oligopolistic firms may reach a tacit understanding not to engage in price competition. Such arrangements may occur because past price wars proved that most of the firms in an industry are strong enough to inflict and sustain considerable damage or because one or more large firms dominate the market and punish price cutters. When individual firms in an oligopoly recognize that price competition is not in their best interests,

Price leadership. A form of oligopoly in which one firm—the leader—initially sets prices and other firms follow with matching increases or decreases. A tacit understanding rather than a formal agreement binds the firms.

they may agree informally to avoid price competition. If they do, how can they establish prices?

The model of **price leadership** describes behavior in industries in which one or more firms eventually emerge to lead. Often the price leader is the strongest firm in the industry (Campbell in the soup industry or Kodak in the film industry, for example). In other cases, a firm brave enough to present an industry response to a change in conditions may become its leader. Regardless of why a price leader assumes that position, its role is basically to assess the effect of economic changes and make the appropriate industry response. Other firms are expected to fall in line.

The price leader must recognize that the best industry price is not necessarily the one that maximizes short-run profits. If barriers to entry are based on cost advantages for existing firms, too high a price will allow less efficient firms to enter the market. The best price may be one that is low enough to keep potential competitors out. This approach can maximize long-run profits by maintaining the current industry structure although short-term profits are lower.

Like cartels, price leadership can work only so long as one firm continues to dominate or others continue to follow. When entry is relatively easy, however, new firms may destroy price stability. This situation occurred in both the steel and automobile industries in the 1970s. The emergence of new and strong competitors in Japan and West Germany caused significant price competition in those industries, which had previously had stable price leadership. The prime beneficiaries of this increased competition were the consumers of steel and autos. The U.S. firms responded by lobbying the federal government to set import quotas to protect their industries from outside competition.

Nonprice Competition in Oligopolistic Industries

As we have noted, firms in oligopolies often decide that price competition is not a good way to maximize profits. Price wars can simply lower total industry profits (and, of course, make consumers very happy). In such cases, competition may be confined largely to nonprice competition. Like other decisions, however, the success of nonprice competition depends on the reaction of other firms.

We can illustrate this point with an industry having only two firms: Addison, Inc., and Wesley Corporation. Each must decide whether to engage in a large-scale or small-scale advertising campaign next year. In Exhibit 12.6 we see that Addison's expected profits depend not only on its choice, but also on Wesley's choice. If both firms decide to advertise only a little, each can expect profits of $100,000 next year. On the other hand, if both advertise a lot, each can expect profits of $60,000 per year. That is, total industry demand will not rise enough to enable the firms to recover the extra costs of their advertising campaigns.

Exhibit 12.6 shows that the firms will earn more if each decides on a limited advertising campaign. But if Addison advertises only a little and Wesley advertises a lot, Addison's profits will fall to only $25,000, while Wesley's increase to $200,000. If it has no way of knowing what Wesley will do, Addison will run a significant risk if it does not advertise a lot.

If Wesley Corporation advertises . . .	If Addison, Inc., advertises . . .	
	a little	a lot
A little	Both firms earn $100,000 per year	Addison earns $200,000 per year Wesley earns $25,000 per year
A lot	Addison earns $25,000 per year Wesley earns $200,000 per year	Both firms earn $60,000 per year

Exhibit 12.6
Payoff Table for Advertising Decision

If neither firm has any knowledge of the other's plans, each will be strongly tempted to undertake a major advertising campaign. This choice will result in the largest minimum payoff each can receive. That is, Addison can receive no less than $60,000 by advertising a lot and may receive more if Wesley does not advertise a lot or is late getting started on a large-scale campaign.

Although we can use this model to predict the amount of advertising the firms will do, it is based on assumptions about the predictability of the firm's behavior. Using different assumptions about their behavior—for example, that both will agree to advertise a little—another decision will be best for Addison.

Oligopoly and Inefficiency

Because the behavior of oligopolies is very different from that of other market structures, we cannot draw precise conclusions about efficiency. The evidence from economic studies does not reveal any consistent finding that industries with only a few firms are more or less inefficient than industries with many firms. The presence of many relatively small firms almost guarantees competitive behavior. And relatively unrestricted entry almost always leads to long-run normal profits. But we cannot draw the opposite conclusions when there are only a few firms or when barriers to entry limit the number of firms.

Although some studies have shown that oligopolistic industries have higher profits, others have presented the opposite conclusion. Getting consistent conclusions is difficult, in part, because data show accounting profits, not economic profits. Moreover, even if higher economic profits are found, this condition may well be only temporary (short-run profits generated by innovative firms) or an indication of superior technical efficiency.

Economists generally agree that oligopolies will seek to avoid competition. When firms can prevent or significantly limit competition—by formation of a cartel, for example—the industry will operate inefficiently. However, any assessment of efficiency requires an examination of the specific circumstances and behavior of a particular oligopoly.

RECAP

In a cartel, firms formally agree to sell at the same price. To raise price the cartel must establish and enforce production limits.

In price leadership, firms tacitly agree not to engage in price competition.

Because of the variety of situations, it is impossible to establish theoretically whether oligopoly necessarily leads to inefficiency.

OLIGOPOLY IN ACTION

The following examples are intended to give you an idea of some oligopolistic situations and the changes that occur in those industries as circumstances change. Although these examples cannot be said to be typical—for there is no typical model—they do provide two real-world examples of oligopolies in action.

Breakfast-Cereal Industry

The market for ready-to-eat breakfast cereals in the United States is an oligopolistic industry in which a few firms are very closely related and act accordingly.[*] The behavior of this industry closely follows the model of a **mature oligopoly**. In a mature oligopoly:

1. Very few interdependent firms dominate (a situation known as "industry concentration").
2. There is little or no price competition.
3. Firms rely on nonprice competition to maintain or increase market share.
4. There is little or no entry or exit of existing firms.
5. The responses of competitors to economic changes are predictable.
6. Existing competitors are tolerated and accepted.

As you can see, in a mature oligopoly firms operate in many respects as a unit. Although formal market sharing is not a feature of the industry, firms do not attempt to eliminate existing rivals or radically change market shares. The result is considerable stability and often a lack of many forms of competition.

The mature-oligopoly model accurately describes the breakfast-cereal industry in the United States over most of its recent history. It is one of the most heavily concentrated industries in the United States: In 1982, the four largest firms accounted for about 85 percent of all industry sales. Kellogg, the largest firm, had 39 percent of industry sales, followed by General Mills with 21 percent, General Foods with 16 percent, and the Quaker Oats Company with 9 percent.

In most such industries, concentration tends to decline as new firms enter in response to economic profits. But the breakfast-cereal industry has actually become more concentrated. In 1935 the four top firms accounted for only 65 percent of all sales. Between 1940 and 1970, no sizable firm entered, despite high average after-tax industry profits. (Between 1958 and 1970, after-tax accounting profits represented an average return on investment of almost 20 percent, compared to less than 9 percent for all manufacturing industries.)

The lack of successful entry can be traced to current advantages of the existing firms and their willingness and ability to respond to new challengers. As in other mature oligopolies, the breakfast-cereal firms do not engage in price competition. Product differentiation precludes one standard price, but because the products

Mature oligopoly. A form of oligopoly in which there is little or no price competition, little or no entry or exit of existing firms, reliance on nonprice competition, predictable responses to economic changes, and mutual tolerance and acceptance among existing rival firms.

---

[*] The material in this section is drawn heavily from F. M. Scherer, "The Breakfast Cereal Industry." In Walter Adams (Ed.), *The Structure of American Industry*, 7th ed. New York: Macmillan, 1986, pp. 172–202.

are close substitutes, prices are confined to a narrow range. In order to stay cost competitive, a firm must build a plant with the capacity to produce some 6 to 7 percent of the total industry output. The substantial initial investment required helps keep new firms out.

However, the industry, in the words of a Kellogg executive, is "virtually free from destructive pricing and promotional practices that—in many similar product categories—have undermined the vitality that is so necessary to their industry's continued progress."[*] Clearly, he viewed the lack of price competition as a good thing (which it is for Kellogg). Other quasi-pricing practices, including coupons, "in-pack premiums," and trade allowances, are used in the industry. However, their use is limited by the principle that what one firm does, the other firms will do shortly. In other words, because all the established firms follow the same practices, they do not undercut each other's position.

However, breakfast-cereal firms do engage in nonprice competition: specifically, in product development and advertising. The industry produces numerous products, with the top four firms alone producing some 65 brands of cereals. But in order to be successful, a product must capture at least 1 percent of total industry sales. Only one of the many new brands introduced in the 1960s (Cap'n Crunch) was able to capture as much as 2 percent of industry sales. While developing or improving products provides some social benefits in the form of wider consumer choice, the difficulty of achieving success has limited the number of successful firms in this industry.

Advertising of established products in the breakfast-cereal industry is unusually high. Advertising expenditures average 3.8 percent of sales for all consumer products, but in the breakfast-cereal industry they amount to an incredible 18.5 percent of sales, a figure exceeded only by the toiletry and soap products industry. Whether the advertising actually helps to increase sales or is necessary simply to maintain them is debatable, as is the effect of advertising on allocative efficiency. What is certain is that advertising costs constitute an important barrier to entry because successful introduction of new products requires significant expenditures for advertising and other product promotions.

We can best illustrate the willingness and ability of the market to respond to outside challengers—even in the face of popular new products—by noting the brief history of the "natural cereals" boom. Beginning in the late 1960s, a number of small or little-known companies began to produce natural granola-type cereals. The sale of these products, ignored at first by the large companies because sales were small, began to skyrocket. By 1972, the big four had introduced their own natural cereals with major advertising campaigns. By 1974, the inroads by outsiders had been halted; the major companies had once again established their dominance.

The lesson for firms considering entry into the breakfast-cereal industry is clear. The established firms not only have cost advantages, but are willing and able to retaliate against new competitors by duplicating their successful products. At best, new firms can expect only limited, short-run success. The existence of strong barriers has resulted in long-run stability and higher-than-normal profits for the major producers of breakfast cereals.

---

[*] From F. M. Scherer, "The Breakfast Cereal Industry." In Walter Adams (Ed.), *The Structure of American Industry,* 7th ed. New York: Macmillan, 1986, p. 183.

Steel Industry

The story of the steel industry differs in important respects from that of the breakfast-cereal industry, despite the oligopolistic nature of both.* Unlike cereals, steel is an undifferentiated product. But more importantly, the breakfast-cereal industry has successfully fought off the entry of new firms and avoided price competition. In contrast, the harmony that once existed in the steel industry has been destroyed recently by several factors, including the rise of successful domestic and foreign competition.

For the purpose of this discussion, we can divide the history of the U.S. steel industry into two periods. Beginning with the creation of the giant U.S. Steel Corporation in 1901 (the result of mergers that put 65 percent of the domestic steel capacity under its control), the industry operated much as the price-leadership model predicts. As the dominant firm in the industry, U.S. Steel set prices for the industry. The industry even raised prices during the 1950s despite stable (and in some years, falling) demand. Indeed, steel prices seldom responded to changes in demand or cost conditions. Despite its dominant position, U.S. Steel did not attempt to eliminate its competitors. In fact, it set prices high enough to enable smaller and sometimes less efficient producers to survive.

With almost no price competition, price rigidity caused wide swings in sales and shifts in demand. Development and promotion of products had limited appeal because of product uniformity. Technical efficiency suffered, since the established steel firms had no interest in competing on any level.

The second period in the steel industry's history began in the 1960s and intensified during the 1970s. By the 1980s U.S. steel producers were no longer a dominant force in the world. Competition for the large steel producers came from both foreign companies and domestic "minimills"—smaller mills that use scrap as their primary resource. Imports accounted for less than 5 percent of total U.S. consumption in 1960 but for almost 27 percent in 1984. Minimills increased their share from less than 2 percent in the mid-1950s to 16 percent in 1984.

The emergence of competitors caused two important changes: (1) pricing became much more flexible; and (2) the large steel companies had to undertake a rapid, large-scale modernization program to cut production costs, using state-of-the-art technology. However, modernizing itself was costly, and competition left U.S. firms with small profits from which to finance modernization efforts.

The case of the steel industry shows some of the potentially harmful side effects of the stability and security that can accompany oligopoly. The relatively long period in which competition was absent was partly responsible for the failure of that industry to keep pace with modern technology. At present there is considerable competition in the steel industry. While this is good for consumers, the large U.S. steel companies have asked for—and received—government protection from foreign competition. But limits on competition, while they may be good for steel producers' profits in the short run, are not likely to lead to long-run technical or allocative efficiency.

---

* The material in this section is drawn heavily from Walter Adams and Hans Mueller, "The Steel Industry." In Walter Adams (Ed.), *The Structure of American Industry*, 7th ed. New York: Macmillan, 1986, pp. 74–125. These authors take issue with the continued classification of the steel industry as oligopolistic because of intense foreign competition.

CONTESTABLE MARKETS AND LONG-RUN ECONOMIC EFFICIENCY

In our discussion of each type of market structure, we have emphasized the number of firms in an industry and their size relative to total market demand. Traditionally, economists have believed that the number of existing firms in an industry determines the behavior of firms with respect to price and nonprice competition. But some economists have challenged this assumption, arguing that ease of entry and exit are far more important in determining behavior than the number of firms currently in an industry.

Consider, for example, a **contestable market**, that is, a market in which entry and exit have no cost and are unrestricted. What can we predict about the behavior of existing firms? First, we expect firms in such markets to earn no more than a normal profit. As we noted earlier, without barriers to entry, economic profits attract new firms. These firms produce goods or services that increase market supply, decrease market price, and drive profits to the normal level. Second, we expect firms in contestable markets to consider both existing and potential competitors. The absence of barriers to entry and exit means that prices will be set so as to yield only normal profits (and thus keep out new entrants), even if there is only one firm in the industry.

The market for airline service between two locations provides an example of a highly contestable market. Many airlines can provide service between any two cities in the United States. Suppose that the prices charged by those currently providing service between Denver and New York are relatively high and yield large profits. It will not take long for other firms to offer new flights that will force prices down to less profitable levels. The airlines currently serving those cities are, of course, aware of this possibility. They may choose to price either high enough to attract new competitors or low enough to earn only normal profits. In either case, the existence of potential rivals and the threat of new ones force competitive-market behavior.

Entry and exit are not costless in most industries and the strong conclusion of contestable market hypothesis does not apply where barriers are significant. But when there are few barriers to entry we can predict that entry and exit will operate to keep profits close to normal and to encourage firms to be technically efficient.

Consider the automobile industry. In the 1960s the large U.S. automobile producers believed themselves to be immune from competition. They enjoyed large economies of scale in production and an established position in U.S. markets. This view proved wrong when Japanese and European producers successfully penetrated the market. The newest entrant is South Korea, and the People's Republic of China may soon enter the market, although the total number of new entrants has not been large. However, profits earned by existing firms have attracted new entrants in sufficient numbers to reduce, if not eliminate, most economic profits.

Contestable market. A market with costless and unrestricted entry and exit.

Other industries, including the computer, video cassette recorder, compact disc player, and calculator industries, have all experienced the effects of increased competition from new entrants. In each case, entry of new firms helped drive down production costs and prices, while also increasing the rate of product innovation—all characteristics of competition.

CONCLUSION

This chapter completes our description of basic market structures. Economists use these models to describe and predict results for real-world industries, even though actual conditions and situations rarely fit the assumptions of the models perfectly. Still, they are useful in studying the economics of operating a firm.

In the last two chapters, we described certain situations in which market solutions can result in allocative and technical inefficiency. In later chapters, we will look at attempts by government to minimize these inefficiencies and to deal with equity issues. When competition has been considered inadequate, government has controlled the structure and behavior of firms in an attempt to improve on imperfect market solutions. These examples suggest that easy entry and exit may be sufficient to force markets to operate efficiently.

SUMMARY

1. In this chapter we discussed how producers make decisions under conditions of monopolistic competition and oligopoly, which are two market structures that fall between the models of competition and monopoly.

2. A monopolistically competitive industry has a large number of relatively small firms. Barriers to entry are quite low. Products are differentiated, however, giving each firm a small degree of market power.

3. The demand curve for a monopolistically competitive firm's product slopes downward, like that of a monopoly. But because many firms produce similar products, demand is quite price elastic, giving each firm very little market power. A firm makes price and supply decisions by comparing marginal revenue and marginal cost. However, marginal revenue is less than demand, so marginal social benefit exceeds marginal social cost at the firm's profit-maximizing level of output. Allocative inefficiency is small, since firms have little market power. Moreover, benefits of product variety may offset inefficiency to some extent.

4. A monopolistically competitive market has few significant barriers to entry or exit. However, entry is not necessarily unrestricted, as it is with the model of pure competition. Since barriers are low, the firm may not expect to earn much more than a normal profit in the long run.

5. Nonprice competition—that is, seeking to gain sales by advertising and product differentiation—is common in monopolistically competitive markets. This practice complicates decision making because the firm must choose not only the best level of output, but also the best product and the best level of advertising. Nonprice competition offers advantages and disadvantages from the social perspective, but economic models cannot adequately assess its impact on an industry's efficiency.

6. An oligopoly market is dominated by a few relatively large firms. Barriers to entry are typically high, some-what isolating existing firms from external competitors.

7. Each firm in an oligopoly market can have a significant impact on other firms, so the actions and reactions of competitors must be considered when making decisions. The results of a price increase or decrease by one firm depend on whether the others follow. Demand becomes very price elastic if only one firm raises its price, and that firm's revenues will fall. If all firms raise prices, total revenues may rise.

8. The risks of price competition are a strong inducement for collusion. In some cases, firms may form a cartel and formally agree to sell at the same price. To the extent that a cartel can also control supply, the firms in effect act like a monopoly, which benefits the firms but not society. But as the case of OPEC indicates, failure to control supply threatens the market power of a cartel. In fact, cartels historically have proved to be unstable.

9. In some cases, oligopolistic firms tacitly agree not to engage in price competition. In the model of price leadership, one firm acts as the leader, establishing a price that others follow. In the model of mature oligopoly, existing firms tolerate and accept current competitors but vigorously bar new firms. In both models, the result is little price competition.

10. Because of the difficulties involved in price competition, oligopolistic firms often rely on nonprice competition when seeking to gain or maintain market position.

11. The variety of situations included within the broad market structure makes it impossible to say whether oligopoly leads to inefficiency. Some oligopolistic markets offer technical efficiency as a result of economies of scale and technical knowledge gained through years of experience. In other cases, such as the steel industry, firms isolated from competition fail to adapt to changes in technology.

12. Some economists stress the importance of barriers to entry and exit over the number of current firms. For example, in a contestable market, entry and exit have no cost and are unrestricted, so long-run profits tend to be at normal levels. Unless existing firms behave competitively and price to earn normal profits, the market attracts new entrants who force profits to normal levels. While few markets are contestable, the lower the barriers to entry, the more likely it is that an industry's behavior will resemble competition.

KEY TERMS

Monopolistic competition, 287
Product differentiation, 289
Nonprice competition, 292
Oligopoly, 296
Cartel, 299
Price leadership, 302
Mature oligopoly, 304
Contestable market, 307

QUESTIONS FOR REVIEW AND DISCUSSION

1. In both of the imperfect market structures presented in this chapter, firms tend to engage in nonprice competition.
   a) What is meant by nonprice competition? What do firms hope to accomplish by using it?
   b) Why do monopolistically competitive firms engage in nonprice competition, whereas firms in competitive markets typically do not? Why, then, do the dairy and cotton industries advertise, since these industries are considered to be competitive?
   c) Why do oligopolistic firms prefer nonprice competition to price competition?
   d) Would a monopolistic firm engage in nonprice competition? Why or why not?
   e) In this chapter we noted that in some oligopolistic markets the products of different firms are relatively uniform. In what ways do these firms engage in nonprice competition?
2. In competitive markets when all firms charge the same price, we say that the result favors allocative efficiency. Why, then, are we concerned when the prices of firms in an oligopoly move together? Can you think of any reasons for common price movement in an oligopoly

that are acceptable from the social perspective? Any reasons that are unacceptable? Explain why in each case.
3. Based on the concepts presented in this chapter, explain why each of the following statements is true, false, or uncertain.
   a) The greater the differentiation of a firm's product, the greater is the firm's market power.
   b) Under oligopoly, a firm is more likely to raise or lower its price when it believes that other firms will follow.
4. Price competition in the airline industry (usually considered an oligopoly) caused prices to fall by 2 percent during a period in which prices overall in the economy rose by 8 percent. At the same time, air travel increased by 18 percent and fuel prices rose faster than the general price level. An airline executive was heard to say, "We have no choice but to pass these charges along to our customers."
   a) Assuming that these figures accurately depict the industry's demand curve, what is the implied price elasticity of demand?
   b) Do you agree with the executive that there is "no choice"? Do you think that the industry as a whole would be better off with higher prices?
   c) If you were the executive of one of the airline companies, what would your pricing strategy be? (Be explicit about any assumptions that you make.)
5. What are the strengths of a monopolistically competitive industry from the standpoint of allocative efficiency? What are its weaknesses? Do you think that society would benefit if more industries adopted this structure? Why or why not?
6. Do you agree with the following statement? "The high rate of failure for small businesses, many of which are in monopolistically competitive industries, is a real waste of resources compared with oligopolistic industries, which are more stable." Why or why not?
7. What are the benefits and costs to society from product differentiation? What market forces tend to limit the amount of product differentiation that occurs?
8. What are the benefits and costs to society of advertising? Would you favor a ban on all advertising? Why or why not? Would you favor banning some advertising? If you answer yes, provide a rule that will allow you to distinguish between acceptable and unacceptable ads.
9. What are the strengths of an oligopolistic industry from the standpoint of allocative efficiency? What are its weaknesses? Would you encourage or discourage adoption of this structure by industries? Why?

PART FOUR

Resource Markets

Demand and Supply in Resource Markets

QUESTIONS TO CONSIDER

☐ How do the principles of rational choice apply to the decision to buy resources?

☐ Why do the conditions of competition in resource markets promote allocative efficiency?

☐ What factors affect demand and supply of resources?

☐ What factors affect the relative efficiency of resources?

☐ How do imperfections in resource markets affect allocative efficiency?

Why do doctors earn more than janitors? Why do workers in the United States earn more than workers in other countries? Why did oil prices rise dramatically in the 1970s? What would happen if a major new supply of oil were discovered?

So far our exploration of microeconomics focused on product markets. But in order to answer the preceding questions and get a complete view of the economy, you must also understand resource markets. In much of this chapter we apply concepts that you have already learned. Thus you will learn how rational choice, demand and supply, production costs, competition, and imperfect competition relate to resource markets.

Why study resource markets? First, the sale of resources—especially labor—is the primary source of household income. Thus resource markets and prices dictate the level and distribution of income. Second, knowledge of resource markets helps economists to understand and predict the effects of economic events. As in product markets, changes in resource markets signal firms to adjust their use of resources and the mix of products they supply. Finally, resource markets affect allocative and technical efficiency. As for product markets, smoothly functioning resource markets promote efficiency. Resource markets that do not operate smoothly create inefficiency and raise questions about equity.

RATIONAL CHOICE AND BUYING RESOURCES

Actually, we have already discussed resource markets to some extent. In Chapter 1 we discussed the three main types of resources: natural, capital, and human resources. Exhibit 13.1 repeats the simple circular-flow model of a market economy that we introduced in Chapter 5. As we noted there with regard to this model, businesses and households interact in both product markets and resource markets. Their roles, however, are reversed in the two markets. In product markets, households demand and businesses supply goods and services. In resource markets, households supply and businesses demand resources.

Products are demanded because they *directly* satisfy consumer wants; resources are demanded because they *indirectly* satisfy consumer wants. That is,

Exhibit 13.1
Circular-Flow Model of Economic Activity
The circular-flow model shows two flows of economic activity. The inner loop is a real flow—the movement of resources from households to businesses, and the movement of goods and services from businesses to households. The outer loop is a money flow—the movement of money from households to businesses in payment for goods and services received, and the movement of money from businesses to households as payment for resources received. The exchange of goods and services for dollars takes place in product markets; the exchange of resources for money takes place in resource markets.

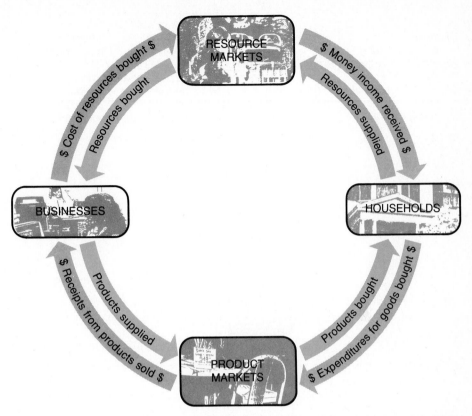

businesses demand resources because they can be used to produce goods and services for sale to consumers. Thus demand for resources in a market economy is directly related to demand for products. Economists say that demand for resources is a *derived demand*, meaning that it is derived from demand for products.

The managers of General Motors do not buy steel because they enjoy looking at piles of steel. They buy steel to produce automobiles that can be sold for a profit. The value of steel to General Motors reflects the value of automobiles that can be produced from steel. In this way, smoothly functioning resource markets help ensure that the best mix of goods and services is produced.

Many items that we refer to as resources are actually products manufactured by businesses for sale to other businesses. For example, aluminum produced by ALCOA is a resource used by Coca-Cola to produce soft-drink containers. However, all the principles discussed in this chapter hold for all resources. It does not matter whether a resource is supplied directly by a household (for example, labor) or through a company, which is, by definition, owned by households.

Optimal Choice of Resources

Regardless of who supplies a resource, an individual firm must decide how much of that resource to use. Economists believe that resource decision making, like product decision making, can best be understood by assuming that businesses apply the principles of rational choice.

Number of workers (E) (workers hired per week)	Total product (TP = Q) (bags of pitons per week)	Product price (P) (dollars per day)	Total revenues (TR = P × Q) (dollars per week)	Marginal revenue product (MRP) (extra revenue in dollars per extra worker hired)	Marginal factor cost (MFC = W) (extra cost in dollars per extra worker hired)	Total costs (TC = TVC + TFC) (dollars per week)	Total variable costs (TVC = W × E) (dollars per week)
0	0	15	0			800	0
				1500	450		
1	100	15	1500			1250	450
				1200	450		
2	180	15	2700			1700	900
				900	450		
3	240	15	3600			2150	1350
				600	450		
4	280	15	4200			2600	1800
				300	450		
5	300	15	4500			3050	2250

Exhibit 13.2
Rational Choice and the Profit-Maximizing Level of Employment

Consider the example of Resourceful Enterprises, a producer of pitons used by rock climbers. To keep this example simple, let's assume that in the short run Resourceful has only one variable resource: production workers. All other resources—such as buildings and machinery—are fixed. Let's also assume that the piton product market is competitive. Thus each bag of pitons that Resourceful produces can be sold at the same price. Finally, let's assume that Resourceful can hire as many workers as it wants to at the same market wage. That is, as we demonstrate in the next section, the labor resource market is competitive.

For its fixed resources and demand for pitons, how many workers should Resourceful hire in order to maximize profits? Following rational choice principles, Resourceful will weigh the extra benefits of hiring another worker against the extra costs of that worker. As long as hiring an additional worker adds more extra benefits than extra costs, the firm can continue to hire and make a profit. We can use the information in Exhibit 13.2 to see how Resourceful, like any profit seeker, measures the extra benefits of hiring another worker. The first two columns show the relationship between number of workers hired per week (E) and total number of bags of pitons produced (TP = Q). If Resourceful hires 3 workers, for example, it can expect to produce 240 bags per week.

But Resourceful is less concerned with the total output associated with hiring workers than with the amount of profit it can earn. That is, how much extra revenue will the firm receive if it hires 3 workers instead of 2? The third column of Exhibit 13.2 shows that Resourceful can sell each bag of pitons for $15 each, therefore total revenues (TR = P × Q) for 2 workers are $2700 per week, or $15(180 bags). Total revenues for 3 workers are $3600, or $15(240 bags). The fifth

Marginal revenue product (MRP). The change in total revenue that results from the use of one additional unit of a variable resource.

Marginal factor cost (MFC). The change in total cost that results from the use of one additional unit of a variable resource.

column shows **marginal revenue product (MRP)**, that is, the extra revenue received when an additional worker is hired. For the third worker hired,

$$\text{Marginal revenue product} = \frac{\text{Change in total revenues}}{\text{Change in workers hired}} \quad \text{or} \quad \text{MRP} = \frac{\text{Change in TR}}{\text{Change in E}}$$

$$= \frac{(\$3600 - \$2700)}{(3 - 2)} \quad \text{or} \quad \$900 \, \text{per week}$$

Marginal revenue product decreases as more workers are hired, reflecting the law of diminishing marginal returns (see Chapter 8). That is, each additional worker hired will add less and less to total output. The first worker can produce 100 bags of pitons. When the second worker is hired, Resourceful's total product increases to 180—a marginal product of 80. Each additional worker adds to total product, but each has an increasingly smaller marginal product. This result is not a comment on the skills or work habits of workers. Rather, it is a result of adding more and more *variable* resources to a *specific amount of fixed* resources. *The declining marginal revenue product curve reflects the declining marginal product curve, which reflects the law of diminishing marginal returns.*

Marginal revenue product measures the extra benefits that Resourceful receives from hiring additional workers. Similarly, **marginal factor cost (MFC)** measures the extra cost of purchasing an additional unit of a variable resource. The sixth column of Exhibit 13.2 shows the marginal factor cost of hiring an additional worker (the only variable cost in our example) as $450 per week.

Using the marginal revenue product and the marginal factor cost in Exhibit 13.2, we can predict that Resourceful Enterprises will hire 4 workers if it wants to maximize profits. Extra costs are greater than extra benefits for the fifth worker. If it hires fewer than 4 workers, profits are less than they could be. We can state this result as a general rule: *As long as marginal revenue product (extra benefit) is equal to or greater than marginal factor cost (extra cost), purchase additional resources to increase profits.* This rule applies to all firms and all resources.

We can derive the same rule from the basic equation for profits.

$$\text{Change in economic profit} = \text{Change in total revenues} - \text{Change in total costs}$$

$$= \text{Change in TR} - \text{Change in TC} \quad \text{or} \quad \text{MRP} - \text{MFC}$$

In other words, the change in profits associated with hiring one more worker (or buying a unit of any other resource) is indicated by comparing marginal revenue product and marginal factor cost. *Profits are maximized by hiring up to the point where MRP = MFC.*

Marginal Revenue Product and Resource Demand

In order to understand and predict a firm's decisions, we must know its demand for resources. What is the maximum wage that Resourceful, as a profit seeker, will pay for each additional worker? For example, what is the most that Resourceful will pay for the third worker?

The data in Exhibit 13.2 indicate that the marginal revenue product of the third worker is $900 per week. Resourceful's profits will increase if it can hire this worker for anything less than $900 per week. That is, marginal revenue product represents both the extra benefits the firm receives from and the maximum price it will pay for another worker. Thus *a firm's demand for resources is determined by its marginal revenue product (D = MRP).*

So far we have focused on the firm's response to changes in the price of one resource. In particular, we have held productivity of the resource and quantity and price of other resources constant. As with product demand, this demand curve is based on the "all-other-things-unchanged" assumption. In the next section we explore how changes other than resource price affect resource demand.

COMPETITIVE RESOURCE MARKETS

Although knowing how a single firm decides the number of workers to hire is interesting, economists are more interested in analyzing the behavior of all the firms in a resource market. For example, what determines how much steel will be sold and at what price?

Like product markets, resource markets can be classified according to the market power of firms—in this case, the firms that are buying. Most firms buy such a small portion of the total market supply that they operate as *price takers*. They have no real influence on price and must *take it or leave it*. A local building contractor, for example, has no real influence on the market for lumber or plumbing fixtures. Even very large firms often fit this model. For example, the U.S. Postal Service, despite its huge fleet of trucks, has very little influence on the total market for gasoline.

Model of Competitive Resource Market

To study the operation of resource markets in which many firms compete to buy available supplies, economists use the model of a **competitive resource market**. The following characteristics define a competitive resource market.

1. Neither buyers nor sellers have any market power.
2. Resources move freely and at low cost.
3. Perfect information exists on available alternatives.

These characteristics are very similar to those we used to define purely competitive product markets. In both cases, the absence of market power means that firms have no influence on market price. The free movement of resources at low cost, as with a lack of barriers to entry and exit, forces the market to respond quickly to changes in demand or supply. Finally, the existence of perfect information means that decision makers will make optimal choices.

These perfect conditions do not accurately describe many resource markets in the real world. But, as we noted before, the true test of a model is whether it can help us to understand and predict the response of price and quantity to changes in market conditions. Later in this chapter we will discuss what happens when these conditions are not met. First, however, let's see how competitive resource markets operate and what factors affect demand and supply in such markets.

Competitive resource market. A resource market in which no individual buyer or seller has any market power, resources move freely, and buyers and sellers have perfect information on available alternatives.

(a) The market

Price
(dollars per pound)

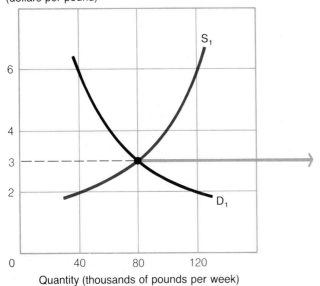

Quantity (thousands of pounds per week)

(b) Numbers Unlimited

Price and cost
(dollars per pound)

Quantity (pounds per week)

Exhibit 13.3
Competitive Resource Markets
Part (a) shows the market for plastic, a competitive resource market. Part (b) shows
demand and supply of plastic by a price taker, Numbers Unlimited. The interaction of
market demand and supply determines the price of plastic. Since Numbers Unlimited
is only a small part of the total market, it cannot influence price. Thus from the company's perspective the supply curve for plastic is horizontal at the market price. The
firm can buy all the plastic it wants to at this price, but none at a lower price. At a
market price of $3 per pound and with its demand for plastic, Numbers Unlimited will
buy 200 pounds of plastic per week.

Demand and Supply: Market and Individual Firm Perspectives

Exhibit 13.3 shows the connection between individual firms and markets.
Exhibit 13.3(a) shows demand for plastic by all firms in the market (D_1) and total
market supply of plastic (S_1). As we would expect, equilibrium in this market
occurs where the demand and supply curves intersect—at $3 per pound. Exhibit
13.3(b) shows demand for and supply of plastic used by Numbers Unlimited, a
manufacturer of hand calculators. The firm's demand for plastic reflects its marginal revenue product schedule: the extra revenue that it can expect to receive
when it uses additional plastic to make more cases for its calculators.

In this competitive resource market, Numbers Unlimited will be a price taker.
Just as a price taker in a product market faces a horizontal (perfectly elastic)
demand curve for its product at market price, so a price taker in a resource market
faces a perfectly elastic *supply* curve. In this case, Numbers Unlimited can buy all

the plastic it wants at the market equilibrium price of $3 per pound, but nothing at a lower price. Because the price of plastic is constant, marginal factor cost is identical to resource price. Following the profit-maximizing rule for resource buying, Numbers Unlimited will choose to buy 200 pounds of plastic per week (where MRP = MFC).

DETERMINANTS OF DEMAND AND SUPPLY

In order to understand how demand and supply interact in a competitive resource market, we must examine the factors that determine demand and supply. As you will see, many of these factors are similar to those affecting demand and supply in product markets.

Supply of Resources

The supply of most resources is determined by five factors: (1) cost of resources; (2) technology; (3) prices of alternative resources; (4) number of suppliers; and (5) expectations of suppliers. These are the same factors listed in Chapter 3 for product markets. The fact that the purchaser is another firm instead of a consumer makes no difference; the price at which a firm can justify supplying a particular quantity for sale remains the same. In Chapters 14 and 15, we explore supply again, taking into account the peculiarities of labor and financial markets.

Demand for Resources

Earlier in this chapter, we related marginal revenue product to resource demand from the individual firm's perspective. In doing so, we made several assumptions, including holding the quantity of all other resources constant. However, demand for resources stems from the firm's desire to make maximum profits. To do so, it must respond to increased demand for its product by increasing output, which means it will want to buy more resources when product demand increases. To maximize profits, the firm must also minimize costs, which means shifting resource combinations in response to changes in relative efficiency. Thus both product demand and relative efficiency of resources are important determinants of resource demand.

Factors affecting demand for a firm's product. As we noted in Chapter 3, five factors affect product demand: (1) tastes and preferences; (2) prices of related goods; (3) income; (4) number of consumers; and (5) expectations of consumers. These factors may affect demand directly or indirectly in resource markets. For example, some companies produce and sell rubber products directly to automobile producers. Demand for resources by rubber companies thus depends on consumer demand for automobiles. Consumer demand is important in determining resource demand in all situations.

But why does demand for a firm's product also determine resource demand? From the firm's perspective, we know that the value of resources is the marginal revenue product, that is, the extra revenue generated when extra resources are purchased. If demand for a firm's product decreases, each unit produced will be

Number of workers (E) (workers hired per week)	Total product (TP = Q) (bags of pitons per week)	Marginal product (MP) (extra bags per extra worker)	Marginal revenue product in dollars if price is . . .	
			$15 per bag ($MRP_1 = \$15 \times MP$)	$10 per bag ($MRP_2 = \$10 \times MP$)
0	0			
		100	1500	1000
1	100			
		80	1200	800
2	180			
		60	900	600
3	240			
		40	600	400
4	280			
		20	300	200
5	300			

Exhibit 13.4
Changes in Product Demand and Revenue

sold at a lower price. Thus the extra revenue that a firm can earn by hiring each extra worker (MRP) will be smaller. The decrease in marginal revenue product will decrease the firm's demand for resources.

Exhibit 13.4 shows how a decrease in demand for pitons affects Resourceful's demand for workers. In this competitive resource market, the decrease in demand drives price down from $15 per bag of pitons to $10. Because marginal revenue product equals price multiplied by marginal product, marginal revenue product also falls. For example, at $15 per bag of pitons, the marginal revenue product of the fourth worker hired is $600, or $15(40). At $10 per bag, it is $400, or $10(40).

If the market price of labor remains constant at $450 per week, Resourceful will decrease its demand for labor from 4 workers to 3. That is, at $10 per bag of pitons, the fourth worker is no longer worth hiring because that worker costs $450 but provides benefits of only $400. In fact, *demand for any firm's product is directly related to its demand for resources; when product demand rises, so does resource demand.*

Relative Efficiency of Resources

So far we have assumed that Resourceful has only one variable resource: workers. You have seen how the firm responds to changes in the price of workers, holding all other resources constant. But in the real world, a change in the price of one resource causes firms to change the quantity of other resources as well.

For example, if the price of computers falls, firms may not only buy more computers but also hire more computer programmers. Computers and programmers are complementary resources. Conversely, a decline in the price of robots may cause firms to buy more robots and less labor. Robots and labor are substitute resources. In other words, demand for any particular resource depends not only on its marginal revenue product, but also on its relative efficiency.

Relative efficiency and equilibrium. We have noted that a profit-seeking firm will hire labor up to the point where MRP = MFC. Technical efficiency requires that a firm do the same for all resources. That is, it must use the optimal mix of resources. Consider, for example, a choice between using unskilled workers and simple machines (combination A) or using skilled workers and sophisticated machines (combination B). The efficiencies of these two combinations are

$$\text{Efficiency of combination A} = \frac{\text{Marginal revenue product of A}}{\text{Marginal factor cost of A}} \quad \text{or} \quad \frac{\text{MRP}_A}{\text{MFC}_A}$$

and

$$\text{Efficiency of combination B} = \frac{\text{Marginal revenue product of B}}{\text{Marginal factor cost of B}} \quad \text{or} \quad \frac{\text{MRP}_B}{\text{MFC}_B}$$

Efficiency is measured as the dollars of revenue generated per dollar of cost. What if combination A (unskilled workers and simple machines) is more efficient than combination B (skilled workers and complex machines)? In that case, a firm can generate more revenue per dollar of cost (and thus more profit) by using more of combination A and less of combination B. A change in any of the terms changes the relative efficiency of the two combinations and the firm's optimal resource mix.

For a firm to achieve maximum technical efficiency, every resource must be utilized to the point where MRP = MFC. As the equimarginal principle (see Chapter 7) predicts, when the two efficiency ratios are equal, the firm has no better option than its current resource combination. That is, the firm reaches equilibrium where

$$\frac{\text{MRP}_A}{\text{MFC}_A} = \frac{\text{MRP}_B}{\text{MFC}_B} = 1$$

Factors affecting relative efficiency. Five factors affect the relative efficiency of a resource: (1) productivity of the resource; (2) productivity and quantity of complementary resources; (3) productivity of substitute resources; (4) prices of complementary resources; and (5) prices of substitute resources. We can relate each of these factors to the preceding equation for relative efficiency and indicate how a change affects demand.

For example, let's consider Apex Manufacturing Company's demand for labor. Apex currently produces hang gliders, using unskilled labor and some simple machines it rents. What will happen if Apex's current workers and those available in the local labor market become more proficient at making hang gliders? This increase in the productivity of labor will directly raise marginal revenue product, with each worker producing more hang gliders per day. As a result, demand for labor will rise.

What will happen, instead, if Apex rents new, more productive machinery for producing hang gliders? This increase in the productivity of a complementary resource will also increase demand for labor. Better machines will lower Apex's costs and increase the quantity of hang gliders that the workers can produce in a day. In effect, this change is an increase in the marginal revenue product of the resource combination of labor and machines. And as marginal revenue product increases, so does demand for labor.

But what if someone invents a robot that can produce hang gliders more cheaply than Apex can with its current technology? The greater productivity of the substitute resource will lower Apex's demand for labor. Although labor is no less productive than before, its *relative* efficiency has fallen.

And what happens if the rental price for the current machines falls? Apex's demand for the machines—and for labor to run them—will increase. In effect, this change is a decline in the marginal factor cost of the resource combination of labor and machines. And as marginal factor cost falls, the best quantity to hire increases.

Finally, what if the price of robots falls? The relative efficiency of robots rises, and the relative efficiency of Apex's current technology falls. As a result, demand for labor falls.

You may wonder why we have ignored the price of labor, even though resource price appears in the relative efficiency formula. Recall the difference between changes in demand and movement along a demand curve (changes in quantity demanded). We have omitted the price of unskilled labor—the resource itself—here because this price does not change demand.

Elasticity of Demand for Resources

From the preceding analysis, we can predict the response of a firm or market to a change in resource supply. But this step is only a starting point for any serious analysis. We also want to predict *how much* prices and utilization of resources will change. This prediction depends on the price elasticity of demand for resources.

For example, suppose that we want to evaluate the impact of a minimum wage on employment. A minimum wage is a minimum price. If it is higher than the equilibrium wage, the quantity of labor demanded will decline. But the extent of this change depends on the price elasticity of demand. If demand is price elastic, the effect on employment will be large. If demand is price inelastic, the effect will be smaller. (Chapter 19 contains an evaluation of minimum wage laws in the United States.)

Price elasticity of demand for resources, like that for products, refers to the responsiveness of quantity demanded to change in price. Four factors affect price elasticity of demand: (1) availability of substitute resources; (2) elasticity of demand for the firm's product; (3) cost of the resource as a percentage of total costs; and (4) time period for adjustment. These factors are useful in predicting whether a given supply change will result in large or small changes in prices and employment.

Availability of substitute resources. As we noted previously, firms have options to consider and choices to make when buying resources. In some cases, however, the options are limited. For example, if a union succeeds in organizing the labor force in a market, a firm may have few good options, especially in the short run. Its demand for labor may be relatively price inelastic. Demand for resources is price inelastic when few close substitutes exist. Demand for resources is price elastic when there are many close substitutes.

Elasticity of demand for a firm's product. When the price of any resource increases, product cost rises. Higher resource costs decrease product supply, resulting in higher product price and smaller quantity sold. As quantity sold decreases, a firm requires fewer resources—such as workers.

How much employment decreases depends on how much sales decrease when price increases. In other words, the price elasticity of demand for a resource depends on the price elasticity of demand for the product. If product demand is price elastic, quantity sold (and thus the volume of resources purchased) is greatly affected. If product demand is price inelastic, neither sales nor utilization of resources is greatly affected. Thus price-inelastic product demand implies price-inelastic resource demand.

For example, demand for telephone service is relatively price inelastic. When AT&T had a monopoly in the telephone industry, it was able to pass along much of any cost increase to its customers. Thus unions for AT&T workers were able to win major raises for their members, but AT&T did not greatly decrease its quantity of labor demanded. In contrast, competition from foreign producers has increased price elasticity in the steel and auto industries. Unions in these industries have sometimes chosen to accept wage cuts in order to avoid layoffs of their members.

Cost of a resource as a percentage of total costs. Economists refer to the relative cost of a resource as the "importance of being insignificant." To illustrate this point, let's consider Resourceful's piton-making machine, which requires a special kind of oil. In an average month, the firm uses a gallon of this lubricant at a cost of $10. Suppose that the only supplier of the lubricant raises its price to $12 per gallon. If Resourceful's monthly total costs are $250,000, the price increase is insignificant. Resourceful probably will not even look for another oil supplier or respond to the price change in any other way. A resource that is an insignificant part of total costs tends to have a price-inelastic demand. On the other hand, if the cost of a resource is a significant part of total costs, the firm will be greatly influenced and respond accordingly.

Time period for adjustment. The final factor considered relevant for price elasticity is the time period. In any market analysis, demand and supply refer to the quantities bought and sold in a specified time period. Whenever demand or supply changes, both resource and product markets must adjust; the longer the time period, the greater the response will be. Thus demand for resources is more price elastic as the time period for adjustment increases.

The case of oil in the 1970s clearly illustrates the difference between long-run and short-run price elasticity of demand. In 1973–1974 the price of oil imported into the United States rose from just under $3 to more than $12 per barrel. As a result, the U.S. economy spent more than $15 billion for imported oil in 1974, compared with $4 billion in 1973. In 1979, the price of imported oil again rose—from $12 to more than $30 per barrel. And spending for that oil rose from $32 billion in 1978 to almost $62 billion in 1980. This increased spending shows that demand for oil is price inelastic in the short run.

But in the long run, demand for oil proved to be quite price elastic. Over a period of time, households and businesses became more energy conscious and energy efficient. In 1982 some 20–25 percent less energy was required to produce a dollar of output than in 1973. In all, by 1982 total energy consumption had fallen by 5 percent and consumption of petroleum products by 12 percent.

RECAP ▮▮▮▮▮

Price elasticity of resource demand determines how much resource use is affected by changes in the price of a resource.

Demand will be more price elastic when more substitutes are available, product demand is more price elastic, resource cost is a large percent of total cost, and a longer period of time is allowed for adjustment.

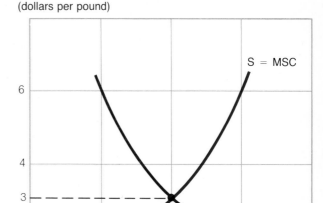

Price
(dollars per pound)

Exhibit 13.5
Competitive Resource Markets and
Allocative Efficiency
The graph shows demand and supply in the market for plastic, a market that we assume to be perfectly competitive. Neither the buyers nor the sellers in this market have any market power. If there are no external costs or benefits, and if buyers sell in competitive product markets, we can equate demand with marginal social benefits (D = MSB) and supply with marginal social cost (S = MSC). This competitive market will tend to adjust to equilibrium, that is, where quantity demanded equals quantity supplied. This market is allocatively efficient because MSB = MSC.

Quantity (thousands of pounds per week)

EFFICIENCY AND INEFFICIENCY IN RESOURCE MARKETS

Perfectly competitive resource markets serve as ideals against which to judge the actions of less competitive markets. But the conditions for competition are not always met in the real world. Thus in this section, we look first at the benefits arising from competitive resource markets—specifically, allocative efficiency. Then we consider imperfections that sometimes occur in real-world markets and how they affect allocative efficiency.

Competitive Resource Markets and Allocative Efficiency

You should not be surprised to learn that competition in resource markets helps the economy achieve allocative efficiency. Exhibit 13.5 shows the market for plastic, a resource used by Resourceful Enterprises in its production of pitons. We assume that this resource market is purely competitive; neither buyers nor sellers have any market power. In addition, we assume that firms demanding resources also sell their output in purely competitive product markets. (Later in this chapter we discuss the implications of changing this assumption.) Finally, we assume that there are no externalities, that is, neither external costs nor external benefits (see Chapter 6).

Using these assumptions, we can equate demand for resources with marginal social benefit (D = MSB). That is, the value to society of using additional resources reflects the value to consumers of the final goods or services those resources help produce. Similarly, we can equate market supply and marginal social cost (S = MSC). That is, the cost to society of using additional resources reflects the alternative uses to which they could be put. As a result, competitive resource markets are allocatively efficient. A competitive resource market reaches equilibrium where the demand and supply curves intersect. Since demand also equals marginal social benefits and supply also equals marginal social costs, market equilibrium also meets a condition for allocative efficiency: MSB = MSC.

Competition in a resource market has the same effect it has in a product market. It forces suppliers to respond to market signals about changes in relative resource supply and relative product demand. For example, oil producers were forced to pay attention to the new competition for oil that developed in the 1970s and 1980s. Competition also forces the economy to produce the mix of goods and services that best satisfies consumer demand and at minimum cost. Knowing that competition in both product and resource markets (in the absence of externalities) leads to allocative efficiency, we are ready to examine some sources of market imperfection and the inefficiency that results.

Imperfect Competition in the Product Market

One market imperfection occurs when a firm buys resources in a competitive market but sells its final product in an imperfectly competitive market. As you saw in Chapters 11 and 12, when a firm has some product market power, its demand curve slopes downward. In order to see the effects of product market power on resource markets, let's return to the case of Resourceful Enterprises. Again, we assume that the firm buys labor at a constant $450 per week in a perfectly competitive resource market and that no externalities exist. But what if Resourceful gains some market power by obtaining a government ban on foreign-made pitons?

The third column of Exhibit 13.6 reflects Resourceful's market power. Note that the product price falls as each additional worker is hired. In a competitive product market, the negative slope reflects only the law of diminishing marginal returns, or the fact that each additional worker hired adds less extra output. In this imperfectly competitive product market, however, the negative relationship also means that Resourceful must lower its price in order to sell more pitons. Under these circumstances, the firm will hire only 3 workers, since marginal revenue product is less than marginal factor cost for the fourth worker.

The sixth column in Exhibit 13.6 shows the **value of the marginal product (VMP)**, which we calculate as price multiplied by marginal product (VMP = P × MP). Product price is what consumers are willing to pay and therefore measures the social benefits of additional units. Thus the value of the marginal product— *not* the marginal revenue product—measures marginal social benefits (VMP = MSB).

The difference between the value of the marginal product and the marginal revenue product reflects the difference between purely and imperfectly competitive product markets. If we are interested in the value to consumers of additional units of a product, we must know the price that consumers will pay. In competitive product markets, price and marginal revenue to the firm are the same, so the value of the marginal product equals marginal revenue product.

Value of the marginal product (VMP). The value to society of using one additional unit of a variable resource; calculated as the marginal product of the additional unit of resource multiplied by the price of the final product it helps to create; equals the marginal revenue product when the firm sells in a competitive product market.

Number of workers (E) (workers hired per week)	Total product (TP = Q) (bags of pitons per week)	Product price (P) (dollars per bag)	Total revenues (TR = P × Q) (dollars per week)	Marginal revenue product (MRP) (extra revenue in dollars per extra worker hired)	Value of marginal product (VMP) (dollars per worker)	Marginal factor cost (MFC = W) (extra cost per extra worker hired)
0	0	—	0			
				1900	1900	450
1	100	19	1900			
				1340	1440	450
2	180	18	3240			
				840	1020	450
3	240	17	4080			
				400	640	450
4	280	16	4480			
				20	300	450
5	300	15	4500			

Exhibit 13.6
Resource Demand When Firms Have Product Market Power

But when a firm sells in imperfectly competitive product markets, these equalities do not hold. In fact, using the value of marginal product as the measure of marginal social benefits, we see that allocative efficiency requires Resourceful to hire 4 workers and produce 280 units of output. Because extra benefits to Resourceful (MRP) are less than the extra benefits to society, the firm hires too few workers and produces too few pitons. The greater the firm's market power, the greater the allocative inefficiency.

Imperfect Competition in the Resource Market

We have assumed so far that firms buy in competitive resource markets. This means that firms are price takers and have supply curves that are horizontal lines. But what if Resourceful Enterprises is such a large employer in a small town that it can hire more workers only if it will pay higher wages? In this case, the firm faces a supply curve that slopes upward, as shown in Exhibit 13.7. The first four columns in this table should look familiar to you. But the seventh column shows that the firm must raise wages if it wants to hire more workers. Because the firm has market power in the resource market, its hiring decision affects the market wage.

Market power in resource markets occurs in this case because Resourceful is no longer one of a large number of relatively small buyers. For example, mining companies were the only employers in some Appalachian towns well into this century. The local population had to accept low wages in the mines or company-run stores if they wanted work in the area. Likewise, Coca-Cola and PepsiCo are large buyers in the sugar, corn syrup, and artificial sweetener markets and have market power in them.

Number of workers (E) (workers hired per week)	Total product (TP = Q) (bags of pitons per week)	Total revenues (TR = P × Q) (dollars per week)	Marginal revenue product (MRP) (extra revenue in dollars per extra worker hired)	Marginal factor cost (MFC) (extra cost in dollars per extra worker hired)	Total variable cost (TVC = W × E) (dollars per week)	Wage (W) (dollars per week)
0	0	0			0	—
			1500	200		
1	100	1500			200	200
			1200	400		
2	180	2700			600	300
			900	600		
3	240	3600			1200	400
			600	800		
4	280	4200			2000	500
			300	1000		
5	300	4500			3000	600

Exhibit 13.7
Hiring in an Imperfectly Competitive Resource Market

Having market power, Resourceful must offer a higher price to *all* prospective workers in order to increase the number it hires. Thus the marginal factor cost that Resourceful pays reflects the new wage paid to the newly hired workers *plus* the increase in wages paid to some of the new workers, who otherwise would have worked for less. As a result, marginal factor cost is greater than wages (as shown in Exhibit 13.7, except when only one worker is hired).

For example, to hire 3 workers instead of 2, Resourceful must raise wages offered from $300 to $400 per week. It must pay $400 to the third worker. But it must also pay $100 more to each of the two workers it could have hired for $300 per week. The increase in total costs, then, is $600 per week. Thus Resourceful will hire only three workers, since marginal revenue product is less than marginal factor cost for the fourth worker.

But is this result allocatively efficient? Since we assume that Resourceful sells in a competitive product market and that no external benefits exist, we can equate marginal revenue product and marginal social benefit (MRP = MSB). Since we also assume that no external costs exist, we can equate marginal social cost and resource supply—in this case, wages (S = W = MSC). As Exhibit 13.7 shows, allocative efficiency (MSB = MSC, or MRP = W) would require Resourceful to hire 4 workers. But, as usual with market power, the firm's desire to maximize profits leads it to underhire and underproduce from society's perspective.

As we stated when first discussing imperfect markets, however, this inefficiency does not result simply because firms seek to maximize profits. As you have seen when competition exists, the profit-maximizing efforts of firms result in allocative efficiency. Allocative inefficiency results from market power—in this case, resource market power. Whenever a firm has market power of any kind, we can expect its actions to lead to allocative inefficiency.

Graphic Representation of Market Power and Efficiency

The graphs in Exhibit 13.8 summarize our conclusions about market power and efficiency. In Exhibit 13.8(a), competition prevails in all markets. Thus the market will buy as many resources as necessary to produce as much as society demands, recognizing costs and demand for other products. It will reach equilibrium where marginal social benefit equals marginal social cost, that is, at the allocatively efficient level.

In Exhibit 13.8(b), product market power means that marginal revenue is less than product price. Thus the value of marginal product curve (VMP = MSB) lies above the firm's demand for resources curve (D = MRP), and extra benefits from the firm's perspective are less than marginal social benefits (MRP < MSB). As a result the firm buys fewer gallons and produces less than is allocatively efficient. The red-shaded area on the graph shows society's gain if resource use were expanded to the point where MSB = MSC.

In Exhibit 13.8(c), resource market power also causes allocative inefficiency because the firm must pay a higher price as it buys more meters of this resource. This causes extra costs to the firm (MFC) to exceed marginal social cost (MFC > MSC). Price paid by firms in this market will be lower than in competitive markets. Again, profit maximizers will buy less than the allocatively efficient number of meters. The red-shaded area shows society's gain if resource use were expanded to the point where MSB = MSC.

Note that the problems we have just discussed arise because firms have market power, *not* simply because they seek to maximize profits. Indeed, profit seeking is allocatively efficient in competitive markets. Most economists believe that resource market power is a less significant social issue today than is product market power. But critics charge that market power is a problem in many resource markets.

Imperfect Information and Resource Immobilities

The final type of imperfection that we will consider results when market information and resource mobility are imperfect. Failure to meet these conditions has major effects on decision making (in the case of information) and on adjusting to economic changes (in the case of resource mobility).

For example, consider the ideal market response when consumers decide to buy fewer cars and more computers. To achieve allocative efficiency, the market must respond to higher demand for computers by increasing the quantity of computers supplied. It must also respond to lower demand for automobiles by reducing the quantity of cars supplied. These changes in product markets require adjustments in resource markets. Automakers must reduce and computer firms must increase resource use. This movement of resources from the auto to the computer industry results in allocative efficiency (market output in line with consumer demand).

Unfortunately, this shift of resources does not always occur smoothly and quickly. For example, unemployed autoworkers may not know about openings in the computer industry (poor information), or they may be unqualified to take the new jobs (resource immobility). Such imperfections slow the shift of resources from one part of the economy to another. The result is unemployment (those who

RECAP

Competition helps direct resources to their best social use. If there were no market imperfections, market equilibrium would also be allocatively efficient (MSB = MSC).

If a firm sells in imperfectly competitive product markets, marginal social benefit (MSB = VMP) will be greater than extra benefits to the firm (D = MRP). The firm will underhire and underproduce from the perspective of allocative efficiency.

If a firm buys in an imperfectly competitive resource market, marginal social cost (MSC = S) will be less than extra costs to the firm (MFC). The firm will underhire and underproduce from the perspective of allocative efficiency.

(a) Competition in resource and product markets

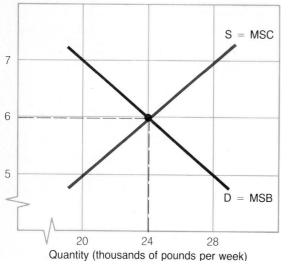

(b) Competitive resource market; imperfectly competitive product market

(c) Imperfectly competitive resource market; competitive product market

Exhibit 13.8
Resource Markets and Allocative Efficiency
Part (a) shows a market in which neither buyers nor sellers have any market power, where buyers sell their products in competitive product markets, and where there are no external benefits or costs. Thus demand reflects marginal social benefits (D = MSB) and supply reflects marginal social costs (S = MSC). Market equilibrium is also allocatively efficient (MSB = MSC). In part (b) the resource market is competitive, but buyers sell their products in imperfectly competitive product markets. As a result, marginal revenue is less than product price and marginal revenue product is less than the value of marginal product. In part (c) buyers in the resource market are large enough to influence resource price. From their perspective, marginal factor cost (MFC) is above the supply curve—that is, they can buy more only if they pay more for all units bought. In both (b) and (c) market equilibrium (where demand equals supply) is allocatively inefficient (MSB > MSC). The red-shaded triangles indicate the extent of inefficiency caused by market power.

lack the information and/or ability to take advantage of job openings) and hence inefficiency.

Such imperfections are more important for some resources (skilled labor, in particular) than for others. But while they can be important causes of unemployment in the short run, they provide only a temporary obstacle to adjustment. Over the long run, we would not expect resource immobility to prevent market adjustments. And whether public policies and programs can speed this flow in a cost-effective manner is hotly debated.

CONCLUSION

Most of the discussion in this chapter applies to any type of resource market. In all cases, optimal resource buying requires a balance between marginal revenue product and marginal factor costs. However, some resource markets are unusual and require additional discussion. In Chapter 14 we examine financial markets and the markets for capital resources (plant and equipment) for which the calculation of marginal revenue product and marginal factor cost are somewhat special. In Chapter 15 we examine labor markets, in which the problems of information and resource immobility are especially important. In Chapter 18 we consider whether resource markets generate an equitable distribution of income.

SUMMARY

1. In this chapter we discussed the operation of resource markets: how demand and supply of resources determine price and the level of resource use.

2. Firms make optimal resource choices following the principles of rational choice. A firm measures extra benefits received from extra resources purchased as marginal revenue product, the extra revenue derived from selling an extra unit of product produced by an extra unit of resource. It measures extra costs as marginal factor cost, the extra cost of buying an extra unit of resource. A firm will maximize its profit by hiring workers up to the point where marginal revenue product equals marginal factor cost (MRP = MFC). Since marginal revenue product is the maximum price the firm will pay to buy a resource, it is also the firm's resource demand schedule.

3. In a perfectly competitive resource market, neither buyers nor sellers have any market power in either resource or product markets. In addition, resources move freely and at low cost, perfect information exists about alternatives, and there are no external costs or benefits. Under such conditions, market demand equals marginal social benefits (D = MSB), and market supply equals marginal social cost (S = MSC). Thus allocative efficiency is achieved (MSB = MSC) when the market reaches equilibrium.

4. Supply of resources is affected by cost of resources, technology, prices of alternatives, number of suppliers, and expectations of suppliers.

5. Demand for resources is directly related to product demand. Product demand is affected by tastes and preferences, prices of related goods, income, number of buyers, and expectations. The relative efficiency of resources is affected by productivity of the resource itself and by productivity and prices of complementary and substitute resources. Relative efficiency of a resource—and hence demand—rises when productivity of the resource or its complements rises, the price of its complements falls, the price of substitutes rises, or productivity of substitutes falls.

6. The extent to which resource price and employment change as supply changes depends on the price elasticity of demand for resources. Demand will be more price inelastic when there are few close substitute resources, demand for the product is price inelastic, the resource cost is a small percentage of total product costs, and when the time period allowed for adjustment is small.

7. The conditions for a perfectly competitive market do not exist in the real world. Imperfect conditions result when the firm sells in an imperfectly competitive product market, the firm has market power as a resource buyer, and less than perfect information and/or resource immobility exist. Each of these three conditions creates some inefficiency.

8. When a firm sells in an imperfectly competitive product market, the value to the firm of additional units sold (marginal revenue) and additional resources purchased (marginal revenue product) is less than the value to society (marginal social benefit), or MRP < MSB. At market equilibrium, marginal social benefits are less than marginal social costs, and fewer resources are purchased (and fewer products produced) than is socially optimal.

9. When a firm has market power as a buyer of resources, its resource supply curve slopes upward. Because the

firm must raise its offer to attract additional resources, marginal factor cost is greater than supply (or the resource price). Extra costs to the firm (marginal factor costs) are therefore greater than marginal social costs (MFC > MSC). Since supply measures marginal social costs and marginal social benefits are greater than marginal social costs, allocative inefficiency results. The firm will buy fewer resources—but at lower prices (because of its market power)—than it would under conditions of perfect competition.

10. Resource mobility and good information are required if resources are to adjust to changes in consumer demand. Lack of these characteristics restricts the movement of resources from declining to growing industries and causes underutilization of resources and inefficiency.

KEY TERMS

Marginal revenue product (MRP), 317
Marginal factor cost (MFC), 317
Competitive resource market, 318
Value of the marginal product (VMP), 326

QUESTIONS FOR REVIEW AND DISCUSSION

1. Corn is used to fatten cattle and is bought and sold in a competitive market. Explain with graphs *and* in words how each of the following events will affect the price of corn and quantity bought and sold.
   a) An increase in consumer income (assuming that beef is a normal good).
   b) A new drug that enables ranchers to fatten their cattle using less corn.
   c) A decrease in the price of chicken, a substitute for beef.
   d) A decrease in the cost of producing corn.
   e) An improvement in the quality of capital resources that are used in combination with corn.
   f) An increase in the supply of soy cake, a substitute for corn.

2. Comment on the statement: "An increase in income raises our standard of living because we can buy more goods, but an increase in prices reduces our standard of living because we can buy fewer goods. Therefore we should hope that prices of goods will fall while incomes rise." (Be sure to explain the connections between income and price.)

3. Is each of the following statements true, false, or uncertain? Why?
   a) If firms sell their products in imperfectly competi-

tive product markets, they're likely also to have market power in resource markets.
   b) Imperfect competition in resource markets causes firms to overproduce from the standpoint of allocative efficiency.

4. Costume Jewelry of Los Angeles faces a competitive labor market. Changes in daily output of bracelets as more workers are hired are as follows:

Number of workers	Daily output of bracelets	Total revenues	Marginal revenue product
0	0	$ 0	>$___
1	12	___	>___
2	19	___	>___
3	24	___	>___
4	28	___	>___
5	30	___	

   a) If the firm's bracelets sell in a competitive product market for $12 each, what is the marginal revenue product associated with hiring the third worker?
   b) If the market wage is $50 per day, how many workers would be hired? (Assume that labor is the only variable resource.)
   c) If fixed costs are $150 per day, how will the firm's demand for labor change over the long run? Why? (*Hint:* Recall the concepts you learned in Chapter 10.) A numerical answer is not expected; state only the direction of change in resource demand.
   d) The data show decreasing marginal productivity as more workers are hired. Does this result mean that the last worker hired is less skilled than the first? How do economists explain declining marginal productivity?

5. Explain the statement: "I can't tell you how much copper ore there is in this mine unless you first tell me the price of copper."

6. Suppose that you own supplies of Dirtinium, a mineral with economic value, for which both resource and product markets are competitive.
   a) How does your personal desire to maximize income lead you to sell Dirtinium in such a way that allocative efficiency is achieved?
   b) What changes could cause the marginal social cost for Dirtinium to increase?
   c) What changes might cause it to fall?
   d) How do changes in the marginal social cost cause

you to respond? How do they affect your personal income?

7. Consider the case of Teak Talk, Inc., a manufacturer of teakwood salad bowls, trays, and furniture. A unique wood, teak grows only in Southeast Asia. Teak Talk thus faces an imperfectly competitive resource market. The supply of this resource to the firm is as follows:

Board feet of teak	Average cost per board foot	Total costs	Marginal factor cost
1	$200	$___	
			$___
2	225	___	
			___
3	240	___	
			___
4	260	___	
			___
5	280	___	

a) What is the marginal factor cost associated with purchasing a second board foot of teak?

b) If each board foot of teak purchased will increase output by 7 trays, each of which can be sold for $50—and if this is the only variable resource—how many board feet will the firm buy?

8. Use the information presented in the appendix to this chapter and the following information to answer questions (a)–(c). Consider the case of The Artisanry, Ltd., which produces art supplies. The firm's demand for labor is

$$\text{Demand:} \quad \text{MRP} = 1050 - 0.4E$$

a) If The Artisanry can hire labor in a competitive market for $330 per week, how many workers will it hire?

b) If the market is imperfectly competitive with the following supply and marginal factor cost relationships,

$$\text{Supply:} \quad W = 150 + 0.1E$$

$$\text{Marginal factor cost:} \quad \text{MFC} = 150 + 0.2E$$

how many workers will it hire? What will the wage be?

c) What level of employment for the market described in (b) is consistent with allocative efficiency (MSB = MSC)?

Appendix to Chapter 13

An Algebraic Look at Resource Markets

In this chapter you saw how a profit-maximizing firm selects the quantity of resources to buy. In this appendix, we consider a firm's resource decision, using an algebraic representation of the firm's demand for resources. In particular, we consider how a firm determines the number of workers to hire. In doing so, we assume that product demand, productivity, and quantity of all other resources remain constant and that labor is the only variable resource.

EQUATION FOR MARGINAL REVENUE PRODUCT

Let's say that the marginal revenue product (MRP) of labor for a firm can be expressed as

$$MRP = 730 - 2E$$

where E is the number of workers hired per week and MRP is the firm's demand for labor. The marginal revenue product indicates how much extra revenue the firm will receive from hiring an additional worker; the firm would pay no more in extra cost than this value.

DECISION MAKING IN COMPETITIVE RESOURCE MARKETS

Firms maximize profits by buying resources up to the point at which extra benefits (MRP) equal extra costs (MFC). When a firm buys labor in a competitive resource market, it has no market power and can buy all it wants to at the current market wage. Marginal factor cost is simply the wage. Hiring an additional worker will raise the firm's costs by the market wage. If the current market wage is $250 per week, we can find the best, or profit-maximizing, number of workers to hire by determining the point at which MRP = MFC.

$$
\begin{aligned}
MRP &= MFC \\
730 - 2E &= 250 \\
2E &= 480 \\
E &= 240 \text{ workers per week}
\end{aligned}
$$

DECISION MAKING IN IMPERFECTLY COMPETITIVE RESOURCE MARKETS

A firm buying in an imperfectly competitive resource market uses the same basic approach, but in order to attract additional workers, it must raise the wage offered. Thus the firm faces a supply curve that slopes upward and an increasing marginal factor cost curve. Suppose that supply and marginal factor cost are given by the expressions

$$
\begin{aligned}
\text{Supply:} \quad & W = 130 + 0.5E \\
\text{Marginal factor cost:} \quad & MFC = 130 + E
\end{aligned}
$$

where W is the wage rate in dollars per week. (To check your understanding, verify that MFC is higher than S by calculating W and MFC at several levels of E.)

The firm makes its resource decision in two steps: First, it equates marginal revenue product and marginal factor cost to determine the optimal number of workers to hire. That is,

$$
\begin{aligned}
MRP &= MFC \\
730 - 2E &= 130 + E \\
3E &= 600 \\
E &= 200 \text{ workers per week}
\end{aligned}
$$

Second, it locates on the supply curve the wage that must be paid to attract that number of workers. At 200 workers per week, that wage is

$$W = 130 + 0.5E$$
$$= 130 + 0.5(200) \quad \text{or} \quad \$230 \text{ per week}$$

ALLOCATIVE EFFICIENCY IN RESOURCE MARKETS

We can determine allocative efficiency in resource markets by relating marginal social benefits and marginal social costs to the preceding expressions. If we assume that no other imperfections exist (no external costs or benefits and a competitive product market), demand equals marginal social benefit and supply equals marginal social cost.

In the first situation (competitive resource markets), the firm's best decision (MRP = MFC) is the same as allocative efficiency (MSB = MSC). When the firm has market power in resource markets, however, the firm's extra costs (MFC) are greater than those for society (S = MSC). Expressed mathematically,

Competition produces allocative efficiency	Market power produces allocative inefficiency
MSB = MSC	MRP = MFC
$730 - 2E = 130 + 0.5E$	$730 - 2E = 130 + E$
$2.5E = 600$	$3E = 600$
$E = 240$ workers per week	$E = 200$ workers per week

CONCLUSION

All profit-seeking firms follow the same rules. First, they find the quantity of resources that equates marginal revenue product and marginal factor cost. Second, the supply curve indicates the price that must be paid for that quantity of resources. Of course, for a firm hiring in a competitive resource market, the second step is trivial because the price the firm must pay is given.

Note, however, that this analysis is only the first step in decision making. We have not bothered to check total revenues against total variable costs to determine whether the firm should shut down or continue to produce. This check is important for a short-run decision. And in the long run, the firm would have to be able to earn at least a normal profit.

We also showed that a firm with market power in resource markets will buy fewer resources (and pay a lower price) than is allocatively efficient. That is, if all other assumptions for a perfect market hold, supply equals marginal social costs (S = MSC), and the firm's demand for resources equals marginal social benefits (D = MRP = MSB). The quantity that is allocatively efficient is found where MSB = MSC, or MRP = S.

CHAPTER 14

Capital Resources and
Financial Markets

QUESTIONS TO CONSIDER

☐ In what ways do markets for capital resources differ from markets for other resources?

☐ How do interest rates affect demand for capital resources?

☐ What role do financial markets play in an economy, and what roles do various economic sectors play in financial markets?

☐ Why is the time value of money important in resource decisions?

☐ What factors affect the presence or absence of economic profits in resource markets?

S hould a company invest in a new machine? If your rich Uncle Sam is willing to give you $1000 in cash, would you care whether you received it today or in five years? What would make you willing to postpone receiving the money? How does a market economy decide whether to produce more capital resources, such as buildings and machinery, or more consumer goods and services? How does a market economy decide which capital resources to produce?

To be able to answer these questions you must understand two special types of markets: capital resource markets and financial markets. Although the rules we developed in Chapter 13 apply to all resource markets, the peculiarities of these two markets require further discussion. For example, capital resources are special because they are long lasting. Unlike materials that are used in making a product for sale, a building or a machine can be used for several or even many years. As you will see in this chapter, the time dimension creates some very special problems, which are not unique to the market for capital resources.

Moreover, as we noted in Chapter 2, an economy that produces more capital resources now can produce an even greater quantity of goods and services in the future. But it can do so only if it is willing to produce and consume fewer goods and services at the present time. By indicating the value to society of satisfying wants today instead of in the future, financial markets help the economy decide how many capital resources to produce.

DEMAND FOR CAPITAL RESOURCES

Physical capital. Long-lasting capital resources, such as buildings and machinery, that yield benefits both in the present and in the future.

Intangible capital. Technological knowledge and legal rights such as patents and trademarks.

Human capital. The skills, education, training, and experience of individuals.

All capital resources are long lasting, yielding benefits not only in the present but also (and perhaps primarily) in the future. But the term *capital resources* actually refers to three types of resources. **Physical capital** includes buildings and machinery. **Intangible capital** refers both to technological knowledge and to legal rights such as patents and trademarks. **Human capital** is the skills, education, training, and experience of individuals. Many of the examples in this chapter refer to physical capital, but the same concepts apply to all capital purchases.

Investment in Capital Resources

In Chapter 13 you learned that firms compare marginal revenue product with marginal factor cost when making decisions about buying resources. To maximize profits, firms buy resources up to the point where marginal revenue product equals marginal factor cost. This principle also applies to capital resources. If a firm buys a machine, it can produce more of its product (or produce at a lower cost). The extra profit that a firm can earn if it owns the machine is the machine's marginal revenue product. The value of capital resources, like other resources, depends on product demand, price and productivity of complementary resources (such as the labor and materials used), and value of substitutes.

But capital resources also have special features. First, capital resources do not generally produce goods by themselves. If a firm is considering buying a new machine in order to increase production, it will have to consider the extra cost of the additional materials and labor that will also be required; holding all other resources constant does not make much sense. Thus marginal revenue product is the extra profit earned after all expected changes in revenues and costs.

Second, capital resources last a long time. If a clothing maker buys material for shirts, its expenditure is returned rather quickly in the form of sales of those shirts. But it can scarcely add the entire price of a new sewing machine to a single shirt. Nor should it, because the firm will benefit from the new machine for years to come. Because some (perhaps most) benefits occur in the future, a firm must compare *current* and *future* costs and benefits when deciding whether to buy a new machine or build a new factory.

Costs and Benefits of Capital Resources

Let's look at how a capital purchase decision might be made. Playtime Toys, Inc., is considering building a new plant so it can manufacture and sell 20,000 more toy robots. Each robot sells for $20 and has an average variable cost (AVC) of $10. The new plant will cost $1.5 million to build and will have annual fixed costs of $50,000. Should Playtime build the plant?

To decide, we must first determine the value of the resource, the new plant. Recall that the value of a resource depends on product demand and costs and productivity of complementary and substitute resources. To Playtime, the value of the new plant is the increased profits the firm expects to earn if it builds the plant. Using the profit equation, we calculate the increase in Playtime's profits to be $150,000 per year, excluding the cost of building the plant, or

$$
\begin{aligned}
\text{Economic profit} &= \text{Total revenue} - \text{Total cost} \\
&= \text{TR} - \text{TVC} - \text{TFC} \\
&= \text{P} \times \text{Q} - \text{AVC} \times \text{Q} - \text{TFC} \\
&= (\$20)(20,000) - (\$10)(20,000) - \$50,000 \\
&= \$400,000 - \$200,000 - \$50,000 \\
&= \$150,000 \text{ per year}
\end{aligned}
$$

Rate of return. The ratio of profits earned from an investment to total dollars invested.

We can also express the value of the plant as a 10 percent annual **rate of return**

Opportunity cost of capital.
The cost of funds used by a firm for investment, expressed as an annual percentage rate; reflects market interest rates, with allowance for future inflation and the risk involved in the investment.

Interest rate. The ratio of the dollars paid in interest charges to total dollars borrowed; usually stated as an annual percentage rate.

on the money invested as construction costs. That is,

$$\text{Rate of return} = \frac{\text{Increase in annual profit}}{\text{Amount of investment}} = \frac{\$150,000}{\$1,500,000}$$

$$= 0.10 \quad \text{or} \quad 10 \text{ percent per year}$$

So far we have determined only the benefits of building the plant. To decide whether building is Playtime's best option, we must also know the true cost of building. That is, we have to determine the opportunity cost of the $1.5 million Playtime must invest to build the plant.

Economists use the term **opportunity cost of capital** to describe this type of cost. If the opportunity cost of capital is 15 percent, Playtime will not build the plant, since the cost is higher than the 10 percent extra benefit that we just calculated. If the opportunity cost of capital fell to 10 percent or below (and the expected rate of return remained at 10 percent), Playtime's best decision would be to build the plant. In general, *a firm will buy additional capital resources only if the expected rate of return is greater than or equal to the opportunity cost of capital.* The expected rate of return is a measure of marginal revenue product, and the opportunity cost of capital represents marginal factor cost.

In Playtime's case the opportunity cost of capital is the sacrifice required to get the money to build the new plant. One option is to borrow the funds. A bank will loan funds to Playtime only if the firm pays the bank enough interest to cover the bank's opportunity cost, that is, what it could earn on other loans. Of course, banks aren't the only source of financing. Playtime could use profits it earned last year. But using profits also involves an opportunity cost. The profits that Playtime earned last year belong to its owners, who also have other opportunities. The owners would want Playtime to invest their profits in a new building only if expected returns are as high or higher than their opportunity cost.

Note that the opportunity cost of capital does not measure a firm's opportunities. Rather, it measures the options of the banks and shareholders whose money the firm uses. These opportunity costs are reflected in the market **interest rate**. As you will see, this rate is determined by demand and supply of loanable funds.

Investment Projects and Demand for Financing

In the real world, firms usually have more than one option. Exhibit 14.1 shows 4 machines that Playtime could buy to produce toys. The purchase price of each machine is the amount of investment required. The expected rate of return for each is the annual profit divided by the purchase price; the expected return varies from 25 percent on machine A, the most profitable one, to only 6 percent for machine D. We can use this information to determine how much Playtime will invest at various interest rates. Following the principles of rational choice, Playtime will seek to maximize profits. Thus it will want to make all investments for which the expected return is equal to or greater than the opportunity cost of capital.

Demand for capital resources depends on the value of the resource to the firm and the current market rate of interest. Thus the lower the market rate of interest, the greater is the market demand for capital resources. For example, if the interest rate is 20 percent, Playtime will buy both machines A and B. Its total investment of $750,000 is both its demand for machinery and its demand for

Investment	Expected increase in annual profits (dollars per year)	Purchase price (dollars)	Expected rate of return (% per year)
Machine A	87,500	350,000	25
Machine B	80,000	400,000	20
Machine C	72,000	600,000	12
Machine D	12,000	200,000	6

Exhibit 14.1
Expected Return and Demand for Loanable Funds

Financial markets. Markets for funds used to make investments and to finance consumption.

loanable funds, since to buy the machines it must obtain $750,000 from financial markets. If the interest rate falls to 12 percent, Playtime will buy 3 machines (A, B, and C) and demand $1,350,000 of investment funds. Exhibit 14.1 therefore represents the firm's demand for loanable funds for each option.

However, businesses are just one part of the market for loanable funds. In the next section we discuss the other participants: households, government, and the foreign sector. Together, the demand for and supply of loanable funds determine the market rate of interest and, as a consequence, demand for capital goods.

RECAP

Capital resources are similar to other resources: The demand for them depends on product demand and the prices and productivity of complementary and substitute resources.

Capital resources differ from other resources because they are long lasting. Decisions to buy them require balancing of costs and benefits for different time periods.

The extra benefit of a capital resource can be measured as the rate of return on the amount of funds invested; it is calculated as the expected increase in annual profits divided by the purchase cost.

The extra cost of a capital resource can be measured as the opportunity cost of capital, that is, the cost of raising the funds required for the investment.

A capital resource should be bought if the expected rate of return equals or exceeds the opportunity cost of capital.

MARKET FOR LOANABLE FUNDS AND MARKET RATES OF INTEREST

Any individual, business, or government that wants to spend more money than it has must obtain the necessary funds from **financial markets**. Bank loans, sales of stocks and bonds, and charges on credit cards all involve exchanges in financial markets. Although there are many types of financial markets, all are connected. Thus we will treat all financial markets as a single market for loanable funds in order to explore the factors that determine the demand and supply of funds and market interest rates.

Market for Loanable Funds

Those who demand loanable funds do so in order to spend more money now than they have. Some households borrow to buy houses, cars, and other goods and services that they cannot pay for in full from current income. Firms borrow to invest in capital resources. Government borrows whenever its expenditures exceed tax revenues. Foreign individuals, businesses, and governments also borrow funds in U.S. financial markets. Mexico, Argentina, and Brazil, for example, currently owe billions of dollars to U.S. banks.

Conversely, the supply of funds represents a willingness to sacrifice some current spending in return for greater future spending. Households are a large source of loanable funds. Any household that saves—that is, puts part of its current income in a savings account or uses it to buy newly issued shares of stock—is a part of the supply of funds. Firms supply funds (mostly to themselves) to finance investments. Government supplies funds to the market when current spending is less than tax receipts. (State governments often add to the supply, although the Federal government has been a large borrower in recent years.) The foreign sector has recently been a large supplier of funds to U.S. financial markets.

Exhibit 14.2 shows a market for loanable funds. Note that demand is *inversely* related to the market rate of interest. This relationship is consistent with our conclusion that firms will buy fewer capital goods—and thus require fewer funds— as the interest rate rises. Similarly, an increase in the interest rate will cause households to buy fewer houses and other commonly financed items. Foreign governments, businesses, and individuals can also be expected to reduce the quantity of borrowing as the interest rate rises. In contrast, the supply of loanable funds is *directly* related to interest rates. That is, as interest rates rise, more funds are supplied. The equilibrium rate of interest—where quantity demanded and supplied are equal—occurs in this case at an interest rate of 12 percent.

Exhibit 14.2
The Market for Loanable Funds
The graph shows demand for and supply of loanable funds. All sectors of the economy are included—households, businesses, and governments, both foreign and domestic. Those who want to spend more than their available resources enter the market to demand funds. Those willing to spend less than they have available supply funds to the market. The quantity of funds demanded is inversely related to interest rates. As rates rise, firms find fewer profitable investments, and households are reluctant to borrow to finance consumption. At the same time, the quantity of funds supplied increases. Households are more willing to wait until the future to spend their income because future rewards will be higher.

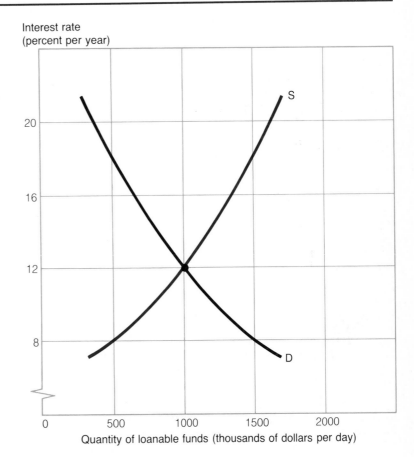

Time Value of Money

One factor that affects interest rates, and thus the supply of loanable funds is the difference between the present value of money and the future value of money. Nearly everyone would rather receive $1000 today than wait a year for it. Why? Because there is an opportunity cost associated with waiting. Economists refer to this cost as the **time value of money**. It affects anyone who supplies loanable funds, such as households that must sacrifice consumption and businesses that must sacrifice profits they could otherwise earn.

Suppose that you have managed to save $1000 and are on your way to the store to buy a compact disc player and stereo system you have been eyeing for some time. On your way, two friends offer the following deal. If you loan them $1000 for 24 hours, they will give you $1050 tomorrow. (To keep this example simple we will assume there is no chance they will not repay you and that you approve of what they plan to do with the money.) Would you gain from making this loan?

It certainly appears that you can make an easy, quick, and guaranteed profit of $50, enough to buy several new compact discs to play on your new sound system. But you have been studying economics long enough to realize there may be some other angle to this story, like our old friend opportunity cost. The opportunity cost that is most important is your having to wait 24 hours before you can enjoy your stereo. For most people, the opportunity cost of waiting would be amply repaid by the $50 bonus.

So far, so good. But what if the deal calls for you to be repaid in a year, instead of 24 hours? Is it still worth waiting? This question is more difficult to answer. We know that the opportunity cost of waiting one year is more than that of waiting one day. As a result, you will require a greater payment. The amount you would charge for the loan to your friends would depend on your time value of money.

If you are willing to loan $1000 to your friends for repayment of $1200 to you next year, you are indifferent about having $1000 today or $1200 next year. That is, your time value of money—your opportunity cost of waiting—is 20 percent, or the bonus you require to postpone consumption. (We usually state the time value of money, like interest rates, as an annual percentage.) Twenty percent is the minimum premium you will accept. If your friends will pay only 15 percent, you would prefer to buy the stereo today.

The time value of money determines how much borrowing occurs. For example, if your time value of money is 20 percent and you can borrow money for one year at 10 percent interest, will you do so? If you follow the principles of rational choice, you will. Borrowing lets you consume today at the sacrifice of future spending. Suppose that you will be given a check one year from today for $1200. If you can borrow $1000 today at 10 percent interest, you can borrow, enjoy the benefits of the money today, repay $1100 and still have $100 left to spend next year.

The time value of money links capital and financial markets. A household's willingness to postpone consumption is directly related to the interest rate it can receive on funds it does not spend. Households will supply funds only if the interest rate is equal to or greater than their time value of money. Higher interest rates promise greater future benefits and cause a greater willingness to forego

Time value of money. The difference between the present and future value of money, expressed as an annual percentage rate.

current consumption, other things being equal. To consumers the time value of money reflects the relative values of consuming now and in the future.

Present value of future dollars. Many decisions require comparing values from different years. Your decision to attend college involves a trade-off between dollars sacrificed at present for larger future income. A firm that buys a machine that will last 10 years is paying out dollars today in return for dollars to be received over the next 10 years.

Dollars received (or paid) in different years cannot be added directly. The discussion of the time value of money indicated that *a dollar received in the future is worth less than a dollar received today*. For individuals whose time value of money is 20 percent, $1200 next year is worth only $1000 today. To make comparisons over a period of time, we must use the time value of money to convert future dollar amounts into their equivalent present values. In doing so, we apply the following principles.

First, *the greater the time value of money, the smaller is the present value of dollars received in the future*. For example, if your time value of money is 10 percent, you are indifferent about having $1000 now and $1100 a year from now. But if your time value of money is 20 percent, $1200 a year from now would equal $1000 now. Each future dollar, therefore, is worth less to you. Second, *the present value of future dollars is smaller the farther into the future they are received*. This principle makes sense if you consider that most people would much prefer to be paid $1000 next year than $1000 in five years.

These principles are sufficient for our present discussion. The appendix to this chapter contains a more rigorous (and mathematical) explanation and example of this concept. To make a decision involving future and current dollars, you must understand the mathematics presented in the appendix (or to hire someone who does). The use of the time value of money in economic decisions is illustrated in A Case in Point: To Buy or Not to Buy a Photocopying Machine?

Interest Rates and Allocative Efficiency

Like other prices, the price of loanable funds—the interest rate—is a signal helping the economy achieve allocative efficiency. If, for example, businesses expected greater gains from capital investments, the demand for loanable funds will increase. The resulting increase in the interest rate signals the greater return to the economy from sacrificing consumer goods for capital investment. The higher rate also acts as an incentive for households to trade current for future benefits.

If the value to households of future consumption rises, the supply of loanable funds will increase. The resulting fall in interest rates is a signal of the change in the relative value of present and future benefits. The lower rate is also an incentive to businesses to increase the production of capital resources. The response of the market for loanable funds thus helps the economy decide how to allocate its current production possibilities between consumer goods and capital resources.

Interest rates also help society allocate loanable funds to the most productive uses at any particular time. The opportunity cost of capital to firms reflects market

A Case in Point
To Buy or Not to Buy a Photocopying Machine?

We can illustrate the essential elements of a capital purchase decision by considering the large demand for photocopying on college campuses. Suppose that the local newspaper advertises a photocopying machine for $1000. If you were to buy one, you could set up a business in your apartment, which is next to a large dorm. You estimate that over the course of a year you will receive $1600 in revenue from sales. Paper and other supplies will cost $400. At the projected level of use, the machine will be completely worn out after one year and will have no remaining value. Should you buy this capital resource and go into business?

First, note that you cannot earn any profits just by buying the machine; it does not produce anything by itself but requires other resources as well. The net benefit of the machine is measured as the increase in profits, that is, additional revenues less additional expenses. Second, the machine is long lasting. A sheet of paper is used up when one copy is made, but you can produce many copies from the one machine. Third, in order to buy the machine you will be making a current sacrifice for a future gain. You must give up $1000 today to receive $1200 next year ($1600 in sales less $400 of expenses).

Let's see what these figures mean. Today you spend $1000 to buy the machine; at the end of next year you expect to have $1200. Since you expect a $200 gain from investing $1000 for one year, your expected rate of return is or $200 ÷ $1000 × 100, or 20 percent.

The expected rate of return measures the extra benefit of the investment. To make a decision, however, you must compare the extra benefit to the extra cost. We have already considered the cost of paper and other supplies, but buying the machine also requires an investment of $1000. To complete the analysis, you have to know the opportunity cost of the money that is invested.

Suppose that your rich Uncle Sam has just handed you $1000, which you could use to purchase the machine. To estimate your opportunity cost of capital you have to know what else you could do with this money. To keep the example simple, let's assume that your only other alternative is to deposit the money in the local bank, which will pay you interest of 8 percent per year. Now we can compare the two options. If you invest in the machine, you will have $1200 next year. If you put the money in the bank, however, you will have only $1080 (the $1000 plus interest of $80). Under these circumstances, would you buy the machine? Although the gain is only $120, this option is better than the alternative.

On the other hand, there is some risk involved in operating a business, whereas there is little risk in putting your money in the bank. To make the final decision, you would have to decide whether the extra reward from purchasing the machine is great enough to compensate you for the extra risk involved.

---

interest rates. Only the most profitable investments—those with an expected return greater than or equal to the market interest rate—will be made.

Real Rate of Interest

Nominal rate of interest. The actual rate of interest in a financial market; includes a premium reflecting the expected rate of inflation.

Real rate of interest. The nominal, or actual, rate of interest less the expected rate of inflation.

So far we have made a crucial but unstated assumption that there is no inflation in the economy—a convenient but often unrealistic assumption. Inflation represents a sustained increase in the average price of goods and services, and we must note here its effect on interest rates.

Economists distinguish between real values and nominal values. The **nominal rate of interest** is the actual market interest rate. The **real rate of interest** is the nominal rate minus a premium reflecting the expected rate of inflation. Real interest rates recognize that inflation reduces the purchasing power of future dollars and thus decreases the sacrifice necessary to pay off a future debt.

To help you understand the distinction in interest rates, consider the following situation: You are willing to loan funds today for one year, as long as the interest rate equals or exceeds your time value of money—10 percent for the next year. That is, you are willing to trade $100 worth of goods and services today for $110 worth of goods and services next year. But suppose that inflation for the next year is expected to be 10 percent. If you are paid $110 next year, you can buy only the same amount of goods that you could have bought today for $100. You would receive no compensation for waiting. Thus if you expect inflation, you will demand a higher interest rate before foregoing current spending.

The nominal rate of interest reflects both compensation for waiting and an adjustment for expected inflation. For you to be able to consume 10 percent more goods and services next year when 10 percent inflation is expected, you must be paid $121 next year. (It takes $110 to buy the original $100 worth of goods. To get 10 percent more in real terms requires an extra $11 since each dollar is worth 10 percent less.) The end result is that expected inflation raises the nominal market rate of interest. Similarly, the opportunity cost of capital to a firm also includes an inflation premium, covering the higher nominal cost of funds.

Usury Laws and Interest Rate Ceilings

In most respects, financial markets are quite competitive. But state governments have long limited the interest that banks and other financial institutions could charge for loans with so-called usury laws. The rationale for usury laws is the desire to protect consumers from the market power of financial institutions. Interest rate ceilings (see Chapter 3) on deposits were first set in the 1930s after a series of bank failures to curb risk taking by banks. In 1986, Congress abolished federal limits on interest rates (except for business checking accounts), but states may still set limits.

Ceilings on loans and deposits. As we have noted, interest rates reflect the value of funds to consumers and businesses. Banks do not deal directly in real goods (either consumer goods or physical capital resources). Banks instead serve an intermediary purpose in financial markets, entering both the demand and supply sides of the market for funds. Banks enter financial markets to demand funds that they can then supply to other individuals or firms. Both usury laws and ceilings on interest rates affect the ability of banks and other regulated financial institutions to compete effectively in the market for loanable funds.

Exhibit 14.3 shows a market for loanable funds in which the ceiling rate (8 percent) is below the equilibrium rate of interest (12 percent). At the lower rate, firms and households find more investments profitable and demand $1,500,000 per day. However, savers find that sacrificing current consumption and investment does not make as much sense and will supply only $500,000 per day. Thus the ceiling rate forces a shortage of $1,000,000 per day.

In addition to creating a shortage, ceiling rates have important effects on efficiency. You can understand those effects by considering the demand side of

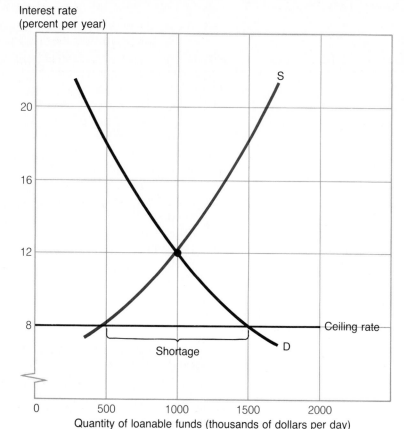

Exhibit 14.3

The Effect of an Interest Rate Ceiling
In this market for loanable funds, the equilibrium interest rate is 12 percent per year (where the demand and supply curves intersect). But government has imposed an interest rate ceiling at 8 percent. Since this maximum rate is below the equilibrium rate, a shortage of funds will result. As the interest rate falls, more funds are demanded but fewer funds are supplied. By distorting the market signal, the ceiling rate may cause allocative inefficiency. Investments that would not be profitable at the equilibrium rate are profitable at the ceiling rate. Moreover, fewer total investments are made than are profitable to both firms and society.

the market. At a relatively low interest rate (8 percent), firms find many investments reasonable. But equilibrium reflects society's opportunity cost of funds. That is, the expected future gain on investments is not as great as society's time value of money. Thus when firms make investments at below equilibrium rates they create allocative inefficiency.

Not only are interest rate ceilings inefficient, but they may also fail to achieve their stated purpose of protecting consumers. Those who can get loans at the artificially low rates will benefit, but because the ceiling rate reduces the available funds, fewer loans will be made than before. As interest rates increased in the 1970s, market rates exceeded ceiling rates in a number of states. As a result, loans were difficult to obtain because lenders were able to find better opportunities in other states.

Although some constraints on interest rates remain, Congress took a significant step toward deregulating financial markets in 1980 by passing the Depository Institutions Deregulation and Monetary Control Act. This act effectively eliminated federal limits on interest rates and also restricted the ability of states to impose interest rate ceilings.

PROFIT: RISK, RENT, AND REWARD

We have already pointed out that economists define profits differently than do accountants. For economists, the total revenues of a firm must be compared with the full value of all the firm's opportunity costs in order to assess its profitability. Suppose that a firm has buildings, equipment, and other assets worth $1 million and earns an accounting profit of $100,000. If the firm's opportunity cost of capital is 15 percent per year, the accounting profit would represent an economic loss of $50,000, that is, the accounting profit of $100,000 minus the time value of money of $150,000.

So far we have not introduced anything new, although associating normal profit with the time value of money is a new way of looking at profit. Can we say, however, that a firm earning more than the time value of money is really making an economic profit? To answer this question we have to know what the opportunity cost of capital measures.

Risk and the Opportunity Cost of Capital

We have been assuming that all options are equally risky, that each project has the same chance of being successful. Yet such is seldom the case. Moreover, most individuals prefer less risk to more risk. They therefore treat the risk of any investment as an additional cost and require an extra benefit to cover the higher possibility of failure. When considering two possible projects requiring identical investments and yielding identical returns, but having different risks, a firm will choose the less risky project. If we consider risk as an additional cost, we can explain this decision as a rational choice. A riskier project has greater costs than a less risky project, but they have equal benefits. A higher rate of return is required when any cost goes up, including the costs associated with higher risk.

In the real world, financial institutions offer funds at many different interest rates. One reason for the difference in rates involves risk. As a consumer with ordinary income and ordinary assets, you will not pay the same interest rate that a major corporation does for a bank loan. Nor will a firm with financial difficulties pay the same interest rate as a firm with more stable earnings. Thus market interest rates include both an inflation premium and a risk premium. The risk premium is the additional return that investors require to cover the extra costs of risk. Firms considering alternative investments having different levels of risk must take risk into account by raising the opportunity cost of capital when figuring expected profits. Unless the firm can anticipate a higher reward, it will not undertake riskier investments.

Economic Rent and Economic Profit

When discussing profits, we noted that economists distinguish between normal profit and economic profit. A normal profit just matches opportunity cost. An economic profit exceeds opportunity cost and, if it persists over time, causes allocative inefficiency. Similarly, economists make a distinction between normal

Economic rent. Payment for a resource in excess of the real opportunity cost of that resource.

payments for resources and economic rents. Normal payments keep resources from moving to their next best use and reflect real opportunity cost. But **economic rent** is a payment over and above opportunity cost.

Recall that when a resource's price equals its opportunity cost, it is being used in an efficient manner. But payment for some resources is much more than the amount necessary to keep them from other uses. Hershel Walker, who signed a multimillion-dollar contract with the Dallas Cowboys, and Larry Bird, who earns more than $1 million a year playing basketball for the Boston Celtics, probably could not earn comparable salaries in other occupations. Prime farmland in Iowa has an actual cost in excess of its value for nonagricultural purposes; prime real estate in growing metropolitan areas has a development value far in excess of its alternative use. Each of these resources commands a larger payment than its opportunity cost and thus earns economic rent.

What causes economic rents? For society, the opportunity cost of a resource reflects the sacrifice involved in using the resource in one way as opposed to another. But this cost does not measure the value of a resource to a particular firm or farmer. Football teams competing for Hershel Walker and farmers seeking prime agricultural land must pay the full value that others in the same industry place on those resources. That is, they must pay both the real opportunity cost to society *and* economic rent if they want to bid the resources away from other teams or farmers.

Economic rent results from the scarcity of a particular talent or activity. It is not easy to duplicate a Hershel Walker or create more prime agricultural land, or create more land in prime residential or commercial locations. Economic rent can also occur when opportunities to increase supply are restricted, as in the case of barriers to entry or occupational licensing in certain industries.

Economic rent and economic profit are also alike in that neither is necessary to keep resource owners in their current use. If we tax away economic rent or economic profit, resource owners and firms will not change their behaviors; they still have no better options. Even when economic rent and economic profit disappear, firms earn normal profits and resources earn their real opportunity cost.

When economic rents are the result of artificial scarcity—such as barriers to entry in occupations or industries—efforts to improve mobility decrease or eliminate rent. In such cases we can ask whether society would be better off if we removed the restrictions and eliminated the economic rent. When the scarcity is real—such as a Hershel Walker or prime agricultural land—mobility is not the answer. The only question is: Who should get the *excess* payment representing economic rent? Should it go to Hershel, to the Cowboys, or to the fans of the Cowboys? This question has no definite answer in terms of economic efficiency, but it requires some consideration in terms of equity.

Profits and Rewards

To conclude our discussion of profits, let's return to the original concept of economic costs and the fundamental problem of scarcity. Normal profits represent the opportunity costs of all resources used and are a necessary and sufficient reward. Firms that receive normal profits over the long run continue to produce desired products and promote allocative efficiency. But in the real world, profits are not always at the normal level. In this section, we discuss the reasons for economic profits, examine the natural role of profits in a market economy, and consider the problems created by imperfect market operations.

The reasons for economic profits. Economic profits occur for many reasons, most of which are beneficial because they lead to allocative efficiency. Understanding the legitimate role of profits—and why unnecessary economic profits arise—is important for many policy questions. Because profits play a vital role in allocating resources, tax policies that restrict profits may create inefficiency.

Shifts in resource supplies and/or product demand. A market economy is never at rest; it is constantly adjusting to changing conditions. For example, if supplies of paper increase, its price falls. Publishing companies, which are heavy users of paper, will have lower costs and may earn economic profits. And when consumer tastes shift, firms whose demand increases may experience economic profits. In both cases, economic profits signal the market economy that these activities should be expanded. As you have seen, under competition the market responds, and economic profits exist for only a short time. But without short-term economic profits, resource adjustments would not take place and allocative efficiency would be impaired.

Rewards for risk. Firms that engage in risky ventures, such as drilling for oil, may appear to receive higher than normal rewards. But as we noted earlier, risks entail higher costs that are related to higher probabilities of failure and the necessity to overcome people's normal reluctance to gamble. Only if rates of return *adjusted for risk* are still higher than normal are economic profits being made. If they are and no restrictions exist, we would also expect to see new firms enter the industry and economic profits disappear. Without extra returns, risky ventures would not be undertaken (possibly to society's loss). Thus the extra accounting profits that risky ventures appear to earn are really just another required return and a part of normal profit.

Incentives for innovation. Innovation—successfully marketing a new idea, product, or method of production—may also produce rewards greater than those earned by the typical venture. In part, the higher rewards reflect a risk premium, since innovation has a higher risk of failure. Innovation profits also reflect a rate of return required to offset research and development costs. Firms will spend money now to discover new and better products or production techniques only if future rewards are high enough to pay the opportunity cost of the investment.

Apple Computers, for example, pioneered the personal computer. The firm's innovative efforts were rewarded with a high level of profits. Without some reward for innovation, less than an optimal amount will be undertaken; new and better products and production techniques will not be developed or produced. Society would suffer in terms of both allocative and technical efficiency. The rationale for granting patents to innovators is to allow them to earn normal profits on the costs of innovation. But as with risk, successful innovators are expected to earn higher than normal returns only in the short run. The success of Apple Computers was followed by the entry of IBM, Tandy, and others attracted by the opportunity to earn profits.

Economic rent and economic power.   Economic rent and economic power may also result in economic profits. But unlike rewards for innovation, risks, and changes in demand and supply, economic profits from rent or market power lead to allocative inefficiency when barriers to entry exist. In addition, taxing away such profits does not cause allocative inefficiency. Firms with market power have no better options when they can earn at least a normal profit. And resources earning economic rents will not be shifted to alternative uses if excess earnings disappear.

Taxation of economic profits.   Because long-run economic profits are often unnecessary, inefficient, and inequitable, taxing them away is frequently proposed. For example, in 1980, Congress imposed a windfall profits tax on the oil industry to prevent what many in Congress saw as large and unjustified profits from rapidly rising oil prices.

When they actually apply to long-run economic profits, such taxes do not reduce efficiency. But if profits only *appear* high and actually reflect rewards for innovation or risk taking, as in the exploration for and discovery of new oil fields, such taxes will cause inefficiency. Certainly oil companies will be less willing to look for and develop new oil supplies if they believe that Congress will impose taxes when prices rise.

Unfortunately, we do not have the tools required to measure precisely economic or normal profits or to account perfectly for risk or innovation. Because they use different methods of measurement, many economists disagree about whether profits for a particular firm or industry (such as the oil industry) exceed normal levels. Thus we cannot state whether the windfall tax is correct or incorrect. We can only point out the issues that must be addressed.

CONCLUSION

In this chapter, you saw how decision making must account for benefits and costs that occur at different times and with different risks. Although we dealt specifically with markets for physical capital, this analysis also applies to other decisions. For example, the value of a patent is the present value of future profits it can generate.

We emphasized that expected profits must allow a firm to earn a return that is at least equal to the opportunity cost of capital. This principle is important to decisions made by both individuals and society, since the opportunity cost of time affects many decisions. We discuss an important application of this principle to investment in human capital—education and job training—in Chapter 15. To determine if a college education is a good investment it is necessary to weigh the current costs against future benefits.

SUMMARY

1. In this chapter we applied the principles of resource demand and supply to capital resources and financial markets.

2. As with other resources, demand for capital resources depends on a firm's ability to use the resources to increase profits. Because capital resources are long last-ing, both benefits and costs must be measured over a period of time. Benefits are measured as the rate of return and costs as the opportunity cost of capital.

3. The opportunity cost of capital must be considered whenever current and future costs and benefits are compared. The greater the opportunity cost of capital,

the lower is the present value of future dollars, since current dollars could be used to earn higher returns. And the farther in the future that dollars are to be paid, the lower is their present value, since a greater sacrifice is required.

4. Interest rates determined in financial markets affect demand for capital resources because they determine the firm's opportunity cost of capital. Firms will buy more capital resources only if the expected return of the investment exceeds the opportunity cost of capital. Higher interest rates mean an increase in the opportunity cost of capital and a reduction in the number of profitable investments.

5. The market interest rate is determined in financial markets by the interaction between demand and supply of loanable funds. All sectors of the economy—households, businesses, government, and foreign—participate on both the demand and supply sides of U.S. financial markets.

6. For decision makers, dollars received now are more valuable than dollars received in the future. Consumers must choose between consuming now or consuming more in the future. Firms must choose between earning profits today or greater profits in the future. The time value of money reflects the degree to which future dollars must exceed current dollars in order to induce firms and consumers to supply financial resources.

7. Interest rates reflect the opportunity cost of capital. They foster allocative efficiency by ensuring that firms make only investments that generate returns equal to or greater than social costs. Interest rates also help society choose how much current consumption to sacrifice in order to expand future productive capacity, thus aiding allocation of resources over a period of time.

8. Inflation decreases the real value of dollars by lessening their purchasing power and thus affects market interest rates. In order to induce individuals and businesses to supply funds, market interest rates must cover both the opportunity cost of time (the real rate of interest) and an inflation premium (reflecting the expected erosion of purchasing power).

9. When ceilings on interest rates are below equilibrium rates, they create a shortage of funds by increasing quantity demanded and reducing quantity supplied. Artificially low interest rates may also cause firms to make investments that do not cover society's opportunity cost of time.

10. All investments are not equally risky. In essence, risks are additional costs. Thus the higher returns required to induce investment in risky projects are not economic profits; they represent opportunity costs associated with risk.

11. Economists distinguish between resource payments reflecting real social opportunity costs and payments in excess of opportunity costs, known as economic rent. Resources may earn economic rent if they have unique qualities not easily duplicated or as a result of artificial barriers such as occupational licensing.

12. Economic profits occur for a number of reasons, most of which are good for the economy. In the short run, economic profits may result from changes in resource prices and/or product demand. These changes signal a preference for different resource allocation. Economic profits also reward risk taking or innovation that would not otherwise occur. The entry of new firms will eliminate economic profits in the long run so long as there are no barriers to entry.

KEY TERMS

Physical capital, 337
Intangible capital, 337
Human capital, 337
Rate of return, 338
Opportunity cost of capital, 339
Interest rate, 339
Financial markets, 340
Time value of money, 342
Nominal rate of interest, 344
Real rate of interest, 344
Economic rent, 348

QUESTIONS FOR REVIEW AND DISCUSSION

1. Comment on the statement: "I can buy a four-year-old truck for $7000; a new one of the same size will cost me $16,000. It only makes sense to buy the used truck."

2. If they are held over a reasonable period of time, fine wines increase in value. Suppose that you have been asked to help a winery determine how long to store its wines before selling them. Assuming that the information you want can be obtained from the winery, how would you determine how long to hold the wine? (Specify the information you require and how you plan to use it.)

3. How would each of the following tend to affect the market rate of interest?
   a) Increase in the expected inflation rate.
   b) Improvement in the prospects for future economic growth.

4. Consider the case of Sun Time Company. Sun Time's managers estimate that the firm could earn a 12 percent rate of return by buying a machine to make a new product: solar-powered miniature radios. How would each of the following factors affect that calculation?
   a) Evidence that the machine will become obsolete two years earlier than expected.
   b) Evidence that new competitors will introduce solar-powered miniature cassette players. (Sun Time's managers had not expected much competition when they estimated the returns.)

5. Jock Starr has been offered $1 million a year to play basketball for the Giants. His next best job opportunity is to work in a local sporting goods store at a salary of $15,000 per year. What do economists call the difference between the two salaries? Which of the two salaries represents his social value? Why?

6. Lazy Bones, Inc., has an opportunity to produce the world's first voice-activated television remote control. It expects to be able to sell 10,000 controls for $50 each. Average variable cost will be $15 per control; total fixed costs will be $175,000 per year. If the firm must invest $875,000 to make the controls and the opportunity cost of capital is 15 percent per year, should Lazy Bones make remote controls?

7. Use the information presented in the appendix to this chapter and the following information to evaluate (a)–(c). A firm is considering buying a machine that costs $80,000 and will be worthless in two years. Should the machine be bought under each of the following conditions?
   a) The machine will add $80,000 to the firm's profits the first year and $20,000 the second year. The firm's opportunity cost of capital is 15 percent.
   b) The machine will add $20,000 to profits the first year and $80,000 the second year. The firm's opportunity cost of capital is 15 percent.
   c) Recalculate (b) if the company's opportunity cost of capital is 10 percent.

Appendix to Chapter 14

Discounted Present Value

In this chapter, we noted that the opportunity cost of time reflects the fact that individuals and firms value dollars they currently receive (or pay) more than dollars they will receive (or pay) in the future. In this appendix we present the mathematical relationship between the value of present and future dollars.

FUTURE VALUE OF PRESENT DOLLARS

Suppose that you have $1000, and the local bank promises to pay you 10 percent interest per year if you put it in a certificate of deposit. If you leave your money in the bank for one year, you will have $1100 to spend next year, or your original

Present value (PV). The current value of money to be received or paid in a future period; the number of dollars that must be invested today at a specified interest rate in order to have a certain sum of money at a particular future time.

Future value (FV). A sum of money to be received or paid at a future time.

$1000 plus $100 in interest. Thus $1000 now equals $1100 next year. In mathematical terms, we can express the relationship between the **present value (PV)** of dollars and the **future value (FV)** of dollars one year from now (FV_1) as follows:

$$FV_1 = PV(1 + r)$$

where r is the market rate of interest, which reflects the time value of money, or the opportunity cost of capital.

If you leave your money in the bank for two years, the future value (FV_2) would be $1210, which we calculate as follows:

$$FV_1 = PV(1 + r) \; = \$1000(1 + 0.10) \quad \text{or} \quad \$1100$$

$$FV_2 = FV_1(1 + r) = \$1100(1 + 0.10) \quad \text{or} \quad \$1210$$

or, substituting for FV_1,

$$FV_2 = PV(1 + r)^2$$

We can generalize this expression to show future value at the end of n years as

$$FV_n = PV(1 + r)^n$$

You can use this general equation to calculate the future value of dollars intended for any number of years at the market rate (or any rate) of interest.

PRESENT VALUE OF FUTURE DOLLARS

Economic decisions often involve comparing present and future dollars. For example, the decision to invest in your education means comparing costs today (for tuition, books, and the opportunity to earn money by working) with returns in the future (higher salary, better living conditions, and the like). To make the decision you should compare benefits and costs measured in present value terms. To translate future dollars into present dollars, we can use the expression we introduced in the previous section. This time we solve for PV, so the expression becomes

$$PV = \frac{FV_n}{(1 + r)^n}$$

To make an investment decision, we first estimate current and future benefits and costs. Then, using the formula and an appropriate value of r, we convert all benefits and costs into present values. Finally, we make the decision by comparing the present values of the benefits and costs.

PRESENT VALUE AND INVESTMENT DECISIONS

Let's consider a firm that has an opportunity cost of capital of 15 percent per year. For $100,000, the firm can buy a machine that will increase its profits in the next three years as follows:

| | Increase in profits in year | | | |
	1	2	3	Total
Actual value	$51,750	$44,965	$36,501	$133,216
Present value	45,000	34,000	24,000	103,000

If we add actual dollars without regard to the time value of money, they total $133,216 over the next three years, or $33,216 more than the original cost of the project. But adding future values is incorrect because future dollars are not equivalent. We have to recognize the time value of money reflected in the opportunity cost of capital.

Applying the present-value formula, we can convert the actual (future) values into present values shown in the second row of the table.[*] If we add the present values, they total $103,000 over the next three years. Since these extra benefits exceed the original cost of $100,000 (allowing for the opportunity cost of capital), the machine is a good investment. Put another way, the future profits the machine will yield are worth $103,000 in present dollars. The value of any capital good is determined by the present value of all increases in profits. Because the value of the machine exceeds its cost, it may be purchased, unless another machine would be worth more.

CONCLUSION

The real cost of making a payment always depends on when that payment is to be made and on the opportunity cost of time. But as the formula for present value indicates, the farther into the future the payment will be made, the lower the real cost will be (the value of n in the denominator increases). The present value is also smaller when the interest rate (r in the denominator) is higher.

---

[*] The conversions to present value are as follows:

Year 1: $PV = \dfrac{FV}{1.15}$ Year 2: $PV = \dfrac{FV}{(1.15)^2}$ Year 3: $PV = \dfrac{FV}{(1.15)^3}$

$= \dfrac{\$51,750}{1.15}$ $= \dfrac{\$44,965}{1.3225}$ $= \dfrac{\$36,501}{1.520875}$

$= \$45,000$ $= \$34,000$ $= \$24,000$

Many economic decisions require us to compare costs and benefits that occur in different years. To make a correct comparison, all values must be converted into common terms, usually by expressing every cost and benefit in present values. Economic options are worth accepting when the present value of current and expected benefits exceed the present value of current and expected costs.

KEY TERMS

Present value (PV), 353
Future value (FV), 353

Economic Encounters
New Strategies on Wall Street

On today's Wall Street, anyone with sharp wits and some money to risk is eligible to join in the speculating. Computers and new trading practices have brought about tremendous change. The Securities and Exchange Commission (SEC), the watchdog of the stock market, is responsible for licensing brokers, enforcing regulations, and protecting investors. But can, or should, the SEC control the new strategies arising on Wall Street?

Wiring Wall Street Less than 20 years ago, securities and money-market traders had few resources to tap in performing their jobs. Traders depended largely on daily newspapers and the telephone to act as middlemen between institutions and brokerages. For years the money market was relatively sluggish and dull; nothing moved quickly enough to merit a rush for information.

Then along came computerized systems—tracking devices that inform traders all over the world of the current international bank interest rates and currency values. Telerate, the first such system, was modeled after centralized stock exchanges. With these computerized systems installed worldwide, information began whizzing around the globe via satellite. Before long, the money market began to zoom with it.

Program Trading: The Latest Craze
During the mid-1980s, a new Wall Street strategy called program trading entered the picture. Program traders use computers to identify opportunities for quick profits based upon differences between actual stock prices and stock price futures.

In futures markets, buyer and seller contract today on the price of a good or stock to be paid for and delivered at a specified future date. Program traders simultaneously buy futures contracts and sell shares or vice-versa.

Profits and losses derive from the price discrepancy between the two.

For example, traders, or their computers, may notice that the cost of a batch of stocks represented in a stock index future may be less than the selling price of the future. By simultaneously buying the actual stock and selling a futures contract, a trader can earn an immediate gain. Although the typical price difference is small, program traders can earn huge profits by buying or selling millions of dollars of stocks.

The Witching Hour All this trading happens at breakneck speed during what is known as "the triple witching hour," the time when options and futures on stock indexes expire. In one half-hour session at the New York Stock Exchange in April 1986, 57 million shares changed hands and the Dow Jones average plunged 36 points.

Some observers have argued that program trading causes large swings in stock prices. This criticism has led them to propose regulations such as "telescoping"—the gradual unwinding of program traders' positions in the week before the triple witching hour—with a goal of softening the impact by spreading it out over a longer period of time. However, recent studies sug-

During "the triple witching hour," pandemonium breaks out as program traders hustle to complete transactions. (Jim Pickerell/Black Star)

Ivan F. Boesky paid a $100-million fine for his role in the 1986 insider trading scandal. (John Chiasson/Gamma-Liaison)

gest that the stability of stock prices has not significantly increased during the period in which program trading has become widespread. This is true even on "triple witching" days.

What does the future hold for the computerized Wall Street? Some experts believe technology will continue to transform the way the stock market functions. Rather than having traders execute transactions on the floors of stock exchanges, individual investors in the future may be able to make their own trades using home computers tapped into a global electronic network. As Walter Wriston, former Citicorp chairman, put it, "A market is not a place; it's a concept."

Insider Trading The 1986 insider trading scandal in which Ivan F. Boesky paid an astronomical $100-million fine sparked lively debate among Wall Street experts. "Insider trading" occurs when individuals who have access to exclusive information about corporations' future plans (consultants, merger experts, and lawyers, among others) use that information for personal gain by buying and selling the stock of those companies, while the general public remains uninformed.

In the 1986 case, Boesky admitted offering Dennis Levine, a merger specialist for Drexel Burnham Lambert, a commission for passing on confidential information about client companies' acquisition plans. Levine gave Boesky names of companies that Drexel clients had targeted for takeover. Boesky then bought stock—often hundreds of thousands of shares—in the target companies. When takeover bids were confirmed, stock prices rose giving Boesky a fortune in profits.

Insider trading is illegal. Why? Opponents of the practice say insiders have an unfair advantage; they make huge profits at the expense of less informed shareholders and the companies themselves. If inside trading were legalized, these people say, investors who didn't have insider information would feel they were playing against a stacked deck. Many investors would pull out of the stock market altogether, injuring publicly traded firms by depriving them of capital.

Proponents of legalizing insider trading say that as long as there are SEC regulations people will continue to break them. Broken rules result in investor distrust and uncertainty, and the stock market suffers accordingly. Therefore, why not do away with the rules? Furthermore, insider proponents claim that existing rules are too vague—exactly how much information is an investor allowed to have? If an investor overhears talk of a merger deal while dining in a public restaurant, is he or she allowed to use that information to make investment decisions? Where do we draw the line?

Proponents argue that insider trading causes market prices to reflect all available information. Thus stock prices would more accurately reflect the true value of a stock. By contrast, SEC rules against insider trading allow only a few unprincipled traders to profit at the expense of others.

Short-term Goals Although millions of individuals own stocks and bonds, financial markets are dominated today by large institutional investors—pension funds, insurance companies, and mutual funds. With over $1 trillion in assets, these institutions own an estimated 60 percent of all corporate stocks and bonds. Moreover, many of these institutions are active traders, buying and selling millions of shares in search of profits.

What does this concentration of power mean for the economy? In effect, critics argue that corporations are being held hostage; unless firms can keep profits spiralling upward, institutional investors will dump their stocks. But if businesses aim only for short-run profits, long-run economic goals may suffer. For example, corporate profits may be improved in the short run by reducing the amount spent on research and development, by postponing purchases of capital resources, or by reducing employee training.

The long-run consequences of these shortsighted strategies could be serious. Some experts believe that the focus on short-run profits has caused

> **Today, anyone with sharp wits and money to risk is eligible to join in the speculating.**

U.S. firms to lag behind such rivals as Japan, both in terms of productivity and in the development of new and improved products. But short-run strategies may also backfire. Some experts argue that companies that underinvest in research and development are the most vulnerable to takeovers.

Not all experts believe that institutional investors should be blamed for the lagging productivity and competitiveness of U.S. businesses. On the contrary, they suggest that, by forcing managers to focus on profits, institutional investors perform a service. Because stock prices reflect both long-run and short-run profits, managers of companies that tend to the future have nothing to worry about. Those who do not deserve their fate.

357

C H A P T E R 15

Labor Markets and
Collective Bargaining

QUESTIONS TO CONSIDER

☐ In what ways do labor markets differ from other resource markets?

☐ What determines demand and supply in labor
markets?

☐ Why do different people earn different wages?

☐ How have the size and power of unions changed in
the United States since 1900?

☐ What effects have unions had on the economy?

I n Chapter 14, we looked at physical capital and financial markets. Another
resource market—labor—also has some unusual features, especially in terms
of supply. In this chapter, you will see how the general principles of resource
markets can be adapted to the special characteristics of labor markets.

More than other resource markets do, labor markets raise both efficiency and
equity questions. The market system uses relative prices to guide resource use;
when demand increases in one industry and falls in another, efficiency requires
resources to move as well. Resource prices and the tie between working (earning
wages) and consuming promote efficiency. Resource prices also determine incomes and thus the levels of consumption by individuals. Inefficiencies caused by
racial or sex discrimination result in inequities.

Debates over economic policies tend to mix efficiency and equity issues. We
treat them separately where possible. However, many policy questions—for example, welfare, in which the tie between work and income is broken—require
trade-offs between efficiency and equity. We return to these issues in Chapter 18,
where both equity and efficiency are addressed.

In this chapter we explore several questions: (1) What are some of the recent
trends and changes in labor markets, and how can we explain them? What do
these trends imply for achieving efficiency and equity? (2) Why do wages vary
among industries and occupations? To what extent does rational choice or efficiency explain these differences? (3) How are wages and other working conditions
determined when unions and management engage in collective bargaining? (4)
What trends and changes are occurring in labor–management relations, and what
do they imply for achieving efficiency and equity?

LABOR MARKETS AND
RATIONAL CHOICE

We can begin to answer these questions by applying resource market principles
to labor markets. However, as we previously noted, labor markets have some
unique features, most of which relate to the simple fact that the labor resource
and its owner are one and the same. This fact affects the market for human
resources in several ways.

First, the efficiency of potential employees is hard to assess and is not totally under the control of the employer. Marginal revenue product is still a sound basis for making decisions about how many and which workers to hire. However, employee productivity depends not only on skill but also on effort. Thus an employer may rationally choose to hire an apparently less talented individual who, in the employer's opinion, will work harder and be a more conscientious employee.

Second, individuals are influenced by more than just the income they can earn from selling the labor resources they own to the highest bidder. Wage rates affect decisions to accept or refuse particular jobs (and whether to work at all). But other, nonprice factors—such as job security, opportunity for advancement, and nature of the job, for example—are also important. An individual may rationally choose to accept a lower paying job because it is located in a more desirable part of the country. In contrast, a firm selling plastic cares little about potential buyers except the price they can and will pay for plastic.

Personal preferences also affect decisions about how much to work. One of society's economic goals is to maintain full employment of all resources, including labor resources. But we also seek to maximize satisfaction with the mix of goods and services produced. If everyone worked 12 hours per day, 7 days per week, more goods and services would be produced. But we would also have far less time for leisure, attending school, and doing housework, among other things.

Finally, although few resources are perfectly mobile, restricted mobility is perhaps most important in labor markets. Efficient allocation of labor resources requires workers to move quickly and easily among geographic regions, occupations, and industries. Yet in reality, geographic mobility is limited by family and social ties and high moving costs; occupational and industrial mobility is limited by training and retraining costs.

Significant long-term immobilities are potential causes of inefficiency. But some resource immobility results from personal preferences. For example, a lumberjack may not want a job assembling computers. Forcing individuals to move from job to job and location to location regardless of their preferences might improve efficiency. But our society also values personal freedom of choice. As is so often the case, we face an economic trade-off: In order to achieve more freedom, our society chooses to sacrifice some efficiency.

LABOR MARKETS: DEMAND AND SUPPLY

The special nature of human resources has led some people to object to classifying people as resources. The American Federation of Labor was successful in having the following statement written into law as a part of the Clayton Act of 1914: "The labor of a human being is not a commodity or article of commerce." People certainly are much more than just resources. But considering labor as a marketable resource lets us examine the forces of demand and supply in that market and learn how wages and employment levels are determined. The operation of labor markets touches most of us directly. Some 75 percent of personal income is derived from labor markets. Demand and supply are impersonal forces but they have important personal effects.

Demand for Labor

Demand for labor is influenced by the same factors that determine demand for any resource: demand for the firm's product, productivity of labor, and price and productivity of complementary and substitute resources (see Chapter 13). In microeconomic terms we are interested in seeing how these factors influence demand for labor in particular industries or occupations.

Examples of changes in product demand or in labor productivity abound. The increased supply of automobiles produced in Europe, Japan, and, most recently, South Korea, decreased demand for automobiles produced in the United States. As a result, U.S. automakers decreased their demand for labor and the wages they are willing to pay. Development of efficient industrial robots also has decreased demand for labor in some manufacturing tasks but has increased demand for labor used to produce the robots.

Henry Ford's development of the assembly line illustrates the importance of complementary resources. The assembly line's efficiency enabled Ford (and later his competitors) to sell cars profitably at a lower price. The expansion of car sales increased demand for labor in the auto industry and led to increased employment and higher wages.

Supply of Labor

To examine labor supply decisions, we will use the **household theory of labor supply**, which recognizes that labor supply decisions take place within a household. Decisions about whether to work and, if so, where and for what wages, take into account the effects of various options for all members of a household.

This theory also divides time into three parts. The first, time spent in market work (paid employment), is the only part that yields dollars that the household can spend in product markets. The second part is nonmarket work, which consists of currently productive but nonpaying activities (such as housework, cutting the grass, and gardening), and activities that yield future benefits (such as education). Leisure, the third part, adds to a household's satisfaction in a consumption sense. The theory of labor supply, then, concerns household decisions about allocating time for these three purposes.

In making rational decisions about how much time its members will spend in market work (the labor-supply decision), a household asks four questions. First, what market wages can each family member earn? Second, how productive are family members in nonmarket work? Third, what are the tastes and preferences of family members for (a) consuming market and nonmarket goods and services, (b) market and nonmarket work, and (c) leisure? And fourth, what other resources does the family have?

How do these factors influence the labor supply? Working backward, you can see that labor supply varies inversely with family resources. For example, mothers of young children are less likely to seek market work if their husbands have high incomes. And the availability of welfare and pensions reduces the labor supply of individuals who have these sources of income.

The tastes and preferences of households have varying effects on labor supply. If a household has a strong preference for nonmarket-produced goods and services—home-cooked meals, family-provided child care, and so on—it will allocate

Household theory of labor supply. A theory suggesting that labor supply decisions are made within households, based on considerations of taste and preferences, market wages, nonmarket productivity, and other family resources.

less time to market work and more time to nonmarket work. However, if a family has a strong preference for market-produced goods and services—cars, vacations, and so on—it will tend to spend more time on market work. The greater the value placed on leisure time, the less time will be spent on market work. Tastes also affect the types of jobs and the wages that household members will accept. Finally, the greater the productivity of household members in nonmarket investment activities, such as schooling, the less time they will spend on market work.

Preference for market work is influenced by nonprice variables, such as social and cultural values. In the United States, for example, we have decided that attending school is a more socially productive activity for children than producing current goods and services. Thus compulsory school-attendance laws and child-labor laws limit market work by those under the age of 16. And until recently, social and cultural values limited the economic role of women. Tastes and social values certainly influence other economic choices, such as what products to demand. But in labor markets they have a direct and significant influence on supply choices.

Market wages and the supply response.   When examining the effects of wages on labor supply, we have to distinguish changes in supply from changes in quantity supplied. A wage increase for one member of a household may well cause the market supply for other members to decrease. Why? First, because the household must purchase substitutes for nonmarket work (someone to do the housework or care for the children). And second, because increased income allows the household to "buy" leisure time for its other members. A wage increase affects the labor supply of other household members, but it affects *quantity supplied* by the one who receives the wage increase.

Unlike that of other resources, quantity of labor resources supplied does not always rise with wages. Higher wages increase the opportunity cost of leisure. For example, if someone is willing to pay you $50 to work next Saturday, refusing and going to the beach instead will cost you $50. Thus higher wages may cause a *substitution effect* (see Chapter 7) by which market work is substituted for other uses of time, and hence more labor is supplied to the market.

But what if you presently have a job and receive a raise? You might choose to spend some of that raise on more leisure. With higher wages, you can work less and still receive more income than before. Thus higher wages may cause an *income effect* (see Chapter 7) by which more leisure is "bought," and hence less labor is supplied to the market.

Given these two contradicting effects from a single act—a wage increase—how can we predict whether the quantity of labor supplied will increase or decrease as wages rise? We must observe what people actually do. For some individuals—and at extremely high income levels—quantity of labor supplied increases only slightly as wages rise. But for most people the substitution effect outweighs the income effect in the short run. Thus in analyzing typical short-run responses, we will continue to draw upward-sloping labor-supply curves.

However, over the long run the average hours worked per week has actually declined while wages paid have increased. Early in the 1900s the typical work week was 50–60 hours; today, a full-time worker is more likely to work only 35–40 hours per week. Over this period of time, wages and the typical standard of living have greatly increased. Thus in the long run, the income effect has outweighed the substitution effect.

Exhibit 15.1

The Decreasing Labor Supply of Older Men, 1955 to 1985

The table indicates that the labor supply of older men has decreased over the 1955 to 1985 period. In 1955 almost 88 percent of all men aged 55–64 were in the labor force; by 1985 only 68 percent were working or looking for work. The percentage of men aged 65 and over who were part of the labor force dropped from almost 40 percent in 1955 to less than 16 percent in 1985.

| | Labor force participation rates | |
| | Ages 55–64 | Ages 65 and over |
Year	(percent)	(percent)
1955	87.9	39.6
1965	84.6	27.9
1975	75.6	21.6
1985	67.9	15.8

Sources: U.S. Department of Labor, *Employment and Training Report of the President, 1982*; *Employment and Earnings,* January 1986.

Demand and Supply: Forces Behind Labor-Market Trends

To illustrate how demand and supply affect labor markets, we can consider explanations for two important trends: (1) decreased market work supplied by older men; and (2) increased market work supplied by women.

Declining participation of older men. During the last 30 years, older men have tended to spend their "golden years" outside the labor market. As Exhibit 15.1 shows, in 1955 almost 40 percent of men aged 65 and over were in the labor force; by 1985, this proportion was less than 16 percent. For men aged 55–64, the proportion dropped from 88 to 68 percent. Several demand and supply factors help to explain these changes. Perhaps the most important factor is the growth of private and public pension plans. Such plans directly affect a key labor-supply variable: family resources. With better incomes available from nonmarket sources, people tend to spend less time on market work. In addition, because of the pension plans, many employers have felt comfortable about forcing older workers to retire, thus creating advancement opportunities for younger workers.

A second factor, this time on the demand side, is the effect of changing technology on the demand for older workers. Changing technology creates new and different jobs, requiring training and adaptation. Because older workers have shorter future worklives, employers can less easily recover the costs of training them, placing older workers at a disadvantage relative to younger ones. Moreover, older workers are less likely to seek employment in a new occupation or by moving to a new location. Thus they tend to be concentrated in declining occupations and industries. If they lose their current jobs, they are less likely to find others; many are forced to choose between unemployment and involuntary retirement.

Despite our ability to explain the situation of older men in terms of labor demand and supply, neither they nor society easily accept their nonparticipation. Even with public and private pensions, the income of the elderly tends to be relatively low. And while life expectancy is increasing, the years during which workers are considered productive are still limited as much by social customs as by statistical evidence of productivity. Thus the decline in the number of older men in the labor market raises efficiency and equity questions.

| | **Labor force participation rates** | | |
Year	Ages 16 and over (percent)	Married women aged 25–34 (percent)	Married women with a child under 6 (percent)
1955	35.7	26.0	16.2
1965	39.3	32.1	23.3
1975	46.4	48.3	36.7
1985	54.5	65.6	53.4

Sources: U.S. Department of Labor, *Handbook of Labor Statistics, 1985*; *Statistical Abstract, 1986.*

Exhibit 15.2
The Increasing Labor Supply of Women, 1955 to 1985
This table shows that market supply of labor by women has increased since 1955. During the period from 1955 to 1985, the overall number of women aged 16 and over who were working or seeking work increased from 36 to 55 percent. The proportion of married women aged 25–34 accounted for a large part of this increase; during the same time period this group increased from 26 to 66 percent. The proportion of mothers with young children also increased substantially, from 16 percent in 1955 to 53 percent in 1985.

Increasing participation of women. In contrast to the situation of older men, women have increased their participation in market work. As shown in Exhibit 15.2, the proportion of women aged 16 and over working or seeking market work rose from less than 36 percent in 1955 to over 54 percent in 1985. Traditionally heavily employed in nonmarket work, married women (even those with young children) have increasingly sought and gained market employment. Although only 26 percent of young married women worked in 1955, almost two-thirds did so in 1985. Only about 16 percent of married women with young children were in the labor-force in 1955, but over 53 percent sought market work in 1985. In all, women have accounted for 60 percent of the labor-force increase since World War II.

Again, an analysis of demand and supply factors helps explain this trend. On the supply side, women appear to have changed their tastes and preferences for market work. Since society tends to judge an individual's worth by income, it is not surprising that many women seek to spend more of their time in market work.

Women also seek market work for economic reasons. Nearly one-half the women in the labor force are not married and therefore are heavily dependent on labor income. Many others are married to men whose earnings are meager and do not have the luxury of choosing whether or not to work. Even women married to men with middle-class incomes have chosen to enter the labor market. In fact, many families would not be part of the economic middle class without the earnings of two of their members. Having two wage earners not only boosts family income, but provides economic protection if either worker becomes unemployed.

In addition to supply-side forces, labor demand for women has increased. Some of this demand is in occupations traditionally filled by women. For example, the growth in demand for medical care, spurred in part by more private and public health insurance plans, has created a growing demand for nurses. However, women have also entered many occupations that were once filled largely by men. Increasing proportions of women occupy managerial, professional, and technical positions from which they were long excluded. Women have gained sizeable entry into some new occupations—in the computer industry, for example. This trend reflects both supply factors (desire to enter new fields) and demand factors (including antidiscrimination laws). Still, women remain concentrated in relatively low-paying service and clerical occupations in which they have traditionally worked.

WAGE DETERMINATION: WHY WAGES DIFFER

By analyzing the forces of demand and supply we can answer questions about labor markets, such as: What determines wages? and Why do various groups of workers receive different wages? These questions are very important, not only for efficiency but also for equity. Equity requires a reasonable way of distributing society's products, which means a reasonable way of determining income. About 75 percent of all personal income is earned in labor markets. Thus for income differences to be reasonable, wage differences must be reasonable. We discuss what is reasonable, or equitable, in more detail in Chapter 18. For now, we want to consider how many wage differences are explained by demand-and-supply analysis and by the principles of rational choice.

To simplify this discussion, let's assume that labor markets are competitive. That is, in this section, we ignore markets in which discrimination, imperfect information, lack of mobility, unions, and governmental regulations exist. We discuss the influence of unions later in this chapter and other imperfections in Chapter 18. But first let's see how competitive labor markets operate.

Equalizing Tendencies of Markets

Before looking at why wages might differ, we must understand how competetive labor markets adjust when wage differentials exist. Consider a group of workers—computer programmers, for example. Suppose all have reasonably uniform training and experience, yet some earn more than others, owing perhaps to their working in different industries. Exhibit 15.3 shows that computer programmers in industry A initially receive $400 per week (where D_{A1} intersects S_{A1}). Programmers working in industry B initially receive $600 per week (where D_{B1} intersects S_{B1}).

Wage differentials are market signals to reallocate resources. When the markets respond, the signals disappear. Thus if there are no labor market barriers between industries A and B, we would expect wages in the two industries to move toward the same level. Some programmers would be attracted to the high-wage industry—increasing supply to S_{B2} and decreasing wages. The programmers would be attracted away from the low-wage industry—decreasing supply to S_{A2} and raising wages. The wage differential will disappear as supply shifts cause the markets to adjust to an allocatively efficient equilibrium. In Exhibit 15.3, wages of computer programmers in the two industries should equalize at $500 per week.

As long as barriers to mobility are slight—as for similarly trained workers in the same geographic area—we would not expect wage differentials to last very

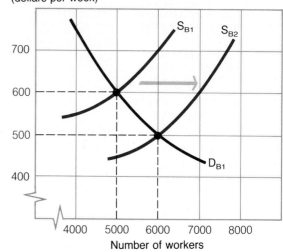

(a) Industry A (low wage)

(b) Industry B (high wage)

Exhibit 15.3
Equalization of Wages in Competitive Labor Markets
Unequal wages in two competitive labor markets will result in a transfer of labor supplied and an equalization of wages. Wages in Industry A are $400 per week, considerably less than the $600 per week wages paid in Industry B. If there are no obstacles to labor mobility between these markets, we can expect some workers to quit jobs in the low-wage market and seek employment in the high-wage market. As a result, labor supply in the low-wage market will decrease (from S_{A1} to S_{A2}), and labor supply in the high-wage market will increase (from S_{B1} to S_{B2}). Changes in labor supply should continue until wages are equal in both markets ($500 per week in this case).

long. When barriers to mobility are more important—as when lengthy training is required for entry-level positions or when jobs are lost in the Northeast and created in the Southwest—wage differentials may persist.

Compensating Wage Differentials

In the real world, wage differentials between two markets (or two employers) may reflect supply decisions. Recall that workers are concerned with both earnings and working conditions. Thus an employer may offer lower wages but better working conditions—less weekend or night work, better job security, safer working conditions, and so on. Workers may be willing to "buy" better working conditions by accepting lower wages.

Conversely, higher wages may reflect less desirable working conditions. Job insecurity, dangerous work assignments, and unpleasant tasks all tend to restrict the labor supply and hence create wage differentials. For example, workers on offshore oil rigs earn high wages to compensate them for the dangers of the job and the inconvenience of spending a lot of time away from their families and regular leisure activities. Such *compensating wage differentials* persist because workers have different preferences for various types of market work. Compensating differentials therefore will not disappear because they represent rational choices.

Productivity and Wage Differentials

Wage differentials may also reflect workers' marginal productivity. As we noted in Chapter 13, the wage differential for two groups of workers having different skills or levels of productivity should be proportional to the difference in productivity. When wage differentials reflect productivity differences, they offer an incentive for workers to train and qualify for the higher-paying jobs. More trained workers will increase the labor supply for those jobs and reduce the differential somewhat. But wages for some occupational groups—doctors, for example—remain relatively high over long periods of time. Why do low-wage workers not move to high-wage occupations in all cases?

Lack of movement may be the effect of compensating differentials. It may also reflect differences in the willingness and ability of workers to acquire the necessary skills. Not everyone has the inherent ability to perform brain surgery, for example, even with many years of training. Moreover, even when ability is not a limiting factor, entering occupations that require extended training has a high opportunity cost. What appears to be a high wage differential may be only enough to justify the opportunity cost of training. When extra benefits expected from higher wages are less than extra costs of training, we expect workers to reject additional opportunities for training and occupational mobility.

Human Capital: Investment in Human Resources

Knowing that skills or productivity differences help explain wage differences raises other questions. For example, how does an individual decide whether to acquire additional skills? How does a firm decide whether to pay for training to increase the skills of its work force? How does society decide whether efficiency and/or equity reasons justify public investments in human resources?

In Chapter 14 we noted that individuals and firms invest in human capital: skills, education, training, and experience. We can analyze investment in human capital the same way we did investment in physical capital. Acquiring more human capital (raising skill levels) generally means higher income for the individual, higher productivity for the firm, and greater production possibilities for society. But increasing human capital also has direct costs—such as paying for instruction and training—and opportunity costs—such as sacrificing income or productivity during training. For example, you probably decided to attend college at least in part because you expect a college degree to improve your earnings potential. But as you are no doubt aware when tuition time comes, a college education is not free. An even more important cost for many is the opportunity cost of not working.

The principles of rational choice tell us that workers invest time and money to increase their human capital only if wage differentials (or other working conditions) are likely to make their investments pay off. Similarly, firms and society invest only if the payoff in terms of improved efficiency warrants the added cost. Because investment in human capital involves costs and benefits over an extended

RECAP

In a competitive labor market with no restrictions on mobility, the wages of similar workers may differ only temporarily. Supply responses tend to equalize wages throughout the market.

However, if jobs differ in terms of working conditions—more job security, safer working conditions, and so on—compensating wage differentials may exist. Because these differentials have rational causes, equalization will not occur.

Most commonly, wage differentials reflect productivity differences. Where training or education is required to qualify for certain jobs, wage differentials must be large enough to convince workers to undertake that training; such differentials will not disappear.

period of time, the investment decision is based on the principles stated in Chapter 14 for investment in physical capital. Benefits and costs occurring in different time periods must be compared, recognizing the opportunity cost of time.

However, investment in human capital differs from investment in physical capital because human capital cannot be separated from the individual. For example, no bank can take away your diploma if you do not pay back your student loans (though they can take other unpleasant actions). As a result, borrowing funds to invest in human capital is more difficult than borrowing funds to finance buildings and machinery. Financial institutions are reluctant to fund individuals' investments in human capital—that is, in the individuals themselves—as you may have found in seeking loans for college.

Similarly, firms may underinvest in training programs for employees, especially when the training increases employee value to both the firm and the market. If an individual trained by one firm quits and goes to work for a second firm, the individual (through higher wages) and the second firm (through higher productivity) gain at the expense of the first firm.

Because the actions of both financial markets and firms may cause investment in human capital to be less than the socially desirable quantity, government policies often supplement private investments. For example, state and local governments fund elementary schools, high schools, and colleges. In this way, government increases the stock of human capital, raises the productivity of one of society's most important resources, and counters the tendency of decision makers in the private sector to underinvest in human capital. We return to consideration of social policies in Chapter 18 because we can apply human-capital analysis to the causes and cures of poverty and the measurement of discrimination.

Barriers to Entry and Wage Differentials

Finally, wage differentials may result from barriers to entry that restrict the supply of workers in a given occupation. For example, individuals must be licensed to practice some occupations, ranging from doctors and lawyers to electricians and beauticians. Unions may also limit entry. By restricting the labor supply, barriers keep wage differentials from falling to levels that just compensate workers for the added cost of training. In addition, barriers can also prevent the supply adjustments necessary to achieve allocative efficiency. Occupational licensing is often justified as protecting consumers from incompetence. But the benefits of such protection must be weighed against the costs of the barriers in order to determine their overall value to society.

Collective bargaining. The process by which a union and management negotiate a mutually acceptable contract and define the meanings of contract terms.

Union. An organization of employees that seeks primarily through collective bargaining with management to secure for its members improvements in wages, hours, and other working conditions.

UNIONS AND COLLECTIVE BARGAINING

Unions also play a role in setting market wages. Thus far we have assumed competitive labor markets. In some markets, however, labor unions and employers determine wages and other working conditions jointly in a process known as **collective bargaining**. In the broadest terms, a **union** is an organization of employees that seeks primarily through collective bargaining with management to secure improvements in wages and other working conditions for its members.

Craft union. A union of workers sharing a common skill, trade, or profession.

Industrial union. A union of workers sharing a common employer; workers may or may not share a common skill or trade.

Labor federation. An organization composed of several unions that provides services to member unions and seeks through political action to improve the status of its workers.

Unions can be divided into two types. In a **craft union** workers share a common skill, trade, or profession. In an **industrial union**, workers share a common employer, regardless of their skills. Carpenters and nurses usually belong to craft unions. Workers in steel foundries and chemical plants generally belong to industrial unions. In both cases, workers organized because they shared common problems and desires and believed that a union would help them to deal more effectively with their employers.

Unions may unite to form a **labor federation**, which is an organization that provides various services to member unions. In particular, labor federations seek to improve the status of union members and the union movement through political action. In this country, most unions belong to the American Federation of Labor–Congress of Industrial Organizations (AFL–CIO). Notable exceptions include the Teamsters Union and the National Education Association. Although heavily involved in political activity, the AFL–CIO continues to stress the achievement of most worker goals through the process of collective bargaining.

Brief History of Unions in America

Today's labor federations came into existence relatively recently. Although labor organizations in one form or another have existed since the 1790s, early unions were usually short-lived, cropping up from time to time to demand higher wages from a single employer and disappearing after the settlement. Not until the second half of the nineteenth century were relatively permanent national unions established.

Knights of Labor. The first major attempt to form a national labor federation, the Knights of Labor, occurred in 1869. At that time the national unions were craft unions. But the Knights tried to enroll the entire working class. Everyone who worked for wages was eligible for membership, except doctors, lawyers, bankers, and bartenders. Unlike U.S. unions today, the Knights of Labor paid little attention to collective bargaining, attempting instead to achieve its goals largely through political action.

Membership in the Knights of Labor peaked at some 700,000 workers in 1886, but faded rapidly thereafter. The organization declined because it lacked internal organization and bargaining strength (its unskilled members were easily replaced during strikes) and it failed to focus on bread-and-butter issues: wages and working conditions. Described by its critics as a political rather than an economic organization, the Knights were an exception to the history of labor unions in this country.

American Federation of Labor. Founded the same year as the Knights of Labor, the American Federation of Labor (AFL) was very different. Its goal was to improve wages and working conditions, mainly through collective bargaining; its membership consisted almost exclusively of craft unions. Although most workers at that time were unskilled laborers in large mass production industries, the AFL had little interest in or involvement with them.

Industrial Workers of the World. Prior to the 1930s, few attempts were made to organize industrial workers, and most of them ended in failure. For example, the Industrial Workers of the World (IWW) was a radical organization that attempted to organize unskilled workers early in the 1900s. Organizers worked with hard-rock miners in the West, lumberjacks in the Northwest, migrant farm workers in the Southwest, and textile workers in the Northeast. Their goal was to fuse these groups into a working-class movement. The IWW did not usually engage in collective bargaining, in part because some of its leaders sought to bring about a socialist revolution. Although it had some success, the IWW never gained the support of the mainstream labor movement represented by the AFL. It was eventually crushed in the "red scare" following World War I.

Congress of Industrial Organizations. Despite previous failures, in the 1930s some leaders in the AFL felt that the time was right to organize the millions of workers in the nation's largest industries. Among these leaders was John L. Lewis, president of the United Mine Workers, one of the few successful industrial unions at that time. Unable to convince other AFL leaders, Lewis and others formed an alternative federation, the Congress of Industrial Organizations (CIO). The CIO launched the largest unionization attempt in the nation's history. With its financial and organizational support, steelworkers, autoworkers, rubber workers, and electrical workers unionized. Despite their differences, the two rival federations merged in 1955 to form the AFL–CIO.

Legal Status of Unions

For many years, the labor movement encountered major legal obstacles. The government—especially the courts—was openly hostile to unions and directly aided the antiunion movement. The courts often declared union activities—especially strikes to raise wages—as illegal.

Perhaps the most frequently used and most successful antilabor device of that time was the **injunction**. Such court orders prohibited a particular action (in labor cases, typically a strike or boycott). When a union organized a strike, usually to gain recognition as the workers' representative, the employer would go to court and ask for an injunction. With little or no consideration of evidence, a court would issue it, jailing anyone who violated the order. Many injunctions were later invalidated, but by that time the strike had lost its momentum and the employer had won.

Norris–LaGuardia Act. Thwarted by the courts, labor leaders sought legislation to prohibit judges from using antitrust statutes and injunctions against unions. Thus AFL president Samuel Gompers hailed the Clayton Antitrust Act (1914) as "labor's Magna Carta." At first its provisions appeared to limit the use of injunctions in labor disputes and to exempt labor unions from antitrust statutes. But subsequently the U.S. Supreme Court ruled that it did not limit the courts' power.

Not until 1932 did labor win its first legislative victory: the Norris–LaGuardia Act, which did restrict the power of courts to issue injunctions. The act also declared illegal the **yellow-dog contract**, which employees signed at the insistence of an employer, stating that they were not and would not become union members.

Wagner Act. Although legal actions had hampered organizing efforts, a major barrier to union success was the workers' lack of economic strength, especially of workers in large industrial plants. In the 1930s, however, industrial unions gained some real economic power using methods such as the sit-down

Injunction. A court order prohibiting a defendant, such as a labor union, from engaging in certain practices, such as striking.

Yellow-dog contract. A contract in which employees stipulated that they were not and would not become a member of a labor union; outlawed in the United States by the Norris–LaGuardia Act (1932).

strike. Workers would occupy the premises of the factory, refusing to leave or allow other workers to enter. Because they occurred just when the country was coming out of the Great Depression and attempts were being made to shore up the American economy, these successful strikes were seen as contrary to the nation's interest. Reflecting a change in the public view of unions, however, government did not attempt to break the unions. Rather, Congress passed the National Labor Relations (Wagner) Act in 1935, laying the foundation for current labor-relations law and policy.

Section 7 of the act gave workers the right to join and support organizations to represent them in bargaining with employers over wages, hours, and other working conditions. To give that promise legal status, the act made two substantial changes. First, it established the National Labor Relations Board (NLRB) to oversee democratic elections by which workers would decide whether they wanted to be represented by a union. Second, the NLRB was empowered to oversee the conduct of employers. Previously, employers had successfully stopped unionization by firing workers simply because they belonged to or supported the union. Now such actions were declared illegal as "unfair labor practices." Under the new law, many new industrial unions were formed and duly certified as the bargaining agents for their members by the NLRB in the 1930s.

War Labor Board. Until the 1940s, unions made demands that were sometimes accepted by employers. However, highly detailed, formal contracts were rarely negotiated. The development of the labor contract was spurred by World War II. Determined to maintain maximum production during the war, the federal government obtained a no-strike pledge from all labor leaders. In return, the War Labor Board was established to settle disputes between unions and management. Typically, a representative of the War Labor Board would come to a plant, hold informal hearings on several disputes, make a decision, and determine a remedy on the spot. As a result, unions and management began to write down and formalize what had been a set of informal rules. The end product was the now-familiar labor–management contract.

Taft–Hartley Act. During the war, wages were frozen in some cases and allowed to rise much less than prices in others. In the immediate postwar period, unions launched a massive wave of strikes in an attempt to regain the financial ground they had lost. However, many Americans opposed these strikes, fearing repetition of the unemployment and depression that had followed World War I.

In 1947, Congress passed the Taft–Hartley Act, amending the National Labor Relations Act in a way that proponents argued made the law neutral (that is, favoring neither unions nor employers). Under the provisions of the new act, the conduct of both unions and management was scrutinized for possible unfair labor practices. Under the Wagner Act, only the conduct of employers had been observed. Taft–Hartley banned discrimination on the basis of union membership by both unions and employers. It barred both from engaging in any action that might "interfere with, restrain, or coerce employees" who were attempting to exercise their rights under the act. And it required both sides to bargain with each other "in good faith," with the hope that agreement would be reached and employment and production continued without interruption.

Current labor-relations law imposes a duty, as well as restrictions, on unions. When a union wins an organizational election, it must now represent all workers, regardless of union membership. But the union does not automatically win the

Union shop. A workplace in which all employees must become members of a labor union within a specified period of time after being hired. Contract provisions establishing a union shop are illegal in states that have right-to-work laws.

Right-to-work laws. State laws that prohibit unions from negotiating union-shop provisions in labor–management contracts. The power to enact such laws was granted to the states by the Taft–Hartley Act (1947).

Closed shop. A workplace in which the employer is obligated to hire only union members; severely limited by the Taft–Hartley Act.

right to require workers to join the union. Unions often seek a contract calling for a **union shop**, which requires workers to become members of the union after working for a specified period of time. Union shops are legal under federal law, but the Taft–Hartley Act allowed states to pass **right-to-work laws** prohibiting union shops. The act also severely limited the use of a **closed shop**, in which the employer is required to hire only union members.

Landrum–Griffin Act. Further restrictions were placed on unions by the Landrum–Griffin Act of 1959. Its goal was to eliminate corruption by opening the internal affairs of unions to public view. The act requires unions to operate as democratic institutions, to hold secret-ballot elections for union officers, to establish written constitutions, and to otherwise act in a noncorrupt manner.

Current status and future trends. The number of union members paralleled the changes in labor-relations law and court decisions. Membership grew dramatically in the 1930s and 1940s, as shown in Exhibit 15.4. Recently, membership has declined from a peak of 22 million members in 1975 to 18 million in 1984. The decline is more significant in relative terms: Union members accounted for over 25 percent of the total labor force in 1970 but only 16 percent in 1984.

One reason for the declining percentage is that union membership varies greatly among industries. Traditionally unionized industries represent a decreasing part of the economy, while traditionally nonunionized industries play an increasing role in the economy. Thus 60 percent of production workers in construction and manufacturing and 80 percent of those in transportation and communications are

Exhibit 15.4
Union Membership as a Percentage of the Total Labor Force

Year	Union membership (total)		Union membership (public sector)	
	Thousands	Percent of labor force	Thousands	Percent of government employees
1930	3,750	7.5	268	8.5
1935	3,650	6.9	312	9.0
1940	7,297	13.1	448	10.7
1945	12,254	22.8	580	9.8
1950	14,294	23.0	744	12.3
1955	16,127	24.8	786	11.4
1960	15,516	22.3	903	10.8
1965	18,269	22.4	2631	26.1
1970	20,990	25.4	4012	32.0
1975	22,207	23.7	5810	39.6
1980	20,968	19.6	5695	35.1
1984	18,306	16.1	5293	33.1

Source: Leo Troy and Neil Sheflin, *Union Sourcebook.* West Orange, N.J.: Industrial Relations Data and Information Services, 1985.

covered by collective bargaining agreements.[*] But relatively few workers in trade and service industries belong to unions.

Union growth in the public sector was especially large from 1960 to 1975. In 1960 only about 11 percent of all government employees belonged to unions, compared to almost 40 percent in 1975. And because the public-sector employment has grown relatively fast, public-sector unions represent an increased share of union members. In 1960, less than 6 percent of union members were in the public sector, compared with 26 percent in 1975. However, in recent years, union membership in the public sector also has begun to decline, both in absolute and relative terms. Much of this decline has occurred in unions representing state and local government employees.[†]

Despite their decline, unions retain influence in the economy. Why? In part because organization gives union members an impact on the economy—especially in the political arena—far beyond their numbers. We discuss later whether this influence benefits or harms the economy. The fact remains that unions are still an important feature of the U.S. economy.

Labor-Relations Environment and Collective Bargaining

Understanding the collective bargaining process means understanding the environment in which labor–management relations operate. This environment results from the goals and objectives of workers and management, economic conditions in the product and labor markets, labor–management law, and many other factors. In this section, we look at how the goals and objectives of both workers and management shape labor–management relations.

Importance of rules. The relationships between managers and workers in a firm are governed by a set of rules that spell out how decisions to promote, discipline, lay off, and so on, are to be made. The set of rules in a particular plant evolves as workers and managers interact over months or years. These rules tend to be those that are acceptable to both parties.

An absence of unions does not mean that management is completely free to manage its labor force, however. Managers who act that way are the ones most likely to face unionization of their plants. Unions seek to write rules into formal written contracts. Unionized plants have more formal processes for modifying existing rules and writing new ones.

In the typical labor-relations environment, both parties usually seek a stable, long-term relationship. For management, stability means lower costs for hiring and training new workers. For workers, stability means job security. A mutual desire for a long-lasting relationship means that, whatever the current conflict, both parties want to reach an agreement. Despite this mutual goal, each side has its own perspective on individual issues, which can lead to conflict. Management wants to control the workplace and to keep costs as low as possible. On the other

---

[*] Richard B. Freeman and James L. Medoff, "New Estimates of Private Sector Unionism in the United States," *Industrial and Labor Relations Review*, January 1979, pp. 143–174.

[†] Leo Troy and Neil Sheflin, *Union Sourcebook*. West Orange, N.J.: Industrial Relations Data and Information Services, 1985.

Arbitration. The settlement of differences between two parties (such as a union and management) by an impartial third party, the arbitrator, whose decision is legally binding on the other two parties.

hand, workers want higher wages and benefits; a say in decisions such as promotions, layoffs, and discipline; and a sense that management decisions are made fairly and consistently. Merging these perspectives is part of collective bargaining.

Bargaining: Negotiating a contract. When most people think of collective bargaining, they think of the process in which union and management representatives sit down in marathon sessions and hammer out the terms of a contract. This process makes newspaper headlines and is a key part of collective bargaining: negotiating a contract.

The issues discussed in the contract-negotiation phase of bargaining cover all rules governing the labor–management relationship. Such rules include wage rates and the mix of pay and fringe benefits. But they also cover seniority and the relative rights of workers to promotions and transfers. Some rules are "effort bargains," which set the speed at which an assembly line will operate or teacher to pupil ratios.

In collective bargaining, both parties expect to give and take. Thus unions typically ask for a greater wage increase and for more new benefits than they will settle for or expect to receive. Management offers less than it will pay. In the bargaining process, both management and the union give in some areas and take in others. The final outcome depends on the relative bargaining strengths and preferences of both parties. For example, in the early 1980s, some unions actually accepted lower wages and benefits than they had previously negotiated in order to preserve jobs.

Bargaining: Interpreting the contract. Negotiating a contract is just the start of collective bargaining. An integral part of the process is the ongoing interpretation of rules and the review of discretionary actions taken by management. Anyone who has attempted to write a completely clear rule knows that the task is impossible. Moreover, many labor–management rules explicitly call for judgments to be made (for example, whether one worker has greater skills than another). When either the union or management objects to an interpretation of a rule, the parties negotiate to settle the dispute.

The procedure used is formally known as a *grievance procedure,* is written into the contract, and is often invoked by unions in reaction to what they feel is a violation of the contract. The intent of grievance procedures is to resolve disputes over rules internally. Both parties meet to discuss and hopefully agree on the precise meaning of the rule or the correct judgment in a particular case. Since workers are concerned that management interpret and apply rules fairly and consistently, a workable grievance procedure is a major union goal.

Most union–management contracts call for outside help in the form of **arbitration** when the parties cannot settle a grievance themselves. A third party is selected jointly by labor and management to ensure neutrality. The arbitrator hears evidence from both sides and interprets the rule or judgment at issue in terms of the contract and the customary meaning of the rule within the spirit and letter of the contract. The arbitrator's decision is legally binding.

This form of arbitration is unique to the United States. National labor-relations policy supports this relatively private means of settling disputes for two important reasons. First, it is clearly in the public interest to avoid unnecessary strikes or other disruptions caused by labor–management disputes. Arbitration settles dis-

RECAP

In craft unions, workers share a common skill, trade, or profession. In industrial unions, workers share a common employer. Unions may also unite to form labor federations, such as the AFL–CIO.

Although initially outlawed, unions eventually won legal protections that have made them a major economic force in the United States.

Collective bargaining extends beyond agreements on wages to include work rules and other conditions of employment. Interpretation of a labor–management contract is an ongoing process, involving arbitration when disputes cannot be settled by the parties themselves.

putes in a manner that avoids interrupting production. Second, arbitration is a private process, which is preferable to having government dictate the outcome.

ECONOMIC IMPACT OF UNIONS

Fair, reasonable, and consistent treatment of employees is a major union goal. But economic goals are also important, both for the workers concerned and for the economy as a whole. In purely competitive labor markets, economic outcomes are determined by the market. When wages are determined by negotiations between unions and management, however, the conditions of a perfect resource market do not exist and allocative inefficiency may result. In this section we explore the impact of unions on wages and allocative efficiency, inflation, technical efficiency, and equity.

Impact on Wages and Allocative Efficiency

Let's consider the effect of a union wage demand, as shown in Exhibit 15.5. In the absence of a union, wages in this market would be $400 per week, and employers would hire 3000 workers. The union seeks wages of $500 per week. But higher wages reduce employment, in this case to 2000 workers. In a competitive market, demand equals supply at an equilibrium that is allocatively efficient. Thus the lower level of employment caused by the union results in allocative inefficiency, shown by the red-shaded area on the graph.

Exhibit 15.5

Impact of a Union Wage Scale in a Competitive Labor Market
In this competitive labor market, wages will be $400 per week (point *a*) in the absence of a union. However, if a union organizes labor, it may seek a wage of $500 per week (point *b*), an amount greater than the equilibrium wage. At the higher wage, employers will hire only 2000 workers, 1000 less than under competitive conditions. When only 2000 workers are hired, the marginal social benefits (measured by demand) exceed the marginal social costs (measured by the supply of labor). The red-shaded triangle indicates the amount of allocative inefficiency.

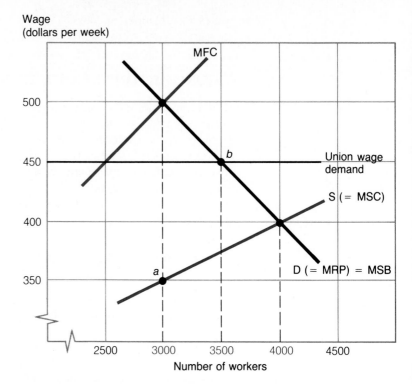

Exhibit 15.6
Bilateral Monopoly: Unions and Firms with Resource-Market Power
In this market, a union faces an employer with market power. Because the firm cannot hire more workers without increasing the wage, its marginal factor cost (MFC) is greater than the market supply (S). In the absence of a union, it would hire only 3000 workers at a wage of $350 per week (point *a*, where MRP = MFC). If the union persuades workers not to work for less than $450 per week, the firm's marginal factor cost will be $450 per week until 3500 workers are hired (point *b*). There is still some allocative inefficiency, but the union's wage demand has reduced the amount of inefficiency.

Collective bargaining and market power. Unions do not bargain just with employers who hire in competitive labor markets, however. They also bargain with employers who have market power in the labor market. In this case we use the model of **bilateral monopoly**, illustrated in Exhibit 15.6, to analyze the impact of a union wage demand on an employer. In the absence of a union, the firm would seek to hire 3000 workers (where MFC = MRP, or D) and would pay wages of $350 per week (from the supply curve). But what if a union seeks a wage of $450 per week?

The union's wage demand causes the employer to face a horizontal supply curve and hire at the wage of $450 or face a strike. If the union wage were accepted, the employer would hire 3500 workers. The effect of the union on allocative efficiency is unclear. In this case, you can see that 4000 workers would be hired in a competitive labor market (where D = S). By seeking wages above $350, but less than $500 per week, the union actually causes employment to increase. This increase moves the market closer to the level of employment associated with allocative efficiency. If the union asked for wages higher than $500, however, employment would fall and inefficiency increase. The point is that when labor markets are not competitive, we cannot be sure whether unions will reduce allocative efficiency.

In the bilateral monopoly model, neither the union nor the employer alone is in a position to dictate terms. Whenever the wage demand exceeds the wage offer, we can use the model of bilateral monopoly to predict only a range of potential outcomes, not a single, unique outcome. Whether the final outcome is closer to the union's demand or the employer's wishes depends on several factors,

Bilateral monopoly. A model of a labor market in which market power exists on both sides of the market; a union with control over the supply of labor and an employer with market power demanding labor.

including bargaining strength, trade-offs between wage issues and other union and management goals, and the negotiating skills and preparation of union and management representatives.

Bargaining strength and strikes. Bargaining strength is a product of many factors. As we noted in Chapter 13, the more price inelastic the demand for a resource, the smaller is the employment impact of higher wages. A price-inelastic demand for union labor lowers the cost (the quantity of unemployment) that will result if a union demands higher wages. Unions thus have more bargaining strength when there are fewer substitutes for union labor. They also benefit when bargaining with employers who have some power in the product market and when labor costs are a relatively small portion of total costs.

Hanging over the negotiation process is the threat of a strike or other form of work stoppage. Unions have more bargaining strength and can win greater concessions when they have demonstrated a willingness to strike and an ability to win a strike. Because it imposes costs on both employers and union members, a strike or the threat of a strike helps to push the parties to reach a settlement.

Public concern about the cost and inconvenience of strikes has led to a number of restrictions on strikes. For example, they are usually illegal during the period when a contract is in effect. Since most contracts cover several years (three years is the most common length), this provision helps minimize the overall disruption of strikes. In addition, the Federal Mediation and Conciliation Service provides mediators, who help the parties to reach an agreement, thereby making a strike unnecessary or minimizing its duration. Finally, strikes by public employees are generally prohibited (or severely limited) because these employees provide essential services for which there are no substitutes.

The direct cost of strikes is actually much less than most people believe. In 1983, for example, strikes resulted in an annual loss of less than 0.1 percent of the potential number of workdays. That is, labor incomes and output produced were lower by that percentage, at most. In many cases, however, the days of work and wages "lost" are not really lost, since inventories are built up in advance or are made up using overtime after the strike ends.

However, we must also consider the indirect cost of strikes. Because a strike is the ultimate weapon of unions, it enables unions to make gains for their members. Economic gains for union members, of course, imply higher costs of production. Strikes may also impose other costs, such as the inconvenience caused travelers by striking airline pilots or bus drivers. But a prohibition on strikes would alter greatly the balance of power between unions and management. Efforts to minimize the incidence and severity of strikes can, however, be in society's interest.

Measuring the impact on wages. If unions actually have limited power, why do most Americans perceive them as a major economic force? Accounts in the newspaper media tend to exaggerate the impact of unions. Moreover, union leaders are perfectly willing to accept all the credit—and management is willing to grant the union all the blame—for any increase in wages.

Economists, however, point to the important economic influences of demand and supply. Measuring union impact on wages requires more than merely noting how much wages will increase under labor–management contracts. The effect of unions on wages must be compared with what would otherwise have occurred.

Union–management negotiations reflect economic concerns and are influenced by economic forces. Whatever demands the union makes for higher wages, the outcome will depend on demand for labor. Whatever management would like to pay its workers, supply of labor establishes a minimum wage.

Overall, economists estimate that unions have created a wage differential of 15–20 percent over what workers would otherwise have received. In addition, unions have increased the fringe benefits of their members by 20–30 percent.[*] However, these effects are not spread evenly across all unions. Strong unions have succeeded in raising wages dramatically. But some weak unions have settled for lower wages than employers would have given workers otherwise, especially in trade-offs for other concessions. The impact is greater for blue-collar workers than for white-collar workers, for younger than middle-aged workers, and for men than for women.

But the influence of unions also extends to nonunion employees and employers. When nonunion and unionized employers compete in the same labor market, the nonunion employers often must pay wages and offer benefits similar to those offered by unionized employers. In addition, nonunion employers often raise wages and other benefits to block union organizing efforts. On the other hand, higher negotiated wages tend to cause unionized employers to hire fewer workers. Thus union wage demands may increase the labor supply in nonunion labor markets thereby lowering wages in those markets.

Impact on Inflation

The last effect mentioned leads most economists to reject the idea that unions, acting as economic institutions, can cause inflation. When a union succeeds in raising wages (and thus costs), some prices may increase in that sector of the economy. However, as workers are let go from that sector, increased unemployment creates downward pressures on labor costs and thus on prices in other sectors. More importantly, because of barriers to mobility, unemployment may persist for some time. Only if government reacts to higher unemployment by trying to raise the total level of employment does inflation result. Thus inflation may be *initiated* by union actions but is actually *caused* by government reactions to unemployment.

Impact on Technical Efficiency

Critics of unions point out that some union work rules lower productivity. When unions restrict the speed of an assembly line or cause management to hire extra workers, the resulting inefficiency is clearly visible. In addition, unions often insist that promotions be based on seniority. Inefficiency can result if more senior, less capable workers advance while younger, more able workers do not.

However, unions may also affect efficiency positively. Craft unions argue that because of rigorous training programs, their members have greater skills and productivity than nonunion workers. Higher wages and better working conditions may reduce employee turnover, saving more on recruiting and retraining than the improvements cost and raising overall efficiency. High worker morale may also

---

[*] Richard B. Freeman and James L. Medoff, *What Do Unions Do?* New York: Basic Books, 1984.

increase productivity. In addition, union demands may cause management to adopt better and more efficient practices. For example, in the face of high union wages, U.S. automakers have begun installing robots to perform many tasks. Japanese manufacturers have long used such mechanized systems, claiming that they keep costs down and provide better quality. Finally, unions improve the flow of information between workers and managers, which may also lead to increased productivity.

In one study researchers found that in manufacturing, unionized firms had 22 percent higher productivity than comparable nonunion firms.[*] However, other examples of both higher and lower productivity can be found. The best evidence suggests that unions on balance have had a detrimental effect on technical efficiency, since profits are somewhat lower in unionized firms. However, the total effect of unions must include an assessment of the benefits they provide their members as well as the costs to society.

Impact on Equity

Union members benefit from the more equitable treatment obtained for them through contract negotiation and interpretation. For example, unions provide a collective voice that tends to protect workers from injustices and gives them an alternative to quitting when working conditions are bad. Union workers express more dissatisfaction than do nonunion workers with various aspects of their jobs, including the physical conditions of the workplace and relations with their supervisors. But union workers are more satisfied with their wages and fringe benefits and are more likely to state that they are unwilling to change jobs under any circumstances.[†]

Politically, unions have supported many social policies to end or reduce discrimination and poverty. Yet, union wage gains are of little benefit to the poor and may even make income distribution more unequal. And the small number of women and minorities in many unions has led to charges that unions perpetuate discrimination. On balance, are unions' noneconomic activities beneficial? Do the benefits that union members receive outweigh the negative economic costs to other groups in society? These are issues that are not easily settled; rather, they remain the basis of rational disagreement.

CONCLUSION

In the six preceding chapters, we have explored the operation of product and resource markets. You have learned that competition in both types of markets leads to allocative and technical efficiency and that imperfections often lead to inefficiency. Correcting for these inefficiencies—and addressing our third economic goal, equity—leads government to intervene in the economy at times. In Chapters 16–19, we discuss how government activities affect the operation of various product and resource markets. As you will see, government also must make trade-offs between efficiency and equity.

---

[*] Charles Brown and James Medoff, "Trade Unions in the Production Process," *Journal of Political Economy*, June 1978.

[†] *See* Freeman and Medoff, *What Do Unions Do?*

SUMMARY

1. In this chapter we applied the basic theory of resource demand and supply to labor markets, taking into account the unique factors affecting labor supply and the role of unions.

2. The issues of equity and efficiency are mixed in labor markets. Wages promote efficiency, causing workers to move from one industry or occupation to another in response to changes in economic conditions. Wages also determine the individual's ability to consume (equity).

3. Labor is a unique resource because it and its owner are one and the same. Thus owners of labor resources care about working conditions; labor quality depends on both skill and effort, making marginal revenue product more difficult to estimate; and mobility is limited by both financial and emotional costs.

4. The laws of demand and supply still apply to labor, however. Demand is based on marginal revenue product, making worker productivity a major factor in wage determination. The household theory of labor supply states that labor supply depends on household preferences for work, for leisure, and for market and non-market goods and services; on the market wages that various family members can earn; on productivity in nonmarket activities; and on other family resources.

5. Higher wages do not necessarily increase quantity of labor supplied because of substitution and income effects. In the short run, the substitution effect outweighs the income effect. In the long run, however, the income effect outweighs the substitution effect.

6. In a competitive labor market with no restrictions on mobility, wages of workers in similar jobs and having similar skills may differ only temporarily. However, wage differentials related to working conditions or productivity are more permanent.

7. Some wage differentials reflect differences in human capital, that is, the skills and training of individual workers. Human capital theory treats investment in training and education like investment in physical capital, comparing benefits and costs and recognizing the opportunity cost of time.

8. Wage differentials can also result from barriers to entry (such as occupational licensing) that restrict supply, artificially increase wages, and lower efficiency.

9. Unions are an important institutional force in some labor markets. In craft unions, workers share a common skill, trade, or profession. In industrial unions, workers share common employers. Unions may also unite to form labor federations, such as the AFL–CIO.

10. Despite the efforts of the Knights of Labor, unions did not become a major force in the United States until formation of the American Federation of Labor. The AFL established collective bargaining, supplemented by political activity, as the best way to achieve worker goals. Efforts of the International Workers of the World to establish industrial unions failed, but the Congress of Industrial Organizations successfully unionized many industries.

11. Legislation such as the Norris–LaGuardia Act (1932) and the Wagner Act (1935) strengthened the position of unions in society. After World War II, union power was limited first by the Taft–Hartley Act (1947), which outlawed "unfair labor practices" by both unions and management, and later by the Landrum–Griffin Act (1959), which opened the operation of unions to public view.

12. Rules governing labor–management relations may be informal and established largely by management (as in nonunion firms) or negotiated periodically by labor and management (as in unionized firms). Interpretation of rules is an ongoing process, often involving arbitration when issues cannot be settled by the parties themselves.

13. Unions seek both economic goals (such as higher wages) and noneconomic goals (such as an effective grievance procedure). By exercising their economic strength, unions influence wages, benefits, hours, and other working conditions.

14. Union activities that increase wages harm allocative efficiency in competitive labor markets, but may harm or help efficiency when employers have market power (the model of bilateral monopoly).

15. Although unions do not directly cause inflation, government unemployment policies in response to union actions may do so.

16. Unions may have both negative and positive influences on technical efficiency. Some union-imposed work rules lower productivity, but productivity is higher in unionized industries in the manufacturing sector as a whole. On balance, however, higher productivity is exceeded slightly by higher wages, resulting in slightly lower efficiency.

17. Many union supporters justify union actions on the basis that they foster greater equity. In the final analysis, the worth of unions is measured by balancing efficiency and equity considerations.

KEY TERMS

Household theory of labor supply, 361
Collective bargaining, 368
Union, 368

Craft union, 369

Industrial union, 369

Labor federation, 369

Injunction, 370

Yellow-dog contract, 370

Union shop, 372

Right-to-work laws, 372

Closed shop, 372

Arbitration, 374

Bilateral monopoly, 376

QUESTIONS FOR REVIEW AND DISCUSSION

1. Evaluate the statement: "Workers' earnings depend on what they do for consumers, not employers."

2. What are the reasons for two workers receiving different wages? Which of these reasons are consistent with efficiency? Which reflect inefficiency? Which are possibly inequitable?

3. College students often earn relatively low wages from summer jobs despite the fact that they have above-average educations. Does this disprove the human capital theory? What explanations can you offer for their relatively low wages?

4. A union bargains with a firm that buys labor in an imperfectly competitive resource market (bilateral monopoly) and succeeds in raising wages above what the employer would have paid. Has the union adversely affected efficiency from society's perspective?

5. Evaluate the statement: "In the absence of unions, management is free to manipulate its labor resources as it pleases" by answering questions (a)–(c).
   a) What are the constraints on managerial discretion in the absence of a union?
   b) What are the costs to a firm whose managers treat workers poorly?
   c) What options do workers have if they believe that they are being treated unfairly?

6. The American Federation of Labor lobbied Congress to include the following statement in the Clayton Act of 1914: "The labor of a human being is not a commodity or article of commerce." What do you think the Federation had in mind? To what extent is labor "an article of commerce"? To what extent do labor markets require special consideration because of concerns about equity?

PART FIVE

Microeconomic Role of Government

CHAPTER 16

Microeconomics of
Public Finance

QUESTIONS TO CONSIDER

☐ What role does government play in a market economy?

☐ Why does government intervene in the economy when external benefits occur and to provide public goods?

☐ How do taxes affect efficiency and equity?

☐ Who pays a tax?

☐ What sources of revenue does the federal government rely on? State governments? Local governments?

T hus far we have concentrated on the private sector of the economy. However, the public sector—government at the local, state, and federal levels—is very much involved in the microeconomy. In 1986, government expenditures in the United States totaled $1.5 trillion dollars. Some 20 percent of total U.S. output was purchased by government; one-fifth of all workers were employed by government. In addition, government laws and regulations have far-ranging effects on the economic decisions of households and businesses.

In this chapter and Chapters 17–19 we look at the U.S. government's role in the microeconomy. We want to find out *why* government is involved, *what* some economists believe government might do to help the economy, and *how* government should determine what to do. Although economists disagree about the appropriate role of government, they do agree that applying the principles of rational choice to government policy decisions is important. Bear in mind that government decisions do not always result in improved economic conditions. Thus we also look at some reasons why government sometimes fails.

GOVERNMENT IN THE MICROECONOMY

In this chapter we focus on **public finance**, that is, the size and distribution of government expenditures and taxes. As you will see, economic principles can help explain government actions and the effect of government expenditures and taxes on the private sector.

Government and the Circular Flow of Economic Activity

Exhibit 16.1 shows some of the impacts of government on the circular flow of microeconomic activity. The loops show the flow of resources, products, and dollars between the government and private sectors of the economy. This activity takes place in resource, product, and financial markets.

Public finance. The size and distribution of government spending and taxation at the federal, state, and local levels.

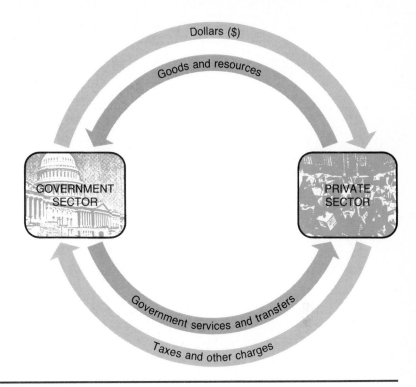

Exhibit 16.1
Circular Flow and the Government Sector
Government affects the circular flow of microeconomic activity in several ways. The government purchases goods and resources from the private sector. The government also imposes regulations, taxes, and other charges. And the government has the power to transfer income and resources from one group in the private sector to another.

In some ways government acts like the private sector. Like businesses, government supplies some products to households in exchange for dollars—state-run liquor stores, for example. Government also purchases resources from households—hiring teachers for the public schools, for example. And like households, government purchases products from businesses—such as computers, airplanes, and, of course, large quantities of paper.

However, government's unique powers and activities set it apart from the private sector. Government has the authority to demand resources without paying full market value—a military draft, for example. (But stories of $640 toilet seats and $2000 hammers indicate that government sometimes pays more than market value. These are not examples, however, of government helping the economy achieve efficiency.) Government can also tax and charge fees that force the private sector to support the public sector. Finally, the flows between the public and private sectors indicate that government uses its powers to transfer income and resources from one group in the private sector to another.

To determine whether government's actions are warranted, we apply the principles of rational choice. That is, we weigh the benefits of the goods and services provided by the government against the opportunity costs. Because of scarcity, every government purchase has *direct* opportunity costs. Resources used by the government require a sacrifice of private goods. But government actions also have *indirect* costs because they affect private decision making.

Government regulations that limit pollution and encourage drug safety may raise producer costs. Tariffs and quotas that restrict imports of foreign goods may give U.S. firms market power. Tax deductions that encourage spending for home ownership, training, and the purchase of machinery and equipment affect resource allocation. Price supports for agricultural products and rent controls on apartments affect prices and output. All are examples of policies that affect private decisions.

Although not indicated in the circular flow, government also affects the economy by participating in financial markets. We noted in Chapter 14 that government can affect the demand for and supply of loanable funds and that government regulations affect the banking system. Other aspects of government's role in the economy involve macroeconomics and are discussed in that portion of this textbook.

FUNCTIONS OF GOVERNMENT

Given the costs involved, why is government involved in the microeconomy? Economists disagree strongly about the effects of particular government economic activities and about how much government activity is desirable. However, most agree that government may improve the microeconomy in certain ways. As we discussed in Chapter 5, the principal microeconomic activities of government are (1) facilitating market activity; (2) correcting for market failures; and (3) redistributing income and economic opportunity.

Facilitating Market Activity

You have seen how private exchanges in smoothly functioning markets generate efficient outcomes. Recall that money helps to facilitate exchanges. Individuals sell their resources—labor, for example—in one market and use the income they receive to buy the goods and services they desire in another market. Government can help markets function smoothly by establishing and protecting the integrity of money.

Moreover, markets function smoothly only when property rights are well-defined and protected. When individuals have property rights in resources, they have a strong incentive to sell those resources to the highest bidder. The result of free exchange of property rights in smoothly functioning markets is allocative efficiency. If property rights do not exist or are not clearly defined, however, efficiency suffers. Through the legal system—laws, police, and courts—government helps establish, protect, and regulate private property rights, thus facilitating market activity.

Correcting for Market Failures

Facilitating market activity is important but is only a small part of government activity. Government activity may also be useful in cases of **market failure**. In other words, there are some circumstances in which market activity may not produce allocative efficiency, technical efficiency, and equity. In such cases, government may try to "correct" for these failures.

Market failure. Inability of a market to achieve allocative efficiency, technical efficiency, or equity.

What circumstances cause markets to fail? What can government policy do to correct the failures? Which policy solutions are desirable and which are undesirable and why? We explore these questions in this chapter and in Chapters 17–19. To begin, though, let's consider some causes of market failures.

Controlling or limiting market power. We have noted that competition is essential to allocative efficiency in a market economy. When market power exists and is exercised, markets will not provide the quantity of goods and services that best matches society's wants. Moreover, firms with market power may not have strong enough incentives to generate technical efficiency. Government actions that reduce or control market power can improve efficiency. We consider government regulation of market power in Chapter 17.

Correcting for externalities. Externalities—external benefits or costs—create market failure because demand and supply do not reflect marginal social benefits and marginal social costs. Government may help the economy correct for externalities and thus help it to achieve allocative efficiency. External benefits are especially important in the case of *public goods*, such as national defense. Unlike private goods (such as pizza or college education), public goods are collectively consumed. The benefits you receive from consuming national defense do not reduce the benefits others can receive. Moreover, it is impractical to exclude any individuals from consuming a public good. How could national defense protect you but not your neighbors? In this chapter we discuss government's role in the case of external benefits and public goods. In Chapter 17 we consider the case of external costs.

Correcting for imperfect information. Market failure also occurs when information available to private decision makers is imperfect or inaccurate. Government may help the market to achieve efficiency by providing information that might not otherwise exist about potential benefits and costs. Warning labels on pesticides, information about potential hazards of drugs, and information about job opportunities are all examples of information provided by government in an effort to assist the market system.

Income Redistribution and Economic Opportunity

In addition to correcting for market failures, government affects the microeconomy through efforts to redistribute income and economic opportunity. Market outcomes, even if efficient, may not generate a distribution of income and opportunity that society collectively believes is equitable. Several government programs are directed to the goal of equity. For example, welfare and Social Security transfer income from one part of the population to another. Antidiscrimination and student-loan programs attempt to improve economic opportunities. Income transfers and equal opportunity programs affect both equity and efficiency, as you will see in Chapter 17.

RATIONAL CHOICE AND GOVERNMENT POLICIES

Most economists agree that the private sector may not always achieve the economic goals of allocative efficiency, technical efficiency, and equity. However, government's role in addressing market failures and redistributing income remains controversial. Even those who strongly support government activities recognize that government also fails at times. Moreover, economists often disagree about the desirability and effects of specific government actions. We cannot expect to resolve normative disagreements over the proper role of government. But we can produce meaningful economic analysis by applying the principles of rational choice. Rational choice helps us to determine how government should operate and to predict the behavior of government and public officials.

Regardless of the success or failure of markets, the principles of rational choice remind us to ask a key question when considering the desirability of government intervention: Is there a government policy that will improve the situation? To answer this question, we must consider both the positive and the negative effects of the policy on the goals of allocative efficiency, technical efficiency, and equity. We first have to identify a type of policy that offers some social benefits by correcting a particular problem. For example, government regulations that reduce the amounts of air and water pollution will provide some social benefits in the form of improved air and water quality. But we must also consider the costs of such a policy, including the potential effects of the policy on economic incentives. For example, pollution-control laws also reduce profitability and may cause firms to spend more time and money to evade government laws than to produce more efficiently.

In addition, we must consider the possibility that government policy may fail. Rational choice principles predict that public officials will act in their own self-interest. Some critics of government regulations, for example, suggest that politicians may be unduly influenced by special-interest groups that seek government regulations to increase their market power. Current producers, for example, may seek to have tougher standards imposed on new firms entering the industry and thus turn pollution-control laws into barriers to entry.

Political debate about policy options often centers on equity because government policies have different effects on different groups in the economy. For example, restricting the use of high-sulfur coal by Midwest utilities may reduce acid rain and benefit residents of the Northeast. But it will also raise the cost of electricity to Midwesterners. Limiting foreign-auto imports will increase the profits of U.S. automakers and provide jobs to U.S. autoworkers. But consumers will pay higher prices for cars.

Economic analysis cannot resolve differences of opinion that are based on value judgments, but it can identify the effects of government policies on economic variables. In addition, even when policies have uneven effects on different groups, economic principles remind us that any policy worth considering should be one for which the extra benefits outweigh the extra costs. Thus the net gain from a policy provides an opportunity to resolve conflicts between those who gain and those who lose.

For example, most economists agree that current restrictions on automobile imports are a net loss to the economy, even though they protect U.S. jobs. But a policy that eliminated restrictions on imports could be coupled with a policy to help retrain and possibly relocate displaced autoworkers. Thus society could gain increased efficiency, but not at the direct expense of one particular group. In this way, the principles of rational choice can help politicians gain support for policies that are economically attractive.

We present a more complete discussion of how the principles of rational choice help to structure the debates over economic policies in the introduction to Chapter 19. These principles, however, represent an outline for the consideration of the policy issues contained in this chapter and Chapters 17–19.

RECAP

Government buys resources and products from households and businesses. It transfers resources from the private sector by imposing taxes.

Government may help the economy to operate smoothly by facilitating market exchanges or correcting market failures. It may improve equity by redistributing income or economic opportunity.

The principles of rational choice indicate that a government action is desirable only if the marginal social benefits of the action outweigh the marginal social costs.

Both direct and indirect costs of government and the potential for government failure must be recognized.

EXTERNAL BENEFITS AND PUBLIC GOODS

In order to apply the principles of rational choice to public finance, we must examine the reasons for and impact of government expenditures and revenues. Many public expenditures and goods and services purchased and/or produced by the public sector offer external benefits. In this section we seek to answer two questions: What are external benefits and how can they justify government support of such goods and services as public health? What characteristics of public goods such as national defense cause market failure?

External Benefits and Allocative Efficiency

As we stated in Chapter 6, when a good or service has external benefits, it provides benefits to individuals other than those who demand or supply it. For example, immunization against communicable diseases—getting shots to prevent measles, for instance—provides private benefits to those who are inoculated by reducing their chances of getting the diseases. However, the benefits of immunization are not limited to those who pay for it. When you are inoculated against measles, not only are you protected, but to some degree so are your family, friends, and economics professor. You will certainly consider the benefits you personally receive from the shots and may also consider the benefits to your family and closest friends. But you are not likely to be willing to pay more for a measles shot because of the benefits your economics professor receives. The benefits to yourself and to the others you consider influence your demand for shots; the benefits received by those you do not consider are external benefits. That is, they are external (and ignored) by people when they decide whether to buy measles shots.

Exhibit 16.2 shows how the external benefits of measles shots create allocative inefficiency. To keep the example simple, we assumed that all product and resource markets are competitive and that there are no external costs. These assumptions allow us to equate the supply curve with marginal social cost (S = MSC). The marginal social benefits (MSB) curve reflects benefits received by all members of society—those who buy and those who benefit because others buy. The market demand curve, however, measures only private benefits received by those who purchase measles shots.

Your demand reflects how much better off you are (and perhaps your family and close friends) but does not reflect benefits received by the rest of society. Thus at each quantity, the MSB curve lies above the demand curve by an amount equal to external benefits. In this case we have assumed constant external benefits of $1 per shot, measured as the vertical distance between the two curves.

Equilibrium output occurs at the intersection of the demand and supply curves, or 15,000 measles shots per year. But allocative efficiency occurs where marginal social benefit equals marginal social cost, or 20,000 measles shots per year. As this example indicates, the market underproduces and society underconsumes immunization because suppliers and consumers ignore external benefits.

To achieve allocative efficiency, government can take one of two steps. As illustrated in Exhibit 16.2, it can subsidize buyers. If buyers receive a subsidy of $1 per shot, demand will increase, as shown on the graph in the shift from D_1 to D_2. Equilibrium will increase to 20,000 shots per year, or the allocatively efficient

Exhibit 16.2
**External Benefits and
Allocative Inefficiency**
When a product generates an external
benefit, market demand no longer equals
marginal social benefits. Demand (D_1)
represents the benefits received by those
who buy measles shots; equilibrium occurs where D_1 = S at 15,000 shots. But
marginal social benefits (MSB) exceed
demand at each quantity by the amount
of the external benefit—in this case, $1
per shot. Allocative efficiency occurs
where MSB = MSC at 20,000 shots per
year. The loss in efficiency is indicated
by the red-shaded triangle. By providing
a subsidy of $1 per shot, government
can either increase demand or lower cost
and thus achieve allocative efficiency.

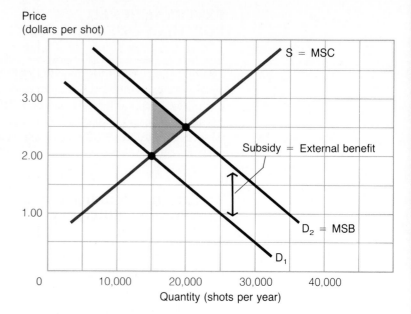

quantity. Note that in either case the 20,000 who buy shots receive no greater
benefits per shot than before. But more people will buy shots because the effective
cost is $1 less per shot.

Alternatively, government can subsidize production of measles shots. If it pays
suppliers $1 for each shot produced and sold, it will effectively lower costs by $1
and increase market supply. The new market supply will be $1 lower than S at
each quantity. The market then will reach equilibrium at 20,000 shots per year
and achieve allocative efficiency. To check your understanding, draw another
supply curve that is $1 lower at each quantity. (This curve will intersect D_1 at the
allocatively efficient quantity of 20,000 shots per year.)

Public subsidies of producers is the more commonly used approach. Note
that the total subsidy paid by the government is the same in both cases: $1 per
shot for 20,000 shots, or $20,000 per year.

Low Transaction Costs and a Private
Market for External Benefits

Government intervention is not the only solution to external benefits. Suppose
that you own an apple orchard and that your next-door neighbor keeps several
hives of bees. The bees benefit both of you. Your neighbor receives honey, and
you receive more apples because of better pollination.

Now suppose that you could increase your apple production and sales by
$300 per year if your neighbor would agree to keep one additional hive of bees.
The extra hive would cost $100 per year. You might offer to pay your neighbor
$200 to keep another hive. Both of you would benefit from this private exchange.

Allocative efficiency would also improve because the gain in value ($300 worth of apples) would exceed the extra cost ($100 to keep more bees). By entering into a private agreement with your neighbor, you internalize what otherwise would be an external benefit from additional bees. The $200 is a private benefit to your neighbor and influences her to keep more bees.

In this simple example, government action was not required to eliminate the externality. But private contracts work only when the transaction costs of arranging and monitoring the contract between the parties are relatively small. Contracts are usually feasible only when few individuals are involved or when individuals are tightly organized into groups formed to negotiate contracts.

In many cases it is difficult, if not impossible, to eliminate externalities with private contracts. Imagine how difficult it would be, for example, to get everyone who benefits from your college education to agree to pay a portion of your tuition each semester. When contracting is impractical, government action is sometimes justified.

Public Goods and Allocative Efficiency

Government almost always provides public goods, such as national defense. Why? First, public goods are *indivisible*. Whatever quantity of national defense is provided, all individuals receive the same amount. Second, regardless of how much national defense you "consume," the same amount is left for me and others to consume. In other words, the marginal cost associated with allowing another individual to consume a public good is zero. Allocative efficiency requires production and consumption up to the point where marginal social benefits equal marginal social costs (MSB = MSC). If marginal social costs are indeed zero, social welfare would be lower if any individual were excluded. For this reason, the appropriate price of a public good is zero. This price reflects the marginal cost of adding another consumer.

Be careful not to confuse *public goods*—an economic term having special meaning—with goods and services supplied by the public sector. It is true that many public goods—such as national defense—are provided by the public sector. But, the public sector also supplies what are essentially private goods—for example, state-operated liquor stores, transportation services, and public utilities. The term *public goods* is a term with a particular and special meaning to economists.

Case against private production of public goods. The private sector could produce and sell public goods in markets, but the characteristics of these goods make it unlikely that a private market would produce the allocatively efficient quantity. Suppose, for example, the government decided to allow private firms to satisfy the demand for national defense. Private firms could certainly produce defense products—in fact, U.S. weapons systems are produced largely by private firms—but there is more to national defense than weapons.

Who would pay companies to produce national defense? Some individuals might be willing to pay. However, economic analysis suggests that the amount individuals are *willing* to pay would be insufficient to provide the quantity that is allocatively efficient. Since it is practically impossible to exclude someone from the protection provided, individuals would have little incentive to pay voluntarily. Many would be "free riders," enjoying the benefits even though they do not pay. Thus when public goods are provided through private markets they tend to be *underproduced.*

Public goods and external benefits are closely related. Because individuals cannot be easily excluded from consuming public goods, there are external benefits when public goods are produced by private markets. Moreover, external benefits can be considered a special case of public goods. For example, public health services such as vaccinations provide some private benefits, but a significant part of the benefits are really public goods, jointly consumed by the rest of society. In both cases, private markets often fail to produce the quantity that is allocatively efficient. When the failures impose significant costs on the economy, government action may be desirable.

Case for private production of public goods.

Government intervention in the economy, however, remains controversial, even in the case of public goods. Some critics charge that government production is always inefficient. Profits motivate managers and firms in the private sector to achieve efficiency. Government officials lack that incentive. They may be motivated instead by a desire to increase their power and influence by increasing the size of their agencies. Those who believe that government enterprises are inefficient are strong supporters of *privatization.* They would prefer to use private contractors instead of public employees to provide such services as fire protection and garbage collection.

However, the evidence about the efficiency of government enterprise is mixed. Some studies have indicated that fire protection and garbage collection can in some cases be provided at lower cost privately than publicly. In 1984, the Grace Commission's report gave some support to the charge of federal government inefficiency. The commission suggested more than 2500 changes that it said would save $424 billion over a three-year period. (Not all of the recommendations sought to obtain the same systems at lower cost; many were directed at eliminating services altogether.) On the other hand, studies have found no consistent difference in the cost of government and private hospitals.

In addition to complaints about efficiency, critics charge that government sometimes provides goods and services that could easily (and perhaps more efficiently) be provided by the private sector. They argue that the postal service, public transportation systems, and publicly operated railroads are not really public goods and have few, if any, external benefits. Critics also suggest that even if private production involves some allocative inefficiency, it also offers important benefits by allowing market prices to direct production and resource allocation.

Problems of public decision making.

While economists and politicians argue over government's role in the economy, in reality government is the largest supplier of public goods. But without the market forces of demand and supply, how can government know how much to produce? In the United States, we rely on political mechanisms to determine the best quantity of public goods. For example, Congress votes on the defense appropriation, state legislatures vote on how much to spend on highways, and local officials vote on how much to spend on county and municipal parks.

Economists hope that politicians will use the principles of rational choice when making these decisions. We cannot justify spending more on national defense simply because it is a public good. Its extra social benefits must outweigh its extra social costs. In some cases, politicians have diverged from the principles of rational choice in order to please special interest groups. For example, a relatively small part of society benefits from municipal golf courses, but a much larger part of society helps to pay for them. Economists generally agree that golf courses do not meet the criteria of public goods, or goods having external benefits, and thus should not be provided at below-market prices.

How is government to finance public goods? Because individuals will not voluntarily pay, public goods are financed through taxes. That is, governments use their taxing powers to force individuals to pay. This process also involves political decisions. Later in this chapter we discuss some of the difficulties of political decision making from the economic perspective. First, we need to explore the U.S. tax system in more detail.

TAXES AND THE GOALS OF EQUITY AND EFFICIENCY

As we discussed in Chapter 5, taxes are the primary means of financing government activities. (Taxes are also used to encourage or discourage activities, but in this section we are concerned with the effects of taxes that are levied solely to raise revenues.) In this section, however, we will consider alternatives to taxes, as well as different types of taxes, and their effects on efficiency and equity. In studying the effects of taxes, we generally consider the expenditure side of a government's budget as fixed. That is, the economic issue for tax policy is not how large the tax burden will be, but the economic consequences of taxes on efficiency and equity.

What Are the Alternatives to Taxes?

If a decision to spend has been made (justified, presumably, by the principles of rational choice), government has several options. First, it can exercise its powers to command a direct transfer of resources from private owners, such as a military draft. In democratic systems, this method is seldom used except during wartime.

Second, the federal government's control over the money supply makes it possible to pay for public expenditures by creating new supplies of money. This option has often been exercised both in the United States and in other countries. Although easy to do, this method results in inflation and destroys the value of the currency. The governments of Argentina and Brazil financed much government spending in this way during the 1970s and, as a result, inflation was as high as 200–600 percent per year. Because most economists agree that the costs of rapid inflation are very high, they seldom recommend this option as a long-term policy.

Third, government can borrow some or all the funds it requires. State and local government often borrow to finance construction of highways and school buildings. Borrowing allows the tax burden to be spread over several years, matching the long-term benefits that such capital expenditures will generate. The federal government borrows when it spends more than it collects in taxes (which it has done every year since 1969). In order to borrow, it must find lenders. The U.S. government has not had too much difficulty finding lenders—especially foreign lenders—because it has been willing to pay relatively high interest rates. However, high interest rates reduce expenditures for capital resources, as we discussed in Chapter 13. Moreover, to make interest payments in the future, government will have to impose taxes.

In the ever-present search for "painless" means of public financing, governments have used a fourth method: lotteries. Long popular in Latin America, they have lately gained favor in much of the United States, including California, Illinois, Massachusetts, and New York. Some states also operate state liquor stores for profit, using the profit (or surplus as it is called) for public expenditures. There is, of course, no painless or costless means of financing. Although taxes also impose costs on the economy, they are the most important means of public financing in the United States. Financing expenditures through taxation forces individuals (and politicians) to recognize the costs of government. And in the long run, taxes are an indispensable means of financing government expenditures.

Efficiency and Incentive Effects of Taxes

Most taxes are imposed in order to raise revenues for government to spend. Economists suggest that such taxes be designed so as to affect individual choice as little as possible (other than to reduce income). To the extent that taxes designed to raise revenues distort the choices that businesses and individuals make, they may impose two costs on the private sector: (1) the opportunity cost of transferring resources to the public sector; and (2) the cost of reduced efficiency.

Effects of an excise tax. Suppose, for example, that the federal government charges brewers a tax of $1 per six-pack of beer produced. Before the tax, consumers bought 2500 six-packs per week at a price of $2.00 per six-pack. This point is the intersection of the market-demand (D) and supply (S_1) curves in Exhibit 16.3. The tax, however, raises the brewers' costs and shifts the supply curve to S_2. Note that the new supply curve is $1 higher at each quantity than before, reflecting the amount of the tax. For the new supply curve, the equilibrium price is higher—$2.50 instead of $2.00—and the quantity exchanged is lower—2000 instead of 2500 six-packs per week. Note also that sellers now do not receive the full price paid by consumers. Of the $2.50 price that consumers pay, $1.00 is paid to the government as tax, leaving only $1.50 per six-pack for the seller. (You find the price received by producers along the original supply curve S_1.)

In this analysis we are interested in the answers to two questions. First, who actually pays the tax? This question may sound silly, since the tax is levied on brewers. However, while brewers are legally responsible for paying it to the government, the tax burden is actually shared by sellers and buyers. Sellers receive $0.50 less for each six-pack than before ($1.50 instead of $2.00). Consumers pay $0.50 more ($2.50 instead of $2.00).

In this example, consumers and sellers share the tax equally, each paying half. But in the real world, the proportion paid by sellers and buyers depends on the price elasticity of demand and supply. The more price elastic the demand, the smaller will be the price increase and the greater the proportion of a tax paid by sellers. The more price elastic the supply, the greater will be the share paid by consumers.

A second question is also important. What is the impact of the tax on efficiency? If the market for beer functioned smoothly before, the tax causes allocative

Exhibit 16.3
Effects of an Excise Tax
The market for beer is initially in equilibrium at a price of $2.00 per six-pack, with 2500 six-packs per week bought and sold. An excise tax of $1.00 per six-pack shifts the supply curve to S_2. As a result, consumers buy less (2000 six-packs per week) and pay more ($2.50 per six-pack). Producers sell less and receive a lower price ($1.50 per six-pack—from curve S_1). Total tax paid is $2000 per week (the area of the blue-shaded rectangle), which is shared by consumers who pay $0.50 more and producers who receive $0.50 less. In addition, society suffers a loss (the area of the red-shaded triangle) by not producing all six-packs that add more to extra benefits than to extra costs.

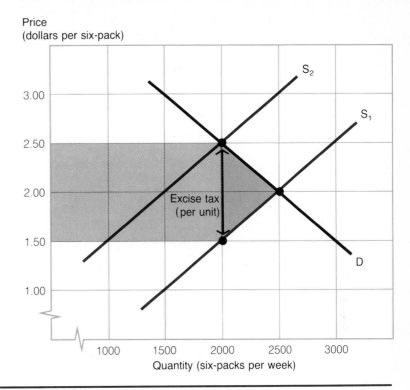

inefficiency. Allocative efficiency requires production of 2500 six-packs per week (where MSB = MSC), but the tax reduces production to below this level. Consumers are willing to purchase more beer at the real opportunity cost of producing it (shown as S_1), but less beer is consumed and produced than before. At the new equilibrium, marginal social benefits exceed marginal social costs.

The red-shaded area in Exhibit 16.3 shows the loss to society from not producing all units that add more to social benefits than to social costs. This cost results because resources are diverted from producing beer to producing other goods that have less value to society. (Recall that the cost to society of producing beer—measured along the supply curve—reflects the value to society of producing other goods.)

The extent of allocative inefficiency caused by a tax reflects the price elasticity of market demand, that is, how much consumers respond to higher prices. When demand is relatively price inelastic (such as for gasoline), quantity consumed decreases only slightly, so effects on allocative efficiency are minimal. Distortion is also less when all goods are taxed equally (such as by a general sales tax), since relative prices of goods are unchanged. By careful consideration of the type of tax and the type of good taxed, government can raise additional revenues with a minimum of market distortion.

Taxing a single item—such as beer—will not create allocative inefficiency if the market is already inefficient. For example, if litter and alcoholism create external costs of $1 per six-pack, then a $1 tax would actually improve allocative efficiency. (In that case, marginal social costs would be associated with S_2.) To the extent that taxes cause choices to reflect marginal social benefits and costs, they can increase allocative efficiency. To the extent that they drive quantities away from the point where MSB = MSC, they cause inefficiency.

Other efficiency effects of taxes. Taxes may also affect efficiency by changing the work efforts of individuals and the investment plans of businesses. Both households and businesses make decisions based in part on the *after-tax* income they can expect. Higher marginal tax rates on additional income may lessen the incentives for individuals to do additional work and businesses to make additional investments. On the other hand, if you must have a certain amount of income (for example, to finance another year of college), higher tax rates will cause you to work more.

How much will individuals change their work efforts and businesses increase their investments if taxes are lowered? Economic principles can only suggest a direction of change—that investment will increase, for example. Additional studies of actual behavior are required to determine how much change will occur. Economists disagree about how sensitive such decisions are to changes in tax rates. Individuals who are the principal income earners in a family appear unlikely to make a significant response, but others (primarily married women) may. Some economists are convinced that businesses will greatly increase their investments if tax rates fall. Others believe that factors such as expectations about economic prospects are more important to investment plans.

Economists have debated the importance of tax rates on economic behavior for years. The academic debate became a political debate in the early 1980s. President Reagan argued that high marginal tax rates were significantly undermining incentives to work, save, and invest. In 1981 Congress responded by significantly lowering tax rates on personal income. It also provided tax relief to businesses in the form of accelerated depreciation. To date, however, there have been no indications that individuals have changed their attitudes or behavior toward work in response.

Taxes can also create inefficiency by encouraging socially unproductive investments. For example, income tax laws prior to 1986 encouraged construction of office buildings. Many of these buildings were profitable to investors—who received large tax breaks—even though they did not attract tenants. The tax changes in 1986 reduced the speculative advantages of many of these socially unproductive investments. Nevertheless, the profitability of investment decisions still depends heavily on tax laws. It is hard to judge the total effect of such laws on allocative efficiency, but any distortions clearly add to the burden of taxes.

What Is a "Good" Tax?

To some the question "What is a 'good' tax?" is a contradiction in terms. After all, taxes reduce incomes and modify behavior. How can a tax be considered good? Taxes are a cost of government and few, if any, individuals enjoy paying taxes. But we should not forget the other side of the equation: Government expenditures also have benefits. In fact, most of the debate over the size of the tax burden is misplaced. A higher level of expenditures is the main cause of high taxes.

Economists judge taxes by their effect on efficiency, that is, how much they distort the allocation of resources. Some economists believe that high tax rates in

All methods of government financing—direct transfers, increases in the money supply, borrowing, and taxes—impose costs on the private sector.

Excise taxes cause fewer taxed goods to be produced and sold. Less quantity reduces allocative efficiency if the markets were functioning smoothly before. The tax is shared by both suppliers and consumers.

High tax rates may reduce work effort and saving to some extent. Taxes may also reduce private investment or cause a change in the type of investments made.

From the economic perspective, a "good tax" is one that raises revenue in an efficient and equitable manner.

the federal income tax system may discourage saving, reduce work effort, and thus decrease efficiency. Certainly, favorable tax treatment of real estate has spurred an oversupply of commercial buildings in some locations. But a "good" tax would raise the desired amount of revenue while creating few undesirable market distortions. A "good" tax is also one that individuals consider fair or equitable. As we have stressed, equity is a normative issue. Positive economic analysis cannot tell us whether a tax is fair. But it can help us to understand the important related question of who actually bears the burden of a tax.

Equity Effects of the Tax Burden

In weighing the effect of taxes, economists can apply one of two alternative principles: the *benefits-received principle* and the *ability-to-pay principle*. Each principle has been proposed as a means of ensuring equitable taxation.

Benefits-received principle. Proponents of the **benefits-received principle** suggest that in fairness those who benefit from public expenditures should pay for those benefits. That is, they believe that government-provided goods should be treated as much like private goods as possible. Because this forces individuals to recognize the costs of financing government benefits, they may weigh benefits and costs when voting for public expenditures.

The benefits-received principle is used when government sets user charges for government services, such as fares for public transportation or fees for hunting and fishing licenses. In other cases, taxes are used to approximate benefits received. For example, gasoline taxes are used to pay for road and highway construction. Even if you never drive on the highway that enters your town, trucks that supply your neighborhood supermarket do. You benefit from construction of a highway, and you pay for it since gasoline taxes affect food prices. Some economists suggest that property taxes reflect the benefits-received principle when those taxes support police and fire protection services, as they do in most municipalities.

Highway and bridge tolls are a means of indirectly taxing residents of other states and localities who do not pay taxes directly to the units of government through which they are traveling. A similar argument is made to support the higher tuition charged to out-of-state residents attending state colleges and universities. In these cases, the fees charged are ways of applying the benefits-received principle.

Even if it sounds fair to tax only those who benefit directly from public expenditures, this approach is not always applicable. We have no practical way to determine the direct benefits received from public goods such as national defense. Moreover, we would find it difficult to use the benefits-received principle for transfer payments, since the purpose of such spending is to raise the income of individuals. Finally, taxes such as highway and bridge tolls discourage consumption even when the marginal cost of an additional consumer is zero. But, when marginal costs are zero, restricting consumption is inefficient.

Ability-to-pay principle. Because the benefits-received principle has limited application, some economists and politicians prefer the **ability-to-pay principle**. According to this principle, those with a greater ability should pay a larger share of taxes. There are two aspects of tax equity from this perspective. First, we want **horizontal equity**; that is, individuals with the same ability to pay should

Benefits-received principle. A theory of taxation that states that individuals should be taxed in proportion to the benefits they receive from government goods and services.

Ability-to-pay principle. A theory of taxation that states that individuals should be taxed in proportion to their income or some other measure of ability to pay.

Horizontal equity. A principle of taxation that suggests that individuals in equal economic circumstances should pay an equal amount of taxes.

Vertical equity. A principle of taxation that suggests that individuals in unequal economic circumstances should pay an unequal amount of taxes.

Marginal tax rate. The percentage of additional income that must be paid in taxes; the ratio of additional tax owed to additional income.

Average tax rate. The proportion of income paid in taxes; the ratio of taxes paid to taxable income.

Progressive tax. A tax for which the average tax rate increases as income increases.

pay the same taxes. In addition, we seek **vertical equity**; that is, individuals with greater ability to pay should pay higher taxes.

Horizontal equity certainly sounds fair; it means that those with equal economic status pay the same. But how do we measure ability to pay and the sacrifice imposed by taxes? And even if we can agree that those who have a greater ability to pay should pay more, how much more in taxes should they pay?

In order to assess either horizontal or vertical equity, we have to measure a household's ability to pay taxes. It seems reasonable to use income to measure ability, but do all households with the same current income have the same ability to pay? Is a single individual with $15,000 of income equivalent to a household of six with the same income? Should we treat a student with low current income but a relatively prosperous future the same as someone with an equal current income but no likelihood of a future increase? These questions strongly suggest that current income is not always a clear indicator of equality of circumstance. Later in this chapter, we examine the current system of taxes from the perspectives of both horizontal and vertical equity.

Distribution of the Tax Burden

When trying to determine whether the tax burden is distributed fairly according to the ability-to-pay principle, economists consider the relationship between income and taxes paid. In order to understand this relationship, we have to distinguish between marginal and average tax rates. The **marginal tax rate** is the tax rate applied to a change in income. The **average tax rate** is the percentage of total income paid out in taxes. We can identify three types of taxes by the way average tax rates are related to income.

Progressive taxes. With a **progressive tax** the average tax rate increases as income rises. That is, the higher one's income, the greater the tax payment is as a percentage of income. We can show how a progressive income tax operates using the data in Exhibit 16.4(a). The second column shows marginal tax rates: on the first $10,000 earned it is 10 percent; on the next $15,000 (from $10,001 to $25,000), it is 20 percent; on additional income above $25,000, the marginal rate is 40 percent. The last two columns show the taxes paid and average tax rate for three individuals with different incomes.

Lindsay earned $10,000 last year and owes $1000 in taxes. All of her income is taxed at the 10 percent rate, and her average tax rate (taxes paid ÷ income) is therefore 10 percent. To calculate the taxes owed by Jenny, who earned $25,000 last year, we must follow the marginal tax rates in the left-hand part of the table. The tax on the first $10,000 of her income is $1000 (10 percent); on the next $15,000—the additional income that falls in the second tax bracket—she pays another $3000 (20 percent of her income above $10,000). Her total tax bill is therefore $4000, and her average tax rate is 16 percent. Note that her average rate is less than the marginal rate because her income is taxed at two different rates. As her income rises above $10,000 she moves into a different tax bracket. But she pays the higher marginal rate only on the portion of her income above $10,000.

Finally, Chris earned $50,000 last year and owes $14,000 in taxes—$1000 on the first $10,000; $3000 on the next $15,000; and $10,000 on the next $25,000 (0.40 × $25,000). His average tax rate is therefore 28 percent ($14,000 ÷ $50,000).

(a) A progressive tax

Income level	Marginal rate	Individual	Income	Tax bill	Average tax rate
$10,000 and below	10%	Lindsay	$10,000	$ 1,000	10%
$10,001–$25,000	20	Jenny	25,000	4,000	16
$25,001 and above	40	Chris	50,000	14,000	28

(b) A proportional tax

Income level	Marginal rate	Individual	Income	Tax bill	Average tax rate
$10,000 and below	20%	Lindsay	$10,000	$ 2,000	20%
$10,001–$25,000	20	Jenny	25,000	5,000	20
$25,001 and above	20	Chris	50,000	10,000	20

(c) A regressive tax

Income level	Marginal rate	Individual	Income	Tax bill	Average tax rate
$10,000 and below	40%	Lindsay	$10,000	$ 4,000	40%
$10,001–$25,000	20	Jenny	25,000	7,000	28
$25,001 and above	10	Chris	50,000	9,500	19

Exhibit 16.4
Progressive, Proportional, and Regressive Taxes

As shown in Exhibit 16.4(a), *for a progressive tax, average tax rates rise as income rises.*

Proportional and regressive taxes. Unlike a progressive tax, the average tax rate is constant for a **proportional tax** and decreases as income rises for a **regressive tax**. That is, individuals pay constant percentages of their incomes when a tax is proportional. They pay declining percentages of their incomes when a tax is regressive.

Exhibit 16.4(b) shows a proportional tax; each dollar of income is taxed at the rate of 20 percent. Lindsay, with an income of $10,000 pays $2000 in taxes; Jenny, $5000 in taxes on her income of $25,000; Chris, $10,000 in taxes on his income of $50,000. *For a proportional tax, the average tax rate is constant.*

Exhibit 16.4(c) illustrates the effect of a regressive tax. Lindsay pays $4000 of her $10,000 income in taxes, for a 40 percent average tax rate. Jenny pays $7000—$4000 on the first $10,000 and $3000 on the next $15,000—for an average rate of 28 percent. Chris, with the highest income, pays only 19 percent of his income in taxes. *For a regressive tax, the average tax rate declines with income.* Note that a regressive tax means that those with lower incomes pay larger *percentages* of their incomes in taxes but not necessarily larger *absolute* amounts.

Many people object to regressive taxes from the standpoint of vertical equity. However, there is no consensus on whether progressive or proportional taxes are

Proportional tax. A tax for which the average tax rate is constant for all income levels.

Regressive tax. A tax for which the average tax rate decreases as income increases.

more equitable. In fact, all three types of taxes could be considered to be equitable under the ability-to-pay principle. All three parts of Exhibit 16.4 show that those with greater incomes (and thus greater ability to pay) will pay more in absolute terms and thus carry a larger share of the total tax burden.

U.S. Tax Systems

Governments in the United States use a wide variety of taxes. Taxes are imposed on spending (sales taxes), earnings (income taxes and payroll taxes), and wealth (property and estate taxes). State governments also receive federal grants for highway, welfare, public education, and urban development programs; and fees such as highway tolls and college tuition payments. And local governments receive fees for water, sewers, garbage collection, parking, and licenses. Exhibit 16.5 shows various taxes and other sources of revenue for local, state, and federal levels of government.

Economists agree that ultimately all taxes are paid by individuals. This statement does not contradict what we said previously about businesses and consumers splitting the cost of an excise tax. They do. But businesses are, in the end, individuals—either individual proprietors or individuals who hold shares in corporations. Thus we are interested in how various types of taxes affect equity as well as efficiency.

Personal income taxes. The most important federal tax—and a large source of revenue for state governments—is the personal income tax. In concept, the personal income tax is simple and is based on the ability-to-pay principle: As your income goes up, so does your tax liability. But the actual tax system is anything but simple.

There are important differences between *actual* income and *taxable* income. Certain types of expenditures—interest paid on home mortgages, for example—are deductible from actual (gross) income in arriving at taxable income. Personal deductions also result in lower taxable income. In 1989 a family will be able to exempt the first $5000 of income plus $2000 for every person claimed as a dependent. In other words, in 1989 a family of four persons will pay no taxes on the first $13,000 of income received. And some types of income are excluded altogether—for example, interest earned on state and local government securities and income from government welfare payments. The amount of income tax owed is based on *taxable* income, that is, income after all exclusions and deductions.

The complexity of the tax code makes assessing either the equity or efficiency of the personal income tax difficult. However, the 1986 tax code reforms seem to have made some improvements in both. By eliminating income taxes for most of the working poor and by closing some questionable "loopholes," these reforms increased the proportion of taxes paid by those with high incomes. By lowering the highest marginal tax rate from 50 to 28 percent, Congress may have increased incentives to work and decreased incentives to cheat on taxes. Efficiency may also benefit from the removal of distortions in the old tax system that made unrentable office buildings, for example, a "tax shelter." Not everyone agrees with all the changes in the tax code, however. Critics argue that gains made in improving the personal income tax code are outweighed by losses caused by increasing corporate taxes.

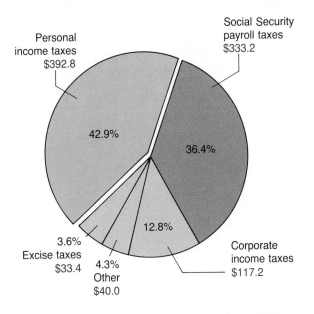

Personal income taxes $392.8 — 42.9%

Social Security payroll taxes $333.2 — 36.4%

Corporate income taxes $117.2 — 12.8%

Other $40.0 — 4.3%

Excise taxes $33.4 — 3.6%

(a) Distribution of federal tax receipts, fiscal year 1988
(in billions of dollars)

Total: $916.6

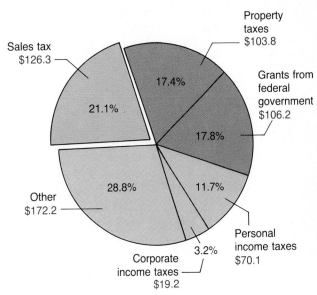

Property taxes $103.8 — 17.4%

Grants from federal government $106.2 — 17.8%

Personal income taxes $70.1 — 11.7%

Corporate income taxes $19.2 — 3.2%

Other $172.2 — 28.8%

Sales tax $126.3 — 21.1%

(b) Distribution of state and local receipts, fiscal year 1984–85
(in billions of dollars)

Total: $597.8

Source: Economic Report of the President, 1987. Part (a) is from Table B-74; part (b) is from Table B-80.

Exhibit 16.5
Sources of Government Revenues
Part (a) indicates that the personal income tax is the most important federal tax, followed closely by the Social Security payroll tax. Part (b) indicates that sales taxes, property taxes, and grants from the federal government are the largest sources of state and local receipts. The category "Other" represents various fees (such as license and auto registration fees and tuition at state universities), lotteries, and "profits" from government enterprises.

Social Security payroll tax. The second most important federal tax is the payroll tax used to finance Social Security. Although the payroll tax rate is constant, it is regressive—not proportional—for several reasons. First, the tax is collected only on income from wages and salaries up to a maximum limit ($42,500 in 1986). Individuals who earn wages or salaries higher than the taxable limit thus pay constant amounts, or declining percentages of their incomes. Moreover, the tax is collected only on wages and salaries. Individuals with relatively high incomes typically receive large portions of their income from sources other than wages and salaries, such as interest and dividends.

The regressive nature of the payroll tax has led some people to question its effect on equity. Payroll taxes obviously violate the principle of horizontal equity because individuals with the same income are not treated the same. If you earn $20,000 in wages, you pay taxes on all income earned. Your neighbor, who receives $20,000 in interest income, will pay no payroll tax.

It is somewhat ironic that charges of inequity should be made against the payroll tax, since it was created to fund Social Security—a program intended to improve equity. Social Security was designed to protect the standard of living of the aged and disabled—and their families—and to redistribute income from higher to lower income individuals and from younger to older generations.

Payroll taxes also have been criticized as harming efficiency. Taxing income from working may lower labor supply to some extent. The prospect of a future government pension may reduce current saving and cause people to retire sooner than they otherwise would.

Are these adverse effects significant? Or are they outweighed by the program's benefits? We have no way of objectively answering such questions, which have produced rational disagreement since the beginning of the Social Security program.

Corporate income taxes. The federal government collected $117 billion in corporate income taxes in 1988, which represents some 12 percent of federal government revenues. Like personal income taxes, corporate income taxes are progressive. The amount each corporation pays depends on its taxable—not actual—profits.

You may be surprised to learn that economists generally agree that corporations do not actually pay taxes. Economists assert that people, not corporations, pay taxes. Although corporations send tax payments to the Internal Revenue Service, the burden of those taxes is borne by their shareholders, customers, and workers. As a result, corporate taxes cause firms to make different (and possibly less efficient) choices than they might otherwise. For example, to some extent the tax on corporate profits is a tax on capital invested. As such, it may cause less than is socially optimal to be invested. And the tax laws treat some types of investment more favorably than others, causing further distortions.

Because of these problems, some economists argue that corporate income taxes should be abolished. Instead, they advocate taxing individual shareholders on their shares of the corporation's earnings, just as proprietors and partnerships are taxed on the earnings of their businesses. Such a change, however, would not automatically eliminate all the complexities and distortions involved in corporate taxation; many laws defining corporate income would probably remain. And economists generally agree that such changes would lower revenues and probably force government to raise other taxes.

Sales and property taxes. The principal forms of taxation used by state and local governments are sales taxes and property taxes. Most studies show sales taxes to be basically regressive. But sales taxes are normally constant-rate taxes (typically, a stated percentage of the purchase price). So how can they be regressive? Statistically, the poor spend a larger portion of their income than do the rich on goods subject to sales taxes. Some states exempt food and medicine, which tend to be a high proportion of a low-income family's budget. This policy reduces, but does not eliminate, the regressive nature of the sales tax, according to most economists. But some economists challenge this conclusion. They argue that transfer payments usually rise to cover higher sales taxes. If so, the real burden of sales taxes falls on the nonpoor.

Property taxes are used mostly by local governments and account for 75 percent of their revenues. Some economists consider property taxes to be a progressive tax on wealth since families with higher incomes usually own more property. Others believe that much of the tax is shifted to renters and view property taxes as either proportional or somewhat regressive.

Progressivity of the U.S. tax systems.   Overall, the tax systems used in the United States are roughly proportional to slightly progressive. In other words, the tax systems do little to redistribute income. Moreover, the current systems overall are less progressive than they were in the 1960s. The decline in progressivity resulted from several changes. Payroll taxes (which are regressive) have become relatively more important. Corporate taxes (which are progressive) have become relatively less important. The federal income tax has become less progressive, largely as a result of decreases in the marginal rates on the highest income groups.[*]

Goals of U.S. Tax Systems

You may think that the goals of taxation are obvious. After all, we have said that taxes are government's main source of revenue. But taxes also play other roles in economic policy. These roles suggest that different types of taxes are appropriate for different purposes.

When taxes are used simply to finance government expenditures, economists suggest that the best tax is one that causes no changes in economic incentives and that is perceived as fair by society. For the sake of efficiency, such taxes should be simple to calculate and administer. (Indeed, many tax reform proposals have been touted as "simplifying" the tax laws.)

Taxes can also be used to discourage certain activities and encourage others. For example, import tariffs are meant to discourage purchases of foreign goods. Taxes on pollution are intended to reduce pollution. Tax credits for insulation are meant to encourage energy-saving investments. In proposing them, however, politicians must keep in mind the possible effects of such taxes on efficiency. If markets are not functioning smoothly, such taxes may improve efficiency. But if markets are functioning smoothly, taxes will probably reduce efficiency.

Taxation can also be used to redistribute income, as with the payroll tax. Such efforts may involve trading off some efficiency for improved equity, however.

There is certainly no consensus among economists on the type of tax that would raise revenues at the lowest possible sacrifice in terms of economic goals. However, most economists recommend one of two forms of taxes: either a tax on income or a tax on consumption, using broad definitions of taxable income and consumption. For example, economists oppose tax-sheltered investments because they distort economic decision making.

---

[*] Joseph A. Pechman *(Who Paid the Taxes, 1966–1985,* Washington, D.C.: The Brookings Institution, 1985) concluded that the U.S. tax systems are almost proportional. Although his finding applies to the pre–1986 federal income tax system, the 1986 changes probably make little difference in the overall conclusion. Pechman's conclusion has been challenged, however. See, for example, Edgar K. Browning and William R. Johnson, *The Distribution of the Tax Burden*, Washington, D.C.: American Enterprise Institute for Public Policy Research, 1979. Browning and Johnson found the overall tax burden in 1976 to be quite progressive, based in part on their belief that transfer payments rise when sales taxes are increased.

Many economists also suggest that a tax system is generally not the best way to achieve certain other goals. For example, economists suggest that direct cash payments are a better way to redistribute income than are complicated provisions in the tax code. They also suggest the use of direct subsidies rather than indirect tax provisions to encourage certain activities.

Tax policy issues are numerous and complex. They include determining what the basic goals should be, how to define income and consumption, and what types of taxes to use. Economic principles can help decision makers to keep the issues in focus and to relate the effects of various policies to the economic goals of efficiency and equity.

CONCLUSION

In this chapter we examined public finance and how government affects the economy through its taxing and spending activities. We also discussed why government activity in the microeconomy may be desirable. In Chapter 17 we consider government regulations aimed at correcting market imperfections caused by market power, external costs, and imperfect information. In Chapter 18 we turn our attention to income distribution and equity, including a discussion of government programs affecting the distribution of income and economic opportunities. In Chapter 19 we complete the discussion of government's role in the microeconomy with an analysis of specific policies and policy issues.

As we continue our discussion of government, keep in mind the principles we use to discuss and evaluate government's role. We always seek to identify the extra benefits and extra costs of government policy and to ask whether the extra benefits outweigh the extra costs. Government's role in the economy is controversial, largely because measuring and interpreting benefits and costs involves value judgments. The economic way of thinking provides an important perspective on public policy and the economy.

SUMMARY

1. In this chapter we considered why and how government in the United States is involved in the microeconomy and looked at the principles of public finance.

2. The circular-flow model shows that government buys resources from households and goods and services from businesses. Government imposes taxes on both households and businesses and transfers income to both.

3. The three major microeconomic functions of government are (a) facilitating market exchange; (b) correcting for market failures; and (c) redistributing income and economic opportunity.

4. Following the principles of rational choice, government actions are justifiable only if marginal social benefits exceed marginal social costs (both direct and indirect). The potential for government failure must also be as-

sessed. Government policies often impose costs on one group but yield benefits to another, which raises questions of equity, as well as of efficiency.

5. When external benefits exist, the market demand curve does not reflect all the benefits society receives from a good. Thus marginal social benefit exceeds demand at each quantity. As a result the equilibrium quantity (where $Q_d = Q_s$) is less than the allocatively efficient quantity (where MSB = MSC). Government subsidies to producers or consumers may help the economy to produce more efficiently.

6. Because public goods are indivisible and cannot be withheld from individuals who do not pay, market demand does not accurately reflect social benefits. Private markets underproduce public goods and services from the perspective of allocative efficiency. Government

production or payment for public goods can improve efficiency.

7. All forms of government financing impose costs on the private sector. Directly transferring resources to the public sector reduces the amount available to the private sector. Increasing the money supply may cause inflation. Borrowing may increase interest rates and decrease private investment. Taxes reduce private-sector income.

8. Excise taxes reduce quantity exchanged, driving up prices paid by consumers and received by suppliers. Reducing quantity below market equilibrium will create allocative inefficiency when markets are otherwise functioning smoothly. If there are external costs, however, a tax may actually improve efficiency. A tax will be shared by both suppliers and consumers, with who pays the most depending on price elasticity.

9. Income taxes may also affect efficiency. High marginal tax rates may reduce work effort and thus overall production. Taxes may also reduce private investment. Tax provisions favoring a specific type of investment may also create inefficiency.

10. Economists define a "good tax" as one that raises revenue with the lowest possible cost, without changing economic incentives, and without harming equity.

11. The equity of taxes is also a concern. According to the benefits-received principle, it is fair to tax individuals according to the benefits they receive. According to the ability-to-pay principle, it is fair to assess higher taxes on individuals who have a greater ability to pay (vertical equity) and to impose equal taxes on those who have equal ability to pay (horizontal equity).

12. Taxes can be classified as progressive (average tax paid increases with income), proportional (average tax paid is a constant percentage of income), or regressive (average tax rate declines as income rises).

13. The federal government obtains 40 percent of its tax revenues from the personal income tax. The second largest tax is the payroll tax, which is used to finance the Social Security system. The corporate income tax accounts for only 12 percent of federal revenues. State governments get most of their tax revenues from sales taxes and personal income taxes; local governments rely heavily on property taxes and service fees.

14. Taxes imposed on businesses ultimately affect their customers (higher prices), workers (less employment and lower wages), or shareholders (smaller profits). Personal income taxes are clearly paid by individuals. More difficult to assess is the burden of other taxes. Studies suggest that, overall, the tax systems in the United States are proportional or slightly progressive.

KEY TERMS

Public finance, 386
Market failure, 388
Benefits-received principle, 399
Ability-to-pay principle, 399
Horizontal equity, 399
Vertical equity, 400
Marginal tax rate, 400
Average tax rate, 400
Progressive tax, 400
Proportional tax, 401
Regressive tax, 401

QUESTIONS FOR REVIEW AND DISCUSSION

1. State whether each of the following statements is true, false, or uncertain. Explain why.
   a) Whenever the market fails, government action will improve the economy's performance.
   b) An unregulated market will tend to overproduce a product that has external benefits.
   c) Municipal libraries are public goods because they are produced by local governments.
   d) Any increase in taxes is a net loss to society because individuals will be able to buy fewer goods to satisfy their wants.

2. State and local governments spend billions of dollars on public education. Evaluate each of the following arguments regarding these expenditures.
   a) Education provides external benefits to society because better educated individuals make better workers.
   b) Free public education is justified because poor families are unable to buy enough education.
   c) Government need not provide free public schools. Low income can be supplemented with transfers; financial market imperfections can be corrected with government loans at market rates.

3. Consider the statement, "Only people pay taxes," and answer (a)–(c).
   a) List some taxes that you and your family pay personally and directly.
   b) If the city council imposes a sales tax of 2 percent to be collected from local merchants, is it correct to say that the merchants pay the tax? What, in fact, determines how much of the tax will be paid by the merchants and how much by their customers?
   c) How will an increase in corporate tax rates affect business activity? Shareholders? Customers? Workers?

4. The following data show how income and taxes paid are related in three different countries.

Annual income	Annual taxes paid by citizens of		
	Jungolia	Mountainia	Desertonia
$ 5,000	$1500	$1000	$2000
10,000	3000	2500	3500
15,000	4500	4500	4500
20,000	6000	7000	5000

a) Identify whether the tax system in each country is progressive, regressive, or proportional.
b) Suppose citizens in a fourth country—Forestia—pay a constant 25 percent of their taxable income to the government. However, the government allows each family to exempt the first $3000 of income from taxes. Using the four income categories shown in the table, calculate taxable income (subtract $3000 from annual income), taxes paid (25 percent of taxable income), and average tax rate (taxes paid divided by annual income). What type of tax system exists in Forestia?

5. Use the following data on demand and supply of toothbrushes to answer the questions in (a)–(g).

Price per toothbrush	Quantity of toothbrushes	
	Demanded	Supplied
$1.50	1400	800
1.75	1300	1000
2.00	1200	1200
2.25	1100	1400
2.50	1000	1600
2.75	900	1800
3.00	800	2000

a) What are the equilibrium price and quantity of toothbrushes in this market?
b) If the government imposes an excise tax of $0.75 per toothbrush, what is the equilibrium quantity? (*Hint:* Add another column showing quantity supplied assuming price includes the tax. For example, after the tax is imposed, 800 toothbrushes will be supplied for $2.25; $1.50 plus the $0.75 tax.)
c) With the tax, what price will consumers pay? What price will producers receive?

d) How much tax will the government collect? How much of the tax do suppliers pay? Consumers?
e) Assuming that the market was functioning smoothly before, explain why the tax causes allocative inefficiency.
f) Explain why it makes no difference to your preceding answers whether the tax is imposed on suppliers or consumers.
g) The following graph shows pretax demand for and supply of toothbrushes. Draw a new supply curve to show the effect of the tax ($0.75 above the original supply curve at each quantity). Indicate on the graph the area representing the total tax paid; the division of the tax between suppliers and consumers; and the area representing the amount of allocative inefficiency.

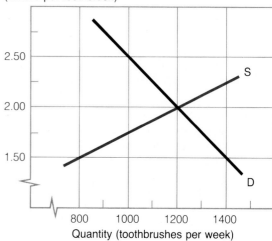

Price (dollars per toothbrush)

Quantity (toothbrushes per week)

6. Should the revenues used to support the activities in (a)–(c) be collected on the basis of benefits-received or ability-to-pay? Explain why. Where you choose the benefits-received principle, explain how the necessary revenues would be raised.
a) Maintenance of a municipal parking lot.
b) Installing street lights in the downtown business district.
c) A food-stamp program for the poor.

7. The personal income tax code contains provisions for allowing individuals to reduce their tax payments if they have certain types of income or make certain types of expenditures. For each of the following examples, explain how a proponent could argue that a public

purpose is served by this provision. Explain how a critic could argue that the public purpose could be better served if the provision were eliminated.

a) No taxes are paid on interest income from state and local government securities.

b) Individuals may deduct large expenditures for medical care (above a certain percentage of their income).

c) Individuals may deduct interest paid on home mortgages.

8. The following data show demand for and supply of deodorant socks.

Price per pair of socks	Quantity of socks	
	Demanded	Supplied
$9.00	1200	2000
8.75	1300	1900
8.50	1400	1800
8.25	1500	1700
8.00	1600	1600
7.75	1700	1500
7.50	1800	1400

a) What are the equilibrium price and quantity of deodorant socks in this market?

b) Suppose that the socks provide external benefits of $0.50 per pair. What quantity would be allocatively efficient (where MSB = MSC)? (*Hint:* Add an MSB column to the table showing quantities associated with price, assuming price reflects MSB. Thus a quantity of 1400 is associated with $9.00; $8.50 of internal benefits and $0.50 of external benefits.)

c) Suppose that the government pays consumers a subsidy of $0.50 per pair. How will this action cause the market to reach the allocatively efficient quantity?

d) Given the subsidy, indicate the total expenditures of consumers (not including the subsidy), the total amount received by producers, and the total subsidy paid by the government. Would your answers to (c) and (d) be different if the subsidy were paid to suppliers instead?

e) The following graph reflects the data. Draw a curve representing marginal social benefits (MSB). (At each quantity MSB is $0.50 more than the price of quantity demanded.) Indicate on the graph the market equilibrium, the allocatively efficient quantity, and the area representing the amount of inefficiency associated with the unregulated market solution.

f) Use the graph to indicate how a subsidy of $0.50 per unit will cause the market to achieve allocative efficiency. (Explain why it does not matter whether the subsidy is paid to consumers or producers.)

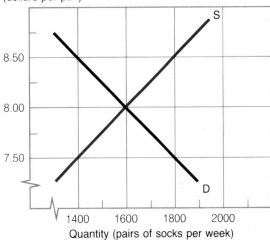

Price (dollars per pair)

Quantity (pairs of socks per week)

Use the information in the appendix to Chapters 3, 10, and 11 to help you answer the following questions.

9. The following equations apply to a certain product.

$$\text{Demand:} \quad P = 155 - 0.005Q$$

$$\text{Supply:} \quad P = 65 + 0.0025Q$$

a) What are the equilibrium price and quantity?

b) Suppose that this product has an external benefit of $15 per unit. What is the marginal social benefit relationship? What quantity is allocatively efficient?

c) What is the supply relationship if a subsidy of $15 is given to suppliers? With this subsidy, show that equilibrium will be allocatively efficient.

d) What is the demand relationship if a subsidy of $15 were given to consumers instead of producers? With this subsidy, show that equilibrium will be allocatively efficient.

10. The following equations apply to a particular product.

$$\text{Demand:} \quad P = 50 - 0.002Q$$

$$\text{Supply:} \quad P = 20 + 0.004Q$$

a) What are the equilibrium price and quantity?

b) Suppose that the government imposed an excise tax of $6 per unit on suppliers. What is the effect on supply? On the equilibrium quantity?

c) Suppose instead that the government imposed the tax on consumers. What is the effect on demand? On the equilibrium quantity?

d) How much total tax will be collected and how much of the tax will be paid by consumers and suppliers, respectively?

Government Regulation and Economic Efficiency

QUESTIONS TO CONSIDER

☐ What types of business activity are restricted by anti-trust policy and why?

☐ When is rate regulation used instead of antitrust policy?

☐ What problems and issues confront those charged with enforcing antitrust policy and setting rates?

☐ Why does government attempt social regulation?

☐ Why do government efforts to regulate business activities sometimes fail?

Chapter 16 covered some of the reasons for government intervention in the microeconomy: market power, external benefits and costs, public goods, and imperfect information. In this chapter you will see how some of these market failures affect efficiency and whether various government policies may be used to achieve better results.

As with every economic choice, policy makers should use the principles of rational choice when considering actions to correct for market failures. That is, they should compare marginal social benefits and marginal social costs, weighing the potential benefits of government regulation against the costs, both direct and indirect. As you will see, it is relatively easy to show that market failures cause inefficiency. It is more difficult, but absolutely necessary, to find practical ways to improve efficiency.

The approach used depends first on the nature of the problem. The government has several options with regard to market power. *Antitrust policy* seeks to prevent the acquisition of market power and to eliminate it when it does occur. In contrast, *rate regulation* and *public enterprise* allow monopolies to exist under government control. When externalities or imperfect information create inefficiency, government policy takes the form of social regulation. Finally, in some cases, the best solution to both market power and external costs may be to *do nothing*. This option is economically preferable when the costs of government action exceed the benefits of overcoming market failures.

In the rest of this chapter, we consider each potential solution, always focusing on how well it has—or has not—addressed market failures. Although economists generally agree that markets sometimes fail, government intervention is controversial. In studying the issues, you will see what the controversy is all about.

ANTITRUST POLICY: LIMITING MARKET POWER

As we showed in Chapter 11, economists agree that the exercise of market power can reduce allocative and technical efficiency. However, economists also recognize that society's utimate goal may not be a perfectly competitive market structure.

Antitrust policy. Government actions that attempt to control market power and monopolistic behavior and to foster competitive behavior.

The question that must be answered in evaluating antitrust policy is whether such laws and regulations meet the test of rational choice theory. That is, do the benefits of such a policy outweigh its disadvantages. Pursuing an **antitrust policy** has its costs. In fact, the legal process is very expensive, both to the government and to firms who must defend themselves.

However, society benefits less and less when the number of firms increases beyond a certain point. Moreover, when economies of scale are important, the entry of many small firms may harm technical efficiency. Finally, if firms are penalized by antitrust policy for normal and efficient business practices, the effect may be less, not greater efficiency. Rational choice theory thus argues for creating only a "sufficient" amount of competition. In practical terms, competition is sufficient whenever the extra costs of an antitrust action outweigh the extra benefits of increased competition.

In evaluating antitrust policy, we must keep in mind that its historical basis goes beyond economics. In 1958, Supreme Court Justice Hugo Black wrote that antitrust policy is

> Aimed at preserving free and unfettered competition as the rule of trade. It rests on the premise that the unrestrained interaction of competitive forces will yield the best allocation of our economic resources, the lowest prices, the highest quality and the greatest material progress, while at the same time providing an environment conducive to the preservation of our democratic political and social institutions.[*]

Most economists would agree with Justice Black that competitive forces are important to achieving efficiency. But what exactly constitutes "free and unfettered competition"? And how can we identify situations in which market power is sufficiently important to warrant government regulation?

Antitrust Laws

Exhibit 17.1 summarizes the major U.S. antitrust laws. The initial antitrust legislation in the United States came in response to the first large-scale enterprises. In the late 1800s, John D. Rockefeller founded the Standard Oil Company, J. P. Morgan's banking activities made and broke fortunes, and Jay Gould controlled much of the railroad industry. Entrepreneur William Vanderbilt fueled the controversy when he arrogantly stated: "The public be damned. I am working for my stockholders."[†] What some saw as blatant abuses of economic power by Vanderbilt and other "robber barons" led to a series of federal laws designed to curb their power.

Sherman Antitrust Act. The first antitrust law—the Sherman Antitrust Act of 1890—has two important parts. The first part outlaws "every contract, combination . . . , or conspiracy, in restraint of trade." This section bans anticompetitive practices. It forbids agreements among firms to fix prices, set production quotas, divide markets, or erect barriers to entry. The second part of the act makes it illegal to "monopolize or attempt to monopolize." This section attempts to control

---

[*] *Northern Pacific Railway Company* v. *United States*, 365 US 1,4 (1958).
[†] Matthew Josephson, *The Robber Barons*. New York: Harcourt, Brace and World, 1962, p. 187.

Title	Date	Major purpose
Sherman Antitrust Act	1890	Section 1: "Every contract, combination, . . . or conspiracy in restraint of trade . . . is hereby declared illegal. . . ."
		Section 2: "Every person who shall monopolize, or attempt to monopolize . . . shall be guilty of a felony. . . ."
Clayton Antitrust Act	1914	Declares illegal various practices, "where the effect . . . may be to substantially lessen competition or tend to create a monopoly. . . ."
Federal Trade Commission Act	1914	Establishes the Federal Trade Commission to prevent ". . . unfair methods of competition . . . and unfair or deceptive acts or practices. . . ."

Exhibit 17.1
Major Antitrust Laws

the growth of market power and to prevent situations in which one firm can control the market for a particular product.

Clayton Act. Perceived flaws in the Sherman Act led Congress to pass the Clayton Act of 1914. Unlike the Sherman Act, the Clayton Act specified the practices that constitute anticompetitive behavior. Among them is price discrimination based on factors other than costs. (This part of the act was strengthened in 1936 with passage of the Robinson–Patman Act.) Also banned were exclusive dealing contracts that bar a buyer from purchasing from competitors; tying contracts, by which buyers are forced to purchase other items in order to obtain the products they want; and interlocking directorates (where the directors of a firm also sit on the boards of competing firms).

Although the Sherman Act had allowed the government to prosecute an existing monopoly, it could not prevent firms from acquiring market power. Section 7 of the Clayton Act made it illegal for firms to obtain monopoly power by acquiring the stock of competing companies. (This provision was strengthened by the Celler–Kefauver Act of 1950, which also made it illegal to obtain the assets of a competing company.) Importantly, the Clayton Act made these practices illegal only when their "effect is to substantially lessen competition or tend to create a monopoly."

Federal Trade Commission Act. That same year, 1914, Congress enacted legislation creating the Federal Trade Commission (FTC) and authorized it to prevent firms from engaging in "unfair methods of competition." Subsequent amendments gave the FTC the power to regulate deceptive advertising, an issue we discussed in Chapter 12.

Antitrust policy at any particular time is the product of three elements. The first element is the body of law that defines generally what constitutes unlawful behavior and illegal situations. The second element is the interpretation of the laws by the courts. The third element is the vigor with which the Antitrust Division of the Justice Department and the FTC enforce the laws and the administrative regulations based on those laws. These two agencies largely determine which cases are brought to the courts and thus significantly influence interpretation of the laws. The agencies deal with three main branches of antitrust policy: (1) *monopolization* policies seek to reduce the market power acquired by large, dominant firms; (2) *collusion* policies seek to eliminate illegal cooperation among potential competitors; and (3) *merger* policies seek to limit the growth of market power.

Monopolization

Although the Sherman Act prohibits *monopolization,* it does not define the term. As you learned in Chapter 11, pure monopoly is rare and usually results from government franchises, but the monopoly model can be applied to markets in which one firm holds a dominant position. In order to apply the law against monopolization, federal prosecutors and the courts have to answer two basic questions. First, is the law violated every time one firm acquires a dominant market position? And second, how do normal (and acceptable) business practices differ from illegal acts that are designed to monopolize?

Standard Oil and the rule of reason. The U.S. Supreme Court dealt with the issue of market structure versus market conduct in 1911. The case involved Standard Oil of New Jersey, a company that at that time controlled some 90 percent of the U.S. petroleum market. The government claimed that Standard Oil had obtained its market power by highly questionable acts. Prosecutors argued that Standard Oil then used its power unscrupulously to preserve its market position. The list of grievances against Standard Oil included creating local price wars to suppress competition and forcing railroads to discriminate against Standard's rivals. Because of its tremendous power, Standard Oil received rebates from railroads, not only on the oil it shipped, but also on oil shipped by its competitors.

In deciding the case, the Court developed the so-called **rule of reason**. That is, the possession of market power in itself is not objectionable, but the undue exercise of that power against rival firms is. In other words, the Court drew a distinction between a "good" monopoly and a "bad" monopoly. The ruling implied that if Standard Oil had obtained its dominant position by normal business practices, it would have been viewed as operating within the law. Because the Court found that it had abused its power, however, Standard Oil was broken up into 33 separate companies. By forcing a more competitive market structure, the Court hoped to force more competitive market behavior.

Should Standard Oil have been penalized? Certainly Standard Oil was an aggressive competitor. But some of its advantage was acquired because it pioneered some cost-efficient ways of refining and successfully intergrated its operations. Moreover, Standard Oil grew largely by buying out potential competitors. Although it clearly acquired a dominant market position, how much of its ultimate power was derived from illegal actions is unclear.

Rule of reason. A legal standard under which the prosecutor must prove not only that an offense has occurred but also that the social welfare will be enhanced by prohibiting, modifying, or punishing the act.

U.S. Steel: The rule of reason again. In a 1920 case involving the United States Steel Corporation, the Supreme Court affirmed the rule-of-reason approach. At that time the company accounted for some 65 percent of the iron and steel output in the United States. The government argued that the size of the company gave it tremendous economic power. Hence breaking up the firm was necessary to yield a market structure compatible with sufficient competition.

The Supreme Court ruled against the government, however, noting that although the company had some market power, it had not used that power to acquire its competitors or to block entry into the industry. In fact, U.S. Steel was acquitted because it helped keep steel prices relatively high, a practice that protected some less efficient firms in the industry. In this and subsequent decisions, the Court established that it was concerned with injuries caused to competitors, not injury to competition. A dominant firm could be either acceptable or unacceptable, depending on its behavior.

ALCOA: A structural test for monopolizing. In 1945 the federal courts dealt with the issue of structure versus conduct once again. ALCOA was the sole domestic producer of virgin aluminum ingots. The government charged the company with monopolizing the market. The company argued that its position was gained through normal business practices and that it had not intended to become a monopolist.

One issue before the U.S. Court of Appeals was determination of the relevant market. The company argued that the market included steel and copper as substitutes, and thus ALCOA had only 33 percent of the market. The Court, however, viewed the market much more narrowly, even ignoring the secondary market for aluminum ingots made from recycled aluminum. By this definition, ALCOA had 90 percent of the market (the other 10 percent was imported aluminum).

The second issue before the Court was the way in which ALCOA had acquired and maintained its market position. Previous decisions had required proof that the firm had acted specifically to forestall competition. The company argued that it had engaged only in normal business activities. In a departure from the rule of reason, the Court ruled that ALCOA's 90 percent control of the market clearly established the firm as a monopolist. The Court declared that specific intent was not required: ALCOA was aware that its business practices effectively barred entry and maintained the firm's virtual monopoly. Subsequent court cases have generally not upheld this strict emphasis on structure, requiring some evidence of monopolizing conduct as well.

Although ALCOA was found guilty, its operations were not touched. The government did, however, provide ALCOA with some competition. Aluminum plants built by the government and operated by ALCOA during World War II were sold to Reynolds and Kaiser. Nevertheless, ALCOA continues to dominate the industry.

Back to the rule of reason. The emphasis in the ALCOA case was purely on structure. Some economists applaud this approach, arguing that market power is undesirable and should be eliminated. But others fear that a purely structural test may stifle competition, innovation, and the technical efficiency possible from economies of scale. They favor the rule-of-reason approach in monopolization cases and view penalizing firms just because they are successful as unfair or inefficient.

Price fixing. Formal agreement among firms in an oligopoly to maintain artificially high prices or to restrict market supply.

Tacit collusion. Informal agreement among firms in an oligopoly not to engage in price competition.

More recently the courts have returned to the rule of reason. In 1972, Eastman Kodak simultaneously introduced a new type of camera, the Instamatic II, along with an improved type of film. The new film was available only in cartridges; it fit Kodak's camera but not any other existing camera. This strategy succeeded in boosting Kodak's share of the camera market. However, another camera manufacturer, Berkey Photo, sued Kodak. Berkey argued that Kodak's dominant position in the film market gave it an unfair advantage in the camera market. Despite Kodak's dominant position, the court ruled in its favor, applying the rule of reason. It termed Kodak's dominance and success in the camera market the result of innovation and perfectly normal business practices.

Collusion

Even harder to define and prove than monopolization is collusion. As Adam Smith observed in 1776, "People of the same trade seldom meet together, even for merriment and diversion, but the conversation ends in a conspiracy against the public or in some contrivance to raise prices."[*] And as noted in Chapter 12, oligopolies benefit by cooperating rather than competing. If firms in an oligopolistic market agree to charge the same price—a practice called **price fixing**—they can increase industry profits. But such cooperative efforts, while they may be profitable to the firms involved, are a form of monopoly.

The Sherman Act makes "every contract, combination . . . , or conspiracy, in restraint of trade" illegal. Because such actions clearly cause inefficiency, the courts have adopted a particularly strict attitude toward restraint of trade. Violations include any action by firms to fix prices, set production quotas, divide markets, or similar types of cooperation. (See, for example, A Case in Point: The Electrical Machinery Conspiracy Case.) However, U.S. law applies only to U.S. companies. Cartels such as OPEC are free to seek price fixing agreements internationally.

In the 1970s, antitrust laws were used to eliminate self-imposed rules that limited price competition among professionals in many fields. Courts struck down prohibitions against advertising by lawyers, as well as published schedules of "suggested minimum fees" for legal tasks. Justice Department efforts eliminated rules against competitive bidding by associations representing architects, accountants, and engineers. In each case, prices appear to have fallen without reducing the quality of service provided.

Although economists generally agree that price fixing is undesirable, they do not agree about whether government policy to control it is necessary. Some point to the basic instability of cartels and other cooperative agreements as evidence that collusion is short-lived and that government actions are unnecessary. Others argue that even if such agreements eventually fail, the benefits of legal constraints are significant.

Tacit collusion. An overt conspiracy to fix prices definitely violates antitrust laws and causes allocative inefficiency. But what about **tacit collusion**, an informal understanding not to engage in price competition? We know that firms in an oligopoly most often find it desirable to avoid price competition. Thus even without a formal agreement, prices in such an industry tend to be similar and to change together in response to market conditions.

---

[*] Adam Smith, *The Wealth of Nations*, Book I, Chapter 10. New York: The Modern Library, 1937, p. 128.

A Case in Point
Electrical Machinery Conspiracy Case

In a 1961 case, the Supreme Court dealt harshly with several manufacturers who conspired to fix prices and share the market for electrical machinery. The case is well-known, not for the legal principles it established—those were long-standing—but for the intricacy and cleverness of the conspiracy.

The price-fixing scheme covered both open and sealed bids. In the case of open bids, the conspirators agreed in advance which company would be the low bidder and what the price would be. Because they wished to share the market, each was allowed a turn at being the low bidder. The conspirators met regularly at trade shows and developed elaborate schemes to contact each other in private. Codes were established and used to identify companies, rather than their names.

Numerous written rules for the conspiracy were found by investigators. The conspirators were not to identify themselves with their companies when registering in hotels. They were to check the wastebaskets before leaving their hotel rooms. And they were to avoid sitting at the same table or conversing with fellow conspirators in the hotel dining room.

Where sealed bids were required, the conspirators showed real ingenuity. In these cases, the low bidder, the low bid, and the bids for the other conspirators were determined by an elaborate chart. To avoid detection and to preserve market shares, the low bidder was changed every two weeks in a regular pattern. In this way, each conspirator knew in advance exactly what to bid and what bids would be submitted by others.

Eventually, several of the coconspirators turned state's evidence, and the secretary of the conspiracy turned over the detailed notes he had maintained to train his future replacement. Thus the government easily proved that the firms had engaged in price fixing. The judge imposed fines totaling $2 million on the companies and individuals involved—and jail sentences on some of the principals in the scheme. In addition, more than 1900 private suits were settled, resulting in additional costs of $400 million to the conspirator firms.

Should the government attempt to prosecute cases of tacit rather than formal agreement on prices? Over the years, the courts have generally ruled that tacit collusion does not violate antitrust laws. Unlike overt collusion, tacit agreements have not aroused universal opposition from economists, in part because such behavior is so similar to normal business practices. When a firm sees its major competitors raising their prices, it can also raise its price without losing a large number of its customers. Such price hikes may appear to be a conspiracy against consumers, but they are also the expected response in an oligopolistic industry when all firms are faced with cost increases.

Mergers: Size or Market Power?

Economists agree that overt collusion harms the economy, but many disagree about how much market power is generated when two or more firms combine, or merge. In the words of the Clayton Act, a **merger** is unlawful if "the effect of such acquisition may be substantially to lessen competition or to create a monopoly." The objective of the law is to prevent situations that would become illegal under other antitrust statutes.

The economic issue is the effect, if any, that a merger will have on market efficiency. Some advocates of strong antimerger policy base their case not only on economic criteria (the effects on competition) but also on political criteria (the effects on political power). This broader interpretation, however, has not been

Merger. The combining of two or more firms under the control of one firm.

Horizontal merger. A merger between firms that produce substitute products and that would otherwise be competitors.

Vertical merger. A merger between firms that would otherwise have a buyer–seller relationship.

Conglomerate merger. A merger between firms that otherwise have no economic relationship; a merger that is neither horizontal nor vertical.

uniformly accepted by the courts, which ultimately determine the legality of mergers.

Antitrust policies distinguish three basic types of mergers. A **horizontal merger** is a combination of firms in the same industry, such as the merger of Texaco and Getty Oil in 1984. A **vertical merger** is a combination of firms that would otherwise have a buyer–seller relationship. Because 80 percent of its chemicals are petroleum-based, du Pont's acquisition of Conoco in 1981 was a vertical merger. Finally, a **conglomerate merger** is a combination of firms that have no clear market relationship. The 1985 merger of Phillip Morris (a tobacco company) and General Foods Corporation was a conglomerate merger.

Horizontal mergers. Legally, the case for using antitrust policy to prevent a merger rests on whether the merger will substantially lessen competition. However, the lack of clear, objective criteria has contributed to the inconsistent treatment of horizontal mergers by the courts. By definition, any horizontal merger reduces the number of competitors, but not every one significantly reduces competition. For example, if one farmer buys out a neighbor and combines the two farms, there is little effect on competition.

Even when a merger occurs between two large firms, the effect may be greater, not less, efficiency. For example, the FTC decided not to challenge the merger between Republic Steel and Jones & Laughlin Steel in 1984. It decided that the combined firm would be better able to compete with other domestic and foreign firms.

Vertical mergers. Firms involved in vertical mergers are not competitors but have a buyer–seller relationship. In fact, if neither of the merging firms has market power, they could hardly gain market power by combining. Moreover, it appears that most vertical mergers occur because of expected cost savings. However, the courts have opposed vertical mergers if the merger threatens to reduce the amount of competition.

For example, in 1961 du Pont was forced to sell its interest in General Motors, a major buyer of du Pont's paints. The Court accepted the claim that du Pont's ownership of 23 percent of General Motors reduced competition in the paint industry. Not all economists agree with the Court's interpretation of the facts in that case or believe that vertical mergers have any significant effect on market power. In fact, the courts and the regulatory agencies have not shown much concern over vertical mergers.

Conglomerate mergers. Conglomerate mergers are even less likely to increase market power. By definition the firms involved are in totally unrelated markets. Opponents of conglomerate mergers argue that an increase in economic size can result in greater economic power and thus create potential market problems.

In addition to purely economic arguments, some people oppose conglomerate mergers on the grounds that concentrated economic power can lead to political power. A large conglomerate may be able to obtain political favors not available to several independent firms. The courts have not accepted the broader political argument. Instead, they have required proof that competition in some particular market would be significantly reduced. As a result, few conglomerate mergers have been challenged successfully.

Reagan administration's merger guidelines. The Reagan administration has been less willing than previous administrations to challenge mergers of all kinds. The administration argues that few mergers have any adverse effects on efficiency and that antitrust policies should not be used to achieve other goals. In 1982, the Justice Department adopted new guidelines on challenging mergers. These guidelines reflected less concern for market structure and more concern for market performance. They utilized the Herfindahl (see A Case in Point: Merger Guidelines). This index identifies industries dominated by a single large firm as a greater public concern than industries in which several firms share market power. In 1984, the guidelines were further revised to recognize that international competition weakens market power and that some mergers may increase efficiency.

Government Regulations that Reduce Competition

Although most public policies seek to increase competition, the government has also acted to reduce competition. In 1936, Congress passed the Robinson–Patman Act to protect small firms from "unfair competition" on the part of larger firms, especially retail chains. The act prohibits practices such as price discrimination and quantity discounts offered to larger buyers when the effect might be to "destroy competition or eliminate a competitor." Most economists argue that the law has been used most often in an anticompetitive way.

The Utah Pie case offers a good example of the law's effects. For many years Carnation Milk, Pet Milk, and Continental Baking had most of the frozen-pie market in Salt Lake City. Then in 1958, the Utah Pie Company opened for business. In a few years the firm had captured some two-thirds of the local frozen-pie market. Carnation, Pet, and Continental responded by lowering prices, and Utah Pie's market share dropped to 45 percent.

Utah Pie sued the three larger firms, charging that they had unfairly and illegally lowered prices. The Supreme Court ruled in favor of Utah Pie, citing evidence of price discrimination. Justice Stewart dissented, however, noting that the majority opinion meant that "Utah Pie's monopolistic position was protected by the federal antitrust laws from effective price competition."

In some cases, government has also created market power by establishing restrictions on entry and allowing firms to cooperate to raise prices above competitive levels. This was the case in the domestic airline industry until 1978. We discuss the general case of such government-sponsored cartels later in the chapter. We consider the airline industry in Chapter 19.

Current Antitrust Issues

Antitrust policy, like all other areas of government regulation, is debated continually. Let's consider four of the main issues currently facing antitrust regulators. What is the relevant market? Are the firm's actions illegal or just normal business practices? Can the government handle the big case? And do the benefits of regulation outweigh the costs?

A Case in Point
Merger Guidelines:
Measuring Market Concentration

In merger cases, antitrust regulators seek some objective measure of the change in market concentration associated with a particular merger. In 1968 the Justice Department introduced standards for challenging mergers based on industry concentration ratios, as well as market shares of the two firms involved. Generally, any merger that caused the four-firm concentration ratio—measured as the total market share accounted for by the four largest firms—to exceed 60 percent was closely examined for a potential challenge.

In 1982 the Justice Department adopted a new set of rules defining when it would challenge mergers. The new guidelines are based on the *Herfindahl index*, which is calculated by summing the squares of the market-share percentages of all firms in a given industry. For example, an industry with four firms, each with a 25 percent market share, would have a Herfindahl index (HI) of 2500, calculated as follows:

$$HI = MS_1^2 + MS_2^2 + MS_3^2 + MS_4^2$$
$$= 25^2 + 25^2 + 25^2 + 25^2 \quad or \quad 2500$$

The table illustrates the calculation of both the concentration ratio and the Herfindahl index. Note that the HI gives greater weight to very large firms. Thus although industry A and industry B both have four-firm concentration ratios of 80 percent, the HI for industry B is 3000 compared to 1800 for industry A, reflecting the existence of the very large firm in industry B.

Experts in industrial organization tend to agree that an industry of 10 equally sized firms would behave competitively. The Herfindahl index for such an industry would be 1000. Under the new guidelines, mergers are not likely to be challenged, unless the merger causes the HI to rise above this level.

Some critics of past merger policies point out that international competition is a significant factor in many industries but is not reflected in the four-firm concentration ratio. They also observe that the presence of a dominant firm is more of a problem than an industry with three or four equally large firms. The Herfindahl index recognizes the presence of international competition and, as the example indicates, gives greater weight to the presence of a dominant firm in an industry. As a result, some mergers that would have been challenged under old guidelines will not be challenged under the new guidelines.

Calculation of Herfindahl Index

| | Industry A | | | Industry B | |
Firm	Market share	Market share squared	Firm	Market share	Market share squared
1	20	400	1	50	2500
2	20	400	2	10	100
3	20	400	3	10	100
4	20	400	4	10	100
5	10	100	5	10	100
6	10	100	6	10	100
Total	100	1800	Total	100	3000

Concentration ratio = 80   Concentration ratio = 80
Herfindahl index = 1800   Herfindahl index = 3000

Note: The concentration ratio is the sum of the market shares of the four largest firms. The Herfindahl index is the sum of the market shares squared of all firms in the industry.

Can a relevant market be established? As you saw in the ALCOA case, prosecuting monopolization cases requires determining the relevant market. Antitrust laws presume that such markets, once determined, are fixed. However, some economists believe that the dynamic changes in the economy—especially technology—continually redefine market boundaries. They argue that the modern corporation is highly flexible and can respond quickly to technological changes. Thus barriers to entry are difficult to establish, and market boundaries are difficult to determine.

If we accept this argument, markets are much more competitive than a static analysis implies, especially when entry barriers are low enough to allow new entrants to earn short-run economic profits. If this view is accurate, government will play a smaller role in the future in ensuring competition through antitrust policy.

Can illegal and normal business practices be distinguished?

Related to the issue of relative markets is the need to distinguish between acceptable, normal business practices and unacceptable, illegal practices. Indirect evidence, such as parallel movements in prices, is difficult to interpret. Direct evidence of collusion is hard to obtain. In addition, law and economic theory conflict. From the economic perspective, all collusion causes economic inefficiency. However, the courts have been reluctant to find a firm guilty of doing what is simply in its own best interest. This problem is particularly difficult in the case of oligopoly pricing, although it also occurs in other antitrust situations. The legal system has yet to develop clear guidelines for businesses that wish to avoid illegal behavior but must necessarily match the competition.

Can the government handle the big case?

The difficulty in knowing what is and is not illegal is one factor that makes government prosecutions of antitrust cases difficult. In recent years, government antitrust authorities have failed in their attempts to prosecute several cases involving large corporations.

Critics of federal antitrust policy point to government's handling of an antitrust suit against International Business Machines (IBM). Despite what some observers saw as fairly strong evidence against IBM, the government finally abandoned the case in 1982, some 13 years after it began. Moreover, by the time the case was dropped, the original reasons for government's action no longer existed, and conditions in the industry had changed radically. As a result, some people now question whether the government is "outgunned" by teams of highly paid private lawyers. The rules governing the collection of evidence may have given IBM an almost unlimited ability to prolong and hence destroy the case.

Do potential benefits outweigh costs?

The costs of antitrust prosecutions are enormous, so we must ask whether the benefits obtained from a successful prosecution would outweigh the costs. This is an important question because the courts have not been able to devise effective remedies. In the IBM case the firm's past conduct was at issue, but the change in market conditions had eroded IBM's market power. What possible remedy could the government have provided? Breaking the company into smaller units certainly was no longer necessary or desirable.

Few economists argue that antitrust actions have accomplished the lofty goals stated in the laws. The potential for antitrust action may have restrained firms in some industries, but the costs associated with major antitrust actions have been large. Moreover, even when the government has won in court, it has not been very successful in reducing market concentration.

As a result, many economists argue for changes in antitrust policies. Those most opposed to market power and concentration suggest streamlining court procedures. They would also change the laws to simply outlaw certain levels of market concentration, thus avoiding the need to prove intent and effect. Others, like those in the Reagan administration, favor limiting antitrust actions to overt collusion and mergers that clearly increase market power.

RECAP

Antitrust policies seek to prevent firms from gaining and exercising significant market power. Policies are aimed at monopolization, collusion, and mergers that reduce competition.

The principal antitrust laws are the Sherman Antitrust Act (1890); the Clayton Act (1914); and the Federal Trade Commission Act (1914). Antitrust policies are administered by the Justice Department and the Federal Trade Commission.

Mergers can be horizontal, vertical, or conglomerate. Horizontal mergers (between competitors) may reduce competition and are the principal focus of merger policy.

Rate regulation. Government actions to set prices in markets as an alternative to antitrust action; may take the form of marginal-cost pricing or average-cost pricing.

Long-run marginal cost (LRMC). The extra cost for an extra unit of output when all resources can be changed.

RATE REGULATION AND PUBLIC ENTERPRISES

Economists generally agree that antitrust policy is inappropriate in the case of natural monopolies. A single firm that can supply an entire market will act in its own best interest, creating allocative inefficiency. But what if the firm is also technically efficient? Breaking up such a natural monopoly into smaller competing firms violates the principles of rational choice: Costs would outweigh benefits. The public policy dilemma is how to take advantage of the technical efficiency of natural monopolies without incurring the costs of allocative inefficiency.

Essentially there are two options: public enterprise or rate regulation. A monopoly can be a public enterprise, that is, a nationalized industry with public managers. European telephone services, utilities, and railroads are usually operated as public enterprises. In the United States, however, the solution has generally been to regulate rates, although some local public utility companies are operated by the government as public enterprises. **Rate regulation** attempts to obtain both allocative and technical efficiency by substituting the "visible hand" of public price regulation for the "invisible hand" of competition. A single, privately owned firm is allowed to build the most technically efficient plant, but it is required to price its product so that it earns only a normal profit.

Mechanisms for Establishing Rates

In rate regulation, a government regulatory agency determines a suitable rate or price, substituting its decisions for price competition. In some cases, such as public utilities and local phone service, the regulatory agencies are state agencies. In others, such as railroads and natural gas, the agencies are federal.

In effect, the regulated price is a ceiling price. The regulated firm can sell all it wants to at that price but nothing at any higher price. In setting the rate, regulators want to ensure allocative efficiency: As you know, there are two conditions for allocative efficiency: From a short-run perspective, marginal social benefits must equal marginal social costs (MSB = MSC); from the long-run perspective, profits must be normal. As you will see, these conditions are not easily achieved, either in theory or in practice.

Rate regulation in theory. Imagine that you are on a regulatory commission in your state and are considering what price to set for Brite Electric, a natural monopoly. Exhibit 17.2 shows demand (D), long-run average cost (LRAC), and **long-run marginal cost (LRMC)**. The last term is the extra cost of an additional unit of output when all resources can be changed. As is often the case for a natural monopoly, long-run average costs decline over the entire range of demand shown because of economies of scale.

If there were no regulation, Brite would produce 2 million kilowatts per month (where MR = LRMC) and charge $10 per thousand kilowatts. At that price Brite would earn an economic profit of $3000 per day (LRAC = $8.50 when 2 million kilowatts are produced). As is typical for monopolies, neither condition for allocative efficiency is met. Marginal social benefit (measured by demand) exceeds marginal social cost (measured by long-run marginal cost). Moreover, the firm earns more than a normal profit.

The objective of rate regulation is to find a (ceiling) price that results in allocative efficiency. You and your fellow commission members might try to

Price and cost
(dollars per thousand kilowatts)

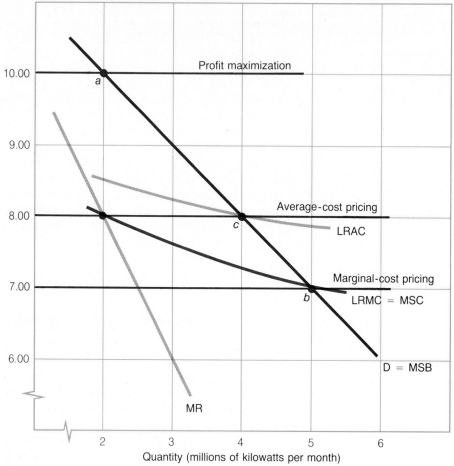

Exhibit 17.2
Rate Regulation in Theory
This graph shows three possible prices for Brite Electric, a natural monopoly. The company maximizes profits by selling 2 million kilowatts per month (where MR = LRMC) and charging $10 per thousand kilowatts (point *a*). Using marginal-cost pricing, rate regulators will want Brite Electric to sell 5 million kilowatts per month (where MSB = MSC) at a set price of $7 per thousand kilowatts (point *b*). Since this price falls below Brite's average cost, a subsidy is required. If regulators use average-cost pricing, Brite will produce 4 million kilowatts at $8 per thousand (point *c*). At this price, Brite earns only a normal profit, but marginal social benefits (D) exceed marginal social costs (LRMC).

Marginal-cost pricing. A price-setting option for rate regulation whereby price is set where demand equals marginal cost (P = MC). As a result, MSB = MSC, but the price may be too low to allow a normal profit.

achieve the short-run requirement for allocative efficiency: Marginal social benefits equal marginal social costs. This option is called **marginal-cost pricing** because the regulated price is determined by the intersection of the demand (representing MSB) and the long-run marginal cost (representing MSC) curves.

In this example, the price would be $7.00 per thousand kilowatts. Your regulatory commission has given Brite Electric a new marginal revenue curve.

Average-cost pricing. A price-setting option for rate regulation whereby price is set equal to average total cost (P = ATC), including an allowance for normal profit; the most commonly used price-setting mechanism.

Rate base. Term used by rate regulators to refer to a firm's total investment. In average-cost pricing, price is set to allow the firm to earn a normal rate of return on the rate base.

Each of the first 5 million kilowatts sold adds $7.00 per kilowatt to Brite's revenue. Applying the profit-maximizing rules, Brite's best output is 5 million kilowatts. This is also the allocatively efficient quantity (where MSB = MSC).

But at $7.00, Brite Electric cannot earn a normal profit, because long-run average cost exceeds the allowable price. When there are significant economies of scale (as in a natural monopoly), long-run average cost declines over a large range of output. But marginal cost is less than average cost when the latter is falling. Under these conditions, marginal-cost pricing will require a public subsidy, or the firm will simply go out of business.

Instead of seeking short-run allocative efficiency, what if you try to set a price that allows Brite to earn only a normal profit? This option is called **average-cost pricing** because the regulated price is determined by the intersection of the demand and the long-run average cost curves. In this example, the regulated price would be set at $8.00 per thousand kilowatts. Brite Electric's marginal revenue is therefore $8.00 per thousand kilowatts for the first 4 million kilowatts sold. Applying the profit-maximizing rules, Brite's best output is 4 million kilowatts. At this quantity it earns only a normal profit, as both price and average cost are $8.00.

However, with average-cost pricing, marginal social benefit exceeds marginal social cost. To check your understanding, verify this gap when 4 million kilowatts are produced. Each of the next 1 million kilowatts produced would be worth more to consumers than the cost of the resources used. But average-cost pricing does meet one condition for allocative efficiency—normal profits—and the firm requires no public subsidy. Neither method of regulation is perfect, as you can see. In practice, average-cost pricing is the most common form of rate regulation.

Rate regulation in practice. The practical aspects of rate regulation also present major obstacles. For example, average-cost pricing involves measurement problems. To earn a normal profit, the firm must be allowed to recover all its operating costs and to earn a fair return on its investment. The problems are (1) to determine the value of the firm's investment (what regulators call the **rate base**; and (2) to establish a fair rate of return. But what is the value of a coal-burning furnace built 10 years ago? What rate of return is fair to both the shareholders and consumers?

In addition to measurement problems, regulators must try to maintain incentives for technical efficiency. If the recovery of all operating costs means that all costs are passed on to consumers, why should the firm minimize costs, that is, strive for technical efficiency? In theory regulators could reject unnecessary or padded expenses. In practice, that is very difficult to do. There is no market test for efficiency and no easy way to identify or enforce it. Use of average-cost pricing also encourages firms to use more than an optimal amount of capital resources. We examine other arguments for and against rate regulation later in this chapter.

Regulation and Deregulation of Potentially Competitive Industries

Government price regulation is not limited to natural monopolies but has been used in industries which are potentially competitive. The earliest government rate regulation occurred in the railroad industry. The Interstate Commerce Commission (ICC) was established in 1886 to offset the local monopolies of some railroads. Its initial regulatory efforts may have been necessary to prevent abuses of economic power. Many rural areas were served by only a single railroad company. The rise of trucking, however, meant increased competition for railroad transportation and eliminated concern over market power. Railroad companies and their associated unions, however, found it more profitable to operate a government-sponsored cartel than to fight it out in a competitive marketplace. They successfully lobbied the ICC and Congress to continue regulation of the railroads and to *extend* regulation to the trucking industry.

Some economists oppose rate regulation when there is no natural monopoly, arguing that such regulation merely protects firms from competition. In fact, government began deregulating a number of industries in the 1970s, abandoning efforts to regulate price and allowing firms to compete. Deregulation of the airline industry, begun in 1978, initially resulted in lower fares. As a result, deregulation spread to other industries. Trucking regulations were eased considerably in 1980, increasing competition and lowering prices. Supporters of deregulation point to these cases as proof that regulation often results in higher, not lower, prices for consumers. We present a more extensive analysis of deregulation in the airline industry in Chapter 19.

The largest case of deregulation came in long-distance telephone service, where technical advances had broken down long-standing natural barriers to entry. Today, local telephone service is still controlled by state public utility commissions. Rates for local service have risen, however, since they are no longer subsidized by revenues from long-distance rates. In contrast, competition in the long-distance market has lowered long-distance rates. Overall, businesses—which use more long-distance service—have gained; households generally have lost, paying overall higher costs.

Issues in Rate Regulation

Economists continue to debate the merits of rate regulation, both in theory and in practice. One debate is over ways to improve the efficiency of rate regulation of natural monopolies. Another looks at whether and how to deregulate industries that do not fit the model of a natural monopoly. The following discussion presents several issues raised by those who favor deregulation in some cases.

Does rate regulation cause inefficiency? As we noted earlier, when a firm is allowed to recover all its costs, it has less incentive to minimize costs. In addition, regulated prices allow a normal rate of return on the rate base (the firm's investment in equipment, plant, and so on). Accordingly, regulation raises the return on capital resources and encourages regulated firms to use more capital-intensive methods than otherwise would be optimal. Thus rate regulation even of natural monopolies may not achieve society's goals of allocative and technical efficiency.

Regulation of potentially competitive industries also raises questions of efficiency. For example, when airline fares were regulated, the airlines competed on the basis of nonprice features. They offered inflight movies, more elaborate meals, painted airplanes bright colors, and so on. These features raised costs but did not make the market more efficient. Although some individual airlines gained, overall industry profits suffered. Because the costs of regulation exceeded the benefits, many airlines welcomed deregulation. (A number of them have also had difficulty earning profits under competitive conditions, however.)

Does rate regulation work? Problems like those of the airline industry lead some economists to question the effectiveness of rate regulation. Prices do not appear to be lower than they would be without regulation (although inefficiencies may occur). In fact, when the trucking and airline industries were regulated, rates were higher than under deregulation.

In a number of cases, regulation appears to benefit affected firms more than society. When an industry resists deregulation, we may assume that it believes itself to be better off with regulation than with competition. For example, both the trucking companies and the Teamsters Union vigorously opposed efforts to deregulate the trucking industry. In addition, critics charge that regulatory agencies are often "captives" of the industries they regulate. Certainly this charge has some merit with regard to the trucking and airline industries, where the regulatory agencies believed that their role was to protect the firms from the effects of "excessive competition."

Regulation may also be ineffective because the regulatory process is complex and the questions it must answer are difficult. It is often impossible to set a price that completely satisfies all the conditions of allocative efficiency, even in theory. Determining a normal rate of return, measuring the rate base, and predicting future directions of technology often involve guesswork. Some economists question the ability of government regulators to know better than private decision makers what direction to take. Others are concerned that political rather than economic criteria often determine regulatory actions.

Is government the cause or the cure? Some opponents of regulation argue that government regulation actually hinders competition. They apply this argument particularly to potentially competitive industries, such as trucking. Critics claim that the rise of trucking should have led to deregulation of the railroads. They believe that if government were to step aside, the return to competitive conditions would provide better results than regulation ever could.

Certainly there is evidence to support this argument. In the early 1980s, AT&T agreed to divide into a regulated component (the local operating companies) and a deregulated component (long-distance service). But prior to that time, the government had worked with the company to extend the company's monopoly into areas in which competition had begun.

How long do natural monopolies last? The AT&T case raises the issue of whether a natural monopoly is permanent. As with antitrust policy, rate regulation is based on the assumption that a relevant market can be defined and considered to hold for long periods of time. Rate regulation is further based on the assumption that there is no competition and none is expected in the future.

Critics respond by stating that the modern corporation has no fixed industry boundaries. Technology especially has created dynamic, not static, boundaries, and what exists today will not resemble what will exist tomorrow. Regulation thus runs against the grain of technology and operates on an assumption that is no longer valid. In addition, the growth of international competition has eroded the power of many U.S. companies, as conditions in the steel and auto industries indicate.

For example, the government created the telephone monopoly to address what it saw as a long-term, clearly defined natural monopoly. (Although, in fact, history suggests that the founder of the Bell System accepted regulation to forestall what he saw as growing competition.) Now, however, the relevant market goes far beyond the telephone itself. Long-distance communication networks using satellites and microwave systems bypass the cables and phone lines of the old technology. What was once a classic case of a natural monopoly is now a highly competitive market.

Public Enterprises: Another Option

As we noted at the start of this section, rate regulation is not the only possible solution to inefficiencies caused by natural monopolies. An alternative is public enterprise. Some local utilities in the United States are operated as public enterprises. At the federal level, the Postal Service and the Tennessee Valley Authority (TVA) are government-run enterprises.

Managers of public enterprises face many of the same problems that regulatory commissions do. They must choose among marginal-cost pricing, average-cost pricing, and monopoly-pricing (profit-maximizing) options. In West Germany, for example, the government-operated telephone company prices to maximize profits. Its profits are then used to subsidize other government services. Each pricing option has its drawbacks. In addition, public enterprises often suffer from technical inefficiency. Public managers, like the managers of a regulated monopoly, have less incentive to operate efficiently.

SOCIAL REGULATION

In addition to the potential problems caused by market power, the market may also fail when there are externalities—external benefits or external costs—and when information is imperfect. Government efforts to deal with these problems are commonly known as **social regulation**. Social regulation differs from antitrust and rate regulation in several important ways. First, social regulation is not confined to a single industry but cuts across industry boundaries and therefore has much wider impact. In addition, while market power can harm society, it does not seem to arouse the emotions of the public as do the issues that bring on social regulation. For example, some social regulations are aimed at health and safety: controlling workplace hazards or protecting the public from pollutants or unsafe drugs.

As with all policy issues, however, policy makers should apply the principles of rational choice to social regulation. This is particularly controversial, however, when the social benefits and social costs involve human life. For example, we know that using seat belts saves lives. Yet even where seat belt use is mandatory, a large percentage of people choose to take greater risks rather than to buckle up. Measuring social benefits and costs inevitably requires value judgments, leading to rational disagreements. But the economic debate must still be focused on the marginal social benefits and marginal social costs of social regulation.

Social regulation. Government regulation aimed at correcting for externalities and imperfect information; concerned with safety and quality of goods, accuracy and completeness of available information, and external benefits and costs.

Government has been involved in social regulation in the United States for a long time. Social regulation expanded tremendously in the 1960s and 1970s, but the 1980s brought a reexamination of government's role. In some areas, regulation has been relaxed. Nevertheless, social regulation will probably continue to play a significant role in the economy. In this section, we examine some of the situations that have led to social regulation and the issues involved in such actions.

External Costs and Allocative Inefficiency

Many cases of social regulation involve markets that have external costs. As we pointed out in earlier chapters, the existence of external costs means that market supply does not fully reflect social costs, and markets are not allocatively efficient. In such cases, social regulation may attempt to improve efficiency.

As an example, consider Shotz, Inc. Its plant buys resources such as chemicals and labor and produces self-developing camera film. Unfortunately, the plant's operation also creates air pollution. Without government regulation, Shotz pays nothing for using up clean air despite the social cost involved. Because clean air is a social good (and hence is not owned by any individual), Shotz can use clean air without incurring any private cost. But since this pollution diminishes society's supply of clean air, society incurs a real cost. In other words, when external costs exist, the marginal cost from the firm's perspective (and thus the market supply) is less than the marginal social cost.

Exhibit 17.3 shows the effects of external costs caused by Shotz's pollution. If we assume that the only market failure is the external cost of the product, market demand equals marginal social benefits (D = MSB). But without regulation, market supply reflects only marginal private costs, not full marginal social costs. In this case, equilibrium occurs when 300,000 packs of film per month are bought and sold. At that point, marginal private costs (measured by S) and marginal social benefits (measured by D) are both $3.00 per pack.

However, the external cost is $1.00 per pack. This cost is the vertical distance between the marginal private cost and the marginal social cost curves. Thus the MSC curve lies above the S curve. At 300,000 packs of film, the marginal social cost is $4.00 per pack, or $1.00 more than the marginal social benefit of $3.00 per pack. Allocative efficiency (MSB = MSC) would require production of only 200,000 packs of film. Whenever there are external costs, market output will exceed optimal output, because private decision makers do not base their decisions on full social costs.

But what if a government regulation limited production to 200,000 packs of film? Marginal social benefits would equal marginal social costs, and allocative efficiency would be achieved. However, there would still be pollution. It may sound strange, but economists term this result the *optimal level of pollution*. Note that the optimal level of pollution is *not* zero. For the social benefits and social costs involved, further reducing production levels and hence pollution would not be economically justifiable. Limiting production to only 100,000 packs of film, for example, would cause marginal social benefits ($4 per pack) to exceed marginal social costs ($3.00 per pack). As long as additional packs of film add more to social benefits than to social costs (including pollution costs), society gains from production.

Exhibit 17.3
External Costs and the Optimal Amount of Pollution
In this market, the equilibrium quantity is 300,000 film packs per month (point *a*), where marginal private cost (S) equals marginal social benefit (D). At that point marginal social cost (MSC) exceeds marginal social benefit because each film pack imposes an external cost of $1 on society (the vertical distance between points *a* and *b*). If government limited production to 200,000 packs, allocative efficiency would be restored (point *c*). Economists term this result the optimal level of pollution. Society's gain in reducing, if not eliminating, pollution is measured by the area of the blue-shaded triangle.

Economists generally agree that external costs cause allocative inefficiency. In addition, most agree that the objective of rational public policy should be to internalize the external cost. That is, they support efforts to have consumers and producers of a product base their choices on society's *full* opportunity costs. The options available to government regulators include: (1) impose taxes; (2) enforce design or performance standards; (3) establish markets; and (4) do nothing. The last option is clearly the best, if the benefits from improved allocative efficiency are less than the costs of government regulation.

Pollution taxes and allocative efficiency.   One way to internalize an external cost is to impose a per-unit tax equal to the external cost. In our film example, the tax should be $1.00 per pack of film, the exact amount of the external cost. Imposing this tax would raise private costs and thus shift market supply so that it equals marginal social costs. As a result, market equilibrium would fall to 200,000 units and restore allocative efficiency (MSB = MSC).

A pollution tax has several attractive economic features. First, it directly internalizes the external cost and causes decision makers to recognize the full opportunity costs of the product. Second, it enables the market to determine the optimal level of pollution. If buyers are willing and able to pay the full social costs, society is better off producing and consuming film, even though one cost is poorer air quality. Finally, the tax gives producers an incentive to purchase and install pollution-control devices, since doing so lowers their pollution tax bill. Such economic incentives can ensure efficient solutions to problems of external costs.

Applying the tax solution to external-cost problems is not quite as easy as our example suggests. It is not easy to establish the dollar value of an external cost. We can measure the chemical composition of air to establish how impure a firm's emissions are, but placing a negative value on the impurities is more difficult. The cost to society depends on such factors as the firm's location, the number of other firms, weather patterns, and the presence of other types of pollution. Thus a great deal of information is required to develop a tax program that enhances efficiency.

In addition, in order to keep the tax rate equal to the external cost, a regulatory agency must constantly monitor the firm's activities, which further adds to costs. As always, we must consider both the costs and benefits of government action in evaluating social regulation. We in the United States have generally rejected pollution taxes, but they have been used with some success in Europe.

Design or performance standards. A more direct approach to external costs, and one more often taken by government regulators, is the use of design or performance standards. Design standards often require firms to use particular devices or technology. For example, regulations might require Shotz to install air scrubbers on the top of smokestacks to reduce the amount of pollution that enters the air. Automakers are required to install emission-control devices on new cars. Design standards require no monitoring, but they do not give firms incentives to improve pollution controls. Design standards also treat all pollution as being equally costly.

Direct controls can also take the form of performance standards. For example, Shotz might be required to reduce its emission of pollutants by 10 percent. Performance standards leave firms free to find the most economical method of meeting the standards. But such standards require monitoring and, like design standards, fail to recognize differences in costs.

Some government regulations completely ban production and use of certain products that have high external costs. For example, the chemical DDT is very effective in insect control. However, it has long-lasting, widespread, and cumulative toxic effects on animals and people, which led to banning of its use in the United States.

Bans may be the best solution in some cases, but eliminating pollution is not generally the best option. For example, would you favor prohibiting cars in order to stop the pollution they cause? The best social choice is to identify the optimal level of pollution. The principles of rational choice tell us that this point occurs when marginal social benefits equal marginal social costs. Many critics charge that the federal Environmental Protection Agency (EPA) and the laws it administers often fail to consider both benefits and costs of pollution and pollution control. But whether the agency gives too much weight to the benefits or to the costs is an area of controversy.

Market-oriented solutions.   The EPA has experimented with approaches that combine performance standards with a "market" for pollution permits. A permit allows the holder to emit a certain amount of pollution of a specified type. Government regulators set a maximum level of emissions for a particular geographical area. Firms within the area are given incentives to negotiate with each other to meet the standard. The EPA grants "emission reduction credits" to firms that reduce pollution. These firms can then sell their credits to other firms in the same area, and the interaction of demand and supply determines who pollutes and at what level. Thus firms that can more easily reduce pollution will gladly sell their rights; firms that find it difficult or expensive to reduce emissions pay highly for pollution rights. The use of market-oriented approaches still has to be monitored, and there is still no precise method of determining a socially optimal standard. However, these approaches offer a flexible and efficient method of meeting set performance standards.

Imperfect Information and Market Failure

Social regulation is not restricted to markets that have external costs. If individuals and businesses are to make decisions that satisfy their personal objectives *and* social objectives also they must have good information. The marketplace provides a lot of information to help individuals judge the quality and safety of products. Most firms rely heavily on repeat business and are greatly affected by information spread by word-of-mouth or the news media about the quality and safety of their products.

Some economists argue that market self-regulation, that is, leaving customers and producers alone to fight it out competitively is the best approach. However, gathering sufficient information for making an informed decision is sometimes difficult and expensive for individuals and small businesses. Most people would prefer not to find out firsthand that a toy can cause an infant's death or that a drug can produce birth defects. Thus government often intervenes to provide good information on product quality and hazards.

The Food and Drug Administration (FDA), for example, has watched over the food, drug, and cosmetic industries since 1906. More recently, the Occupational Safety and Health Administration (OSHA) and the Consumer Product Safety Commission have worked to counteract imperfect information. Supporters of such agencies argue that consumers cannot competently evaluate potential hazards. However, critics charge that consumer-affairs agencies often establish regulations or prohibitions rather than simply providing information. Most economists believe that when consumers receive adequate and easily understood information, bans on products cause allocative inefficiency. The benefits of the product are eliminated along with potential costs. We examine the role of the FDA in promoting drug safety in Chapter 19.

Social Regulation: Issues for the Future

Arguments over the merits of social regulation have become major political issues in recent years. Opponents stress the economic drawbacks—government's failure to weigh both costs and benefits—and a desire to restore lost "freedoms." In this section, we consider some of these criticisms as issues for the future. The objective is not to resolve the debate or to present the "correct" answer, but rather to provide some food for thought.

How are benefits and costs to be measured? In economic terms benefits are not infinite, and rational choice involves measuring costs in terms of opportunity cost. Then we can consider whether (1) to achieve some level of safety while sharply decreasing or eliminating certain benefits, or (2) to trade some risks for some benefits.

Critics charge that government regulators count only the direct costs of regulation—those measured by agency budgets, for example. These direct costs represent only the tip of the iceberg. Filling governmental requests for information and testing and implementing government-mandated procedures and processes impose costs on businesses and thus on the consumer. Compliance costs must also be included in the rational-choice equation.

Many people reject the idea that an exact monetary value can (or should) be put on everything. Moreover, as we discussed earlier, placing precise dollar amounts on the benefits and costs to society is difficult, if not impossible. Thus perceptions of costs and benefits of many social problems vary and are debatable. Nevertheless, policy makers must try to approach these problems from a rational-choice—not an emotional—point of view.

Should design standards or performance standards be used? Even assuming that consensus could be reached on the desirability of government intervention, debate would still rage over the methods to be used. The performance-standard approach is almost universally accepted by economists. However, regulators in this country rarely use it, perhaps because many believe that only by forcing firms to adopt the best available technology can pollution be reduced, for example.

While the performance-standards approach seems to be called for by rational economic thinking, it is always dangerous to argue that only one approach to a particular problem is correct. And even when performance standards are implemented, questions remain: What should the standards be? How can we measure and encourage compliance?

Who should make decisions regarding social regulation? At the root of the debate over social regulation is another question: Who decides? Some economists (generally those who believe that there are few social problems to be corrected) advocate leaving decisions to the individual consumer or worker. But others (who generally support government regulation) believe that government must address the problem of equating social benefits and costs.

If government is to decide, are the decisions likely to be better if they are made at the local level (cities and towns), the state level, or the federal level? Are local and state governments in a better position to assess local conditions and concerns (that is, costs and benefits)? The small, congested eastern states generally supported the national 55-mile-per-hour speed limit. The same speed limit was considered to be nonsense by some large, sparsely populated western states. In 1987, Congress reacted by increasing the limit to 65 in rural areas. Are federal controls desirable in some cases? A midwestern state might find it desirable to place fewer restrictions on smokestack emissions. But eastern states might suffer from the external costs of acid rain as a result. Because of such difficulties, the debate over local versus central control over social regulation seems likely to continue.

What are the other effects of social regulation? Most attention has centered on agency effectiveness in solving a particular set of problems. However, social regulation, like most economic policy issues, has broader effects. Social regulation may contribute to industrial concentration by raising barriers to entry. For example, the drug-testing procedures required by the FDA may help protect current drug manufacturers from new competition. And requiring expensive pollution-control equipment may raise fixed costs enough to create at least some barriers for new entrants in a number of industries.

Like many other problems, social regulation also has international repercussions. The costs imposed by government regulation of U.S. manufacturers of steel, autos, and chemicals may have contributed to their inability to compete in international markets. However, the choices are complex. If we relax environmental standards, we may reduce unemployment, but at the expense of diminished environmental quality. Or we can buy steel, chemicals, and other goods from foreign manufacturers, thus reducing pollution but raising domestic unemployment.

Finally, some people question whether social regulation stifles innovation, lessens efficiency, and adds to inflation. If the answer is yes, then these effects must also be treated as costs of social regulation and considered when policy choices are debated.

GOVERNMENT FAILURE: WHY REGULATION IS IMPERFECT

Thus far we have observed that when the market fails government *may* act in an attempt to correct the situation. However, as critics of governmental regulation point out, government, too, may fail. Just as it is incorrect to assume that markets always operate perfectly, it is incorrect to assume that government always makes the perfect response to market failure. In this section we consider several reasons for government failure. The objective is not to discredit public officials or employees, many of whom are interested in achieving effective solutions to complex public issues. But public officials and employees are subject to personal benefits and costs associated with their tasks. By looking at what economic principles have to say about *how* government works, we can better understand both the benefits and costs of relying on government solutions to economic problems.

Difficulty of Measuring Social Benefits and Costs

Government failure may result from the difficulties involved in discovering what the "public interest" actually is. In a smoothly functioning market system without imperfections, markets reflect consumers' relative values and thus the public interest. In the absence of markets or when they fail, discovering the social benefits and social costs is difficult. How much are consumers willing to pay for cleaner air or water? Even more difficult is balancing the benefits to one group with the costs to other groups. For example, to solve the problem of acid rain in the Northeast, some people want to impose higher costs on the utilities that provide power for the Midwest. The lack of clear-cut ways to measure social benefits and costs hampers government decision makers when they attempt to apply the principles of rational choice.

On the other hand, government regulators have sometimes acted as though their role was to *eliminate* market failures. As a result, they may have overestimated the social benefits of regulation while underestimating the social costs.

Rational Ignorance

Political choices are most often made by elected officials. But studies indicate that many voters do not know the positions of their own representatives on economic issues. Economic analysis suggests that this "rational ignorance" may result from weighing benefits and costs. Few voters expect their individual votes to influence the outcome of a political election or their individual voices to influence the vote of their representatives. Thus the individual may judge the benefits of becoming informed and involved to be small relative to the costs. While this choice may be rational for an individual, it may lead to poor public choices and government failure.

Special-Interest Effect

In many cases, governmental policies provide relatively large private benefits to a relatively small group. Those so-called special interests rationally spend time, energy, and money to win favorable legislation or administrative rulings. The rest of society must bear the costs. Government agencies and legislators are subject to considerable pressure from special-interest groups, but there are few lobbies for the "public interest." Politicians may rationally pay more attention to the special interests who can help them gain reelection than to the rest of society. Policies developed in response to special-interest pressures may benefit elected officials politically. However, such policies result in government failure if the total social costs outweigh the total social benefits.

You should be especially alert for the special-interest effect when you hear someone argue for government policies that restrict competition or the opportunities for individual choice. Part of any good analysis of a public issue is to identify those who win and those who lose.

Short-Sighted Effect

Economic issues often involve trade-offs between long-run and short-run effects. For example, restricting foreign imports of shoes will have immediate effects on those who own and those who work in shoe factories. The gains from free trade come from the long-run effects of competition. But long-run results are often complex and vague to the average voter and politician. Thus elected officials favor policies that yield immediate benefits and have costs only in the future. They oppose policies that impose immediate, visible costs—such as a tax increase— even if there are significant future benefits. In holding these views, voters and politicians are simply acting in their own self-interest as they recognize it. However, such self-interested actions may not best meet the economic goals of society as a whole.

Lack of Incentives for Efficiency

Finally, critics often observe that government administrators and elected officials do not face the penalties for inefficiency that private managers do. For public managers, spending below budgeted levels usually results only in a lower future budget—hardly a reward. Thus public managers may actually be motivated to avoid efficient solutions. This criticism of government may apply even to public managers who strive to serve the public interest.

The recognition that government may fail, just as the market sometimes fails, does not mean that government has no role to play. When market failures are significant, government action may be the best option. Although agencies such as the EPA and OSHA may be flawed, not all government regulation has failed. The important point is that all government policies, whether regulation or inaction, have both costs and benefits. Economists who suggest reasons for government failure, however, add the potential for government failure to the costs of government action. They suggest we consider factors such as rational ignorance or the special-interest effects when proposing political solutions to economic problems.

CONCLUSION

In this chapter we looked at government responses to market failures associated with market power, external costs, and imperfect information. In exploring its theory and practice, we have considered some of the current issues in government regulation. As you have seen, some critics want government to significantly reduce its regulatory role in the economy. Others want to continue government regulation, but with regulators using the principles of rational choice to determine what and how to regulate. The specific examples of government regulation contained in the minichapters of Chapter 19 provide a closer look at government regulation in action.

Thus far our examination of government's role in the microeconomy has focused on situations in which markets fail to generate allocative or technical efficiency. In Chapter 18 we look at government's role with respect to equity issues. We have noted before that the market system distributes income (and therefore output) based on the value of resources owned and supplied by households. But sometimes society may view the resulting distribution as inequitable. In Chapter 18 we also look at the actual income distribution in the United States and at programs designed to change it.

SUMMARY

1. In this chapter we explored the use of government regulation—antitrust policies, rate regulation, and social regulation—to correct market failures. We also saw how government regulations may sometimes fail.

2. If a business gains significant market power, it may cause the economy to operate inefficiently. Preventing growth in market power and fostering competition are the benefits of government antitrust policies. The principal antitrust laws are the Sherman Antitrust Act (1890), the Clayton Act (1914), and the Federal Trade Commission Act (1914). The Justice Department and the Federal Trade Commission (FTC) administer antitrust policy.

3. Some antitrust policies are aimed at monopolization—when one firm gains enough market power to dominate an industry. Some are aimed at collusion—when two or more firms agree not to compete and thereby jointly exercise market power. And some are aimed at mergers—when the combining of two companies threatens to substantially reduce competition.

4. Beginning with the Standard Oil case in 1911, the courts have usually taken a "rule-of-reason" approach in monopolization cases. That is, the courts are less concerned with the presence of market power than with the anticompetitive behavior of the firm.

5. The courts have been strict in ruling against firms that agree to fix prices. But the courts have required direct evidence of collusion and have not ruled against tacit collusion.

6. Mergers between firms may be horizontal (between firms in the same industry), vertical (between firms with a buyer–seller relationship), or conglomerate (between firms with no direct connection). Antitrust policies have been aimed largely at preventing horizontal mergers where the effect would be to lessen competition.

7. Current issues for antitrust policy are: (a) Can a relevant market be established? (b) Can illegal practices be distinguished from normal business practices? (c) Can the government handle the big cases? (d) What should be the goals of antitrust policy?

8. Natural monopolies present a public-policy dilemma. Allowing only one firm to operate in a market is best from the standpoint of technical efficiency. But a monopolist will charge more and produce less than is desirable. In the United States, rate regulation by state and federal commissions has been the principal regulatory method used. The use of public enterprises is more common in Europe and other countries. In trying to set rates that produce the same results as would competition, regulatory commissions may set price equal to marginal cost (marginal-cost pricing). If substantial economies of scale exist, however, this rate may require a public subsidy. The more common option, average-cost pricing, is an attempt to set rates that allow a monopoly to earn only a normal profit.

9. Issues in rate regulation are: (a) Is there a legitimate reason to use rate regulation in potentially competitive industries? (b) Does rate regulation cause inefficiency? (c) Does rate regulation work? (d) Is government the cause of or cure for monopoly power? (e) How long do natural monopolies last? (f) Is public enterprise a desirable alternative?

10. When there are external costs, as in the case of pollution, market supply does not reflect marginal social costs. Too much of the product (and too much pollution) is produced. In such cases, social regulation may improve allocative efficiency. Economists stress that the social objective is not to eliminate external costs. Rather, it is to find the optimal amount, that is, the point where marginal social benefits equal marginal social costs. Many economists favor market-based solutions—taxes or marketable pollution rights—because they preserve incentives. Much government regulation, however, has taken the form of design standards or performance requirements.

11. When information is difficult to obtain or evaluate, social regulation may improve market efficiency. This is the rationale for the regulatory efforts of the Food and Drug Administration, the Occupational Safety and Health Administration, and the Consumer Product Safety Commission. Whether these and other agencies should only provide information, enforce regulations, or ban some products altogether is controversial.

12. Current issues for social regulation are: (a) How can social benefits and costs be measured? (b) Should market-based solutions be used in place of design or per-

formance standards? (c) Who should make decisions in the cases of external costs and imperfect information? (d) What are the other effects of social regulation (such as on market power or international competitiveness)?

13. There are both benefits and costs to government regulation. One cost is the potential that government might fail. Measuring social benefits and costs is difficult, as is determining what the "public interest" actually is. Legislators and regulators may be overly influenced by special interests. And government administrators may have insufficient incentive to achieve efficiency. Individuals often fail to participate in politics because of rational ignorance; that is, if the personal costs of a problem are likely to be small, it does not pay to collect information or lobby for a cure.

KEY TERMS

Antitrust policy, 413
Rule of reason, 415
Price fixing, 417
Tacit collusion, 417
Merger, 418
Horizontal merger, 419
Vertical merger, 419
Conglomerate merger, 419
Rate regulation, 423
Long-run marginal cost (LRMC), 423
Marginal-cost pricing, 424
Average-cost pricing, 425
Rate base, 425
Social regulation, 428

QUESTIONS FOR REVIEW AND DISCUSSION

1. Economists often state that antitrust policy aims to eliminate artificial barriers to entry. Give some examples of artificial barriers. Give some examples of genuine barriers. Why, if either type of barrier leads to market power, is antitrust policy aimed only at artificial ones?

2. Sometimes, regulated firms are required to supply products or services that do not generate a normal profit. For example, under regulation, airlines had to provide service to some areas that they later abandoned under deregulation. Do you think any firm should be required to provide unprofitable services? What criteria

would you use to determine whether a product should be supplied, assuming that your goal is to be allocatively efficient? In particular, is the profit that a firm can make the best or only measure of a product's social value?

3. Large firms often charge lower prices in markets in which they face substantial competition than in less competitive markets. Is this an example of predatory pricing or are there other, rational explanations for the behavior? What guidelines would you suggest for distinguishing predatory pricing from good business practices?

4. Explain the statement: "In regulated industries in which prices are set on a cost-plus basis, the normal incentives for technical efficiency are reversed."

5. Consider the statement: "Critics have charged the Postal Service with declining service, but the decline is the result of management's efforts to deliver mail at the least possible cost. Since mail delivery is a public service, it should be required to break even." In what sense do we require public services to break even? Should management be faulted for attempting to deliver mail at the least possible cost? What trade-offs are important to consider?

6. Based on the following data, answer the questions in (a)–(d).

Q	P	TR	MR	MC	TC
4000	$1.30	$5200			$4900
			0.80	0.80	
5000	1.20	6000			5700
			0.60	0.90	
6000	1.10	6600			6600
			0.40	1.00	
7000	1.00	7000			7600
			0.20	1.10	
8000	0.90	7200			8700

a) What price would this firm set to maximize its profits? How much profit would it make?

b) If the government regulated this firm using marginal-cost pricing, what price would it set? How much profit would the firm make? What problems would the government (and the firm) face under this pricing policy?

c) If the government regulated the firm using average-cost pricing, what price would it set? How much profit would the firm make? Is the result allocatively efficient?

d) Suppose that this firm is a monopoly that gained market power as the result of a government-granted patent (an exclusive right to produce and sell the product). How much would you say the patent is worth to the firm? If the government had auctioned the patent rights, how much economic profit would the winning bidder be able to make?

7. Repeat Question 6 using the data shown in following graph.

Price
(dollars per unit)

Quantity (thousands of units per week)

8. Is each of the following statements true, false, or uncertain? Explain why.
   a) The problem with market power is that the firm tends to underproduce; that is, greater output is required to achieve allocative efficiency.
   b) Under conditions of natural monopoly, the market will tend to achieve technical efficiency but will fail to achieve allocative efficiency.
   c) Because the exercise of market power is inefficient, efforts to restrict it will result in increased efficiency.

9. An owner of a large appliance store states, "I welcome government efforts to regulate the appliance repair business. Too many consumers are cheated by amateurs who promise low prices but deliver shoddy work." Do you share these sentiments? Why or why not?

10. Market failure (and social regulation) does not affect all groups in the economy equally. In each of the following cases, which groups in the economy are hurt and which benefit from the indicated market failure or social regulation?
    a) The air pollution caused by producing steel.
    b) Poor information about health hazards for workers in chemical plants producing pesticides.

c) A government regulation requiring public utilities that burn coal to install air scrubbers on their smokestacks.
d) A law making firms liable for any problems that result from worker exposure to potential health hazards.

11. Consider the following data for a market in which each unit of output produces $2 worth of external costs.

Price	Quantity demanded	Quantity supplied
15	5,000	25,000
14	10,000	20,000
13	15,000	15,000
12	20,000	10,000
11	25,000	5,000
10	30,000	0

a) What will be the equilibrium level of output in the market if the external costs are not recognized?
b) What level of output would be consistent with allocative efficiency?
c) What will happen to market output and market price if a $2 tax is placed on each unit produced?
d) What will happen to market price and market output in the short run if each firm is assessed a yearly fee of $2000? In the long run?

12. Do you agree or disagree with the following statements? Why?
    a) Government tends to take a long-run point of view, representing both present and future generations. Firms, on the other hand, aren't motivated to consider long-run interests. Their behavior leads to market failure and a need for government regulation.
    b) Pursuing self-interest in the marketplace tends to result in allocative efficiency. In the political arena it has the opposite effect.

13. Is each of the following statements true, false, or uncertain? Explain why.
    a) In the long run, competition tends to drive out firms producing products that have high external costs, since it forces firms to maintain low costs.
    b) In the long run, the costs of government-imposed social regulation will be paid by consumers if an industry is competitive.
    c) If external costs are associated with a particular product, prohibiting its production will improve allocative efficiency, since the external costs are eliminated.

14. In what sense is the word *efficiency* used in the following two statements? Do the statements indicate an understanding of the principles presented in this chapter? Explain.

    a) The efficiency of U.S. industries is severely affected by current social regulation. If we reduced (or, better yet, eliminated) regulation, efficiency would improve. And because social regulation affects most industries, all consumers would benefit.

    b) Businesses claim to be interested in efficiency but would, if left to their own devices, ignore the problems addressed by social regulation. A real accounting of efficiency requires a recognition of the costs of worker safety and health, pollution, and other social costs.

15. Why do the principles of rational choice lead economists to reject both of the following statements?

    a) Market participants pursue self-interest. Government regulation is therefore necessary to ensure that social benefits and social costs are properly recognized.

    b) Government regulators cannot measure social benefits and social costs with precision. Thus government regulation can't lead to improved allocative efficiency.

CHAPTER 18

Income Distribution
and Equity

QUESTIONS TO CONSIDER

☐ How are sources of personal income related to distribution of income?

☐ In what ways do the absolute, relative, and official measures of poverty differ?

☐ What are the causes of poverty?

☐ Why may individuals "rationally" choose to discriminate?

☐ Why have antipoverty programs not eliminated poverty?

R ecall that in previous chapters we concentrated on the goals of technical and allocative efficiency, that is, on how effectively the economy utilizes its scarce resources. In this chapter we expand the analysis to consider the third economic goal: equity. Is the distribution of goods and services determined by rules that society believes are fair and just? Bear in mind that economic analysis cannot tell us whether the rules or outcomes are fair. But understanding the factors that determine income distribution can allow us to predict the outcomes of various policies.

Most people realize that income in the United States is distributed unequally. The wealthiest individuals have incomes of more than a billion dollars per year. On the other hand, if it were not for a variety of private and public programs, the poorest would not have sufficient income to satisfy their most basic demands for food and shelter. But just how unequal is the distribution on income? What economic and noneconomic factors determine the distribution? What is poverty and why are individuals poor? What does the government do about poverty and inequality? What effects do these government policies have on inequality, poverty, and efficiency? We address each of these questions in this chapter.

RATIONAL CHOICE: EFFICIENCY AND EQUITY

A rational approach to the issues of inequality of income and poverty requires an understanding of the important connection between inequality and efficiency in a market economy. Efficiency, for example, requires economic resources to be fully utilized. Individuals in a market economy receive income from the sale of productive resources they own. Thus individuals have an incentive to utilize fully the economic resources under their control. Government transfers—payments to individuals that are unrelated to goods and services provided—redistribute income. As a result, transfers can reduce the incentive to work, total economic output, and economic efficiency. This effect does not mean that transfers should not be made, but we must be aware that reduced efficiency is an important opportunity cost of such payments.

Efficiency also requires that resources be put to their most valuable use. A market system relies on price signals to indicate where resources can be employed most efficiently. It relies on economic incentives to cause resources to respond. But the talents, skills, experience, and preferences of individuals differ. We expect these differences to result in an appropriate allocation of all resources. Giving everyone the same income, regardless of how they use their resources, destroys economic incentives to achieve efficiency.

Inequality sometimes enhances overall efficiency. However, society's goals require not only maximizing economic output but also an *equitable* distribution of that output. The existence of programs that redistribute income suggests a political determination that the market-determined distribution is not always equitable. Still, heated debates over the size and characteristics of such programs point to significant disagreements over how much and to whom additional income should be redirected. Because defining equity is a political (not an economic) issue, such arguments involve rational disagreements based on subjective value judgments.

Of course, not all inequalities increase efficiency. For example, discrimination may prevent highly qualified individuals from gaining employment opportunities. It may limit their willingness or ability to obtain useful skills. Thus discrimination is inefficient, and most people also find it inequitable. In addition, individuals with insufficient incomes may be unable to function effectively in the economy. That is, poverty may restrict the development of human capital, lowering the total level of economic resources. Clearly, individuals lacking sufficient food and other necessities cannot contribute fully to social output.

Sometimes society cannot achieve all its economic goals simultaneously. For example, inequality often has a positive influence on efficiency but may also lead to inequity. In such instances, the principles of rational choice tell us that society must weigh the extra benefits (greater efficiency) against the extra costs (greater inequity). Economic analysis cannot tell us how much redistribution is fair. But it can help us understand how the distribution occurs. By showing us the effects of policies on inequality and efficiency, economic analysis can help us make the debate rational.

DISTRIBUTION OF INCOME: THE FACTS

Rational economic discussion centers on the facts. To understand inequality in the United States, we have to describe income distribution in the United States and how it has changed. Because of the connection between efficiency and inequality, you should not be surprised to find that income distribution is unequal.

Sources of Personal Income

Exhibit 18.1 shows that three-fourths of all personal income is derived from wages and salaries, that is, from the sale of labor services. In fact, the true proportion is higher because some proprietor income also represents returns from the sale of labor services. Such is the case for businesses owned by a single individual, such as lawyers, farmers, and many small businesses. An additional

Source	Personal income ($ billions)	Percent of nontransfer income	Percent of total income
Wages and salaries	2282.6	72.8	65.5
Proprietor income	278.9	8.9	8.0
Dividends and interest	556.6	17.8	16.0
Rental income	15.6	0.5	0.4
Total nontransfers	3133.7	100.0	
Plus transfers	353.3		10.1
Total personal income	3487.0		100.0

Source: Economic Report of the President, 1987, Table B-24.

Exhibit 18.1
Distribution of Personal Income by Source, 1986

one-fifth of income is generated from returns on land, buildings, and other forms of wealth. Exhibit 18.1 shows income from these sources as dividends, interest, and rent. Although income from wealth may be an important source for the very wealthy, these data suggest that income for most households depends largely on the success of their members in labor markets. Thus labor markets are important in explaining income inequality.

Inequality of Income

One rough indication of the extent of income inequality is to compare the share of income received by families with high incomes with the share received by families with low incomes. Exhibit 18.2(a) shows the share of income received by each fifth of the families in the United States in 1985. If income were equally distributed, the percentage of families and the percentage share of income would be identical. That is, the share of income in each category would be one-fifth, or 20 percent.

However, in 1985 the 20 percent of families with the lowest incomes received only 4.6 percent of the total income in the United States. That represents about one-fourth of the share they would have received if income had been equally distributed. On the other hand, the 20 percent of families with the highest incomes received 43.5 percent of the total, or more than double their proportionate share. The top 5 percent of families received 16.0 percent of the total, or more than three times the share they would have received if income had been equally distributed.

Despite this evidence of inequality, income distribution in the United States cannot be described in terms of a few wealthy families at one end of the income scale and most families clustered at the opposite end. A large middle class (in terms of income) receives nearly its proportionate share of income. In 1985 the middle 60 percent of families received 52 percent of the total income.

Economists often display information about income distribution on a graph like that shown in Exhibit 18.2(b). The horizontal axis shows the percentage of

(a) Distribution of income in the United States, 1985

Income group	Percentage of total income received by	
	Families in this income group	Families in this and lower income groups
Lowest 20%	4.6	4.6
Second 20%	10.9	15.5
Middle 20%	16.9	32.4
Fourth 20%	24.2	56.6
Highest 20%	43.5	100.0
Top 5%	16.0	

Source: U.S. Bureau of the Census, Current Population Reports, P-60 Series, No. 154, *Money Income and Poverty Status of Families and Persons in the United States: 1985.*

(b) Lorenz curve for the distribution of income in the United States, 1985

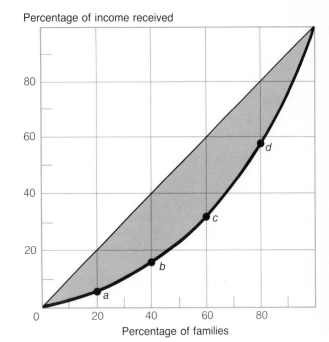

Exhibit 18.2
Distribution of Income in the United States, 1985
The income distribution data in part (a) is plotted as a Lorenz curve in part (b). The diagonal line indicates a perfectly equal income distribution. The difference between the Lorenz curve and the line of absolute equality measures the degree of inequality in the income distribution.

all families, the vertical axis the percentage of income received. Point *a* corresponds to the 20 percent of families having the lowest incomes who received 4.6 percent of the total income, as shown in Exhibit 18.2(a). Point *b* indicates that 15.5 percent of the total income received in 1985 went to the bottom 40 percent of families (the first two income groups considered together). The other points also correspond to the data in the last column of Exhibit 18.2(a). If we connect these points with a smooth curve, we have a **Lorenz curve**.

Note that the diagonal line on the graph represents the Lorenz curve if income were distributed equally. Along that line the percentage share of income and the percentage of families are identical. The difference between the Lorenz curve of absolute equality and the actual curve in this case (the shaded area on the graph) indicates the extent of inequality. The larger the shaded area, the larger is the difference between the share actually received and the equal-distribution share.

Changes in income distribution. Exhibit 18.3 shows the percentage of income earned by each fifth of the population for selected years since 1950. The data reveal little change in the distribution for the years shown. The bottom 20 percent received about one-fourth of their proportional share, whereas the top 5

Lorenz curve. A graphic representation of the actual income distribution obtained by plotting the cumulative percentage of income received against the cumulative percentage of families or individuals. The greater the deviation of the actual Lorenz curve from a diagonal straight line, the greater is the degree of inequality.

Income group	1950	1960	1970	1980	1985
Lowest 20%	4.5%	4.8%	5.4%	5.1%	4.6%
Second 20%	12.0	12.2	12.2	11.6	10.9
Middle 20%	17.4	17.8	17.6	17.5	16.9
Fourth 20%	23.4	24.0	23.8	24.3	24.2
Highest 20%	42.7	41.3	40.9	41.6	43.5
Top 5%	17.3	15.9	15.6	15.3	16.7
Median family income (constant dollars)	$14,829	$20,413	$27,336	$27,446	$27,735

Sources: Economic Report of the President, 1984 and 1982; Current Population Reports, P-60 Series, No. 154, *Money Income and Poverty Status of Families and Persons in the United States: 1985.*

Exhibit 18.3
U.S. Income Distribution, 1950–1985

percent received more than three times their share in each of those years. In addition, the middle 60 percent consistently received about one-half of the total income.

Exhibit 18.3 also shows median income in constant dollars, that is, after removing the effects of changes in price levels (inflation). Between 1950 and 1985, median family income increased from $14,829 to $27,735. So, in real terms (the ability to purchase a certain quantity of economic goods and services) the median family is better off than it was in 1950. In addition, the real income earned by the typical family in each income group shown has increased. Thus while inequality has remained relatively constant, the standard of living of families in all income groups shown has increased.

Income inequality and income mobility. Note, however, that the apparent lack of change in income distribution does *not* mean that the same people are in the same income group year after year. In fact, recent evidence from the Institute for Social Research at the University of Michigan reveals considerable income mobility.[*] Fewer than one-half of all individuals remained in the same income group from the late 1960s to the late 1970s. One-third of the group studied dramatically improved their incomes. Another 20 percent had dramatic decreases. Even year-to-year variations in income are quite large. Less than one-half of the young adults whose parents were poor remained poor after leaving home.

This mobility means that we must be careful when we interpret a "snapshot" of the economic status of the population in any particular year. It also reinforces the importance of distinguishing between those people who have temporarily low incomes and those who have persistently low incomes. For example, in any one year some portion of the poorest group may be students who are making investments in their human capital, which will lead to high incomes later.

[*] Greg Duncan, *Years of Poverty, Years of Plenty.* Ann Arbor: University of Michigan Press, 1984. The study reports on data collected from the same households over a ten-year period.

RECAP

A market economy relies on work incentives to achieve efficiency. Some inequalities in income encourage individuals to train for new jobs or move to industries and locations where labor demand is increasing.

Breaking the connection between work effort and income may cause inefficiency. In considering income redistribution, the trade-off between efficiency and equity must be recognized.

Income distribution has changed little since 1959. The poorest 20 percent of U.S. families have consistently received about 5 percent of the total income. The richest 5 percent have received over 15 percent. But there is considerable income mobility from year to year and between generations.

International comparisons of income distribution. Exhibit 18.4 shows the distribution of income in several countries, including the United States. Inequality in the more industrialized countries tends to be less pronounced than in countries with low average incomes. Partly this reflects the greater use of government redistribution programs in the more-developed countries. In addition, wealth in the less-developed countries is more unequally distributed and the opportunities to develop human resources are severely limited. In the last chapter in this textbook, we provide an in-depth look at the economic situation of less-developed economies.

POVERTY: DEFINITION AND FACTS

Those concerned with unequal income distribution often are concerned with the plight of the poor. But just how should we define poverty? Using a commonsense approach, we could probably agree that poverty means insufficient income or insufficient access to economic goods. The problem with this definition is its vagueness. What constitutes "insufficient" income? In this section, we review some of the definitions of poverty used by economists. Later in this chapter, we analyze the official definition used by the Census Bureau, as well as some criticisms of this definition. Differences in definition are important not only for what they reveal about the extent of poverty in this country, but also for what they imply about appropriate policies to "cure" poverty.

Two Approaches: Absolute versus Relative Poverty

Absolute poverty approach.
Poverty defined by an income below the level necessary to maintain a minimum standard of living.

Basically, there are two ways of defining poverty. The **absolute poverty approach** defines poverty on the basis of some minimal standard of living. That is, a certain quantity of goods and services are deemed essential for a family's welfare. Using the absolute approach, a family (or individual) is considered poor

---

Exhibit 18.4
International Comparisons of Income Distribution

Income group	United States	Brazil	Japan	France	West Germany	Mexico	Zambia	Kenya	Canada	India
Lowest 20%	5.3%	2.0%	8.7%	5.3%	7.9%	2.9%	3.4%	2.6%	5.3%	7.0%
Second 20%	11.9	5.0	13.2	11.1	12.5	7.0	7.4	6.3	11.8	9.2
Middle 20%	17.9	9.4	17.5	16.0	17.0	12.0	11.2	11.5	18.0	13.9
Fourth 20%	25.0	17.0	23.1	21.8	23.1	20.4	16.9	19.2	24.9	20.5
Highest 20%	39.9	66.6	37.5	45.8	39.5	57.7	61.1	60.4	40.0	49.4
Top 10%	23.3	50.6	22.4	30.5	24.0	40.6	46.3	45.8	23.8	33.6
Income per capita (in 1984 dollars)	$15,390	$1,720	$10,630	$9,760	$11,130	$2,040	$470	$310	$13,280	$260

Source: The World Bank, *World Development Report, 1986.*
Note: The data are considered by the World Bank to be the best available, but are not necessarily consistent from country to country.

Relative poverty approach. Poverty defined by an income below some fraction of the average income; focuses on inequality of income.

Poverty threshold. A sliding income scale, adjusted according to family characteristics and the general level of prices, below which poverty is officially considered to exist.

when its income is too low to allow it to attain that minimum standard of living. As we discuss later in this chapter, the absolute approach is the basis for the official (government) definition of poverty.

In contrast, the **relative poverty approach** defines poverty on the basis of income inequality. That is, poverty is defined relative to the average standard of living. Using the relative approach, a family is considered poor if its income falls below some fraction of the average income level. Relative poverty thus exists whenever income is very unequally distributed. This approach is based on a concept of equity, or fairness, that suggests that members of society should receive relatively equal income.

Both approaches have strengths and weaknesses that spark debate. The absolute approach requires the setting of an absolute standard. Whether this standard should be relatively low—a minimum level for survival—or relatively high—a minimum level for comfort is controversial. The relative approach to poverty requires elimination of inequality, yet the market system depends on incentives created by inequality to operate efficiently.

Critics of the relative approach also argue that it provides no useful guides for policy formulation. We can define the poverty population as the 20 percent of families with the lowest income (a common relative poverty measure). But this definition does not tell us how desperate their situation is or how much income they require to maintain a minimally acceptable standard of living. Without these facts, it is difficult to come up with an appropriate policy to combat the effects of poverty.

Official Definition of Poverty

With regard to the inequality of income distribution, we discussed poverty in the United States from a relative standpoint. In setting policies to cure poverty, however, the federal government has used the absolute approach, defining poverty as income below a specified level. In this section, we take a look at the official definition of poverty and the magnitude and characteristics of poverty as measured by it.

How many poor are there? Policies to deal with any problem begin with data defining the size and nature of the problem. The effort to measure poverty in the United States dates only from the 1960s. At that time, Michael Harrington's book, *The Other America*, focused the nation's attention on the problems of poverty. Poverty was, of course, widespread in the 1930s during the Great Depression. But the United States in the 1950s was a nation of plenty, an abundant society. Harrington's book revealed that poverty remained in this country and was, perhaps, a much greater problem than many people believed it to be.

Following the debate stirred by the book, an effort was made to quantify poverty using the absolute poverty approach. As a base, officials used the minimal nutritional requirements determined by the U.S. Department of Agriculture. One study suggested that $1000 per year would buy enough food to satisfy this minimal requirement for a family of four. Evidence showed that in 1955 the typical family spent approximately one-third of its income on food. Combining both studies, the Council of Economic Advisors adopted a **poverty threshold** of $3000 for a family of four in 1963. Families with incomes below the threshold were classified as

Incidence of poverty. The percentage of the population that falls into the poverty group by official standards.

In-kind transfers. Noncash government transfers, such as Food Stamps, subsidized housing, and medical care.

poor. The standard was adjusted to account for differences in normal family requirements. For example, a two-person family required less income than a four-person family in order to be "nonpoor." Currently, there are 48 official poverty thresholds, classifying families by age of household head, family status, and number of children.

The poverty threshold is also adjusted each year to reflect changes in prices. In 1985 the poverty threshold for a family of four (two adults and two children) was $10,989, up 3.6 percent from 1984. This increase reflected a rise in the Consumer Price Index, a measure of changes in average prices. If the threshold had not been increased, the standard of living associated with the poverty threshold would have declined as prices rose. (The same income buys fewer goods at higher prices.) In all, some 33 million persons in the United States had incomes below the poverty threshold in 1985. Put another way, the **incidence of poverty** was 14.0 percent of the total population. It is important to note that poverty statistics are based on family income *including cash transfers*. That is, the 14.0 percent of the population classified as poor are those who remain so despite receiving cash transfer payments from the government.

Opponents of the absolute approach make numerous arguments against poverty thresholds which, they believe, are too low. The original contention that three adequate meals for a four-person family could be purchased in 1955 for a total of $2.74 per day is termed unrealistic. They also note that the poverty threshold has fallen as a percentage of the median family income. In 1959 the poverty threshold for a four-person family was 49 percent of the median income; by 1985 it had fallen to 40 percent.

Criticisms also focus on the omission of those who barely cross the threshold. Officially classified as nonpoor, their standard of living is not significantly better than that of those classified as poor. Counting those whose incomes fell below 125 percent of the threshold would increase the poverty population by one-third to 44.2 million in 1985, and the incidence of poverty to 18.7 percent. Many of those who escape poverty do so by finding employment, but remain just above the threshold income. A single long spell of unemployment is enough to push such families back into official poverty.

Other critics suggest that the current approach may overstate poverty and inequality. They note that both poverty figures and income distribution data are based on *pretax income*. They argue that the income distribution data would probably reveal slightly less inequality if income were measured on an after-tax basis.[*] However, one study concluded that the poverty rate would have increased by about 10 percent in 1979 if federal and state income and payroll taxes had been considered.

More importantly, official income figures do not include **in-kind transfers** such as the value of subsidized housing, Food Stamps, and medical care. This exclusion is important because of the tremendous growth in such transfers. More-

---

[*] As we noted in Chapter 16, many economists believe that the overall tax system is roughly proportional, which is why the income distribution is relatively equal in the middle range. We also noted that Browning suggested that, prior to 1986, the overall tax system was somewhat progressive at both ends of the distribution and somewhat reduced equality. For evidence on the effect of taxes on poverty, see Timothy Smeeding, *Testimony Before the House Ways and Means Committee*, Institute for Research on Poverty, Discussion Paper No.740-83. The 1986 revisions in the tax code effectively removed most of the working poor from the tax roles.

Category and group	Number of persons below poverty threshold (in thousands)			Percentage of group with income below poverty threshold		
	1959	1973	1985	1959	1973	1985
All persons	39,490	22,973	33,064	22.4	11.1	14.0
65 and over	5,481	3,354	3,456	35.2	16.3	12.6
Children, under 18	17,208	9,453	12,483	26.9	14.2	20.1
In families headed by women	10,390	11,357	16,365	50.2	34.9	33.5
Blacks	9,927	7,388	8,926	55.1	31.4	31.3
65 and over	711	620	717	62.5	37.1	31.5
Children, under 18	5,022	3,822	4,057	65.6	40.6	43.1
In families headed by women	2,906	4,564	6,215	70.0	55.4	53.2
Hispanic	n.a.	2,366	5,236	n.a.	21.9	29.0
65 and over		95	219		24.9	23.9
Children, under 18		1,364	4,605		27.8	39.6
In families headed by women		971	2,338		55.5	55.7

Source: U.S. Bureau of the Census, Current Population Reports, P-60 Series, No. 154, *Money Income and Poverty Status of Families and Persons in the United States: 1985.*

Exhibit 18.5
Poverty by Population Group, 1985

over, such transfers enable a family to increase its standard of living. In 1984 some 82 percent of those officially classified as poor received at least one type of in-kind transfer payment. Including the market value of food and housing subsidies as income would have reduced the poverty population by about 10 percent to 30.1 million, and the incidence of poverty from 14.4 to 12.9 percent. Including the market value of medical care lowers the poverty population to 22.6 million, or 9.7 percent of the population.[*]

There is widespread agreement that food and housing subsidies should be recognized along with cash transfers. The inclusion of medical services is more controversial, since only those who require medical care receive direct assistance. Moreover, these payments, while certainly helpful, cannot be used to put food on the table or heat the home.

Who are the poor? Although it is important to know how many people are poor, it is also important to know whether poverty exists more within certain parts of the population than in others. Exhibit 18.5 shows that the incidence of poverty among various groups is uneven, which is another indication of inequality. A slightly higher than average percentage of persons under 18 years of age are poor. The differential is considerably higher for blacks. Over one-third of all black

---

[*] Data on noncash benefits can be found in U.S. Bureau of the Census, Current Population Reports, Series P-60, *Characteristics of Households and Persons Receiving Selected Noncash Benefits: 1984.* The effect of including noncash benefits on poverty statistics is found in U.S. Bureau of the Census, Technical Paper 55, *Estimates of Poverty Including the Value of Noncash Benefits, 1985.*

families are poor, and almost one-half of black children are members of poor families.

Poverty is also a greater problem for single-parent families headed by women. More than one-third of all persons living in such families are poor, as are more than one-half of all black and Hispanic families headed by women. This group constitutes a growing percentage of the poor population. In 1959, about one-fourth of the poor lived in single-parent families headed by women. In 1985, these families accounted for about one-half the poverty population. Many of these poor fell into poverty as a result of the death or departure of a working man. Many are only temporarily poor and manage to escape poverty when the head of the household finds full-time work, remarries, or both. For others, the change in family structure begins a significant period of low income.

Not all the groups shown in Exhibit 18.5 have experienced increased rates of poverty, however. As you can see, the overall incidence of poverty and the number of poor persons decreased greatly between 1959 and 1973. In 1959, over 20 percent of the population, or nearly 40 million persons, were below the poverty threshold. Since that time, the incidence of poverty for the aged, for blacks, and for persons living in families headed by women has been substantially reduced. The federal government's "war on poverty," begun in the 1960s, won less than a complete victory. But the reduced incidence of poverty in the 1960s and 1970s is certainly in part the result of government transfer programs.

On the other hand, the number of persons living in low-income households and the incidence of poverty have not declined further from their low point in 1973. In fact, the sluggish performance of the economy in the late 1970s and early 1980s caused the number of poor and the incidence of poverty to rise to levels not seen since the mid-1960s. Perhaps as important are demographic changes, especially the rise in the number of households headed by women. Some improvement in the poverty statistics has occurred as the economy recovered from its low of the early 1980s. But the general persistence of poverty in specific groups suggests that eliminating or even reducing it below the level of the 1970s may be difficult.

Dynamics of poverty. There is an important drawback to the official statistics on poverty: They do not distinguish the temporarily poor from the persistently poor.[*] About one-fourth of the population will fall into the poverty population in any ten-year period. But there is a large turnover in the poverty population: About one-half the poor of one year escape from poverty the following year.

The temporarily poor are virtually indistinguishable from the general population. Their poverty generally stems from short-term unemployment, birth of a child, divorce, or illness. But about one-half of the poor—approximately 5 percent of all households—are persistently poor. Individuals in this group are more likely to be elderly, black, and in families headed by women.

The distinction between the temporarily and persistently poor has important implications for antipoverty policies. The temporarily poor seem quite able to escape from poverty rather quickly. Persistent poverty appears to be a smaller, but perhaps more difficult, problem than official statistics would indicate.

RECAP

Poverty can be defined and measured either in absolute terms—the number of individuals with less than a minimum standard of living—or in relative terms—the degree to which income is unequally distributed. The official U.S. government definition of poverty is based on the absolute approach.

Both the number of poor in absolute terms and the incidence of poverty have decreased since 1959, but significant numbers of poor people remain. Poverty is unequally distributed. The incidence of poverty is considerably higher than average among blacks and individuals in families headed by women.

About one-half of the poor in any year are only temporarily poor and can expect to escape from poverty in a short period of time; the other one-half are persistently poor.

---

[*] Duncan, *Years of Poverty, Years of Plenty.*

CAUSES OF POVERTY
AND INEQUALITY

One of our objectives in this chapter is to assess current and past public efforts to reduce poverty and inequality. But we must first consider the causes of poverty because rational policies must address these causes. In fact, the different causes of poverty have led various economists to propose widely varying policies. Although the data that we have presented so far reveal the extent of poverty, they do little to help us identify its causes, although they do identify particular groups that have specific problems. As you will see, the causes of poverty are also the causes of inequality.

Distinguishing causes from correlates. As you read about the causes of poverty, be careful not to confuse the *correlates* of poverty with its *causes*. To illustrate, consider that children make up a large portion of the poor population. That is, age is correlated with poverty. However, age does not necessarily explain or cause poverty. Similarly, we know that blacks are more likely to be poor. That is, race and poverty are correlated. But why? Does discrimination limit opportunities both to invest in and to use human capital? We know that blacks have less education than whites. But is less education a cause of poverty? We might better ask why blacks have less education. When discussing poverty and discrimination, we must be careful to distinguish causes from correlates. Causes provide an explanation; correlates merely raise additional questions.

Inadequate Income from Labor

We know that income and resource markets are directly linked and that some three-fourths of all household income comes from wages and salaries. Thus it is natural to examine the labor market for causes of poverty and inequality. To explain poverty, then, we must understand why labor incomes for some groups are low.

Contrary to popular myth, a large percentage of the people aged 18 and over who live in poverty *do* work. About 40 percent of the poor aged 15 and above worked during 1985. In fact, almost one-third of the poor adults who worked had full-time, year-round employment. However, both the percentage who work and the percentage who work full-time are significantly lower for the poor than for the nonpoor. Clearly, a full explanation of poverty must include reasons why the poor have relatively little work experience and receive relatively low wages.

We can identify only a few factors that might explain why some individuals receive low income from work. Labor income is a product of the wage level and the quantity of labor sold. Thus explanations of low incomes must account for either low wages or low quantities of labor sold.

Inadequate Demand for Labor

The decline in the incidence of poverty in the 1960s was partly the result of strong economic growth, which provided high employment and many new jobs. The failure of the incidence of poverty to decline further in the 1970s and 1980s is related in part to relatively slow economic growth and periods of high unemployment. In 1980–1981, unemployment reached its highest level since the 1930s. High unemployment was a major reason why 8 million more persons were

Percent in poverty

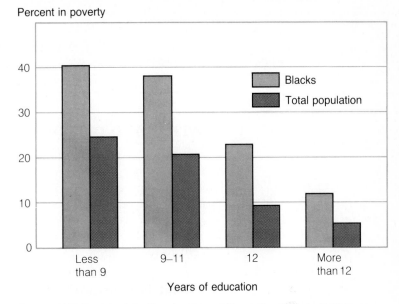

Exhibit 18.6
Correlation of Education and Poverty by Race, 1984 (for persons aged 22 and above)
This graph indicates a correlation between education and poverty. The more education an individual has, the lower the probability is of that person being poor. The greatest drop in the poverty rate is associated with high school graduation. Blacks have a high incidence of poverty in each educational group.

Source: U.S. Bureau of the Census, Current Population Reports, P-60 Series, No. 152, *Characteristics of the Population Below the Poverty Line: 1984.*

classified as poor in 1982 than in 1979. It also helps to explain why the incidence of poverty rose from 11.4 percent to 15 percent, the highest since 1965. As the economy recovered, the poverty rate fell slightly.

Poverty and Human-Capital Deficiencies

Low wages and high unemployment may be the result of low human capital. Exhibit 18.6 shows how education (number of years of schooling) correlates with poverty. The greater the amount of education completed, the lower is the percentage of poverty. The greatest drops in the incidence of poverty are related to graduating from high school and to attending college. This pattern is true for blacks as well as whites, although a higher percentage of blacks are poor, regardless of educational attainment.

It seems clear that some individuals are poor because they have little education. About 50 percent of the poor, but more than 70 percent of the nonpoor, have at least a high school education. Educational levels help to determine a person's marginal productivity and hence wage level. Education is also used to ration scarce job opportunities among various applicants. On the other hand, higher education is not a guarantee against poverty. Some 5.3 percent of those with at least one year of college are also poor.

In searching for the causes of poverty, we have to consider educational differences between the poor and the nonpoor. But we also must explain both why educational differences exist and why an education does not guarantee income security. Low levels of education and poverty are correlated, but lack of education per se is not a cause of poverty. Education may be an individual cure,

Economic discrimination. Income inequality caused by hiring, firing, promoting, or paying a wage differential on the basis of some factor, such as race, sex, or age, that has no direct relationship to marginal productivity.

but addressing poverty on a massive scale also requires high employment in the economy as a whole. Education does help us explain the distribution of unemployment: Those with less education experience more unemployment. It also helps us understand the occupational distribution: Those with more education are concentrated in the highest paying jobs.

POVERTY AND DISCRIMINATION

Earlier in this chapter, we showed that the incidence of poverty is significantly different for men and women and for whites and nonwhites. (For example, the incidence of poverty in 1985 was 11.4 percent for whites but 31.3 percent for blacks and 29.0 percent for Hispanics.) These and other data suggest that economic discrimination may be a cause of poverty. In this section, we explore the meaning of economic discrimination and examine some evidence on the relationship of poverty to race and sex.

What Is Economic Discrimination?

Throughout this textbook we have focused on rational economic decision making. A rational employer, seeking maximum profits, would hire the best-qualified person and promote (or at least give a raise to) the individual with the greatest marginal productivity on the job. **Economic discrimination** exists when an employment decision is based on some factor not directly related to marginal productivity. For example, hiring, firing, promotion, and wages have no direct relationship to race, sex, or age. An employer who acts as if they are related is practicing economic discrimination.

Occupational differences by race and sex. Exhibit 18.7 shows significant occupational differences by race and sex. A higher percentage of women than men are employed in administrative support (clerical) and service occupations. Moreover, black women are more heavily concentrated than white women in service occupations. Black men are much less likely than white men to be executives, administrators, or managers. They are more likely than white men to be service workers and operatives, fabricators, and laborers.

Because earnings vary greatly by occupation, differences in the distribution of occupations contribute to overall income differences. In general, occupations in which women and blacks are clustered have lower weekly earnings than those in which white men predominate. And women and blacks are typically clustered in the lowest-paying categories *within* each of the broad occupational groups. Women in professional specialties are more likely to be nurses or elementary school teachers than doctors, lawyers, or college professors. Neither occupational differences nor the resulting income differences are clear evidence of discrimination, but the data certainly makes us ask why these patterns exist.

Discrimination: Inefficient and inequitable. Economic discrimination is both inefficient and inequitable from society's perspective. Inefficiency results when individuals with superior economic productivity are rejected in favor of those with poorer qualifications. In addition, most people believe that discrimination is inequitable. Whatever our feelings may be about equality of income as

Occupational category	Men		Women		Median weekly earnings
	White	*Black*	*White*	*Black*	
Executive, administrative, and managerial	13.9%	6.2%	10.0%	6.0%	$511
Professional specialty	11.9	6.6	14.6	10.7	500
Technicians	3.0	2.1	3.2	3.1	416
Sales	11.9	5.2	13.7	8.7	351
Administrative support	5.4	8.6	29.8	26.5	300
Service	8.5	17.6	17.0	28.3	223
Precision production, craft, and repair	20.7	16.0	2.3	2.6	408
Operatives, fabricators, and laborers	19.8	34.0	8.2	13.7	301
Farming, forestry, fishing	4.9	3.7	1.2	0.4	217

Source: U.S. Department of Labor, Bureau of Labor Statistics, *Employment and Earnings,* January 1987, Tables 21 and 56.

Exhibit 18.7
Occupational Distribution by Sex and Race, 1986

a desirable goal, equality of opportunity most often is part of our concept of equity. We believe that individuals using comparable skills and talents and seeking similar jobs should be treated equally. Discrimination violates this standard and is therefore viewed as being inequitable by most people.

Reasons for economic discrimination. Since discrimination is inefficient and inequitable, why does it exist? The reasons vary and are complex. Some individuals may discriminate because of personal prejudices. In addition, some employers discriminate because either the majority of their present work force or their customers demand it. In that case, the employer may well be acting rationally (that is, maximizing profits) by practicing what appears to be economic discrimination.

As we have consistently noted, markets provide strong incentives for efficiency. However, the economic power of other employees or customers can create inefficiency, as you have seen in other contexts. What we observe as discrimination, then, may be an attempt by some groups to exercise economic power. If economic power does not exist, discrimination cannot be maintained without economic sacrifices.

Institutional Discrimination

Institutional discrimination.
Any practices in social institutions that result in differential and inequitable treatment of individuals on the basis of race, sex, age, or some other characteristic not related to economic productivity.

In addition to economic discrimination, where equally qualified individuals receive unequal treatment, economists also study institutional discrimination. **Institutional discrimination** refers to economic and social forces that *create* inequality. For example, if Hispanics are systematically excluded from some educational opportunities, the educational system may be guilty of institutional discrimination. Social forces (not individual acts) may establish an economic role for women that limits their access to training. The resulting income, wage, or occupational differences thus stem from institutional discrimination, even if no overt individual acts of economic discrimination take place.

Differences versus Discrimination

In order to relate any form of discrimination to occupational differences, we must answer several questions. How much are the differences in occupational distribution the result of (1) less education or other elements of human capital and (2) personal preferences? If women voluntarily seek occupations that allow for a dual role as breadwinner and homemaker, is this discrimination? If blacks voluntarily choose to acquire less education and thus get poorer jobs, is this discrimination?

These questions can be answered both *yes* and *no*. Some economists believe that occupational differences largely reflect personal preferences or talents. Others believe that discrimination, not personal preference, is the principal explanation. Different explanations lead to different policy proposals. Some economists take a narrow view, supporting only the notion that equally qualified individuals should be given a reasonably equal chance in the labor market. Others would attack all forms of discrimination—economic, educational, or social.

The government's answer to these questions has been to regulate private decisions. Both the labor market and related institutions, such as educational systems, are regulated in an effort to ensure that individuals get "a fair chance and a fair shake." (The entire blame for discrimination, however, cannot be placed on the private sector. Government itself has been guilty of discriminatory employment practices.) We explore some government policies aimed at reducing discrimination in the next section.

ANTIPOVERTY AND ANTIDISCRIMINATION POLICIES

In the 1960s many new government programs were designed and implemented to ease the plight of the poor and to reduce, if not eliminate, economic and institutional discrimination. In this section we briefly discuss some of the government policies that deal with poverty and discrimination. Both policy areas are a source of continuing debate. Some people feel that government efforts in these areas are inadequate and that more could and should be done. Others, including members of the Reagan administration, are critical of past efforts and argue that government actions are often unnecessary, ineffective, and too extensive. Public opinion and public policy appear to be swinging toward less, not more, governmental action—at least for the time being.

Antipoverty Policies: The Range of Options

Government has two policy options for antipoverty efforts. One is transfer programs, both cash transfer payments and in-kind transfers. The second is labor-market programs, including employment and training programs and antidiscrim-

RECAP

Poverty results from a variety of factors. Inadequate demand for labor—poor economic growth and high unemployment—cause higher rates of poverty. Individuals who have limited human capital experience higher poverty rates. Temporary poverty can also result from divorce, death of a spouse, or illness.

Overt or economic discrimination is the differential treatment of two individuals on the basis of some factor, such as race or sex, that has no relationship to productivity. It offers a possible reason why two equally qualified individuals might be treated unequally in the labor market.

Institutional discrimination, which refers to social customs or forces that might, for example, result in excluding some groups from educational opportunities, offers a possible explanation for why two individuals might enter the labor market with unequal human capital.

Discrimination on any basis other than productivity results in inefficiency and is generally thought to be inequitable. Discrimination may reflect personal preferences of employers or a response to consumer preferences and employee pressure.

ination efforts. As you will see, government has used both options in its war on poverty.

The policy option—or a mix of the two—that society chooses depends on the characteristics of the people it seeks to help. The largest single group (almost 50 percent) of the pretransfer poor consists of individuals over the age of 65. Since few people expect this group to earn a significant amount of money by working, most programs aimed at helping the elderly poor are transfer programs.

The same expectation holds for two other groups: the disabled and single women with one or more children under the age of six (one-eighth and one-sixth of the pretransfer poor, respectively). While their problems differ, both the disabled and the single mother have handicaps. Some disabled people have severe labor-market limitations and are candidates for transfer payments; others can profit from job training programs. The high cost and scarcity of day care keep many single mothers of young children from working.

Taken together, these three groups account for almost two-thirds of the pretransfer poor. As a result, transfer payments appear to be a rational policy option for the majority of the poor. However, as children grow older the single mother can benefit from job training and job assistance programs.

The remainder of the poor are expected by society to be able to earn income and pay their own way. Some of these individuals are faced with inadequate labor demand, either in general or for their particular skills. Others work full-time but earn low wages. If society wants to aid these poor, labor-market programs can be used to improve their human capital and hence the income they can receive from working. For this group, the important policy questions are whether transfers, job training, and employment assistance should be available.

Transfer Policies: Efforts and Results

As we have noted, transfer payments can be in cash or in kind. Both approaches are used in the United States. In this section, we examine current transfer programs and discuss their effectiveness in reducing poverty.

Cash transfers. By simply transferring a sufficient amount of income, we could raise every family above the poverty threshold. Our society has not taken this simple approach, however, in part because it would violate some of our basic values. It would also break the connection between work and reward, reducing work incentives and efficiency. However, the federal government and the states do provide several important cash transfer programs.

The largest cash transfer programs are the Old Age, Survivors, and Disability and Health Insurance Programs—known collectively as Social Security. In 1986 some 37 million persons received monthly Social Security payments totaling $192 billion. Most of these payments do not go to the poor but to persons who have never been poor. Not specifically designed as an antipoverty program, Social Security pays individuals who contributed to the system in the past (or their dependents). But because many older Americans have little income other than Social Security payments, this program has been effective in reducing poverty. Social Security is the major source of income for over 60 percent of the elderly who receive payments; it represents 90 percent of the income for one-fourth of this group.

Some cash transfer programs are specifically designed to help the poor. More than $26 billion was transferred to a monthly average of 16 million persons in 1985 under the three major welfare programs: Aid to Families with Dependent Children (AFDC), Supplemental Security Income (SSI), and General Assistance (GA). The first two are funded by the federal government, the third by the states; all are administered by the states.

Aid to Families with Dependent Children.

Started in the 1930s as part of the New Deal, the government expected this program to last only until the economy recovered from the Great Depression. Instead, it is still operating and has increased dramatically in size. This is the program that most people think of as "welfare." It is directed largely to single-parent households, but about one-half the states have a similar program for two-parent households. No transfers are made to families without children. As of December 1985, more than 3.7 million families (nearly 11 million individuals, including 7.5 million children) were receiving an average payment of $348 per month.

Supplemental Security Income.

This program is designed to aid both the aged poor and the disabled poor. In 1985 an average of 4 million persons per month received SSI payments. About two-thirds of this group are blind or disabled.

General Assistance.

This program is the smallest in dollar terms and is directed at those not covered by other programs. Totally state run, it varies considerably from state to state. In 1984 about 1.3 million individuals received general assistance payments.

In-kind transfers.

As noted earlier, not all government transfer programs give cash to the poor. In-kind transfers include Food Stamps, Medicare, Medicaid, the school lunch program, and subsidized housing, to name some of the larger programs. In 1984 a total of 76.7 million households—88 percent of all households in this country—received at least one type of in-kind transfer. Some of these transfers—school lunches, for example—benefit the middle class as well as the poor. Expenditures for in-kind transfers aimed at the poor amounted to $51.5 billion—over one-half for Medicaid—and reached 61 percent of the poor.

Effects of transfers on poverty.

Cash transfers to the poor, although large, do not eliminate poverty. All of the official income and poverty statistics include cash transfer payments as income. To eliminate poverty in 1985 (at least by official standards) would have required additional cash transfers of almost $48 billion.

Although transfer programs treat only the symptoms of poverty, they are highly progressive, reducing the number of people classified as poor by about 65 percent. Social Security, unemployment compensation, and other transfers not aimed specifically at the poor raise about one-third of the poor above the poverty threshold. In-kind transfers do the same for another 25 percent. But cash transfers to the poor—AFDC, SSI, and GA—reduce the poverty population by less than 5 percent.

The failure of cash transfers to do a better job of reducing poverty reflects in part the fact that only about 50 percent of the poor typically receive cash assistance payments. In addition, the typical monthly payment is only about one-half of the amount necessary to bring the average family up to the poverty threshold. Both these facts reflect a policy choice that trades off some generosity in welfare assistance for some incentives to work.

The importance of transfers varies for different groups. The official poverty rate of the elderly, for example, is currently below that for the rest of the population, resulting almost entirely from cash transfers. As the percentage of poor who are children or persons in single-parent families headed by women increases, the importance of transfers to the poor is likely to increase as well.

Transfer Programs: Problems and Issues

Not surprisingly, income transfers are a source of considerable debate. From recent efforts to reform the system, we can easily identify the major issues for transfer programs.

Are current levels of cash and in-kind transfers appropriate?   Some critics argue that current transfer payments are inadequate. They claim that in most states payments do not bring individuals up to the official poverty threshold, a level they view as barely adequate to begin with. Others suggest that transfers are more than generous and should be reduced. The issue of transfer adequacy is complicated by the effects of transfers on work efforts and by the direct relationship between adequacy and overall costs. The more generous the transfers, the greater is their contribution to poverty reduction, but the weaker are the work incentives and the greater the costs.

In addition to the total amount of transfers, economists and politicians dispute the propriety of in-kind transfers instead of cash transfers. Advocates of in-kind transfers argue that this policy ensures that the poor receive what society deems necessary. Critics charge that in-kind transfers deprive the poor of the right to make decisions about their lives.

Is the current transfer system equitable?   Some critics see gaps in current transfer programs, especially the limited transfers available to the working poor and single, nonelderly individuals. Others criticize the inequity of low transfers paid by some states compared with the high transfers paid by other states. Finally, some people suggest that equity considerations should include the effects on those who pay for the transfers. Is it fair, they ask, for some to work and pay for those who do not? These critics argue that some individuals receiving transfers have a higher standard of living than many who work.

How do transfers affect work incentives?   A major issue in the debate is the extent to which transfers reduce the willingness of individuals to work and thus cause inefficiency. Some argue that the present welfare system provides adequate work incentives to many of the poor. They point to low payments and the fact that many poor people, especially those in families headed by men under the age of 65, are ineligible for most cash transfer programs. On the other hand, work incentives are weakened because welfare payments are greatly reduced when

Threshold income (dollars)	Pretransfer income (dollars)	Negative income (dollars)	Negative tax transfer (dollars)	Posttransfer income (dollars)
10,000	0	−10,000	−5,000	5,000
10,000	2,000	−8,000	−4,000	6,000
10,000	6,000	−4,000	−2,000	8,000
10,000	10,000	0	0	10,000

Exhibit 18.8
Example of a Negative Income Tax

the recipients work. Attempts to modify transfer programs involve major debates over the necessity and strength of work incentives.

Do transfers create welfare dependency? Some people are concerned that present welfare policies may create a cycle of dependency. However, the evidence from the Institute of Social Research shows that only 2 percent of those receiving welfare are dependent on it for extended periods of time. Most use welfare as it was intended, as temporary relief. Moreover, most of the children reared in families receiving welfare did not receive welfare once they left home and established households of their own.

Negative Income Tax

Because of the controversy surrounding transfer programs, many economists and politicians have sought alternative solutions. One economic solution is a transfer of income using a **negative income tax**. Under this approach, a family's (or individual's) actual income is compared to an official poverty threshold. To the extent that the income is above that threshold, the family would pay income taxes in the usual manner. However, if the income is below that amount, the family or individual would report a *negative income* on its tax return, and the government would transfer income to the family.

Consider the example presented in Exhibit 18.8. With an official poverty threshold of $10,000, a family with no actual income would have a negative income of $10,000. If the negative income tax rate is 50 percent, the family would receive a negative tax, or transfer, of $5000 (50 percent of their negative income). Thus $5000 would be the minimum income level after transfers. A family with a pretax income of $6000 would have a negative income of $4000 and would receive a transfer of $2000. Thus the family's income would be $8000, or $6000 from nontransfer sources and $2000 from the transfer. When earned income reached or exceeded the threshold level, a family would be subject to regular income taxes.

The negative income tax offers several advantages over the present system. The negative tax would be comprehensive (a large number of the poor are currently ineligible for most welfare programs). It would be simple, offering possible savings in current administration costs. And the negative tax supports

Negative income tax. A system that guarantees a minimum income to the poor through government income transfers, the amount of which depends on how far below the poverty threshold a family's income is.

work incentives: Individuals would have more income if they worked than if they did not.

If the negative income tax is so ideal, why has it not been implemented? The major problem is not the general concept but the specific details. A number of the proposed welfare reforms suggested in recent years have been modeled on the negative income tax. However, the specific threshold income, once specified, becomes a target both for those who want to raise the levels and those who want to lower them. In 1978 the Carter administration proposed a reform along the lines of a negative income tax. The proposal died in Congress because the committee considering it could not agree on the specifics of the legislation.

Reagan programs: Some new directions.

During the 1960s and 1970s, a number of changes in the system of federal transfers increased the support provided to the poor. In contrast, the 1980s have seen cutbacks in many programs that President Reagan viewed as overly generous and undermining work incentives. Eligibility standards were tightened and many of the poor actually received lower benefits. For example, individuals cannot receive AFDC payments if the value of their assets, excluding their home and car, exceeds $1000. In addition, a maximum limit on total income was established at 150 percent of the amount that each state sets as a standard of need, which in most states, is below the federal poverty threshold. These changes were designed to focus the programs on those whom President Reagan referred to as the "truly needy," limiting eligibility to the lowest-income groups.

However, these changes have also reduced work incentives. Previously, the working poor could deduct expenses for child care and work-related costs from actual earnings before any reductions in welfare payments were made. The Reagan administration limited the deduction to $75 per month in work expenses and $160 per month for child care. In addition, under the old rule, individuals who worked lost only $2 in welfare payments for every $3 earned. The new rules call for a 100 percent reduction in welfare payments for every $1 earned (after a four-month period). Thus this rule has reduced incentives for individuals to take part-time or low-paying full-time jobs.

To offset these disadvantages the Reagan administration proposed compulsory work, or "workfare." This plan would have required welfare recipients to work (on community service projects, for example) in order to continue receiving payments. Although Congress did not require states to adopt workfare programs, it did authorize them to adopt such programs if they wished. By 1986 almost one-half the states had done so, but in most cases workfare has been used in only a few counties on a trial basis. Two notable programs are those in California and Massachusetts. In both cases the programs appear to be moderately successful in helping those receiving welfare—principally young single mothers—to obtain employment. The success of the Massachusetts program is due in part to the fact that it is not compulsory. Thus those most motivated and likely to succeed are the most likely to participate.

Finally, President Reagan proposed that the federal government turn over responsibility for AFDC and Food Stamps to the states. Opponents countered that federal participation in these programs helps to even out differences among state programs and in incomes from state to state. Poorer states, which often have a higher proportion of poor people, would have a difficult time maintaining current payments, adding to the disparities. To date, Congress has shown little interest in relinquishing the federal role in the welfare system. Complaints about the current system abound, however, suggesting that the debate about welfare reform will also continue.

Although not specifically a welfare reform, the changes in the federal income tax system in 1986 did offer some help to the working poor, many of whom are ineligible for current welfare assistance. The new system raised the amount of income a family can earn before paying any income tax. By eliminating income taxes for them, the changes effectively raised the income of the working poor.

Labor-Market Programs that Aid the Poor

We noted earlier that the low wages earned and quantity of labor sold by the poor sometimes relate to labor-market problems. Income transfers may help the poor live better, but transfers do not address the reasons for their poverty. Since the early 1960s, government has tried to improve the success of the poor in the labor market in two ways: (1) it has provided employment and training programs; and (2) it has attempted to reduce discrimination. Judging from studies of income mobility, these programs may be very important in aiding the long-term, or persistently, poor.

Employment and training programs. If the poor have inadequate human capital, solving this problem may help reduce poverty. The first government employment program for the poor started in 1962. The total number of persons served by such programs has always been small relative to the total number of poor people. And evidence of program effectiveness is somewhat mixed. Over the past 25 years, some employment programs have succeeded, while others have failed.

The extent and types of training programs offered is another policy area in which the Reagan administration made changes. In 1982 Congress approved the Job Training Partnership Act. This new program is much smaller than the Comprehensive Employment and Training Act (CETA) program it replaced and is aimed primarily at helping to train individuals for jobs in the private sector. Moreover, most of the administrative responsibility for the program rests with state and local governments, which may be a precedent for future training and employment programs.

Antidiscrimination programs. As with employment and training, the government has played a role in reducing economic discrimination in the labor market for many years. The first major piece of legislation, the Civil Rights Act of 1964, has been amended and extended. For the most part, public policy declares that economic discrimination is illegal. When employers or other parties are found guilty in court of specific acts of discrimination, they can be required to pay restitution for past actions.

Because of our earlier discussion about the inefficiency and inequity of economic discrimination, you may wonder why antidiscrimination programs are controversial. One point of debate is the proper extent of government action. Most people believe that government should declare discriminatory acts illegal.

Affirmative action programs.
Government requirements that employers adopt programs and make extraordinary efforts to recruit, hire, and promote individuals from specific groups, such as women, blacks, and Hispanics, that have been subjected to past economic or institutional discrimination.

But should government also require **affirmative action programs**? That is, should private employers, colleges, and others have to increase the proportion of persons previously excluded by economic and institutional discrimination that they employ or admit?

Those who define discrimination only as overt acts based on prejudice often reject affirmative action programs as inappropriate. Those who seek to eliminate both economic and institutional discrimination generally support such programs. Because these disagreements focus on interpretation of facts and differences in values, the controversies over these programs are likely to continue.

CONCLUSION

As you have seen, much of the poverty in the United States reflects failures in labor markets. However, separating the amount of poverty that results from individual failures (poor occupational choices or decisions about how much to work) and the amount that results from market inefficiencies is not easy. To the extent that market failures such as economic discrimination exist, corrective action may be justified in order to improve efficiency.

However, many programs are meant to correct perceived inequities, which involve trade-offs between efficiency and equity. The principles of rational choice apply to such decisions, forcing us to recognize benefits and costs in terms of both equity and efficiency. Moreover, we must recognize the benefits and costs of governmental policies aimed at correcting poverty and discrimination. As always, we should compare the cost of a government program to the benefits and effectiveness of alternatives, including that of doing nothing. However, even the principles of rational choice cannot end rational disagreements over the direction and extent of public policies that address the problems of poverty and discrimination. These issues involve value judgments and interpretations of facts, which will continue to be debated.

SUMMARY

1. In this chapter we examined the meaning and significance of poverty and discrimination in the United States, including their effects on efficiency and equity.

2. Inequality is tied to efficiency in a market economy because wage differences provide incentives to use labor resources efficiently. Thus the goal of equity sometimes conflicts with that of efficiency.

3. Income in the United States is unequally distributed. However, the inequality exists largely at the two ends of the distribution. Middle-income households receive almost their proportionate share of total income. Economists use a Lorenz curve to display graphically the distribution of income.

4. Income distribution changed little from 1950 to 1985.

However, income mobility is significant: One-half of those living in poverty one year usually escape poverty during the next year.

5. There are basically two approaches to defining poverty. The absolute approach considers a family (or individual) to be poor if its income does not allow it to attain some minimum standard of living. The relative approach considers a family (or individual) to be poor if its income is significantly below average.

6. By the official definition of poverty in the United States (based on the absolute approach), 33 million persons (14 percent of the population) were classified as poor in 1985. Both the total number of poor people and the incidence of poverty have declined since 1959. How-

ever, the recession in 1980–1981 and slow economic growth subsequently pushed the number of poor people in the 1980s to levels not seen since the 1960s.

7. In seeking to understand the causes of poverty, it is important to distinguish causes from correlates. Causes provide explanations; correlates tend to suggest additional questions.

8. Because individuals in our society earn income primarily through the sale of their labor resources, we can examine the labor market to find causes of poverty. Low wages can be explained as the result of either low productivity (limited human capital) or discrimination. Limited quantity of work sold may be the result of high unemployment in the economy as a whole or of lack of demand for particular skills. Although the poor as a group have less work experience than the nonpoor, a significant percentage of the poor do work or seek work.

9. Economists distinguish between two types of discrimination. Overt, or economic, discrimination occurs when equally qualified individuals are treated unequally in the labor market. Institutional discrimination may cause individuals to enter the labor market unequally prepared. To the extent that discrimination exists in either form, the economy will fail to achieve maximum efficiency; moreover, discrimination is now generally considered inequitable in our society.

10. One type of antipoverty effort in the United States—income transfers—includes cash transfer programs, such as Supplemental Security Income, Aid to Families with Dependent Children, and General Assistance. In-kind transfer programs include Food Stamps, subsidized housing, Medicare, Medicaid, and subsidized school lunches. Antipoverty transfer programs are aimed primarily at those whom society recognizes cannot work.

11. Three questions are raised about the current transfer system: (a) Are transfer payments at an appropriate level? (b) Is the current system equitable? (c) How do transfers affect work incentives and therefore efficiency?

12. The second type of antipoverty effort seeks to increase the skills of the poor and eliminate discrimination, enabling the poor to earn enough income to escape from poverty. Questions about this approach relate to the extent to which government should be involved in employment training, and affirmative action programs.

KEY TERMS

Lorenz curve, 445
Absolute poverty approach, 447
Relative poverty approach, 448
Poverty threshold, 448
Incidence of poverty, 449
In-kind transfers, 449
Economic discrimination, 454
Institutional discrimination, 455
Negative income tax, 460
Affirmative action programs, 463

QUESTIONS FOR REVIEW AND DISCUSSION

1. Why might two individuals have different incomes? To what extent does this difference raise questions about efficiency? To what extent does it raise questions about equity? To what extent does it reflect choices made by the individuals? To what extent does it suggest that society is at fault?

2. Explain why you agree or disagree with each of the following statements.
   a) Without the potential for inequalities, a market system couldn't function efficiently.
   b) Because economists stress that inequality is connected to efficiency, the more inequality there is, the more efficient the economy will be.

3. In-kind transfers are not included when incomes are calculated for comparison with the poverty threshold. Do you think that either of the following should be counted as income for the poor? (a) Food Stamps. (b) Medicare and Medicaid payments. Why? How would their inclusion give a more accurate picture of the income distribution and incidence of poverty? How might their inclusion overstate the income of the poor?

4. Assuming that a certain number of transfers are to be made, what are the relative merits of cash versus in-kind transfers? Consider both from the standpoints of society and of the recipients.

5. Suppose that society wanted to eradicate poverty today and for the future *at a minimum cost*. Would it be desirable to have both transfer and labor-market programs in the mix of policies? Could one or the other do the job alone?

6. A negative income tax has three features: (a) a threshold income level; (b) a negative income tax rate; and (c) a break-even income level. Using the example in the chapter,
   a) calculate the break-even income level if the income tax rate increases to 75 percent;
   b) explain how a change in the tax rate affects work incentives;

c) determine the threshold income level if a proposed negative income tax has a break-even income level of $8000 and a tax rate of 50 percent; and

d) explain why legislators (and economists) would be concerned with keeping the threshold level of income reasonably low.

7. Comment on the statement: "If the economy functions efficiently and if individuals are given a reasonably equal opportunity to invest in human capital, there is likely to be little concern over equity."

8. Explain why economic discrimination is inefficient. Is institutional discrimination also inefficient?

9. What arguments would you use to support the position: "The distribution of income created by the marketplace is equitable." What arguments would you use to criticize that position?

Economic Encounters
South Africa: A National Policy of Discrimination

South Africa, a country built on the remnants of white empires, is 70 percent black. However, a national policy of apartheid, or "separateness," puts the political and economic power in the hands of the white minority. Although blacks outnumber whites by more than four to one, apartheid efficiently keeps the black people in an economic straitjacket in terms of poor education, low-paying menial jobs, and poverty-level living conditions. How does this national system of discrimination affect the country's economy?

Sagging Economy In 1984 South Africans lost jobs at a rate of 1000 per week because of the falling price of gold (a major export), a decline in the value of the rand (South Africa's currency), a prolonged drought in agricultural regions, and inflation. Experts say that the South African government could greatly aid its economy by dropping its costly policy of discrimination.

First of all, the cumbersome apartheid system requires duplicate salaries and benefits. For example, South Africa currently pays one minister of education for whites, one for each of the colored groups, one for each of the Indian tribes, and one each for the ten black homelands. Multiply these figures by all the government ministers and their related staffs and the burden that apartheid places on the South African economy becomes evident.

Second, according to some reports, more than 8 percent of the black South African workforce was unemployed in 1985—about 506,000 people. Other estimates go as high as 3 million. Experts predict rising unemployment rates will lead to more violence and destruction of property. In turn, the government will spend more money on security forces to control rioters—money that could be put to better use within the economy.

Most importantly, apartheid virtually guarantees that the South African economy will fail to achieve its full economic potential. Discrimination in the educational system denies blacks the opportunities to develop talents and increase productivity. Discrimination in the labor market confines blacks to the most menial jobs. The majority of blacks still work in service jobs as butlers, doormen, nannies, and maids, or as laborers in industries such as mining. These jobs are low-paying and offer little opportunity for advancement.

Apartheid puts political and economic power in the hands of the white minority.

As a result, the talents of blacks are underutilized and they are unable to receive the experience and education to improve their productivity. Although the income of South Africans, black and white, is relatively high by African standards, black incomes are only 30 percent of white incomes, with few opportunities for significant improvements.

Frustration Mounts The apartheid system is increasingly resented by blacks. Not only are black communities separated from white ones, but often blacks of different social and tribal backgrounds are walled off in "townships" of shanties, sometimes with no water or sewage systems. Such social divisions make it almost impossible for blacks to join forces to gain any political or economic control.

Since 1984, when blacks began a more organized movement of racial unrest, more than 2300 people have been killed. Surprisingly, nearly three quarters of the victims were blacks killed by other blacks. Experts think that this "black-on-black" violence stems from their fury at being segregated in ghetto townships where traditional authority has given way to chaos. Born in poverty and racial discrimination, black youths devote themselves to violence instead of education and employment.

The Controversy over American Involvement For years, the United States attempted to ease the effects of apartheid in South Africa, pouring in dollars to subsidize jobs and social programs for blacks. Between 1983 and 1986 alone, U.S. corporations spent an estimated $150 million in South Africa, including funds for medical care, schools, and housing. Between 1976 and 1986, U.S. firms followed the Sullivan Code, a policy of nondiscriminatory employment. During this period, U.S. companies were often seen as enclaves of open hiring practices, offering managerial and technical jobs to blacks on the basis of merit.

Unfortunately, even well-intentioned U.S. involvement had its limitations. Needs of the companies' various constituencies—shareholders, the antiapartheid lobby at home, and South Africa's black community—were not always compatible. Blacks' resentment grew over a policy they perceived as a shortsighted, scattergun approach to social development.

Their resentment was fueled by American corporate blunders such as installing computer workshops in schools where many youngsters were still illiterate, and erecting the $10 million, ultramodern Pace Commercial College in the midst of the poverty-stricken Soweto township. In 1986 that school closed its doors following a demonstration during which black students burned an American flag and sent the U.S. Chamber of Commerce spokesman fleeing with the flag's remnants draped over his shoulders.

U.S. Corporate Help Grinds to a Halt As change came slowly—or not at all—to South Africa, blacks became disillusioned with America's limited ability to cause lasting reforms. U.S. corporations were equally frustrated by the apparent invulnerability of the apartheid system.

Beginning in 1985, under pressure of divestiture movements back home, American companies—among them IBM, Kodak and Coca-Cola—withdrew investments of about $2.8 billion from the South African economy. Some South African blacks responded by accusing the U.S. of raising blacks' expectations for beating apartheid and then letting them down. Even South Africans who supported divestment criticized the way American companies departed—like "thieves in the night," without grooming any black managers to take over.

The no-win situation has left black and mixed race communities feeling betrayed by Americans. Some black community leaders, headed by the U.S.S.R.-backed African National Congress argue that the West cannot be trusted and that capitalism brings only ruthless exploitation of native peoples. Such suspicion may make communism, not free enterprise, the economic force shaping South Africa's future.

Mother and child, residents of Crossroads township, draw water from a single neighborhood tap. Township households commonly have no running water or sewage systems. (Mark Peters/Black Star)

U.S. Economic Sanctions To place pressure on South Africa's white government to rethink its national policy of discrimination, the United States joined in a world boycott of South African goods in 1986. South Africa, a country rich in minerals, diamonds, and rare metals, has always been proud of its healthy economy. By attacking that economy, the United States and other antiapartheid nations hoped to encourage change.

As part of the sanction movement, the United States curtailed the import of many South African goods, placed a ban on sale of computers to South African agencies that enforce apartheid, and restricted loans to South African banks and companies. Other nations banned trade on a variety of products, from fruit and vegetables to coal and steel. These sanctions forced South Africa to bypass normal channels for foreign trade and greatly increased the country's cost of trade.

What Next? Have divestment and sanctions really put significant pressure on the white minority? Many observers feel these policies have not had the desired impact. South African products continue to be marketed internationally. Moreover, the South African economy is quite self-sufficient; it can feed itself—indeed, it exports food. It has abundant raw materials and has long made gasoline and other fuels by crushing coal from its large reserves. While the sanctions have been costly to South Africa, the economy is far from collapsing; the government appears willing to bear the costs rather than abandon apartheid.

While there have been costs, the government of South Africa appears willing to bear these costs rather than abandon apartheid. South African President P.W. Botha, remaining adamant despite economic sanctions, said in 1986, "Let it be. We have the faith, the inherent ability and the natural resources to ensure our future. South Africa will not crawl before anyone."

So, the white South African government tightens its belt for more battle, this time not just against its own blacks, but the world; and many observers still ask, "How much longer before outright civil war tears South Africa apart?"

CHAPTER 19

Microeconomic Issues and Government Policies

T he importance of economics is in the way it helps us understand the real world and analyze real-world problems and issues. Economic analysis is especially important in understanding the effects of economic policies. In this section we consider several particular microeconomic policy issues. These issues are not abstract. They apply to real situations in which government plays an important role in determining prices and resource allocation.

In presenting these issues we show you (1) how to apply economic principles to real-world problems; and (2) how to analyze the efficiency and equity effects of alternative economic policies. After studying this introduction and the cases that follow, you should understand the methods of economic analysis. You will also see how lost we would be in trying to explain or predict outcomes and effects without economic principles to guide our thinking.

Applying the Principles of Rational Choice to Policy Analysis

If we apply the principles of rational choice, first introduced in Chapter 2, we can structure economic policy analysis in terms of a series of questions. The answers we obtain help us to determine whether a policy helps the economy achieve its economic goals.

Why is government action being proposed? It is useful to begin with an analysis of why government action is proposed. In theory, a smoothly functioning market economy, left to its own devices, should be able to achieve allocative and technical efficiency. In addition, some economists also believe that distribution of income would be reasonably equitable. In the real world, however, things are not so simple. For a variety of reasons that we discuss in this textbook, markets sometimes fail to operate smoothly. When markets fail—and even sometimes when they do not—government may step in to try to correct the failure. The job of economic analysis is to determine whether such intervention is desirable.

In order to determine whether government action is desirable, we must first ask why it is being proposed. Has the market failed to function efficiently? Is the goal of equity not being achieved by the market's distribution of income? What is the particular issue that requires addressing? (Note that we say *issue*, not problem, because *problem* implies that government action is necessarily desirable and helpful.)

We can often understand why policies are being proposed by asking: "Who stands to gain if the policy is implemented?" For example, we must be suspicious of U.S. shoemakers when they propose high tariffs (taxes) on imported shoes "to protect consumers from poor-quality shoes produced by foreign competitors." Not all situations require government action, and to decide whether government intervention is appropriate, we must apply the principles of rational choice.

What are the extra benefits and costs of the proposed policy? As we note throughout this textbook, the principles of rational choice require that you identify and compare the extra benefits and extra costs of a proposed policy. Thus you do not begin with a statement, "In my opinion . . . ." Rather, you must analyze facts and apply economic principles, keeping several points in mind.

Sunk costs are irrelevant.   You should not consider sunk costs, that is, resources already invested. Thus when deciding whether to spend more money to complete a nuclear power plant, for example, you would ignore money already spent; it cannot be "unspent." In economic analysis, it is important to concentrate on likely *future* benefits and costs. If the plant will generate $500 million in future benefits but cost an additional $1 billion to complete, it is not worth the effort.

Economic decisions are rarely all-or-nothing choices.   For example, the choice does not have to be between eliminating pollution or living with current levels. You can analyze the extra benefits and extra costs associated with reducing pollution a little bit, a lot, or by stages.

All extra costs are relevant.   Direct costs of government actions—salaries of government administrators, for example—are relatively easy to identify but are only part of the costs. You must also weigh the indirect costs incurred by businesses and individuals who must comply with the regulations. Further, some policies have a cost known as a *moral hazard*—the danger that government action will undermine economic incentives. For example, high Social Security benefits may reduce the incentive for private pensions and lower the incentive for older citizens to work. Government insurance against crop failure may lower the incentive for farmers to protect their crops or to obtain private insurance. Moral hazard and other indirect costs of government policies do not necessarily mean that government action is unwarranted. But sound economic analysis requires that you weigh *all* costs against expected benefits.

Policies that do not work can be eliminated.   To be useful, a proposed policy should improve the economy's performance. That is, you measure the benefits of policies by the resulting improvements in efficiency and/or equity. For example, a policy that provides information about health risks associated with food products or occupations may enable consumers and workers to make more informed and thus efficient choices. But not all government programs help the economy achieve its goals. A program that trains poor people for nonexistent jobs will not reduce the incidence of poverty. Moreover, it is not enough that a policy provide *some* benefits. The extra benefits must *exceed* the extra costs.

Economic policies inevitably involve trade-offs.   As the principles of rational choice imply, any decision involves costs and benefits. Some groups will benefit and others lose under any policy. Thus all policies involve trade-offs, often between efficiency and equity. For example, a government regulation that requires steel mills to install pollution-control devices will raise the cost of steel produced in the United States. As a result, U.S. steelmakers may lose sales to foreign steel producers and some steelworkers may lose their jobs. The policy forces a trade of jobs and steel production for improved air quality. Economic analysis is helpful in identifying how a policy affects efficiency. But it cannot determine whether the trade-offs required by a policy are equitable. However, economic reasoning can help establish who will benefit and who will be harmed. Without that information, rational decisions cannot be made.

Are there superior alternative policies?   In addition to deciding whether the benefits of a government action outweigh its costs, you must also ask whether another policy might address the problem more efficiently or equitably. Likewise, rejecting one particular policy does not necessarily mean rejecting all government action; an acceptable alternative policy may be available. But no government action is an alternative that must always be considered. The best policy option, whether action or doing nothing, is the one that will most improve the economy's performance.

Why Economists Disagree about Government Involvement

It is often said (in jest) that if you laid all the economists on earth end-to-end, they would never reach a conclusion. Economists generally agree that efficiency and equity are the economic goals against which actual performance should be judged. Why, then, do they disagree on the appropriate role of government?

Some economists disagree because of difficulties with measuring economic performance. It is not always easy to establish whether a market has failed or the exact size of the benefits and costs of a government policy. Economists who expect certain results from a proposed policy may therefore rationally disagree with those who expect different results. In addition, recall from Chapter 2 the distinction between *positive* and *normative* statements. Many disagreements between economists reflect different personal opinions. Thus even when they agree on the expected results of some policy, economists may propose different solutions.

Economists who recommend limited government intervention usually stress two major costs: (1) reduced economic efficiency; and (2) restricted personal freedom and individual choice. In contrast, economists who support broad government involvement sometimes accept efficiency costs for what they believe are more equitable outcomes. Different values, emphases, or interpretations of equity often lead to formulation of different policies.

Despite their disagreements, economists have much in common. Importantly, they agree on the validity and importance of economic analysis and evidence. When economic theories and evidence are conclusive, economists tend to join ranks. For example, a large majority of economists agree that international trade restrictions reduce efficiency and that ceiling prices on rents eventually reduce the quantity and quality of apartments.[*]

Conclusion

In the cases that follow, we use the preceding framework when examining the issues and evaluating policy alternatives. We take a positive (rather than a normative) approach to policy analysis, forecasting potential outcomes rather than advocating solutions. In the final analysis government policies are determined by political judgment. The role of economic analysis is to identify potential benefits and costs and winners and losers—and to keep the discussion centered on a rational approach to the issues.

---

[*] See, for example, Kearl, *et al.* "A Confusion of Economists?" *American Economic Review,* May 1979, pp. 28–37.

19.1 THE FARM "PROBLEM" AND AGRICULTURAL PRICE SUPPORTS

Agriculture is one of the most competitive industries in the United States but also one in which government plays a major role. There are over 2 million farms in the United States. Even within a more narrowly defined product area—such as beef or apples or eggs—there are thousands of farmers. As a result, an individual farmer cannot affect market price.

Because agricultural markets are very competitive, you might expect little government regulation of the industry. However, since 1933, government has used a system of price supports, direct subsidies, and production controls to attempt to raise and stabilize farm income. Between 1986 and 1990, the government is expected to spend as much as $70 billion on these programs. But is government regulation of agriculture desirable? Do its benefits outweigh its costs? Are there alternatives to current policies that would improve agricultural performance?

Why Is Government Involved in U.S. Agriculture?

Current U.S. farm policies are rooted in the characteristics of demand and supply of agricultural products and the historical experience of the 1920s and 1930s. Since that time, farm policies have attempted to address two issues: unstable short-run farm prices and low long-run farm incomes. But why are farm prices particularly unstable? Why are farm incomes low? Can we connect these issues to one or more economic goals?

Promoting price stability and allocative efficiency. Farming has always been risky in part because farm prices and farm income vary widely from year to year. Price and income instability result from two factors: (1) unpredictable year-to-year shifts in demand and supply caused by weather conditions in both the United States and the rest of the world; and (2) price inelasticity of both demand and supply of farm products.

Supply of agricultural products depends on biological processes. Regardless of demand, another growing season is required to produce another crop. Unpredictable changes in weather conditions occur frequently. Good weather in the United States means an increase in the supply of domestic farm produce. Poor weather in other countries means an increased demand for U.S. farm products. Weather and the growing season limit farmers' ability to respond to changes in demand. Those two conditions make supply quite price inelastic in the short run. In addition, demand for most farm products is also price inelastic; that is, people do not eat much more when prices fall.

As we discussed in Chapter 4, a change in demand causes a relatively large change in price when supply is price inelastic. Similarly, price changes resulting from changes in supply are greater when demand is price inelastic. Thus even small shifts in demand and supply cause large changes in farm prices. Of course, demand for specific farm products can be highly price elastic. Consumers will switch from beef to chicken when relative prices change. Demand for wheat and other farm products traded internationally is also price sensitive. However, studies do indicate significant price inelasticity of demand for farm commodities in general.

The price inelasticity of demand also makes farm income unstable. In fact, good production years can be disasters in terms of farm income. When the weather cooperates and U.S. farmers produce a bumper crop, supplies increase and prices fall. Because demand is price inelastic, prices fall (in percentage terms) more than quantities sold increase. As a result, farmers receive lower total revenues but incur higher costs for harvesting, storing, and marketing their products. Thus farm incomes may fall substantially. Government has responded with programs that attempt to stabilize farm prices.

In terms of the economy as a whole, there is no real reason to favor stable prices. In a market economy, prices are signals. For example, falling prices resulting from less demand should signal farmers to produce less. But some economists argue that the variations in farm prices are extreme and may therefore cause producers to overreact. Because overreaction is inefficient, some efforts to stabilize prices may be warranted. Moreover, stabilizing prices also benefits consumers, especially low-income consumers, who otherwise face large swings in food prices.

Promoting higher farm incomes and equity.   In addition to stabilizing prices, government action in agricultural markets has been proposed as a way to improve equity. Farm programs were first implemented in the 1930s, when the Great Depression and a series of droughts hit farmers very hard. As a result, the average income of farm families was only 40 percent that of the rest of the families in this country. Farmers complained that this discrepancy was inequitable. They demanded that government help them achieve a "fair price" for their products and government responded.

Nevertheless, low farm incomes persisted for several reasons. First, the income elasticity of demand for farm products is quite low. That is, people do not eat a great deal more as their incomes rise. Thus as the U.S. economy grew steadily in the 1950s and 1960s, the demand for farm products rose more slowly. At the same time, significant improvements in farm productivity sharply increased supply. The number of farms dropped significantly, but total farm production increased steadily. The slow increase in demand and the large increase in supply combined to exert downward pressure on farm prices.

But falling prices and low incomes are also a signal that too many resources are devoted to agriculture. In a smoothly functioning market, low prices and income would cause some farmers to leave the industry, thus decreasing market supply and increasing agricultural prices and farm incomes. When the number of farms has declined enough, remaining farmers should be able to earn enough income to justify continuing to farm. Hence persistent low income must reflect either immobility of resources or a willingness to accept lower income in return for the benefits of being a farmer.

In fact, there *has* been a tremendous exodus from farming. In the 1930s there were 6.8 million farmers, or about three times as many as today. But many economists believe that government farm programs—because they raised farm income—have slowed down the transfer of resources. Farm income increased in the 1970s as worldwide demand for U.S. farm products increased. Under these pressures (and on the advice of some government agencies), many farmers expanded operations, borrowing heavily to do so. But in the early 1980s, a drop in demand caused farm incomes to drop sharply. Some of the farmers who had taken on large debts were unable to survive the drop in farm prices, prompting many midwestern legislators to press for farm "bailout" measures.

Critics of current and past farm programs are skeptical of programs that seek to raise the income of any special group. Why, they argue, should farms be treated differently from other businesses that fail when demand cannot justify their existence?

What Are the Benefits and Costs of Farm Programs?

Whether raising farm income *should* be a goal of government policy is not an economics question. But economists can analyze the benefits and costs of alternative ways of achieving price stability and income support. Government policies to raise and stabilize farm prices may take one of three forms: (1) price supports; (2) target prices and deficiency payments; and (3) production controls. In this section, we consider who benefits from each of these programs. These programs do not apply to all farm products, however. The major crops affected are wheat and other grains, milk and other dairy products, cotton, tobacco, and sugar. Moreover, each of these programs involves costs to society.

Price-support system. In the Agricultural Adjustment Act of 1933, Congress established a system of price supports and the Commodity Credit Corporation (CCC) to oversee the price-support system. When the act was passed, most people expected the price-support system to be temporary. They assumed that the economy would recover from the Great Depression and that farm prices would return to "reasonable levels." Further government help would then be unnecessary. Instead, downward pressure on farm prices continued. The "temporary" price-support system remains in place today, with only minor variations from the original system.

The price-support program guarantees farmers a specified minimum price for their crops. For example, suppose that the government sets a price support of $3.50 per bushel on the agricultural commodity shown in Exhibit 19.1.1. Because the price support is above the equilibrium price of $3.00 per bushel, buyers respond by reducing quantity demanded. At the same time, farmers respond by producing larger quantities. As you would expect from any price support above the equilibrium level, a surplus results. In this case the surplus is 60 million bushels per year (the difference between the 280 million bushels bought and the 340 million bushels produced).

Because the goal is to raise farm incomes, it is not enough to simply set a minimum price. Any price above the equilibrium price simply reduces the amount that farmers can sell. In fact, for farmers to sell all that they have produced (340 million bushels), the market price would have to fall to $2.50 per bushel. (Note on the demand curve that the public will buy 340 million bushels only if the price is $2.50.) To raise farm income, the Commodity Credit Corporation will buy any portion of a crop that cannot be sold at the support-price level.

Actually, the CCC has two approaches. It purchases butter, cheese, and nonfat dry milk, buying directly some $1.8 billion of dairy products in 1985. In the case of grains, however, the CCC makes loans at the support-price level. If the market price rises above the loan price, farmers can sell their products at the higher price and repay the loan. If the price remains below the support level, the CCC accepts the farmer's wheat or corn as repayment without any penalty. Both policies guarantee a minimum price for all production and result in the purchase of surpluses by the federal government.

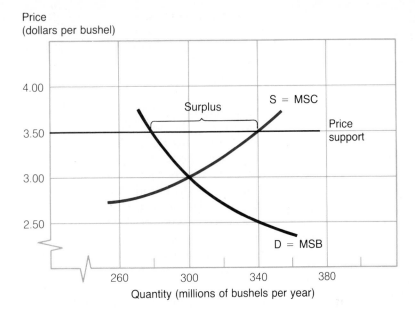

Exhibit 19.1.1
Effect of Farm Price Supports
Setting a support price of $3.50 per bushel—above the equilibrium price of $3.00 per bushel—will create a surplus of 60 million bushels per year. Allocative inefficiency results because the actual production—340 million bushels—exceeds the quantity for which marginal social benefit (measured by the demand curve) equals marginal social cost (measured by the supply curve).

Exhibit 19.1.1 shows the effects of CCC price supports. As you can see, support prices raise farm revenues. Without the program, farmers would have produced and sold 300 million bushels at $3 per bushel, receiving $900 million. With the program, they produce and sell 340 bushels at $3.50 per bushel, receiving $1190 million. Of this figure, consumers pay $980 million ($3.50 per bushel for 280 million bushels). The government (CCC) pays $210 million ($3.50 per bushel for 60 million bushels).

Price supports, in effect, transfer income from consumers and taxpayers to farmers. (Note, however, that the transfers do not affect all farmers equally. Larger, more successful farmers receive the majority of all transfers.) But gains to farmers come at a cost to others in the economy. Consumers pay more for less. As taxpayers, they also pick up the government's share of the bill. In addition, some farmers also lose. Meat producers must pay higher prices for feed grains but do not receive supports for beef, pork, and chicken production.

Price supports create both short-run and long-run resource misallocation. In the short run, farmers tend to grow more of what the government supports and less of other products that could be sold in unsupported markets. Production fails to match social benefits and social costs, as represented by market demand and supply curves. Expanding production beyond market equilibrium means producing goods that add more to social costs than to social benefits. In addition, price supports do not eliminate the basic problem. As we noted earlier, despite a large reduction in the number of farms over the past 50 years, too many resources are still devoted to farming. Price supports have slowed the rate at which farmers have gone out of business in response to market signals.

Finally, what is the CCC to do with the acquired surplus? It cannot sell without forcing prices down to $2.50. And if it drives prices down, the CCC will have to buy the whole crop—domestic and international. Who would pay farmers $3.50 per bushel when the government is selling at $2.50 per bushel? Critics of government farm programs note that the United States has lost a significant share of the world market because support prices exceed market prices. In theory, the CCC sells the surplus from good production years during lean production years to keep prices from rising. In this way, CCC actions should help stabilize prices. However, farmers have successfully fought these efforts, knowing that such sales would drive prices down. The price-support system was designed to protect farmers against severe price declines and consumers against severe price increases and shortages. The result has been constant surpluses (except during the 1970s when demand was very high) and increased prices for consumers.

Despite these problems, many farmers (and their representatives) strongly favor price supports. Indeed, for many years farm groups have lobbied for *parity pricing*, that is, setting farm prices according to resource costs. In particular, they would like to use the same price-to-cost ratio that occurred spontaneously in 1910–1914 (an excellent time for farm incomes). However, opponents of these measures—including most economists—point to the potential inefficiencies of such a price system.

Target-price deficiency-payment system. In 1973 the Nixon administration introduced a variation of the price-support system. That administration wanted agricultural markets to reach equilibrium (especially in good years) so that U.S. farm products would be more competitive internationally and consumers would pay less for food. To achieve this goal, the government established a system of target prices and deficiency payments. A *target price* is a government-guaranteed price to the farmer. However, in this program the government does not buy any surplus. Farmers sell whatever they produce on the open market. The government then gives the farmer a *deficiency payment* equal to the difference between the price received and the target price.

Exhibit 19.1.2 shows the effect of a target price of $3.50 per bushel. Farmers base their production decisions on this guaranteed price. As a result, they produce 340 million bushels (40 million more than if they had to rely only on market demand). The demand curve indicates that they can sell this quantity only at $2.50 per bushel or less. Farmers thus receive $850 million from market sales. The government then pays farmers the $1.00 per bushel difference between the price received and the target price. The blue-shaded area represents the total deficiency payment of $340 million.

The target-price system differs from price supports in three ways. First, government does not acquire any surplus commodities. Second, consumers do not pay higher prices. Third, more of a product can be sold, especially internationally. But target prices do pose problems similar to those of price supports. Both systems encourage excess production and allocative inefficiency when the guarantee price is consistently above the equilibrium price. And both systems transfer income from taxpayers to farmers. As with price supports, the farmers who receive the most in deficiency payments are usually the successful farmers, not the rural poor.

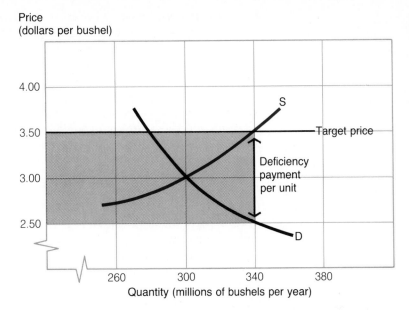

Exhibit 19.1.2
Effect of Target Prices and Deficiency Payments
A target price of $3.50 per bushel will cause 340 million bushels per year to be produced. Farmers must sell this quantity for $2.50 per bushel, the price at which 340 million bushels can be sold. Farmers receive a deficiency payment of $1.00 per bushel from the government, equal to the difference between the price at which they sell and the target price. The blue-shaded area indicates the total amount of deficiency payments made.

Production controls. You have seen that both the price-support system and the target-price system encourage surplus production when prices are set above the equilibrium price. Surplus production requires government purchases in the price-support system and government deficiency payments in the target-price system. These negative consequences for taxpayers and for the government's budget can be reduced somewhat if farmers will reduce production. Policies aimed at getting farmers to do so have been a consistent part of government farm programs since their inception.

In some cases government has restricted the number of acres of a particular crop that farmers may plant in order to be eligible for government supports. In 1985, for example, wheat farmers had to agree not to plant 30 percent of their acreage to be eligible for the target price. They received a payment of $2.70 for each bushel *not* produced on 10 percent of their idle land.

Production controls, especially when they involve cash payments, have the same drawbacks as price supports and target prices. All encourage inefficiency, transfer income, and have little success in reducing surpluses. Farmers naturally choose to leave the least productive portions of their farms idle. In addition, farmers often farm their remaining acres more intensively, using more fertilizer, for example. Thus average yields have actually risen under production controls.

Overall benefits and costs of agriculture policies. Studies indicate that the benefits of government agricultural programs—measured as the gains to farmers—have been less than the costs to taxpayers and consumers. According to the President's Council of Economic Advisors, the programs have increased farm incomes by some $9.5–$12.2 billion per year. However, the cost to taxpayers has been $10.3–$11.4 billion per year and the cost to consumers an additional $5.1–$7.6 billion per year. Comparing the benefits with the costs, it appears that the programs generate a net loss of $6–$7 billion per year. (The 1985 farm bill resulted in somewhat lower costs, but there is still a net loss.)

Are There Superior Alternatives to Current Farm Policies?

The government policies that have been in effect for many years are not the only possible approaches to the issues of low farm incomes and wide fluctuations in farm prices and incomes. Most economists agree that current policies have been quite expensive, in terms of both the government expenditures required and the inefficiency created. There are various alternatives, some government-based, some market-based.

Cash transfers. If it is desirable to raise the income of farmers and the rural poor, direct cash transfers (independent of farm production) would be simpler and more efficient than current farm programs. Such transfers would not encourage surplus production and excess capacity. They would also apply to the rural poor (who gain little under current programs) but not to wealthy and successful farmers who receive the most from current farm programs. Cash transfers would address concerns about income equity directly.

Lower price supports. The goal of protecting farmers from large price drops can also be achieved with alternative policies. If price supports were set below expected long-run equilibrium price levels, farmers would base their production decisions more on projected demand and supply rather than on government policies. Surpluses would be minimized, but farmers would be protected against large-scale price declines in any one year. Based on this idea, Congress lowered the level of price supports in the 1985 farm bill. It is still too early to know how the new price-support levels will compare with long-run equilibrium price levels (especially with regard to the international market for agricultural products). If price supports are indeed established below long-run equilibrium price levels, they should encourage efficiency and avoid the huge surpluses created by past programs.

Futures markets. Another alternative is for government to take no action at all. If farmers want to reduce the risk that prices will fall, they can sell their crops in *futures markets* before planting time. That is, a farmer can contract with a potential buyer and agree to sell a certain quantity at a specific price at some fixed date. For example, a wheat farmer could contract in February to supply 10,000 bushels of wheat at a price of $3.50 per bushel in November. In this way, farmers know in advance the price they will receive. Thus they do not require government price supports to avoid the risk of a price decline.

But farmers cannot avoid all risks if they utilize the futures markets. There is still the risk that prices may rise. In fact, when the Soviet Union agreed to buy

Warehousemen and truckers stand on a mountain of grain before the Walla Walla Grain Growers' elevator near Eureka, Washington. Government price-support programs have created huge surpluses of commodities such as this wheat—most of which was eventually shipped to Asia. (Michael Melford/Wheeler Pictures)

large quantities of wheat in the early 1970s, many farmers had already sold their crops in futures markets. They got the prices they had agreed on, but the buyers of the futures contracts made huge profits because of the increase in demand. In addition, there is the risk that the actual crop may be less than the quantity that a farmer has promised to deliver. If the overall harvest of a commodity is poor, the market price may be much higher than contracted prices. As a result, farmers risk substantial loss because they would have to pay premium prices to buy enough of the commodity to meet the terms of their contracts.

What has prevented implementation of alternative programs? With all the drawbacks of current farm programs, you may wonder why more alternative approaches have not been tried. Most critics of current programs believe that the persistence of farm programs is the result of lobbying by the special interest group that benefits most: large farmers. Farms with annual sales of $100,000 or more account for only 14 percent of all farms. But in 1984 they received 66 percent of all direct government payments, an average of $16,600 per farm. Smaller farmers, by contrast, receive very little support from current programs. Farm-program lobbyists also recognize that removing price supports would decrease the value of farmland, transferring even more wealth from landowners to taxpayers.

Unlike wealthy farmers, who gain much under current programs and stand to lose much under changes, consumers are not as well-organized and vocal. Moreover, while farm programs are expensive to taxpayers and consumers as a group, their effects on individual taxpayers and consumers are relatively small. With consumers not motivated to organize and push for changes, it seems likely that the farm lobby will continue to shape farm legislation in the future.

Conclusion

Many economists would like to see the system of price supports abandoned entirely. While this change may be in our society's best long-run interest, it would face considerable political opposition from farm groups. Moreover, it would certainly result in some difficult adjustments for farmers. Farmland prices—and the wealth of owners of farmland—would drop. Some farmers would lose their farms and be forced out of agriculture. These problems may justify smaller and slower decreases in price-support levels and efforts to smooth the transition to a smaller agricultural industry. But transition costs are not a sound reason to keep programs indefinitely. A long-run policy aimed at stabilizing farm prices and income must be more market-oriented to avoid compounding the problems of the past.

QUESTIONS FOR REVIEW AND DISCUSSION

1. To understand the effects of price supports on agriculture, consider how the industry would behave in the absence of government programs. Explain whether the following statements are true, false, or uncertain—*assuming that there are no government price-support policies.*
    a) Wheat farmers would be able to earn more if each one burned a tenth of each year's crop. (Why does economic analysis predict that farmers are *not* likely to do this?)
    b) In the long run, technological progress in agriculture will benefit consumers more than farmers.
    c) Farmers are always complaining that high costs of operation lower their profits. But they're unlikely to earn greater profits if fertilizer prices drop 10 percent.

2. One objective of price-support policies is to stabilize the prices of farm commodities. Recognizing this objective, answer the following questions.
    a) Why do economists argue that constant farm prices are generally undesirable?
    b) What are the social benefits of stabilizing farm prices? Would it also be desirable to stabilize the price of TV sets? (Are there differences that make stabilizing farm prices more desirable?)
    c) If Congress decides to stabilize farm prices with a price-support system, would it be more efficient to set price-support levels above or below the long-run equilibrium price level? Why?
    d) Farmers want protection against unexpected price declines. Critics of current farm programs argue that such protection is available in futures contracts. How do futures contracts work and how do they provide protection for farmers? Do they protect farmers against all risks?

3. Explain how (and why) government price-support policies have affected the price of farmland. What would happen to the value of farmland if the government announced that government price supports were being discontinued? Who would gain and who would lose as a result of such a policy change?

4. State the arguments in favor of eliminating government's role in determining farm prices and quantities produced. State the arguments in favor of continuing government's role (although not necessarily in its current form). If it were decided that government should help to stabilize prices, how should the program operate? (Consider the level of price supports, whether target or support prices are better, what the CCC should do with surpluses it may acquire, and other issues that you feel are important.)

19.2 DEREGULATION OF THE AIRLINE INDUSTRY

Almost from its beginning, the airline industry was highly regulated. In 1938, Congress passed the act creating the Civil Aeronautics Board (CAB). For the next 40 years, the CAB set prices and controlled entry into the industry. In 1978, Congress passed legislation that eliminated the CAB and the regulation of price and entry. Currently airline competition is virtually unrestricted. Was regulation ever really necessary? Did its benefits ever exceed its costs? Has deregulation been a better approach?

Why Did Government Become Involved in Airline Regulation?

We have noted that, in general, competition helps markets function smoothly and thus promotes allocative and technical efficiency. But regulation of airlines was proposed to prevent "excessive competition." Many costs of flying are fixed per flight (cost of the plane and salaries of pilots and flight attendants, for example). The marginal cost of adding another passenger to an existing flight is quite low. Proponents of regulation argued that without policies to prevent price competition, some airlines would set prices below long-run costs in order to drive out competitors. The result would be a small number of economically powerful airlines. Congress accepted this argument in 1938, and the airlines and CAB soon became strong supporters of continued regulation. They even argued that regulation was in the best interest of consumers, an argument that most economists now reject.

What Were the Benefits and Costs of Regulating the Airline Industry?

In response to the belief that competition would destroy the airline industry, the CAB set price floors to keep competition from forcing prices down and virtually prevented the entry of new competitors. The costs of this policy were higher prices for consumers and higher costs and lower profits for airlines. (If you are surprised that the airlines supported regulation, given these effects, so were most economists. Apparently, airline managers truly believed they were better off under regulation.)

Higher prices for consumers.   There is a lot of evidence that regulated prices were higher than competitive prices would have been. In the first place, the CAB often rejected requests by airlines for lower rates. In addition, the differences in rates charged by regulated and unregulated airlines were significant. Airlines that had no interstate flights were outside the jurisdiction of the CAB and could set prices as they saw fit. The price of a flight from Washington, D.C., to Boston (regulated) was twice that of a flight from San Francisco to Los Angeles (unregulated), although the distances were nearly identical. Similarly, it cost twice as much to fly from Washington, D.C., to New York (regulated) as from Houston to Dallas (unregulated).

Higher costs and lower profits for airlines.   You might think that with higher prices the airlines were able to earn economic profits. However, profits

(a) The market for air travel

Price
(dollars per passenger mile)

Quantity (millions of passenger miles per year)

(b) Costs for Skyhigh Airlines

Price and cost
(dollars per passenger mile)

Quantity (thousands of passenger miles per year)

Exhibit 19.2.1
Regulation and Nonprice Competition
In the absence of government price regulations, market price would be $10 per pas-senger mile (where D and S_1 intersect) and the typical airline would earn only a normal profit. A price floor of $15 per passenger mile initially makes each airline more profitable. But airlines may seek to attract travelers by offering more frequent flights and in-flight movies, for example. If all airlines do so, costs will increase—indicated by the shift in ATC and in market supply. This nonprice competition raises costs, reduces air travel, and eliminates economic profits.

under regulation were actually lower. To learn why, let's consider Exhibit 19.2.1, which compares market prices and Skyhigh Airlines' costs.

Exhibit 19.2.1(a) shows that in the absence of government regulation, market price would be $10 per passenger mile (where D intersects S_1). At that price, Skyhigh would supply 50,000 passenger miles per year (where MR_1 intersects MC_1 in Exhibit 19.2.1 b). The price is just enough to enable Skyhigh to earn a normal profit. What would happen if the CAB set rates at $15 per passenger mile? If Skyhigh continues to supply 50,000 passenger miles per year, it will earn an economic profit (the area of the blue-shaded rectangle).

But Skyhigh can increase its profits if it can attract additional passengers from its competitors. Its maximum profits occur when it supplies 70,000 passenger miles per year (where MR_2 intersects MC_1). To attract customers from its compet-itors by nonprice means, Skyhigh might (as many airlines actually did) offer more frequent flights, movies, meals, and other "frills." These extras would drive Sky-high's costs up, but the increased benefits of more passenger miles might more than offset these costs initially.

Unfortunately for Skyhigh, other airlines will no doubt counter by offering similar frills. Because these frills may have very little (if any) effect on total market demand for air travel, Skyhigh's flights will probably drop back to 50,000 passenger miles per year. At that point, the extra costs of frills will simply reduce Skyhigh's profits. If costs rise to ATC_2, as shown in this case, economic profits will be totally eliminated.

Although the Skyhigh example is hypothetical, airlines actually behaved in much the same way. Profits remained low because the costs of frills was high. Frills were the only means of competition; to survive, all airlines had to offer comparable services. But the airlines had little incentive to hold costs down because the CAB was willing to approve fare increases when costs increased. When wage costs rose—with the CAB willing to grant higher fares to cover the higher labor costs—the airlines had little incentive to accept losses from strikes.

Has Deregulation Been a Better Approach?

Problems in the airline industry under regulation provided strong support for deregulation, and in 1978 deregulation began. As economists had expected, one result was the entry of new airlines. Some, like People Express, emerged as nationwide competitors. Others entered to offer more regional and commuter services. In 1986 there were 100 airlines, compared with 36 before deregulation.

The entry of new firms and the end of CAB price floors also spurred price competition, lowering fares and raising industry profits. (One study estimated that travelers saved about $6 billion per year, while annual profits of the industry rose $2.5 billion.)[*] Competition also increased efficiency, as airlines were forced to watch costs closely. Fuller flights, lower labor costs, and more fuel-efficient planes have been some of the results.

Fears that deregulation would end services to small airports have proved to be unfounded. Larger airlines have reduced services, but smaller airlines have filled many gaps. In fact, in many cases, service is actually more frequent and more convenient than before. And because the smaller airlines generally buy smaller aircraft, their service is provided more efficiently than was the case when larger airlines were forced to serve these airports.

Deregulation has not been a total success, however. Some routes are still served by only two or three airlines. In part, this limited competition reflects limited gate space and landing rights at airports. Of concern to economists is that these rights are often controlled by older airlines and are a barrier to entry of new airlines. Moreover, prices on routes with limited competition appear to be somewhat higher than prices on more competitive routes. Proposals to solve these problems often focus on having the government market airport gate and landing rights. Such a policy would allow increased competition and would increase the efficiency of airport-space utilization.

In addition, the transition from a regulated to an unregulated industry has not been completely smooth for the airlines themselves. Since 1978, the airline industry has experienced numerous mergers, bankruptcies, and labor disputes. Between 1980 and 1982, the industry lost some $1.4 billion. Some of this turmoil is directly related to the effect of increased competition. But increased fuel prices in 1979 and the recessions in 1980–1982 also contributed. Mergers have already

---

[*] Steven Morrison and Clifford Winston, *The Economic Effects of Airline Deregulation.* Washington, D.C.: The Brookings Institution, 1986.

reduced the number of airlines from peak levels. In the long run the number of airlines is likely to be even smaller than it was in 1986. But economists disagree about whether this increase in concentration is cause for concern.

Conclusion

Despite the transition problems, the long-run economic results of airline deregulation appear economically desirable. Some economists believe that antitrust regulators must carefully monitor mergers to prevent significant concentration in the airline industry. But few economists argue for a return to the old system of regulation. Most agree that rate regulation in any largely competitive industry causes more problems than it solves.

QUESTIONS FOR REVIEW AND DISCUSSION

1. The CAB sought to prevent "excessive competition" by maintaining minimum prices. But by all accounts, prices were higher than they would have been without regulation.
   a) Why did airlines not benefit from these higher prices? Who did benefit?
   b) Why do economists generally agree that "excessive competition" did not justify rate regulation in the airline industry?
   c) Why did individual airlines continue nonprice competition if it did not increase profits?

2. The CAB also limited entry into the industry. In fact, between 1950 and 1974 it received 79 applications from companies that wanted to enter the industry; all were denied.
   a) If existing airlines were not earning economic profits, why did additional firms want to enter the market?
   b) Does the fact that existing airlines had excess capacity suggest that additional firms were undesirable? If so, from whose perspective?

3. There is evidence that the demand for airline travel is relatively price elastic, at least in the price range that existed under CAB regulations.
   a) If this is true, why would the airlines have preferred lower fares?
   b) What problems would the CAB have faced in trying to determine how much to lower fares?

4. Airports control the number of planes that can take off and land in the interests of safety. How would efficiency improve if the government were to market landing and takeoff rights? Who would stand to lose from such a policy?

19.3 DRUG SAFETY AND THE FOOD AND DRUG ADMINISTRATION

The history of government regulation of drugs is tied closely to tragedy. In 1938 the Massingale Company marketed a new, liquid form of sulphanilamide. The company had already sold the drug in tablet and capsule form. However, the key ingredient used to make the liquid form—diethylene glycol—caused the painful death of some 100 people before the drug was withdrawn from the market. The publicity surrounding this event spurred Congress to pass the Food, Drug, and Cosmetic Act of 1938. This law requires drug producers to demonstrate the safety of a new drug to the Food and Drug Administration (FDA).

In 1960 the Merrell Corporation sought FDA permission to market a tranquilizer known as thalidomide, which was already being widely used in Europe.

Under its procedures at that time, the FDA could have approved the drug automatically, since it had no evidence that the drug was unsafe. However, an FDA examiner, Dr. Frances Kelsey, kept returning the application to Merrell on the grounds of insufficient information, preventing the drug's approval. In late 1961, evidence linked the use of thalidomide by pregnant women to birth defects, and Merrell withdrew its application. Congress amended the Food, Drug, and Cosmetic Act to strengthen the FDA's role in testing for drug safety. The amendment also required the FDA to certify that approved drugs are effective.[*]

Does the fact that current laws and regulations resulted from past tragedies mean that government regulation is desirable? From an economic viewpoint, do current rules promote efficiency and/or equity? Has the market failed, requiring government intervention?

Why Is Government Involved in the Drug Industry?

Those who support government regulation of drugs argue that imperfect information creates a market failure. That is, without government regulation, consumers (and their physicians) would not have enough information about safety and effectiveness to make informed and rational decisions.

Not everyone agrees that government action is necessary, however. Critics of government regulation counter that market forces protect consumers. They argue that a company that markets lethal, defect-causing, or ineffective drugs will be penalized by buyers. Both the threat of lawsuits and the long-term damage to its reputation thus cause a drug company to be interested in marketing only safe products. Supporters of this view point to the actions of companies to withdraw and repackage many over-the-counter capsule medications in 1986 after a series of product-tampering cases.

However, none of us want to find out *after* the fact that using a drug can produce birth defects and other terrible side effects or even cause death. And no one would choose to waste money on a drug they knew was ineffective. Yet the safety and effectiveness of drugs are not obvious. Most physicians cannot keep up with the most recent pharmaceutical research and tend to rely on information supplied by drug companies. When information is difficult to obtain or interpret—as in the case of drugs—the market may fail.

Because of the health risks involved in market failure, many economists believe that government must play some role in the drug market. But they disagree sharply over the best approach for government action. Some take what can be called a *consumer-sovereignty view*. They believe that government should limit its role to ensuring the provision of adequate information and argue that individual consumers and their physicians are willing to accept different degrees of risk. According to this view, informed consumers are better judges of whether the risks are acceptable than are government regulators.

In contrast, other economists take what can be called a *consumer-protection view*. They argue that information on drug safety and effectiveness is difficult to assess, even for trained physicians. According to this view, it is impossible to be an "informed consumer," and government must limit the market to safe and effective products in order to protect consumers.

---

[*] A good summary of the issues and history of drug regulation is presented in Kenneth J. Meier, *Regulation: Politics, Bureaucracy, and Economics.* New York: St. Martin's Press, 1985.

What Are the Benefits and Costs of FDA Regulation?

As you would expect, economists who hold different views about methods of government drug regulation also disagree about the benefits and costs of such regulation—and thus about the appropriate role of the FDA. Debate centers on three points: (1) the agency's regulatory strategy; (2) whether the FDA should actually prohibit the marketing of drugs or limit its role to providing information; and (3) whether the FDA should even be concerned with effectiveness.

FDA's regulatory strategy. The FDA's current strategy is the result of 1962 amendments to the Food, Drug, and Cosmetic Act. Congress directed the FDA to approve only those drugs determined to be safe and effective by stringent testing. The FDA thus requires extensive (and expensive) testing of new drugs before allowing them to be marketed. This consumer-protection approach results in lower risks, but higher costs. Prior to 1962, the FDA had allowed drugs to be marketed unless there was proof that they were unsafe or ineffective. Expenses for testing and the opportunity cost of waiting for drugs to reach the market were both lower. That policy was closer to the consumer-sovereignty approach, but its lower costs (as the thalidomide case showed) also involved higher risks.

Both approaches have strengths and weaknesses. Following the consumer-protection approach, the FDA may provide too much safety and keep some very useful drugs off the market, or at least delay their entry. Using the consumer-sovereignty approach, the FDA may provide too little safety and allow too many unsafe products to reach the market. But which approach is better? There is no clear-cut answer. As always, we must weigh the benefits and the costs of each approach. The annual cost of testing new drugs rose from about $4 million in 1962 to $50 million in 1986, while the number of new drugs marketed each year declined. In almost every case, a new drug is marketed in Europe long before it is available in the United States. Clearly, regulations can sometimes discourage the development of new drugs. And there is little doubt that safety standards impose high costs on U.S. consumers. But the life-and-death nature of drugs makes it very difficult to put a price tag on the benefits of a cautious approach or the costs of a less-regulated approach.

In terms of news-media attention, an unsafe drug that causes numerous deaths attracts far more coverage than do the deaths of people denied unapproved drugs that might have saved them. Although such attention is obviously one of the reasons for the FDA's approach, it does not mean that the approach is the most rational economic choice. The FDA has been sensitive to criticisms of its delays, especially when a new drug promises benefits unavailable with current drugs. In recent years the FDA has established a "fast-track" testing procedure for drugs with potentially great benefits. But reduced delays increase risks. For example, the FDA allowed marketing of Oraflex (an antiarthritic medicine) and Zomax (a painkiller) under the fast-track procedures. Both were later linked to deaths, and the subsequent publicity gave support to those who favor high standards and a cautious approach.

Should the FDA only provide information or ban unsafe products? The FDA is very much concerned with drug safety. No drug is 100 percent safe, and there is always a risk that an individual will have an adverse reaction to some particular drug. The principles of rational choice remind us that from the standpoint of allocative efficiency, government regulations should *not* increase safety without limitation.

Rather, the principles of rational choice suggest that there is an "optimal" amount of safety. Thus the FDA must consider the extra benefits of greater safety when setting standards. But it must balance these benefits against the extra costs of rejecting new prescription drugs that fail to meet its standards. The stricter the safety standards, the more drugs the FDA will reject. Rejecting drugs as unsafe provides benefits in the form of greater safety; but the *extra* benefits decline as standards are raised further and more safety is provided.

Tighter standards also mean higher costs and fewer drugs. Rejecting a drug means that it will not be available to individuals who might, in fact, benefit from the drug. The "optimal" quantity of drug regulation, or drug safety, occurs when the extra benefits of additional safety equal the extra costs. This safety level may vary from drug to drug and from individual to individual. The terminally ill may be quite willing to risk the long-term complications of a drug that can prolong their lives, for example. Proponents of a consumer-sovereignty approach thus argue that regulations may be both inequitable and less efficient than a market approach by forcing all consumers to buy more safety than they want.

In general, economic principles suggest that banning drugs may impose high costs on some individuals. Banning is the correct approach only when the social benefits are less than social costs for even the first unit produced. This may be the case with drugs that are clearly toxic to all individuals, but is not generally true.

Should the FDA require proof of effectiveness? Even more controversial is the legal requirement that drugs be effective. Critics of this policy believe that the FDA should concentrate on safety, leaving consumers and physicians to determine effectiveness. Requiring proof of effectiveness causes delays and raises costs which, to the critics, are not justified by extra benefits. The FDA's role, if any, should be limited to providing information about potential effectiveness.

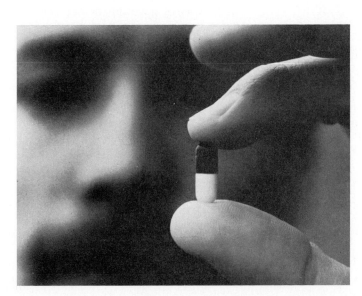

As required by the federal government, the FDA must protect consumer welfare by submitting new drugs to stringent and lengthy tests; a procedure that results in lower risk but higher costs. However, in 1987, public concern over AIDS persuaded the FDA to bypass its usual extensive testing and expedite approval of AZT, an experimental drug used in treatment of the virus. (Steve Kagan/Gamma-Liaison)

Supporters of the effectiveness requirement point out that ineffective drugs are not harmless. Even the best drugs have side effects. Moreover, if someone is treated with an ineffective drug instead of one that works, the opportunity cost could be high. Reasonable arguments can be made on both sides of the issue, so the requirement for effectiveness continues to be controversial.

Are There Superior Alternatives to Current Drug Policies?

Because of the controversial nature of drug regulation, it is not surprising that alternatives have been suggested. Major concerns are the high costs and long delays caused by the required testing procedures. What can be done to lower cost and speed availability without unduly compromising the goals of safety and effectiveness?

Proponents of the consumer-sovereignty approach suggest that government officials or outside review committees examine the evidence on safety and effectiveness submitted by drug producers. When this evidence is sufficient, the drugs would be given government certification. When the evidence is not convincing, certification would not be granted. However, physicians could still choose to prescribe uncertified drugs. This alternative would certainly speed up availability, reduce costs, and probably increase the number of new drugs marketed. But it would also increase risks. Since public policy has historically favored low risks, use of this alternative may be politically unacceptable.

Other FDA critics believe that safety and effectiveness could be reasonably assured with fewer premarketing tests. Some argue that using outside review groups to arbitrate disputes between the FDA and drug manufacturers would provide more-balanced decisions. As an alternative, the FDA could make greater use of provisional releases of new drugs. Such releases might restrict the drugs' use to certain institutions or require more intensive monitoring. Each of these proposals would provide some protection without the absolute ban on entry that the FDA currently uses. Again, however, the FDA's concern that unsafe drugs not reach the market makes use of such alternatives unlikely.

However, not all FDA actions to protect consumers have drawn fire from opponents of government regulation. In 1982, after poison was discovered in Tylenol capsules, the FDA required nonprescription drugs to be packaged in tamper-resistant containers. This action won widespread approval even from traditional opponents of government regulation for several reasons. First, the FDA decision came at the urging and with the cooperation of manufacturers. Second, by requiring tamper-resistant rather than tamper-proof packaging, the FDA rejected the notion of providing absolute safety. Third, by allowing manufacturers to choose the actual design, the regulations provide producers with incentives to develop technically efficient solutions. And finally, allowing a reasonable period of time for phasing in the new requirements recognized the consumer's desire for both safer products and uninterrupted access to nonprescription drugs.

Conclusion

Drug regulation is a particularly emotional issue because human health and lives are clearly at stake. However, the same is true of many other public policy issues, where establishing values is so complex that rational thinking is extremely difficult. Those on both sides of the drug regulation issue use the protection-of-human-life argument: Those favoring extensive testing point to lives saved; those arguing against it point to lives lost before useful drugs can be marketed. The principles of rational choice suggest that both benefits and costs must be considered. The issues are not whether to have safety or whether the government has a role to play because information is imperfect. Rather, the economic issues are how much safety is best and what type of role the government should play.

QUESTIONS FOR REVIEW AND DISCUSSION

1. Most economists agree that there are reasonable arguments in favor of some role for government in the drug market. What are the market failures in the drug market? How, in the face of these market failures can government improve the efficiency of the market?

2. The debate over drug regulation can be viewed as a debate between advocates of the consumer-sovereignty and consumer-protection approaches.
   a) What does each approach say about the extent and direction of government regulation?
   b) What are the benefits and costs to drug producers of considering safety and effectiveness? Do you think that the incentives are strong enough to warrant *no* government regulation? Less regulation than now exists?
   c) Consider the case of automobile safety. What would each consumer approach say about what government should do? Current government regulations require auto manufacturers to build in safety features—padded dashboards and seat belts, for example. What would each approach say about this method of government regulation?

3. Why do Congress and the FDA tend to overestimate the benefits of safety and underestimate the costs? Would a greater reliance on nongovernment committees to review and approve new drugs change this bias and make more drugs available? Do you think that this change would significantly lower safety standards?

4. What are the benefits and costs of government regulations to ensure drug effectiveness? What changes would you foresee if the FDA concerned itself only with safety? (Consider both benefits and costs to consumers.)

19.4 IMPACT OF MINIMUM WAGE LAWS

In 1938 Congress passed the Fair Labor Standards Act, establishing a minimum wage of $0.25 per hour. Subsequent revisions to the law have raised the minimum. The last change, in 1981, increased the minimum wage to $3.35 per hour.

In the past, Congress raised the minimum wage as other wages rose. Because the minimum has not been changed since 1981 as other wages and prices have risen, the *relative* value of the minimum wage has fallen. In 1981 the minimum wage was 46 percent of the average wage of workers in private nonagricultural industries. By 1986 it represented only 38 percent. As a result, the market wage is above the legal minimum even in many industries that employ large numbers of low-wage workers—such as fast-food restaurants.

Some politicians have suggested a further increase in the minimum wage. Would such a policy be desirable? What are the benefits and costs of minimum wage laws? Why do many economists believe that there are better alternatives that affect efficiency less?

Why Has Government Set a Minimum Wage?

Proponents of minimum wage laws view them as enhancing equity. They argue that without the protection of government, competition in the labor market would drive wages of some workers down, perhaps to mere subsistence levels. This argument—like all arguments about equity issues—is normative. Thus economic analysis cannot support or refute it. But economic principles can show us the benefits and costs of minimum wages and alternative policies.

What Are the Benefits and Costs of a Minimum Wage?

The benefits of minimum wage rates are clear: Some workers earn more than they would without regulation. But what about the costs? The costs of minimum wages, like those of any price floor, follow the rules of resource demand and supply (see Chapter 13). Although wages are income to those employed, they are a cost to employers. Profit-seeking employers will be willing to hire additional workers only if the value of additional output (marginal product) is greater than the wage. Because marginal product declines as each extra worker is hired, a higher wage will reduce the number of workers hired.

The effects of a minimum wage are likely to be greater for those who currently work for low wages. (The employment prospects and salary of a doctor or college professor are unlikely to be directly affected, for example.) Thus Exhibit 19.4.1 focuses on demand for and supply of low-wage workers. From the graph we can conclude that without a minimum wage law, a total of 200,000 workers would have jobs paying $3.00 per hour (where D intersects S). But with a legal minimum wage of $3.50 per hour, only 190,000 workers will have jobs (where D intersects P_{min}). These changes also cause allocative inefficiency. The area of the red-shaded

---

Exhibit 19.4.1
Demand for and Supply of Unskilled Workers
A minimum wage of $3.50 per hour set above the equilibrium wage of $3.00 per hour will raise the wages of the 190 thousand workers still employed. But some 20 thousand workers will be unemployed. The red-shaded area represents the reduction in allocative efficiency compared with the results of a competitive market.

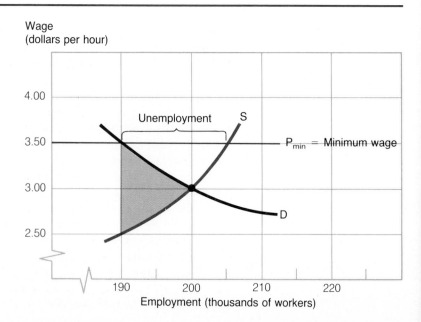

triangle indicates how much society loses by hiring 190,000 instead of 200,000 workers.

Ironically, minimum wage laws tend to do the most harm to low-wage workers. Note that minimum wage laws cause a labor surplus: More individuals are seeking work than there are jobs. Employers therefore can afford to be choosy about which workers they select. The least productive workers more than likely will be rejected. As critics of the minimum wage also observe, employers are better able to indulge their prejudices, if they so desire. Of course, not all low-wage workers lose. The 190,000 workers who still have jobs earn $0.50 per hour more. Moreover, the increase in the relative price of low-wage workers should increase the demand for substitutes, including more skilled workers.

But minimum wage laws also have other effects on the economy. Some experts trace the rise of self-service gasoline stations to the minimum wage. Home delivery services have virtually disappeared. Minimum wages also cause employers to substitute adults for teenagers. Indeed, one study found that minimum wages had little effect on adults, but reduced teenage employment by 1–3 percent.[*] Higher wages also induce some substitution of machinery for labor. Employers of low-wage workers may reduce nonwage benefits, such as vacations or health insurance, or seek to get more output out of fewer workers by raising production standards. However, in most cases these responses only reduce—not eliminate—the effect of minimum wages on product costs. As a result, minimum wage laws usually increase product prices.

Are There Superior Alternatives to a Minimum Wage?

As you might expect, the normative nature of the debate about labor-market policies leads economists to very different opinions about appropriate wage policy. Those who believe that wages in unregulated labor markets are equitable argue for no government regulation. Evidence certainly supports the notion that minimum wage laws have not raised the income of many of the working poor. As many as one-half of the low-wage workers appear to be members of families with above-average incomes. Others are poor not because of low wages but because they do not work, cannot find jobs, or work only part time.

Because of these findings, even advocates of government involvement have suggested doing away with or reducing the effect of minimum wage laws and substituting other policies. For example, many economists believe that it is more efficient to simply give cash directly to those whose incomes are to be raised. Of course, cash transfers will reduce total output if some individuals work less as a result. However, a minimum wage greater than the equilibrium level will affect efficiency more.

Others support job-training programs. They argue that low wages are the result of both demand and supply factors. A minimum wage law does nothing to increase the market value of the working poor. If, instead, those individuals were to obtain job training, their skills and productivity would improve. Job training policies would, proponents argue, increase efficiency *and* address equity issues. Job-training programs also have costs, but they may be a more efficient way of improving the incomes of the poor.

---

[*] Charles Brown, Curtis Gilroy, and Andrew Kohen, "The Effect of the Minimum Wage on Employment and Unemployment," *Journal of Economic Literature,* June 1982, pp. 497–528.

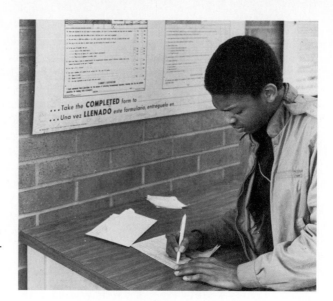

Although minimum wage laws raise wages for some workers, other groups—particularly teenagers—may experience increased unemployment. (Peter Menzel/Stock, Boston)

Finally, proposals have been made to establish a lower minimum wage for teenagers—those who are most affected by the current law. Opponents point out that such wage laws might encourage employers to substitute teenagers for adult workers. Supporters observe that teenagers, especially low-income teenagers, are hurt the most under the current policy. Restrictions on their employment not only cost them current income, but job experience that may help them get better jobs as adults.

Conclusion

With the strong economic arguments against minimum wage laws, why do they remain the wage policy of choice? Consider who benefits and who loses. Low-wage workers who retain their jobs benefit. They are likely to recognize that minimum wage laws increase their wages. Those who are unemployed because of minimum wages are less likely to connect their situation with the policy. And although minimum wage laws raise costs, and thus prices, few consumers see the connection. Most believe that the minimum wage actually helps the poor at little or no cost to themselves. Finally, minimum wage policy may prevail because it is more acceptable politically than alternative policies, such as cash transfers and job training.

QUESTIONS FOR REVIEW AND DISCUSSION

1. Explain how and why each of the following groups are affected by a minimum wage greater than the equilibrium level.
   a) Teenagers with summer jobs.
   b) Firms that employ low-wage workers.
   c) Members of labor unions.
   d) Consumers.

2. Explain whether each of the following statements is true, false, or uncertain.
   a) Employers of low-wage workers are likely to respond to a minimum wage by hiring more skilled workers and utilizing more machinery. Both these changes increase efficiency. As a result, society gains.

b) Employers of low-wage workers don't have to reduce employment when the minimum wage rises. They could either pass along the costs to their customers or simply accept lower profits.

3. Explain whether each of the following statements is true, false, or uncertain.
   a) Minimum wage laws will be opposed politically by those who stand to lose the most.
   b) Those who gain from minimum wage laws are likely to be strong political supporters of increases in the minimum wage.

4. Rational policy analysis requires considering both policy objectives and alternative programs. Apply this principle to answer the questions in (a)–(d).
   a) What arguments would you use to support government assistance to the working poor? What arguments would you use against such support? (Be sure to distinguish normative from positive arguments.)
   b) What are the major costs to society of minimum wage laws?
   c) What are the major costs to society of government-subsidized job training? What are the benefits?
   d) What are the benefits and costs of cash transfers to the working poor? (Consider the effects on those individuals most likely to be low-wage workers.)

19.5 ECONOMIC REGULATION IN THE OIL MARKET

Energy plays an essential role in the economy. We use energy to heat and light our homes, to manufacture goods and furnish services, and to transport people and products. Oil continues to be the single most important source of energy, accounting for 40 percent of total energy used. Is government involvement in the oil market desirable? Do the costs of such actions outweigh the benefits? Or would other energy policies be preferable?

Why Is Government Involved in the Oil Market?

Many arguments in favor of government intervention in the oil market have been advanced. The three most prevalent are: (1) national defense; (2) efficiency; and (3) stable prices. Oil is undoubtedly important to national defense. Aircraft, ships, and tanks all run on oil products. But national defense is a public good, collectively consumed and indivisible. As discussed in Chapter 16, private markets thus may not reflect the benefits of national defense. If private markets fail to reflect the full social benefits of oil consumption, government intervention in the market may improve efficiency.

Most economists agree that prices in smoothly functioning markets usually signal producers and consumers to respond to changing demand and supply conditions. The result is generally allocatively efficient. But proponents of government activity in the oil market point out that major price increases in both 1973 and 1979 were caused primarily by a group of oil-producing countries exercising market power. As a result, the U.S. economy experienced some severe and painful adjustments. If government policies can prevent or reduce the effects of such disruptions, they can be beneficial. Finally, economists generally agree that the principal objective of these policies is to help the economy achieve efficiency.

Thus government action is justified only in case of market failure and if government policies can provide sufficient extra benefits to cover their extra costs.

What Are the Benefits and Costs of U.S. Oil Policies?

U.S. oil policies have differed greatly over the years. Thus any meaningful economic analysis must focus on one of two periods of time.

Pre–1973 policies. Before 1973, U.S. policies were generally proproducer. (Antitrust action taken against the Standard Oil Company in 1911 was a notable exception.) A combination of policies served to encourage exploration for and production of domestic oil and to maintain prices above world market levels.

Tax policies encouraged oil exploration and production in the United States and benefitted many firms. But many oil wells tap the same pool of oil, and the owner of any one well can gain an advantage over others by pumping as fast as possible. (You may have faced a similar problem if you have ever tried to share a pizza with others.) Accordingly, domestic oil supply rose, driving price down.

As a result consumers benefitted, but not without some future cost. The faster that oil is pumped from a well, the smaller is the total volume of oil that can be recovered from a given pool. Moreover, producers were upset about lower prices and were willing (even anxious) to have government control production. As a result, state regulatory agencies—especially the Texas Railroad Commission—controlled production tightly.

The federal government ultimately entered the regulatory arena when the future of domestic oil production was threatened by the discovery of large deposits of foreign oil that could be produced more cheaply. Because the oil is closer to the surface, the marginal cost of pumping oil in the Middle East is lower than in U.S. fields. Arguing that reliance on foreign oil could harm the nation's ability to defend itself in time of war, the federal government set limits on the quantity of oil that could be imported. These limits benefitted the domestic producers who had lobbied for them. But in the long run, they may have *increased* U.S. dependency on foreign oil, since they led to more rapid use of domestic supplies.

Post–1973 policies. By 1971 the United States no longer had any surplus capacity. Although producers and government policy makers no longer worried about excess supply driving price down, the economy was quite vulnerable to any supply disruption. Two years later, we discovered the full extent of this vulnerability. In 1973 oil prices skyrocketed when members of the Organization of Petroleum Exporting Countries (OPEC) halted shipments of oil to the United States. Over the next six months, oil prices rose from less than $3 to $12 a barrel. Expenditures for imported oil rose from $4 billion in 1973 to more than $15 billion in 1974.

These conditions led to a dramatic turnaround in U.S. oil policy. Instead of being aimed at keeping prices from falling, new policies were put into effect to hold down price increases. Instead of a proproducer bias aimed at keeping profits high, the new, proconsumer policies were aimed at preventing "windfall profits." Government price ceilings on oil were a major part of the new policy approach. Although the ceilings did not keep prices from rising, they did slow the rate of increase. Supporters of the price ceilings argued that the ceilings would shelter the economy from some of the disruptive effects of vastly higher oil costs.

Price ceilings were also seen as a way to prevent a transfer of wealth from consumers (who would have to pay higher prices) to owners of existing oil supplies (suddenly worth four times as much because the price of oil had quadrupled). Therefore the ceiling price on existing supplies ("old oil") was set lower than on newly discovered oil to prevent "windfall" gains. In addition, Congress enacted a *windfall profits tax* to capture some of the increased value for government programs to increase alternative supplies of energy and reduce vulnerability to even further price increases.

While price ceilings offered benefits to some parts of the economy, they also imposed costs. For example, price ceilings create shortages (see Chapter 3). If prices are not allowed to resolve the shortage, some other method must be used. In this case the federal government set up an elaborate allocation system in an attempt to try fairly and efficiently to distribute oil supplies (primarily gasoline and home heating oil). As is typical of such schemes, the administrative costs and the potential for misallocation were high. In addition, pricing oil below market value discouraged production of U.S. oil and thus actually *increased* demand for imported oil.

Are There Superior Oil-Policy Options?

Citing many of these policy costs, in 1981 President Reagan and the U.S. Congress ended price controls on oil. In most respects, the oil market today is unregulated. Problems with past policies—especially price controls—have made many economists and politicians cautious about suggesting new government regulations.

Some economists question whether any policies are necessary. They argue that a free market can make efficient allocation and pricing decisions. They point out that high prices in the 1970s—not government policies—stimulated businesses and households to reduce energy consumption. The United States decreased its dependence on unstable Middle East oil supplies, and new discoveries in Mexico, Alaska, and the North Sea increased worldwide supplies. By 1986 the world market became glutted, and oil prices fell dramatically.

Some proponents of government intervention in the oil market argue that market failures, such as OPEC's market power, *require* government correction. Although OPEC's power now seems to be less than it was in the 1970s, some experts see this group as a continued threat. If market prices do not correctly signal consumers to conserve or oil producers to supply, government policies may improve efficiency. But most economists believe that it would be very difficult—perhaps impossible—to effectively but efficiently prevent supply disruptions stemming from political factors or the exercise of market power.

Vulnerability to sudden oil price increases can be reduced by government stockpiles of oil. By releasing supplies from the stockpile, the government could counteract supply disruptions. In 1980, Congress authorized the federal government to establish a Strategic Petroleum Reserve. Under this program, the government bought some 500 million barrels of oil—a one month's supply. Unlike taxes or price controls, a stockpile does not seriously distort the incentives of oil producers and consumers.

Nearly all economists agree that the stockpile should not be used to offset price increases caused by fundamental demand and supply changes. Some also argue that the market already provides ample incentives for private individuals and businesses to consider the future and to protect themselves from potential disruptions. As we noted in Chapter 3, expectations influence current demand and supply. Owners of oil supplies will decide whether to sell now or in the future, depending on their expectations about demand and supply. If they expect another oil shortage to occur, they will decrease current supply, driving prices up. Businesses and households will take expected shortages into account when making their private decisions.

Conclusion

A review of regulation in the oil market leads to a strong conclusion that government policies have imposed large costs on the economy. Although motivated in most cases by reasonable objectives, price controls are generally recognized as a poor policy option. In many respects, the results were the exact opposite of the intended goals. Economists tend to favor market-directed solutions, given smoothly functioning markets. In the case of oil, however, there are some reasonable arguments that some protection against contrived supply disruptions and price increases is desirable.

QUESTIONS FOR REVIEW AND DISCUSSION

1. Each of several competitive firms drawing oil from the same pool has an incentive to pump as much oil as it can, even if the effect is to reduce the total amount that could be pumped. Why? Does this situation create external costs for society? What options exist for handling this issue? (Discuss the benefits and costs of each option, including the option of doing nothing.)

2. What are the effects of a general tax on oil imports? (Consider the effects on domestic consumption, on domestic exploration, on domestic production, and on incentives to develop substitutes for oil.) Do you think that this policy would increase or reduce dependence on foreign oil?

3. Some people argue that government must intervene in the oil market to ensure that adequate supplies are available for future generations.
   a) What incentives does a private producer have to consider future generations in deciding how much oil to produce today? (Give examples of events that may increase or decrease these incentives.)
   b) What changes occur in a smoothly functioning market as known oil reserves decrease?
   c) How do these changes help to make the reserves last longer than might otherwise be expected?
   d) What actions might a firm not in the oil business take if it expected supplies of oil to decrease? What actions would you expect individuals to take?

4. Currently the government has some 500 million barrels of oil stored in its Strategic Petroleum Reserve. An important policy question is how that reserve should be used.
   a) Under what circumstances should the government release oil from its reserve? (Consider in particular whether it would be desirable for the government to sell some of its reserve anytime the price of oil increases.)
   b) What are the advantages and disadvantages of each of the following ways of releasing stockpiles: (1) giving each major oil refinery a quantity based on its total use of oil over the past year; (2) selling a specified amount to the individual or firm that will pay the most for it.
   c) How would countries in Europe or Asia benefit from the release of oil from U.S. stockpiles? Why would any of those countries have an incentive to take advantage of the U.S. stockpile without being willing to make a monetary contribution?

PART SIX

Macroeconomic Measures and Models

Introduction to
Macroeconomics

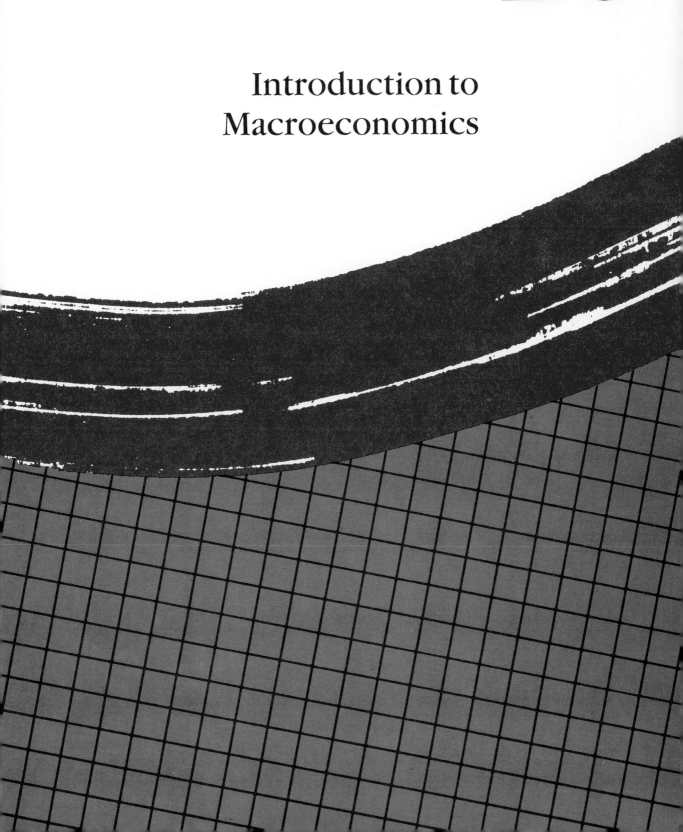

QUESTIONS TO CONSIDER

☐ How do microeconomics and macroeconomics differ?

☐ What do economists mean by *full employment,* and why is it an important macroeconomic goal?

☐ What do economists mean by *price stability,* and why is it an important macroeconomic goal?

☐ How well has the United States met its goals of full employment and price stability since 1900?

☐ Why do macroeconomists focus on changes in aggregate demand and aggregate supply?

We discussed some of the basic principles of economics in Chapters 1–6, noting how individual markets operate and what the basic overall economic goals of the economy are. With this chapter we begin to explore the economy from a macroeconomic viewpoint.

Macroeconomic topics—unemployment, inflation, interest rates, and economic growth—are constantly in the news. If you are a typical college student, however, your experience in the job market and with the general price level has probably been limited. As you will discover in this chapter—and in the world of work after college—unemployment and inflation can severely affect the way people live. Consider how you and your family would have to change your lifestyles if one or both of your parents were out of work for a year. Or if you are trying to live on last summer's income but prices jump 10 percent, you may wonder what caused the inflation that has curtailed your social life.

Macroeconomics is concerned with describing, understanding, and predicting the performance of an entire economy. Economists judge an economy's performance in terms of three basic macroeconomic goals: price stability, full employment, and economic growth. In this chapter we consider some measures of how well the U.S. economy has met these goals. As you will see, it has fallen far short of them at times, and we have experienced high inflation and/or unemployment.

The problems that develop when macroeconomic goals are not met are extremely complex. Thus this chapter is just a first look at them. We return to these problems again and again in later chapters, as you learn more about macroeconomics.

MACROECONOMIC CONCEPTS AND GOALS

As you begin your study of macroeconomics, you should understand what macroeconomics is and how it differs from microeconomics. You will also have to learn some new concepts, which are useful in viewing the economy from the macroeconomic perspective.

Microeconomics versus Macroeconomics

Both microeconomists and macroeconomists study the actions of individuals, firms, and governments in both domestic and foreign economies. But the questions they ask and the perspectives they take differ. The terms *micro* and *macro* come from words meaning *small* and *large*. The terms refer to perspective, not to size. Thus we use the tools and concepts of microeconomics to study the behavior of a firm, regardless of whether the firm is as small as a local grocery store or as large as General Motors. We use macroeconomic concepts and analyses to study output, unemployment, and inflation in an economy as a whole, whether the economy is as small as that of Grenada or as large as that of the United States.

We use microeconomics to explain changes in the mix of goods and services produced—why we are producing more personal computers and fewer large automobiles, for example. We use macroeconomics to explain changes in the total level (quantity) of all goods and services produced. Economists measure this level, called **aggregate output**, as **gross national product (GNP)**. Macroeconomics thus may explain why GNP in 1982 was $83 billion less than in 1981 and why GNP increased at a faster rate in the 1960s than it has since.

Using microeconomics we also explore the distribution of jobs across industries and occupations—why there are more jobs in medical care and fewer in steel production, for example. Macroeconomics explores the total level (quantity) of employment (and unemployment). Why were 1.5 million more people unemployed in 1980 than in 1979? Why were over 9 percent of the workers in the United States unemployed in 1982–1983?

Finally, we use microeconomics to study relative prices of products and resources in an economy—why prices of compact disk players have fallen while college tuitions have risen, for example. But we use macroeconomics to study changes in the **general price level**, that is, the average price of all goods and services produced. Why did the general price level increase by over 10 percent per year from 1979 to 1981 but by under 4 percent per year from 1982 to 1986?

Microeconomic–macroeconomic interrelationships. Although it is convenient (and traditional) to study microeconomic and macroeconomic principles separately, such a division is artificial when we analyze real-world situations. After all, an economy's macroeconomic performance reflects choices in individual product markets. In exploring the effect of microeconomic decisions on macroeconomic results, however, we must avoid the *fallacy of composition*: What is true for an individual consumer or an individual market may not be true for the economy as a whole. For example, if you decide to spend more of your current income, prices and output in the economy will not be affected. But if all households in the economy do the same thing, prices will rise and total output will increase.

We must also avoid the *fallacy of division*: What is true for the economy as a whole may not be true for its each and every part. When unemployment increases, for example, only some individuals lose their jobs. When the average level of prices increases, some prices will rise, but some may stay the same and others may fall.

Nevertheless, you should always keep in mind that microeconomics and macroeconomics are two halves of the complete picture. Thus when economists

Aggregate output. The total quantity of all goods and services produced in the economy in a given period of time.

Gross national product (GNP). A measure of the total market value of all final goods and services produced in the economy during a given period of time.

General price level. The average price of all goods and services in the economy.

were exploring the potential effects of changes in the income tax law enacted in 1986, they considered the effects on macroeconomic factors, such as economic growth and inflation. But they also considered the effects on microeconomic factors, such as demand for U.S. exports and distribution of income. Both economic perspectives are important; they complement rather than substitute for each other.

In the rest of this chapter we turn our attention to the basic macroeconomic goals of full employment, economic growth, and price stability. You will learn how economists describe the ideal macroeconomic performance of the economy. Is it desirable, for example, to eliminate all unemployment? Does price stability mean that all prices remain constant? Economists would say the answer to both of these questions is no.

FULL EMPLOYMENT, UNEMPLOYMENT, AND ECONOMIC GOALS

Full employment is an important macroeconomic goal. The production possibilities curves presented in Chapter 2 show that at any particular time the economy has a certain potential to produce goods and services. This potential can only be realized if resources are fully employed. When they are not, aggregate output falls below the potential level and fewer wants can be satisfied.

Ideally, then, an economy should achieve full employment. But is all unemployment bad for the economy? What causes different types of unemployment? What policies should be used to address them? In this section, we answer these questions and explore government measures of unemployment and a practical goal for full employment.

Official Definition of Unemployment

Calvin Coolidge once remarked that when people are out of work, unemployment results. While not incorrect, this observation is not sufficient for our purposes. We must have a clearer definition and a better explanation of causes of unemployment. Although any resource can be employed or unemployed, the term *unemployment* is most often used to refer to the number of individuals out of work. But we certainly would not consider all idleness to be an economic problem. After all, no human being can work 24 hours a day, seven days a week.

If we want to know the extent to which unemployment is an economic problem, we have to make a distinction between voluntary and involuntary idleness. For example, a retired person who does not want to work should not be considered unemployed. We want to limit the definition to those who are actively seeking work but are unable to find jobs. However, it is not always easy to distinguish voluntary from involuntary choices statistically. In fact, defining and measuring unemployment (and its opposite, full employment) is partly a matter of judgment.

Despite the difficulties, we must be able to measure the magnitude of unemployment in order to evaluate the economy's performance. The Bureau of Labor Statistics, an agency of the federal government, officially measures employment and unemployment. The Bureau conducts the Current Population Survey, which is the basis for the labor-force statistics that are reported monthly in the

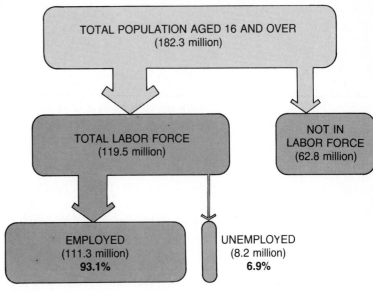

Exhibit 20.1
Population and Labor Force, 1986

Source: Economic Report of the President, 1987.

news media. Each month interviewers survey some 60,000 households that have been chosen statistically to represent the total U.S. population.* Interviewers ask about the activities of each household member during a given week, seeking to learn whether the individual was working, going to school, looking for a job, or retired.

Based on the responses, the bureau assigns individuals to one of three categories: (1) *employed* individuals—those who worked for one hour or more for pay during the survey week (or 15 hours or more without pay in a family-owned enterprise); (2) *unemployed* individuals—those who are without work but are actively looking for market work; and (3) individuals *not in the labor force*—those who are out of work but are not looking for work. The total number of people who are either employed or unemployed constitutes the **labor force**. Exhibit 20.1 shows the population aged 16 and over divided into these three categories for 1986. (Because individuals below the age of 16 are typically in school, labor force statistics are based only on those who are 16 and over.)

The labor-force statistic that gets the most public attention is the **unemployment rate**, or the percentage of the labor force that is unemployed. In 1986 the unemployment rate of 6.9 percent was calculated as follows:

$$\text{Unemployment rate} = \frac{\text{Number of unemployed}}{\text{Total labor force}} \times 100$$

$$= \frac{8.2 \text{ million}}{119.5 \text{ million}} \times 100 \quad \text{or} \quad 6.9\%$$

Labor force. The total number of individuals classified by government statistics as either employed or unemployed.

Unemployment rate. The number of individuals unemployed, expressed as a percentage of the labor force.

Interpreting changes in the unemployment rate is not always easy. Some reflect

---

* Despite the relatively small number of households surveyed, statisticians believe the overall unemployment rate generated from the sample is accurate to within 0.1 percent.

Discouraged workers. Individuals who are out of work and who currently are not looking for work because they believe that they cannot find it. They are not officially classified as unemployed.

Underemployed. Individuals who have jobs but either work part-time when they would prefer full-time work or work at jobs below their capabilities and skills.

seasonal factors. For example, in the summer many young people are out of school and seeking summer jobs. Because such jobs are very hard to find (as all who have tried to find one will testify), the level of unemployment is somewhat exaggerated during the summer. The government therefore adjusts for seasonal factors in its published statistics. Other seasonal adjustments are made in September to reflect students' return to school and in December and January to reflect employment activity during the holiday season.

Who Is unemployed? In order to understand better the official measure of unemployment, let's consider how government statistics classify several representative individuals. Hal Lerner goes to school full-time; he has no job and no time for one at present. Rita Tyre retired last year at age 65; she has no further interest in working. Most people would agree with the official government definition in these cases: Neither Hal nor Rita is unemployed because neither wants a job. They have chosen to spend their time in other ways and are considered—in official government statistics—to be "not in the labor force."

The government measure of unemployment also excludes Chris Kerr. Chris is raising six children and caring for the family's home. Certainly Chris is working, but he is not considered part of the official labor force because he is not exchanging his services in any market—nor is he seeking to.

What about individuals who are out of work and want jobs? Should all of them be counted as unemployed, or should they have to demonstrate that they are job hunting before being counted? Consider the case of Craig Eisweil, a freezer salesman in Nome, Alaska. Craig is a **discouraged worker**. He would like to have a job, but has given up looking because he does not think he can find one. Because the official definition requires that an unemployed individual be actively seeking work, Craig is not classified as unemployed.

Not all economists agree that discouraged workers should be excluded from government unemployment statistics. Critics argue that many discouraged workers do return to the job market when economic conditions improve. Thus their exclusion from the statistics may cause the official rate to understate unemployment when the economy slumps. Even though the government does not classify discouraged workers as part of the labor force, it does collect statistics on them. In the fourth quarter of 1986, the official unemployment rate was 6.8 percent; if discouraged workers had been included as unemployed, the rate would have been 7.6 percent.

And what about Amy Kau? Amy has a Ph.D. in agriculture, but after a long search could only find a part-time job in a local florist's shop. Amy would be considered **underemployed** because she is not working as much as she wants to or fully utilizing her skills. But Amy does have a job and is therefore considered employed in the official statistics. Some economists challenge this classification, arguing that it, too, understates the unemployment problem.

In other cases, official statistics may overstate the unemployment problem. For example, consider Russell Hack, the teenage son of a successful surgeon. In the past year, Russ has been looking off and on for a job. He has turned down a number of jobs as not "meaningful" enough. His older sister, Lena, graduated from college last month with a degree in philosophy. She has made it clear to potential employers that her minimum salary requirement is $100,000 per year. Should Russ and Lena be counted as unemployed?

Many people say no, but government statistics will count both as unemployed as long as they actively search for work. But should we include those who have rejected job offers, have a low labor-market commitment, or could be employed if they would accept the market wage? Obviously, the official government definition is, in some respects, a compromise.

Types of Unemployment and Economic Goals

Defining, measuring, and interpreting unemployment is difficult in part because individuals are unemployed for different reasons. Some are unemployed because they have been fired or laid off. Others have just begun looking for a job for the first time or after being out of the labor force for several years. Some are unemployed because they are searching for a better job. Others may lack the skills that employers are seeking or might be the victims of racial, sexual, or religious discrimination. Sometimes there may not be enough jobs in the economy as a whole.

Economists have developed several classifications of unemployment based on the reasons for unemployment. Each type of unemployment has a different effect on the goals of efficiency and equity and a different meaning for the goal of full employment. In fact, some unemployment actually benefits the economy as a whole (even though affected individuals are still harmed). Despite the definitions of these different types of unemployment, dividing the measured unemployment rate into separate parts is not possible.

Frictional unemployment.   When interpreting government statistics, we must recognize that even in the best of times there is some unemployment. In fact, what economists call **frictional unemployment** is a natural and beneficial part of a market economy. When consumer demand changes, resources should move. For example, if demand for video cassette recorders increases and demand for paperback novels declines, resources (including labor) should shift from producing paperback novels to producing video cassette recorders.

But labor resources cannot move instantaneously, and information about job opportunities does not reach unemployed workers immediately. Thus we can expect some individuals to be unemployed for a short time when demand shifts. In addition, some workers, especially those for whom unemployment is not a terrible hardship, may be very particular about the type of work they will accept. As a result, they may choose an extended job search over any of the currently available jobs.

Because it is temporary and society receives benefits from resource mobility, frictional unemployment is not a major target of unemployment policy. A match between a frictionally unemployed worker and a job is simply a matter of time and job-search effort. Nevertheless, there are benefits to lowering even frictional unemployment. Improved labor-market information or efforts to speed job and geographic mobility may reduce frictional unemployment. Although *some* frictional unemployment serves a useful social purpose, unemployment beyond a certain level—whatever its cause—is a problem. The challenge to policy makers is to determine when unemployment is too high, that is, when higher unemployment involves extra social costs that exceed extra social benefits.

Structural unemployment.   Unlike frictional unemployment, structural unemployment may persist over long periods of time. **Structural unemployment** results when unemployed individuals lack the necessary skills to fill available

Frictional unemployment. Unemployment resulting from normal job-search activities, or from imperfect knowledge and imperfect mobility. Although a permanent feature of a dynamic economy, frictional unemployment is temporary for any individual.

Structural unemployment. Unemployment resulting from a mismatch in the labor market between the location and skills of unemployed workers, the location and skill requirements of available jobs; may also reflect discrimination. Unlike with frictional unemployment, unemployment for individuals may be prolonged.

Cyclical unemployment. Unemployment resulting from decreases in aggregate economic output. Cyclical unemployment increases during recessions and decreases during recoveries.

Business cycle. The recurring but irregular swings in aggregate economic activity. A complete cycle has four phases: recession, trough, recovery, and peak.

Recession. The phase of the business cycle in which real aggregate output of the economy is decreasing.

jobs or live far away from areas where job vacancies exist. Discrimination may also cause structural unemployment. Structural unemployment has no real social benefits. But it cannot be easily or efficiently attacked by macroeconomic policies that are aimed simply at creating additional jobs. The only solutions involve relocating and/or retraining individuals, relocating or restructuring jobs, and reducing discriminatory barriers. Whether structural unemployment should be a social responsibility and whether efficient policies to reduce it can be found are strongly debated.

Business cycles and cyclical unemployment.   The existence of frictional and structural unemployment means that even in the best of times we cannot expect the measured unemployment rate to be zero. However, changes in the level of GNP and in the rate of unemployment are indirectly related. For example, when GNP fell by 2.5 percent in 1982, the unemployment rate increased from 7.5 percent to 9.5 percent. The increase in unemployment associated with a decrease in GNP is what economists call **cyclical unemployment**.

Changes in cyclical unemployment are generally related to overall fluctuations in aggregate output called the **business cycle**. As shown in Exhibit 20.2, a business cycle has four phases: (1) during a **recession** the economy slows down and GNP

Exhibit 20.2
Phases of the Business Cycle
This graph shows a representative cycle for the U.S. economy. The *peak* of the business cycle corresponds to the maximum level of economic activity. As shown here, peaks occurred in the U.S. economy in 1973 and 1980. Note that the second peak is higher, indicating that the economy has grown. Following a peak, economic activity declines during the *recession* phase (1973–1975). At the *trough* (1975), economic activity reaches its lowest point. Following the trough, economic activity increases during the *recovery* phase of the cycle (1975–1980), culminating again in a peak.

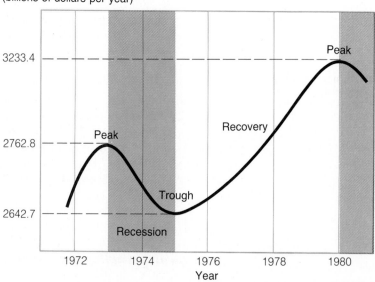

Length of previous recovery (months)	Dates of recessions			Length of preceding recession (months)
	Peak	to	Trough	
37	November 1948	–	October 1949	11
45	July 1953	–	May 1954	10
41	August 1957	–	April 1958	8
24	April 1960	–	February 1961	10
104	December 1969	–	November 1970	11
36	November 1973	–	March 1975	16
58	January 1980	–	July 1980	6
12	July 1981	–	November 1982	16

Exhibit 20.3
Business Cycles Since World War II

drops; (2) at the **trough** GNP stops declining; (3) a **recovery** begins when GNP starts to rise; and (4) at the **peak** GNP stops rising. These fluctuations in aggregate activity have recurred in all market economies throughout history. Some economists, however, find the term *cycle* a bit misleading because it gives the impression that the fluctuations occur regularly. In fact, both their length and size are very irregular.

The National Bureau of Economic Research (NBER) unofficially designates recessions. Many economists define a recession as two consecutive quarters in which aggregate output declines. But the NBER, using a more complicated method, has identified eight recessions since the end of World War II. Exhibit 20.3 shows the dates of official recessions and associated peaks in business activity. Note that periods of recession are typically much shorter than periods of expansion or recovery.

We can view cyclical unemployment—too few jobs available at the current market rate for the number of individuals seeking employment—from at least two perspectives. First, we might conclude that the current market wage is too high; that is, it is above an equilibrium rate. If so, the obvious solution would be to lower wages to allow the labor market to reach equilibrium. When this occurs, everyone who seeks a job at the market wage will be able to find work. (There will still be frictional and structural unemployment, but no cyclical unemployment.)

Or, second, we can view cyclical unemployment as a result of a declining GNP. From this perspective cyclical unemployment represents too few jobs at the current wage. The obvious solution is to increase GNP and thus the number of jobs.

Trough. The end of the recession phase; the point at which real aggregate output reaches its lowest level.

Recovery. The phase of the business cycle in which real aggregate output of the economy is increasing.

Peak. The end of the recovery phase; the point at which real aggregate output reaches its highest level.

Most economists agree that, unlike frictional unemployment, cyclical unemployment is a problem, offering few benefits to balance against its costs. However, as the two possible views of cyclical unemployment suggest, economists do not agree on whether government should intervene or allow the economy to correct itself.

Unemployment and equity. Regardless of its causes, unemployment always has costs for those who are unemployed and face lower income. Equity concerns led to the federal government's unemployment insurance program. This program reduces the cost of unemployment to individuals by paying those who have lost a job a portion of the wage they would otherwise have received. However, as with many programs, there is a trade-off between equity and efficiency. To some extent, paying individuals to look for jobs may prolong their job search and thus lead to higher unemployment.

Equity issues are also raised because different groups are affected differently by unemployment. For example, the unemployment rate for blacks has consistently been twice that for whites. The unemployment rate for women has consistently been higher than that for men. The reasons behind these differentials are complex and not easily measured.

To the extent that such differentials reflect discrimination, they are an equity concern. However, they may also reflect differences in education, experience, and intensity of job search. Because value judgments are required, economists cannot scientifically calculate the equity costs of unemployment. Nevertheless, concern about equity is a major reason why unemployment is perceived as an economic and a political problem.

Natural, or "Full-Employment," Unemployment Rate

Just as the definition of unemployment is a compromise, so too is the definition and measurement of its opposite: full employment. In Chapter 2, we associated full employment with operating on the production possibilities frontier. That is, full employment is achieved when the economy produces at its full potential.

But does the economy reach full employment only when the measured unemployment rate is zero? Economists generally answer *no*. In fact, as we noted earlier, some frictional unemployment is useful and efficient because it is a response to changes in consumer demand and worker preferences. But what about structural and cyclical unemployment? As we defined it, structural unemployment reflects a mismatch between unemployed workers and job vacancies. It is not a temporary condition and is not easily reduced by macroeconomic policies. For this reason, economists generally agree that some structural unemployment is also consistent with the concept of production possibilities and thus with full employment. In contrast, economists generally agree that cyclical unemployment is inconsistent with full employment.

The unemployment that remains when all cyclical unemployment has been eliminated is known as the **natural rate of unemployment**. In theory, this rate is the expected level of frictional and structural unemployment when the economy is producing at its full potential. Thus the natural rate of unemployment could also be called the *full-employment* unemployment rate. As with many economic variables, measurements of the natural rate are debatable. Current estimates range from 5 to 7 percent.

Natural rate of unemployment. The unemployment rate achieved when the economy has eliminated all cyclical unemployment; sometimes referred to as the *full-employment* unemployment rate.

Defining the full-employment unemployment rate as "natural" does not mean that it represents some law of nature. Rather, it reflects the typical or normal functioning of the market economy. Moreover, defining full employment to include some frictional and structural unemployment does not mean that economists believe that all such unemployment cannot and should not be attacked. If remedies that provide greater extra benefits than extra costs can be found, they should be used to lower frictional or structural unemployment.

Potential GNP. The aggregate output that could be produced with the available technology if labor and other economic resources were fully employed.

GNP gap. The difference between real GNP and potential GNP for a specific period of time. When positive, it measures the output lost as a result of unemployment.

Inflation. A sustained upward movement in the general level of prices.

Price index. A measure of price level in a given year as a percentage of the price level in some specified base, or reference, year.

Consumer price index (CPI). A price index reflecting changes in the prices of consumer goods; involves the use of a constant market-basket approach.

RECAP

The official definition of the unemployed is an individual without a job who is actively looking for a job. Retired individuals, full-time students, and full-time homemakers are excluded.

There are three types of unemployment: frictional, structural, and cyclical. Frictional unemployment occurs when individuals first enter or leave the job market or move from industry to industry. Structural unemployment occurs when the skills of the unemployed do not match the skills required by vacant jobs. Cyclical unemployment occurs when the number of unemployed exceeds the number of jobs available.

Full employment—the natural rate of unemployment—is the level of unemployment that would occur if the economy were producing at its potential GNP level. Full employment is consistent with some frictional and structural unemployment but not with any cyclical unemployment.

The GNP gap is the difference between potential and actual GNP. A positive gap indicates that potential GNP is more than actual GNP. A negative gap indicates that potential GNP is less than actual GNP.

Full Employment and Potential GNP

We can use the concept of the natural rate of unemployment to define and measure full employment. It is the employment level in an economy that has fully adjusted to all existing macroeconomic conditions. Thus **potential GNP** is the level of aggregate output that would be produced if the economy eliminated cyclical unemployment (where actual and natural unemployment rates are equal). By comparing actual GNP in any year to potential GNP, we can measure the amount of output lost when the economy fails to maintain full employment.

The difference between actual and potential GNP, called the **GNP gap**, is often expressed as a percentage of potential GNP. For example, in the fourth quarter of 1986 the GNP gap was estimated to be $176.4 billion, or 4.6 percent of potential. That is, the economy lost $176.4 billion of aggregate output because it failed to attain full employment. In other words, the economy produced only 95.4 percent of the output it could have produced if cyclical unemployment had been zero.

Potential GNP and the natural rate of unemployment give economists a framework for defining and measuring the admittedly ambiguous term *full employment.* But as with almost all economic measures, we are unable to precisely measure potential GNP and the natural rate of unemployment. Thus although economists generally find these concepts useful, they often disagree about the accuracy of any particular measure. Despite this difficulty, we will use the concepts of potential GNP and the natural rate of unemployment as a standard against which to judge the economy's performance.

PRICE STABILITY, INFLATION, AND ECONOMIC GOALS

Another macroeconomic goal, price stability, refers to stability in the general price level. Macroeconomists want to know the significance of changes in the price level for the economy as a whole and for particular groups within the economy. Since World War II, the general price level has consistently moved upward. Such a sustained upward movement is what economists call **inflation**. Inflation was especially high in the United States in the 1970s. Although recent experience has been good (by comparison), inflation is still a potential concern.

Measuring the General Price Level

Economists measure the general price level by constructing a **price index**. A price index measures the price level in a given period of time as a percentage of the price level in a selected *base* (reference) *year*. The most publicized price index is the **consumer price index (CPI)**. As its name implies, this index reflects changes in the prices of a wide range of consumer goods and services. The index is calculated and published monthly by the Bureau of Labor Statistics.

To construct the index the Bureau first identifies a "market basket," reflecting what a "typical" urban family might buy. Currently the CPI market basket is based on a 1982–1984 survey of consumer buying habits. Each month, surveyors shop 85 urban areas to see how much it would currently cost a family to buy the designated items. The limited nature of the items in the market basket means that

Year	CPI (1967 = 100)	Inflation rate (% change in CPI)	Year	CPI (1967 = 100)	Inflation rate (% change in CPI)
1960	88.1	1.6	1974	147.1	11.0
1961	89.6	1.0	1975	161.2	9.1
1962	90.6	1.1	1976	170.5	5.8
1963	91.7	1.2	1977	181.5	6.5
1964	92.9	1.3	1978	195.4	7.7
1965	94.5	1.7	1979	217.4	11.3
1966	97.2	2.9	1980	246.8	13.5
1967	100.0	2.9	1981	272.4	10.5
1968	104.2	4.2	1982	289.1	6.1
1969	109.8	5.4	1983	298.4	3.2
1970	116.3	5.9	1984	311.1	4.3
1971	121.3	4.3	1985	322.2	3.6
1972	125.3	3.3	1986	328.4	1.9
1973	133.1	6.2			

**Exhibit 20.4
Consumer Price Index and
Annual Inflation Rates**

Source: Economic Report of the President, 1987.

the CPI does not measure all price changes. (We illustrate the calculation of price indexes in the appendix to this chapter.)

Price-level changes and the rate of inflation.   Exhibit 20.4 shows the CPI from 1960 to 1986. The rate "1967 = 100" indicates that the base year for CPI is 1967. Thus the CPI in any year indicates how much more or less it cost to buy the same items than it would have cost in 1967, the base year. For example, the 1985 CPI value was 322.2. Thus the average price of the items in the CPI market basket in 1985 was 322.2 percent of the average price in 1967. In other words, an item that cost $100 in 1967 would have cost $322.20 in 1985, if its price had increased at the average rate of the CPI.

Economists are concerned mainly with *changes* in the CPI, not in its actual value. The percentage change in the CPI can be used to measure the percentage change in the general price level. Technically, a one-year increase in the general price level is not inflation—economists use the term *inflation* to refer to *sustained increases* in the general price level. However, following normal terminology, Exhibit 20.4 shows inflation rates calculated as the percentage change in the price level from one year to the next. For example, between 1984 and 1985 the CPI increased from 311.1 to 322.2, a 3.6 percent increase or inflation rate. We calculate this figure as follows:

$$\text{Inflation rate, 1984–1985} = \frac{\text{CPI}_{1985} - \text{CPI}_{1984}}{\text{CPI}_{1984}} \times 100$$

$$= \frac{322.2 - 311.1}{311.1} \times 100 \quad \text{or} \quad 3.6\%$$

We multiply the ratio by 100 to change the decimal fraction to a percent. Each of the inflation rates shown in Exhibit 20.4 was calculated the same way. To check your understanding of this formula and this concept, calculate some of the other rates shown.

Price-level changes and the value of money. The data in Exhibit 20.4 clearly indicate that the general price level has increased rather significantly over the period shown. In order to understand why inflation is bad, you must first understand the implications of a change in the price level. Economists recognize that a change in the price level means a change in the value of money. We have not said much about money so far other than using a monetary unit—the dollar—to express price and to measure other economic variables such as income and government expenditures. But what is a dollar worth? In economic terms, the value of a dollar is measured by the amount of economic goods and services that it will buy. For this reason, an increase in the general price level will lower the value of a dollar.

For example, in 1975 a single-dip ice cream cone cost about 25 cents; in 1985 one cost about 50 cents. Thus a dollar was worth 4 ice cream cones in 1975 but only 2 cones in 1985. The same was true for prices in general. Between 1975 and 1985 the general price level (CPI) also doubled, indicating that a dollar bought about half as much in 1985 as in 1975. *An increase in the general price level decreases the purchasing power of money, that is, the amount of economic goods and services or resources that you can buy with a given number of dollars.*

Economic Facts and Changes in the General Price Level

Changes in the purchasing power of money create a problem in measuring economic variables. When the value of the dollar changes, we have to translate values into constant units to obtain a valid measurement. The following example may help you see the problem.

You want to know how much your nephew has grown in the last two years. You know that two years ago, he was one-half as tall as the small pine tree in your sister's front yard. If you learn that he is now only one-fourth as tall as the tree, would you believe that he has shrunk? Probably not. After all, you have been comparing the height of your nephew with a measure—the pine tree—that is not a constant size. In order to learn how much he has grown, you must compare his height with something that has remained a constant size, such as the height of the rock wall in the back yard.

We cannot use the height of a rock wall to measure economic variables, such as income or expenditures. It is important, however, to have a method of expressing value in constant terms. When variables are measured in **nominal** terms, they refer to actual dollars and actual prices. To adjust from nominal to **real** terms, economists remove the effects of changes in the price level and express the variables in terms of dollars of constant purchasing power. Economists call this translation or adjustment "deflating" nominal values.

Nominal. A term used to identify economic variables measured in terms of current prices.

Real. A term used to identify economic variables measured in terms of constant prices of some base year.

Nominal income. The actual number of dollars of income earned, expressed in terms of current dollars unadjusted for changes in the general price level.

Imagine a very simple economy in which the only product offered for sale is postcards. Suppose that in 1987 you had $200 of income and postcards cost $1 each. In real terms—the maximum number of postcards you can buy—is 200. Suppose that in 1988 your income increases to $300. However, because the price of a postcard increases to $2.00, you can now buy only 150 postcards. The increase in the price of a postcard caused a decline in the value of a dollar. A dollar in 1987 was worth one postcard; in 1988 it was worth only one-half a postcard.

We can express your income in 1988 in two ways. Your **nominal income** (the number of actual dollars) increased by $100, or 50 percent. However, because

Real income. Income expressed in terms of its purchasing power; nominal income adjusted to remove the effects of changes in the general price level.

the price of a postcard increased by 100 percent, your **real income** (the number of postcards you can buy) fell. If nominal income (or any other nominal value) increases more slowly than the average price of goods and services, its real value will fall. On the other hand, if prices and nominal income rise at the same rate, real income will be unchanged.

In a more complex economy, we use price indexes to translate from nominal to real terms. When we use the CPI, we are in effect translating nominal income or expenditures into "market-basket" equivalents. That is, if the CPI increases by 25 percent, it will take 25 percent more real dollars to purchase the same market

A Case in Point
Using Price Indexes

When the general price level changes, so does the real dollar value of economic variables. Price indexes can be used in two ways: (1) to translate values from nominal into real terms; and (2) to adjust nominal values of pensions or wages in order to preserve their purchasing power.

Using the CPI to Deflate Nominal Values

The data in Exhibit 20C.1 illustrate how the income of the Frieze household can be deflated (translated from nominal into real terms) using the consumer price index. The second column shows the family's nominal income in each of three years. The third column shows the corresponding values of the CPI index (from Exhibit 20.4). The fourth column shows the family's real income, that is, their income after correcting for changes in the purchasing power of the dollar. Because 1967 is used as the base year for the CPI, the family's real income is expressed in terms of the purchasing power of 1967 dollars.

Exhibit 20C.1
Deflating Nominal Income

Year	Nominal income (current dollars)	CPI (1967 = 100)	Real income (constant dollars)
1983	30,000	298.4	10,054
1984	30,600	311.1	9,836
1985	33,660	322.2	10,447

To deflate the Frieze's income, we want to remove the influence of changes in prices. The CPI tells us how much we have to change nominal income to put all figures on a price-adjusted basis. The value of the CPI in 1983 was 298.4. That is, it took $298.40 in 1983 to buy what $100 would have bought in 1967, or in equation form,

$$\frac{\$298.40 \text{ of income}}{\text{at 1983 prices}} = \frac{\$100.00 \text{ of income}}{\text{at 1967 prices}}$$

Dividing both sides by $298.40, the value of the CPI in 1983, we have

$$\frac{\$1.00 \text{ of income}}{\text{at 1983 prices}} = \frac{\$0.3351 \text{ of income}}{\text{at 1967 prices}}$$

In other words, the purchasing power of a dollar in 1983 was only 33.51 percent of that in 1967. Thus to translate the family's income in 1983 into the equivalent purchasing power in 1967 dollars, we can use the following relationship:

$$\frac{\text{Real income in 1967 dollars}}{} = \frac{\text{Nominal income in 1983 dollars}}{\text{CPI in 1983}} \times 100$$

$$= \frac{\$30,000}{298.4}(100) \text{ or } \$10,054$$

We used a similar procedure to translate the Frieze's income in each of the other two years into real terms. The family's nominal income increased by 2 percent from 1983 to 1984; however, prices increased by 4.3 percent. Because the price level increased faster than nominal income, the family's real income fell. Between 1984 and 1985, prices rose by 3.6 percent; the family's

Nominal GNP. The value of the gross national product measured by current quantities and current prices.

Real GNP. The value of the gross national product measured by current quantities and constant prices.

basket of goods contained in the CPI. Any nominal value that increases by less than 25 percent will fall in real terms. (See A Case in Point: Using Price Indexes, which indicates how such adjustments are made.)

Similarly, we make a distinction between **nominal GNP** and **real GNP**. Only by adjusting nominal GNP for changes in the general price level can we know how much of any change reflects increased production and how much reflects changes in the general price level. (We discuss the specific index used to adjust from nominal to real GNP in Chapter 21, but all indexes remove the distorting effect of price-level changes.)

nominal income increased by 10 percent. Because nominal income increased faster than the price level, the family's real income increased. To check your understanding of the deflation process, apply the same procedure to the other two years.

Using the CPI to Index Nominal Values

To prevent the real value of wages from falling, some labor unions have negotiated indexing clauses in their contracts. Some government transfers, such as Social Security, and some private pensions are also indexed. A price index such as the CPI can be used to determine how much the nominal values of wages, transfers, or pensions must increase to maintain their real values.

The data in Exhibit 20C.2 show how indexing affects the finances of John Elderidge. John retired on December 31, 1982. He was entitled to a monthly, fully

Exhibit 20C.2
Indexing a Pension

Year	CPI as of December	Percentage change in CPI	Real value of pension	Nominal value of pension in January
1982	292.4	—	$171.00	$500.00
1983	303.5	3.80	171.00	519.00
1984	315.5	3.95	171.00	539.50
1985	327.4	3.77	171.00	559.85

Note: The nominal pensions are as of January of the following year. That is, $519.00 is the nominal pension as of January 1984, which reflects the inflation that occurred in 1983.

indexed pension that in January 1983 had a nominal value of $500. Using the December 1982 value of the CPI, his pension had a real value of $171. According to the terms of his pension plan, John's nominal pension changes each January by the same percentage as the CPI in the previous year.

We can calculate the nominal pension values in January in one of two ways. First, we can calculate the percentage increase in the CPI and apply this percentage increase to the previous nominal value. For example, between December 1982 and December 1983, the CPI increased by 3.8 percent. Thus his nominal pension will increase to $519 per month as of January 1984. Second, the increase can be calculated as

$$\text{Real pension in base year dollars} = \frac{\text{Nominal pension in January}}{\text{CPI in previous December}} \times 100$$

$$\$171.00 = \frac{\text{Nominal pension in January 1984}}{\text{CPI in December 1983}} \times 100$$

Thus,

$$\text{Nominal pension in January 1984} = \$171 \times \frac{\text{CPI in December 1983}}{100} \times 100$$

$$= \$519$$

The other values in Exhibit 20C.2 can be calculated in the same way. Note that this type of indexing (a common form) will not prevent John's real monthly income from falling *during* the year. The lag in the adjustment will cause some erosion of purchasing power during the year. To check your understanding of indexing, verify the nominal pension that John received in January 1985 and January 1986.

Standard of living. The quantity of wants that can be satisfied, or the quantity of goods and services that can be purchased, with current income.

The important point here is that values expressed in terms of actual dollars, that is, in nominal terms, are potentially misleading whenever the general price level has changed. Throughout your study of macroeconomics you must be careful to distinguish between nominal and real values and between higher dollar prices and higher relative prices. Otherwise, you will find it impossible to correctly interpret economic "facts."

Inflation and the Standard of Living

Having seen how a change in the price level affects the interpretation of economic measurements, you are now ready to consider an important question: Is inflation necessarily a problem? Many people believe that inflation is a problem because they think that it automatically means a decline in their **standard of living**. But in economic terms, a decline in the standard of living occurs only when most households (or an identifiable group of households) cannot satisfy as many of their wants as before. Thus the standard of living depends on the quantity of economic goods and services that households can consume. Changes in the price level and changes in the standard of living are not necessarily connected.

Similarly, people often believe that inflation increases their cost of living. This is true only if we define cost in nominal terms, that is, as the average *dollar* cost of purchasing the goods and services required to maintain a certain standard of living. If a higher dollar cost is matched by an equal change in nominal (dollar) income, the *average* standard of living remains unchanged.

It is important to distinguish between a change in the purchasing power of money and the standard of living. A decline in purchasing power occurs whenever the general level of prices increases. A decline in the standard of living occurs only to the extent that nominal income does not rise enough to offset the change in prices.

Sometimes, however, price levels and income do not move at the same rate. For example, between 1929 and 1933, average prices fell by nearly 25 percent, but nominal income fell by over 50 percent. In this case lower prices did not improve the standard of living. Individuals who *had the same income* could purchase more because of lower prices. However, most people suffered a decline in real income and thus could afford to buy less. And between 1970 and 1979, the general price level increased by 80 percent, while nominal income increased by 147 percent. Although prices increased, nominal income rose faster. As a result, real income and the real standard of living went up. These examples indicate that the average standard of living for the economy as a whole is not affected in any consistent manner by changes in the general price level. What is important is whether real income and real output in the economy are increasing.

Inflation and Equity

If inflation does not necessarily mean that the average standard of living is lower, why are government officials, economists, and consumers so concerned about inflation? In the first place, inflation is always a problem for those whose income does not rise as fast as the general price level rises. It is also a problem when the prices of some goods rise more than others, as is often the case. In both situations, inflation raises equity issues.

For example, suppose that you lease an apartment for one year at a fixed rent of $500 per month. If the general level of prices increases during the year, the

Indexation. Adjusting the nominal values of wages, transfer payments, income tax brackets, or other economic variables in direct proportion to changes in the general price level.

real cost of your rent will decrease. You will gain but your landlord will lose. Of course, your landlord is likely to be aware of the potential effect of inflation and has probably considered it when determining your rent. If so, your landlord will lose only if prices rise more than anticipated.

Who wins and who loses from inflation is especially important to borrowers and lenders. In the 1950s and early 1960s, for example, home mortgage loans were available at interest rates of 3–4 percent. But inflation in the late 1960s rose to over 5 percent and averaged 7 percent from 1968 to 1982. With interest payments less than the rate of inflation, borrowers paid for their homes with "cheaper" dollars. Borrowers were pleased, but banks were not. However, inflation in the mid-1980s fell more rapidly than expected. Some people who had borrowed in the late 1970s and early 1980s were forced to pay the banks more, in real terms, than they had planned. Repayment became a very large problem for many farmers, whose real income was falling at the same time their real debt payments were increasing.

Finally, inflation raises equity questions because the nominal incomes of some individuals may not increase as fast as prices. For example, if retired individuals depend on fixed pensions, they will be hurt by inflation. Congress has *indexed* many federal benefit programs, raising payments as the CPI rises. **Indexation** refers to the procedure of adjusting the nominal value of something in order to maintain its real value. It has had a major impact on government transfer payments. Each 1 percent increase in the CPI causes an estimated $4.6 billion increase in federal transfers to Social Security, military, and civil service retirees and food stamp recipients.

Some politicians defend indexation as protecting the real value of government transfers for the recipients. Others oppose automatic spending increases, pointing to the already enormous federal budget deficit and the possibility that the CPI may overstate inflation. To the extent that the CPI overstates inflation, using it to index government transfers and pensions increases their real cost to the economy and the real income of those receiving payments.

Inflation and Efficiency

Rapid and unpredictable changes in the general price level may also decrease efficiency in the economy. For example, if your boss gives you a 10 percent raise at the same time the general price level increases 15 percent, you have actually received a wage cut. In hindsight, you can easily see whether you have gained or lost, but you may not have been able to when you got the raise. If you misunderstand the real economic meaning of your raise, you may not respond appropriately. Decreased real wages signal resources (including you) to seek other employment. If they do not, efficiency suffers (and your real income will fall).

In addition, when virtually all prices in the economy are changing, a business manager may not be sure whether a price rise signals increased demand or merely a rise in the general price level. A manager who mistakes changed demand for simple price inflation will respond inappropriately, and efficiency will suffer. Inefficiency is most likely when the rate of inflation is high and fluctuating, since such inflation creates considerable uncertainty.

Many costs of inflation stem from uncertainty. However, inflation imposes costs on the economy even when it is correctly anticipated. For example, many individuals buy gold, real estate, or works of art in expectation of inflation. If, as buyers hope, the prices of these products rise at rates equal to or above that of inflation, the buyers' wealth is protected. Although these purchases are not necessarily harmful, they may direct attention away from more productive uses of time, human energy, and financial assets. To the extent that they do, efficiency suffers. When inflation is both high and uncertain, individuals and businesses spend considerable amounts of time and energy seeking ways to "beat inflation." Although it may pay for individuals to do this, such activities rarely add to the country's overall productivity.

Businesses may also be misled by actual increased consumer demand during inflationary periods. Since inflation reduces the purchasing power of money, individuals who anticipate inflation may try to beat it by spending before the purchasing power of their money declines. That is, they may reduce current saving in order to buy products today that they will not consume until much later. This change in buying habits is not necessarily bad, but it may give businesses false signals about demand for certain products and may lower efficiency.

Price Stability: What Should Be the Goal?

If you are a typical college freshman, you probably have not lived in a year without inflation. Almost every political leader in recent times has worried about inflation and has wanted (or at least stated a desire) to control it. When we speak of achieving price stability, however, we do not mean that all prices should remain constant. Because changes in the prices of individual products and resources are the sources of the market system's information, we expect and even desire changes in relative prices. The goal of price stability is stable *average* prices. To accomplish this goal, prices of goods for which demand is decreasing must fall to offset the rising prices of goods for which demand is increasing.

However, some economists believe that the cost of absolute price stability may be too high. The connection between inflation and unemployment is that an increasing demand for goods results in more jobs and less employment, but greater demand also puts upward pressure on prices. Some economists argue that, in the short run, it may be preferable to trade somewhat higher rates of inflation for somewhat lower rates of unemployment. Politicians who set policy seem to prefer this option, fearing the wrath of an unemployed electorate. As you will discover in your study of macroeconomics, it is rarely possible to work on all of the macroeconomic goals at once. Trade-offs—whether between price stability and unemployment or between price stability and economic growth—may be inevitable.

MACROECONOMIC PERFORMANCE: THE U.S. ECONOMY

We would not expect any real-world economy to perform perfectly. But we are interested in knowing how closely the U.S. economy has come to meeting the goals of price stability, full employment, and economic growth. As you will see in this section, the historical record shows both successes and failures.

Aggregate output (real GNP)
(billions of dollars per year)

Exhibit 20.5
The Level of Aggregate Output: 1909–1986
The graph shows aggregate output (measured as real GNP) from 1909–1986. Data is plotted on a ratio or log scale in which the intervals represent equal percentage changes. Over the period shown, aggregate output has generally increased: The average growth rate has been 3.2 percent per year. There are also periodic fluctuations, the most severe of which occurred in the pre–World War II era.

Economic Stability and Economic Growth

Exhibit 20.5 shows the level of aggregate output from 1909 to 1986. Typically, aggregate output is shown as real GNP. We get several general impressions from Exhibit 20.5. First, despite a generally upward trend, the graph shows clear and persistent fluctuations (both upward and downward). These fluctuations are more frequent and more severe in the years before World War II (1909–1941) than after the war. Nevertheless, aggregate output has generally risen. In fact, we could approximate growth in aggregate output from 1950 to the present by a straight line. Over that period the average rate of increase has been about 3.2 percent per year.

Full Employment

Exhibit 20.6 shows that the unemployment rate fluctuated greatly prior to World War II. At the peak of the Great Depression in the 1930s, one of every four workers was unemployed. While this represented the worst case of unemployment in the United States in this century, unemployment has been a fairly constant source of concern.

Unemployment rate
(percent)

Exhibit 20.6
The Aggregate
Unemployment Rate:
1900–1986
This graph indicates that the unemployment rate in the U.S. economy has fluctuated widely. The fluctuations are more pronounced in the pre–World War II era. In the post–World War II era, the rate has shown an upward trend.

Year

Sources: *Historical Statistics of the United States; Economic Report of the President, 1987.*

Unemployment during recent business cycles. Exhibit 20.7 shows changes in both real GNP and the overall unemployment rate from 1955 to 1986 and the peaks in the business cycles during this period. From this information we can make two observations: First, changes in real GNP seem to be inversely related to changes in unemployment; when GNP grows, unemployment falls. Second, the unemployment rates associated with peaks in the business cycle have increased (except for the peak in 1969). Indeed, as the economy recovered following the recession in 1982, unemployment fell—but remained above 7 percent for almost 4 years.

What does this second observation mean in terms of macroeconomic performance? You might expect that full employment accompanies peaks in business activity. Do the data then imply that we have been less and less successful in reaching full employment? Do they mean that the natural rate of unemployment has changed over the years? Economists disagree strongly about the meaning of these data. Some believe that the natural rate of unemployment has increased greatly since the 1960s and may now be as high as 6–7 percent. Others, even those who accept some increase in the natural rate, believe that the economy has failed to reach its full employment potential in the 1980s.

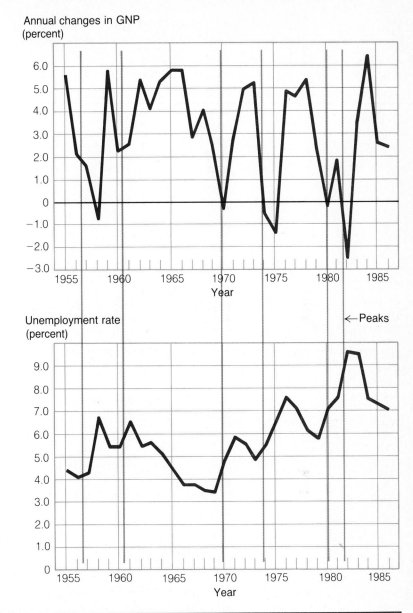

Exhibit 20.7
Changes in GNP and the
Unemployment Rate: 1955–1986
The two graphs indicate that the unemployment rate is inversely associated with changes in real GNP: When real GNP increases, the unemployment rate falls. However, the unemployment rate associated with *peaks* in the business cycle appears to have increased over time. Many economists associate at least part of this phenomenon to increases in the natural rate of unemployment.

GNP gaps as measures of full employment.   Exhibit 20.8 shows one estimate of the GNP gap, both in dollars and as a percentage of potential output, for the years 1955–1986. As you can see, in most years the GNP gap was positive, indicating that actual GNP was below potential GNP. For much of the last two decades, the GNP gap has been substantial. In 1982, for example, the GNP gap was estimated to be $290.4 billion, or 8.4 percent below potential output.

For a few years, however, especially in the late 1960s, the GNP gap was negative. That is, actual GNP exceeded potential GNP. That actual output could exceed potential output may sound strange. However, potential output and the natural rate of unemployment both reflect the behavior of the labor force under

Year	Gap in billions of 1982 dollars	As a percent of potential GNP	Year	Gap in billions of 1982 dollars	As a percent of potential GNP
1957	4.9	0.3	1972	−22.5	−0.9
1958	66.8	4.2	1973	−69.1	−2.6
1959	29.2	1.8	1974	35.1	1.3
1960	46.9	2.7	1975	151.5	5.3
1961	59.3	3.4	1976	103.4	3.5
1962	26.2	1.4	1977	57.6	1.9
1963	12.1	0.6	1978	−10.5	−0.3
1964	−47.8	−2.5	1979	2.9	0.1
1965	−64.4	−3.2	1980	94.2	2.9
1966	−111.8	−5.3	1981	118.9	3.5
1967	−98.9	−4.6	1982	290.4	8.4
1968	−114.4	−5.1	1983	268.4	7.6
1969	−90.5	−3.9	1984	151.0	4.1
1970	0.3	0.0	1985	151.6	4.1
1971	15.2	0.6	1986	160.3	4.2

Exhibit 20.8
GNP Gap: 1957–1986

Sources: Natural GNP data excerpted from Robert J. Gordon, *Macroeconomics,* 4th ed., Table A-1. Copyright © 1987 by Robert J. Gordon. Reprinted by permission of Little, Brown; actual GNP obtained from *Economic Report of the President, 1987,* Table B-2.

"normal" conditions. That is, individuals normally engage in a certain amount of job searching and are willing to trade only a certain amount of leisure for market work.

But such constraints are not absolute. Individuals may be induced to work a few more hours a week for a period of time, or employers may accept workers they might otherwise reject if demand is temporarily high. Potential GNP can be exceeded temporarily since it does not represent a *physical* or *technological* maximum.

Price Stability

Exhibit 20.9 shows how the general price level has fluctuated during the period 1909–1986. (The specific price index graphed, called the GNP deflator, functions much like the CPI; we explain it in Chapter 21.) However, since World War II (1946–1986), prices have consistently moved upward, accelerating rapidly in the 1970s. Thus inflation has been a major fact of economic life for some time.

Two Periods in Recent Macroeconomic History

Looking more closely at the data, we can divide the post–World War II years into two periods. Between 1945 and 1970, policy makers saw a straightforward trade-off between high prices and high economic growth. When the economy grew rapidly and unemployment was low, as in the late 1960s, inflation increased. When unemployment was high and economic growth low, as in the late 1950s, inflation was low. Thus policy makers generally opted for moderate growth in aggregate output and slowly rising prices.

Price-level index

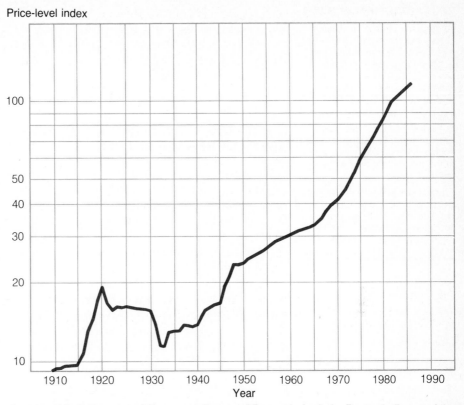

Sources: U.S. Department of Commerce, Bureau of Economic Analysis; *Economic Report of the President, 1987.*

Exhibit 20.9
The General Level of Prices: 1909–1986
This graph indicates how the general price level of the U.S. economy has fluctuated. In the pre–World War II period, prices sometimes rose and sometimes fell. However, since World War II, there has been a consistent upward trend in prices, with an acceleration in the 1970s. The graph is drawn on a ratio scale in which the units on the vertical axis represent equal percentage changes in prices, not equal absolute changes. *Note:* This is a plot of the GNP deflator, a particular measure of the general price level. We discuss the meaning and construction of this measure in Chapter 21.

In the 1970s, however, the economy experienced both rising unemployment and increased inflation. Twice in the decade—in 1970–71 and in 1974–75—aggregate output decreased while inflation accelerated. Unemployment averaged 30–40 percent higher than in the 1950s or 1960s. The average rate of inflation was more than twice as high. Economists termed this double whammy **stagflation**, indicating the combination of stagnation (or recession) and inflation. In dealing with stagflation, the macroeconomic policies chosen in the 1970s appear to have failed. But the economy's performance does not depend solely on such policies. Twice during the 1970s (1973–1974 and 1979–1980), energy prices skyrocketed. The macroeconomic consequences of these events must also be considered when judging the policies used.

Controversy over interpretation of macroeconomic data is typical. As you have seen, some economists even question whether measures such as the unemploy-

Stagflation. A period of time during which the total output of the economy falls, while the levels of general prices and unemployment rise.

ment rate and the CPI are accurate. What causes macroeconomic outcomes is even more controversial. In the following chapters, we identify and describe the basic factors that, we believe, determine macroeconomic outcomes. Only with this background will you be able to rationally consider the likely results of different macroeconomic policies.

A PREVIEW OF AGGREGATE DEMAND AND AGGREGATE SUPPLY

Economists generally agree that demand and supply are useful tools for exploring both microeconomic and macroeconomic issues. Recall that microeconomists use demand and supply to analyze changes in price and output for individual goods. Macroeconomists use **aggregate demand (AD)** and **aggregate supply (AS)** to study changes in the general price level and aggregate output.

Aggregate demand in the U.S. economy is the relationship between price level and quantity of all goods and services demanded. It reflects the spending plans of all U.S. households, businesses, and governments, as well as those of foreign households, businesses, and governments for U.S. goods and services. Aggregate supply is the relationship between U.S. price level and total output supplied by all U.S. businesses. The interaction of these two forces determines the level of aggregate output and the general price level.

Graphic Representation

Exhibit 20.10(a) shows demand and supply of doughnuts (see Chapter 3), and Exhibit 20.10(b) shows aggregate demand and aggregate supply for an economy. The two graphs are alike in several ways. Both demand for doughnuts and aggregate demand have a negative slope (downward and to the right). Both supply of doughnuts and aggregate supply have a positive slope (upward and to the right). In both graphs, the vertical axis represents price, and the horizontal axis represents quantity; both graphs show quantity demanded and supplied in a particular period of time.

The two graphs are different in important respects, as well. The microeconomic graph (Exhibit 20.10a) shows the output of a single good. The macroeconomic graph (Exhibit 20.10b) shows general price level as measured by a price index (vertical axis) and aggregate output for the economy (horizontal axis). Of course, no one actually buys a unit of aggregate output. (If you add 2 doughnuts and 3 cups of coffee, what would you call the sum—breakfast?) As we describe more completely in Chapter 21, economists measure aggregate output by adding the market values of all goods and services produced in the economy. For the United States, this amount is rather large. Note that aggregate output in Exhibit 20.10(b) is measured in billions of dollars.

Aggregate demand (AD). Demand for all goods and services in the economy; relationship between total quantity of goods and services demanded and general price level.

Aggregate supply (AS). Supply of all goods and services in the economy; relationship between total quantity of goods and services supplied and general price level.

Shapes of aggregate demand and aggregate supply curves. The reasons for the shapes of the aggregate demand and aggregate supply curves also differ from the reasons for the shapes of microeconomic curves. The negative slope of demand for doughnuts reflects the law of demand: A higher price will cause consumers to buy substitutes. The positive slope of supply of doughnuts reflects the law of supply: As prices fall, producers will supply fewer doughnuts

(a) Microeconomic view

(b) Macroeconomic view

Exhibit 20.10
Two Views of Demand and Supply
The graph in part (a) is a microeconomic view of demand and supply of a single product: doughnuts. The graph in part (b) is a macroeconomic view of aggregate demand and supply of all goods and services produced in the economy. In both graphs, price appears on the vertical axis and quantity on the horizontal axis. While the microeconomic view shows the output of a single good, the macroeconomic view shows the general price level (the average price of all goods and services) and aggregate output (the value of all goods and services produced). Demand and supply curves have similar shapes in both graphs, but the explanation behind the shape and the factors that shift the curves are very different.

and more substitutes. But if the price of all goods (that is, aggregate output) changes, there may be no cheaper substitutes.

The shape of the aggregate demand curve reflects the operation of three forces. First, a decrease in price level will increase the wealth of households. For example, suppose that you have $2000 in the bank that you are saving to pay some of next year's college expenses. If prices of all goods (including college expenses) drop by 10 percent, the purchasing power of your $2000 will have increased. You can spend some of this money and still be able to pay as much of next year's expenses as before. As price level decreases, real wealth of households increases and quantity of aggregate output demanded increases.

Second, a drop in the price level in the United States causes a change in the relative price of U.S. and foreign products. Foreigners will buy more U.S. products and U.S. residents will buy fewer foreign products (and more U.S. products) as

U.S. price level falls. Finally, a fall in the price level tends to reduce the rate of interest, that is, the cost of borrowing. As a result, households will borrow more to finance house and automobile purchases. Businesses will borrow more to invest in machinery and buildings.

The positive slope of the aggregate supply curve suggests that businesses will increase total quantity of goods produced when the general price level increases. As we discuss more completely in Chapter 26, this change often occurs because some costs (wages, for example) may increase more slowly than product prices as price level rises. Thus an increase in the general price level will raise business profits and induce businesses to offer more for sale.

Interactions

The concept of equilibrium is also used in both microeconomics and macroeconomics, but in somewhat different ways. We have already described how individual product markets reach equilibrium where quantity demanded equals quantity supplied, that is, where the demand and supply curves intersect. Similarly, macroeconomic equilibrium lies at the intersection of the aggregate demand and aggregate supply curves. In Exhibit 20.10(b), equilibrium output is $1950 billion per year. The equilibrium price level is 120, which means that prices are (on the average) 120 percent of those in the base year. This equilibrium point tells us the level of aggregate output and the current price level. But in macroeconomics, we are also interested in understanding why price level, aggregate output, and unemployment *change*. Macroeconomists associate these changes with shifts in aggregate demand and supply.

Consider, for example, Exhibit 20.11(a), which shows an increase in aggregate demand (from AD_1 to AD_2). It predicts that both aggregate output and price level will rise. This increase is exactly what happened in the U.S. economy between 1964 and 1966. Aggregate output increased at the rate of 4 percent per year—a very high rate by historical standards. Unemployment fell from over 5 percent to under 3 percent—the lowest level since World War II. At the same time, price level increased at twice its rate of the preceeding five years.

Exhibit 20.11(b) shows a decrease in aggregate supply (from AS_1 to AS_2). It predicts that aggregate output will fall and price level will rise. This pattern describes the performance of the U.S. economy from 1973 to 1975. Aggregate output fell by 0.5 percent in 1974 and 1.3 percent in 1975. Unemployment increased by almost 3 percent. The general price level increased by over 12 percent in 1974 and 7 percent in 1975.

CONCLUSION

We showed how the performance of the economy has certainly been less than ideal, with regard to the goals of full employment, price stability, and economic growth. But the more important (and very controversial) question is what, if anything, the government can do to improve economic performance? Economists disagree sharply on whether such *stabilization policies* are possible and desirable or unnecessary and impractical.

(a) An increase in aggregate demand

(b) A decrease in aggregate supply

Exhibit 20.11
Changes in Aggregate Demand and Aggregate Supply
Part (a) shows the effects of an increase in aggregate demand from AD_1 to AD_2. Note that at each price level, quantity of aggregate output demanded is greater. As a result, the general price level increases and quantity of aggregate output bought and sold increases. (Compare point *a* with point *b*.) Part (b) shows the changes that occur when aggregate supply decreases. Note that at each price level, quantity of aggregate output supplied is less. As a result, the general price level increases and quantity of aggregate output bought and sold decreases. (Compare point *c* with point *d*.)

In addition, economists do not agree on the conclusions to be drawn from the historical record. The period from 1945 to the present, in which the government became an active participant in efforts to stabilize the economy, is particularly controversial. Some economists believe that this experience indicates how little faith can be placed in macroeconomic policies. Others see benefits from using macroeconomic policies and believe that the economy's recent performance compares favorably with that of earlier periods.

Although macroeconomics involves a lot of controversy, economists generally agree on the validity and usefulness of some basic tools of macroeconomic analysis. In Chapters 26–31 we use the tools of aggregate demand and supply introduced in this chapter and expand on them. As you will see, interactions between aggregate demand and supply help us to see how the macroeconomy functions. And different interpretations of how they interact help explain why economists have reached such different conclusions.

SUMMARY

1. In this chapter we explored macroeconomic perspectives on unemployment, inflation, and aggregate demand and supply.

2. Microeconomics focuses on the relative prices of individual products and resources. Macroeconomics focuses on the economy as a whole: aggregate output and the general price level. Both macroeconomic and microeconomic perspectives are important when considering any economic policy.

3. Full employment is a macroeconomic goal, but definitions of unemployment and full employment are controversial. The official definition of an unemployed person is someone without a job who is actively engaged in looking for work. Official statistics may underestimate the true unemployment rate by ignoring discouraged individuals who have stopped looking for a job and underemployed workers. Official statistics may overestimate the true unemployment rate by counting workers who are voluntarily unemployed.

4. Economists identify three types of unemployment. Frictional unemployment occurs when individuals move into or out of the job market or from industry to industry. Such unemployment is a normal part of the economy and promotes efficiency but at some cost to the temporarily jobless. Structural unemployment occurs when unemployed individuals do not qualify for jobs that are vacant or perhaps because of discrimination. This mismatch serves no useful social purpose but is difficult to overcome. Cyclical unemployment is associated with declines in GNP. Additional jobs are required to reduce cyclical unemployment.

5. Economists define full employment—the natural rate of unemployment—as the level of unemployment that would exist if the economy were producing at the level of its potential GNP. It is the level of unemployment consistent with frictional and structural unemployment, but reflecting zero cyclical unemployment.

6. Potential GNP is the maximum level of output that an economy can produce without putting upward or downward pressure on the general price level. The difference between potential and actual GNP is called the GNP gap. A positive gap occurs when actual GNP is less than potential GNP. A negative gap occurs when actual GNP is more than potential GNP.

7. Economists measure the general price level using price indexes, such as the Consumer Price Index. The CPI is calculated by comparing the cost of a market basket of certain goods with the cost in a specified base or reference year. The percentage change in the price index from one year to the next is called the inflation rate.

8. When the general price level rises, the purchasing power of money falls. To correctly interpret changes in economic variables (such as income or GNP) that are measured in dollar terms requires translation from nominal terms (actual dollars) to real terms (purchasing power). Changes in real income or real GNP represent changes in the standard of living.

9. Inflation represents a sustained increase in the general price level. It erodes the purchasing power of income and some forms of wealth and, especially when unanticipated, redistributes wealth. Inflation may lower efficiency by distorting price signals and causing individuals to spend time and energy trying to offset its effects.

10. Economists define the goal of price stability in terms of a relatively stable general price level because relative price changes are important signals for the economy.

11. The U.S. economy has had varying rates of growth, unemployment, and inflation. Since 1950, the growth rate has fluctuated less than before. But since 1960, the unemployment rate has risen, possibly as a result of a higher natural rate of unemployment. And since 1950, the general price level has generally risen.

12. Aggregate demand and aggregate supply reflect the relationship between aggregate output demanded and supplied and the general price level. Aggregate demand has a negative slope because lower prices raise the real wealth of households, increase the relative price of foreign goods and services, and lower interest rates. Aggregate supply has a positive slope because some resource prices (costs) rise more slowly than product prices. Increases in aggregate demand raise the general price level, increase aggregate output, and lower unemployment. Decreases in aggregate supply raise the general price level, decrease aggregate output, and raise unemployment.

KEY TERMS

Aggregate output, 501
Gross national product (GNP), 501
General price level, 501
Labor force, 503
Unemployment rate, 503
Discouraged worker, 504
Underemployed, 504
Frictional unemployment, 505
Structural unemployment, 505
Cyclical unemployment, 506
Business cycle, 506
Recession, 506
Trough, 507
Recovery, 507

Peak, 507
Natural rate of unemployment, 508
Potential GNP, 509
GNP gap, 509
Inflation, 509
Price index, 509
Consumer price index (CPI), 509
Nominal, 511
Real, 511
Nominal income, 511
Real income, 512
Nominal GNP, 513
Real GNP, 513
Standard of living, 514
Indexation, 515
Stagflation, 521
Aggregate demand (AD), 522
Aggregate supply (AS), 522

QUESTIONS FOR REVIEW AND DISCUSSION

1. Comment on the statement: "*Micro* means small, and microeconomics is what economists use to study the operations of a small grocery store or the aggregate activity of a small economy such as New Zealand's. *Macro* means large, and macroeconomics is what economists use to study the aggregate economic activity of a large country such as the United States or the operations of a large corporation such as IBM."

2. If the price of an average restaurant meal rises by 5 percent during a period when the general price level rises by 8 percent, are restaurant meals really more expensive? Would you expect more or fewer restaurant meals to be purchased? Why is it important to adjust prices, incomes, and other economic variables for changes in the general price level?

3. Do you believe that inflation or unemployment is the more serious problem today? Why?

4. Between 1982 and 1986, the after-tax income of John Adams, proprietor of the Yankee Doodle Company, increased from $37,500 to $40,000. (Note that in Exhibit 20.4 the consumer price index increased from 289.1 in 1982 to 328.4 in 1986.)

   a) Did John's income increase in real terms?
   b) If John's income was fully indexed to the consumer price index (that is, a 1 percent increase in the CPI meant a 1 percent increase in his income), what would his income have been in 1986?

   c) If John's income rises by exactly the same rate as the CPI, does this necessarily mean that his standard of living is unchanged? Why or why not?

5. Based on the official definitions of unemployment, would the following individuals be classified as employed, unemployed, or not in the labor force?

   a) John Youngblood, age 15, worked 20 hours last week in a local grocery store.
   b) Mildred Elderberry, a retiree, worked 20 hours last week without pay in her son's paint store.
   c) Robert Pickney, a recent college graduate, was offered three different jobs last week but continued to look for a better job.
   d) Hilda Kraft, a former elementary school art teacher, was laid off last spring because of budget cuts, would like a similar job, but is not currently looking for work.
   e) Bill Bluestone, a factory worker, is not working this week because of illness but will return to work next week.

6. The government publishes indexes showing industrial production for the economy as a whole and for individual product groups. The following table shows some index numbers for July 1981 and November 1982, the start and end of the most recent recession.

	Indexes of industrial production for				
Date	All final products	All consumer products	Autos	Consumer staples	Business equipment
7/81	153.9	150.7	147.6	151.6	184.8
11/82	134.9	141.3	120.7	152.0	146.4

   a) Calculate the percentage change in each index.
   b) Why do you suppose that the index for autos changed more than the index for consumer staples? (*Hint:* Consider a recession as a change in national income and use the concept of income elasticity from Chapter 4.)
   c) What do these data suggest about the distribution of unemployment across industries during a recession?
   d) What do these data suggest about the effect of a recession on consumption spending and fixed investment?

7. What changes in aggregate demand or aggregate supply would explain the following conditions?

   a) An increase in aggregate output.
   b) A decrease in the general price level.
   c) An increase in the general price level and a decrease in aggregate output.
   d) Lower unemployment and a higher general price level.

8. Use the information presented in the appendix to this chapter and the following data, which show prices and quantities consumed of three products over two years, to help you find the answers to (a)–(d).

Product	1988		1989	
	Quantity consumed	Price per unit	Quantity consumed	Price per unit
Bananas	100 lb	$0.50/lb	110 lb	$0.55/lb
Cloth	200 yd	3.00/yd	250 yd	3.10/yd
Books	10	2.00/book	20	2.50/book

a) Use the constant market-basket approach and calculate an index of the price level for each year, using 1988 as the base year.
b) Use the current market-basket approach and calculate an index of the price level for each year, using 1988 as the base year.
c) Calculate the percentage change in the price level using each index. Explain the difference.
d) What can you say about the change in the relative prices of the three items?

Appendix to Chapter 20

Measuring Price Levels

As we noted in this chapter, economists measure average prices by constructing a *price index* that measures the price level as a percentage of the price level in a selected base, or reference, year. There are two basic approaches to constructing a price index: the *constant market-basket* approach and the *current market-basket* approach. Each is used to calculate average prices; each results in a common measure of the general price level.

We can contrast the two approaches using a simple economy with only two products—apples and wooden spoons—and limiting our discussion to two years—1988 and 1987. Exhibit 20A.1 shows this economy. How should we calculate the average price in each year? We could, of course, simply take the average of the two prices. But doing so would not recognize the relative importance of the two goods. The market value of apples in 1987 was $80 (40 pounds × $2 per pound). The market value of spoons was $40 (40 spoons × $1 per spoon).

To recognize the greater importance of apples in the economy, we want the average price to be a *weighted average*. The market value of the goods consumed weights the prices by the quantity consumed. But we cannot compare the total market values in the two years. The increased market value in 1988 is only partly the result of higher prices. Quantities produced and consumed are also greater.

To calculate how much average price has changed, we want to compare the cost of buying a certain number of apples and wooden spoons. If quantities are fixed, then all changes in market value must be caused by changes in price. The constant market-basket approach tells us how much more (or less) it costs to buy

(a) Basic information on prices and quantities

	1987		1988	
Product	*Quantity*	*Price*	*Quantity*	*Price*
Apples	40 lb	$2.00/lb	60 lb	$2.20/lb
Wooden spoons	40 spoons	$1.00/spoon	80 spoons	$1.25/spoon

(b) Constant market basket (Consumer Price Index)

	Market value of 1987 quantities	
Product	*In 1987 prices*	*In 1988 prices*
Apples	$ 80	$ 88
Wooden spoons	40	50
Total	$120	$138

$$\text{Price index, 1988} = \frac{\text{Cost of 1987 quantities in 1988 prices}}{\text{Cost of 1987 quanities in 1987 prices}} \times 100$$

$$= \frac{\$138}{\$120}(100) \quad \text{or} \quad \underline{\underline{115}}$$

(c) Current market basket (GNP deflator)

	Market value of 1988 quantities	
Product	*In 1987 prices*	*In 1988 prices*
Apples	$120	$132
Wooden spoons	80	100
Total	$200	$232

$$\text{Price index, 1988} = \frac{\text{Cost of 1988 quantities in 1988 prices}}{\text{Cost of 1988 quanities in 1987 prices}} \times 100$$

$$= \frac{\$232}{\$200}(100) \quad \text{or} \quad \underline{\underline{116}}$$

Exhibit 20A.1
Calculating Price Indexes

the same quantities in the current year as in the base year. The current market-basket approach tells us how much more (or less) it would have cost to buy today's quantities at base-year prices.

CONSTRUCTING A PRICE INDEX: THE CONSTANT MARKET-BASKET APPROACH

The constant market-basket approach is the one used for the Consumer Price Index. The first step is to select a base, or reference, year. The base year for the CPI is 1967. In this example we use 1987 as the base year. The second step is to determine quantities for the market basket using quantities consumed in the base year. In this case, the quantities are the 40 pounds of apples and 40 wooden spoons purchased in 1987. Using 1987 prices, it would have cost $120 to buy this market basket. In 1988, the price of apples went up by 10 percent (from $2.00 to $2.20 per pound). The price of wooden spoons increased by 25 percent (from $1.00 to $1.25 per spoon). But what was the average increase?

In using this approach, we calculate the increase in average price as the percentage increase in the cost of the constant market basket. To determine this increase, we calculate the cost of the market basket—40 pounds of apples and 40 spoons—using 1988 prices. As shown in Exhibit 20A.1, we would have paid $138 in 1988 to buy the market basket. That is, the cost of the constant market basket (average price) increased by 15 percent.

As we also noted in this chapter, economists generally use a price index to indicate the general price level. They construct a constant market-basket price index by dividing the current cost of the market-basket price level by the cost for the base year (then multiply the ratio by 100 to express the index as a *percentage*). Expressed as a formula, the current-year price index is

$$\text{Current-year price index} = \frac{\text{Cost of base-year market basket in current-year prices}}{\text{Cost of base-year market basket in base-year prices}} \times 100$$

The price index will always have a value of 100 in the base year because the numerator and the denominator in the formula are identical. In our example, the constant market-basket price index for 1988 has a value of 115, calculated as

$$\text{1988 price index} = \frac{\text{Cost of 1987 market basket in 1988 prices}}{\text{Cost of 1987 market basket in 1987 prices}} \times 100$$

$$= \frac{\$138}{\$120}(100) \quad \text{or} \quad 115$$

The 1988 price index of 115 means that the price level in 1988 is 115 percent of the price level in 1987. In other words the price level, a measure of average price, increased by 15 percent. To check your understanding of this formula, find the price index for 1986 if 35 apples were bought at $1.80 per pound and 30 wooden spoons were bought at $0.75 each. Keep 1987 as your base year. (Your answer should be 85.)

CONSTRUCTING A PRICE INDEX: THE CURRENT MARKET-BASKET APPROACH

The second method of calculating a price index is based on the current cost of the market-basket quantities. We calculate the price index by comparing the market-basket cost in current and base-year prices. As shown in Exhibit 20A.1, this constant-price approach results in an index for 1988 that is based on 1988 prices. We can state this relationship in a formula as

$$\text{Current-year price index} = \frac{\text{Cost of current market basket in current-year prices}}{\text{Cost of current market basket in base-year prices}} \times 100$$

Using the data from our example, we calculate the current market-basket price index for 1988 as 116. That is,

$$1988 \text{ price index} = \frac{\text{Cost of 1988 market basket in 1988 prices}}{\text{Cost of 1988 market basket in 1987 prices}} \times 100$$

$$= \frac{\$232}{\$200}(100) \quad \text{or} \quad 116$$

Again, the 1988 price index of 116 means that the price level in 1988 is 116 percent of the price level in 1987. That is, the price level (average price) increased by 16 percent. To check your understanding of this formula, find the price index for 1986 if 35 apples were bought at \$1.80 per pound and 50 wooden spoons were bought at \$0.90 each. Keep 1987 as your base year. (Your answer should be 90.)

Economists use the current market-basket approach to calculate a price index known as the GNP deflator. (We discuss the GNP deflator in detail in Chapter 21.) Actually, the GNP deflator is the ratio of nominal GNP to real GNP. That is, the numerator in the current market-basket approach represents the market value of the current quantities at current prices (nominal GNP). The denominator represents the market value of the current quantities after removing the effects of the change in prices (real GNP).

Some economists favor using the GNP deflator instead of the CPI because the former covers a wider range of goods and services in the economy. (The CPI is based only on consumer goods and services.) Even more important, the constant market basket used in the CPI does not reflect changes in tastes and preferences or substitutions of relatively less for relatively more expensive items over time.

CONCLUSION

The two methods shown are alternative ways to calculate an index of the general price level. Both types of indexes hold quantity consumed constant, so that only price change is measured. In the constant market-basket approach, current- and base-year costs of the quantities from the base year are compared. In the current market-basket approach, current- and base-year costs of the quantities of the current year are compared. Each method yields an index, changes in which measure annual inflation rates. The Consumer Price Index follows the constant market-basket approach. The GNP deflator uses the current market-basket approach.

Gross National Product:
Measuring Aggregate Output

QUESTIONS TO CONSIDER

☐ What does GNP measure?

☐ How do economists measure GNP?

☐ What do the accounting identities tell us about the circular flow in a private-sector economy?

☐ In what ways do the government and foreign sectors affect the circular flow?

☐ How do national income accounting definitions differ from accounting identities?

I n Chapter 20 we introduced gross national product (GNP) as the statistical measure of aggregate output. In 1970, real GNP in the United States was $2.4 trillion, or an average of $11,800 per person. By 1986, real GNP had grown to $3.7 trillion, or $15,300 per person. In this chapter we consider how GNP is calculated and how useful it is as an indicator of economic activity.

Why do economists spend so much time defining and measuring gross national product? Because GNP is a key indicator of whether the economy as a whole is progressing toward society's economic goals. Government policy makers use past values of GNP to determine how well their policies worked. They use forecasts of future GNP to determine the potential effects of policies they are considering. Businesses use forecasts of GNP to predict future demand for their products. Economists use GNP to test the correctness of macroeconomic theories.

In addition, the measurement of GNP reveals a great deal about the relationships between resource markets and product markets. In Chapter 6 we showed how households, businesses, governments, and the foreign sector interact. As we discuss how GNP is calculated, you will learn how the interactions of these sectors, especially in financial markets, explain the operation of the macroeconomy.

DEFINING AND MEASURING AGGREGATE OUTPUT

In Chapter 20 we defined gross national product as the total *market value* of the *final* goods and services that an economy *produces during a particular period of time*. Each of the italicized phrases is important to your understanding the meaning of GNP.

GNP Measures Market Values

Measuring aggregate output—the quantity of all goods and services produced in the economy—presents a problem unlike that of measuring the output of individual markets. In Chapter 3 we used a physical measure of output (dozens of doughnuts) in studying the market for doughnuts. But to measure aggregate output (GNP) we must count not only the quantity of doughnuts but also the

	Apples	Wooden spoons	Gross national product (GNP)
Price (P)	$2.00/apple	$1.00/spoon	
Quantity produced (Q)	200 apples	600 spoons	
Market value (P × Q)	$ 400 +	$ 600 =	$1000

Exhibit 21.1
Calculating Gross National Product for a Two-Good Economy

quantities of shoes, apples, and all other products. We cannot simply add physical quantities of different products and obtain a meaningful number. But we can calculate the market values (market price multiplied by physical quantity) of doughnuts, shoes, apples, and other products and then add these values to obtain total market value. Total market value is aggregate output, or GNP.

Exhibit 21.1 provides a simple example of how GNP is calculated. This hypothetical economy produces only two goods—apples and wooden spoons. Using the market-value approach, we first determine the total market value of each good by multiplying the market price and quantity produced (P × Q). To calculate GNP we add the market values of each product. In this example, $400 worth of apples and $600 worth of wooden spoons were produced during the period, giving a GNP of $1000.

Economists generally believe that market prices reflect the relative benefits consumers receive from different products. Thus a change in market values can help us determine whether the economy has satisfied more or less of society's wants. Of course, no measure—including GNP—is perfect. But economists generally believe that it is a good measure of aggregate output.

GNP Measures Output of Final Goods and Services

When calculating GNP, economists distinguish between final goods and intermediate goods. **Final goods** are (or will be) sold to their ultimate user. **Intermediate goods** are either used up completely in producing other goods or are purchased for resale. The value of intermediate goods is excluded from GNP. Including intermediate goods would double-count the value of resources used, since intermediate goods ultimately become part of the value of final goods.

For example, if you buy a new car produced in the United States this year for $8000, we can say that a final good worth $8000 was produced. But several market transactions occurred before you purchased the car. The local car dealer purchased it from the manufacturer for $6000. At that stage, your car was an intermediate good because it was purchased for resale. If we added the $6000 and $8000 together we would overstate the value of goods produced. Only the $8000 value of the final good—the car purchased by its ultimate consumer—is counted in GNP. By the same logic, we exclude the value of steel and tires purchased by the car manufacturer. These, too, are intermediate goods because they are used to produce the car. They are already a part of the final $8000 value, and to count their purchases also would overstate GNP.

Final goods. Products and services that are (or will be) sold to their ultimate user. GNP is a measure of the value of final goods produced.

Intermediate goods. Products and services that are used to produce other goods and services or are purchased for resale. The value of intermediate goods is excluded from GNP.

GNP Measures Goods and Services Produced in the Current Period

The definition of GNP also indicates that we want to calculate the economic value that an economy *produces in a particular period of time*, such as the current year. Thus GNP for this year does not count the $200 you paid for a new bicycle yesterday if the bicycle was produced last year. If your bicycle was produced in 1988, it is counted as part of GNP for 1988 even if it was not finally sold until 1989.

In addition, GNP is a measure of economic value *produced*, not *sold*, so we do not count the sale of secondhand items. The original sale of an item represents the value of the good produced. The $400 you paid for a new video cassette recorder in February is a part of GNP. But if you sell it to your roommate in June for $175, the value of VCRs produced does not increase. There are no additional VCRs, just a different owner.

Finally, GNP excludes financial transactions because they do not represent goods and services produced. Your purchase of 100 shares of common stock of a new corporation for $1000 or a bank loan of $50,000 to a business are purely financial exchanges. Neither transaction represents the production of additional goods or services. GNP focuses only on exchanges that occur in product markets, not financial markets.

Measuring GNP: Real versus Nominal GNP

Although market prices help us estimate the value of goods and services produced, market prices are a somewhat unstable measuring scale, as you saw in Chapter 20. When the general price level rises, average market price increases, but the higher price level does not necessarily reflect the production of more real economic value. (If the price of a pizza increases from $5 to $8, do you get more satisfaction from eating it?)

Thus if we use current market prices, measured GNP may increase, even if the economy's performance has not improved. Thus we must clearly distinguish changes in *nominal GNP* from changes in *real GNP*. (Recall that nominal values are expressed in current dollars. Real values are expressed in terms of dollars of constant purchasing power.) An increase in nominal GNP can occur even when fewer economic goods and services are produced. For example, nominal GNP increased by 3.7 percent in 1982. However, 1982 was a year of recession and real GNP actually decreased by 2.5 percent.

Exhibit 21.2 again illustrates a simple economy that produces only apples and wooden spoons. In the top half of the exhibit, current prices and current quantities are used to calculate *nominal GNP*. In this example, nominal GNP increased from $1000 in 1988 to $1320 in 1989, a 32 percent increase. But did the economy actually produce 32 percent more goods and services? We cannot use nominal GNP to answer that question because both output and price may increase (as they did in this example). You can see in the table that the quantity of apples produced increased by only 20 percent. The rest of the increase in the market value of apples occurred because the price of apples rose.

Year	Apples			Wooden spoons			Gross national product
	Price (P_a)	Quantity (Q_a)	Market value $(P_a \times Q_a)$	Price (P_s)	Quantity (Q_s)	Market value $(P_s \times Q_s)$	
Nominal GNP: Current quantities and current prices							
1988	$2.00	200	$400	$1.00	600	$600	$1000
1989	2.20	240	528	1.10	720	792	1320
Real GNP: Current quantities and 1988 prices							
1988	$2.00	200	$400	$1.00	600	$600	$1000
1989	2.00	240	480	1.00	720	720	1200

**Exhibit 21.2
Nominal and Real GNP for a Two-Good Economy**

GNP deflator. The ratio of nominal GNP to real GNP expressed as a percentage; a measure of the general price level.

Since higher prices do not mean that more of society's wants have been satisfied, economists distinguish between changes in nominal GNP and changes in real GNP. To measure *real GNP,* economists use a constant set of prices. Because prices are held constant, real GNP changes only when the quantities produced rise or fall. We calculated real GNP in Exhibit 21.2 by determining how much GNP would have been in 1989 if prices had remained the same as they were in 1988. Using the 1988 price of apples and wooden spoons we calculated the real GNP for 1989 to be $1200, compared with $1320 for nominal GNP. Nominal GNP increased by $320 (32 percent). Of that increase, $200 represents a 20 percent increase in higher real value; $120 reflects the 10 percent increase in the average price of goods and services.

As we noted in Chapter 20, macroeconomic analysis often requires us to translate from nominal to real terms. As you saw, the CPI is sometimes used to deflate economic variables. When dealing with GNP, however, economists use the **GNP deflator**, that is, the ratio of nominal GNP to real GNP in a given year. In our example,

$$\text{GNP deflator, 1989} = \frac{\text{Nominal GNP, 1989}}{\text{Real GNP, 1989}} \times 100$$

$$= \frac{\$1320}{\$1200}(100) \quad \text{or} \quad 110$$

The value of the GNP deflator, like the value of the CPI, expresses the price level in any year as a percentage of the price level in a base year. In our example, we used 1988 prices to calculate real GNP; thus 1988 is the base year. The value of 110 for the GNP deflator indicates that the general price level increased by 10 percent between 1988 and 1989. (We can verify this rise, since Exhibit 20.2 shows that the price of each of the two products increased by 10 percent. However, it would be unusual for all prices to increase at the average rate.)

Currently, 1982 is used as the base year for the GNP deflator for the United States. We can calculate the value of the GNP deflator for 1985 by using the preceding formula and the value for nominal GNP ($3992.5 billion) and real GNP ($3573.5 billion). The GNP deflator for 1985 was 111.7, indicating that the general price level increased by 11.7 percent from 1982 to 1985. To check your understanding, verify this calculation using the same formula and the values given for nominal and real GNP in 1985.

First and Second Accounting Identities

The United States did not always have a measure of aggregate output. Many of the concepts and techniques used to measure GNP were developed in the 1930s, largely as a result of the efforts of Simon Kuznets. For his work, Kuznets was later awarded a Nobel Prize in Economics. Fundamental to Kuznets's measurements are two **accounting identities**, which are expressions that are *always true* by definition.

First accounting identity. The first identity states that aggregate output is always equal to actual aggregate expenditures. **Aggregate expenditures (AE)** are the total expenditures by all sectors of the economy on final goods in a specific period of time. Expressed in equation form,

First accounting identity

Aggregate output = Actual aggregate expenditures

Clearly, the amount spent on final goods sold is equal to the value of goods sold. (If you spend $300 to buy a color-TV set, the $300 represents both the amount you spent and the market value of what you bought.) But GNP is the value of final goods *produced*, not *sold*. What happens if businesses are unable to sell all that they have produced? Economists consider all final goods produced but not sold as though they had been bought by the business sector. This convention preserves the accounting identity and the objective of measuring the value of final goods produced in a particular period of time.

You may suspect (correctly) that aggregate expenditures are related to aggregate demand. But two differences are important. First, aggregate demand is a *relationship* between quantity of GNP demanded and general price level. Actual aggregate expenditures are a *single quantity* produced at the current price level. Second, actual aggregate expenditures may include "unplanned spending," or spending by businesses for goods produced but not sold. *Planned* aggregate expenditures at a certain price level and quantity of aggregate output demanded at that price level are, in fact, identical. (We discuss planned aggregate expenditures in detail in Chapter 22.)

Accounting identities. Relationships between macroeconomic variables that are always true by definition.

Aggregate expenditures (AE). Total expenditures on final goods by all sectors of the economy during a particular period of time.

National income (NI). Total income earned by the household sector; the sum of wages, rent, interest, and profits. It represents payment for resources used to produce final goods during a particular period of time.

Second accounting identity. The second identity recognizes that any market transaction involves two parties and can be examined from two perspectives. All dollars spent on aggregate output become dollars of income received by households in the economy. Thus aggregate output equals national income. **National income (NI)**—the total income earned by the household sector—is the sum of wages, rent, interest, and profits. Thus it represents payment for the resources used to produce final goods during a particular period of time. Expressed in equation form,

Second accounting identity

Aggregate output = National income

Together, the two accounting identities express fundamental macroeconomic relationships that help us understand how GNP is determined. Expressed in equation form, these relationships are

Accounting identities

Aggregate expenditures = Aggregate output = National income

$$AE = GNP = NI$$

Because of some real-world measurement problems, GNP as actually measured is not identical to national income. We identify these complications as we come to them in the following sections. Nevertheless, these problems do not disturb the fundamental equality between the concepts of aggregate output and national income.

Two Ways to Measure GNP

The equation combining the two accounting identities indicates that there are two ways to calculate GNP: (1) actual *expenditures* on final goods produced; and (2) total *income* received by owners of resources.

Exhibit 21.3 shows the values connected with the manufacture and final sale of a chair. The chair began life as a tree, which was harvested by the landowner and sold to a lumber mill. The tree became lumber, which was sold to the furniture manufacturer. The lumber was made into a chair, which was sold to a furniture store. Finally, the chair was sold for $55 to a family that put it in their living room.

Exhibit 21.3
Gross National Product: Expenditure or Income

Revenues and costs of businesses			Income earned	
Landowner:				
Selling price		$ 5		
Less: Wages of lumberjack		2	Lumberjack	$ 2
Profit to landowner		$ 3	Landowner	3
Lumber mill:				
Selling price		$13		
Less: Cost of timber	$ 5			
Wages of mill workers	4	9	Mill workers	4
Profit to mill owner		$ 4	Mill owner	4
Furniture mfg.:				
Selling price		$35		
Less: Cost of lumber	$13			
Wages of factory workers	15	28	Factory workers	15
Profit to factory owner		$ 7	Factory owner	7
Furniture store:				
Selling price		$55		
Less: Cost of chair	$35			
Rent on building	4		Building owner	4
Wages of store employees	11	50	Store employees	11
Profit to store owner		$ 5	Store owner	5
			Total income earned	$55
Summary of incomes earned, all stages:			Wages	$32
			Rent	4
			Profit	19
			Total	$55

GNP equals actual aggregate expenditures. The first—and most obvious—way to arrive at the value of GNP associated with the chair is to equate the value to the amount spent by the family who bought it. After all, this amount is clearly the market value of a final good produced this year. What is true in this simple example is also true for the economy as a whole. We can determine the market value of final goods produced (GNP) by adding up the total amount that the household, business, government, and foreign sectors spent on the final goods produced in a particular year. We can use total spending as a measure of GNP because the first accounting identity, GNP equals actual aggregate expenditures, is always true.

GNP equals income received. We can also calculate GNP using the second accounting identity. That is, we add the income earned by owners of all the resources used to make the chair. In stage 1, the lumberjack earned $2 in wages and the landowner earned $3 in payment for her land and timber. In stage 2, the mill workers earned $4 in wages and the mill owner earned $4 in profits. In stage 3, the factory workers earned $15 in wages and the factory owner earned $7 in profits. In stage 4, the store employees earned $11 in wages, the building owner received $4 in rent, and the store owner earned $5 in profits. If we total the income earned by each person associated with producing and selling the chair—from landowner to furniture store worker—we arrive at the $55 value of the chair. This second accounting identity is true not only in this simple example, but also for the economy as a whole. (Actually, there are some measurement complications, as we discuss later in the chapter, but the basic relationship remains true.)

GNP: Does It Measure Social Value?

Before leaving the discussion of how GNP is measured, we should consider what it actually does and does not measure. Like any other economic measure, GNP is only one indicator of the economy's performance. Although economists generally believe that it is a good measure of aggregate output, GNP excludes certain factors that may cause it to inaccurately reflect how many of society's wants are satisfied.

GNP excludes nonmarket exchanges. First, GNP excludes values produced outside the marketplace, even if they add to social welfare. When individuals pay someone else to take care of their children or clean their houses, the expenditures are reflected in GNP. However, if individuals take care of their own children or clean their own houses, they satisfy wants but do not add to GNP. Likewise, almost all direct exchanges of services—you help me paint my house, I help you construct a garage for your house—satisfy wants but are not a part of GNP.

GNP also excludes some of the value of leisure time. If you go to the movies or play racketball in a local club, the payments you make are included in GNP. But if you watch TV or go for a walk in the woods, no market exchange occurs and no value is added to GNP. In fact, if each worker in the economy received one afternoon off (without pay) each week and spent it walking in the woods, measured GNP would fall. Fewer goods and services would be produced and less money would be exchanged in markets. Whatever value an afternoon in the woods might have, it is not reflected in GNP.

Such activities are not excluded from GNP because economists view them as unimportant or less valuable than goods and services exchanged in the market. Their exclusion is based on practical considerations: How can they be identified and what is their value? Even though their exclusion may underestimate the true wealth of a nation, it does not make GNP a less valuable measure. As long as such activities do not fluctuate much, GNP is still a good measure of how well the economy is performing.

GNP ignores external costs. In addition, GNP fails to subtract external costs (see Chapter 6) from market value. Pollution and other external costs reduce social well-being but are not costs that producers or consumers pay for directly. Thus they are not reflected in the marketplace. As a result, measured GNP may somewhat overstate economic welfare.

GNP ignores the underground economy. Some economists feel that the values exchanged in the underground economy are among the most important omissions from GNP. Statisticians measuring GNP must use recorded information to estimate actual expenditures and actual output. However, many economic exchanges are not a matter of public record.

Some underground exchanges are payments for illegal products or services such as drugs and prostitution. In addition, a significant amount of income received is never reported. For example, individuals working in restaurants or bars may not report all the tips they receive. Similarly, owners of retail stores may not record all their cash receipts. And individuals may perform various services for which they receive but do not report cash income. The size of this underground economy is difficult to estimate, but estimates run as high as $100 billion per year, or almost 3 percent of measured GNP. Its significance in distorting measures of economic activity is difficult to estimate.

GNP uses cost to value government goods and services. Although most products are valued by their market prices when included in GNP, goods and services produced and consumed by government, such as highways and public education, are valued at their cost. But do government expenditures always reflect increases in social well-being? Some individuals question whether all the dollars spent on the latest weapon systems really add to social value. Others question the value of government expenditures to protect the environment or consumers. Since there is no direct market for these goods and services, economists must rely on costs to measure their contribution to GNP. Note, however, that this reliance deviates from the use of consumer demand to determine the economic values totaled to obtain GNP.

GNP does not indicate distribution or equity. Finally, like most aggregate measures, GNP does not tell us whether various groups are better or worse off. That is, as a measure of aggregate output, it tells us nothing about the distribution of output and therefore nothing about equity. This difference is especially important in some of the poorer countries of the world. In considering whether these countries have improved or developed economically, economists watch not only the size but also the distribution of national income.

The first accounting identity states that aggregate output always equals actual aggregate expenditures.

The second accounting identity states that aggregate output always equals national income.

GNP can be measured in three ways: as aggregate expenditures, value added, or income earned.

GNP excludes most nonmarket exchanges, ignores external costs and the underground economy, values government goods and services at cost, and does not indicate distribution or equity. Although a good measure of aggregate output, it is an imperfect measure of social welfare.

Despite the drawbacks, GNP remains an important indicator of an economy's growth or decline. Moreover, most economists agree that significant increases in real GNP in the United States over the past 50 years represent significant increases in the average standard of living. To this extent, the economy today appears to satisfy more of society's wants than before. But most economists agree that other indicators, such as the distribution of income, should also be used in any attempt to assess whether individuals are, in fact, better off.

CIRCULAR FLOW OF INCOME AND OUTPUT: A PRIVATE-SECTOR ECONOMY

Now that you have a better understanding of GNP, let's consider some of the fundamental macroeconomic relationships it reflects. We can use the circular-flow model introduced in Chapter 5 to illustrate how the household, business, government, and foreign sectors are related. This model will help you to see how the economy's gross national product is defined and measured. We can also use the model to indicate the fundamental truth of the two accounting identities.

A Simple Private-Sector Economy

Exhibit 21.4 shows a model of a simple economy that has no government or foreign sector. The household sector owns all the resources and spends all the income it receives. The business sector sells all the goods it produces to households. The bottom half of the model shows **consumption expenditures (C)**, which is the total amount spent by the household sector to purchase the final goods in product markets. With our simplifications, these dollars represent the only source of aggregate expenditures; that is, AE = C. According to the first accounting identity, these actual expenditures represent the value of the final goods produced during the period; that is, AE = GNP.

The top half of Exhibit 21.4 shows dollars flowing from the business sector to the household sector. In other words, dollars received by the business sector become dollars of income for people in the household sector. Revenues received by businesses either pay for labor (wages) and other resources (rent, for example) or pay the owners of businesses for the resources they supply (profits). With our simplifications, this dollar flow is also equal to national income; that is, NI = Wages + Rent + Interest + Profits.

The second accounting identity tells us that the flow in the bottom half of Exhibit 21.4 (GNP) and the flow in the top half (NI) are identical amounts (GNP = NI). Thus we can view the flow in this economy as either the dollar amount of expenditures (the value of final goods exchanged) or as the dollar amount of income received (the value of resources exchanged).

Numerical example. We can illustrate these points using the example shown in Exhibit 21.5. The household sector has an income of $1000 (NI = $1000), and according to our assumptions, the household sector spends all its income (AE = C = $1000). These expenditures are received by the business sector as revenues, or receipts from sales. Because they measure the value of goods produced, these expenditures equal GNP (AE = C = GNP).

Consumption expenditures (C). Expenditures of households on final goods during a particular period of time.

Exhibit 21.4
The Circular Flow of Economic Activity: GNP and National Income
In the top half of this simplified circular-flow diagram, payments to resource owners by the business sector become income to the household sector. The total dollar amount is therefore national income. In the bottom half of the diagram, consumption expenditures by the household sector represent the total market value of goods and services produced by the business sector, or GNP. In this simplified model, all dollars received by households are spent and all dollars received by businesses become payments for resources used. Thus the total value of goods produced can be calculated either by adding expenditures in the product markets (GNP) or by adding incomes received (national income).

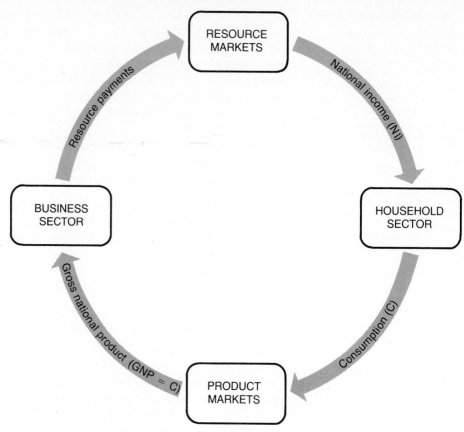

Exhibit 21.5 also shows that the business sector pays $1000 for resources such as labor, materials, buildings, and machinery used to produce final goods. The payments also include the profits paid to owners of businesses for the resources they contribute. In total, these resource payments are the $1000 of national income received by the household sector. Thus the example shows the fundamental accounting identity between aggregate expenditures, GNP, and national income: AE = GNP = NI = $1000. Although the relationships among the various sectors get more complicated in our later discussions, these fundamental equalities are always true.

A More Realistic Private-Sector Economy

Although the basic accounting identities hold in all situations, a more realistic circular-flow model of economic activity requires that we complicate our example. We now add the factors of saving and investment to the model.

Income, consumption, and saving. Households do not typically spend their entire incomes. Most spend only a portion of what they earn and save the rest. When we relax our simplifying assumption to recognize saving, we must

Exhibit 21.5
Simple Circular Flow: A Numerical Example

modify the circular-flow model. Exhibit 21.6 differs from our simple circular-flow model, reflecting the two possible uses for income. As you can see, the dollars that households receive as income are split into two flows: consumption expenditures (C) and **saving (S)**. Saving represents dollars received as income but not spent on consumer products. In other words, the income of the household sector flows out as consumption expenditures or saving. Expressed in equation form,

$$\text{National income} = \text{Consumption} + \text{Saving}$$
$$\text{NI} \quad = \quad \text{C} \quad + \quad \text{S}$$

Saving (S). The portion of income received by households during a particular period of time that is not spent on final goods.

Fixed investment. Expenditures by businesses for capital resources, such as new plants, equipment, or commercial buildings, and by households for residential construction during a particular period of time.

Business investment. Another simplification that we have used so far is the assumption that businesses produce only consumer goods for the household sector and that all goods produced are sold. However, some businesses produce capital resources (such as machinery and equipment) that are purchased by others in the business sector. Business expenditures for capital resources are called **fixed investment**. Like the purchase of consumer goods by the household sector, purchases of capital resources by the business sector are considered expenditures for final goods. (Household spending on residential construction is also included in fixed investment in government statistics. This fact does not affect the analysis or conclusions we reach, however.)

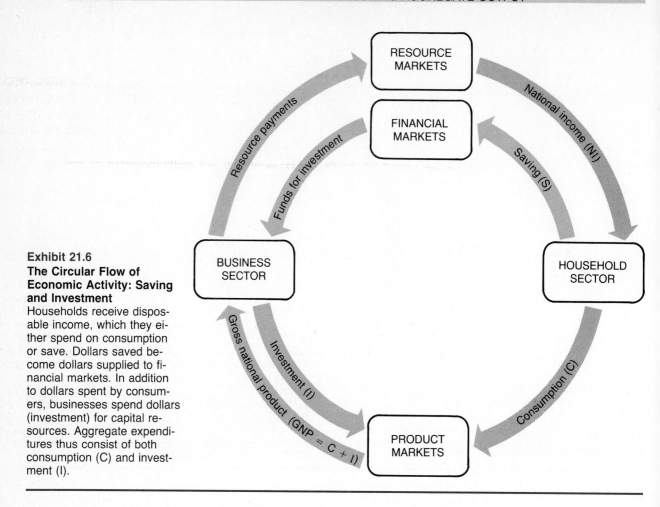

Exhibit 21.6
The Circular Flow of Economic Activity: Saving and Investment
Households receive disposable income, which they either spend on consumption or save. Dollars saved become dollars supplied to financial markets. In addition to dollars spent by consumers, businesses spend dollars (investment) for capital resources. Aggregate expenditures thus consist of both consumption (C) and investment (I).

Depreciation (capital consumption allowance). A business cost representing the value of capital resources used to produce goods; the fractional cost charged each year over the life of the resource to reflect both physical wear and tear and obsolescence. Unlike other costs, no payment is made for depreciation.

Why are capital resources not considered to be intermediate goods? After all, machinery, like materials, is used to produce final goods. Capital resources differ from intermediate goods in an important respect: They last for many years and are not completely used up in producing a batch of goods. Because capital resources last for years, expenditures on them—fixed investment—are considered to be expenditures on final goods and hence a part of GNP.

For example, a baker buys flour, yeast, and an oven. When the baker makes bread, the flour and yeast are completely used up. The total value of these products becomes part of the value of bread, as is true with any intermediate good. Although the oven is used, it is not used up and remains useful to the baker. By convention, we count only a fraction of the oven's value as a cost of producing the bread during a specific period of time. This amount, called **depreciation (capital consumption allowance)**, represents not only physical wear and tear but also the decrease in value when resources become outdated.

Depreciation is the second reason that national income and GNP are different numbers *as measured*. National income is calculated by adding up wages and salaries, rent, interest income, and profits. But profits equal revenues received *minus* all business costs. When capital resources wear out and become obsolete,

Net national product (NNP).
Gross national product minus depreciation (capital consumption allowance).

Inventory investment. The value of final goods produced in a particular period of time but not sold. The unsold goods are considered to have been "bought" by the businesses that produced them, and thus are counted as part of business investment expenditures.

Investment (I). Expenditures for fixed investment and inventory investment.

Financial markets. Markets in which lenders supply and borrowers demand loanable funds. In these markets, dollars saved become dollars invested.

the business assets are reduced. Thus depreciation is definitely a cost to the business sector.

Unlike other costs, however, depreciation does not also represent a payment to any resource owner and is not, therefore, a part of national income. Thus in order for GNP to equal national income, we must first subtract depreciation (the capital consumption allowance) from GNP. The resulting figure, called the **net national product (NNP)**, is in some ways a better measure than GNP of how much the economy has grown. To the extent that investment goes into replacing worn-out capital resources, the economy has not really increased its capacity to produce. We consider depreciation further, later in this chapter. But, in general, we continue to use GNP as our measure because it is difficult to measure depreciation and because GNP and NNP change together.

Another simplifying assumption that we have to reexamine is that of when final goods are sold. The fact is that businesses do not always immediately sell the final goods they produce; some goods are warehoused for future sale. As we mentioned earlier, economists by convention consider that businesses "buy" this inventory in the period in which it is produced. Any final goods produced but not sold are considered to be **inventory investment**.

In our more realistic economy, then, aggregate expenditures consist of two components: consumption (C) and **investment (I)**. Exhibit 21.6 shows investment—total fixed and inventory investment—as a second expenditure in the product-market portion of the model. Thus the first accounting identity can be expressed in this model as

$$\text{Aggregate output} = \text{Aggregate expenditures} = \text{Consumption} + \text{Investment}$$
$$\text{GNP} \quad = \quad \text{AE} \quad = \quad \text{C} \quad + \quad \text{I}$$

Financial Markets: The Link between Saving and Investment

One final and important complexity involves the link between saving and investment. Real-world economies contain financial markets, as well as product and resource markets. In **financial markets** borrowers and lenders exchange dollars for financial claims. Thus financial markets link dollars saved and dollars invested.

For example, if you save $1000 next year and decide to buy newly issued shares of stock in a corporation, you have exchanged savings for ownership claims in the business. If you put your money in a bank, you have exchanged savings for a claim on the assets of the bank. If the bank lends the money to a business, the bank exchanges funds for a claim on the business's assets.

Financial markets exist for two primary reasons. Individuals who save generally do not want to hide their savings in a mattress. Instead, they want their savings to grow. By trading their savings for claims in financial markets, households can earn additional income, either in the form of interest payments or growth in the value of their claims. Also, as the second accounting identity indicates, the revenues that businesses receive from selling their products represent income earned by households. If businesses want to make investments—buy additional equipment or build a new plant—they must acquire the necessary funds. Financial markets link households that want to save with businesses that require funds to make investments.

Note that we show all saving as originating from the household sector in Exhibit 21.6. However, businesses also save. Business saving is the sum of retained

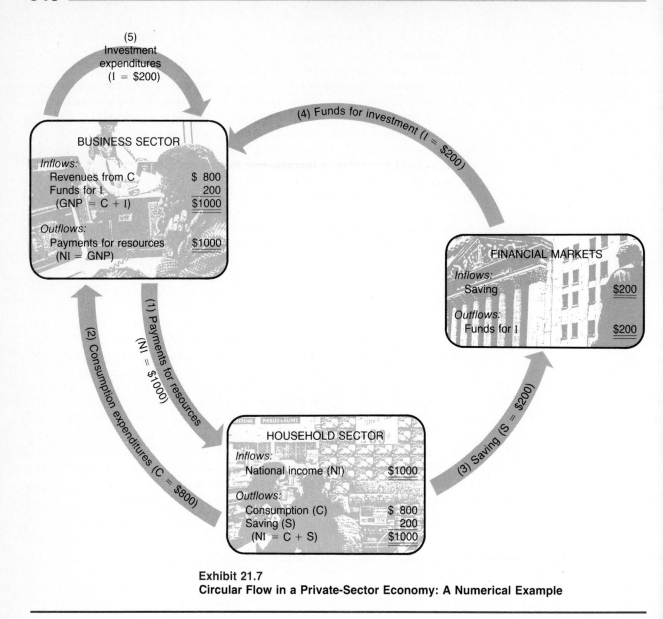

Exhibit 21.7
Circular Flow in a Private-Sector Economy: A Numerical Example

earnings—income earned but not paid out as dividends to stockholders—and depreciation—which is considered a cost but is not a cash payment. In fact, business saving is the largest source of funds used by the business sector to finance its investments.

We discuss financial markets in greater detail in the microeconomic portion of this textbook. For now, you should know that in financial markets, as in other markets, demand and supply of funds achieve equilibrium. In our simple economy, financial-market equilibrium equates the amount saved with the amount invested.

Numerical example. Exhibit 21.7 illustrates flows in a private-sector economy that includes both saving and investment. In this example you can see the equalities represented by the two accounting identities. Businesses producing

Stock. A quantity existing at some moment in time, such as the stock of capital resources or the stock of inventory possessed by the business sector on December 31 of any year.

Flow. A quantity or activity measured over a period of time, such as the gross national product produced in a particular year or the amount of income earned in a specific month.

consumer goods receive revenues of $800, which equal consumption expenditures (C). Businesses producing capital goods receive revenues equal to the $200 of investment (I).

As the first accounting identity indicates, GNP equals aggregate expenditures, which equals the sum of consumption and investment (GNP = AE = C + I). Exhibit 21.7 also shows that the entire $1000 of revenues received by the business sector for goods produced are matched by $1000 of payments to resource owners and therefore national income (GNP = NI = $1000). (This equality holds only if there is no depreciation, a simplification that we make here and in the following numerical examples.) Finally, the flows into and out of financial markets are equal. The household sector has income of $1000 and decides to spend $800 and save $200. The $800 spent flows into product markets and becomes $800 in revenues for businesses. The $200 saved flows into the financial market, where it becomes $200 of funds available for investment.

Stocks and Flows: Totals and Changes

The term *investment* has a special meaning in economics. Noneconomists often use the word to mean the total value of a firm's assets, or the stock of capital possessed by the firm. A **stock** is a quantity that exists at some moment in time—the stock of capital resources that businesses possessed on December 31, 1987, for example. In economics, however, investment refers to a **flow**, such as the total expenditure for new capital resources during the year 1987.

As you will see, macroeconomists focus on flows of economic activity, such as national income and gross national product. But flows are often related to stocks. For example, the quantity of products that businesses can produce in a year is a function of the stock of capital resources they possess during that year. The amount of interest income a household receives in a month depends, in part, on how much of its stock of wealth is in bank accounts, bonds, or other interest-paying forms of savings.

RECAP

A private-sector economy has two types of aggregate expenditures: consumption (C) and investment (I). Thus GNP = C + I. The two private sectors (households and businesses) are connected by financial markets. The portion of income not spent, saving (S), flows through financial markets to become funds for investment (I).

Stocks refer to amounts that exist on a specific date; flows refer to amounts measured over a period of time. Economists use the terms *investment* to refer to the flow of expenditures for new capital resources or inventory and *saving* to refer to that part of the flow of income not spent on final goods.

CIRCULAR FLOW: GOVERNMENT AND FOREIGN SECTORS

Thus far we have ignored the influence of the government and foreign sectors. Although we present a full discussion of how the government and the foreign sectors influence the economy in later chapters, we can illustrate their general effects in terms of our circular-flow model. We can also restate the accounting identities in view of the expanded circular-flow model.

Government and the Circular Flow

You can see the impact of government on the economy by relating the circular-flow model in Exhibit 21.8 to the basic elements of the government budget that we discussed in Chapter 6. On the receipts side, government obtains most of its ability to spend from tax payments made by individuals. (For simplicity, we ignore here all taxes not collected directly from households. We consider the effects of sales and other indirect taxes later in this chapter, however.) There are two kinds of government spending: transfer payments and purchases of goods and services.

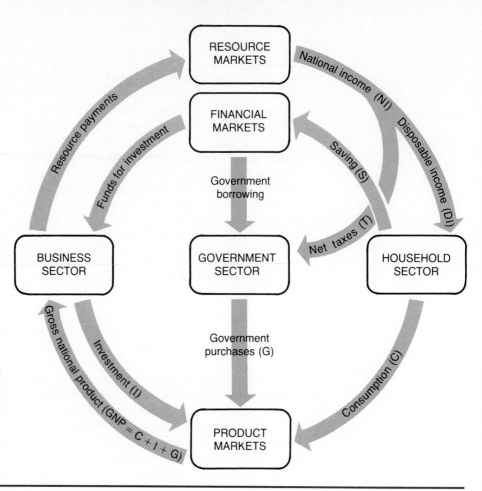

Exhibit 21.8
The Circular Flow of Economic Activity: The Role of Government
Government constitutes a third sector in the circular flow. Government reduces the flow of national income at the top of the circular flow through taxes but injects additional income in the form of transfer payments. Dollars received by households (disposable income) therefore are national income less net taxes (taxes less transfer payments). Government is also a third source of expenditures in product markets at the bottom of the circular-flow diagram. With government considered, then, GNP is the sum of consumption, investment, and government expenditures. Finally, government participates in the financial markets.

Disposable income (DI). Income received by households in a particular period of time and available to be spent or saved; household income after taxes have been deducted and transfer payments have been added.

Government purchases (G). Expenditures by the government sector to purchase final goods; a part of aggregate expenditures.

As we noted in Chapter 6, transfer payments represent payments to individuals for the purpose of redistributing income. They are not payments for resources provided.

In the top part of Exhibit 21.8, you can see that the flow to the household sector is decreased by the amount of taxes paid to government. The flow is increased by the transfer payments that government gives to households. Because taxes generally exceed transfer payments, national income is usually greater than disposable income. **Disposable income (DI)** is the income received by the household sector after taxes and transfer payments are accounted for. When considering how much households spend or save, we start with disposable income, not national income. We explore this difference in greater detail later in this chapter, but it does not affect the two accounting identities.

Government also buys goods and services, such as airplanes and missiles for national defense and asphalt and concrete for roads and sidewalks. **Government purchases (G)** are a third type of expenditure to be considered along with consumption and investment. Thus the first accounting identity between aggregate output and actual aggregate expenditures becomes

Aggregate output = Actual aggregate expenditures
Gross national product = Consumption + Investment + Government purchases
GNP = C + I + G

Note that this equation excludes transfer payments, although in Chapter 6 we included both transfer payments and government purchases as government expenditures. Transfer payments are excluded from GNP because they are not expenditures that are made to purchase final products. Their effect is to change the *distribution* of household income.

Finally, Exhibit 21.8 shows how government participates in financial markets. As in other sectors, funds entering and leaving the government sector are balanced. If outflows (for purchases and transfers) are less than inflows (taxes), government has a budget surplus. Government will then supply funds to financial markets to balance inflows and outflows. If outflows are greater than inflows, government has a budget deficit (as it has in recent years). The government budget deficit averaged $125 billion from 1982 to 1986. Government will then demand funds from the financial markets to balance inflows and outflows. We explain this impact of government on financial markets more fully in later chapters. For now you should recognize only that its role in financial markets greatly influences the macroeconomy's performance.

Numerical example.   Exhibit 21.9 provides a numerical example of government's effect on the economy. Government directly affects the household sector in two ways: taxes and transfer payments. Net taxes (T), that is, taxes minus transfer payments (in this example, $125), are a flow from the household sector to the government. The government sector also affects the business sector in this example by purchasing goods and services. This expenditure on final products is a part of GNP. It adds $175 to the revenues of the business sector, just as consumption expenditures by the household sector do.

Finally, you can see the effect of government on financial markets. In this example, government has a budget deficit. Net taxes are $125; government purchases are $175, leaving a deficit of $50. The government will enter financial markets to borrow funds to make up this difference. Note that this action causes government to compete with the business sector for available funds. Of the $200 of saving available, the government takes $50 to finance its deficit, leaving $150 available for investment.

Foreign Trade and the Circular Flow

To complete our overview of the economy, we add the foreign sector to the circular-flow model. Individuals, governments, and businesses of foreign countries comprise this sector. Flows to and from foreign economies are shown in a separate sector, but as Exhibit 21.10 indicates, foreign and domestic economies are closely related.

You can see the three effects of the foreign sector in Exhibit 21.10. First, some household expenditures flow to the foreign sector when households purchase **imports (M)**. (Domestic businesses and governments also buy foreign goods and

Imports (M). Expenditures by U.S. households, businesses, and governments for goods and services produced in other countries. These expenditures must be deducted from aggregate expenditures in order to measure GNP; they represent aggregate spending that is not used to purchase domestically produced goods.

Exhibit 21.9
Circular Flow in a Closed Economy: A Numerical Example

Exports (X). Expenditures made by foreign households, businesses, and governments for goods produced domestically. Exports must be added to aggregate domestic expenditures when measuring GNP; they represent spending to purchase domestically produced goods.

services. We show all imports as consumer items only to keep the example simple.) Second, some goods and services produced by domestic businesses are sold to foreign households, businesses, and governments in the form of **exports (X).** Finally, you can see the foreign sector also participates in domestic financial markets.

We want GNP to measure *domestic* aggregate output and must therefore measure spending on domestic goods and services. Thus we subtract the amount that U.S. households, businesses, and governments spend on foreign goods and services. We also add the amount spent by foreign households, businesses, and governments on goods and services produced in the United States. The difference between exports and imports (X − M) is called *net exports*. By subtracting imports and adding exports, we count expenditures on domestic products. The accounting identity of output and expenditures becomes

Aggregate output = Actual aggregate expenditures

$$\begin{matrix} \text{Gross national} \\ \text{product} \end{matrix} = \text{Consumption} + \text{Investment} + \begin{matrix} \text{Government} \\ \text{purchases} \end{matrix} + \begin{matrix} \text{Net} \\ \text{exports} \end{matrix}$$

$$\text{GNP} \quad = \quad \text{C} \quad + \quad \text{I} \quad + \quad \text{G} \quad + (\text{X} - \text{M})$$

Exhibit 21.10
The Circular Flow of Economic Activity: The Foreign Sector
Dollars flow into the foreign sector in payment for imported goods. Dollars flow into the U.S. economy in payment for exported goods. The addition of these two dollar flows makes total spending (GNP) equal to the sum of consumption, investment, government purchases, and net exports (exports less imports). In addition, the foreign sector participates in U.S. financial markets.

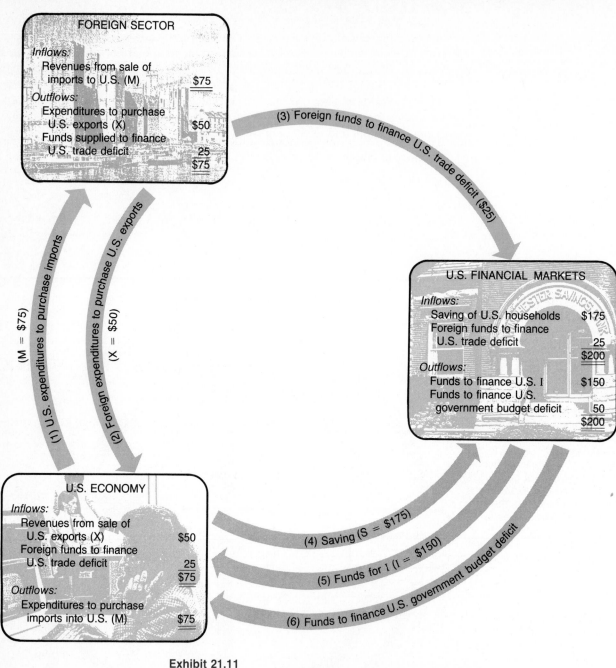

Exhibit 21.11
Circular Flow in an Open Economy: A Numerical Example

The foreign sector also affects financial markets. Foreign individuals, businesses, and governments may demand loanable funds (as Mexico, Brazil, Argentina, and other countries have done in recent years). They may also supply additional funds to U.S. borrowers. The net effect of the foreign sector in U.S. financial markets depends on the value of net exports. As in the other sectors, inflows and outflows must balance. (No sector can spend more than it receives without borrowing.) If net exports are positive, that is, exports exceed imports, the foreign sector will, on balance, borrow from U.S. financial markets to finance these additional purchases. If net exports are negative, that is, imports exceed exports, the foreign sector will, on balance, supply funds to U.S. financial markets. See A Case in Point: Additional Accounting Identities for other ways of looking at these relationships.

Numerical example. Exhibit 21.11 illustrates the impact of the foreign sector on the domestic economy. At the left of the exhibit we see the trade flows. The $75 spent by U.S. individuals, businesses, and governments on imports represents a flow of dollars from the U.S. economy to the rest of the world. The $50 spent by foreign residents on U.S. exports is a flow of dollars into the domestic economy. Net exports are a negative $25, representing a trade deficit. As shown in the bottom of the exhibit, the trade deficit is matched by a $25 flow of funds supplied to U.S. financial markets from the foreign sector. Foreign-supplied funds, along with saving by U.S. households, are then available to finance investment and a government budget deficit.

The foreign sector has become increasingly important to the U.S. economy because the volume of imports and exports has grown. In 1986, over 11 percent

A Case in Point
Additional Accounting Identities

The two accounting identities that we have already introduced can be supplemented by a third one. It recognizes that the circular flow must be balanced overall. In the aggregate, if national income is $1000, then aggregate spending must be $1000.

Several of the flows that we have identified can be considered "leakages." For example, households do not spend all they receive as income. Saving constitutes a leakage from the circular flow. All of national income does not reach the household sector; government taxes represent a leakage. Imports represent a portion of consumption spending that leaks from the circular flow.

At the same time, inflows or "injections" add to the circular flow. Exports to the foreign sector and business investment inject spending, as do government purchases and transfer payments. These inflows or "injections" balance the outflows or "leakages." This idea is stated in the third accounting identity: actual leakages must equal actual injections. Expressed in equation form,

Third accounting identity

Actual leakages = Actual injections

As we noted, the leakages from the system are saving (S) and net taxes (T). The injections are investment (I), government purchases (G), and net exports (X − M). Thus for the full circular-flow model, the third accounting identity is

Actual leakages = Actual injections

$$\text{Saving} + \text{Net taxes} = \text{Investment} + \text{Government purchases} + \text{Net exports}$$

$$S + T = I + G + (X - M)$$

Leakages and injections are also related to inflows and outflows in financial markets. Saving, for example, is an inflow; funds for investments is an outflow. Negative net exports (a trade deficit) means an inflow; positive net exports (a trade surplus) means an outflow. A government budget deficit (purchases exceed net taxes) means an outflow; a budget surplus means an inflow. These relationships can be expressed in a fourth identity as

Fourth accounting identity

$$\text{Financial market inflows} = \text{Financial market outflows}$$

$$\text{Saving} + \text{Trade deficit} = \text{Investment} + \text{Budget deficit}$$

$$S + (X - M) = I + (G - T)$$

of all U.S. final goods were exported, compared to less than 5 percent in 1960. In the mid-1980s, imports exceeded exports by a sizable amount; in 1986, for example, net exports were $106 billion. Thus the foreign sector helped to finance the large budget deficits of the federal government. We do not formally study the foreign sector until much later in this textbook. Learning some of the basic macroeconomic principles is easier when you study an economy without a foreign sector. Meanwhile, we point out, when appropriate, how the foreign sector influences the macroeconomy.

NATIONAL INCOME ACCOUNTING

As we noted earlier in this chapter, we can calculate GNP in two ways: (1) as a sum of expenditures on final goods; and (2) as a sum of income received by owners of resources. Combining the two accounting identities, we can express the GNP relationships as

Actual aggregate expenditures = Gross national product = National income

Using the first identity and referring to Exhibit 21.12, you can see that GNP in 1986 is equal to the sum of consumption, investment, government purchases, and net exports. According to the second identity, we should be able to calculate GNP by adding up various forms of income. That is, GNP should equal the sum of employee compensation (wages and salaries), rent, interest, and business prof-

Exhibit 21.12
Gross National Product and National Income in 1986 (billions of nominal dollars)

Expenditures approach			Income approach	
Consumption:			Employee compensation	$2498.3
Durable goods	$ 388.3		Rental income	15.6
Nondurable goods	932.7		Net interest	294.9
Services	1441.3		Business profits*	578.6
Total		$2762.4	National Income	$3387.4
Investment:			Plus: Indirect business taxes	366.0
Fixed investment	$ 675.1		Net National Product	$3753.4
Inventory investment	11.4		Plus: Capital consumption allowance	455.1
Total		686.4	Gross National Product	$4208.5
Government purchases:				
Federal	$ 367.2			
State and local	498.1			
Total		865.3		
Exports and imports:				
Exports	$ 373.0			
Less: Imports	− 478.7			
Net exports		− 105.7		
Gross National Product		$4208.5		

*Business profits include both corporate profits and proprietor income.
Source: Economic Report of the President, 1987 (Tables B-1, B-21, and B-23).

its. But this sum, national income, is less than GNP in Exhibit 21.12. If they are supposed to be identical, the logical question is: Why don't they add up? In Exhibit 21.12 you can see that the two differences between national income and gross national product are depreciation (the capital consumption allowance) and indirect business taxes.

We noted earlier that indirect business taxes, such as sales taxes, also cause GNP not to equal national income. They do not represent payments to resource owners and thus are not part of national income. But they are a part of actual aggregate expenditures and thus part of GNP. Exhibit 21.12 shows that in 1986, indirect business taxes amounted to $366.0 billion. (This figure also includes small adjustments for business transfers and net surpluses earned by government enterprises.) Adding these to national income gives net national product, that is, net of depreciation.

We also noted earlier that GNP includes all production of goods and services in a specific period of time—even production of capital resources that merely replaces those that are worn-out or obsolete. But because depreciation cost does not involve any payments, it is not income to anyone and so is excluded from national income. Thus we add the capital consumption allowance (total depreciation) to national income to get gross national product. The amount is not insignificant, as Exhibit 21.12 indicates: The capital consumption allowance in the U.S. economy amounted to $455.1 billion in 1986, or about 11 percent of total output.

National, Personal, and Disposable Income

We also gave little attention in our initial discussions to the distinction between national income and disposable income. *Income earned* by resource owners—the concept behind national income—differs from *income received*—the concept behind personal income (see Chapter 6)—in several ways. These differences are shown in Exhibit 21.13.

First, all business profits represent income earned and are therefore part of national income. But corporations usually do not distribute all their profits as dividends. Only the portion of corporate profits paid out as dividends counts as income received by the household sector. Thus to calculate personal income, we subtract corporate profits from national income and add dividends. Second, payments by businesses to help fund workers' social insurance (Social Security, for example) are counted in national income because they are payments for resources. Because the payments go to the government and not to households, however, they are excluded from personal income. Finally, personal income includes transfer payments, since such income can be spent or saved. But transfer payments are not income earned and thus are not included in national income.

Having accounted for the differences between national income and personal income, we next consider how personal income and disposable income differ. If you examine the definitions of these two terms side by side, the difference is obvious:

Personal income	**Disposable income**
Household income after transfer payments have been added but before personal income taxes have been subtracted.	Household income after transfer payments have been added and personal income taxes have been subtracted.

Gross National Product			$4208.5
Less: Capital consumption allowance			455.1
Net National Product			$3753.4
Less: Indirect business taxes			366.0
National Income			$3387.4
Less: Corporate profits	$299.7		
Contributions to social insurance	376.1		
		$675.8	
Plus: Dividend income	$ 81.2		
Transfer payments	513.7		
Other adjustments*	180.5		
		775.4	
			99.6
Personal Income			$3487.0
Less: Personal taxes			513.4
Disposable Income			$2973.6

*Other adjustments correct for the difference between net interest paid and interest income received by households.
Source: Economic Report of the President, 1987 (Tables B-21 and B-22).

Exhibit 21.13
Relationship of GNP to Disposable Income, 1986 (billions of nominal dollars)

In 1986, personal income taxes and other nontax payments to government (such as payments for automobile license plates) in the United States amounted to $513.4 billion, or 15 percent of personal income.

CONCLUSION

In this chapter, we previewed in general terms many of the basic economic relationships necessary to understand macroeconomics. We identified the major sectors of the economy—household, business, government, and foreign—and their most important interactions in product, resource, and financial markets. In Chapter 22 we begin to explore how decisions are made in each sector and how those decisions determine the macroeconomic performance of the economy. We also begin to show how different groups of economists have explained the workings of the macroeconomy.

SUMMARY

1. In this chapter we discussed the general concepts, definition, and measurement of aggregate output and some of the relationships among key macroeconomic variables.

2. Gross national product (GNP) is the market value of final goods produced in the economy in a particular period of time. Although market values are used to measure the value of the various products produced,

GNP is a measure of production—not sales. Goods and services produced in previous periods, goods that are resold, and intermediate goods are not included.

3. Nominal GNP is measured using current quantities and current prices. Changes in nominal GNP reflect changes in both prices and quantities. Real GNP is measured using a constant set of prices; it therefore reflects changes in quantities only. The GNP deflator, calculated as the ratio of nominal to real GNP, is a measure of the general price level.

4. Fundamental relationships between macroeconomic variables can be expressed in accounting identities that are always true. The first accounting identity states that aggregate output equals actual aggregate expenditures. It expresses the definition of GNP as the market value of final goods produced. To preserve the identity, any inventory produced but not sold is assumed to have been bought by the business sector.

5. The second accounting identity—aggregate output equals national income—expresses the concept that each dollar spent can be traced to a dollar of income. Although we use this identity for simplicity, technically we must subtract both depreciation and indirect business taxes from measured GNP in order to equate aggregate output and national income.

6. Gross national product can be calculated in two ways: (a) the sum of aggregate expenditures, or GNP = C + I + G + (X − M); or (b) the sum of incomes earned by resource owners, that is, GNP = Wages + Interest + Rent + Profits. The accounting identities show that the two ways are equivalent.

7. Although generally accepted as an important indicator of economic activity, GNP is not an accurate measure of social welfare for several reasons: (a) GNP does not measure all activity; (b) GNP does not subtract external costs such as pollution; (c) GNP does not account for the underground economy; (d) GNP does not count the costs of government services; and (e) GNP tells us nothing about the distribution of output or whether particular groups are better or worse off. Despite its limitations, GNP can be used to provide some direction for economic policy and to help determine whether economic activity is increasing or decreasing.

8. A purely private economy—one with no government and foreign sectors—has two types of aggregate expenditures: consumption (C) and investment (I). Thus GNP = C + I. The household and business sectors are related in that (a) household consumption expenditures become business revenues; (b) business costs and profits become household income; and (c) saving by households yields funds for business investment.

9. Financial institutions such as banks, savings and loan associations, and insurance companies help to channel saving into investment. They provide the link between those who save (and thus supply loanable funds) and those who demand loanable funds for investment, to finance government budget deficits, or to finance negative net exports.

10. A stock is an amount measured at some specific time; flows are amounts measured over a period of time. National income and GNP are flows.

11. A closed economy—one without a foreign sector—has three types of aggregate expenditures: consumption (C), investment (I), and government purchases (G). Thus AE = GNP = C + I + G. Disposable income received by households is less than national income because of net taxes (taxes minus transfer payments) paid to the government. Government demands funds from financial markets to finance budget deficits. Government supplies funds to financial markets when it has budget surpluses.

12. An open economy—one with a foreign sector—has four types of aggregate expenditures: consumption (C), investment (I), government purchases (G), and net exports (X − M). Thus GNP = C + I + G + (X − M). Imports are subtracted because part of domestic expenditures go to purchase foreign products and thus do not indicate domestic goods and services produced. Exports are added because some domestic goods and services produced are purchased by residents, businesses, and governments of other countries. If exports exceed imports (a trade surplus), the foreign sector will demand funds from financial markets. If imports exceed exports (a trade deficit), the foreign sector will supply funds to financial markets.

13. National income accounting requires us to account for depreciation and business taxes in order to make gross national product equal to national income.

KEY TERMS

Final goods, 534
Intermediate goods, 534
GNP deflator, 536
Accounting identities, 537
Aggregate expenditures (AE), 537
National income (NI), 537
Consumption expenditures (C), 541
Saving (S), 543
Fixed investment, 543
Depreciation (capital consumption allowance), 544

Net national product (NNP), 545
Inventory investment, 545
Investment (I), 545
Financial markets, 545
Stock, 547
Flow, 547
Disposable income (DI), 548
Government purchases (G), 548
Imports (M), 549
Exports (X), 550

QUESTIONS FOR REVIEW AND DISCUSSION

1. How much, if anything, do the following activities contribute to gross national product?
   a) A worker earned $300 working in a factory.
   b) A teenager mowed the family lawn; otherwise, the family would have had to hire someone for $10.
   c) An appliance store finally sold, for $200, a refrigerator that had been sitting in its warehouse for two years.
   d) A business produced $600 worth of consumer goods, but sold only $500 worth.
   e) An individual bought a new car produced this year in February for $8000. Not wishing to keep the car, she sold it for $6000 during the summer of the same year.
   f) An individual bought 100 shares of Zenon Corporation for $1500.
   g) A manufacturer of TV sets sold $3000 worth to Ned's Appliance Store.

2. How do you think GNP would be affected if the economy became more technically efficient? Can you think of any ways in which GNP can increase as a result of either allocative or technical inefficiency?

3. In each of the following cases, solve for the unknowns.

Case	Nominal GNP	Real GNP	GNP deflator
1	$3000	$2500	___
2	4000	___	125
3	___	3000	150

4. The owner and operator of Ned's Appliance Store decides to take off for a week and hires Kay Maree (who would have otherwise been unemployed) to operate the business. Is GNP affected?

5. Use the accounting relationships from the chapter to solve for the unknowns in each of the following cases and to answer questions (a) and (b). Note that these cases refer to a *closed economy*, that is, there is no foreign sector.

	Case 1	Case 2
Gross national product	$2000	$___
Consumption	1500	___
Net taxes	___	550
Saving	___	400
Investment	___	500
Disposable income	1700	___
Government purchases	350	___
National income	___	3700

   a) What is the size of the government budget deficit or surplus in each case?
   b) What are the inflows and outflows in the financial markets in each case?

6. Explain how whole-wheat flour can be either an intermediate good or a final good, depending on who purchases it and for what purpose.

7. The items in (a) and (b) are examples of costs that are not currently included in measuring GNP. For each example, answer the following questions: Should it be? If it were included, how would you measure it? Does its omission make any difference in our ability to determine whether economic activity has increased from one period to another? Why or why not?
   a) The value of services provided by homemakers.
   b) The external costs of pollution.

8. Use the accounting relationships from the chapter to solve for the unknowns in each of the following cases and to answer questions (a)–(c). Note that these cases refer to an *open economy*, that is, there is a foreign sector.

	Case 1	Case 2
Gross national product	$___	$4200
Exports	300	___
Government purchases	400	700
Saving	___	500
Net taxes	___	900
National income	___	___
Consumption	1500	___
Imports	200	450
Disposable income	2150	___
Investment	500	800

   a) What is the size of the government budget deficit or surplus in each case?
   b) What is the size of the trade deficit or surplus in each case?
   c) What are the inflows and outflows in the financial markets in each case?

Aggregate Expenditures and Equilibrium Output

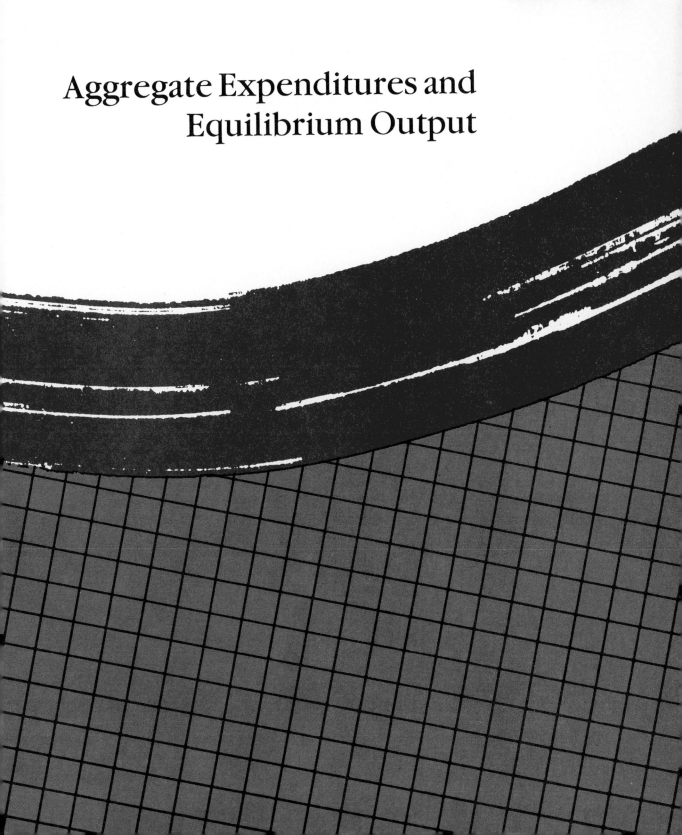

QUESTIONS TO CONSIDER

☐ How do the classical and Keynesian views of macroeconomic equilibrium differ?

☐ Why are economists interested in the marginal propensities to consume and save?

☐ What factors affect household consumption?

☐ What factors affect business investment?

☐ How does equilibrium output differ in the classical and Keynesian theories?

Thus far you have been exposed to several basic concepts of macroeconomics: aggregate demand and supply, gross national product, unemployment, and inflation. In Chapter 20 you learned that aggregate demand and supply determine macroeconomic equilibrium. In Chapter 21 you learned that actual aggregate expenditures always equal gross national product. But what is the connection between aggregate demand and actual aggregate expenditures? What determines aggregate supply? When an economy reaches equilibrium does it have stable prices and full employment? In order to answer these questions you must learn what affects aggregate demand and supply and how they determine macroeconomic equilibrium.

TWO VIEWS ON MACROECONOMIC EQUILIBRIUM

Over the years, economists have given different answers to those same questions. In this section, we consider two of the dominant theories: that of the classical economists and that of John Maynard Keynes and his followers. As you will see later in this textbook, modern economic theory incorporates elements of both the classical and Keynesian theories.

Classical View: Full-Employment Equilibrium

Prior to the 1930s, mainstream economic theory concluded that an economy would automatically reach macroeconomic equilibrium at the full-employment level of output. Keynes referred to economists who held this view as classical economists. (Actually, he applied that term to any economist who held views counter to his own. Not all economists at the time held precisely the same views that we generally attribute to this group.)

To simplify our explanation of **classical economic theory**, let's consider an economy having only a business sector and a household sector. We consider the roles of the government and foreign sectors in later chapters, but the explanation is easier to follow when there are only two sectors.

Classical economic theory.
Macroeconomic theories of economists in the late 1800s and early 1900s who assumed that interest rates, wages, and prices were flexible; this theory predicts that the economy will tend to operate at full employment.

Say's law. The proposition, popularized by nineteenth-century French economist Jean Baptiste Say, that supply creates its own demand.

Say's law. Why did the classical economists believe that an economy would reach a full-employment equilibrium? Why would businesses produce that particular amount and why would households demand the same amount? We can summarize the classical school's conclusion by stating **Say's law**, named for Jean Baptiste Say (1767–1832), to whom it is attributed. Simply put, Say's law says that *supply creates its own demand.*

That is, as the accounting identities indicate, when businesses produce $1000 billion of goods, they simultaneously create an equivalent amount of income (GNP = NI). In other words, households receive enough income to buy all that is produced. For example, when businesses produce $1000 billion of output, households receive $1000 billion of income in wages, rent, interest, or profits. If there is no saving, households will spend all $1000 billion of their income, exactly the amount necessary to buy all that is produced. If businesses increase production to $1500 billion, income and expenditures will rise to match. Say's law, in effect, says that total spending (demand) is determined by total output (supply).

But the classical economists were aware that households tend to save a portion of their incomes. When there is saving, the economy cannot reach macroeconomic equilibrium unless saving equals investment (S = I). For example, if households save $200 billion of their $1000 billion of income, consumption will be only $800 billion, or $200 billion less than output. For equilibrium to occur, businesses must be willing to invest the same amount that households save—in this case, $200 billion. But if businesses invest only $150 billion, total spending will be only $850 billion, which is not enough to buy all that is produced. Classical economists believed that saving would equal investment because financial markets make household saving available to businesses for investment, as you learned in Chapter 21.

Flexible interest rates mean that saving equals investment. Exhibit 22.1 shows household saving flowing through financial markets to supply funds for business investment. Classical economists viewed saving as positively related to interest rates and investment as negatively related to interest rates. An increase in interest rates means a greater reward for saving, that is, greater interest income in the future. Thus saving increases as interest rates rise and decreases as interest rates fall. A decline in interest rates lowers the cost of borrowing and increases the profits that businesses expect from investing. Thus investment increases as interest rates fall and decreases when interest rates rise.

If interest rates are flexible, as classical economists believed, the rate will adjust to make the quantity of funds supplied (saving) equal to the quantity demanded (investment). Any change in supply (or demand) will cause adjustments that return financial markets—and therefore the economy—to equilibrium. Thus flexible interest rates help make Say's law true.

Flexible wages and prices guarantee full employment. Classical economic theory is also based on the assumption that wages and prices are flexible. Classical economists concluded that an economy tends to produce at its potential, or full-employment, output level. To see why, let's consider what flexible wages and prices mean in the labor market and in the macroeconomic model of aggregate demand and supply.

Businesses demand labor to produce goods and services; households supply labor to obtain income. Both labor demand and supply decisions are influenced

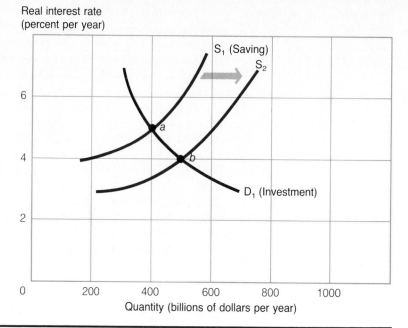

Exhibit 22.1
Financial Market Equilibrium and Classical Theory
In classical economic theory flexible interest rates automatically equate saving and investment in the market for loanable funds. Initially this market is in equilibrium at point *a*, where S_1 intersects D_1. An increase in saving shifts the supply of loanable funds to S_2. The initial surplus of funds is eliminated as the interest rate falls, restoring the market to equilibrium at point *b*.

by the level of *real wages*. If real wages increase, higher wage costs will cause businesses to demand less labor. But higher wages also mean greater rewards for working, so households will supply more labor. If wages are flexible, the labor market will reach equilibrium where quantity of labor supplied equals quantity demanded. The classical economists associated this result with "full employment" because everyone who wants to work for the existing wage is employed. Anyone still without a job is, according to the classical economists, voluntarily unemployed.

If the labor market is operating at full employment, the business sector is also producing at the full-employment level of output, or at what we called potential GNP in Chapter 20. No more could be produced without additional labor, but labor is fully employed. Will this quantity of output be bought? The answer, according to the classical school is *yes*. The flexibility of interest rates and prices ensures the necessary adjustment to "full-employment" equilibrium.

Full-employment equilibrium in classical theory. Exhibit 22.2 illustrates the classical theory of aggregate demand and supply. Note that aggregate supply in this model is a vertical line at the economy's potential GNP of $3000 billion per year. If wages are flexible, the labor market will adjust to full employment and the business sector will tend to produce at the "full-employment" level of output, or potential GNP. This result will occur regardless of price. Real, not nominal, wages determine the level of employment and therefore the level of output.

With flexible interest rates, wages, and prices, equilibrium will occur at an economy's potential GNP. Classical economists did not suggest that the economy would operate constantly at full-employment equilibrium. They recognized that various "shocks" to the system might occur. Consumers, for example, might decide to save more or save less; businesses might change the level of their desired investments. But classical economists did believe that full employment was the "normal," or equilibrium, condition of an economy. They believed that a departure from equilibrium would result in *automatic adjustments* that would return the economy to full-employment equilibrium. And they believed that these adjustments would occur rapidly enough for the economy to be considered self-correcting. As a result, they considered government intervention both unnecessary and undesirable.

Suppose, for example, that households decide to spend less and, as a result, aggregate demand decreases (from AD_1 to AD_2 in Exhibit 22.2). The economy is no longer in equilibrium. At the old price level (115), quantity of output demanded ($2900 billion) is less than quantity supplied ($3000 billion). However, this disequilibrium is only temporary. The economy would automatically and rapidly begin to adjust and restore equilibrium. The decline in spending causes saving to increase, driving down interest rates and causing investment spending to rise. As output falls, so does demand for labor. Surpluses in labor and product markets force wages and prices to fall. As these changes occur, the general price level falls (to 110), and output returns to the full-employment level.

Most economists today believe that automatic adjustment mechanisms will eventually restore an economy to full-employment equilibrium. But unlike classical economists, not all modern theorists assume that interest rates, wages, and prices are perfectly flexible, nor do they all believe that the adjustment will be rapid.

Exhibit 22.2
Macroeconomic Equilibrium and Classical Theory
In classical economic theory aggregate supply equals potential GNP. Changes in aggregate demand affect the general price level but not real output. If aggregate demand falls to AD_2, a temporary surplus is created in both labor and product markets. But as real wages fall, the labor market returns to full employment. As prices fall, the economy adjusts to produce at potential GNP. With flexible wages and prices, the economy returns to full employment quickly and automatically.

Keynesian View: Equilibrium below Full Employment

Doubts about the speed of automatic adjustment mechanisms were generated by events of the Great Depression. Between 1929 and 1933, real output in the United States fell by 30 percent, and unemployment rose to 25 percent. Prices and interest rates fell, as classical economic theory predicted. But still the economy lingered in a deep and prolonged depression.[*] To the classical assertion that the economy would automatically adjust to full employment in the long run, economist John Maynard Keynes replied: "In the long run we are all dead."

Faced with circumstances that seemed to contradict the classical view, Keynes challenged the very premises of classical theory. First, he turned Say's law upside down. In Keynesian theory, aggregate demand determines the quantity of output businesses produce. If aggregate demand is insufficient, the economy will not achieve full employment. Keynes argued that demand creates supply, not the other way around as Say's law suggests.

But what of the automatic adjustments that supposedly lead to full employment, according to the classical view? Keynes attacked the notions that wages, prices, and interest rates were flexible enough to guarantee full employment. Unions, for example, may strongly resist nominal wage cuts, even if theory suggests that falling prices will keep real wages the same. If wages are not flexible enough, the labor market may not adjust to full employment. Keynes disagreed that saving and investment respond to interest rates. In the **Keynesian theory**, saving depends most heavily on current income. Investment is largely determined by expected future demand. Under these conditions, financial markets may fail to adjust to a full-employment equilibrium.

Keynes's theory can be expressed in terms of the aggregate demand and supply diagram in Exhibit 22.3. Note that the Keynesian aggregate supply (AS) curve is horizontal across a considerable range of output. It is vertical at the full-employment, or potential GNP, output level.

The horizontal portion of the aggregate supply curve reflects Keynes's view of an economy in the midst of a deep depression. With many people out of work, businesses could hire more workers at the current wage. With many plants and factories operating well below their capacity, producing more at the same cost would be possible. Thus output is determined by aggregate demand. If wages and prices do not fall, the economy will reach equilibrium (where AD_1 intersects AS) below the full-employment level. Without flexible wages and prices, the economy has no automatic mechanism to return it to full employment.

Keynes placed great stress on aggregate demand. In the Great Depression he saw proof that aggregate demand could be inadequate and that the economy could reach equilibrium despite considerable unemployment. Classical economists classified this unemployment as voluntary because they believed that the unemployed could get jobs if they were willing to accept a lower wage. Keynes classified this unemployment as involuntary, expressing his belief that low aggregate demand was not the fault of the unemployed. Keynes suggested that increases in aggregate demand, not lower wages, was the best way to return the economy to full em-

Keynesian theory. The economic propositions of John Maynard Keynes, including the belief that fluctuations in aggregate output are generally caused by changes in private-sector demand. Keynesian economists generally recommend government policies to boost aggregate demand during recessions.

---

[*] The difference between a depression and a recession (a fall in GNP as defined in Chapter 20) is a matter of semantics. A depression is just a severe and prolonged recession. A classic economics joke is that the economy is in a recession when your neighbor is out of work. It is in a depression when you lose your job.

Exhibit 22.3
Macroeconomic Equilibrium and the Keynesian Model
In the simple Keynesian model a fall in aggregate demand causes a drop in real output. Because wages and prices are inflexible, the general price level is unaffected. The downward inflexibility of prices makes the Keynesian aggregate supply curve horizontal below full-employment output. However, as with classical theory, aggregate supply becomes vertical when the economy reaches full employment.

ployment. To raise aggregate demand, he suggested that government increase its spending, an idea that remains controversial.

In the rest of this chapter, we follow the Keynesian approach to macroeconomic equilibrium. For simplicity, we continue to describe the operation of a private-sector economy (no government or foreign sectors). Since Keynesian theory focuses on aggregate demand, let's begin by considering factors that influence the spending decisions of households and businesses.

CONSUMPTION AND SAVING: THE HOUSEHOLD SECTOR

We begin our survey of aggregate demand by looking at the household sector. To keep our analysis simple, we temporarily make several simplifying assumptions:

1. The economy consists of business and household sectors only. (That is, we ignore the influence of the government and foreign sectors.)

2. The general price level is constant.

3. There is no capital consumption allowance, nor are there any business taxes. (This allows us to equate real GNP, aggregate output, and national income, in keeping with the accounting identity introduced in Chapter 21.)

Although we relax some of these assumptions later, they make understanding macroeconomic principles a bit easier. After you have grasped some of the essentials of macroeconomic analysis, using this simplified economy, we can consider a more realistic and complete model of the economy. In particular, we can consider what happens when the price level varies.

When looking at the effect of households on aggregate demand, we have to consider the determinants of household consumption expenditures. As we noted in Chapter 21, household expenditures for final consumer goods and services are a component of aggregate demand. In fact, consumption accounts for over 60 percent of the total purchases of final goods. An understanding of what determines consumption is crucial to understanding what determines aggregate demand.

Consumption, Saving, and Disposable Income

Among the factors that influence household consumption and saving decisions, the most important by far is the level of disposable income (DI). Since we are ignoring government at this point, disposable income (income less taxes plus transfer payments) is equal to national income. As you might suspect, *the greater the level of disposable income, the greater is the level of consumption.* Keynes argued that this relationship between consumption and disposable income was a "fundamental psychological law." Households, he said, "are disposed, as a rule and on the average, to increase their consumption as their income increases, but not by as much as their income increases."[*]

Exhibit 22.4 illustrates the basic relationship between disposable income and consumption as a **consumption schedule**. You can see that the household sector spends more as disposable income increases, as Keynes observed. When income increases from $1200 billion to $1600 billion, for example, consumption rises from $1100 billion to $1400 billion per year. Note that we singled out disposable income and made the "all-other-factors-unchanged" assumption. We consider other factors that affect the level of consumption—such as wealth and the availability of credit—later in this chapter.

Marginal propensity to consume.   Exhibit 22.4 also supports Keynes's second proposition: Households spend only part of any increase in disposable income. While disposable income increases from $1200 billion to $1600 billion— a $400 billion increase—consumption increases by $300 billion—from $1100 billion to $1400 billion per year. Because of its importance, Keynes gave the relationship between a change in disposable income and a change in consumption a specific name: the **marginal propensity to consume (MPC)**. In Exhibit 22.4, when disposable income rises from $1200 billion to $1600 billion, the marginal propensity to consume is 0.75, calculated as

Consumption schedule. A table showing the level of consumption expenditures at various levels of disposable income.

Marginal propensity to consume (MPC). The ratio of changes in consumption to changes in income; indicates the proportion of any additional income that will be spent on consumption.

$$\text{Marginal propensity to consume} = \frac{\text{Change in consumption}}{\text{Change in disposable income}} \quad \text{or} \quad \frac{\text{Change in C}}{\text{Change in DI}}$$

$$\text{MPC} = \frac{(\$1400 - \$1100)\,\text{billion}}{(\$1600 - \$1200)\,\text{billion}}$$

$$= \frac{\$300\,\text{billion}}{\$400\,\text{billion}} \quad \text{or} \quad 0.75$$

---

[*] John Maynard Keynes, *The General Theory of Employment, Interest, and Money.* New York: Harcourt, Brace & World, 1936, p. 96.

Disposable income (DI)	Consumption (C)	Saving (S = DI − C)
0	200	− 200
400	500	− 100
800	800	0
1200	1100	100
1600	1400	200
2000	1700	300

Exhibit 22.4
Consumption, Saving, and Disposable Income (billions of dollars per year)

The marginal propensity to consume shows what proportion of a change in disposable income will be spent. The MPC of 0.75 in this example means that every $100 billion of extra disposable income will cause consumption to increase by $75 billion. To check your understanding of this concept, apply the formula to other data in Exhibit 22.4 and calculate the marginal propensity to consume for several changes in disposable income. (We assumed a constant MPC, so you should obtain 0.75 in each case.)

Average propensity to consume. It is important to distinguish the marginal propensity to consume from the average propensity to consume. The marginal propensity to consume indicates how much a *change* in disposable income will *change* consumption. The **average propensity to consume (APC)** is the ratio of consumption to disposable income at some specified level of income. Or if you divide the *level* of consumption in any year by disposable income in that same year, you get the average propensity to consume. In Exhibit 22.4, the average propensity to consume is 0.85 when disposable income is $2000 billion per year, calculated as

$$\text{Average propensity to consume} = \frac{\text{Level of consumption}}{\text{Level of disposable income}} \quad \text{or} \quad \frac{C}{DI}$$

$$\text{APC} = \frac{\$1700 \text{ billion}}{\$2000 \text{ billion}} \quad \text{or} \quad 0.85$$

The average propensity to consume shows how much of a specified level of disposable income will be spent. In this case, the household sector will spend 85 percent of disposable income if it is $2000 billion per year. Although the marginal propensity to consume is the same at each level of income, the average propensity to consume is not. If disposable income is $800 billion, consumption will also be $800 billion, and the average propensity to consume will be 1.0.

In this example, when disposable income falls below $800 billion, the average propensity to consume exceeds 1.0. For example, average propensity to consume is 1.25 when disposable income is $400 billion. This figure indicates that the household sector is *dissaving,* that is, spending more than its current income. To

Average propensity to consume (APC). The ratio of consumption to income at some specified level of income; indicates the proportion of a specified level of income that will be spent on consumption.

Saving schedule. A table showing the level of saving for various levels of disposable income.

Marginal propensity to save (MPS). The ratio of changes in saving to changes in disposable income; shows the proportion of any additional disposable income that will be saved.

check your understanding, calculate the average propensity to consume when disposable income is $1600 billion. (You should find APC to be 0.875.)

Saving Schedules and the Marginal Propensity to Save

Exhibit 22.4 also shows a **saving schedule**, that is, the amounts that will be saved at various levels of disposable income. By definition, households have only two options for their disposable income: consumption or saving. That is, disposable income always equals consumption plus saving, or DI = C + S.

Note that by rearranging terms in the equation, we can calculate saving as the difference between disposable income and consumption, or S = DI − C. For example, when disposable income is $1600 billion per year, the household sector will consume $1400 billion. Saving, therefore, is $200 billion. Because of this relationship, the factors that determine saving are really the same as those that determine consumption.

The data in Exhibit 22.4 show that households not only spend more when their disposable income rises, but they also save more. The change in saving, like the change in consumption, is less than the change in disposable income. As for the marginal propensity to consume, we can define the **marginal propensity to save (MPS)** as the relationship between changes in disposable income and changes in saving.

In Exhibit 22.4, the marginal propensity to save for an increase in disposal income from $1200 billion to $1600 billion per year is 0.25, calculated as

$$\text{Marginal propensity to save} = \frac{\text{Change in saving}}{\text{Change in disposable income}} \quad \text{or} \quad \frac{\text{Change in S}}{\text{Change in DI}}$$

$$\text{MPS} = \frac{(\$200 - \$100) \text{ billion}}{(\$1600 - \$1200) \text{ billion}}$$

$$= \frac{\$100 \text{ billion}}{\$400 \text{ billion}} \quad \text{or} \quad 0.25$$

The marginal propensity to save shows the proportion of a change in income that will be saved. In this example, the MPS of 0.25 indicates that a $100 billion change in disposable income will cause a $25 billion change in saving. You should verify that the marginal propensity to save is 0.25 at each level of disposable income shown in Exhibit 22.4.

Because any change in disposable income will be either spent or saved, the sum of the proportion consumed (MPC) and the proportion saved (MPS) always equals 1 (MPC + MPS = 1). For example, if your marginal propensity to consume is 0.75, you will spend $0.75 of every $1 of additional disposable income you receive and save the balance of $0.25.

Consumption and Saving: A Graphic View

The relationship between disposable income and consumption in Exhibit 22.4 is shown graphically in Exhibit 22.5(a). The horizontal axis shows disposable income in billions of dollars. The vertical axis shows consumption expenditures

(a) Consumption

Consumption expenditures
(billions of dollars per year)

(b) Saving

Saving
(billions of dollars per year)

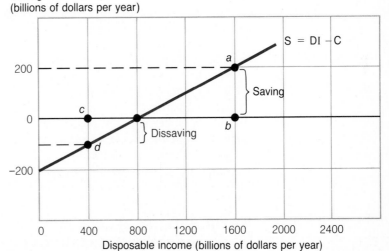

Exhibit 22.5
Consumption and Saving: A Graphic View
Part (a) shows consumption and saving at various levels of disposable income. The red 45° line indicates points at which expenditures and income are identical. For example, at $800 billion of income where C intersects the 45° line, consumption will also be $800 billion, indicating zero saving. At $1600 billion of income, consumption is $1400 billion—the difference between points *a* and *b*—indicating saving of $200 billion. At $400 billion of income, consumption is $600 billion—the difference between points *c* and *d*—indicating dissaving of $200 billion. The amount of saving is shown in part (b).

Disposable income is the most important component of consumption. Consumption tends to rise as disposable income rises, but not as quickly.

The marginal propensity to consume (MPC) indicates the proportion of any additional disposable income that will be spent. The average propensity to consume (APC) indicates the proportion of some specified level of income that will be spent. The aggregate consumption line indicates how the level of consumption varies with disposable income for the entire household sector.

The marginal propensity to save (MPS) indicates the proportion of any additional income that will be saved. The 45° line indicates how the level of saving varies with disposable income for the entire household sector.

in billions of dollars. You can read the level of consumption spending at any level of disposable income from the blue line (labeled C) on the graph.* For example, locate disposable income of $1600 billion per year on the horizontal axis. Then move vertically from that point to the consumption line, and from there horizontally to the vertical axis. Consumption expenditures are $1400 billion per year. To check your understanding, try reading other points on the graph.

Another line on the graph is also important to our analysis. Because of its angle, this line is labeled "45° line." Its significance for graphic analysis is that each point on the line is the same distance, measured in dollars, from both the vertical and horizontal axes. Thus the height of the 45° line (above the horizontal axis) measures disposable income. Using the 45° line and the consumption line, we can identify the level of saving for any level of disposable income. For example, suppose that disposable income is $1600 billion. The height of the 45° line at that level of income is also $1600 billion. We can divide that height into two parts: consumption and saving. Consumption, indicated by the height of the consumption line, is $1400 billion. The vertical distance between consumption and the 45° line, $200 billion in this case, indicates the amount of disposable income saved.

Where the consumption line intersects the 45° line (at $800 billion), consumption and disposable income are equal and saving is zero. When disposable income is above the point of intersection, the consumption line lies below the 45° line, indicating that the household sector is saving some portion of its current disposable income. When disposable income is below the point of intersection, however, the consumption line lies above the 45° line, indicating that consumption exceeds disposable income.

In this example, when disposable income is $400 billion, consumption is $500 billion. Thus saving is −$100 billion. Negative saving (called *dissaving*) means that households are spending more than their current disposable income. If you are like many college students, you work during the summer, putting at least part of your earnings in the bank. By saving during the summer, you are able to spend more than your income during the school year. During the summer you save; during the school year, you dissave.

Although they can read the level of saving from a consumption graph, economists sometimes find it convenient to display saving as shown in Exhibit 22.5(b). Again the horizontal axis represents the level of disposable income. The vertical axis shows the level of saving. The graph indicates, for example, that saving will be $200 billion if disposable income is $1600 billion and that dissaving of $100 billion will occur if disposable income is $400 billion.

Other Determinants of Consumption Expenditures

Although disposable income is the most important determinant of consumption, several other factors influence consumption. These factors include wealth, the general price level, and expectations about future income and price levels. They are the "all-other-things-unchanged" factors that we have held constant while

---

* The ratio of the change in consumption to the change in disposable income is the marginal propensity to consume. Hence the slope (see the Appendix to Chapter 1) of the consumption line measures MPC. The intercept (see also the Appendix to Chapter 1) shows the portion of consumption spending that depends on factors other than current disposable income, that is, the factors held constant along the consumption line. A change in any of these factors will change the intercept and shift the consumption line.

discussing the relationship between consumption and income. Let's now consider their effects.

Wealth. If you or your family have put aside some income in past years, you have accumulated wealth. Your wealth may include a savings account in a local bank, stocks and bonds of corporations, and equity in a house (the part of the house that belongs to you, not the bank). If you have wealth, you can spend more than your current income. Individuals who lose their jobs and thus their current income, for example, often spend more than their income by withdrawing funds from their savings.

The determinants of consumption are also determinants of saving. Households save for many reasons, but two of these are to build up security against job losses and to provide for retirement. The more wealth a household has, the greater its financial security. Thus we can expect that *greater wealth will decrease saving, and therefore increase consumption at each level of income*.

Two historical examples show the relationship between wealth and consumption. Between 1973 and 1975, the value of stocks traded on the New York Stock Exchange declined significantly, lowering the real wealth of the household sector. For that reason (and perhaps others), consumption expenditures were $17–$20 billion per year lower than might have been expected for the level of income.

During World War II, production of war materials had high priority. The economy produced few consumer durable goods, especially cars and household appliances. With few goods to buy, households saved nearly 25 percent of their disposable income (compared to an average of about 6 percent in the past 10 years). A backlog of demand for durable goods grew, and when the war ended and production of consumer goods resumed, consumption expenditures increased dramatically. Saving fell to a historic low of only 3.1 percent of disposable income in 1947 as households spent accumulated wealth. Some economists and politicians had been concerned that the economy might slip into a depression after the war. Instead, increased consumption made inflation and excess demand a more serious concern.

Price level. Consumption expenditures are also affected by price level because a change in the general price level causes a change in real wealth. Households hold a great deal of their wealth in the form of **monetary assets**, such as bonds or other debt obligations of businesses and governments. Such assets are essentially promises to make payments that are fixed in nominal terms.

For example, suppose that you hold a $1000, 10-year government bond with an 8 percent interest rate. The government has promised to pay you, the holder of the bond, $80 each year for the next 10 years and to return your $1000 at the end of the 10-year period. The *nominal* value of the interest and principal payments is fixed, but the *real* value of these promised payments depends on the general price level. If it increases, the purchasing power of money falls. As we noted in Chapter 20, you then would not be able to buy as much with the $80 interest payment as you could before. An increase in the general price level reduces the purchasing power of a dollar and therefore the real value of the promised payments. As a result, *an increase in the general price level reduces the real wealth of bondholders and consequently reduces consumption expenditures*.

Monetary assets. Bonds or other debt obligations that promise the holders future payments that are fixed in nominal terms.

Expectations. Household spending is also affected by expectations about income and prices. Expected changes in income cause households to change their consumption patterns in the same direction as do changes in current income. Thus if households are pessimistic about the future—for example, if they believe that a recession is coming and income will fall—they tend to save more and spend less current income. On the other hand, if households have confidence in the future, consumption will rise. *If future income is expected to rise, current consumption will also rise.*

The aggregate response to expectations of future price levels is not easy to predict. Usually, consumption is lower than normal during bursts of inflation, perhaps in part because people expect government to invoke policies to reduce prices. But during the burst of inflation in 1979–1980, consumption was higher than usual. Some economists viewed this reaction as household fears that even higher prices were coming. Although economists have some difficulty understanding exactly how expectations are determined, they agree that consumer and business expectations have important effects on the economy.

Cost and availability of credit. A change in *real* interest rates can have two conflicting effects on consumption. On the one hand, a higher interest rate means an increased reward for saving. At the same time, the higher rate increases the cost to consumers who borrow to finance cars, appliances, and other purchases. As a result of the higher rate, saving will increase and consumption will decrease.

On the other hand, consider the effect on a family that is saving with a particular objective in mind: to buy a car or put a son or daughter through college. For that family, a higher interest rate would raise future interest income and reduce the amount of saving required to achieve their objective. Although Keynes did not believe that consumption or saving was strongly influenced by interest rates, classical economists did. More recent studies of interest effects and the availability of credit have reached conflicting conclusions.

Movement along Consumption Curve versus Shifts in Consumption

The factors affecting the level of consumption can be grouped into two categories: disposable income and all others. Recall that Exhibit 22.5(a) focuses on the relationship between consumption and disposable income and that all other factors—wealth, price level, and expectations—remain constant. In Chapter 3 we made a similar distinction with regard to demand. We concentrated on the relationship between price and quantity consumed while holding prices of substitutes and complements, income, and other factors constant. Recall that we distinguished movement along a curve from a shift in the curve. Movement along a product demand curve occurs when product price changes. A shift in a product demand curve results from a change in one of the other factors that we assume are unchanged along any demand curve.

Similarly, we distinguish movement along a consumption line from a shift in the line. When drawing a consumption line, we hold factors other than income constant. A change in consumption caused by a change in the level of disposable income results in *movement along* the consumption line. This change is called

Consumption expenditures
(billions of dollars per year)

Exhibit 22.6
Movement along versus a Shift in the Consumption Line
The consumption line shows the response of households to a change in GNP, all other factors affecting consumption remaining constant. When GNP increases from $1200 to $1600 billion, consumption rises from $1100 to $1400 billion as the economy moves along C_1 from point a to point b. If autonomous consumption increases (greater wealth, more optimistic expectations, lower interest rates), the consumption line shifts upward (to C_2) indicating more consumption at each level of income. Compare point b on C_1 to point c on C_2, for example.

induced consumption because additional consumption is *induced* by the change in disposable income. On the other hand, changes in wealth, price levels, or expectations cause a shift in the consumption line, also known as a change in **autonomous consumption**. When the consumption line shifts, more or less is consumed at every level of disposable income.

In Exhibit 22.6, C_1 is the initial consumption line. If all other factors remain constant as disposable income rises from $1200 billion to $1600 billion, consumption will rise from $1100 billion to $1400 billion. That is, we *move along* C_1 from a to b. We can also predict the size of the change in consumption by knowing that the marginal propensity to consume is 0.75. Since each $100 increase in disposable income results in a $75 increase in consumption, a $400 billion rise in disposable income (from $1200 billion to $1600 billion) will increase consumption by $300 billion. Using the formula for MPC,

Induced consumption. A change in consumption in response to a change in income (holding other factors constant); results in a movement along a consumption line.

$$\text{Marginal propensity to consume} = \frac{\text{Change in consumption}}{\text{Change in disposable income}}$$

$$\text{MPC} = \frac{\text{Change in C}}{\text{Change in DI}}$$

Thus

Autonomous consumption. The portion of consumption that is independent of the level of income. A change in a factor other than income causes a change in autonomous consumption and results in a shift in a consumption line.

$$\text{Change in C} = \text{MPC} \times \text{Change in DI}$$

$$= 0.75(\$400 \text{ billion}) \quad \text{or} \quad \$300 \text{ billion}$$

By contrast, suppose that households simply become more optimistic about the future, based perhaps on Wall Street analyst Rosie Scenario's forecast of strong economic growth. With the expectation that *future* income will be greater, households are likely to spend more *now* at each level of income. Exhibit 22.6 shows that households will spend $1600 billion per year if disposable income is $1600 billion (point *c* on C_2), compared to $1400 billion (point *b* on C_1) under the old expectations. This change causes the consumption line to *shift* from C_1 to C_2, indicating that consumption will be $200 billion higher *at each level of disposable income*. This change in one of the other factors results in a $200 billion change in the intercept of the consumption line. The intercept represents the portion of consumption that does not depend on current income. As we noted earlier, economists refer to spending that is independent of the level of income as *autonomous*. Therefore the intercept represents autonomous consumption.

Long-Run and Short-Run Views of Consumption

Exhibit 22.7 shows the historical relationship between consumption and disposable income for the years 1929–1986. It supports the idea that consumption rises with income but by less than the increase in disposable income. For example, between 1972 and 1982, disposable income increased by $1421.8 billion and consumption expenditures by $1293.1 billion. Using the formula for marginal propensity to consume, we obtain an MPC of about 0.91. This figure has remained fairly steady over time. Although the consumption line is not exactly straight, the relationship between consumption and disposable income appears to be reasonably stable and predictable.

However, there is a major difference between this plot of historical data and the consumption lines shown in Exhibit 22.6. That graph shows that households will maintain some minimum level of spending even if they must dissave to do so, and observations of individual households confirm such a relationship. In contrast, the historical graph in Exhibit 22.7 shows no significant dissaving at any income level. (In fact, for the entire period shown, dissaving occurred only in 1932–1933, and even then it was less than 2 percent of income.)

Economists have explained this puzzle by distinguishing between long-run and short-run consumption. The historical relationship measures long-run reactions; the hypothetical consumption line indicates short-run reactions. This difference explains the extent of dissaving shown in both graphs. When disposable income declines temporarily, households can maintain some level of spending by dissaving. However, if disposable income remains quite low for a long period of time, households will deplete much or all of their savings. Thus they will be unable to consume more than their current disposable income (without borrowing).

You can see the distinction by considering how you might react to a long-run increase in your income—a $1000 per year raise—and a short-run change—a legacy of $1000 from your rich Uncle Sam. In either case, your income this year is $1000 greater than last year's. However, the check from Uncle Sam is a temporary change that affects only your current income. In contrast, the raise affects your permanent (long-run) income, so you can expect higher disposable income not only this year but also in the future. A change in your permanent income is obviously worth more to you and thus tends to result in a greater increase in spending. Economists generally agree that *a change in permanent income will stimulate a greater change in consumption than will a change affecting current income only*.

Exhibit 22.7
Historical Consumption Function, 1929–1986

Historically, the marginal propensity to consume has been a relatively consistent 0.91, indicating that increases in disposable income cause smaller increases in consumption. For example, between 1972 and 1982, consumption increased by $1293.1 billion, while disposable income increased by $1421.8 billion. Unlike the hypothetical relationship, the historical relationship does not indicate dissaving at low levels of income (although dissaving did occur in 1932–1933). Economists believe that the historical relationship indicates how consumption responds to long-run or permanent changes in disposable income.

Sources: U.S. Department of Commerce, *The National Income and Product Accounts of the United States, 1929–82* (Table 2.1); *Economic Report of the President, 1987* (Table B-26).

RECAP

Long-run or permanent changes in income cause greater changes in consumption than do short-run or temporary changes.

In addition to the level of income, consumption spending is affected by wealth, the general price level, expectations, interest rates, and availability of credit.

Induced changes in consumption result from an increase or a decrease in income. They cause movement along a given consumption line, with all other factors held constant. Autonomous changes in consumption result from a change in a factor other than income. They cause the aggregate consumption line to shift.

Two historical examples illustrate the importance of distinguishing between temporary and permanent changes in income. In 1964, Congress approved a permanent tax cut. In estimating its effect—how much consumption spending would increase initially—economists used a marginal propensity to consume of roughly 90 percent, based on the historical, or long-run relationship. The actual results were not very different from that prediction.

In 1968, Congress enacted a temporary tax increase. The initial decrease in consumption spending was far less than would have been projected by the long-run relationship. Because the 1964 cut was a permanent change (or as permanent as any tax changes ever are), it increased the household sector's estimate of its permanent income. The 1968 tax increase, clearly labeled as a temporary increase, affected only current income and thus caused a smaller change in consumption. Despite the economic lessons of the 1968 temporary tax increase, a temporary tax cut was approved in 1975. The results were disappointing to the politicians who expected a greater increase in consumption but were perfectly understandable to those familiar with economic analysis.

INVESTMENT AND THE BUSINESS SECTOR

As consumers of most final goods, households are clearly a major force in determining aggregate demand. However, investment spending by the business sector is another significant part of aggregate demand. Businesses make *fixed investments* in capital resources, such as buildings and equipment, and *inventory investments* in quantities of goods held for future sale. To understand aggregate demand, we must examine the factors that influence business investment decisions.

Autonomous Nature of Investment Decisions

Unlike household consumption decisions, business investment decisions are not greatly affected by current levels of output. Once resources such as labor hours and materials are purchased and used, they are gone. Thus demand for such resources is based largely on *current* levels of aggregate output and expected levels of *current* sales. But capital resources are by definition long-lasting; they provide services both now and in the future. Thus demand for them is based largely on expected *future* sales.

Similarly, decisions to change inventory levels are influenced mostly by expected future sales, not just by current levels of income and sales. Businesses typically add to inventories at the beginning of the recovery phase of a business cycle, for example. Even though current sales and income are low, businesses build up inventories because they anticipate an increase in future sales (or perhaps higher future costs).

Neither demand for fixed investment nor demand for inventory investment is closely related to current sales. For simplicity, then, we assume that investment in both capital resources and inventory is completely autonomous. In other words, we assume that the business sector will invest the same amount at all levels of GNP. Although current sales may have some influence on investment, historical data support the assumption that the influence is small.

Historical relationship between investment and real GNP. When we looked at the historical data on consumption, we found a fairly stable relationship between consumption and disposable income. In contrast, the relationship between investment and real GNP is anything but stable. Exhibit 22.8 shows percentage changes in real GNP and in investment from 1955 to 1986. We can draw two conclusions from these data: (1) there is no consistent relationship between investment and real GNP; and (2) investment is much more volatile than real GNP. Over the 1955–1986 period, annual changes in real GNP ranged from a low of −2.6 percent to a high of 6.4 percent. Changes in investment ranged from a low of −20.4 percent to a high of 29.4 percent.[*]

Economists differ sharply over the cause of this instability. Keynesians believe that these fluctuations reflect unstable spending by the private sector and support

---

[*] As we noted in Chapter 21, investment in national income and product accounts includes not only business spending for capital resources and inventory but also housing investment by households. Although the level of investment in housing is very unstable, eliminating this category would not greatly change the central point of the graph.

Percentage change

Exhibit 22.8
Volatility of Investment Spending, 1955–1986
This graph shows annual percentage changes in real GNP and investment. Note that there is no consistent relationship between investment and real GNP and that investment is much more volatile than real GNP. Between 1955 and 1986, annual changes in real GNP ranged from a low of −2.6 percent to a high of 6.4 percent. During the same period, changes in investment ranged from a low of −20.4 percent to a high of 29.4 percent.

Sources: U.S. Department of Commerce, *The National Income and Product Accounts of the United States, 1929–82* (Table 1.2); *Economic Report of the President, 1987* (Table B-1).

government policies to correct for the instability. Other economists, however, believe that government policies are themselves an important source of the instability. We return to this controversy when we have given you the necessary tools to analyze the arguments.

Determinants of Investment Expenditures

Although investment is not closely related to current levels of aggregate output, it is sensitive to several factors. These factors are expectations, real interest rates, current capacity and future demand, technological change, and tax policies.

Expectations (business confidence). As we noted previously, both fixed investment and inventory investment decisions are heavily influenced by expected

Nominal interest rate. The actual or market interest rate charged for borrowed funds; determines how many dollars must be paid in interest.

Real interest rate. The cost of borrowed funds stated in real terms; the nominal rate of interest minus the expected rate of inflation; reflects the amount of real purchasing power a borrower can expect to pay in interest.

sales. Investment tends to rise when businesses expect sales to increase in the future.

Real interest rates. Another important determinant of investment spending is the real interest rate. The **nominal interest rate** is the market rate and indicates the actual or nominal cost of financing. The **real interest rate** has been adjusted for expected inflation and shows the real cost of financing.

Why is the real interest rate important? Businesses often borrow to purchase capital resources or more inventory. When they obtain funds from their shareholders, the interest rate represents the opportunity cost of using those funds. In either case, an increase in real interest rates means greater real costs for funds. As a result, investment will decrease.

Although nominal interest rates determine how many dollars of interest must be paid, an increase in the general price level reduces the real value of a dollar. Both borrowers and lenders are aware of this fact, so nominal interest rates are not accurate estimates of real costs. Remember that it is real—not nominal—interest rates that influence business investment.

Current capacity and future demand. An expected increase in aggregate demand also increases investment spending for new plant and equipment. When considering how much to invest, businesses compare current capacity to expected sales. If they have significant unused capacity, they can meet increased sales without further investment. But if they have no excess capacity, businesses must make additional investments if they are to meet future demand.

Rate of technological change. As you might expect, a firm having machines or other equipment that is in danger of becoming obsolete in the near future is likely to invest in new capital resources. When new technology allows for either lower costs or better quality products, firms that want to remain in business have little choice but to invest. But when technological change is very rapid, firms may hesitate to invest large sums in equipment that may soon become obsolete.

Government tax policy. Although we are not ready to bring the government sector into our analysis, we should note that government tax policy can affect investment decisions. In the past, businesses have been granted special tax incentives to encourage new investment. The tax changes in 1986 removed some of these incentives and caused some economists to predict a decline in investment.

RECAP

Unlike consumption, investment is not very responsive to changes in the current level of aggregate output or income.

Investment spending by the business sector is influenced by expectations (business confidence), interest rates, current capacity and future demand, the rate of technological change, and government tax policies.

Historically, investment has been much less stable than real GNP, but economists disagree over why.

EQUILIBRIUM OUTPUT IN THE SIMPLE KEYNESIAN MODEL

Now that you have a better understanding of two of the determinants of aggregate demand—consumption and investment—we can consider the determination of macroeconomic equilibrium. As the title of this section indicates, we explore equilibrium in terms of the simple Keynesian model of the economy. Thus we assume that the general price level is fixed. For the moment we also ignore the effects of the government and foreign sectors.

Although we relax these unrealistic assumptions later, you can learn a great deal about macroeconomic equilibrium from this over-simplified model. In particular, we consider why Keynes believed that the economy could reach equilibrium below the full-employment, or potential output, level.

Macroeconomic Equilibrium

Before seeing how equilibrium is achieved in this Keynesian model, you must understand what macroeconomic equilibrium means. This requires that you clearly distinguish between the *accounting identity* we used in Chapter 21 to measure GNP and the *equilibrium condition* we use in this chapter to determine equilibrium GNP.

In Chapter 21 you saw that GNP, the level of output produced, is by definition identical to the level of *actual* aggregate expenditures. In the purely private-sector economy that we are considering, there are three components of actual aggregate expenditures: consumption expenditures (C), *planned* (or desired) investment (I), and *unplanned* (or undesired) inventory investment (I_u). To make the relationship between GNP and actual expenditures an identity, economists count unplanned inventory investment as an expenditure by the business sector. In equation form,

Accounting identity

Aggregate output = Actual aggregate expenditures

$$= \text{Consumption} + \frac{\text{Planned}}{\text{investment}} + \frac{\text{Unplanned}}{\text{inventory investment}}$$

$$\text{GNP} = C + I + I_u$$

However, macroeconomic equilibrium occurs only when quantity produced equals quantity *demanded*. Businesses are forced to make unplanned inventory investments when the quantities they supply are different from quantity demanded. We would not expect businesses to be satisfied, however, if they produced more (or less) than could be sold at current prices. The economy will not be in macroeconomic equilibrium unless unplanned inventory investment (I_u) is zero. Thus

Equilibrium condition

Aggregate output = Planned aggregate expenditures

= Consumption + Planned investment

$$\text{GNP} = C + I$$

Keynesian Equilibrium

We can use the data in Exhibit 22.9 to see how equilibrium is reached in the simple Keynesian model. Exhibit 22.9(a) shows planned aggregate expenditures at several levels of output. In this private-sector economy, planned aggregate expenditures are the sum of planned spending by the household and business sectors (AE = C + I). Note the assumption that planned investment (I) is $400 billion at each level of GNP. That is, following the assumptions of Keynesian theory, we assume that investment is unrelated to current output. Planned aggregate expenditures increase as output increases because consumption spending increases.

Exhibit 22.9
Equilibrium in the Simple Keynesian Model (billions of dollars per year)
For the economy to attain macroeconomic equilibrium in the simple Keynesian model, quantity of output demanded must equal quantity of output supplied. The aggregate expenditures curve (AE = C + I) shows planned spending, or quantity of output demanded. If actual GNP is $3200 billion, planned spending is only $3000 billion; that is, $200 billion of planned inventory investment exists (the difference between points *a* and *b*). Businesses will reduce output to $2400 billion to achieve equilibrium. If actual GNP is $1600 billion, planned spending is $1800 billion; that is, $200 billion of unplanned inventory disinvestment exists (the difference between points *c* and *d*). Businesses will increase output to $2400 billion to restore equilibrium.

(a)

| Aggregate output (GNP) | Planned expenditures | | | Unplanned inventory investment $(I_u = GNP - AE)$ |
	Consumption (C)	Planned investment (I)	Aggregate expenditure (AE = C + I)	
0	200	400	600	−600
800	800	400	1200	−400
1600	1400	400	1800	−200
2400	2000	400	2400	0
3200	2600	400	3000	200
4000	3200	400	3600	400

(b)

Expenditures
(billions of dollars per year)

Both consumption (C) and planned aggregate expenditures (AE) are plotted in Exhibit 22.9(b). Planned investment (I) is not plotted, but if it were, it would appear as a horizontal line at $400 billion. The vertical distance between the consumption and planned aggregate expenditures lines represents that $400 billion of investment. As we discuss the determination of equilibrium, you should be sure you understand the reasoning in terms of both the graph and the table.

The last column in Exhibit 22.9(a) shows *unplanned inventory investment* at each level of output. Unplanned inventory investment represents output produced but not sold. We can calculate it as the difference between aggregate output and planned aggregate expenditures ($I_u = GNP - AE$). For example, when GNP is $3200 billion, planned expenditures are only $3000 billion. That is, $200 billion of output produced would not be sold, and warehouses would be filled with products that could not be sold at existing prices. (In Exhibit 22.9(b), unplanned inventory investment is the vertical distance between aggregate expenditures and the 45° line. Recall that expenditures are equal to output on the 45° line.)

At this point, the economy clearly is not in equilibrium because businesses do not want this extra inventory. What can they do to get rid of the surplus? One possible action is to reduce quantity produced. If businesses reduce output from $3200 billion to $2400 billion, unplanned inventory investment would disappear. (Recall that in this simple Keynesian model, the general price level is fixed. While you might expect to see businesses lowering price to achieve equilibrium, we have assumed that this option is unavailable. Keynes assumed that workers would not accept a cut in nominal wages. Thus businesses would be reluctant to lower prices, because their profits would fall.)

Similarly, the economy would not be in equilibrium if GNP were only $1600 billion per year because planned spending ($1800 billion) exceeds aggregate output. As a result, unplanned inventory investment is a − $200 billion, or what economists call unplanned inventory *disinvestment*. (Note in Exhibit 22.9(b) that planned aggregate expenditures are $200 billion above the 45° line at a GNP of $1600 billion.)

The resulting good news for businesses is that sales are high. But the bad news is that warehouses are not holding the quantity of goods that businesses want. Businesses can expand production by hiring unemployed workers and putting idle capacity to use. Because we are assuming costs do not increase, the increase in output will not require higher prices. When output is increased to $2400 billion, unplanned inventory investment is zero. The stock of goods held in warehouses is exactly what businesses want. Aggregate output is equal to planned aggregate expenditures (GNP = AE = C + I) and macroeconomic equilibrium has been reached. An alternative way of finding equilibrium is given in A Case in Point: Equilibrium—Planned Leakages and Injections.

EQUILIBRIUM OUTPUT AND FULL EMPLOYMENT

We have just shown that businesses adjust quantity of output to match quantity demanded. This adjustment produces macroeconomic equilibrium in the simple Keynesian model. But what about the macroeconomic goal of full employment? In this section we indicate why, in this model, the equilibrium level of output may not be the same as the full-employment level of output.

A Case in Point
Equilibrium—Planned Leakages and Injections

We can determine the conditions for equilibrium using the concept of leakages and injections presented in A Case in Point in Chapter 21. There we noted that according to the third accounting identity, *actual leakages* always equal *actual injections*. If we consider a simple private-sector economy, saving is the only leakage and investment the only injection. Thus

Accounting Identity

Actual leakages = Actual injections

$$\text{Saving} = \begin{array}{c}\text{Planned}\\\text{investment}\end{array} + \begin{array}{c}\text{Unplanned}\\\text{inventory}\\\text{investment}\end{array}$$

$$S = I + I_u$$

This identity is always true, but the economy cannot achieve equilibrium unless unplanned inventory investment is zero. That is, equilibrium requires that *planned leakages* equal *planned injections*. Thus

Equilibrium condition

Planned leakages = Planned injections
Saving = Planned investment
S = I

In the table below, we show planned saving as the difference between GNP and consumption (C) because we are using a private-sector economy only. (To consider an economy that also has a government sector, we would have to distinguish between GNP and disposable income.) We also use the accounting identity to find unplanned inventory investment.

In the graph, unplanned inventory investment is the difference between the saving (S) curve and the investment (I) curve. When saving is above investment (when

Leakages and injections
(billions of dollars per year)

GNP is $3200 billion, for example), unplanned inventory investment results. When saving is below investment, unplanned inventory disinvestment results. When the saving and investment curves intersect (where GNP equals $2400 billion), unplanned inventory investment is zero. Planned investment, the only planned injection, equals planned saving, the only planned leakage. Thus the economy is in equilibrium.

Equilibrium: Leakages and Injections (billions of dollars per year)

Actual output (GNP)	Consumption (C)	Planned leakages: Saving (S = GNP − C)	Planned injections: Investment (I)	Unplanned inventory investment (I$_u$ = S − I)
0	200	−200	400	−600
800	800	0	400	−400
1600	1400	200	400	−200
2400	2000	400	400	0
3200	2600	600	400	200
4000	3200	800	400	400

GNP Gaps and Cyclical Unemployment

Exhibit 22.10 shows the same planned aggregate expenditures (AE = C + I) that we used in Exhibit 22.9. As noted, we can express equilibrium as planned expenditures equal actual output. Thus the equilibrium level of aggregate output is the intersection of the planned aggregate expenditures curve (AE = C + I) and the 45° line. In this case, equilibrium output is $2400 billion per year.

But what if the full-employment level of output (the level of potential output) is $3200 billion per year? The difference between the equilibrium level of output ($2400 billion) and potential output ($3200 billion) is what we called the GNP gap in Chapter 20. In this case the GNP gap is $800 billion. A positive GNP gap is called a **contractionary gap**.

Why will the economy not reach full employment? Note that at full employment, actual aggregate output ($3200 billion) is greater than planned aggregate expenditures ($3000 billion). As a result, unplanned inventory investment equals $200 billion. Businesses would try to eliminate unplanned inventory investment by reducing aggregate output. The economy will not be in equilibrium unless output falls to $2400 billion per year. A decline in output is what happens when the economy contracts, hence the term *contractionary gap*. In the Keynesian view, this decline in output also results in cyclical unemployment, as output and employment fall below their full-employment levels.

Contractionary gap. The amount by which potential GNP exceeds the equilibrium level of aggregate output.

Exhibit 22.10
A Contractionary Gap: Equilibrium at Less than Full Employment
In this graph, full employment, or potential GNP, is shown as $3200 billion. However, for current planned spending (AE = C + I), the economy reaches equilibrium at a GNP of $2400 billion, which falls below full employment. The result is a positive GNP gap of $800 billion (the difference between potential GNP and equilibrium GNP). In this simple Keynesian model, which assumes a constant general price level, the economy has no automatic way of adjusting to full employment. Therefore Keynes predicted that the economy could be stuck for an indefinite period operating below full employment.

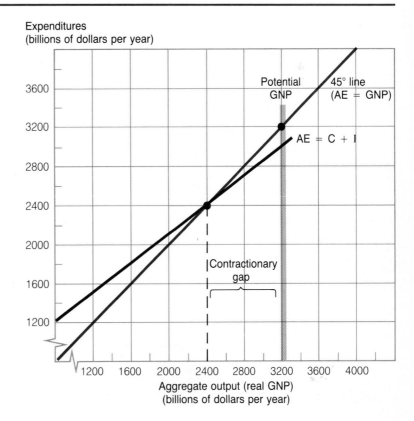

Expenditures
(billions of dollars per year)

Aggregate output (real GNP)
(billions of dollars per year)

Equilibrium Adjustments: Keynes and the Classical Economists

The classical economists agreed with Keynes that the economy might contract as a result of a decline in aggregate demand. But they disagreed with Keynes's analysis of how the economy would react. And they strongly disagreed with Keynes about whether government action was necessary or desirable.

What causes a contractionary gap at a particular price level? Keynes viewed inadequate aggregate demand as the cause of such gaps. He argued that equilibrium falls below the full-employment level because planned spending by households and businesses is too low. If planned aggregate expenditures were greater, the economy would achieve full employment. To close the gap and achieve full employment, aggregate demand must be increased.

Note that this conclusion rests on two assumptions of the simple Keynesian model: (1) wages and prices will not fall; and (2) saving depends on the level of income and not on interest rates. With these assumptions, there is only one way for the economy to achieve equilibrium: Businesses must adjust output to match the level of planned spending. But there is no guarantee that the economy will achieve full employment. The mechanisms that produce full employment in the classical view—flexible interest rates, wages, and prices—are assumed not to operate.

Actually, Keynes (and current Keynesians) recognized that wages and prices are likely to adjust. But he also believed that these adjustments may be slow and uncertain. In Keynes's view, there was no reason for the economy to endure a lengthy recession. His solution? Add government spending to private-sector spending to increase aggregate demand.

The classical economists (and their modern counterparts) did not accept Keynes's conclusion or his solution. Instead of inadequate demand, they suggested that a contractionary gap is a temporary situation in which the existing price level is too high. If wages and prices are flexible, as classical theory assumes, the contractionary gap will close automatically as the general price level falls. Government action is unnecessary because the economy is self-correcting.

The models of Keynes and the classical economists begin with different assumptions and lead to different conclusions. Because Keynes assumed wages and prices were inflexible, he concluded that the economy may require an occasional prod from the government to attain full-employment equilibrium. The classical economists assumed flexible wages and prices and concluded that the economy is self-correcting.

Which of these analyses best represents the economy? That question is still being debated by economists. In fact, modern variations of both the Keynesian and classical arguments are not quite as simple as we have indicated here. We can, however, trace the assumptions and analysis of modern economists to those roots. We continue the comparison of the classical and the Keynesian views as we build our economic model in the following chapters.

CONCLUSION

In this chapter, you saw how the economy achieves equilibrium in the models of both Keynes and the classical economists. In the Keynesian analysis, a change in one of the factors that determine planned consumption and planned investment will cause a change in planned aggregate expenditures. But *how much* will a change in planned aggregate expenditures change the equilibrium level of aggregate output? As you will see in Chapter 23, an initial change in autonomous spending causes aggregate output to expand by more than just the initial change in spending.

We also introduced you to an important, but highly controversial macroeconomic question: Does the economy have quick and automatic adjustment mechanisms that will help to achieve full employment? The answer to this question is very important for determining the desirability of various macroeconomic policies. Although neither Keynes or his contemporaries are alive today, the debate they engaged in is very much alive. Modern economists who believe, as Keynes did, that the adjustment mechanism is slow and uncertain, continue to argue for government action to stabilize the economy. Economists who believe that automatic adjustment mechanisms are strong and quick side with the classical economists and argue that government should play a passive role in the macroeconomy.

SUMMARY

1. In this chapter we discussed some of the differences between the models of Keynes and the classical economists. We discussed the factors that determine consumption and investment and showed how a private-sector economy reaches macroeconomic equilibrium in the simple Keynesian model.

2. Classical economists viewed interest rates, wages, and prices as flexible. They expected interest rates to adjust automatically to equate saving and investment at any level of output and real wages to adjust automatically to create full employment. In the classical model, output is determined strictly by the factors that determine the economy's potential output. The classical aggregate supply curve is a vertical line at potential GNP.

3. Keynes disputed the classical assumptions. He believed that saving was largely determined by current income and investment by expected future demand. He saw no reason to believe that the two would necessarily coincide at potential GNP. He also believed that during a depression, wages and prices might not fall, which could lead to equilibrium at less than full employment. In the simple Keynesian model, aggregate supply is a horizontal line below full employment, but a vertical line at potential GNP.

4. The most important determinant of consumption spending is disposable income. Consumption tends to increase as income rises but at a slower rate. Saving is the difference between income and consumption. The marginal propensity to consume (MPC) indicates what proportion of any change in disposable income will be spent. The marginal propensity to save (MPS) indicates what proportion will be saved.

5. When the consumption–income relationship is shown on a graph, an additional line—the 45° line—is added to show points at which expenditures equal income. The difference between the 45° line and the consumption line measures the amount of saving (or dissaving if income is less than consumption) at any level of income.

6. Based on historical data, the marginal propensity to consume for the U.S. economy appears to be 0.91 on the average. However, historically there has been no tendency for dissaving to occur at low levels of income. Households will change consumption more if a change in disposable income is considered to be permanent or long run. Consumption will change less if the change in disposable income is considered to be short run or temporary.

7. Consumption also responds to wealth, the general price level, expectations, interest rates, and the availability of credit.

8. Economists distinguish between induced and autonomous changes in consumption. Induced changes result from a change in the level of disposable income and cause a movement along a consumption line. Autonomous changes result from a change in a factor other than disposable income and cause a shift in the consumption line. An increase in autonomous consumption means higher consumption at every level of income.

9. Investment spending by the business sector is influenced by expectations, interest rates, current capacity and future demand, the rate of technological change, and government tax policies. Historically, changes in

investment spending have been more volatile than changes in real GNP.

10. Accounting identities are always true. Equilibrium conditions are true only when equilibrium exists. By the first accounting identity, aggregate output is always identical to actual aggregate expenditures because unplanned inventory investment is considered to be an actual expenditure. Aggregate output is equal to planned aggregate expenditures (equilibrium condition), only if unplanned inventory investment is zero. If unplanned inventory investment is not zero, an adjustment can be expected in output to return the economy to equilibrium.

11. In the simple Keynesian model, the equilibrium output may not be the full-employment, or potential, output. A contractionary gap exists if potential GNP is greater than the equilibrium output. In the classical model, a contractionary gap will cause wages and prices to fall. This automatic adjustment returns the economy to full-employment equilibrium. In the simple Keynesian model, wages and prices will not fall (or at least not quickly). Government spending may be desirable to return the economy quickly to full employment.

KEY TERMS

Classical economic theory, 560
Say's law, 561
Keynesian theory, 564
Consumption schedule, 566
Marginal propensity to consume (MPC), 566
Average propensity to consume (APC), 567
Saving schedule, 568
Marginal propensity to save (MPS), 568
Monetary assets, 571
Induced consumption, 573
Autonomous consumption, 573
Nominal interest rate, 578
Real interest rate, 578
Contractionary gap, 583

QUESTIONS FOR REVIEW AND DISCUSSION

1. Why was consumption in 1932–1934 (during the Great Depression) higher than the long-run relationship would predict? Why was consumption much lower between 1942 and 1945 (during World War II) and somewhat higher between 1946 and 1947 than the long-run relationship would predict?

2. The average propensity to consume (APC) tends to change along the short-run consumption line. Would you expect it to rise or fall during a recession? Why?

3. Answer the following questions for an economy for which the marginal propensity to consume has a value of 0.80.
   a) What does a marginal propensity to consume of 0.80 mean?
   b) What change would you expect in consumption if disposable personal income increased by $400 billion? What change in saving?
   c) What change in saving would you expect if disposable personal income decreases by $300 billion? What change in consumption?

4. Consider the data for the hypothetical economy shown in the following table. (In answering the questions that follow, use the assumptions of the simple Keynesian model as in the chapter.)

Aggregate output (GNP)	Consumption (C) (billions per year)
400	$ 520
800	840
1200	1160
1600	1480
2000	1800
2400	2120

   a) If planned investment is $120 billion, what will the equilibrium level of output be? What will the level of saving be when aggregate output is $800 billion? When aggregate output is $1600 billion?
   b) What will unplanned inventory investment be when aggregate output is $1200 billion? When aggregate output is $1600 billion?
   c) What will the average propensity to consume be when aggregate output is $2000 billion? When aggregate output is $800 billion? What does it mean if the average propensity to consume exceeds 1.0?
   d) What is the marginal propensity to consume in this economy? (*Hint:* Use the formula for the marginal propensity to consume, choose any two levels of output, and remember that aggregate output equals income in this simplified economy.) What is the marginal propensity to save? Below what level of income does dissaving occur?
   e) If potential GNP is $2000 billion, what is the size of the contractionary gap?
   f) For equilibrium level of output to be $2000 billion, what change in autonomous consumption or planned investment is necessary?

5. Use the graph below to answer the questions in (a)–(c).

Expenditures
(billions of dollars per year)

Aggregate output (real GNP)
(billions of dollars per year)

a) What is the equilibrium level of output?
b) What is the level of unplanned inventory investment (or disinvestment) when aggregate output (real GNP) is $1850 billion? What automatic adjustment would you expect to happen in this simple Keynesian model to bring the economy to equilibrium?
c) If potential GNP (full-employment output) is $2000 billion, what is the size of the contractionary gap? What is the level of unplanned inventory investment (or disinvestment) at full-employment output? What

automatic adjustment would you expect in this Keynesian model if the economy were currently producing this full-employment output?

6. Investment spending tends to increase as interest rates fall. In the 1930s—during the Great Depression—however, investment spending and interest rates fell at the same time. What factors explain the fall in investment? Does this situation mean that investment does not respond to interest rates?

7. Explain why each of the following statements is false.
   a) An increase in the general price level tends to raise the real wealth of households and thus increases consumption.
   b) If planned aggregate expenditures exceed actual aggregate output, the current level of aggregate output is above the equilibrium level.
   c) If actual aggregate expenditures are greater than planned aggregate expenditures, there is currently unplanned inventory disinvestment.
   d) If planned investment is greater than planned saving, the current level of aggregate output is below the equilibrium level.

8. Use the information presented in the appendix to this chapter and the consumption relationship for a hypothetical economy expressed below to answer questions (a)–(d).

$$C = \$320 \text{ billion} + 0.60GNP$$

   a) If planned investment is $400 billion, what is the equilibrium level of GNP?
   b) If equilibrium GNP is $1200 billion, what is the level of investment?
   c) What is the equation for saving?
   d) Using the equilibrium condition that planned leakages must equal planned injections, calculate the equilibrium value if planned investment is $240 billion.

Appendix to Chapter 22

Algebra of Keynesian Equilibrium

In this chapter, you learned to determine macroeconomic equilibrium in the simple Keynesian model and to locate the equilibrium level of aggregate output both in a table and on a graph. In this appendix we examine the same concepts using algebraic representations of consumption, investment, and saving. As in the chapter, we assume a private-sector economy with a constant price level.

EXPRESSION FOR CONSUMPTION

Holding all other factors constant, we express consumption in terms of GNP. We can express algebraically the same consumption relationship we used in Exhibit 22.9(a) and (b) as

$$C = 200 + 0.75 \text{ GNP}$$

where C is consumption expenditures and GNP is aggregate output (in billions of dollars per year). The 0.75 in the expression is the value of the marginal propensity to consume. To check your understanding, verify that this expression is the same as the one used in the chapter. Plug in several values for aggregate output (GNP) and compare the values you obtain for consumption expenditures (C) with the data in Exhibit 22.9.

EXPRESSION FOR PLANNED AGGREGATE EXPENDITURES

As we did in the chapter, we assume that planned investment is completely autonomous (that is, unrelated to aggregate output) and has a given value of 400. Since consumption and investment are the only expenditures in this simple economy, we can write the expression for planned expenditures as

$$
\begin{aligned}
\text{Aggregate expenditures} &= \text{Consumption} + \text{Planned investment} \\
\text{AE} &= C + I \\
&= 200 + 0.75\text{GNP} + 400 \\
&= 600 + 0.75\text{GNP}
\end{aligned}
$$

EQUILIBRIUM: PLANNED EXPENDITURES EQUAL AGGREGATE OUTPUT

As noted in the chapter, we can express equilibrium in one of several ways. First, recognizing that there can be no unplanned expenditures when equilibrium is reached, we equate planned aggregate expenditures (AE) with aggregate output (GNP). Thus we can determine equilibrium as follows:

$$\text{Aggregate output} = \text{Planned aggregate expenditures} \quad \text{or} \quad \text{GNP} = C + I$$
$$\text{GNP} = 600 + 0.75\,\text{GNP}$$
$$(1 - 0.75)\,\text{GNP} = 600$$
$$0.25\,\text{GNP} = 600$$
$$\text{GNP} = 2400$$

In this case, the equilibrium level of aggregate output—the level at which planned expenditures equal aggregate output—is 2400.

EQUILIBRIUM: PLANNED LEAKAGES EQUAL PLANNED INJECTIONS*

We can also express the equilibrium condition in terms of leakages and injections. In this simple model, saving is the only leakage and investment the only injection. We already have the value of 400 for investment. We must now derive an expression for saving.

First, we recognize that our simplifying assumptions make GNP identical to national income and national income identical to disposable income (GNP = NI = DI). (We continue to ignore depreciation, and with no government there are no taxes and transfers.) Second, we know that households will either spend (C) or save (S). Thus we can conclude that GNP is equal to the sum of consumption expenditures (C) and saving (S). That is,

$$\text{GNP} = C + S$$
$$= (200 + 0.75\,\text{GNP}) + S$$

Solving for S, we have

$$S = 0.25\,\text{GNP} - 200$$

Note that the value 0.25 in the expression for saving represents the marginal propensity to save, or the same value we obtained in the chapter. To check your understanding, plug a few values for aggregate output into the expression and compare the values you calculate with those in Exhibit 22.9.

We now have expressions for planned leakages since saving is the only actual or planned leakage in this case. There are two possible actual injections: planned investment (I) and unplanned inventory investment (I_u). We noted in Chapter 21 that there is a third accounting identity: Actual leakages equal actual injections.

---

* Before reading this section, be sure to read A Case in Point: Equilibrium—Planned Leakages and Injections, which appears on p. 585.

Thus it is always true that

Accounting identity

Actual leakages = Actual injections

Saving = Planned investment + Unplanned inventory investment

$$S = I + I_u$$

But in equilibrium, unplanned inventory investment is zero, and planned leakages equal planned injections. Using this condition and the expressions for saving and investment,

Planned leakages = Planned injections

$$S = I$$

$$0.25\,\text{GNP} - 200 = 400$$

$$0.25\,\text{GNP} = 600$$

$$\text{GNP} = 2400$$

This is the same equilibrium level of aggregate output we obtained previously, supporting the notion that equilibrium can be expressed in two ways.

CONCLUSION

In this appendix we demonstrated algebraically equilibrium in a simple Keynesian model for a private-sector economy. We obtained equilibrium values by using two different forms of the equilibrium condition: Planned expenditures equal aggregate output, and planned leakages equal planned injections.

We can demonstrate algebraically that the two equilibrium conditions are really the same by recognizing the following identity:

$$\text{GNP} = C + S \quad \text{or} \quad C = \text{GNP} - S$$

If we substitute the expression for C into the first equilibrium condition, we get the second equilibrium condition:

Aggregate output = Planned expenditures

$$\text{GNP} = C + I$$

$$\text{GNP} = \text{GNP} - S + I$$

or

$$S = I$$

Planned leakages = Planned injections

Changes in Spending and the Multiplier Effect

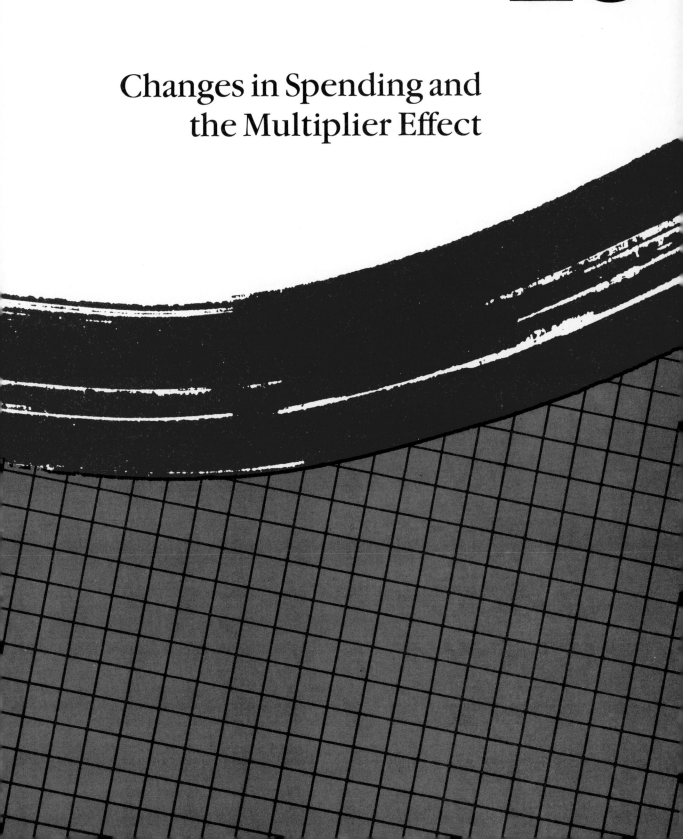

QUESTIONS TO CONSIDER

☐ What is the multiplier and what does it predict about an initial change in spending?

☐ Why did Keynes conclude that the absolute level of saving cannot be increased?

☐ How do government fiscal policies affect the equilibrium level of output in an economy?

☐ What does the multiplier predict about government attempts to close a contractionary gap with discretionary fiscal policies?

☐ How do imports and exports affect the equilibrium level of output in an economy?

R ecall that in Chapter 22 we discussed how the economy adjusts to equilibrium in the simple Keynesian model. We observed that a change in a factor such as wealth, expectations, or interest rates would change planned aggregate expenditures and thus equilibrium output (GNP). In this chapter you will see *how much* equilibrium output will change. We can expect equilibrium output to increase by more than the initial change in spending. Using this principle, we can answer the following questions: Why did a $116 billion decrease in investment between 1929 and 1933 result in a $211 billion decrease in GNP? Why did President Kennedy's advisors recommend a $15 billion tax cut to increase GNP by $30 billion?

MULTIPLIER EFFECT

For the time being, we continue to examine an economy having only household and business sectors. In addition, we continue to follow the simple Keynesian model and assume that the general price level is constant.

Multiplier Effect of a Change in Investment

Before examining the effect of a change in aggregate expenditures on the total economy, let's consider the effect that a single firm has on the economy when it changes its spending plans. Suppose Dynamic Enterprises expects the economy to grow rapidly. As a result, the firm decides to invest in a new plant—at a cost of $1 million. The $1 million that Dynamic pays to have the plant built will, from the macroeconomic perspective, raise GNP *initially* by $1 million. In addition the accounting identity between GNP and national income indicates that the $1 million expenditure causes income to increase by $1 million *to begin with*. That is, the expenditure becomes income for the owners and workers of the construction company and the owners and workers of firms supplying building materials.

Multiplier. The amount that equilibrium GNP will change as a result of a change in autonomous expenditures. Measured as the ratio of the change in equilibrium GNP to the change in autonomous expenditures. The simple multiplier effect, assuming a constant price level, can also be calculated as $1 \div (1 - MPC)$.

Thus far we have gone around the circular flow once—from an increase in spending to an increase in national income. But the flow continues because we can expect the individuals who received the $1 million to spend part of their new income. If the marginal propensity to consume is 0.75, each dollar of extra income results in an additional $0.75 worth of consumption. The $1 million initial increase in income causes consumption to rise by $750,000 (0.75 × $1 million). At this point the initial $1 million increase in investment has induced additional consumption of $750,000, making a total increase in aggregate expenditures and GNP of $1.75 million.

As Exhibit 23.1 illustrates, the process does not stop there. The $750,000 increase in consumption raises GNP and national income by $750,000. This increase in income, in turn, induces additional consumption of $562,500 (0.75 × $750,000) in the third round, which induces an additional $421,875 (0.75 × $562,500) of consumption in the fourth round, and so on. Although the process has no end, the effects eventually become quite small. In Exhibit 23.1, for example, you can see that the increase in consumption in the twenty-fifth round is only $1003.

Exhibit 23.1 shows that the process ultimately means a $4 million increase in aggregate expenditures, GNP, and national income. In other words, the increase in GNP was four times as large as the initial increase in investment expenditures by Dynamic. The total change in aggregate expenditures represents the sum of the initial (autonomous) increase in investment ($1,000,000) and the subsequent (induced) increase in consumption ($3,000,000).

The principle that an initial increase in autonomous spending results in an even greater change in equilibrium output, is called the *multiplier effect*. The **multiplier** is the ratio of the change in equilibrium GNP to the change in autonomous spending. Thus it indicates how much equilibrium GNP changes because of a change in autonomous spending. Any change in autonomous spending—whether consumption, investment, government purchases, or net exports—can have a multiplier effect.

Now that you have some understanding of why a multiplier effect occurs, let's consider *how strong* the effect is by measuring a multiplier for a change in

Exhibit 23.1
The Multiplier Effect of a Change in Autonomous Spending

Round	Initial increase in investment	Additional induced consumption	Increase in income this round	Cumulative increase in aggregate expenditures and GNP
1	$1,000,000	$ 0	$1,000,000	$1,000,000
2	0	750,000	750,000	1,750,000
3	0	562,500	562,500	2,312,500
4	0	421,875	421,875	2,734,375
.	.	.	.	.
.	.	.	.	.
25	0	1,003	1,003	3,997,742
.	.	.	.	.
Total	$1,000,000	$3,000,000	$4,000,000	$4,000,000

Exhibit 23.2
Multiplier Effect of a Change in Planned Investment
Initially, the economy's equilibrium GNP is $1600 billion. Part (a) shows that a $200 billion increase in investment raises aggregate expenditures by $200 billion at each level of output. In part (b) the aggregate expenditures curve shifts upward by $200 billion from AE_1 to AE_2. As a result, equilibrium GNP increases to $2400 billion. Thus the $200 billion increase in planned investment causes an $800 billion increase in equilibrium GNP, indicating a multiplier of 4.0. That is, equilibrium GNP increases by $4 for each $1 increase in autonomous spending.

(a) Output and expenditures data
(billions of dollars per year)

| Aggregate output (GNP) | Planned expenditures | | | Unplanned inventory investment (I_u) |
	Consumption (C)	Planned investment (I)	Aggregate expenditures (AE = C + I)	
Original investment (I = $200); Equilibrium GNP = $1600				
0	200	200	400	−400
800	800	200	1000	−200
1600	1400	200	1600	0
2400	2000	200	2200	200
3200	2600	200	2800	400
New investment (I = $400); Equilibrium GNP = $2400				
0	200	400	600	−600
800	800	400	1200	−400
1600	1400	400	1800	−200
2400	2000	400	2400	0
3200	2600	400	3000	200

(b) Output–expenditures graph

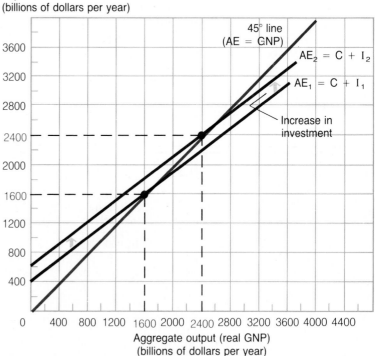

Expenditures
(billions of dollars per year)

autonomous spending. We begin with an economy in equilibrium. Exhibit 23.2 shows that, initially, equilibrium GNP is $1600 billion—where the aggregate expenditures line intersects the 45° line on the graph, and where unplanned inventory investment is 0 in the table.

Suppose that businesses expect demand to increase, and as a result, they want to invest in new machinery. Exhibit 23.2(a) shows that if investment spending increases by $200 billion, aggregate expenditures will also increase by $200 billion at each level of output. In Exhibit 23.2(b), the planned expenditures line shifts upward by $200 billion (from AE_1 to AE_2). The increase in autonomous expenditures raises equilibrium GNP to $2400 (where the AE and 45° lines intersect). In other words, businesses decided to spend an additional $200 billion, but this increase ultimately resulted in an increase of $800 billion in output and spending. Thus the multiplier has a value of 4.0, calculated as

$$\text{Multiplier} = \frac{\text{Change in equilibrium GNP}}{\text{Change in autonomous expenditures}}$$

$$= \frac{\$800 \text{ billion}}{\$200 \text{ billion}} \quad \text{or} \quad 4.0$$

The value of the multiplier measures the additional aggregate output resulting from each dollar of initial spending. In this case, the value of 4.0 indicates that for each $1 increase in planned investment, aggregate output will increase by $4. Check your understanding by returning to Exhibit 23.2 and raising investment spending by $400 billion instead of $200 billion per year. (You should find that equilibrium GNP will increase to $3200 billion, an increase of $1600 billion, or four times the increase in autonomous expenditures.)

This example shows that when businesses spent only an additional $200 billion, total output and spending increased by $800 billion. The important question is: Where did the other $600 billion come from and what determines the size of the multiplier effect?

Marginal propensity to consume and the multiplier.   The multiplier effect depends on how much new spending is generated in each round. As the example of Dynamic Enterprises indicated, this depends on the marginal propensity to consume. If the marginal propensity to consume in that example had been 0.80 instead of 0.75, $800,000 of consumption would have been induced in the second round instead of $750,000. Each round would have increased consumption even more than it did. Ultimately, aggregate expenditures and GNP would have increased by five times.

We can express the relationship between the autonomous expenditures multiplier and the marginal propensity to consume (MPC) mathematically. For example, when the marginal propensity to consume is 0.75, the multiplier is 4, which we calculate as follows:

$$\text{Multiplier} = \frac{1}{1 - \text{Marginal propensity to consume}} \quad \text{or} \quad \frac{1}{1 - \text{MPC}}$$

$$= \frac{1}{(1 - 0.75)}$$

$$= \frac{1}{0.25} \quad \text{or} \quad 4.0$$

The appendix to this chapter explains how we arrived at this formula. From the formula we can see an important economic principle: *The larger the value of the marginal propensity to consume, the larger is the value of the multiplier*. This relationship is logical because a greater proportion of each dollar of income is spent in each round and thus in total. To check your understanding of this point, calculate the value of the multiplier when the marginal propensity to consume is 0.80. (Your answer should be 5.0.)

The multiplier is important because we can use it to predict the change in output caused by a change in autonomous expenditures. If the multiplier has a value of 4.0, we can predict that a $100 increase in autonomous expenditures will result in a $400 billion increase in equilibrium GNP. We can express this relationship as

$$\text{Change in equilibrium GNP} = \text{Change in autonomous expenditures} \times \text{Multiplier}$$

$$= \$100 \text{ billion} \times 4.0 \quad \text{or} \quad \$400 \text{ billion}$$

The multiplier effect also works in reverse. That is, a $100 *decrease* in autonomous expenditures will cause a $400 *decrease* in equilibrium GNP when the multiplier has a value of 4.0. See A Case in Point: Keynesian Analysis of the Great Depression for an example of the multiplier effect in reverse.

Saving and the Paradox of Thrift

We have seen how a change in autonomous investment has a multiplier effect. The same is true for a change in autonomous consumption or saving, a fact that is helpful in answering the following question: Individuals may increase their personal wealth by saving more, but can an economy also increase its wealth through saving? If the household sector overall attempts to save more, will the level of saving actually rise?

The obvious answer, *yes*, is the answer that economists typically gave prior to the 1930s. The classical economists emphasized that an economy grows when it produces more capital resources. If the economy is operating at full employment, more capital resources can be produced only by sacrificing current consumption. In other words, the economy must save in order to grow. In fact, classical economists believed that if most households saved more (that is, more at each level of income) the economy would grow faster.

Recall, however, that the classical economists assumed that saving and investment are directly linked through financial markets: More saving reduces interest rates and causes investment to rise. In the classical model total output does not change; only the mix changes—more capital resources and fewer consumer goods and services. By producing fewer video cassette recorders and clothes and more machines and factories, the economy's future production possibilities increase.

In contrast, Keynes suggested that the classical model reflected the *fallacy of composition*: What is true for an individual is not necessarily true for the whole economy (see Chapter 1). Let's consider Exhibit 23.3, for example. Under the original conditions (AE₁), equilibrium GNP is $2400 billion. At that level of output, the actual level of saving is $200 billion per year.

Now suppose that households decide to save $200 billion more at the current level of output. This change shifts the planned expenditures line down by $200 billion (to AE₂). At each level of output, saving is $200 billion more and con-

A Case in Point
Keynesian Analysis of the Great Depression

Together, the simple Keynesian model and the multiplier provide an easily understood (but incomplete) description of what actually happened to the U.S. economy during the early years of the Great Depression. In order to use the multiplier we have to know its value. As we have stated, the multiplier depends on the marginal propensity to consume. Between 1929 and 1933, real GNP decreased by $211.1 billion—from $709.6 billion to $498.5 billion. During the same period, consumption declined by $92.7 billion—from $471.4 to $378.7 billion. Using the formulas for MPC and the relationship between MPC and the multiplier, we can estimate the multiplier for the years 1929–1933 at 1.8, calculated as

$$\frac{\text{Marginal propensity}}{\text{to consume}} = \frac{\text{Change in consumption}}{\text{Change in GNP}}$$

$$= \frac{471.4 - 378.7}{709.6 - 498.5}$$

$$= \frac{92.7}{211.1} \quad \text{or} \quad 0.44$$

and

$$\text{Multiplier} = \frac{1}{1 - \text{MPC}}$$

$$= \frac{1}{1 - 0.44}$$

$$= \frac{1}{0.56} \quad \text{or} \quad 1.78$$

The multiplier helps us connect two important facts about the Great Depression: (1) real GNP fell by $211 billion; and (2) real investment fell by $116 billion. (Other components of aggregate expenditures were fairly stable, falling less than $2 billion.) The multiplier effect suggests that a $118 billion change in autonomous expenditures would result in a $212 billion ($118 × 1.8) change in real GNP, which is almost identical to the change that actually occurred.

While this example shows the usefulness of the multiplier, it does not fully explain the Great Depression. Why did investment decrease by $116 billion? Did other important changes occur? Why did the economy not adjust as classical theory predicts? We consider the answers to these questions as we develop a more complete model of the macroeconomy. Economists have had much to say about the causes of the Great Depression and disagree sharply on the best explanation for it. While the simple Keynesian approach is incomplete, it did seem to explain the Great Depression better than the classical approach. As a result, Keynesian economics became, for a time, the mainstream of U.S. economic thought.

sumption is $200 billion less. The new equilibrium GNP is $1600 billion. But what happened to the absolute level of saving? In this example, the level of saving remained the same. But why? If income had been unchanged, there would have been $200 billion more in saving. Because higher saving means lower consumption, however, equilibrium output and income decreased. As a consequence, the absolute amount saved by the household sector was unchanged.

This conclusion depends on the assumption that investment remains constant as saving increases. In fact, Keynes argued that the drop in consumption might make businesses pessimistic about future demand for their products. If this occurs, investment may actually fall, leading to even lower output and a decrease in the level of saving. In the simple Keynesian model, the household sector cannot increase the absolute amount of saving because any attempt to do so reduces equilibrium output. This result is known as the *paradox of thrift.*

Who is right? Modern economists agree and disagree with both theories. Most economists now agree with the classical economists that higher saving leads to

Exhibit 23.3
Paradox of Thrift
Initially, equilibrium GNP is $2400 billion and saving is $200 billion. If households increase saving by $200 billion at each level of GNP, the Keynesian model predicts that equilibrium GNP will fall (to $1600 billion in this case). Thus the actual level of saving is unchanged, a result known as the paradox of thrift. This result depends on the assumption that investment will be unchanged.

(a) Output and expenditures data
(billions of dollars per year)

Aggregate output (GNP)	Planned expenditures				Unplanned inventory investment (I_u)
	Consumption (C)	Saving (S = GNP − C)	Planned investment (I)	Aggregate expenditures (AE = C + I)	
Original consumption and saving; Equilibrium GNP = $2400					
0	400	−400	200	600	−600
800	1000	−200	200	1200	−400
1600	1600	0	200	1800	−200
2400	2200	200	200	2400	0
3200	2800	400	200	3000	200
New consumption and saving; Equilibrium GNP = $1600					
0	200	−200	200	400	−400
800	800	0	200	1000	−200
1600	1400	200	200	1600	0
2400	2000	400	200	2200	200
3200	2600	600	200	2800	400

(b) Output–expenditures graph

Expenditures
(billions of dollars per year)

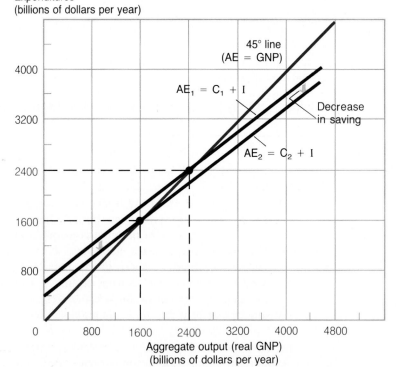

Aggregate output (real GNP)
(billions of dollars per year)

greater investment and economic growth in the long run. But some economists believe that the link between saving and investment is imperfect. They argue that these imperfections may cause the short-run response of investment to be slow or limited. As a consequence, the immediate effect of higher saving may be a decrease in planned spending and a drop in output.

The key point is that to be effective, any increase in saving must be channelled into investment. This channelling is easily done in a planned economy like the Soviet Union, where government officials control both the level of investment and the level of saving. It is more uncertain in a market economy, where the individuals who save and those who invest are not the same.

GOVERNMENT FISCAL POLICIES AND EQUILIBRIUM

Until now we have explored macroeconomic theory by focusing only on the private sector. Although we are not yet ready to tackle all the important questions about government's impact on the economy, we can take a first look. In this section we again utilize the simple Keynesian model. And again we assume that the general price level is constant and that investment is determined independently from saving.

Government and the Circular Flow

To begin, let's reexamine the circular-flow diagram from Chapter 20, as shown in Exhibit 23.4. Adding government to the circular flow changes three elements in the analysis. First, disposable income (DI)—the income received by the household sector—no longer equals aggregate output and national income. Recall that the government takes part of national income in the form of net taxes (T), or the difference between taxes and transfer payments. Second, government purchases of final goods and services are a part of planned aggregate expenditures (AE = C + I + G). Finally, government demands funds in the financial market when it has a budget deficit and supplies funds when it has a budget surplus.

Government Purchases and Equilibrium Output

Most economists agree that government can affect the overall economy by changing the size of elements in its budget. To illustrate how, let's look at the elements one at a time, beginning with government purchases (G). As the circular-flow diagram indicates, government purchases represent demand by the public sector for final goods and services. Exhibit 23.5(a) shows that the addition of government purchases to private sector expenditures means that AE = C + I + G. Equilibrium GNP initially is $1600 billion, where the aggregate expenditures line intersects the 45° line.

Multiplier effect of a change in government purchases. An increase in government purchases (with all other factors unchanged) will increase planned aggregate expenditures—and thus equilibrium GNP. Like a change in investment,

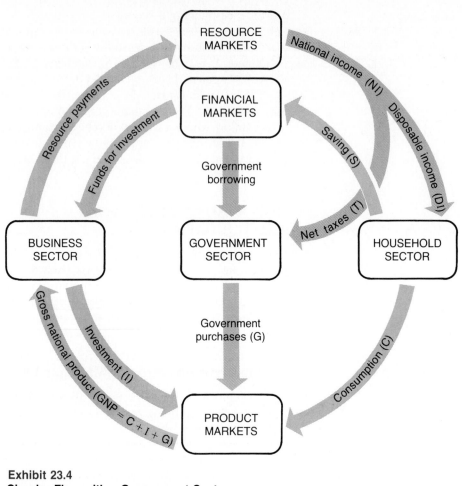

Exhibit 23.4
Circular Flow with a Government Sector

a change in government purchases will have a multiplier effect. Exhibit 23.5(b) shows that increasing government purchases by $400 billion—from $200 billion to $600 billion—shifts aggregate expenditures from AE_1 to AE_2. That is, aggregate expenditures increase by $400 billion at each level of aggregate output. The new equilibrium GNP is $3200 billion, or $1600 billion more than it was initially.

We can use the multiplier to predict this change in GNP. As shown earlier, when MPC is 0.75 the multiplier is 4.0. In this case the only change we made was to add government purchases, so the change in aggregate output will be $1600 billion, which we calculate as

Change in equilibrium GNP = Change in autonomous expenditures × Multiplier

$$= \text{Change in G} \times \text{Multiplier}$$

$$= (\$600 \text{ billion} - \$200 \text{ billion}) \times 4.0$$

$$= \$400 \text{ billion} \times 4.0 \quad \text{or} \quad \$1600 \text{ billion}$$

Exhibit 23.5
Multiplier Effect of a Change in Government Purchases
A $400 billion increase in government purchases will increase planned aggregate expenditures by $400 billion at each level of output. In part (b) this change shifts the aggregate expenditures line upward (from AE_1 to AE_2). The $400 billion increase in government purchases causes a $1600 billion increase in equilibrium GNP, indicating a multiplier of 4.0.

(a) Output and expenditures data
  (billions of dollars per year)

| | Planned expenditures | | | |
Aggregate output (GNP)	*Consumption (C)*	*Planned investment (I)*	*Government purchases (G)*	*Aggregate expenditures (AE = C + I + G)*
Original government purchases (G = $200); Equilibrium GNP = $1600				
0	50	150	200	400
800	650	150	200	1000
1600	1250	150	200	1600
2400	1850	150	200	2200
3200	2450	150	200	2800
New government purchases (G = $600); Equilibrium GNP = $3200				
0	50	150	600	800
800	650	150	600	1400
1600	1250	150	600	2000
2400	1850	150	600	2600
3200	2450	150	600	3200

(b) Output–expenditures graph

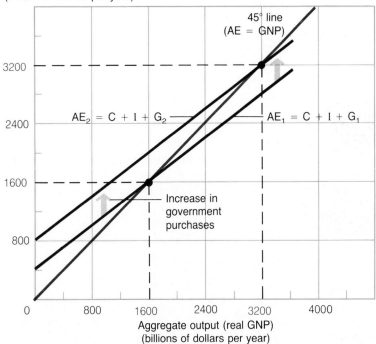

Expenditures
(billions of dollars per year)

Taxes, Consumption, and Aggregate Expenditures

Let's also consider the effects of a change in net taxes.[*] The basic effect of higher taxes is straightforward: They lower disposable income received by the household sector and thus consumption at each level of output. When taxes are zero, as shown in the top part of Exhibit 23.6(a), aggregate output, national income, and disposable income are identical. When taxes are imposed, as in the bottom part of Exhibit 23.6(a), we must recognize that a part of national income flows to the government sector as taxes. Thus we subtract taxes from output to get disposable income. If taxes are $400 billion, disposable income is $400 billion less than GNP at each level. In Exhibit 23.6(b) the taxes cause a downward shift in the aggregate expenditures line from AE_2 to AE_1.

Note that consumption is lower at each level of aggregate output because taxes reduce disposable income. The relationship between consumption and disposable income is the same in both the top and bottom parts of Exhibit 23.6(a). In both cases consumption is $1550 billion when disposable income is $1600 billion and $1850 billion when disposable income is $2000 billion. But consumption at each level of aggregate output falls when taxes are imposed because disposable income is lower. For example, at $2000 billion of output, disposable income is $1550 billion with taxes but is $1850 billion without taxes.

This example shows the effect of a **lump-sum tax**. Unlike a sales or income tax, the amount of lump-sum taxes paid is not affected by the level of aggregate output or income. The property tax, a major source of state and local government revenues, is an example of a lump-sum tax.

Multiplier effect of a change in taxes. Exhibit 23.6 also shows that a change in lump-sum taxes, like changes in spending, has a multiplier effect. To calculate the effect, we first determine the change in autonomous expenditures, that is, the change in planned spending at each level of output when taxes change. Second, we multiply this change by the multiplier to obtain the change in equilibrium GNP.

In the example shown in Exhibit 23.6, a $400 billion increase in lump-sum taxes produces a $300 billion change in consumption at each level of GNP. Why does a $400 billion increase in taxes cause only a $300 billion decrease in consumption? Because a change in taxes does not affect aggregate expenditures directly (as a change in investment or government purchases does). Rather, by changing disposable income at each level of output, it reduces consumption. But with a marginal propensity to consume of 0.75, each $100 of lump-sum taxes causes only a $75 decline in consumption. Thus the multiplier effect of a change in taxes is less than that of a change in investment or government purchases.

With a multiplier of 4.0, we can predict that a $300 billion drop in autonomous expenditures will result in a $1200 billion drop in equilibrium GNP. That is,

$$
\begin{aligned}
\text{Change in equilibrium GNP} &= \text{Change in autonomous expenditures} \times \text{Multiplier} \\
&= (\text{Change in taxes} \times \text{MPC}) \times \text{Multiplier} \\
&= (\text{Change in disposable income} \times \text{MPC}) \times \text{Multiplier} \\
&= -\$400 \text{ billion} \times 0.75 \times 4.0 \\
&= -\$300 \text{ billion} \times 4.0 \quad \text{or} \quad -\$1200 \text{ billion}
\end{aligned}
$$

Lump-sum tax. A tax, such as the property tax, that is unaffected by the level of aggregate output.

[*]Note that an increase in net taxes can represent either higher taxes or lower transfer payments. We make no distinction between them in this analysis because the effects are the same.

(a) Output and expenditures data
  (billions of dollars per year)

Aggregate output (GNP)	Net taxes (T)	Disposable income (DI = GNP − T)	Consumption (C)	Investment (I)	Government purchases (G)	Aggregate expenditures (AE = C + I + G)
Original equilibrium (No lump-sum taxes); Equilibrium GNP = $3200						
1600	0	1600	1550	50	400	2000
2000	0	2000	1850	50	400	2300
2400	0	2400	2150	50	400	2600
2800	0	2800	2450	50	400	2900
3200	0	3200	2750	50	400	3200
3600	0	3600	3050	50	400	3500
New equilibrium (Lump-sum taxes = $400); Equilibrium GNP = $2000						
1600	400	1200	1250	50	400	1700
2000	400	1600	1550	50	400	2000
2400	400	2000	1850	50	400	2300
2800	400	2400	2150	50	400	2600
3200	400	2800	2450	50	400	2900
3600	400	3200	2750	50	400	3200

(b) Output–expenditures graph

Exhibit 23.6
Multiplier Effect of a Change in Lump-Sum Taxes
Lump-sum taxes are the same at each level of GNP. Disposable income is less than GNP by the level of net taxes. As lump-sum taxes increase from zero to $400 billion, equilibrium GNP falls from $3200 billion to $2000 billion. The $400 billion increase in taxes causes a $400 billion decrease in disposable income and an initial decrease in consumption of $300 billion because the marginal propensity to consume is 0.75. The $300 billion reduction in autonomous expenditures causes a $1200 billion decrease in equilibrium GNP.

Government purchases are another part of aggregate expenditures. When they are included, aggregate expenditures become AE = C + I + G. Changes in government purchases have a multiplier effect as do changes in autonomous consumption and investment.

Changes in net taxes have a smaller multiplier effect than do government purchases. A change in net taxes changes disposable income, but only part of any increase in disposable income is spent.

The change in autonomous expenditures caused by a change in lump-sum taxes equals the change in taxes multiplied by the marginal propensity to consume.

Because income taxes increase with GNP, a smaller increase in aggregate expenditures is associated with a change in GNP as is a smaller multiplier effect than with lump-sum taxes.

Multiplier effect of income taxes. Thus far we have focused on lump-sum taxes—taxes that are independent of the level of aggregate income. But both income taxes and sales taxes increase with the level of GNP. And these taxes account for most of the federal government's revenues and a large part of state and local government revenues. Both income taxes and lump-sum taxes reduce disposable income to less than aggregate output. However, lump-sum taxes are a constant amount at all levels of income; income taxes increase with income. Because income taxes change the relationship between consumption and GNP, income taxes change the multiplier effect.

In Exhibit 23.7, the marginal propensity to consume—the relationship between disposable income and consumption—is 0.75. Every $400 billion increase in disposable income results in $300 billion of additional consumption ($400 billion × 0.75). However, with an income tax of 20 percent, each $500 billion increase in GNP results in $100 billion more in taxes and only $300 billion more in consumption. In other words, an income tax means that a smaller change in consumption is associated with each change in GNP. Because the consumption change is smaller, the multiplier effect is also smaller.

We can observe the multiplier effect by noting the increase in equilibrium GNP associated with an increase in investment. In Exhibit 23.7 you can see that equilibrium GNP increases from $2000 billion to $3000 billion when investment increases by $400 billion. In other words, the $400 billion increase in autonomous expenditures resulted in a $1000 billion increase in real GNP. The effect is a multiplier of 2.5, which we calculate as follows:

$$\text{Multiplier} = \frac{\text{Change in equilibrium GNP}}{\text{Change in autonomous expenditures}}$$

$$= \frac{\$1000 \text{ billion}}{\$400 \text{ billion}} \quad \text{or} \quad 2.5$$

Note that the marginal propensity to consume has not changed, but the multiplier is smaller than in the earlier example because tax revenues increase as GNP increases.

Fiscal Policy and a Contractionary Gap

So far we have shown that a change in government purchases or a change in taxes can have a multiplier effect on aggregate output. In other words, government can increase aggregate expenditures by deliberately changing taxes and/or government purchases. Economists call such actions **discretionary fiscal policy**.

Keynes and his followers argued that changes in fiscal policy can and should be used to stabilize the economy. Most (but not all) economists today believe that changes in the government's budget *can* affect the level of planned spending. But not all of them believe that government *should* use discretionary fiscal policies. We return to this important debate in Chapter 26. But for the moment we ask why, according to Keynes, would an increase in government spending (or a decrease in taxes) close a large contractionary gap, such as the one that occurred in the Great Depression?

Discretionary fiscal policy. Deliberate changes made in elements of the federal government's budget—taxes, transfer payments, and/or government purchases of goods and services—to affect the level of aggregate demand. The aim of such policies is to achieve macroeconomic stabilization—full employment and stable prices.

(a) Output and expenditures data
  (billions of dollars per year)

Aggregate output (GNP)	Income taxes (T = 0.20 × GNP)	Disposable income (DI = GNP − T)	Consumption (C)	Investment (I)	Government purchases (G)	Aggregate expenditures (AE = C + I + G)
Original equilibrium (Investment = $100); Equilibrium GNP = $2000						
1000	200	800	900	100	400	1400
1500	300	1200	1200	100	400	1700
2000	400	1600	1500	100	400	2000
2500	500	2000	1800	100	400	2300
3000	600	2400	2100	100	400	2600
3500	700	2800	2400	100	400	2900
New equilibrium (Investment = $500); Equilibrium GNP = $3000						
1000	200	800	900	500	400	1800
1500	300	1200	1200	500	400	2100
2000	400	1600	1500	500	400	2400
2500	500	2000	1800	500	400	2700
3000	600	2400	2100	500	400	3000
3500	700	2800	2400	500	400	3300

(b) Output–expenditures graph

Exhibit 23.7
Multiplier Effect of Income Taxes
Income tax receipts, unlike lump-sum tax receipts, rise as GNP increases. As a result, the change in consumption associated with a change in GNP is smaller. That is, the multiplier effect is reduced. In this case, a $400 billion increase in investment causes equilibrium GNP to increase by $1000 billion (from $2000 billion to $3000 billion), a multiplier effect of 2.5.

Expenditures
(billions of dollars per year)

Exhibit 23.8
Closing a
Contractionary Gap
Initially, equilibrium GNP is $2400 billion (where AE_1 intersects the 45° line). With potential GNP at $3600 billion, however, there is a contractionary gap of $1200 billion. Keynes suggested that discretionary fiscal policy—deliberate changes in government purchases or taxes—be used to close the gap. A $300 billion increase in government purchases or a $400 billion decrease in lump-sum taxes would shift the aggregate expenditures line to AE_2. With a multiplier of 4.0, government policies that increase autonomous expenditures by $300 billion will close the contractionary gap of $1200 billion.

Consider the situation in Exhibit 23.8. Initially, real (equilibrium) GNP is $2400 billion. Full employment, or potential GNP, however, is $3600 billion. As we noted in Chapter 22, when potential GNP is greater than real GNP, a contractionary gap exists (in this case, a gap of $1200 billion). Keynes believed that in the Great Depression the economy had reached such a position.

Recall that Keynes assumed that wages and prices would not fall in a recession. Thus he believed that the economy has no automatic mechanism to quickly restore the economy to full-employment equilibrium. However, he believed that either a decrease in taxes or an increase in government purchases (or a combination of both) could be used to close a contractionary gap. In this example, we know the multiplier—4.0, as in our earlier examples—and the desired change in equilibrium GNP—$1200 billion, or the size of the contractionary gap. Using the multiplier formula, we can show that a $300 billion change in autonomous expenditures would increase equilibrium GNP by the required amount. That is,

Change in equilibrium GNP = Change in autonomous expenditures × Multiplier

$1200 billion = Change in AE × 4.0

Change in AE = $300 billion

The government could generate the required increase in autonomous expenditures by either a $300 billion increase in government purchases (G) or a $400 billion decrease in lump-sum taxes. (A $400 billion decrease in lump-sum taxes leads to an initial $300 billion change in consumption, if the marginal propensity to consume is 0.75.) As discussed in A Case in Point: The 1964 Tax Cut, a similar analysis of the position of the U.S. economy in the early 1960s, led Keynesian economists to suggest a tax cut in 1964.

A Case in Point
The 1964 Tax Cut

One of the factors that helped elect John F. Kennedy president in 1960 was general dissatisfaction over economic conditions. During the preceding four years (1956–1960), there had been two recessions and relatively slow economic growth. Kennedy's advisors were Keynesians; they argued that aggregate demand was inadequate to maintain full employment. They believed that the economy was facing a contractionary gap, that is, that actual output was below potential output.[*]

To develop what they saw as a desirable change in fiscal policy, the president's advisors had to have two basic measures: (1) an estimate of the size of the contractionary gap; and (2) an estimate of the multiplier effect. They attacked the first problem by attempting to estimate full-employment output. Their studies suggested that the full-employment unemployment rate (what economists later came to call the natural rate of unemployment) was 4 percent. They then estimated potential GNP at that rate of unemployment and, comparing actual and potential GNP, estimated the contractionary gap at $30 billion.

In addition, the president's advisors estimated the multiplier to be 2.5.[†] Putting these two estimates together—and assuming a marginal propensity to consume of 0.80—they suggested that a tax cut of $15 billion would completely close the contractionary gap. That is,

$$\begin{array}{c} \text{Change in} \\ \text{equilibrium} \\ \text{GNP} \end{array} = \begin{array}{c} \text{Change in} \\ \text{autonomous} \\ \text{expenditures} \end{array} \times \text{Multiplier}$$

---

[*] For more details about the 1964 tax cut, see Charles McClure, Jr., "Fiscal Failure: Lessons of the Sixties," in *Economic Policy and Inflation in the Sixties*. Washington, D.C.: American Enterprise Institute, 1972. Although basically a critical analysis of the 1964 tax cut, the article explains the Keynesian rationale for it.

[†] The Council of Economic Advisors did not actually provide an estimate of the multiplier but did indicate that every dollar of tax cut would generate two dollars of extra output. Assuming that the marginal propensity to consume is 0.80, the multiplier is 2.5.

$$\begin{array}{c} \text{Change in} \\ \text{equilibrium} \\ \text{GNP} \end{array} = \left(\begin{array}{c} \text{Change} \\ \text{in taxes} \end{array} \times \text{MPC} \right) \times \text{Multiplier}$$

$$\$30 \text{ billion} = \left(\begin{array}{c} \text{Change} \\ \text{in taxes} \end{array} \times 0.80 \right) \times 2.5$$

$$\begin{array}{c} \text{Change} \\ \text{in taxes} \end{array} = \$30 \text{ billion} \div 2.0$$

$$= \$15 \text{ billion}$$

Of course, the president's advisors could also have proposed a $12 billion increase in government expenditures to obtain a $30 billion increase in GNP. However, they believed that they could more easily get Congress to agree to a tax cut than to an increase in spending. Many of those who supported the tax cut did so for other reasons. Some—using arguments similar to those used by President Reagan in the 1980s—wanted a tax cut to boost incentives to work, save, and invest. Others hoped that the tax cut would reduce the overall size of the government.

Although the motives of its supporters in Congress differed, the bill gathered enough support to be enacted into law. The tax cut reduced personal taxes by 20 percent and corporate taxes by 10 percent. The contractionary gap was effectively closed by 1965. Unemployment, which had been at over 5 percent in the early 1960s, stood below the full employment target, prompting *Time* magazine to put John Maynard Keynes on its cover.

Although the tax cut clearly increased aggregate demand, it now appears to have been too much for the economy to handle. Coupled with rising government expenditures to pay for the Vietnam War, the tax cut helped create excess demand, which fueled the fires of inflation. There are at least two lessons to be learned from this experience: (1) tax cuts can increase aggregate demand; and (2) predicting the effects of discretionary fiscal policies is more difficult than the architects of the 1964 tax cuts believed at the time.

Fiscal Policy and Timing of the Multiplier Effect

Any attempt to use discretionary fiscal policy must be based on an estimate of the multiplier, the size of the gap to be closed, and the speed with which the multiplier works. The quicker and more certain the response of the economy to policy action, the better is the case for discretionary fiscal policy. The slower and less certain the response, the weaker is the case.

When we introduced the multiplier earlier in this chapter, we discussed its effects in terms of *rounds* of the circular flow. But how long does a round of spending take to work its way around the circular flow. Some economists suggest that, roughly, a round might take three or four months. Thus the full impact of a change in fiscal policy is not immediately felt, but is spread over a considerable period of time. As we discuss in Chapter 26, the delayed effect weakens the case for fiscal policy action to close contractionary gaps.

EQUILIBRIUM IN AN OPEN ECONOMY

To complete our model of the economy we must also include the foreign sector. As we noted in Chapter 20, the impact of this sector on spending is measured as *net exports* (X − M), the difference between imports (M) and exports (X).

Exhibit 23.9 shows the effects of adding net exports to our model (maintaining the Keynesian assumptions). Planned aggregate expenditures is greater by the

Exhibit 23.9
Keynesian Equilibrium in an Open Economy
Adding net exports (X − M) to total planned aggregate expenditures (AE = C + I + G + X − M) shifts the aggregate expenditures line. Equilibrium GNP will rise to $2400 billion in this case because exports exceed imports.

amount of net exports (AE = C + I + G + X − M). We add spending by foreign individuals, businesses, and governments on domestic goods and services (exports) because the goods are produced in the United States. We subtract spending by domestic households, businesses, and government (imports) because those goods and services are produced in other countries. The net result shows spending for domestically produced goods and services, that is, domestic GNP.

Equilibrium is still the point at which planned aggregate expenditures equal aggregate output. Note, however, that in this example we show net exports as a constant amount, unaffected by the level of output. In the real world, imports tend to rise as output (GNP) and income increase. Why? When GNP increases, businesses buy and use more foreign resources (such as tin from Bolivia). Households buy and consume more foreign goods (such as coffee from Brazil and automobiles from Japan and South Korea).

CONCLUSION

In this chapter, you learned that changes in spending have a multiplier effect on equilibrium GNP. An initial boost in spending creates more income and therefore even more spending. Our analysis of the multiplier was based on the simple Keynesian model. The simplifications—especially the fact that the general price level is held constant—made the introduction of macroeconomics easier. To study the actual behavior of the U.S. or any other modern economy, however, we must use a more complete and realistic model.

One important factor that we have ignored so far is money. To complete our macroeconomic model we have to consider the role of money and how a change in the amount of money supplied affects economic activity. Moreover, if we are to study inflation, we must allow the price level to vary. Thus we must discuss the factors behind the full-scale aggregate demand and supply model introduced in Chapter 20 and how we can use that model.

As we proceed, you will encounter the multiplier effect again and again. As we modify our model, you will find that many elements reduce the overall multiplier effect in the real world. Only after making the model more realistic and complete can we return to the idea of government policies and whether they can improve economic performance—a controversial but exciting issue.

SUMMARY

1. In this chapter we discussed how a change in autonomous expenditures has a multiplier effect on equilibrium GNP, based on the Keynesian assumptions of inflexible wages and investment which is independent of current income and saving.

2. The multiplier is the ratio of the change in equilibrium GNP to the change in autonomous expenditures. The multiplier effect results from an initial increase in spending that causes an increase in income and therefore generates further increases in spending. But because the household sector spends only a portion of the increase in income, subsequent rounds of spending are smaller and smaller. The greater the marginal propensity to consume, the greater is each round of spend-

ing and the larger the eventual multiplier effect. The product of the multiplier and the change in autonomous expenditures predicts the change in equilibrium GNP.

3. Classical economists believed that more saving increases investment and therefore the economy's potential GNP. In the simple Keynesian model, investment is constant; an initial increase in saving reduces consumption, causing equilibrium GNP to decline and thus the total level of saving to be unchanged. This effect is called the paradox of thrift. But if investment falls as firms become pessimistic about the future, the level of both saving and GNP may fall.

4. When the government sector is added to the model, disposable income is less than national income (and GNP) by the amount of net taxes (taxes less transfer payments). And government purchases are added to consumption and investment to determine planned aggregate expenditures (AE = C + I + G).

5. Changes in government purchases and in net taxes, like changes in other autonomous expenditures, have a multiplier effect. A change in lump-sum taxes (taxes unrelated to aggregate output) first affects disposable income. Because households spend only a portion of any change in income, the initial change in spending is the product of the change in taxes and the marginal propensity to consume.

6. The amount of income taxes paid increases with aggregate output, as does the difference between GNP and disposable income. A smaller increase in aggregate expenditures is associated with a change in GNP and the multiplier effect is less.

7. Because wages and prices are inflexible in the simple Keynesian model, the economy could reach equilibrium at less than full employment. Using discretionary fiscal policy—deliberate changes in government purchases and/or taxes—the government can increase expenditures and push the economy to the full-employment, or potential GNP, level.

8. Adding the foreign sector to the simple Keynesian model requires adding net exports (X − M) to aggregate expenditures. Exports represent foreign spending on domestic goods and services; imports represent domestic spending on foreign goods and services. In this expansion of the model, AE = C + I + G +(X − M).

KEY TERMS

Multiplier, 593
Lump-sum tax, 602
Discretionary fiscal policy, 604

QUESTIONS FOR REVIEW AND DISCUSSION

1. A small city is considering trying to attract additional industry. A city council member argues: "If we attract a firm with an annual payroll of $2 million, local merchants will find their sales rising by $2 million as well." Based on the concepts presented in this chapter, how would you respond to the city council member and help the council analyze the effect of a new firm on the local economy? How would the closing of a similar plant affect the local economy?

2. Suppose that the marginal propensity to consume is 0.80. Complete each of the following statements.

a) If disposable income increases by $400 billion, consumption will (increase/decrease) by $_____ billion.

b) If disposable income decreases by $300 billion, saving will (increase/decrease) by $_____ billion.

c) If there is no government or foreign sector and if investment is unaffected by current output, the multiplier will have a value of _____.

d) Based on the answer to (c), a $150 billion increase in planned investment would increase equilibrium GNP by $_____.

e) If equilibrium GNP increases by $300 billion because of a change in planned saving, then saving must have (increased/decreased) by $_____ billion.

3. Use the following graph to complete the statements in (a)–(f).

Expenditures
(billions of dollars per year)

Aggregate output (real GNP)
(billions of dollars per year)

a) The change in planned expenditures caused equilibrium GNP to increase from $_____ billion to $_____ billion.

b) Autonomous expenditures increased by $_____ billion.

c) The multiplier is _____.

d) If government purchases were to decline by $50 billion, equilibrium GNP would (increase/decrease) by $_____ billion.

e) Suppose that potential GNP is $1400 billion. The contractionary gap that initially existed (AE₁) was $_____ billion. Indicate the size of the gap on the graph.

f) Draw a new AE line that shows the level of planned aggregate expenditures required to close the gap. Planned aggregate expenditures would have to increase by $_____ (from AE_2) to close the gap and bring the economy to full employment.

4. The following table shows planned aggregate expenditures by the household and business sectors in the economy of Orcam, both before (case 1) and after (case 2) an increase in investment.

Aggregate output (GNP) (millions)	Planned aggregate expenditures (millions)	
	Case 1	Case 2
$ 500	$ 600	$ 650
750	800	850
1000	1000	1050
1250	1200	1250
1500	1400	1450

Answer the following questions, assuming that there is no government or foreign sector.
a) What is the equilibrium GNP in each case?
b) By how much did autonomous expenditures increase between case 1 and case 2?
c) What is the marginal propensity to consume?
d) What is the value of the multiplier?
e) If potential GNP is $1500 million, what is the size of the contractionary gap in each case? By how much must autonomous expenditures be increased to close the gap?

5. The macroeconomy of Lower Bakpayne is described as follows:

Aggregate output (GNP) (millions)	Planned aggregate expenditures (millions)
	Current
$ 600	$640
700	720
800	800
900	880
1000	960

a) What is the current equilibrium level of GNP?
b) If investment, government purchases, taxes, and net exports are fixed, what is the value of the marginal propensity to consume? What is the value of the multiplier?

c) If net taxes are $125 billion, what is disposable income when GNP is $1000 billion? What is consumption?
d) If potential GNP is $1000 billion, how big is the current contractionary gap? By how much would government purchases have to increase to close the gap? What change in lump-sum taxes would close the gap?
e) What would the new equilibrium GNP be if government purchases decreased by $20 billion? (Answer this part both by adding another column to the table and using the formula for the multiplier.)
f) Starting from the initial conditions given, what will be the new equilibrium GNP if net taxes decreased by $50 billion? (Answer this part both by adding another column to the table and by using the formula for the multiplier.)

6. Explain whether each of the following statements is true, false, or debatable in the context of the simple Keynesian model.
a) The greater the marginal propensity to consume, the smaller is the multiplier.
b) An increase in lump-sum taxes has the same effect on equilibrium GNP as a change in government purchases.
c) The multiplier effect tends to be smaller when the government relies on income taxes instead of lump-sum taxes.

The following questions are based on the appendix to this chapter.

7. Suppose that planned investment and planned consumption are expressed as follows:

$$C = 650 + 0.60GNP \quad \text{and} \quad I = 150$$

a) If this is a purely private-sector economy, what is the equilibrium level of GNP?
b) What is the marginal propensity to consume? What is the multiplier?
c) If planned investment rises by $50, how much will equilibrium GNP increase? (Answer this part both by using the multiplier and by solving for the new equilibrium level of aggregate output.)

8. Suppose that planned expenditures are expressed as

$$C = 250 + 0.75DI \quad G = 150 \quad X = 100$$
$$I = 125 \quad T = 100 \quad M = 75$$

a) What is the equilibrium level of GNP?
b) If potential GNP is $2320, what is the size of the contractionary gap?
c) By how much would government purchases (G) have to increase to close the contractionary gap? How much would net taxes (T) have to fall?

Appendix to Chapter 23

Algebra of the Multiplier Effect

In this chapter, you saw that a change in autonomous expenditures has a multiplier effect, increasing the equilibrium level of aggregate output by more than the initial change in spending. In this appendix, we demonstrate the multiplier effect and derive the multiplier using an algebraic representation of aggregate expenditures.

AGGREGATE EXPENDITURES: A NUMERICAL EXAMPLE

In the Appendix to Chapter 22, we used the following consumption (C) function:

$$C = 200 + 0.75GNP$$

where C is consumption and GNP is aggregate output. As we noted in that appendix, the figure 200 represents autonomous consumption (the portion that does not vary with aggregate output). As before, the coefficient of GNP (0.75) is the value of the marginal propensity to consume (MPC).

If we assume an initial value of investment (I_1) of 400, we derive the formula for aggregate expenditures (AE_1) as follows:

$$\text{Aggregate expenditures} = \text{Consumption} + \text{Investment}$$
$$AE_1 = C + I_1$$
$$= 200 + 0.75GNP_1 + 400$$
$$= 600 + 0.75GNP_1$$

Note that the figure 600 in the equation represents total autonomous expenditures, that is, the sum of autonomous consumption and autonomous investment. If businesses become more optimistic about the future and investment rises to 600 as a result, we can express the new aggregate expenditures (AE_2) as

$$AE_2 = 800 + 0.75GNP_2$$

Note that the $200 billion increase in planned investment raised the autonomous portion of aggregate expenditures (the part not related to GNP) from $600 to $800 billion.

CHANGE IN EQUILIBRIUM: THE MULTIPLIER EFFECT

As in the chapter, we want to know how the change in investment affects equilibrium. Equilibrium requires that

$$\text{Aggregate output} = \text{Planned aggregate expenditures}$$
$$GNP = AE$$

Thus

$$\text{When } I = 400: \quad GNP_1 = 600 + 0.75GNP_1$$
$$\text{When } I = 600: \quad GNP_2 = 800 + 0.75GNP_2$$

Solving each equation, we find that equilibrium GNP will increase from $2400 to $3200. That is

When I = 400

$$GNP_1 = 600 + 0.75GNP_1$$
$$(1 - 0.75)GNP_1 = 600$$
$$GNP_1 = 600/(0.25)$$
$$= \$2400$$

When I = 600

$$GNP_2 = 800 + 0.75GNP_2$$
$$(1 - 0.75)GNP_2 = 800$$
$$GNP_2 = 800/(0.25)$$
$$= \$3200$$

This analysis indicates that the multiplier is 4.0 because a $200 increase in investment increased equilibrium GNP by $800.

We can also find the change in equilibrium GNP directly by subtracting the expression for GNP_1 from that for GNP_2, or

$$(GNP_2 - GNP_1) = (800 + 0.75GNP_1) - (600 + 0.75GNP_2)$$
$$= 200 + 0.75(GNP_2 - GNP_1)$$
$$(1 - 0.75)(GNP_2 - GNP_1) = 200$$
$$(GNP_2 - GNP_1) = 200/0.25 \quad \text{or} \quad 800$$

ALGEBRAIC DERIVATION OF THE MULTIPLIER

We can derive a more general expression for the multiplier by first rewriting the expression for aggregate expenditures, substituting general terms for the numbers we used previously.

Original expression

$$AE_1 = 200 + 0.75GNP_1 + I_1$$

General expression

$$AE_1 = AC + (MPC \times GNP_1) + I_1$$
$$= (AC + I_1) + (MPC \times GNP_1)$$

where AC represents autonomous consumption, MPC represents marginal propensity to consume, and AE represents aggregate expenditures. Then using the general expression and the equilibrium condition, we obtain a general expression of the multiplier, assuming an increase in investment from level I_1 to level I_2.

Original expression

$$GNP_2 - GNP_1 = 200 + (0.75)(GNP_2 - GNP_1)$$

General expression

$$GNP_2 - GNP_1 = (I_2 - I_1) + MPC(GNP_2 - GNP_1)$$
$$(1 - MPC)(GNP_2 - GNP_1) = I_2 - I_1$$

and

$$\text{Multiplier} = \frac{GNP_2 - GNP_1}{I_2 - I_1} = \frac{1}{1 - MPC} \quad \text{or} \quad \frac{1}{MPS}$$

Note that any change in income will either be spent or saved. As a result, the proportion spent (MPC) plus the proportion saved (MPS) equals 1. Thus

$$1 - \text{MPC} = \text{MPS} \quad \text{and} \quad \frac{1}{1 - \text{MPC}} = \frac{1}{\text{MPS}}$$

EQUILIBRIUM IN A PUBLIC-SECTOR ECONOMY

When we add the public sector to our model we must make two important changes. First, we subtract net taxes (T) from aggregate output (GNP) to obtain disposable income (DI). That is,

$$C = 200 + 0.75(\text{GNP} - T)$$
$$= 200 + 0.75\text{DI}$$

Note that this expression assumes lump-sum, not income, taxes. That is, the amount of net taxes is unaffected by changes in income.

Second, we add government purchases to consumption and investment to obtain aggregate expenditures. Thus if investment (I) is 350 and both government purchases (G) and net taxes (T) are 200, planned aggregate expenditures (AE) are

$$AE = C + I + G$$
$$= 200 + 0.75(\text{GNP} - 200) + 350 + 200$$
$$= 600 + 0.75\text{GNP}$$

For these conditions equilibrium GNP will be $2400, calculated as

$$\text{Aggregate output} = \text{Planned aggregate expenditures}$$
$$\text{GNP} = \text{AE}$$
$$(1 - 0.75)\,\text{GNP} = 600$$
$$\text{GNP} = \frac{600}{0.25} \quad \text{or} \quad \$2400$$

CONCLUSION

In this appendix we showed how to use the equilibrium condition and expressions for planned aggregate expenditures to derive the multiplier. You saw that in a simple, private-sector economy the value of the multiplier is determined by the value of the marginal propensity to consume (MPC).

PART SEVEN

Money, Banking, and Economic Activity

Money and the
Banking System

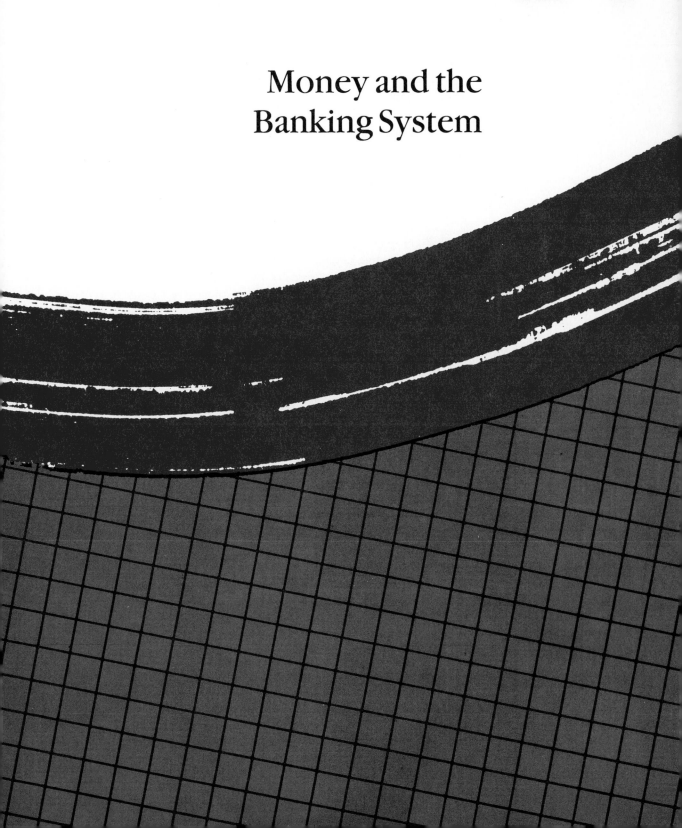

QUESTIONS TO CONSIDER

☐ In what ways have definitions of money changed from time to time and place to place?

☐ How do banks create money?

☐ What are the functions of the Federal Reserve System?

☐ How and to what degree does the Fed control the money supply?

☐ What does the deposit multiplier predict about a change in the money supply?

We take a look at money and its effects on a macroeconomy in this chapter and Chapter 25. In previous chapters we stated values of certain economic variables in terms of dollars (prices and GNP, for example). But we did not define money or discuss its role in the economy. You might think that everyone knows what money is. But in this chapter you will discover that economists use the term *money* in a special, technical way. So, what is money and what functions does it serve? Where does money come from? How do banks create money?

As we answer these questions you will learn that economists generally agree that money can play an important role in our quest for macroeconomic stability. When we lose control of money, we face serious economic consequences. For example, economists generally agree that too fast a growth in the supply of money causes high rates of inflation. And most severe economic recessions (depressions) have been accompanied by a collapse of the banking system and a sharp reduction in the supply of money. But to understand why, you must first learn what money is and how its supply is determined.

WHAT IS MONEY?

We begin our discussion with a simple question: What is money? As you will see, the answer to this question depends on the time and place, as well as the person you ask.

Commodity Money

Commodity money. An item used as a medium of exchange that also has significant value for other uses.

Money. Any item used as a medium of exchange.

The earliest forms of money were items such as cattle, animal hides, large stone wheels, and salt. The Case in Point in Chapter 5 showed how prisoners in World War II POW camps used cigarettes as money. Economists call such items **commodity money**. Various types of commodity money may have very different physical characteristics, but they all meet the broad economic definition of **money**: They serve as a medium of exchange. That is, buyers may use these items to purchase goods and services and sellers will accept them in payment.

Consider for a moment how an economy without a system of money might function. If you wanted to buy a shirt, for example, you would still go to a store and pick one out. But when you asked the clerk how much it cost, he might reply, "I'll trade you the shirt for 2 history textbooks. You're actually getting a bargain. Last week the price was 3 bushels of apples." In this moneyless economy, there is no standard unit of account; last week it was apples, this week textbooks. Regardless of what you receive in payment for your work, you are going to have trouble buying what you want. If you are paid in apples and want to buy a shirt this week, you must first find someone who will trade you history textbooks for apples and then go back to the store and buy the shirt. If this process takes a while, by the time you get back, the clerk may now want razors instead of textbooks.

Arranging trades can be difficult and time-consuming. But if any one item is generally accepted in exchange, these costs can be greatly reduced. That is, instead of trading apples for textbooks and textbooks for a shirt, you can, like the Roman legionnaires, be paid in salt and use salt to buy the things you want. *By serving as a standard unit of account and a medium of exchange, money makes trading much easier.* As a result, money improves the efficiency of the economic system.

To be a useful medium of exchange, an item must be relatively standardized and easily transported. It must be easily divisible, so that it can be used for both small and large purchases. However, many commodities have drawbacks as media of exchange. No two cows or pelts are identical; stone wheels are heavy and bulky; and a tenth of a cigarette is of little use. Money also offers a way to store wealth. By saving some of what you earn today, you can buy more-expensive items—houses, cars, education—tomorrow. But salt is subject to moisture, apples rot, cigarettes go stale, and cows grow old and die.

Because of these difficulties, gold and silver historically have been the most common forms of commodity money. Gold and silver coins have been minted for at least 2500 years. However, like all commodities used as money, gold and silver have other valuable uses. Thus if the value of the gold in $10 gold coins increases to $15, the coins will be melted down and the gold used to make candlesticks, jewelry, or other products. Moreover, significant amounts of real resources are required to discover, mine, and smelt gold and silver. Those resources cannot then be used in other ways.

These two problems point out another drawback to commodity money. In order to serve as a medium of exchange, money must maintain a relatively stable or predictable value. If the value of money falls dramatically—as occurs during very rapid inflation—it may not be accepted in exchanges. But in order to maintain a stable value, the **money supply**—the quantity of money in circulation at any time—cannot fluctuate wildly. And it is very difficult to control the supply of most commodities. For example, Spanish looting of the New World in the sixteenth century dramatically increased the supply—and decreased the value—of gold.

Goldsmiths and the First Bank Money

Some of the disadvantages of commodity money led to the creation of the first paper currency and early banking. In the fifteenth and sixteenth centuries, gold and silver coins were common forms of money. But traders soon discovered that transporting gold over large distances was expensive and the risks of theft high.

Money supply. The total quantity of money in circulation at any time.

(a) 100 percent reserve system

Balance sheet at 12/31/1578			
Assets		Liabilities	
Gold in vault (reserves)	$1000	$1000	Bank money (receipts)

(b) Fractional reserve system

Balance sheet at 12/31/1588			
Assets		Liabilities	
Reserves	$1000	$5000	Bank money (paper currency)
Loans	4000		

Exhibit 24.1
Financial Position of A. U. Smith

Assets. Items of value.

Liabilities. Claims on assets.

Reserves. Funds held by banks in order to meet the demands of their depositors and the legal requirements of the Federal Reserve System.

European goldsmiths, however, had relatively secure locations in which to store the gold they used in their work. Individuals began depositing their gold at goldsmiths' shops for safe keeping. In return, they were given a receipt that was, in effect, an IOU or a claim from the goldsmith for so many ounces of gold. Soon traders found it more convenient to trade the receipts than to exchange quantities of gold. Thus goldsmiths' receipts became an early form of paper money.

Paper money has several advantages as a medium of exchange. First, it is easy to transport and store. Second, it has a constant nominal value. (However, as you will see later, its real value can change.) And third, it need not depend on the supply of any commodity, even though the earliest paper money was based on gold.

Exhibit 24.1(a) shows a balance sheet for A. U. Smith, which illustrates these early banking activities. The balance sheet, as we discussed it in Chapter 6, is simply a listing of a business's **assets**—items of value—and **liabilities**—claims against the assets. It is a useful way both to view the current financial position of any business and to follow the evolution of money and banking.

Smith's assets are the $1000 of gold stored in his vault. The gold is identified as **reserves**, indicating that he is holding this amount of gold to pay anyone who presents a claim against the gold. The other side of the balance sheet shows Smith's liabilities. In this case, his only liabilities are the receipts representing claims to the gold in his vaults. Anyone holding $100 of Smith's currency could present it to Smith and receive $100 worth of gold in exchange. The paper money has been identified as *bank money.* Later in this chapter when we discuss modern banking, you will see that Smith and banks operate in much the same way.

The balance sheet shows the effect of having a banking system with a 100 percent reserve. As long as Smith holds $100 of gold in reserve for every $100 of claims on his gold, his activities do not affect the money supply. At first, goldsmiths and traders simply used one form of money (goldsmiths' notes or bank money) for another (gold or commodity money). However, there is an important difference. Although both gold and paper money are assets (items of value) to those who hold them, paper money is a liability to the bank (goldsmith) that issued it. Whether these pieces of paper are acceptable in exchanges depend on the reliability of the issuer. As long as traders believed that Smith would make good his promises, his paper money was acceptable.

Creating Money in a Fractional Reserve System

Eventually, some enterprising goldsmith noticed that depositors typically demanded only a fraction of the amount of gold held on deposit. Thus it was possible—and profitable—for "bankers" like A. U. Smith to loan out some of the "extra" gold. The interest they earned on loans increased their income. Moreover, those seeking loans did not always demand gold. Many were willing to trade a financial claim on their own assets (their promise to pay the goldsmith back with interest) for a financial claim on the goldsmith's assets (the goldsmith's paper money).

The balance sheet in Exhibit 24.1(b) shows Smith's position 10 years after he learned how profitable it was to make loans. He now has two types of assets: $1000 of gold in his vaults and $4000 in loans. Loans are promised future payments of interest on and the return of principal to Smith.

Although Smith has only $1000 of gold on reserve in his vaults, he has issued $5000 of paper money. This arrangement is what economists refer to as a **fractional reserve banking system**. In this case, Smith's reserves are only 20 percent of the deposits, or the claims against reserves. The fraction of bank money backed by reserves (0.20, or 20 percent, in this case) is called the *reserve ratio*. (We return to the idea of a reserve ratio later in this chapter when we consider current legal requirements for reserves.)

Moving from a 100 percent reserve to a fractional reserve system has two important implications. First, in a fractional reserve banking system, *banks create money and increase the money supply*. Smith accepted $1000 in gold but issued $5000 in paper money. As a result, he increased the money supply by $4000. (The money in Smith's vault is not in the hands of the public, that is, not in circulation, and thus is not part of the money supply.)

Second, because banks hold insufficient reserves to pay all claims at one time, *banks and their depositors are exposed to risks*. Smith holds only $1000 in reserves. If all $5000 of claims (paper money) were presented at the same time, Smith could not pay the full amount of those claims. A large·part of his assets are loans, which represent *future* cash payments. The value of the money issued by Smith now depends on trust—trust that Smith is a competent manager, that he has not made too many loans, and that the loans will be repaid.

This example of a fractional reserve banking system, also illustrates two difficulties in controlling the quantity of money in circulation. First, to a large degree, the quantity of bank money depends on the risks Smith and other bankers are willing to accept. Note that Smith's income depends on accepting risks—both the risk that depositors may want all their gold at once and the risk the loans may not be repaid. The more risks that Smith is willing to accept, the smaller is the fraction of reserves he will hold and the greater the amount of bank money he will issue.

Second, the money supply depends on public trust in banks. For example, if depositors learned that Smith had loaned $2000 to finance a ship lost at sea, they might rush down to Smith and demand their gold. But there would be only $1000 with which to satisfy their claims. Smith might be able to get some borrowers to pay early, or he might borrow from another goldsmith and thus pay off some of his depositors.

Fractional reserve banking system. A system in which banks hold reserves that are only a fraction of their deposits.

If Smith cannot raise enough gold to satisfy his depositors, he will be forced to close his doors. His paper money would then be worthless, and no one would accept it as a medium of exchange. As a result, the money supply would fall by $4000 ($1000 in gold would return to circulation but $5000 of paper currency would disappear). If distrust of banks spread, the entire banking system could fail. Only confidence in Smith and in the system as a whole can prevent such problems.

Checking Deposits: Modern Bank Money

The example of the goldsmiths is true and is one way banks in the United States created money in the first half of the 1800s. At that time, U.S. banks accepted deposits of gold, made loans, and issued paper money just like their earlier European counterparts, the goldsmiths. Just prior to the Civil War there were over 9000 different types of banknotes, as well as 3000 known types of counterfeit notes. Some of them were not worth much more than the paper on which they were printed.* Then in 1864, Congress passed the National Banking Act, effectively eliminating private banknotes. At the same time it restricted the power to issue paper money to the Federal government. (Currently all paper money is issued by the Fed and all currency is minted by the U.S. Treasury Department.)

In place of paper notes, banks in the nineteenth century expanded the use of another form of bank money: **checking deposits**. A check is essentially an order to your bank to pay funds that you have previously placed in a checking deposit at the bank. Most of the time when you pay by check, no coins or paper bills are involved at all. If you write a check to pay the bookstore for your textbooks, the bookstore will probably deposit the check in their account at the same or another bank. The bank (or banks) will make bookkeeping entries that decrease the funds in your checking account and increase the funds in the bookstore's account.

A check is a very good substitute for cash, and, for many purposes, is actually superior. Checks are a relatively safe form of payment because it is difficult for someone who finds a lost or stolen check to get funds from your account. Checks also provide a record of payments. Because checks are widely used to make payments and are easily converted into cash, checking deposits, like the paper money that banks used to issue, are recognized as money. In fact, almost 90 percent of the dollar amount of payments in the United States are now made by check. Checking deposits (bank money) account for most of the money in circulation.

Official measures of the money supply. The growth in use of checking accounts changed the way economists measure the money supply, that is, the quantity of money in circulation at any time. Measuring the money supply is important because changes in it affect the number and type of economic exchanges. However, economists do not agree on the best measure of the money supply for purposes of predicting economic activity.

Most economists accept currency (coins and paper money) in circulation and checking deposits as money. Indeed, this definition is the **M-1** measure of money, one of several official measures of the money supply. The term *in circulation* is important; cash held in bank vaults is not considered part of the money supply. Although checking deposits are a medium of exchange, the distinction between a

Checking deposits. Funds held in checking accounts by banks; may be transferred by writing a check; included in the M-1 definition of money.

M-1. The narrow official definition of money, which includes only currency held by the public and checking deposits.

---

*Robert Puth, *American Economic History*. New York: Dryden Press, 1982, p. 175.

A Case in Point
Financial Innovation and the Supply of Bank Money

In this and subsequent chapters, we focus on how money is created and why it is important that a nation control its money supply. In order to control its money supply, a nation must be able to define and measure that supply. As we noted in the text, one official measure is based on the M-1 definition of money. But changes in financial institutions and the characteristics of deposit accounts they offer have caused substantial changes in the M-1 money supply in recent years.

Prior to the 1930s, government regulation of the banking industry made it relatively easy to define money. Commercial banks were permitted to provide checking deposits, but could not pay interest on those deposits. Thrift institutions—savings-and-loan associations, credit unions, and mutual-savings banks—could not offer checking accounts. As a result, the money supply was simply the currency held by the public plus checking deposits in commercial banks, which paid zero interest.

Financial institutions are in business to earn profits, which they do by attracting funds that they can in turn lend or invest. Thus an institution that can attract more funds can earn more profits. During the 1970s and 1980s, high inflation rates led the public to demand high interest payments as an incentive to deposit their funds. But government regulations limited the rate of interest that thrift institutions could pay. In order to remain competitive, these institutions sought ways around the restrictions. In particular, they wanted to offer the services of a commercial bank, while paying interest on deposits.

In 1972, courts in Massachusetts and New Hampshire ruled that savings banks could set up *NOW accounts*. Like savings deposits, NOW accounts pay interest. But as with checking accounts, NOW depositors can write "negotiable orders of withdrawal" that are, for all practical purposes, checks. In 1974, credit unions started providing comparable services in the form of *share draft accounts*. Finally, in 1978 some savings banks began to offer *automatic transfer services (ATS)*, which automatically transfer funds from savings accounts to cover checks written.

These new substitutes for commercial bank checking deposits caused many people to withdraw their funds from commercial banks. In response, in 1980 Congress empowered all types of depository institutions to offer NOW and ATS accounts. As a result, the government definition of M-1 now includes all such accounts. Commercial banks and thrift institutions are not the only financial institutions, however. Investment firms also compete for the public's funds. To counteract the surge of interest in new bank accounts, in the 1970s investment firms established *money market mutual funds.* Buying shares in a money market mutual fund enabled small investors to earn higher rates of interest than they could on savings accounts. From 1977 to 1982 these funds grew from $4 billion to $232 billion, largely because individuals withdrew funds they had formerly deposited in commercial banks and savings-and-loan associations. In 1982, banks were allowed to compete with these new funds by offering *money market deposit accounts*.

The addition of money market accounts complicated the measuring of the money supply. Both money market mutual funds and money market deposit accounts offer only limited checking privileges. Although these are certainly close substitutes for checking deposits, they are included in the M-2 but not the M-1 definition of money. These and other innovations have so blurred the dividing line between M-1 and other definitions of money that the Fed has decided to stop using M-1 as its principal measure of the money supply.

---

checking deposit and other kinds of deposits is not as clear-cut as it might seem. In A Case in Point: Financial Innovation and the Supply of Bank Money, we discuss how innovations in financial services have created many new forms of deposit accounts. Exhibit 24.2 shows the money supply as defined by M-1 in 1986. As you can see, checking deposits account for approximately 75 percent of the M-1 money supply.

Liquidity. How quickly and inexpensively an asset may be turned into money without risk of loss of value. Money has perfect liquidity; other assets, less liquidity.

The currency and checking deposits that make up M-1 are not only interchangeable, they also share a common characteristic: high **liquidity**, or spendability. We noted earlier in this chapter that in an economy without money, you might find it difficult to use the assets you own to buy the goods and services you

	1970		1986	
	Billions of dollars	Percentage	Billions of dollars	Percentage
Components of M-1				
Currency	49.2	22.7	183.5	25.1
Checking deposits	167.4	77.3	546.9	74.9
Total M-1	216.6	100.0	730.4	100.0
Components of M-2				
Total M-1	216.6	34.5	730.4	26.1
Savings deposits	261.0	41.5	371.5	13.2
Small time deposits	151.1	24.0	852.4	30.4
Money market mutual funds	0.0	0.0	207.2	7.4
Money market deposit accounts	0.0	0.0	570.7	20.3
Other	−0.5	0.0	72.5	2.6
Total M-2	628.2	100.0	2804.7	100.0

Source: *Economic Report of the President, 1987* (Tables B-64 and B-65).

Exhibit 24.2
The Money Supply, 1970 and 1986 (at December 31)

want. The easier it is to convert an asset to immediately spendable form *without risk of loss of value*, the more liquid the asset is. Currency is perfectly liquid, checking deposits only slightly less so, stocks still less so, and land and jewelry even less so.

Exhibit 24.2 also shows a broader official measure of the money supply, **M-2**. This measure includes all items that are in M-1 plus savings deposits, small time deposits, money market mutual fund shares, and money market deposit accounts. Some economists believe that M-2 is a better measure of the money supply because there is very little difference between funds held in these accounts and the items included in M-1.

For example, savings deposits are part of M-2 but not M-1. You cannot directly spend funds held in your savings account, but they are very close substitutes for M-1 money. Technically, a bank may require 30 days notice before allowing a withdrawal from a savings account. In practice, such rules are rarely enforced. Most banks allow depositors to withdraw cash immediately at the bank, at automatic teller machines, or even over the telephone.

Similarly, money market mutual fund shares and money market deposit accounts are almost as spendable as checking deposits because most mutual funds and banks allow some check-writing privileges. (They often place limits on the minimum size of the check or the number of checks than can be drawn per month, however.) Because these accounts allow ready access to funds and pay higher interest rates than conventional checking deposits, they are attractive substitutes for M-1 money. These and other financial innovations have blurred the distinction between M-1 and M-2.

Even broader measures of the money supply, known as M-3 and L, include additional, progressively less liquid, items. Economists continue to debate which

M-2. A broader official definition of money, including not only currency held by the public and checking deposits (M-1 money) but also savings deposits, small time deposits, money market mutual fund shares, and money market deposit accounts.

measure is the best predictor of changes in economic activity. For our purposes the simplest definition and measure of money is the best. Thus in this textbook *money is defined as items used as media of exchange and is measured as M-1, or currency in the hands of the public and checking deposits.*

Whether banks issue paper currency or accept checking deposits, they still create bank money—M-1—just as the goldsmiths did. Moreover, because the modern banking system is a fractional reserve system, it is subject to the same potential problems that the goldsmiths faced. Because the quantity of bank money (checking deposits) depends on the willingness of banks to accept risks, controlling the money supply can be difficult. In addition, widespread concern over the integrity of several banks can cause individuals to lose confidence in bank money. As a result, the money supply may fall rapidly. Several such "panics" and runs on banks in the latter part of the 1800s caused serious economic recessions.

THE FEDERAL RESERVE SYSTEM

The panic of 1907 finally prompted Congress to seek a way to avoid such problems. In 1913, a new financial institution was created: the Federal Reserve System, commonly referred to as the Fed.

Structure of the Fed

The Federal Reserve System has several components. The 12 regional Federal Reserve Banks are located in Atlanta, Boston, Cleveland, Chicago, Dallas, Kansas City, Minneapolis, New York, Philadelphia, Richmond, St. Louis, and San Francisco. These regional banks have only limited authority to act independently. Actually, they are more like branches of a single central bank.

The Board of Governors sets policy for the Fed and is headed by a chairman, who is the most powerful member of the board. The chairman and the other six board members are appointed by the president for 14-year terms of office. The original intent behind the long terms was to give the Fed's officers experience and independence. But while it is theoretically independent and is generally considered to act professionally, the Fed is not immune to political pressure. Moreover, because most board members have resigned before completing a full 14 years of service, the Fed has not had the depth of experience originally envisioned.

The Federal Open Market Committee (FOMC) consists of the Board of Governors and five of the 12 presidents of the regional banks. The president of the New York regional bank is always on the FOMC; the other presidents serve on a rotating basis. All 12 regional presidents usually meet with the Open Market Committee, although only five may vote on committee business. The FOMC is perhaps the most powerful committee of the Fed. The committee meets regularly to decide whether to change the money supply and, if so, by how much.

Functions of the Fed

The Federal Reserve System is the nation's central bank. Like central banks in other countries, the Fed has two principal responsibilities: (1) to help the banking system operate smoothly and safely; and (2) to control the supply of money.

Helping the financial system work. When it established the Fed in 1913, Congress's objective was to help ensure the smooth and safe functioning of the nation's financial system. In doing so the Fed provides banking services for the federal government. The Treasury Department and other federal agencies have checking deposits at the Fed. The Fed is also your banker's bank. Banks maintain deposit accounts at the Fed. A bank that is temporarily short of reserves can get a temporary loan from the Fed. (However, nonbank businesses and private citizens cannot have accounts at the Fed.)

The Fed also provides check-clearing services. For example, suppose that you write a $100 check on your account at the Northeast Bank to pay for some clothes you bought at the Farout Place. The owner of the Farout Place deposits your check in her account at the Southwest Bank. The Southwest Bank will send your check to the Fed. The Fed will then add $100 to the deposit account of the Southwest Bank, subtract $100 from the deposit account of the Northeast Bank, and send your check to the Northeast Bank. In this way the Fed helps to transfer $100 from your account to that of the Farout Place.

To help the financial system function safely, the Fed also oversees the activities of member banks (in conjunction with various other government agencies). When discussing the goldsmiths, we noted that risks and bank profits are linked; so too are risks and bank failures. To keep these risks within acceptable limits, agents of the government periodically (usually once a year) conduct financial audits of banks. They check on the quantity of cash on hand, the riskiness of loans, and generally assess the performance of the bank's management. These activities are designed to spot banks that may be headed for trouble before they actually fail.

However, even the closest monitoring cannot prevent all failures. Recognizing that, Congress established two independent federal agencies, the Federal Deposit Insurance Corporation (FDIC) and the Federal Savings and Loan Insurance Corporation (FSLIC), to insure most deposit accounts at banks. Currently, this insurance covers accounts up to $100,000. Thus most depositors will suffer no loss even if their banks fail, and so are less likely to try to withdraw all their funds, which could cause a bank failure. This protection does not extend by law to accounts larger than $100,000. Recently, large depositors in some large banks were given full protection. But similar protection has not been extended to large depositors in smaller banks. As a result, smaller banks have complained they have lost large accounts.

Controlling the money supply. When it established the Fed, Congress appeared to be most concerned about preventing panics in the banking system that would result in large-scale contractions in the money supply. Now, however, economists believe that the Fed's most important macroeconomic role is implementing **monetary policy**, that is, controlling the size and growth rate of the money supply.

Why are economists concerned about the size of the money supply? The size of the money supply determines the value of money. The value of money determines how much you can buy with a dollar (or franc, or pound, or lira, or yen, depending on the nation involved). A $20 bill will always buy $20 worth of goods and services, but the quantity of such products may vary. For example, a $20 bill that bought two sacks full of groceries 10 years ago can buy only one sack full today.

Monetary policy. Federal Reserve System actions taken to influence the size or growth rate of the money supply.

When the money supply grows rapidly, the purchasing power of money declines. If the money supply grows extremely rapidly, people may lose confidence in the value of paper money and refuse to accept it in exchange. If so, it will cease to be money and exchanges will be less efficient. (This, in fact, occurred in Bolivia in the mid-1980s when prices rose by several hundred percent *per month*.) To maintain the dollar's value, the Fed uses a variety of economic tools to control the money supply, which we discuss in the next section.

MONETARY POLICY AND THE MONEY SUPPLY

How does the Fed control the M-1 money supply in the United States? How complete is that control? As is so often the case in economic discussions, the answer to the first question is easy, the answer to the second is debatable.

Factors Determining the Quantity of Checking Deposits

In considering the Fed's control of the money supply, we focus on its control of checking deposits. Although the Fed is responsible for issuing currency—one other part of M-1—it readily supplies currency on demand. For example, in peak trading months (such as December) the quantity of currency in circulation expands. Thus to control the size of the money supply, the Fed seeks to influence the quantity of checking deposits, or bank money. But if bank money is created by banks, how does the Fed influence the quantity of checking deposits?

To understand how, recall the two factors that determined how much bank money A. U. Smith created in our earlier example: the size of his reserves and the reserve ratio. Smith had $1000 in reserves, which represented 20 percent of his bank money. Reserves, the reserve ratio, and the quantity of bank money are related as follows:

$$\text{Reserves} = \text{Bank money} \times \text{Reserve ratio}$$
$$\$1000 = \$5000 \times 0.20$$

Although the Fed cannot directly increase or decrease the quantity of bank money, it can change the reserve ratio and the quantity of reserves in the banking system. In response, banks will change the quantity of bank money. By influencing the quantity of bank money, the Fed's monetary policy changes the money supply.

Monetary-Policy Tools of the Fed

Required reserve ratio. The minimum portion of deposits that must be legally held as reserves, as set by the Fed.

Legal reserves. Reserves held by banks to satisfy legal minimums imposed by the Fed. They include currency held in bank vaults and banks' deposits held at the Fed.

Open-market operations. The buying and selling of government securities by the Fed; used to change the quantity of bank reserves and hence the supply of money.

The Fed has three basic monetary-policy tools. First, it has the legal power to establish and enforce a **required reserve ratio**, which is the minimum percentage of deposits that banks must maintain in **legal reserves**. (Both currency held in a bank's vault and the bank's deposits at the Fed are counted as part of its legal reserves.) Second, the Fed can increase banks' reserves by granting them loans. But the most common monetary policy tool is **open-market operations**, which involves changing the quantity of bank reserves by buying or selling government securities from the public.

(a) Initial balance sheet

Assets		Liabilities	
Reserves	$1000	$5000	Deposits
Loans	4000		

Reserves:	Actual	$1000	
	Required	1000	(= 5000 × 0.20)
	Excess	$ 0	

(b) Deposit of Fed's $200 check

Assets		Liabilities	
Reserves	$1200	$5200	Deposits
Loans	4000		

Reserves:	Actual	$1200	
	Required	1040	(= 5200 × 0.20)
	Excess	$ 160	

(c) After $160 loan to Ms. MacBeth

Assets		Liabilities	
Reserves	$1040	$5200	Deposits
Loans	4160		

Reserves:	Actual	$1040	
	Required	1040	(= 5200 × 0.20)
	Excess	$ 0	

Exhibit 24.3
Effect of Open-Market Operations on the Goldsmith National Bank

Creating Money in the Banking System by Open-Market Operations

To see how the money supply increases, let's consider how the Goldsmith National Bank reacts to an initial increase in its deposits. In tracing these effects we will consider reserves and loans as the only two assets of the bank and checking deposits as the only liability. This simplification allows us to focus on the important elements of the process. In addition, we make three assumptions:

1. The public—individuals and nonbanking businesses—does not want to hold any additional currency.

2. Banks do not want to hold any excess reserves.

3. The required reserve ratio is 20 percent.

Open-market operations—First round. Initially, Goldsmith National Bank has $1000 of reserves, $4000 in loans, and $5000 of checking deposits, as shown in Exhibit 24.3(a). With a required reserve ratio of 20 percent, the bank's actual and required reserves are equal, and it has no excess reserves.

Suppose that the Fed wants to increase the money supply through open-market operations. To initiate the increase, the Fed purchases $200 of government securities held by Mr. H. I. Roller, paying him with a check. Mr. Roller deposits the Fed's check in the Goldsmith National Bank. The bank sends the check back to the Fed, which increases Goldsmith National Bank's deposits at the Fed by $200. The effect of this initial (first-round) action is shown in Exhibit 24.3(b). The Goldsmith National Bank now has $200 more of actual reserves (since deposits at the Fed are reserves) and $160 of excess reserves. The amount of currency in circulation did not change, but the $200 increase in checking deposits increased the money supply by $200.

Second-round increase in money and reserves.
The money creation process is not over, however, because Goldsmith National Bank does not want to hold any excess reserves. To increase its profits, the bank loans the $160 of excess reserves to Ms. MacBeth, who runs the local dry cleaners. To keep the example simple, we assume that she receives $160 in cash. With this exchange of cash (reserves) for a financial claim (the loan), Goldsmith has eliminated its excess reserves as shown in Exhibit 24.3(c).

Ms. MacBeth did not take out the loan so she could carry $160 around in her purse. She took out the loan to spend it, as borrowers typically do. Suppose that she spends the money on an elaborate macrame wall-hanging made by Shirley Knott, a local artist. Because Ms. Knott does not want to hold cash, she deposits the money in her bank account at the Silversmith National Bank. With her deposit, the second round ends.

What is the effect on the money supply so far? The Fed's initial action increased checking deposits and the money supply by $200. But the Goldsmith National Bank ended up with excess reserves, which it loaned out, causing the money supply to grow by another $160. Thus far the money supply has grown by a total of $360: the $200 in Mr. Roller's checking account plus the $160 in Ms. Knott's checking account. Note that the Fed is directly responsible for the first $200 of new money created. But the profit-seeking activities of the Goldsmith National Bank led it to make a new loan, which led to the creation of $160 of new deposits.

Before moving on, we might ask: What would happen if Goldsmith National Bank had created new money by giving Ms. MacBeth a loan in the form of a checking deposit? Wouldn't this maintain the bank's reserves and allow it to create more money? Giving Ms. MacBeth checking deposits instead of cash would *temporarily* keep the bank's reserves from decreasing. But Ms. MacBeth wants to spend the money she has borrowed. If the person receiving Ms. MacBeth's money has an account in another bank (as in our example), the Goldsmith National Bank will eventually lose reserves, just as if the loan had been made in cash. Thus *in a banking system that has many banks, a single bank can increase loans only to the extent that it has excess reserves.*

Third-round increase in money and reserves.
The money creation process continues beyond the second round. Exhibit 24.4 shows changes in Silversmith National Bank's balance sheet. The bank had no excess reserves initially. However, the $160 deposit by Ms. Knott increases the bank's deposits and reserves by $160, as shown in Exhibit 24.4(b). The increase in deposits raises the bank's required reserves by $32 (0.20 × $160), but leaves it with $128 in excess reserves. To eliminate this excess and increase its profits, the bank makes a $128 loan to Ed Satera. Mr. Satera takes the loan in cash, thus eliminating Silversmith National Bank's excess reserves. He then uses the cash to buy a curio cabinet from Hu's Whatnots. When Mr. Hu deposits the $128 in the store's account at the Coppersmith National Bank, the third round ends.

What is the effect on the money supply so far? At the end of the second round it had grown by $360. During the third round, it grows another $128 for a total of $488 in additional deposits at the end of the third round.

(a) Initial balance sheet

Assets		Liabilities	
Reserves	$ 800	$4000	Deposits
Loans	3200		

Reserves:	Actual	$800	
	Required	800	(= 4000 × 0.20)
	Excess	$ 0	

(b) Deposit of $160 by Shirley Knott

Assets		Liabilities	
Reserves	$ 960	$4160	Deposits
Loans	3200		

Reserves:	Actual	$960	
	Required	832	(= 4160 × 0.20)
	Excess	$128	

(c) After loan of $128

Assets		Liabilities	
Reserves	$ 832	$4160	Deposits
Loans	3328		

Reserves:	Actual	$832	
	Required	832	(= 4160 × 0.20)
	Excess	$ 0	

Exhibit 24.4
Effect of Open-Market Operations on the Silversmith National Bank

Multiplier Effect on Deposit Expansion

After accepting Hu's deposit, Coppersmith National Bank holds $26 in excess reserves. We can expect the bank to loan out this excess, which will again increase deposits and excess reserves. The deposit-expansion process, like that of the expenditures multiplier in Chapter 23, goes on endlessly.

As Exhibit 24.5 indicates, however, changes in excess reserves and deposits get smaller with each round. Why? Because the 20 percent required reserve ratio means that in each round excess reserves and subsequent expansion in loans and the money supply are only 80 percent as large as in the previous round. By the end of the twenty-fifth round, there will be virtually no increase in deposits and in the money supply.

What is to be learned from this example? First, an initial increase in deposits and reserves leads to a multiple expansion in deposits and therefore in the money supply. In this case, the ultimate increase in deposits (roughly $1000) is five times larger than the initial increase in bank reserves ($200). We can express this relationship using the **deposit multiplier**, calculated as

Deposit multiplier. The ultimate change in checking deposits (bank money) caused by a $1 initial change in bank reserves; in a simple banking system, equal to 1 ÷ required reserve ratio.

$$\text{Deposit multiplier} = \frac{\text{Total increase in deposits}}{\text{Initial increase in reserves}}$$

$$= \frac{\$1000}{\$200} \quad \text{or} \quad 5.0$$

Economists—especially those at the Fed—use the deposit multiplier to predict the increase in deposits in response to an initial change in reserves. For example, if the deposit multiplier is 5.0, an increase of $300 million in reserves will result in a $1500 million increase in deposits, calculated as

$$\text{Deposit multiplier} = \frac{\text{Total increase in deposits}}{\text{Initial increase in reserves}}$$

$$5.0 = \frac{\text{Total increase in deposits}}{\$300 \text{ million}}$$

$$\$1500 \text{ million} = \text{Total increase in deposits}$$

In order to use this formula to predict changes in deposits, economists first have to determine the deposit multiplier. In the example above, a deposit multiplier of 5.0 resulted from a required reserve ratio (rrr) of 20 percent. We can state this relationship mathematically as

$$\text{Deposit multiplier} = \frac{1}{\text{Required reserve ratio}} \quad \text{or} \quad \frac{1}{\text{rrr}}$$

Thus the deposit multiplier is inversely related to the required reserve ratio. The larger the required reserve ratio, the smaller is the multiplier. To check your understanding, calculate the deposit multiplier if the required reserve ratio is 25 percent. (Your answer should be 4.) And the smaller the deposit multiplier, the smaller is its effect on growth of the money supply, since in each round a bank would have to hold back more and lend out less of new deposits. For example, at a 20 percent required reserve ratio, a bank can lend $80 of each $100 of deposits. At a 25 percent required reserve ratio, it can lend only $75 of each $100 of deposits.

Exhibit 24.5
Summary of Deposit Expansion Process

	Changes in				Money supply	
Round	Actual reserves	Checking deposits	Required reserves	Loans	(This round)	(Cumulative)
1	$200.00	$ 200.00	$ 40.00	—	$ 200.00	$ 200.00
2	—	160.00	32.00	$ 160.00	160.00	360.00
3	—	128.00	25.60	128.00	128.00	488.00
.	.	.	.	.	.	.
.	.	.	.	.	.	.
.	.	.	.	.	.	.
25	—	0.76	0.15	0.76	0.76	996.98
.	.	.	.	.	.	.
.	.	.	.	.	.	.
Total	$200.00	$1000.00	$200.00	$1000.00	—	$1000.00

(a) Initial balance sheet

Assets		Liabilities	
Reserves	$1000	$5000	Deposits
Loans	4000		

Reserves:	Actual	$1000	
	Required	1000	(= 5000 × 0.20)
	Excess	$ 0	

(b) After the Fed cashes Mr. Roller's $100 check

Assets		Liabilities	
Reserves	$ 900	$4900	Deposits
Loans	4000		

Reserves:	Actual	$ 900	
	Required	980	(= 4900 × 0.20)
	Excess	$ −80	

(c) After Goldsmith reduces its loans by $80

Assets		Liabilities	
Reserves	$ 980	$4900	Deposits
Loans	3920		

Reserves:	Actual	$980	
	Required	980	(= 4900 × 0.20)
	Excess	$ 0	

Exhibit 24.6
Deposit Contraction Process

Multiplier Effect on Deposit Contraction

The deposit-multiplier process also works in reverse. Suppose, for example, that the Fed sells Mr. Roller $100 of government securities, accepting his check drawn on the Goldsmith National Bank. The Fed will decrease the bank's deposits at the Fed by $100 and send the check to the bank. The bank will deduct $100 from Mr. Roller's checking deposit.

But this transaction decreases reserves and deposits at Goldsmith National Bank by $100, leaving the bank with *negative* excess reserves (− $80), as shown in Exhibit 24.6. That is, the bank does not have enough reserves to meet the legal requirement. To remedy this situation, the bank will reduce its outstanding loans enough to meet the reserve requirement. For example, suppose that the next customer to enter the Goldsmith National Bank, Ernie Frankly, gives the bank a check drawn on the Silversmith National Bank for $80, representing the last payment on his car loan. The Goldsmith National Bank sends his check to the Fed, which transfers $80 from the Silversmith National Bank's deposit account to Goldsmith's account. This action brings Goldsmith's reserves back to the required level, but leaves Silversmith $64 short of the required reserve ratio.

So far deposits (and the money supply) have decreased by $180 ($100 from Mr. Roller's account and $80 from Mr. Frankly's account). As with the expansion process, the contraction process continues until the banking system has eliminated all negative excess reserves. Since the required reserve ratio is 0.20, the deposit multiplier is 5.0, so the $100 initial decrease in reserves will lead to a $500 decrease in deposits, calculated as

$$\text{Deposit multiplier} = \frac{\text{Total decrease in deposits}}{\text{Initial decrease in reserves}}$$

$$5.0 = \frac{\text{Total decrease in deposits}}{\$100}$$

$$\$500 = \text{Total decrease in deposits}$$

Other Monetary-Policy Tools

The Fed has two other monetary policy tools that it can use: loans to banks and changes in reserve requirements. Typically, the Fed makes loans only to banks requiring temporary help, acting as a lender of last resort. But additional loans would, like the purchase of securities in the open market, inject additional reserves into the banking system.

Exhibit 24.7(a) shows the effect on Goldsmith National Bank of a $200 loan from the Fed. The loan adds $200 to the bank's actual and excess reserves and $200 to its liabilities. We can expect the bank to loan out its excess reserves, an action that will trigger the deposit-multiplier process. Exhibit 24.7(a) does not trace all the steps in the process but for a deposit multiplier of 5.0, the final increase in the money supply will be $1000—the $200 initial increase in reserve times 5.0, the deposit multiplier.

The Fed may also affect the money supply by changing the required reserve ratio. Exhibit 24.7(b) shows that if the Fed raises the required reserve ratio from 20 to 25 percent, Goldsmith National Bank will have negative excess reserves (-250). Thus the increase in the required reserve ratio means that it must decrease its loans by $250. The cash it receives when the loan is repaid will add $250 to its reserves. Once again this initial action is only the first step in the deposit-expansion process. Note that the change in the required reserve ratio to 25 percent decreases the deposit multiplier to 4.0. Thus the initial drop of $250 will eventually cause the money supply to contract by $1000 ($250 × 4.0).

Some Real-World Complications

What we have illustrated is the simplest form of the deposit multiplier. In deriving the formula, we made two important assumptions. First, we assumed that *the public does not want to hold additional currency*. This assumption means that every additional dollar the public receives will be deposited in the banking system. However, if individuals and businesses hold some or all of the increase in currency, the change in reserves will be smaller and deposits will expand less.

Second, we assumed that *banks do not want to hold excess reserves*. This assumption is reasonable, in terms of normal banking practices. But banks sometimes do maintain excess reserves. To the extent that they do so, the value of the deposit multiplier is lowered. For example, what if Goldsmith National Bank holds reserves equal to 22 percent of deposits (despite a required reserve ratio of only 20 percent)? In the first round, the bank would have increased loans by only $156

(a) Effect of a Fed loan of $200 to the Goldsmith National Bank

Initial balance sheet		
Assets		*Liabilities*
Reserves	$1000	$5000	Deposits
Loans	4000		

Reserves:	Actual	$1000	
	Required	1000	(= 5000 × 0.20)
	Excess	$ 0	

After the Fed's $200 loan		
Assets		*Liabilities*
Reserves	$1200	$5000	Deposits
Loans	4000	200	Fed's loan

Reserves:	Actual	$1200	
	Required	1000	(= 5000 × 0.20)
	Excess	$ 200	

(b) Fed raises required reserve ratio from 20 to 25 percent

Initial balance sheet		
Assets		*Liabilities*
Reserves	$1000	$5000	Deposits
Loans	4000		

Reserves:	Actual	$1000	
	Required	1000	(= 5000 × 0.20)
	Excess	$ 0	

After the Fed raises the reserve ratio		
Assets		*Liabilities*
Reserves	$1000	$5000	Deposits
Loans	4000		

Reserves:	Actual	$ 1000	
	Required	1250	(= 5000 × 0.25)
	Excess	$ − 250	

Exhibit 24.7
Effects of Other Monetary Policies

instead of $160 (see Exhibit 24.3). If other banks also hold higher reserves, expansions in later rounds will also be smaller.

In fact, the simple deposit-multiplier formula that we used indicates only the *potential* change in the money supply. The *actual* multiplier effect depends on real-world actions. However, the ultimate effect of Fed policies on the money supply cannot be predicted as precisely as our examples might suggest. This uncertainty is an important limitation on the Fed's policy making, which we discuss in Chapter 27. Nevertheless, the basic principle remains true: Any excess reserves (whether positive or negative) in the banking system will cause a multiple change in deposits and thus in the money supply.

CONCLUSION

In this chapter we began to explore the role of money in macroeconomic analysis. We showed how the quantity of money in circulation at any time depends on the current size of bank reserves, the required reserve ratio, and banks' desire to create excess reserves. As we have seen, the Fed has a major influence on each of these factors through its various monetary-policy tools.

In Chapter 25 we consider a fourth factor affecting the quantity of money in circulation at any time: the public's desire to hold currency. Here, too, the Fed plays a role by instilling public confidence in the banking system and the economy in general. By considering demand for money we can demonstrate how the money market reaches equilibrium and how changes in the money supply affect aggregate expenditures.

Once we make that connection, we can fully explore the operation of aggregate demand and aggregate supply (Chapter 26). We return to the topic of monetary policy in Chapter 27. There we discuss how the Fed decides how much money to supply and consider how and why economists disagree about monetary policy. As you will see, the Fed's inability to directly change the supply of money has important implications for monetary policy.

SUMMARY

1. In this chapter we explored the history, functions, and definition of money and how the actions of banks and the Federal Reserve System determine the quantity of money in circulation.

2. Some early forms of money actually were commodities: tobacco, cattle, or stone wheels. For many centuries gold and silver were used as money. The basic function of money is to facilitate exchanges, reducing the difficulty and time required in bartering. Any item used as a medium of exchange is considered money. To be most useful as a medium of exchange, however, an item must be relatively standardized, easily stored and transported, and easily divisible so that it can be used for both small and large purchases. For money to be an acceptable medium of exchange, its supply and value must remain relatively stable.

3. Goldsmiths in the fifteenth and sixteenth centuries stored gold in their vaults and issued receipts that could be exchanged for a given quantity of gold. Traders found it convenient to trade these receipts rather than the actual gold, and the receipts became the first form of bank money. The value of this bank money depended on the honesty and reputation of the goldsmiths who issued it.

4. Because only a fraction of the gold was ever demanded at one time by depositors, goldsmiths began to loan out their "extra" gold. The quantity of reserves maintained became only a fraction of the bank money issued. This fractional reserve banking system allowed goldsmiths to expand the money supply. Fractional reserve systems involve risks, since a bank has insufficient reserves to meet the claims of all depositors at any one time. The total quantity of bank money depends on the reserve ratio (proportion of bank money represented by reserves) and the level of reserves.

5. Banks today act in much the same way that the early goldsmiths did. Instead of paper money, banks today create checking deposits, which is simply another form of bank money. The value of this bank money depends on the integrity and skills of bank management. Official definitions of money reflect liquidity. Liquidity expresses the ease and expense of converting an asset into money with little risk of loss of value. The most narrow official definition of money (M-1) indicates high liquidity: only currency in circulation and checking deposits. A broader, somewhat less liquid official measure of the money supply (M-2) includes all items in M-1 plus savings deposits, deposits in money market mutual fund shares and money market deposit accounts, and small time deposits.

6. The Federal Reserve System (the Fed) was created by Congress in 1913 to help the banking system function smoothly and safely and to control the money supply. There are 12 regional Federal Reserve Banks, but power in the Fed is centralized. The Board of Governors is the chief policy-making committee; the Federal Open Market Committee is the group most responsible for setting monetary policy.

7. The Fed issues all paper money, supplies currency as demanded, provides banking services for the federal government, clears checks, holds bank reserves, makes loans to banks, and oversees banking activity. The FDIC and FSLIC insure most types of deposits in member banks and savings and loan associations.

8. The Fed's major economic role is to control the money supply, which it does by regulating the quantity of bank money represented by checking deposits. The quantity of bank money created can be expressed by the following relationship: Reserves = Bank money × Reserve ratio. The smaller the reserves and the larger the ratio

of bank money to reserves, the smaller is the quantity of bank money.

9. The Fed's three monetary-policy tools are (a) changes in the required reserve ratio; (b) increasing reserves through loans; and (c) open-market operations, that is, buying and selling government securities. The principal tool is open-market operations.

10. Excess reserves in the banking system lead to a multiple expansion of loans and deposits. If the public does not want to hold additional currency and banks do not want excess reserves, the deposit multiplier is equal to 1 ÷ required reserve ratio. The deposit multiplier will overstate the actual expansion in the money supply if the public increases its desire for currency and/or if banks wish to hold some excess reserves. The deposit-multiplier process also works in reverse to contract the money supply when there are negative excess reserves.

KEY TERMS

Commodity money, 618
Money, 618
Money supply, 619
Assets, 620
Liabilities, 620
Reserves, 620
Fractional reserve banking system, 621
Checking deposits, 622
M-1, 622
Liquidity, 623
M-2, 624
Monetary policy, 626
Required reserve ratio, 627
Legal reserves, 627
Open-market operations, 627
Deposit multiplier, 630

QUESTIONS FOR REVIEW AND DISCUSSION

1. If you were to ask people how much money they have in the bank, do you think they would differentiate between money held in savings and checking accounts? In what way are savings accounts like currency and checking deposits? In what way are they different? Substituting shares of common stock for savings deposits, answer the same questions.

2. Comment on the statement: "The concept of scarcity certainly applies to money. I could never have enough." If you had more money (as economists define it) today than you did 10 years ago, would you necessarily be better off? Explain. (Be sure to distinguish money from income and real from nominal income.)

3. Almost anything can serve as money. If you were choosing a commodity to use as money, what physical attributes would be important? What limitations do the following commodities have as money: rice, carved stones, whiskey, personal IOUs, and furs?

4. Comment on the statement: "Banks can create money from nothing." Explain how banks create money. What limits the amount of money that a bank can create? What is the connection between the amount of money banks create and their income?

5. Explain why each of the following statements is true.
   a) An individual bank reduces its reserves when it makes a new loan.
   b) The banking system as a whole can't change the quantity of actual reserves.
   c) Banks can eliminate excess reserves.

6. Explain whether the money supply will increase, decrease, or be unaffected by each of the following actions.
   a) The Fed sells $100 million of government securities.
   b) The public decides to hold less currency (and the Fed takes no offsetting action).
   c) A business in California sends a large check to a business in New York, which deposits the check in its local bank.
   d) Banks decide to hold more excess reserves.
   e) The Fed lowers the required reserve ratio.
   f) The Fed prints new paper money and stores it in its vaults.
   g) New supplies of gold are discovered in Vermont.

7. Suppose that the public does not want to hold additional currency and that the banking system does not want to hold excess reserves.
   a) If the required reserve ratio is 0.25 and the Fed buys $50 billion worth of securities from the public, what happens to the money supply?
   b) If the required reserve ratio is 0.15 and the Fed sells $75 billion worth of securities to the public, what happens to the money supply?
   c) If the required reserve ratio is 0.15 but banks decide to hold 0.20 in reserves, what happens to the money supply if the Fed sells $150 billion in securities?

8. Explain how the following statement can be true: "Financial claims are both liabilities and assets at the same time." For which groups are the following claims either liabilities or assets: checking deposits, U.S. government

securities, bank loans, a $5 bill held by the public, deposits held at the Fed?

9. How would you explain the fact that during the 1930s (the period of the Great Depression) banks held significant excess reserves? Why do banks typically hold almost no excess reserves today? Are banks with no excess reserves safe places to keep your money?

10. Explain the statement: "The quantity of checking deposits in the banking system depends on the quantity of loans made by banks and the confidence the public has in the security of bank deposits." Between 1929 and 1933 (the period of the Great Depression) the U.S. money supply dropped by 25 percent (although currency in the hands of the public increased). How does the statement explain why the quantity of bank money (checking deposits) may have fallen?

11. Use the following information to answer the questions in (a)–(e).

Loans issued by banks	$2600 billion
Currency held in bank vaults	90 billion

Checking deposits	1600 billion
Currency held by the public	450 billion
Savings deposits	500 billion
Bank deposits held by the Fed	150 billion
Currency in the Fed's vaults	50 billion
Government securities held by banks	600 billion
Small time deposits	800 billion

a) Using the M-1 definition, what is the stock of money?

b) What is the amount of actual reserves held by banks? If the required reserve ratio is 0.125, what are the amounts of the required reserves and excess reserves? (Assume there are no required reserves for savings deposits.)

c) Based on your answer to (b), by how much would you expect the money supply to change if banks do not want to hold excess reserves (assuming no change in the public's desire to hold currency)?

d) How would your answers to (b) and (c) change if the required reserve ratio were 0.20?

e) What steps can an individual bank take to eliminate negative excess reserves?

Economic Encounters Inside the Underground Economy

The underground economy isn't just organized crime, like gambling or prostitution. It's the street vendor peddling sunglasses and watches outside your office building. It's farmers selling home-grown vegetables from roadside stands. It's musicians playing in subways and city squares for spare change, and it's fairly ordinary people who work "under the table" as waitresses, carpenters, or babysitters.

Estimates place the worth of the underground economy at around $500 *billion* annually, a figure that, because it cannot be verified, is not included in the GNP. This segment of the economy has two basic components: money earned from illegal activity (such as drug trafficking or prostitution) and nonreporting of money earned legally (for example, by cab drivers who don't run their meter, or by waiters who don't report tips). The Internal Revenue Service estimates that unreported income from *legal* sources grew by 13 percent per year from 1973 to 1981—or from $94 billion to $250 billion. Unreported income from three *illegal* activities—prostitution, drug trafficking, and gambling—grew even more rapidly: by 18 percent per year, or from $9 billion to $34 billion.

The only good news about this situation is that we therefore may be overestimating national unemployment (of the 20 million estimated underground workers in the U.S., 1 million may be listed on official records as unemployed) and underestimating our actual GNP. But the good news ends there.

Sources: "A Monetary Perspective on Underground Economic Activity in the United States," *Federal Reserve Bulletin,* March 1984, pp. 174–190; "Inching Down the Capitalist Road," by James O. Jackson. *Time,* May 4, 1987, p. 42; and "In Defense of the Black Market," by Mario Vargas Llosa. *The New York Times Magazine,* February 22, 1987.

Playing by Their Own Rules In many of the nation's cities, hundreds of thousands of people have dropped out of the legitimate economy to earn a living in any number of illegal ways: prostitution, street vending, drug dealing, or petty theft. One expert estimates that 30 percent of youths in Boston, Philadelphia, and Chicago claim that crime (like running numbers and other gambling activities) is more lucrative than legitimate work. Shoplifting and mugging are also high on the list of "careers" in the underground economy.

A Worldwide Underground The underground economy is a problem everywhere, not just the U.S. In Bolivia, a country wracked by economic troubles, experts estimate that a whopping 60 percent of the labor force works in the underground economy, many in illegal drugs, like cocaine.

Sometimes the underground economy results from frustration with the myriad rules and regulations set down by a nation's government. For instance, Peru's 500,000 laws and executive orders seem to favor the already privileged. With no education, no training, and no chance of obtaining credit, the poor find occupations outside the mainstream of Peru's society. By one estimate, 95 percent of Lima's

> **The underground economy isn't just organized crime, like gambling and prostitution.**

public transportation is provided by underground businessmen.

The U.S.S.R.'s underground economy is estimated to include 40 percent of all household services; the average citizen, it is estimated, obtains about 12 percent of his income from underground activities. To discourage moonlighters and other underground workers by giving them a share of the legitimate economic pie, the Soviets

Street vendors are an integral part of the New York City scene. They, too, are a part of the underground economy. (Naoki Okamoto/Black Star)

began to lean more toward capitalism than ever before, approving plans to allow for some small private enterprises—"mom and pop" operations like shoe repair shops, jewelry studios, or vegetable markets.

The actual success of the Soviet measures to coax the underground economy above ground is in question, especially since the government plans to tax legitimized businesses that register with authorities. One moonlighter, an interior decorator, explained, "This law is for old ladies who knit socks, not for people doing real jobs. We don't plan to register."

Avoiding Uncle Sam Of Ben Franklin's two "certainties" of life—death and taxes—at least one seems avoidable by some people. Tax evasion occurs most frequently when taxes are deemed too high by potential taxpayers. In Sweden—where tax rates skyrocket to about 80 percent of income—citizens often resort to nonmonetary types of income, or payments "under the table." For example, a plumber might repair a carpenter's plumbing in return for repairs on his home. When asked to bid on a job, a worker might submit two figures: a high one if the transaction is to be reported to the government, a much lower one if the job is to be paid for in cash.

Even if a person's entire income isn't obtained "underground," he or she might easily be tempted to temporarily join the ranks when receiving an unexpected cash windfall from gambling at cards or horses. A day at the races or a night in Las Vegas may never be reported to the IRS—cold cash without taxation.

In 1981, the IRS estimated that unreported legal income totalled 250 billion dollars. Government agencies have almost no recourse because people who work off the books are almost impossible to trace. One New York auto mechanic claims to earn $30,000 yearly in unreported income; the owner of the body shop where he

Police destroy the plunder of a recent cocaine bust in Columbia by dumping the drug into the Caribbean Sea. Drug traffickers comprise a sizeable portion of the underground economy. (Matthew Naythons/Gamma-Liaison)

works pays him, in cash, 60 percent of the bill for each car he repairs. With his earnings (and remember, none of it goes to Uncle Sam), he's bought a three-bedroom home with hot tub and Jacuzzi, rents a two-bedroom apartment in Greenwich Village, and drives a snazzy foreign car. No disadvantages to the mechanic's situation, you say? He says there *are* a few—he gets no health benefits or pension program.

A day at the races or a night in Las Vegas may never be reported to the IRS.

Because they cannot list legitimate jobs and don't want to leave a trail of records behind, participants in the underground economy can't apply for credit cards or use checks. Cash is the lifeblood of the underground economy. Transactions paid in cash are easy to hide from authorities and difficult to trace. Some economists believe the increased demand for currency in recent years—especially large-denomination bills—is evidence of a growing underground economy. Currency as a percentage of the total money supply increased from 20 percent in 1960 to 28

percent in 1984, despite the growing popularity of interest-paying checking accounts during this period.

The IRS and other concerned agencies say that income tax evaders not only damage the government, but they cheat honest taxpayers and erode national morals. As one solution, authorities have proposed a shift from income tax to a tax on spending. That means every time anyone made a purchase, they would pay a tax. This way, whether our money came from "honest" labor or underground activities, we'd all contribute to the government's coffers—at an estimated rate of $20 billion a year. In addition, proponents argue that a consumption tax would encourage saving, and could allow lower-income Americans to be eliminated from the income tax rolls.

Remember, the next time you buy a pair of earrings or necklace from a street vendor, or pay your gardener under the table, you are contributing to an underground network that has large repercussions for the entire economy. One last statistic: The underground economy in the U.S. causes tax revenues to be underpaid by as much as $100 billion yearly—an amount that, if channeled properly, could make a substantial dent in the national deficit.

C H A P T E R 25

Money and
Economic Activity

QUESTIONS TO CONSIDER

- ☐ Why do individuals and businesses hold money?
- ☐ What factors influence the demand for money?
- ☐ How does the market for money adjust to achieve equilibrium?
- ☐ What did the classical economists conclude from the equation of exchange?
- ☐ How do modern economists believe the economy responds to a change in the money supply?

Our discussion of money is continued as we answer the following questions: Can you ever have too much money? Can the economy ever have too much money? What happens if there is more money in circulation than households and businesses demand? How does a change in the supply of money affect economic activities such as spending, lending, and output decisions?

In Chapter 24 you learned what money is and how the Fed and the banking system can expand or contract the money supply. To study the market for money, however, we must consider why money is demanded and what factors affect that demand. Only then can we consider how demand for and supply of money interact and answer the preceding questions.

RATIONAL CHOICE AND DEMAND FOR MONEY

Beginning students in economics sometimes believe that money is one item with unlimited demand. Part of that confusion comes from a failure to distinguish money—currency and checking deposits—from income. We do, of course, receive much of our income in the form of money. And all of us want more income so we can buy more goods and services and increase our stock of savings. But a desire for more income is not the same as a desire to hold more money. In fact, the fraction of our income we hold as money—currency and checking deposits—is quite small.

As you study this chapter, do not confuse wanting more income with wanting to hold additional quantities of money. When economists talk about demand for money, they mean the *willingness to hold currency and checking deposits*—the two items in the M-1 definition of money. But why do individuals and businesses demand money? What causes demand for money to change? Economists believe that demand for money can best be predicted by assuming that households and businesses apply the principles of rational choice. That is, households and businesses weigh the extra benefits against the extra costs of holding money.

Benefits of Holding Money

Two of the principal uses of money suggest benefits of holding it. Because money is a medium of exchange, there is a **transactions motive** for holding

Transactions motive. The desire to hold money in order to make economic transactions, that is, to buy resources and products in economic markets. This motive is related to money's function as a medium of exchange.

641

Precautionary motive. Holding money to meet unexpected expenditures; related to money's function as a liquid store of value.

money. That is, individuals and businesses want to hold money so they can exchange it for goods and services. The more you expect to spend in the coming week, the more money you are likely to hold. For example, if you expect to spend $100 on groceries during the next week, you are likely to hold $100 of money, either in cash or in your checking account.

Not all expenditures can be fully anticipated, of course. Because money is a liquid store of value, there is a **precautionary motive** for holding it. For example, you may choose to hold more money in your checking account than you expect to spend next week in case your car suddenly breaks down and must be repaired. Businesses also maintain precautionary balances because they cannot predict exactly when they will receive money from their customers, yet they must have money to pay their own bills.

GNP or national income.

The transactions motive helps explain why demand for money depends in part on nominal GNP (nominal national income). Think about how you might change your transactions demand for money as your income rises. Suppose that each Friday you deposit your weekly earnings of $350 in the bank. If you spend your income at a rate of $50 each day, you hold an average of $175 (three and one-half days of expenditures) in the bank as money.

What will happen to your demand for money if your nominal income doubles to $700 per week? You will probably spend more each week. If you deposit $700 each Friday and spend $100 each day, you will hold an average of $350 (still three and one-half days of expenditures) in the bank as money. In this case, your demand for money has doubled because your income (and your spending) has doubled. Even if your spending does not exactly double, we would expect your demand for money to vary directly with changes in your nominal income.

Note that spending should increase regardless of how your real income is affected. If your real income is rising—say, prices increase by 5 percent while your paycheck increases by 10 percent—you may spend more because you buy more steak and less hamburger or more-expensive clothes. If your real income declines—say, prices increase by 10 percent and you receive a 5 percent raise—you will have to spend more money (write a larger check) to buy hamburger and a less expensive brand of clothes.

What is true for an individual is, in this case, true in the aggregate. As nominal national income increases, the dollar volume of aggregate expenditures will increase. In response, more money will be demanded to support the greater volume of transactions. Thus we can conclude that *an increase in nominal GNP will increase the quantity of money demanded.*

Frequency of payment.

The average balance in your checking account will also depend on how often you are paid. In the preceding example, we said that if you deposited your salary of $700 every week and spent it at $100 per day, your average checking deposit balance would be $350. If you receive the same annual salary but are paid $1400 every two weeks, your average checking account balance (the money you hold) will be $700. In general, *the more frequently that individuals are paid, the less money they will hold.* Similarly, businesses that expect to receive frequent cash payments will hold less money.

Costs of Holding Money

As much as we all like money, economists recognize that people may some-times have more money than they want to hold. To understand why, we must recognize that there are costs to holding money. The costs depend on current interest rates, expected inflation rates, and availability of close substitutes for money.

Nominal interest rates. A major cost of holding money is the opportunity cost of not earning interest, or some other return, on that portion of your wealth. Even interest-bearing checking accounts (such as NOW accounts) involve some costs because they pay lower interest rates than time deposits and money market accounts. We can expect that *higher interest rates will cause a decrease in the quantity of money demanded* because higher rates increase the opportunity cost. In other words, higher interest rates offset the inconvenience and risk of not holding assets in a more liquid form.

Expected price levels. In Chapter 24 we observed that the real value of money (its purchasing power) decreases when the general price level rises. In contrast, the nominal value of some assets, such as stocks and real estate, typically increases along with the price level, often by enough to maintain their real value. *Thus an expected increase in the general price level will raise the cost of holding money and thus lower demand for money.*

But we said in Chapter 22 that nominal interest rates typically reflect expected changes in the general price level. However, economic studies show that nominal interest rates on checking deposits tend to adjust more slowly than other interest rates. As a result, the opportunity cost of holding money increases when the general price level increases.

In the United States, the annual increase in the general price level in the mid-1980s has been less than 5 percent, making the cost of holding money relatively low. But in Bolivia, where consumer prices rose by 12,000 percent in 1985, people began leaving work early on payday and spending their income before prices rose further. Under such unusual circumstances, there is virtually no demand for money.

Availability of close substitutes. Rapid price-level increases also increase demand for highly liquid, interest-earning alternatives to money. In the late 1970s, the relatively high rates of inflation (by U.S. standards) led banks and other financial institutions to create many new substitutes for money. For example, money market mutual funds and money market deposit accounts both emerged during this period of time. These accounts allow limited check writing but pay higher interest rates than standard checking deposits. Although somewhat less liquid than cash or checking deposits, they offered higher interest as a protection against inflation.

Credit cards are another substitute for money. Credit cards allow you to spend your income before you receive it. And if you pay your bill in full each month, the cost of using the card is just a small annual fee. Credit cards have reduced both transactions demand and precautionary demand for money. By paying with "plastic" you can hold very little cash and maintain small amounts in your checking account. In many cases unused credit is also a very good substitute for holding precautionary money. Similarly, a business that has arranged to borrow money (a line of credit) as necessary to meet its bills can satisfy its demand for liquidity without holding money. As these examples indicate, *increased availability of close substitutes decreases demand for money*.

EQUILIBRIUM IN THE MARKET FOR MONEY

You should not be too surprised to learn that economists study the interaction between demand for and supply of money in the money market. As in product markets, equilibrium in the money market occurs when quantity demanded equals quantity supplied. Moreover, the market automatically adjusts to equilibrium as individuals and businesses respond to shortages and surpluses. In this section we describe how the money market reaches equilibrium and what this process means for aggregate spending.

Supply of Money

Before we can consider equilibrium, however, we must expand on our discussion of the money supply. In Chapter 24 we said that the money supply depends on the current size of bank reserves, the required reserve ratio, and the banking system's desire to create excess reserves. We also noted that the Fed seeks to control the money supply, using its monetary-policy tools. The Fed sets required reserve ratios and manipulates bank reserves primarily through open-market operations.

But the supply of money also depends on the public's desire to hold currency. The Fed can influence this demand (by assuring confidence in the security of the banking system, for example). Because factors other than Fed policies affect the money supply, the Fed's control is incomplete. In the following discussion, however, we will assume that the money in circulation is the quantity decided on by the Fed. (You can believe that the Fed wishes this assumption were true.) Although a simplification, this assumption lets us focus on the relationship between changes in the money supply and changes in aggregate spending and output. In Chapter 27 we will consider the implications of the Fed's inability to control the money supply exactly.

What Is the Money Market?

Exhibit 25.1 shows a hypothetical money market, illustrating the relationship between quantity of money demanded and supplied and nominal interest rates. (There are many interest rates in an economy, and they all tend to move up and down together, though not always at the same speed.) Because we assume that the Fed fixes the supply of money, the money supply curve (Ms) is a vertical line at $600 billion. And since we expect quantity of money demanded to fall as the interest rate rises, the money demand curve (Md) slopes downward and to the right, like a typical demand curve. The money market is in equilibrium when quantity demanded equals quantity supplied (where Md intersects Ms). As shown in Exhibit 25.1, equilibrium occurs when the interest rate is 8 percent.

For any money demand curve we again make the all-other-things-unchanged assumption. That is, we hold constant the level of nominal GNP, expectations, and

Nominal interest rate
(percent per year)

Quantity of money (billions of dollars)

Exhibit 25.1
Market for Money
The market for money indicates how the demand and supply of money determines
the nominal rate of interest. Although the Fed's control over the money supply is
imperfect, we assume here that the quantity of money supplied will be established by
the Fed's monetary policies. Thus the money supply (Ms) is a vertical line. An increase in the nominal interest rate means an increase in the opportunity cost of holding money and causes quantity of money demanded to fall. When drawing the demand for money curve (Md), we hold all other factors constant—especially nominal
GNP and price level expectations. The money market will reach equilibrium when
quantity of money demanded equals quantity supplied, or at an interest rate of 8
percent in this case.

---

the other factors that affect demand. A change in any of these factors will cause a
shift in the money demand curve. For example, an increase in nominal GNP will
increase demand of money, shifting the curve to the right.

To understand the market for money you must be able to answer the following
question: If the Fed's policies determine how much money is supplied, what
forces will automatically adjust quantity demanded to match quantity supplied? As
you will discover, there are actually two adjustments that can bring the money
market to equilibrium. One involves changes in the interest rate; the other involves
changes in nominal GNP.

Before we go into detail about the adjustments, ask yourself what you would
do if you had too much money? (Recall, we are *not* talking about having too much
income or wealth.) Suppose that your rich Uncle Sam just handed you a nice
surprise—a $1000 bill. But this is more money than you want to hold as cash or
in your checking account. What can you do with it? To oversimplify, you can either

spend the money—perhaps buy a new stereo system—or *lend* it—perhaps put it in a money market account or buy some shares of common stock. (Note that we use the term *lend* broadly here. Lending includes a loan you make to your roommate whose allowance check has not arrived. But it also includes your purchase of savings bonds or shares of common stock.)

By either spending or lending the money, you can eliminate the excess money you are holding. But the money you spend or lend does not disappear; it winds up in the hands of others. If they do not want more money, they will also spend or lend the excess. The important principle is that the spending and lending actions of the household and business sectors do not affect the quantity of money in circulation. These actions just move the existing quantity of money around. The public as a whole cannot get rid of money (except by using paper currency to start fires or as wallpaper).

How, then, does the money market ever reach equilibrium? As you will see shortly, spending and lending activities change nominal GNP and interest rates and thus the demand for money. (In the following discussion we continue to hold constant expected price levels, frequency of payment, and substitutes for money.)

Adjusting to a Surplus of Money by Increasing Spending

Exhibit 25.2(a) shows a market initially in equilibrium at 8 percent interest and $600 billion supplied (where Md_1 intersects Ms_1). But what if the Fed lowers the reserve ratio or buys government securities in the open market? Either of these actions would give banks excess reserves and set in motion an expansion of loans and checking deposits. In this case the money supply would increase to $620 billion (step 1, a shift from Ms_1 to Ms_2).

As a result of the Fed's policy change (and the banks' response), the money market is not in equilibrium. A surplus of $20 billion exists at the current nominal GNP and interest rate. Anyone holding too much money will either spend it or lend it. By tracing both paths, you can see how each action increases quantity of money demanded and brings the money market into equilibrium. At the same time, you can see how money affects aggregate expenditures.

What happens if households and businesses spend the $20 billion surplus? More spending means an increase in planned aggregate expenditures—more consumption and/or investment—shown as step 2, the shift from AE_1 to AE_2 in Exhibit 25.2(b). An increase in aggregate expenditures raises nominal GNP. As nominal GNP increases, so will the number of transactions and transactions demand for money. (Although we will continue to refer to nominal GNP, the graphs in Exhibits 25.2 and 25.3, like all our Keynesian output–expenditures graphs, show output as real GNP. Higher real GNP is also higher nominal GNP because we are holding the general price level constant.)

As long as there is a surplus of money, aggregate expenditures and nominal GNP will rise. The result will be a new money demand curve—step 3, the shift from Md_1 to Md_2 in Exhibit 25.2(a)—and a new equilibrium in the money market. The adjustment process can be summarized as:

Spending response to an increased supply of money

Increased money supply	*causes*	Increased aggregate expenditures	*causes*	Increased nominal GNP	*causes*	Increased demand for money

(a) Money market

(b) Market for final goods

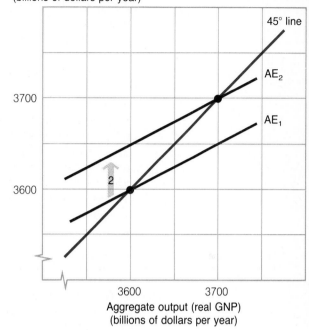

Exhibit 25.2
Spending Response to Increased Supply of Money
If Fed policies increase the money supply (step 1, shift from Ms_1 to Ms_2), a surplus of money will exist at the initial interest rate (8 percent). If the public attempts to get rid of the surplus by increased spending, planned aggregate expenditures increase [step 2, shift from AE_1 to AE_2 in part (b)] raising the equilibrium level of GNP. The increase in GNP, in turn, increases money demand (step 3, shift from Md_1 to Md_2) and restores equilibrium.

The adjustment process works in a similar fashion when the money supply decreases. That is, a smaller money supply reduces aggregate expenditures and decreases nominal GNP. As a result, demand for money decreases, returning the money market to equilibrium. (You might test your understanding of this process by drawing the shifts in money supply, aggregate expenditures, and money demand that illustrate this adjustment.)

Adjusting to a Surplus of Money by Increasing Lending

Instead, what if households and businesses *lend* the excess $20 billion? As we noted earlier, we are using the term lend broadly to reflect not only a direct loan to a friend but also the purchase of a government bond or new shares of common stock. In an important way all such purchases are alike: Any increase in lending can be considered an increase in demand for financial claims, such as government bonds. And as in any market, we can expect an increase in demand for bonds to

Yield. The interest rate (return) received from the purchase of a financial claim; varies inversely with the price of the financial claim. Market interest rates are yields.

raise their price. But what is the relationship between the price of a bond and interest rates?

Suppose that you decide to buy a bond representing the government's promise to pay you a fixed sum of $100 in interest each year. If you can buy the bond for $1000, you will earn a 10 percent return on your purchase ($100 ÷ $1000 = 0.10, or 10 percent). Economists call the return actually earned on a bond the **yield**. The yield on a bond is *inversely* related to the price of the bond. Suppose, for example, that the price of the bond for sale increases to $1250. In that case, the fixed annual interest payment of $100 represents a yield of only 8 percent per year ($100 ÷ $1250 = 0.08, or 8 percent).

The yield on any particular bond partially reflects the risk the bondholder accepts in holding that bond (which can be substantial for some corporate or foreign securities). It also reflects the real return that bondholders require to justify parting with their money. The yield is the same as the money market interest rate.

We can now state how lending helps the money market reach equilibrium. *A surplus of money increases lending and therefore the demand for financial claims. As a result, the prices of financial claims rise and the yield or interest rate falls. A drop in the interest rate reduces the opportunity cost of holding money, making people willing to hold more money.* Exhibit 25.3(a) shows this effect as step 2, a movement along the money demand curve (Md).

Although we show the money market in equilibrium, the economy has not finished its adjustments. Because we have assumed that the general price level will remain constant, a drop in the nominal interest rate represents a drop in the *real interest rate*. Lower real interest rates decrease the cost of borrowing. Thus businesses will find more investment projects profitable, and households can afford to borrow money to buy durable goods, such as cars and appliances. (Demand for housing is particularly sensitive to changes in interest rates, but housing purchases are part of investment spending in GNP accounting.) In other words, as interest rates fall we can expect an increase in aggregate expenditures and an increase in nominal GNP, shown as step 3 in Exhibit 25.3(b).

Lending response to an increased supply of money

Increased money supply	*causes*	Decreased interest rates	*causes*	Increased aggregate expenditures	*causes*	Increased nominal GNP

Comparison of Spending and Lending Responses

The reactions of households and businesses to an increase in the money supply—either spending or lending—cause the money market to adjust to equilibrium. In addition, both spending and lending increase aggregate expenditures and nominal GNP. Higher spending directly increases aggregate expenditures and nominal GNP. The money market adjusts as higher nominal GNP increases money demand. Higher lending reduces interest rates (yields), indirectly stimulating an increase in aggregate expenditures. Lower interest rates result in a movement along the money demand curve, helping to restore money market equilibrium.

(a) Money market

Nominal interest rate
(percent per year)

Quantity of money
(billions of dollars)

(b) Market for final goods

Aggregate expenditures
(billions of dollars per year)

Aggregate output (real GNP)
(billions of dollars per year)

Exhibit 25.3
Lending Response to Increased Supply of Money
An increase in the money supply (step 1, shift from Ms_1 to Ms_2) leaves a surplus in
the money market at the initial interest rate (8 percent). If the public uses the surplus
to buy financial claims—savings bonds or shares of stock, for example—the increased demand for financial claims raises their price and lowers their yield (the interest rate). That persuades the public to hold more money (step 2, shown as movement
along the money demand curve) and restores equilibrium in the money market. But
the lower interest rate also stimulates additional investment and interest-sensitive
consumption spending. The consequent rise in aggregate expenditures [step 3, shift
from AE_1 to AE_2 in part (b)] causes GNP to increase.

Although we have discussed the responses separately, most economists believe
that an increase in the supply of money will cause both more spending and more
lending. That is, actual adjustment to equilibrium appears to result from a combination of a shift in the demand curve *and* movement along the money demand
curve. But as we discuss in the next section, economists differ in the emphasis
they place on the two adjustment processes.

Finally, it is important to note that the economy will continue adjusting until
both the money market and the market for final goods are in equilibrium. That
is, quantity of money demanded must equal quantity supplied *and* aggregate
expenditures must equal quantity of output supplied. Moreover, these two markets
are interrelated. An increase in nominal GNP will increase demand for money.
Increased demand for money increases interest rates, which in turn decreases

An increase in the money supply will create a surplus. If individuals do not want to hold more money, they will spend it or lend it. Lending activities include the purchase of any financial claim—savings bonds or shares of stock, for example.

Additional spending—more planned aggregate expenditures—raises nominal GNP, which in turn increases demand for money (shifts the money demand curve), helping to restore equilibrium in the money market.

Additional lending raises the price of financial claims and lowers their yields, or interest rates. As interest rates fall, the quantity of money demanded increases (movement along the curve), helping to restore equilibrium in the money market. Lower interest rates also stimulate additional spending and raise nominal GNP.

Full macroeconomic equilibrium requires that both the money market and the market for final goods be in equilibrium simultaneously.

planned aggregate expenditures. In other words, changes in the money market cause changes in nominal GNP, and changes in nominal GNP cause changes in the money market. Economists are well aware of these interconnections. (In the appendix to this chapter we describe how interest rates and nominal GNP are determined simultaneously.)

MONEY AND ECONOMIC ACTIVITY: CLASSICAL AND MODERN VIEWS

You now know something about demand, supply, and equilibrium in the money market. But two important questions remain unanswered. First, how much will aggregate expenditures increase when the money supply is increased? Second, how much of any increase in nominal GNP represents higher real GNP and how much represents higher prices?

The modern answer to the second question is presented in Chapter 26. However, the classical economists believed that these questions had fairly simple answers. Their analyses suggested that an increase in the money supply would not affect real GNP but would cause a proportional increase in the general price level. To understand this conclusion, we must consider yet another accounting identity.

Equation of Exchange

We can view any market exchange from two perspectives: what is bought and what is spent. For example, suppose that you go to the local music shop and buy 3 tapes for $20, giving the sales clerk a $20 bill. We can look at this exchange as your *buying* $20 worth of tapes. (Since tapes are a final good, you have also added $20 to nominal GNP.) We can also look at this exchange as your *spending* one $20 bill.

Of course, the $20 bill that you gave the clerk will be spent over and over again during a year. For example, the store owner may put the same $20 bill (along with a few more) into the clerk's pay envelope on Friday. On Saturday, the clerk may go to a clothing store and exchange the same $20 bill for a new sweater. Again, the same $20 bill is exchanged for $20 of final goods. The two purchases—yours and the clerk's—represent a total of $40 of consumption, or $40 of nominal GNP. But it was the same $20 bill that was spent twice. The number of times the average dollar of money in the economy is spent to buy a final good in a year is what economists call **velocity (V)**.

The two ways of looking at exchanges give us two identical dollar values. On the one hand, we have $40 of final goods bought—3 tapes for $20 and 1 sweater for $20. On the other hand, we have $20 of money spent twice, which also equals $40. If we followed the circulation of every dollar in the economy, we would find that the value of what is spent *always* equals the value of what is bought. We can express this relationship as an accounting identity (which is always true by definition) called the **equation of exchange**:

Velocity (V). The average number of times each dollar in the money supply is spent during a specific period of time; calculated as the ratio of nominal GNP to the money supply, that is, $V = (P \times Q) \div Ms$.

Equation of exchange. The identity of total spending and nominal GNP, or

$$Ms \times V = P \times Q$$

Value of money spent = Value of goods bought   or   nominal GNP
Money supply × Velocity = General price level × Real GNP

$$Ms \quad \times \quad V \quad = \quad P \quad \times \quad Q$$

Classical quantity theory. The proposition of the classical economists that changes in the money supply cause proportional changes in the price level; based on the equation of exchange ($M \times V = P \times Q$) assuming velocity (V) is constant and real GNP (Q) equals potential GNP.

It is possible to estimate the size of the money supply, real GNP, and the general price level. But velocity cannot be directly measured. (How much time and effort would it take to trace the flow of even a few dollar bills for one year?) Instead economists calculate velocity by rearranging the equation of exchange. Thus in 1986 the M-1 money supply averaged $672.5 billion and real GNP was $3674.9 billion. The general price level (the GNP deflator in proportionate, *not* percentage terms) was 1.145. So the velocity of money (the number of times an average dollar was spent on final goods and services) was 6.26, calculated as

$$\text{Velocity (V)} = \frac{\text{Nominal GNP}}{\text{Money supply}} \quad \text{or} \quad \frac{P \times Q}{M\text{-}1}$$

$$= \frac{1.145(\$3674.9)}{\$672.5} \quad \text{or} \quad 6.26$$

Classical Quantity Theory

The equation of exchange is an identity, not a theory. To construct a theory from the equation of exchange, we have to specify which variables affect which other variables. The classical economists turned the equation of exchange into **classical quantity theory** by assuming that both velocity and real GNP are constant in the short run.

You may be wondering why the classical economists believed velocity and real GNP to be constant. They thought that velocity was determined largely by how often people were paid, how long banks took to process checks, and personal preferences for holding and spending money. These factors generally change quite slowly, so classical economists assumed that velocity was constant. Recall that classical economists also believed that flexible wages, prices and interest rates would cause the economy to produce at its potential GNP level. Potential GNP can be considered constant in the short run, and the classical economists assumed that real GNP was also fixed.

Accepting these assumptions for the moment, we can see why changes in the money supply are directly related to changes in the general price level. For example, suppose that potential GNP is $2000 billion. Because the classical assumption is that the economy will adjust to full employment, real GNP is also $2000 billion. If the supply of money is $500 billion and velocity is 5, the equation of exchange indicates a general price level index of 1.25, calculated as

The equation of exchange (Ms × V = P × Q) is an identity. It recognizes the fact that the total value spent and received on final goods are equal. Total value spent (Ms × V) is the product of the money supply (Ms) and velocity (V). Total value received—nominal GNP—is the product of the general price level (P) and real output (Q).

Classical quantity theory is based on the assumptions that velocity is constant and that real GNP equals potential GNP. It predicts that increases in the money supply will result in proportional increases in prices.

The modern view of money recognizes that velocity can change as nominal interest rates change. It also recognizes that increases in the money supply can cause real GNP to increase in the short run, although increases in the money supply cause a higher general price level in the long run.

Money supply	×	Velocity	=	General price level	×	Real GNP
Ms	×	V	=	P	×	Q
$500 billion	×	5	=	P	×	$2000 billion
1.25			=	P		

Classical economists were very much impressed by indications that the money supply and the general price level fluctuated together. This relationship is approximately true, but unfortunately for classical quantity theory, changes in the money supply are not *always* exactly proportional to changes in prices. The classical version of the quantity theory is, in fact, too simple to explain the relationship between the money supply and the general price level.

Modern Monetary Theories

The simple theory of the classical economists has been replaced by modern monetary theories. These theories recognize that velocity is not constant. Changes in nominal interest rates may change money demand, thereby offsetting part or all of any change in money supply and reducing the impact on nominal GNP. In addition, modern theories recognize that the economy does not always operate at full employment and that a change in money supply may increase real GNP in the short run. Although most modern monetary theories are based on these principles, economists do not agree on some important details, as you will see.

Changes in velocity.   Economists now maintain that velocity is not constant because demand for money is not constant and money and velocity are linked. At the beginning of this chapter, we noted that demand for money depends on how frequently people are paid—a factor that also affects velocity. Consider that if you spend $36,000 per year and are paid once a month, your average demand for (holding of) money is $1500. If you are paid twice a month, your demand for money falls to $750. But your personal velocity of money—the number of times you spend essentially the same dollar—rises from 24 ($36,000 ÷ $1500) to 48 ($36,000 ÷ $750). Thus we can conclude that *velocity is inversely related to quantity of money demanded*.

Historically, the evidence supports the modern economic contention that velocity is not constant. Exhibit 25.4 shows two measures of velocity: one based on the M-1 definition of money and one based on the M-2 definition. (In each case, velocity is calculated by dividing yearly averages of nominal GNP by the average supply of money, either M-1 or M-2.) The graphs reveal several interesting facts.

First, the velocity of M-1 money increased during most of the period shown, rising from 3.5 in 1959 to peak at 7.1 in 1981. This increase reflects declining demand for M-1 money, which many economists attribute to the increased availability of interest-paying substitutes. In addition, households have held less and less money for transactions and precautionary purposes by relying increasingly on credit cards. Finally, because nominal interest rates generally increased, businesses reduced the quantity of money they held.

The velocity of M-2 money fluctuated within a fairly narrow range during the same period. The stability of the M-2 velocity reflects the fact that many substitutes for M-1, especially money market mutual funds and money market deposit accounts, are included in the M-2 measure of the money supply. Thus a switch of funds from checking deposits to these new funds decreased M-1 but had no effect on M-2.

However, since 1981, M-1 velocity has fallen significantly, representing an increase in demand for money. Economists do not agree on whether this change represents a temporary or more permanent change in money demand. Whatever the cause, M-2 velocity has been more stable than M-1 velocity during this period. How important is the change in velocity of money? For economists who want to predict changes in the money supply, the more important question is whether changes in velocity are predictable. To the extent that changes in velocity are predictable, the effects of a change in the money supply on nominal GNP are also predictable. But if velocity changes are erratic, the Fed has difficulty knowing how much to change the money supply to achieve the results it seeks.

Velocity of circulation

Exhibit 25.4
Velocity of Circulation: 1959–1986
The graph indicates that velocity, as measured by the ratio of nominal GNP to the M-1 stock of money, has a clear upward trend until 1981, reflecting in part the development of substitutes, especially money market mutual funds and money market deposit accounts. Velocity based on the M-2 stock of money is more stable, although certainly not constant.

Sources: Economic Report of the President, 1987; U.S. Department of Commerce, *The National Income and Product Accounts of the United States, 1929–1982;* Federal Reserve Bank of Boston.

Some economists prefer to focus on M-2, which has been relatively stable. They argue that updating classical quantity theory to use M-2 as a measure of money makes the effect of velocity change predictable. But economists are very much divided on the question of how accurately velocity can be predicted.

Short-run changes in real output. A second difference between the classical and modern views of money is the classical assumption that the economy operates at full employment. Based on that assumption, the classical economists concluded that changes in the money supply primarily affect the general price level. However, most modern theories consider a change in the general price level to be the most significant *long-run* effect of a change in the money supply. But modern theories also recognize that changes in the money supply can have important short-run effects on real GNP, especially if the economy is operating below potential GNP.

As we noted in Chapter 23, if an economy is operating below its potential GNP level, a contractionary gap exists. Increasing the money supply can help close the gap by increasing aggregate expenditures. Although an increased money supply means a higher general price level, it also means lower interest rates and greater real output, at least in the short run. Those who advocate monetary policy to offset falling demand during recessions want to take advantage of this short-run effect.

Monetarists and Keynesians: A contrast. Economists now generally agree with the modern theories that we have stated, although complete agreement

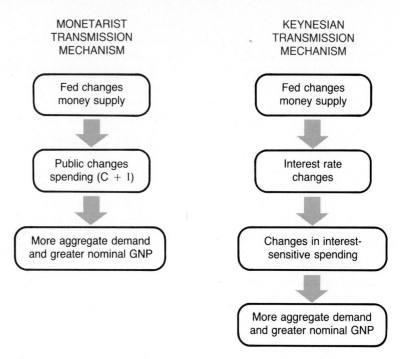

MONETARIST TRANSMISSION MECHANISM

KEYNESIAN TRANSMISSION MECHANISM

Fed changes money supply

Fed changes money supply

Public changes spending (C + I)

Interest rate changes

More aggregate demand and greater nominal GNP

Changes in interest-sensitive spending

More aggregate demand and greater nominal GNP

Exhibit 25.5
Monetarist and Keynesian Monetary Transmission Mechanisms

does not exist. During the 1950s and 1960s, however, economists disagreed strongly about the importance of money. Economists who followed the Keynesian tradition argued that monetary policy was largely ineffective. A rival school of economists, the **monetarists**, countered with the argument that changes in the money supply were the most significant cause of short-run changes in nominal GNP.

Both monetarists and Keynesians now believe that money matters. However, as Exhibit 25.5 shows, the two groups tend to differ over how a change in the money supply affects aggregate expenditures. Monetarists generally emphasize the direct connection between changes in the money supply and changes in aggregate expenditures. In their view—based on a modern version of classical quantity theory—interest rates do not have to fall to stimulate additional spending. In contrast, Keynesians emphasize lending, stressing the connection between changes in spending and changes in interest rates caused by changes in the money supply. Both groups contend that more money leads to more aggregate expenditures. But the link between money and spending is somewhat weaker and looser in the Keynesian view. As a result, Keynesians are more likely to look for changes in factors other than the money supply when seeking to explain short-run changes in output.

While consensus was being reached on some issues, new controversies emerged. Most economists agree that Keynesian theory focused attention on the short-run behavior of the economy in contrast to the long-run behavior analyzed by the classical theories. Indeed, much of modern macroeconomics, as you will

Monetarists. Economists who believe that fluctuations in aggregate output are generally caused by changes in the money supply.

see in the remaining chapters, is devoted to analyzing the short-run behavior of the economy. Although monetarists recognize the importance of short-run analysis, they often accuse Keynesians of not emphasizing the long run enough. As part of this difference in focus, Keynesians are generally more supportive of the use of monetary and fiscal policies to correct short-run problems. Monetarists and their allies tend to stress that most problems will be taken care of automatically in the long run. They show less enthusiasm for policies to smooth out economic fluctuations. We return to this argument when we consider monetary and fiscal policies in Chapter 27.

CONCLUSION

In this chapter we showed that economists generally agree that changes in the supply of money will increase aggregate expenditures, hence nominal GNP. Thus we know that the money supply is important. But our model so far is inadequate to address an important question: How much of any change in nominal GNP will be a general price-level change and how much will reflect a change in real GNP?

Throughout this chapter, we have assumed that the Fed can increase the money supply without affecting general price-level expectations. But in fact, an increase in the money supply tends to raise the general price level. If households and businesses react to an increase in the money supply with expectations of higher prices, interest rates may not fall and the Fed's policy may have less impact than we have suggested. To consider this most important issue, we explore in some detail in Chapter 26 the modern macroeconomic model of aggregate demand and supply.

Moreover, we have to consider how the Fed can best use its monetary-policy tools to help the economy achieve full employment, price stability, and growth. Economists generally agree that both monetary and fiscal policies affect aggregate spending. However, they do not agree on how, or if at all, these policies should be used. We explore these issues in Chapter 27.

SUMMARY

1. In this chapter we explored the factors affecting demand for money; how equilibrium is achieved in the money market; and how economic views of the effects of money have changed over the years.

2. Demand for money reflects the willingness of households and businesses to hold money. They hold money for transactions and precautionary reasons. That is, they hold money to make purchases and to guard against unforeseen expenses. When nominal GNP increases, so does demand for money. When individuals or businesses receive more frequent payments, demand for money decreases.

3. When nominal interest rates rise and when the general price level is expected to increase, the opportunity cost of holding money rises and demand for money falls.

When good substitutes for money—such as money market funds and credit—are developed, demand for money decreases.

4. The money supply depends on the current size of bank reserves; the banking system's desire to hold reserves in excess of the required reserve ratio; and the public's desire to hold currency. The Fed's control of the money supply, while not absolute, is extensive.

5. The economic model of the money market shows the relationship between the nominal rate of interest and quantity of money demanded and supplied. If there is too much money in the economy, individuals and businesses will either spend it on final goods or lend it by purchasing a financial claim. Either activity results in money market equilibrium.

6. Additional spending on final goods (more planned aggregate expenditures) causes nominal GNP to increase, which in turn increases demand for money (shifts the demand curve), restoring equilibrium in the money market.

7. Additional lending increases prices and lowers interest rates (yields) on financial claims, lowers the cost of holding money, and increases the quantity of money demanded (a movement along the money demand curve), restoring equilibrium. In addition, lower interest rates stimulate more investment and interest-sensitive consumption, increasing aggregate expenditures and thus nominal GNP.

8. The money market and the market for final goods are related. A change in the money market affects planned spending (by affecting spending and/or lending) and thus affects the market for final goods. Changes in the market for final goods cause changes in nominal GNP and therefore in money demand. For an economy to reach equilibrium, both markets must achieve equilibrium simultaneously.

9. The equation of exchange ($Ms \times V = P \times Q$) is an identity, expressing the fact that identical values are spent and received in market exchanges. The total value spent ($Ms \times V$) depends on the quantity of money (Ms, the money supply) and the average number of times it is spent (V, the velocity). The total value received ($P \times Q$) is the product of the general price level (P) and real output (Q), that is, nominal GNP.

10. The classical economists assumed that velocity and real GNP were constant in the short run. Thus classical quantity theory concludes that increases in the money supply result in proportional increases in prices.

11. The modern view of money recognizes that velocity (and demand for money) can change in response to changes in nominal interest rates. It also recognizes that an economy may operate below potential GNP in the short run. And finally, it recognizes that increases in the money supply may cause higher real output in the short run, although most of the long-run influence is on prices.

12. Both Keynesians and monetarists agree that changes in the money supply can change nominal GNP. Keynesians tend to stress lending, emphasizing that an increase in the money supply lowers interest rates and stimulates interest-sensitive spending. Monetarists tend to stress spending, emphasizing that an increase in the money supply leads to more aggregate expenditures.

KEY TERMS

Transactions motive, 641
Precautionary motive, 642
Yield, 648
Velocity (V), 650
Equation of exchange, 650
Classical quantity theory, 651
Monetarists, 654

QUESTIONS FOR REVIEW AND DISCUSSION

1. Consider each of the following statements. Using the concepts of this chapter, explain why the person making each statement is confused.
   a) How can economists believe that there can ever be too much money? This notion could only apply to the richest people in our society.
   b) Economists speak of a demand for money, but the only reason I want money is to spend it as fast as I get it. After all, I can't eat, wear, or enjoy money. But I can eat, wear, and enjoy the things I can buy with money.
   c) Economic theory shows that increases in the supply of money result in greater aggregate output. Thus the solution to the problem of scarcity is for Congress to require the Fed to increase the supply of money.

2. What effect will each of the following changes have on quantity of money demanded? On velocity?
   a) An increase in interest rates.
   b) An increase in credit card use.
   c) Growth in real output.
   d) Expectations of a higher general price level.
   e) An increase in the general price level (assuming that expectations do not change).

3. Is each of the following statements true, false, or uncertain? Explain why.
   a) An increase in the money supply will result in a smaller increase in nominal GNP if velocity increases as well.
   b) An increase in bond prices will increase the yield on bonds and thus result in higher market interest rates.
   c) An increase in velocity means the demand for money has decreased.

4. Suppose that the U.S. government sends each of its citizens five newly printed $100 bills. (That would total some $125 billion, or represent about a 20 percent increase in the money supply.)
   a) Predict the effect of this action on demand for goods and services. The general price level. Nominal interest rates.
   b) Would you be any better off than you were the day before? (Explain why your answer might depend on whether the economy were producing at its level of potential GNP.)

5. Suppose a business is considering selling some bonds to finance a new plant. Explain how each of the following would affect the price of its bonds. The yield received by someone buying the bonds.
   a) The Fed increases the money supply (but does not cause individuals to expect an increase in the price level).
   b) The Fed increases the money supply setting off expectations that future price levels will increase.
   c) The firm announces its new plant will be built in a foreign country with a highly unstable economy.
6. Ambrose Bierce, an American short-story author (but not an economist), defined money as "a blessing that is of no advantage to us excepting when we part with it." Would you expect economists to accept or reject Bierce's definition? Why?
7. Use the information presented in the appendix to this chapter, as well as the following equations, to answer questions (a)–(c). Suppose that the money market and

market for final goods of the economy can be described as follows:

Final goods market

C = 150 + 0.7GNP
I = 75 − 4r
G = 100

Money market

Ms = 500
Md = 160 − 8r + 0.4GNP

where C, I, G, Md, and Ms are expressed in millions of dollars.
a) What is the equilibrium level of GNP and the interest rate?
b) What will the equilibrium level of output and the interest rate be if the money supply rises by $20 million?
c) What will the equilibrium level of output and the interest rate be if government expenditures rise by $10 million? Explain why the expenditures multiplier cannot be expressed as 1 ÷ (1 − MPC). [*Hint:* What is investment (I) at the new equilibrium?]

Appendix to Chapter 25

Algebra of Joint Equilibrium in the Final Goods and Money Markets

In this chapter we observed that macroeconomic equilibrium requires that both the final goods and money markets be in equilibrium. In this appendix, we demonstrate how these two markets achieve equilibrium simultaneously. In doing so, we will show how interest rates and aggregate output connect the final goods and money markets.

EQUILIBRIUM IN THE FINAL GOODS MARKET

As we noted in Chapters 22 and 23, equilibrium in the final goods market is reached when GNP = C + I + G, where C is consumption, I is investment, and G is government expenditures. (For simplicity we ignore the foreign sector.)

Consumption is directly related to GNP, if we ignore consumption sensitive to interest rates.

In previous appendixes we considered investment to be constant. But now that we have included the money market in our model, we must recognize the relationship between investment and the interest rate, r. Since money markets have a major influence on interest rates, interest rates link final goods and money markets. We continue to assume that government expenditures (G) are not related to other variables in the model.

In the final goods market, equilibrium requires that the quantity of output produced be equal to the quantity of planned expenditures (GNP = AE). Thus, if

$$C = 100 + 0.75GNP$$
$$I = 100 - 5r$$

we can express *equilibrium in the final goods market* as

$$
\begin{aligned}
\text{Aggregate output} &= \text{Planned aggregate expenditures}\\
\text{GNP} &= \text{AE}\\
&= C + I + G\\
&= (100 + 0.75GNP) + (100 - 5r) + G\\
&= 200 + 0.75GNP - 5r + G\\
0.25GNP &= 200 - 5r + G
\end{aligned}
$$

EQUILIBRIUM IN THE MONEY MARKET

As noted in the chapter, equilibrium in the money market requires that quantity of money supplied equals quantity of money demanded (Ms = Md). To keep the analysis simple, we continue to assume that the Fed determines the supply of money. But we must recognize that demand for money varies directly with aggregate output (GNP) and indirectly with the rate of interest r. Thus if

$$Md = 200 - 10r + 0.30GNP$$

we can describe *equilibrium in the money market* as

$$
\begin{aligned}
\text{Supply of money} &= \text{Demand for money}\\
\text{Ms} &= \text{Md}\\
\text{Ms} &= 200 - 10r + 0.30GNP\\
0.30GNP &= -200 + 10r + \text{Ms}
\end{aligned}
$$

MACROECONOMIC EQUILIBRIUM

To reach macroeconomic equilibrium, the final goods and money markets must reach equilibrium simultaneously. Since both equilibrium equations contain the same variable, r, we first solve each for r, as follows:

Final goods market	**Money market**
$0.25GNP = 200 - 5r + G$	$0.30GNP = -200 + 10r + \text{Ms}$
$5r = 200 + G - 0.25GNP$	$10r = 200 - \text{Ms} + 0.30GNP$
$r = 40 + 0.2G - 0.05GNP$	$r = 20 - 0.1\text{Ms} + 0.03GNP$

If the economy is to reach equilibrium, r must have the same value in each equation. And assuming that government purchases (G) are 75 and the money supply (Ms) is 450, the equilibrium level of GNP is 1000, calculated as

$$\text{Interest rate in money market} = \text{Interest rate in final goods market}$$
$$20 - 0.1\text{Ms} + 0.03\text{GNP} = 40 + 0.2\text{G} - 0.05\text{GNP}$$
$$20 - (0.1)(450) + 0.03\text{GNP} = 40 + (0.2)(75) - 0.05\text{GNP}$$
$$0.08\text{GNP} = 80$$
$$\text{GNP} = 1000$$

We can then determine the interest rate at this equilibrium level of output by using either the equation for money market equilibrium (shown below) or the equation for final goods market equilibrium. Thus

$$r = 20 - 0.1\text{Ms} + 0.03\text{GNP}$$
$$= 20 - (0.1)(450) + (0.03)(1000)$$
$$= 5\%$$

To check your understanding, verify this equilibrium level by substituting the equilibrium values for GNP and r into the final goods and money markets equilibrium equations.

CONCLUSION

In this appendix we considered a more complete model of the economy than those in previous appendixes. We demonstrated how macroeconomic equilibrium requires that both final goods and money markets be in equilibrium and showed how interest rates and aggregate output link these two markets. Thus a policy change—an increase in the money supply by the Fed, for example—will affect both markets and macroeconomic equilibrium. We explore the issues involved with such policies in Chapter 27.

Aggregate Demand and
Aggregate Supply

QUESTIONS TO CONSIDER

☐ How are aggregate expenditures and aggregate demand related?

☐ What factors affect aggregate demand?

☐ In what ways do long-run and short-run aggregate supply and equilibrium differ?

☐ How does an economy respond to an expansionary or contractionary gap?

☐ Why do economists disagree about the speed of the economy's automatic response to a contractionary gap?

Recall that in Chapters 22–25 we explored aggregate expenditures, including the role of money in the economy. At this point you know that changes in spending—caused by changes in the money supply or other factors—will change aggregate expenditures and lead to changes in nominal GNP. But *how much* does real output change when aggregate expenditures change? And *how much* of any change in aggregate expenditures is simply a change in the general price level? Why did the U.S. economy experience both higher prices and lower output in 1974–1975? Why did the high growth in real output in the mid-1960s have little effect on inflation? Why did both real output and inflation fall in the early 1980s?

To be able to answer these and similar questions we must have a model of the economy that incorporates both real output and the general price level. In this chapter, we return to the aggregate demand/aggregate supply diagram introduced in Chapter 20. By looking more closely at aggregate demand and supply and how they interact, we can develop a model to use in looking at the economic history of the United States. More importantly, the model can help us predict the types of changes that will accompany future economic events.

AGGREGATE DEMAND

In Chapter 20 we introduced the aggregate demand curve and some of the reasons for its shape. Now that we have considered the role of money in the economy, we can return to these reasons and consider them in greater detail. Moreover, we can now consider the factors that cause aggregate demand to increase or decrease. First, however, you must understand how aggregate expenditures and aggregate demand are linked.

Connecting Aggregate Expenditures and Aggregate Demand

Before exploring their details, take a quick look at Exhibit 26.1. Exhibit 26.1(a) shows the familiar output–expenditures model that relates planned aggregate expenditures to the level of aggregate output (real GNP). The aggregate expen-

Exhibit 26.1
Relating Aggregate Expenditures to Aggregate Demand
Along each aggregate expenditures curve shown in part (a) the price level is held
constant. (Note that AE_1 corresponds to the price level of 125.) Only one point on
each aggregate expenditures curve–where AE intersects the 45° line—represents a
potential point of equilibrium. These intersections represent points on the aggregate
demand curve shown in part (b).

ditures curve (AE$_1$) indicates how much the economy—household, business, government, and foreign sectors combined—will be willing and able to spend on real output.

Exhibit 26.1(b) shows aggregate demand. As defined in Chapter 20, aggregate demand shows *the relationship between the total quantity of goods and services demanded and the general price level*. The definitions of the two relationships indicate their close connection. The total quantity of aggregate output demanded at any price level is the same as the total amount of planned expenditures at that price level. In other words, both curves represent the output demanded by all sectors of the economy combined. But what is the precise connection between the two curves?

First, you should recognize that any point along an aggregate demand curve could be a point of equilibrium, where quantity of output demanded and supplied are equal. However, only one point along an aggregate expenditures curve satisfies this condition for equilibrium. For example, at the intersection of AE$_1$ and the 45° line (point *a*), the economy is willing to buy $1950 billion of real output if $1950 billion is supplied. But at any other level of output, quantity produced would not match quantity demanded. There would be unplanned inventory investment or disinvestment—too much or too little supplied.

Second, recall that along an aggregate expenditures curve, *the price level is constant*. In deriving AE$_1$, for example, we asked how much planned spending would be associated with a price level of 125 (which is why you see P = 125 in parentheses after AE$_1$). Exhibit 26.1(a), then, indicates that if the price level were 125, planned spending would equal aggregate output at $1950 billion. Since we know that the economy demands $1950 of output at a price level of 125, we know one point on the aggregate demand curve. Note that point *a* in Exhibit 26.1(a) is directly related to point *a* in Exhibit 26.1(b).

Changing the price level will shift the planned expenditures curve in Exhibit 26.1(a) and cause movement along the aggregate demand curve in Exhibit 26.1(b). For example, if the price level falls to 120, the aggregate expenditures curve shifts upward to AE$_2$ (P = 120). At the higher level of planned spending, the new quantity demanded is $2000 billion, or point *b* on both graphs. If the price level falls to 115, the aggregate expenditures curve shifts again, this time to AE$_3$ (P = 115). The new quantity of output demanded ($2100 billion) is represented by point *c* on both graphs.

This analysis shows that higher price levels are associated with lower spending levels and vice versa. But why? What is it about a higher price level that makes planned spending (and quantity of output demanded) fall?

Negative Slope of the Aggregate Demand Curve

The aggregate demand curve shown in Exhibit 26.1(b) has the same downward slope as the aggregate demand curves we drew in Chapter 20. This negative slope—an inverse relationship between the price level and quantity of aggregate output demanded—results from three effects of a change in the price level. First, an increase in the price level decreases the purchasing power of money and wealth held by the household sector. Second, an increase in the price level increases the nominal interest rate in the money market. And third, an increase in the price level decreases the relative prices of foreign goods.

To understand aggregate demand, you must understand how and why an increase in the price level leads to lower planned spending—less output demanded—by all sectors of the economy combined.

Real wealth or real balances effect. The wealth of the household sector is held in many forms: houses, land, stocks, bonds, and money, to name a few. What happens to this wealth when the price level increases? Typically, an increase in the price level brings an increase in the price of many assets. For example, housing and land are often viewed as inflation-proof assets because their market value tends to rise with the general price level. However, households also hold part of their wealth as money, checking deposits, and bonds. These monetary assets represent a claim that is fixed in *nominal* terms. Thus a rise in the price level means a drop in the *real* value of monetary assets and real wealth.

For example, suppose that your wealth consists of $500 in a checking account and a government bond that promises you $100 in interest payments over the next five years plus a final payment of $1000. What happens to the real value—the purchasing power—of your wealth if the price level doubles? You will still have a $500 nominal balance in your checking account and can still buy $500 worth of goods and services. But with most items costing twice as much, you can buy only one-half as much with $500 as you could before. The *real balance* in your account has decreased. Similarly, you will still receive the promised interest and return of principal on the bond. But these sums are also worth only half as much as before. Your *real wealth*—what you can buy with the assets you own—is only one-half as large as before.

As we noted in Chapter 22, consumption is directly related to wealth: More wealth means more spending. Because households hold much of their wealth as monetary assets, household wealth falls when the price level rises. Thus *if the price level rises, real wealth and hence consumption will fall, and less aggregate output will be demanded.* In Exhibit 26.1, the effect on real wealth is one reason that an increase in the price level from 120 to 125 would shift the aggregate expenditures curve from AE_2 to AE_1. This shift would also cause a movement along the AD curve from point *b* to point *a*. Conversely, *a decline in the price level will increase real wealth and hence consumption, causing quantity of aggregate output demanded to rise.* In Exhibit 26.1, a decline in the price level from 120 to 115 shifts the aggregate expenditures curve from AE_2 to AE_3 and results in movement along the AD curve from point *b* to point *c*.

Interest-rate effect. An increase in the price level also means a greater nominal GNP at every level of real output. (Recall that nominal GNP represents the price level times real GNP.) But, as you learned in Chapter 25, higher nominal GNP means a greater volume of transactions and therefore an increase in demand for money. If the money supply remains fixed, greater money demand will cause real interest rates to rise. Higher interest rates, in turn, reduce both business investment and interest-sensitive household consumption. Thus *an increase in the price level raises nominal GNP and hence demand for money. The consequent increase in interest rates reduces quantity of aggregate output demanded.* The interest-rate effect is thus another reason for the downward slope of the aggregate demand curve.

Foreign-prices effect.   Finally, a change in the U.S. price level changes the *relative* prices of foreign goods and services. Higher prices for U.S. products means that foreign products are relatively less expensive. For example, as foreign cars become relatively less expensive, you may buy a Toyota instead of a Ford. And U.S. businesses may buy more German steel and less U.S. steel. But foreigners will also buy fewer U.S. products. That is, *an increase in the U.S. price level will raise imports (M) and lower exports (X). This reduction in net exports (X − M) represents a drop in planned spending—less U.S. output demanded.*

Factors that Shift the Aggregate Demand Curve

When drawing an aggregate demand curve, we want to focus only on the changes in spending caused by a change in the price level. Thus we make an all-other-things-unchanged assumption, holding monetary and fiscal policies, expectations, foreign income, and price levels in other countries constant. Changes in any of these factors will cause a change in planned spending *at each and every price level.* That is, changes cause a shift in the aggregate demand curve.

Monetary and fiscal policies.   In Chapter 25 we noted that changes in the money supply cause changes in the level of aggregate expenditures. If Fed policies increase the money supply, households and businesses will increase their spending at each and every price level. Thus an increase in the money supply means an increase in aggregate demand (a shift to the right of the AD curve).

Conversely, if Fed policies decrease the money supply, households and businesses will decrease their spending at each and every price level, causing a decrease in the aggregate demand curve (a shift to the left). Thus to draw an aggregate demand curve, we hold monetary policy constant because a change in monetary policy causes a shift in the aggregate demand curve.

We also hold fiscal policies—both taxes and government purchases—constant. Any change in fiscal policies changes the level of spending at any given price level, that is, shifts the aggregate demand curve. For example, a decrease in tax rates raises household income and the profits businesses can expect to earn on any new investment. As a result, decreased tax rates will increase consumption and investment at all price levels. A change in government purchases directly changes planned spending and aggregate demand; thus if government purchases increase, so will aggregate demand.

Expectations.   Spending decisions are strongly influenced by expectations. Suppose that the Fed announces plans to reduce the money supply. As we showed in Chapter 25, the reduction in money supply will reduce planned spending. Thus businesses may expect the demand for their products will fall. As a result, businesses may reduce their inventories and halt plans to build new plants and buy new machinery, that is, investment will fall. Households may expect the reduction in the money supply to raise unemployment and lower future prices. If so, current consumption will decrease.

To draw any particular aggregate demand curve, therefore, we hold expectations constant—expectations both about future price levels and future real income. Note that a change in expectations causes a reduction in investment and consumption even before the Fed actually takes any action to reduce the money supply.

Income and price levels in foreign economies.   You have already seen how changes in net exports affect aggregate expenditures and thus aggregate demand. Net exports might increase, for example, if price levels in Western Europe increase rapidly, making U.S. goods relatively less expensive. Net exports might fall if income in Latin America falls, decreasing the quantity of U.S. exports purchased. Any change in foreign income and foreign price levels will shift the aggregate demand curve.

All these factors—monetary and fiscal policies, expectations, and foreign income and price levels—are held constant for an aggregate demand curve. Be alert for these factors. When they change, they shift the aggregate demand curve and cause adjustments in the macroeconomy.

Changes in Aggregate Demand: The Multiplier Effect

In Chapter 23, we noted that a change in planned expenditures (a shift in the AE curve) has a multiplier effect. That is, an initial change in spending causes a much larger final change. For example, if businesses expect the economy to boom in the next several years, they may increase their investments in new machinery now. As a result, they will earn more profits, create more jobs, and generate more household income and more consumption spending. In Exhibit 26.2(a) the $50 billion increase in investment causes a $100 billion increase in total spending. (Note that AE_2 is $50 billion above AE_1 at each level of output and that AE_2 intersects the 45° line at $100 billion more output.) This movement from point *a* on AE_1 to point *b* on AE_2 represents a multiplier effect of 2.

Importantly, both the initial increase in investment and the resulting increase in consumption represent greater output demanded *at the current price level*. (Note that both AE_1 and AE_2 refer to planned spending at a price level of 125.) As you can see in the bottom graph, this increase in aggregate expenditures causes aggregate demand to increase (a shift from AD_1 to AD_2).

The amount by which the aggregate demand curve shifts is determined by the multiplier effect. That is, the curve will shift by the full amount of the final change in spending. In other words, *the multiplier indicates how much the aggregate demand curve shifts as a result of a change in planned aggregate expenditures*. Note that in both graphs movement is from point *a* to point *b*, and output demanded increases by $100 billion. However, as you will discover when we add aggregate supply to the diagram, the actual change in real output will be less than this change in planned expenditures.

Note that any change in planned expenditures affects the quantity of output demanded. When aggregate expenditures change because the price level changes, there is a movement along an aggregate demand curve. A change in aggregate expenditures caused by changes in monetary policies, expectations, or factors other than the price level results in a shift in the aggregate demand curve.

RECAP

The aggregate demand curve (AD) is directly related to the aggregate expenditures curve (AE). Each AE curve is drawn for one particular price level. The intersection of an AE curve and the 45° line represents a single point on an AD curve. A change in the price level shifts the AE curve but causes movement along the AD curve.

An increase in the price level lowers the real value of money and monetary assets held by households, raises demand for money and real interest rates, and raises the relative prices of U.S. versus foreign goods and services. These changes reduce spending and cause movement along the AD curve.

An increase in the money supply, lower taxes, higher government purchases, expectations of price level increases or real income increases, and higher income and price levels in foreign countries all increase aggregate demand (shift the curve to the right).

An initial change in spending has a multiplier effect. The multiplier effect determines how much the aggregate demand curve shifts.

(a) Shift in aggregate expenditures

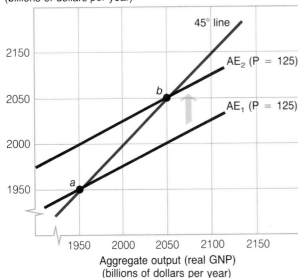

(b) Shift in aggregate demand

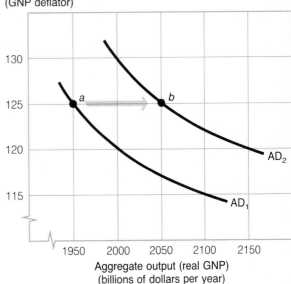

Exhibit 26.2
The Multiplier Effect: Changing Aggregate Demand
In part (a) a $50 billion increase in planned investment shifts the aggregate expenditures line upward by $50 billion. The quantity of aggregate output demanded increases by $100 billion—a multiplier effect of 2. In part (b) we see that this shift represents a $100 billion increase in the quantity of aggregate output demanded at the (constant) price level of 125. Aggregate demand shifts by the full extent of the multiplier effect.

LONG-RUN AGGREGATE SUPPLY AND EQUILIBRIUM

So far in our study of macroeconomics we have concentrated on the demand side of the economy. But as we noted in Chapter 20, the equilibrium level of real GNP and the price level lies at the intersection of the aggregate demand and aggregate supply curves. To complete our model, then, we must consider aggregate supply: how the quantity of aggregate output produced and the price level are related.

Macroeconomists distinguish *two* aggregate supply curves. One, following classical theory, describes the *long-run* relationship between the price level and aggregate output. The other, following the Keynesian tradition, describes the *short-run* relationship. In this section we consider the long-run aggregate supply curve and in the following section, the short-run aggregate supply curve. Both supply curves are useful in describing and predicting macroeconomic events.

According to classical economics, the level of aggregate output is completely determined by factors on the supply side. Regardless of the level of aggregate demand, classical economists believed that automatic adjustment mechanisms— changes in wages, prices, and interest rates—would restore the economy to full employment (potential GNP). Many present-day economists argue that classical theory does not describe the short-run behavior of the economy. But most accept the classical conclusion that the economy tends to produce at its potential GNP level in the long run, that is, after making a full and complete adjustment to current economic conditions. To understand the long-run aggregate supply curve, then, we must answer two questions: What determines the level of the economy's potential GNP? Why is the level of output produced unrelated to the price level in the long run?

Factors that Change Potential GNP

In Chapter 20 we associated potential GNP with the economy's production possibilities curve. Economists also identify four factors that determine the economy's potential GNP: supplies of natural resources, supplies of labor, supplies of capital resources, and technology.

Supplies of natural resources. The amount and types of final goods an economy can produce are affected by the available supplies of natural resources. This factor includes the amount and quality of land and water, as well as supplies of oil, iron ore, and other important minerals. Although an economy can import natural resources, it must pay for them, reducing its ability to produce goods and services to satisfy domestic demands.

Supplies of labor. The size and skills of the labor force affect potential output. Thus education and job training can increase the potential GNP of an economy. Indeed, much of the growth in potential output in the U.S. economy has been credited to the increased skills of its work force. Attitudes about who should work and how much they should work also affect the amount of labor supplied. For example, the United States has laws requiring children under 16 to attend school and forbidding them to hold most jobs. And how many hours per week do you associate with a full-time job? Many individuals view full-time work as 40 hours per week. But 100 years ago the normal workweek was closer to 60 hours. The more hours that individuals are willing to work the larger the supply of labor. Similarly, the increasing proportion of women seeking work in the labor market in the 1960s and 1970s added to the economy's potential GNP.

Supplies of capital. The economy's potential output is also limited by the quantity and quality of existing capital resources—machinery, buildings, and transportation and communications systems. However, these resources can certainly be changed over time. Increases in capital resources allow more output to be produced with the same amounts of labor and natural resources. In fact, private and public investments in capital resources are a major source of economic growth.

Technology. The final factor affecting potential output is technology. Technology determines how much output can be obtained from the supplies of other resources that are available. Technological progress can increase potential output even if supplies of resources remain constant.

We will explore the determination of potential output further in Chapter 30. Economic growth—the subject of that chapter—depends on the steps an economy takes to increase its potential output. In this chapter, our interest is in aggregate supply—how the quantity of aggregate output supplied changes with the price level.

Long-Run Aggregate Supply and Potential GNP

Now that you understand the factors that affect potential GNP (output), we can consider how potential GNP affects the economy's long-run aggregate supply curve. We can also show why quantity of aggregate output supplied is unrelated to the price level in the long run.

When discussing the shape of the economy's long-run aggregate supply curve, we hold the factors that determine potential GNP constant. Then we ask how, if at all, the quantity of aggregate output produced is related to the price level when the economy has adjusted completely to current economic conditions. To understand the shape of the long-run aggregate supply curve we must ask, as the classical economists did: Does a change in aggregate demand affect quantity of output produced? Suppose, for example, the economy shown in Exhibit 26.3 is initially operating where aggregate demand (AD_1) intersects the potential GNP line (point *a*). Because the quantity produced (2000 billion) is equal to the quantity demanded at the initial price level of 120, the economy is in equilibrium.

What happens, however, if aggregate demand increases to AD_2? At the original price level, quantity of aggregate output demanded exceeds the economy's potential GNP. Thus many, if not most, markets will experience shortages which put upward pressures on wages and prices. Employers will bid against each other for available workers; consumers will bid against each other for available products. As wages and prices increase the price level will rise. At the same time, higher prices reduce quantity of aggregate output demanded. When the price level reaches 130, the aggregate shortage disappears and the economy once again produces and sells its potential output of $2000 billion (point *b*). The increase in aggregate demand has increased the price level, but had no effect on GNP.

What if aggregate demand decreases to AD_3? At the original price level (120), quantity of aggregate output demanded will be less than the economy's potential GNP. Thus many, if not most, markets will experience surpluses which put downward pressure on wages and prices. Rather than face unemployment, workers will accept lower nominal wages. As labor costs fall, businesses will lower prices to keep sales from falling. As wages and prices decrease, the price level will fall. At the same time, lower prices increase quantity of aggregate output demanded. When the price level reaches 110, the surplus disappears and the economy once again produces and sells at its potential output of $2000 billion (point *c*). Again, the change in aggregate demand affects only the price level, not real GNP.

Long-run equilibrium. A position in which quantity of aggregate output demanded at the current price level equals the economy's potential output; graphically, when the aggregate demand and short-run aggregate supply curves intersect at the potential output level. The position the economy will achieve if wages and prices fully adjust to aggregate demand.

What does this analysis tell us? First, it suggests that changes in aggregate demand set in motion automatic adjustments, principally changes in wages and prices. When the economy has made a full and complete adjustment, it will produce and sell its potential GNP. In the view of most economists, this full and complete adjustment does not take place instantly, but it does occur eventually. Reflecting the period of time this adjustment may take, economists say that the economy has reached **long-run equilibrium** when quantity of output demanded equals potential GNP.

Exhibit 26.3
Long-Run Aggregate Supply and Potential GNP
An increase in aggregate demand (from AD_1 to AD_2) creates excess demand pressures. Shortages put upward pressure on input prices. The price level rises (to 130 in this case) but the economy produces and sells its potential GNP. Similarly, a decrease in aggregate demand (from AD_1 to AD_3) creates surpluses and puts downward pressure on wages and prices. As the price level falls, the economy returns to long-run equilibrium at the potential GNP level (although at a lower price level). Hence the economy's long-run aggregate supply curve is a vertical line at potential GNP.

RECAP

The long-run aggregate supply curve is a vertical line at the economy's potential GNP. Given time to make a full adjustment, the economy will produce this full-employment level of output.

Potential GNP will change when supplies of natural, capital, or labor resources change or when technology changes.

Potential GNP is not a technological maximum. More than this level of output can be produced in the short run. In the long run, potential GNP is the only level of output that can be sustained.

Second, in the long run an economy's equilibrium output is its potential GNP, regardless of the level of demand and the price level. There is no long-run relationship between the price level and real GNP. That is, *the economy's long-run aggregate supply curve is a vertical line at potential GNP*.

SHORT-RUN AGGREGATE SUPPLY AND EQUILIBRIUM

Our analysis in the previous section followed classical economic theory. Most economists now generally accept the notion that the economy will produce its potential GNP when the economy has fully adjusted to economic conditions. But there is clear evidence that the economy does not always produce at its potential GNP level. Thus economists—at least since Keynes—have explored factors that may explain why the general price level appears to be directly related to quantity of output supplied in the short run.

Factors that Shift the Short-Run Aggregate Supply Curve

To derive a short-run aggregate supply curve, we must first define the short-run relationship between aggregate output supplied and the general price level. We focus only on the response to changes in the price level by holding the other factors that influence quantity supplied constant. We expect the short-run aggregate supply curve to shift if there is a change in the prices of resources, price-level expectations, or the economy's potential GNP.

Resource prices.   There is some evidence to indicate that resource prices, especially labor prices, in the short run are reasonably constant. That is, the economy can produce somewhat more or less aggregate output without having a serious impact on resource prices. In the case of materials and intermediate goods, the adjustment may be slow because many producers will have existing contracts with suppliers that specify resource price levels and must be honored. Automakers, for example, may have already contracted for next month's supplies of steel.

Many wages are also fixed in the short run. In unionized companies, wage rates are written into formal contracts. And many nonunion workers have their wages reviewed and adjusted only once a year, during an annual performance appraisal. Thus the assumption that resource prices are fixed is realistic for the short run, and we hold them constant when drawing a short-run aggregate supply curve. However, it is unrealistic to believe that resource prices will remain unchanged for very long. And when resource prices change, the short-run aggregate supply curve shifts: *Increases in resource prices decrease aggregate supply, and decreases in resource prices increase aggregate supply in the short run.*

Price-level expectations.   Economists believe that quantity of labor supplied depends on the *real wages* that workers receive. In other words, people work to earn income in order to consume. Higher real wages increase the quantity of goods and services that can be purchased. Thus more labor will be supplied when real wages increase, and less labor will be supplied when real wages fall.

However, workers are typically promised a certain nominal, or dollar, wage over the next year. How much the real wage is, therefore, depends on how the price level changes over the next year. While the future price level is unknown to those of us without accurate crystal balls, individuals tend to translate nominal wage offers into real terms based on what they *expect* average prices to be. The higher the expected price level, the lower is the expected real value of any nominal wage offer.

In drawing an aggregate supply curve, we hold both price-level expectations and nominal wages constant. We assume that workers believe that they are facing a specific and constant real-wage offer. Workers are likely to change their expectations, however, if they observe that actual price changes are slower or faster than they expected. If they expect a greater increase in prices, they will recognize that their expected real wage is lower than anticipated. They may therefore refuse to work unless they receive a matching increase in nominal wages.

Higher wages raise costs to businesses, which respond by raising prices. Thus a change in expectations about future prices will cause the short-run aggregate supply curve to shift: *An increase in the expected price level will cause a decrease in aggregate supply; a decrease in the expected price level will cause an increase in aggregate supply.*

Potential GNP. When drawing a short-run aggregate supply curve we also assume that the economy's productive potential is constant. We noted earlier in the chapter that potential GNP depends on supplies of natural resources, supplies of labor, supplies of capital resources, and technology. A change in any of these factors also shifts an economy's short-run aggregate supply curve. That is, *increases in potential GNP increase the short-run aggregate supply curve. Decreases in potential GNP decrease the short-run aggregate supply curve.*

Slope of the Short-Run Aggregate Supply Curve

Although potential GNP is fixed in the short run, businesses can supply a wide range of aggregate output. In fact, quantity supplied in the short run depends on the price level. The higher the price level, the more output businesses will offer for sale. As a result, the short-run aggregate supply curve drawn by most economists slopes upward and to the right, as shown in Exhibit 26.4. (Note that the short-run curve is labeled AS. Long-run supply curves are labeled Potential GNP.)

Following the principles of rational choice, we can expect businesses that seek to maximize profits to supply more when real profits rise and to supply less when real profits fall. But, as we noted in Chapter 20, real profits are linked to both cost and price. Thus the shape of the short-run aggregate supply curve depends on how businesses respond in the short run to changes in aggregate demand.

Consider what happens to profits if aggregate demand increases (holding resource prices, price-level expectations, and potential GNP constant). Businesses first observe the increase in demand when inventories fall and orders for their products increase. More demand puts upward pressure on product prices. With resource prices fixed, however, a higher product price means a greater real profit for producers, who are then willing to supply more for sale. That is, higher demand results in an increase in both price and real output in the short run. This response is consistent with a short-run aggregate supply curve having a positive slope.

Similarly, a decrease in aggregate demand puts downward pressure on product prices. But with resource prices fixed, lower product prices mean lower real profits for producers. Their short-run response is to lower quantities offered for sale. Thus the positive slope of the short-run aggregate supply curve reflects the positive relationship between profits and product prices when resource prices are fixed.

Note that, like the Keynesian view of aggregate supply presented in Chapter 22, the curve in Exhibit 26.4 is relatively flat at very low levels of output. At higher levels of output, it has a relatively steep slope, like the classical supply curve in Chapter 22. The overall·shape also reflects costs and profits. For any short-run aggregate supply curve, the economy's production possibilities are fixed. At very low levels of output, many machines and factories are unused and many workers are unemployed. In such circumstances, we can predict that businesses and work-

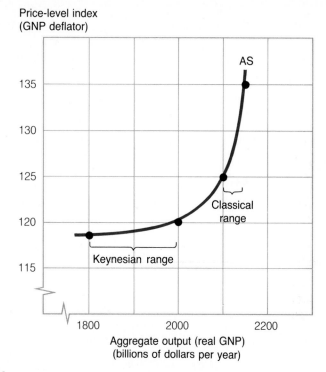

Exhibit 26.4
Shape of the Short-Run Aggregate Supply Curve
The short-run aggregate supply curve (AS) shows the relationship between output supplied and price level in the short run. At low levels of output (from $1800 to $2000 billion in this case), the AS curve indicates that changes in aggregate demand largely affect real GNP. This portion of the curve is labeled the Keynesian region because Keynes' theory suggested that in a recession, when there are substantial unemployed resources, increases in output could be obtained with relatively little or no increase in cost. At relatively high levels of output (above $2100 billion on this curve), the AS curve is quite steep. This portion of the curve is labeled the classical region because the theories of the classical economists stressed that, when the economy is near full employment, an increase in aggregate demand would largely result in higher prices. Increases in output in this region can be obtained only by employing less-efficient machinery and labor, and thus at sharply rising costs. Therefore more will be supplied only with substantial increases in prices.

ers will be eager to respond to higher demand, even if prices increase only a small amount.

On the other hand, at high levels of output most resources are employed. Thus increases in output are likely to require the use of some less efficient—and hence more expensive—resources. Businesses will demand higher prices to cover this increase in costs.

Short-Run Equilibrium

The short-run aggregate supply curve does not tell us how much real output the economy will produce or what the price level will be. But it does tell us how the economy can be expected to react in the short run to changes in aggregate

Short-run equilibrium. A position in which quantity of aggregate output demanded at the current price level equals quantity supplied; graphically, where the aggregate demand and short-run aggregate supply curves intersect.

demand. The price level and quantity of real GNP produced are jointly determined by aggregate demand and the short-run aggregate supply curve.

For example, consider Exhibit 26.5. Under the initial conditions (AD_1 and AS_1), the economy is in **short-run equilibrium**; aggregate output is $2000 billion and the price level is 120 (point a). But what if planned investment increases by $25 billion per year (perhaps because lower interest rates make purchases of capital resources more profitable)? If the multiplier is 4.0, planned aggregate expenditures (quantity of aggregate output demanded at the current price level) will increase by $100 billion, shifting the aggregate demand curve to the right (to AD_2).

Because demand has increased, the economy is no longer in equilibrium at the old price level of 120. Quantity of aggregate output demanded *at the current price level* is greater than quantity supplied. In response, producers will expand

Exhibit 26.5
Short-Run Equilibrium
The intersection of aggregate demand and the short-run aggregate supply curve determines short-run equilibrium. A change in aggregate demand (a shift in the curve from AD_1 to AD_2) will cause the economy to move along its short-run aggregate supply curve (from point a to point b). The simple multiplier indicates how much aggregate demand shifts (in this case, by a factor of 4). The real-output multiplier is smaller (a factor of 2) because the price level absorbs part of the change in demand.

The short-run aggregate supply curve shows the economy's initial response to a change in aggregate demand.

Changes in resource prices, price-level expectations, and potential GNP shift the short-run aggregate supply curve. For any short-run AS curve, these factors are held constant.

Short-run equilibrium occurs at the intersection of the aggregate demand and the short-run aggregate supply curves. Increases in aggregate demand cause the economy to move along the short-run aggregate supply curve. Both real GNP and the price level will increase.

output. But the slope of the aggregate supply curve means that costs rise as output increases causing producers to raise prices. To restore short-run equilibrium, both aggregate output and the general price level will increase. The changes that occur represent movement along the short-run aggregate supply curve from point *a* to point *b*.

This example shows why the simple multiplier we used in Chapters 22 and 23 overstates the short-run effect of spending changes on real output. In Exhibit 26.5 the $25 billion increase in investment increased aggregate demand by $100 billion. Because the short-run aggregate supply curve is positively sloped, however, the change in aggregate demand affected both real output and the price level. After the economy adjusted to equilibrium, real GNP increased by only $50 billion, a real-world multiplier effect of only 2.

This real-world multiplier effect depends on the shape of the short-run aggregate supply curve. If the economy is operating at far below its full-employment level, the short-run aggregate supply curve is, as you have seen, relatively flat. In that case a change in demand primarily affects real output. But if the economy is operating somewhere on the sharply upward sloping portion of the aggregate supply curve, an increase in demand primarily affects the price level.

We showed that in the short run, changes in aggregate demand result in movement along the short-run aggregate supply curve. An increase in aggregate demand raises both real output and the price level. A decrease in aggregate demand lowers both aggregate output and the price level. These adjustments explain how the economy reaches short-run equilibrium. But, as you have also seen, most economists expect further adjustments to take place in the long run. In order to predict the long-run adjustments that may occur, we have to compare current output to potential GNP, as indicated in the next section.

ADJUSTMENTS TO GNP GAPS

The short-run response of the economy depends on the short-run aggregate supply curve, which in turn depends on holding resource prices and price-level expectations constant. We showed earlier that after the long-run adjustments are complete the economy will produce its potential GNP. But how quickly can the economy adjust? To see how and why economists give different answers to this question, let's consider how the economy makes first a short-run, then a long-run, response to a change in aggregate demand.

Adjustments to an Expansionary Gap

What changes can we expect if aggregate demand increases? Exhibit 26.6 shows an economy initially in a long-run equilibrium position (point *a*). If aggregate demand increases (from AD_1 to AD_2), the short-run response of the economy is to move along the initial short-run aggregate supply curve (AS_1) to a new *short-run* equilibrium (point *b*). This short-run equilibrium is not likely to last, however, since actual output is greater than potential output. In Chapter 20 we introduced the concept of a GNP gap, which we defined as the difference between potential

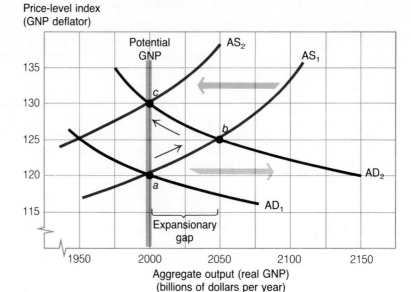

Exhibit 26.6
Long-Run Response to an Expansionary Gap
If the economy begins from a long-run equilibrium position (point *a*), an increase in aggregate demand will cause the economy to move along its short-run aggregate supply curve (to point *b*). Real GNP increases along with the price level, opening an expansionary gap (actual GNP exceeds potential GNP). This gap is possible in the short run, but excess demand pressures will cause input prices to rise, decreasing aggregate supply (shifting the curve to AS$_2$). As the economy makes a full adjustment, it will return to long-run equilibrium and produce and sell its potential GNP (point *c*).

output and the current level of GNP. In its current position (point *b*) the GNP gap is −$50 billion, calculated as

$$\begin{aligned} \text{GNP gap} &= \text{Potential GNP} - \text{Actual GNP} \\ &= \$2000 \text{ billion} - \$2050 \text{ billion} \\ &= -\$50 \text{ billion} \end{aligned}$$

We refer to a negative GNP gap—when actual GNP exceeds potential GNP— as an **expansionary gap** because it occurs as the economy attempts to expand beyond potential GNP. We can also describe this situation as one of *excess aggregate demand*. That is, the level of output demanded at the existing price level (125 in our example) exceeds the full-employment, or potential GNP, level.

Although the economy has reached short-run equilibrium, we still have to answer two important questions: Just how can the economy produce more than its potential output? What adjustments can we expect the economy to make in the long run?

Expansionary gap. When actual GNP exceeds potential GNP; a negative GNP gap. When actual unemployment is below the natural rate of unemployment.

Recall that potential GNP is not a physical maximum. An economy can produce more than this level if workers temporarily agree to work longer than normal hours or if higher nominal wages attract additional people to jobs that they would normally reject. This higher level of output may also be reached if employers are temporarily willing to take on workers they might normally refuse to hire and thus accept temporarily lower profits. Although these measures allow the economy to reach short-run equilibrium above its potential output, excess demand pressures will put upward pressure on prices.

Note that as output expands beyond potential GNP, unemployment falls below the natural rate of unemployment we associated with the frictional and structural unemployment in Chapter 20. Jobs are plentiful, but workers are relatively scarce. As businesses compete against each other for available resources, resource prices will rise. Moreover, workers will realize that the increase in the price level has reduced their real wages. Accordingly, they will revise their expectations and ask for higher nominal wages in order to restore real wages to their former level. In other words, we can expect increases in both resource prices and price-level expectations, two factors that we had assumed to be constant for any particular short-run supply curve.

As resource prices increase, short-run aggregate supply will decrease; that is, the curve will shift to the left. This pattern of upward pressure on prices—raising costs and lowering supply—will continue until there is no longer any excess demand. In Exhibit 26.6 excess demand—the expansionary gap—is gone when aggregate supply reaches the level of AS_2. The economy will thus reach long-run equilibrium at a price level of 130 (where AD_2 intersects AS_2).

This analysis indicates that the economy cannot reach a stable equilibrium position beyond potential GNP. Left to its own devices, the economy will automatically adjust to relieve excess demand pressures. Although both real GNP and the price level increase in the short run, the increase in aggregate demand affects only the price level in the long run. This result usually occurs when the economy starts from a long-run equilibrium position.

Note also that this one-time increase in aggregate demand causes only a one-time increase in the price level. There is no reason to expect such a change to cause inflation, that is, a sustained increase in the price level. However, if demand increases continually, the economy may experience a series of expansionary gaps and a series of price level increases, as A Case in Point: Expansionary Gaps indicates.

Adjustments to a Contractionary Gap

Economists basically agree that adjustments to expansionary gaps are relatively quick. In contrast, economists are sharply divided over how quickly and easily an economy adjusts to a contractionary gap. Let's first consider the adjustment process and then why some economists believe that the economy adjusts quickly, while others believe that adjustment is long and costly.

Consider, for example, the economy shown in Exhibit 26.7. Under initial conditions (AD_1 and AD_2), the economy is operating at its potential output level of $2000 billion (point a). If aggregate demand decreases to AD_2, the economy

Exhibit 26.7
Long-Run Response to a Contractionary Gap
As aggregate demand decreases (as the curve shifts from AD₁ to AD₂), the economy
moves along its short-run aggregate supply curve. Real GNP falls, along with the
price level, opening a contractionary gap (actual GNP is less than potential GNP).
This gap puts downward pressure on wages and prices. A fall in wages and other
input prices will increase aggregate supply (to AS₂) and restore long-run equilibrium.

will move along the AS_1 curve to reach short-run equilibrium at point *b*. But at
this point, potential output exceeds actual output by $100 billion. This positive
gap between potential and actual GNP is a **contractionary gap**. (Use the formula
for the GNP gap and the data in Exhibit 26.7 to demonstrate that there is a positive
gap of $100 billion.)

As output demanded falls, producers will cut back on production, laying off
or firing some of their workers. As unemployment rises, workers may be willing
to accept lower nominal wages. The surpluses in product markets and other
resource markets put downward pressure on prices. Eventually, resource costs
(including wages) and prices—which we held constant in the short run—will
begin to fall. Moreover, the downward movement in prices should cause workers
to lower their price-level expectations. Together, these changes cause aggregate
supply to increase; that is, the curve will shift to the right. The pressures of the
contractionary gap continue until the short-run aggregate supply curve reaches
AS_2 and the economy returns to long-run equilibrium at point *c*.

Contractionary gap. When potential GNP exceeds actual GNP; a
positive GNP gap. When the actual
unemployment rate is greater than
the natural rate of unemployment.

Automatic Adjustments—
Fast or Slow?

The preceding description of the economy's response to a contractionary gap basically reflects the classical viewpoint. Indeed, if wages and prices are flexible, the economy should make the adjustment to long-run equilibrium rather quickly. For classical economists, the contractionary gap was merely a short-run surplus of labor (and other resources). They believed that workers would recognize that if both nominal wages and prices fall at the same rate, they could return to work at the same real wages.

But the experience of the U.S. and British economies during the Great Depression in the 1930s suggested that the classical view was incorrect. That prolonged and deep recession suggested that the automatic adjustment mechanism operated slowly in the face of a contractionary gap—if it worked at all. Keynes concluded that wages and prices were not flexible enough to permit rapid adjustment,

A Case in Point
Expansionary Gaps: A Historic Example

Economic events during 1966–1969 provided a real-world example of adjustments to an expansionary gap. In this period, U.S. government spending increased. More was spent on social programs—President Johnson's War on Poverty—and on national defense—the Vietnam War. The increase in government expenditures was supported by an increase in the money supply. The increase in both government expenditures and the money supply caused aggregate demand to increase. As a result, the economy was pushed beyond its potential output level. The expansionary gap in 1968 is shown in the graph. From 1966 to 1969 the GNP gap averaged −$103.9 billion per year or 4.7 percent of potential GNP. As a result, the rate of inflation (as measured by the GNP deflator) more than doubled, rising from 2.7 percent in 1965 to 5.6 percent in 1969.

We noted in this chapter that a one-time increase in aggregate demand should cause only a one-time increase in the price level. As the economy returns to its potential output level, the expansionary gap is eliminated. To get inflation—a sustained upward movement in prices—requires continued excess demand pressure. But such sustained excess demand is exactly what happened in 1966–1969. Continued increases in government spending and in the money supply kept increasing aggregate demand beyond the potential output level. The result was a high rate of inflation.

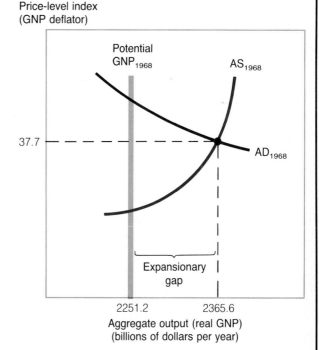

Price-level index
(GNP deflator)

perhaps because workers may believe that lower nominal wages would mean a decline in real income. This reluctance to accept lower nominal wages—a necessary condition for shifting the short-run aggregate supply curve—may cause the economy to remain in a recession for an indefinite (or prolonged) period of time.

Since Keynes, most economists have recognized that wages and prices do not respond quickly enough to prevent significant short-term reductions in output. However, many economists now reject Keynes's conclusion that the inflexibility reflects irrational behavior by workers. Some economists put the blame on inaccurate price-level expectations. Others point to contracts and other arrangements that limit short-run adjustments in wages and prices. These arguments deserve further explanation because each results in different policy recommendations.

Sluggish adjustment: Expectations theory. Workers are presumed to respond to changes in real wages. Because wage and salary offers are stated in nominal (not real) terms, however, workers must translate a nominal wage offer into an expected real wage. Suppose that workers are promised a 5 percent increase in nominal wages. If they expect the price level to rise 3 percent, they will consider this offer to represent higher real wages. If they expect prices to rise 8 percent, they will consider the offer to represent lower real wages. The response of workers to a change in nominal wages, then, depends on their price-level expectations.

But what if workers' price-level expectations are wrong? For example, what if workers are offered a 10 percent increase in nominal wages and the general price level increases by 10 percent? In real terms, wages are unchanged. Workers will certainly notice the increase in nominal wages, but may not immediately or correctly notice the increase in prices. If they believe that prices are rising more slowly than 10 percent, they will believe real wages are rising and respond by increasing the quantity of labor they supply. As a result, the economy will be able to produce more.

However, this increase in labor supplied and output will only be temporary. Eventually, workers will realize that real wages are unchanged. They will then respond by offering the initial quantity of labor, and output will fall back to the original level.

Likewise, businesses seek real profits, but their forecasts of the price level may also be incorrect. Thus they may reject nominal wage or other resource prices that actually represent constant or lower real costs to the firm. As for workers, however, we can predict that such behavior will be corrected when better information is available.

The economy should operate at the potential GNP level whenever expectations match reality. If the price level is expected to rise faster than it actually does, workers may believe that real wages are falling, and businesses may believe that real profits are falling. As a result, real output may drop below the potential GNP level. If price-level expectations are lower than actual changes, workers may view real wages as rising, and businesses may view real profits as rising. As a result, real output may increase above the potential GNP level.

Expectations theory provides an explanation for why a decrease in demand lowers real output and increases unemployment in the short run. It attributes this relationship to inaccurate perceptions about actual changes in the price level. But it predicts that the fall in output will be only temporary. As expectations adjust to reality, the short-run aggregate supply will increase, bringing the economy back to potential GNP.

Expectations theory has been used to explain the economy's behavior in 1969 and 1970. Increased government spending in 1966–1969 fueled inflation. The Fed reacted by reducing the money supply, and the economy went into a recession. However, prices and unemployment continued to rise. Milton Friedman and others argued that this behavior reflected incorrect expectations. Friedman suggested that workers and businesses believed that the inflation of the late 1960s would continue, in part because they expected government to continue to increase aggregate demand. Expecting higher price levels, workers continued to demand higher nominal wages and producers kept raising prices despite the recession.

Sluggish adjustment: Contracts theory.

Other economists, while not rejecting the importance of expectations, argue that wages are often set by contract. Union contracts may fix nominal wages for two or even three years. Some wage contracts call for indexing nominal wages to changes in the general price level, but these adjustments occur only once or twice a year. Even nonunion employees not covered by formal wage contracts often have their salaries set once a year at performance-review time. These arrangements may be viewed as informal wage contracts.

Whether wage contracts are formal or informal, changes in aggregate demand have a much greater effect on employment (and real output) than on wages and prices in the short run. Wages eventually adjust to reflect labor-market conditions, but the speed of the adjustment is slowed by the length of time that wages are fixed by contracts. Although expectations may be important, changes in expectations can affect only those contracts that are up for change.

Contracts and expectations theories compared.

Both the contracts and expectations theories are consistent with a short-run aggregate supply curve that slopes upward. However, their implications for macroeconomic adjustments and policy are quite different.

According to expectations theory, the obstacle to a return to full-employment is inaccurate expectations. Because of the publicity given to inflation rates by the news media, it is unlikely that many people can hold incorrect expectations for long. Thus advocates of expectations theory believe that the short run is only a brief period of time. And since the economy's automatic adjustment mechanism works quickly, the economy will not remain below full employment for very long. Costs to the economy—both opportunity costs of lost production and associated costs to individuals of unemployment—should be reasonably small according to expectations theory.

According to contracts theory, however, adjustment to full employment depends on the length of wage contracts. Advocates of contracts theory thus believe that the short run may be a relatively long period of time. Because the adjustment is slow, the costs to the economy—lost output and unemployment—are high. As you will see in Chapter 27, some economists use the likelihood of slow adjustment to justify macroeconomic policies to shift the aggregate demand curve.

Does the economy adjust quickly or slowly to contractionary gaps? Can past experience help us choose between the two competing theories? Since the 1950s,

RECAP

If short-run equilibrium occurs beyond potential GNP, an expansionary gap results. This excess demand pressure causes increases in input prices and/or upward adjustments in price-level expectations. As the economy automatically adjusts, aggregate supply decreases, closing the gap.

If short-run equilibrium occurs below potential GNP, a contractionary gap results. This excess supply pressure causes decreases in wages and prices and/or downward adjustments in price-level expectations. As the economy automatically adjusts, aggregate supply increases, closing the gap.

Economists agree that the economy adjusts quickly to expansionary gaps. They disagree about whether contractionary gaps are quickly and easily closed. Some attribute contractionary gaps to temporarily incorrect expectations; others attribute such gaps to contracts that limit short-run changes in resource prices.

the largest initial effects of an actual decrease in demand have been a drop in output and a rise in unemployment. Moreover, the price level stubbornly resists an actual decline. (The GNP deflator last fell in 1949.) Thus history would seem to support those who believe that the adjustment process is slow.

But proponents of expectations theory believe that at least some of this price level behavior reflects private-sector expectations that government policies will increase demand and push prices up. This expectation prevents the downward adjustment in aggregate supply necessary to automatically restore full employment. These economists also point to the rapid fall in inflation rates in 1981–1982, when the Fed's monetary policies were clearly aimed at slowing price increases. Who, then, is right? The contradictory evidence and the difficulty of measuring expectations may make agreement impossible.

A Case in Point
Aggregate Demand and Supply in Action

We can use aggregate demand and supply to answer some of the real-world questions raised in the introduction to this chapter. Why did real output grow in the mid-1960s without causing much inflation? Why did both real output and the rate of inflation fall in the early 1980s?

The late 1950s and early 1960s were a period of slow and erratic growth, with low rates of inflation. With a few exceptions, the annual change in the Consumer Price Index was less than 2 percent. But the economy appeared to be operating below its potential output level.

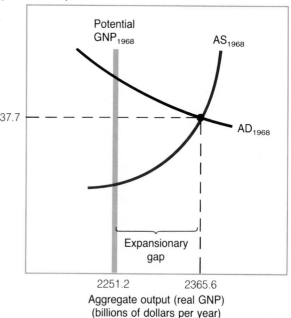

(a) The economy in 1962

Price-level index (GNP deflator)

Potential GNP$_{1962}$

AS$_{1962}$

31.9

AD$_{1962}$

Contractionary gap

1799.4   1825.6

Aggregate output (real GNP) (billions of dollars per year)

(b) The economy in 1968

Price-level index (GNP deflator)

Potential GNP$_{1968}$

AS$_{1968}$

37.7

AD$_{1968}$

Expansionary gap

2251.2   2365.6

Aggregate output (real GNP) (billions of dollars per year)

Exhibit 26C.1
The 1964 Tax Cut

Supply Shocks: Double Whammy

Thus far we have focused on how the economy adjusts to changes in aggregate demand. In some cases, however, it must also adjust to changes in aggregate supply. As A Case in Point: Aggregate Demand and Supply in Action indicates, economies have experienced **supply shocks**, or sudden and sharp increases in resource prices. Exhibit 26.8 shows how a supply shock decreases aggregate supply, causing real GNP to fall and the price level to rise. A supply shock also opens a contractionary gap, as real GNP falls below the potential GNP level.

Supply shocks. Sharp declines in aggregate supply caused by a decrease in the supply of key resources; may cause a decline in potential output.

The long-run effect of a supply shock depends in part on the policy response. As you will see in Chapter 27, monetary and fiscal policies can be used to increase demand, or the economy can be allowed to adjust on its own. If higher prices are

---

The economy's position in 1962 is shown in Exhibit 26C.1(a). Between 1958 and 1962 the economy experienced a contractionary GNP gap averaging $45.7 billion or 2.6 percent of potential GNP. The remedy suggested by President Kennedy's Keynesian advisors was a tax cut, which was finally passed in 1964.

A tax cut tends to raise aggregate demand, resulting in movement along the short-run aggregate supply curve. The 1964 tax cut closed the contractionary gap that had existed and caused real GNP to grow at an average rate of 4.5 percent between 1964 and 1967. As the economy moved along the short-run aggregate supply curve, the price level also rose, causing the rate of inflation to increase from 1.9 percent in 1965 to 3.4 percent in 1966. Unfortunately, as Exhibit 26C.1(b) shows, the economy was stimulated beyond the point of potential output. As the graph indicates, this can (and did) cause excess aggregate demand, resulting in the rapid inflation of the late 1960s.

The U.S. economy was rocked again in 1979 by a second oil-induced supply shock, this time caused by the revolution in Iran that disrupted oil supplies and doubled oil prices. Inflation accelerated into double digits, averaging 13.3 percent in 1979 and 12.4 percent in 1980. Opinion polls indicated that the general population believed inflation to be the country's major economic problem.

In an effort to bring down inflation, the Fed reduced the growth of the money supply. Exhibit 26C.2 shows the effects of this policy change on the economy's position in 1982. Decreased aggregate demand opened up a sizable contractionary gap. Unemployment rose significantly, exceeding 10 percent for several months.

But the policy change also put significant downward pressure on wages and prices. As a result, inflation, which had averaged nearly 9 percent in 1981, fell below 4 percent in 1982. The policy was clearly successful in eliminating inflationary pressures, although at a cost of high unemployment and lower output for a period of time.

Exhibit 26C.2
Fed Policies and the Economy in 1982

Price-level index
(GNP deflator)

Exhibit 26.8
Supply Shock—A Decrease in Aggregate Supply
A sharp increase in input prices causes a supply
shock—a decrease in aggregate supply (a shift in the
curve from AS_1 to AS_2). As a result, real output falls and
the price level rises. The supply shock also opens a
contractionary gap. The economy will have to adjust by
increasing aggregate supply (back to AS_1) unless aggregate demand is increased.

paid to foreign owners for resources (as they were in the 1970s), real wages and
profits may have to fall before aggregate supply can increase. Whatever policy is
followed, the effects of a supply shock will be unpleasant.

The U.S. economy was subjected to supply shocks in 1973–1975. In 1973–
1974 the price of imported oil quadrupled as a result of OPEC action. The result
was a recession that lasted from November 1973 until March 1975. In many respects
it was the worst recession since the Great Depression of the 1930s. Real output
fell by almost 5 percent, and unemployment climbed to nearly 9 percent. In early
1975, real output was $140 billion below potential output. At the same time, the
price level increased by nearly 9 percent in 1973 and over 12 percent in 1974.
(As we noted in Chapter 20, this double dose of bad news is termed *stagflation*.)

CONCLUSION

In this chapter we considered how the macroeconomy reaches equilibrium in the
face of changing aggregate demand and supply. In doing so, we took special note
of the difficulty the economy may have in adjusting to a contractionary gap. We
know that monetary and fiscal policies can increase aggregate demand and bring
about faster adjustment to long-run equilibrium. But should government try to
speed the adjustment process? Or is the short run so short that intervention is
unnecessary? In the next part of this textbook, we consider the issues surrounding
macroeconomic policy. Only then can you understand why economists disagree
strongly over the desirability of government intervention.

SUMMARY

1. In this chapter we explored aggregate demand and supply and how the macroeconomy adjusts to equilibrium in both the short run and the long run.

2. For any aggregate expenditures (AE) curve we hold the price level constant. Each point of equilibrium between an AE curve and the 45° line is a single point on the aggregate demand (AD) curve, since such points represent quantity demanded at some particular price level. A change in the price level shifts the AE curve and results in movement along the AD curve.

3. Three factors explain why quantity of aggregate output demanded falls when the price level rises. Higher prices lower the real value of money and monetary assets held by the household sector, causing wealth and thus consumption to fall. Higher prices also increase nominal GNP and thus transactions demand for money and interest rates, lowering investment and interest-sensitive consumption. And higher prices in the United States make foreign goods more attractive, which decreases exports and increases imports.

4. For any aggregate demand curve we hold monetary and fiscal policies, expectations, and income and price levels in foreign countries constant. A change in any of these factors will increase or decrease aggregate demand and shift the AD curve.

5. An initial change in spending has a multiplier effect that determines how much more or less aggregate output will be demanded at the current price level, that is, how much the aggregate demand curve will shift.

6. The long-run aggregate supply curve is a vertical line at the economy's potential GNP level. Given sufficient time to adjust, the economy will reach a long-run equilibrium at potential GNP. Potential GNP changes when technology or resource supplies change.

7. The short-run aggregate supply curve shows how the economy will initially respond to a change in aggregate demand. The curve will shift if resource prices, price-level expectations, or potential GNP change.

8. Short-run equilibrium occurs at the intersection of the aggregate demand and short-run aggregate supply curves. An increase in aggregate demand causes movement along the short-run aggregate supply curve. Both real GNP and the price level will rise. The simple multiplier predicts how much aggregate demand increases as a result of an increase in planned spending. The real-world multiplier effect—the final change in real output—will be less because price increases absorb a part of the demand impact.

9. If short-run equilibrium occurs at the economy's potential GNP level, the economy is also in long-run equilibrium. If short-run equilibrium occurs beyond potential GNP, an expansionary gap results. This gap will be closed by excess demand pressures that raise resource prices and/or price-level expectations and decrease aggregate supply. If short-run equilibrium occurs below potential GNP, a contractionary gap results. This gap will be automatically closed by excess supply pressures that lower wages and prices and raise aggregate supply, returning the economy to long-run equilibrium.

10. Economists generally agree that the economy adjusts quickly and automatically to close an expansionary gap. But they disagree about how quickly the economy's automatic adjustments will close a contractionary gap. Proponents of a speedy reaction believe that the gap occurs because households and businesses incorrectly forecast price-level changes for a brief time. Proponents of a slow reaction argue that many resource prices are fixed by contracts for longer periods.

11. Sharp increases in resource prices—such as the oil-price increases in the 1970s—result in supply shocks. As aggregate supply decreases, real GNP falls and the price level rises. How the economy adjusts depends in part on government economic policies.

KEY TERMS

Long-run equilibrium, 669
Short-run equilibrium, 674
Expansionary gap, 676
Contractionary gap, 678
Supply shocks, 683

QUESTIONS FOR REVIEW AND DISCUSSION

1. Explain the effect that each of the following changes will have on aggregate demand, aggregate supply, the price level, and equilibrium GNP level in the short run. If the effect is uncertain, state why. Draw a graph showing the changes in aggregate demand and/or aggregate supply that illustrate your answer.
   a) The money supply increases.
   b) Workers demand higher real wages.
   c) Households and businesses expect the economy to expand in the near future.
   d) Real interest rates increase.
   e) The real cost of resources increases.
   f) An increase in the price level is expected for the future.
   g) Foreign incomes increase.

2. Explain how, if at all, potential GNP is affected by the following:
   a) An improvement in production technology.
   b) A significant decrease in resource supplies.

c) An increase in the number of skilled workers.

d) An increase in the general price level.

3. What change in aggregate demand and/or aggregate supply would explain each of the following:
   a) Aggregate output increases.
   b) The general price level falls.
   c) Real GNP increases and the price level falls.
   d) Both real GNP and the price level increase.

4. Use the following graph to help you answer the questions in (a)–(e).

a) What is the current equilibrium GNP and general price level?

b) Is this economy in long-run equilibrium? How do you know?

c) Indicate on the graph the existing GNP gap. Is this a contractionary or an expansionary gap? Is this a positive or a negative GNP gap?

d) On the graph, draw the changes that will occur as the economy's automatic adjustment mechanism operates. Describe the changes, that is, what is happening in the labor and product markets.

e) Suppose that instead of relying on the automatic adjustment mechanism, the Fed takes action to eliminate the gap. Would the Fed increase or decrease the money supply? What specific actions might the Fed take to accomplish this change?

5. Explain whether each of the following statements is true, false, or debatable.
   a) An increase in the price level decreases planned spending. Therefore aggregate demand will fall.

b) If aggregate demand doesn't rise as fast as potential output, the economy can't maintain full employment unless the price level falls.

c) Starting from a position of long-run equilibrium, an increase in aggregate demand will be followed by a decrease in short-run aggregate supply as the economy adjusts to long-run equilibrium.

d) Changes in aggregate demand affect the price level less in the short run than in the long run.

6. The following table shows aggregate supply and demand both before and after a change in demand.

General price level	Aggregate supply	Aggregate demand	
		AD_1	AD_2
80	800	1200	1400
90	1000	1000	1200
100	1100	900	1100
110	1150	800	1000

a) Did aggregate demand increase or decrease? How do you know?

b) What is the equilibrium level of output under both the original and new conditions?

c) If potential GNP is $1000, will there be a contractionary or expansionary gap under the new aggregate demand conditions? Of what size? What do you predict about the economy's future adjustment to long-run equilibrium?

d) If potential GNP is $1200, will there be a contractionary or expansionary gap under the new aggregate demand conditions? Of what size? What do you predict about the economy's future adjustment? How, if at all, does your prediction depend on what you assume about the flexibility of wages and prices?

7. Explain how a contractionary gap can be created by a decrease in aggregate demand or an increase in potential output. (Draw two graphs: one depicting a decrease in aggregate demand, the other showing an increase in potential output.) Explain how a contractionary gap can be closed by either an increase in aggregate demand or an increase in aggregate supply. Why might economists who stress the contracts theory recommend an increase in aggregate demand in response to a contractionary gap?

8. For each of the following situations, start by drawing aggregate demand and aggregate supply curves for an economy in equilibrium. Then add curves as needed to reflect the following conditions:
   a) The economy experiences an increase in real output, but the price level falls (short-run analysis only).
   b) The economy experiences an increase in both the price level and real output (short-run analysis only).
   c) The economy experiences a decline in output and the price level (short-run analysis only).

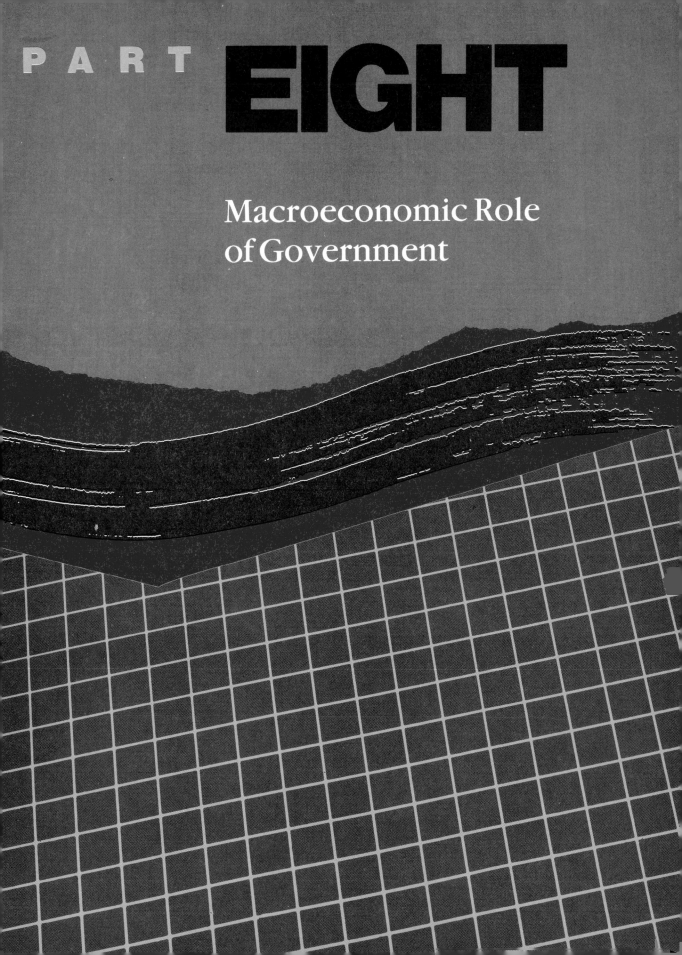

PART EIGHT

Macroeconomic Role of Government

CHAPTER 27

Macroeconomic Policy: Theory and Practice

QUESTIONS TO CONSIDER

☐ How do macroeconomic government policies affect the federal budget and government's interaction with the private sector?

☐ What types of fiscal and monetary policies might be used to close GNP gaps and what are the alternatives?

☐ How do the effects of automatic stabilizers, crowding out, and rational expectations limit discretionary fiscal policy?

☐ Why do economists disagree about whether the government should take an active role in counteracting business-cycle fluctuations?

☐ Is the growing national debt a macroeconomic problem and, if so, what can be done about it?

In Chapter 26 we showed how the automatic adjustment mechanism eventually stabilizes prices and returns an economy to equilibrium at its potential or full-employment GNP. But we also noted that the U.S. economy has suffered through periods of recession and inflation. Could government actions have avoided some of these problems? Or were they a cause? What policies should government pursue in the future in order to obtain what the Employment Act of 1946 called "maximum employment, production, and purchasing power"?

In this chapter, we consider issues surrounding the use of macroeconomic policies to counteract the business cycle. We first consider the underlying economic principles, that is, the theory behind macroeconomic policies. How does a government budget deficit affect the economy? How does the economy's performance affect the federal government's budget? What can the Fed do to stabilize the economy?

After considering the theory of macroeconomic policy, we can turn to practical questions and problems facing policy makers and the subject of economic policy debates. *Can* government affect macroeconomic conditions? *Should* it try to? These are important and controversial questions. In fact, they are the very questions that led to the development of macroeconomics. Keynes got economists and politicians interested in the notion that government could and should play an active role in managing the macroeconomy. Macroeconomists since then have been busy either defending or attacking his assertion.

GOVERNMENT AND MACROECONOMIC POLICY

The public sector—government at the local, state, and federal levels—is very much involved in the macroeconomy. In 1986, total government expenditures in the United States were almost $1.5 trillion dollars. At the same time, government receipts—taxes and other fees—totaled $1.34 trillion. Some 20 percent of total output in the United States was purchased by government. One-fifth of all working individuals were employed by government. Governments establish laws and regulations with far-reaching effects on economic decisions of households, banks and other businesses, and the foreign sector. Recall that an agency of the federal government—the Federal Reserve System (the Fed)—has the power to increase or decrease the money supply, which has important effects on the economy.

Government and the Circular Flow

Exhibit 27.1 shows an overview of the macroeconomic roles of government. The flows at the bottom show the effects of government interactions in financial markets. These include the sale of government bonds to finance a budget deficit as well as monetary policies affecting the supply of money. The flows at the top and the summary in the box at the right show the effects of government's *fiscal policies,* that is, its taxing and spending activities. Government purchases are, of course, a component of and directly affect aggregate demand. Transfer payments and taxes directly affect income in the private sector and, consequently, consumption and investment. Interest payments on the national debt are another source of income for the private sector. Purchases, taxes, and transfer payments are elements of government's current fiscal policies. But interest payments reflect the effects of past policies, as you will see.

Government Budget Deficits and Surpluses

The federal government's budget summarizes the receipts and expenditures resulting from its fiscal policies. We are particularly interested in the **budget balance**, that is, the difference between receipts (taxes and fees) and expenditures (purchases, transfers, and interest paid), or

$$\text{Budget balance} = \text{Receipts} - \text{Expenditures}$$
$$= \text{Taxes} - (\text{Purchases} + \text{Transfers} + \text{Interest})$$

If the government's budget balance is positive (receipts exceed expenditures) government has a **budget surplus**. If the balance is negative (expenditures exceed receipts) government has a **budget deficit**. Large federal budget deficits have been common in recent years. As shown in Exhibit 27.1, the government sector—including state, local, and federal governments—had a combined budget deficit of $143.1 billion in 1986. The federal government ran a deficit of $204 billion, but state and local governments collectively had a $61 billion surplus. At the end of 1986, the public held approximately $1750 billion of federal government debt representing an average of $7250 per person in the United States.

Methods of financing government spending. The government—like individuals or households—cannot spend more money than it receives. But if you have a personal deficit (spend more than your current income), you may convince someone to lend you money. In contrast, the government can raise money by taxing or by printing more money, as well as by borrowing.

Local, state, and federal governments all have the power to impose and collect taxes. In fact, taxes and other fees provide over 90 percent of the money that government spends. However, in the United States, only the federal government

Budget balance. The difference between government receipts (taxes and fees) and expenditures (purchases, transfers, and interest payments on national debt).

Budget surplus. A positive budget balance, when receipts exceed expenditures.

Budget deficit. A negative budget balance, when expenditures exceed receipts.

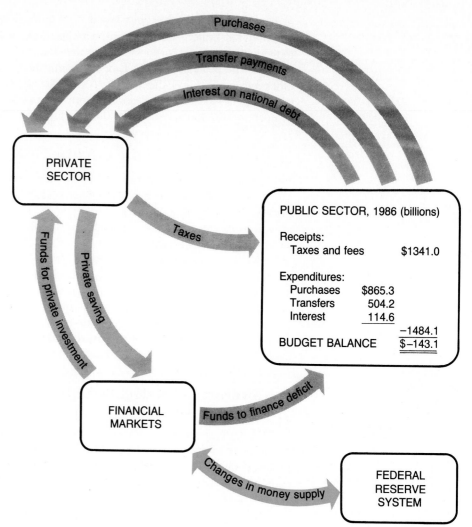

Exhibit 27.1
Government's Impact on the Macroeconomy
The government has a direct impact on the private sector through its purchases, transfer payments, taxes, and interest payments on the national debt. Purchases add directly to aggregate demand. Taxes, transfer payments, and interest payments directly affect income and indirectly affect aggregate demand. These flows represent the government's fiscal policies.

Source: Economic Report of the President, 1987, Table B-77.

has an option of "printing" its way out of a deficit. That is, it can mint coins and print paper money. As we discussed in Chapter 24, the Federal Reserve System has control over *monetary policy* in the United States. The Fed determines how much government money (coins and paper money) circulates. It also influences the quantity of bank money (checking deposits). By changing the money supply the Fed can affect aggregate demand.

Although the Fed is a government agency, it operates independently. Congress and the president determine fiscal policy, but the Fed determines monetary policy. This separation of powers is important: In the United States, that part of government responsible for spending cannot simply print money to spend. Congress and the president can (and have) put pressure on the Fed to "monetize" a deficit by purchasing some of the government's debt. As we explained in Chapter 24,

National debt. The total amount owed by the federal government; the cumulative effect of past budget deficits and surpluses.

when the Fed buys government securities it sets in motion a deposit expansion process that increases the money supply. Fiscal and monetary powers are not separate in all other countries, however. Where government directly controls the "printing press" it can easily create government money. The result is often a continual rapid increase in the money supply and, consequently, inflation.

But if the Fed is unwilling to lend enough to cover the deficit, the government must enter the financial market and borrow from U.S. households or businesses. (The federal government increasingly has also borrowed from the foreign sector.) Borrowing is the only alternative to taxing for state and local governments. And these governments are often strictly limited by state law in their ability to spend more than they receive in taxes and other receipts. Typically, borrowing is limited to funding capital expenditures—to finance a new school building, for example—by issuing bonds.

Additional borrowing to finance a federal government deficit adds to the **national debt**, that is, the total amount owed by the government. The federal debt ceiling is set—and, in recent years, raised—by Congress each year. Government borrowing often reduces the amount of saving available to finance private-sector spending. (A budget surplus has the opposite effect: reducing the national debt and increasing the funds available for private investment.)

Do not confuse the terms deficit and debt. They are connected, but different. A deficit refers to the excess of expenditures over receipts during one budget (fiscal) year. The national debt is the total amount owed by the federal government as of a particular date. A deficit financed by borrowing increases the national debt. The national debt reflects the cumulative effect of all past deficits and surpluses.

Historically, the national debt increased primarily during wartime and recessions. During World War II, the national debt increased from $43 billion in 1940 to $235 billion in 1945. During the Great Depression, the national debt increased from $17 billion in 1929 to $48 billion in 1939. However, the federal government has run huge budget deficits in the 1980s, only a small part of which can be attributed to the recession of 1982. As a result, the national debt increased by over 250 percent from fiscal year 1980 to fiscal year 1987. The size of the budget deficits has created special problems, as you will see later in this chapter.

Each method of financing government expenditures has, to some extent, a negative effect on the economy. Taxes reduce private spending directly. Increases in the money supply may lower the purchasing power of money and monetary assets held by households. Borrowing raises interest rates and indirectly reduces private spending. On the other hand, government spending also offers benefits to society. To identify the best level of spending and the best means of financing, these benefits and costs must be considered.

RECAP

The federal government's budget summarizes its fiscal policies. Taxes and fees are receipts; expenditures include purchases of final goods, transfers, and interest paid on the national debt.

The budget balance is the difference between receipts and expenditures. A positive balance is a budget surplus; a negative balance is a budget deficit.

Governments have three ways to raise money to spend: taxes, borrowing, and printing new money. Because the Fed has independent responsibility for the money supply, Congress, the president, and state and local governments can spend only by taxing and borrowing.

Although government spending may be beneficial, each method of financing government spending has a negative effect on the economy. Taxes directly reduce private spending; borrowing raises interest rates and indirectly reduces private spending; increases in the money supply may lower the purchasing power of money and monetary assets held by households.

Government Stabilization Policies

With this background on the federal government's budget, we can now consider how government policies—both fiscal and monetary—affect the budget and the economy as a whole. Government macroeconomic policies can influence the economy in both the short run and the long run. The long-run macroeconomic goal of economic growth is the topic of Chapter 30. In this chapter we focus mostly on the short-run goals of price stability and full employment. To achieve these goals, the economy must avoid contractionary and expansionary GNP gaps.

Recall that the macroeconomy is subject to sudden changes or shocks. A sudden, large increase in investment or in the money supply will increase aggregate demand, creating a demand shock. The increase in aggregate demand may open an expansionary gap (actual GNP rises above potential GNP). Although this results in a temporary increase in real GNP and a fall in unemployment, the expansionary gap puts upward pressure on prices. A sudden decrease in aggregate supply (a supply shock) or in aggregate demand will open a contractionary gap (actual GNP falls below potential GNP) and cause unemployment to increase.

When either a contractionary or an expansionary gap opens, policy makers have two basic options. First, they can *do nothing* and allow the economy's automatic adjustment mechanism to operate; eventually, the economy will return to full employment. Second, government can *enact fiscal or monetary policies* that shift aggregate demand and reduce or eliminate the gaps.

Exhibit 27.2
Policy Responses to a Contractionary Gap
The initial equilibrium (point *a*) shows the economy in a contractionary gap; actual GNP ($1900 billion) is $100 billion below potential GNP. If no action is taken, automatic adjustment mechanisms decrease wages and prices and ultimately increase aggregate supply (to AS_2). If government uses expansionary fiscal and/or monetary policies, aggregate demand will increase (to AD_2). Either response will eventually restore the economy to long-run equilibrium, producing and selling at its potential GNP. Automatic adjustments will result in lower prices (to point *b*) but may take considerable time and result in higher unemployment. Expansionary policies produce rapid adjustments but put upward pressure on prices (point *c*).

(a) Rely on automatic adjustment

(b) Use expansionary policies

Expansionary policies. Changes in fiscal and/or monetary policies that increase aggregate demand. Lower taxes and higher spending are expansionary fiscal policies; reducing the required reserve ratio and buying government securities are expansionary monetary policies.

Eliminating contractionary gaps with expansionary policies. Exhibit 27.2 shows an economy initially facing a contractionary gap. Actual GNP ($1900 billion) is $100 billion less than potential GNP, and the actual unemployment rate is more than the natural rate. If the government did nothing, relying on the automatic adjustment mechanism, the contractionary gap would put downward pressure on wages and prices. This pressure would eventually cause an increase in aggregate supply (to AS_2), as shown in Exhibit 27.2(a).

Some economists argue that automatic adjustments take too long. They suggest that government use **expansionary policies** to increase aggregate demand (to AD_2 in Exhibit 27.2b). If Congress and the president agree to increase purchases or lower taxes to stimulate private-sector spending, they are using expansionary *fiscal* policies. If the Fed buys government securities in the open market or lowers the required reserve ratio to increase the money supply and stimulate private-sector spending, it is using expansionary *monetary* policies. As illustrated in A Case in Point: Closing a Contractionary Gap, an expansionary policy, such as a tax cut, can increase aggregate demand enough to close a contractionary gap and restore full employment. Although expansionary policy may enable the economy to return to full employment more quickly, the price level will rise as well.

A Case in Point
Closing a Contractionary Gap:
The 1964 Tax Cut

One of the factors that helped elect John F. Kennedy to the presidency in 1960 was a general dissatisfaction with economic conditions. In particular, two recessions and relatively slow economic growth had occurred during the preceding four years (1956–1960). At the time, Keynesian economists dominated economic thought. Kennedy's advisors were no exception. They argued that aggregate demand was generally inadequate to maintain full employment. In other words, they believed that the economy was facing a contractionary gap. Because they assumed that wages and prices would fall too slowly to allow a return to full employment, they recommended that government enact expansionary fiscal policies to stimulate aggregate demand.[*]

As a first step in developing such a fiscal policy, the economists required two basic measures: (1) an estimate of the size of the contractionary gap; and (2) an estimate of the multiplier effect. They attacked the first problem by attempting to discover what full-employment output would be. Based on their studies, they concluded that full employment could be roughly measured as the output associated with a 4 percent unemployment rate. Translating this figure into the level of output that could be produced with full employment, they arrived at a contractionary gap of $30 billion.

In addition, they estimated the multiplier effect to be 2 for the change in taxes. (Although the multiplier they used is not the simple multiplier we discussed in Chapter 23, it is based on the same principles.) Putting these two estimates together, they recommended a tax cut of $15 billion to close the contractionary gap. That is,

Change in GNP = Change in taxes × Multiplier

$30 billion = Change in taxes × 2.0

$15 billion = Change in taxes

President Johnson and Congress accepted the argument, enacting the 1964 tax cut. Initially, the tax cut met its goals: The contractionary gap closed and unemployment fell. However, over the next several years, the stimulus of the tax cut—coupled with increases in spending for the Vietnam War and for President Johnson's War on Poverty—opened an expansionary gap.

[*] For more details about the 1964 tax cut, see Charles McClure, Jr., "Fiscal Failure: Lessons of the Sixties" in *Economic Policy and Inflation in the Sixties*. Washington, D.C.: American Enterprise Institute, 1972. McClure is critical of the tax cut but explains the thinking of the Keynesian advisors who recommended this fiscal policy.

(a) Rely on automatic adjustment

(b) Use contractionary policies

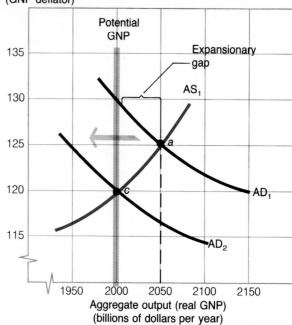

Exhibit 27.3
Policy Responses to an Expansionary Gap
The initial equilibrium (point *a*) shows the economy in an expansionary gap; actual GNP ($2050 billion) is $50 billion above potential GNP. If the government takes no action, automatic adjustment mechanisms increase wages and prices and ultimately decrease aggregate supply (to AS$_2$). If the government uses contractionary fiscal and/or monetary policies, aggregate demand will decrease (to AD$_2$). Either response will eventually restore the economy to long-run equilibrium, producing and selling at its potential GNP. Automatic adjustments result in higher prices (point *b*). Contractionary policies reduce the upward pressure on prices (point *c*).

Eliminating expansionary gaps with contractionary policies. Similarly, the government has two policy options when an increase in aggregate demand opens an expansionary gap, as shown in Exhibit 27.3. The initial short-run equilibrium (where AD$_1$ intersects AS$_1$) is $50 billion above potential GNP, indicating that actual unemployment is less than the natural rate. If government takes no action, as illustrated in Exhibit 27.3(a), automatic adjustments will eventually decrease aggregate supply (to AS$_2$) as wages and prices adjust upward.

On the other hand, government may use **contractionary policies**, as illustrated in Exhibit 27.3(b). If Congress and the president increase taxes or decrease government purchases to lower aggregate demand, they are using contractionary *fiscal* policies. If the Fed sells securities or raises the required reserve ratio (thereby lowering bank reserves, the money supply, and hence aggregate demand), it is using contractionary *monetary* policies. Contractionary policies will also

Contractionary policies.
Changes in fiscal and/or monetary policies that decrease aggregate demand. Higher taxes and lower spending are contractionary fiscal policies; raising the required reserve ratio and selling government securities are contractionary monetary policies.

The government has two options when the economy is not in long-run equilibrium: do nothing and rely on the automatic adjustment mechanism, or take discretionary action using fiscal or monetary policies to change aggregate demand and close the GNP gap.

In response to a contractionary gap, automatic adjustments lower wages and prices and increase aggregate supply.

Expansionary fiscal policies (increased spending or lower tax rates) or expansionary monetary policies (lower reserve requirements or buying government securities) increase aggregate demand. Expansionary policies may cause change more quickly than automatic adjustment, but they raise the price level.

In response to an expansionary gap, automatic adjustments increase wages and prices and decrease aggregate supply.

Contractionary fiscal policies (higher taxes or lower spending) or contractionary monetary policies (higher reserve requirements or selling government securities) decrease aggregate demand. Contractionary policies lower the price level.

Discretionary policies. Deliberate changes in monetary and/or fiscal policies to counteract cyclical changes in economic activity, that is, to reduce or eliminate expansionary and contractionary gaps. Also called countercyclical policies.

restore the economy to its potential output, but at a lower price level than the do-nothing policy.

MACROECONOMIC POLICY: SOME COMPLICATIONS

The belief that government can take effective action to reduce the swings in the business cycle dates from the Great Depression. Before then, most economists believed that the economy's automatic adjustment mechanism was sufficient to restore full employment. But the experience of the Great Depression shook the faith of many economists and politicians in the automatic adjustment process. Keynes and his followers argued that government could and should take action in a deep recession to boost aggregate demand and help the economy recover to full employment. In fact, during the 1960s many economists believed that government policies could be changed easily and quickly to counterbalance virtually any shift in aggregate demand.

Today few economists believe that it is desirable or even possible for government to react to every fluctuation in the economy. But economists continue to debate whether government should rely exclusively on the automatic adjustments or, under some circumstances, take discretionary policy actions. The following questions are important to this debate: To what extent will changes in actual GNP *automatically* result in stabilizing changes in the federal government's budget? To what extent will expansionary fiscal policy reduce private-sector spending? And to what extent will households and businesses take rational actions that offset the effects of anticipated policies? These complications, discussed in this section, affect the benefits and costs of discretionary policy actions.

Budget Deficits and the Business Cycle

An increase in the budget deficit results from greater expenditures (purchases, transfers, and interest payments) and/or lower receipts (taxes and fees). Either change is expansionary, but an increase in the deficit can occur for two different reasons.

Discretionary fiscal policies and budget deficits.   First, the deficit will increase if Congress and the president decide to increase government spending or lower tax rates. Because these budget changes require deliberate decisions, economists refer to them as **discretionary policies**. Discretionary fiscal policies that are expansionary will increase aggregate demand and the size of the government's budget deficit (or lower its budget surplus) *at the existing level of GNP*.

Contractionary policies can also be discretionary, as, for example, a decision by government to cut spending or increase tax rates. Discretionary fiscal policies that are contractionary tend to reduce a budget deficit at the existing level of GNP. To check your understanding, refer to the budget equation at the beginning of this chapter. Demonstrate how expansionary fiscal policies would increase (and contractionary policies reduce) a budget deficit.

Automatic stabilizers. Taxes and expenditures that automatically change when economic activity changes. Stabilizers cause a decrease in the actual budget balance when GNP falls and an increase when GNP rises. These changes reduce cyclical changes in aggregate demand. Important stabilizers are income taxes, unemployment compensation, and welfare.

Automatic stabilizers and budget deficits. But discretionary fiscal policies are only one cause of a change in the deficit. The deficit will also increase if the level of GNP falls, because lower GNP means lower income and higher unemployment. Thus a drop in GNP automatically lowers tax receipts and increases government transfer payments. Because income taxes, unemployment compensation, welfare, and other government revenue and transfer programs respond spontaneously *to a change in GNP*, economists refer to them as **automatic stabilizers**. That is, these programs automatically cause changes in aggregate demand that offset contractionary and/or expansionary gaps. Do not confuse automatic stabilizers with the automatic adjustment mechanism. The automatic adjustment mechanism works in a private-sector economy. Automatic stabilizers are aspects of government policy.

To see the effect of automatic stabilizers, let's suppose that aggregate demand falls and the economy slips into a recession. Unemployment will rise, and GNP and national income will fall. Because federal government revenues are largely dependent on income taxes (both individual and business), the decline in income will lower tax receipts even if tax rates remain constant. Since 1960, government tax receipts have been approximately 20 percent of GNP. If this relationship was constant, tax receipts would fall from $440 billion to $400 billion as GNP falls from $2200 billion to $2000 billion.

At the same time—because unemployment is increasing—government transfer payments for unemployment compensation and welfare will rise. This increase in transfer payments happens even if the policies that determine eligibility and the level of individual benefits remain constant. Both the decline in tax receipts and the increase in transfer payments will increase a budget deficit. But these automatic changes in the budget are also expansionary. Thus they offset to some extent the decline in private-sector income, helping to lessen the decrease in aggregate demand.

Automatic stabilizers also help close an expansionary gap caused by an increase in aggregate demand. Rising income and falling unemployment automatically increase tax receipts and lower transfer payments. These automatic changes in the budget will somewhat offset the rise in private-sector income, limiting the increase in aggregate demand and reducing excess demand pressures.

Discretionary policies and automatic stabilizers compared. The distinction between automatic and discretionary changes in the government's fiscal policies is important. An increase in the federal budget deficit may result from either a change in tax or spending policies or from a decrease in GNP unrelated to changes in fiscal policy. But the meaning of and appropriate response to the deficit are quite different.

Suppose, for example, that aggregate demand drops, reducing output and employment. Automatic stabilizers will increase the budget deficit. If Congress responds with contractionary policies—raising taxes or lowering spending—aggregate demand will decrease. As a result, the recession will worsen, increasing the deficit. A similar failure to recognize the distinction between discretionary policies and automatic stabilizers caused a serious policy mistake in 1932, as A Case in Point: Response to a Budget Deficit illustrates.

Full-employment budget. Government receipts and expenditures that would occur under existing fiscal policies if the economy were producing at its potential GNP level. Changes in the full-employment budget reflect discretionary changes in fiscal policies.

Full-employment budget and fiscal policies.   To distinguish discretionary fiscal policy changes from the operation of automatic stabilizers, economists use the concept of a **full-employment budget**. This budget is an estimate of what government expenditures and receipts would be *under existing tax and spending laws if the economy were producing at its potential GNP level*. The full-employment budget gets its name from the relationship of potential GNP to full employment (the natural rate of unemployment). Because a full-employment budget eliminates the effects of cyclical changes in GNP—movement above and below potential GNP—it is sometimes called a *cyclically adjusted* budget. (Like potential GNP, the concept of a full-employment budget is widely accepted, although there is considerable debate over how to measure it.)

Expansionary fiscal policies will worsen the full-employment budget balance (a deficit will increase or a surplus will decrease). Contractionary fiscal policies will improve the full-employment budget balance (a deficit will decrease or a surplus will increase). On the other hand, because the full-employment budget

A Case in Point
Response to a Budget Deficit:
The 1932 Budget Changes

In 1930 the federal government's budget was nearly in balance. In 1931, however, government expenditures were twice the size of tax receipts, leaving a budget deficit of $2.1 billion. In today's world of $200 billion deficits, $2.1 billion may sound like a rather small amount. However, that deficit was 2.8 percent of nominal GNP in 1931 and therefore was equivalent to a $112 billion deficit in 1985.*

President Herbert Hoover and his economic advisors—like most classical economists—viewed the deficit as poor fiscal management and were determined to eliminate it. Hoover pushed for and Congress accepted an increase in taxes and a decrease in government expenditures in 1932. But Hoover and his advisors did not realize that the deficit was caused largely by the recession and consequent fall in income tax receipts.

Hoover's choice of a contractionary fiscal policy helped to turn the recession into the Great Depression. The deficit fell only to $1.4 billion because tax receipts decreased as GNP fell. Personal tax receipts in 1932 were only one-half those in 1931. In fact, if transfer payments had not fallen (unemployment compensation and other automatic stabilizing expenditure programs

did not exist at that time), the deficit would have been almost identical in 1931 and 1932.

By November 1932, U.S. citizens had begun to blame Hoover for their economic woes and voted him out of office in favor of Franklin Delano Roosevelt, who promised action. Interestingly, Roosevelt agreed with Hoover's fiscal policy. In fact, during the 1932 campaign Roosevelt criticized Hoover for not taking more drastic measures to reduce the deficit. Roosevelt wanted government action but he (and his advisors) did not have the concept of the full-employment budget balance to guide their thinking.

Two lessons are to be learned from this example. First, when an actual budget deficit is caused by a fall in GNP, contractionary policies (increasing taxes and reducing expenditures) will cause further decreases in GNP. Second, the actual budget deficit (or surplus) is a poor measure on which to base fiscal policy actions and a poor measure of whether government policies are expansionary or contractionary. Increases in actual budget deficits can either reflect decreases in GNP (as they did during the Great Depression) or expansionary fiscal policies (tax cuts or increases in government spending). Only the full-employment budget balance—which removes any effect of changes in real GNP—can give a clear signal.

* All data in tis example are expressed in nominal terms.

balance is estimated at potential GNP, it is unaffected by changes in actual GNP, that is, by changes in automatic stabilizers. Thus changes in the full-employment budget are clear signals of discretionary policy changes. *A rise in the full-employment budget surplus means that contractionary fiscal policies have been adopted. A decline in the full-employment budget surplus means that expansionary fiscal policies have been adopted.* By contrast, changes in the actual budget are ambiguous signals. A rising deficit may reflect either expansionary fiscal policies or the effects of automatic stabilizers as the economy slips into a recession.

In addition to providing a way to distinguish discretionary policy changes from the effects of automatic stabilizers, the full-employment budget is important to debates over federal budget deficits. In 1986 the full-employment deficit was estimated to be 4–5 percent of potential GNP, or almost as high as the actual deficit. If this estimate is accurate, automatic stabilizers will not reduce the actual deficit much, even if the economy operates at full employment. Discretionary fiscal policy changes—reducing spending and/or raising taxes—will be necessary to significantly reduce the budget deficits. The effects of these deficits and policies to reduce them are discussed in a policy case in Chapter 31.

Crowding-Out Effect

Another fiscal policy issue is the degree to which expansionary fiscal policy actually raises aggregate demand. There are reasons to believe that the effects of higher government spending may be partially or fully offset by lower private spending. Economists call this result the **crowding-out effect**.

To see why the crowding-out effect occurs, let's consider what happens when government expenditures increase. Recall that in order to increase spending, government must borrow more, raise taxes, or print more money. Because we want to see the effect of fiscal policy alone, we hold the money supply constant.

Effect of borrowing. To borrow more money, the government must sell bonds in the financial market. But doing so increases the supply of bonds, lowering bond prices and increasing real interest rates, as we have already shown. (Put another way, an increase in demand for borrowing will increase the cost of borrowed funds, that is, raise interest rates.) Higher real interest rates cause households and businesses to consume and invest less. Thus higher government purchases are offset to some extent by lower private-sector spending. Because government borrowing effectively *crowds* some private-sector borrowers *out* of financial markets, the effectiveness of expansionary fiscal policies is reduced.

Crowding out is a serious issue in terms of economic growth. To the extent that crowding out slows private investment in new machinery, plants, and technology, it may limit an economy's ability to expand its potential output, that is, to grow. We consider the importance of private-sector investment to growth in more detail in Chapter 30.

Crowding-out effect. A decrease in investment and consumption resulting from the increase in interest rates caused by expansionary fiscal policies (holding the money supply constant). This effect is strongest when the economy is close to potential GNP, and it reduces the effect of expansionary fiscal policies.

Effect of raising taxes. Higher taxes directly reduce private-sector income and thus lower private-sector spending. But, as we noted in Chapter 22, households will reduce consumption by less than the decline in income (because the marginal propensity to consume is less than 1). But to keep spending from falling as much as their incomes, households must either borrow more or sell some of the bonds they own.

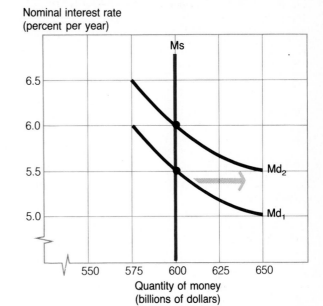

(a) Government crowds out private-sector spending

(b) Greater money demand raises interest rates

Exhibit 27.4
Crowding-Out Effect of Increased Government Spending
Expansionary fiscal policies increase aggregate demand (to AD_2), ignoring the crowding-out effect. But higher spending also raises demand for money and, consequently, the interest rate, as shown in part (b). As the interest rate rises, investment and interest-sensitive consumption spending fall—crowded out of financial markets—so aggregate demand increases only to AD_3. The difference between AD_2 and AD_3 is an indication of the extent of the crowding-out effect.

Either way, we can expect interest rates to rise and, consequently, private-sector spending will fall. Because private-sector spending is affected by both the decline in income and the crowding-out effect, the expansionary effect of government spending financed by higher taxes is generally quite small. Indeed, *the greater the crowding-out effect, the smaller will be the impact of expansionary fiscal policy*. In fact, if crowding out is large enough, fiscal policy may not raise aggregate demand at all.

Exhibit 27.4 illustrates the crowding-out effect if government raises spending or reduces taxes but the money supply remains unchanged. The direct effect of the expansionary fiscal policy (before considering crowding out) is shown in Exhibit 27.4(a) by the dashed curve AD_2. But with the money supply fixed, higher spending raises the demand for money and therefore the interest rate (to 6 percent), as shown in Exhibit 27.4(b). The higher interest rate lowers investment and interest-sensitive consumption. Taking into account the crowding-out effect, expansionary fiscal policies can be expected to raise aggregate demand only to AD_3. The reduction in aggregate demand from AD_2 to AD_3 reflects the strength of the crowding-out effect.

How strong is the crowding-out effect? Economists do not all agree on the answer to this question. But the evidence suggests that the crowding-out effect is more important when the economy is operating close to its potential GNP level. When there is considerable slack in the economy, expansionary fiscal policies may raise income and consequently the total level of saving. If saving rises enough, public-sector borrowing will not have to crowd out private-sector borrowing. Moreover, an increase in the funds supplied to the U.S. financial market by foreign individuals and businesses may, as it has in recent years, offset the crowding-out effect. But borrowing from the foreign sector has other negative effects, as discussed in Chapter 33.

Rational Expectations: Are Fiscal and Monetary Policies Ineffective?

In addition to the crowding-out effect, some economists believe that the effectiveness of fiscal and monetary policies is reduced because they change expectations. The strongest advocates of this position, the **new classical macroeconomists**, argue that neither fiscal nor monetary policy will affect the economy *if the policy change is fully anticipated*. These economists base their theory on the belief that individuals are rational and have **rational expectations**. That is, individuals can be expected to consider all available information and adjust their expectations to known future events.

Suppose that Congress increases government spending, financing this expansionary fiscal policy by additional borrowing. What effect would this policy have on your expectations? According to rational expectations theory, you would recognize that there is no essential difference between spending financed by borrowing and spending financed by current taxes. Government borrowing today means that higher future taxes will be required to meet interest payments and eventual repayment of the principal. Borrowing does not change the total amount of taxes that will be paid, but it does change the timing. The real wealth of the household sector declines, just as though current taxes were used instead of borrowing. As wealth falls, so does consumption.

In the view of the new classical macroeconomists, the rational response of individuals (less consumption and more saving) makes an increase in borrowing equivalent to an increase in taxes. As we have noted, tax-financed increases in spending have a small effect anyway. If expectations are adjusted, reducing the effect even more, discretionary tax policies may be totally ineffective. The new classical macroeconomists also argue that rational reactions will offset discretionary monetary policies. Suppose that the Fed announces an increase in the money supply. We can expect this action to increase aggregate demand and, consequently, the price level. What kinds of reactions can we expect if the increase in the price level is anticipated?

Anyone lending money will want a higher *nominal* interest rate to cover the anticipated loss in the purchasing power of money. (Instead of falling as the money supply increases, the *real* interest rate may not change at all.) Workers and other resource suppliers will want higher nominal wages and prices to cover the expected price-level increase. As resource prices rise, aggregate supply decreases. If individuals succeed in protecting real wages and real incomes, the drop in aggregate supply will completely offset the higher demand. Although the price level will rise, real GNP will not change.

New classical economists. Economists who assume that wages and prices are very flexible, a theoretical approach similar to that of classical economists. Their theories suggest that rational responses to anticipated policy actions will make policies completely ineffective.

Rational expectations. An assumption that individuals utilize all available information, including their understanding of the effects of fiscal and monetary policy, in anticipating future economic conditions.

Higher government spending financed by borrowing will raise demand for credit and cause interest rates to rise. Higher interest rates reduce investment and interest-sensitive consumption spending. This crowding-out effect reduces the impact of expansionary fiscal policies.

Government spending financed by taxes directly reduces household income. Consumption falls less than income (because of the marginal propensity to consume) and households must either borrow or sell bonds they hold. Either way, interest rates rise, crowding out private-sector spending. The larger the crowding-out effect, the smaller will be the effect of fiscal policies on aggregate demand.

The new classical macroeconomists argue that fiscal and monetary policies are ineffective in changing real GNP because individuals with rational expectations will take offsetting actions. Expansionary fiscal policies financed with borrowing will lead to expectations of higher taxes and an increase in current saving. Expansionary monetary policy will lead to expectations of a higher price level and higher nominal (not real) interest rates. Aggregate supply decreases, and only the price level (not real output) is affected.

Nonactivists. Economists who believe it unnecessary, undesirable, and impractical to employ discretionary monetary and fiscal policies to stabilize the economy. They recommend stable policies—a constant growth in the money supply and a balanced full-employment budget—and reliance on the economy's automatic adjustment mechanism.

Activists. Economists who believe it necessary, desirable, and practical to use discretionary monetary and fiscal policies to stabilize the economy.

Note, however, that this conclusion applies only to *anticipated* policies. When the economy is surprised by policy actions, short-run output may change. But once the policy action is recognized, the economy should, according to the new classical macroeconomists, adjust immediately.

Not all economists accept this strong conclusion that anticipated policy actions have *no* effect. They observe that it is not enough for individuals to adjust their expectations; they must also adjust their behavior. To the extent that contracts set wages and other resource prices for some specified period of time, for example, the response may be delayed. However, most economists do accept that private-sector responses due to changed expectations may weaken the impact of anticipated policies.

MACROECONOMIC POLICY: ACTIVISM VERSUS NONACTIVISM

Is it necessary to "correct" departures from full employment or price stability with discretionary policies, or will the economy correct itself? Is it practical to use discretionary policies or are there serious problems with them that must be overcome? Should government policy makers be allowed to use their own discretion in setting policies or should they be required to follow fixed rules? Most economists agree that fiscal and monetary policies *can* affect aggregate economic activity. But there is still considerable debate about whether such policies *should* be used to reduce or eliminate swings in the business cycle.

We have observed that government has two alternative policy choices when the economy is not currently operating at its potential output level. It can take no action and rely on the economy's automatic adjustment mechanism. Or it can take discretionary action to shift aggregate demand and close the gap. We can identify proponents of these two policies as **nonactivists** and **activists**, respectively. To a large extent activists are associated with Keynesian beliefs; nonactivists include both monetarists and the new classical macroeconomists.

Franco Modigliani, a Keynesian and a leading proponent of activism, says that activists

> Accept what I regard to be the fundamental practical message of *The General Theory* (of John Maynard Keynes): that a private enterprise economy . . . *needs* to be stabilized, *can* be stabilized, and therefore, *should* be stabilized by appropriate monetary and fiscal policies.[*]

In contrast, Milton Friedman, the founder of modern monetarism, argues that

> We simply do not know enough to be able to recognize minor disturbances when they occur or to be able to predict either what their effects will be with any precision or what monetary policy is required to offset their effects.[†]

These quotations indicate that the disagreement has little to do with whether government policies *can* affect the economy. (The new classical macroeconomists, as we have noted, dispute the effect of policies announced in advance.) The more crucial and controversial question is whether the effects of these policies are

---

[*] Franco Modigliani, "The Monetarist Controversy, or Should We Forsake Stabilization Policies?" *American Economic Review*, March 1977, p. 1.

[†] Milton Friedman, "The Role of Monetary Policy," *American Economic Review*, March 1968, p. 14.

beneficial. Will they actually stabilize the economy? Those who answer *no* to this question stress practical problems in designing and implementing policies, as you will see.

Are Discretionary Policies Necessary?

Activists believe that the economy is inherently unstable. They observe that there are wide swings in two elements of private-sector spending: consumer spending on durable goods and fixed investment. (Durable goods include automobiles, microwave ovens, and other appliances. Fixed investment includes business investment in plant and equipment and residential construction.) Activists also note that demand and supply shocks can create severe economic problems. Certainly, increased spending for national defense during the Vietnam War and the oil-price supply shocks in the 1970s hurt the economy. Activists argue that government fiscal and monetary policies are vital to minimizing instability and the negative effects of such economic upheavals.

Nonactivists counter that durable goods and fixed investment are the two most unstable portions of consumption. They argue that spending on other goods and services is very stable, making total consumption spending more stable. Moreover, nonactivists believe that what appears to be unstable private-sector spending is really a response to unstable government policies. They explain the drop in investment spending in the late 1960s, for example, as a response to the high interest rates caused by tight monetary policy and high government borrowing. They blame the inflationary bias in the economy since World War II on instability in monetary policies.

On balance, the evidence is not conclusive. Some poorly designed and implemented government policies *have* created instability. But the supply shocks of 1973 and 1979 have little to do with macroeconomic policies. (However, they do raise a question of which policy response is best, an issue we address in Chapter 31.) Moreover, the case for government policies depends on more than private-sector instability. Instability would not be a serious problem if the economy's automatic adjustment mechanism were able to restore stability quickly and smoothly.

How Fast Does the Automatic Adjustment Mechanism Work?

Following in the tradition of Keynes, activists believe that wages and prices fall slowly when a contractionary gap opens. Activists note that resource prices are often fixed for substantial periods of time by contracts or by the custom of adjusting wages and salaries annually. Because resource costs do not respond immediately, changes in aggregate demand will have a stronger short-run effect on quantity—both output and unemployment—than on prices. As a result, activists argue that the automatic adjustment mechanism works slowly and that the costs of relying on it are high. Thus the benefits of discretionary policies are also high.

Recent historical data support this view. Wages and prices *have* been slow to respond during nearly every recession since the late 1960s. For example, the rate of inflation continued to rise throughout the 1969–1970 recession. Although price levels rose more slowly in response to the 1981–1982 recession, it was the most severe recession in the last 40 years.

In contrast, nonactivists blame the slow response of wages and prices on government policies. Because workers and businesses expect expansionary policies, they have little reason to reduce wages and prices during a recession. Were it not for the effect of expected government policies, nonactivists believe that workers and businesses would respond rapidly. Any delay would be brief: the time required to get accurate information on which to base price-level expectations.

What Is the Historical Evidence?

As you can see in Exhibit 27.5, the U.S. economy has been more stable in the post–World War II era than in the pre–World War II period. Annual changes in real GNP have been smaller and recessions have been shorter. Activists observe that the postwar period was when the federal government recognized its ability and responsibility to stabilize the economy. They attribute much of the stability to active government policies.

Such reasoning, however, is not proof. Nonactivists attribute the greater stability to other causes. For example, the increasing size of the federal budget increased the importance of automatic stabilizers. Reforms in the banking system— government deposit insurance, for example—helped prevent the financial panics that had characterized the pre–World War II period. In their view, stability is not the result of discretionary government policies.

Exhibit 27.5
Macroeconomic Stability: A Historical View
The graph shows annual percentage changes in real GNP from 1909 to 1986. The shaded areas indicate periods of recession. Note that the fluctuations prior to World War II (1941–1945) are larger and the recessions longer, indicating that the economy has been more stable since the war.

Annual percentage change in real GNP

Year

Can we know who is right? Unfortunately, it is difficult to separate cause and effect, so statistical tests have proved inconclusive. However, the debate between activists and nonactivists is not just a dispute over whether discretionary policies are necessary. They also disagree on the question of whether the government can, in fact, make appropriate responses to contractionary and expansionary gaps.

What Information Is Required for Discretionary Policy Action?

Early in this chapter we showed how government policies might shift aggregate demand enough to close any contractionary or expansionary gap that might occur. Making such changes may have appeared easy to do (and they are easy to draw on graphs). But the real world is much more complicated. A large amount of information is required to formulate and implement economic policy. Consider, for example, what you would have to know in order to develop an ideal policy response to a contractionary gap.

Any discretionary fiscal policy requires an estimate of how much aggregate expenditures have to change. In order to make this estimate, we have to know the current level of real GNP and potential GNP. In addition, because it takes time for the full effect of fiscal policies to be felt, we must have some idea of future values of the GNP components. Because fiscal policies have a multiplier effect, we also have to estimate how much total expenditures would rise as a result of an initial policy change. To do so requires that we estimate the effects of crowding out and changes in expectations, as well as the size of the multiplier.

Discretionary monetary policies are also complex to develop. In order to decide how many government securities to buy on the open market, the Fed would have to estimate the deposit expansion multiplier. The Fed would also have to determine how much, if any, excess reserves the banking system might want to hold. Developing a monetary policy is further complicated by the fact that the Fed controls the *money supply*, but the goal of monetary policy is to change *aggregate demand*. The connection between changes in the money supply and short-run changes in aggregate demand are not exact or constant.

The knowledge required for an ideal policy response to cyclical fluctuations is not easy to come by. Economists accept the concept of potential GNP but have no way of directly observing or precisely measuring it. Forecasting future levels of aggregate demand, aggregate supply, and potential GNP is far from an exact science. Nonactivists believe that these difficulties strongly support their position. Activists recognize the information limitations, but they believe that policy makers can know enough to give the economy a push in the right direction.

How Significant and Uncertain Are Policy Lags?

Another practical difficulty in developing discretionary policy is the effect of time lags. Throughout this textbook we have drawn graphs on which aggregate demand shifts from an initial gap to a final equilibrium position. These shifts are not immediate; rather, several time lags, or delays, occur. First, it takes time for policy makers to recognize that a problem exists and additional time to develop a policy response to the problem. In addition, the effects of policy actions are not instantaneous, which creates an additional lag.

Recognition lag. The delay between when a macroeconomic problem occurs and when it is recognized.

Action lag. The delay between when a problem is recognized and when policy actions are taken.

Recognition and action lags. No discretionary policy response can be developed until a problem is recognized. For example, information on GNP is produced only once a quarter, and economists are reluctant to say that a recession exists unless real GNP has declined for two consecutive quarters. Thus the **recognition lag**, the time that passes before a recession can be recognized, might be as long as 4–8 months. Although data on unemployment and prices are available somewhat more frequently, a recognition lag of at least four months for fiscal policies seems a reasonable estimate.*

Monetary policy is also subject to recognition lags, although they are shorter than for fiscal policies. Monetary policy usually aims at intermediate targets, such as interest rates or the supply of money. Data on interest rates are available daily. Money supply figures can be obtained weekly but are subject to such extensive revisions that accurate figures are generally obtainable only monthly. Moreover, economists disagree about which measure of money supply to use and what intermediate target is the best goal for monetary policy.

The recognition lag can be shortened if future events can be forecast with reasonable accuracy. Although forecasts are inexact, activists argue that forecasts do not have to be perfect to be useful. However, some major economic events—such as the oil-price increase in 1979—are not predictable. And some changes are not well understood even after several years. (For example, economists are still unclear about how deregulation of banks and changes in the Fed's operation in the early 1980s affected demand for money.) Forecasts that do not take into account changes in relationships between policy variables and economic activity will be particularly inaccurate and unreliable.

After a problem has been identified, there is an **action lag** while a policy response is being developed and implemented. The action lag is a major obstacle, especially for fiscal policy. To implement a discretionary fiscal policy, Congress must pass and the president approve changes in tax laws or spending programs. Even when there is general agreement that a problem exists, there is apt to be disagreement over the best size and type of fiscal policy response. Which group should be given a tax cut? On which program should more be spent? The short-run economic impact does not depend on the type of government spending. But the political consequences of changing taxes or spending make it difficult for Congress and the president to act swiftly.

In addition, critics observe that fiscal policy tends to be very one-sided. That is, legislators typically are willing to vote for expansionary fiscal measures but not for contractionary fiscal measures. That is, they are willing to spend more and/or tax less (issues of enormous budget deficits aside) but not to cut programs or raise taxes. Indeed, voting for contractionary fiscal measures is often considered to be political suicide.

While monetary policy also is subject to action lags, they are much briefer than for fiscal policy for several reasons. First, the Federal Open Market Committee, the Fed's policy-making group, is small. Thus members can more easily reach consensus. And compared with legislators, board members face less political pressure. Moreover, monetary policy can be implemented quickly when agreement to expand or contract the money supply is reached. The shorter action lag is a

---

*Note also that data on GNP are constantly being revised. Many times the revisions are substantial: as much as 1 or 2 percent, or a potential variation of as much as $70 billion in real GNP. As a result, it is difficult for anyone to know for sure how much change, if any, has occurred until well after the fact.

Impact lag. The delay between when policy actions are taken and when they fully affect aggregate demand.

point in favor of using monetary policy as a stabilizer, assuming that stabilizing policies are desired.

Impact lag. Perhaps even more important is the long and uncertain **impact lag** between the time a policy is implemented and the time its full effect is felt. Fiscal policy changes involve the multiplier effect. Economists estimate that it takes about three months for a round of spending to occur. Thus the economy may not feel most of the multiplier effect for a year or longer. Moreover, the estimated period for a spending round is an average. The actual effect may take more (or less) time, again increasing the uncertainty of the effect. The timing and extent of the crowding-out effect and adjustments in expectations are also uncertain.

Changes in the money supply also suffer from long and variable impact lags. For the Fed's action to have its full effect, banks must receive the new deposits and turn them into new loans. Like the spending multiplier, the deposit expansion process takes time. Most economists believe that this response is quite slow. Because the effect of monetary policy depends on so many other decisions, the impact lag for such policies may run from six months to two years.

Policy implications of lags. Nonactivists note that because of lags, discretionary policies are likely to *destabilize* the economy. Exhibit 27.6 shows potential GNP growing at a constant rate (indicated by the straight line). However, actual GNP at times is below potential GNP (creating a contractionary gap) and at other times is above it (creating an expansionary gap).

Suppose that the economy is initially at point *a*. Actual output is beginning to fall below potential GNP, opening a contractionary gap. If there were no lags, discretionary policies might halt this downward slide. Because of the recognition lag, however, policy makers may not actually recognize the problem until a later time (point *b*). Because of the action lag, the actual policy response may not begin until point *c*. But at that point, the economy's automatic adjustment mechanism has already kicked in, recovery has started, and the contractionary gap has begun to shrink.

Worse still, from the nonactivist's point of view, the discretionary policy may finally have its full effect at point *d*, while the economy is experiencing an expansionary gap. The path of the economy if no policy were implemented is indicated by the smooth line on the graph. The path caused by poorly timed action is shown by the dotted line. Far from stabilizing the economy (reducing the length and depth of the recession), the policy destabilizes the economy (increasing inflation).

Nonactivists' Case for Fixed Rules

Because of the many problems involved in taking action and obtaining expected results, nonactivists have little faith in discretionary policies. Instead, they believe that the private sector is basically stable, that the economy's automatic adjustment mechanism works well, and that automatic stabilizers are a sufficient policy response to cyclical changes in demand. In addition, they believe that policy makers often use discretionary policies for political rather than economic purposes.

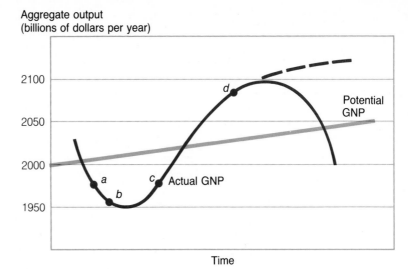

Exhibit 27.6
Discretionary Policy: Lags and Potential Instability
Nonactivists argue that lags may cause discretionary policies to be destabilizing. Suppose that the economy is initially at point *a* where a contractionary gap is beginning to open. If there were no lags, expansionary policy action at this point might prevent further declines. The recognition lag, however, may mean that the problem is not recognized until point *b*, when the gap is nearly at its maximum. The action lag may mean that policy makers do not respond until point *c* when the automatic adjustments have already begun to close the gap. The impact lag may mean that the policy has its full effect on the economy at point *d*. As a result, the policy increases the size of the expansionary gap (following the dashed line), when the automatic adjustment would have been closing the gap.

Instead of leaving policy decisions to politicians, they advocate fixed policy rules that they believe would stabilize the economy. Nonactivists do not all agree on the best rules, but two rules have broad acceptance: (1) a constant rate of growth in the money supply; and (2) a balanced full-employment budget.

Constant growth of the money supply.   To stabilize monetary policy, nonactivists favor a rule requiring the Fed to increase the money supply at a constant rate regardless of current economic conditions. In support of this rule they offer several arguments. First, if the money supply grows at a constant rate that is equal to the long-run rate of growth in potential output, the economy could grow *and* prices would be stable. Second, because monetary policy is subject to long and variable impact lags, nonactivists believe it to be impractical to develop and implement short-term policy responses to close GNP gaps. And third, fixed rules would prevent potential mistakes by the Fed.

History is full of such errors by the Fed. In 1958–1959, the Fed cut back the money supply just in time to "help" the economy slide further into recession. In 1968–1969, the Fed increased the money supply even though the economy was already experiencing inflationary pressures. The most serious mistakes occurred during the Great Depression. From 1929 to 1933, the Fed reduced the money supply by 25 percent, adding to contractionary pressures in the middle of the most severe recession in U.S. history. In 1937, as the economy appeared to be struggling toward recovery, the Fed raised the reserve requirements, halting growth in the money supply and extending the Great Depression it had helped to create.

Nonactivists also observe that having the money supply grow at the same rate as long-run real GNP provides an element of automatic stabilization. During a brief recession, the money supply would grow more rapidly than real GNP, helping to close a contractionary gap. And if an increase in aggregate demand opened an expansionary gap, the money supply would grow less rapidly than real GNP, helping to close the gap.

Activists charge that such responses would be inadequate to counterbalance sharp changes in money demand or events such as a major supply shock. Non-activists, however, believe that demand for money is basically stable and that short-run changes are generally mild and short-lived (and therefore much less of a problem). Individuals would not have to worry about protecting themselves from erratic changes in the money supply, and stable expectations would reduce erratic shifts in aggregate demand. Moreover, nonactivists view the short-run costs of any shift in aggregate demand or aggregate supply as less important than the potential long-run destabilizing effects of discretionary policies.

Balanced full-employment budget. To stabilize fiscal policy, nonactivists generally favor a rule requiring Congress and the president to balance the full-employment budget.[*] Congress would determine the optimal amount of government spending in terms of allocative efficiency and then adjust tax rates to bring the full-employment budget into balance. The case for this rule is based on arguments similar to those for the constant monetary growth rate. Lags, imperfect knowledge, and opportunity for political judgments to prevail make discretionary fiscal policies unreliable and ineffective in the view of nonactivists.

It is important for you to recognize that we are talking about balancing the full-employment budget, not the actual federal budget. The economy's automatic stabilizers would still function, offsetting instability in private-sector spending to some extent. Thus the actual budget would show a deficit during a recession and a surplus when inflation occurred. But there would be no attempt to adjust the full-employment budget balance to reduce either a contractionary or an expansionary gap. Because the nonactivists believe that the private sector is relatively stable, they also believe that automatic stabilizers are a sufficient policy response to any GNP gaps.

Activists' Case for Discretionary Policies

Activists recognize that imperfect information and lags make it impractical to try to eliminate minor fluctuations in real GNP. They also recognize that policy mistakes in the past have made the economy perform poorly. But they are not

---

[*] Some nonactivists believe that the government should strive for a full-employment budget surplus. In this way government could pay off some of its outstanding debt, freeing up funds for private-sector investment and thus spurring economic growth. The important point for this discussion is that the full-employment budget balance be constant, not what it is.

When developing discretionary policies, policy makers face the difficulty of measuring actual and potential GNP and predicting the size and timing of the effects of policies.

Discretionary policies are subject to lags. A recognition gap occurs until a problem is recognized. An action gap occurs between recognition of a problem and formulation of a response to it. An impact gap occurs between implementation of a policy and its full effect. Nonactivists argue that lags can cause discretionary policies to further destabilize an economy.

Because of problems in developing and implementing discretionary monetary and fiscal policies, nonactivists propose fixed policy rules: a stable growth of the money supply and a balanced full-employment budget.

Activists recognize the problems of implementing discretionary monetary and fiscal policies, but believe that such policies can give the economy a push in the right direction and prevent major, costly GNP gaps.

ready to abandon the idea of taking action to offset some of the business cycle instability that they believe is inevitable. They believe that discretionary actions should be taken to point the economy in the right direction when problems arise. In their view, the slow response of wages and prices makes reliance on the automatic adjustment mechanism too costly.

No policy approach is perfect, and thus any policy approach is unlikely to provide complete stability. The best approach is the one that will result in the greatest benefits for the least cost. Nonactivists believe that fixed rules are best. Activists believe that moderate actions should be taken. Despite agreement on some important principles, economists continue to be divided over the crucial question of whether discretionary fiscal and monetary policies are necessary, desirable, and practical.

DEFICITS AND DEBT: ISSUES AND OPTIONS

Now that we have considered some of the theoretical and practical problems facing policy makers, we can examine a major policy issue regarding the U.S. economy: the size of federal budget deficits and of the national debt. We noted at the beginning of this chapter that both have grown dramatically in recent years. Moreover, the deficits since 1983 cannot be attributed to war or recession—the traditional causes of deficits. But is the national debt a serious problem? What options do we have for reducing it?

Myths and Realities about the National Debt

Myth and reality are combined in the notion that federal budget deficits and the national debt are cause for concern. In some circumstances moderate deficits and debt may have some desirable effects. But the magnitude of the current deficits and the fact that they largely reflect a deficit in the full-employment budget raise some serious concerns.

Does a growing deficit mean a growing burden? Before we can consider whether they are a burden to the economy, we must put debts and deficits into perspective. That is, we must compare an increase in debt to changes in the ability to service and repay that debt. For example, you may have borrowed to finance your college education. But if your future income rises as a result, your ability to pay the interest and repay the principal also increases. Similarly, comparing federal budget deficits and the size of the national debt to GNP tells us whether the nation is able to pay interest and repay principal and hence how burdensome the debt is.

Exhibit 27.7(a) shows the federal government's budget balance expressed as a percentage of GNP from 1951 to 1986. What do these data suggest? First, budget deficits are certainly not unusual. In fact, deficits occurred in 28 of the last 37 years. The last surplus occurred in 1969.

But deficits in the 1980s have been extraordinarily large. For most of the period shown, federal deficits were about 1–2 percent of GNP. (The primary exception before the 1980s occurred during the major recession in 1975.) By contrast, recent deficits have been over 4.5 percent of GNP and are expected to

(a) Federal budget balance

Percentage of GNP

(b) National debt

Percentage of GNP

Exhibit 27.7
Deficits and Debt: A Historical View
Part (a) shows the federal budget balance expressed as a percentage of GNP. Areas shaded red correspond to budget deficits. Deficits occurred in 28 of the 37 years shown. For most of the period deficits averaged 1–2 percent of GNP. But since 1980, deficits have run 4–5 percent. Part (b) shows the national debt as a percentage of GNP. From 1951 to 1974, the national debt grew more slowly than GNP, although it increased in absolute terms. Since 1974 the relative size of the debt has increased.

remain almost that large for the rest of the 1980s. To finance a deficit equal to 5 percent of GNP, government borrowing will use up about two-thirds of private saving, which could otherwise be used for business investment or household consumption. As we have stated, such crowding out seriously affects long-run economic growth.

What about the national debt? It has grown in absolute size, increasing by 50 percent between 1951 and 1970. The deficits in the 1970s caused the debt to *double* in a single decade. However, as Exhibit 27.7(b) shows, from 1951 to 1979 the national debt fell from 96 percent of GNP to 34 percent of GNP. That is, the debt grew more slowly than national income, so the nation was better able to afford it. (Just as you can afford to carry more debt—for a bigger house, perhaps—if you earn more.)

However, between 1980 and 1985 the debt doubled once again and the debt grew from one-third of GNP to nearly one-half. Some of that increase was caused by the two recessions between 1980 and 1982. But much of the change and most of the projected increases are the result of fiscal policies that lowered tax receipts while spending continued to increase. This change raises questions about the nation's ability to afford such a debt.

Is debt a future burden? The current size of the national debt is not necessarily a cause for alarm. But its growth raises questions about whether the debt will seriously burden future generations economically. Those who believe that it will usually argue that the present generation is enjoying the benefits of government spending, while future generations will have to pay taxes to eliminate the debt. In evaluating this argument, we have to recognize that for the most part, we owe the debt to ourselves. This *internal debt* is not really an aggregate burden, although it will redistribute income in the future. That is, future interest payments will transfer income from one group (taxpayers) to another (debt holders).

In contrast, 15 percent of the national debt is *external debt*, held by the foreign sector. Interest and principal payments on the external debt require a transfer of resources from U.S. taxpayers to foreigners. The foreign sector bought more than $90 billion of the new government debt issued from 1980 to 1985. An increase in external debt is not necessarily bad. If the funds allow an increase in productive capacity, the economy may grow fast enough to repay the debt and increase domestic standards of living.

On the other hand, some economists fear that the foreign funds are being used to finance government spending that adds little to future growth. In this case, additional foreign-owned debt *does* represent a future burden, as it does already in Brazil, Argentina, and Mexico. Foreign debt in 1984 represented nearly 50 percent of the GNP in each of those countries, much of it owed to U.S. banks. In seeking to pay off their debts, they are having to make real sacrifices. From 1980 to 1984 the debt burden was partly responsible for a drop in average income in these countries. Although the U.S. debt is not that large a problem now, continued increases in external debt could produce such problems in the future.

Will debt bankrupt the nation? Even if the debt burden increases, there is no reason for the government to go bankrupt and default on its debt. After all, the U.S. national debt represents a promise to pay U.S. dollars. (The problem is not so simple for Mexico and Brazil because their external debt is owed in dollars.) In other words, the U.S. government could always pay off its debt by printing more money (unless it runs out of paper). It is unlikely to do so, however, because the large increase in the money supply would be highly inflationary. (Moreover, under current law, debt cannot be "monetized" unless the Fed is willing to buy the debt.)

Do deficits cause higher real interest rates? Deficits financed by borrowing result in increased demand for credit which tends to raise interest rates. But historical evidence suggests that real interest rates and deficits are *not* related. This lack of connection may reflect the fact that, historically, deficits have occurred mostly during recessions. If government borrows during a recession—when overall demand for credit is weak—the borrowing may have little effect on real interest rates. Moreover, prior to 1979 the Fed typically increased the money supply when interest rates began to rise, "monetizing" much of a deficit. In the 1980s, however, the Fed has often declined to finance government debts, forcing government to borrow in the money market, driving up real interest rates.

Do deficits cause inflation? There is little reason to believe that deficits financed by borrowing cause the price level to rise, especially when deficits occur during recessions. During a recession, aggregate demand is relatively weak. Deficits caused by automatic stabilizers or discretionary fiscal policies add to aggregate demand but have little impact on the price level. Because the crowding-out effect is relatively strong, deficits may have little effect on aggregate demand when the economy is near full employment.

However, there is some evidence that over the long run higher deficits in the United States have been accompanied by more growth in the money supply. Such expansionary monetary policies can result in a higher price level. The exact reason for this relationship is debatable. But some economists believe that it results from the Fed's historical interest in keeping interest rates low. Because the Fed has been willing to allow real interest rates to rise in the 1980s, the rate of inflation has dropped, but deficits have been high.

What are the opportunity costs and the benefits of a deficit? Federal budget deficits and large and growing national debt that cause higher real interest rates and/or expectations of higher inflation may have serious opportunity costs. Higher real interest rates may reduce private investment, reducing future growth and output—a real cost to future generations. Moreover, if the economy is at full employment, any increase in government spending transfers resources away from the private sector. Conversely, many resources are not utilized by the private sector during recessions. Deficits that stimulate aggregate demand during recessions may enable the economy to avoid the opportunity costs of unused economic resources.

Government spending also can provide benefits. Some spending—to improve roads or education, for example—may increase the economy's potential output. A deficit caused by financing a war or to provide greater national defense may yield present and future benefits. Finally, some deficits result from government policies that also create higher output and employment. As with most economic issues, the important question is whether the extra costs associated with debt or debt reduction are balanced by extra benefits.

Current Situation: What Are the Options?

When we have considered all the positive and negative effects of budget deficits, the national debt, and fiscal and monetary policies, the question still remains: What should government do? Many economists believe that the high current and projected budget deficits will raise real interest rates, crowd out private-sector investment, and reduce future economic growth. They also fear that such high deficits may tempt the Fed to increase the growth of the money supply (and thus cause higher inflation rates) to avoid the crowding-out effect. Finally, the federal budget deficits have caused a heavy inflow of foreign funds, which means that real resources will have to be transferred to the foreign sector in the future.[*]

Despite these drawbacks, not all economists agree that deficits *should* be reduced, let alone *how* to reduce them. Some express hope that the economy will grow fast enough to eliminate the deficit. As the economy grows, so will income and therefore tax receipts. If the economy grows fast enough, the deficit will automatically be eliminated. This claim was made originally when the 1981 tax cut was passed, but its achievement appears unlikely in the foreseeable future.

Congress apparently agreed with those who believe that the deficit will not decrease without changes in fiscal policies. Passage of the Gramm–Rudman–Hollings bill in 1985 committed Congress (and the president) to reducing the deficit to zero by 1991. A key provision in the original legislation would have *automatically* cut spending as necessary to meet the targeted deficits. Although this provision was declared unconstitutional by the Supreme Court in 1986, Congress has continued to set deficit-reduction targets and work toward meeting them in their budget deliberations.

Some economists are skeptical of the Gramm–Rudman–Hollings law. They note that it fails to distinguish between actual budget deficits and a full-employment budget deficit. Thus it requires contractionary fiscal policies even if the economy is experiencing a contractionary gap—the type of change that makes the budget a destabilizing influence on the economy. The same economists also note that there is nothing necessarily magic about a balanced budget. After all, if the economy grows faster than the debt, the debt burden will decline. Other critics argue that the law is not really macroeconomic policy but a political attempt to reduce the overall size of the federal government.

Many economists, even those skeptical of Gramm–Rudman–Hollings, want to see the deficit reduced but realize that it is no easy task. We noted earlier that the current deficits are structural, that is, full-employment budget deficits. They will not be erased automatically by the elimination of a contractionary gap. To lower such deficits requires either higher taxes or less spending.

Tax increases traditionally meet strong political opposition, especially in election years. Other arguments against tax increases suggest that they have negative effects on work and investment incentives, reducing future growth in potential output. Cutting expenditures is also difficult politically. To some extent, those who favor spending cuts also favor reducing the size of government. Moreover, a large portion of the federal budget appears to be politically immune to spending cuts. Few politicians are willing to cut Social Security, national defense, or Medicare, which together represent over one-half the budget. Another significant portion— nearly 16 percent—is interest payments and veterans' benefits, which represent promised payments. In order to eliminate the budget deficit in 1986, the rest of the budget would have had to be cut by 70 percent. Clearly, there are both costs and benefits to reducing deficits.

---

[*] The inflow of foreign funds also causes the value of the U.S. dollar to rise. As we discuss in Chapter 33, when the U.S. dollar is stronger than other currencies, U.S. exports are less competitive on world markets, and foreign imports are more attractive to U.S. buyers. Thus U.S. goods and services are "crowded out" of foreign markets and foreign goods "crowd out" U.S. goods and services in the U.S. market.

CONCLUSION

In this chapter we explored both the theory and practice of macroeconomic policy. We showed how such policies could, in theory, be used to close both expansionary and contractionary gaps. But we also showed that discretionary policies have some theoretical and practical limitations and are hotly debated. Although the debate will likely continue, it does not hide the consensus among economists that macroeconomic policies play an important role in the economy.

In Chapters 28 and 29 we continue to discuss macroeconomic policies, looking more specifically at the problems of unemployment and inflation. As you study those chapters, you will see again the debates over the "correct" policy to help society reach its macroeconomic goals of full employment and price stability. A further analysis of the policy options is contained in Chapter 31.

SUMMARY

1. In this chapter we considered the role of government in the macroeconomy and the issues involved in government policies to counteract fluctuations of the business cycle.

2. Government interacts with the private sector, competing for goods, resources, and money. The government's budget balance is the difference between its receipts (taxes and fees) and expenditures (purchases, transfers, and interest paid on national debt). A positive balance is a budget surplus; a negative balance is a budget deficit. The cumulative result of deficits and surpluses over the years is the total national debt.

3. To finance spending, governments can tax and borrow, and the federal government can print money. In the United States, Congress and the president determine the federal government's fiscal policies while the Fed controls monetary policy. Each method of financing government spending has negative effects that must be weighed against the benefits of government spending.

4. Government fiscal and monetary policies are sometimes used to counteract fluctuations in the business cycle. Expansionary policies (more government spending or selling government bonds, for example) can close a contractionary gap. Contractionary policies (higher taxes or reserve requirements, for example) can close an expansionary gap. Another option is for the federal government to take no action, relying on the economy's automatic adjustment mechanism to restore equilibrium. Automatic adjustments may act more slowly than government policies. But contractionary policies tend to lower the price level, and expansionary policies tend to raise the price level while restoring equilibrium.

5. Changes in the budget balance may occur as a result of either discretionary fiscal policies or the actions of automatic stabilizers. The full-employment budget changes only when discretionary fiscal policies change.

6. Effects of discretionary fiscal policies may be limited by the crowding-out effect when the money supply is fixed. Increased government spending or lower taxes raises interest rates, crowding out private investment and consumption. The larger the crowding-out effect, the smaller will be the increase in aggregate demand from expansionary fiscal policies.

7. The new classical macroeconomists argue that anticipated policies are ineffective because rational individuals take offsetting actions. Recognizing that current increases in government borrowing mean higher future taxes, individuals increase saving, offsetting expansionary fiscal policy. Anticipated higher prices lead to decreased aggregate supply, offsetting expansionary monetary policy.

8. Problems confronting policy makers include the difficulty of obtaining accurate measures of economic variables and time lags. Recognition lags occur before problems are recognized. Action lags occur between problem recognition and policy implementation. Impact lags occur between implementation and full effects of a policy.

9. Nonactivists oppose the use of discretionary policies because of measurement problems, time lags, the crowding-out effect, rational expectations, and the political nature of such policy decisions. Instead, they propose that stable policies—constant rate of growth in the money supply and maintaining a balanced full-employment budget—and reliance on the automatic adjustment mechanism be used.

10. Activists view the economy as inherently unstable, that is, subject to unexpected changes in aggregate demand and/or supply. They also believe that the automatic adjustment mechanism closes contractionary gaps slowly. While most activists recognize the problems of developing and implementing effective policies, they remain convinced that discretionary policies are nec-

essary to prevent major GNP gaps and to push the economy in the right direction.

11. Many myths have sprung up regarding the national debt. The growth of the national debt is of concern only to the extent that it grows faster than national income, which it has in recent years. The debt is burdensome only to the extent that it is external (owed to foreigners) and does not fund enough new economic growth to pay the interest costs. The debt cannot bankrupt the nation because it requires payment in U.S. dollars, of which more could always be printed (but at the cost of inflation). Deficits occurring during recessions put little pressure on prices or on real interest rates.

12. Current deficits are large by historical standards and mostly represent deficits in the full-employment budget. They will not fall much even if the economy reaches potential GNP. Future growth should increase tax receipts (as income rises) and help reduce deficits, as long as spending does not also rise. Most economists, however, believe that it will take fiscal actions—either cuts in total spending or increases in taxes—to significantly reduce the deficits.

KEY TERMS

Budget balance, 691
Budget surplus, 691
Budget deficit, 691
National debt, 693
Expansionary policies, 695
Contractionary policies, 696
Discretionary policies, 697
Automatic stabilizers, 698
Full-employment budget, 699
Crowding-out effect, 700
New classical macroeconomists, 702
Rational expectations, 702
Nonactivists, 703
Activists, 703
Recognition lag, 707
Action lag, 707
Impact lag, 708

QUESTIONS FOR REVIEW AND DISCUSSION

1. In 1983 and 1984, the best monetary policy for the Fed to follow was subject to much debate. The economy was emerging from a rather severe recession and was growing somewhat. Inflation had dropped significantly but both nominal and real interest rates remained high. Some economists and politicians argued that if the Fed did not boost the rate of growth in the money supply, the recovery would be threatened. Others argued that the Fed should restrain the rate of growth in the money supply to prevent inflation from recurring. How would too little monetary growth threaten to bring on a recession? How would too much growth threaten to cause inflation? How can the Fed decide whether the monetary growth rate is too low or too high?

2. Consider the statement: "One of the difficulties with fiscal policy is the long action lag required for legislative agreement on tax and spending changes. This lag could be reduced significantly if the president were given the authority to change tax rates or spending on certain types of public works projects (highway and building construction, for example)." State whether this proposal would significantly improve the chances that discretionary fiscal policy could stabilize the economy. Explain. Are there other effects that should be considered?

3. In 1983 and 1984, important issues were the nominal rate of interest and the extremely large federal budget deficits projected through the 1980s. What are the possible connections between large budget deficits and nominal interest rates? Under what circumstances will budget deficits also affect real interest rates?

4. Explain how each of the following actions will affect investment. (*Note:* Most affect more than one factor that determines investment.)
   a) Contractionary monetary policy.
   b) An increase in the full-employment budget deficit.
   c) Contractionary monetary policy and expansionary fiscal policy at the same time.
   d) Expansionary monetary policy and contractionary fiscal policy at the same time.

5. In each of the following cases, indicate (a) the type of stabilization policy that activists would favor; and (b) the short-run effects of following the rules approach (constant growth of the money supply and a balanced full-employment budget).
   a) A decrease in velocity, that is, an increase in the quantity of money demanded at each level of nominal GNP.
   b) A drop in autonomous investment spending.

6. From mid-1980 to 1981, nominal interest rates on long-term financial claims (such as 10-year corporate bonds) rose by nearly 4 percent. Why did some economists suggest that an expansion in the money supply would be necessary to lower interest rates? Why did others suggest that a reduction in the growth rate of the money supply would be required? (*Hint:* Recall that nominal interest rates have both a real and an inflation premium component.)

7. Because federal deficits in the mid-1980s were largely full-employment deficits, economists generally believe that it will be necessary to increase taxes or reduce spending to significantly reduce deficits.
   a) Why would the deficits not be reduced by the economy's automatic adjustment mechanism?
   b) How will future economic growth affect the deficits, assuming no changes in spending? What are the effects of large deficits on future economic growth?
   c) What arguments could be used by those who believe that an increase in taxes is better than a decrease in spending. Be sure to note whether these arguments are normative or positive.
   d) What arguments could be used by those who believe that a decrease in spending is better than an increase in taxes. Be sure to note whether these arguments are normative or positive.
   e) Why would economists suggest that a significant reduction in budget deficits be accompanied by faster growth in the money supply (an expansionary monetary policy)?

8. As we noted in this chapter, if the federal government wants to spend more than it receives, it can borrow (sell bonds) or increase the money supply (print money).
   a) What happens to interest rates in either case? Why? (How does your answer depend on price-level expectations?)
   b) Which of the two ways will be more likely to lead to inflation? Why?
   c) Which of the two ways would be politically easier to implement?
   d) In the United States, the agency responsible for the money supply (the Fed) is independent. Is this independence good for the economy? Why or why not?

9. A number of costs are involved in financing a government budget deficit.
   a) How does the cost of a government budget deficit financed by borrowing depend on the strength of the crowding-out effect?
   b) What costs are involved if a government budget deficit is financed by increasing the money supply? (Contrast the effects during periods of relatively full employment and periods of recession.)
   c) What are the costs of eliminating government budget deficits by raising taxes? By reducing government spending? (Contrast the effects during periods of full employment and during periods of recession.)

Unemployment: Some Microeconomic Foundations

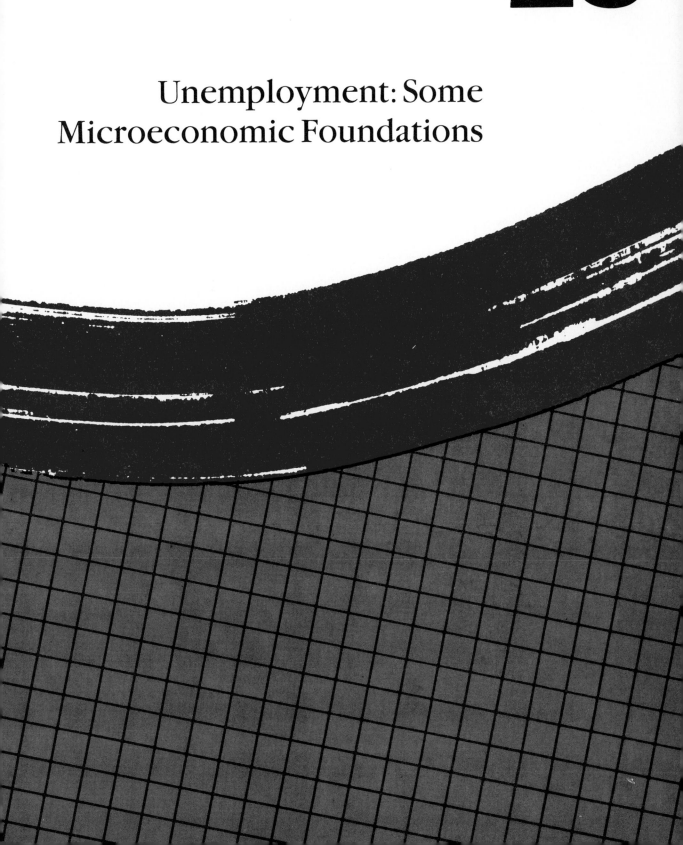

QUESTIONS TO CONSIDER

☐ How does the microeconomic view of unemployment differ from the macroeconomic view?

☐ Why does job-search theory hold that most unemployment is voluntary?

☐ Why does contracts theory hold that most unemployment is involuntary?

☐ What factors have caused the natural rate of unemployment to rise in recent years?

☐ How do various policy options to reduce unemployment differ?

Achieving full employment is an important economic goal. But economists do not agree on how it can best be accomplished. Will the economy quickly and smoothly adjust to contractionary gaps? Or will the adjustment be slow and costly in terms of unemployment? As you have already learned, these questions are at the heart of economic debates over the proper macroeconomic role for government. In large part the answers depend on the microeconomic behavior of labor markets. In this chapter we explore some of the microeconomic theories developed by economists to explain how labor markets operate. Using different theories, economists have arrived at conflicting conclusions about the speed of the economy's automatic adjustment mechanism.

In drawing these conclusions, economists had to compare actual unemployment rates with some standard. As we noted in Chapter 20, a common but controversial economic measure of unemployment is the natural rate of unemployment, that is, the rate that would exist if the economy were operating at its potential GNP level. But how high (or low) is the natural rate? In this chapter, we explore the microeconomic changes that economists generally believe have caused the natural rate to rise in recent years. Only then can we evaluate macroeconomic policies for lowering the natural rate of unemployment.

LABOR MARKETS: A CLOSER LOOK AT THE UNEMPLOYMENT RATE

Before considering theories about labor markets, however, we should examine the nature of employment and unemployment more closely. Labor-force statistics indicate that at the aggregate level the labor force is reasonably stable. For example, the overall unemployment rate generally changes little from month to month (a 0.2 percent change is often viewed as significant). However, a closer, microeconomic look indicates a great deal of instability. The labor-force status of millions of individuals changes every month. In this section, we explore this apparent instability in order to see the effect of unemployment on the macroeconomy and consider alternative policies to address unemployment.

Flows into and out of Labor Markets

Exhibit 28.1 shows that the labor-market status of a large number of individuals changes in an average month. These data—based on averages for the period 1968–1984—indicate that an average of 4.7 million individuals previously unemployed or out of the labor force found jobs each month. But 4.5 million who had been employed in the previous month became unemployed or dropped out of the labor force (flows 2 and 3). Overall, the flows had little effect on the unemployment rate. But with 8 percent of the population changing status in a typical month, the labor market is clearly dynamic. (In fact, if we count individuals who change jobs without experiencing unemployment, labor-market activity is even higher.) Unfortunately, economists do not fully understand these dynamics, especially flows into and out of the labor force. Thus economists interpret the data differently and suggest a variety of policies to reduce unemployment.

Most economists attribute at least part of the apparent instability to the difficulty in clearly distinguishing between the "unemployed" and those "not in the labor force." Statistics show that nearly one-half of those who withdraw from the labor force in any one month say that they want a job, although they are not actively looking for work. And many of those who withdraw from the labor force reenter it within less than three months. As a result, some economists believe that much of the measured unemployment is largely voluntary. This view suggests that government action to reduce unemployment is unnecessary and probably unworkable.

Exhibit 28.1
Labor-Market Flows, Monthly Averages for the Period 1968–1984
This diagram illustrates the large monthly flows between labor-force categories. In a typical month some 1.6 million individuals who were unemployed the previous month found jobs (flow 1), while another 1.3 million moved from jobs to unemployment (flow 2). A total of 3.1 million moved from being out of the labor force (flow 4) to jobs, while another 1.3 million unsuccessfully searched for work (flow 5). A total of 4.7 million left the labor force (flows 3 and 6). Because the flows in and out of each category are nearly balanced, there is not much monthly change in labor-force status. But beneath that apparent stability is considerable movement.

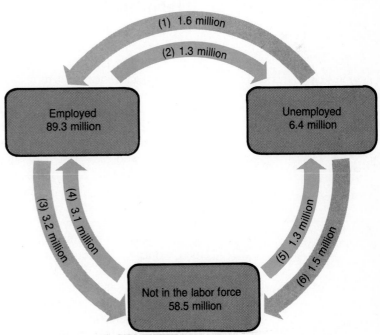

Source: Michael C. Keeley, "Cyclical Unemployment and Employment: Effects of Labor Force Entry and Exit," Federal Reserve Bank of San Francisco, *Economic Review, Number 3,* Summer 1984, p. 10.

	Percentage of the unemployed			Percentage of the total labor force		
Reason	1978 (low unem- ployment)	1983 (high unem- ployment)	1986	1978 (low unem- ployment)	1983 (high unem- ployment)	1986
Job losers	41.7	58.4	49.0	2.5	5.6	3.4
Job leavers	14.1	7.7	12.3	0.9	0.7	0.9
Reentrants	29.9	22.5	26.2	1.8	2.2	1.8
New entrants	14.3	11.4	12.5	0.9	1.1	0.9
Total	100.0	100.0	100.0	6.1	9.6	7.0

**Exhibit 28.2
Unemployment by Reason:
1978, 1983, and 1986**

Source: *Employment Report of the President, 1987* (Table B-33).

Other economists believe that the official unemployment rate understates the full extent of unemployment. They note that the official statistics do not include discouraged workers: those who have quit looking for work because they do not believe they can find jobs. This view suggests that government action may be desirable. We cannot hope to resolve this dispute. But the competing theories of unemployment that we discuss later in this chapter partially reflect these different interpretations of the data.

Reasons for Leaving and Entering Labor Markets

Exhibit 28.2 shows some of the reasons why individuals are unemployed. To indicate how important these reasons are across the business cycle, we show data for two years. In 1978 the unemployment rate was 6.1 percent, a figure that some believe was close to the natural rate of unemployment at the time. In 1983 the unemployment rate was 9.6 percent, well above any estimate of the natural rate. Individuals who leave their jobs voluntarily represent a relatively small portion of both the unemployed and the labor force. Even in 1978 when there was little unemployment, such individuals accounted for only 14 percent of the unemployed. Individuals who have lost their jobs make up both the largest portion of the unemployed and the bulk of the cyclically unemployed. Such individuals account for over 80 percent of the increase in unemployment between 1978 and 1983.

In addition, there appears to be a core of unemployed workers in each category in both the best and worst economic circumstances. In the good times of 1978, some 2.5 percent of the labor force still lost a job. In the bad times of 1983, some 3.3 percent were able to enter or reenter the labor force. Many economists suggest that core unemployment reflects frictional unemployment. Others believe that it also includes structural unemployment. And most economists associate core unemployment with the natural rate of unemployment, or the level of unemployment when the economy is producing at its potential GNP level. Thus understanding changes in core unemployment is important to understanding changes in the natural rate of unemployment.

Exhibit 28.2 also shows data for 1986. (You can obtain more recent data from two government publications, the *Monthly Labor Review* or *Employment and Earnings*, if you want to update the table and make your own analysis.) What do these data suggest about the economy? Do the numbers look more like 1978 (a year of low unemployment) or 1983 (a year of high unemployment)? The data reflect the economic recovery that was well under way in 1986. The overall unemployment rate was lower than in 1983, and the relative size of the most cyclically sensitive portion—those who had lost jobs—had fallen. However, that proportion (almost 50 percent) is somewhat higher than it was in 1978. In addition, those who had lost jobs made up a higher proportion of the labor force: 3.4 percent as opposed to 2.5 percent. This analysis is not conclusive, but it does suggest that unemployment in 1986 was somewhat above the natural rate.

Duration of Unemployment

As we noted earlier, one of our main objectives is to understand how quickly and easily the automatic adjustment mechanism operates. In addition, we are concerned with whether the burden of adjusting to equilibrium is widely shared or falls on only a relatively few people. Data on the duration of unemployment are therefore of considerable interest to policy makers. Relatively short-term unemployment is perhaps an acceptable cost for a dynamic economy, especially if this cost is widely shared. But long-term unemployment involves greater personal costs which some economists and politicians believe should be treated with government policies.

Data such as those in Exhibit 28.3 are often used to support the contention that most unemployment is short term and that society should rely on the economy's automatic adjustment mechanism. In 1978 (a relatively good year) nearly one-half the unemployed had been looking for work for 5 weeks or less and less than one-fourth for as long as 15 weeks. Even during the relatively bad year of 1983, one-third of the unemployed had been looking for work for less than five weeks. In fact, on average, 60 percent of the unemployed are out of work for less than one month. Comparing 1983 to 1978, you can see that the long-term unem-

**Exhibit 28.3
Unemployment by
Duration: 1978, 1983,
and 1986**

Weeks unemployed	Percentage of the unemployed			Percentage of the total labor force		
	1978 (low unemployment)	1983 (high unemployment)	1986	1978 (low unemployment)	1983 (high unemployment)	1986
Less than 5	46.2	33.3	41.9	2.8	3.2	2.9
5–14	31.0	27.4	31.0	1.9	2.6	2.2
15–26	12.4	15.4	12.7	0.8	1.5	0.9
More than 26	10.4	23.9	14.4	0.6	2.3	1.0
Total	100.0	100.0	100.0	6.1	9.6	7.0

Source: Employment Report of the President, 1987 (Table B-33).

	Percentage of total weeks of unemployment for individuals	
Duration of unemployment	1974	1975
Less than 2 months	31	25
2–3 months	35	30
4–5 months	16	18
6 months or more	18	27
Total	100	100
Aggregate unemployment rate	5.6	8.5

Exhibit 28.4
Distribution of Total Weeks of
Unemployment: 1974–1975

Source: Kim B. Clark and Lawrence H. Summers, "Labor Market Dynamics and Unemployment: A Reconsideration," Brookings Papers on Economic Activity, 1979:1, Table 1, p. 19.

ployed (26 weeks or more) represent more than twice as large a proportion of the total unemployed when overall unemployment is high. But long-term unemployment accounts for only one-half of the increase in the unemployment rate; a larger percentage of the labor force experiences unemployment in all categories. As we found earlier, 1986 resembles a period of low unemployment, although long-term unemployment was a more serious problem in 1986 than in 1978.

These data suggest that most individuals experience unemployment for only a short period of time. But in some respects the data may be misleading. First, they do not indicate how unemployment for individuals ends. In fact, about one-half of all unemployment ends when an individual withdraws from the labor force. But we noted earlier that many of those who have withdrawn from the labor force (according to the official statistics) still want work and eventually return to work. Thus official statistics may understate the average length of unemployment. In fact, some studies suggest that long-term structural unemployment is the most important aspect of unemployment.

Exhibit 28.4 shows the distribution of those unemployed by total weeks of unemployment based on a study by Clark and Summers.[*] In these data, individuals who have been unemployed longer (two months or more) are given greater weight in the distribution. The result is very different from that shown in Exhibit 28.3, which emphasized short-term unemployment. The long-term unemployed appear to account for a significant portion of the total weeks of unemployment. In 1974, a year of relatively low unemployment, short-term unemployment (durations of less than two months) accounted for only one-third of all unemployment. Long-term unemployment (durations of four months or longer) accounted for more than one-third of the total. During a recession, such as in 1975, long-term unemployment increases; about 45 percent of all unemployment was long term.

Clark and Summers also demonstrate the significance of long-term unemployment in another way. They estimate that the 1974 unemployment rate would have fallen from 6.0 to 5.75 percent if short-term unemployment (five weeks or

---

[*] Kim B. Clark and Lawrence H. Summers, "Labor Market Dynamics and Unemployment: A Reconsideration," Brookings Papers on Economic Activity, Vol. 1, 1979, p. 16.

less) had been eliminated. However, eliminating long-term unemployment (six months or longer) would have reduced the rate from 6.0 to 3.5 percent.

What can we conclude from this discussion? First, most unemployed individuals experience only a short period of unemployment. Second, the long-term unemployed account for a significant portion of total weeks of unemployment. Third, much of any cyclical rise in unemployment represents an increase in individuals who have lost their jobs and an increase in long spells of unemployment. Fourth, even in the best of times the labor force is much more dynamic than overall unemployment statistics indicate. But what accounts for these facts? How do economists explain labor-market behavior? In the next section we take a close look at two theories that attempt to explain unemployment.

EXPLAINING UNEMPLOYMENT: JOB-SEARCH AND CONTRACTS THEORIES

The overall unemployment rate and dynamics of the labor market reflect, in part, the choices of individuals. For this reason, economists use theories based on microeconomic principles to try to understand and explain the labor market. The two theories we discuss here—the job-search and contracts theories—offer explanations for cyclical changes in unemployment and predictions about the speed of the economy's automatic adjustment mechanism.

Job-Search Theory and Unemployment

The **job-search theory** is an application of the principles of rational choice to unemployment. Unemployed individuals are considered to be engaged in a search for a job that matches what they expect (and want) to find. How long individuals remain unemployed depends on their preferences, expectations about wages and other job characteristics, and overall labor market conditions. Individuals have different skills and job preferences. Some seek part-time or temporary work; others want career jobs. Some have specialized skills; others have very general skills. Some have unrealistic expectations about jobs for which they are qualified. Available jobs offer different wages and other working conditions. To find a match between preferences and jobs, individuals must engage in job search.

Job-search theory identifies both the benefits and the costs of searching for a job. Initially, the major benefit is that you will learn more about available jobs, wages, and working conditions. When you have received a job offer, however, the benefits of continuing your job search depend on the probability of finding another job with higher pay or better working conditions. Likewise, initially the costs of conducting a job search are those connected with search activities. For example, you must scour the newspapers and other ads, call for appointments, travel to interviews, and face the frustration of being rejected. When you have received a job offer, however, the costs of continuing your job search include the opportunity cost of rejecting income that you could have earned by accepting the offer. Following the principles of rational choice, individuals will continue to search for a job (remain unemployed) as long as the expected extra benefits outweigh the extra costs.

Job-search theory. A view of unemployment as a search for information. Unemployed individuals make rational choices, weighing extra benefits of a continued job search (the prospects of finding a better job) against extra costs (accepting a lower paying job).

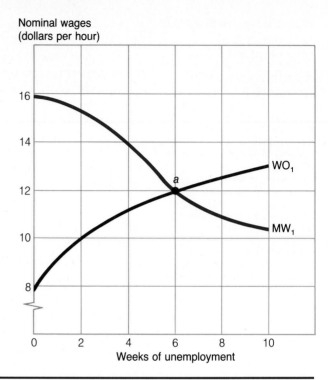

Exhibit 28.5
Job Search and the Duration of Unemployment
The minimum acceptable wage (MW$_1$) for Anita Braique, a typical unemployed worker, will decline as she gathers information about potential jobs and as the cost of continuing to look for a job increases. She encounters higher and higher job offers, as shown by the wage offer curve (WO$_1$). The curve shows the rising opportunity cost of rejecting offers to keep searching for a better job. Anita will stop searching when she encounters a job that pays the minimum wage that she is willing to accept. In this case her job search can be expected to last 6 weeks (point a).

Individuals begin their job search with some preconceived notion of how much they are worth. They know the types of jobs they like, and they have a perception of current and future prices. These expectations establish the individual's minimal acceptable standards for a job and a nominal wage. Exhibit 28.5 illustrates the job-search process. It shows how the minimally acceptable nominal wage, MW$_1$—also called the reservation wage—varies with length of job search for Anita Braique, an average unemployed individual. If Anita finds a job offering that wage, she will take the job. (Note that although other aspects of jobs are certainly important to the employment decision, we use the wage to represent all benefits. This simplification does not detract from the basic point of the analysis.) The MW$_1$ curve slopes downward, indicating that Anita will eventually recognize the market wage that she can reasonably expect and will, accordingly, revise any unrealistic expectations.

Exhibit 28.5 also shows the wage offer (WO$_1$) curve, which indicates the best offer Anita has received up to that time. Note that this curve slopes upward because the longer her search continues, the greater is Anita's chance of being offered a higher wage. At some point, however, Anita's expectations and the reality of labor market conditions will be the same, and she will take a job. This occurs when Anita has been unemployed 6 weeks and receives a job offer at $12 per hour (point a, where WO$_1$ intersects MW$_1$). If Anita is a typical unemployed person, and if these curves represent the normal functioning of the economy, six weeks of unemployment is associated with the natural rate of unemployment and with potential GNP. However, any factor that temporarily raises the minimally acceptable nominal wage (such as anticipation of an increase in prices) will lengthen the unemployment period. So will any factor that lowers wage offers (such as a drop in aggregate demand).

Job-search theory and reduced aggregate demand. To understand this last connection, you must know how job-search theory predicts the economy's reaction to a contractionary gap caused by decreased aggregate demand. Job-search theory recognizes that employers respond to a decrease in aggregate demand by lowering product prices and offering correspondingly lower nominal wages. As shown in Exhibit 28.6(a) and (b), the decline in aggregate demand results in a new, lower nominal wage offer curve (WO_2). Unless unemployed workers recognize that product prices are also falling, they will not immediately change their minimally acceptable nominal wage curve (MW_1). Since labor then will be relatively more expensive, employers will reduce the number of workers they hire, increasing unemployment.

In Exhibit 28.6(a), the duration of unemployment rises from six to eight weeks (point *b*, where MW_1 intersects WO_2). This higher level of unemployment is partly normal, or frictional (the six weeks), and partly cyclical (the extra two weeks). The increase in unemployment is also associated with the opening of the contractionary gap in Exhibit 28.6(b). Aggregate output falls and unemployment rises as the economy moves along the initial short-run aggregate supply curve (AS_1) to point *b*. Job-search theory associates this *temporary* rise in unemployment with cyclical unemployment resulting from misperceptions about current and future prices. But as we discussed in Chapter 26, information about actual prices and forecasts of future prices should quickly correct misperceptions and expectations.

As workers revise their expectations to meet reality, the minimally acceptable nominal wage curve falls (to MW_2). Workers accept lower nominal wage offers, recognizing that real income is not affected, since prices have fallen. This downward adjustment in nominal wages causes the short-run aggregate supply curve to increase (to AS_2). This automatic adjustment returns the economy to full employment. The normal job-search process for the individual shown in Exhibit 28.6(a) will again result in six weeks of unemployment (point *c*, where WO_2 intersects MW_2). At that point, the economy again produces at its potential GNP ($2000 billion) and unemployment is again at the natural rate.

By tying search behavior to expectations, job-search theory suggests that cyclical unemployment is only a temporary concern. The automatic adjustment mechanism requires only a revision of expectations about future prices in order to restore equilibrium in the labor market. Because the economy's response to cyclical changes is not instantaneous, some unemployment will result. But if expectations are quickly revised (and the theory assumes that they can be), full employment can be quickly restored.

Job-search theory and characteristics of unemployment. Job-search theory considers unemployment to be the outcome of a rational choice, a weighing by the individual of the benefits and costs of continuing to look for a job. As you have just seen, the theory is consistent with one of the facts about unemployment: For most people unemployment lasts only a short period of time.

The theory also provides a reason why new labor force entrants and reentrants experience higher-than-average unemployment. These individuals are less likely to have much information about what jobs are available. They are also more likely to have incorrect and overly optimistic wage demands. Thus they will end up spending more time trying to find a match between what they feel they are worth and what they are offered in the labor market.

Exhibit 28.6
Job Search: Response to Decreased Aggregate Demand
Initially, Anita Braique will be unemployed for 6 weeks (point *a*, where WO_1 and MW_1 intersect). We associate this with the natural rate of unemployment and with potential GNP in part (b). If aggregate demand decreases (to AD_2) in part (b), nominal wage offers also decrease (to WO_2) in part (a). The increase in Anita's unemployment period (to 8 weeks, point *b*) corresponds to the contractionary gap in part (b). As Anita's expectations adjust to the falling price level, her minimum acceptable wage offer decreases (to WO_2), a change reflected in the increase in aggregate supply (to AS_2) in part (b). These adjustments return unemployment to the natural rate and real output to its potential GNP level (point *c* in both graphs).

(a)

(b)

In general, job-search theory offers a plausible explanation for normal frictional unemployment. But a complete theory must also provide some explanation for long-term unemployment. As we noted earlier in this chapter, a significant number of individuals remain unemployed for long periods of time even when the economy is booming. However, because it treats unemployment as a rational choice, job-search theory explains long-term unemployment only as a voluntary decision to keep rejecting suitable job offers. Some economists reject this explanation and believe that job-search theory, while useful for some purposes, is not a complete theory of labor-market behavior. Moreover, some reject the notion that expectations are the major explanation for temporary unemployment and the cyclical rise in unemployment during recessions. Their alternative, contracts theory, is based on the existence of labor contracts.

Contracts Theory and Unemployment

Whereas job-search theory focuses on the relatively short-term unemployment of most individuals, **contracts theory** explains the relative stability of employment for much of the labor force. Proponents of contracts theory divide labor markets into *career* and *casual* markets. In career labor markets, workers and their employers seek a relatively long-lasting employment relationship. This type of relationship describes employment of faculty in colleges and universities, as well as supervisors and production workers in most manufacturing facilities. In casual labor markets, neither employers nor workers necessarily expect the employment relationship to last. Examples of casual labor markets include summer jobs for students.

Career labor markets. Career labor markets are most often characterized by jobs that require highly specialized skills and/or training and education. Because of the difficulty of finding and training suitable workers, employers may be willing to pay a premium to current employees to retain their skills. By offering a long-term relationship, the employer can avoid some of the costs of recruiting, screening, and training new employees. In return, workers in career labor markets receive the benefits of greater job security and opportunities for advancement.

To stabilize employment in career labor markets, employers and employees enter into *contracts* that define their relationships. In unionized organizations, these contracts are usually formal and explicit. Many of the rules covering working conditions are written down and result from formal bargaining between management and union representatives. Written contracts are not very common in non-union organizations, but informal and implicit contracts are widespread and no less important. Whatever their form, contracts usually restrict managerial options. For example, employers typically agree to promote present workers rather than hire new workers to fill jobs.

Contracts theory. A view of employment based on the existence of explicit or implicit contracts defining worker–employer relationships. Contracts provide long-term benefits to both workers and employers but fix nominal wages, slowing short-run adjustments in wages.

Career labor markets and reduced aggregate demand. If a decline in aggregate demand reduces demand for a firm's product, an employer may want to lower prices by cutting costs, including employee wages. But contracts typically require employers to maintain nominal wages, at least in the short run. Therefore employers in career labor markets are more likely to lay off some employees temporarily, while maintaining the current nominal wage for those who remain.

Union contracts usually require that those laid off must first be rehired before new employees can be hired. Thus layoffs protect the firm from losing its most experienced and trained workers and give laid-off workers a valuable right to be rehired. Such contract terms not only protect the employer from the greater costs of replacing skilled, experienced workers but also provide workers with a measure of job security. However, the firm is prevented from taking advantage of the increase in aggregate unemployment to hire lower priced workers, at least in the short run. Contracts are not necessarily ideal for either employers or workers, but they represent a compromise between the interests of each and between short-run and long-run considerations. Contracts trade higher short-run costs (higher product costs and more unemployment) for better long-run results (less turnover and greater job security).

Although these aspects of the career labor market benefit both workers and employers, they also slow down the economy's adjustment to a decline in aggregate demand. Because contracts do not allow nominal wages to adjust quickly, the short-run aggregate supply curve will not shift until current contracts expire and can be renegotiated. Eventually, however, new contracts will be written, adjusting wages as necessary to return the economy to full employment. But depending on contract lengths, the adjustment process may be slow.

Contracts theory does not rely on incorrect perceptions about real wages or faulty expectations about future prices by workers to explain the slow response of the automatic adjustment mechanism. Expectations influence the wages that are set when contracts are negotiated. The response to changes in aggregate demand is delayed because nominal wages paid under contracts do not change frequently—and usually not at all in response to temporary changes in demand.

Casual labor markets. In contrast to those in career labor markets, jobs in casual labor markets require little or no skill. Employers thus have low costs for and little difficulty in hiring new workers. Accordingly, they have little incentive to enter into long-term contracts with workers. Most jobs in casual labor markets offer low pay, poor working conditions, and little job security. The dead-end nature of such jobs also contributes to relatively high turnover. Unemployment for workers is usually short-term, but occurs frequently. As a result, average unemployment rates are higher than average.

Supporters of job-search theory argue that these effects reflect individual preferences (not to obtain more education, for example) and that high turnover contributes to economic efficiency. But advocates of contracts theory see low wages and other unpleasant characteristics of casual labor markets as evidence of structural problems. Employers in career labor markets will incur the costs of hiring and training only for individuals they feel are suitable for a long-term employment relationship. Individuals who lack basic skills and the desire to make a long-term commitment, will be judged unqualified and therefore not suitable for the career labor market.

Some workers may prefer casual markets. But contracts theory argues that other workers are stuck in casual labor markets because they lack—and cannot obtain—the skills required for jobs in career labor markets. The unemployment of such workers is structural, resulting from a mismatch between their skills and the demands of employers in career labor markets. This type of structural unemployment is included in the natural rate of unemployment along with the more "natural" frictional unemployment.

Job-Search and Contracts Theories Compared

Both the job-search and contracts theories offer interesting and helpful views of the operation of labor markets. For example, job-search theory argues that most unemployed workers could find work if they lowered their wage demands to realistic levels. Their refusal to accept offered wages is viewed as a voluntary, rational choice. However, the theory also recognizes that some cyclical unemployment may result from misperceptions of real wages, which is a short-term problem. In either case, it is the failure of real wages to adjust that causes unemployment.

In contrast, contracts theory views much unemployment as involuntary. Because contracts force employers in career labor markets to stop hiring when aggregate demand drops, even those willing to work for less cannot get jobs in those markets. For this reason, proponents of contracts theory suggest that cyclical unemployment may be more accurately viewed as inadequate aggregate demand. Moreover, workers in casual labor markets suffer high unemployment because the jobs offer few incentives for stable work, not because workers are unwilling to work for lower wages. And structural problems prevent many such workers from finding jobs in career labor markets.

These differences between the job-search and contracts theories lead to different attitudes toward unemployment policy. Proponents of job-search theory tend to oppose government attempts to reduce unemployment. They argue that the automatic adjustment mechanism can work both smoothly and quickly if inflationary expectations do not interfere. In contrast, supporters of contracts theory often advocate government policies to reduce unemployment. They believe the automatic adjustments as slow and more unemployment as involuntary. As you will see in Chapter 29, these contrasting theories also lead to different recommendations for policies to fight inflation.

In an important sense, however, neither theory alone offers a complete explanation for unemployment. Neither explains the existence of long-term unemployment very well. And neither provides a convincing explanation of the large-scale monthly fluctuations in the labor market.

On the other hand, both theories add to our understanding of the labor market. Most economists recognize that short-term unemployment responds to the factors included in job-search theory. Policies that lower the cost of looking for a job (such as unemployment compensation) can add to unemployment. Policies that improve information about jobs and reasonable wage offers can lower unemployment. Moreover, job-search theory can help us explore some of the factors responsible for the rise in the natural rate of unemployment. In contrast, contracts theory offers a rationale for some past labor-market behavior—especially the short-term response of unemployment to decreases in aggregate demand. It offers one explanation for why labor markets may fail to adjust quickly, even when information about future prices and government policies is available.

RECAP

According to contracts theory, workers and employers in career labor markets seek a long-term employment relationship. They agree to operate under long-term (formal or informal) contracts, which provide job security for senior employees and lower turnover costs for employers.

Contracts require employers to respond to declining demand by laying off workers, maintaining nominal wage rates, and not hiring new workers. Because nominal wages fall slowly, the economy's automatic adjustment mechanism will operate slowly. According to contracts theory, contract provisions and lack of skills may keep some workers from leaving casual labor markets and finding jobs in career labor markets.

Because job-search theory views most unemployment as short run and voluntary, its supporters oppose government attempts to reduce unemployment. Because contracts theory views unemployment as long run and involuntary, its supporters advocate government attempts to reduce unemployment.

INCREASES IN THE NATURAL RATE OF UNEMPLOYMENT

At the beginning of this chapter we noted that economists generally agree that the natural rate of unemployment has increased during the last 20 years. In this section, we examine the evidence and explanations for this belief. We also discuss some of the policies proposed to reduce the natural rate of unemployment.

Unemployment: Official and Natural Rates

Exhibit 28.7 shows the official unemployment rate and one estimate of the natural unemployment rate for the 1955–1986 period. Note that the official rate has increased in recessions and decreased during recoveries. At the same time, the unemployment rate associated with peaks in the business cycle has increased. In the early 1960s, economists associated this upward drift with a growing GNP gap (shown by the gap between the actual and natural rates of unemployment). But the 1970s were a period of high inflation. If the GNP gap had been growing, there should have been downward, not upward, pressure on prices. (The fact that some of the price-level increases reflect supply shocks complicates the picture.)

Most economists now believe that some part of the increase in official unemployment rates during peaks in the business cycle represents a rise in the

Exhibit 28.7
Actual and Natural Rates of Unemployment: 1955–1986
This graph shows both the actual rate of unemployment and one estimate of the natural rate of unemployment. The actual rate rises and falls with the business cycle but also shows an upward trend. (Note that the peaks of the actual unemployment rate coincide with troughs in the business cycle—that is, with recessionary periods shown by the red bands.) The natural rate shows an upward trend, which is associated with demographic changes in the labor market, government programs, structural changes in industrial demand, and international competition.

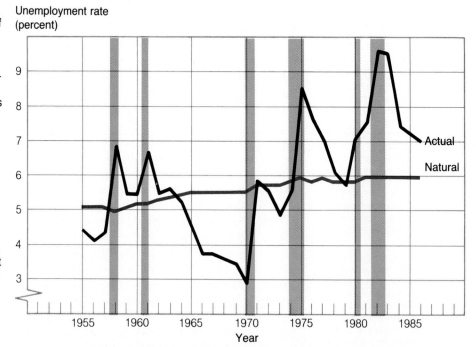

Sources: Actual unemployment rates from *Economic Report of the President, 1987,* Table B-31. Natural rate of unemployment from Robert J. Gordon, *Macroeconomics,* 4th Ed., Table A-1. Copyright © 1987 by Robert J. Gordon. Reprinted by permission of Little, Brown.

natural rate of unemployment. This conclusion is shown in Exhibit 28.7 as the upward-sloping natural rate line. This estimate of the natural rate increases from 5.0 in 1955 to 6.0 percent in 1986. As we have noted before, the natural rate cannot be observed, only estimated. Other estimates of the natural unemployment rate in the early 1980s range from 5 percent to 7 percent.

Factors that Increase the Natural Rate of Unemployment

Whatever the current natural rate of unemployment is, economists generally agree that it did increase in the 1960s and 1970s. Why did it rise? The reasons most often given are demographic changes in the labor force and the use of certain public policies.

Demographic changes.   Earlier in this chapter, we showed how job-search theory explains unemployment among workers just entering or reentering the labor market. We noted that such individuals may be unemployed longer because they have unrealistic expectations about available jobs, wages, and working conditions. Thus if new entrants and reentrants become a more important part of the labor force, the natural rate of unemployment will rise.

Two demographic changes increased the proportion of entrants and reentrants in the 1960s and 1970s. First, young workers (below the age of 25) became a larger percentage of the labor force in the 1970s. Since this group contained more than the average proportion of new entrants, this change increased the natural unemployment rate. In addition, many of these young workers sought work in the casual labor market, especially while still in school. (Summer jobs, such as flipping burgers or cleaning up parks are part of the casual labor market.) Casual labor markets, as we have noted, have higher job turnover and more unemployment than career labor markets.

A second demographic change was the increasing proportion of women in the labor force. Statistically, women are more likely to be reentrants or new entrants. Thus their average unemployment rate will be higher than that of men. In addition, married women with a working husband can be more selective about jobs. On average therefore they may spend a longer time looking for a job. To some extent, these factors may become less important over time, since women are increasingly entering the career labor market, seeking the same opportunities as men.

These demographic trends help explain the rise in the natural rate in the 1960s and 1970s. But, as we noted in Chapter 6, those historical trends have largely ended. Teenagers have represented a declining proportion of the labor force since the mid-1970s, a trend expected to continue in the future. And while projections show that the percentage of women in the labor force will continue to increase, future changes will be much smaller than past changes.

Government policies.   In addition to demographic changes, economists note that several government policies may have contributed to the rise in the natural unemployment rate. An often cited example is the unemployment compensation program, which provides cash payments to workers who have been laid off or whose jobs have been eliminated. (Note that it is not available to new entrants.) In 1986, government payments for unemployment compensation totaled $14.5 billion.

Most economists recognize three impacts of unemployment compensation on frictional unemployment and hence on the natural rate. First, unemployment payments lower the cost of looking for a job. Thus we can anticipate longer searches, more frictional unemployment, and a higher natural rate. Second, unemployment benefits reduce the costs of layoffs. Thus unions often press for contracts that specify layoffs, rather than nominal wage reductions, as the employers' response to temporary decreases in demand. Finally, the level of benefits provided and the number of the unemployed who were eligible increased during the 1960s and 1970s.

Other economists believe that periodic increases in the minimum wage law have increased the natural rate of unemployment in two ways. First, it has encouraged new entrance into the labor-force. At the same time, it has lowered the number of job openings. Some economists also blame increasing welfare benefits. But in the early and mid-1980s, real benefits (adjusted for price-level rises) fell and some eligibility requirements were stiffened. If these programs did add to the natural rate in the past, they no longer do.

Structural changes and international competition. Structural shifts from manufacturing to services and increased international competition have also been blamed for a rising natural rate of unemployment. These structural shifts have been quite large: Between 1980 and 1986, manufacturing industries lost some 800,000 jobs, while service industries gained some 4 million jobs. Many manufacturing industries resemble the career labor market with steady employment and low job turnover. But many service industries resemble the casual labor market with high rates of job turnover and many part-time or temporary jobs. Thus this shift from manufacturing to service employment may have increased the amount of frictional unemployment, adding to the natural rate.

In addition, international competition, along with the reluctance of workers to accept lower real wages, undoubtedly contributed to the loss of U.S. manufacturing jobs. A number of large plants have closed, eliminating thousands of jobs in local labor markets. Competition may also have caused U.S. firms to change some of the contract rules that formerly provided stable long-term jobs. Thus the major adjustments required of many workers—geographical and occupational mobility and accepting lower real wages—may lead to longer periods of unemployment. Whatever the long-run implications, international competition has probably raised both frictional and structural unemployment and, consequently, the natural rate of unemployment.

Policies to Lower the Natural Rate of Unemployment

As you might expect, economists are divided over whether government policies can—or should—be used to reduce the natural rate of unemployment. Because the natural rate is not likely to be affected by aggregate demand, attempts to lower it have usually involved microeconomic rather than macroeconomic policies. Such policies attempt to reduce the length of the typical job search or to better match the skills of the unemployed with the skills that employers want. In these ways, some economists and politicians hope to lower both the frictional and structural unemployment that are part of the natural rate.

Employment assistance and job training programs. We noted earlier that many women and young people who are first entering or reentering the job market may experience unemployment because they lack accurate information about wages. We also pointed out that some individuals in casual labor markets (including many young workers) usually lack the skills necessary to enter career markets. To the extent that the natural rate of unemployment results from imperfect information or a lack of skills, employment assistance and job training programs may lower the rate. Some information about available jobs, wages, and similar characteristics has been provided for many years through state-run, federally supported employment services. But existing programs have been of only limited help to the unemployed. Many employers inform the state services of openings for only the lowest paying, lowest skilled jobs.

Structural unemployment is the target of job training programs. Modest, federally funded programs were started in the early 1960s. Overall, they succeeded in increasing the skills and job potential of the individuals enrolled. However, they apparently had no effect on the natural rate of unemployment. Many of these programs were cut from the federal budget by the Reagan administration. Some economists argue that the programs failed to provide realistic training and significant job skills. Others suggest that the effort failed because of the modest scale of the programs. It is also possible that job training changed the distribution, but not the level, of unemployment.

Reforming the unemployment insurance program. Because the unemployment compensation program may have contributed to the rise in the natural rate of unemployment, some economists suggest altering this program. They advocate reducing benefits, requiring those eligible for benefits to look harder for jobs, and eliminating payments for those who refuse job offers. These reforms are aimed at increasing efficiency in the economy.

But such efforts are opposed by those who are concerned with equity. Supporters of current programs point out that unemployment compensation may lessen workers' demands for long-term contracts which provide job security. Thus the unemployment program allows producers to respond to shifts in product demand, improving efficiency. Moreover, they argue that by providing time for job searches, the program may allow workers to find more suitable jobs. Workers forced to accept low-wage jobs may soon be unemployed again.

Like all other economic policies, efforts to reduce the natural rate of unemployment require careful consideration of benefits and costs. Because benefits and costs are difficult to measure (especially benefits associated with equity), rational disagreement is inevitable. Moreover, it should be clear from the brief discussion of the causes and possible policies that it is not easy to lower the natural rate of unemployment.

CONCLUSION

In this chapter we explored the nature of unemployment and two theories—the job-search and contracts theories—that economists have developed to help them understand and predict changes in unemployment. While neither theory provides a complete description of unemployment, each offers a view of at least part of the problem. Because their explanations differ, however, economists reach different conclusions about the speed of the automatic adjustment mechanism.

In addition, we noted that while economists generally accept the notion of a natural rate of unemployment, they disagree about appropriate policies to reduce unemployment to this level. Most agree that changes in aggregate demand will affect the actual rate of unemployment in the short run. But aggregate demand policies cannot successfully maintain unemployment below the natural rate over the long run. The effect of attempting to do so, as we discuss in Chapter 29, is inflation.

SUMMARY

1. In this chapter we examined some of the microeconomic foundations of labor markets and their implications for the macroeconomic problem of unemployment.

2. Although the aggregate unemployment rate usually changes slowly, a significant number of people change their labor-force status every month. The largest proportion of the unemployed—those who have lost jobs—are the most cyclically sensitive unemployed. Most unemployment lasts a month or less, but the long-term unemployed account for a significant proportion of total unemployment.

3. Job-search theory views unemployment as a rational choice of individuals, who compare the benefits of continuing to look for a job (the prospects of finding a better job) to the opportunity costs (rejecting a current job offer or leaving the labor force). A decline in aggregate demand may temporarily increase unemployment until individuals can adjust their wage demands to reflect more accurate information and expectations. According to job-search theory, high unemployment rates among teenagers and women reflect the fact that many are new entrants and reentrants who may have unrealistic ideas about wages and working conditions.

4. According to the contracts theory, workers and employers in career labor markets seek a long-term employment relationship and agree to operate under long-term (formal or informal) contracts. Contracts provide job security for senior employees and lower turnover costs for employers. But they require employers to respond to declining demand by laying off workers, maintaining nominal wage rates, and not hiring new workers. Since nominal wages are slow to fall, the economy's automatic adjustment mechanism will operate slowly.

5. Supporters of job-search theory view most unemployment as short run and voluntary; they reject the use of government policies to reduce unemployment. Proponents of contracts theory view a significant part of unemployment as long run and involuntary; they support government attempts to reduce unemployment.

6. Economists generally agree that the natural rate of unemployment has increased in the last 25 years. Demographic factors—the increased proportion of young workers and women—have raised the proportion of unemployed in the new entrant and reentrant categories. In addition, the natural unemployment rate may have been raised by some government programs—such as the unemployment compensation program—that prolong job searches or encourage new entrants.

7. The size of the change in the natural rate of unemployment and the importance of various factors in accounting for it are debatable. Changes in the demographics of the labor force, government policies such as unemployment insurance, structural changes in demand, and international competition have all received attention as possible causes.

8. Proposals to reduce the natural rate of unemployment include job training, employment assistance, and alteration of the unemployment compensation program.

KEY TERMS

Job-search theory, 725
Contracts theory, 729

QUESTIONS FOR REVIEW AND DISCUSSION

1. Using the wage offer and minimum acceptable wage curves shown in this chapter, describe how the actual unemployment rate might be pushed below the natural rate for a short period of time, but how it would adjust to the natural rate in the long run.

2. Why do proponents of job-search theory believe that the automatic adjustment mechanism works quickly and effectively? Why do proponents of contracts theory believe that it operates slowly? According to the contracts theory, can the mechanism be speeded up significantly? Why or why not?

3. Classical economists tended to view unemployment as voluntary, meaning that individuals who wanted to work could find employment if they were willing to accept wages that reflected their value to employers. However, Keynes suggested that in a recession, some unemployment was involuntary. Do you think that public policy should be directed to reducing all unemployment, or simply aimed at involuntary unemployment? Explain how cyclical unemployment can be viewed either as nominal wages that are too high or as aggregate demand that is too low. With which view would you associate activists? Nonactivists?

4. Which of the following individuals would you classify as voluntarily unemployed? Involuntarily unemployed? What criteria makes unemployment voluntary?
   a) A teenager looking for a part-time summer job.
   b) A laid-off worker who draws unemployment compensation and confines her job search to jobs with comparable pay.
   c) An unemployed head of household who refuses to accept a job in the casual labor market.
   d) A person whose spouse is well-paid and who is looking for a "meaningful" job.

5. Some economists favor lowering the minimum wage for teenagers who work during the summer in order to reduce the high unemployment rate for this group. Why would this policy tend to reduce the unemployment rate of teenagers? What are the arguments against this proposal?

6. The closing of a large plant can create a significant amount of local unemployment. What are the costs and benefits of each of the following possible policies?
   a) Subsidizing the company in order to keep the plant open.
   b) Restricting foreign competition that may be responsible for the plant's low profits.
   c) Providing retraining and/or relocating the affected workers.
   d) Doing nothing.

7. What is the relationship between the natural rate of unemployment and potential GNP? Explain the effects of the changing work patterns of women in the 1960s and 1970s on the natural rate and on potential GNP.

Inflation and Unemployment

QUESTIONS TO CONSIDER

☐ How do economists measure inflation?

☐ What causes—and does not cause—inflation?

☐ Why did economists once believe that some increase in inflation could be traded for a reduction in unemployment?

☐ What is the consensus among present-day economists on the trade-off between unemployment and inflation?

☐ How do the expectations and sticky-price views of inflation lead to differing policy proposals?

T hose of you who are 20 years old or younger probably do not remember a year when the price level did not increase. In this chapter we want to see why the price level increases (and decreases). Why have we experienced the sustained increases that economists call inflation? To what extent are government monetary and fiscal policies a cause and/or a cure for inflation?

In Chapter 28 we considered explanations and effects of unemployment. In this chapter we do the same for inflation. At times unemployment and inflation appear to be connected: Reducing unemployment may cause prices to rise and reducing inflation may cause unemployment to rise. But why does this trade-off occur, and can macroeconomic policies be used to trade lower unemployment for higher inflation? In this chapter we consider some of the different ways that economists have answered this question. Understanding why economists disagree will help you to understand why the use of aggregate demand policies to fight inflation or to lower unemployment remains controversial.

INFLATION

In Chapter 20 we considered some of the reasons why inflation is usually considered to be undesirable. Inflation harms some people (those on fixed incomes, for example) more than others. Moreover, individuals living in inflationary economies spend a lot of time and energy trying to protect themselves from inflation. Since these conditions threaten both equity and efficiency, why has almost every modern economy experienced inflation? Before you can answer that question, you have to know more about inflation and the economic forces that cause it.

Measuring Inflation

Inflation rate. The annual rate of increase in the price level.

What you usually hear called inflation is actually the **inflation rate**, that is, the annual percentage change in some price-level index. For example, the GNP deflator increased from 111.5 in 1985 to 114.5 in 1986. This is an annual inflation rate of 2.7 percent, calculated as

$$\text{Inflation rate} = \text{Percentage change in GNP deflator}$$

$$= \frac{\text{Deflator, 1986} - \text{Deflator, 1985}}{\text{Deflator, 1985}} \times 100$$

$$= \frac{114.5 - 111.5}{111.5} \times 100$$

$$= 2.7\% \text{ per year}$$

That is, the average price of goods and services as measured by the GNP deflator increased by 2.7 percent in 1986. To check your understanding, verify some of the inflation rates provided in the Appendix at the back of this textbook.

In recent years forecasting the direction of change in prices has been easy. The last annual *decline* in the CPI occurred in 1955, and the GNP deflator has increased every year since 1949. Nevertheless, from time to time and especially in recession periods, there have been monthly declines in the price level. Moreover, there were both large price-level increases and decreases in years prior to the 1940s. The inflation in the U.S. economy, even during periods of recession, actually started after World War II.

Increases in the General Price Level: A Short-Run View

The inflation rate tells us what has happened to prices, but not why. More importantly, the inflation rate for any one year does not indicate whether the increase in prices is temporary or part of a sustained increase. That is, does it represent the effects of a one-time change in economic conditions? Or does it indicate a sustained upward movement in the general price level?

Later in this chapter we consider what economists generally agree is the principal cause of sustained movements in prices: changes in the money supply. First, however, we want to consider the factors that cause short-run changes in the price level. Put simply, *an increase in the price level can be caused by either an increase in aggregate demand or a decrease in aggregate supply*.

Exhibit 29.1 shows changes in actual GNP for the United States. From 1967 to 1968, real GNP (output) rose by more than 4 percent (or faster than the long-run average of 3.2 percent). Exhibit 29.1(a) shows this change as a shift in the aggregate demand curve (from AD_1 to AD_2). As a result, the economy moved along its short-run aggregate supply curve, and the general price level increased from 35.9 to 37.7. That is, the annual inflation rate was 5.0 percent (using the formula previously given), or more than twice the annual rate of the previous five years.

A change in any of the factors that increase aggregate demand will cause the price level to rise. Increases in planned consumption or investment, government spending, the money supply, or net exports can all increase aggregate demand and hence the price level. Thus price-level increases caused by increases in aggregate demand are sometimes referred to as **demand-pull inflation**. Higher aggregate demand is said to be pulling the price level up.

Such was the case in 1967–1968, when government spending, both for the Vietnam War and for President Johnson's War on Poverty, increased dramatically. The large tax cut passed by Congress in 1964 had also helped boost both consumption and investment. And, the Fed increased the money supply in 1968 by 7

Demand-pull inflation. Increases in the price level caused by increases in aggregate demand.

(a) Increase in aggregate demand, 1967–1968

Price-level index
(GNP deflator)

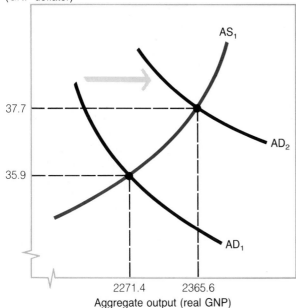

Aggregate output (real GNP)
(billions of dollars per year)

(b) Decrease in aggregate supply, 1973–1974

Price-level index
(GNP deflator)

Aggregate output (real GNP)
(billions of dollars per year)

Exhibit 29.1
Increases in the Price Level—Two Causes
An increase in the price level can be caused by either an increase in aggregate demand, as shown in part (a), or by a decrease in aggregate supply, as shown in part (b). Both changes cause excess demand at the old equilibrium price level and thus put upward pressure on prices. They have different effects on real GNP, however. An increase in aggregate demand causes real GNP to rise; a decrease in aggregate supply causes real GNP to fall.

percent, compared to a 4 percent average increase during the preceding five years. All these factors contributed to higher aggregate demand and the consequent increase in both real output (GNP) and prices.

In contrast, between 1973 and 1974, real GNP fell by 0.5 percent. Exhibit 29.1(b) shows this change as a shift in the aggregate supply curve (from AS_1 to AS_2). As a result of this change, the economy moved along its aggregate demand curve, and the price level increased from 49.5 to 54.0. That is, the annual inflation rate was 9.1 percent (using the formula previously given).

We can expect a higher price level to result from an increase in any factor that decreases aggregate supply. Increases in the prices of resources or in expected future price levels will decrease aggregate supply. Thus a rise in the price level that is caused by a decrease in aggregate supply is sometimes called **cost-push inflation**. Higher costs are said to be pushing the price level up.

Such was the case in 1973–1974, when the price of oil—a major resource—increased from $3 to more than $12 a barrel. The increased price of oil raised the cost of production in many industries. In this same period, poor harvests in many parts of the world caused a sharp increase in food prices. Food prices in

Cost-push inflation. Increases in the price level caused by decreases in aggregate supply. Most economists believe that sustained decreases in aggregate supply are unlikely.

the United States increased an average of 12–14 percent. The prices of many other resources and goods also increased because the federal government removed general price ceilings early in 1974.

Faced with higher costs for home heating, transportation, and food, workers demanded higher wages, further increasing costs of production and thus reducing aggregate supply. Finally, businesses and workers became concerned about future inflation and raised their price-level expectations, which also decreased aggregate supply. The overall result was a decrease in real GNP and an increase in prices.

Note that in both 1967–1968 and 1973–1974, the initial change resulted in excess demand (more demanded than supplied) at the old price level. Excess demand drove the price level up as the economy adjusted to a new equilibrium position. But conditions during these two periods also differed in an important respect. When aggregate demand increased, real GNP (in the short run) rose along with prices. But when aggregate supply decreased, real GNP fell as prices rose. By noting how real GNP changes, we can decide whether a particular price-level increase was caused by shifts in aggregate demand or by shifts in aggregate supply.

Inflation: What Does *Not* Cause It

Short-run changes in the price level reinforce the basic macroeconomic principles that have been the focus of our discussion in previous chapters. But short-run changes, such as a single increase in demand or decrease in supply, have only a limited effect on the economy. As we have discussed before, the economy's automatic adjustment mechanism will eventually restore long-run equilibrium. The price level may be higher, but once the economy has fully adjusted, there is no reason for any further increase.

Of far greater importance to economists, politicians, and individuals are the effects of inflation, that is, a sustained upward movement of the price level. Can inflation, like a short-run price-level increase, be caused by shifts in either aggregate demand or supply? In this section we demonstrate why most economists agree that continual increases in aggregate demand are the main cause of inflation. We also show why they believe that there is a long-run connection between inflation and the growth rate of the money supply.

Consider Exhibit 29.2, which shows the price level increasing from 120 to 128 because of two decreases in aggregate supply. Note that each decrease in aggregate supply causes the price level to increase. But to get sustained increases in prices from this source, aggregate supply must continue to decrease. Although such decreases are theoretically possible, they are virtually unheard of. Why? Suppose that the decreases in aggregate supply represent an attempt by oil producers to force oil prices up. An initial decrease in oil supplies will indeed decrease aggregate supply and raise the general price level. But sustained price-level increases require sustained supply shocks. Generally, economists believe that oil producers would not find it in their best interests to continue to reduce the supply of oil.

Once oil prices have risen to their profit-maximizing level, only changes in economic conditions—such as reductions in the supplies of substitutes—would justify further price increases. Moreover, the more oil prices are raised, the faster producers can expect substitutes to develop, reducing the economic power that allowed them to raise prices in the first place. In addition, as you can see in Exhibit 29.2, each decrease in aggregate supply pushes the economy farther away from potential GNP (output). The increase in the size of the contractionary gap increases the downward pressure on wages and prices in general. And, as real

Price-level index
(GNP deflator)

Exhibit 29.2
Decreases in Aggregate Supply
The initial equilibrium (point *a*) shows the economy in long-run equilibrium, producing and selling at its potential GNP of $2000 billion. The first "supply shock" decreases aggregate supply (to AS₂), raising the price level and opening a contractionary gap. Actual output at point *b* is $1950 billion, a gap of $50 billion below potential GNP. A second decrease in aggregate supply further increases the price level and further widens the contractionary gap. The widening gap puts downward pressure on prices and tends to make further price increases unprofitable.

GNP falls, so will demand for and sales of the product. Eventually, downward pressures on prices will make further decreases in aggregate supply unprofitable. Thus *decreases in aggregate supply may produce short-run increases in the general price level, but they are unlikely to lead to continuing inflation.*

This sequence of events, in fact, is what occurred in the 1970s with the oil price shocks. The members of the Organization of Petroleum Exporting Countries (OPEC) succeeded in pushing oil prices up in 1973–1974 and again in 1979. Although both events raised the general price level, OPEC did not continually raise oil prices. Actually, the higher oil prices stimulated conservation efforts and the development of substitutes. The fall in oil consumption and decreased demand during the 1981–1982 recession pushed oil prices from more than $35 per barrel in 1980 down to less than $11 per barrel in 1986. Although these supply shocks caused the price level to increase in the mid-1970s and early 1980s, they added only temporary upward pressure on prices.

If decreases in aggregate supply do not cause inflation, what about increases in aggregate demand, the second reason for a short-run increase in the price level? In Exhibit 29.3 we show only changes in potential GNP and aggregate demand because we want to focus on long-run changes in prices. We also assume that the economy moves from one long-run equilibrium position to the next. Both parts (a) and (b) show that potential GNP increases over a period of time, but whether or not the price level increases depends on how much aggregate demand increases.

Exhibit 29.3(a) shows an economy with no inflation. From year to year, aggregate demand and potential GNP both increase at the same rate. The economy

(a) No inflation: Aggregate demand matches increases in potential GNP.

(b) Inflation: Aggregate demand increases faster than potential GNP.

Exhibit 29.3
Inflation: A Dynamic View
Both graphs show a growing economy; that is, potential GNP (potential output levels, shown as PO_1, PO_2, and PO_3) increases over time. In part (a) the increases in potential GNP are just matched by increases in aggregate demand as the economy moves from point a to point b to point c. As a result, there is no pressure on the price level and no inflation. In part (b) aggregate demand is growing faster than potential GNP, opening expansionary gaps as the economy moves from point a to point b to point c. (Note that at the price level of 120, AD_2 shows $2050 billion demanded, or more than the new potential GNP (PO_2) of $2000.) This excess demand puts upward pressure on the price level and the result is inflation, or a steady, sustained increase in the price level.

moves from one long-run equilibrium position to the next (from a to b to c) without experiencing excess demand. Thus the economy grows without affecting the price level. In contrast, Exhibit 29.3(b) shows an economy with inflation. Each year, aggregate demand increases faster than potential GNP, opening an expansionary gap at the old price level. Thus each year there is excess demand pressure. Although we do not show the short-run adjustment, as long as aggregate demand continues to grow faster than potential GNP, the price level will continue to increase. That is, the economy will experience inflation.

Implicit in this explanation of inflation is the assumption that aggregate demand grows faster than potential GNP. How can such excess demand be sustained? The factors that can cause excess demand are those that can shift aggregate demand. But with one exception—increases in the money supply—these factors are not likely to cause persistent inflation. For example, an increase in government spending tends to boost aggregate demand and may push prices up temporarily. But can the government continue to increase spending faster than real GNP grows? If the money supply is fixed, higher government spending will crowd out private-sector spending, as you saw in Chapter 27. And, as you have also seen, this crowding-out effect is strongest when, as here, the economy is operating at or near its potential GNP level.

Similarly, other components of real domestic spending are limited by the total amount of GNP available. Thus spontaneous increases in planned spending can be expected to cause only temporary increases in the price level if the money supply is fixed. (How long such "temporary" increases can go on is, however, the subject of much debate.) Moreover, it seems highly unlikely that any spontaneous change in spending could account for a 50 or 200 percent increase in prices in a single year. Long before such a spending change could generate that type of demand pressure, the limits on spending would be reached. Thus if we want to explain large, sustained increases in prices, we must find another explanation.

Inflation: What *Does* Cause It

The limits that apply to other aggregate-demand factors do not apply to increases in the money supply. History has shown that there are few realistic limits to how fast and how long the money supply can be increased. The money supply can easily be doubled in a very short period of time. Large increases in the money supply can last for an extended period of time and, in fact, provide the only reasonable explanation for continuing high rates of inflation. In 1985, Bolivia experienced an inflation rate of 11,750 percent! This inflation was fueled by such large increases in the money supply (almost 8000 percent) that Bolivian currency printed in West Germany and Great Britain was Bolivia's third leading import. (See A Case in Point: Money Supply versus Inflation for more on international links between money and inflation.)

Bolivia obviously is an extreme example, but most economists agree that any large, sustained increase in the price level lasting several years is the result of "too much money chasing too few goods." That is, high inflation rates are caused by excessive growth in the money supply. Milton Friedman wrote that "Inflation is everywhere and always a monetary phenomenon."* Most economists agree with Friedman, but some believe that this statement is too strong.

Exhibit 29.4 reinforces this conclusion by showing growth of the money supply (M-1) and annual inflation rates (increases in the GNP deflator) in the United States from 1960 to 1986. As you can see, in the early 1960s low rates of inflation were accompanied by slow growth rates in the money supply. From 1950 to 1964 the money supply grew at an average annual rate of 2.1 percent. During the same period, the annual inflation rate was 2.5 percent. From 1968 to 1973, the money supply grew at an average annual rate of 6.3 percent; the rate of inflation increased to 5.1 percent. During the 1976–1979 period, the inflation rate averaged 7.3 percent, while the money supply grew at an average rate of 7.6 percent.

Exhibit 29.4 shows a clear, but far from perfect, long-run relationship between changes in the money supply and the rate of inflation. But what about the short run? From 1973 to 1976 and from 1980 to 1982, the price level increased faster than the money supply. In those periods, supply shocks had a major effect on the

---

* Milton Friedman, *Dollars and Deficits*. Englewood Cliffs, N.J.: Prentice-Hall, 1968, p. 39.

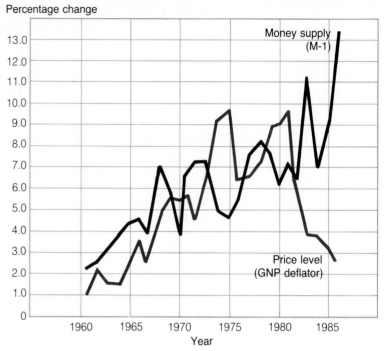

Percentage change

Exhibit 29.4
Changes in the Money Supply and the Price Level: 1960–1986
The graph shows percentage changes in the money supply (measured by M-1) and the price level (measured by the GNP deflator). The two series move together for most of this period. The increases in the growth rates of the money supply from 1960 to 1975 is matched by similar increases in inflation rates. The relationship is not exact. This is particularly true in the 1980s, when money-supply growth was increasing while the inflation rates fell.

Sources: Money supply from Federal Reserve Bank of Boston; GNP deflator from *Economic Report of the President, 1987.*

price level. What about the 1983–1986 period, when money growth was higher than growth in GNP but inflation fell? Economists disagree about the cause. Some view it as reflecting a major increase in demand for money (M-1) as households reacted to falling interest rates on nonchecking accounts and began to hold more money in NOW accounts, for example.

The important point is that *short-run variations in the rate of inflation can be caused by any factor that shifts aggregate demand or the short-run aggregate supply curve. Long-run trends in the rate of inflation are generally associated with trends in the growth rate of the money supply.* No large, sustained upward movement in the price level can occur without a large, sustained growth in the money supply. A slowly growing money supply will eventually lead to a low rate of inflation.

Lingering Effects of Demand and Supply Shocks

The differences that we have pointed out between temporary and long-run changes in the inflation rate are sometimes difficult to sort out in the real world. We have noted that the effects of a single shift in aggregate supply (a supply shock) or aggregate demand (a demand shock) are temporary. When the effects have run their course, prices will stabilize unless additional shocks occur. But in the real world, the effects of a major demand or supply shock may affect the price level for a substantial period of time.

Consider, for example, the supply shocks that hit the United States in 1973–1974. We noted earlier that increases in oil and food prices decreased aggregate supply and real GNP while the inflation rate nearly doubled in 1974. But the United States experienced further severe inflation in 1975, as the supply shocks of 1973–1974 affected electric rates and transportation costs, driving up product prices. And, as noted, workers raised their price-level expectations and demanded higher wages. These reactions also fueled inflation. The initial boost in oil and food prices occurred in a relatively short period of time. But studies show that it took the economy several years to fully adjust to higher resource prices.

Similarly, we must be careful in interpreting the large drop in inflation in the early and mid-1980s. The economy was again rocked by an oil-price shock in 1979. Inflationary expectations rose again in the face of double-digit inflation rates in 1979 and 1980. But by 1982 the rate of inflation had declined significantly. In part, we can attribute this drop to the Fed's efforts to restrain the growth of the money supply. But part of the decline occurred because the effects of the supply shock had finally ended. The initial shock and its aftereffects left the price index at a much higher level. But once the economy adjusted to the shock, the upward pressure on prices ended. The rate of inflation was high, only temporarily, just as we would have expected from a single supply shock.

A Case in Point
Money Supply versus Inflation:
A Look at International Conditions

The connection between changes in the money supply and the price level becomes obvious when we examine other economies. The table at right shows that those countries in which the growth of the money supply was most rapid—such as Argentina and Brazil—had the highest rates of inflation. Countries with more modest increases in the money supply—Switzerland, for example—had more modest increases in the price level.

But the correlation between the growth of the money supply and inflation is not perfect for any of the countries shown, nor do economists expect it to be. For one thing, monetary growth has no effect on the price level if it simply causes aggregate demand to increase along with potential GNP. For another, demand for money may decline because of the development of substitutes or, in high inflation economies, because of expectations of a rising price level. In such cases, prices may increase faster than money-supply changes indicate. Although other factors also affect the price level, changes in the money supply are one of the most important. When the money supply grows very rapidly over a period of time, inflation can certainly be expected to result.

Country	Period	Average annual percentage change in	
		Money supply	Price level
West Germany	1960–1985	7.7	3.8
Switzerland	1960–1985	6.3	4.1
United States	1960–1985	5.7	5.2
Canada	1960–1985	8.0	5.6
Japan	1960–1985	14.7	6.4
Sweden	1960–1982	8.6	6.9
France	1960–1985	10.5	7.3
India	1960–1985	12.5	7.4
United Kingdom	1960–1985	8.8	8.3
Italy	1960–1984	16.1	9.7
South Korea	1960–1985	25.3	13.5
Mexico	1960–1985	22.6	19.7
Brazil	1960–1984	61.1	72.6
Israel	1975–1985	97.3	129.7
Argentina	1973–1985	218.4	248.8
Bolivia	1960–1985	360.2	528.1

Source: International Monetary Fund, *International Financial Statistics Yearbook,* 1986 (Washington, D.C., 1987).

Change	1964–1971	1972–1980	1981–1984
Demand pressure	+3.28%	−2.44%	−2.76%
Food and energy prices	−0.08	+2.90	−0.81
Import prices	−0.13	+1.59	−0.67
Other	+0.42	+3.92	−0.19
Change in inflation rate	+3.49%	+5.97%	−4.43%

Source: Robert J. Gordon, "Understanding Inflation in the 1980s," *Brookings Papers on Economic Activity*, 1985:1, p. 286.

Exhibit 29.5
Factors Responsible for Changes in Inflation

Disinflation. A decline in the rate of increase of the general price level; the price level continues to rise, but more slowly.

RECAP

It is important to distinguish between a one-time change in the price level and sustained increases in it. After a one-time increase in aggregate demand or decrease in aggregate supply, the economy returns to equilibrium and price stability. Continual increases in aggregate demand create inflation.

Changes in aggregate supply cannot explain inflation because continued decreases in aggregate supply cause contractionary gaps and thus put downward pressure on prices.

Most determinants of aggregate demand cannot explain inflation because they involve spending limits, beyond which the household, business, government, and foreign sectors cannot go to cause continued upward movement of the price level.

Most economists agree that inflation is the result of increases in the money supply that exceed increases in real GNP.

In the real world, it is not always easy to distinguish short-run changes in the price level from inflation because supply shocks and changes in other factors that affect aggregate demand may effect the economy for significant periods of time.

History of Factors that Influence Inflation

We have seen that a change in the price level can be caused by both temporary changes—such as supply shocks—and long-term changes in macroeconomic policies. But which factors have been most significant in terms of the U.S. economy? Exhibit 29.5 shows the results of a study of the influences of various factors on changes in U.S. inflation rates. The last line indicates that the inflation rate (the average annual increase in the price level) was almost 3.5 percent higher in 1971 than in 1964. Almost all of this increase is attributed to excess demand pressures.

From 1972 to 1980 increases in food and energy prices (the supply shocks discussed earlier) combined with increased prices of other imports to raise the inflation rate. At the same time, the macroeconomic policies followed were contractionary, as indicated by the negative sign on the demand pressure variable. (The effect of "other variables"—price level expectations, for example—was also quite significant during this period.)

Finally, you can see that 1981–1984 was a period of **disinflation**. That is, inflation rates decreased. (For more on this topic, see A Case in Point: History of Inflation and Disinflation.) The 1981–1984 disinflation reflects both lower food and energy prices and the Fed's efforts to keep the economy growing slowly. In addition, the increase in the value of the dollar during this period allowed U.S. households and businesses to pay less for foreign imports. For example, a West German product that would have cost $55 in 1980 could have been purchased for $34 in 1984, just because the value of the dollar was higher.

This study supports our conclusion that many factors affect the rate of inflation during any specific period of time. Changes in demand (as in the first and third periods shown) are often the most significant influences. But other factors can have significant short-run effects on the rate of inflation.

UNEMPLOYMENT AND INFLATION: IS THERE A TRADE-OFF?

In the preceding section you saw once again how important it is to distinguish between short-run and long-run views of the economy. This distinction is also very important in determining the connection between unemployment and inflation and whether macroeconomic policies can trade higher prices for lower unemployment.

A Case in Point
History of Inflation and Disinflation

The concepts presented in this chapter help to explain changes in inflation and unemployment rates in the United States and in other countries since 1965. In analyzing the situation, we want to examine evidence on inflation and unemployment and seek explanations for the changes we observe.*

For the United States, Europe, and Japan, the late 1960s were a period of slowly rising but relatively moderate rates of inflation. The annual rate of inflation in the United States in the first half of the 1960s averaged only 1.6 percent. In the last half of that decade, inflation increased to 3.9 percent. Similar increases were felt in many countries.

At least a part of the increase was attributed to increased wage demands. France suffered a general strike in 1968; Italian unions struck often in 1969. But in the United States, much of the increase resulted from expansionary fiscal policies to finance the Vietnam War, and the War on Poverty, and a corresponding expansionary monetary policy. The inflation in the United States soon spread to other countries. Higher prices for U.S. exports raised the cost of living in other countries. Increased U.S. spending on foreign-made goods (imports) increased aggregate demand in other nations and helped push prices up.

Although inflation worsened, the 1960s were good times in terms of unemployment and economic growth. But the moderate (creeping) inflation of the 1960s was replaced by sharply rising (galloping) inflation in the 1970s. In Japan, the rate of inflation in 1974 was 5 times the 1972 rate. In the United States, inflation averaged

---

* The data and analysis are based largely on the work of George A. Kahn, "Inflation and Disinflation: A Comparison Across Countries," *Economic Review*, Federal Reserve Bank of Kansas City, February 1985.

over 9 percent in 1974 and 1975. The major causes of these bursts of inflation were the supply shocks caused by higher oil and food prices. But some economists argue that the supply shocks produced inflation (not just short-term price increases) only because overly expansionary macroeconomic policies fueled inflationary expectations.

Following the peak in inflation in 1979–1980, inflation in many countries fell dramatically. Although price levels continued to rise, the rates of increase—the inflation rates—dropped. In contrast to "double-digit" inflation rates in 1980, the United States experienced disinflation in 1983, as the inflation rate fell to less than 4 percent. At least some credit for the slowing of inflation can be given to U.S. antiinflationary monetary policies. However, the United States experienced a severe recession in the early 1980s. As the United States economy slowed, so too did the economies of its trading partners. Less spending by the United States on European and Japanese goods decreased aggregate demand abroad.

In addition, some credit can be given to the absence of any additional momentum from supply shocks. In fact, prices of oil, food, and other important commodities actually fell. The United States also benefitted from the relative increase in the value of the dollar. As the dollar's value in foreign trade rose, the cost to U.S. residents of buying Japanese, European, and other foreign goods fell.

The record on inflation through 1986 looks good, but the important question is whether higher inflation will return. The value of the dollar has fallen, which most economists predict will put upward pressure on U.S. prices. Moreover, the huge federal budget deficits in the United States are a major potential threat to the present economy. The deficits are one reason why some economists are predicting higher inflation in the future.

Unemployment and Prices: A Short-Run View

We can easily see a short-run connection between unemployment and the price level. The current unemployment rate reflects the current level of economic activity (real GNP). An increase in real GNP requires an increase in employment (a decrease in unemployment). When aggregate supply is stable, an increase in aggregate demand tends to cause both an increase in the price level and a decrease in unemployment. A decrease in aggregate demand tends to cause a decrease in the price level and an increase in unemployment.

Phillips curve. A plot of the relationship between the rate of inflation and the rate of unemployment. Current theory recognizes an inverse short-run relationship but no long-run relationship.

This inverse relationship between inflation and unemployment is evident in the performance of the U.S. economy. In the 1950s inflation was low, but unemployment was relatively high. In the mid to late 1960s, unemployment fell but inflation rose. In the early 1980s unemployment rose while inflation fell. In each of these cases, changes in aggregate demand (and movement along a short-run aggregate supply curve) appear to explain the facts.

Phillips Curves: Promise and Failure

The connection between inflation and unemployment just described has not always been accepted by economists. Classical economists did not emphasize such a relationship. They believed that employment (and hence unemployment) was determined in labor markets in which wages were flexible. In the classical view, there was only one equilibrium level of employment—that associated with full employment—regardless of the rate of inflation. Aggregate demand determined the inflation rate but had no effect on real wages or on unemployment.

In 1958, however, a New Zealand-born economist, A. W. Phillips, published an article that showed a *long-run* statistical connection between unemployment and inflation. Phillips plotted the rate of change in nominal wages against unemployment on a graph and fitted a curve to the points. Most importantly, he noted that the relationship between inflation and unemployment seemed to be stable for various periods of time. For example, a curve drawn to fit data from 1861 to 1913 also fit data from 1948 to 1957.

Exhibit 29.6(a) shows changes in the general price level (the GNP deflator) and the unemployment rate in the United States for the years 1950–1968. Each point on the graph represents the change in prices and the unemployment rate for a single year. (We show changes in the general price level rather than in wages as Phillips did because we are interested in inflation. However, changes in nominal wages will change product costs and hence change product prices.) As with Phillips's data, most of the points appear to lie on or near the so-called **Phillips curve** shown on the graph.

Although Phillips was not the first economist to notice this relationship, his article popularized the apparent trade-off. Economists and politicians were intrigued by what the Phillips curve suggested. If the relationship was stable (an idea supported by analyses at that time), policy makers might be able to pick a point along the curve that fit their own preferences or biases. Then, by using expansionary macroeconomic policies to increase aggregate demand, they could produce lower unemployment at the expense of a somewhat higher rate of inflation.

For example, the Phillips curve in Exhibit 29.6(a) suggests that an inflation rate of zero could be realized if we accept an unemployment rate of about 6 percent. However, if we are willing to live with a 4 percent inflation rate, the unemployment could be reduced to about 3 percent. In the early and mid 1960s, unemployment averaged 5.5–6 percent. But many economists considered full employment to be a 4 percent unemployment rate. They argued for expansionary policies to stimulate aggregate demand enough to reach this lower unemployment target. Based on the Phillips curve, the cost appeared to be a minimal rise in the inflation rate *as long as aggregate supply remained stable*.

The United States Congress accepted this argument and passed a large tax cut in 1964. This tax cut, complemented by a growth in the money supply, did boost

(a) 1950–1968: A stable relationship (?)

(b) 1969–1986: An unstable relationship

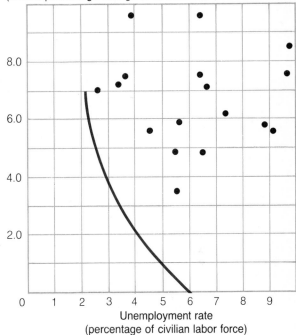

Exhibit 29.6
The Phillips Curve: An Unstable Relationship
The points in part (a) show the unemployment rate and the price level from 1950 to 1968. Most of the points lie on or near the Phillips curve (PC) shown on the graph. Although the relationship is not perfect, it does suggest a trade-off between unemployment and inflation. The points in part (b) show data for the years 1969 to 1986. For these years, most of the points lie above the Phillips curve of part (a), suggesting that there is no stable relationship between inflation and unemployment.

aggregate demand. As the Phillips curve had predicted, unemployment fell to 3.8 percent in 1966 and 1967, while the inflation rate rose to a modest 2.6 percent in 1967. It appeared at the time that macroeconomic policy had achieved a great triumph: full employment with only mild inflation. Some optimistic economists actually predicted that it might be possible to use economic policies to end the business cycle. That is, they hoped to maintain the economy at full employment while at the same time maintaining reasonable price stability. That prediction proved premature, partly because the Phillips curve proved to be far from stable.

Problems with the Phillips curve. The expansion of demand in the late 1960s was generally recognized to be excessive, leading to concern about serious inflation. In response, contractionary policies were implemented in 1969 and 1970. The Phillips curve predicted that such policies would increase unemployment and decrease the rate of inflation. The prediction was only half right: between 1969 and 1971, both inflation and unemployment increased.

Exhibit 29.6(b) shows the annual changes in the GNP deflator and rates of unemployment for 1969–1986. Note that these points all lie above the Phillips curve for 1950–1968. Economists recognized that the points for the 1970s could not be on the old Phillips curve. Although the curve had apparently shifted, some economists remained convinced that the relationship was still fairly stable.

However, the points in Exhibit 29.6(b) do not appear to lie along *any* single line or curve. As Arthur Okun put it, "Since 1970, the Phillips curve has been an unidentified flying object and has eluded all efforts to nail it down."* In fact, economists now believe that the original analysis was flawed because Phillips and other economists failed to recognize the importance of inflationary expectations.

The Phillips Curve and Expectations: The Accelerationist Argument

The expectations complication, which fooled most economists in the 1960s, had been predicted by Milton Friedman and Edmund Phelps. As they explained, the basic problem with the analyses was that other economists had confused short-run and long-run relationships. Friedman and Phelps noted that the apparent trade-off of the Phillips curve is only a short-run possibility that corresponds to movement along the short-run aggregate supply curve.

In the long run, output and unemployment are limited by the economy's potential GNP, so no long-run trade-off is possible. To keep the unemployment rate below the natural rate would require continual acceleration (increases) in the money supply. The resulting increases in aggregate demand would result in more and more inflation. The Friedman–Phelps "accelerationist" critique of the trade-off between inflation and unemployment is based on the role that expectations play in determining short-run aggregate supply.

The Phillips curve and aggregate demand. Exhibit 29.7(a) shows aggregate demand and supply in an economy with a potential GNP of $2000. Exhibit 29.7(b) shows a Phillips curve and a vertical line at this economy's natural rate of unemployment (6 percent). The natural rate of unemployment is related directly to potential GNP, since potential GNP is the level of real output the economy will produce if unemployment is at the natural rate. When unemployment is at the natural rate, there is no GNP gap and therefore no tendency for the price level to either rise or fall. Thus point *a* on the Phillips curve—unemployment at the natural rate and no change in prices—corresponds to point *a* in the aggregate demand and supply diagram. In neither case is there any excess demand or supply or any tendency for prices to rise or fall.

But what if aggregate demand increases to AD_2? Aggregate demand has grown too fast, and Exhibit 29.7(a) shows that the economy has been pushed beyond its potential GNP (point *b*). The result is an expansionary GNP gap of $50 billion. At AD_2 higher demand will cause the price level to rise by 8 percent (from 100 to 108). In Exhibit 29.7(b) point *b* is also associated with an 8 percent increase in prices. But unemployment is 5 percent, or below the natural rate, just as actual GNP is above potential GNP in Exhibit 29.7(a). In both diagrams, point *b* does not represent long-run equilibrium. Excess demand will cause higher prices, driving GNP down to its potential level and unemployment up to the natural rate.

*Arthur Okun, in Martin S. Feldstein (ed.), *The American Economy in Transition*. Chicago: University of Chicago Press, 1980, p. 166.

(a) Aggregate demand and supply

(b) Phillips curve relationship

Exhibit 29.7
Changes in Aggregate Demand and Movement along a Short-Run Phillips Curve
The two graphs show the link between the aggregate demand and supply diagram
and the Phillips curve. The unemployment rate associated with producing potential
GNP in part (a) is the natural rate of unemployment shown in part (b). In part (a) if
aggregate demand increases to AD_2, an expansionary gap of $50 billion opens and
moves the economy to point *b* on the Phillips curve, or below the natural rate of
unemployment. Thus the higher price level in part (a) means a higher inflation rate in
part (b). A decrease in aggregate demand to AD_3 opens a contractionary gap of $50
billion and moves the economy to point *c* in part (b). Thus the lower price level in part
(a) means a lower inflation rate in part (b).

What if aggregate demand grows more slowly than potential GNP? The result
is a contractionary GNP gap of $50 billion. Exhibit 29.7(a) shows this condition as
point *c*, when aggregate demand is AD_3. Here excess supply has caused the price
level to fall by 4 percent (from 100 to 96). Exhibit 29.7(b) also shows that point
c is associated with a 4 percent decrease in prices. But unemployment is 8 percent,
or above the natural rate, just as actual output is below the potential level in the
aggregate demand and supply diagram. In both diagrams, point *c* does *not* represent long-run equilibrium. Excess supply puts downward pressure on wages
and prices, driving GNP up to its potential level and unemployment down to the
natural rate.

This analysis indicates that the relationship between unemployment and inflation shown by the Phillips curve is only temporary. Higher aggregate demand
tends to temporarily lower unemployment. This trade-off shows as movement
along either the short-run aggregate supply curve or the short-run Phillips curve.
But in the long run the economy will not continue to produce beyond its potential

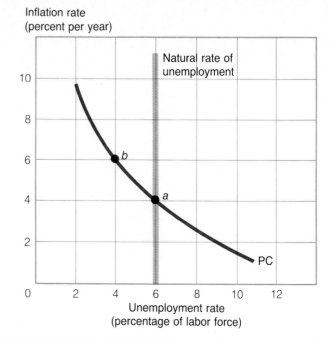

Inflation rate
(percent per year)

Exhibit 29.8
Short-Run Adjustment along a Phillips Curve
The economy is initially at long-run equilibrium at point *a* on the short-run Phillips curve, with unemployment at a natural rate of 6 percent and the actual and expected inflation rates at 4 percent per year. If aggregate demand increases too rapidly, an expansionary gap will open. In the short-run, wages may rise more slowly than prices, in part because workers are slow to adjust their inflationary expectations. This movement along the Phillips curve from *a* to *b* reduces unemployment below the natural rate. (For aggregate demand and supply, the economy would move along its short-run aggregate supply curve beyond potential GNP.) But in the long-run, as prices and expectations adjust, the economy will return to equilibrium with unemployment at the natural rate.

GNP level. Only the natural rate of unemployment is consistent with long-run equilibrium. This long-run relationship indicates that any constant and fully anticipated rate of inflation is compatible with long-run equilibrium. There are, as we have noted elsewhere, significant costs to very high rates of inflation. As a result, many economists believe that government should adopt fiscal and monetary policies that keep the inflation rate reasonably low. But how low? And should government actually force price-level *decreases*? The answers to these questions are sharply debated.

Short-run adjustment: Role of expectations. As Friedman and Phelps noted, the short-run aggregate supply curve and the Phillips curve are stable only as long as inflationary expectations are constant. A change in inflationary expectations will shift both the aggregate supply curve and the Phillips curve.

We have often observed that demand for and supply of labor are sensitive to real wages. When workers expect inflation to be 4 percent next year, they want nominal wages to rise 4 percent. But if both nominal wages and the price level rise 4 percent, real wages and real product costs will not change. Exhibit 29.8 shows a short-run Phillips curve (PC) intersecting the natural rate of unemployment when the inflation rate is 4 percent (point *a*). We can interpret this curve to mean that if real wages and prices both rise 4 percent, as expected, the economy should produce at its potential GNP level and unemployment should be at the natural rate (6 percent in this case).

Suppose, however, that aggregate demand increases faster than expected, and actual inflation increases to 6 percent. If actual inflation is not immediately observable, households and businesses may continue to expect 4 percent inflation. Businesses may incorrectly view this change as increased demand for their products and seek to increase output. They may even increase nominal wages. If workers do not immediately perceive the increase in prices, they will interpret higher nominal wages as higher real wages and offer to work more. But if nominal wages rise by 4 percent while prices rise by 6 percent, real wages will actually be falling and businesses will offer more for sale.

Thus incorrect expectations cause the economy to move along its short-run aggregate supply curve. On a Phillips curve, this change shows as movement to the left (to point *b* in Exhibit 29.8). Unemployment falls below the natural rate, which results in greater real GNP than potential GNP. According to the accelerationist argument, unemployment falls below the natural rate only because expected inflation (4 percent) is less than actual inflation (6 percent).

Incorrect inflationary expectations can yield a short-run trade-off between unemployment and inflation, as shown by the Phillips curve. But as Friedman and Phelps note, the trade-off is only temporary. Eventually, producers and workers will realize that actual inflation is higher than they expected. As they revise their expectations, workers will demand nominal wage increases to match the actual inflation rate. But higher nominal wages will raise producers' costs and thus prices, causing short-run aggregate supply to decrease. This process—the automatic adjustment mechanism—results in a return to the potential GNP level, reducing unemployment to the natural rate.

Long-run view. Because there is no long-run trade-off, what we have been calling the Phillips curve is really a short-run Phillips curve. The long-run relationship between unemployment and inflation is simply a vertical line at the natural rate of unemployment. To see why, let's consider the response of an economy if government tries to lower unemployment below the natural rate. In Exhibit 29.9, inflation is initially expected to be 2 percent per year and the natural rate of unemployment is 6 percent. If actual inflation equals expected inflation, the economy will be in long-run equilibrium at point *a*, where PC_1 intersects the natural rate. However, policy makers may decide to use expansionary policies, such as a tax cut or an increase in the money supply, to reduce unemployment. If so, aggregate demand will grow faster than potential GNP and an expansionary gap will open.

In the short run, if actual inflation goes unrecognized, real GNP may rise and unemployment may fall below the natural rate, as we have noted. In Exhibit 29.9 this change shows as movement from point *a* to point *b* along PC_1. This movement corresponds to movement upward and to the right along a short-run aggregate supply curve. In the long run, however, households and businesses will revise their expectations to match the actual inflation rate of 4 percent, shifting the short-run Phillips curve from PC_1 to PC_2. Note that PC_2 intersects the natural rate of unemployment line at point *c*, where actual and expected inflation are 4 percent. Left alone, the economy will adjust to its potential GNP level at the natural rate of unemployment (6 percent).

What if government continues to try to lower unemployment to 4 percent? Aggregate demand once more will increase, causing the economy to move along PC_2 to point *d*, where actual inflation is 6 percent. In the long run, when expectations are revised to account for this higher inflation, the short-run Phillips curve shifts upward once again (to PC_3). As Exhibit 29.9 indicates, expansionary policies cannot maintain unemployment below the natural rate. In the long run, those policies will only increase inflation. Conversely, attempts to lower inflation by decreasing aggregate demand have no long-run effect on unemployment. Thus in the long run the Phillips curve is vertical; there is no long-run trade-off. Only at

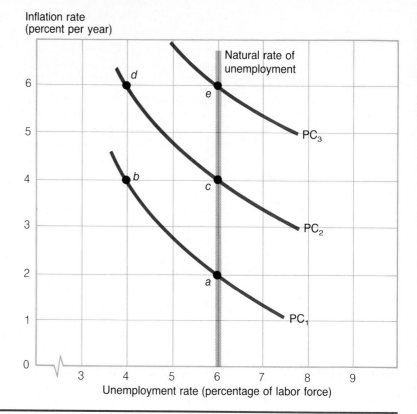

Exhibit 29.9
Long-Run Adjustment to Changes in Demand Pressure
The economy is initially in long-run equilibrium at point *a* on the short-run Phillips curve PC_1, where the actual and expected inflation rates are both 2 percent per year. Attempts to reduce unemployment by using expansionary policies will temporarily push the economy along the Phillips curve to point *b*. If demand pressures are maintained, inflationary expectations will adjust, shifting the Phillips curve (to PC_2). The economy adjusts to point *c* where actual and expected inflation are again equal. Further attempts to lower unemployment below the natural rate cause additional upward shifts in the Phillips curve. In the long-run, unemployment cannot be maintained below the natural rate and there is no long-run trade-off between inflation and unemployment.

the natural rate of unemployment are actual and expected inflation the same; only at this rate will the economy reach long-run equilibrium.

Rational Expectations and the New Classical Macroeconomists

Friedman and Phelps's analysis rests on a particular view of how price-level expectations change. (For more on the effect of expectations, see A Case in Point: Effect of Expectations on Inflation and Unemployment Policies.) Their arguments are based on the same kind of analysis we used in Chapter 26 when drawing the short-run aggregate supply curve. That is, we assume that expectations adjust to a change in actual inflation—but always after the change, adapting to historical information. Thus an increase in aggregate demand always causes a temporary expansion in real GNP, since decision makers consistently underestimate price rises. For example, if workers observe that the price level has risen 4 percent per year in the past, they will assume that this trend will continue—until new information suggests that their expectation is wrong.

Some economists criticize the idea that expectations depend largely, if not exclusively, on past events. Would it not be more reasonable, they ask, to assume that individuals utilize all available information when forecasting future price levels? In place of Friedman's *adaptive expectations*, these economists maintain that individuals have *rational expectations*. When forming rational expectations about inflation, individuals do not just look at past inflation rates; they consider any and all information that may affect future price levels. Why, they argue, would individuals make consistent mistakes in forecasting the effects of macroeconomic policies? Why would they always underestimate increases in inflation and overestimate decreases, as they do in Friedman's model? According to the hypothesis of rational expectations, rational individuals would not form their inflationary expectations by looking only at past inflation rates. Rather, they would consider any and all information that may affect future price levels, including the expected effects of announced or anticipated macroeconomic policies.

Note that the hypothesis of rational expectations does not assume that decision makers *always* accurately forecast the rate of inflation or any other significant economic factor. But it does assume that they learn from past events and are as likely to overestimate as underestimate the effects of economic changes. Importantly, the hypothesis suggests that once a policy change is announced or anticipated, expectations will adjust immediately. Many economists currently base their economic models on rational expectations. But the new classical macroeconomists—following the lead of Robert Lucas, Thomas Sargent, and Neil Wallace—also assume (like the classical economists) that wages and prices are very flexible. This assumption, combined with the hypothesis of rational expectations, leads to

A Case in Point
Effect of Expectations on Inflation and Unemployment Policies

Most economists now accept the notion that no long-run trade-off between inflation and unemployment is possible. But why did the Phillips curves drawn for both the United States and England in the 1960s suggest that the relationship was stable in the long run? The answer, according to Milton Friedman, is that there was no consistent expectation of inflation. Prior to the 1960s, government had not tried to increase aggregate demand. Inflation had rarely occurred, so long-run expectations of zero (or at least very low) inflation were reasonable. But the expansionary policies of the 1960s increased not only the price level, but also expectations of inflation.

This analysis also explains why both unemployment and inflation rose in 1969–1971. By 1969 policy-makers recognized that expansionary policies had not only lowered the unemployment rate dramatically but also increased inflation. They expected contractionary policies to raise unemployment and decrease inflation. But when they implemented these policies, they got an unpleasant surprise: Unemployment fell as expected, but inflation continued to rise.

To see why, we must recognize that unemployment in the late 1960s was below the natural rate and that

actual inflation was above the expected level. (Not surprising since many economists had been convinced that inflation would not be greatly affected by expansionary policies. They realized that the expansionary actions in the late 1960s were excessive, but they had not considered the role of expectations.) Eventually, expectations caught up with actual inflation, causing the short-run Phillips curve to shift. As the economy adjusted to this new relationship, unemployment rose along with inflation.

But why did inflation continue to rise? Although economists initially rejected Friedman and Phelps's conclusion, most now accept their assessment that workers and producers had come to expect increasing inflation. The private sector expected government to boost aggregate demand in the face of cyclical unemployment. Thus people had every reason to believe that the price level would continue to increase. Increased inflationary expectations decreased short-run aggregate supply (and shifted the short-run Phillips curve). As a result, prices and unemployment continued to increase while GNP decreased.

a prediction that the economy will quickly and smoothly adjust to any change in demand or supply.

Suppose that the Fed publicly announces that it is increasing the growth rate of the money supply. Most economists would recognize that this announcement will increase aggregate demand. They would predict that there would be a short-run decrease in unemployment until expectations and actual wages and prices change. But they would recognize that faster growth in the money supply (assuming that the growth exceeds that of potential GNP) would lead to higher inflation in the long run.

There is little controversy over the long-run effect of an increase in the growth rate of the money supply. But the new classical macroeconomists would argue that this long-run effect occurs immediately. Because wages and prices are very flexible in their models, they predict immediate shifts in the short-run aggregate supply curve and the short-run Phillips curve. As a result, the announced change in the growth rate of the money supply should raise the price level without affecting real GNP or unemployment. That is, the new classical macroeconomists do not believe that there is even a short-run trade-off between inflation and unemployment when policy changes are known or anticipated. (To see their point, return to Exhibit 29.9 and consider the effect of an increase in aggregate demand that would eventually raise inflation to 4 percent. Note that the economy would move immediately from point a to point c if an increase in expected inflation immediately shifted the Phillips curve from PC_1 to PC_2.) However, many economists are unconvinced that the economy's automatic adjustment mechanism operates as quickly as the new classical economists believe or that short-run trade-offs are impossible.

AGGREGATE DEMAND POLICIES: FIGHTING INFLATION

In our analysis of inflation and unemployment, we have concluded that most economists attribute large, sustained increases in the price level to excessive growth in the money supply. Moreover, most (although, as you just saw, not all) economists believe that there can be short-run trade-offs between unemployment and inflation, but not long-run tradeoffs. However, economists remain divided on how short the short run is. Depending on their view of the short run and how quickly the economy's automatic adjustment mechanism works, they have different views about the appropriateness of policies used to fight inflation. Wage and price controls, which we cover in Chapter 31, are a particularly controversial policy.

The Expectations View and the "Cold Turkey" Approach

Both the new classical macroeconomists and the monetarists (including Milton Friedman) share the view that short-run responses to changes in aggregate demand depend largely on expectations. Most economists agree that, to the degree that short-run responses do depend on expectations, the automatic adjustment mechanism can provide a swift return to full-employment equilibrium. In our society, good information is readily available, making long-term incorrect expectations unlikely.

Their emphasis on expectations leads both monetarists and the new classicists to favor a "cold turkey" approach. That is, they support major, but consistent, reductions in growth of the money supply in order to fight inflation. For example, they would have the Fed announce a new policy of a constant growth rate in the money supply of 3 or 4 percent per year and stick to it. The faster the cycle of inflationary expectations is broken, the sooner the economy can return to full employment and price stability, they argue. As they see it, it is a matter of "pay me now or pay me later." The costs associated with higher current unemployment are, in their opinion, lower than the costs of continued inflation over a longer period of time.

To be effective, policies must be consistent and believable. Otherwise, workers and producers cannot accurately forecast price-level changes. With a consistent policy, households and businesses will quickly adjust their expectations to new, lower rates of inflation. Because this adjustment occurs quickly, the economy would not, in this view, have to suffer a long or deep recession. (The new classical view is similar, but predicts an almost instant adjustment to an announced and believable policy change.)

We noted in Chapter 27 that the monetarists and new classical macroeconomists do not believe that government should intervene to try to offset demand or supply shocks. However, they do advocate using monetary policies to fight inflation. The policy that they propose—slower growth in the money supply—is *not* a discretionary policy for counterbalancing temporary economic fluctuations. Rather, it is a fixed rule meant to bring long-run inflationary pressures under control. If a particular growth rate in the money supply is not enough to bring inflation down to an acceptable level, a slower but still constant rate can be tried.

The "Sticky-Price" View and the Gradual Approach

For the short-run aggregate supply curve to shift, it is not enough for expectations to adjust; actual wages and prices must also adjust. According to economists who hold the expectations view, a change in expectations will cause a shift. But other economists, in the Keynesian tradition, believe that the automatic adjustment mechanism operates slowly because wages and prices are "sticky," not flexible. They generally support the contracts theory we discussed in Chapters 26 and 28, which suggests that many wages are set by explicit or implicit long-run contracts. Thus in the short run, workers cannot respond to changes in aggregate supply by changing wage demands and employers cannot respond by adjusting labor costs.

If actual adjustments are slow, the unemployment costs of large-scale contractionary policies may be high. Economists who believe that the economy adjusts slowly are not against reducing inflation. They agree that lower inflation requires a slower rate of growth in the money supply, but suggest a gradual reduction, not the "cold turkey" approach. A gradual adjustment will take longer to lower inflation, but it may prevent high unemployment and large contractionary gaps.

The Historical Record

The argument of the monetarists and new classical macroeconomists that the automatic adjustment mechanism works swiftly appears to be contradicted by historical evidence. For example, the inflation rate continued to rise during the 1969–1970 recession even though the unemployment rate rose sharply. The recessions in 1974–1975 and again in 1980–1982 also showed the economy's short-run response to reduced aggregate demand included higher unemployment. These recessions—largely traceable to contractionary policies—were the deepest since the 1930s. But the recessions in the early 1980s offer some support for the monetarists' and new classical macroeconomists' point of view. The evidence suggests that the Keynesians underestimated the speed and degree of inflation reduction that occurred. However, the monetarists and new classicists underestimated the resulting amount of unemployment.

As in many real-world situations, both sides claim partial victory and are quick to explain away their faulty predictions. The Keynesians blame their miscalculation on having underestimated the speed with which OPEC would collapse (and thus energy prices would fall). The monetarists and new classicists note that at the time, households and businesses had every reason to expect the government to abandon any inflation-fighting program as soon as unemployment began to rise. At no time since the 1950s had policy makers allowed contractionary policy to run its course and purge the economy of inflationary expectations. Indeed, on some occasions in which contractionary policies were used (1969–1970 and 1974–1975), expansionary policies quickly followed the rise in unemployment.

Historically, policies followed a stop-and-go pattern, with quick and dramatic changes in direction and speed. If we compare managing the economy to driving a car, these policy changes were like alternately flooring the accelerator and slamming on the brakes. Thus in some ways, the economy suffered from the worst of both worlds: Unemployment was consistently high and inflationary expectations were continually fed. Workers and businesses expecting expansionary policies had little reason to settle for lower nominal wage and price increases. A little more restraint at the appropriate time, critics argue, might have broken the inflationary cycle. Antiinflation policies in the 1970s definitely lacked credibility. The monetarists and new classicists note that this historical failure does not mean that the automatic adjustment mechanism would not work quickly if the inflation-fighting policy were believed to be sincere. In fact, they observe that when inflation-fighting policies became believable in the 1980s, the inflation rate fell rapidly.

The Keynesians, however, see the deep recession of 1982 as evidence in support of their position. They credit the rapid fall in inflation to several factors. First, they observe that the effects of earlier supply shocks ended in 1979–1980. Second, they note that oil prices fell in the early 1980s—a sort of "favorable" supply shock. Finally, they point to the decline in the prices of other imports because of the strong relative value of the U.S. dollar. Since that time, there have been no unfavorable supply shocks, and the Fed by its monetary policies has kept the economy operating below its potential GNP level. As a result, the Keynesians argue, it is not surprising that inflation has remained low.

Supply Shocks and Aggregate Demand Policies

So far we have focused on the use of contractionary policies to reduce inflation caused by too much growth in aggregate demand. But what about the price-level increases caused by supply shocks? We explore this issue in more detail in Chapter 31, but the basic dilemma is that supply shocks put upward pressure on price levels while opening contractionary gaps. Their influence on prices is temporary, as we have shown. But what policies are best?

Contractionary policies might prevent an increase in inflationary expectations. But reducing aggregate demand would lead to even higher unemployment. Expansionary policies might reduce the impact on unemployment. But increasing

RECAP

There is general agreement that slower monetary growth will result in lower inflation over the long run.

Some economists believe that the automatic adjustment process can work quickly and favor a "cold turkey" policy of large-scale reduction in growth of the money supply. These economists, including most monetarists and new classicists, stress the importance of expectations in response to changes in aggregate demand.

Other economists, primarily Keynesians, believe that the automatic adjustment process will respond slowly and argue for a more gradual reduction in growth of the money supply.

aggregate demand will lead to even higher prices and a risk of raising inflationary expectations. Doing nothing might be reasonable if the economy's automatic adjustment mechanism operates quickly. But adjustment to a supply shock is more difficult than are adjustments to most contractionary gaps. Because shocks can represent a transfer of real resources out of the country (as was true for higher oil prices), real income has to fall. But who will quickly volunteer to accept lower real wages? There are no easy answers and all policies have considerable costs.

Popularity of Inflationary Policies

We have devoted much of this chapter to showing why excessive growth in the money supply is responsible for inflation. We have emphasized that this effect is widely recognized as the culprit by economists. Why, then, do governments continue to implement inflationary policies? We can offer two explanations for the political popularity of inflationary policies: (1) politicians have a strong preference for high employment; and (2) increasing the rate of growth in the money supply can help finance government spending.

In the United States, the political goal of low unemployment came out of the experience of the Great Depression. The image of a 25% unemployment rate is still vivid, and no elected official can afford to be indifferent to rising unemployment. (Herbert Stein, chairman of the Council of Economic Advisors under President Nixon, said that Nixon was "allergic to unemployment." He had in mind a political allergy, no doubt.) Moreover, the Great Depression introduced the United States to the Keynesian notion that government could do something to reduce unemployment. Later the Phillips curve promised that that "something" would cost nothing (or very little), which economists—but not all voters and politicians—now reject.

In addition, political leaders like to promise government spending on certain programs (ranging from national defense to welfare to local highways). Recall that, unlike the rest of us who must be content with spending what we earn or what we can borrow, national governments have a third option: printing money. Choosing this option is easier politically than raising taxes. Moreover, in countries with underdeveloped financial markets, the ability to borrow substantial funds is limited. In the long run, large-scale monetary expansion will lead to inflation, perhaps even to hyperinflation. But politicians sometimes see these costs as offset by short-run political advantages (especially near election time).

In the United States, monetary growth is under the direct control of the Federal Reserve System. This separation of fiscal and monetary controls is one reason why we have not experienced the hyperinflation that other countries have. But political pressures to minimize unemployment influence both monetary and fiscal policies in this country. As a result, inflation in the United States in the 1970s was greater than that experienced in Japan, for example, where very restrictive macroeconomic policies were used.

CONCLUSION

In this chapter we demonstrated the connection between unemployment and inflation. Economists generally agree that there is no long-run trade-off, but most concede that a short-run trade-off is possible. However, they disagree over the reasons for the relationship and the speed with which the automatic adjustment mechanism operates.

These disagreements are at the heart of the current economic debate over how to fight inflation and respond to future supply shocks. As our discussion of alternative policies clearly indicates, the economic and political dilemmas caused by inflation are serious and have no easy solutions. Inflation was cited as the "number-one enemy" of the economy in the 1970s but has decreased substantially. Has the battle been won? Will inflation remain low? These important questions are as yet unanswered. But by applying the concepts presented in this chapter, you can learn to read the signs of inflation and explain changes in future inflation rates.

So far in our exploration of macroeconomics we have focused largely on the short run and on long-run adjustments to a given level of potential GNP. In Chapter 30 we turn our attention to the long run, to see how potential GNP is determined, how fast it grows, and what policies might increase its rate of growth. Although we must consider the short run, we cannot discuss economic policies intelligently without considering the long run.

SUMMARY

1. In this chapter we examined the causes of inflation, the debate over trade-offs between inflation and unemployment, and the use of macroeconomic policies to reduce either inflation or unemployment.

2. The annual percentage change in the price level is referred to as the inflation rate. But it is important to distinguish between temporary changes and sustained upward movement in the price level. Either an increase in aggregate demand or a decrease in aggregate supply can cause a one-time increase in the price level. But once the economy has adjusted to either change, prices would not continue to rise unless additional shifts in demand or supply occur.

3. Over the long run, inflation is the result of continued excess demand. That is, inflation results from excessive growth of the money supply, causing aggregate demand to grow faster than potential GNP. But any other factor affecting aggregate demand or aggregate supply can change the price level, making it hard to separate the exact causes of a price-level change in the short run.

4. Distinguishing the causes of inflation is further complicated by the length of time that the aftereffects of demand and supply shocks affect the economy.

5. In the early 1960s observations led many economists to believe in a stable relationship between the rate of unemployment and the rate of inflation. Graphs expressing this relationship are known as "Phillips curves," after the economist who popularized the concept. Experience in the 1970s suggested that this relationship was not stable. Economists now generally believe that there is a short-run relationship but that no long-run trade-off is possible.

6. Theoretical support for the lack of a stable long-run trade-off between unemployment and inflation is based on the assumption that expectations adjust to actual inflation. Lowering unemployment below the natural rate causes rising inflation. Increased inflation causes a revision of expectations and a return to the natural rate of unemployment, at which actual and expected inflation are the same.

7. The new classical macroeconomists believe that wages and prices are highly flexible and that households and businesses change their expectations immediately in response to changes in the inflation rate. Thus they maintain that even short-run trade-offs between inflation and unemployment are impossible.

8. There is general agreement among economists that slower monetary growth results in lower inflation over the long run. Some monetarists and new classicists, believing that the automatic adjustment process can work quickly, favor a "cold turkey" policy of large-scale reduction in the growth of the money supply. Keynesians, believing that the automatic adjustment mechanism will respond slowly, argue for a more gradual reduction.

9. The "correct" policy response to a supply shock depends on the resulting trade-off between unemployment and inflation and the speed of the economy's automatic adjustment mechanism. But any policy implemented will have some costs.

10. Despite the inflationary effects of policies that expand the money supply, this "solution" remains a popular political alternative to raising taxes or to high unemployment.

KEY TERMS

Inflation rate, 739
Demand-pull inflation, 740
Cost-push inflation, 741
Disinflation, 748
Phillips curve, 750

QUESTIONS FOR REVIEW AND DISCUSSION

1. Explain how a short-run change in the price level can be caused by either a change in aggregate demand or aggregate supply. Explain why economists tend to agree that sustained increases in the money supply provide the only explanation for high rates of inflation.

2. What short-run change in inflation and unemployment would you expect from each of the following events?
    a) An increase in consumer and business confidence.
    b) A one-time increase in the money supply.
    c) An increase in the rate of growth of the money supply.
    d) An increase in the prices of important resources.
    e) An expectation of a higher rate of inflation.

3. Many economists argue that policy makers created problems for the U.S. economy by the stop-and-go nature of the macroeconomic policies used in the 1960s and 1970s. Some critics argue that the reason is that finding support for contractionary policies to fight inflation is politically more difficult than finding support for expansionary policies to fight recessions and high unemployment. Explain why this belief might be true. (*Hint*: Consider the policies that are required in each case and the effects they have.) Do you think that the political choices made reflect the values of voters, a lack of understanding of economics on the part of voters and politicians, or a basic failure of government?

4. We noted in this chapter that most economists now believe that there is no stable short-run Phillips curve. But the data in Exhibit 29.6(a) suggest there was a stable relationship that existed for many years. Explain why. In particular, consider whether the stability of the observed relationship in Exhibit 29.6(a) might be connected with the absence of government stabilization policies that sought to improve on the economy's au-

tomatic adjustment mechanism. How do supply shocks affect the short-run Phillips curve?

5. In the mid-1980s, the size of projected annual federal budget deficits was an important economic and political issue. Is there necessarily any connection between a budget deficit and inflation? Why were some economists worried that the deficits would be inflationary? What are the Fed's policy options in the face of such deficits? Explain the benefits and costs of each option.

6. Because the short-run Phillips curve suggests that unemployment and inflation are inversely related, some economists have argued that economic theory cannot explain why unemployment and inflation increase together at times. How would you explain increases in both unemployment and inflation? What does your answer mean in terms of the short-run Phillips curve?

7. The long-run Phillips curve indicates that there is no long-run relationship between unemployment and inflation. Explain the reasoning behind the absence of a long-run trade-off. What policies, if any, can you suggest that may shift the position of the Phillips curve?

8. The identity expressed by the equation of exchange ($M \times V = P \times Q$) indicates that changes in the money supply (M) should be proportional to changes in the price level (P), unless either velocity (V) or real GNP (Q) changes. Using this equation and the graph in Exhibit 29.4, explain the relatively slow growth of the money supply in the early 1960s. The relatively fast growth in the price level from 1975 to 1977 and again from 1980 to 1982? The slowing of inflation in the 1980s?

9. Comment on the statement: "Macroeconomic policies based on the assumption that the automatic adjustment mechanism and expectations are slow to respond to the pressures of a contractionary gap guarantee a slow response."

10. In each case below, explain what change in prices you would expect. (You may find it helpful to explain your answer in terms of the equation of exchange.) State explicitly what variables you must hold constant to reach your conclusions.
    a) The supply of money grows more slowly than real output.
    b) The supply of money grows at the same rate as real output, but the public wants to hold more money.
    c) The supply of money grows, and the public expects this growth to lead to a higher rate of inflation.

Economic Growth:
Increasing Potential GNP

QUESTIONS TO CONSIDER

☐ What is economic growth?

☐ How have economists' views of economic growth changed?

☐ What factors can result in economic growth?

☐ Why has economic growth in many industrialized nations slowed?

☐ What government policies have been used in attempts to stimulate growth?

So far out exploration of macroeconomics has focused on how the economy adjusts to changes in aggregate demand and supply assuming potential GNP remains constant. But in the real world, potential GNP can (and does) increase, resulting in economic growth. Economic growth does not eliminate scarcity. Wants will always exceed an economy's ability to produce. But by increasing its potential GNP, an economy can produce more goods and services and, as a consequence, satisfy more of its wants. We noted the factors that determine potential GNP in Chapter 26. But which of those factors are most important to economic growth? Can economic policies increase the rate of economic growth? These are the questions we address in this chapter.

ECONOMIC GROWTH: DEFINITION AND CAUSES

The most important benefit to a society of economic growth is raising the standard of living by increasing the amount of real goods and services available for consumption. Economists therefore measure economic growth as an increase in **real GNP per capita**, that is, the ratio of real GNP to total population. For example, real GNP in the United States in 1986 was $3674.9 billion, and the total population was 241.5 million. Thus real GNP per capita in 1986 was $15,217, calculated as

$$\text{Real GNP per capita, 1986} = \frac{\text{Real GNP}}{\text{Population}} = \frac{\$3674.9 \text{ billion}}{241.5 \text{ million}} = \$15,217 \text{ per person}$$

Exhibit 30.1 shows percentage changes in real GNP, population, and real GNP per capita for several countries. Note that an increase in real GNP per capita means that the economy has produced more output per person. But we cannot be sure that every person in the economy has more output to consume. Nor can we be sure that every increase in GNP makes us better off. As we noted in Chapter 21, GNP does not take into account costs such as those of air and water pollution. Because GNP includes both consumer and military goods, an economy may show increases in real GNP per capita, but its citizens may not be better off. Nevertheless, most economists equate an increase in real GNP per capita with a higher *average* standard of living.

Real GNP per capita. The average quantity of real output produced per person, calculated by dividing real GNP by total population.

765

Country	1965–1973 Percentage changes in			1973–1984 Percentage changes in		
	GNP	Population	GNP per capita	GNP	Population	GNP per capita
United States	3.2	1.1	2.1	2.3	1.0	1.3
Japan	9.8	1.2	8.6	4.3	0.9	3.4
UK	2.8	0.4	1.4	1.0	0.0	1.0
Canada	5.2	1.4	3.8	2.5	1.2	1.3
France	5.5	0.8	4.7	2.3	0.5	1.8
West Germany	4.6	0.7	3.9	2.0	−0.1	2.1
China	7.8	2.7	5.1	6.6	1.4	5.2
India	3.9	2.3	1.6	4.1	2.3	1.8
Bolivia	4.4	2.4	2.0	0.8	2.6	−1.8
Brazil	9.8	2.5	7.3	4.4	2.3	2.1
Mexico	7.9	3.3	4.6	5.1	2.9	2.2
Hong Kong	7.9	2.0	5.9	9.1	2.4	6.7
South Korea	10.0	2.2	7.8	7.2	1.5	5.7
Singapore	13.0	1.8	11.3	8.2	1.3	6.9

Exhibit 30.1
International Growth Rates

Source: The World Bank, *World Development Report, 1986,* Washington, D.C.: Oxford University Press, 1986, Tables 2 and 25, pp. 182–183 and pp. 228–229.

Growth: Increased Real GNP per Capita

Our definition of growth has three components. Growth represents an *increase;* it is measured in *real* terms; and it is generally expressed on a *per-capita* basis. That growth is an increase is fairly obvious, but why must it be stated in real and per-capita terms?

Real versus nominal GNP. It is relatively easy to see why we measure economic growth as a change in real rather than nominal output. Real GNP is the quantity of economic goods and services available to the economy. But nominal GNP reflects both changes in quantities and changes in the price level. (Remember that nominal GNP is the product of the price level and real GNP.)

For example, per capita nominal GNP in the United States grew by 7.5 percent between 1974 and 1975—from $6887 to $7401. During the same period, the price level increased by 9.8 percent—from 54.0 to 59.3—as measured by the GNP deflator. Thus real GNP per capita actually *declined* by 2.3 percent. *Only if nominal GNP per capita rises faster than the price level will real GNP per capita increase.* And only increases in real GNP enable more wants to be satisfied.

Real GNP per capita versus real GNP. The reasons for defining growth in terms of per capita GNP are also straightforward. Sometimes economists do discuss economic growth in absolute terms. For example, if we wanted to compare the overall influence of the United States and the Soviet Union on the world economy, it might be better to use real GNP, not real GNP per capita. But comparing real GNPs can conceal important differences in average standards of living. For example, in 1984 India's real GNP was $194.8 billion, while Switzerland's was

$104.5 billion. However, India's population was 749 million, while Switzerland's was 6 million. Thus real GNP per capita in India was $260, while in Switzerland it was $16,330. *An economy's average standard of living will increase only if real GNP per capita rises.*

For real GNP per capita to increase, real GNP has to rise faster than population. Many poor countries experience large increases in real GNP, but at the same time they experience large increases in population. As a result, their standards of living improve only slightly or not at all. For example, between 1973 and 1984, real GNP in India increased 4.1 percent, a rate that compares favorably with Japan's 4.3 percent growth rate. However, India's population increased 2.3 percent per year, compared to 0.9 percent per year in Japan. As a result, real output per capita grew only 1.8 percent per year in India, compared to 3.4 percent per year in Japan. Because of this relationship between population and standard of living, many poor nations have tried to improve living standards by reducing birth rates.

When discussing growth, you should recognize that even seemingly small differences in economic growth rates can have tremendous long-run effects on the standard of living. For example, in 1870 real GNP per capita in the United Kingdom was 21 percent higher than in the United States. Between 1870 and 1985 the average annual growth rate in the United States was 1.84 percent per year, apparently not much greater than the 1.24 percent per year in the United Kingdom. However, over the 115-year period, this 0.6 percent difference in growth rates resulted in a real GNP per capita that was 62 percent higher in the United States than in the United Kingdom.[*]

Another way of expressing the effects of economic growth is by the length of time required for real GNP to double if the growth rate remains constant. A formula called the *rule of 72* is used to calculate the number of years it takes for GNP to double as the ratio of 72 to the annual growth rate. Let's use the U.S. growth rate of 1.8 percent and the British growth rate of 1.2 percent. We can then approximate the length of time required for the U.S. GNP to double as 40 years and that for the United Kingdom as 60 years, calculated as

$$\text{Years to double} = \frac{72}{\text{Annual growth rate}}$$

$$\text{Years to double, U.S.} = \frac{72}{1.8\% \text{ per year}} \quad \text{or} \quad 40 \text{ years}$$

$$\text{Years to double, UK} = \frac{72}{1.2\% \text{ per year}} \quad \text{or} \quad 60 \text{ years}$$

Changes in Real GNP—Short-Run and Long-Run Views

At the beginning of this chapter, we noted that increases in potential GNP can cause economic growth, or increases in real GNP per capita. But must potential GNP increase—that is, must the production possibilities curve shift outward—for an economy to grow? To answer this question we must distinguish short-run changes in real GNP from sustained increases, just as in Chapter 29 we distinguished short-run changes in price levels from inflation.

---

[*] Based on Robert J. Gordon, *Macroeconomics,* 4th ed. Boston: Little, Brown, 1988, pp. 555–556.

(a) An increase in aggregate demand

(b) An increase in aggregate supply

Exhibit 30.2
Short-Run Changes in Real GNP
A short-run increase in real GNP can occur as a result of a change in either aggregate demand or aggregate supply. In part (a) an increase in aggregate demand (from AD₁ to AD₂) increases real output from $2000 billion to $2050 billion. In part (b) an increase in aggregate supply (from AS₁ to AS₂) also increases real GNP from $2000 billion to $2050 billion.

Short-run changes in real GNP. In the short run, real GNP changes in response to changes in either aggregate demand or short-run aggregate supply. Exhibit 30.2(a) shows how an increase in aggregate demand (a shift of the curve from AD_1 to AD_2) increases real GNP. Exhibit 30.2(b) shows how an increase in short-run aggregate supply (a shift of the curve from AS_1 to AS_2) also increases real GNP. Note that because this is a short-run view, we can assume a constant population. Thus higher real GNP means higher real GNP per capita. Real GNP increases from $2000 billion to $2050 billion, an increase of $50 billion (or 2.5 percent), calculated as

$$\text{Growth rate in real GNP} = \frac{\text{GNP}_2 - \text{GNP}_1}{\text{GNP}_1} \times 100 \quad \text{or} \quad \frac{\text{Change in GNP}}{\text{GNP}_1} \times 100$$

$$= \frac{\$2050 - \$2000}{\$2000} \times 100$$

$$= \frac{\$50}{\$2000} \times 100 \quad \text{or} \quad 2.5\%$$

Similarly, a decrease in aggregate demand or a decrease in aggregate supply will cause real GNP and/or the growth rate of real GNP to decline from one year to the next.

Short-run changes in real GNP: A historical example. This short-run view of real GNP changes is supported by historic events. For example, from 1962 to 1966, real GNP per capita in the United States increased at an average annual rate of 3.9 percent, or well above the long-run trend of 1.8 percent. Most economists attribute this high growth to increases in aggregate demand, especially increases in government spending. Exhibit 30.3(a) shows changes in aggregate demand, aggregate supply, and potential GNP during this period of time.

Note that actual GNP grew by $409 billion between 1962 and 1966—from $1799 to $2208 billion. (Actual GNP is indicated by the intersection of the aggregate demand and short-run aggregate supply curves.) At the same time, potential GNP grew by $270 billion. How did actual GNP grow by $139 billion more than potential GNP? In 1962 actual GNP ($1799 billion) was below potential GNP ($1826 billion). Part of the increase in real GNP from 1962–1966 reflected the closing of this contractionary gap. In addition, aggregate demand increased fast enough to push actual GNP in 1966 ($2208 billion) above potential GNP ($2096), opening a $112 billion expansionary gap. Economists separate the growth that occurred into two parts: (1) the temporary changes in real GNP resulting from the closing and opening of gaps; and (2) the long-run changes in potential GNP. But long-run economic growth should be measured as increases in potential GNP. To see why, consider what happened in the years after 1966, as shown in Exhibit 30.3(b).

Between 1966 and 1970, real GNP grew by $208 billion (from $2208 billion to $2416 billion). During the same period, potential GNP increased by $320 billion. The slower growth in actual GNP partly reflects the economy's attempt to close the expansionary gap in 1966. Had there been no change in potential GNP, aggregate supply would have decreased. However, because potential GNP increased, aggregate supply continued to increase, although more slowly than before. At the same time, the inflation rate, which averaged only 1.7 percent per year from 1958 to 1964, increased to 3.6 percent in 1966 and to over 5 percent in 1968 and 1969. In addition, real GNP increased at an average annual rate of 2.7 percent from 1966 to 1970. By contrast, potential GNP grew at an average annual rate of 3.7 percent in the same period. As shown in Exhibit 30.3(b), the economy was operating at its potential GNP level in 1970.

Long-run changes in real GNP. The preceding example illustrates an important point about changes in real GNP: *In the short run, real GNP can grow faster or slower than potential GNP. But in the long run, real GNP growth is limited by potential GNP growth.* If real GNP grows faster than potential GNP, an expansionary gap results. If real GNP grows more slowly than potential GNP, a contractionary gap results. In either case, the automatic adjustment mechanism closes the gaps. Thus only increases in potential GNP translate into sustainable increases in real GNP per capita.

If there are two reasons why real GNP might increase, we must distinguish between two basic policy issues: (1) stabilization policy to close GNP gaps; and (2) growth policies to increase potential GNP. If real GNP grows more slowly than potential GNP, a contractionary gap will open. To close the gap, government may use stabilization policies (discretionary fiscal or monetary policies to increase aggregate demand) or allow the economy to stabilize itself. But stabilization

Exhibit 30.3
Changes in Real GNP: 1962–1970
The graphs illustrate changes in real GNP that occurred between 1962 and 1970. Part (a) shows that in 1962 there was a contractionary gap (actual GNP was less than potential GNP). But from 1962 to 1966 aggregate demand grew faster than potential output, causing a significant expansionary gap (actual GNP was larger than potential GNP). While some of the increase in real GNP from 1962 to 1966 represented growth in potential output, another part reflected short-run changes resulting from closing and opening GNP gaps. Part (b) shows that from 1966 to 1970, actual GNP grew more slowly than potential output as the increase in aggregate supply slowed, closing the expansionary gap by 1970.

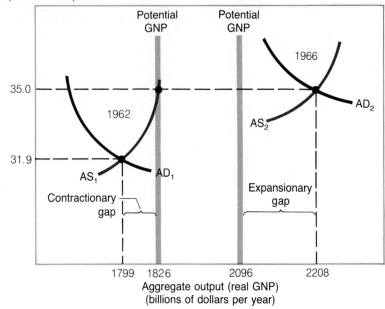

(a) Fast growth from 1962 to 1966

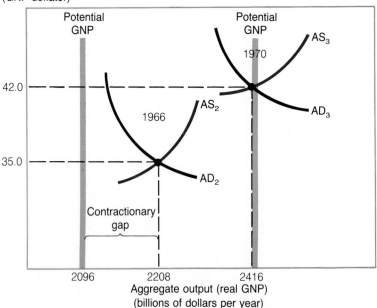

(b) Slower growth from 1966 to 1970

policies and the closing of GNP gaps are short-run issues. In this chapter, we want to focus on long-run issues and policies to achieve economic growth, that is, long-run, sustainable increases in potential GNP. Thus we concentrate on factors that help explain the growth rate of potential GNP.

FACTORS IN ECONOMIC GROWTH

Basically, there are two ways of obtaining increases in economic output: putting more resources to work and getting more output from available resources. Thus increased potential GNP requires an increase in the quantity or productivity of one of four factors: (1) supplies of natural resources, such as land, water, and minerals; (2) supplies of labor; (3) supplies of capital resources, such as machinery and buildings; or (4) technology.

Economists currently assume that increases in the availability of virtually all these factors are possible. However, for many centuries economists assumed that only labor supplies could change. The results of these different assumptions help explain why classical economists expected no economic growth, whereas economists now worry about the recent decline in the rate of U.S. economic growth.

Classical Assumptions and Doomsday Predictions

Although modern industrial economies experience regular increases in real GNP per capita, economic growth is relatively recent. Until 1750 or so, neither aggregate economic output nor the population in Western Europe had grown over the long run. Thus it was natural for the classical economists of the eighteenth and nineteenth centuries to search for a theory to explain why economies have a zero growth rate.

Fixed supplies and diminishing returns. Classical economists reached their conclusion about zero growth by assuming that supplies of important resources, especially land, were fixed and that technology changed very slowly, if at all. These were not unreasonable assumptions at the time. Agriculture accounted for most, but not all, economic activity. What manufacturing existed focused largely on processing certain agricultural products, such as cotton or wool. In such an economy land was naturally seen as a major limiting factor.

Moreover, farming was largely labor intensive. There were little capital equipment and few significant scientific advances in farm production. Increases in agricultural output could be achieved only by adding additional labor resources to fixed land supplies. Thus increases in output were limited by the economic **law of diminishing returns**. This law states that less and less extra output can be obtained by adding more and more labor to fixed supplies of land and capital.

To see this effect on a small scale, consider a single farm. A farmer may be able to increase total output by 1000 bushels by hiring a single helper. He may obtain even more output by adding a second and a third helper. But with fixed amounts of land and capital, each additional helper hired will increase output by less and less. As economists are fond of saying, were it not for the law of diminishing returns, we could grow the world's food supply in a flowerpot just by adding enough labor and other resources.

Law of diminishing returns. The proposition that adding labor to a fixed quantity of land and capital will eventually result in smaller and smaller increases in total output if technology is constant.

Thomas Malthus and the "dismal science". In his famous book, *An Essay on the Principle of Population* (first published in 1798), Thomas Malthus saw a conflict between population growth and what he believed to be a fixed supply of natural resources. He concluded that population tends to grow faster over the long run than the economy's ability to support it.

Malthus recognized that if a country's population is small relative to its land resources, additional workers may increase per capita output. (Even today, labor-intensive agricultural societies view having many children as creating workers who produce more than they eat.) But if population growth continues unchecked, more and more workers are added to the same quantity of land. If capital and technology do not change, the law of diminishing returns means that additional workers eventually will produce less than they consume. At that point, the average standard of living will fall. According to Malthus, population growth will eventually push the average standard of living down to a subsistence level. Beyond that point, starvation, disease, and wars will limit population growth. No wonder economics back then was called the "dismal science"!

Modern Assumptions and Expectations of Economic Growth

Since Malthus's time, the world's population has grown enormously. But its standard of living, especially in the industrialized nations, has also risen dramatically. Modern economists believe Malthus was wrong because he made the wrong assumptions. Since his time, major advances in technology have expanded supplies of capital resources and land for agricultural production. (Note that the world still has the same amount of land as in Malthus's time, but far more of it is now put to agricultural use, particularly in North America.)

Malthus's assumptions were reasonable to him at the time. He had no reason to expect the growth of technology and increase in capital resources to come. Technological change was extremely important to economic growth during the Industrial Revolution in the nineteenth century. And in the United States, technological change may account for as much as 40 percent of the country's economic growth since World War II.

Linked to technological advances are increased supplies of capital resources that have substantially increased **labor productivity**, that is, average output per employed worker. Increases in the *quality* of labor (through education and training) have also contributed to economic growth. As a result, growth in the production of food and other economic goods and services has outstripped population growth, which is not the result Malthus predicted.

However, the world is not completely free from the conditions about which Malthus wrote. As Malthus observed, we cannot view an increase in population as just an increase in labor resources (and thus in aggregate supply). Whenever population grows faster than real output, the average standard of living will decline. As we noted earlier, in poor countries rapid population growth offsets many gains in real output. And some nations with abundant labor resources—the People's Republic of China, for example—have had relatively slow economic growth because of difficulties in putting those resources to effective use.

Moreover, in some African countries such as Ethiopia, the quantity of arable (farm) land has shrunk greatly in recent decades because of severe droughts. In some of these nations, the average standard of living is quite close to or at the subsistence level, and starvation is not a remote possibility but a recurring fact of

Labor productivity. The average output per unit of labor input, most often measured as real output per hour of work.

life. But for most of the world, economic growth is a reality. To understand why and what, if anything, we can do to increase the rate of economic growth, we must consider the factors that contribute to economic growth.

Changes in Natural Resources

Although the world's total supply of any natural resource is fixed, the quantity available for particular purposes may change. Damming rivers can turn water power into electric power and provide energy for economic use. Discoveries of new reserves—oil in the North Sea and in Alaska—or the development of substitutes for natural resources—synthetic rubber—can also add to an economy's potential GNP. Improved transportation systems—the building of the transcontinental railroad in the United States, for example—can make more resources available to the economy.

Changes in the Labor Supply

In Chapter 26, we noted that an increase in the labor supply can raise potential GNP. The increase in the labor supply might occur because of an increase in population. But as we just stated, a larger population not only means more workers, but also more people to feed, house, and clothe. Unless output per worker also increases, real GNP per capita will not increase, although total output may rise. Thus in considering changes in the labor supply, economists now believe that economic growth will occur only if the proportion of the population that contributes to GNP (the employment/population ratio) increases or if labor productivity increases.

The employment/population ratio. An increase in the proportion of the population that is employed—that is, the employment/population ratio—increases the quantity of labor supplied by the same population. Reducing the proportion of the population not in the labor force adds to output just as reducing unemployment does. Thus economists observe that an increase in the employment/population ratio adds to the economy's potential GNP and to real GNP per capita. In the United States, the increasing proportion of women seeking work in the 1960s and 1970s increased both the employment/population ratio and the rate of economic growth. However, changes in the employment/population ratio can have only a limited effect on economic growth. After all, we cannot expect 100 percent of the population to be employed. Moreover, with a few exceptions—efforts to reduce population growth rates or eliminate mandatory retirement programs—little can be done to change this factor.

Changes in the employment/population ratio may reflect changes in the age distribution of the population. In less-developed countries with high birth rates, children account for an increasing proportion of the population. As a result, employment/population ratios are declining, making economic growth more difficult. In the United States, an increasing proportion of the population is reaching age 65 and retiring from the active labor force. This trend may make increases in real GNP per capita more difficult in the future.

Moreover, we can't lose sight of the element of truth in Malthus's gloomy predictions. Without improvements in technology and/or increase in capital resources, the law of diminishing returns would indeed apply. That is, we would expect an increase in labor supply to result in a fall in labor productivity—the average output per employed worker. As a result, the average standard of living would decrease. To achieve significant long-run economic growth, labor productivity must improve.

Quality of labor. One factor affecting labor productivity is the quality of labor, that is, the skills, training, experience, and mobility of labor. An increase in the quality of labor raises the output per worker and therefore raises real GNP per capita. Although we cannot measure precisely the contribution of this factor, some economists believe that as much as 15–20 percent of the past economic growth in the United States can be attributed to growth in the quality of the labor force.

In any economy, expenditures on education and training can pay off in terms of future economic growth. However, as with all economic decisions, investment in labor quality requires sacrifices. More should be invested only if the extra benefits (higher future growth) are worth the extra costs (less current consumption). However, education, training, and experience of the labor force are just the tip of the labor-quality iceberg. Many economists believe that such intangibles as entrepreneurship, the work ethic, inventiveness, and "Yankee ingenuity" are as or more important. They believe that much of the past economic success of the United States relative to the rest of the world resulted from these unmeasurable but powerful factors.

If these intangibles really are important to economic growth, can an economy somehow foster them? The answer to this question is highly controversial. Some economists suggest that high marginal tax rates in the United States and Western Europe may have stifled innovation. (This argument was offered as a reason for the substantial cuts in the marginal tax rates in both 1981 and 1986.) Others take the same stand on centrally planned economies such as the Soviet Union's. They question whether the U.S.S.R. can continue to grow at its current rate because managers and workers in that system have little incentive to innovate or adopt new technology.

Changes in Capital Resources

In our discussion of Malthus and more recent economic-growth theory, you saw that changes in capital resources—an increased number of machines, for example—can affect economic growth. Such changes actually cause growth indirectly. That is, they increase the productivity of labor, which causes economic growth.

Capital/labor ratio. Economists measure the effect of changes in capital resources on labor productivity as the **capital/labor ratio**, or the average quantity of capital resources per worker. As this ratio rises, we can anticipate more output per worker because they have more machinery and other capital resources to work with.

A rising capital/labor ratio appears to have played a major role in the economic growth of industrialized nations. For example, the use of more and larger agricultural equipment is credited for much of the tremendous increase in agricultural productivity in the United States. In fact, some economists believe that economic growth requires an increase in capital. That is, it does little good to have a larger and better educated work force if that work force lacks the necessary capital resources to maintain and increase their productivity. Without an increase in

Capital/labor ratio. The average quantity of capital resources per worker, calculated by dividing the stock of capital by the number of employed workers.

Extensive growth. Economic growth achieved by increasing the quantity of economic resources, such as labor and capital resources.

capital, the law of diminishing returns would apply, and output per worker would fall.

Interaction of saving and investment. To increase the capital/labor ratio the economy must increase its investment in capital resources. In fact, investment (over and above the amount necessary to replace worn-out or obsolete capital resources) must grow faster than the labor force. But we said in Chapter 21 that GNP is the sum of consumption, investment, government purchases, and net exports. Thus if the economy is operating at its potential GNP level, an increase in investment requires a decrease in another component of GNP.

For example, a decrease in consumption (that is, an increase in private saving) or a reduction in government purchases would free resources for investment, as would lowering net exports. That is, we could lower the quantity of goods we ship to other countries (exports) and increase the quantity of goods we import. By lowering our exports, we have more potential to produce capital resources domestically. By increasing our imports, we can purchase more capital resources such as machines. Or we can import consumer goods, freeing domestic industries to produce capital resources.

But the foreign sector cannot be relied on indefinitely. For an economy to increase imports faster than exports, it must borrow from other countries. That is, purchases must either be paid for now (with export earnings) or later. But paying later for goods consumed now means borrowing. Inflows of foreign capital can increase output in the short run. Funds supplied by the World Bank, the International Monetary Fund, and by individual countries such as the United States have been important sources of temporary financing in less-developed nations. But, ultimately, economic growth is limited by the amount of internal saving an economy can generate. Eventually nations must trade off current consumption for economic growth and future consumption.

Economists refer to growth caused by an increased supply of capital resources as **extensive growth**. The Soviet Union, which has given a high priority to economic growth, has achieved much of its past growth by allocating a large share of production to capital resources. By fostering extensive growth, central planners in the Soviet Union have managed to increase real output faster than has the U.S. economy in the last 40 years. But extensive growth requires saving, that is, a sacrifice of consumption. Thus while the Soviet Union has grown, it has done so at the expense of satisfying demand for consumer goods.

Keep in mind that in arguing for nations to save today in order to grow tomorrow, we assume that their economies are already producing at the potential GNP level. If there is a contractionary gap, increasing saving or decreasing government spending may reduce aggregate demand unless it is matched by an equal increase in investment. That is, more saving may decrease real GNP in the short run, or what we called the paradox of thrift in Chapter 23. But what happens to demand in the short run can have important effects on long-run supply. If an economy operates at below its potential GNP, it will fail to produce all the goods and services that it can. The result will be less actual saving and investment and thus less growth. Thus maintaining full employment can help an economy grow in the future.

Changes in Technology

Another factor in economic growth—changes in technology—works by increasing the productivity of both labor and other resources. As we noted earlier,

Intensive growth. Economic growth achieved by increasing the productivity of economic resources, that is, by technological progress.

Economies of scale. A situation in which long-run average cost decreases as a firm increases the size (or scale) of its plant and output; implies that larger plants are more technically efficient than small plants if large quantities of goods are produced.

technological changes are credited with a great deal of nineteenth- and twentieth-century economic growth. Economists use the term **intensive growth** to describe growth generated by changes in technology.

We can identify two broad types of technological change that can lead to intensive growth. Some technological changes directly improve methods of production. For example, better soil management, erosion control, and pesticide control have contributed to greater agricultural production throughout the world. Other technological changes take the form of new products such as computers and telecommunications systems. Both types of technological change have been important in the past. Whether they can continue to spur economic growth remains to be seen.

Reallocation of Resources

Finally, increases in productivity and potential GNP may occur if resources are reallocated. As we noted earlier, having more resources is of little direct benefit unless they are effectively organized and used. In many less-developed countries, productivity in the agricultural sector is still relatively low, while individuals are severely underemployed. If surplus labor resources can be moved from the low-productivity agricultural sector to the high-productivity industrial sector, average productivity will increase. The opportunity to make such transfers may be limited, of course, especially if there are few industrial jobs. Moreover, such transfers often require education and training of workers. In addition, transfers may also require increases in capital resources to make workers more productive.

An economy can achieve a limited amount of growth through labor reallocation. The transfer of labor from agricultural to nonagricultural industries was a significant factor in U.S. economic growth in the 1940s and 1950s. And this type of change could still increase economic growth in many less-developed nations. Unfortunately, these countries often do not have many capital resources or the income to invest in labor reallocation.

Reallocating resources may allow countries to employ technology and capital equipment that is productive only when the volume of output is large. Although not every increase in size generates greater productivity, when **economies of scale** do exist, larger firms will be more productive than smaller firms. In such cases, reallocating resources from smaller, less efficient plants to larger, more efficient ones can raise average productivity.

RECAP

Economic growth can occur because of increases in resources or increases in productivity.

Discovery or development of natural resources can add to the economy's potential GNP.

Labor supplies can increase because of a higher employment/population ratio; population growth; increased skills; or more-efficient work habits and inventiveness.

An increase in the capital/labor ratio resulting from investment in additional capital can increase productivity. Greater investment requires additional saving or an inflow of foreign capital if the economy is operating at full employment. Growth caused by increased capital is called extensive growth.

Technological progress increases productivity, enabling the economy to obtain more output from the same quantity of resources. Such growth is called intensive growth.

ACCOUNTING FOR ECONOMIC GROWTH

In the preceding discussion we identified the factors responsible for economic growth. In this section we want to explore the actual growth of the U.S. economy. What factors contributed the most to economic growth in the past? How can we explain the growth rate of the U.S. economy relative to two of its main economic rivals, West Germany and Japan? What accounts for the fact that the growth rate of the U.S. economy in the 1970s and early 1980s was far below its historical average?

Source	1929–1948	1948–1973	1973–1979	1980–1982
Quantity of labor	1.07%	1.21%	1.73%	1.49%
Quality of labor	0.38	0.25	0.17	0.27
Quantity of capital	0.11	0.77	0.76	0.51
Technology	0.49	1.09	0.22	−0.58
Resource allocation	0.53	0.57	0.13	0.07
Other	−0.01	0.00	0.00	0.06
Potential GNP	2.57%	3.89%	3.01%	1.82%
Less: Population growth	0.98	1.48	1.01	1.06
Real GNP per capita	1.59%	2.41%	2.00%	0.76%

**Exhibit 30.4
Sources of Economic
Growth in the United
States: 1929–1982**

Source: Edward Denison, *Accounting for Slower Economic Growth.* Washington, D.C.: Brookings Institution, 1985, Table 8-2, p. 112.

Sources of U.S. Economic Growth, 1929–1973

Growth of the U.S. economy from 1929 to 1973 was impressive. Real GNP per capita more than doubled, rising from $5830 in 1929 to $12,950 in 1973. Exhibit 30.4 compares sources of economic growth in potential GNP in four periods. These figures are from a study by economist Edward Denison, who attempted to track and explain U.S. economic growth.*

The first two columns in Exhibit 30.4 show that potential GNP grew faster immediately after World War II than before the war—3.89 percent versus 2.57 percent—and suggests the reasons for it. In both periods, increases in the *quantity* of labor accounted for over 1 percent of growth annually. *Quality* changes in the labor force (rising educational levels and the changing age–gender mix of workers) also contributed significantly to total growth in both periods.

But improved labor quality accounts for less of the growth in the more recent period, which Denison attributes to the rising proportion of young and women workers in the labor force. As Denison points out, these groups were concentrated in low-skilled (and low-paid) occupations, but were not inherently less productive. Thus the faster growth attributed to higher quantities of labor in 1948–1973 was offset by a smaller contribution from improvements in the quality of labor.

Improvements in resource allocation were also responsible for much of the growth. In both the 1929–1948 and 1948–1973 periods, growth occurred because production was transferred to larger plants (economies of scale). Labor transfers— from farm to industrial employment, for example—also resulted in growth. But neither labor nor other resource allocation accounts for the large difference between the two periods. Rather, as Exhibit 30.4 indicates, higher growth after World War II resulted from two factors. First, the quantity of capital contributed more to growth from 1948 to 1973 than from 1929 to 1948. Second, technology— or what Denison calls "advances in knowledge"—added greatly to postwar growth.

---

* In his study Denison actually uses potential national income, not output. As we have noted before, however, national income and aggregate output, although not identical, are very closely related. We can expect that the changes Denison observed in potential national income will apply also to potential GNP. Moreover, Denison, like most economists who have tried to account for growth, does not directly calculate the contribution of technology. Rather, he explains as much of the growth as he can by using other factors. Technology is assumed to account for the rest.

Reasons for the lower rate of capital growth between 1929 and 1948 are obvious. The Great Depression of the 1930s slowed capital investment considerably (which illustrates the importance of high employment to economic growth). Moreover, private investment was postponed during World War II, when the economy concentrated on production of war materiel. The faster growth rate of technology since 1948 may also reflect somewhat the same two events. Expenditures on private research and development during the Great Depression and World War II were small compared to those of the postwar period. Research and development expenditures do not always pay off, but when they do, the result is reflected in economic growth through technological progress. (See A Case in Point: Sources of Growth for a comparison of economic growth in the United States, Japan, and West Germany.)

Slowdown in Economic Growth Since 1973

Since 1973 the rate of economic growth in the United States has slowed considerably. Real GNP per capita grew by only 2.00 percent per year between 1973 and 1979 and by only 0.76 percent per year from 1980 to 1982. The slowdown in real GNP growth reflects economically troubled times. As we noted in Chapter 27, major supply shocks in both 1973–74 and 1979 triggered recessions. The 1981–82 recession in the United States also reflected contractionary policies used to bring down the rate of inflation.

However, our interest in this chapter is not in the temporary changes in GNP that reflect recessions. Rather, we want to know how changes affect the growth rate of potential GNP. Denison's analysis, as shown in Exhibit 30.4, indicates that potential GNP growth has slowed since 1973 in part because of a slight decline in the growth of capital. But the slowdown resulted primarily from less technological progress and the end of resource-allocation contributions to growth.

According to Denison's calculations, technology accounted for a much smaller part of growth in the late 1970s and did not make a positive contribution at all in the early 1980s. In addition, resource allocation, a significant factor in earlier periods, had virtually no effect on the growth rate after 1973. As we suggested earlier, even in the immediate postwar period, the United States had nearly reached the limit of resource allocation as a source of growth. The 1973–1982 period saw other nations reach the limit, too.

Denison believed that labor-productivity growth had fallen—a conclusion confirmed by other data. Since 1890, labor productivity has grown at an average rate of 2 percent per year. From 1950 to 1965 productivity growth was 2.7 percent per year, or well above the long-run trend. Between 1965 and 1973, productivity grew at just under 2 percent per year. Since 1973, however, productivity growth has averaged less than 1 percent per year. Even after the economy rebounded from the recession in 1981–82, productivity growth remained disappointing. In fact, productivity growth averaged less than 1 percent in 1986.

As with many economic variables, productivity growth follows the business cycle. That is, it generally falls during a recession and rises during a recovery. This pattern occurs partly because employers are reluctant to lay off all their most skilled workers for fear of losing them permanently. Thus businesses keep some skilled workers on the payroll, even though there is not enough work to keep

A Case in Point
Sources of Growth:
An International Comparison

Edward Denison also analyzed the high economic-growth rates in West Germany and Japan since World War II. The table below shows that growth in both countries greatly exceeded that of the United States. In all three countries, increases in labor supplies were significant. However, this factor accounts for little of the difference in growth rates.

The biggest difference is the faster increase in capital resources in Japan and West Germany. Some attribute the capital growth to the higher saving rates in Japan

Sources of Economic Growth in the United States, Japan, and West Germany: 1929–1973 (percentage contributions to total growth in national income)

Source	United States 1948–1969	Japan 1953–1971	West Germany 1950–1962
Quantity of labor	0.99%	1.37%	1.22%
Quality of labor	0.31	0.48	0.15
Quantity of capital	0.79	2.10	1.41
Technology	1.19	1.97	0.87
Resource allocation	0.72	2.88	2.52
Other	0.00	0.01	0.10
Potential output	4.00%	8.81%	6.27%

Source: Edward Denison and William Chung, How Japan's Economy Grew So Fast. Washington, D.C.: Brookings Institution, 1976, Table 4-8, pp. 42–43.

and West Germany. Because saving and investment are connected, some economists believe that the United States must seek policies to increase saving if growth rates are to increase again. But both Japan and West Germany also received aid from the U.S. economy which helped them modernize and rebuild.

A second important difference is the contribution of resource allocation, including movement out of agriculture and self-employment, and economies of scale. As we noted earlier, the contribution of this factor is limited. The United States simply appears to have reached its limits earlier than the other two countries.

Finally, Denison's calculations indicate that technology is responsible for a relatively large share of the difference in the growth rate between the United States and Japan. These statistics have led some economists to suggest that efforts to increase the rate of technological progress may be necessary to close this gap.

Since 1973, the rate of economic growth in the United States has slowed considerably. Real GNP per capita grew by 2.65 percent per year between 1960 and 1973, but by only 1.46 percent from 1973 to 1985. Because the United States is a major buyer and seller of internationally traded goods, the slowdown in U.S. economic activity was reflected in other countries as well. Growth also slowed in Western Europe and Japan in the latter period, largely as a result of oil-supply shocks. But the economies of both Japan and West Germany experienced greater growth than the U.S. economy.

them fully occupied. In order to see the true impact of productivity on potential GNP, we have to adjust our figures to remove cyclical effects. But even after making these adjustments, we find that productivity growth still averaged only 1 percent per year in the first half of the 1980s, or only one-half the long-run average. Why has productivity growth fallen? We explore some possible explanations in the following sections. Unfortunately, none of them fully explains what happened to productivity.

Declining technological progress.   As we noted earlier, Denison attributed part of the decline in real GNP growth to a lower rate of technological progress. Other studies draw similar conclusions. But these studies, like Denison's, measure technological progress as the amount of growth that cannot be explained by other factors. Indirect evidence also indicates that efforts to improve technology may have decreased, however. For example, the percentage of GNP devoted to research and development appears to have fallen.

Declining capital/labor ratio. Recall that an increase in the capital/labor ratio tends to increase labor productivity because workers have more and better machinery with which to work. However, the actual capital/labor ratio in the United States has declined in recent years. Why did it decline? One explanation is that the economy has operated well below the potential GNP level during many of the years since 1973, experiencing three recessions. Recessions tend to slow the rate of capital investment for two reasons: (1) businesses have lower profits with which to finance such spending; and (2) the short-run payoff of new investments is low when business conditions are uncertain and unfavorable.

The rapid increase in energy prices that occurred during this period may also explain part of this change. According to this argument, capital and energy are complements, whereas energy and labor are substitutes. Therefore higher energy costs increase the use of labor and decrease the use of capital, lowering the capital/labor ratio. Higher energy costs—and the consequent decrease in the short-run aggregate supply curve—have also been suggested as causes of the recessions in 1973–1975 and 1980.

Economists generally conclude that the change in the capital/labor ratio accounts for part but not all of the slowdown in productivity. However, many economists still believe that efforts to increase capital growth are a key to increasing labor productivity and, consequently, potential GNP.

Government regulations. Some economists blame part of the productivity slowdown on increased government regulation during the 1970s. Government increasingly regulated the environment, worker health and safety, auto safety, and other areas of social concern during that decade. And these policies did divert some capital resources from investments that could have increased productive capacity or the capital/labor ratio. Moreover, managerial efforts devoted to satisfying government regulations might have been used instead to increase productivity.

But while these policies may have lowered measured productivity, they also offered some benefits. For example, diverting labor and capital resources to pollution control can improve air and water quality and thus the standard of living. Such benefits are not fully measured by GNP, but they may provide a reason not to completely abandon policies that may lower measured growth.

Management problems. Mistakes on the part of managers—and their failure to solve management problems—may also have contributed to lower economic growth. Critics charge that U.S. managers are more interested in short-run results than in long-term gains, leading to too little investment in research and development. Major mistakes may also have made the United States a noncompetitor in some world markets. Certainly, U.S. automakers have paid for responding slowly to changing consumer demands. And the U.S. steel industry has lost sales by failing to invest in modern, cost-cutting technology.

But is this apparent shortsightedness a management problem, or is it related to uncertainties in the economy? Did mistakes by U.S. manufacturers or govern-

RECAP ▤▤▤▤▤▤▤▤

Studies of economic growth in the United States attribute the growth to an increased supply of labor, a rise in the capital/labor ratio, technological progress, and improved allocation of resources.

The higher growth rate from 1948 to 1973 than from 1929 to 1948 principally reflects an increase in the capital/labor ratio and a higher rate of technological progress.

The slowdown in economic growth in the United States since 1973 has been attributed to a combination of factors, including less technological progress, a declining capital/labor ratio, government regulations, management problems, and misguided macroeconomic policies.

ment regulations divert resources away from investment in capital resources and research and development? To what extent are labor unions also responsible for businesses' shortsightedness and low productivity growth? Unfortunately, we do not have conclusive answers to any of these questions.

Macroeconomic policies.   Finally, some critics argue that macroeconomic policies in the 1970s caused high and variable inflation. High inflation, in turn, resulted in less saving and investment because of the tax system. When inflation occurs, individuals receive higher nominal income and pay higher taxes, lowering their real income. If they try to maintain the same real level of consumption, their saving must decline. Similarly, businesses are taxed on inflated profits and will decrease investment. Higher taxes on nominal interest earned also discourages saving.

Advocates of supply-side policies pushed for—and won—some changes in the federal tax system in 1981. (See A Case in Point: Supply-Side Effects of Tax Cuts for more on their views.) Individual tax rates are now indexed (as of 1985), that is, they will be adjusted automatically for changes in the price level. The tax reforms in 1986 lowered tax rates and made the tax rates less progressive. Whether these changes will lead to higher future growth remains to be seen. There is not much evidence that the tax changes in 1981 influenced either saving or growth.

Other economists also blame macroeconomic policies but for different reasons. Keynesians such as James Tobin argue that overly restrictive monetary policies in the 1970s and early 1980s kept the economy operating at below its potential GNP level. When output falls, so does saving and investment, further lowering output. As Tobin observes, maintaining output close to the potential level not only maximizes current production, but also adds to investment and potential GNP growth.

This survey of possible causes has not enabled us to draw any final conclusions about why the U.S. economy's growth has slowed. In fact, most economists believe that the slowdown stems from a combination of the factors we presented and discussed. But because the slowdown seems to have several causes, economists have also suggested a number of possible policies to again speed up the rate of economic growth.

IMPROVING ECONOMIC GROWTH: POLICY OPTIONS

The slowdown in the rate of economic growth that has occurred in recent years is troubling for what it implies, not so much about the present but about the future. For this reason, policies to raise this growth rate are believed to be important. Indeed, the Reagan administration's economic policies have been devoted in large part to this economic goal. As we explore the policies of this and other administrations, keep in mind the following point: *In the long run, economic growth requires an increase in the capital/labor ratio and/or technological progress. Policies to change the rate of economic growth will work if they can affect at least one of these two factors.*

A Case in Point
Supply-Side Effects of Tax Cuts

In most of our discussion of government policy and the macroeconomy, we have stressed the demand side of the economy, especially the demand-side orientation of Keynesian economists. But government policies can also affect the supply side of the economy, that is, aggregate supply and potential GNP. How significant are these effects?

Supply-side economists believe that government policies can make a measurable difference. They advocate government policies to enhance private incentives to work, save, and invest. Most argue for the removal of government regulations, which they believe have stifled economic incentives, and cutting income tax rates.

Lower tax rates increase the rewards of working, thereby increasing the incentive to work. A wage rate of $10 an hour before taxes adds only $4 an hour to after-tax income if the marginal tax rate is 60 percent. But lowering the rate to 25 percent raises the effective wage to $7.50 per hour. As we discussed in Chapter 26, additional work effort on the part of the same population increases aggregate supply and potential GNP.

Lower taxes also increase the incentive to save. A 10 percent interest rate on savings means only a 4 percent after-tax return if the marginal tax rate is 60 percent. Lowering the marginal rate to 20 percent raises the after-tax return on savings to 8 percent. Similarly, lower taxes on business increases the profits that can be earned on investments in factories and equipment and in research and development of new technologies. As we noted in this chapter, an economy must invest to grow, and to invest it must either save or borrow from foreign economies. Lower taxes may increase both domestic saving and investment and, consequently, increase aggregate supply and potential GNP.

Most economists believe that such policies have relatively small short-run effects on aggregate supply. In fact, supply-side economics is, for the most part, aimed at making small increases in the rate of economic growth. But even small increases add up to significant gains over the long run. However, some ardent supporters of supply-side policies argue that the economy can make a significant short-run response to improved incentives. In supporting the large tax cuts of 1981, for example, they predicted that total tax revenues would actually increase despite lower tax rates.

Actual evidence from the 1981 tax cuts, however, suggests that the effects of tax cuts on aggregate supply are modest at best. Work effort, measured by the labor-force participation rate, has grown more slowly since 1981 than before. The decline in tax revenues was very much as predicted by traditional economic models. While there may be some small long-run effects of tax cuts, the claims of the ardent supply-siders appear to have been exaggerated.

Raising Saving and Investment

The capital/labor ratio can rise only if the growth of capital exceeds that of the labor force. As we noted earlier, in the long run greater investment must be matched by greater saving. Thus policies to improve the capital/labor ratio focus on increasing saving and investment.

Increasing the rate of saving. The rate of saving is lower in the United States than in other industrialized nations that have had faster growth rates. As a result, some economists (including advisors to the Reagan administration) argue that the United States must increase its rate of saving if it is to again experience greater economic growth.

Policies to increase saving are directed both to personal saving (disposable income minus consumption) and to saving by business (retained earnings). Government can encourage both private and business saving through tax policies. For example, some economists argue for replacing the income tax with a consumption tax. Under such a policy, only the portion of income spent would be taxed, providing a strong incentive for saving. This tax is used in some European countries, but has not yet attracted the attention of many politicians in the United States.

The tax changes passed in 1981 and 1986 included some policies aimed at increasing the rate of saving. Tax rates fell significantly, raising the return on saving. Since income tax rates are now indexed, only changes in real income are taxed. Individuals may no longer deduct interest paid on consumer loans but may continue to deduct interest on home mortgages.

Increasing the rate of investment. As we observed earlier, the objective of growth policies is not higher saving as such but higher investment. Increased saving is important because it raises the supply of funds available for investment. Some economists have also proposed policies to directly increase demand for investment funds. Because investment spending is influenced by the after-tax rate of return, a reduction in taxes stimulates more investment, assuming that all other factors remain the same.

But as you well know by this time, all other things do not always remain unchanged. The 1986 tax changes lowered overall corporate tax rates. But the new tax laws allow much less generous deduction for depreciation. Moreover, a provision that allowed an immediate tax credit for new investment was eliminated. These changes work in opposite directions but appear to be more favorable to service industries (where capital investment is small). They appear to be less favorable to manufacturing industries (where capital investment is large). Some industries that face stiff foreign competition and want to renovate plant and buy new equipment—steel and automobiles, for example—may be harder pressed to make those investments.

Some economists have even argued that corporate taxes should be eliminated entirely. But if receipts from corporate taxes were eliminated, the federal government would either have to find another source of revenue or cut spending significantly. The political battle would be bloody because of existing budget deficits and likely objections that such a change favors affluent stockholders. Moreover, although increased investment in fixed capital is important, some government expenditures also increase potential GNP. Public expenditures on transportation and communication systems, public health, education and training, and research and development are social investments. As with any government spending, there is a short-run trade-off: The more resources the government uses, the fewer are the resources available for the private sector. But some government investments may be as important to long-run growth as additional private investment.

Increasing Technological Change

Another factor that we noted as important, and one that has apparently contributed to the declining growth rate, is technological change. Technological progress cannot be directly controlled, but it can be indirectly stimulated by increasing the resources devoted to research and development of new technologies. Government policies to spur technological progress thus take one of three approaches. First, government spending or subsidies may be targeted to specific projects or ideas. Second, favorable tax treatment of privately funded research and development can provide indirect government encouragement. And third, government can remove potential obstacles to technological growth.

Direct government spending and subsidies. Proponents of direct government subsidies and spending argue that recent declines in technological progress reflect market failures. To the degree that private returns on investment in research fail to capture total social returns, such policies may be warranted. In fact, it is often difficult for a private firm to capture the returns from technological breakthroughs because of the speed with which competitors may imitate them. The best case for direct government subsidies and spending appears to be in the area of basic research, in which the risks of market failure are greatest.

Indirect government support. One form of indirect government support for research and development is the patent system. This system increases the chance that an inventor will be able to capture the returns from innovation by granting a 17-year monopoly on an invention. Another indirect support is the favorable tax treatment of research and development expenditures compared with other forms of investment. Some economists who are concerned about recent declines in technological progress suggest that further support should be given in the form of tax credits. But as we noted earlier, reducing one form of taxes would force government either to cut spending or to find a new source of revenues.

Removing barriers. Other economists believe that government regulations have seriously impeded technological progress. They consider the money and effort that businesses spend to comply with government regulations as diverting resources away from productive uses. Government regulations on pollution, health, and safety appear to have increased both the length of time it takes to turn research into profits and the uncertainty of future returns.

Supporters of deregulation argue that it would have desirable effects on technological progress. They note that current government regulations impose costs on the economy, especially by reducing economic growth. Critics of deregulation acknowledge these costs but argue that regulations also force private decision makers to recognize external costs, thus providing social benefits. The principles of rational choice tell us that only those regulations that add more to social benefits than social costs should be implemented. But the often normative nature of measuring benefits and costs explains why economists rationally disagree about the "correct" policy.

Industrial Policy

Some economists believe that economic growth can be increased by means of a consciously designed and applied **industrial policy**. Actually a set of microeconomic policies, it includes tax rules, research and development grants, direct subsidies, international trade restrictions, and labor-training programs. Supporters of an industrial policy argue that Japan's use of one to redirect resources into industries with growth potential has been a major reason for that nation's high growth rate. They propose that the United States establish a counterpart to Japan's Ministry of International Trade and Industry (MITI) to set industrial priorities. Industries that show promise of growth would be given public support. Workers in other industries would be retrained to improve their mobility.

Supporters of this centralized process note that current industrial policies in the United States are likely contributing to less efficiency and economic growth.

Industrial policy. A set of microeconomic policies designed to affect economic growth; includes tax rules, research and development grants, direct subsidies, international trade restrictions, and labor-training programs.

These policies are a hodgepodge of special favors that have been given to industries having political clout. In many cases industries receiving government support have little growth potential. In contrast, a conscious, centralized process of selecting and supporting growth industries would assist the orderly transfer of resources to them from declining industries. Advocates of changes in U.S. industrial policy include Keynesians, monetarists, new classicists, and supply-siders. Indeed, most economists believe that special favors currently accorded specific industries—such as agriculture, textiles, and steel—are often inefficient.

However, the notion of a centralized, government-set industrial policy has many critics. Some argue that a government agency could not pick winning industries any better than do market forces. Many critics fear that bureaucrats in such an agency would give in to lobbyists, just as they have in the past. A number of the critics, especially some supply-siders, believe that government's role should be limited to assisting the market. They advocate general incentives to saving, investment, and research and development, and elimination of existing barriers to growth. But they believe that the market—not government—should determine where resources can be best utilized.

The issues raised by proponents of industrial policy are important even if their proposed solutions are controversial. Whether the best alternative to the current hodgepodge is a centralized system of specific supports or a decentralized system of general supports will continue to be strongly debated. Policy options to improve international competitiveness of the U.S. economy—including industrial policy—are considered in Chapter 31.

Stabilization Policies and Economic Growth

Economic-growth policies are designed to increase potential GNP. In contrast, stabilization policies are designed to keep the economy operating at close to its potential output (GNP) level while maintaining price stability. Although their aims are different, the two types of policies are closely related.

Supply-side economists note that poor stabilization policies may lead to high and variable rates of inflation. In turn, inflation creates uncertainty and potential distortions through a tax system that discourages saving and investment. Thus poorly designed stabilization policies can lead to slower economic growth. Keynesian economists note that poor stabilization policies may leave the economy operating below its potential output (GNP) level. Because real output is lower, saving and investment will fall, which will also slow economic growth.

Both groups raise valid points. In the long run, the total quantity of saving and investment can be raised only by increasing the proportion of real output that is both saved and invested. In the short run, higher real output associated with lower GNP gaps can raise total saving and investment even if there is no change in the portion of real output saved.

CONCLUSION

Economic growth, like the other economic goals, is not as easy to achieve in the real world as we might wish. Moreover, achieving greater economic growth is not inexpensive. Basically, economists understand how to achieve economic growth, as we have described in this chapter. Indeed, economists disagree less about what causes economic growth than they do about what causes inflation and unemployment. But they do not all agree that government policies have played—or can play—a very positive role in aiding economic growth.

It is not easy to balance the desire for greater economic growth with the desire to achieve other economic objectives. Thus there is no shortage of debate over the "best" policy. Much of this debate centers on the rate of economic growth that can be attained in the short run and the long run and how these rates can be reached. We have become accustomed to economic growth, and political policies intended to support continued growth are likely. But in the final analysis, many growth factors, including technological change, may not be easily manipulated by government policies.

SUMMARY

1. In this chapter we examined the meaning and causes of economic growth, as well as historical growth rates and policies designed to increase economic growth.

2. Economic growth is generally measured as an increase in real GNP per capita and is desired because it represents an increase in the average standard of living. Although real GNP per capita can increase in the short run due to a reduction in the GNP gap, over the long run economic growth requires an increase in the economy's potential GNP.

3. Classical economists, such as Malthus, assumed that land, capital, and technology were fixed. Thus they concluded that long-run economic growth was impossible. They believed that following the law of diminishing returns, increases in the population would eventually cause the standard of living to fall to subsistence levels. Economists now recognize the contribution of increases in land, capital, and technology to economic growth.

4. Growth may occur because of increased availability of natural resources, increased quantity and quality of labor resources, an increase in the capital/labor ratio, improved technology, or improved allocation of resources.

5. Studies of economic growth in the United States attribute this growth to an increase in the quantity and quality of labor resources, an increase in the capital/labor ratio, technological progress, and improved allocation of resources. The higher growth rate from 1948 to 1973 than in 1929 to 1948 principally reflects an increase in the capital/labor ratio and a higher rate of technological progress.

6. The slowdown in economic growth in the United States since 1973 has been attributed to a combination of factors, including a declining capital/labor ratio, government regulations, a lower rate of technological

change, management problems, and the failure of stabilization policies.

7. Economists generally agree that in the long run, greater economic growth requires more saving and investment. Some believe that tax incentives to encourage saving and investment can be important. Others argue that the actual effect of tax incentives on saving has been quite small.

8. Technological progress has been important to past economic growth but has apparently slowed in recent years. Some suggest that government policies—direct subsidies and favorable tax treatment—may help to encourage research and development that will lead to technological change.

9. Some economists believe that economic growth can be increased by a centralized government agency coordinating industrial policy. The agency would identify and support industries with the greatest growth potential and encourage transfers of resources away from industries with little growth potential. Critics favor a reliance on market forces, with government's role limited to removing barriers to economic growth.

10. Stabilization and economic-growth policies are closely related. In order to achieve both price stability and economic growth, we must be careful to distinguish short-run problems from long-run problems. Controversies over the length of the short run and the effects of different policies are the focus of continuing economic debate.

KEY TERMS

Real GNP per capita, 765
Law of diminishing returns, 771
Labor productivity, 772
Capital/labor ratio, 774

Extensive growth, 775
Intensive growth, 776
Economies of scale, 776
Industrial policy, 784

QUESTIONS FOR REVIEW AND DISCUSSION

1. Explain how a decline in the supply of an important energy source can slow economic growth.

2. Suppose that a major technological development results in a dramatic increase in the capital/labor ratio in an industry employing a large number of workers. How will this change affect the long-run growth of output in the industry? What are the potential short-run problems? What are the benefits of developing policies to solve these short-run problems? Can you think of any costs?

3. The success of a centralized industrial policy requires selecting and assisting industries that can contribute the most to economic growth. If you were in charge of such a process, what criteria would you use to make the selection? How, if at all, do your criteria differ from those a bank might use to grant a loan?

4. Three important elements of the Reagan administration's economic policies were (a) reducing the size of government, (b) lowering marginal income tax rates, and (c) using restrictive monetary policy to fight inflation. In what way would a supply-side economist argue that each element adds to economic growth? In what way might a Keynesian economist argue that in the short run aggregate demand might be most affected? Does the record of the early 1980s confirm either or both positions?

5. From the standpoint of growth, what are the impacts of each of the following policies? What are their impacts on other economic goals, including allocative efficiency and equity? For each policy develop both a supporting and an adverse argument.
   a) Cutting taxes by lowering rates more for high-income than for low-income taxpayers.
   b) Reducing a full-employment budget deficit by raising taxes.
   c) Reducing a full-employment budget deficit by reducing government spending.
   d) Combining a full-employment budget surplus with an expansionary monetary policy.
   e) Combining a full-employment budget deficit with a contractionary monetary policy.

Economic Encounters
Living With and Curing Hyperinflation

You are probably familiar with the problems caused by inflation. But the inflation most of us have experienced is relatively mild in comparison with that in an economy experiencing *hyperinflation*. In post-World War I Germany, price levels rose by over 100,000,000 percent in just a 14-month period. Although the inflation in Argentina, Bolivia, Brazil, and Israel has not reached these heights (or depths), each has faced hyperinflation in the 1980s.

Runaway Inflation According to the World Bank, the annual rate of inflation in these four countries from 1980 to 1985 ranged from 148 percent in Brazil to 569 percent in Bolivia. Like most averages, these figures hide some periods of even more rapid inflation. In January 1985 Bolivia's price level rose by 80 percent, equivalent to an annual inflation rate of 116,000 percent had prices continued to rise at this rate. But inflation slowed during the rest of the year and rose by *only* 20,000 percent for the year.

Under these conditions money ceases to have much real value at all. People try to spend their money as fast as they get it. Individuals are reluctant to invest in businesses in such an uncertain environment and instead buy real estate, gold, or jewels (items expected to increase in value) or put their savings into foreign economies (where they can expect to receive real returns on their money).

Hyperinflation causes inefficiency; but curing hyperinflation is not painless. Traditional cures for inflation require belt-tightening. Reducing the rate of growth of the money supply—which most economists agree is necessary—slows the economy, increasing unemployment and decreasing output.

Brazil, Bolivia, Argentina, and Israel have experimented in recent years with alternative policies hoping to beat inflation without plunging the ecnomy into a recession. Their plans included direct controls on prices and/or income as well as the more traditional contractionary fiscal and monetary policies. But can hyperinflation be cured without causing an economic slump? So far the results are mixed.

Latin American Woes In 1983, when he became the first democratically elected president of Argentina after years of military rule, Raul Alfonsin hoped to improve the economy. Instead, economic growth was slow and inflation jumped from 250 percent per year to over 2000 percent in 1985. These conditions created an economic and a political crisis for the Argentinian government and led to the announcement in June 1985 of the Austral plan (named for the new currency created to replace the discredited peso.)

The theory behind this new plan was that high inflation rates have a way of sustaining themselves. Workers expecting high inflation continually ask for large wage increases to keep their real incomes from falling. But faced with higher costs, businesses continually raise product prices. The theory suggests that inflation might continue to increase even after monetary growth is reduced as long as individuals expect it to continue. Thus the Austral plan coupled a freeze on wages and prices with restrictive monetary policy. According to the theory, this combination should halt the momentum of inflation without a costly period of unemployment.

The immediate effects of the Austral plan were in line with predictions. As monetary growth slowed, inflation fell dramatically, in part because of the wage and price freeze. However, in April 1986 the government had to take a backward step. Actual prices (as opposed to officially controlled prices) continued to increase. Unions and consumers protested the consequent fall in their real income. The government relaxed the controls for a period of time but reinstituted them in Septem-

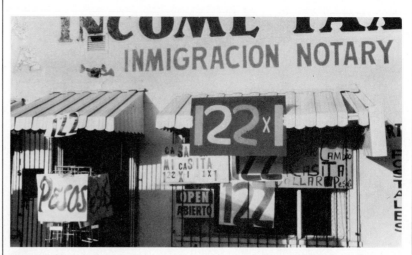

Signs of the times: exchange rates posted in San Ysidro, California. (Danuta Otfinowski/Black Star)

ber. By the end of 1986 prices were increasing at an annualized rate of approximately 30 percent—not a low rate but certainly a dramatic improvement in a short period of time. However, inflation surged again in January 1987, and in February a new freeze was imposed. Thus the Austral plan has had

only moderate success and is certainly not a blueprint for a painless cure for inflation.

In February 1986 Brazil instituted its anti-inflation program. Modeled on the Austral plan, it attacked the 250 percent annual inflation by freezing prices and wages (after allowing for an 8–15 percent increase in wages) and by creating a new currency—the cruzado. As in Argentina, the Cruzado plan had dramatic and immediate effects on inflation. But within nine months, Brazil's plan was in chaos. Because the money supply growth was not significantly reduced, demand in the economy continued to grow. Inflation was suppressed, not reduced. Consumers faced shortages in regular markets while prices in black markets soared. This failure to control demand was a serious economic mistake, although it did create a short-term political victory for the Brazilian leaders. Once price controls were removed, inflation again shot up and Brazil was engulfed in a quagmire of economic problems.

Bolivia's Black Market Blues Bolivia had the dubious distinction in 1985 of having the world's highest inflation rate—some 20,000 percent. Under the weight of this staggering hyperinflation the Bolivian currency lost virtually all value, leading to some ludicrous situations. Banks did not bother to count money that customers deposited, either taking their word for the amount or weighing the currency

to get an approximate amount. The 1000 peso bill—the most common denomination—cost more to print than it was worth. Currency printed in West Germany and Britain was Bolivia's third most significant import in 1985. Prices rose so fast that the last people waiting in line at a movie theater paid thousands of pesos more than those at the front of the line. Black-market moneychanging became a full-time occupation for many. The Bolivian economy was on the verge of complete collapse.

The Bolivian government entitled its anti-inflation package the New Economic Policy, but in most respects the plan contained traditional anti-inflation remedies—contractionary monetary and fiscal policies. The budget deficit fell from 28 percent of domestic output in 1984 to 4 percent in 1986 as the government imposed a new wealth tax, froze public-sector wages, and eliminated gasoline subsidies. In contrast to the Austral and Cruzado plans, the Bolivian plan removed controls on prices, interest rates, and goods.

From the perspective of inflation the New Economic Policy was successful. Inflation in Bolivia fell from 20,000 percent in 1985 to only 10 percent in the second half of 1986. But all the economic news was not good. Unemployment rose to almost 20 percent. Real wages of public-sector workers (who account for almost 40 percent of the labor force) fell. Real output fell by 3 percent in 1986.

Not Just a Latin American Problem In Israel, consumer prices rose by more than 100,000 percent between 1978 and 1985. But most wages and prices were cushioned from this hyperinflation by indexation—automatic increases in wages and interest rates as the price level increases.

By 1985 it was clear that Israel's economy was in trouble. The annual inflation rate surged up to 2000 percent. Israel tackled the problem in a manner closely resembling the Austral plan. Wages and prices were frozen

and indexation of prices and wages was suspended. Steps were taken to reduce the government's budget deficit, which fell from over 10 percent of domestic output in 1985 to around 3 percent in 1986. These policy measures helped to bring inflation down to only 20 percent in 1986, although unemployment increased. Since then inflation has begun to rise, but not yet at the rates of the previous period.

No Quick and Painless Solutions Economists are generally agreed that hyperinflation is caused by excessive growth in the money supply. In many less-developed economies it is difficult for government to raise money through taxation. At the same time there are tremendous demands for government spending to improve education, social welfare, transportation, and communication services—programs considered important to economic development. Faced with size-

able deficits, these governments sometimes simply printed money to spend. Such policies, however, are dangerously inflationary. Most economists would agree that curtailing monetary growth is essential to curing rapid inflation, even if the immediate consequences of such policies are somewhat higher unemployment, slower economic growth, and less public-sector support for economic development.

There is some disagreement among economists about whether wage and price controls might be useful in slowing the upward momentum in wages and prices. But price controls create another set of problems. As the experience in Brazil clearly indicates, there is little hope for an end to hyperinflation without monetary restraint.

CHAPTER 31

Macroeconomic Issues and Government Policies

The importance of economics is in the way it helps us to understand the real world and analyze real-world problems and issues. Economic analysis is especially important to an understanding of the effects of economic policies. In this section we consider several particular macroeconomic policy issues. The issues and policies we discover are examples of real situations in which government action has been proposed and used.

By exploring these issues, we seek to learn (1) how to apply economic principles to real-world situations; and (2) how to analyze the effects and effectiveness of alternative economic policies. After studying this introduction and the policy cases that follow, you should better understand the methods of economic analysis. You will also see how lost we would be in explaining or predicting economic outcomes without economic principles to guide our thinking.

Applying the Principles of Rational Choice to Policy Analysis

If we apply the principles of rational choice, which we first introduced in Chapter 2, we can structure the analysis of economic policy in terms of a series of questions.

Why is government action being proposed? It is useful to begin any analysis by considering why government action is being proposed. In other words, is the policy intended to lower unemployment, increase economic growth, or reduce inflation? Implicit in any new policy is a belief that current policies are inadequate. We should ask what supposed failure—either of current policy or of the private sector—suggests that government action is desirable. Before attempting to answer this question, we must establish criteria to judge a policy against.

The macroeconomy is capable of adjusting itself to economic changes. But its speed of adjustment is important to policy decisions. The faster the economy adjusts itself, the weaker the economic arguments for government intervention. Economists who believe that the economy adjusts itself very slowly or incompletely often view government actions as preferable to doing nothing. But government policies can be imperfect. Thus, as Charles Kindleberger has observed, in deciding whether government policies are desirable:

> The trick is to apply the appropriate adage: "If it ain't broke, don't fix it," or "A stitch in time saves nine."*

What are the extra benefits and costs of the proposed policy? To decide whether government policies are appropriate, we must apply the principles of rational choice. These principles require that we identify and compare the extra benefits and extra costs of a proposed policy. Thus we do not begin with the normative statement, "In my opinion. . . ." Rather, we must analyze facts and choose only those options for which the extra benefits outweigh the extra costs. In the case of macroeconomic policies, we identify and measure benefits and costs in terms of society's economic goals. These goals include the macroeconomic goals of full employment, price stability, and economic growth, as well as the micro-

---

* Charles Kindleberger, "Reversible and Irreversible Processes in Economics," *Challenge*, September/October 1986, pp. 4–10.

economic goals of allocative and technical efficiency, and equity. But in weighing the benefits and costs, you should keep several points in mind.

Economic policies may affect economic behavior. In making choices, individuals and businesses take into account expected government policies. If they expect government to create more jobs in response to a recession, workers will be reluctant to accept wage cuts and managers reluctant to cut prices. As a result, the economy will adjust more slowly than it would otherwise. Similarly, higher taxes may cause households to work and save less. When identifying the benefits and costs of alternative policies, policy makers must be careful to look for potential changes in economic behavior.

Economic policies do not require an all-or-nothing approach. Faced with high unemployment, policy makers do not have to choose to do absolutely nothing or to enact policies that completely eliminate unemployment. Faced with inflation, policy makers do not have to either eliminate all inflation or allow it to continue at the same rate. In these and similar cases, they can use policies that partly address the problem.

Economic policies inevitably involve trade-offs. As the principles of rational choice imply, any decision involves benefits and costs. Government policies to reduce unemployment may raise prices. Waiting for the economy to adjust itself may mean high unemployment for a longer period of time. When considering what policy to pursue, policy makers must be careful to include both benefits (lower unemployment) and costs (price instability).

Economic policies have distributional effects. Macroeconomic policy choices also affect various groups in the economy differently. For example, government policies that create new jobs may also drive prices up. While individuals who gain employment benefit from such a policy, retirees on fixed incomes lose. Just because some individuals gain and others lose under a particular policy is not reason enough to automatically reject it. Few policies—including doing nothing—could pass such a test. But in weighing benefits and costs, policy makers must consider the equity of imposing costs on one group and benefits on another. As we have noted previously, economic analysis cannot determine the equity of policies. But it can help to identify potential winners and losers and the size of gains and losses.

Economic policies that do not work can be eliminated. To be useful, a proposed policy must improve the economy's performance. A policy designed to reduce unemployment is acceptable only if it will, in fact, cause unemployment to fall. That there are *some* benefits to a policy choice is not enough. The extra benefits must *exceed* the extra costs.

Political pressures may affect policy makers. When considering whether policies will work, policy makers may consider political objectives to be as (or more) important than economic objectives. For example, presidents and the Congress often prefer higher inflation to higher unemployment, fearing the wrath of unemployed voters.

Are There Superior Alternative Policies?

In addition to deciding whether the benefits of one policy outweigh its costs, policy makers must also ask whether another policy might be more efficient or equitable. Similarly, rejecting one particular policy does not necessarily mean rejecting government action, if an acceptable alternative policy can be found. But no government action is an alternative that must always be considered. The best policy option—action or doing nothing—is the one that will most improve the economy's performance.

Why Economists Disagree about Government Involvement

It is often said in jest that if you laid all the economists on Earth end to end, they would never reach a conclusion. Economists generally agree that full employment, price stability, and economic growth are the macroeconomic goals against which actual policy performance should be judged. Why, then, do they disagree on the appropriate role of government?

Some disagreements result from inadequate methods of measurement. We cannot directly measure either potential GNP or the natural rate of unemployment, for example. Thus in the mid-1980s, estimates of the natural rate of unemployment ranged from 5 to 8 percent, but the actual unemployment rate was between 6.5 and 8 percent. Economists who accepted the lower natural rate were concerned that the economy was operating at below its potential. Economists who accepted the higher figure feared that faster economic growth would be inflationary.

In addition, some disagreements reflect *normative* economics, or matters of personal values (see Chapter 2). Economic analysis can help us make *positive* statements about predicted effects of a policy. But even when economists can agree on the positive statements, they often suggest different policies because of different values. There is no scientific way to judge normative statements, but economic analysis can help us to avoid answering every economic question with an opinion.

Although economists disagree a lot, they also have a lot in common. They agree on the validity and importance of economic analysis and economic evidence. When economic theories and evidence are conclusive, economists tend to join ranks. For example, most economists agree that sustained, rapid increases in the money supply leads to inflation.

Conclusion

In the following policy cases, we use the analytical framework that we have just discussed. We take a positive approach to policy analysis, concentrating on forecasting potential outcomes rather than advocating particular solutions. Government policies are, in the final analysis, often political judgments. The role of economic analysis is to identify the benefits and costs, and the winners and losers, and to approach the discussion of the issues rationally.

31.1 DEREGULATION OF BANKING: IS THE SYSTEM SAFE?

Banks perform important services for the economy. By offering checking services—a safe and efficient means of payment—they facilitate market exchanges. In addition, they serve as financial intermediaries, moving funds between savers and investors. Banks are also the channel for monetary policy. As we noted in Chapter 24, a safe and stable banking system is important to a smoothly functioning economy. But what government regulations, if any, are desirable?

Why and How Had the Banking System Been Regulated?

Between 1930 and 1933 some 10,000 banks in the United States failed. As a result, many people lost their life savings. Moreover, bank failures resulted in a sharp contraction in the money supply, disrupting the national economy. At the time some economists and politicians believed that excessive competition and fraud were the principal causes of bank failures. Competition for funds, they argued, drove costs up and forced banks to take great risks in order to earn higher returns. By taking large risks, banks became more vulnerable to depositor panics, and the banking system became less stable.

There was also concern that banks had engaged in some activities that were more risky than business loans. Perhaps the riskiest of these activities was the underwriting of new stock issues. Stock underwriters agree to purchase at a certain price a large block of a new stock being issued. They then resell it to their customers—at a profit to themselves, of course. Underwriting created many po-

Anxious customers, eager to withdraw their savings, gather outside the Delaney Street branch of the Bank of the United States on March 4, 1933. Such bank runs were a common occurrence during the Great Depression. To safeguard depositors' funds, the federal government imposed regulations on banks. (UPI/Bettmann Newsphotos)

tential conflicts of interest in banks. In the 1930s, banks were accused of forcing customers, their trust departments, and others to buy securities that they had underwritten. In some cases banks concealed relevant facts, such as the difficulty firms were having repaying loans to the underwriting banks.

A final concern was a fear that large banks would control the financial market. With their greater assets, they were able to offer more services and attract more business than could smaller banks. In addition to threatening the competitive nature of the banking business, the concentration of banking in major metropolitan areas worried some economists and politicians. Local banks had been viewed as supporting local industries. Would farmers and small-town businesses get the same loans from banks in the big cities that they got from their local banks?

As a result of these concerns, three types of regulation emerged from Congress and state legislatures. First, to eliminate competition for deposits, banks were not allowed to pay any interest on checking deposits. In addition, the interest they could pay on savings deposits was limited. Second, to keep them out of risky activities and to limit conflicts of interest, banks were prohibited from offering services such as underwriting securities, selling insurance, and acting as real estate brokers. Finally, to protect local banks and reduce concentration of power, interstate banking was restricted, and in some cases, large metropolitan banks were prevented from operating branches in rural areas. In addition to these regulations, a system of federal deposit insurance was implemented.

Why and How Was Banking Partially Deregulated in the Early 1980s?

From the 1930s to the late 1960s, there were relatively few bank failures. While deposit insurance probably deserves the major credit for reducing bank failure, some economists also believe that the other regulations were helpful. But increased rates of inflation, beginning in the late 1960s and continuing through the 1970s, made continued interest-rate regulations impractical. As inflation rose, new substitutes for checking and savings deposits emerged. Money market mutual funds, for example, paid market interest rates and permitted limited check writing. Unable to offer competitive interest rates, banks began to lose deposits.

In response, banks began to circumvent the regulations. For example, to get around regulations prohibiting them from paying interest on checking accounts, banks invented a new type of account: the automatic transfer service (ATS). Technically these are savings accounts on which banks were allowed to pay interest. But for all practical purposes they are checking accounts, since funds are automatically transferred to a checking account as checks are written.

The new types of financial instruments and services made defining a bank and money more difficult. Because many of the new types of accounts were not subject to reserve requirements, the Fed felt its control of the money supply was inadequate. In response, Congress enacted two reform bills: the Depository Institutions Deregulation and Monetary Control Act of 1980 and the Garn–St. Germain Depository Institutions Act of 1982. These acts essentially legitimized changes that had effectively deregulated the banking industry already.

The new acts eliminated restrictions on interest rates (except for businesses' checking accounts). They also allowed banks of all kinds to offer similar services, make similar types of loans, and subjected all types of banks to similar deposit restrictions. Even so, banking remains a highly regulated industry.

What Are the Benefits and Costs of Deregulation?

Economists generally agree that there are benefits to deregulation. The banking system is more efficient, and individuals can now receive market interest rates on funds held in checking accounts. At the same time, some economists have expressed concern about the safety of banks and the banking system. By removing regulatory barriers, banks are forced to pay more to attract funds. Repeating the argument used in the 1930s, these critics argue that deregulation has led banks to engage in activities that involve more risk but pay higher returns. But have these higher risks compromised the system's stability and soundness? Are these costs of deregulation excessive?

Economists who attribute these costs to deregulation point to the large number of bank failures in the 1980s. During the 1970s fewer than 15 banks failed or were merged out of existence in an average year; fewer than 2 percent were considered to be in danger of failing. In the 1980s, an average of almost 4 banks per week have failed or have been merged out of existence; over 10 percent of all banks are in danger of failing.

But other economists attribute recent problems to regulations that remain, not to deregulation. For example, many banks that have failed were small banks concentrated in geographical areas that were hard hit by problems in the oil industry and agriculture. They argue that regulations restricting banks to small geographical areas increase risk by not allowing banks to diversify. Diversifying lowers risks, as the old economic proverb—"Don't put all your eggs in one basket"—suggests.

Are There Superior Alternatives to Further Deregulation?

Where do we go from here? Any future policy must address two issues: control of the money supply and safety of the banking system. Nearly all economists believe that the Fed must retain the power to set required reserve ratios to control the money supply. Many advocate extending the Fed's power to money market mutual funds and other types of financial institutions in order to control the money supply more completely. But economists have widely different ideas about the desirability of regulating bank safety.

Some economists propose eliminating all regulations regarding bank safety. They argue that the market can best determine the optimal amount of safety and the services that banks and other financial institutions offer. But fears of a return to a time of massive bank failures make use of this option unlikely. At the opposite extreme, other economists argue that we should return to a system of close regulation. To do so, however, regulations would have to extend to all businesses that offer financial services—Sears and Merrill Lynch, for example not just banks. Most economists believe that this option is both impractical and undesirable. The financial marketplace continues to change rapidly. Constant revisions of regulations would be necessary both to accommodate new entrants and to prevent those currently in the industry from exploiting loopholes, as they have in the past.

Fortunately, as we noted in the introduction, policy makers do not have to choose between total regulation and no regulation. They can remove those regulations that seem unjustified and leave others intact. For example, because of the relatively large number of bank failures in the oil and farm belts, economists are increasingly supporting removal of barriers to interstate banking. Such an action might actually reduce risks. But, as we noted above, most also believe that the Fed's control of the money supply should be broadened, not reduced.

There is also strong support among economists for reducing some of the constraints on services provided by banks. Many economists believe that banks can take on such activities as real estate brokerage, stock brokerage, and selling insurance to households without seriously increasing their risks. Government supervision of banks and legal penalties could minimize conflicts of interest without directly prohibiting such otherwise legitimate business activities.

There is less support among economists for banks gaining the right to underwrite securities and to sell commercial risk insurance to businesses. These ventures involve much higher risks and a greater potential for conflicts of interest. But the boundaries between acceptable and unacceptable risks is fuzzy and likely to change. Moreover, banks can and do currently make high-risk loans, such as those made to Latin American governments.

There is strong support among economists for continued government monitoring of bank assets and liabilities. In part, such supervision is a means of providing public information and ensuring some confidence in the banking system. Continued monitoring is also important because most deposits are federally insured. But relaxing regulations somewhat would enable banks to earn greater income without compromising the soundness necessary to an efficient banking system and a stable money supply.

Conclusion

The banking system is an important part of the economy. Because of its special role as a financial intermediary and in the creation of money, banking has been subject to considerable regulation. Changes in the system have resulted from new technology and competition from other financial service institutions and foreign banks. Limits on interest rates and, in some cases, on the types of services that banks can offer have been lifted.

But what type of bank regulatory system—if any—will best serve the U.S. economy in the future? Economists offer different recommendations, but most believe a return to the old style regulation is neither likely nor desirable. Many favor a continued relaxation of restrictions, including allowing interstate banking and a broader range of bank services. There is strong support, however, for continuing the role of regulators in monitoring the quality of bank assets and in setting reserve requirements to assist in monetary control.

QUESTIONS FOR REVIEW AND DISCUSSION

1. Determine whether each of the following statements is true, false, or uncertain and explain why.
   a) A bank that accepts deposits and makes loans within a small geographical area has less risk than one that has loans all over the country and in foreign countries.
   b) A loss of confidence in any one bank will inevitably cause a run on all banks.
   c) When banks must pay higher interest on deposits, they will be tempted to take greater risks.

2. Regulations prohibiting the payment of interest on checking deposits and limiting the interest paid on savings deposits led banks to try other means of attracting customers.
   a) How is offering free checking services like paying interest on deposits? How is it different?

    b) If offered a choice, would you prefer free services or actual interest payments on money held in a deposit account? Why?

    c) Use your answer to part (b) to explain why free services and other premiums (toasters, television sets, and other products sometimes offered to new depositors) are less efficient than simply paying interest.

3. The historical rationale for regulating banks is based on the special nature of banks compared to other forms of businesses. To have special regulations for banks, it is necessary to distinguish banks from other businesses.

    a) What services are provided by banks? How is a bank like a manufacturing company and how is it different? An insurance company? An investment services company, such as Merrill Lynch?

    b) Use your answer to (a) to write a definition of a bank that distinguishes it from other businesses.

    c) In what ways are banks special (according to your definition)? Do these characteristics provide a rationale for government regulation of banks? Why or why not?

31.2 POLICY RESPONSES TO A SUPPLY SHOCK

Prior to 1973, discussions of macroeconomic policy focused on how best to respond to shifts in aggregate demand. Although some economists believed that powerful unions or producers could raise wages and prices somewhat, most expected aggregate supply to grow slowly over time. However, the experiences of the United States and other countries in 1973–1974 and again in 1979 made it clear that sharp decreases in aggregate supply (supply shocks) were indeed possible.

Poor harvests worldwide in 1972 and 1973 caused the food component of the Consumer Price Index (CPI) to increase by 20 percent in 1973. In addition, the Organization of Petroleum Exporting Countries (OPEC) imposed an oil embargo that resulted in major oil-price increases. As a result, the energy component of the CPI rose by almost 17 percent in 1973 and an additional 22 percent in 1974. Another serious supply shock hit the U.S. economy in 1979, again in the form of higher oil prices, which increased by 45 percent. Thus aggregate supply decreased significantly in both 1973–1974 and 1979.

For the first time, economists and politicians were faced with the question of what government could—and should—do in response to a supply shock. In this policy case we consider their answer, as well as the benefits and costs of alternative macroeconomic policies.

Why and How Might Government Respond to a Supply Shock?

Government intervention was proposed because the supply shocks had a significant effect on the economy. The oil-price increases in 1973-1974 and 1979 had immediate and powerful effects on oil consumers. But oil and other energy supplies are also important resources for almost every sector of the economy. Higher energy prices raised production costs of manufactured goods. Higher

A long line of cars winds through the streets of New York City in February, 1974. Similar lineups occurred throughout the United States after the oil embargo by OPEC. Increased scarcity of gasoline was only one manifestation of the supply shocks during this time. (UPI/Bettmann Newsphotos)

transportation costs further added to retail prices. Even service industries, such as life insurance companies, were affected by increased electricity and heating costs. As a result, the price of almost every product in the economy increased.

Because higher prices reduced real wages, workers demanded higher nominal wages, further increasing costs and causing a secondary decrease in aggregate supply. Secondary effects on real income and nominal wages occur over time and may give the false impression that price increases will be sustained. The Consumer Price Index initially increased rapidly for many months after both the 1973–1974 and 1979 shocks. Almost three-fourths of the CPI's 14.2 percent increase in 1979 was caused by the rise in energy prices. But the CPI also increased by over 11 percent in 1980, although energy prices had leveled off. The continued spiral reflected secondary effects of the supply shock.

Exhibit 31.2.1(a) indicates the two supply-shock problems that macroeconomic policies may attempt to correct. First, a supply shock causes aggregate supply to shift (from AS_1 to AS_2), real GNP to fall, and the price level to increase. In fact, if individuals expect inflation to continue, those expectations may further decrease aggregate supply. Second, a supply shock opens a contractionary gap, and pushes unemployment above the natural rate. The result is higher prices and higher unemployment—the double whammy of stagflation.

In response to an increase in the price level, government might use an *extinguishing policy*. That is, government might use contractionary policies to decrease aggregate demand, thereby extinguishing inflationary pressures, as shown in Exhibit 31.2.1(b). Or, in response to rising unemployment, government might use an *accommodating policy*. That is, it might use expansionary policies to increase aggregate demand, thereby reducing the short-run impact of unemployment, as shown in Exhibit 31.2.1(c). Alternatively, government might do nothing. This *neutral policy* relies exclusively on the economy's automatic adjustment mechanism to restore long-run equilibrium, as shown in Exhibit 31.2.1(d).

(a) Initial effect of a supply shock

(b) Extinguishing policy

Exhibit 31.2.1
Policy Options for a Supply Shock
A supply shock causes a decrease in aggregate supply (from AS_1 to AS_2), raising the price level and opening a contractionary gap, as shown in part (a). To reduce high prices brought on by inflationary pressures, policy makers may use an extinguishing policy, decreasing aggregate demand (from AD_1 to AD_2) as in part (b). While this

What Are the Benefits and Costs of Taking Policy Action?

In deciding which option is best, economists consider two factors: (1) the speed of the automatic adjustment mechanism; and (2) the relative costs of inflation and unemployment.

Accommodating policies. Some economists believe that the economy's automatic adjustment mechanism is slow to close contractionary gaps. Fearing that supply shocks will cause unacceptably high unemployment and prolonged recessions, these economists therefore recommend accommodating policies. They also note that major supply shocks, such as those of 1973–1974 and 1979 cause a decline in real income for the economy as a whole. Because foreign interests succeeded in imposing higher real costs for imported oil, less real output was available for domestic use. Thus real income had to fall. But workers and businesses sought to maintain real income, which slowed the required adjustments in nominal wages and prices.

If the economy adjusts slowly, as these economists maintain, high unemployment may well be a long-term result, and an accommodating policy may be the

(c) Accommodating policy

(d) Neutral policy

action puts downward pressure on prices, it opens a larger contractionary gap and slows return to full employment. To reduce unemployment, policy makers may turn to an accommodating policy, increasing aggregate demand (from AD_1 to AD_3) as in part (c). However, this action puts additional upward pressure on prices. If no action is taken—a neutral policy—the economy's automatic adjustment mechanism will eventually close the gap as indicated in part (d).

best policy. But in deciding in favor of such a policy, policy makers must be aware that an accommodating increase in aggregate demand will cause larger increases in the price level. And these increases may fuel expectations of continued inflation.

Extinguishing policies. However, some economists reject an accommodating policy response to a supply shock. They believe that an increase in the price level resulting from a supply shock may trigger expectations of continued inflation and thus reduce aggregate supply. In addition, supporters of extinguishing policies argue that use of accommodating policies causes individuals to expect such government action whenever a supply shock occurs. This expectation further slows the economy's automatic adjustment mechanism and raises the cost of future antiinflation efforts. Fearing that increased inflationary expectations may further decrease aggregate supply and delay the return to long-run equilibrium, they recommend extinguishing policies.

By increasing the contractionary gap, such policies may cause somewhat higher unemployment in the short run. But proponents of extinguishing policy believe that the economy's automatic adjustment mechanism operates quickly. A quick response makes the costs of an extinguishing policy—higher unemployment and lost output—relatively small.

Would No Action Be a Better Policy?

As we noted in the introduction, policy makers must always consider the option of a neutral policy, that is, taking no action. Unlike inflation which results from rapid and sustained growth in the money supply, price increases that result from a supply shock cause only a *one-time* increase in the general price level. Eventually, aggregate supply will increase because unemployment forces wages and prices to fall. Given sufficient time to adjust, aggregate supply will fall enough (back to AS_1 in Exhibit 31.2.1a) to restore long-run equilibrium. At that point, the economy will produce at its potential GNP level and unemployment will return to the natural rate.

Is a neutral policy a superior option? Some economists who believe that the automatic adjustment mechanism works reasonably well think so. So do those who believe that policy makers do not have the knowledge or ability to apply any macroeconomic policy accurately. A neutral policy tends to have neutral long-run effects on inflation and unemployment; it makes them neither better nor worse. Unemployment costs with a neutral policy may be higher than with an accommodating policy. But if the automatic adjustment mechanism operates quickly, unemployment may not be a serious problem. The short-run increase in the price level with a neutral policy may be higher than with an extinguishing policy. But if individuals do not raise their price-level expectations, a neutral policy may be the best.

Why Do Economists Disagree about Appropriate Policy Actions?

Now that you understand some of the pros and cons of various policy options, let's consider the historical record and why economists disagree about the decisions that were made. The United States responded to the supply shocks of both 1973–1974 and 1979 with extinguishing policies. That is, contractionary monetary and fiscal policies were used to reduce aggregate demand and dampen inflationary expectations. There is little doubt that these policies resulted in a lower price-level increase than would have occurred with either neutral or accommodating policies. At the same time, those policies helped cause the two most severe recessions since the Great Depression.

Was it worth it? This question is very important, but different economists have answered it differently. Some economists argue that extinguishing actions were unnecessary and undesirable. They note that a supply shock causes only a one-time increase in the general price level, not long-run inflation. The short-run increase in the price level is the unavoidable result of a supply shock, and in the long run no action is needed. Moreover, they point to high unemployment and large contractionary gaps as evidence that the cost of reducing the price level was extremely high.

Some of those who disagree with the actual policy responses would have preferred an accommodating policy response. They would gladly have accepted a somewhat higher increase in the price level in return for lower unemployment and more real GNP. Others who disagree with the actual policies would have preferred a more neutral policy.

But some economists support the government's actions. They note that a short-run rise in unemployment is also an unavoidable result of a supply shock. They blame the prolonged high unemployment rate and major recessions in both 1975 and 1981–1982 in part on individuals' expectations that government would use accommodating policies. This expectation was based on such policy actions in the 1960s and early 1970s. Supporters of extinguishing policies argue that the high economic price paid in 1981–1982 was worthwhile in the long run. They maintain that it established the credibility of policy makers and an unwillingness to tolerate inflation.

Conclusion

Economists do not agree on the best policy reponse to a supply shock, although they do agree that all policies have both costs and benefits. The debate continues because we cannot accurately measure the speed of the automatic adjustment mechanism or the costs of inflation and unemployment. In addition, we do not yet know—nor are we likely to be able to quantify—the long-run costs of various policies' effects on expectations. Finally, economists (and politicians) put different values on the costs of inflation and unemployment.

QUESTIONS FOR REVIEW AND DISCUSSION

1. Japan responded to the 1973–1974 supply shock with extinguishing policies. Great Britain applied accommodating policies. In which of these countries would you expect that the price level increased more? In which would you expect that more output was lost?

2. The following data show some annual economic indicators for an eight-year period.

	Annual percentage changes in			Size of GNP gap as a percentage of potential GNP
Year	Nominal GNP	Real GNP	GNP deflator	
1	8.6	2.8	5.7	0.6
2	10.0	5.0	4.7	−0.9
3	12.1	5.2	6.5	−2.6
4	8.3	−0.5	9.1	1.3
5	8.5	−1.3	9.8	5.3
6	11.5	4.9	6.4	3.5
7	11.7	4.7	6.7	1.9
8	13.0	5.3	7.3	−0.3

a) In which year(s) do you see evidence of a supply shock? Explain which indicators are significant.

b) What evidence suggests that the effects of a supply shock are temporary but lingering?

3. The following table shows changes in the money supply and the size of the actual and full-employment federal budget balances (see Chapter 27) expressed as a percentage

of potential GNP. (The negative numbers indicate budget deficits.) The years shown correspond to those in the table in Question 2.

Year	Percentage change in money supply (M-1)	Size of federal budget surplus as a percentage of potential GNP	
		Actual	Full employment
1	5.2	−1.5	−2.0
2	6.6	−1.3	−1.4
3	9.2	−1.0	−0.4
4	5.5	−0.6	−0.8
5	4.4	−2.5	−4.1
6	4.9	−1.8	−2.9
7	6.6	−1.7	−1.7
8	8.0	−1.5	−1.3

a) For the year(s) you tied to a supply shock in Question 2, were monetary and fiscal policy neutral, accommodating, or extinguishing? On what evidence in the table of Question 3 do you base your conclusions?

b) What evidence of the effects of these macroeconomic policy actions can you find in the data in Question 2?

4. Some labor-union contracts index members' wages to the Consumer Price Index. As prices rise in response to a supply shock, nominal wages automatically increase.

a) Does indexing protect the real income of workers? Why or why not?

b) How does indexing affect the economy's automatic adjustment mechanism?

c) Suppose that in Charybdis there is no indexation, while in Scyllia the nominal wages of all workers are indexed. Compare the effects of a supply shock (a decrease in aggregate supply) on the two countries. In which will prices rise more? In which will unemployment and lost output be greater? Why?

31.3 REDUCING THE FEDERAL BUDGET DEFICIT

From 1980 to 1986 the portion of the U.S. national debt held by the public increased by more than $1.2 trillion dollars. Debt as a percentage of GNP increased from 27 to 51 percent. This increase was the result of unprecedented peacetime budget deficits. The federal government's budget deficit in 1986 was $204 billion, 4.8 percent of GNP. Moreover, the full-employment budget deficit was over 4 percent, indicating that major reductions in the deficit are unlikely to occur automatically. But what can—and should—government do?

Why and How Should the Deficit Be Reduced?

All deficits are not the same. Because of automatic stabilizers, the federal government tends to have a deficit when the economy is in a recession. These deficits have expansionary short-run effects and may help bring the economy out of recession. But large full-employment budget deficits have created serious economic problems for both the United States and other countries.

A deficit must be financed somehow. If a deficit is financed by increases in the money supply, inflation is a serious concern. (The high rates of inflation experienced in some Latin American countries clearly indicate the dangers.) If a deficit is financed by borrowing, real interest rates tend to rise and investment may fall, thus slowing long-run economic growth.

High U.S. interest rates are also attractive to foreign individuals and businesses. Accordingly, they may choose to buy U.S. businesses, stocks, and government bonds. As we describe in Chapter 33, foreign investments in the U.S. economy drive up the value of the U.S. dollar, which raises the relative price of U.S. goods and services. As a result, U.S. consumers and businesses will buy more foreign-produced goods and services (imports rise). At the same time, U.S. producers have trouble selling their products abroad (exports fall). The high value of the dollar also makes it difficult for countries with large international dollar debts—Mexico, Brazil, and Argentina, for example—to repay those debts. To avoid such problems, then, the United States must reduce future federal budget deficits. In theory, we can reduce deficits in two ways: by either reducing expenditures or increasing tax revenues.

What Are the Benefits and Costs of Taking Policy Action?

Both cutting spending and raising taxes can help to reduce deficits. But both approaches have economic and political costs. (Although a combination of spending cuts and tax hikes is also possible, in this section we explore the benefits and costs of relying mainly on one or the other of the two alternatives.)

Spending cuts. One way to reduce future deficits would be to cut federal government expenditures. As shown in Exhibit 31.3.1, between 1979 and 1986 federal government receipts in the full-employment budget—as a percentage of potential GNP—fell only 0.3 percent, while expenditures increased by 3.1 percent. Thus most of the 3.4 percent increase in the full-employment budget deficit can be attributed to spending increases. However, a major problem with cutting expenditures to reduce deficits is deciding which expenditures to cut. The principles of rational choice tell us that we should eliminate any expenditure that results in more costs than benefits. But there is no economic or political consensus

Exhibit 31.3.1
Changes in the Federal Budget, 1962–1986

	Full-employment federal budget (percentage of potential GNP)			Nominal federal expenditures by type (percentage of actual GNP)				
Year	Receipts	Expenditures	Surplus	National defense	Nondefense purchases	Transfer payments	Net interest	Other
1962	18.7	19.4	−0.7	9.1	2.2	4.9	1.2	2.0
1979	20.1	20.9	−0.8	4.9	2.2	8.4	1.7	3.6
1986	19.7	24.5	−4.8	6.6	2.1	9.5	3.2	3.1

Sources: Economic Report of the President, 1987; U.S. Department of Commerce, Bureau of Economic Analysis.

on which expenditures fail to meet this test. Three major targets for cuts—national defense, transfer payments, and interest payments on the national debt—all have supporters and detractors.

Advocates of defense cuts note that expenditures in this category have grown the most since 1979. Opponents counter that such cuts would jeopardize national security and note that spending for national defense is a smaller percentage of GNP than it was in 1962. Some people argue for cuts in transfer payments, since this category accounted for most of the increase in spending between 1962 and 1986. But others believe that transfer payments, such as Social Security, are essential to equity. Net interest on the national debt cannot be directly cut by Congress. Interest payments will fall only if the debt is reduced or interest rates fall.

What about the expenditures that make up the other one-third of the federal budget? Many of these programs also have their advocates. Student-loan programs, improved highways, and basic scientific research, for example, are all supported as public investments that foster long-run economic growth. Moreover, to have eliminated the deficit in 1986, while leaving national defense and transfer and interest payments unchanged, Congress would have had to reduce other expenditures by 90 percent.

Some proponents of large spending cuts want to reduce deficits by eliminating what they see as an unnecessary and undesirable intrusion of the public sector into the private sector. They propose "privatization"—that is, selling off government enterprises such as Conrail or using educational vouchers to ensure access to education without government provision of services. Similarly, they argue for further reducing government regulatory agencies and activities.

Tax increases. National defense, Social Security, and Medicare (which together account for almost one-half of total spending by the federal government) are politically untouchable. And to reduce interest payments the government must first reduce deficits. The seemingly obvious alternative to spending cuts is to raise taxes. But politicians, fearing voter outcry, are slow to adopt this solution.

The political costs of raising taxes are obvious, but what are the economic costs? Some economists argue that incentives to work, save, and invest will be reduced significantly if taxes are increased. Because the U.S. economy already has a very low saving rate and productivity growth, they argue that we cannot afford to reduce incentives. In addition, they worry that tax increases will relieve the pressure on Congress to eliminate unnecessary and wasteful expenditures. Other economists believe that tax increases will have only small effects on incentives. Moreover, they doubt that there is much "fat" in the budget that can be trimmed to reduce the deficit. Some expenditures targeted for cuts—student loans, highways, or scientific research—are, they argue, useful public investments that add to long-run economic growth. They believe that the benefits of reducing the deficit will outweigh the costs of a tax increase.

Would No Action Be a Better Policy?

As we noted in the introduction to this chapter, the likely outcomes of policy actions must be contrasted with those of no action. But most economists view government failure to act on large full-employment deficits as a poor policy choice. Such deficits have high costs to society and can be reduced only through some combination of changes in taxes and expenditures.

Why Do Economists Disagree about the Appropriate Policy Response?

Although they are nearly unanimous in their desire to see deficits reduced, economists disagree sharply about the correct policy action to take. As usual, some of these disagreements are normative—whether cuts in social programs are equitable, for example. In addition, accurately measuring the benefits of many programs and the full costs of higher taxes is impossible. Thus economists also rationally disagree about whether the benefits of spending cuts or raising taxes outweigh the costs.

Despite the political difficulty of agreeing on spending cuts and voting for tax increases, in 1985 Congress voted for the Gramm-Rudman-Hollings Act. This act requires Congress to eliminate the actual deficit by 1991 and to achieve specified deficit-reduction targets for each year until then. If the estimated deficit in the budget passed by Congress does not meet the target, equal cuts in defense and nondefense spending are supposed to be made. (Some nondefense spending, such as Social Security, is exempt from these automatic cuts.) Although a federal court of appeals declared the automatic cuts to be unconstitutional, Congress and President Reagan have continued to try to reduce the deficit. However, the actual budget deficits in fiscal years 1987 and 1988 exceeded the targets, in part because the economy grew more slowly than predicted, and in part because there was no consensus on expenditure cuts or tax increases.

Some economists consider this act to be a political attempt to force necessary consensus. No one really favors cutting expenditures across the board as the act requires. Those who favor spending cuts hope that the act will pressure Congress to agree on some cuts in spending. Others apparently hope that the act may cause some to recognize the necessity of a tax increase.

Conclusion

Economists generally agree that the large full-employment budget deficits experienced in the mid-1980s are costly to the economy and must be reduced. But there is no consensus on the best way to reduce deficits. Some economists argue for expenditure cuts and against tax increases. Typically they stress the negative effects of tax increases on economic incentives and the desirability of cutting unnecessary expenditures to promote economic efficiency. Other economists disagree, pointing out the political difficulties and potential equity problems associated with major spending cuts. In contrast, they view the negative effects of higher taxes on economic incentives as small.

QUESTIONS FOR REVIEW AND DISCUSSION

1. Government can finance spending in three ways: taxing, borrowing, and increasing the money supply.
   a) Explain the effects of each method of financing on the economy.
   b) Assuming that there is general agreement that a certain level of spending is desirable, which method of financing would you recommend? Why?

2. Using the data in Exhibit 31.3.1, explain whether fiscal policy was expansionary or contractionary between 1979 and 1986.

3. One problem that economists see with the recent large federal budget deficits is that they seriously handicap the Fed and monetary policy.
   a) Why would these deficits make the Fed reluctant to increase the rate of growth of the money supply?

b) What are the effects on the economy if the Fed slows the rate of growth of the money supply? (Note the effects on unemployment, growth of real GNP, the price level, and interest rates.) How does this policy affect the actual budget deficit?

c) What are the resulting effects on international capital flows and the exchange rate value of the U.S. dollar if fiscal policy is expansionary and monetary policy contractionary?

4. Keynes argued that under the right circumstances, an actual budget deficit would have favorable effects on the economy. What were the "right circumstances" to which he referred and how is a deficit favorable? Do these circumstances fit the current situation?

31.4   INCOMES POLICIES: A CURE FOR INFLATION?

The traditional policy response to inflation is contractionary policy, especially reducing the rate of growth of the money supply. However, contractionary policy also causes a temporary increase in unemployment. As a result, economists and politicians have looked for less painful methods to lower inflation.

In this example we explore the use of *incomes policies*, which intervene directly in the processes of setting wages and prices. Incomes policies include mandatory and voluntary wage and price controls and tax-based incomes policies (TIP), which offer tax reductions to firms that follow specified wage and price guidelines.

Incomes policies are not a new idea. In fact, an incomes policy was used during the reign of the Roman emperor Diocletion in A.D. 300. (The Romans really tried to enforce it—violators were sentenced to death—but still were unable to get full compliance.) But are such policies effective? Can they reduce the costs of reducing inflation? Are they a substitute for traditional policies?

Why and How Might Government Impose Incomes Policies?

Incomes policies are based on a belief that some wage and price increases are not "justified" by economic forces. That is, they do not represent a response to fundamental demand and supply conditions. Rather, they are unwarranted attempts by strong unions and/or strong businesses to exercise economic power by forcing wages and/or prices up. Some proponents argue that incomes policies would prevent such wage and price increases from occurring, or at least slow wage and price increases. In either event, upward pressure on the price level would diminish.

Some economists also propose incomes policies as a way to speed up the economy's adjustment when contractionary policies are utilized to lower inflation. They believe that wages and prices are heavily influenced by past inflation rates and thus are slow to adjust as necessary to close contractionary gaps. By forcing wage and price adjustments, incomes policies may decrease inflationary expectations. As a result, incomes policies may help reduce the unemployment costs of contractionary policies.

Incomes policies can take a variety of forms. The mildest form is *jawboning*, or what some call an "open-mouth" policy. Jawboning is an attempt to talk unions and businesses out of planned or announced wage and price increases. For example, in 1962 President Kennedy publicly chastised U.S. steel companies for announcing a large price increase. Coupled with threats to cancel outstanding defense contracts, jawboning worked; the steel companies rescinded the announced price increase. Presidents Johnson, Nixon, and Carter also employed jawboning in their struggles with inflation.

A more formal approach to incomes policies is the use of *wage and price controls*. Wage and price "guideposts" or "voluntary" controls, were used in 1962–1967 and in 1978–1979. More formal, "mandatory" wage and price controls with legal penalties were first used in the United States during World War II. They were also enacted during the Korean War and most recently in 1971–1974. Wage and price controls have also been used in Brazil, Argentina, Israel, and Bolivia as part of their fights against inflation rates that averaged several hundred percent per year.

Wage and price controls pressure workers and businesses to hold down costs and prices. One alternative, *tax-based incomes policies (TIP)*, instead provides tax incentives for complying with wage and price controls. Under TIP, government sets an aggregate wage target—perhaps a 5 percent average increase in wages. Employers who give larger average wage increases are required to pay higher taxes. Those who give smaller wage increases can earn tax reductions. By holding wages down, TIP seeks to hold down product costs and thus reduce pressures for higher prices.

What Are the Benefits and Costs of Incomes Policies?

Inflation clearly imposes costs on an economy. Price stability—an economic goal—is sacrificed. Moreover, wages and/or prices that exceed market rates cause allocative inefficiency. If inflation becomes a way of life, individuals expect more inflation and make their economic plans accordingly. They may change their expectations only slowly, even if government begins using contractionary policies. As a result, unemployment and lost output may be high for a long time. But incomes policies can slow actual wage and price increases. Thus such policies may speed the economy's adjustment, reducing the duration of unemployment and restoring long-run equilibrium.

Incomes policies can also impose significant costs on the economy. In the first place, there is no sure way to determine a reasonable or acceptable wage or price increase. To remedy this problem, some economists suggest limiting wage increases to gains in productivity, or output per worker. When wage increases match productivity gains, product costs are unaffected. But productivity is very difficult to measure in service industries. (How would you measure the output of your economics professor? By the number of students that passed economics? By the grade-point average in economics classes?) Moreover, productivity standards make no allowance for changes in wages and prices that may be warranted by changes in demand.

As we noted in Chapter 5, unless the *relative* prices of products and resources adjust, the economy cannot operate efficiently. General wage and price controls inevitably distort price signals. The results of distorted price signals are shortages and surpluses and a tendency for *actual* and *official* prices to differ. In Chapter 3, you learned that a price ceiling in a single market creates a shortage. Although prices cannot legally rise above a ceiling, actual prices often do. Illegal or black markets commonly develop when legal markets cannot adjust.

Members of the Price Commission named by President Nixon are sworn into office in October, 1971. This commission was charged with implementation of general wage and price controls in the period from 1971 to early 1974. (UPI/Bettmann Newsphotos)

Are incomes policies effective?   In the introduction to this chapter, we noted that policies are judged in part by whether they meet their objectives. Incomes policies have both succeeded and failed. As utilized in the early 1960s, they appeared to work well, but more recent outcomes have been less satisfactory. Overall, incomes policies do not appear to be effective when there is excess aggregate demand. The apparent success of such policies in the early 1960s, for example, may have resulted from the lack of excess demand pressures at the time. When such pressures were present in 1966–1967, however, incomes policies were unsuccessful.

Price controls imposed in 1971–1974 likewise failed. At the time, the Nixon administration wanted to reduce inflation and unemployment. A general freeze on wages and prices was followed by a series of formally administered controls. The freeze and the controls did reduce the price level while they were in operation. But when the controls were lifted in 1974, prices rose to the level they probably would have reached if the controls had never been enacted.

Wage and price controls imposed by Brazil and Argentina during the mid-1980s also failed. Although they caused a spectacular drop in inflation when imposed, they were not accompanied by controls on growth of the money supply; high rates of inflation returned when controls were removed.

Is There a Better Alternative?

As we noted in Chapter 26, most economists consider inflation to be the result of excess growth in the money supply. Accordingly, they believe that reducing the rate of money-supply growth is vital to slowing inflation. Even those who believe that incomes policies may be useful suggest them only as a complement to—not a substitute for—policies that slow money-supply growth.

Israel was successful in bringing inflation down from 1000 to 20 percent in a very short period of time, using a combination of limited money-supply growth and wage and price controls. But not all of its success can be attributed to incomes policies. And when incomes policies are used instead of the more painful limits on the money-supply's growth—as in Brazil—the result has been still worse inflation when the incomes policies are ended.

Why Do Economists Disagree about Incomes Policies?

As is so often the case, disputes about incomes policies revolve around the speed with which the economy adjusts on its own and on the costs of inflation and unemployment. Proponents of incomes policies believe that they speed up an otherwise sluggish adjustment. And a slow adjustment implies long periods of inflation—the high cost of taking no action.

In contrast, some opponents of incomes policies argue that they are at best unnecessary. These economists believe that the economy adjusts rapidly to changes. Because they believe that high price levels will last only a short time, they see the cost of allowing the economy to adjust on its own as low. Conversely, they view the cost of incomes policies as high because such policies distort prices, causing resources to be inefficiently utilized. In addition, these economists argue that incomes policies—by fueling expectations that policies to limit the growth of the money supply will not be used—may in fact slow the economy's adjustment.

Conclusion

Incomes policies have been proposed as one tool in the fight against inflation. If they are successful in holding wages and prices to levels justified by demand and supply conditions, they may reduce inflationary pressures without serious effects on efficiency. By forcing actual wages and prices down, they may complement money-supply controls. But there is widespread agreement among economists that incomes policies are ineffective if there are significant excess demand pressures in the economy. Opinion is more mixed about their use under other circumstances. Many economists remain quite skeptical. They tend to believe that incomes policies are impractical and potentially expensive, even when combined with credible money-supply controls.

QUESTIONS FOR REVIEW AND DISCUSSION

1. The economic czar of Fortunia wants to ensure that wage and price increases throughout the economy put no upward pressure on the price level.
   a) Workers producing plastic dinner plates have increased their output from 100 to 110 plates per hour. Can the czar give them a wage increase from $10 to $11 per hour without increasing product costs and prices?
   b) Is there any legitimate reason for wages in any industry to rise faster than productivity? Why or why not?
   c) Can strong businesses and unions create sustained increases in the price level by continually raising prices and wages? Why or why not?

2. Proponents of the new classical macroeconomics (see Chapter 27) argue that incomes policies are unnecessary. Other economists disagree.
   a) In an economy in which wages and prices are very flexible, why could limiting the growth of the money supply end inflation at very little cost?
   b) What arguments would the new classical macroeconomists use to explain why the Fed's tight money controls during the early 1980s successfully reduced inflation but, at the same time, caused a serious recession?
   c) If wages and prices are slow to adjust and if individuals' expectations are heavily influenced by past inflation, explain how wage and price controls might be useful.

3. Economists generally agree that incomes policies can only temporarily suppress inflation, if there is continued excess demand pressure.
   a) Why is suppressing inflation temporarily not the same as reducing it more permanently?
   b) What long-run effects would you anticipate if wage and price controls suppress inflation while excess demand pressures continue?

31.5 THE TRADE DEFICIT AND GLOBAL COMPETITIVENESS

Since 1980, the United States has experienced an extremely large trade deficit. In 1986, exports were almost $150 billion less than imports in real terms. By historical standards this trade deficit is unprecedented. Trade deficits and surpluses of 1–2 percent of GNP are quite common, but the 1986 trade deficit was over 4 percent of real GNP. The deterioration in the trade balance has raised concern that U.S. industries have lost their "global competitiveness," that is,

> The degree to which a nation can, under free and fair market conditions, produce goods and services that meet the test of international markets while simultaneously maintaining or expanding the real incomes of its citizens.*

As we have noted throughout this textbook, competitiveness is highly desirable in and among market economies. But what can and should government do to improve competitiveness?

Why and How Might Government Policies Improve Competitiveness?

Economists generally agree that the size of the current trade deficit is a cause for concern. Trade deficits must be financed by borrowing from foreigners, and eventually such borrowing must be repaid—with interest. The higher that debt is, the less domestic production can be used to satisfy domestic wants. Some forecasters believe that the United States may soon owe foreigners as much as $1 trillion. If large trade deficits continue, the United States will have to devote a significant portion of its domestic production to paying interest on its foreign debt, a problem that already plagues the Mexican, Brazilian, and Argentinian economies.

Fiscal and monetary policies. Any policy to reduce the trade deficit requires an analysis of the cause(s) of that deficit. There is little question that fiscal and monetary policies are an important part of the problem. In the early 1980s the federal government borrowed heavily to finance its large budget deficits. At the same time, the Fed limited the growth of the money supply in order to lower inflation. In combination, these policies resulted in high real interest rates in the United States, which attracted large capital inflows. Capital inflows increased demand for the dollar and caused the U.S. dollar to rise in value.

This rise in the value of the dollar reduced the competitiveness of U.S. businesses by increasing the relative price of U.S. goods and services. The "strong

---

* *Global Competition: The New Reality*, The President's Commission on Industrial Competitiveness, 1985, p. 6.

dollar" made it more difficult for U.S. exporters to sell abroad and easier for foreign producers to sell in the United States. Although the value of the U.S. dollar began to fall in 1985, some economists believe that its value will have to continue to fall well below 1980 levels to recapture the market for U.S. goods and services.

To the extent that the decline in U.S. competitiveness stems from fiscal and monetary policies, the solution must involve those policies. Reducing the federal budget deficit would help to lower real interest rates, as would a more expansionary monetary policy (unless matched by a similar policy abroad). Similarly, fiscal policy changes in other countries—lowering tax rates or otherwise stimulating investment—would raise real returns on investment there. Although changes in fiscal and monetary policies may not be the only policy response necessary, they are part of nearly all proposed solutions to the trade deficit.

But is competitiveness strictly a macroeconomic issue? Some economists believe that the problem is at least partly the result of a microeconomic problem: declining productivity. Growth in productivity has averaged less than 1 percent in the United States since 1973, which is well below the average rate in the 1950s and 1960s and far below the rates of our major trading partners. Slow productivity growth means rising labor costs and downward pressure on real wages. It also creates a danger that more and more U.S. industries will be underpriced by foreign competitors.

Industrial policy. One proposed solution to this microeconomic problem is the so-called *industrial-policy* approach. Government would take an active role in directing and fostering improved U.S. competitiveness. Advocates view the recent loss of competitiveness as stemming in part from ineffective and inefficient private-sector responses. They argue that managers focus on short-run results to satisfy impatient shareholders.

Proponents of an industrial policy for the United States often suggest a cooperative relationship among industry, labor, and government, with the initiative and much of the funding coming from the private sector. A national development bank and a planning council would help identify and support "sunrise" industries—those industries considered important for future U.S. competitiveness. Firms in sunrise industries would develop plans for improved competitiveness and would be rewarded with some public financing to help them develop new products and improve production processes. The planning council would also provide retraining and relocation assistance to help move resources out of "sunset" industries—those industries in which the United States has lost its comparative advantage.

Free-market policies. In contrast, *free-market policies* would decrease the role of government. Advocates view the decline in U.S. competitiveness as the result of excessive government regulation and poorly designed tax policies. They suggest reducing government regulation of pollution control, health and safety, and pensions. Such regulation, they argue, creates barriers to firms entering and exiting industries and thus causes allocative inefficiency. If antitrust laws permitted more mergers and allowed firms to engage in joint research and development projects, U.S. firms would be stronger competitors. Lifting trade restrictions that now shelter U.S. firms would force them to become more competitive worldwide. Lower tax rates and greater tax incentives for research and development would increase investment and encourage more product development.

Fair-trade policies. Finally, many economists and politicians favor a *fair-trade approach*. They believe that the lack of U.S. competitiveness is partly caused by "unfair trading practices." Dumping—that is, selling goods below cost—is an issue, as are direct and indirect government subsidies to producers. Import restrictions—tariffs, quotas, and other nontariff restrictions—are a special target. Some of the countries with the largest trade surpluses—Japan, South Korea, and Taiwan—are those in which U.S. firms have had great difficulty penetrating trade barriers. Reducing or eliminating these barriers would, according to proponents, allow U.S. businesses to compete on a "level playing field."

What Are the Benefits and Costs of Trade-Deficit Policies?

As always, in choosing the "best" policy, policy makers must weigh the benefits and costs of different approaches and select the one for which benefits most outweigh its costs. (Note that although we discuss each policy approach separately, many economists believe that a *combination* of policies should be followed.)

Fiscal and monetary policies. As we discussed more fully in the policy case on federal budget deficits, reducing these deficits means raising taxes or cutting spending. Both actions have political and economic costs. Tax increases direct resources toward the public sector and may stifle saving and work effort. Reducing "unnecessary" government expenditures is universally accepted, but there is much disagreement over which expenditures are unnecessary. Moreover, reducing expenditures and raising taxes are both contractionary policies. But if government eases monetary policy to reduce this contractionary effect, inflation may result.

Industrial policy. Advocates of an industrial-policy approach argue that this is a more systematic, rational way of reducing the trade deficit. In a way, the United States already has an implicit industrial policy of sorts. Tax policies, direct and indirect subsidies, and various trade restrictions already enacted into law provide support (and discouragement) of industrial development. But Congress passes a lot of legislation to satisfy domestic special interest groups rather than to specifically improve global competitiveness.

Supporters of industrial policy point to agricultural policies as an example of the benefits of a cohesive industrial policy. In the 1930s U.S. agriculture was a dying industry. With the help of government research funds, cooperative marketing arrangements, and government help in promoting exports, agriculture became a highly technical, highly productive industry. Agriculture currently accounts for almost 20 percent of the nation's exports and enjoys a comparative advantage in international trade.

But industrial policies also involve costs. One potential cost is that government planners may be less capable than the marketplace in picking individual winners and losers. And an agency responsible for industrial policy would be subject to the same political pressures that affect any government agency.

Free-market policies. The free-market approach also involves both benefits and costs. Relaxing regulations lowers production costs; lowering taxes raises profitability; and allowing more mergers increases financial strength and market position. Although each of these policies may increase the global competitiveness of U.S. firms, there are costs to be considered. Relaxing regulations may increase pollution and reduce worker safety; lower taxes may increase the federal budget deficit; and mergers may reduce competition among U.S. firms.

Fair-trade policies.   Economists generally favor lower trade barriers because free trade allows each country to produce efficiently and to satisfy more wants. Proponents of fair-trade policies argue that the United States should take action to pressure other countries to lower tariffs, remove quotas, and eliminate subsidies and other restrictions. But the United States sometimes uses the same policies it opposes: subsidizing exports of grain and imposing tariffs and quotas to restrict imports of steel, textiles, and automobiles. Almost all economists support negotiations to eliminate restrictions. But some argue for retaliation when negotiations fail. In early 1987, threats of retaliation by the United States caused some European countries to drop plans to restrict U.S. grain imports. The United States also imposed retaliatory tariffs when Japanese manufacturers of semiconductor chips were accused of violating an antidumping agreement. But retaliation is a risky strategy because it may only escalate protectionism.

Would No Action Be a Better Policy?

The problem of a trade imbalance is, according to economic theory, likely to correct itself over time. The ability of the United States to import more than it exports depends on the willingness of foreigners to continue to loan us money. But eventually they will want to be repaid. When foreigners are unwilling to loan us more, demand for U.S. dollars will fall and the dollar will depreciate. If it falls far enough (and remains low long enough), the trade imbalance will correct itself.

However, few economists recommend waiting for this self-correction. In the first place, it will likely take some time to occur. In the meantime, the United States will run up a sizable debt to foreigners, and just financing this debt will be very expensive. Although there is no consensus on the policies that should be used, most economists suggest that efforts be made to decrease the trade deficit now.

Japanese cars on the dock await shipment to United States markets. Increased imports of foreign automobiles during the 1980s were a visible symbol of decreased international competitiveness of U.S. manufacturers. (UPI/Bettmann Newsphotos)

Why Do Economists Disagree about Trade-Deficit Policies?

Economists generally agree that the high value of the dollar helped to cause very large U.S. trade deficits in the early 1980s. Most believe that lowering the federal budget deficit and, consequently, interest rates is essential to improving competitiveness. There is also widespread agreement among economists on the desirability of removing trade barriers both by the United States and by other countries.

Economists do not agree, however, on whether government should take any other steps to improve the competitiveness of U.S. businesses. Some economists recommend no additional government action. Others recommend active support of emerging industries and steps to ease the transition from dying industries. Others suggest removing what they see as government obstacles to competitiveness. These disagreements stem in part from subjective, normative elements in the debate and in part from the difficulty of assessing the degree to which various proposals would increase competitiveness.

Conclusion

The U.S. trade deficit has grown tremendously in recent years. Even though some of the blame may lie with federal budget deficits, the decline in competitiveness of U.S. industries also appears to be an important factor. A wide variety of solutions have been proposed, ranging from removing the influence of government to adding new government programs. But the difficulty of getting political and international agreement makes a quick end to the debate unlikely.

QUESTIONS FOR REVIEW AND DISCUSSION

1. Many economists argued that U.S. firms faced competitive disadvantages in the early 1980s as the value of the U.S. dollar increased significantly.
   a) Explain how a sufficiently large reduction in the value of the U.S. dollar would give U.S. businesses a competitive advantage in international markets.
   b) What are the disadvantages of allowing the dollar's value to fall? (Note who bears the costs of this fall.)

2. In 1987 President Reagan imposed tariffs on some Japanese products because Japanese manufacturers of semiconductor chips (used in computers) were accused of unfairly "dumping" the chips below cost.
   a) What are the benefits (and who receives them) if chips are "dumped" in the United States?
   b) What are the costs (and who pays them) if "dumping" occurs?
   c) How would you determine whether chips (or any other product) were being sold "below cost"? (That is, what costs would you consider? How does the principle of opportunity cost apply?)

3. The industrial-policy approach suggests the use of direct subsidies and other means to support selected industries.
   a) What criteria would you use to determine which industries to support?
   b) Would the criteria you use be like or different from those used by private financial firms (such as banks)?
   c) Explain how critics of the industrial-policy approach argue that the real criteria used are more likely to be political rather than economic.

PART NINE

International Economics

CHAPTER 32

International Trade

QUESTIONS TO CONSIDER

☐ How important is international trade to the U.S. economy?

☐ Why do nations engage in international trade?

☐ What are the benefits and costs of international trade?

☐ Why do nations sometimes impose restrictions on international trade?

☐ What alternatives to trade restrictions do economists recommend and why?

E conomic news in the United States increasingly concerns international trade and finance. International trade accounts for a smaller part of goods and services produced and consumed in the United States than in most other noncommunist countries. Nevertheless, some $331 billion worth of U.S. goods and services were sold to other countries in 1986, and U.S. residents bought almost $496 billion worth of goods and services produced abroad that year.

Why do countries trade? You would probably find life very different without Italian shoes, French wines, German automobiles, and Japanese electronic products. But international trade involves costs as well as benefits. For example, U.S. shoemakers, vintners, car companies, and stereo producers often lose the battle for consumers' dollars to foreign producers. In this chapter we present the benefits and costs of trade in more detail and show why some producers, workers, and politicians support trade restrictions—and why most economists don't.

INTERNATIONAL TRADE AND THE UNITED STATES

Trade is the very essence of market transactions. Every time you go to work or to the grocery store you are engaging in trade; that is, you are trading your services for income and the income for food. As you will see, the principles governing international trade and the reasons why trade is beneficial are the same whether we are considering nations within the world economy or individuals within a nation's economy. First, however, we must consider the extent of international trade.

International trade is big business. As Exhibit 32.1 indicates, about $1.8 trillion worth of goods flowed among countries in 1985. But the importance of international trade varies by country. Some 7 percent of all U.S. goods and services produced are sold in other countries. As we noted in Chapter 6, these products are considered to be exports by the U.S. economy and imports by the countries that buy them. A number of other countries export a much larger percentage of their total production. West Germany, for example, exported about one-third of its total production. In the Netherlands, exports accounted for nearly 65 percent of all goods and services produced, and in Belgium they represented 76 percent.

Country	Exports of goods (billions of U.S. dollars)	Imports of goods (billions of U.S. dollars)	Exports as a percentage of domestic GNP
United States	213.1	361.6	7.0
Japan	177.2	130.5	16.4
United Kingdom	101.2	109.0	29.3
Canada	90.6	81.1	29.8
West Germany	183.9	158.5	36.7
Netherlands	68.3	65.2	64.5
Belgium	53.7	56.2	75.7*
Total World	1782.9	1879.0	

* Figure is for 1984.
Source: International Monetary Fund, *International Financial Statistics, 1986 Yearbook.*

Exhibit 32.1
Volume of International Trade, 1985

However, the importance of international trade to the United States is much greater than the relatively small amount of total production that is exported. The U.S. economy depends heavily on imports of natural resources, such as oil. And as we have already noted, imported goods such as shoes, steel, and automobiles are important competitors for products made in the United States.

Volume of U.S. International Trade

Trade balance (balance on merchandise trade). The difference between the values of exports and imports of goods only (excludes imports and exports of services).

Trade deficit. A negative trade balance; occurs when the value of imports exceeds the value of exports.

Trade surplus. A positive trade balance; occurs when the value of exports exceeds the value of imports.

Another important aspect of international trade is the balance (or imbalance) of imports and exports of goods and services. As Exhibit 32.2 shows, in 1986 the United States exported $221.7 billion worth of goods (excluding services) but imported $369.5 billion worth. Thus the **trade balance (balance on merchandise trade)**—the difference between the values of goods exported and imported—for 1986 was −$147.7 billion. That is, the United States had a $147.7 billion **trade deficit**. However, the U.S. trade balance has not always been negative. Indeed, for many years, exports exceeded imports, giving the nation a **trade surplus**.

Exhibit 32.2
U.S. International Trade, 1986 (in billions of U.S. dollars)

Exports of goods	221.7
Less: Imports of goods	369.5
Trade balance	−147.7
Exports of goods and services	370.7
Less: Imports of goods and services	496.1
Balance on goods and services	−125.4

Source: U.S. Department of Commerce, *Survey of Current Business,* March 1987, Table 1-2, p. 44.

Category	Exports of goods (billions of U.S. dollars)	Imports of goods (billions of U.S. dollars)	Net exports (billions of U.S. dollars)
Foods and feeds	22.6	24.0	−1.4
Industrial supplies	63.4	103.1	−39.7
Energy products	8.2	38.1	−29.9
Capital goods	79.2	75.7	3.5
Automobiles	23.9	78.1	−54.2
Consumer goods	14.5	78.0	−63.5
Other goods	18.2	10.6	7.6
Total merchandise trade	221.8	369.5	−147.7
Services	148.9	126.6	22.3
Trade of goods and services	370.7	496.1	−125.4

Source: U.S. Department of Commerce, *Survey of Current Business,* March 1987, Tables 2 and 3.

Exhibit 32.3
U.S. International Trade by Category, 1986

Balance on goods and services. The difference between the value of exports and imports of both goods and services.

In addition to trading goods, countries also import and export services. As a resident of the United States, if you travel to Europe on British Airways, for example, you are buying a service made in Great Britain. Your expenditure is counted as an import in the United States and an export in Great Britain. Services traded internationally include not only expenditures for travel and transportation, but also international investments. In 1986, the U.S. **balance on goods and services**, including imports and exports of both goods and services, showed a $125.4 billion deficit.[*]

Exhibit 32.3 shows exports and imports by category. As you can see, the United States is a net exporter of both agricultural products and capital resources. It is a net importer of industrial supplies and consumer goods. Indeed, net imports of petroleum products alone were $29.9 billion in 1986. Exhibit 32.3 also indicates that the United States had a significant surplus of trade in services.

The volume of international trade has increased significantly over the past 25 years. In 1960, total trade in the United States (exports plus imports) was $200 billion, equivalent to 12 percent of all goods and services produced.[†] The volume in 1986 ($892 billion) was equal to 24 percent of total U.S. production. The rising volume and relative importance of international trade is an important trend. It means that U.S. businesses face increasing competition for the dollars spent by U.S. households and businesses. In addition, U.S. businesses are increasingly looking to foreign markets for sales.

---

[*] If you have studied macroeconomics, you may find it useful to remember that the balance on goods and services is roughly equal to net exports as used in accounting for national income and gross national product.

[†] If you have studied macroeconomics, you may be interested in knowing that the data in this paragraph are stated in real terms; that is, the effect of inflation have been removed.

Changing Pattern of U.S. International Trade

The pattern of U.S. international trade in goods has changed substantially over the past 10 years as shown in Exhibit 32.4. Europe and Canada remain our largest trading partners and account for virtually the same proportion of total trade at the beginning and end of the period. But U.S. trade with Japan and the developing Asian countries, including Hong Kong, Singapore, and South Korea, has increased dramatically. Total volume of trade with these countries quadrupled between 1975 and 1985.

As a result, trade with the major oil-exporting nations of the Middle East (from the U.S. perspective, mostly imports of oil) became relatively less important. In 1975 trade with these nations represented 14 percent of all U.S. trade; in 1985 it was only 6 percent. Imports from these countries increased dramatically in 1980, reflecting the large oil-price increases that occurred in 1979–1980. But the dollar volume of trade with these nations declined as oil prices dropped and the United States imported more oil from other countries, such as Mexico.

Another significant change in the U.S. trade pattern is the nation's rising trade deficit. In 1986 the U.S. trade deficit represented over 4 percent of the nation's total production of goods and services. In the 25 years prior to 1980, the largest deficit—equal to 1.9 percent of the nation's total production—occurred in 1972.

Why are the deficits so large? As Exhibit 32.4 indicates, the value of U.S. exports has grown more slowly than that of its imports. Average annual growth in exports between 1975 and 1985 was 7 percent. Over the same period, imports increased at a rate of 13 percent per year. This pattern held for nearly all the world regions shown, but was strongest in U.S. trade with Japan and the developing Asian countries. Exports to this region increased by 9 percent, but imports increased by 19 percent. We consider other reasons for U.S. trade deficits and possible solutions in Chapter 33. (This topic is also explored in Chapter 31.)

Exhibit 32.4
Shifting Pattern of U.S. Trade (billions of U.S. dollars, nominal terms)

Region	Total trade (imports + exports)		Exports from United States		Imports into United States		Trade deficits	
	1975	1985	1975	1985	1975	1985	1975	1985
Europe	49.7	135.5	28.2	53.6	21.5	81.9	6.6	−28.3
Canada	44.5	116.7	21.7	47.3	22.8	69.4	−1.0	−22.2
Oil exporters	30.3	33.6	10.4	12.0	19.9	21.6	−9.5	−9.6
Latin America	34.3	80.1	17.1	31.0	17.2	49.1	0.1	−18.1
USSR and Eastern Europe	3.1	3.8	2.5	2.9	0.6	0.9	1.9	2.0
Developing Asia	22.7	90.2	11.0	29.0	11.7	61.2	−0.7	−32.2
Japan	21.9	95.0	9.6	22.6	12.3	72.4	−2.8	−49.8

Source: Joseph A. Whitt, Jr., Paul Kuch, and Jeffrey Rosenweig, "The Dollar and Prices: An Empirical Analysis," *Economic Review,* Federal Reserve Bank of Atlanta, October 1986.

GAINS FROM INTERNATIONAL TRADE

Clearly, international trade is an important part of the U.S. economy—and that of most nations. But why? We can summarize the reasons for trade as follows: *Countries trade with each other because each country can benefit*. This principle is basic to understanding why economists generally agree that trade restrictions are usually not in a nation's best long-run interest. Trade can be beneficial when two countries possess different natural and/or capital resources. It can be beneficial when they have different preferences. And it can be beneficial when the efficiency with which they produce a given set of goods differs. Studying the benefits of trade can help you identify the factors that determine which goods a country will import and which it will export.

Differences in Resources

Countries are often motivated to trade because they have different natural resources. The United States, for example, has an abundant quantity of fertile land. In 1986 we exported $27 billion worth of agricultural products. Saudi Arabia, on the other hand, has few natural resources other than sand and oil. The Saudis rely heavily on exports of petroleum products.

Similarly, the capital/labor ratio—which measures the value of capital resources such as machinery and equipment per worker—helps to predict trade flows. For example, the United States has a high capital/labor ratio compared to India, meaning that the United States has more abundant capital resources. Thus we would expect the United States to export goods for which capital resources are relatively important but India to export goods that require relatively more labor.

We trade with Brazil to get coffee and with Honduras to get bananas, neither of which grow in North America. We travel to the Caribbean, trading for sunshine, beautiful beaches, and warm water. Citizens of many countries attend U.S. colleges and universities, trading for educational services.

Differences in Preferences

Trade would also tend to occur even if all countries had identical resources because countries have different preferences. The British, for example, prefer tea to coffee; Americans have the opposite preference. Even if each country had the same quantities of tea and coffee, trade would be beneficial. By trading coffee for tea, the British would be sacrificing something of less value to them (coffee) for an item they value more (tea). At the same time, Americans would also gain. Even though the total quantity of goods would be the same, both countries would have increased their satisfaction by trading.

Differences in Productivity: Absolute Advantage

Differences in resources and preferences create opportunities for gains through trade and explain some trade patterns. Even more significant, however, trade offers an opportunity for countries to specialize—to produce the goods that they can produce most efficiently. Thus trade allows countries to escape the limits imposed by their own production possibilities. As a result, trade enables the world

Absolute advantage. The ability to produce a good or service with fewer resources; refers only to relative productivity.

to satisfy more wants because it allows resources to be used more efficiently. A country that is more productive in making a certain good—that can produce the good with fewer resources—has an **absolute advantage** in producing that good. Thus, because of its climate, Brazil has an absolute advantage in growing coffee beans.

Assume for the moment that there are only two countries in the world: the United States and Tradesia. Assume also that only two products are produced: computers and applesauce and that both nations can produce both products. Exhibit 32.5 indicates that U.S. workers can produce more applesauce in a week than workers in Tradesia (100 cases per week compared to 50 cases). Greater productivity gives the United States an absolute advantage in producing applesauce. On the other hand, Tradesia has an absolute advantage in producing computers because its workers produce more computers per week (25 compared to 10).

This simple example shows why absolute advantage means that trade will increase efficiency. If one U.S. worker switches from producing computers to producing applesauce, the United States will produce 100 more cases of applesauce and 10 fewer computers per week. If one Tradesian worker stops producing

Exhibit 32.5
Gains from Trade: Absolute Advantage

(a) Labor productivity

	Quantity produced by one worker in one week	
Product	*in the United States*	*in Tradesia*
Applesauce	100 cases	50 cases
Computers	10 computers	25 computers

(b) Opportunity cost

	Opportunity cost per unit produced	
Product	*in the United States*	*in Tradesia*
Applesauce	0.10 computer	0.50 computer
Computers	10 cases of applesauce	2 cases of applesauce

(c) Gains from trade

	Cases of applesauce		
Country	*Changes in output*	*Goods traded*	*Final result*
United States	+100 cases	−60 cases	+40 cases
Tradesia	− 50	+60	+10
Net effect	+ 50 cases	0 cases	+50 cases

	Number of computers		
Country	*Changes in output*	*Goods traded*	*Final result*
United States	−10 computers	+12 computers	+ 2 computers
Tradesia	+25	−12	+13
Net effect	+15 computers	0 computers	+15 computers

applesauce and starts producing computers, that country will have 50 fewer cases of applesauce and 25 more computers. From a worldwide perspective (in this two-country world), this change results in a net increase in production of both goods: 50 more cases of applesauce and 15 more computers. Because more goods have been produced using the same amount of resources, using absolute advantages has increased efficiency.

The world has benefited, but what about the United States and Tradesia? Suppose that Tradesia agrees to ship 12 computers to the United States in exchange for 60 cases of applesauce. Compared to the position before switching resources and trading, the United States is better off. It has 40 more cases of applesauce—100 more were produced but 60 traded—and 2 more computers—10 were not made, but 12 were received in trade. Tradesia is also better off. It has 10 more cases of applesauce—it sacrificed making 50 cases but received 60 U.S. cases—and 13 more computers—it made 25 more but traded 12 to the United States. *When each country specializes in what it can produce most efficiently, trading can result in greater worldwide output and can benefit all countries involved.*

Gains from specialization reflect different opportunity costs of production in the United States and Tradesia. A U.S. worker can produce *either* 100 cases of applesauce or 10 computers in a week. Thus in the United States each computer has an opportunity cost of 10 cases of applesauce (100 cases of applesauce ÷ 10 computers). In Tradesia the opportunity cost is 2 cases of applesauce per computer (50 cases of applesauce ÷ 25 computers). Thus it is more efficient to produce computers in Tradesia, where the opportunity cost is lower.

Similarly, the U.S. opportunity cost of producing applesauce is 0.10 computer compared to 0.50 computer in Tradesia. Thus the United States can produce applesauce more efficiently than Tradesia. As this example indicates, if each country produces with its efficiency advantage (lower opportunity cost), more goods can be produced from the same amount of resources. Because the size of the "pie" for the world is larger as a result of this specialization, each country can have a bigger "slice."

Differences in Opportunity Cost: Comparative Advantage

It is not difficult to see that trading can be beneficial when each country has an absolute advantage in one commodity. (If you are better in economics and your friend is better in biology, you can both make better grades by helping each other study.) However, you may be surprised to learn that *both countries can gain from trade even if one country has an absolute advantage in producing both goods.*

Suppose, for example, that a U.S. worker can produce more computers or more applesauce in a week than a Tradesian worker, as Exhibit 32.6 shows. The key word in that sentence is the word *or*. A worker cannot produce both a week's worth of applesauce and a week's worth of computers in a single week. To produce a week's worth of applesauce, a week's worth of computer production must be sacrificed. The opportunity cost of producing applesauce is thus the quantity of computers that must be sacrificed.

If we measure efficiency in terms of opportunity cost, we see that the U.S. opportunity cost of a case of applesauce is 0.10 computer. The Tradesian opportunity cost is 0.40 computer per case. Thus the United States is more efficient in producing applesauce. But Tradesia has a lower opportunity cost of producing

(a) Labor productivity

	Quantity produced by one worker in one week	
Product	*in the United States*	*in Tradesia*
Applesauce	100 cases	20 cases
Computers	10 computers	8 computers

(b) Opportunity cost

	Opportunity cost per unit produced	
Product	*in the United States*	*in Tradesia*
Applesauce	0.10 computer	0.40 computer
Computers	10 cases of applesauce	2.5 cases of applesauce

(c) Gains from trade

	Cases of applesauce		
Country	*Changes in output*	*Goods traded*	*Final result*
United States	+100 cases	−60 cases	+40 cases
Tradesia	− 40	+60	+20
Net effect	+ 60 cases	0 cases	+60 cases

	Number of computers		
Country	*Changes in output*	*Goods traded*	*Final result*
United States	−10 computers	+12 computers	+2 computers
Tradesia	+16	−12	+4
Net effect	+ 6 computers	0 computers	+6 computers

Exhibit 32.6
Gains from Trade: Comparative Advantage

computers: 2.5 cases of applesauce per computer compared with 10 cases per computer in the United States.

In other words, although the United States has an absolute advantage in producing both applesauce and computers, Tradesia has a **comparative advantage** in producing computers. A country has a comparative advantage when it can produce a good for a lower opportunity cost. Workers in Tradesia produce fewer computers in a week than workers in the United States, but the opportunity cost is lower. Put another way, a U.S. worker can produce 5 times as many cases of applesauce but only 25 percent more computers. Relatively speaking, U.S. workers are better—have a comparative advantage—at producing applesauce but are at a relative disadvantage when producing computers.

When countries use the principle of comparative advantage to select which goods to produce and trade internationally, more goods are produced worldwide. To see why, look again at Exhibit 32.6. If one U.S. worker stops producing computers and starts producing applesauce, the United States will produce 10 fewer

Comparative advantage. The ability to produce a good or service at a smaller opportunity cost; refers to relative efficiency.

International trade occurs because it is possible for both countries involved in trade to gain. Gains are possible because of differences in resource supplies, preferences, and, most importantly, relative efficiency.

Absolute advantage is the ability to produce a good using fewer resources, that is, with greater productivity. Comparative advantage is the ability to produce a good at a lower opportunity cost, that is, more efficiently.

Comparative advantage determines which country can most efficiently produce a particular good. Because every use of resources involves an opportunity cost, every country has a comparative advantage in at least one good.

If countries specialize in producing goods for which they have a comparative advantage and then engage in trade, total worldwide production can be increased, meaning that it is possible for all nations to gain from trade.

computers but 100 more cases of applesauce. At the same time, if two Tradesian workers quit producing applesauce and begin making computers, Tradesia will produce 16 more computers and 40 fewer cases of applesauce. The result is increased efficiency because 6 more computers and 60 more cases of applesauce are produced from the same resources. *When countries specialize in producing products for which they have a comparative advantage, efficiency improves worldwide.*

Again, both the world and the two nations benefit from trade. Suppose that Tradesia agrees to trade 12 computers to the United States for 60 cases of applesauce. Compared to its initial position, Tradesia has 4 more computers (16 were made but 12 traded away) and 20 more cases of applesauce. The U.S. has 40 more cases of applesauce and 2 more computers.

Absolute versus comparative advantage. Although both absolute advantage and comparative advantage support the idea that trade benefits both nations, comparative advantage is the more reliable guide to decision making. Absolute advantage shows only the benefits obtained from producing. To make decisions about what goods to produce, the extra costs must also be considered.

As in our two-country example, a country's resources may be more productive (have an absolute advantage) in two tasks. But they cannot be more efficient (have a comparative advantage) at both tasks because using resources to produce one good requires the sacrifice of another good. The more productive resources are, the greater is the sacrifice or opportunity cost involved. That is, the better a country is at producing any good, the greater the sacrifice required to produce another good.

This important conclusion does not depend on the particular numbers we used in the example. No country can have a comparative advantage in producing all goods. There is always some comparative advantage and hence gains to be made from specializing and trading. These gains are a major reason why economists generally agree that trade is beneficial and that trade restrictions are not in a country's best economic interests.

Terms of Trade

As you have just seen, specialization along the lines of comparative advantage means greater worldwide efficiency and production. As a result, countries can gain through trade. But how much will each country gain? In the last part of our example, we assumed that the United States exchanged 60 cases of applesauce for 12 computers. This means that the **terms of trade**—the relative price expressed in terms of physical commodities—were 5 cases of applesauce per computer. But what, if anything, can we say about the terms of trade in the real world?

In our simple example, suppose that the terms of trade were set at 15 cases of applesauce per computer. Would the United States be willing to trade applesauce for computers with Tradesia on these terms? The answer is *no*. To see why, let's suppose that the United States traded for 10 computers. To do so, it would have to make 150 cases of applesauce to export (10 computers × 15 cases of applesauce). To produce 150 cases of applesauce, however, the United States would have to sacrifice making 15 computers (because every 10 cases of applesauce means that one less computer can be made). In other words, after trading, the United States would have the same amount of applesauce but 5 fewer computers.

Terms of trade. The relative prices of goods and services involved in international trade expressed in physical terms (for example, 5 cases of applesauce per computer).

Because it would be worse off, the United States would not be willing to trade. The terms of trade are too high to make trading profitable for the United States.

Why are the terms of trade too high? Because the United States *can* make computers, it attains an economic gain by trading only if computers can be imported more cheaply than they can be made. That is, the terms of trade—the price of imports—must be more favorable than the domestic opportunity cost. In our example, it costs the United States 15 cases of applesauce to trade for one computer. But it costs only 10 cases of applesauce to make one computer.

The terms of trade can also be too low to tempt nations to produce goods for export. Tradesia will gain economically by exporting computers only if it can make a profit, that is, if the terms of trade exceed the opportunity cost of production. (Nations also may or may not trade with certain countries for political reasons, as is the case in U.S. trade relations with the Soviet Union, Eastern Europe, and Cuba. Economic analysis cannot easily predict the direction of political actions, but it can identify the economic costs of restricting trade.)

These principles allow us to calculate the maximum and minimum terms of trade for the example given in Exhibit 32.6. The maximum terms of trade are 10 cases of applesauce for one computer, or the opportunity cost of making a computer in the United States. Unless the terms of trade (price of a computer) are less than 10 cases of applesauce, it will not be economically profitable for the United States to import computers. The minimum terms of trade are 2.5 cases of applesauce per computer, or the opportunity cost of making a computer in Tradesia. If the terms of trade are lower, it would not be economically profitable for Tradesia to export computers. To check your understanding, express the minimum and maximum terms of trade in number of computers. (Your answers should be a maximum price of 0.40 computer per case and a minimum price of 0.10 computer per case.)

The closer the terms of trade are to the maximum, the greater are the gains received by Tradesia. The closer the terms are to the minimum, the greater are the gains received by the United States. In the example in Exhibit 32.6, the terms are 5 cases of applesauce per computer. *Because these terms fall between the minimum and maximum levels, both nations find trade profitable.* To check your understanding, calculate the gains to each nation if the terms of trade are 3 cases per computer and 12 computers are traded. (Because the price of computers declines relative to applesauce, the United States, the importer, gains more. Tradesia, the exporter, gains less.)

Demand and Supply: International Equilibrium

Minimum and maximum terms of trade are linked to costs. But we cannot predict whether actual terms will be closer to the maximum or minimum values by looking only at relative costs. To understand how the terms of trade are determined, we must also consider demand and supply conditions in each country. As we first noted in Chapter 3, demand and supply determine the price of a product in a market economy. Exhibit 32.7 shows domestic demand and supply of applesauce in the United States and Tradesia. We can compare the price and quantity of applesauce produced and consumed both with and without trade.

If there is no trade, the applesauce market in Tradesia, shown in Exhibit 32.7(a), will reach equilibrium at a price of $5 per case (where D_T and S_T intersect).

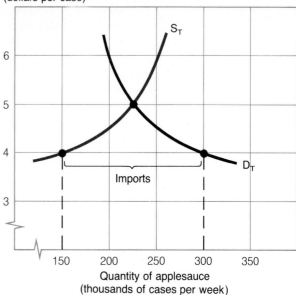

(a) Market for applesauce in Tradesia

Price of applesauce
(dollars per case)

Exhibit 32.7
World Market for Applesauce
Part (a) shows that with no trade the market for applesauce in Tradesia will reach equilibrium at a price of $5
per case. Part (b) shows that the U.S. market will
achieve equilibrium at a price of $3 per case. If interna-
tional trade is allowed, applesauce will be exported from
the United States, where it can be produced more
cheaply. When demand for and supply of applesauce in
both countries are combined, worldwide equilibrium occurs at a price of $4 per case, as part (c) indicates. At
that price, exports from the United States equal imports
into Tradesia.

At this price, 225,000 cases will be bought and sold. Similarly, Exhibit 32.7(b)
indicates that the equilibrium price of applesauce in the United States will be $3
per case if there is no trade.* Because the price in Tradesia is higher than the
price in the United States, however, worldwide equilibrium is not achieved. If
trading between the countries is not restricted, a firm can earn a profit simply by
buying U.S. applesauce and selling it in Tradesia (if shipping costs do not eliminate
profits). Such trading gains would be possible as long as there is a difference in
price.

When international trade is allowed, there are two conditions for equilibrium.
First, the price in both countries must be the same (except for transportation
costs). And second, quantity supplied worldwide must equal quantity demanded
worldwide. That is, the quantity exported from the United States must equal the
quantity imported by Tradesia and bought by Tradesian residents.

The first condition is not met when there is no trade because the price of
applesauce is higher in Tradesia than in the United States. But examining the
world market in Exhibit 32.7(c), you can see that both conditions are met when
the world price (and the price in each country) is $4 per case. Not only are the
prices the same (condition 1) but the quantity demanded and supplied worldwide
are both 550,000 cases (condition 2).

---

* In this example, prices in both countries are expressed in dollars. In the real world, countries use
different currencies. However, because our interest here is in the relative price of applesauce in the
two countries, we have translated the foreign prices into dollar prices. In Chapter 33 we discuss how
the relative "prices" of currencies of two countries are determined.

(b) Market for applesauce in the United States

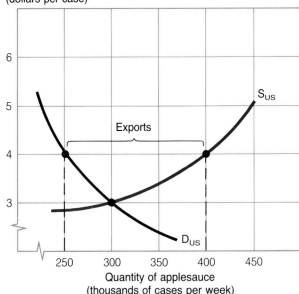

(c) World market for applesauce

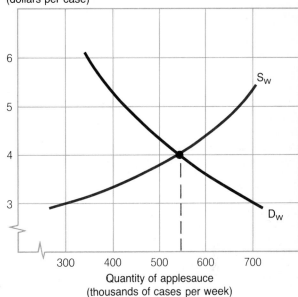

Note that equilibrium does not mean that the quantity produced in each country is equal to the quantity bought. Tradesia produces only 150,000 cases but consumes 300,000. Imports from the United States are part of the available supply in Tradesia. They make up the difference between quantity produced domestically and quantity consumed. Similarly, in the United States, total demand represents demand by U.S. residents (D_{US}) together with demand by Tradesians (D_T) for U.S. exports.

How do the U.S. and Tradesian markets adjust to reach this price and level of production? Adding demand by Tradesian residents to that of U.S. residents causes U.S. applesauce prices to rise from $3 to $4 per case. In response, U.S. applesauce producers increase quantity offered for sale from 300,000 to 400,000 cases per week. Although U.S. customers buy less applesauce as the price rises, U.S. producers export 150,000 cases to Tradesia. In Tradesia, the market price of applesauce falls from $5 to $4 per case when the supply from the United States is added to the domestic supply. Although Tradesian applesauce producers offer less for sale, imports from the U.S. allow Tradesian residents to increase the quantity of applesauce consumed from 225,000 to 300,000 cases per week.

This example illustrates several important points. First, when there is international trade, we cannot predict prices or quantities exchanged simply by looking at domestic demand and supply. The available supply in any country depends on quantities supplied by both domestic and foreign producers. Likewise, demand by foreign residents must be added to demand by domestic residents. Second, as you saw in this example, international trade does not mean complete specialization. The Tradesian demand for applesauce is met partly by Tradesian firms and partly by imports from the United States. This situation—where foreign producers compete against domestic producers in the same markets—is typical. The lack of complete specialization partly reflects preferences; some U.S. residents, for example, prefer Fords and Chevrolets to Toyotas and Volvos.

INTERNATIONAL TRADE: GAINS AND LOSSES

So far we have indicated how it is possible for countries to gain through international trade. We have also shown how demand and supply determine a worldwide equilibrium price for a single product. But our references to gains are from the perspective of the country as a whole. Not all individuals in a country stand to gain from trade. And of those who do gain, some gain more than others. Like most other economic activities, international trade involves both benefits and costs. In this section, we examine these benefits and costs, paying special attention to which groups in the economy tend to benefit and which tend to lose. This distinction is important because those who stand to lose often argue for trade restrictions, seeking to avoid the costs associated with trade.

Higher Prices for Exported Goods

Looking at the price of applesauce in the United States, we can see one of the costs of trade. Before trade, the price was $3 per case, based on domestic demand and supply. After trade, it is $4 per case. In general, a price increase accompanies most goods that are exported. Demand for U.S. applesauce is higher when both the domestic and foreign demand are combined. Higher demand drives prices up, causing U.S. consumers to pay more and buy less applesauce.

Thus it appears that U.S. residents lose by trading internationally. But trade is not a one-way street. At the same time, Tradesian suppliers are offering computers to U.S. buyers at lower prices than before. Overall, as you saw earlier, more is available and consumers in both countries gain as a group. Those who consume more applesauce than computers, however, may be worse off as individuals.

Decreased Demand in Import-Competing Industries

Another major cost of trade is the decline in Tradesian applesauce production from 225,000 cases before trade to 150,000 cases after trade. In other words, trade means that less applesauce will be produced in Tradesia (and sold at a lower price). Thus profits of Tradesian applesauce firms are lower, wages paid Tradesian applesauce workers are lower, and fewer Tradesian workers will be employed in this industry. From the standpoint of producers and workers in the Tradesian applesauce industry, then, imports are a threat. In response, they may seek government protection from imported applesauce. In the United States, efforts to restrict imports of automobiles, steel, shoes, and textiles have been supported both by producers and unions representing workers in those industries.

Lower Prices for Imports and Greater Demand for Exports

However, trade involves benefits as well as costs. Although prices of exported goods are higher because of trade, prices of imports are lower. Thus consumers of imported goods gain. Although trade reduces demand for goods and labor in import-competing industries, demand in export industries rises, resulting in higher profits, increased employment, and higher wages in such industries. In addition, we must not forget the first lesson of trade: By increasing efficiency worldwide, total production and consumption are greater in the world (and in each country) than without trade. These benefits must be compared to costs to estimate the net gain to an entire country. Economists generally believe that the extra benefits of trade are greater than the extra costs.

Distributional Effects of Trade

The greater efficiency associated with trade means greater output worldwide. Moreover, countries are willing to trade only when the terms of trade benefit each, improving their overall economic positions. On the other hand, not every firm or individual is better off. That is, trade has distributional effects. Those who consume above-average amounts of imported goods gain more because of lower prices. Those who consume above-average amounts of exported goods lose more because of higher prices. Moreover, producers and workers in export industries gain, whereas producers and workers in import-competing industries lose. These distributional effects are a major reason why some individuals seek restrictions on trade.

Concentrated costs. Note, however, that the distributional effects of trade have several important characteristics. First, *the costs of trade are often more highly concentrated and more directly visible than the benefits*. For example, a growing percentage of shoes sold in the United States is imported. We gain from lower shoe prices as a result. But our individual gains are small, even if the total gain is large. On the other hand, many U.S. shoemakers have suffered substantially lower profits. As a result, many have closed factories and laid off workers.

The concentration of costs and the diffusion of benefits are important for two reasons. They help explain why politicians often seek to restrict trade. Moreover, they suggest a possible way of dealing with the distributional problem without resorting to trade restrictions. A part of the gains from trade could be used to compensate those who lose, by subsidizing job training or job relocation for displaced workers, for example. If the net gain from trade were shared, support for free trade might be easier to win.

Costs and mobility. Second, *the costs of trade are smaller when labor and capital are highly mobile and greater when mobility is restricted*. As we have noted, some losers under unrestricted trade are workers and producers in import-competing industries, such as shoes. Their losses reflect the decrease in demand which suggests that resources be reallocated—away from import-competing industries to other industries—in the interest of efficiency. If workers in shoe factories can quickly and easily find other employment, the unemployment costs related to free trade will be small.

But if workers left unemployed by free trade lack the skills to move to other jobs, or if other jobs require a move across country, the costs are significant, at least to unemployed shoeworkers. This cost may justify distributional aid. However, it also suggests that such aid might best take the form of programs to increase labor mobility, including retraining and/or relocation assistance, rather than restricting trade. Such programs would help society to improve the allocation of resources (efficiency), while reducing the distributional costs (equity) of free trade. As we discuss later in this chapter, such programs have been a part of U.S. economic policy for many years.

Long run versus short run. And third, *benefits tend to be greater and costs lower when considered over the long run; the opposite is true for the short run.* In some respects, this point is much like the second one. Given enough time, workers will find other employment even if it means some retraining or relocation. Thus in a long-run analysis, the benefits of greater efficiency worldwide outweigh the costs. Bear in mind, however, that a meaningful economic analysis must recognize both the short-run costs and the long-run benefits. If, as most economists believe, the long-run benefits outweigh the short-run costs, trade should be encouraged. However, it is still reasonable to suggest, as many do, that short-run costs should be shared by those who benefit from trade.

TRADE RESTRICTIONS AND ALTERNATIVE TRADE POLICIES

Most economists agree that free trade—that is, unrestricted trade—is beneficial to an economy overall. They also recognize that trade restrictions are common in the real world. In this section we consider several questions: What are the effects of trade restrictions? Are there legitimate reasons for proposing restrictions? What are the alternatives?

Import Tariffs

A common form of trade restriction is an **import tariff**, which is a tax on imported goods. You can see the results of an import tariff by returning to our example of demand for and supply of applesauce in Tradesia. Like Exhibit 32.7(c), Exhibit 32.8 shows that in the absence of trade restrictions, applesauce will sell for $4 per case. Tradesians will buy 300,000 cases per week, including 150,000 cases imported from foreign countries.

What if Tradesian applesauce producers and workers successfully lobby their legislators for an import tariff of $0.50 per case? Tradesian applesauce producers and workers will then gain at the expense of Tradesian consumers and foreign producers. The tariff will raise the price of foreign applesauce in Tradesia to $4.50 per case. Even if they charge the same price as foreign producers will have to charge, Tradesian producers can increase their sales from 150,000 to 200,000 cases per week, as shown in Exhibit 32.8. Sales, profits, and employment in the applesauce industry will increase. Tradesian applesauce producers and their employees will be better off.

Import tariff. A tax placed on imported goods.

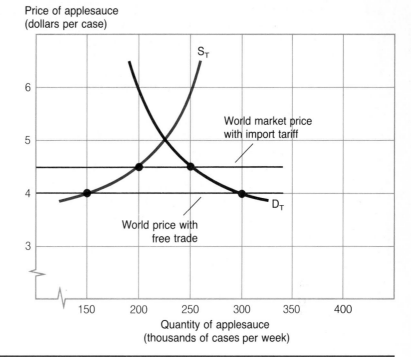

Exhibit 32.8

Effects of Import Tariffs on Market for Applesauce in Tradesia

With free trade, the world price of applesauce will be $4 per case. At that price, Tradesia will import 150,000 cases per week (the difference between quantity demanded and quantity supplied). But Tradesian applesauce producers and their workers may argue for a protective tariff. If a tariff of $0.50 per case is imposed, the market price in Tradesia will increase to $4.50 per case, and the quantity of imports will fall to 50,000 cases per week. Tradesian producers will sell more, but Tradesian consumers will pay more for fewer cases of applesauce. The Tradesian government will collect $25,000 per week from the tariff ($0.50 × 50,000 cases imported).

In addition, imports fall from 150,000 cases (the difference between quantity demanded and domestic supply at a price of $4 per case) to 50,000 cases. Thus part of the gain to Tradesian producers and workers is paid by foreign producers and workers. The tariff also gives the Tradesian government additional receipts. With a $0.50 per case tariff on imported applesauce, the Tradesian government collects $25,000 per week (50,000 cases × $0.50 per case).

However, the Tradesian consumer would have to pay more for less. The price of applesauce rises by $0.50 per case and quantity consumed falls by 50,000 cases. Thus part of the gain to Tradesian producers and workers will come at the expense of Tradesian consumers. Other Tradesian producers and workers also stand to lose. Tradesian bakers making applesauce cakes and restaurants serving applesauce will pay more for applesauce, and their profits will fall. Moreover, if many products are subject to tariffs, workers in many industries may seek higher wages in an effort to maintain their standard of living in the face of rising prices.

Tariffs also damage efficiency. Protected industries produce more than they would in the absence of tariffs. Thus they use more resources (such as labor) than they would otherwise. As a result, nonprotected industries will be forced to pay higher prices for resources. Some economists also note that industries may be somewhat less efficient producers when they are protected against the efficiency-stimulating effects of greater competition. Nobody benefits from goods not produced because of inefficiency.

Restrictions on trade also harm efficiency indirectly. Because foreign countries can sell fewer of their goods to Tradesia, they have less to spend on Tradesian goods. Hence quantities of goods demanded and supplied internationally will fall.

Import quota. A limit on the quantity of a particular good that can be imported.

These effects are often multiplied as one nation retaliates for another's tariffs by establishing its own tariff system. For example, the United States might respond to a Tradesian tariff on applesauce by placing a tariff on Tradesian computers. In general, economists believe that the domestic economy suffers a net loss as a result of an import tariff. That is, a few gain but not as much as the rest of the economy loses. However, the short-run costs and distributional effects can be significant.

To illustrate, let's consider the U.S. shoe industry, which responded to a significant loss in profits because of foreign competition by pressuring Congress to impose a tariff on foreign-made shoes. Domestic shoe manufacturers and their employees have benefited from higher production, profits, wages, and employment. But consumers have paid higher prices for shoes, foreign producers have sold fewer shoes, and China has restricted imports of U.S. agricultural products, hurting U.S. farmers. Moreover, U.S. resource allocation has suffered since resources that could be more efficiently utilized elsewhere remain in the shoe industry. There may very well be legitimate concerns about the short-run costs to U.S. shoeworkers who lose their jobs and producers who lose profits. However, tariffs and other protectionist measures are not efficient policy responses to this concern because they result in a net loss to the economy as a whole.

Import Quotas

Another common form of trade restriction is an **import quota**, which is a limit on the quantity of a particular good that may be imported. In some ways the effects of quotas and tariffs are alike. In fact, Exhibit 32.8 also shows what would happen if Tradesia limited imports of applesauce to 50,000 cases per week. The quota causes imports to fall from 150,000 to 50,000 cases per week, and like a tariff, it also causes prices to rise. Tradesian consumers again pay more for less. In fact, consumers may actually lose more from quotas than from tariffs, since quotas also restrict consumer choice.

Tradesian producers and workers benefit from increased demand for domestic applesauce. Tradesian companies benefit from reduced competition and, as a result, may actually be able to charge more and produce less. The lack of competition may also harm technical efficiency, as Tradesian producers have less incentive to use the best technology. And allocative efficiency will suffer if quotas enable Tradesian applesauce producers to ignore or delay responding to changing consumer tastes.

A major difference between quotas and tariffs is that a quota does not increase Tradesian government receipts. Moreover, foreign producers may gain as a result. Although they can sell fewer cases of applesauce, the price per case is higher. There is some evidence, for example, that Japanese car manufacturers have increased their profits while complying with U.S. import quotas by selling more expensive models at higher prices.

"Voluntary" quotas. In recent years, certain U.S. industries especially hard hit by foreign imports—shoes, steel, autos, and textiles—have put increased pressure on the government for protection. In some cases, the U.S. government has negotiated "voluntary" quotas. For example, Japan agreed to voluntarily restrict exports of automobiles to the United States in return for a U.S. agreement not to raise the import tariff on imported automobiles. Voluntary quotas, however, yield the same results as mandatory quotas: fewer imports, higher import prices, and protection of the domestic industry. And, like other restrictions, they invite retaliation, further increasing restrictions on trade worldwide and further reducing potential gains. One study estimated that voluntary quotas on Japanese automobiles cost U.S. consumers $4.3 billion in 1983, not counting any loss caused by restrictions on choice. That is, each job saved by the quota cost $160,000. It seems that another policy approach would surely be more desirable.

Other Nontariff Barriers

In addition to tariffs and quotas, imports are sometimes restricted by other nontariff barriers. For example, automobiles imported into the United States are required to meet standards for safety and pollution control. Imported drugs must meet standards of safety and effectiveness imposed by the U.S. Food and Drug Administration. For the most part, the United States has imposed these restrictions on imports to force them to meet standards that apply to U.S. products. These restrictions are not strictly intended to reduce foreign competition. However, U.S. automakers and other U.S. producers complain that Japan imposes restrictions on imports that are not required of Japanese producers. To the extent that these barriers are selectively applied to imports, they are trade restrictions with effects similar to those of tariffs and quotas.

Arguments for Trade Restrictions

Despite the problems with trade restrictions, they remain politically popular. In fact, the political pressures for the United States to increase trade restrictions have been particularly strong recently. In this section, we consider some of the arguments used to justify trade restrictions and the reasons why economists reject some of these arguments.

Promoting national security. In some cases, proponents of trade restrictions argue that such measures are necessary to protect an industry vital to national security, regardless of the effects on efficiency. What do the principles of rational choice tell us about this argument? As always, we must consider not only the benefits but the costs of a particular policy. The United States once restricted oil imports on the grounds that it was important to national security to encourage domestic exploration and production of oil. The limits on oil imports into the United States actually resulted in faster use of domestic oil reserves and higher oil prices at the same time. The national security argument has also been used to prohibit or restrict exports. The United States limits trade in some technologically advanced products—such as some computer technology—and in certain military goods. The reasons for such restrictions are political, not economic, although they impose economic costs as do all other restrictions.

The U.S. steel industry, which has been hard hit by foreign imports, has argued that steel production is essential to national security. While this may be true, some economists are skeptical that steel producers protected from competition will again become strong and efficient. The critics argue that U.S. steel producers did not use the opportunity granted by protection in the past to do so.

Protecting infant industries. Comparative advantage suggests that it is in the long-run interest of a country to import items that can be produced more efficiently abroad. But what about the short run? Supporters of the "infant-industry" argument note that sometimes it is difficult for a new industry to compete initially with established foreign companies. They argue that short-run protection will allow the industry to develop to the point where it can compete.

Economists have several problems with this approach. First, they note that it is often difficult to identify industries capable of long-run survival that would not survive without protection. Many question the notion that an industry could be profitable in the long run but unable to survive short-run losses without *government* assistance. They observe that private financing is normally sufficient to cover short-run losses in successful industries. And if government assistance is necessary, direct subsidies may be better than trade restrictions. Finally, they argue that assistance to infant industries must be short term, but government policies often fail to set reasonable end dates for assistance.

Supporting domestic industries.

The "buy American" argument has been popularized in TV ads, by politicians, and on bumper stickers. Supporters argue that "If we buy from abroad, we get goods but foreigners get our money. If we buy at home, we get both goods and money." This argument, however, fails to recognize that the objective of economic activity is to satisfy the greatest quantity of society's wants. Money by itself satisfies no significant wants. Only economic goods can satisfy wants.

Whether foreigners have more of our money or not is irrelevant to the issue for several reasons. First, foreigners as a group have little else to do with our money (and no reason to seek it) except to use it to buy goods in exchange. If we could convince foreigners to continually accept money in exchange for real economic goods, we could exchange something that costs little to produce for something of significant value. This type of exchange is unlikely, however, because foreigners also want goods, not money. Ultimately, trade involves the exchange of goods for goods, a notion we explore in more detail in Chapter 33.

Retaliating for other nations' restrictions.

There is actually some economic support for the notion that trade restrictions may be necessary to protect the U.S. economic position in the face of other nations' restrictions. Proponents argue that only in this manner can we limit the actions of other nations who gain at our expense by imposing trade restrictions on U.S. exports. Economists generally agree that an absence of all trade barriers would be preferable. If retaliatory measures succeed in reducing trade restrictions they may be a useful tactic. But retaliation is also risky, and may only lead to further retaliation.

In 1986, for example, the United States imposed a 35 percent tariff on Canadian cedar shingles. Canada responded with "compensating tariffs" on U.S. computer parts, novels, and oatmeal. The United States then slapped tariffs on oil-well piping. The immediate effects of such trade wars are reduced trade and inefficiency. But supporters of such get-tough policies argue that such tariffs are necessary to force reluctant countries to lower their own barriers. They point to the success of U.S. threats in 1987 that forced some European countries to relax restrictions on U.S. grain exports.

Protecting domestic workers from cheap foreign-labor competition.

Some who favor trade restrictions argue that, without protection, U.S. workers would be forced to accept the same low wages as workers in less-developed nations. This argument fails in two respects. First, the level of wages paid to foreign labor does not, by itself, establish whether the products they make are cheaper. To make this calculation, we must compare both the relative wages and the relative productivities of workers in the two countries. To the extent that higher paid U.S. workers are more productive than their foreign counterparts, they are also more efficient and can compete without accepting lower wages.

And second, even if U.S. workers cannot compete with foreign labor in one industry, they probably have a comparative advantage in another industry. As our earlier discussion shows, it is impossible for even "cheap" foreign labor to have a comparative advantage in the production of all goods. Thus economists argue that trade restrictions cause inefficiency by keeping labor resources from their best use. The industries hit hardest by foreign imports—shoes, textiles, steel, and autos—appear to be industries in which other countries have a competitive advantage, in part because wages and living standards are low. In fact, the United States may *not* be able to effectively compete in those areas. But it does seem to have a comparative advantage in producing chemicals, industrial machinery, and scientific instruments.

Preventing high unemployment.   There is an element of truth in the argument that free trade can cause unemployment, at least in the short run. Trade will reduce demand for some domestic products and hence lower employment in those industries. However, as we have pointed out elsewhere, unutilized resources are not without value as long as we live in a world of scarcity. In the absence of trade restrictions, export industries will demand more labor, which should offset the lower demand in import-competing industries. In other words, to the extent that unemployment results from free trade, it should be only a short-run problem of labor resources moving from import to export industries. And as you will see in the next section, economists believe that policies other than trade restrictions can more efficiently address the short-run unemployment problem.

Alternatives to Trade Restrictions

In proposing alternatives to trade restrictions, economists focus on policies that offer greater benefits than costs. As a result, some economists support direct subsidies as opposed to trade restrictions, when legitimate reasons exist to support domestic industries.

Subsidies and efficiency.   These economists believe that direct subsidies do not raise product prices. Thus consumers do not experience high costs directly. Domestic industries that use imported products do not experience higher costs. (Subsidies do impose indirect costs in the form of higher taxes, however.) Economic studies suggest that direct subsidies impose smaller costs than do trade restrictions. Although economists view direct subsidies as being more efficient than trade restrictions, they do not argue for direct subsidies whenever free trade decreases profits and employment in an industry. They recognize that subsidies can raise the profits of firms that are not efficient enough to compete on their own. But the benefits of direct subsidies must be balanced against the costs before they can be justified.

Subsidies and equity.   As we noted earlier, some economists also favor subsidies to help retrain or relocate workers in import-competing industries. That is, rather than trying to save jobs in a particular industry, they favor helping workers make a smooth and equitable transition from one job to another. In this way, both equity and efficiency can be addressed.

Until recently, workers displaced because of reductions in trade barriers were given additional unemployment insurance payments under the Trade Adjustment Assistance (TAA) Program. Most studies of this particular program have concluded that it met its equity goals, despite the difficulty of determining whether specific workers were displaced because import policies changed. However, the program appeared to be inefficient. Critics argue that it spent too much on cash grants that were not tied to adjustment efforts. Rather than increase mobility, the grants tended to slow it. Many economists believe that future legislation should put greater emphasis on educational and relocation programs that provide efficiency gains, as well as help to the displaced.

Economists disagree over the extent to which such help is desirable, however. Some argue that most workers who lose their jobs find new ones without government help and that special assistance for those affected by import policies is unnecessary. Others argue that workers in the industries most affected—shoes, textiles, steel, and autos—will be hard pressed to find new jobs, especially if adjustments involve closing large plants.

Reasons for the Popularity of Trade Restrictions

Despite these problems, economists generally agree that subsidies are a more efficient solution than are trade restrictions. Why, then, do trade restrictions remain the most common policy? One reason is that a direct subsidy appears to be a handout. Some firms and individuals are reluctant to accept such direct help, and policy makers are often reluctant to give it.

By contrast, trade restrictions most visibly and directly harm foreign producers and workers; they most visibly and directly benefit domestic producers and workers. Foreign producers and workers do not vote, whereas domestic producers and workers vote and lobby their legislators. Consumers and producers in other industries are often unaware of the extra costs they pay. Indeed, they may view rising prices and falling demand as the result of "unfair" foreign competition, not a shift in comparative advantage.

U.S. Trade Policy

As we noted earlier, one serious problem with trade restrictions is that countries tend to counterattack with their own restrictions. That is, a Japanese tariff on U.S. products is likely to be followed by a U.S. tariff on Japanese goods. As a result, trade wars may develop and the resulting loss in efficiency worldwide may be great.

Tariff barriers have generally declined since the 1930s, a time in which trade wars reached epidemic proportions. (Some economists believe that the trade restrictions were an important factor in the Great Depression of the 1930s.) In 1930, goods imported into the United States paid an average tariff of 53 percent. By 1967, the average tariff was only 8.3 percent. Much of this reduction resulted from negotiations between countries, which were spurred by the General Agreement on Tariffs and Trade (GATT) signed by the United States and 23 other countries in 1947. The most recent conference, the "Tokyo Round," led to an agreement in 1979 to reduce tariffs by nearly one-third and eliminated a large number of nontariff barriers. In 1986, trading nations began negotiations in Ponte del Este, Argentina, which may produce even lower trade barriers.

Despite the trend toward freer trade, however, restrictions continue to play an important role in trade. Moreover, Congress continues to debate (and sometimes to pass) trade restrictions. Serious discussions about limiting trade on shoes, textiles, steel, and autos continue. When countries such as Japan continue to impose import restrictions on U.S. products, Congress is more tempted to erect competing barriers to trade.

On taking office, President Reagan clearly stated his policy objective: to reduce trade barriers. He vetoed legislation that would have imposed additional restrictions on shoe and textile imports and prevented additional controls on imported steel and automobiles. But Reagan was not immune to the retaliatory argument. He encouraged the 1986 retaliatory tariffs against Canadian cedar shingles. In early 1987, he threatened to impose a 200 percent tariff on brandy, white wine, and soft cheese exported by European countries unless they reduced some of the trade barriers he blamed for falling grain sales. And he imposed tariffs on some Japanese products when the Japanese were accused of selling semiconductor chips below costs.

Moreover, you should recognize that the United States has many policies that restrict trade. Some—such as import controls on certain agricultural products—support domestic price controls. In other cases—such as with textiles and automobiles—a wide range of policies from tariffs and quotas are used to restrict trade. The United States and other nations have been reluctant to reduce or abolish restrictions by themselves, despite generally favoring free trade.

CONCLUSION

Economists generally believe that the benefits of free trade outweigh the costs and problems it creates. Although the adjustments required by free trade involve some costs, the country as a whole benefits from greater efficiency and satisfies more of its wants. Thus economists generally recommend a minimum of trade restrictions. Instead, they favor direct subsidies if problems arise that require government assistance.

The flow of goods and services has important consequences for the international economy, but so does the flow of funds. In Chapter 33 we consider the reasons for and implications of financial flows: the flow of funds from the United States to foreign financial markets and of foreign funds into U.S. financial markets. In addition, we look at how the relative prices of currencies are determined. Why did the value of the U.S. dollar increase dramatically in the early 1980s, and plunge in the mid-1980s? To completely understand the foreign sector of the economy, you must understand the effects of these financial flows.

SUMMARY

1. In this chapter we examined the reasons for and the benefits and costs of international trade, as well as the reasons for and arguments against trade restrictions.

2. International trade occurs because both countries involved in trade can gain from the exchange. Gains are possible because of differences in resources, preferences, and, most important, relative efficiency.

3. Comparative advantage—the ability to produce a good at a lower opportunity cost—not absolute advantage—the ability to produce a good using fewer resources—

determines which country can produce a certain good most efficiently. Because every use of resources has an opportunity cost (other goods not produced), a country will always have a comparative advantage in producing at least one good. If countries specialize in producing goods for which they have a comparative advantage and then engage in trade, total world output can be increased, enabling all nations to gain from trade.

4. The terms of trade express in physical terms the relative prices of traded goods. For a country to gain from trade, the terms of trade must be favorable relative to domestic opportunity costs. That is, a product will be imported only if the quantity of products that must be sacrificed is less than the opportunity cost of producing them domestically. A product will be exported only if the quantity of products received in trade is greater than the opportunity cost of production.

5. The world price of a traded good depends on demand and supply in all trading countries. The price of an imported product will be lower than the price of a domestic product (if there were no trade) because imports increase supply. The price of an exported product will be higher than the price of a domestic product (without trade) because exports increase demand.

6. The costs of trade include higher prices for exported goods, as well as decreased demand and lower employment in import-competing industries. The benefits from trade include lower prices for imported goods, greater demand and employment in export industries, and increased total production.

7. Trade has distributional effects, benefiting some workers and industries and increasing costs to others. Import-competing industries and workers with lower short-run mobility are the most adversely affected. Because costs are highly concentrated and visible, politicians often support trade restrictions.

8. Common forms of trade restrictions include import tariffs, import quotas (both mandatory and "voluntary"), and nontariff barriers, such as required standards of safety and/or pollution control.

9. Rationales for trade restrictions include protecting national security interests, allowing "infant industries" to become established, supporting domestic industry, retaliating for other nations' restrictions, protecting U.S. wage rates, and maintaining high employment. Economists generally reject these arguments, favoring direct subsidies if problems arise from free trade.

KEY TERMS

Trade balance (balance on merchandise trade), 821
Trade deficit, 821
Trade surplus, 821

Balance on goods and services, 822
Absolute advantage, 825
Comparative advantage, 827
Terms of trade, 828
Import tariff, 834
Import quota, 836

QUESTIONS FOR REVIEW AND DISCUSSION

1. Some early economists (known as the mercantilists) called a trade surplus a "favorable balance of trade," implying that a country with a trade surplus was better off than one with a trade deficit.
   a) Based on the mercantilists' reasoning, what types of trade policy do you think they favored?
   b) Adam Smith argued in his book, *The Wealth of Nations*, that the wealth of a nation was greater when free trade was encouraged. In what way does free trade increase total wealth? What are the costs of free trade?
   c) Does the U.S. economy gain more from exporting $1 million worth of goods or from importing $1 million worth of goods? Explain.

2. Consider the statement: "A U.S. worker who produces goods exported to West Germany makes a product that helps the United States import West German steel. Thus in a fundamental way, we can say that the U.S. worker is producing steel for the U.S. economy."
   a) Does this statement express a fundamental truth or a fallacy?
   b) What difference does it make to the U.S. economy whether steel is produced by U.S. workers in the steel industry or obtained by trading U.S. exports for foreign steel?
   c) Does this difference help explain why politicians from steel-producing areas tend to support restrictions on imported steel?

3. The following data show the relative productivity with which beer and TV sets can be produced in Tropicola and Temperania.

| Product | Quantity produced per worker per day in | |
	Tropicola	Temperania
Beer	200 barrels	400 barrels
TV sets	5 sets	8 sets

a) For which product(s) does Temperania have an absolute advantage?
b) What is the opportunity cost of a TV set in each country?

c) For which product(s) does Tropicola have a comparative advantage?

d) Would both countries benefit from trade if the terms of trade were 45 barrels of beer per TV set? What terms would make trade unprofitable for Temperania? For Tropicola?

e) What factors might explain why Temperanian workers can produce more TV sets per day?

4. Explain how each of the following situations would likely affect the relative price of beer and TV sets (or the terms of trade) in Tropicola and Temperania.

a) Improved technology that allows Tropicolan workers to produce more TV sets per day than before.

b) A switch in Tropicolans' preferences from local fruit juices to imported beer.

c) An increase in the price of Temperanian beer.

d) A decrease in the quality of TV programs in Tropicola.

e) An import tariff on imported TV sets in Tropicola.

f) In each case, the terms of trade will worsen for one of the two countries. In which cases will the residents of Tropicola be worse off after the change than before?

5. A U.S. manufacturer makes the following argument: "Our industry has difficulty competing with foreign producers not because we are less productive but because of the maze of government regulations governing worker safety and pollution. If these were eliminated, we could expand our business and provide many more jobs for U.S. workers."

a) Explain why government regulations such as those mentioned would place a U.S. manufacturer in a less competitive position.

b) Would the U.S. economy be better off if such regulations were eliminated? Be sure to consider both private and social benefits from and costs of the regulations in your answer.

6. The United States currently imposes a tariff on imported automobiles. If the tariff were eliminated, what would you expect to happen to

a) prices of automobiles in the United States?

b) prices of automobiles in Japan?

c) profits of U.S. automakers?

d) employment in the U.S. auto industry?

e) demand for U.S. exports?

7. Discuss the statement: "Trade restrictions are necessary to protect the wages of U.S. workers. Without protection, the standard of living of U.S. workers would fall to the low levels of workers in other countries."

International Finance

QUESTIONS TO CONSIDER

☐ How do exchange rates affect international trade?

☐ Why do individuals and businesses in one nation demand the currency of another nation?

☐ What factors affect international monetary flows?

☐ How does a gold standard operate and why did the United States go off the gold standard?

☐ What were the restrictions of the Bretton Woods system and why does the United States now allow the dollar to "float"?

In Chapter 32 we discussed the flow of goods and services from one country to another. But not all international transactions are trades of goods or services. Japanese and French businesses buy U.S. companies and build factories in the United States. Egyptians and Argentinians buy stock in U.S. firms and U.S. government bonds. Many U.S. corporations, such as IBM, Coca-Cola, and Exxon, operate throughout the world. Sometimes they produce goods and services in the United States for export to other countries. But they also build or buy plants and other facilities in foreign countries. (There seems to be a McDonald's in every major city in Europe, for example.) In this chapter we show how these international transactions, along with trade in goods and services, affect the U.S. economy.

In addition, you must recognize that international transactions involve more than one currency. For example, prices are stated in marks in West Germany and in pounds in Great Britain. When international transactions occur, the flow of goods and services (or financial claims such as stocks and bonds) in one direction is matched by a flow of currency in the opposite direction. When U.S. residents buy Japanese cars, for example, dollars flow out of the United States to Japan. But Japanese car manufacturers want yen to pay their workers. Someone—either the U.S. buyer or the Japanese seller—will have to exchange dollars for yen. In this chapter you will see how international currency exchanges determine the relative values of two currencies. You will also learn something about systems that have been used to set currency values.

EXCHANGE RATES AND INTERNATIONAL TRADE

International trade is in many respects like the trade that occurs entirely within a country. Buyers and sellers agree on a price and exchange currency for goods and services. But international trade often involves more than one language and more than one set of legal, cultural, and institutional factors. In addition, because each country uses a different monetary unit, international trade involves the exchange of two currencies.

		Exchange rate	
Country	Currency	Dollars per unit of foreign currency	Units of foreign currency per dollar
Australia	Dollar	0.6864	1.4569
Belgium	Franc	0.0263	37.9600
Canada	Dollar	0.7646	1.3079
France	Franc	0.1642	6.0910
India	Rupee	0.0776	12.8900
Italy	Lira	0.0007	1300.5000
Japan	Yen	0.006605	151.4000
Mexico	Peso	0.000912	1097.0000
Netherlands	Guilder	0.4833	2.0690
Portugal	Escudo	0.007107	140.7000
Sweden	Krona	0.1564	6.3940
Switzerland	Franc	0.6527	1.5320
United Kingdom	Pound	1.6040	0.6234
West Germany	Mark	0.5469	1.8285

Exhibit 33.1
Foreign Currency Exchange Rates, March 1987

Exhibit 33.1 shows the monetary units used by a number of countries. Many give their currency a unique name—the rupee in India, the yen in Japan, the krona in Sweden, for example. Currencies of different countries may have the same name but are really different currencies with different values. For example, the monetary unit in both the United States and Canada is the dollar. But the U.S. dollar and the Canadian dollar are different currencies and can have very different values. Similarly, the Swiss franc and the French franc are different currencies having different values, even though they have the same name.

Currencies are not usually exchanged on a one-for-one basis. The rate at which one currency trades for another—the number of yen received in exchange for one French franc, for example—is what economists call an **exchange rate**. Exchange rates between the dollar and various other currencies are also shown in Exhibit 33.1. An exchange rate between two currencies can be stated in terms of either currency. For example, the exchange rate between the Indian rupee and the U.S. dollar is shown as 12.89 rupees per dollar (fourth column), and as $0.0776 per rupee (third column). Note that these are not two different rates, only two way of expressing the same rate.

Exchange rates also reflect relative prices. Let's say that you are visiting in France and see a bottle of wine you like selling for 45.68 francs. If you can buy the same wine in the United States for $9 per bottle, would it be cheaper to buy it in France or wait until you get home? Using the data in Exhibit 33.1, you can convert francs into dollars (or dollars into francs). With an exchange rate of 6.091 francs per dollar, the French price is equivalent to $7.50 U.S. dollars. You can save money by buying the wine in France. To check your understanding, determine the price in francs that would be equivalent to the $9 price in dollars. (Your answer should be 54.82 francs.)

Exchange rate. The price of one currency in terms of another; the quantity of one currency that must be given up to obtain a unit of another currency (for example, 150 yen per dollar).

In the current international monetary system, exchange rates are not fixed, and when they change, they make products in one country more or less expensive.

Currency appreciation. An increase in the exchange rate for the domestic currency (for example, from 150 to 160 yen per dollar); each unit of the domestic currency buys more units of the foreign currency; makes imports from foreign countries less expensive to domestic residents but exports to foreign countries more expensive to foreign residents.

Currency depreciation. A decline in the exchange rate for the domestic currency (for example, from 150 to 140 yen per dollar); each unit of the domestic currency buys fewer units of the foreign currency; makes imports from foreign countries more expensive to domestic residents but exports to foreign countries less expensive to foreign residents.

For example, if the value of the French franc falls relative to the U.S. dollar, it will be even less expensive to buy the French wine in France instead of in the United States. Conversely, if the value of the dollar falls, there may be no price differential, or it may be relatively cheaper to wait and buy the wine when you get home. To check your understanding, determine whether it is cheaper to buy the wine in France or the United States if the exchange rate is 4.5 francs per dollar. (You should find that the U.S. price is equivalent to 40.5 francs, and therefore it is cheaper to buy in the United States.)

Economists refer to changes in the relative value of currencies as **currency appreciation** (when the exchange rate rises) and **currency depreciation** (when the exchange rate decreases). For example, between 1975 and 1980 the U.S. dollar depreciated against the West German mark, falling from 2.46 marks per dollar to 1.82 marks per dollar. From 1980 to 1985, however, the dollar appreciated, rising from 1.82 marks per dollar to 2.92 marks per dollar. *When the dollar appreciates, foreign goods become less expensive to U.S. residents.* You may think that having the U.S. dollar appreciate would be wonderful and having it depreciate would be terrible. But there are pluses and minuses to changes in both directions. As the U.S. dollar appreciates, U.S. residents will buy more foreign-made goods because they are less expensive than before. But because other currencies must have depreciated at the same time, foreign residents will buy fewer U.S.-made goods. Thus *appreciation of the U.S. dollar decreases exports and increases imports to this country and thus can worsen a trade deficit; depreciation has the opposite effects.*

FOREIGN-EXCHANGE MARKETS

As you have seen, exchange rates affect the relative prices of imports and exports. But what determines exchange rates and what causes them to change? Economists find it useful to treat the exchange rate as a price: the price of one currency in terms of another. In this way they can consider how the price is determined by the interaction of demand and supply of currency in foreign-exchange markets. But why would anyone demand marks or yen or dollars? As we show in this section, currencies are demanded and supplied every time there is an international exchange of goods, services, or financial claims.

International Exchanges and the Flow of Dollars

The circular-flow model in Exhibit 33.2 shows the types of international exchanges that can occur and how they are connected to exchanges of foreign currencies. At the top are the elements of international trade: exports and imports. At the bottom are international capital flows: financial investment in physical and financial assets such as factories, stocks, and bonds. Connected with each international exchange is a flow of dollars into or out of the United States.

Note that the flow of exports is matched by a flow of dollars into the United States. That is, if IBM sells computers to a firm in France, the French firm must pay IBM in dollars. To obtain these dollars, the French firm must exchange francs for dollars. The French firm will therefore demand dollars from (and supply francs

An exchange rate expresses the price of one currency in terms of another. A change in the exchange rate also means a change in relative prices of goods in the two countries.

If the exchange rate of one currency rises (appreciates), that of another currency must fall (depreciate) relatively.

If a currency appreciates, that country can afford more imports but will sell fewer exports. The reverse is true if the currency depreciates.

Trade and capital flows are matched by demand and supply of currency. Foreigners demand dollars to pay for U.S. exports and to buy U.S. physical and financial assets. Similarly, U.S. residents supply dollars to buy foreign imports or physical and financial assets.

to) the foreign-exchange market. Thus *U.S. exports will be matched by demand for U.S. dollars in foreign-exchange markets.*

Conversely, the flow of imports is matched by a flow of dollars out of the United States. That is, if you buy a Japanese car from a U.S. car dealer, you pay for the car in dollars. But the car dealer had to pay its Japanese supplier in yen. To obtain these yen, the car dealer had to exchange dollars for yen. The dealer will therefore demand yen from (and supply dollars to) the foreign-exchange market. Thus *U.S. imports will be matched by supply of U.S. dollars in foreign-exchange markets.*

The same principles apply in international capital markets. When a U.S. firm purchases a foreign company or builds a plant in another country, it is demanding foreign physical assets. (Economists refer to these purchases as direct foreign investment.) And U.S. residents and businesses may also buy financial claims—stock in foreign firms or the bonds of foreign governments, for example. To purchase foreign assets, U.S. firms and residents must exchange dollars for foreign currency. And when foreign firms buy U.S. companies, factories, stocks, or bonds, they must exchange foreign currencies for dollars. Thus, *demand by foreign residents for U.S. physical and financial assets leads to a demand for U.S. dollars. Demand by U.S. residents for foreign investments leads to a supply of U.S. dollars.*

Exhibit 33.2
The Flows of International Exchanges
This exhibit shows the international economic exchanges between the United States and the rest of the world. The top part of the exhibit shows trade flows; exports and imports of goods and services are matched by an equal but opposite flow of dollars. The bottom part shows international financial or capital flows, representing financial investments in foreign assets by U.S. residents and financial investments by foreigners in U.S. assets.

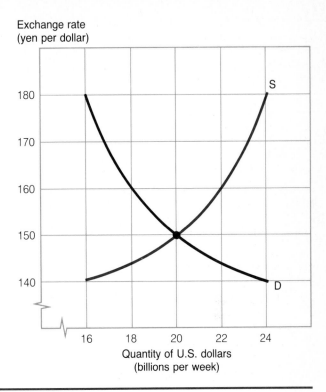

Exhibit 33.3

Demand for and Supply of U.S. Dollars in Foreign-Exchange Markets

International economic exchanges between the United States and the rest of the world result in demand for and supply of dollars in foreign-exchange markets. When U.S. residents purchase foreign imports or make financial investments in foreign countries, they supply U.S. dollars in exchange for foreign currencies to purchase foreign imports or make financial investments in foreign countries. Foreign residents demand dollars in exchange for foreign currencies to purchase U.S. exports or to make financial investments in U.S. assets. In this graph, the exchange rate of the U.S. dollar is expressed in terms of yen (the currency of Japan). Equilibrium occurs at an exchange rate of 150 yen per dollar, with $20 billion exchanged per week.

Demand for and Supply of Foreign Exchange

As you just saw, trade and capital flows lead to demand for and supply of dollars to be used for international exchanges. In Chapter 3, we introduced the idea that the forces of demand and supply determine price in a market economy. In the international economy, demand for and supply of different currencies determines an exchange rate, that is, the price of one currency in terms of another.

For simplicity let's initially assume that exchange rates are determined only by demand and supply. That is, as economists put it, we assume that the system is one of **flexible (or freely floating) exchange rates**, which, for the most part, characterizes the current international monetary system. (Later in this chapter, we consider systems in which rates cannot freely adjust to market conditions.) Exhibit 33.3 shows how demand for and supply of foreign currencies interact in a foreign-exchange market.* The horizontal axis shows the quantity of dollars. The vertical axis indicates the price of a dollar, or its exchange rate—in this case the exchange rate between the dollar and the Japanese yen. As in other markets, the foreign-exchange market determines an equilibrium price (exchange rate)—in this case 150 yen per dollar. At any higher rate, there is a surplus. At any lower rate, there is a shortage.

Flexible (or freely floating) exchange rates. A system in which exchange rates are determined by demand and supply without government intervention in foreign-exchange markets.

---

* For those who have studied macroeconomics, note that this market is not the same as the demand for and supply of money, although they are closely related. The demand for and supply of dollars here are related to international exchanges. Thus the demand for dollars does not reflect the demand by U.S. residents to hold cash in a bank, but rather the demand by foreign residents to obtain dollars, which they can use to buy U.S. goods and services or to invest in U.S. assets.

Since this market is free to adjust, the exchange rate will always move to equilibrium, eliminating any shortage or surplus. In general, foreign-exchange markets work like other markets. An increase in demand increases the price (or exchange rate). An increase in supply causes the exchange rate to fall. Note that *as the exchange rate (yen per dollar) rises, the dollar appreciates in value and the yen depreciates.*

Shapes of demand and supply curves.   A decline in the exchange rate (yen per dollar) means that foreigners can buy dollars more cheaply. A specific quantity of yen buys more dollars and hence more U.S. products. That is, depreciation of the dollar reduces the prices of U.S. exports to Japanese residents and should cause U.S. exports to increase. As exports increase, more dollars will be demanded in the foreign-exchange market. Thus the demand for dollars curve slopes downward, as do most demand curves, because changes in the exchange rate affect relative prices.

At the same time, a decrease in the exchange rate reduces the value of the dollar and makes Japanese products more expensive to U.S. residents. Because of the effect on relative prices, U.S. consumers (and businesses) will demand fewer Japanese goods and will supply smaller quantities of U.S. dollars as the exchange rate falls. Thus the supply of dollars curve slopes upward, as do most supply curves.*

Factors that change imports and exports.   Clearly, demand for and supply of currencies in foreign-exchange markets reflect international transactions: exports, imports, and foreign investments. But what changes the willingness of U.S. and foreign firms and individuals to make such transactions? Why would U.S. residents buy more Japanese or French products? Why would U.S. firms buy more raw materials from African countries or more products from Brazil? What would cause Canadian residents or British firms to buy more goods and services from U.S. firms? The same factors that influence demand for any good affect demand for imports and exports: (1) tastes and preferences; (2) income; and (3) relative prices.

Changes in tastes and preferences, including those stimulated by changes in product quality, increase or decrease demand for exports and imports. Thus they change demand for and supply of U.S. dollars in foreign-exchange markets and hence exchange rates. Tastes and preferences partly account for increased U.S. demand for Japanese products in recent years. In particular, U.S. buyers have liked the quality and performance of Japanese automobiles. At the same time, other nations have a strong preference for U.S. capital resources, especially those involving advanced technology.

Similarly, a change in the income of U.S. residents will cause increased or decreased demand for goods and services. If income rises, demand increases not only for goods produced by U.S. firms, but also for foreign goods and services—Swedish automobiles and travel in Asia, for example. More imports will increase the supply of dollars. And lower income in foreign countries will lessen demand for U.S. exports and thus demand for dollars. By affecting demand and supply of dollars, changes in income can affect exchange rates.

---

* Technically, the slope of the supply curve is positive only if the demand by U.S. residents for foreign goods is price elastic (see Chapter 4). We assume for simplicity—and reflecting reality—that the supply curve has its usual positive slope.

In addition, the relative prices of domestic and foreign goods are important factors in international trade. If U.S. computer makers improve their production methods, for example, the price of U.S. computers will fall relative to computers made abroad. This change—reflecting a new comparative advantage—will increase the quantity of computers exported and demand for U.S. dollars. In fact, we expect the price of identical goods traded internationally to be the same in all trading nations, as we noted in Chapter 32. This principle, known as *purchasing power parity*, means that exchange rates should adjust so that equivalent goods are equivalently priced throughout the world.

Suppose that the price of wheat is $3 per bushel in the United States and 12 marks in West Germany. If the exchange rate is 3 marks per dollar, wheat will cost the equivalent of $4 per bushel in West Germany. Because the U.S. price is lower, U.S. exports will rise and imports will decline. Greater U.S. exports increase demand for dollars. Reduced imports decrease supply of dollars. As a result, the price (exchange rate) of a dollar will increase. If the exchange rate rises to 4 marks per dollar, purchasing power parity is restored, so that wheat costs the equivalent of $3 per bushel in both the United States and West Germany. In the real world, of course, U.S. prices would also change, and the adjustment of exchange rates would thus be less. But the basic principle holds true regardless.

Purchasing power parity also suggests that exchange rates adjust to eliminate the effects of different inflation rates—increases in the average price of goods and services—in two nations. If the inflation rate is higher in Japan than in the United States, the prices of Japanese goods will rise relative to U.S. goods. As a result, Japanese exports will fall and foreign imports into Japan will rise. These changes in trade flows mean an increased supply of and a decreased demand for Japanese yen. Consequently, the yen will depreciate. But depreciation of the yen lowers the price of Japanese exports and raises the price of foreign goods to Japanese residents. According to purchasing power parity, the yen will continue to depreciate until the effects of higher inflation have been eliminated.

We want to emphasize several important points about purchasing power parity and the importance of trade flow in determining exchange rates. First, purchasing power parity applies only to the average prices of goods and services traded internationally. Tariffs and other restrictions on trade can prevent parity from being achieved. Second, parity prices change when tastes and preferences or comparative advantage change. And third, the rule of purchasing power parity predicts only general movements in exchange rates over the long run, largely in response to sustained differences in overall prices or inflation rates. To understand short-run changes in exchange rates, you have to consider changes in international capital flows.

Factors that change international capital flows. Foreign investment in the United States and U.S. investment in foreign economies depend largely on real interest rates. Individuals and firms will invest in another country only if they expect to earn more profit than they could by investing the same amount in their own country. Thus if real interest rates in France are 12 percent while U.S. rates are 8 percent, more U.S. businesses will invest in France. To invest they will have to exchange dollars for francs, increasing the supply of dollars in foreign-exchange markets. As a result, the value of the dollar will fall relative to the franc. That is, *when a country's real interest rate is high relative to interest rates in the rest of the world, its currency's value will appreciate.*

Under a system of floating exchange rates, the equilibrium exchange rate is determined by demand for and supply of foreign exchange.

If demand for dollars increases, the exchange rate increases, representing an appreciation of the dollar's value. If supply of dollars increases, the exchange rate decreases, representing a depreciation of the dollar's value.

In the long run, changes in tastes and preferences, income, and relative prices affect demand for and supply of imports and exports and thus demand and supply of currencies.

In the short run, interest rates affect demand for and supply of other nations' financial assets and thus demand for and supply of currencies.

Evidence indicates that as much as $200 billion held by banks, multinational corporations, and wealthy individuals is continually in search of the highest possible short-run return. Because of this so-called "hot money," a change in relative interest rates can result in a substantial change in the international flow of funds. Economists generally believe that international capital flows are the cause of most short-run fluctuations in exchange rates. Thus short-run changes in trade flows (exports and imports) are strongly influenced by changes in exchange rates caused by changes in relative interest rates. For example, many economists believe that high real interest rates in the United States are the reason for the very large trade deficits experienced in the 1980s.

When evaluating potential investments, investors also consider risk. The greater the risk, the higher is the interest rate required by investors. Some economists believe that demand for U.S. financial assets has been relatively strong in recent years because the U.S. government is relatively stable compared to the governments of many nations. There is little risk that a change in the U.S. government will cause the seizure of private firms or property, for example, as has happened in some Third-World nations.

Finally, the return that an investor can expect to receive also depends on expectations of future exchange rates. For example, suppose that investors can choose between a one-year U.S. government bond paying 12 percent interest and a one-year West German government bond paying 5 percent. If investors expect the exchange rate between the two countries to remain steady, funds will flow out of West Germany and into the United States.

But what if the exchange rate is expected to change from an initial value of 4 marks per dollar to 3.75 marks per dollar at the end of one year? If you buy a $1000 bond in the United States, you will have $1120 after one year—your original $1000 plus $120 of interest. Alternatively, you could exchange your $1000 for 4000 marks at the initial exchange rate and buy a West German bond for 4000 marks. In one year, you will have 4200 marks. At the expected exchange rate at that time—3.75 marks per dollar—this amount equals $1120 (4200 marks ÷ 3.75 marks per dollar).

Although the West German bond pays a lower interest rate, each mark that you receive will have increased in value. Part of the return expected from buying the West German bond is the anticipated appreciation of the mark relative to the dollar. Under the current and expected exchange rates, a 5 percent real interest rate in West Germany is equal to a 12 percent interest rate in the United States. Because these interest rates are equivalent, we would not expect any additional capital flows.

Changes in the dollar's value: Historical examples. Recent fluctuations in the value of the dollar show that it has responded to changes in demand and supply. For example, we noted that differences in inflation from nation to nation affect demand for a nation's goods. In 1975–1976, inflation rates were generally lower in the United States than in other countries. As a result, the dollar appreciated in value. From 1977–1979, U.S. inflation rates were relatively high and the value of the dollar depreciated.

Inflation rates are not the only factors that affect demand and supply and thus the value of the dollar. Interest rates are also important. From 1980–1985, U.S. real interest rates were high relative to those in most of the world. The result was a large net capital inflow and appreciation of the dollar. But in 1986–1987, U.S.

interest rates moved closer to those of other countries, in part because of increased belief that the U.S. federal budget deficit would be reduced. As a result, the value of the dollar depreciated again.

Balance of Payments Accounting

To trace the components of the demand for and supply of foreign exchange, economists have developed a system of accounts corresponding to different types of international transactions. Each international transaction leads to a payment either to or by U.S. residents. Thus U.S. imports are matched by payments from U.S. residents. Foreign investments in the United States are matched by payments to U.S. residents. Balances between payments to and from U.S. residents for different types of transactions are the basis for international accounting systems. Thus the accounts are referred to as *balance of payments accounts.*

Balance on current account. The top part of Exhibit 33.4 shows the calculations leading to the **balance on current account** figure. The first line shows exports and imports of economic goods. The difference between exports and imports, shown on the right, is the trade balance. To obtain the balance on goods and services, we also add exports and imports of various services, including transportation and travel. Note that dollars spent by U.S. residents for food and hotels in foreign nations or travel on foreign airlines is counted as an import of foreign services. Just like imports of foreign goods, these transactions result in a supply of dollars to foreign-exchange markets. Even if you pay for your foreign travel with U.S. dollars or traveler's checks, the hotel or restaurant will exchange the dollars into foreign currency.

Another substantial component of current account is income earned on foreign investments. Interest payments that you receive on a bond issued by a French firm and the income Coca-Cola receives from a plant it owns in West Germany are treated as payments for services exported. Both result in a flow of dollars into the United States, just as exported goods do. When Egyptian residents receive interest on U.S. government bonds they hold and when Toyota or Volvo receive income from factories they own in the United States, dollars are supplied to foreign-exchange markets, just as when goods are imported.

The final item in the balance on current account is transfers, including gifts, grants, and foreign aid. Exhibit 33.4 indicates that the United States had a substantial negative trade balance of $147.7 billion in 1986. To some extent this deficit was offset by a surplus of trade in services. But the final balance on current account was still a deficit of over $140 billion.

Note that in balance of payment accounts, transactions that result in a flow of dollars into the U.S. economy (such as exports of goods and services) are shown with a positive sign. Transactions with a negative sign represent flows of dollars out of the economy (such as imports). In terms of demand for and supply of foreign exchange, inflows (positive exchanges) represent demand for dollars by the foreign sector. Outflows (negative exchanges) indicate a supply of dollars by the domestic sector.

Balance on capital account. The bottom part of Exhibit 33.4 shows the calculations leading to the **balance on capital account** figure. Foreign investments in U.S. physical assets—Honda's building of an automobile plant in the United States, for example—are direct foreign investment. These investments,

Balance on current account.
Net exports of goods and services less net transfers (gifts and foreign aid) to foreign residents and foreign governments; a negative balance indicates that imports plus transfers to domestic residents exceed exports plus transfers to foreign residents.

Balance on capital account.
The net flow of funds used to purchase physical and financial assets; a positive balance indicates that purchases of domestic assets by foreigners exceed purchases of foreign assets by domestic residents.

	Demand for U.S. dollars	Supply of U.S. dollars	Balances
Current account transactions:			
Exports of goods	221.8		
Imports of goods		−369.5	
Trade balance			−147.7
Exports of transportation and travel services	31.0		
Imports of transportation and travel services		−41.1	
Income from U.S. investments abroad and other services	117.9		
Income from foreign investments in the U.S. and other services		−85.5	
Balance on goods and services			−125.4
Private and public transfers, net		−15.2	
Balance on current account			−140.6
Capital account transactions:			
Direct foreign investment in U.S.	25.6		
Direct U.S. investment abroad		−31.9	
Foreign financial investment in U.S.	154.3		
U.S. financial investment abroad		−68.2	
Balance on capital account			79.8
Official asset transactions:			
Change in assets of foreign governments	33.4		
Change in assets of U.S. government	0.3		
Balance on official transactions			33.7
Statistical discrepancy			27.1
Balance of payments			0.0

**Exhibit 33.4
Balance of Payments
Accounts, 1986 (in billions
of U.S. dollars)**

Source: U.S. Department of Commerce, *Survey of Current Business,* March 1987 (Table 1-2, p. 44).

along with purchases of U.S. financial assets (such as stocks and bonds), result in an inflow of dollars. They represent a demand for dollars by the foreign sector. Similarly, U.S. investments in foreign physical and financial assets result in an outflow of dollars. Thus they represent a supply of dollars by the domestic sector.

Official asset transactions. Balance of payments accounts also include transactions by U.S. and foreign governments. In 1986 both U.S. and foreign governments added to the demand for dollars. We have more to say about these transactions later in the chapter, since they are more significant under a system in which exchange rates do not adjust freely.

Statistical discrepancies. Under a system of freely floating exchange rates, the market for foreign exchange tends to be in equilibrium. That is, quantity of dollars demanded equals quantity of dollars supplied. From an accounting standpoint, then, the positive and negative totals should always be identical, so the final balance of payments should always be zero. Any one balance—on current account or capital account, for example—may not be zero, but when all are considered together, equilibrium requires that the balance be zero.

Why then do the numbers in Exhibit 33.4 not balance? In the real world, international transactions are difficult to measure precisely. Thus the balance of payments accounts include a final category: the *statistical discrepancy*. This number is simply the amount required to make the quantity of dollars demanded and supplied equal. In this case the statistical discrepancy is shown as a surplus of $27.1 billion, the amount necessary to make the final balance zero.

Note, however, that *equilibrium in the market for dollars does not mean that there will be a balance between exports and imports or between inflows or outflows of capital flows. It does mean that any trade deficit will be offset by a net inflow of investment funds, and that any trade surplus will be matched by a net outflow of investment funds.* Thus, if a nation experiences a net inflow of investment funds, this will be offset by a rising trade deficit—more imports and fewer exports.

Indeed most economists believe that the U.S. trade deficits in the 1980s have been the result of very large inflows of foreign capital attracted by relatively high real interest rates in the United States. The large capital inflow increased demand for U.S. dollars and the value of the dollar. Foreign goods accordingly became relatively inexpensive to U.S. residents and U.S. goods relatively expensive to foreign residents. Thus while an imbalance in current accounts did occur, it was the result of capital flows.

FIXED EXCHANGE-RATE SYSTEMS

So far we have focused on foreign-exchange markets in which exchange rates float freely. In this system, demand and supply are the only forces that determine exchange rates. Indeed, the current international finance system is based largely on floating exchange rates. However, foreign-exchange systems that rely on **fixed (or pegged) exchange rates** have existed in the past and have supporters who suggest their return. In this section, we consider the benefits and costs of two systems that have been used in the past—the gold standard and the Bretton Woods system.

Fixed Rates under the Gold Standard

Fixed (or pegged) exchange rates. A system in which exchange rates are not allowed to adjust in response to changes in demand for and supply of currency.

When nations agree to use a gold standard to fix exchange rates, they must follow three basic rules. First, each country must define its currency in terms of a certain quantity of gold. Second, each country must be willing to buy and sell gold at the fixed price. Third, each country must maintain a fixed ratio between its domestic money supply and its stock of gold. When these three rules are agreed upon and followed, the gold system provides an automatic mechanism for establishing an equilibrium in balance of payments.

(a) Initial equilibrium

(b) Adjustment to equilibrium

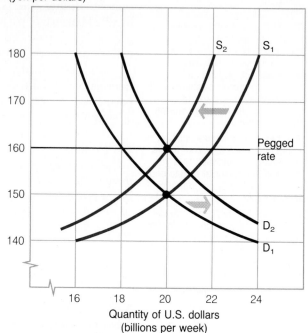

Exhibit 33.5
Equilibrium Adjustments under a Gold Standard
Under a gold standard, every currency exchanges for a fixed quantity of gold. Thus the exchange rate of every currency is fixed or pegged. Part (a) shows the U.S. dollar pegged at 160 yen per dollar, or higher than the equilibrium rate. By the rules of the gold standard, the U.S. government would have to sell $4 billion of gold (equal to the surplus) and, because it owns less gold, reduce the domestic money supply. As the money supply declines, U.S. interest rates rise, spending by U.S. residents falls, and U.S. prices fall. These changes will decrease imports and financial investments in foreign countries, decreasing supply of U.S. dollars (from S_1 to S_2). In addition, exports increase and financial investment in the United States rises, increasing the demand for U.S. dollars (from D_1 to D_2). As a result of these adjustments, a new equilibrium is achieved at the pegged rate of 160 yen per dollar.

Disequilibrium and adjustment under a gold standard. We illustrate the operation of a gold standard in Exhibit 33.5(a). In this market, the equilibrium exchange rate (where D_1 intersects S_1) is 150 yen per dollar. However, the fixed (pegged) rate is 160 yen per dollar. If the United States follows the established rules, it must be willing to buy and sell gold at the pegged price. To eliminate the surplus, the U.S. government will have to sell $4 billion of gold. By selling gold for dollars, the U.S. government will "demand" enough dollars to satisfy quantity supplied at the pegged rate. (In the balance of payments account this would show as part of the official asset transactions of the U.S. government.)

But selling gold is only the first stage in the gold standard's automatic adjustment mechanism. According to the rules, the United States must maintain a fixed ratio between its domestic money supply and its stock of gold. Because it had to sell some gold to cover the surplus of dollars in the foreign-exchange market, the U.S. government must reduce the domestic money supply. With less money available, U.S. residents will demand and consume fewer goods, including imports. Prices of all goods, including exports, will fall. The decrease in the money supply will also cause interest rates to rise, at least temporarily. (Interest rates rise because a decrease in the money supply reduces the supply of loanable funds.)

With more foreign funds flowing into the U.S. economy as foreign residents buy U.S. exports, stocks, and bonds, demand for U.S. dollars rises (to D_2 in Exhibit 33.5b). At the same time, lower imports and smaller outflows of investment funds reduce the supply of dollars (to S_2). Following these changes, the equilibrium exchange rate equals the *pegged rate*, and no further adjustments are necessary. Note that this adjustment mechanism works only if all three rules for a gold standard are followed. The willingness to buy and sell gold at the agreed-on price keeps exchange rates fixed. The strict relationship between the domestic money supply and the quantity of gold held allows the system to adjust to equilibrium. As you will see later in this chapter, when the gold standard was actually used, countries often violated these rules, blocking the automatic adjustment mechanism.

Both floating-rate and gold-standard systems have automatic adjustment mechanisms. In a floating-rate system, exchange rates provide an automatic adjustment mechanism. Under the gold standard, adjustments depend on changes in the domestic money supply, which requires government policy changes.

Advantages and disadvantages of a gold standard.   Proponents of a gold standard point to several advantages. First, when they are uncertain about future exchange rates, businesses face an additional risk (an exchange-rate risk) when engaged in international trade. For example, suppose that a U.S. company contracts to buy steel from a Japanese manufacturer at a price of 420 million yen, with the steel to be delivered and paid for in yen in six months. But what if the exchange rate between the Japanese yen and the U.S. dollar falls from 150 to 140 yen per dollar? The U.S. company, which agreed to the transaction when the price was equivalent to $2.8 million, must now pay $3.0 million for the steel. Because of increased risk, businesses may be less willing to engage in international trade. But exchange-rate risk can be avoided when exchange rates are fixed.

Second, the rules of a gold-standard system automatically restore equilibrium in the foreign-exchange market. Gold-standard proponents argue that, while floating-rate systems also create equilibrium, they do so by allowing currency values to change. Finally, supporters of the gold standard note that fixed rates prevent governments from constantly increasing the money supply. Rapid growth in the money supply will raise the prices of all goods and services; that is, it will cause inflation. Limiting the growth of the money supply can prevent inflation. Any inflation that does occur would not last long, since exports would fall and imports would rise. As a result, the government would have to buy dollars, reducing the money supply and lowering inflation.

Since it has these advantages, why did the trading nations agree to abolish the gold standard? Some critics charge that fixed rates, by limiting money supply, limit a country's ability to stimulate spending in response to economic downturns (recessions). Since increased spending causes increased production and hiring of workers, limits on the money supply may interfere with the macroeconomic goals of economic growth and full employment.

Some opponents of a gold standard also fear that the quantity of gold mined in the world is not enough to allow the money supply to grow in proportion to production. If so, a gold standard would force economies to deflate their currency, that is, to lower overall prices. But this type of adjustment can be slow and requires some unemployment, making the adjustment painful and expensive. The reliance on a single physical resource is another weakness of the gold standard, since a major new discovery of gold would create economic turmoil. Indeed, in the sixteenth century European prices rose dramatically when the Spanish began importing gold from the New World. Other opponents of a gold standard are concerned about the potential economic power that it would give to South Africa and the Soviet Union, the major producers of gold.

The Gold Standard in Practice

Critics of the gold standard find other support in the historical record. Certainly, the last attempt at a gold standard was less than an outstanding success. It began in 1879, when the United States and other major trading nations adopted it. But in 1914, World War I broke out. Nations promptly abandoned the rules for the gold standard, expanding their money supplies in excess of their gold supplies in order to finance the war effort.

Even during its relatively brief existence, the gold standard suffered from a lack of international agreement on acceptable fixed rates. England, for example, wanted a rate for the pound that was too high, that is, likely to cause a continual surplus in the foreign-exchange market. Any attempt to reinstitute a gold standard today would face similar problems. Countries with major international debts favor relatively high prices for their currency, which allows them to repay debts with appreciated currency. Countries to which the debts are owed favor the opposite.

In the years after World War I, some countries (including the United States) continued to follow the rules selectively. Many countries sought to gain a competitive edge in international trade by reducing the price of their currency and by erecting tariff and other trade barriers. The result was international uncertainty and a failure of the automatic mechanism to bring foreign-exchange markets into equilibrium. By the time the Great Depression struck most of the world in the 1930s, the international monetary system was a shambles.

Fixed Exchange Rates under the Bretton Woods System

Near the end of World War II, many nations began planning for the reestablishment of economic order. In 1944, representatives of most of the countries that were heavily involved in international trade met in Bretton Woods, New Hampshire, to establish a new international monetary system based on fixed exchange rates. That system went into effect in 1946 and prevailed until the early 1970s.

Fixed rates and exchange-rate policies. Like the gold standard, the Bretton Woods system established exchange rates in terms of the price of an ounce of gold. The price of gold was set at 12.5 British pounds or 35 U.S. dollars per ounce, implying an exchange rate of 2.80 U.S. dollars per British pound ($35 ÷ £12.5). Under the Bretton Woods system, each country was supposed to set a value for its currency as close to a long-run equilibrium level as possible. If each country's exchange rate remained at or very near this equilibrium rate, the system functioned as intended. A country might run deficits in one period but would run offsetting surpluses in another.

Adjustment to temporary disequilibrium.   The Bretton Woods system, like any fixed-rate system, required a mechanism to respond to changes in demand for and supply of currencies. In a floating-rate system, the exchange rate adjusts. In a gold system, the domestic money supply adjusts. Under the Bretton Woods system, a government was supposed to buy and sell enough of its currency to eliminate any shortages or surpluses that arose. As you learned from the discussion of balance of payments accounting, such official asset transactions can either add to demand or to supply. The Bretton Woods system was based on the assumption that most disequilibriums were only small, temporary deviations from equilibrium. Thus the nations that created the system did not consider making adjustments in the money supply or allowing fluctuations in the exchange rate to be necessary.

Adjustments to "fundamental disequilibrium."   But what happens if a country's currency is pegged above the long-run equilibrium rate? The result will be a continual surplus of currency. A country could not continue to buy its own currency because it would run out of gold or supplies of some other currency with which to buy. (Continuing to respond to a shortage of foreign exchange would not be difficult, of course, unless the supply of paper used to print more money became scarce.)

A country that experienced a long-run surplus or shortage position in the market for its currency was faced with what the Bretton Woods system called a *fundamental imbalance*. That is, demand for and supply of currency were apt to be continually unbalanced. A country facing a long-run surplus (a balance of payments deficit) had three basic options. First, it could impose tariffs, quotas, or other trade restrictions. By reducing imports, the surplus in the foreign-exchange market would fall. However, trade restrictions violated one of the principal objectives of the Bretton Woods agreement: to expand and encourage trade.

A second option for a nation facing a long-run surplus was to decrease its domestic money supply until prices fell and interest rates rose, as under the gold standard. Falling prices increase exports and reduce imports. Higher interest rates attract capital inflows. Demand for the currency will rise, supply will fall, and equilibrium will be restored. However, this type of adjustment sometimes interfered with a nation's domestic economic and political goals. For example, in the 1950s, the United States adhered to the Bretton Woods rules by slowing the growth rate of the money supply in order to keep the surplus of dollars in the foreign-exchange market from worsening. But in doing so, the government restricted the nation's ability to expand its production and caused higher unemployment.

As a last resort, a nation with a continuing currency surplus might choose **devaluation**, or a reduction of its fixed exchange rate. (Do not confuse devaluation with depreciation. Devaluation is a deliberate, planned reduction in a fixed rate. Depreciation is the natural result of adjustments in a floating-rate system.) Under the Bretton Woods system, devaluation was generally forced by high inflation caused by a government's failure to control its domestic money supply.

Advantages and disadvantages of the Bretton Woods system.   Many of the arguments for and against the Bretton Woods system are like those for and against the gold standard. In theory, both are fixed-rate systems. And if countries adjust their macroeconomic policies when there is a fundamental disequilibrium,

Devaluation. A deliberate, planned reduction in the exchange rate under a system of fixed exchange rates.

both systems can reduce the likelihood of inflation. But when official rates are out of line, there are incentives to create black markets. In Brazil and Argentina, the black market is so well established that the "unofficial" black-market exchange rate is published in the newspapers.

Moreover, as with the gold standard, participating nations often broke the rules of the Bretton Woods system when it served their domestic economic or political purposes. As a result, exchange rates were not really fixed and speculation about future devaluations often created major problems. For example, in the early 1970s, persistent surpluses indicated that the U.S. exchange rate was too high for long-run equilibrium. Those who expected the United States to devalue the dollar because of this problem began to sell large amounts of dollars in foreign-exchange markets. This increase in the supply of dollars pushed the market into a greater surplus position. Such speculation worsened the problem and eventually caused the system to collapse.

President Nixon twice devalued the dollar, first in 1971 and again in 1973, but these actions did not solve the problem. This failure by one of the major trading nations led to the breakdown of the Bretton Woods system. By 1973 several countries had abandoned the attempt to maintain a fixed rate for their currency, preferring instead to allow the currencies to float. The system ended because it was not possible to maintain a system of fixed exchange rates when the foreign-exchange markets were very unstable. The required adjustments in macroeconomic policies were considered politically, if not economically, undesirable.

The Current International Monetary System

After the devaluation of 1973, the Nixon administration decided to allow the dollar to float, and many other nations followed suit. However, the current system is not totally a freely floating system. First, some countries, notably some Third-World nations, still maintain fixed exchange rates in terms of the dollar or some other currency. Second, the United States, Japan, the United Kingdom, West Germany, and France have agreed to let governments intervene in foreign-exchange markets to smooth out minor changes in demand or supply. As a result, the current system is often termed a *managed-float system*.

In fact, balance of payments data indicate that governments intervene extensively in foreign-exchange markets, buying and selling currencies. In 1985, representatives of the United States, France, West Germany, Japan, and the United Kingdom agreed to encourage depreciation in the value of the dollar. These countries subsequently intervened in foreign-exchange markets, selling dollars and buying other currencies to accomplish this task. In the short run, this intervention did cause the dollar to depreciate. However, many economists suggest that intervention is not effective in the long run and cannot substitute for changes in basic economic policies.

Some supporters of the Bretton Woods system were concerned that a floating-rate system would stifle trade, but these fears proved to be groundless. Exchange rates have fluctuated more under this system than they did when rates were pegged. And the rise of oil prices in the late 1970s did cause some uncertainty in the foreign-exchange market. But international trade has generally increased since the floating-rate system was adopted. The seeming success of the current system has won the support of most economists although some still fear that fluctuations may be excessive. Most of the controversy now centers on whether a fixed exchange-rate system—a gold standard, for example—might be a useful way to control money supply growth and hence inflation. But support for this position is not widespread among economists, and few politicians will concede national control of the money supply.

CONCLUSION

In this chapter we considered various ways of determining exchange rates and noted the changing attitudes toward fixed-rate and floating-rate systems. But not all countries are part of the current floating-rate system. Those who manage planned economies—such as that of the Soviet Union—have vastly different views on exchange rates. And, as noted, some Third-World nations continue to use fixed rates.

In Chapter 34 we consider some of the distinctive features of planned economies and less-developed nations. These economies not only provide an interesting contrast to the developed market economies on which we have focused thus far, but they also have a major effect on the U.S. economy.

SUMMARY

1. In this chapter we considered the meaning and determination of exchange rates in both floating-rate and fixed-rate systems. We also explored some of the advantages and drawbacks of these approaches.

2. An exchange rate expresses the price of one currency in terms of another. A change in the exchange rate also results in a change in the relative prices of goods and services in the two countries. If the exchange rate of one currency rises relative to another currency, the rising currency is said to appreciate and the other currency to depreciate. When a nation's currency appreciates, we can expect its exports to fall and its imports to rise. When its currency depreciates, we can expect its exports to rise and its imports to fall.

3. Every international exchange leads to demand for or supply of currency in foreign-exchange markets. To pay for U.S. exports, foreigners demand dollars. To pay for foreign imports, U.S. residents supply dollars. When foreigners buy U.S. physical or financial assets, they demand dollars. When U.S. residents buy foreign physical or financial assets, they supply dollars.

4. Under a system of floating exchange rates, the interaction of demand and supply determines the rate. Foreign residents seeking to buy U.S. goods and services or U.S. physical or financial assets demand dollars while supplying foreign currencies. And U.S. residents seeking to buy foreign goods and services or foreign physical or financial assets supply dollars while demanding foreign currencies. Demand and supply forces will automatically eliminate currency surpluses and shortages.

5. Changes in tastes and preferences, income, and relative prices of goods and services affect international trade and thus demand and supply of currencies in the long run. Relative real interest rates affect financial capital flows and hence short-run demand and supply of currencies.

6. Balance of payments accounting reflects demand for and supply of foreign exchange. The trade balance is the difference between dollars demanded to purchase U.S. exports and dollars supplied to purchase foreign imports. The balance on capital account is the difference between dollars demanded to purchase U.S. physical and financial assets and dollars supplied to purchase foreign assets. When government asset transactions are also considered, the *net* balance should be zero (except for any statistical discrepancy) because we expect the foreign-exchange market to reach equilibrium.

7. A gold standard is an international monetary system in which three rules are followed: (a) each country fixes the price of gold in terms of its currency; (b) each country is willing to buy or sell gold at the fixed price; and (c) each country maintains a fixed ratio between the domestic supply of money and its stock of gold. Shortages and surpluses in the market for foreign exchange force a government to adjust its domestic money supply, which restores equilibrium at the fixed rate.

8. The Bretton Woods system also involved fixed rates but had no automatic adjustment mechanism. Temporary shortages and surpluses were to be offset with official government purchases or sale of currency. Long-term

shortages and surpluses were to be offset with changes in domestic money supplies. Instead, many countries chose to devalue their currency rather than change fiscal and monetary policies when faced with long-run "fundamental disequilibrium."

9. Proponents of fixed-rate systems believe that international trade is stimulated as uncertainty about future exchange rates is reduced. They also believe that fixed rates reduce the chance of inflation. The gold system also has an automatic adjustment mechanism. Floating-rate proponents point to difficulties in establishing and maintaining fixed rates, especially when the system requires governments to control their domestic money supplies. They observe that, in practice, rates do not remain fixed for very long and that even a gold standard requires government action, while the automatic adjustment mechanism in a floating-rate system does not.

KEY TERMS

Exchange rate, 846
Currency appreciation, 847
Currency depreciation, 847
Flexible (or freely floating) exchange rates, 849
Balance on current account, 853
Balance on capital account, 853
Fixed (or pegged) exchange rates, 855
Devaluation, 859

QUESTIONS FOR REVIEW AND DISCUSSION

1. The early economists (known as mercantilists) believed that a nation's wealth would be increased if it held more gold.
   a) What trade policies do you believe the mercantilists would recommend (recognizing that during their time, a nation that imported more than it exported had to pay out gold to cover the difference)?
   b) Why are present-day economists critical of the mercantilists?
   c) Under a system of floating exchange rates, what happens when a country exports more than it imports (including the "export" of financial capital used to purchase foreign assets)?

2. Answer the following questions to show your understanding of exchange rates.
   a) If the exchange rate between the Japanese yen and the U.S. dollar is 200 yen per dollar, what is the exchange rate between the dollar and the yen?
   b) If the exchange rate between the U.S. dollar and the Swedish krona is $0.12 per krona, how much will a

U.S. resident have to pay for a Volvo priced at 150,000 krona? How much will a Swedish firm have to pay (in krona) for a U.S. machine priced at $27,000?
   c) If a case of French wine costs either $75.00 or 525 francs, what is the exchange rate between the franc and the dollar (expressed as francs per dollar)?

3. The following table shows the approximate exchange rate of the U.S. dollar in terms of the West German mark for four years.

Year	Marks per dollar	Dollars per mark
1968	4.0	
1978	2.0	
1983	2.5	
1987	1.8	

   a) Calculate the exchange rate of the mark in terms of the dollar for each year.
   b) In which period(s) did the dollar depreciate? What happened to the mark at the same time?
   c) How much would a West German automobile priced at 30,000 marks cost in dollars in each year? How much would a U.S. automobile priced at $15,000 cost in marks in each year?
   d) What might explain the change in the exchange rate from 1968 to 1978? From 1978 to 1983? From 1983 to 1987?
   e) In any issue of the Wall Street Journal you can find the current exchange rate of the mark. Look up the most recent rate you can find. Has the mark appreciated or depreciated since 1987? What might explain why?

4. Perhaps you have heard someone refer to the existence of a balance of payments "problem." In the context of a system of fixed rates, what do you suppose this means? What meaning, if any, could it have under a system of floating rates?

5. Suppose that you could set the exchange rate of the U.S. dollar against other foreign currencies at any level you wanted to.
   a) What are the advantages and disadvantages of a higher rate? Of a lower rate?
   b) Could you determine a "best" rate? Why or why not?
   c) What changes occur as a country's currency depreciates?

6. What effect would each of the following changes have on the exchange rate of the U.S. dollar, that is, its price in terms of the Japanese yen? (Express each as a change in demand for and/or supply of currency.)
   a) Improved quality of U.S. consumer goods.
   b) Higher real interest rates in Japan.
   c) Reducing the growth rate of the U.S. money supply.

d) Increased foreign aid on the part of the U.S. government (included as part of net transfers).

e) An increase in the number of Japanese tourists to the United States.

7. Explain how each change in Question 6 would affect (a) the balance on current account and (b) the balance on capital account.

8. In the early 1980s the U.S. dollar appreciated against the Japanese yen and other major currencies.
   a) What reasons might account for this change? (Check them against facts that you can find in a recent *Employment Report of the President*.)
   b) Why were some analysts concerned about the effects of the "strong" dollar on the U.S. economy?
   c) What options would the U.S. government have for dealing with this "problem"?
   d) What ramifications did the U.S. dollar's appreciation have for Latin American countries (such as Argentina and Brazil) with large foreign debts that had to be paid in U.S. dollars?
   e) What factors could have caused the dollar to depreciate since 1985? (Check your answers against facts that you can find in a recent *Employment Report of the President*.)

9. In recent years several Asian economies—Taiwan, South Korea, and Hong Kong—have closely tied their currencies to the U.S. dollar, in effect, fixing the exchange rate.
   a) What are the advantages to those countries of fixing the exchange rate relative to the dollar?
   b) Would they be better off fixing the value of their currency at a high or low value relative to the dollar? Why?
   c) What are the disadvantages of fixing rates? (Note especially the effects on the economy of having a rate that is too high and one that is too low.)

10. Large U.S. trade deficits in the 1980s coincided with large capital inflows into the U.S. economy.
    a) What are the major causes of the inflows of foreign capital? (Economists do not agree, so you should give several possible explanations, indicating the logic supporting each.)
    b) Why do many observers believe that inflows of foreign capital are a potential problem for the U.S. economy? (Explain what problems may arise and why.)
    c) The United States also received a large quantity of foreign capital in the nineteenth century. In contrast to the current situation, however, inflows of foreign capital in the nineteenth century were seen as useful, not as a problem. What is different about current inflows and those in the last century?

Economic Encounters
Third-World Debt: Can It Ever Be Repaid?

Less-developed countries (LDCs) of the Third World are up to their necks in foreign debt—by some estimates as much as $1 trillion worth. About half of this debt is owed by Latin American countries—especially Brazil, Mexico, Argentina, and Venezuela—and much of the foreign debt is owed to banks in the United States. Not only have these countries not reduced their debt, many have had to resort to additional borrowing just to meet scheduled interest payments. Just how did these countries get into this mess, and where will the debt crisis lead?

increased relative to the currencies of the LDCs. Together, these events raised the real burden of the LDC debt.

At the same time, the ability to service the debt fell. The growth rate of the LDCs fell in the early 1980s. Moreover, slow growth in the industrialized countries and the worldwide recession in 1982 also dramatically reduced the demand for LDCs' exports. Exports of the large Latin American

Why So Much Debt? Foreign borrowing is helpful to less-developed countries (LDCs) if used to finance projects that add to the economy's potential output. The consequent growth in income allows the debt to be repaid and the standard of living increased. But the buildup of debt to large-scale proportions in the 1970s was largely attributable to the oil price shocks that hit the world in 1973 and 1979. Oil-importing LDCs (Brazil, for example) increased their debt from $4 billion in 1973 to $15 billion in 1974. The second shock in 1979 raised their debt to the $50-billion level. Higher oil prices encouraged some oil-exporting LDCs (Mexico, for example) to borrow. Initially, such borrowing was used to finance the development of oil production. However, some LDCs also borrowed against expected future oil receipts to diversify and broaden their industrial base.

This initial borrowing did significantly increased the debt of these countries but did not create a debt crisis. Indeed, most of the heavy borrowers also were experiencing substantial economic growth—an average of 4.7 percent per year for LDCs compared with 2.5 percent for industrial countries over the 1973 to 1982 period. Moreover, exports in Brazil, Argentina, Mexico, and Venezuela grew by 17.5 percent per year between 1973 and

IMF restrictions angered Brazilian workers, who took to the streets to protest stiff wage cuts. (Abril Editoria/Gamma-Liaison)

1982. With rapid economic growth and relatively low interest rates, the ability of the LDCs to repay was growing faster than the increase in debt payments. But changes in the economic environment in the early 1980s highlighted the inherent risks of the debt both to the lenders and the LDCs.

The Debt Crisis Emerges Much of the LDC debt—and a very large percentage of the debt of Mexico, Argentina, and Brazil—is owed to U.S. banks and is tied to U.S. interest rates. Between the end of 1977 and the end of 1980, U.S. interest rates rose from just over 6 percent to almost 15 percent. Moreover, the value of the U.S. dollar

borrowers—Brazil, Argentina, Mexico, and Venezuela—fell by almost 12 percent in 1982. Mexico and Venezuela, both of which rely heavily on oil exports, experienced a severe shock as oil prices dropped sharply in the mid-1980s.

Although an important part of the debt crisis can be blamed on external factors, poor internal economic policies in the LDCs also contributed to the problems. Inflationary macroeconomic policies and artificially high exchange rates strongly encouraged imports while reducing the quantity of exports. Moreover, high inflation and an uncertain economic environment discouraged both local and foreign investment and encouraged "capital flight." That is, individuals with savings preferred to store their wealth in foreign banks and buy stocks of foreign businesses. Finally, in some cases the funds borrowed were squandered—used to finance poorly designed projects, make political payoffs, or subsidize inefficient government enterprises.

What Can Be Done? The LDCs appear to be increasingly frustrated by the burdens of debt and the consequences of that debt on their economies. Most of the largest borrowers have at one time or another threatened to default. In 1985 Peru announced that it would not limit debt payments to 10 percent of its export revenues. In 1987 Brazil announced that it would suspend all payments until a more acceptable debt package was negotiated. But is default the only way out?

The ideal solution to the debt crisis is fast growth in the LDCs. But the LDCs cannot grow unless they can sell more exports, especially to the industrialized economies. Thus macroeconomic and trade policies in the industrialized economies are important. If the industrialized economies grow slowly or impose trade barriers, the debt crisis will likely continue. Moreover, restrictive monetary policies in the industrialized economies also keep real interest rates high, thereby adding to the burden of existing debt.

Many observers note that LDCs will require additional foreign financing to enable them to make the investments in plant and equipment—and in

---

Much of the LDC debt is owed to U.S. banks and is tied to U.S. interest rates.

---

education and training—that are essential to growth. This new financing need not create a new concern as long as the exports grow fast enough to enable the LDCs to service and eventually repay both the old and the new debt.

But to stand eventually on their own, the LDCs must be able to gener-

ate funds for investment without relying as heavily on foreign borrowing. This will require the discipline to adopt appropriate macroeconomic policies to set a climate for profitable investment, thereby reducing capital flight and encouraging direct foreign investment.

To some extent, LDCs have made attempts to restore order to their economies—with mixed results. Virtually all the debtor nations have, at one time or another, tried the traditional austerity measures suggested by the International Monetary Fund (IMF). The largest Latin American borrowers cut imports by an average of 50 percent from 1981–1983. Some made bold attempts to reduce the size of government budget deficits and to cut monetary growth rates to slow inflation.

But these traditional remedies are often painful. Imports of capital resources were significantly reduced as were public investments in education and training. In 1986 investment in Brazil was 30 percent lower than in 1981; in Argentina it was 50 percent less. While there may be useful short-run policies, they may also jeopardize future economic growth. Moreover, the traditional remedies are contractionary, causing higher unemployment and lower real wages. Such measures often result in large-scale political protests.

Many economists argue that additional foreign funds are needed to generate economic growth in the LDCs. But they also recognize that it is desirable for much of this financing to come from direct foreign investment, not more borrowing. To attract this investment and to reverse capital flight, the LDCs will have to use appropriate macroeconomic policies, avoiding rapid inflation and economic instability.

The debt burden could also be lowered through so-called "debt-equity swaps." Under these schemes, a private business buys LDC debt from a bank and exchanges it for local currency, which it uses to acquire a factory and equipment in the LDC. As a result, the LDC gets new foreign investment and reduces its outstanding loans. Al-

though these swaps have benefits, they are not without costs. Unless the foreign business actually constructs a new factory, there is no net addition to the LDC's capital resources, but merely a

---

The ideal solution to the debt crisis is fast growth in the LDCs.

---

new owner. If the government simply prints new money to buy back its loan, the increase in the money supply will be inflationary. Moreover, as some LDCs note, the net result of these swaps is that foreign businesses acquire a larger stake in their economies.

Should the debt simply be forgiven? After all, at least a part of the buildup can be attributed to policies in the industrialized countries, and much of the debt will not be repaid, anyway. Critics of this policy argue that it creates a bad precedent. If all LDCs decided they wanted forgiveness, the transfer of wealth would be substantial. Moreover, the LDCs will continue to depend on foreign financing. What country or private bank would want to make future loans if there was a high probability that such ventures would turn out to be worthless?

Muddling Through the Crisis Outside of the worst cases (largely confined to some of the African nations), the LDC debtors have managed to continue to pay at least a part of the required interest payments on their debt. Some economists are optimistic that the LDCs will be able to muddle through this crisis if they are given the necessary temporary financing and if they make the necessary policy adjustments to strengthen their economies. These economists believe that future growth in the LDCs will eventually enable repayment of most of the debt. In the meantime, these countries remain highly vulnerable to events, many of which are not under their control. Muddling through may eventually work, but the potential for continued crises continues.

Comparative Economic Systems and Economic Development

QUESTIONS TO CONSIDER

☐ What features distinguish a market capitalist economic system from a planned socialist economic
  system?

☐ Which system is superior?

☐ How well has the planned socialist system worked
  for the Soviet Union?

☐ What features characterize the economies of the
  less-developed countries?

☐ How might these nations improve the economic
  well-being of their citizens?

Throughout this textbook we have concentrated on the economy of the
United States. Most of what you have learned directly applies to the
economies of Western Europe and Japan. But the economies of the Soviet
Union, China, and Eastern Europe—representing about one-third of the world's
population—are vastly different. As we noted in Chapter 1, these are planned
socialist economies, not the market capitalist economies with which you are now
familiar. In the first part of this chapter we explore the differences between these
two types of economic systems in more detail and the operation of the Soviet
Union's economy specifically.

In addition, nearly three-fourths of the world's population lives in countries
with significantly less industry and lower standards of living than either the United
States or the Soviet Union. As you will see in the second part of this chapter, these
nations share certain common problems that have caused them to be less developed. A wide variety of economic strategies have been proposed to strengthen
the economies of these countries.

MARKET CAPITALISM VERSUS PLANNED SOCIALISM

In Chapter 1 we noted that in market capitalist economies, most resources are
privately owned. In planned socialist economies, most resources are owned by
the government. As you have seen throughout this textbook, the interaction of
demand and supply determines how resources are allocated in market economies.
In planned socialist economies, central government agencies make allocation and
distribution decisions. That is, the "invisible hand" of markets is replaced by the
"visible hand" of government planning.

In this section, we describe "pure" models of market capitalism and planned
socialism. In the real world, of course, no economy fits either model perfectly.
However, as Exhibit 34.1 shows, the economy of Hong Kong is very close to pure
market capitalism and that of Albania is very close to pure socialism. Although the
U.S. economy is close to pure market capitalism, the role of government is very

Exhibit 34.1
Range of Economic Systems
Real-world economies utilize a mixture of capitalism and socialism, of market operations and planning. This exhibit indicates that the economies of Hong Kong and the United States closely resemble market capitalism. At the other extreme, the economies of Albania, the Soviet Union, and China closely resemble planned socialism. France, Sweden, and the United Kingdom utilize more planning and government ownership than does the United States, but less than do China and the Soviet Union.

significant. But planning and state ownership are much more important in France and the United Kingdom. However, recent sales of some state-owned enterprises in both countries have moved those economies closer to market capitalism.

The economies of both the Soviet Union and China are close to pure planned socialism. But recent changes in both countries have increased the importance of the private sector and quantity of goods sold in markets. Not all countries fit neatly into these categories. For example, Yugoslavia actually combines heavy reliance on markets with government ownership. Nevertheless, most nations fit one of the two patterns closely enough for economists to make some useful predictions based on these models.

Moreover, you should bear in mind that the pure forms of these economic systems reflect the ideals held by the nations that utilize them. For example, although the economy of the United States may fall short of being a pure market capitalist economy, many economists and politicians in this country believe that system to be the ideal. They argue for minimal government intervention in the economy and for limiting government activities to those that help markets to function better. In the Soviet Union, the situation is reversed. Although that country's economy has some capitalistic elements, they are considered to be less desirable economic options than is a centralized, planned approach.

Market Capitalism and Planned Socialism: A Comparison

Exhibit 34.2 shows the basic characteristics of market capitalism and planned socialism. These systems represent two very different methods of answering the fundamental economic questions of what, how, and for whom to produce. In this section, we consider three additional questions: Who sets an economy's goals? Who decides how to meet those goals? And what incentives do individuals have to make the system work?

Setting goals. The basic goal of any economic system is to satisfy society's wants. We have defined this goal as allocative efficiency: producing the mix of goods and services that yields the greatest satisfaction. In a market economy, however, the goal is often more specifically stated as satisfying *individual* wants. Markets can aid in achieving this goal by providing the goods and services most in demand (within the limits of technology and resource supplies).

In planned socialist economies, collective wants are deemed more important than individual wants, although they could be the same. Central government planners decide what the economy will produce, even though that may not be the mix of goods and services that satisfies the most individual wants. Preferences are established by central planners, with no specific reference to the preferences of individuals.

Every economic system, whatever its goals, must have good information on which to base activities to achieve those goals. Decision makers must know the relative availability of resources and the relative wants of society. In market capitalism, decision makers rely on prices to signal changes in the relative scarcity of resources and changes in relative wants. Businesses do not have to collect information about total demand or supply—prices tell them what and how to produce. However, when market failures occur—external benefits and costs, for example—prices may not be completely satisfactory guides.

When government planners set goals with little regard for individual wants, they do not require information on consumer demand. They must, however, determine the resources they have for meeting the goals they have set. Thus to plan for the economy as a whole, government officials must know a great deal about the quantities of resources available and the capacities of plants and farms. Central planners must collect this information from the thousands of factories and farms in that country. They must then consolidate the information and analyze it.

Meeting goals. Every economy has limited resources and must decide how to allocate resources to produce the goods and services desired. In a market capitalist economy, resource ownership is largely private. Thus most decisions about what and how to produce and how much to invest are made by private businesses. But profit-seeking businesses are guided by market demand which reflects the preferences of households. And individuals have a lot of freedom to decide where and how much to work. As a result, economic decision making is highly decentralized in a market economy. Although government regulations influence these decisions, ultimately individuals decide what will be produced.

In planned socialist economies, government owns most of the nonhuman resources. Government planners allocate those resources and set goals for the managers of production facilities. Individual choice about where and how much

Exhibit 34.2
Characteristics of
Economic Systems

Type of economic system	Who owns most resources?	Who makes most economic decisions?	How is information acquired?
Market capitalism	Households	Households and business managers	Prices signal changes in wants and resource scarcity
Planned socialism	Government	Government planners	Planners determine preferences and collect information on available resources

to work is often severely limited. Thus there is little room for individual consumer wants to influence basic decisions about what is produced.

Incentives to meet economic goals. Regardless of the economic system, many decisions will be made by individuals, either as business managers or workers. Even in a centrally planned economy, workers must decide how hard to work, and managers must translate centrally established goals and plans into goods and services produced. For an economic system to work, individuals must have some incentive to make it work.

In market capitalism, incentives are basically material. Individual choices about where to work, how much to work, and what occupations to choose are heavily influenced by expected incomes. Profits provide the incentives for producers to satisfy consumer demand in the most technically efficient manner possible. Workers and managers in planned socialism are also influenced to some extent by material rewards. But those who control most planned economies attempt to minimize income differentials. As a result, they reduce material incentives to some extent. In the real world, most such economies have experienced severe shortages of consumer goods. The incentive to earn greater income is less when individuals have few ways to use income to improve their standard of living.

How Well Do the Two Systems Work?

In the preceding discussion, we highlighted how the two systems might operate in theory. In practice, neither system operates without problems. Market capitalist economies have experienced high unemployment and unstable prices. Planned socialist economies have had more stable prices and employment, but have often lacked innovation and efficiency.

In short, there is no simple answer to which system is better. It may be fairest to say that each system has advantages in meeting its own goals. History has shown that market economies are better able to meet individuals' demand for goods and services. But some planned economies—most notably that of the U.S.S.R.—have been successful in meeting their goal of high economic growth. However, by allocating a high percentage of resources to capital resources, they have not met as many demands for consumer goods and services. And many Third-World nations that have chosen planned socialism have not experienced the hoped-for growth. Indeed, the failures of planned socialist economies outnumber the successes.

A comparison of real economies is very complicated. The type of economic system is only one of many factors that determine economic outcomes. A nation's supplies of natural resources, labor, and capital also influence the goals it can set and meet. For example, China and the Soviet Union have lower GNP per capita than the United States. But to what extent is a lower GNP per capita the result of different economic systems? Perhaps the best way to discuss the issues involved is to consider the pros and cons of each system from the perspective of their proponents.

Views of proponents of market capitalism. Proponents of market capitalism see the difficulty of gathering accurate information on an entire economy's resources (and wants, if consumer goods and services are to be produced) as a great weakness of planned socialism. As a result, they argue, planners may not respond appropriately to changes in relative scarcity and wants. In contrast,

RECAP

In market capitalism most resources are privately owned and markets are the principal mechanism that determine resource allocation.

In planned socialism most resources are collectively owned and central plans are the principal mechanism that determine resource allocation.

Proponents of market capitalism believe that markets are the most efficient way of providing information; that profits and income create the best incentives; and that decentralized economic power leads to the greatest amount of individual freedom.

Proponents of planned socialism believe that capitalism concentrates economic power; that the drive for maximum profits creates inequities; and that central planning can reduce unemployment and increase economic growth.

prices determined in smoothly functioning markets communicate nearly all the information necessary to ensure efficient responses.

Similarly, they argue that planned economies provide few incentives for individuals to help the economy reach its goals, let alone to innovate. Market economies—through higher incomes and profits—provide these incentives. Thus market economies automatically promote allocative and technical efficiency. Finally, supporters of market capitalism argue that it is the economic system most consistent with political and economic freedom. Concentrating power in the hands of central government planners, on the other hand, is more consistent with authoritarian control. Thus market capitalism promotes equity.

Views of proponents of planned socialism. Proponents of planned socialism believe that market capitalism often concentrates economic power in the hands of a few wealthy individuals. As a result, they argue, it creates major inequalities and inequities that can be only partially remedied through public redistribution policies. In their quest for maximum profits, businesses tend to create undesirable working conditions. Socialism eliminates unequal ownership of property and can put worker safety ahead of profits. Thus planned socialism promotes equity.

Further, they charge that because wealth and income are unequally distributed in market economies, resources are not used to meet society's most important wants. Price instability and high unemployment cause economic waste (as well as human hardship). By focusing on fulfilling the wants of the broader society (not individual desires for more chrome on their cars, for example) and avoiding unemployment and price fluctuations, central planners make better use of a country's resources. Thus planned socialism promotes allocative and technical efficiency.

In summary, the proponents of each system conclude that theirs is more efficient and equitable. Their conclusions, however, involve many value judgments, especially in the argument over equity. Because of the normative aspects of these positions, economists will always disagree about which system is "best." However, other disagreements arise when a theoretical model of one system is compared with real-world examples of the other. In such a contest, the model wins every time. After all, theoretical models are designed to describe the operation of an ideal system. If you are to make valid comparisons of economic systems, you should learn something about the operation of a real planned economy. Thus in the next section, we consider how the Soviet Union's economy functions.

ECONOMY OF THE SOVIET UNION

In the Soviet Union, as in any centrally planned socialist economy, the government owns and controls most resources and the vast majority of output is produced by public enterprises.* Most economic activity is directed according to a centrally determined and administered plan. As a real-world economy (not a model), it has had both failures and successes. Moreover, the Soviet system is a product of its

* Although the Soviet Union is often called a communist country, it does not meet the definition of Communism set down by Karl Marx: "From each according to ability, to each according to need." Rather, it fits the socialist definition: "From each according to ability, to each according to contribution." While some socialists argue that socialism requires a free discussion of public wants—which is not characteristic of Soviet life—most economists describe the economy of the U.S.S.R. as socialist.

history. In many ways, it still operates as it did in the 1930s. To try to understand it, we have to examine its historical roots. Then we can consider the centralized planning function as it now operates and some of the problems the system has encountered. Finally, we will attempt to draw some basic conclusions about the Soviet economy.

Early History of the Soviet Economy

In 1917 when the communists seized control of the Russian government, the economy was a disaster. Russia lagged behind most of Western Europe in industrialization and had a very inefficient system of agriculture. World War I and the revolution brought further economic chaos. The country's new rulers abolished much of the old economic order. But preoccupied with eliminating political opposition to their government, they did not replace it with a new economic system until 1928. At that time the Soviet government issued its first Five Year Plan but with little idea of how a planned socialist economy might operate. Nevertheless, they plunged ahead, developing the theory and practice as they went along.

The first economic plan called for nationalization of industry and agriculture, both of which were to be controlled by a central plan. Moreover, in line with the priorities of communist leader Joseph Stalin, the plan called for a massive transfer of resources from agriculture to heavy industry. Stalin believed that industrialization was necessary both for economic development and increased military strength. The plan called for the Soviet economy to become as independent and self-sufficient as possible. At that time the Soviets had the only socialist economy in the world and felt (correctly, no doubt) that they had few allies on which to depend.

The essential objectives of this first economic plan remain a part of Soviet planning even today. First priority is given to industry, both to increase economic capacity and to provide military goods. Agriculture is valued, but has been a consistent problem. Expansion of farming into marginal lands in the 1950s and 1960s was designed to boost total output, but production has been erratic, with massive crop failures in some years. While these failures may be good news to U.S. farmers (because of increased exports), they have caused difficulties for the Soviet economy. Finally, consumer goods receive the lowest priority. In Stalin's earliest years, per capita consumption actually fell. Even now, consumer goods are scarcer than in many market economies.

Because of its emphasis on investment in heavy industry, however, the Soviet economy achieved very high rates of growth from 1928 until World War II broke out in 1939. According to official Soviet statistics, the annual growth rate averaged nearly 15 percent. Western observers calculate the growth more conservatively: somewhere in the range of 5–12 percent per year. But even 5 percent per year growth is remarkable. Few countries ever achieve that rate of growth over such an extended period of time. (By contrast, the U.S. growth rate in the 1960s—considered to be a strong growth period—was less than 4 percent per year.) In addition, the Soviet Union's rapid economic growth was achieved while the rest of the world was experiencing the Great Depression.

Developing the Economic Plan

Neither the overall Soviet economic priorities nor the basic structure of the Soviet economy has changed much over the years. Since the 1930s, it has been

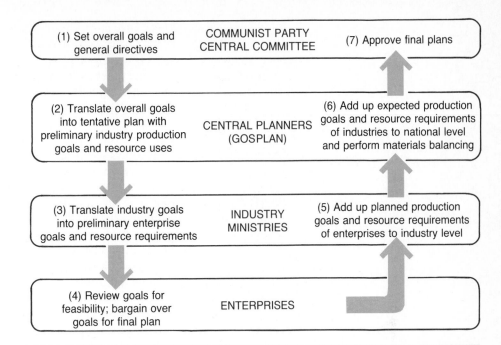

**Exhibit 34.3
Economic Planning
Process in the
Soviet Union**

tightly controlled by a central plan. Exhibit 34.3 provides a simplified version of the Soviet economic planning process.* Overall economic goals are set by the Communist Party's Central Committee (the top officials in the Communist Party). The goals specify how much to allocate to production of consumption goods, how much to invest in capital goods, and which industries to expand and which to reduce. At this level, however, few details are provided.

The next step of the process involves the central planning bureaucracy, in particular the agency known as Gosplan. This group is responsible for converting the goals into operational plans. It establishes preliminary production quotas, or targets, and allocates resources by industry. The size of the planning task is enormous. The Soviet economy produces an estimated 20 million different products. The central plan actually covers *only* a few thousand items. Even so, most planning at this level is done by product groups—molded plastic or shoes, for example. Many different products are included in each group, but centralized planning on a more detailed level would be impossible.

The preliminary central plan is submitted to the Industrial Ministries—a group of planning agencies—each of which is responsible for a particular industry. (In some cases, Regional Ministries rather than Industrial Ministries are involved because production of certain items—such as consumer goods and housing—is organized geographically. The principles remain the same, however.) Ministry planners translate industry goals into plans or production targets for each "enterprise"—the Soviet equivalent of a firm. Enterprise managers review the plans, noting whether all necessary supplies have been allocated.

---

*An organizational chart that accurately displayed all elements in just the central planning system would fill a large wall poster. See, for example, Paul K. Cook, "The Political Setting," in *Soviet Economy in the 1980s: Problems and Prospects*. Washington, D.C.: U.S. Government Printing Office, 1983, selected papers submitted to the Joint Economic Committee, 97th Congress, 2nd session, part 1, pp. 18–21.

Although managers do not have any ultimate authority, their influence can be significant. Because they are evaluated on whether they meet the targets assigned to them in the plan, managers and ministers alike try to obtain more supplies and lower production quotas. Central planners in the Soviet Union, however, tend to drive hard bargains and planning is generally tight. The final plan is then submitted to political authorities for approval, ending the planning process.

Materials balancing. The central plan establishes targets for production, investment, and costs. But the critical element is the plan for *materials balancing*: allocating resources so as to achieve the desired level of output. In the Soviet Union, Gosplan is responsible for ensuring that resources required by industries to meet their planned output goals are available to them. There are three sources of resources: (1) existing supplies; (2) supplies produced during the period; and (3) imports.

As the final plan begins to take shape, Gosplan calculates the total sources and uses of each resource. It is possible that they will balance, but usually, Gosplan must adjust sources and/or uses. Because the Soviets aim for maximum growth and full employment, Gosplan typically must either increase sources or reduce uses. For example, if total uses for steel exceeds the planned sources, Gosplan could order steel factories to increase production. But increasing steel production will require more coal, iron ore, electricity, and other resources. In fact, a change in the amount of any one good produced will have far-reaching effects on resources. The Soviet goal of self-sufficiency also limits Gosplan's use of imported resources and products.

As a result, materials balancing in the Soviet Union often means reducing uses of resources. To reduce uses, Gosplan can either cut back on the resources given to factories (or force them to use substitutes) or it can reduce production of consumer goods. In the past, Gosplan has used both options, but most often it has reduced consumer goods, reflecting Soviet economic priorities.

Implementing the Plan

Actual implementation of the central plan falls to managers of Soviet enterprises. These managers are responsible for operating industrial plants, state-run agricultural farms, and retail establishments. Each manager is given a plan, which amounts to a quota, and an indication of the resources they will receive. Managers are charged with carrying out the plan—not with developing alternatives—but generally they are not told how to operate their enterprises.

As an incentive to make the plans work, enterprise managers are rewarded with large bonuses—amounting to 25 to 50 percent of their salaries if they meet their assigned goals. But their options and controls are limited. For example, Gosplan and the ministries not only determine what supplies an enterprise receives, but also matches up suppliers and customers. The managers of the two enterprises must then determine grade of product, delivery date, and other important but unplanned specifics. Since neither supplier nor customer has an option, supplying managers have little incentive to satisfy customer managers. But they do have major incentives to meet the quantitive goals of the plan in any way possible.

Two characteristics of the planning and implementation process create problems for the Soviet economy. First, the planners operate on the principle that managers will be more efficient if planned targets are difficult (but not impossible) to achieve. Second, managers receive large bonuses for reaching their targets but none if they do not. To understand the problems that can arise as a result, try to imagine how you might act if you were a manager trying to meet a production target.

First, you would probably try to build some slack into the plan. Thus you might underreport the resources you have on hand (ensuring enough to meet the production goal). Or you might understate your factory's capacity (to keep the production goal low). Once you begin implementing the plan, you might refuse to slow down or halt production to try new technology or new ideas to improve productivity. Moreover, since your "customers" have no choice but to accept whatever you produce, you can reduce quality, use inferior materials, or change the grade of a product if necessary to meet the quantity target.

You can also manipulate the target. If the plan calls for producing 1 million cans of shaving cream, for example, you might order each can filled one-fourth of an ounce less full. If the goal is to produce $1 million worth of dresses, you might choose to make them out of silk instead of cotton. Finally, you might decide to employ people who specialize in obtaining supplies on quick notice—even though they may use threats, bribes, or other such means. Although these actions may help you achieve your production goals, each of these responses creates a problem for the economy.

The "Second Economy"

The preceding description of the planning and implementation process describes most—but by no means all—economic activity in the Soviet Union. A complete picture of the Soviet economy must include the *second economy,* a combination of legal and illegal economic activities. The most important and best known legal part of the second economy is private agricultural production. Workers on state and collective farms are allowed to farm relatively small plots (usually one acre or less) and to sell what they produce. Although such plots account for only 3 percent of all agricultural land, they produce nearly one-fourth of all agricultural commodities. Such plots are especially important for livestock and vegetable production.

Other parts of the legal private sector include certain personal services, such as physicians and teachers who are allowed to sell their after-work services. Although these and other legal private activities are tolerated, they are not completely accepted. In fact, they violate the principles of the Soviet economy because they are unplanned. Moreover, it is sometimes difficult to clearly distinguish between legal and illegal activities. For example, farm workers may "divert" supplies from the collective farm for use on the private plot, or they may "borrow" equipment. Although private farming is permitted, the use of state-owned equipment and supplies is not. But there is little doubt such use occurs.

Some activities are clearly illegal, such as producing goods for sale on the black market. Severe shortages, lack of variety, and relatively poor quality of the consumer goods provided by the state leave ample room for a black market to function. Smuggling and stealing from warehouses is also an important industry. Of course, similar activities occur in the United States and all other countries, where the underground economy is a place for illegal activities (such as drug trafficking) and tax evasion.

In fact, some illegal aspects of the Soviet "second economy" appear to be tolerated by the authorities. Certainly, the second economy helps to provide some of the consumer goods that make wage and other material incentives effective. Moreover, the ability to acquire supplies on the black market—by hook or crook or both—helps to overcome poor resource allocation. But such activities undoubtedly channel resources and efforts away from the targets of the official economic plan. In addition, the existence of the second economy is, at least in part, an indication of system failure.

Success and Failure

Drawing firm conclusions about the Soviet economy is somewhat difficult because impartial and accurate information is scarce. Moreover, the goals of the Soviet Union's economic system are different from those of the U.S. and other market economies. Still, observers of the Soviet system have reached several general conclusions.

Economic-growth rate has been high. We noted earlier the high growth rate of the Soviet economy prior to World War II. Since the war, the rate of growth has continued to be high. Between 1950 and 1979, the Soviet economy grew at just under 5 percent annually, according to Western calculations (Soviet figures put it higher still). In contrast, the U.S. economy grew only about 3.5 percent annually. Over this period, only the growth rate of the Japanese economy exceeds that of the Soviet Union's.

The high rate of Soviet economic growth has several explanations. First, by severely restricting the production of consumer goods, central planners have forced a high rate of capital growth. Then by maintaining almost zero unemployment, they have further increased production. In addition, Russia started at a lower level of economic development, making high percentage increases in production easier to attain. Finally, the Soviet economy grew in part by importing or imitating technology developed in other parts of the world.

Despite its past record, however, some economists question whether the Soviet economy can continue to grow at the same rate. In fact, the economy has slowed considerably in the late 1970s and 1980s, and several problems seem to have emerged. First, much of the growth in the past was the result of increased supplies of labor and capital. However, population growth has slowed, and central planners have begun to give more priority to consumer goods. Moreover, future Soviet economic growth appears to depend heavily on technology, as in most developed economies. But the Soviets lag in adopting the most advanced technology: information processing, computers, and similar technological areas. Limited incentives for innovation at the plant level may not only have contributed to the slowdown in growth, but may pose a major obstacle to future growth.

Degree of equity is unclear. Proponents of socialism argue that it produces a more equal distribution of income. Comparative data are scarce but there appears to be little difference between income-distribution patterns in the Soviet Union and in many market economies. Top Soviet political officials are a privileged class. They receive finer houses, shop in special stores, have access to better educational institutions for their children, and enjoy many other privileges not available to others in Soviet society.

Labor income—wages and salaries—seems to be distributed about as unequally in the Soviet Union as in the United States, probably because wages and bonuses are important incentives in both countries. Moreover, Soviet citizens do not have other sources of income, such as rent and interest. Thus, overall, income distribution in the United States is more unequal. However, many goods and services—health care, education, and housing—are provided at no direct cost or at low cost in the Soviet Union. The standard of living of the lowest income groups in the Soviet Union is therefore somewhat higher than indicated by income distribution.

Innovation and quality have suffered.   In discussing implementation of the central plan, we noted several problem areas: managers misrepresenting resources or capacity and producing low-quality products. There are strong incentives to "beat the system," but few incentives to produce more high-quality products at less cost. Indeed, managers who succeed in raising productivity often find their reward to be a higher quota in subsequent periods.

Managers in many market economies—especially in the United States—have also been criticized for focusing on meeting short-term goals and failing to make the best long-run decisions. (Some economists have suggested that this behavior occurs because large corporations are controlled by corporate plans and, like planned economies, have difficulty developing appropriate incentives for managers.) But the problem appears to be particularly pronounced in planned socialist economies.

Full employment and price stability may be myths.   The Soviets point proudly to full employment and stable prices. However, some Western observers believe that these claims are exaggerated. In their opinion, many workers are underemployed even though few individuals are without a job. Managers hold on to workers who are not busy full time in order to ensure that they will meet their production quotas. Government allocation of resources—including labor—may also result in some individuals working in jobs for which they are overqualified. And although official statistics show little or no inflation, they disregard prices on the black market, a major force in the Soviet economy. Moreover, rubles (the Soviet currency) are not the only way of measuring prices. The hours spent waiting in line to purchase the few consumer goods available also has an economic cost.

RECAP

Until recently, the Soviet economy had experienced rapid economic growth. A high rate of population growth, transfer of resources from agricultural to industrial production, high rates of capital investment, and imported technology were the source of past growth.

Slower population growth, limited technological progress, and the lack of incentives to develop and implement new technology have been cited as reasons for a slower growth rate more recently.

Is there a bottom line?   Ultimately the evaluation of a system becomes a matter of personal judgment and preference. Is the price that the Soviets pay for full employment too high? Has it been worth the sacrifice of consumer goods to build up industrial and military strength? Nearly everyone has an opinion on these and other aspects of the Soviet system.

Those who study comparative economics are cautious about comparisons, but they do agree on two points. Either type of economic system can be made to operate and both have experienced successes and failures. Whether the Soviet Union can make the necessary reforms to continue its economic progress is debatable. Other planned socialist economies—especially those of Hungary and China—have introduced more decentralized decision making, placed more emphasis on markets, and improved efficiency as a result. But the Soviet Union believes that such changes would violate the very premise of its economic system and therefore resists them.

ECONOMIC DEVELOPMENT AND THE THIRD WORLD

The United States and the Soviet Union have quite different economic systems, as you have seen. But in some respects they are alike. Each has the characteristics of a **developed economy**. Both are highly industrialized, have average standards of living far above subsistence levels, and maintain sophisticated institutions (government, education, transportation, and communication). Economists often refer to the developed market capitalist economies—the United States, Canada, Western Europe, Japan, and Australia—as the economic "First World." And they often refer to the developed planned socialist economies—the Soviet Union and Eastern Europe—as the economic "Second World."

In contrast, **less-developed countries (LDCs)**—Ethiopia, Sudan, Zaire, Sri Lanka, and Bolivia, to name only a few—are often called "Third-World" nations. Unlike the developed nations, they have little industry and very limited educational and communication systems. Poverty is not an isolated phenomena but the typical way of life, encompassing the majority of the population and persisting from year to year, generation to generation.

There is no neat dividing line between the developed and less-developed countries. Moreover, like all classifications, there is much diversity within the Third World—from the near-destitute situation in Ethiopia to moderate success in South Korea. (For more on some of the newly industrialized economies, see A Case in Point: The Dragons Are Coming!) But less-developed countries do face similar problems that justify grouping them together. As you will see, however, there are no simple ways to relieve their absolute and relative poverty.

Dimensions of Poverty

Exhibit 34.4 shows the relative and absolute poverty of Third-World nations. Following the classification scheme of the World Bank, less-developed countries are divided into two groups: low-income and middle-income. Middle-income countries are more developed in important ways than are low-income countries. But they are still less developed than the industrial market economies. (Centrally planned economies other than China are not included because of the lack of comparable data.)

Low output per capita. The extent of poverty in Third-World economies is evident from the low levels of output per capita in the low-income countries. Output per capita in 1984 ranged from a low of $110 per year in Ethiopia to a high of $360 per year in Sudan. You probably cannot imagine trying to exist for a year on $200–$400 of income. Indeed, in 1984, four-person families with incomes below $10,609—over ten times the average income in many LDCs—were officially classified as poor in the United States. Although GNP statistics may not accurately reflect actual standards of living, they do reflect *relative* standards of living.

Moreover, as we noted earlier, in most Third-World nations nearly everyone is poor. The situation is better in some of the middle-income countries, especially Israel and Hong Kong, but these are exceptional cases. The poorest countries also suffer from income inequalities. Most have a successful upper class, but almost no middle class and little chance for upward mobility.

Developed economy. An economy that is industrialized, has relatively high standards of living, and has sophisticated institutions (government, education, transportation, and communication).

Less-developed countries (LDCs). Nations that have relatively low standards of living, limited industrialization, and minimal education, transportation, and communication systems; collectively known as the Third World.

Country	GNP per capita (dollars per year)	Average life expectancy (years)	Daily calorie supply (percent of required)	Population per physician
Low income				
Ethiopia	110	44	93	81,120
Bangledesh	130	50	81	9,010
Zaire	140	51	96	13,940*
Tanzania	210	52	98	17,740*
India	260	56	96	2,610
China	310	69	111	1,730
Sri Lanka	360	70	106	7,620
Sudan	360	48	90	9,070
Middle income				
Bolivia	540	53	82	1,950
Nigeria	730	50	86	10,540
Thailand	860	64	105	5,020
Turkey	1,160	64	123	1,500
Colombia	1,390	65	110	1,700*
Chile	1,700	70	105	950
Brazil	1,720	64	106	1,200
South Korea	2,110	68	118	1,440
Mexico	2,040	66	126	1,140
Hungary	2,100	70	135	320
Yugoslavia	2,120	69	141	670
Greece	3,770	75	144	390
Israel	5,060	75	121	400
Hong Kong	6,330	76	122	1,260
Industrial market				
Italy	6,420	77	140	750
United Kingdom	8,570	74	128	680
Austria	9,140	73	132	580
Japan	10,630	77	113	740
France	9,760	77	139	460
West Germany	11,130	75	130	420
Canada	13,280	76	130	510
Sweden	11,860	77	116	410
United States	15,390	76	137	500
Switzerland	16,330	77	129	390

**Exhibit 34.4
Indicators of Economic
Status**

* These numbers are from The World Bank, *World Development Report, 1985.*
Source: The World Bank, *World Development Report, 1986.*

High birth and death rates. With a few exceptions, life expectancy in the less-developed countries is below that in the developed countries. Poverty is a major reason: The daily calorie supply per person is *on average* below the subsistence level in some countries and only just above it in others. And health care, as indicated by the number of persons per physician, is far below the standard

A Case in Point
The Dragons Are Coming!

In Oriental tradition China is known as the *big dragon*. Economists have nicknamed the fast-growing economies of South Korea, Taiwan, Singapore, and Hong Kong the *little dragons*. Using a strategy of export promotion, these areas have increased the output of their economies by an average of 9 percent per year over the past two decades. Although they all experienced slower growth in 1985—an average of only 2.3 percent—they are expected to grow at a 6–8 percent pace within the next few years. They have become a force to be reckoned with in international product markets, including textiles, electronics, and automobiles.

In the past the little dragons have relied on low-cost labor to attract foreign investment and foreign sales. Taiwan's exports to the United States are largely labor-intensive goods produced directly for U.S. firms. General Motors was attracted to South Korea by labor costs of $2.16 per hour, compared to $24.40 in the United States. Two Japanese companies—Matsushita and Sanyo—have recently built new plants in Singapore to take advantage of cheap labor.

A symbol of the growing economic strength of the little dragons, however, is their decision to invest in foreign economies and to undertake joint ventures with foreign companies. A Singapore electronics company, Singatronics, bought a U.S. company in order to acquire its brand name and its distribution network. Uaewoo, a South Korean firm, has entered into several joint ventures with General Motors, including manufacturing a new model Pontiac to be sold in the United States.

Much of this past growth has been virtually invisible in the United States. For the most part the little dragons have acted as subcontractors, manufacturing goods for U.S. and, more recently, Japanese firms. The vast majority of their exports to the United States have been sold under U.S. or Japanese labels. But South Korea, the strongest of the little dragons, is seeking to do to the Japanese what the Japanese did to U.S. firms in the 1960s: take over the low-cost end of many markets. Hyundai is successfully battling the Japanese in the subcompact auto market with its Excel. While South Korea sold only 65 cars to the United States in 1985, in 1986 this figure was more like 140,000. Projected sales for 1987 should top 300,000. Uaewoo, another South Korean conglomerate, manufactures Leading Edge computers, a successful IBM look-alike. South Korean firms have captured as much as 10 percent of the market for VCRs, a figure that is expected to increase.

Although they have not yet earned full status as First-World economies, the little dragons can no longer be counted among the less-developed countries. In fact, these "newly industrialized countries" hope to make the transition from developing to developed economies. If they don't succeed—and many economists believe that they will—it won't be for lack of trying. As U.S. firms seek to regain some of the international competitiveness lost over the last few years, they had better keep a sharp eye on the Far East. The dragons are coming!

---

of the developed countries. At the same time, population growth in many Third-World nations is rapid. There is no simple correlation between population growth and poverty, but most economists believe that rapid population growth makes it difficult to improve standards of living.

Economic Growth versus Economic Development

A low standard of living is clearly one of the most significant problems in less-developed countries. In order to raise their standards of living, Third-World nations must increase their total production of goods and services. That is, economic growth is perhaps their most important economic goal. But achieving economic growth is not a simple matter, especially in nations with poor transportation and education systems and unstable or outmoded social and political sys-

Economic development. The process of changing economic, social, and political systems in order to sustain economic growth and overcome mass poverty.

tems. These features are both products of nations' less-developed status and obstacles to their progress.

To achieve economic growth, an economy must increase resources supplied—especially capital resources—and/or improve technology. But many economists believe that **economic development** in Third-World nations will also require changes in social, political, and institutional systems. As you will see, the failure of some proposed solutions can be attributed to failure to address these fundamental—and essential—aspects of development.

Dimensions of Economic Development

We can identify the systems that must be changed by considering how Third-World nations differ from First-World and Second-World countries. As Exhibit 34.5 shows, the typical less-developed country is more dependent on agriculture, is more rural, has lower educational achievement, and is more dependent on primary exports, such as largely unprocessed minerals and agricultural products. In addition, these nations have had a history of political and economic instability.

Heavy concentration in agriculture. In many Third-World countries, 75 percent of the population is engaged in agriculture, much of it subsistence farming. (Among the industrialized market economies, only Japan and Italy have as much as 10 percent of the population in agriculture.) In some ways agriculture is a key industry for less-developed countries. Improvements in agricultural technology can increase yields per acre dramatically and raise the standard of living. By reducing the demand for farm labor, this step can also free workers for industrial production.

Low degree of urbanization. In the more advanced industrialized countries, most of the population lives in urban areas. In the less-developed countries, most of the population still lives in rural areas. Rural life, of course, reflects the concentration in agriculture. In developed countries, urbanization reflects industrialization and a large number of service jobs. However, urbanization can create problems in a less-developed country. In many Third-World nations, people have been attracted to urban areas faster than new industrial jobs have been created. Not only has this shift caused declines in agricultural output, but it has also resulted in heavy unemployment in urban areas and even greater poverty.

Low educational attainment. Educational services are poor in many less-developed countries. Teachers are scarce, and relatively few of the population attain even a high school diploma, much less attend college. Although workers without high school diplomas can perform most industrial jobs, education and training are related. Most Third-World economies have too few trained individuals. One result is low labor productivity (units produced per worker).

Dependency on primary exports. Most less-developed countries are too small to ever be totally self-sufficient. Indeed, the economics of comparative advantage discussed in Chapter 32 suggest that all nations are better off when they trade. For Third-World nations, successful trade can provide income not only to buy manufactured products, but also to finance investment in capital resources and thus increase their capacity to produce.

Country	Agricultural output as percent of total	Percent of labor force in agriculture	Urban population as percent of total	Percent of age group in secondary school	Primary commodities as percent of merchandise exports
Low income					
Ethiopia	48	80	15	13	99
Bangledesh	48	75	18	19	39
Zaire	36*	72	39	23*	—
Tanzania	52*	86	14	3	87*
India	35	70	25	34	47
China	36	69	22	35	43
Sri Lanka	28	53	21	56	70
Sudan	33	71	21	18	98*
Middle income					
Bolivia	25	46	43	35	—
Nigeria	27	68	30	16*	—
Thailand	20	70	18	29	68
Turkey	19	58	46	38	54
Colombia	20	34	67	49	81
Chile	6	16	83	65	92*
Brazil	13	31	72	42	59
South Korea	14	36	64	89	9
Mexico	9	37	69	55	73
Hungary	20	18	55	74	37
Yugoslavia	15	32	46	82	24
Greece	18	31	65	82	50
Israel	5	6	90	78	19
Hong Kong	1	2	93	68	8
Industrial market					
Italy	6	12	71	75	15
United Kingdom	2	3	92	85	35
Austria	4	9	56	74	15
Japan	4	11	76	94	3
France	—	9	81	89	26
West Germany	2	6	86	50	13
Canada	3	5	75	101	45
Sweden	3	6	86	85	22
United States	2	4	74	97*	30
Switzerland	—	6	60	—	7

* These numbers are from The World Bank, *World Development Report, 1985.*
Source: The World Bank, *World Development Report, 1986.*

Exhibit 34.5
Indicators of Economic Development

But to succeed in trade, a nation must be able to compete and to diversify. Many less-developed nations instead depend on the export of minerals and agricultural products—called *primary exports.* When a country is very heavily dependent on the export of one or two main products, it is highly vulnerable to changes in demand and supply that occur frequently in international markets. And when a nation exports many of its raw materials, it loses the opportunity to gain income by processing those materials and selling more finished goods.

Inadequate transportation and communication systems. Economic development, as we indicated, requires an economic system with adequate transportation and communication systems. We tend to take them for granted in the United States, but in many Third-World nations, it is difficult and expensive to transport goods from one part of the country to another. Inadequate transportation and communication systems hamper industrial growth, reduce efficiency, and virtually isolate some members of an economy.

Political and economic instability. Economists generally agree that less-developed countries have a history of economic and political instability. Economic instability is most visible as high unemployment and highly unstable prices. Political instability is observed as turnover of governments and radical changes in economic goals.

Political and economic instability hamper economic development. Private individuals and firms worry about not recovering their investments. Indeed, in many countries businesses have lost some or all of their investments as a result of political decisions. Price instability makes individuals reluctant to put their savings to work in domestic financial markets, which also lowers private investment. Many of these problems and symptoms are related, presenting a major challenge for the less-developed countries. But what is required and what strategies are useful for economic development? We address these questions in the next several sections.

Conditions for Economic Development

Economic development is a process that is complicated and has many dimensions. A high priority for Third-World nations seeking economic growth is to increase their investment in capital resources—that is, machines and factories. Not only can such investment spur industrial growth but it can also help increase agricultural productivity. Moreover, even though many jobs in modern industries require few skills, almost every industry requires some skilled labor. In addition, management and entrepreneurial skills are required. In order to grow, then, less-developed nations must improve the education and training of their work forces.

Similarly, Third-World nations must increase agricultural and industrial productivity if their economies are to grow. Adopting improved technologies would increase productivity, lowering the cost of goods and making them more competitive in world markets. Unfortunately, not all technology used in the United States and other developed economies can be instantly adopted by less-developed nations. Some modern equipment is extremely expensive; some modern techniques require a highly skilled labor force. In addition to investing in new machines, technology, and worker training, less-developed nations must invest in transportation, communication, health, and education. As we noted, these aspects of what economists call the *social infrastructure* are underdeveloped in most Third-World nations.

All these investments, of course, cost money. Unfortunately, the low incomes of the less-developed countries limit the possibility of generating substantial investment funds from domestic saving. And political and economic instability tends to cause any private saving to be put into gold, jewelry, or foreign bank accounts where they are available to finance new investment. Thus Third-World nations must raise investment funds in one of four other ways: (1) running a trade surplus; (2) attracting foreign investment; (3) borrowing from foreign financial institutions or governments; or (4) obtaining grants from foreign governments. The most successful less-developed nations have used a combination of these sources. But none is easy or without potential problems.

Strategies for Economic Development

Because of the many problems and complexity of economic development, there is no single or easy way to make it happen. Moreover, most economists argue that a country should pursue several options at the same time to reduce the risk of failure. In searching for a strategy, less-developed countries must address some of the questions that follow.

Import substitution or export promotion? Successful trade is essential for most Third-World nations, as it is for the more industrialized countries. Most developing economies have to import at least some, if not all, of the capital resources they require. International trade can generate funds to pay for capital resources, but only if the nation can run a trade surplus on noncapital goods.

To create a surplus, a nation may choose import substitution or export promotion. *Import substitution* is the domestic production of some goods that were previously imported. If successful, it will free export earnings to pay for capital resources. Import substitution has been a popular strategy for many less-developed countries, who see it both as a way to develop domestic industries and to become more self-sufficient. Efforts to improve productivity in local industries—including agricultural production—can increase total production and raise the standard of living.

Nevertheless, import substitution as normally practiced has not always been a success. Some Third-World nations have tried to produce locally what they can more cheaply buy abroad. (The relatively large number of inefficiently operated steel mills in less-developed countries is an example.) And some poorer nations have imposed trade restrictions to protect domestic industries from foreign competition. As we noted in Chapter 32, economists believe that free trade offers greater benefits than trade restrictions.

In contrast, *export promotion* requires that a nation make its goods more attractive to foreign buyers. Revenues from greater exports can then be used to pay for imported capital resources. South Korea, Hong Kong, Taiwan, and Japan all used this strategy successfully. Economists generally consider export promotion to be consistent with the principle of comparative advantage and increased worldwide trade. They suggest that less-developed economies should try to find some niche in the world marketplace. Ideally, this niche should not be just the production of raw materials, but one that will allow the country to process raw materials to some degree and thus increase its income. Moreover, they reject as shortsighted the strategies of some nations, notably Japan, that combine export promotion with trade restrictions.

Industry or agriculture? Noting the difference in focus on agriculture between developed and less-developed nations, many Third-World nations tried shifting most of their attention to industrialization. Although industrialization is important, an exclusive focus on it can cause agricultural output to fall and urban unemployment to rise at the same time.

Economists now suggest that less-developed nations also increase their efforts to develop agriculture. As we noted earlier, greater agricultural productivity will improve the food supply, making the economy less dependent on imported food and improving the standard of living. It will also free workers for jobs in industry. A more balanced policy toward the two sectors, and more efforts to provide industrial jobs in rural areas are seen as crucial to sound economic growth and development.

Private foreign investment? Less-developed countries must also decide whether to encourage private foreign investment. Foreigners can provide funds for capital purchases and help a nation industrialize, modernize, and provide training for its workers. Foreign-owned businesses may also provide a market for domestic raw materials and intermediate goods (such as steel).

Many Third-World nations are reluctant to allow foreign investment, however. They view foreign investors as exploiters of local labor and contributors of little of their profits to the domestic economy. Countries that have allowed foreign investment have often required local ownership of a substantial percentage of the company and limited the transfer of profits out of the country. In some cases governments have taken over private businesses. Needless to say, such restrictions and uncertainty limit foreign investments. The challenge for less-developed nations, then, is to find a way to encourage foreign investment, while at the same time ensuring that they receive the benefits from it.

Foreign loans? Although foreign loans can be used to finance economic development, this strategy can be dangerous. A number of less-developed countries, especially in Latin America, are heavily in debt. They borrowed substantial sums of money, much of it from U.S. banks. But they currently find it virtually impossible to pay interest charges, much less repay any of the principal owed. In some cases, this debt crisis may reflect poor investment decisions or the use of borrowed funds to finance consumption rather than investment. But the worldwide recessions in the 1980s followed by slow economic growth have made it difficult for Third-World countries to increase their exports. Third-World countries also claim that trade restrictions in First-World countries have further limited their ability to export goods profitably. In addition, rising interest rates and falling prices of major exports have increased the less-developed nations' burden of debt. And both the rise and fall of oil prices in the 1980s hurt debtor nations. Increased oil prices in the early 1980s hurt oil importers, such as Brazil; the decline in oil prices in the mid-1980s hurt oil exporters, such as Mexico.

Foreign aid? Another possible source of funds—foreign aid—also has costs as well as benefits. Is accepting foreign aid a useful way to begin economic development, or does it create a dependency and stifle self-reliance? As usual, the answer depends on the situation. In some countries, most notably Tanzania, foreign aid has been badly used, resulting in overly ambitious plans and acquisition of complex machinery that the country has been unable to maintain. But examples of successful aid can be found and are, in fact, more numerous. The issue is less whether aid is granted but how it is used and for what purposes. If aid is used to fund poorly designed projects or to build palaces for the ruling elite, success cannot be expected. On the other hand, well-chosen and well-designed projects can be highly successful.

Free markets or centralized planning? Finally, the governments of developing countries have to choose a type of economic system. Should they opt for a centrally planned economy? Or should they allow markets to make economic decisions? Some economies, including those of the Ivory Coast, Singapore, and Hong Kong, have stressed international trade, private investment, and market capitalism. Others—Cuba, Vietnam, and North Korea, for example—have adopted planned socialist economies. Most, however, have followed a mixed strategy, although many utilize centralized economic planning more than do most developed nonsocialist economies.

For example, governments in most developing nations have chosen to intervene to improve the social infrastructure, that is, transportation and communication systems, schools, hospitals. Many economists accept this type of intervention as useful for economic development. But many are skeptical of other government activities. There are numerous examples of government mistakes, such as large-scale projects—dams or steel mills—that remain incomplete, and examples of state-operated enterprises that are highly inefficient.

In addition, the role of government in Third-World trade policies remains controversial. Some of the success of Hong Kong and South Korea may have resulted from policies that violate the principles of free trade. Other countries—Brazil and Chile, for example—have burdened their economies with trade restrictions. The problems arising from poor government decisions underscore the importance of developing flexible and efficient political and social institutions as a part of economic development.

What Will the Future Bring?

As you have seen, Third-World economies face many problems. Can they succeed with so many handicaps? Can development strategies help them? The experience of the past 30 years is inconclusive. Some economies are no better off now than then. But the growth record of many less-developed countries is good—exceeding that of the developed economies.

A few economies have almost made it over the hump—South Korea and Hong Kong, for example. Others, including Brazil, Mexico, China, and Argentina have made great strides, although progress has not been sure and steady. But economists have learned a great deal about obstacles and options from the experiences of these economies. The evidence is ample that the future is far from hopeless. Whether it is bright remains a point of contention among economists.

Most economists believe the Third-World nations will continue to require the help of industrialized economies. Some of this help may be in the form of foreign aid or private investments, but equally, if not more importantly, the industrialized economies can help by keeping their economies healthy, growing, and free of trade restrictions. In this way, the Third-World countries can earn the funds required to import capital goods, improving economic growth and standards of living.

Finally, even under the best of circumstances, economic development does not happen quickly. The developed economies have a tremendous head start and, despite problems, they continue to grow. Thus even remarkable progress in raising per capita output levels—such as in South Korea and Hong Kong—will not close the gap. Less-developed countries appear likely to lag behind in relative terms for a long time to come.

CONCLUSION

We end as we began, noting that all economies face the fundamental problem of scarcity. But you have learned that not all take the same approach to allocating society's scarce resources and goods. The approaches that different nations have taken have produced radically different outcomes. What system is best and what system less-developed countries should use to improve their standards of living remain controversial. But whatever path Third-World nations choose, it seems likely that they will require the help of the First-World and Second-World nations if they are to raise significantly their standards of living. And in watching the progress of less-developed countries, it may be that the more developed countries will also find a key to continued growth.

SUMMARY

1. In this chapter we compared planned socialist and market capitalist economies, discussed the economy of the Soviet Union, and explored the problems of less-developed countries.

2. In market capitalism, most resources are privately owned and most allocation decisions are directed by market forces. In planned socialism, most resources are owned by the government and most allocation decisions are directed by government plan.

3. In market capitalism, the economy seeks to satisfy individual wants, as expressed by market demand. Although government policies and regulations are influential, the market is the preferred mechanism for answering the fundamental economic questions of what to produce, how to produce, and to whom to distribute. In planned socialism, satisfying collective wants, as defined by central planners, is the primary goal. Although markets are sometimes permitted, the plan is the preferred mechanism for answering the fundamental economic questions.

4. Proponents of market capitalism believe that markets are a more efficient way to obtain information about demand and resource scarcity; that private property rights and the connection between income and consumption provide the best incentives to utilize resources efficiently; and that decentralized economic and political power make market capitalism most consistent with personal freedom.

5. Proponents of planned socialism believe that market capitalism often results in concentrated economic and

political power; that the drive for maximum profits creates inequity and inattention to important social wants; that inflation and unemployment significantly reduce the efficiency of market economies; and that planning leads to more economic growth.

6. The Soviet Union is a centrally planned socialist economy. In 1928, the Soviets launched their first Five Year Plan, emphasizing industrialization and the production of military and capital resources. This emphasis on industrial and military goods as opposed to consumer goods remains true today.

7. The top economic goals for the Soviet economy are determined by the leaders of the Communist party. Gosplan, the central planning bureau, is responsible for developing an economic plan to achieve these goals. In cooperation with industry planning bureaus and enterprise managers, Gosplan develops the plan and allocates resources and other materials. Actual implementation of the plan is the responsibility of enterprise managers.

8. In addition to planned activities, there is a "second economy" in the Soviet Union: a combination of legal and illegal activities. Some private-enterprise activities are permitted, although generally they are not encouraged.

9. The Soviet economy has historically achieved a very high rate of growth. High population growth, large-scale transfer of resources from agricultural to industrial production, high rates of capital investment, and imported technology have been the source of past

growth. Slow population growth, limited technological progress, and the lack of incentives to develop and implement new technology have been cited as reasons for slower growth rates more recently.

10. Some of the less-developed countries have serious structural problems: high poverty, heavy concentration on agriculture, low urbanization, poor education, limited industrialization, heavy dependence on the export of primary products, inadequate transportation and communication systems, and political and economic instability. These structural problems make economic progress difficult and complex.

11. In order to develop, less-developed countries must invest in capital and human resources. Funds for these investments may be earned through exports, borrowed from foreign banks or governments, or obtained as gifts from foreign governments.

12. Less-developed countries must decide whether to promote exports or to produce goods that substitute for foreign imports, whether to emphasize agriculture instead of developing industry, whether to encourage or limit foreign investment, whether to rely heavily on foreign aid and foreign loans, and whether to utilize a free-market or planned-socialist economy.

KEY TERMS

Developed economy, 878
Less-developed countries (LDCs), 878
Economic development, 881

QUESTIONS FOR REVIEW AND DISCUSSION

1. Suppose that you were an enterprise manager in the Soviet Union. You are promoted and receive a bonus based only on meeting the quota you negotiate with the industry ministry.
   a) Explain the steps you would take to ensure your promotion and bonus.
   b) How important are the following to decisions you make? Producing a quality product. Satisfying the demands of firms and individuals who use your product. Making sure that your plant uses the most efficient technology.
   c) What are the long-run implications of such an incentive system?
   d) What changes in the evaluation system can you suggest that would improve efficiency?

2. Some critics of U.S. business argue that managers focus too much on short-run goals. In many large firms, managers can expect to stay in any particular job for less than two years. They are evaluated on the basis of profits that they can generate during that period of time.
   a) Explain how this system of evaluation may lead to a purely short-run focus.
   b) Explain how short-run profits may be affected by reducing expenditures for training employees, maintaining equipment, and buying new machinery. What are the long-run implications of these actions?
   c) What changes in the evaluation system can you suggest that would improve efficiency?

3. Every economy faces similar issues, although different economic systems address them differently. Compare and contrast the economies of the United States and the Soviet Union by explaining how each system would approach the following issues. When answering, consider the mechanisms used, the relative importance of various economic goals, and the ease with which reasonably satisfactory results can be obtained.
   a) Maintaining full employment.
   b) Achieving a high rate of saving and investment.
   c) Determining the quantities of automobiles, heavy machinery, housing, and clothing to produce.
   d) Setting the wages of college professors, farmers, and factory workers.

4. In the early nineteenth century the United States had some of the same characteristics that we now associate with less-developed countries. How were the problems faced by the United States at that time similar to those of today's LDCs? How were they different?

5. Some LDCs have placed significant constraints on businesses operated by foreigners. What are some of the benefits of foreign manufacturing facilities? What are some of the potential costs?

6. Some LDCs are heavily dependent on exports of one commodity—copper in Chile and oil in Mexico and Nigeria, for example.
   a) What problems are caused by such dependency?
   b) What are the advantages and disadvantages of using trade restrictions to develop local industry?
   c) What are the advantages and disadvantages of trying to develop substitutes for foreign imports?
   d) What are the advantages and disadvantages of trying to develop export industries?
   e) If you were in charge of selecting the best new industry to develop, what factors would influence your choice?

A P P E N D I X

AGGREGATE OUTPUT AND NATIONAL INCOME: 1929–1986

Year	Nominal Gross National Product (current dollars)	Real Gross National Product (1982 dollars)	Net National Product (1982 dollars)	National income (1982 dollars)	Real GNP per capita (1982 dollars)	Annual change in real GNP per capita (1982 dollars)
1929	103.9	709.6	622.8	574.0	5828.0	—
1930	91.1	642.8	554.1	517.7	5243.0	−10.0
1931	76.4	588.1	499.1	454.4	4735.0	−9.7
1932	58.5	509.2	420.9	381.7	4111.0	−13.2
1933	56.0	498.5	412.0	369.0	3952.0	−3.9
1934	65.6	536.7	451.5	409.1	4276.0	8.2
1935	72.8	580.2	496.1	455.8	4632.0	8.3
1936	83.1	662.2	578.3	524.2	5216.0	12.6
1937	91.3	695.3	611.0	564.2	5481.0	5.1
1938	85.4	664.2	579.5	530.0	5164.0	−5.8
1939	91.3	716.6	632.2	575.1	5554.0	7.6
1940	100.4	772.9	687.9	630.7	5850.0	5.3
1941	125.5	909.4	823.1	766.5	6817.0	16.5
1942	159.0	1080.3	993.4	952.8	8011.0	17.5
1943	192.7	1276.2	1190.5	1162.3	9333.0	16.5
1944	211.4	1380.6	1295.7	1242.9	9976.0	6.9
1945	213.4	1354.8	1269.4	1204.9	9682.0	−2.9
1946	212.4	1096.9	1008.9	947.4	7758.0	−19.9
1947	235.2	1066.7	975.0	904.7	7401.0	−4.6
1948	261.6	1108.7	1011.9	950.0	7561.0	2.2
1949	260.4	1109.0	1007.3	933.2	7434.0	−1.7
1950	288.3	1203.7	1097.1	1015.0	7905.0	6.3
1951	333.4	1328.2	1216.4	1123.4	8576.0	8.5
1952	351.6	1380.0	1263.0	1169.0	8759.0	2.1
1953	371.6	1435.3	1313.2	1211.2	8960.0	2.3
1954	372.5	1416.2	1288.8	1183.0	8687.0	−3.0
1955	405.9	1494.9	1362.3	1251.5	9009.0	3.7
1956	428.2	1525.6	1387.3	1284.6	9032.0	0.3
1957	451.0	1551.1	1407.7	1298.7	9019.0	−0.1
1958	456.8	1539.2	1391.5	1276.2	8801.0	−2.4
1959	495.8	1629.1	1477.2	1358.8	9161.0	4.1
1960	515.3	1665.3	1508.9	1390.5	9217.0	0.6
1961	533.8	1708.7	1548.1	1421.8	9302.0	0.9
1962	574.6	1799.4	1634.3	1497.3	9646.0	3.7
1963	606.9	1873.3	1703.0	1561.9	9899.0	2.6
1964	649.8	1973.3	1797.0	1650.2	10284.0	3.9
1965	705.1	2087.6	1903.9	1746.9	10744.0	4.5
1966	772.0	2208.3	2016.1	1840.6	11235.0	4.6
1967	816.4	2271.4	2070.3	1896.2	11431.0	1.7
1968	892.7	2365.6	2155.8	1972.9	11786.0	3.1
1969	963.9	2423.3	2203.4	2019.1	11956.0	1.4
1970	1015.5	2416.2	2186.4	1989.0	11783.0	−1.4
1971	1102.7	2484.8	2245.3	2032.5	11966.0	1.6
1972	1212.8	2608.5	2355.2	2137.3	12428.0	3.9
1973	1359.3	2744.1	2480.5	2255.0	12949.0	4.2
1974	1472.8	2729.3	2453.2	2227.6	12762.0	−1.4
1975	1598.4	2695.0	2408.0	2172.0	12478.0	−2.2
1976	1782.8	2826.7	2529.4	2278.9	12964.0	3.9
1977	1990.5	2958.6	2649.0	2393.3	13434.0	3.6
1978	2249.7	3115.2	2791.5	2526.7	13996.0	4.2
1979	2508.2	3192.4	2851.1	2582.3	14185.0	1.4
1980	2732.0	3187.1	2831.0	2562.6	13995.0	−1.3
1981	3052.6	3248.8	2879.1	2610.4	14123.0	0.9
1982	3166.0	3166.0	2782.8	2518.5	13626.0	−3.5
1983	3405.7	3279.1	2884.7	2603.7	13975.0	2.6
1984	3765.0	3489.9	3082.8	2794.8	14754.0	5.6
1985	3998.1	3585.2	3159.6	2866.8	14963.0	1.4
1986	4206.1	3674.9	3233.9	2917.5	15218.0	1.7

Sources: U.S. Department of Commerce, *The National Income and Product Accounts of the United States, 1929–1982; Survey of Current Business* (various issues).

AGGREGATE EXPENDITURES: 1929–1986

Year	Consumption (1982 dollars)	Investment (1982 dollars)	Government purchases (1982 dollars)	Net exports (1982 dollars)
1929	471.4	139.2	94.2	4.7
1930	439.7	97.5	103.3	2.3
1931	422.1	60.2	106.8	−1.0
1932	384.9	22.6	102.2	−0.5
1933	378.7	22.7	98.5	−1.4
1934	390.5	35.3	110.7	0.1
1935	412.1	60.9	113.0	−5.9
1936	451.6	82.1	132.5	−4.2
1937	467.9	99.9	127.8	−0.3
1938	457.1	63.1	137.9	6.0
1939	480.5	86.0	144.1	6.1
1940	502.6	111.8	150.2	8.2
1941	531.1	138.8	235.6	3.9
1942	527.6	76.7	483.7	−7.7
1943	539.9	50.4	708.9	−23.0
1944	557.1	56.4	790.8	−23.8
1945	592.7	76.6	704.5	−18.9
1946	655.0	178.1	236.9	27.0
1947	666.6	177.9	179.8	42.4
1948	681.8	208.2	199.5	19.2
1949	695.4	168.8	226.0	18.8
1950	733.2	234.9	230.8	4.7
1951	748.7	235.2	329.7	14.6
1952	771.4	211.8	389.9	6.9
1953	802.5	216.6	419.0	−2.7
1954	822.7	212.6	378.4	2.5
1955	873.8	259.8	361.3	0.0
1956	899.8	257.8	363.7	4.3
1957	919.7	243.4	381.1	7.0
1958	932.9	221.4	395.3	−10.3
1959	979.4	270.3	397.7	−18.2
1960	1005.1	260.5	403.7	−4.0
1961	1025.2	259.1	427.1	−2.7
1962	1069.0	288.6	449.4	−7.5
1963	1108.4	307.1	459.8	−1.9
1964	1170.6	325.9	470.8	5.9
1965	1236.4	367.0	487.0	−2.7
1966	1298.9	390.5	532.6	−13.7
1967	1337.7	374.4	576.2	−16.9
1968	1405.9	391.8	597.6	−29.7
1969	1456.7	410.3	591.2	−34.9
1970	1492.0	381.5	572.6	−30.0
1971	1538.8	419.3	566.5	−39.8
1972	1621.9	465.4	570.7	−49.4
1973	1689.6	520.8	565.3	−31.5
1974	1674.0	481.3	573.2	0.8
1975	1711.9	383.3	580.9	18.9
1976	1803.9	453.5	580.3	−11.0
1977	1883.8	521.3	589.1	−35.5
1978	1961.0	576.9	604.1	−26.8
1979	2004.4	575.2	609.1	3.6
1980	2000.4	509.3	620.5	57.0
1981	2024.2	545.5	629.7	49.4
1982	2050.7	447.3	641.7	26.3
1983	2146.0	504.0	649.0	−19.9
1984	2246.3	652.0	675.2	−83.6
1985	2324.5	647.7	721.2	−108.2
1986	2418.7	657.2	746.8	−147.8

Sources: U.S. Department of Commerce, *The National Income and Product Accounts of the United States, 1929–1982; Survey of Current Business* (various issues).

POTENTIAL GNP AND GNP GAP: 1955–1986

Year	Potential GNP (billions of 1982 dollars)	GNP gap (Billions of 1982 dollars)	GNP gap (Percent of potential GNP)
1929	—	—	—
1930	—	—	—
1931	—	—	—
1932	—	—	—
1933	—	—	—
1934	—	—	—
1935	—	—	—
1936	—	—	—
1937	—	—	—
1938	—	—	—
1939	—	—	—
1940	—	—	—
1941	—	—	—
1942	—	—	—
1943	—	—	—
1944	—	—	—
1945	—	—	—
1946	—	—	—
1947	—	—	—
1948	—	—	—
1949	—	—	—
1950	—	—	—
1951	—	—	—
1952	—	—	—
1953	—	—	—
1954	—	—	—
1955	1465.7	−29.2	−2.0
1956	1510.1	−15.5	1.0
1957	1556.0	4.9	0.3
1958	1606.0	66.8	4.2
1959	1658.3	29.2	1.8
1960	1712.2	46.9	2.7
1961	1768.0	59.3	3.4
1962	1825.6	26.2	1.4
1963	1885.4	12.1	0.6
1964	1925.5	−47.8	−2.5
1965	2023.2	−64.4	−3.2
1966	2096.5	−111.8	−5.3
1967	2172.5	−98.9	−4.6
1968	2251.2	−114.4	−5.1
1969	2332.8	−90.5	−3.9
1970	2416.5	0.3	0.0
1971	2500.0	15.2	0.6
1972	2586.0	−22.5	−0.9
1973	2675.0	−69.1	−2.6
1974	2764.4	35.1	1.3
1975	2846.5	151.5	5.3
1976	2930.1	103.4	3.5
1977	3016.2	57.6	1.9
1978	3104.7	−10.5	−0.3
1979	3195.3	2.9	0.1
1980	3281.3	94.2	2.9
1981	3367.7	118.9	3.5
1982	3456.4	290.4	8.4
1983	3547.5	268.4	7.6
1984	3640.9	151.0	4.1
1985	3736.8	151.6	4.1
1986	3835.2	160.3	4.2

INDUSTRIAL PRODUCTION: 1929–1986

Year	Index of Industrial Production (1967 = 100)
1929	—
1930	—
1931	—
1932	—
1933	—
1934	—
1935	—
1936	—
1937	—
1938	—
1939	16.0
1940	18.4
1941	23.3
1942	26.7
1943	32.4
1944	34.9
1945	29.9
1946	25.8
1947	29.0
1948	30.2
1949	28.6
1950	33.1
1951	35.9
1952	37.2
1953	40.4
1954	38.2
1955	43.0
1956	44.9
1957	45.5
1958	42.6
1959	47.7
1960	48.8
1961	49.1
1962	53.2
1963	56.3
1964	60.1
1965	66.1
1966	72.0
1967	73.5
1968	77.6
1969	81.2
1970	78.5
1971	79.6
1972	87.3
1973	94.4
1974	93.0
1975	84.8
1976	92.6
1977	100.0
1978	106.5
1979	110.7
1980	108.6
1981	111.0
1982	103.1
1983	109.2
1984	121.4
1985	123.8
1986	125.1

Sources: Potential GNP data based on Robert J. Gordon, *Macroeconomics*, 4th ed., Table A-1. Copyright © 1987 by Robert J. Gordon. Reprinted by permission of Little, Brown and Company. Updated by author. Real GNP used to calculate GNP gap from *Economic Report of the President, 1987*, Table B-2, and *Survey of Current Business* (various issues).

Source: Economic Report of the President, 1987 (Table B-45).

PRICE INDEXES: 1929–1986

Year	GNP deflator (1982 = 100)	Annual changes in GNP deflator (percent per year)	Consumer Price Index (1967 = 100)	Annual changes in CPI (percent per year)	Misery Index (change in CPI plus unemployment rate)
1929	14.6	—	51.3	—	—
1930	14.2	−2.7	50.0	−2.5	0.7
1931	13.0	−8.5	45.6	−8.8	−0.1
1932	11.5	−11.5	40.9	−10.3	5.6
1933	11.2	−2.6	38.8	−5.1	18.5
1934	12.2	8.9	40.1	3.4	28.3
1935	12.5	2.5	41.1	2.5	24.2
1936	12.5	0.0	41.5	1.0	21.1
1937	13.1	4.8	43.0	3.6	20.5
1938	12.9	−1.5	42.2	−1.9	12.4
1939	12.7	−1.6	41.6	−1.4	17.6
1940	13.0	2.4	42.0	1.0	18.2
1941	13.8	6.2	44.1	5.0	19.6
1942	14.7	6.5	48.8	10.7	20.6
1943	15.1	2.7	51.8	6.1	10.8
1944	15.3	1.3	52.7	1.7	3.6
1945	15.7	2.6	53.9	2.3	3.5
1946	19.4	23.6	58.5	8.5	10.4
1947	22.1	13.9	66.9	14.4	18.3
1948	23.6	6.8	72.1	7.8	11.6
1949	23.5	−0.4	71.4	−1.0	4.9
1950	23.9	1.7	72.1	1.0	6.3
1951	25.1	5.0	77.8	7.9	11.2
1952	25.5	1.6	79.5	2.2	5.2
1953	25.9	1.6	80.1	0.8	3.7
1954	26.3	1.5	80.5	0.5	6.0
1955	27.2	3.4	80.2	−0.4	4.0
1956	28.1	3.3	81.4	1.5	5.6
1957	29.1	3.6	84.3	3.6	7.9
1958	29.7	2.1	86.6	2.7	9.5
1959	30.4	2.4	87.3	0.8	6.3
1960	30.9	1.6	88.7	1.6	7.1
1961	31.2	1.0	89.6	1.0	7.7
1962	31.9	2.2	90.6	1.1	6.6
1963	32.4	1.6	91.7	1.2	6.9
1964	32.9	1.5	92.9	1.3	6.5
1965	33.8	2.7	94.5	1.7	6.2
1966	35.0	3.6	97.2	2.9	6.7
1967	35.9	2.6	100.0	2.9	6.7
1968	37.7	5.0	104.2	4.2	7.8
1969	39.8	5.6	109.8	5.4	8.9
1970	42.0	5.5	116.3	5.9	10.8
1971	44.4	5.7	121.3	4.3	10.2
1972	46.5	4.7	125.3	3.3	8.9
1973	49.5	6.5	133.1	6.2	11.1
1974	54.0	9.1	147.7	11.0	16.6
1975	59.3	9.8	161.2	9.1	17.6
1976	63.1	6.4	170.5	5.8	13.5
1977	67.3	6.7	181.5	6.5	13.6
1978	72.2	7.3	195.4	7.7	13.8
1979	78.6	8.9	217.4	11.3	17.1
1980	85.7	9.0	246.8	13.5	20.6
1981	94.0	9.7	272.4	10.4	18.0
1982	100.0	6.4	289.1	6.1	15.8
1983	103.9	3.9	298.4	3.2	12.8
1984	107.9	3.8	311.1	4.3	11.8
1985	111.5	3.3	322.2	3.6	10.8
1986	114.5	2.7	328.4	1.9	8.9

Sources: Economic Report of the President, 1987 and *Survey of Current Business* (various issues) for GNP deflator; Bureau of Labor Statistics for Consumer Price Index.

MONEY SUPPLY AND VELOCITY: 1929–1986

Year	M-1 Billions of dollars	M-1 Percentage change	M-1 Velocity (% of nominal GNP)	M-2 Billions of dollars	M-2 Percentage change	M-2 Velocity (% of nominal GNP)
1929	26.6	—	3.9	46.6	—	2.2
1930	25.8	−3.0	3.5	45.7	−1.9	2.0
1931	24.1	−6.6	3.2	42.7	−6.6	1.8
1932	21.1	−12.4	2.8	36.0	−15.7	1.6
1933	19.9	−5.7	2.8	32.2	−10.6	1.7
1934	21.9	10.0	3.0	34.4	6.8	1.9
1935	25.9	18.3	2.8	39.1	13.7	1.9
1936	29.5	13.9	2.8	43.5	11.2	1.9
1937	30.9	4.8	3.0	45.7	5.1	2.0
1938	30.5	−1.3	2.8	45.5	−0.4	1.9
1939	34.2	12.1	2.7	49.3	8.4	1.9
1940	39.7	16.1	2.5	55.2	12.0	1.8
1941	46.5	17.1	2.7	62.5	13.2	2.0
1942	55.4	19.1	2.9	71.2	13.9	2.2
1943	72.2	30.3	2.7	89.9	26.3	2.1
1944	85.3	18.1	2.5	106.8	18.8	2.0
1945	99.2	16.3	2.2	126.6	18.5	1.7
1946	106.5	7.4	2.0	138.7	9.6	1.5
1947	111.8	5.0	2.1	146.0	5.3	1.6
1948	112.3	0.4	2.3	148.1	1.4	1.8
1949	111.2	−1.0	2.3	147.5	−0.4	1.8
1950	114.1	2.6	2.5	150.8	2.2	1.9
1951	119.2	4.5	2.8	156.5	3.8	2.1
1952	125.2	5.0	2.8	164.9	5.4	2.1
1953	128.2	2.5	2.9	171.2	3.8	2.2
1954	130.3	1.6	2.9	177.2	3.5	2.1
1955	134.5	3.2	3.0	183.7	3.7	2.2
1956	136.0	1.1	3.1	186.9	1.7	2.3
1957	136.8	0.6	3.3	191.8	2.6	2.4
1958	138.4	1.2	3.3	201.1	4.8	2.3
1959	141.4	3.6	3.4	293.3	4.7	1.6
1960	141.4	0.0	3.6	304.3	3.8	1.7
1961	144.3	2.1	3.7	324.9	6.8	1.6
1962	147.9	2.5	3.9	350.2	7.8	1.6
1963	152.4	3.1	4.0	379.7	8.4	1.6
1964	158.3	3.9	4.1	409.4	7.8	1.6
1965	165.1	4.2	4.3	442.6	8.1	1.6
1966	172.7	4.6	4.5	471.5	6.5	1.6
1967	179.6	4.0	4.5	503.7	6.8	1.6
1968	192.1	7.0	4.6	545.4	8.3	1.6
1969	203.5	5.9	4.7	579.1	6.2	1.7
1970	211.2	3.8	4.8	603.2	4.2	1.7
1971	225.2	6.8	4.9	676.4	12.1	1.6
1972	241.6	7.1	5.0	760.9	12.5	1.6
1973	259.2	7.3	5.2	836.2	9.9	1.6
1974	272.2	5.0	5.4	887.2	6.1	1.7
1975	285.0	4.7	5.6	970.1	9.3	1.6
1976	301.0	5.6	5.9	1095.7	12.9	1.6
1977	324.0	7.6	6.1	1234.4	12.7	1.6
1978	350.5	8.2	6.4	1339.6	8.5	1.7
1979	377.6	7.7	6.6	1450.2	8.3	1.7
1980	401.1	6.2	6.8	1566.7	8.0	1.7
1981	429.5	7.1	7.1	1714.6	9.4	1.8
1982	457.6	6.6	6.9	1874.5	9.3	1.7
1983	508.9	11.2	6.7	2109.3	12.5	1.6
1984	544.5	7.0	6.9	2277.9	8.0	1.7
1985	593.9	9.1	6.7	2484.6	9.1	1.6
1986	672.5	13.2	6.3	2683.2	8.0	1.6

Sources: Data from 1929 to 1958 from U.S. Department of Commerce, *Historical Statistics of the United States: Colonial Times to 1970;* data from 1959 to 1986 from Federal Reserve Bank of Boston.

FEDERAL GOVERNMENT BUDGET: 1929–1986

| | Actual federal government budget | | | | |
| | (in billions of 1982 dollars) | | | (as % of real GNP) | |
Year	Receipts	Expenditures	Budget surplus	Expenditures	Budget surplus
1929	26.0	18.5	7.5	2.6	1.1
1930	21.8	19.7	2.1	3.1	0.3
1931	16.2	32.3	−16.2	5.5	−2.7
1932	15.7	27.8	−12.2	5.5	−2.4
1933	24.1	35.7	−11.6	7.2	−2.3
1934	29.5	52.5	−23.0	9.8	−4.3
1935	32.0	52.8	−20.8	9.1	−3.6
1936	40.8	69.6	−28.8	10.5	−4.3
1937	54.2	57.3	−3.1	8.2	−0.4
1938	50.4	67.4	−17.1	10.2	−2.6
1939	53.5	70.9	−17.3	9.9	−2.4
1940	66.9	76.9	−10.0	10.0	−1.3
1941	112.3	148.6	−36.2	16.3	−4.0
1942	156.5	381.6	−225.2	35.3	−20.8
1943	260.3	568.9	−308.6	44.6	−24.2
1944	268.6	624.8	−356.2	45.3	−25.8
1945	272.0	539.5	−267.5	39.8	−19.7
1946	209.8	191.8	18.0	17.5	1.6
1947	199.5	139.4	60.2	13.1	5.7
1948	186.0	150.4	35.6	13.6	3.2
1949	167.7	178.7	−11.1	16.1	−1.0
1950	210.9	172.4	38.5	14.3	3.2
1951	257.4	231.5	25.9	17.4	1.9
1952	265.5	280.0	−14.5	20.3	−1.1
1953	271.8	299.6	−27.8	20.9	−1.9
1954	244.1	267.3	−23.2	18.9	−1.6
1955	268.8	252.2	16.5	16.9	1.1
1956	279.4	258.0	21.4	16.9	1.4
1957	283.5	275.6	7.9	17.8	0.5
1958	267.0	301.7	−34.7	19.6	−2.3
1959	298.0	301.6	−3.6	18.5	−0.2
1960	313.6	303.9	9.7	18.2	0.6
1961	317.3	329.8	−12.5	19.3	−0.7
1962	336.1	349.2	−13.2	19.4	−0.7
1963	356.8	355.9	0.9	19.0	0.0
1964	353.2	363.2	−10.0	18.4	−0.5
1965	372.2	370.7	1.5	17.8	0.1
1966	410.0	415.1	−5.1	18.8	−0.2
1967	425.1	461.8	−36.8	20.3	−1.6
1968	469.2	485.1	−15.9	20.5	−0.7
1969	501.8	480.7	21.1	19.8	0.9
1970	465.2	494.8	−29.5	20.5	−1.2
1971	456.5	506.3	−49.8	20.4	−2.0
1972	499.4	535.5	−36.1	20.5	−1.4
1973	532.7	544.0	−11.3	19.8	−0.4
1974	544.3	565.7	−21.5	20.7	−0.8
1975	497.3	614.2	−116.9	22.8	−4.3
1976	539.0	623.9	−84.9	22.1	−3.0
1977	570.7	639.1	−68.4	21.6	−2.3
1978	611.4	651.9	−40.6	20.9	−1.3
1979	642.5	663.0	−20.5	20.8	−0.6
1980	646.2	717.7	−71.5	22.5	−2.2
1981	680.3	748.2	−67.9	23.0	−2.1
1982	635.3	781.2	−145.9	24.7	−4.6
1983	635.1	804.5	−169.4	24.5	−5.2
1984	673.3	830.9	−157.6	23.8	−4.5
1985	705.7	883.3	−177.7	24.6	−5.0
1986	722.1	899.8	−177.7	24.5	−4.8

Budget figures were deflated using the GNP deflator.

Sources: U.S. Department of Commerce, *The National Income and Product Accounts of the United States, 1929–1982; Survey of Current Business* (various issues).

FEDERAL GOVERNMENT BUDGET: 1929–1986

| | Full-employment budget | | | | |
| | (in billions of 1982 dollars) | | | (as % of potential GNP) | |
Year	Receipts	Expenditures	Budget surplus	Expenditures	Budget surplus
1929	—	—	—	—	—
1930	—	—	—	—	—
1931	—	—	—	—	—
1932	—	—	—	—	—
1933	—	—	—	—	—
1934	—	—	—	—	—
1935	—	—	—	—	—
1936	—	—	—	—	—
1937	—	—	—	—	—
1938	—	—	—	—	—
1939	—	—	—	—	—
1940	—	—	—	—	—
1941	—	—	—	—	—
1942	—	—	—	—	—
1943	—	—	—	—	—
1944	—	—	—	—	—
1945	—	—	—	—	—
1946	—	—	—	—	—
1947	—	—	—	—	—
1948	—	—	—	—	—
1949	—	—	—	—	—
1950	—	—	—	—	—
1951	—	—	—	—	—
1952	—	—	—	—	—
1953	—	—	—	—	—
1954	—	—	—	—	—
1955	259.9	251.5	8.4	17.2	0.6
1956	274.5	258.0	16.5	17.1	1.1
1957	284.5	276.3	8.2	17.8	0.5
1958	285.1	297.3	−12.2	18.5	−0.8
1959	298.4	301.0	−2.6	18.2	−0.2
1960	319.1	303.6	15.5	17.7	0.9
1961	326.3	326.9	−0.6	18.5	0.0
1962	336.7	349.5	−12.9	19.1	−0.7
1963	355.2	356.2	−0.9	18.9	0.0
1964	344.7	364.7	−20.1	18.9	−1.0
1965	353.8	374.3	−20.4	18.5	−1.0
1966	380.0	421.1	−41.1	20.1	−2.0
1967	399.7	468.0	−68.2	21.5	−3.1
1968	439.3	492.8	−53.6	21.9	−2.4
1969	478.9	488.9	−10.1	21.0	−0.4
1970	470.2	496.0	−25.7	20.5	−1.1
1971	467.3	505.2	−37.8	20.2	−1.5
1972	502.2	535.5	−33.3	20.7	−1.3
1973	518.4	545.7	−27.3	20.4	−1.0
1974	550.4	567.0	−16.7	20.5	−0.6
1975	531.4	603.7	−72.3	21.2	−2.5
1976	562.9	616.0	−53.1	21.0	−1.8
1977	582.5	634.0	−51.6	21.0	−1.7
1978	604.8	651.1	−46.3	21.0	−1.5
1979	638.2	663.0	−24.8	20.7	−0.8
1980	668.0	711.7	−43.6	21.7	−1.3
1981	710.0	739.3	−29.3	22.0	−0.9
1982	705.2	764.7	−59.5	22.1	−1.7
1983	697.9	791.3	−93.5	22.3	−2.6
1984	700.0	825.9	−125.9	22.7	−3.5
1985	726.7	879.8	−153.1	23.5	−4.1
1986	740.6	897.5	−156.9	23.4	−4.1

Sources: Potential GNP and full-employment budget from Robert J. Gordon, *Macroeconomics*, 4th ed., Table A-1. Copyright © 1987 by Robert J. Gordon. Reprinted by permission of Little, Brown and Company. Updated by author. Real GNP and actual expenditures from *Economic Report of the President, 1987* and U.S. Department of Commerce, *Survey of Current Business* (various issues).

STATE AND LOCAL GOVERNMENT BUDGET: 1929–1986

	Actual state and local government budget (in billions of 1982 dollars)			(as % of real GNP)	
Year	Receipts	Expenditures	Budget surplus	Expenditures	Budget surplus
1929	52.1	53.4	−1.4	7.5	−0.2
1930	54.9	59.2	−4.2	9.2	−0.7
1931	59.2	65.4	−6.2	11.1	−1.0
1932	63.5	66.1	−2.6	13.0	−0.5
1933	64.3	64.3	0.0	12.9	0.0
1934	70.5	66.4	4.1	12.4	0.8
1935	72.8	68.8	4.0	11.9	0.7
1936	68.8	64.8	4.0	9.8	0.6
1937	69.5	64.1	5.3	9.2	0.8
1938	72.1	69.8	2.3	10.5	0.4
1939	75.6	75.6	0.0	10.5	0.0
1940	76.9	71.5	5.4	9.3	0.7
1941	75.4	65.9	9.4	7.3	1.0
1942	72.1	59.9	12.2	5.5	1.1
1943	72.2	55.6	16.6	4.4	1.3
1944	72.5	55.6	17.0	4.0	1.2
1945	73.9	57.3	16.6	4.2	1.2
1946	67.0	57.2	9.8	5.2	0.9
1947	69.7	65.2	4.5	6.1	0.4
1948	75.0	74.6	0.4	6.7	0.0
1949	83.0	86.0	−3.0	7.8	−0.3
1950	89.1	94.1	−5.0	7.8	−0.4
1951	93.2	95.2	−2.0	7.2	−0.1
1952	99.6	100.0	−0.4	7.2	0.0
1953	105.8	105.4	0.4	7.3	0.0
1954	110.3	114.8	−4.6	8.1	−0.3
1955	116.5	121.0	−4.4	8.1	−0.3
1956	124.6	127.8	−3.2	8.4	−0.2
1957	132.3	136.8	−4.5	8.8	−0.3
1958	141.4	149.5	−8.1	9.7	−0.5
1959	153.3	154.6	−1.3	9.5	−0.1
1960	161.8	161.5	0.3	9.7	0.0
1961	173.4	174.7	−1.3	10.2	−0.1
1962	183.7	182.4	1.3	10.1	0.1
1963	195.7	194.1	1.5	10.4	0.1
1964	212.2	209.1	3.0	10.6	0.2
1965	223.4	223.4	0.0	10.7	0.0
1966	243.4	242.0	1.4	11.0	0.1
1967	262.1	265.2	−3.1	11.7	−0.1
1968	286.2	285.9	0.3	12.1	0.0
1969	303.5	299.7	3.8	12.4	0.2
1970	323.3	319.0	4.3	13.2	0.2
1971	345.9	340.1	5.9	13.7	0.2
1972	385.6	356.6	29.0	13.7	1.1
1973	396.8	369.5	27.3	13.5	1.0
1974	394.6	381.3	13.3	14.0	0.5
1975	404.0	396.6	7.4	14.7	0.3
1976	428.1	404.0	24.1	14.3	0.9
1977	445.9	405.9	40.0	13.7	1.4
1978	457.5	417.2	40.3	13.4	1.3
1979	452.0	416.9	35.1	13.1	1.1
1980	455.1	423.8	31.3	13.3	1.0
1981	452.8	416.4	36.4	12.8	1.1
1982	449.4	414.3	35.1	13.1	1.1
1983	469.4	423.7	45.7	12.9	1.4
1984	501.2	437.8	63.4	12.5	1.8
1985	517.9	471.6	46.4	13.2	1.3
1986	542.3	487.2	55.0	13.3	1.5

Budget figures were deflated using the GNP deflator.

Sources: U.S. Department of Commerce, The National Income and Product Accounts of the United States, 1929–1982 and *Survey of Current Business* (various issues).

CIVILIAN POPULATION AND LABOR FORCE: 1929–1986

Year	Civilian noninstitutional population aged 16 and over (millions)	Civilian labor force (millions)	Civilian employment/ population ratio (percent)	Civilian unemployment rate (percent)
1929	85.6	49.2	55.6	3.2
1930	87.1	49.8	52.2	8.7
1931	88.2	50.4	48.1	15.9
1932	89.3	51.0	43.6	23.6
1933	90.5	51.6	42.8	24.9
1934	91.7	52.2	44.6	21.7
1935	92.9	52.9	45.5	20.1
1936	94.1	53.4	47.2	16.9
1937	95.2	54.0	48.6	14.3
1938	96.5	54.6	45.8	19.0
1939	97.8	55.2	46.8	17.2
1940	100.4	55.6	47.6	14.6
1941	101.5	55.9	50.4	9.9
1942	102.6	56.4	54.5	4.7
1943	103.7	55.5	57.6	1.9
1944	104.6	54.6	57.9	1.2
1945	105.6	53.9	56.1	1.9
1946	106.5	57.5	53.6	3.9
1947	101.8	59.4	56.0	3.9
1948	103.1	60.6	56.6	3.8
1949	104.0	61.3	55.4	5.9
1950	105.0	62.2	56.1	5.3
1951	104.6	62.0	57.3	3.3
1952	105.2	62.1	57.3	3.0
1953	107.1	63.0	57.1	2.9
1954	108.3	63.6	55.5	5.5
1955	109.7	65.0	56.7	4.4
1956	111.0	66.6	57.5	4.1
1957	112.3	66.9	57.1	4.3
1958	113.7	67.6	55.4	6.8
1959	115.3	68.4	56.0	5.5
1960	117.2	69.6	56.1	5.5
1961	118.8	70.5	55.4	6.7
1962	120.1	70.6	55.5	5.5
1963	122.4	71.8	55.4	5.7
1964	124.5	73.1	55.7	5.2
1965	126.5	74.5	56.2	4.5
1966	128.1	75.8	56.9	3.8
1967	129.9	77.3	57.3	3.8
1968	132.0	78.7	57.5	3.6
1969	134.3	80.7	58.0	3.5
1970	137.1	82.8	57.4	4.9
1971	140.2	84.4	56.6	5.9
1972	144.1	87.0	57.0	5.6
1973	147.1	89.4	57.8	4.9
1974	150.1	91.9	57.8	5.6
1975	153.2	93.8	56.1	8.5
1976	156.2	96.2	56.8	7.7
1977	159.0	99.0	57.9	7.1
1978	161.9	102.3	59.3	6.1
1979	164.9	105.0	59.9	5.8
1980	167.7	106.9	59.2	7.1
1981	170.1	108.7	59.0	7.6
1982	172.2	110.2	57.8	9.7
1983	174.2	111.6	57.9	9.6
1984	176.4	113.5	59.5	7.5
1985	178.2	115.5	60.1	7.2
1986	180.6	117.8	60.7	7.0

Data from 1929–1946 are for persons 14 years of age and over; data from 1947 to 1986 are for persons 16 years of age and over.

Source: U.S. Department of Labor, *Employment and Earnings* (various issues).

GLOSSARY

A

Ability-to-pay principle. A theory of taxation that states that individuals should be taxed in proportion to their income or some other measure of ability to pay.

Absolute advantage. The ability to produce a good or service with fewer resources; refers only to relative productivity.

Absolute poverty approach. Poverty defined by an income below the level necessary to maintain a minimum standard of living.

Accounting identities. Relationships between macroeconomic variables that are always true by definition.

Accounting profit. The difference between revenues and explicit costs, ignoring implicit costs.

Action lag. The delay between when a problem is recognized and when policy actions are taken.

Activists. Economists who believe it necessary, desirable, and practical to use discretionary monetary and fiscal policies to stabilize the economy.

Affirmative action programs. Government requirements that employers adopt programs and make extraordinary efforts to recruit, hire, and promote individuals from specific groups, such as women, blacks, and Hispanics, that have been subjected to past economic or institutional discrimination.

Aggregate demand (AD). Demand for all goods and services in the economy; relationship between total quantity of goods and services demanded and general price level.

Aggregate expenditures (AE). Total expenditures on final goods by all sectors of the economy during a particular period of time.

Aggregate output. The total quantity of all goods and services produced in the economy in a given period of time.

Aggregate supply (AS). Supply of all goods and services in the economy; relationship between total quantity of goods and services supplied and general price level.

Allocative efficiency. Producing the combination of goods and services that satisfies society's wants to the greatest degree.

"All-other-things-unchanged" assumption. The assumption commonly made in demand-and-supply analysis that all determinants of quantity demanded and quantity supplied, except price, are held constant.

Antitrust policy. Government actions that attempt to control market power and monopolistic behavior and to foster competitive behavior.

Arbitration. The settlement of differences between two parties (such as a union and management) by an impartial third party, the arbitrator, whose decision is legally binding on the other two parties.

Assets. Items of value.

Automatic stabilizers. Taxes and expenditures that automatically change when economic activity changes. Stabilizers cause a decrease in the actual budget balance when GNP falls and an increase when GNP rises. These changes reduce cyclical changes in aggregate demand. Important stabilizers are income taxes, unemployment compensation, and welfare.

Autonomous consumption. The portion of consumption that is independent of the level of income. A change in a factor other than income causes a change in autonomous consumption and results in a shift in a consumption line.

Average-cost pricing. A price-setting option for rate regulation whereby price is set equal to average total cost (P = ATC), including an allowance for normal profit; the most commonly used price-setting mechanism.

Average fixed cost (AFC). Total fixed costs divided by the quantity of goods or services produced (total product). Mathematically, AFC = TFC ÷ Q.

Average product (AP). The ratio of total quantity produced (total product) to units of variable resources used to produce those goods. Mathematically, AP = Q ÷ Units of variable resources.

Average propensity to consume (APC). The ratio of consumption to income at some specified level of income; indicates the proportion of a specified level of income that will be spent on consumption.

Average tax rate. The proportion of income paid in taxes; the ratio of taxes paid to taxable income.

Average total cost (ATC). Also called *unit cost*; calculated as total costs divided by the quantity of goods or services produced (total product). Mathematically, ATC = TC ÷ Q or ATC = AVC + AFC.

Average variable cost (AVC). Also called *unit variable cost*; calculated as total variable costs divided by the quantity of goods or services produced (total product). Mathematically, AVC = TVC ÷ Q.

B

Balance on capital account. The net flow of funds used to purchase physical and financial assets; a positive balance indicates that purchases of domestic assets by foreigners exceed purchases of foreign assets by domestic residents.

Balance on current account. Net exports of goods and services less net transfers (gifts and foreign aid) to foreign residents and foreign governments; a negative balance indicates that imports plus transfers to domestic residents exceed exports plus transfers to foreign residents.

Balance on goods and services. The difference between the values of exports and imports of both goods and services.

Barriers to entry. Legal, technological, or economic factors that make it impossible or very difficult for a new firm to enter a particular market; examples include control of key resources, economies of scale, and government patents or licenses.

Barter. An exchange of one product or service for another; an exchange not involving money.

Benefits-received principle. A theory of taxation that states that individuals should be taxed in proportion to the benefits they receive from government goods and services.

Bilateral monopoly. A model of a labor market in which market power exists on both sides of the market; a union with control over the supply of labor and an employer with market power demanding labor.

Bonds. IOUs of a business or government representing a promise to pay a specified sum of interest at regular intervals (usually every four or six months) for a specified period of time. At the end of the loan period, the borrower is obligated to repay the original amount loaned.

Budget balance. The difference between government receipts (taxes and fees) and expenditures (purchases, transfers, and interest payments on national debt).

Budget constraint. In indifference-curve analysis, a line indicating the combinations of two goods that a buyer can purchase, given the price of each good and the buyer's income.

Budget deficit. A negative budget balance, when expenditures exceed receipts.

Budget surplus. A positive budget balance, when receipts exceed expenditures.

Business cycle. The recurring but irregular swings in aggregate economic activity. A complete cycle has four phases: recession, trough, recovery, and peak.

Business firm. An organization that produces goods and services for sale.

C

Capital/labor ratio. The average quantity of capital resources per worker, calculated by dividing the stock of capital by the number of employed workers.

Capital resources. The buildings, machinery, roads, transportation equipment, and other long-lasting items that can be used to produce goods and services. Also called *capital goods*.

Cartel. A form of oligopoly in which firms formally agree to establish a common price, in effect acting as a monopoly.

Causation. The presumption that a change in one factor causes a change in another factor with which it is statistically correlated.

Ceiling price. A legal maximum price established by government for a specific market.

Checking deposits. Funds held in checking accounts by banks; may be transferred by writing a check; included in the M-1 definition of money.

Circular-flow model. A model of a market economy that shows the interaction of households and businesses in product and resource markets.

Classical economic theory. Macroeconomic theories of economists in the late 1800s and early 1900s who assumed that interest rates, wages, and prices were flexible; this theory predicts that the economy will tend to operate at full employment.

Classical quantity theory. The proposition of the classical economists that changes in the money supply cause proportional changes in the price level; based on the equation of exchange (M × V = P × Q) assuming velocity (V) is constant and real GNP (Q) equals potential GNP.

Closed shop. A workplace in which the employer is obligated to hire only union members; severely limited by the Taft–Hartley Act.

Collective bargaining. The process by which a union and management negotiate a mutually acceptable contract and define the meanings of contract terms.

Commodity money. An item used as a medium of exchange that also has significant value for other uses.

Comparative advantage. The ability to produce a good or service at a smaller opportunity cost; refers to relative efficiency.

Competitive resource market. A resource market in which no individual buyer or seller has any market power, resources move freely, and buyers and sellers have perfect information on available alternatives.

Complements. Goods that can be used with other goods, such as hot dogs and hot-dog rolls. When two goods are complements, an increase in the price of one leads to a decrease in demand for the other.

Conglomerate merger. A merger between firms that otherwise have no economic relationship; a merger that is neither horizontal nor vertical.

Constant-cost industry. An industry in which entry and exit of firms has no effect on product costs; characterized by a horizontal long-run supply curve.

Constant returns to scale. A situation in which long-run average cost is constant; implies that large and small plants have equal technical efficiency.

Consumer price index (CPI). A price index reflecting changes in the prices of consumer goods; involves the use of a constant market-basket approach.

Consumer products. Goods such as autos, food, appliances, and movies, and services such as health care that directly satisfy consumer wants.

Consumer surplus. The difference between the total benefits buyers receive and the total expenditures they make for all units of a product they consume.

Consumption expenditures (C). Expenditures of households on final goods during a particular period of time.

Consumption schedule. A table showing the level of consumption expenditures at various levels of disposable income.

Contestable market. A market with costless and unrestricted entry and exit.

Contractionary gap. When potential GNP exceeds actual GNP; a positive GNP gap. When the actual unemployment rate is greater than the natural rate of unemployment.

Contractionary policies. Changes in fiscal and/or monetary policies that decrease aggregate demand. Higher taxes and lower spending are contractionary fiscal policies; raising the required reserve ratio and selling government securities are contractionary monetary policies.

Contracts theory. A view of employment based on the existence of explicit or implicit contracts defining worker–employer relationships. Contracts provide long-term benefits to both workers and employers but fix nominal wages, slowing short-run adjustments in wages.

Corporation. A firm created as a legal entity separate from the persons who established it. It is usually owned by many individuals, whose liability is limited to their investment in the firm.

Correlation. The statistical relationship between two factors and the extent to which changes in one factor are accompanied by changes in the other.

Cost-push inflation. Increases in the price level caused by decreases in aggregate supply. Most economists believe that sustained decreases in aggregate supply are unlikely.

Craft union. A union of workers sharing a common skill, trade, or profession.

Cross elasticity of demand. A measure of the responsiveness of quantity demanded for one product to a change in the price of another product, usually expressed as the percentage change in quantity demanded for one product divided by the percentage change in the price of another product.

Crowding-out effect. A decrease in investment and consumption resulting from the increase in interest rates caused by expansionary fiscal policies (holding the money supply constant). This effect is strongest when the economy is close to potential GNP, and it reduces the effect of expansionary fiscal policies.

Currency appreciation. An increase in the exchange rate for the domestic currency (for example, from 150 to 160 yen per dollar); each unit of the domestic currency buys more units of the foreign currency; makes imports from foreign countries less expensive to domestic residents but exports to foreign countries more expensive to foreign residents.

Currency depreciation. A decline in the exchange rate for the domestic currency (for example, from 150 to 140 yen per dollar); each unit of the domestic currency buys fewer units of the foreign currency; makes imports from foreign countries more expensive to domestic residents but exports to foreign countries less expensive to foreign residents.

Cyclical unemployment. Unemployment resulting from decreases in aggregate economic output. Cyclical unemployment increases during recessions and decreases during recoveries.

D

Demand. All the quantities of a product that individuals are both willing and able to buy at every possible price during a specified period of time.

Demand curve. A graphic representation of the demand schedule; the demand curve always slopes downward and to the right.

Demand function. An algebraic expression showing how quantity demanded is affected by market price and other factors influencing demand.

Demand-pull inflation. Increases in the price level caused by increases in aggregate demand.

Demand schedule. A table showing quantities of a product that consumers are willing and able to buy at various prices during a specified period of time.

Dependent variable. In any given relationship, an element that is affected by a change in the value of an independent variable.

Deposit multiplier. The ultimate change in checking deposits (bank money) caused by a $1 initial change in bank reserves; in a simple banking system, equal to 1 ÷ Required reserve ratio.

Depreciation (capital consumption allowance). An estimate of that part of the original cost of capital goods, such as machinery and buildings, that has been used up or worn out during a specific period of time. A business cost representing the value of capital resources used to produce goods; the fractional cost charged each year over the life of the resource to reflect both physical wear and tear and obsolescence. Unlike other costs, no payment is made for depreciation.

Devaluation. A deliberate, planned reduction in the exchange rate under a system of fixed exchange rates.

Developed economy. An economy that is industrialized, has relatively high standards of living, and has sophisticated institutions (government, education, transportation, and communication).

Diminishing marginal returns. A situation in which each additional unit of a variable resource has a smaller marginal product than the previous unit; total product increases, but at a decreasing rate.

Discouraged workers. Individuals who are out of work and who currently are not looking for work because they believe that they cannot find it. They are not officially classified as unemployed.

Discretionary fiscal policy. Deliberate changes made in elements of the federal government's budget—taxes, transfer payments, and/or government purchases of goods and services—to affect the level of aggregate demand. The aim of such policies is to achieve macroeconomic stabilization—full employment and stable prices.

Discretionary policies. Deliberate changes in monetary and/or fiscal policies to counteract cyclical changes in economic activity, that is, to reduce or eliminate expansionary and contractionary gaps. Also called countercyclical policies.

Diseconomies of scale. A situation in which long-run average cost increases as a firm increases the size (or scale) of its plant and output; implies that larger plants are less technically efficient than smaller plants.

Disinflation. A decline in the rate of increase of the general price level; the price level continues to rise, but more slowly.

Disposable income (DI). Income received by households in a particular period of time and available to be spent or saved; household income after taxes have been deducted and transfer payments have been added.

Dividends. The portion of a corporation's profits paid out to its shareholders.

E

Economic development. The process of changing economic, social, and political systems in order to sustain economic growth and overcome mass poverty.

Economic discrimination. Income inequality caused by hiring, firing, promoting, or paying a wage differential on the basis of some factor, such as race, sex, or age, that has no direct relationship to marginal productivity.

Economic growth. An increase in society's production possibilities.

Economic model. A simplified verbal, tabular, graphic, or mathematical representation of a real economy that is used to analyze and predict how the economy would work under the specified conditions.

Economic profit. The difference between revenues and the full opportunity costs of all resources used, including both explicit and implicit costs.

Economic rent. Payment for a resource in excess of the real opportunity cost of that resource.

Economics. The study of how individuals and societies, faced with the problem of scarcity, choose how to produce, exchange, and consume goods and services.

Economic system. The institutions and mechanisms used to determine what and how to produce and who will receive the goods and services produced.

Economies of scale. A situation in which long-run average cost decreases as a firm increases the size (or scale) of its plant and output; implies that larger plants are more technically efficient than small plants if large quantities of goods are produced.

Equation of exchange. The identity of total spending and nominal GNP, or Ms × V = P × Q.

Equilibrium price. The price at which quantity supplied equals quantity demanded; graphically, the point of intersection of the demand and supply curves.

Equimarginal principle. The principle that for equilibrium to exist, the ratio of extra benefits to extra costs for each product (or resource) must be equal. For consumer choice it means that for each product consumed, buyers will receive the same marginal utility per dollar. Mathematically,

$$\frac{\text{Marginal utility of product A}}{\text{Price of product A}} = \frac{\text{Marginal utility of product B}}{\text{Price of product B}}$$

Equity. Distributing goods and services in a manner considered by society to be fair.

Exchange rate. The price of one currency in terms of another; the quantity of one currency that must be given up to obtain a unit of another currency (for example, 150 yen per dollar).

Expansionary gap. When actual GNP exceeds potential GNP; a negative GNP gap. When actual unemployment is below the natural rate of unemployment.

Expansionary policies. Changes in fiscal and/or monetary policies that increase aggregate demand. Lower taxes and higher spending are expansionary fiscal policies; reducing the required reserve ratio and buying government securities are expansionary monetary policies.

Explicit costs. Costs involving direct payment for resources used by a firm. The only costs considered in calculating accounting profit.

Exports (X). Expenditures made by foreign households, businesses, and governments for goods produced domestically. Exports must be added to aggregate domestic expenditures when measuring GNP; they represent spending to purchase domestically produced goods.

Extensive growth. Economic growth achieved by increasing the quantity of economic resources, such as labor and capital resources.

External benefits. Benefits from a product received by individuals other than those who demand and supply it.

External costs. Costs of a product that are borne by individuals other than those who demand and supply it.

Externalities. Benefits and costs from any product that affect individuals other than those who demand and supply the product.

F

Fallacy of composition. Incorrectly concluding that what is true of the part is also true of the whole.

Fallacy of division. Incorrectly concluding that what is true of the whole is also true of every part.

Final goods. Products and services that are (or will be) sold to their ultimate user. GNP is a measure of the value of final goods produced.

Financial markets. Markets for funds used to make investments and to finance consumption. Markets in which lenders supply and borrowers demand loanable funds. In these markets, dollars saved become dollars invested.

Fixed costs. Costs associated with fixed resources; they are constant in the short run. Examples include rental payments on buildings, interest paid on debt, and property taxes.

Fixed (or pegged) exchange rates. A system in which exchange rates are not allowed to adjust in response to changes in demand for and supply of currency.

Fixed investment. Expenditures by businesses for capital resources, such as new plants, equipment, or commercial buildings, and by households for residential construction during a particular period of time.

Fixed resources. Resources that in the short run do not vary directly with output; that is, output can be increased (within limits) without using more fixed resources. Typical examples are buildings and machinery.

Flexible (or freely floating) exchange rates. A system in which exchange rates are determined by demand and supply without government intervention in foreign-exchange markets.

Flow. A quantity or activity measured over a period of time, such as the gross national product produced in a particular year or the amount of income earned in a specific month. (*See* Shock.)

Foreign sector. The part of a nation's economy made up of foreign individuals, businesses, and governments that participate in the nation's product, resource, and financial markets.

Fractional reserve banking system. A system in which banks hold reserves that are only a fraction of their deposits.

Frictional unemployment. Unemployment resulting from normal job-search activities, or from imperfect knowledge and imperfect mobility. Although a permanent feature of a dynamic economy, frictional unemployment is temporary for any individual.

Full-employment budget. Government receipts and expenditures that would occur under existing fiscal policies if the economy were producing at its potential GNP level. Changes in the full-employment budget reflect discretionary changes in fiscal policies.

Future value (FV). A sum of money to be received or paid at a future time.

G

General price level. The average price of all goods and services in the economy.

GNP deflator. The ratio of nominal GNP to real GNP expressed as a percentage; a measure of the general price level.

GNP gap. The difference between real GNP and potential GNP for a specific period of time. When positive, it measures the output lost as a result of unemployment.

Government purchases (G). Expenditures by the government sector to purchase final goods; a part of aggregate expenditures.

Gross national product (GNP). A measure of the total market value of all final goods and services produced in the economy during a given period of time.

H

Horizontal equity. A principle of taxation that suggests that individuals in equal economic circumstances should pay an equal amount of taxes.

Horizontal merger. A merger between firms that produce substitute products and that would otherwise be competitors.

Household. Any person or group of people living together and functioning as a single economic unit.

Household theory of labor supply. A theory suggesting that labor supply decisions are made within households, based on considerations of taste and preferences, market wages, nonmarket productivity, and other family resources.

Human capital. The skills, education, training, and experience of individuals.

Human resources. The strength, skills, training, and talents of society's population that can be used to produce goods and services.

I

Impact lag. The delay between when policy actions are taken and when they fully affect aggregate demand.

Imperfect competition. Any market structure that does not have the characteristics of pure competition; monopoly, oligopoly, and monopolistic competition are imperfect competition market structures.

Implicit costs. Opportunity costs for resources that a firm owns and uses; benefits not received from the next best use of the resource. Costs considered in calculating economic profit but not in calculating accounting profit.

Import quota. A limit on the quantity of a particular good that can be imported.

Imports (M). Expenditures by U.S. households, businesses, and governments for goods and services produced in other countries. These expenditures must be deducted from aggregate expenditures in order to measure GNP; they represent aggregate spending that is not used to purchase domestically produced goods.

Import tariff. A tax placed on imported goods.

Incidence of poverty. The percentage of the population that falls into the poverty group by official standards.

Income effect. The change in quantity demanded resulting from a change in real income caused by a change in price.

Income elasticity of demand. A measure of responsiveness of quantity demanded to a change in income; usually expressed as percentage change in quantity demanded divided by percentage change in income.

Increasing-cost industry. An industry in which entry of new firms raises the price of resources and product costs; characterized by an upward sloping long-run supply curve.

Increasing marginal returns. A situation in which each additional unit of a variable resource has a greater marginal product than the previous unit; total product increases at an increasing rate.

Independent variable. In any given relationship, an element that is subject to independent change. A change in the value of an independent variable affects the value of the dependent variable.

Indexation. Adjusting the nominal values of wages, transfer payments, income tax brackets, or other economic variables in direct proportion to changes in the general price level.

Indifference curve. A graphic representation of the indifference set.

Indifference map. A graph displaying several indifference curves representing different levels of satisfaction, or total utility.

Indifference set. A table showing several combinations of goods and services that would give a buyer the same total utility.

Induced consumption. A change in consumption in response to a change in income (holding other factors constant); results in a movement along a consumption line.

Industrial policy. A set of microeconomic policies designed to affect economic growth; includes tax rules, research and development grants, direct subsidies, international trade restrictions, and labor-training programs.

Industrial union. A union of workers sharing a common employer; workers may or may not share a common skill or trade.

Industry. A group of firms producing the same or similar products.

Inferior goods. Goods for which demand varies inversely with income, decreasing as income rises and increasing as income falls—for example, margarine.

Inflation. A sustained upward movement in the general level of prices.

Inflation rate. The annual rate of increase in the price level.

Injunction. A court order prohibiting a defendant, such as a labor union, from engaging in certain practices, such as striking.

In-kind transfers. Noncash government transfers, such as Food Stamps, subsidized housing, and medical care.

Institutional discrimination. Any practices in social institutions that result in differential and inequitable treatment of individuals on the basis of race, sex, age, or some other characteristic not related to economic productivity.

Intangible capital. Technological knowledge and legal rights such as patents and trademarks.

Intensive growth. Economic growth achieved by increasing the productivity of economic resources, that is, by technological progress.

Intercept. The point at which a line on a graph touches one of the axes.

Interest rate. The ratio of the dollars paid in interest charges to total dollars borrowed; usually stated as an annual percentage rate.

Intermediate goods. Products and services that are used to produce other goods and services or are purchased for resale. The value of intermediate goods is excluded from GNP.

Inventory investment. The value of final goods produced in a particular period of time but not sold. The unsold goods are considered to have been "bought" by the businesses that produced them, and thus are counted as part of business investment expenditures.

Investment (I). Expenditures for fixed investment and inventory investment.

Isocost. A curve showing combinations of two resources that result in the same total costs; the slope of an isocost is the ratio of the prices of the two resources.

Isoquant. A curve showing combinations of two resources that will produce the same level of output.

J

Job-search theory. A view of unemployment as a search for information. Unemployed individuals make rational choices, weighing extra benefits of a continued job search (the prospects of finding a better job) against extra costs (accepting a lower paying job).

K

Keynesian theory. The economic propositions of John Maynard Keynes, including the belief that fluctuations in aggregate output are generally caused by changes in private-sector demand. Keynesian economists generally recommend government policies to boost aggregate demand during recessions.

L

Labor federation. An organization composed of several unions that provides services to member unions and seeks through political action to improve the status of its workers.

Labor force. The total number of individuals classified by government statistics as either employed or unemployed.

Labor productivity. The average output per unit of labor input, most often measured as real output per hour of work.

Law of demand. The principle that as the price of any product decreases (increases), the quantity of the product demanded will increase (decrease).

Law of diminishing marginal returns. The principle that beyond a certain point, additional variable resources added to a constant quantity of fixed resources will result in smaller and smaller increases in total product.

Law of diminishing marginal utility. The principle that beyond a certain point, the marginal utility of the last unit declines as more is consumed.

Law of diminishing returns. The proposition that adding labor to a fixed quantity of land and capital will eventually result in smaller and smaller increases in total output if technology is constant.

Law of supply. The principle that as the selling price of any product increases (decreases), the quantity of the product supplied also increases (decreases).

Legal reserves. Reserves held by banks to satisfy legal minimums imposed by the Fed. They include currency held in bank vaults and banks' deposits held at the Fed.

Less-developed countries (LDCs). Nations that have relatively low standards of living, limited industrialization, and minimal education, transportation, and communication systems; collectively known as the Third World.

Liabilities. Claims on assets.

Liquidity. How quickly and inexpensively an asset may be turned into money without risk or loss of value. Money has perfect liquidity; other assets, less liquidity.

Long run. A period of time in which a firm can alter all its resources. In the long run, a firm can change all resources.

Long-run average cost (LRAC). The minimum average total cost for each level of output when a firm can change all its resources.

Long-run equilibrium. A position in which quantity of aggregate output demanded at the current price level equals the economy's potential output: graphically, when the aggregate demand and short-run aggregate supply curves intersect at the potential output level. The position the economy will achieve if wages and prices fully adjust to aggregate demand.

Long-run marginal cost (LRMC). The extra cost for an extra unit of output when all resources can be changed.

Long-run supply curve (LRS). The long-run relationship between price and quantity supplied by all firms.

Lorenz curve. A graphic representation of the actual income distribution obtained by plotting the cumulative percentage of income received against the cumulative percentage of families or individuals. The greater the deviation of the actual Lorenz curve from a diagonal straight line, the greater is the degree of inequality.

Lump-sum tax. A tax, such as the property tax, that is unaffected by the level of aggregate output.

M

M-1. The narrow official definition of money, which includes only currency held by the public and checking deposits.

M-2. A broader official definition of money, including not only currency held by the public and checking deposits (M-1 money) but also savings deposits, small time deposits, money market mutual fund shares, and money market deposit accounts.

Macroeconomics. That level of economic analysis concerned with the activity of the entire economy and the interactions between large sectors of it.

Marginal. A term used by economists to denote *extra* or *additional*.

Marginal cost (MC). The additional cost associated with producing one additional unit of output; calculated as change in total costs divided by change in quantity of goods or services produced (change in total product). Mathematically, MC = Change in TC ÷ Change in Q.

Marginal-cost pricing. A price-setting option for rate regulation whereby price is set where demand equals marginal cost (P = MC). As a result, MSB = MSC, but the price may be too low to allow a normal profit.

Marginal factor cost (MFC). The change in total cost that results from the use of one additional unit of a variable resource.

Marginal product (MP). The extra quantity of goods produced (change in total product) per unit of variable resource added. Mathematically, MP = Change in Q ÷ Change in variable resources.

Marginal propensity to consume (MPC). The ratio of changes in consumption to changes in income; indicates the proportion of any additional income that will be spent on consumption.

Marginal propensity to save (MPS). The ratio of changes in saving to changes in disposable income; shows the proportion of any additional disposable income that will be saved.

Marginal rate of substitution. The quantity of one product that may be sacrificed to obtain one unit of another product for the same total utility; the slope of an indifference curve, or mathematically,

$$\frac{\text{Marginal utility of product A}}{\text{Marginal utility of product B}}$$

Marginal rate of technical substitution. The ratio of marginal products of two substitute resources; the slope of an isoquant measures the marginal rate of technical substitution.

Marginal revenue (MR). The extra revenue obtained from the sale of one extra unit, calculated as

$$\text{Marginal revenue} = \frac{\text{Change in total revenue}}{\text{Change in total product}}$$

Marginal revenue product (MRP). The change in total revenue that results from the use of one additional unit of a variable resource.

Marginal social benefit (MSB). The extra benefit society receives from one additional unit of some good.

Marginal social cost (MSC). The extra cost to society of producing one more unit of some good.

Marginal tax rate. The percentage of additional income that must be paid in taxes; the ratio of additional tax owed to additional income.

Marginal utility (MU). The additional satisfaction derived from consuming one additional unit of a good or service; the increase in total utility associated with a one-unit increase in quantity.

Market. The interaction of buyers (market demand) and sellers (market supply) which determines a price and quantity exchanged.

Market capitalism. An economic system in which most resources are privately owned by individuals and most economic interactions occur in markets.

Market economy. An economy in which households and businesses interact in markets to determine prices and thus answer the fundamental economic questions of what and how much to produce, how to produce it, and to whom to distribute goods and services.

Market equilibrium. A state in which neither buyers nor sellers have any reason to change quantity demanded or supplied; the market in balance, with quantity demanded equal to quantity supplied at the existing market price.

Market failure. Inability of a market to achieve allocative efficiency, technical efficiency, or equity; for example, poorly defined property rights or lack of competition.

Market power. The ability to influence market price.

Market structure. The characteristics of an industry, including number of buyers and sellers, uniqueness of goods and services produced, and ease of entry and exit.

Mature oligopoly. A form of oligopoly in which there is little or no price competition, little or no entry or exit of existing firms, reliance on nonprice competition, predictable responses to economic changes, and mutual tolerance and acceptance among existing rival firms.

Merger. The combining of two or more firms under the control of one firm.

Microeconomics. That level of economic analysis concerned with the activity of individual units of the economy and their interrelationships.

Monetarists. Economists who believe that fluctuations in aggregate output are generally caused by changes in the money supply.

Monetary assets. Bonds or other debt obligations that promise the holders future payments that are fixed in nominal terms.

Monetary policy. Federal Reserve System actions taken to influence the size or growth rate of the money supply.

Money. Items such as coins, paper bills, and checking account deposits that are widely accepted in market exchanges. Any item used as a medium of exchange.

Money supply. The total quantity of money in circulation at any time.

Monopolistic competition. A market structure in which a relatively large number of relatively small firms each produces a somewhat distinctive or differentiated product. Barriers to entry and exit usually are small. The distinctive nature of the products gives each firm a small amount of market power.

Multiplier. The amount that equilibrium GNP will change as a result of a change in autonomous expenditures. Measured as the ratio of the change in equilibrium GNP to the change in autonomous expenditures. The simple multiplier effect, assuming a constant price level, can also be calculated as $1 \div (1 - \text{MPC})$.

N

National debt. The total amount owed by the federal government; the cumulative effect of past budget deficits and surpluses.

National income (NI). Total income earned by the household sector; the sum of wages, rent, interest, and profits. It represents payment for resources used to produce final goods during a particular period of time.

Natural monopoly. An industry in which a single producer, operating the most technically efficient plant, can supply the entire market demand; a result of economies of scale.

Natural rate of unemployment. The unemployment rate achieved when the economy has eliminated all cyclical unemployment; sometimes referred to as the *full-employment* unemployment rate.

Natural resources. The land, water, minerals, climate, and other products of nature that can be used to produce goods and services.

Negative income tax. A system that guarantees a minimum income to the poor through government income transfers, the amount of which depends on how far below the poverty threshold a family's income is.

Net national product (NNP). Gross national product minus depreciation (capital consumption allowance).

New classical macroeconomists. Economists who assume that wages and prices are very flexible, a theoretical approach similar to that of classical economists. Their theories suggest that rational responses to anticipated policy actions will make policies completely ineffective.

Nominal. A term used to identify economic variables measured in terms of current prices.

Nominal GNP. The value of the gross national product measured by current quantities and current prices.

Nominal income. The actual number of dollars of income earned, expressed in terms of current dollars unadjusted for changes in the general price level.

Nominal interest rate. The actual rate of interest in a financial market; includes a premium reflecting the expected rate of inflation. The actual or market interest rate charged for borrowed funds; determines how many dollars must be paid in interest.

Nonactivists. Economists who believe it unnecessary, undesirable, and impractical to employ discretionary monetary and fiscal policies to stabilize the economy. They recommend stable policies—a constant growth in the money supply and a balanced full-employment budget—and reliance on the economy's automatic adjustment mechanism.

Nonprice competition. Competing with other firms using approaches such as advertising and product differentiation instead of changing price.

Normal goods. Goods for which demand varies directly with income, rising as income rises and decreasing as income decreases—for example, steak.

Normal profit. Opportunity cost of owner investment, the minimum level of profit necessary to justify a decision to produce in the long run, or an economic profit of zero; considered an implicit cost when calculating economic profit but ignored when calculating accounting profit.

Normative statement. A statement involving value judgments of what ought to be.

O

Oligopoly. A market structure in which a relatively small number of relatively large firms each produces goods or services that are close substitutes or are somewhat differentiated. Barriers to entry are typically high. Firms must consider the actions and reactions of competitors when making decisions.

Open-market operations. The buying and selling of government securities by the Fed; used to change the quantity of bank reserves and hence the supply of money.

Opportunity cost. The value of the next best option that must be sacrificed when a choice is made.

Opportunity cost of capital. The cost of funds used by a firm for investment, expressed as an annual percentage rate; reflects market interest rates, with allowance for future inflation and the risk involved in the investment.

Origin. The point on a graph representing a zero value for both variables; the intersection of the horizontal and vertical axes, generally the lower left corner of a graph.

P

Partnership. A form of business organization in which two or more individuals share the ownership, profits, and liabilities of the firm.

Patent. The legal right to produce a specified product or to use a specified process exclusively; granted for 17 years in the United States.

Peak. The end of the recovery phase; the point at which real aggregate output reaches its highest level.

Personal income. The total amount of income, before taxes, received by all households from all sources.

Phillips curve. A plot of the relationship between the rate of inflation and the rate of unemployment. Current theory recognizes an inverse short-run relationship but no long-run relationship.

Physical capital. Long-lasting capital resources, such as buildings and machinery, that yield benefits both in the present and in the future.

Planned socialism. An economic system in which most resources are owned by government and their use is controlled by a government plan.

Positive statement. A statement limited to a factual description of what is or what will be.

Potential GNP. The aggregate output that could be produced with the available technology if labor and other economic resources were fully employed.

Poverty threshold. A sliding income scale, adjusted according to family characteristics and the general level of prices, below which poverty is officially considered to exist.

Precautionary motive. Holding money to meet unexpected expenditures; related to money's function as a liquid store of value.

Present value (PV). The current value of money to be received or paid in a future period; the number of dollars that must be invested today at a specified interest rate in order to have a certain sum of money at a particular future time.

Price. The amount of one item that an individual will sacrifice in order to obtain another item and often stated in terms of the quantity of money that must be sacrificed.

Price discrimination. Selling identical goods and services at different prices to different groups of buyers.

Price elastic. A situation in which the percentage change in quantity is larger than the percentage change in price, giving an elasticity coefficient greater than 1 (ignoring the sign).

Price-elasticity coefficient. The number obtained by using the price elasticity formula. When its absolute value (ignoring the sign) is greater than 1, the demand (or supply) is price elastic; when it is less than 1, the demand (or supply) is price inelastic; when it equals 1, the demand (or supply) has unitary elasticity.

Price elasticity of demand. A measure of the response of buyers to a change in price, usually expressed as the percentage change in quantity demanded, divided by the percentage change in price.

Price elasticity of supply. A measure of the response of sellers to a change in price, usually expressed as the percentage change in quantity supplied, divided by the percentage change in price.

Price fixing. Formal agreement among firms in an oligopoly to maintain artificially high prices or to restrict market supply.

Price index. A measure of price level in a given year as a percentage of the price level in some specified base, or reference, year.

Price inelastic. A situation in which the percentage change in quantity is smaller than the percentage change in price, giving an elasticity coefficient less than 1 (ignoring the sign).

Price leadership. A form of oligopoly in which one firm—the leader—initially sets prices and other firms follow with matching increases or decreases. A tacit understanding rather than a formal agreement binds the firms.

Price searcher. Any firm that is not a price taker; a firm that can influence price and must search for the price that maximizes profits.

Price taker. A firm in a purely competitive market; a firm facing a horizontal (perfectly price elastic) demand curve; a firm that can sell all it wants to at the market price but nothing at any higher price. A price taker has zero market power.

Private goods. Goods and services that benefit only those people who purchase them. People who are unwilling or unable to pay for them can be prevented from receiving their benefits.

Private sector. The part of a nation's economy made up of households and businesses.

Product differentiation. The strategy of making a product appear to be different from similar products, regardless of whether it actually is. It may be achieved by varying product design, features and service, or through advertising.

Production function. The relationship between the quantity of resources used and the quantity of goods produced; the maximum amount of goods that can be produced using various combinations of resources and the best available technology.

Production possibilities curve. A curve showing the various combinations of output that an economy can produce with its existing resources when operating at maximum technical efficiency.

Productivity. The relationship between the quantity of goods or services produced and the quantity of a variable resource used.

Product markets. Markets in which businesses sell and households buy goods and services.

Profits. The difference between the total of all revenues received from the sales of goods and the total of all costs of producing those goods.

Progressive tax. A tax for which the average tax rate increases as income increases.

Proportional tax. A tax for which the average tax rate is constant for all income levels.

Proprietorship. A firm in which one person owns all the productive property, receives all the profits, and is personally responsible for all the liabilities.

Public choice theory. An economic theory based on rational choice principles that attempts to explain how choices are made in the public (government) sector.

Public finance. The size and distribution of government spending and taxation at the federal, state, and local levels.

Public goods. Goods and services that cannot benefit one person without benefiting all. People who cannot or will not pay for them cannot be prevented from receiving their benefits.

Public sector. The part of a nation's economy made up of federal, state, and local governments.

Pure competition. A model of a market with a very large number of firms, each producing virtually identical products. Perfect information exists and entry and exit are unrestricted.

Pure monopoly. A market structure in which a single firm produces a product for which there are no close substitutes; entry and exit are very restricted; model used to predict behavior of a firm with significant market power.

Q

Quantity demanded. The amount of a product that consumers are both willing and able to buy at a specified price.

Quantity supplied. The quantity of a product that suppliers are both willing and able to offer for sale at a specified price.

R

Rate base. Term used by rate regulators to refer to a firm's total investment. In average-cost pricing, price is set to allow the firm to earn a normal rate of return on the rate base.

Rate of return. The ratio of profits earned from an investment to total dollars invested.

Rate regulation. Government actions to set prices in markets as an alternative to antitrust action; may take the form of marginal-cost pricing or average-cost pricing.

Rational choice. Selecting among economic alternatives by comparing extra benefits expected to be received with extra costs expected to be incurred; an economic model used to explain the choices made by individuals, businesses, and government.

Rational expectations. An assumption that individuals utilize all available information, including their understanding of the effects of fiscal and monetary policy, in anticipating future economic conditions.

Real. A term used to identify economic variables measured in terms of constant prices of some base year.

Real GNP. The value of the gross national product measured by current quantities and constant prices.

Real GNP per capita. The average quantity of real output produced per person, calculated by dividing real GNP by total population.

Real income. Income expressed in terms of its purchasing power; nominal income adjusted to remove the effects of changes in the general price level.

Real interest rate. The nominal, or actual, rate of interest less the expected rate of inflation. The cost of borrowed funds stated in real terms; reflects the amount of real purchasing power a borrower can expect to pay in interest.

Recession. The phase of the business cycle in which real aggregate output of the economy is decreasing.

Recognition lag. The delay between when a macroeconomic problem occurs and when it is recognized.

Recovery. The phase of the business cycle in which real aggregate output of the economy is increasing.

Regressive tax. A tax for which the average tax rate decreases as income increases.

Relative poverty approach. Poverty defined by an income below some fraction of the average income; focuses on inequality of income.

Relative price. The price of one good in comparison to the prices of other goods.

Required reserve ratio. The minimum portion of deposits that must be legally held as reserves, as set by the Fed.

Reserves. Funds held by banks in order to meet the demands of their depositors and the legal requirements of the Federal Reserve System.

Resource markets. Markets in which households sell and businesses buy resources used to produce goods and services.

Resources. The human, capital, and natural resources that can be used to produce goods and services.

Retained earnings. The portion of a corporation's profits not paid out to its shareholders but retained by the corporation to finance future production.

Right-to-work laws. State laws that prohibit unions from negotiating union-shop provisions in labor–management contracts. The power to enact such laws was granted to the states by the Taft–Hartley Act (1947).

Rule of reason. A legal standard under which the prosecutor must prove not only that an offense has occurred but also that the social welfare will be enhanced by prohibiting, modifying, or punishing the act.

S

Saving (S). The portion of income received by households during a particular period of time that is not spent on final goods.

Saving schedule. A table showing the level of saving for various levels of disposable income.

Say's law. The proposition, popularized by nineteenth-century French economist Jean Baptiste Say, that supply creates its own demand.

Scarcity. The fundamental conflict between unlimited human desires and limited availability of resources.

Shortage. A situation in which quantity demanded exceeds quantity supplied at the existing market price; excess demand.

Short run. A period of time in which a firm cannot alter all its resources. In the short run, a firm can change only variable, not fixed, resources.

Short-run equilibrium. A position in which quantity of aggregate output demanded at the current price level equals quantity supplied; graphically, where the aggregate demand and short-run aggregate supply curves intersect.

Slope. The ratio of the change in the vertical direction to the change in the horizontal direction between two points along a graph of a straight line.

Social benefits. Benefits measured from the perspective of society; include both private benefits and external benefits.

Social costs. Costs measured from the perspective of society; include both private costs and external costs.

Social regulation. Government regulation aimed at correcting for externalities and imperfect information; concerned with safety and quality of goods, accuracy and completeness of available information, and external benefits and costs.

Stagflation. A period of time during which the total output of the economy falls, while the levels of general prices and unemployment rise.

Standard of living. The quantity of wants that can be satisfied, or the quantity of goods and services that can be purchased, with current income.

Stock. (1) Shares of ownership in a corporation. (2) A quantity existing at some moment in time, such as the stock of capital resources or the stock of inventory possessed by the business sector on December 31 of any year. (*See* Flow.)

Structural unemployment. Unemployment resulting from a mismatch in the labor market between the location and skills of unemployed workers, the location and skill requirements of available jobs; may also reflect discrimination. Unlike with frictional unemployment, unemployment for individuals may be prolonged.

Substitutes. Goods that satisfy similar desires and therefore compete for the consumer's dollar. When two goods are substitutes, an increase in the price of one leads to an increase in demand for the other.

Substitution effect. The change in quantity demanded resulting from a change in the price of a product relative to the price of substitute products.

Sunk cost. Cost incurred as a result of a past decision; historical cost that cannot be recovered and that is irrelevant to economic decisions.

Supply. All the quantities of a product that suppliers are both willing and able to offer for sale at every possible price during a specified period of time.

Supply curve. A graphic representation of the supply schedule; the typical supply curve slopes upward and to the right.

Supply function. An algebraic expression showing how quantity supplied is affected by market price and other factors influencing supply.

Supply schedule. A table showing quantities of a product that suppliers are willing and able to offer for sale at various prices during a specified period of time.

Supply shocks. Sharp declines in aggregate supply caused by a decrease in the supply of key resources; may cause a decline in potential output.

Support price. A legal minimum price established by government for a specific market.

Surplus. A situation in which quantity supplied exceeds quantity demanded at the existing market price; excess supply.

T

Tacit collusion. Informal agreement among firms in an oligopoly not to engage in price competition.

Technical efficiency. Producing goods and services for the least possible cost while maintaining full utilization of resources.

Terms of trade. The relative prices of goods and services involved in international trade expressed in physical terms (for example, 5 cases of applesauce per computer).

Time value of money. The difference between the present and future value of money, expressed as an annual percentage rate.

Total costs (TC). The sum of total variable costs and total fixed costs. Mathematically, TC = TVC + TFC.

Total fixed costs (TFC). The sum of all costs associated with a particular quantity of fixed resources; they are typically constant over a given range of total product in the short run.

Total product (TP or Q). The total quantity of goods that can be produced with a given quantity of resources in a specific period of time.

Total revenue (TR). The total number of dollars received from sales, calculated as the product of price and quantity sold, or TR = P × Q.

Total utility. The total amount of satisfaction obtained from all units of a good or service consumed.

Total variable costs (TVC). The sum of all costs for the quantity of variable resources used; they increase as total product increases.

Trade balance (balance on merchandise trade). The difference between the values of exports and imports of goods only (excludes imports and exports of services).

Trade deficit. A negative trade balance; occurs when the value of imports exceeds the value of exports.

Trade surplus. A positive trade balance; occurs when the value of exports exceeds the value of imports.

Transaction cost. The time, effort, and other costs of arranging and negotiating an exchange.

Transactions motive. The desire to hold money in order to make economic transactions, that is, to buy resources and products in economic markets. This motive is related to money's function as a medium of exchange.

Transfer payments. Payments, usually made by government, to individuals for the purpose of redistributing income.

Trough. The end of the recession phase; the point at which real aggregate output reaches its lowest level.

U

Underemployed. Individuals who have jobs but either work part-time when they would prefer full-time work or work at jobs below their capabilities and skills.

Unemployment rate. The number of individuals unemployed, expressed as a percentage of the labor force.

Union. An organization of employees that seeks primarily through collective bargaining with management to secure for its members improvements in wages, hours, and other working conditions.

Union shop. A workplace in which all employees must become members of a labor union within a specified period of time after being hired. Contract provisions establishing a union shop are illegal in states that have right-to-work laws.

Unitary price elasticity. A situation in which the percentage change in quantity demanded (or supplied) equals the percentage change in price or income; the absolute value of the elasticity coefficient is 1.

Utility. A measure of the satisfaction obtained from consuming a good or service.

V

Value of the marginal product (VMP). The value to society of using one additional unit of a variable resource; calculated as the marginal product of the additional unit of resource multiplied by the price of the final product it helps to create; equals the marginal revenue product when the firm sells in a competitive product market.

Variable costs. Costs associated with variable resources; they increase directly with total product in the short run. Examples include costs of labor and materials.

Variable resources. Resources that vary directly with output; that is, any increase in output requires greater use of variable resources. Typical examples are labor and raw materials.

Velocity (V). The average number of times each dollar in the money supply is spent during a specific period of time; calculated as the ratio of nominal GNP to the money supply, that is, V = (P × Q) ÷ Ms.

Vertical equity. A principle of taxation that suggests that individuals in unequal economic circumstances should pay an unequal amount of taxes.

Vertical merger. A merger between firms that would otherwise have a buyer–seller relationship.

Y

Yellow-dog contract. A contract in which employees stipulated that they were not and would not become a member of a labor union; outlawed in the United States by the Norris–LaGuardia Act (1932).

Yield. The interest rate (return) received from the purchase of a financial claim; varies inversely with the price of the financial claim. Market interest rates are yields.

INDEX

The boldfaced numbers indicate the pages on which key terms are defined in the margins.

A

Ability-to-pay principle, **399**–400
Absolute advantage, **825**, 824–828
Absolute poverty approach, **447**–448
Accelerationist argument of Friedman and Phelps, 752–757
Accommodating policies, 799–801, 803
Accounting:
  balance of payments, 853–855
  national income, 554–556
Accounting identities, **537**–538, 554–555, 579, 582, 590, 650–651
  in circular-flow model, 541–547
  types of:
    first, 537, 539, 548–549, 554
    second, 537–539, 554–555
    third, 553, 582
    fourth, 553
Accounting profit, **175**–176, 244
Action lags, **707**–708
Activism in economic policy, 703–711
Activists, **703**
Actual aggregate expenditures, 538–539
Actual income, 402

Actual inflation, 755–757
Actual leakages and injections, 582, 589–590
Actual unemployment rates, 732
Adams, Walter, 296n, 304n–306n
Adaptive expectations, 756
Advantage:
  absolute, **825**, 824–828
  comparative, **827**, 826–828, 851, 884
Advertising, 292, 302–303, 305
AFDC (Aid to Families with Dependent Children), 458, 461
Affirmative action programs, **463**
AFL (American Federation of Labor), 360, 369
AFL–CIO (American Federation of Labor–Congress of Industrial Organizations), 369
Africa:
  debts of, 865
  South, apartheid policy of, 466–467
African National Congress, 467
Age:
  and employment, 118, 119
  in labor market, 363
  in population, 773
  and unemployment, 733, 735
Aggregate demand, **522**–525, 661–667, 682–683
  and automatic stabilizers, 698

  and career labor markets, 729–730
  and contractionary gaps, 584
  excess (expansionary gaps), 675–677, 679, 693–700
  expectations in, 665–666
  and expenditures:
    aggregate, 661–663
    investment, 578
  and government policies:
    accommodating, 799–801, 803
    extinguishing, 799–803
    fiscal, 665
    monetary, 665
  households in, 565–575
  and inflation, 742–745
  long-run, 669–670
  and multiplier effect, 666–667
  and Phillips curve, 752–754
  and price levels, 740–742
  and real GNP, 768–769
  in theories:
    classical economic, 561–563
    job-search, 727, 728
    Keynesian economic, 561–563
Aggregate demand curves, 522–525, 674
  shifts in, 665–667
  slopes of, 663–665
Aggregate demand policies, 758–761
Aggregate expenditures, **537**
  and aggregate demand, 661–663

Aggregate expenditures *(cont.)*
  calculating, 612
  and consumption expenditures, 541
  and contractionary gaps, 604, 606–607
  and equilibrium output, 560–584, 602–605
  and real interest rates, 648–650
  types of:
    actual, 538–539
    planned, 537, 588, 589, 664–665
Aggregate output, **501**, 517, 533–541. *See also* GNP *entries*; Gross national product
  in long run, 667–668
  and planned aggregate expenditures, 589
  in short run, 667, 671
  types of:
    equilibrium. *See* Equilibrium output
    potential. *See* Potential GNP
    real, 653, 680–681. *See also* Real GNP
Aggregate supply, **522**–525, 682–683
  in economic theories:
    classical, 561–563
    Keynesian, 564–565, 672–673
  and inflation, 742–743
  in long run, 667–670
  and price levels, 740–743
  in short run, 670–675, 768–769
  and tax cuts, 782
Aggregate supply curves, 522–525, 674
  shifts in, 671–672
  slopes of, 672–673
Agricultural Adjustment Act of 1933, 474
Agricultural markets, 252
Agricultural productivity, 774, 776, 883
Agriculture:
  as economic activity, 771
  economic profit in, 189
  efficiency in, 472–473
  equity in, 473–474
  income from, 473–474
  in international trade, 824
  in less-developed countries, 774, 776, 881–883, 885
  price stability in, 472–473
  price supports for, 66, 474–478
  regulation of, 472–480
  and resource reallocation, 776, 777
  in Soviet Union, 872, 875

Aid to Families with Dependent Children (AFDC), 458, 461
Airline industry, 299, 300, 420
  deregulation of, 426–427, 483–484
  profits of, 481–483
  regulation of, 481–483
ALCOA (Aluminum Company of America), 261, 275–276, 416
Alfonsin, Raul, 788
Allocative efficiency, **27**–29
  in agriculture, 472–473
  and competition, 335. *See also* of monopolies; of resource markets, competitive, *below*
    monopolistic, 293–295
    pure, 250–252
  as economic goal, 868–870
  and external benefits, 391–393
  government in, 137. *See also* and public goods; of social regulation; and taxes, *below*
  and interest rates, 343–344
  in long run, 251–252
  in market economies, 107–109. *See also* of resource markets, *below*
  and market power, 273–275, 282, 335
  of monopolies, 273–275, 423–425
  and public goods, 393–395
  of resource markets, 329, 330, 335
    competitive, 325–326, 335
  in short run, 250–251
  of social regulation, 429–432
  and taxes, 396–398, 430–431
  and union impact on wages, 375–378
"All-other-things-unchanged" assumption, **49**–50
Alternative goods, prices of, 58–59
Aluminum Company of America (ALCOA), 261, 275–276, 416
Aluminum industry, 261, 275–276
American Federation of Labor (AFL), 360, 369
American Federation of Labor–Congress of Industrial Organizations (AFL–CIO), 369
American Telephone and Telegraph (AT&T), 324, 427
Anticipation. *See* Expectations *entries*
Antidiscrimination programs, 462–463
Antipoverty policies, 456–462
Antitrust laws, 360, 413–415, 494, 813
Antitrust policy, **413**

on collusion, 417–418
  issues in, 420–422
  in market power limitation, 412–422
  on mergers, 418–420
  on monopolies, 415–417
Apartheid in South Africa, 466–467
Apple Computers, 349
Appreciation of currency, **847**
Arbitration, **374**–375
Argentinean inflation, 788, 809, 810
Assets, 129, **620**. *See also* Capital resources
  liquidity of, 623–625
  monetary, **571**
Asset transactions, official, 854
AT&T (American Telephone and Telegraph), 324, 427
ATS (automatic transfer services), 623, 795
Austral plan in Argentina, 788
Automatic adjustment mechanism, 698, 708–710, 758–760, 799–802
  in economic theories:
    classical, 563, 564, 584–585
    Keynesian, 584–585
  in exchange-rate systems, 857, 859
  operation of, 723
  speed of, 704–705
Automatic stabilizers, **698**–700
Automatic transfer services (ATS), 623, 795
Automobile industry, 205, 307, 361, 390, 780
Autonomous consumption, **573**–574, 596–599, 612
Autonomous expenditures, 593
Autonomous expenditures multiplier, 595–597. *See also* Multiplier effect
Average-cost pricing, **425**
Average costs, 183–186
  fixed, **183**–185
  long-run, 191, 192, 194
  total, **183**–186
  variable, **183**–185
Average fixed costs, **183**–185
Average product, **179**, 178–180
Average propensity to consume, **567**–568
Averages, weighted, 528
Average tax rates, **400**
Average total costs, **183**–186
Average variable costs, **183**–185
Axes, horizontal and vertical, 19

B

Balanced budgets:
full-employment, 710
in Gramm–Rudman–Hollings law, 715, 807
Balance of payments accounting, 853–855
Balance of trade (net exports), 551–554, 608–609, 666, 775, 812–816, **821**–822. *See also* Trade deficits; Trade surpluses
Balance on capital account, **853**–854
Balance on current account, **853**, 854
Balance on goods and services, **822**
Balance on merchandise trade (balance of trade; net exports), 551–554, 608–609, 666, 775, 812–816, **821**–822. *See also* Trade deficits; Trade surpluses
Balances, budget, **691**
Balance sheets, 128, 129, 620
Ballpoint pen industry, 113
Bank deposits. *See* Deposits
Bank failures, 794–796
Banking:
and goldsmiths, 619–621
interstate, 796–797
Banking systems:
deregulation of, 707, 794–797
functioning of, 626
money creation in, 628–630
regulation of, 623, 794–796
types of:
fractional reserve, 620–622
100 percent reserve, 620
Bank money, 620–625
Bank panics, 625
Banks:
balance sheets of, 620
as Federal Reserve System members, 626
loans to, by Federal Reserve System, 633, 634. *See also* Loans
in money supply increases, 621–622
reserves of. *See* Reserve ratios; Reserves
in stock issue underwriting, 794–795
types of:
central, 625. *See also* Federal Reserve System
Federal Reserve, 625
mutual-savings, 623
Barriers to entry, **261**–262, 421–422

into labor markets, 368
into monopolies, 261–262, 273, 277
pure, 288, 297
in monopolistic competition, 288, 295
in pure competition, 288, 297
Barriers to exit from markets, 288, 295, 297
Barriers to trade. *See* Trade restrictions
Barter, **100**
Beer industry, 296
Bell Telephone, 261, 277
Benefits:
external, **136**, 389, 391–395
marginal, 36–39, 250
private, 136
social, **136**, 250, 433, 435, 469–470
Benefits-received principle, **399**
Benham, Lee, 292*n*
Berkey Photo, 417
Bilateral monopolies, **376**–377
Bird, Larry, 348
Birth rates, 879–880
Black, Hugo, 413
Black markets, 66, 789, 875–876
Board of Governors of Federal Reserve System, 625
Boards of directors, 125–126
Boesky, Ivan F., 357
Bolivia:
inflation in, 745, 788, 789, 809
interest rates in, 643
underground economy of, 638
Bonds, **129**, 571
government, 700. *See also* Government securities
Borrowing. *See* Debt *entries*; Government borrowing
Botha, P. W., 467
Boycott of South African goods, 467
Brazilian inflation, 788–789, 809, 810, 811
Break-even analysis, 227–228
Breakfast-cereal industry, 304–305
Bretton Woods system, 858–860
Brown, Charles, 379*n*, 491*n*
Browning, Edgar K., 405*n*, 449*n*
Budget balances, **691**
Budget constraints, **167**–168
Budget deficits, **691**–693
and business cycles, 697–700
dealing with, 714–715, 804–807, 813
automatic stabilizers in, 698

and discretionary fiscal policy, 697
and expansionary monetary policy, 714
full-employment, 804, 805, 807
and government expenditures, 805–807
and inflation, 714, 749
monetizing, 692–693, 714
and money supply, 714
myths and realities about, 711–714
versus national debt, 693
and net exports, 554
and oil prices, 205
opportunity costs and benefits of, 714
and real interest rates, 714
timing of, 699, 711–712
Budgets, 805
balanced. *See* Balanced budgets
cyclically adjusted (full-employment), **699**–700, 710. *See also* Full-employment budget deficits
Budget surpluses, **691**, 693
full-employment, 700, 710*n*
Burger King, 119
Business confidence, 577–578
Business cycles, **506**–507
and budget deficits, 697–700
and economic policy, 697. *See also* Discretionary policies
elements of:
peaks, 506, **507**, 732–733
recessions. *See* Great Depression; Recessions
recoveries, 506, **507**, 732, 778–779
troughs, 506, **507**. *See also* Great Depression; Recessions
and labor productivity, 778–779
and unemployment, 518, 519, 724, 732–733
Business firms, **98**
in circular-flow model, 98–99, 102–114, 121–129, 314–315, 541–551, 600
in classical economic theory, 560–563
classification and grouping of, 126–127
in economic systems, 869
elements of. *See specific entries, for example:* Costs; Output, of business firms; Profits
expenditures of:

Business firms *(cont.)*
  for capital resources (fixed investment), 543–545, 576–578, 704
  and monetary and fiscal policy, 665
  and money surpluses, 646–650
finances of, 127–129
instability of, 109
investment by. *See* Investment
loans by, 646–650
management problems of, 780–781
practices of, illegal and normal, 422
price levels affecting, 664–665
rational choice by, 103
risks by, 122–123
saving by, 545–546
shutting down by, 214–217, 222
sizes of, 123–124
in South Africa, 466–467
taxes on. *See* Corporate income taxes; Indirect business taxes
types of:
  corporate. *See* Corporate *entries*; Corporations
  monopolistic, 262–270, 280–282. *See also* Monopolies
  mutually interdependent, 296. *See also* Oligopolies
  partnership, 125
  proprietorship, 124, 125
"Buy American" argument for trade restrictions, 838
Buyers. *See* Consumer *entries*

C

CAB (Civil Aeronautics Board), 481–483
Cady, John F., 292*n*
Capacity (in investment expenditures), 577, 578
Capital:
  flows of, 141–142, 812–813, 847–853
  mobility of, 833–834
  opportunity costs of, 339, 347
  types of:
    foreign, 775
    human, **337**, 367–368, 453–454. *See also* Human resources
    intangible, **337**
    physical, **337**
Capital account, balance on, 853–854
Capital consumption allowance (de-

preciation), 127–129, **544**–546, 555, 783
Capital flight, 864
Capital flows, 141–142, 812–813, 847–853
Capital goods. *See* Capital resources
Capitalism, 7, 27–28, 867–871, 886
Capital/labor ratio, **774**–775, 780–783, 824
Capital resources, **9**
  demand for, 337–340
  depreciation of, 127–129, 544–546, 555, 783
  in economic growth, 33–35, 774–775, 777
  expenditures for (fixed investment), 543–545, 576–578, 704
  investment in, 338, 775, 780, 883
    fixed. *See* expenditures for (fixed investment), *above*
  supply of, 668
  types of. *See* Capital, types of
Career labor markets, 729–730
Cartels, **299**–301, 417. *See also* Organization of Petroleum Exporting Countries
Carter, Jimmy, 809
Cash transfers, 449, 457–459, 478, 491, 806
Casual labor markets, 729–731
Causation, **13**
CCC (Commodity Credit Corporation), 474–476
Ceiling prices, **66**, 68, 73, 423–425, 494–495, 742
Ceilings on interest rates, 345–346
Celler–Kefauver Act of 1950, 414
Cellophane monopoly, 262
Central banks, 625. *See also* Federal Reserve System
Central Committee of Communist Party, 873
Central planning (planned socialism), 7, 27–28, 867–871, 886
  in Soviet Union, 871–877
CETA (Comprehensive Employment and Training Act), 462
Cheap foreign labor argument for trade restrictions, 838–839
Check-clearing services of Federal Reserve System, 626
Checking deposits, **622**–625, 627, 642, 795. *See also* Money *entries*
  contraction of, 632–633
  expansion of, 630–632

Checks, 622
Choice, 6, 35–41
  in long run, 257
  in monopolies, 273
  of resources, optimal, 315–317
  types of:
    consumer. *See* Consumer choice
    equilibrium, 168–169
    producer, 174–195, 207–224
    rational. *See* Rational choice
CIO (Congress of Industrial Organizations), 370
Circular-flow model, **98**, 97–102
  capital flows in, 141–142
  fiscal and monetary policy in, 690, 691
  foreign exchange in, 847–848
  gross national product in, 542
  international trade in, 141–142
  leakages from and injections into, 553, 582, 589–590
  markets in:
    financial, 544–552, 600
    product, 314–315, 542, 600
    resource, 314–315, 542, 600
  and multiplier effect, 593. *See also* Multiplier effect
  national income in, 542
  sectors in:
    business, 121–129, 314–315, 541–551, 600
    foreign, 140–142, 549–554, 608–609
    government, 133–140, 386–388, 547–549, 551, 599–608, 691, 692
    household, 121, 129–132, 314–315, 541–551, 600
    private, 541–549. *See also* business; household, *above*
Civil Aeronautics Board (CAB), 481–483
Civil Rights Act of 1964, 462
Clark, Kim B., 724–725
Classical economic theory, **560**–563. *See also* Classical quantity theory; New classical macroeconomists
  automatic adjustment mechanism in, 584–585
  contractionary gaps in, 679
  economic growth in, 771–772
  and Great Depression, 699
  interest rates in, 572
  price level and aggregate output relationship in, 667–668

saving and investment in, 596–599
unemployment in, 750
Classical quantity theory, 650, 651
    modern version of (monetarism),
        653–655, 703, 758–760
Clayton Antitrust Act of 1914, 360,
    370, 414, 418
Closed shops, **372**
Coal as resource, 28–29
Cold turkey approach to inflation
    fighting, 758–759
Collective bargaining, **368**–379. *See
    also* Union contracts
Collective farms, 875
Collective wants, 869
Collusion, 417–418
Commodity Credit Corporation
    (CCC), 474–476
Commodity money, **618**–620
Communication systems in less-devel-
    oped countries, 883, 886
Communism, defined, 871*n*. *See also*
    Planned socialism
Communist Party in Soviet Union, 873
Comparative advantage, **827**, 826–828,
    851, 884
Compensating wage differentials,
    366–367
Compensation. *See* Unemployment in-
    surance; Wage *entries*
Competition:
    algebra of, 255–257
    and efficiency, 234–252, 335
    in market economies, 111–113
    and market failures, 135
    and rationing, 26–27
    reduction of, 420
    types of:
        imperfect, **259**, 287–307, 326–
            329
        international, 734, 812–816
        monopolistic, 235, **287**–295
        nonprice, **292**–293, 295, 302–
            303, 305, 482–483
        price, 299
        pure (perfect), **235**–236, 248,
            250–252, 288, 297
        unfair, 420
Competitive industries, potentially,
    425–426
Competitive markets, 235–238. *See
    also* Competitive resource
    markets
    and economic goals, 248–252
    efficiency of, 248–252

and reasonable prices, 248
wage differentials in, 365–366
Competitive resource markets, **318**–
    325
    decision making in, 334
    efficiency of, 322, 325–331, 335
    imperfectly, 334–335
Complements, **52**–53
Composition, fallacy of, 13–14, 501,
    596
Comprehensive Employment and
    Training Act (CETA), 462
Computers in securities markets, 356–
    357
Concentrated costs of international
    trade, 833–834
Concentration ratios, 421
Conglomerate mergers, **419**–420
Congress of Industrial Organizations
    (CIO), 370
Constant-cost industries, **245**–247
Constant market-basket approach,
    528–530
Constant returns to scale, 192, **193**
Consumer behavior, 10
Consumer choice:
    and economic costs, 149
    and equimarginal principle, 155–
        159
    and indifference theory, 164–171
    and law of demand, 161–162
    theory of, 148–162
Consumer demand, 150–161, 170–
    171
Consumer price index (CPI), **509**–
    513, 529–531, 798, 799
Consumer products, **33**–35
Consumer Product Safety Commis-
    sion, 432
Consumer-protection view, 485, 486
Consumers, 53–54
Consumer-sovereignty view, 485, 486
Consumer surpluses, **160**, 159–161,
    249
Consumption, 602–605. *See also* Aver-
    age propensity to consume; Mar-
    ginal propensity to consume
    autonomous, **573**–574, 596–599,
        612
    induced, **573**
Consumption expenditures, **541**–543.
    See also Saving
    and aggregate demand, 565–575
    in aggregate expenditures, 588
    and credit, 572

in crowding-out effect, 700–702
on durable goods, 704
graphic view of, 568–570, 572–574
and gross national product, 588
and income, 566–570, 572–574. *See
    also* Disposable income
long-run versus short-run, 574–575
and monetary and fiscal policy, 665
and money surpluses, 646–650
and price levels, 570–574
and wealth, 570, 571
Consumption function, 574, 575, 612
Consumption line, 572–575
Consumption schedule, **566**–568
Consumption taxes, 782–783
Contestable markets, **307**
Contractionary gaps, **583**–584, 653,
    678, 677–680, 682–683, 799–801
    and automatic stabilizers, 698
    avoiding, 693–694
    and economic policies:
        fiscal, 604, 606–607
        stabilization, 769, 771
    eliminating, 695, 697–700
    in job-search theory, 727
    and supply shocks, 694
Contractionary policies, **696**–697, 759,
    760, 778
    extinguishing, 799–803
    fiscal, 696–697, 699
    monetary, 696–697, 759
Contracts theory:
    of unemployment, **729**–731
    of wage-setting, 681
Cook, Paul K., 873*n*
Coolidge, Calvin, 503
Core unemployment, 722
Corporate income taxes, 404, 405,
    783. *See also* Indirect business
    taxes
Corporate raiders, 284–285
Corporations, **125**–126
    earnings of, retained, 129, 546. *See
        also* Profit maximization;
        Profits
    financial statements of, 127–129
    mergers of, 284–285, 418–421, 813
    sizes of, 123
    South Africa divestment by, 467
    stocks of. *See* Stocks (corporate)
    takeovers of, 284–285
Correlation, **13**
Cost curves, short-run, 183–186
Cost minimization, 36–39, 188. *See
    also* Profit maximization

Cost of living, 514
Cost-push inflation, **741**–742
Costs:
  concentrated, 833–834
  economic, 149
  explicit, **175**, 176
  external, **136**, 389, 429–432, 540
  fixed. *See* Fixed costs
  implicit, **175**, 176
  long-run, 188–195
  marginal. *See* Marginal-cost pricing;
    Marginal costs
  opportunity. *See* Opportunity costs
  private, 136
  production, 174–195
  short-run, 176–186, 195
  social, **136**, 250, 433, 435, 469–470
  transaction, **100**, 122, 392–393
Countercyclical policies. *See* Discretionary policies
CPI (consumer price index), **509**–
  513, 529–531, 798, 799
Craft unions, **369**
Credit, 572
Credit cards, 643–644
Credit unions, 623
Cross elasticity of demand, **91**–92
Crowding-out effect, **700**–702, 712
Crown jewels of corporations, 284
Cruzado plan in Brazil, 788–789
Currency, 622, 639, 644. *See also* Ex-
  change rates; Foreign exchange
  entries; Money *entries*
Currency appreciation, **847**
Currency depreciation, **847**, 859, 860
Currency devaluation, **859**
Current account, balance on, 853, 854
Current market-basket approach, 528,
  530–531
Current Population Survey, 502–503
Cycles, economic. *See* Business cycles
Cyclically adjusted (full-employment)
  budgets, 699–700, 710
Cyclical unemployment, **506**–507,
  583–584, 731

D

Death rates, 879–880
Debt, government. *See* Budget deficits; Government borrowing;
  Less-developed countries, debt
  of; National debt

Debt-equity swaps, 865
Decision making:
  economic approach to, 37–39, 195
  government, 394–395
  in production, 174–176
  in resource markets, 334–335
  in short run and long run, 177, 195
Decisions:
  economic, 207–224, 262–270
  investment, 576–577
  long-run, 217–224, 241–248
  pricing, 289–291
  short-run, 207–217, 289–291
  supply, 207–224
Decreasing-cost industries, 248*n*
Defense spending, 704, 806, 807
Deficiency payments, 476–477
Deficits. *See* Budget deficits; Trade deficits
Demand, **47**–55
  changes in, 50–51, 54, 62–63, 106–
    107
    equation for, 72–73
  determinants of, 51–55
  elasticity of. *See* Price elasticity of
    demand
  equation for, 71
  for exports, 833, 850–851
  for financing, 339–340
  in import-competing industries, 832
  for imports, 850–851
  law of, **48**, 161–162
  in monopolies, 270–271, 273
  in oligopolies, 298
  and prices, 236–238
  and supply. *See* Supply and demand
  types of:
    aggregate. *See* Aggregate demand
      entries
    consumer, 170–171
    derived, 315
    individual, 154–155
    labor. *See* Labor demand
    market, 154–155
    product, 320–321, 349
    resource, 317–318, 320–321,
      326–327, 337–340
    revenue, 320–321
Demand curves, **48**–50, 264–265, 294
  aggregate. *See* Aggregate demand
    curves
  slopes of, 81–82, 850
Demand functions, **71**
Demand-pull inflation, **740**–741

Demand schedules, **48**–50
Demand shocks, 694, 704, 746–747
Denison, Edward, 777–779
Dependent variables, **18**–19
Deposit accounts, money market, 623,
  624, 643
Deposit insurance, 795
Deposit multipliers, **630**–634
Depository institutions, 623. *See also*
  Banks
Depository Institutions Deregulation
  and Monetary Control Act of
  1980, 346, 795
Deposits:
  contraction of, 632–633
  expansion of, 630–632
  at Federal Reserve System, 626
  insurance on, 795
  interest rates on, 795
    ceilings on, 345–346
  types of:
    checking. *See* Checking deposits
    savings, 623, 624
    time, 624
Depreciation:
  of capital resources, **127**–129, **544**–
    546, 555, 783
  of currency, **847**, 859, 860
Depressions, 564*n*. *See also* Great
  Depression; Recessions
Deregulation. *See* Government deregulation
Derived demand, 315
Design standards, 431–433
Desired investment. *See* Planned inventory investment; Planned in-
  vestment
Devaluation of currency, **859**
Developed countries (economies),
  774–775, **878**–880
Diamond puzzle of Adam Smith, 153–
  154
Diminishing marginal returns, **180**,
  183
  law of, 180, 193–194
Diminishing marginal utility, law of,
  150–152, 166
Diminishing returns:
  law of, 771–775
  marginal, **180**, 183
    law of, 180, 193–194
Diocletion, 808
Discounted present value, 352–354
Discouraged workers, **504**

Discretionary policies, **697**–700, 703–711
  fiscal, **604**, 606–607, 697–700, 706, 769, 771
  monetary, 697–700, 706, 769, 771
Discretionary policy lags, 706–709
Discrimination:
  economic, **454**–456, 462–463, 508
  employment, 454–456, 462–463, 466–467, 508
  institutional, 455–456
  and poverty, 454–456
  price, **269**–270
  racial, in South Africa, 466–467
Diseconomies of scale, 192, **193**
Disinflation, **748**, 749. *See also* Inflation *entries*
Dismal science of economics, 772
Disposable income, **548**, 566–570. *See also* Consumption *entries*
  changes in, temporary versus permanent, 574–575
  and equilibrium output, 614
  and national income, 555–556
  versus personal income, 555–556. *See also* Personal income
  and saving, 568–570
  and taxes, 602–605
Dissaving (negative saving), 567–568, 570
Divestment from South African corporations, 467
Dividends, **129**, 131
Division, fallacy of, 14, 501
Dollar(s). *See also* Currency *entries*; Exchange rates; Foreign exchange *entries*; Money *entries*
  appreciation and depreciation of, 852–853
  future, present value of. *See* Present value
  present, future value of, 352–353
Domestic industry argument for trade restrictions, 838
Doomsday predictions about economic growth, 771–772
Drexel Burnham Lambert, 357
Driving, fixed and variable costs of, 218–219
Drug safety regulations, 484–488
Dumping, 814, 815
Duncan, Greg, 446*n*, 451*n*
Du Pont de Nemours, E. I., 262, 419
Durable goods, 704

E
Earnings, retained, **129**, 546
Eastman Kodak, 261, 277, 417
Economic activity. *See* Circular-flow model; Classical quantity theory
Economic approach to decision making, 37–39
Economic behavior and government policies, 792
Economic concepts, 4–10, 500–525
Economic costs, 149
Economic decision making, 37–39, 195
Economic decisions, 207–224, 262–270
Economic development, **881**
  versus economic growth, 880–881
  in less-developed countries, 878–886
    conditions for, 883–885
    dimensions of, 881–883
    strategies for, 884–885
Economic discrimination, **454**–456, 462–463, 508
Economic efficiency. *See* Efficiency
Economic goals, 27–29, 114, 500–525, 693–697, 868–870. *See also* Allocative efficiency; Economic growth; Equity (fairness); Full employment *entries*; Price stability; Technical efficiency
  and competitive markets, 248–252
  meeting, incentives for, 870, 871
  and taxation, 395–406
Economic growth, **33**
  accounting for, 776–781
  assumptions and predictions about, 771–772
  and consumer products, 33–35
  and crowding out, 700, 712
  definition and causes of, 765–771
  versus economic development, 880–881
  and economic stability, 517
  and employment/population ratio, 773–774
  expectations of, 772–773
  of Far East, 880
  and labor supply, 773–774, 777
  and oil prices, 204
  in planned socialism, 870, 872, 876
  and production possibilities curve, 32–33
  rates of, 766–767

  and resource allocation, 776–778
  resources in:
    capital, 33–35, 774–775, 777
    natural, 771–773
  slowdown in, 778–781
  sources of, 771–776
    government, 138, 781–785
    investment, 775, 783
    saving, 775, 782–783
    technological change, 772, 775–778, 783–784
    by year, 777–781
  of Soviet Union, 774, 775, 872, 876
  types of:
    extensive, 775
    intensive, 776
Economic losses, 219, 223, 241–243
Economic models, **10**–14
Economic opportunity, 137–138, 389
Economic organization, forms of. *See* Economic systems
Economic outcomes, predicting, 11–12
Economic performance, history of, 516–522
Economic planning of Soviet Union, 872–875
Economic policies, 469–471, 690–715
  alternative, 793
  analysis of, 791–793
  complications of, 697–703
  in economic growth improvement, 781–785
  in economic growth slowdowns, 781
  economist disagreements on, 793
  fixed rules for, 708–710
  and inflation, 758–761, 799–803, 808–811
  lags in, 706–709
  and supply shocks, 798–803
  types of:
    accommodating, 799–801, 803
    activist versus nonactivist, 703–711
    aggregate demand, 758–761
    contractionary. *See* Contractionary policies
    countercyclical (discretionary). *See* Discretionary policies
    expansionary. *See* Expansionary policies
    extinguishing, 799–803
    fiscal. *See* Fiscal policy

Economic policies *(cont.)*
  free-market, 813–815
  incomes, 808–811
  industrial, 784–785, 813, 814
  microeconomic, 784–785
  monetary. *See* Monetary policy
  neutral, 799–802
  stabilization, 577, 693–697, 709–
    710, 769, 771, 785
  supply-side, 781, 782
  tax, 577, 578, 781, 782
Economic power, 350
Economic profit, **176**, 208–209, 217–
    221, 243–244, 257
  in agriculture, 189
  and economic rent, 347–348
  in monopolies, 271–273, 281–282
  in monopolistic competition, 291–
    292
  and opportunity costs, 175–176,
    347
  of price takers, 244
  and rewards, 348–350
  and risk, 347
  taxation of, 350
Economic rents, 347–**348**, 350
Economics, 7–**8**
  as dismal science, 772
  language of, 9–10
  study of, 4–8
  types of:
    macro- and micro-, **8**, 501–502
    normative, 793
    viewpoints on, differences in, 14–
      16, 114, 793, 816
Economic stability, 113–114, 138, 517,
    705–706, 708, 709, 883–884. *See
    also* Automatic stabilizers
  price, 472–473, 509–516, 520–522,
    693–697, 877
Economic systems, **7**–8, 867–877
  goals of, 868–870
  types of:
    market capitalism, 7, 27–28, 867–
      871, 886
    mixed, 28
    planned socialism. *See* Planned
      socialism
Economic theories. *See specific en-
    tries, for example:* Classical eco-
    nomic theory; Keynesian eco-
    nomic theory; Monetarism
Economic value of goods produced,
    535

Economies. *See* Economic systems;
    specific entries, for example: De-
    veloped countries (economies);
    Market economies; Underground
    economy
Economies of scale, 122, **191**, 188–
    195, 261, **776**
Economizing, 36
Education:
  in economic growth, 774
  and employment, 119
  in less-developed countries, 881–
    883, 886
  and poverty, 453–454
  in South Africa, 467
Educational vouchers, 806
Efficiency:
  and competition, 234–252, 335
    monopolistic, 293–295
  in competitive markets, 248–252,
    322, 325–331
  and economic discrimination, 454–
    455
  incentives for, 436
  in income distribution, 442–443
  and inflation, 515–516
  in international trade, 825–826,
    835–836, 839
  long-run, 307
  and market equilibrium, 322
  and market power, 276, 329, 330
  of monopolies, 271, 273–275
  of oligopolies, 303, 306
  of resources, 321–323
  and subsidies, 839
  and taxes, 396–398
  and transfer payments, 459–460
  types of. *See* Allocative efficiency;
    Technical efficiency
  and unemployment, 507–508
Elasticity. *See* Price elasticity *entries*
Elasticity coefficients, 80–81, 89–92
Electrical machinery conspiracy, 418
Elzinga, Kenneth, 296*n*
Emission reduction credits, 432
Employed individuals, 503, 721–725
Employment. *See also* Labor *entries*;
    Unemployment *entries*; Wage *en-
    tries*; Work *entries*
  and age, 118, 119
  discrimination in, 454–456, 462–
    463, 466–467, 508

and education, 119
full. *See* Full employment *entries*
in government, 373, 691
in imperfectly competitive resource
    markets, 327–328
by industry, 127
and race, 454, 455, 466–467
by sex, 454, 455
Employment assistance programs,
    462, 735. *See also* Job training
    entries
Employment contracts, 681, 729, 730
Employment/population ratio, 773–
    774
Energy. *See* Oil *entries*
"Enterprises" in Soviet Union, 873,
    874
Environmental Protection Agency
    (EPA), 431–432
Equality versus equity, 28. *See also*
    Equity (fairness); Income ine-
    quality
Equation of exchange, **650**–651
Equilibrium:
  in international trade, 829–832
  long-run, 669–670
  macroeconomic. *See* Equilibrium
    output
  market. *See* Market equilibrium
  short-run, 673–675
Equilibrium choice, 168–169
Equilibrium condition, 579, 582
Equilibrium output, 579, 658–659
  adjustments in. *See* Automatic ad-
    justment mechanism
  and aggregate expenditures, 560–
    584, 602–605
  and aggregate supply, 667–675
  and consumption, 602–605
  and disposable income, 614
  in economic theories:
    classical, 560–563
    Keynesian, 564–565, 578–584,
      588–590, 599–608
  in economies:
    open, 608–609
    public sector, 614
  and fiscal policy, 599–608
  and full-employment level of out-
    put, 560–563, 581–584
  below full-employment level of
    output, 564–565, 578–584
  and government purchases, 599–
    601

and multiplier effect, 592–609, 612–613
planned leakages and injections in, 582
and taxes, 602–605, 614
Equilibrium prices, **60**–65, 72
Equimarginal principle, **156**, 155–159, 168–169, 188
Equities of corporations, 129
Equity (fairness), **28**, 29, 137–138
in agriculture, 473–474
and economic discrimination, 454–455
and gross national product, 540
and income distribution, 442–463
and inflation, 514–515
in international trade, 839–840
in market economies, 109–110
and pure competition, 252
in Soviet Union, 876–877
and taxes, 399–400
in transfer programs, 459
types of:
horizontal, 399–400
vertical, 400
and unemployment, 507–508
union impact on, 379
Essay on the Principle of Population, An (Malthus), 772
Excess aggregate demand (expansionary gaps), 675–677, 679, 693–700
Excess reserves, 628–634
Exchange, 6–7
equation of, 650–651
foreign, 847–853
markets for, 847–855, 859
market, 101–102, 122
money as medium of, 618–620
nonmarket, 539–540
Exchange rates, **846**, 845–847
fixed (pegged), **855**–861
flexible (freely floating), **849**–853, 857, 859–861
Excise taxes, 396–398
Expansionary gaps, **676**, 675–677, 679, 693–700
Expansionary policies, 694–**695**, 760
accommodating, 799–801, 803
fiscal, 694, 695, 697, 699–702, 749
monetary, 694, 695, 714, 749
Expectations, 53–54, 59
of economic growth, 772–773
about income, 570, 572–574, 665–666

of inflation, 752–757, 788
in inflation fighting, 758–759
and investment expenditures, 577–578
in job searches, 726, 727
about price levels, 570, 572–574, 643, 665–666, 671–672, 680, 742
types of:
adaptive, 756
rational, 36, **702**–703, 756–758
Expectations theory, 680–682
Expenditures. *See specific entries, for example:* Aggregate expenditures; Government expenditures
Explicit costs, **175**, 176
Export promotion, 884
Exports, **140**–142, **550**–551, 553, 832, 881–883. *See also* Balance of payments accounting; Imports; International trade
demand for, 833, 850–851
net (trade balances), 551–554, 608–609, 666, 775, 812–816, 821–822. *See also* Trade deficits; Trade surpluses
Export subsidies, 815. *See also* Subsidies, in international trade
Extensive growth, **775**
External benefits, **136**, 389, 391–395
External costs, **136**, 389, 429–432, 540
External debt, 713
Externalities, **136**–137, 389
Extinguishing policies, 799–803

F
Fair Labor Standards Act of 1938, 489
Fairness. *See* Equity (fairness)
Fair-trade policies, 814, 815
Fallacy of composition, 13–**14**, 501, 596
Fallacy of division, **14**, 501
Far Eastern economic growth, 880
Fast-food eateries, 119
FDA (Food and Drug Administration), 432, 434, 484–488, 837
Federal deposit insurance, 795
Federal Deposit Insurance Corporation (FDIC), 626
Federal Mediation and Conciliation Service, 377
Federal Open Market Committee (FOMC), 625, 707
Federal Reserve Banks, 625

Federal Reserve System (Fed), 625–634
bank deposits at, 626
bank loans by, 633, 634
banks as members of, 626
Board of Governors of, 625
check-clearing services of, 626
checking deposit control by, 627
Federal Open Market Committee of, 625, 707
functions of, 625–627
government securities bought by, 693
independence of, 692–693
money holding control by, 644
money supply control by, 623, 626–634. *See also* Monetary policy
open market operations of, 627–630
paper money issued by, 622
required reserve ratios of, 627–633, 796
structure of, 625
Federal Savings and Loan Insurance Corporation (FSLIC), 626
Federal Trade Commission (FTC), 414–415
Federal Trade Commission Act of 1914, 414–415
Feldstein, Martin S., 752*n*
Final goods, **534**, 537
Final goods markets, 657–659
Finance:
international, 845–861, 864–865
public, 386. *See also* Government expenditures; Tax *entries*
Financial claims, returns on, 648
Financial institutions, 623. *See also* Banks
Financial markets, **340**–350, 356–357, **545**–547
in circular-flow model, 544–552, 600
equilibrium in, 561, 562
government in, 548, 549, 691–693, 700
in Keynesian economic theory, 564
Financial statements, 127–129, 620
Financial system, functioning of, 626
Financial transactions and gross national product, 535
Financing demand, 339–340
Firms. *See* Business firms; Corporations

First accounting identity, 537, 539, 548–549, 554
"First-World" countries, 878
Fiscal policy, 690–693, 702–703. *See also* Automatic stabilizers; Government expenditures
and aggregate demand, 665
and contractionary gaps, 604, 606–607
and equilibrium output, 599–608
and full-employment budgets, 699–700
in Keynesian economic theory, 599–608, 655
lags in, 707, 708
and multiplier effect, 604, 606–607
and trade deficits, 812–814
types of:
contractionary, 696–697, 699
discretionary, 604, 606–607, 697–700, 706, 769, 771
expansionary, 694, 695, 697, 699–702, 749
stabilization, 693–697, 710
Five Year Plans of Soviet Union, 872
Fixed costs, **181**, 182, 218–219, 268–269
average, 183–185
total, 181, 182
Fixed exchange rates, **855**–861
Fixed investment, **543**–545, 576–578, 704
Fixed resources, **177**
Fixed supply of natural resources, 771–772
Flexible (freely floating) exchange rates, **849**–853, 857, 859–861
Floor (support) prices, 66–68, 474–478
Flows, **547**, 553. *See also* Circular-flow model
of capital, 141–142, 812–813, 847–853
of investment, 547
into and out of labor markets, 721–722
real versus money, 99
FOMC (Federal Open Market Committee), 625, 707
Food, Drug, and Cosmetic Act of 1938, 484–486
Food and Drug Administration (FDA), 432, 434, 484–488, 837
Food prices, 741–742, 749
Food Stamps, 458, 461

Ford, Henry, 361
Foreign aid, 885–886
Foreign exchange, 847–853
Foreign-exchange markets, 847–855, 859
Foreign investment in less-developed countries, 865, 885
Foreign labor argument for trade restrictions, 838–839
Foreign loans to less-developed countries, 885
Foreign sector, **121**, 665, 693, 713, 715, 775
in circular-flow model, 140–142, 549–554, 608–609
Foreign trade. *See* International trade
45° line, 570
Fourth accounting identity, 553
Fractional reserve banking systems, **620**–622
Franchises, government, 261–262, 277
Freely floating exchange rates, **849**–853, 857, 859–861
Freeman, Richard B., 373n, 378n, 379n
Free-market policies, 813–815
Free markets for less-developed countries, 886
Free riders, 394
Free-trade costs, 833–834
Frictional unemployment, **505**, 722, 729, 731, 734
Friedman, Milton, 681, 703, 745, 752, 757, 758
Friedman–Phelps accelerationist argument, 752–757
FSLIC (Federal Savings and Loan Insurance Corporation), 626
FTC (Federal Trade Commission), 414–415
Full employment, 693–697
as economic goal, 502, 508–509, 517–520
and GNP gaps, 519–520
and potential GNP, 509
in Soviet Union, 877
Full-employment budget deficits, 804, 805, 807
Full-employment budgets, **699**, 699–700, 710
Full-employment budget surpluses, 700, 710n
Full-employment level of output:
in economic theories:
classical, 560–563

Keynesian, 564–565, 578–584
and equilibrium output, 560–563, 581–584
equilibrium output below, 564–565, 578–584
and wage and price flexibility, 561–565
Full-employment unemployment rate (natural rate of unemployment), 508, 722, 723, 731–735
Fundamental imbalance in foreign-exchange markets, 859
Future dollars, present value of. *See* Present value
Futures markets, 356, 478–479
Future value (of present dollars), 352–**353**

G
GA (General Assistance), 458
Game theory, 299
Garn–St. Germain Depository Institutions Act of 1982, 795
General Agreement on Tariffs and Trade (GATT), 840
General Assistance (GA), 458
General Motors, 205, 419, 880
General price levels, **501**, 509–516, 520–522, 663, 750, 751. *See also* Aggregate demand; GNP deflator; Price levels
Germany:
economic growth of, 779
hyperinflation in, 788
Gilroy, Curtis, 491n
GNP. *See* Gross national product
GNP deflator, 520, **536**, 739–741, 750, 751. *See also* General price levels
GNP gaps, **509**, 519–520, 583–584, 675–684
contractionary. *See* Contractionary gaps
expansionary, **676**, 675–677, 679, 693–700
Goals. *See* Economic goals
Gold as commodity money, 619–620
Golden parachutes, 284
Goldsmiths and banking, 619–621
Gold standard, 855–858, 861
Gompers, Samuel, 370
Goods and services. *See also* Product *entries*
balance on, 822
distribution of, 28

measuring, 535
mix of, determining, 27–28
types of. *See specific entries, for example:* Complements; Final goods; Public goods
Gordon, Robert J., 732, 748, 767*n*
Gosplan, 873, 874
Gould, Jay, 413
Government, 138–140, 388–389, 784, 816. *See also* Public *entries*
  in circular-flow model, 133–140, 386–388, 547–549, 551, 599–608, 691, 692
  in economic systems, 869–870
  in financial markets, 548, 549, 691–693, 700
  in income redistribution. *See* Income redistribution; Transfer payments
  and market power, 389, 412–422
  state and local, 691, 693
  taxation by. *See* Tax *entries*
Government bonds, 700
Government borrowing, 395–396, 693, 700, 713. *See also* Budget deficits; Less-developed countries, debt of; National debt
Government budgets. *See* Budget *entries*
Government decision making, 394–395
Government deregulation, 425–426, 784
  of airline industry, 426–427, 483–484
  of banking industry, 707, 794–797
Government employment, 373, 691
Government enterprises, 428
  privatization of, 394, 806
Government expenditures, 138–140, 690, 704, 714, 740–741. *See also* Fiscal policy; Government purchases
  in economic growth policy, 784
  and expansionary gaps, 679
  financing, 691–693. *See also* Budget deficits; National debt
  increasing, 700–703
  in Keynesian economic theory, 584
  reducing, 699, 715, 805–807, 814
Government franchises, 261–262, 277
Government policies:
  benefits and costs of, 469–470, 791–792
  disagreements about, 471

and rational choice, 138, 389–390, 469–471, 791–793
  reasons for, 791
  types of. *See specific entries, for example:* Antitrust policy; Economic policies; Unemployment policy
Government purchases, **548**–549, 553, 599–601, 606–607, 691. *See also* Government expenditures
Government regulation, 412–436. *See also* Government deregulation
  of agriculture, 472–480
  in competition reduction, 420
  failure of, 434–436
  of industries:
    airline, 481–483
    banking, 623, 794–796
    drug, 484–488
    potentially competitive, 425–426
  and labor productivity slowdowns, 780
  of market power, 389
  in oil market, 493–496
  of prices (ceiling), 66, 68, 73, 423–425, 494–495, 742
  of rates, 423–428
  of safety, 484–488, 543
  social, 428–434
  and trade balances, 813
  of wages, 489–492. *See also* Minimum wages
Government regulatory agencies. *See specific entries, for example:* Civil Aeronautics Board; Occupational Safety and Health Administration
Government revenues, 402–405, 690–691. *See also* Tax *entries*
Government securities, 693. *See also* Government bonds
Government subsidies. *See* Subsidies
Grace Commission, 394
Gramm–Rudman–Hollings Act of 1985, 715, 807
Graphs:
  in economic models, 11, 12
  use of, 18–24
Great Depression, 564
  agriculture in, 474
  and contractionary fiscal policy, 699
  as contractionary gap, 679–680
  and economic growth, 778
  and economic policy, 697
  in Keynesian economic theory, 597
  money supply errors in, 710

national debt during, 693
  and trade restrictions, 840
  unemployment during, 517, 761
Greenmail, 284
Grievance procedures, 374–375
Gross national product (GNP), **501**, 533–556. *See also* Aggregate output; GNP gaps
  in circular-flow model, 542
  and consumption expenditures, 588
  minus depreciation (net national product), 545
  as measure:
    of aggregate expenditures, 538–539
    of goods and services produced in current period, 535
    of income of resource owners, 539
    of market value, 533–534
    of output of final goods, 534
    of social value, 539–541
  measuring, 535–536. *See also* GNP deflator; Nominal GNP; Real GNP
  and multiplier effect, 593. *See also* Multiplier effect
  and national income, 554–556
  per capita, 878–879
  and transfer payments, 549
  types of. *See* Nominal GNP; Potential GNP; Real GNP

H

Harrington, Michael, 448
Herfindahl index, 421
Hoffman-LaRoche, 277
Hong Kong economy, 880
Hoover, Herbert, 699
Horizontal axis, 19
Horizontal equity, **399**–400
Horizontal mergers, **419**
Hot money, 852
Households, **98**
  in aggregate demand, 565–575
  in circular-flow model, 98–99, 102–114, 121, 129–132, 314–315, 541–551, 600
  in classical economic theory, 560–563
  in economic systems, 869
  expenditures of. *See* Consumption expenditures
  housing investments by, 576*n*

Households *(cont.)*
  income of, 130–132, 443–445, 555–556. *See also* Disposable income; Wages
  lending by, 646–650
  price levels affecting, 664–665
  rational choice by, 103
  saving by. *See* Saving
  wealth of, 664
Household theory of labor supply, **361**–362
Housing:
  household investment in, 576*n*
  price supports for, 68
  subsidized, 458
Human capital, **337**, 367–368, 453–454
Human resources, **9**, 367–368
100 percent reserve banking system, 620
Hyperinflation, 788–789
Hyundai, 880

I

IBM (International Business Machines), 261, 422
Icahn, Carl, 284
ICC (Interstate Commerce Commission), 425–426
Illegal activities, 638, 639, 875–876
IMF (International Monetary Fund), 775, 865
Impact lags, **708**
Imperfect competition, **259**, 287–307, 326–329
Imperfect information, 137, 329–330, 389, 432, 485
Imperfectly competitive resource markets, 334–335
Implicit costs, **175**, 176
Import-competing industries, 832
Import quotas, 389, 814, 815, **836**–837
Import restrictions, 814, 815
Imports, **140**–142, **549**–550, 775. *See also* Balance of payments accounting; Exports; International trade
  demand for, 850–851
  and inflation, 749
  as leakage from circular flow, 553
  prices of, 665, 760, 833
Import substitution, 884

Import tariffs, 814, 815, **834**–836, 838, 840–841, 851
Incentives:
  for economic goals, 870, 871
  for efficiency, 436
  for innovation, 349
  in Soviet Union, 877
  and taxes, 396–398
  for work, 459–462
Incidence of poverty, **449**
Income. *See also* Wages; Wealth
  from agriculture, 473–474
  and consumption expenditures, 566–570, 572–574
  of countries, 878, 879, 882
  and demand, 52
    aggregate, 666
    import and export, 850
  in economies:
    market, 871
    underground, 638–639
  expectations about, 570, 572–574, 665–666
  versus money, 641
  and output, circular flow of. *See* Circular-flow model
  and prices, 87, 92–93
  of resource owners, 539
  types of:
    actual versus taxable, 402
    after-tax, 398
    disposable. *See* Disposable income
    household (personal), 130–132, 443–445, 555–556. *See also* Disposable income
    labor, 130–131, 877
    national. *See* National income *entries*
    nominal, **511**–513
    real, 512–513, 665–666
Income distribution, 110, 132, 442–463. *See also* Income redistribution; Transfer payments
  in Soviet Union, 876–877
Income effect, **161**–162, 362
Income elasticity of demand, **91**, 90–93, 473
Income inequality, 445–447, 452–454
Income mobility, 446
Income redistribution, 137–138, 389
Incomes policies, 808–811
Income statements, 127–129
Income taxes:
  as automatic stabilizers, 698

  evading, 638–639
  indexation of, 781–783
  and multiplier effect, 604, 605
  reform in, 40, 402, 462, 781, 783
  replacing, 782–783
  types of:
    corporate, 404, 405, 783. *See also* Indirect business taxes
    negative, 460–462
    personal, 402–403, 405, 781–783
Increasing-cost industries, **247**–248
Increasing marginal costs, 183
Increasing marginal returns, **179**
Independent variables, 18–**19**
Indexation, **515**, 781–783
Indifference curves, **165**–166
Indifference maps, **166**–167
Indifference sets, **165**–166
Indifference theory, 164–171, 198–203
Indirect business taxes, 554, 555
Induced consumption, **573**
Industrialization of less-developed countries, 883, 885
Industrialized countries, 774–775, 878–880
Industrial market economies, 878, 879, 882
Industrial Ministries in Soviet Union, 873
Industrial policies, **784**–785, 813, 814
Industrial Revolution, 772
Industrial unions, **369**
Industrial Workers of the World (IWW), 369–370
Industries, **126**–127. *See also specific industries, for example:* Automobile industry; Restaurant industry; Steel industry
  and economies of scale, 193, 194
  employment in, 127
  nationalization of, 872
  types of:
    constant-cost, **245**–247
    decreasing-cost, 248*n*
    domestic, 838
    increasing-cost, **247**–248
    infant, 837–838
    potentially competitive, 425–426
Infant industry argument for trade restrictions, 837–838
Inferior goods, **52**
Inflation, **509**–516, 739–749. *See also* Stagflation
  and aggregate demand, 742–745
  and aggregate supply, 742–743

in bank deregulation, 795
and budget deficits, 714, 749
causes of, 742, 745–747. *See also*
    influences on, *below*
and economic policies, 758–761,
    799–803, 808–811
and efficiency, 515–516
and equity, 514–515
expectations of, 752–757, 788
fighting, 758–759. *See also* reduc-
    ing, *below*
and imports, 749
influences on, 378, 748. *See also*
    causes of, *above*
and investment, 781
measuring, 739–740
and money substitutes, 643
and money supply growth, 747
reducing, 799–803, 808–811. *See*
    also fighting, *above*
and saving, 781
and standard of living, 514
and taxes, 781
timing of, 572, 748–750, 757, 761
types of:
    actual versus expected, 755–757
    cost-push, **741**–742
    demand-pull, **740**–741
    hyper-, 788–789
and unemployment, trade-off be-
    tween, 748–761
and wages, 749, 788
Inflation rates, **739**–740
and demand and supply shocks,
    746–747
history of, 679, 681–683, 748, 749,
    852
and money supply growth, 745–747
and price-level changes, 510–511
and unemployment rates, 750–758
Information. *See also* Rational choice
for discretionary policy action, 706
in goal-setting, 869–871
imperfect, 137, 329–330, 389, 432,
    485
in market economies, 112
Injections into circular flow, 553, 582,
    589–590
Injunctions, **370**
In-kind transfers, **449**–450
Innovation, 349, 877. *See also* Techno-
    logical change
Insider trading in stock markets, 357
Institutional discrimination, **455**–456
Institutional investors, 357

Insurance:
    of bank deposits, 795
    unemployment, 507–508, 698, 733–
        735, 840
Intangible capital, **337**
Intensive economic growth, **776**
Intercepts of lines, **23**
Interest rates, **339**, 852–853. *See also*
    Rate of return; Yields (returns)
and allocative efficiency, 343–344
on bank deposits, 795
    ceilings on, 345–346
increasing, 700–702
in Keynesian economic theory, 564
lowering, 806
and price levels, 664–665
types of:
    flexible, 561, 562
    market, 340–350
    nominal, **344**, 345, **578**, 643–646
    real, **344**–345, 572, 577, **578**,
        648–650, 714
Intermediate goods, **534**
Internal debt, 713
International Business Machines
    (IBM), 261, 422
International capital, flows of, 847–
    853
International competition, 734, 812–
    816
International finance, 845–861, 864–
    865
International Monetary Fund (IMF),
    775, 865
International trade, 820–841. *See also*
    Balance of payments accounting;
    Exchange rates; Foreign ex-
    change *entries*; Trade *entries*
advantage in:
    absolute, 824–828
    comparative, 826–828, 851
benefits of, diffusion of, 833
capital mobility in, 833–834
in circular-flow model, 141–142,
    549–554, 847–848
competitiveness of, 734, 812–816
costs of:
    concentrated, 833–834
    opportunity, 825–828
distributional effects of, 833–834
efficiency in, 825–826, 835–836,
    839
flows of, 847–853. *See also* in circu-
    lar-flow model, *above*
gains from, 824–834

for less-developed countries, 884
losses in, 832–834
and natural resources, 824
patterns of, 823
and preferences, 824
relative prices (terms of trade) in,
    828–829
restrictions on. *See* Trade restric-
    tions
subsidies in, 815, 839–840
supply and demand equilibrium in,
    829–832
volume of, 821–822
Interstate banking, 796–797
Interstate Commerce Commission
    (ICC), 425–426
Inventory disinvestment, 581
Inventory investment, **545**, 576–578
planned (desired), 579–582
unplanned (undesired), 579–583
Investment, **545**, 576–578
in crowding-out effect, 700–702
in economic growth, 775, 778, 783
in education and training, 774
financial markets in, 545–547
and flexible interest rates, 561, 562
flows of, 547
in housing, 576*n*
and inflation, 781
as injection into circular flow, 553
in Keynesian economic theory, 564
and present value, 354
in resources:
    capital, 338, 775, 780, 883. *See*
        also types of, fixed, *below*
    human, 367–368
in stocks, 356–357. *See also* Stocks
    (corporate)
types of:
    fixed, 543–545, 576–578, 704
    inventory. *See* Inventory disin-
        vestment; Inventory invest-
        ment
    planned (desired), 588–590
    private, 778, 865, 885
    unplanned (undesired), 589–590
Investment decisions, 576–577
Investment expenditures, 576–578
multiplier effect of, 592–597, 612–
    613
stability of, 704
Investment projects, 339–340
Investment tax credits, 783
Invisible hand (of Adam Smith), 102,
    110–114

Involuntary unemployment, 564
Isocosts, **200**–201
Isoquants, **198**–200
Israeli inflation, 788, 789, 809, 810
IWW (Industrial Workers of the World), 369–370

J

Jackson, James O., 638
Japan:
  economic growth in, 779
  in international trade, 784, 836, 837
Jawboning as incomes policy, 808–809
Jevons, W. S., 13
Job-search theory, **725**–731
Job training, 119, 774, 834, 839–840
Job Training Partnership Act of 1982, 462
Job-training programs, 462, 491, 735
Johnson, Lyndon, 809
  War on Poverty of, 679, 695, 740–741, 749
Johnson, William R., 405n
Josephson, Mathew, 413n

K

Kahn, George A., 749
Keeley, Michael C., 721
Keister, Douglas C., 295n
Kelsey, Frances, 485
Kennedy, John F., 607, 683, 695, 809
Keynes, John Maynard, 560, 607
Keynesian economic theory, **564**–565, 703
  aggregate supply in, 672–673
  automatic adjustment mechanism in, 584–585, 759, 760
  contractionary gaps in, 679–680
  government policy in:
    fiscal, 599–608, 655
    industrial, 785
    monetary, 653–655, 781
    stabilization, 785
  households in, 565–575
  interest rates in, 572
  investment expenditures in, 577
  investment in, 596–599
  net exports in, 608–609
  output in:
    aggregate (and price level), 667, 671
    equilibrium, 578–584, 588–590, 599–608

full-employment level of, 564–565, 578–584
  recessions in, 584, 597, 697
  saving in, 596–599
  and tax cut of 1964, 695
  unemployment in, 761
Kindleberger, Charles, 791
Knights of Labor, 369
Kodak, Eastman, 261, 277, 417
Kohen, Andrew, 491n
Korean War, 809
Kuch, Paul, 823
Kuznets, Simon, 537

L

Labor, 35
  and capital, ratio of, 774–775, 780–783, 824
  cheap foreign, as trade restriction argument, 838–839
  in economic growth, 774, 776, 777
  in international trade, 833–834
  quality and quantity of, 777
  quantity supplied of, 361–363
Labor demand, 118–119, 361, 452–453, 561–562
Labor federations, **369**
Labor force, 129, 130, 502–**503**, 733
  unemployed in, 503–505, 720–725
Labor income, 130–131, 877
Labor markets. *See also* Employment *entries*; Wage *entries*
  age in, 363
  bilateral monopolies in, 376–377
  entry into, 722–723
    barriers to, 368
  exit from, 722–723
  flows into and out of, 721–722
  operation of, 731
  and poverty, 452, 462–463
  and rational choice, 359–360
  by sex, 363–365
  supply and demand in, 360–365
  types of:
    career, 729–730
    casual, 729–731
    competitive, 365–366
Labor mismatches, 118–119
Labor productivity, **772**–774, 776, 778–780, 809, 825
  marginal, 367
Labor-relations environment, 373–375
Labor-relations law, 370–374

Labor supply, 118–119, 361–363, 561–562, 668, 773–774, 777
  household theory of, **361**–362
Land in economic growth, 771–772
Landrum–Griffin Act of 1959, **372**
Latin America:
  debt of, 864–865, 885
  inflation in, 745, 788–789
Law of demand, **48**, 161–162
Law of diminishing marginal returns, **180**, 193–194
Law of diminishing marginal utility, **150**–152, 166
Law of diminishing returns, **771**–775
  marginal, **180**
Law of supply, **55**
Layoffs, 730
LDCs. *See* Less-developed countries
Leakages from circular flow, 553, 582, 589–590
Legal reserves, **627**–633
Leisure time, 539
Less-developed countries (LDCs), **878**–886
  agriculture in, 881–883, 885
  birth and death rates in, 879–880
  debt of, 205, 864–865, 885. *See also* financing in, *below*
  economic development in. *See* Economic development, in less-developed countries
  education in, 881–883, 886
  financing in, 775. *See also* debt of, *above*
  future of, 886
  gross national product per capita in, 878–879
  inflation in, 745, 788–789
  instability of, 883–884
  poverty in, 878–880
  primary export dependence of, 881–883
  productivity in, 776
  standard of living in, 880–881
  transportation and communication systems in, 883, 886
  urbanization of, 881, 882
Levine, Dennis, 357
Lewis, John L., 370
Liabilities, 129, **620**
Liability, limited, 126
Life expectancy, 879–880
Liquidity, **623**–625
Little dragons of Far East, 880
Living:

cost of, 514
standard of. *See* Standard of living
Llosa, Mario Vargas, 638
Loanable funds, markets for, 340–350
Loans:
    to banks, by Federal Reserve System, 633, 634
    ceilings on, 345–346
    by households and business firms, 646–650
    to less-developed countries, 885
Local government, 691, 693
Long run, **177**
    quantity supplied in, 220–223
Long-run adjustments:
    to economic losses, 241–243
    to economic profit, 243–244
Long-run aggregate demand, 669–670
Long-run aggregate output, 667–668
Long-run aggregate supply, 667–670
Long-run average costs, **191**, 192, 194
Long-run benefits of trade, 834
Long-run choice, 257
Long-run consumption expenditures, 574–575
Long-run costs, 195
    and economies of scale, 188–195
    of trade, 834
    types of:
        average, **191**, 192, 194
        marginal, **423**
Long-run decisions, 195, 241–248
Long-run economic goals. *See* Economic growth
Long-run efficiency:
    allocative, 251–252
    economic, 307
Long-run equilibrium, **669**–670
    market, 241–248, 290–292
Long-run inflation-unemployment relationship, 750; 755–757. *See also* Long-term unemployment
Long-run marginal costs, **423**
Long-run price levels, 667–670
Long-run real GNP, 767, 769, 771
Long-run supply:
    aggregate, 667–670
    market, 245–248
Long-run supply curves, **245**–248
Long-run supply decisions, 217–224
Long-term unemployment, 729, 731
Lorenz curves, 444, **445**
Losses, economic, 219, 223, 241–243
Loss minimization, 212–217. *See also* Profit maximization

Lotteries, 396
Low-income countries, 878, 879, 882. *See also* Less-developed countries
Lucas, Robert, 757
Lump-sum taxes, **602**–604, 607, 614
Luxuries versus necessities, 88

M

M-1, **622**–625, 652
M-2, **624**–625, 652, 653
McClure, Charles, Jr., 695*n*
McDonald's, 119
Macroeconomic concepts, 500–525. *See also* Economic growth; Full employment *entries*; Price stability
Macroeconomic equilibrium. *See* Equilibrium output
Macroeconomic goals, 500–525
    long-run. *See* Economic growth
    short-run, 693–697. *See also* Full employment *entries*; Price stability
Macroeconomic policy. *See* Economic policy
Macroeconomics, **8**
    versus microeconomics, 501–502
Macroeconomic stability. *See* Economic stability
Macroeconomic theories. *See specific entries, for example:* Classical economic theory; Keynesian economic theory; Modern economic theories; Monetarists
Malthus, Thomas, 772
Management problems, 780–781
Manufacturing as economic activity, 771
Manufacturing industries, 783
Marginal, defined, **36**
Marginal benefits, 36–39, 250
    social, **250**
Marginal-cost pricing, **424**–425
Marginal costs, 36–39, **181**–183, 211–212, 238–239
    equations for, 256, 280
    long-run, 423
    social, **250**
Marginal factor cost, **317**
Marginal product, **179**, 178–180
    value of the, **326**–327
Marginal productivity, 367
Marginal propensity to consume,

566–567, 570*n*, 573–575, 595–597, 604, 605
Marginal propensity to save, **568**
Marginal rate of substitution, **166**
Marginal rate of technical substitution, **198**–199
Marginal returns:
    diminishing, **180**, 183
    law of, 180
    increasing, 179
Marginal revenue, **209**–212, 264–265, 280
Marginal revenue product, **317**–318, 326–328, 334
Marginal social benefits, **250**
Marginal social costs, **250**
Marginal tax rates, **400**, 774
Marginal utility, **150**–161
    diminishing, law of, **150**–152, 166
Market activity, government in, 134–135, 388
Market-basket approaches for price indexes, 528–531
Market capitalism, **7**, 27–28, 867–871, 886
Market concentration, 421
Market conditions and equilibrium prices, 62–65
Market demand, 154–155, 236–238
Market economies, **46**, 96–114
    circular flow in. *See* Circular-flow model
    competition in, 111–113
    efficiency in:
        allocative, 107–109
        technical, 108–109
    equity in, 109–110
    industrial, 878, 879, 882
    production in, 107–110
    rational choice in, 103–107
    and resource allocation, 104–114
    self-interest in, 102–107
    wealth and income in, 871
    workings of, 121–142
Market equilibrium, **61**, 60–65, 71–73
    and efficiency, 322
    long-run, 241–248, 290–292
    short-run, 240, 289–291
    types of:
        final goods, 657–659
        financial, 561, 562
        foreign exchange, 855–857
        money, 644–650, 658–659
Market exchanges, 101–102

Market exchanges (cont.)
    foreign, 847–855, 859
    transaction costs of, 122
Market failures, **110**–114, 135–137,
    388–389, 432, 434, 435
Market interest rates, 340–350
Market power, **236**
    and collective bargaining, 376–
        377
    and efficiency, 276, 329, 330
        allocative, 273–275, 282, 335
    and government, 389, 412–422
    and mergers, 418–421
    and monopoly markets, 259–262
    and price discrimination, 269–270
    and resource demand, 326–327
Market prices, 103–104, 236–240, 534
Markets, 7, **46**
    entry into, 722–723
        barriers to. See Barriers to entry
        unrestricted, 307
    exit from, 722–723
        barriers to, 288, 295, 297
        unrestricted, 307
    types of, 234–235
        agricultural, 252
        black, 789, 875–876, 879–880
        competitive. See Competitive
            markets; Competitive re-
            source markets
        contestable, **307**
        final goods, 657–659
        financial. See Financial markets
        foreign-exchange, 847–855, 859
        free, 886. See also Free-market
            policies
        futures, 356, 478–479
        labor. See Labor markets
        loanable funds, 340–350
        monopoly, 259–262
        oil, 493–496
        pollution permits, 431
        product. See Product markets
        relevant, 416, 421–422
        resource. See Resource markets
        stock, 356–357
Market structures, **234**–235, 260. See
    also Monopolies; Monopolistic
    competition; Oligopolies; Pure
    competition
Market supply, 238–240, 245–248
Market values, 533–534
Market wages, 362–363
Marx, Karl, 871n
Massingale Company, 484

Materials balancing in Soviet Union,
    874
Mathematical models, 23–24
Matsushita, 880
Mature oligopolies, **304**–305
Mediation, 377
Medicaid, 458
Medicare, 458
Medoff, James L., 373n, 378n, 379n
Meier, Kenneth J., 485n
Merchandise trade, balance on (trade
    balances; net exports), 551–554,
    608–609, 666, 775, 812–816, 821–
    822. See also Trade deficits;
    Trade surpluses
Mergers, 284–285, **418**–421, 813
Merrell Corporation, 484–485
Mexico, debt repayment by, 205
Microeconomics, **8**, 386–388
    versus macroeconomics, 501–502
Middle-income countries, 878, 879,
    882
Minimum wage laws, 489–492
Minimum wages, 66, 734
Ministry of International Trade and
    Industry (MITI), 784
Mobility:
    of capital, 833–834
    of income, 446
    of labor, 833–834
    of resources, 112–113, 329–330
Models, economic, **10**–14
Modern economic theories, 597–599,
    680–682, 772–773
Modern monetary theories, 650, 652–
    655, 703, 758–760
Modigliani, Franco, 703
Monetarists, **654**, 653–655, 703, 758–
    760
Monetary assets, **571**
Monetary policy, **626**–634, 665, 702–
    703
    in circular-flow model, 690, 691
    determination of, 692
    in Keynesian and monetarist eco-
        nomic theories, 653–655
    lags in, 707–708
    and recessions, 653
    in trade deficit reduction, 812–814
    types of:
        contractionary, 696–697, 759
        discretionary, 697–700, 706, 769,
            771
        expansionary, 694, 695, 714, 749
        stabilization, 693–697, 709–710

Monetary-policy tools, 627–634
Monetary systems, international, 845–
    861, 864–865
Monetizing budget deficits, 692–693,
    714
Money, **100**–101, **618**–634. See also
    Checking deposits
    creation of:
        in fractional reserve system, 621–
            622
        by open-market operations, 628–
            630
    holding, 641–644. See also Money
        demand
    versus income, 641
    as medium of exchange, 618–620
    printing, 692, 693
    purchasing power of, 511–514
    as standard unit of account, 619
    substitutes for, 643–644
    theories of:
        classical quantity, 650, 651
        modern, 650, 652–655, 703, 758–
            760
    types of:
        bank, 620–625
        commodity, 618–620
        foreign, 715
        hot, 852
        paper, 620, 622. See also Cur-
            rency
    value of, 511
        time, 342–344. See also Present
            value
    velocity of, 650–653
Money demand, 641–646, 652–655,
    710
Money flows, 99
Moneyless economies, 619
Money market deposit accounts, 623,
    624, 643
Money market equilibrium, 644–650,
    658–659
Money market mutual funds, 623, 624,
    643, 795, 796
Money supply, **619**, 624
    and budget deficits, 714
    and currency holding, 644
    decreases in, 683, 709–710, 758–
        759
    Federal Reserve System control of,
        623, 626–634. See also Mone-
        tary policy
    and foreign-exchange markets, 859,
        860

growth in, 740–741
  adjusting to, 646–650
  and banks, 621–622
  constant, 709–710
  control of, 761
  and expansionary gaps, 679
  and inflation, 742, 745–747, 788
  in inflation fighting, 759, 810
  measures of, 622–625. *See also* M-1; M-2
  and nominal interest rates, 644–646
  and price levels, 650–651, 653–655, 746
  versus taxes, 395
  theories of:
    classical quantity, 650, 651
    modern monetary, 650, 652–655, 703, 758–760
Money surpluses, 646–650
Monopolies, 235
  in antitrust policy, 415–417
  barriers to entry into, 261–262, 273, 277
  demand in, 270–271, 273
  economic profit in, 281–282
  economies of scale in, 261
  inefficiency of, 271, 273–275
  marginal revenue and marginal cost in, 280
  myths about, 270–272
  price searching in, 281–282
  short-run output in, 281
  types of:
    bilateral, 376–377
    natural, **261**, 423–428
    pure, 260
    utilities as, 262, 275–276
Monopolistic business firms, 262–270, 280–282
Monopolistic competition, 235, **287**–295
Monopoly markets, 259–262
Moral hazards, 470
Morgan, J. P., 284, 413
Morrison, Steven, 483*n*
Mueller, Hans, 306*n*
Multiplier effect, 592–609, 612–614
  of changes:
    in aggregate demand, 666–667
    in autonomous consumption, 596–599
    in government purchases, 599–601
    in investment expenditures, 592–597, 612–613

in planned investments, 594, 595
    in saving, 596–599
    in taxes, 602–605, 695
  defined, 593
  on deposit contraction, 632–633
  on deposit expansion, 630–632
  and fiscal policy, 604, 606–607
  impact lags in, 708
  and marginal propensity to consume, 595–597
  real-world, 675
Multipliers, **593**, 613–614
  autonomous expenditures, 595–597
  deposit, 630–634
Mutual funds, money market, 623, 624, 643, 795, 796
Mutual-savings banks, 623

N

National Banking Act of 1864, 622
National Bureau of Economic Research (NBER), 507
National debt, **693**, 711–714, 804. *See also* Budget deficits; Government borrowing; Less-developed countries, debt of
National defense spending, 704, 806, 807
National Education Association, 369
National income, **537**, 542, 554–556
  nominal. *See* Nominal GNP
  potential, 777*n*. *See also* Potential GNP
National income accounting, 554–556
Nationalization in Soviet Union, 872
National Labor Relations Act of 1935, 370–371
National Labor Relations Board (NLRB), 371
National product:
  gross. *See* Gross national product
  net, **545**
National security argument for trade restrictions, 837
Natural monopolies, **261**, 423–428
Natural rate of unemployment, **508**, 722, 723, 731–735
Natural resources, **9**, 668, 771–773, 824
NBER (National Bureau of Economic Research), 507
Necessities versus luxuries, 88
Negative income taxes, **460**–462
Negative slopes, 23
Negotiable order of withdrawal

(NOW) accounts, 623
Net exports (trade balances), 551–554, 608–609, 666, 775, 812–816, 821–822. *See also* Trade deficits; Trade surpluses
Net national product (NNP), **545**
Net taxes, 602–605, 614
Neutral economic policies, 799–802
New classical macroeconomists, **702**–711, 756–760, 785
New Economic Policy in Bolivia, 789
Newly industrialized economies, 878–880
New York Stock Exchange, 356, 571
Nixon, Richard M., 476, 761, 809, 810, 860
NLRB (National Labor Relations Board), 371
NNP (net national product), **545**
Nominal, defined, **511**
Nominal GNP, **513**, 642, 648–655
  per capita, 766
  versus real GNP, 535–536, 766. *See also* GNP deflator
Nominal income, **511**–513
Nominal interest rates, **344**, 345, **578**, 643–646
Nominal wages, 671, 680–681, 726–727
Nonactivism in economic policy, 703–711
Nonactivists, **703**
Nonmarket exchanges, 539–540
Nonprice competition, **292**–293, 295, 302–303, 305, 482–483
Nontariff trade restrictions, 814, 815, 836–837
Normal goods, **52**
Normal profits, **218**, 217–221, 244–245
Normative economics, 793
Normative statements, **14**
Norris–LaGuardia Act, 370
Not in labor force, 721–725
NOW (negotiable order of withdrawal) accounts, 623

O

Occupational Safety and Health Administration (OSHA), 543
Occupations. *See* Employment; Work *entries*
Official asset transactions, 854
Oil embargo in 1970s, 798
Oil industry taxation, 350

Oil market regulation, 493–496
Oil prices, 301
    ceilings on, 494–495
    decreases in, 204–205, 743, 760,
        885
    increases in, 204–205, 350, 494,
        495, 742–743, 749
        1970s, 204, 683, 684, 704, 741,
            743, 747, 780, 798–799, 823,
            864
        1980s, 743, 780, 823, 885
Oil supply shocks, 683, 684, 704, 743,
    747, 864
Okun, Arthur, 752
Old Age, Survivors, and Disability and
    Health Insurance Programs. *See*
    Social Security *entries*
Oligopolies, 235, **296**–306
    barriers to entry and exit in, 297
    efficiency of, 303, 306
    mature, 304–305
    nonprice competition in, 302–303,
        305
    price leadership in, 301–302
    pricing in, 297–299
100 percent reserve banking system,
    620
OPEC (Organization of Petroleum Ex-
    porting Countries), 204–205,
    270–271, 300–301, 494, 495, 684,
    743, 760, 798
Open economies, 608–609
Open market operations (of Federal
    Reserve System), **627**–630
"Open-mouth" policy, 808–809
Opportunity, economic, 137–138, 389
Opportunity costs, 9–**10**
    of budget deficits, 714
    of capital, **339**, 347
    and economic profit, 175–176
    in international trade, 825–828
    of money holding, 643
    in monopolistic competition, 291–
        292
    and prices, 46, 103–104
    and scarcity, 30–31, 40–41
Optimal level of pollution, 429–431
Optimal plant size, 244–245
Optimal resource mix, 186–188, 198–
    203, 315–317
Organization of Petroleum Exporting
    Countries (OPEC), 204–205, 270–
    271, 300–301, 494, 495, 684, 743,
    760, 798
Origins in graphs, **19**

OSHA (Occupational Safety and
    Health Administration), 543
Other America, The (Harrington), 448
Output:
    of business firms, short-run, 177–
        179, 281, 667, 671
    of economy. *See* Aggregate output;
        Equilibrium output; Full-em-
        ployment level of output; GNP
        entries; Gross national product;
        Potential GNP; Real output
    and income, circular flow of. *See*
        Circular-flow model

P

Pace Commercial College, 467
Panics (bank), 625
Paper money, 620, 622. *See also* Cur-
    rency
Paradox of thrift, 596–599, 775
Parity pricing, 476
Partnerships, **125**
Patents, **261**, 277, 349, 784
Payroll taxes, 403–405
Peaks in business cycles, 506, **507**,
    732–733
Pechman, Joseph A., 405*n*
Pegged (fixed) exchange rates, 855–
    861
Peres, Shimon, 789
Perfect (pure) competition, 235–236,
    248, 250–252, 288, 297
Performance, economic,, 516–522
Performance standards, 431–433
Personal income, **130**–132, 443–445,
    555–556. *See also* Disposable in-
    come; Wages
Personal income taxes, 402–403, 405
Personal services in Soviet Union, 875
Peruvian underground economy, 638
Phelps, Edmund, 752–757
Phillips, A. W., 750
Phillips curves, **750**–758
Photocopying machine purchase, 344
Physical capital, **337**
Planned aggregate expenditures, 537,
    588, 589, 664–665
Planned investment, 588–590, 594,
    595
    inventory, 579–582
Planned socialism, **7**, 27–28, 867–871,
    886
    in Soviet Union, 871–877
Plant size, 244–245

Poison pills for corporations, 284
Polaroid, 261, 277
Policy lags, 706–709
Political instability of less-developed
    countries, 883–884
Political pressures on policy makers,
    792–793
Pollution, optimal level of, 429–431
Pollution control, 429–432
Pollution taxes, 430–431
Population:
    characteristics of, 129–130
    and employment, ratio of, 773–774
    and labor force, 502–503, 733
Population growth, 129–130, 772
Positive slopes, 23
Positive statements, **14**
Postal Service, 428
Potential GNP, **509**, 668–670, 682–
    683. *See also* Full-employment
    level of output
    and aggregate demand, 669–670
    and aggregate supply, 669–670, 672
    and contractionary gaps, 678
    and economic growth, 765, 767–
        785. *See also* Economic
        growth; Real GNP, per capita
    and expansionary gaps, 676
    and real output, 680–681
Potential national income, 777*n*
Poverty, 447–463
    approaches to, 447–448
    causes of, 452–454
    correlates of, 452, 453
    definitions of, 447–451
    and discrimination, 454–456
    dynamics of, 452
    fighting, 456–462
    incidence of, 449
    and labor markets, 452, 462–463
    in less-developed countries, 878–
        880
    War on, 679, 695, 740–741, 749
Poverty threshold, **448**
POW camps, 100–101
Precautionary motive (for holding
    money), **642**
Preferences, 51–52, 106–107, 361–
    362, 824, 850
Present dollars, future value of, 352–
    353
Present value, 343, 344, **353**
    discounted, 352–354
Price ceilings, **66**, 68, 73, 423–425,
    494–495, 742

Price changes, 78–80, 161–162, 204–205. *See also* Price levels
  and consumer demand, 170–171
  in oligopolies, 297–299
  of resource mixes, 202–203
Price competition, 299
Price controls, 788, 808–810
Price discrimination, **269**–270
Price elastic demand, **77**–78, 84–85
Price-elasticity coefficient, **80**–81, 89–92
Price elasticity of demand, **76**–89
  in agriculture, 472–473
  versus demand curve slope, 81–82
  determinants of, 85–88
  for resources, 323–324
  and total revenue, 82–87
  types of:
    cross, 91–92
    income, 90–93, 473
    unitary, 81
Price elasticity of supply, **89**–90, 92–93
Price elastic supply, 89
Price fixing, **417**–418. *See also* Cartels
Price floors (supports), 66–68, 474–478, 481–483
Price indexes, **509**, 512–513, 528–531
  consumer, **509**–513, 529–531, 798, 799
Price inelastic demand, **77**–78, 84–85
Price inelastic supply, 89
Price leadership, 301–**302**
Price levels. *See also* Price changes
  and aggregate demand, 666, 740–742
  and aggregate supply, 671–672, 740–743
  and contractionary gaps, 584, 680–681
  in economic theories:
    classical, 667–668
    Keynesian, 667, 671
    modern monetary, 653–655
  and equilibrium output, 670–675
  expectations about, 570, 572–574, 643, 665–666, 671–672, 680, 742
  and expenditures:
    consumption, 570–574
    planned, 664–665
  in GNP deflator, 536
  increases in, 510–511, 664–665, 740–742. *See also* Inflation *entries*

long-run, 667–670
measuring, 528–531
and money supply, 650–651, 653–655, 746
and money value, 511
and potential GNP, 669–670
short-run, 667, 670–675, 740–742, 749–750
types of:
  foreign, 666
  general, **501**, 509–516, 520–522, 663, 750, 751. *See also* Aggregate demand; GNP deflator
and unemployment rates, 749–750
Price making, 265–267
Price (rate) regulation , 423–428
Prices, **46**
  agreements on, 299–301, 417. *See also* Price fixing
  of alternative goods, 58–59
  and demand, 236–238
  and income, 87, 92–93
  and marginal revenue, 238–240
  and marginal utility, 153–154
  and quantity supplied, 55, 56, 267–269
  during recessions, 704–705
  types of:
    equilibrium, **60**–65, 72
    flexible, 561–565
    foreign, 665
    market, 103–104, 236–240, 534
    reasonable, 248
    relative, **54**–55, 106–107, 157–158, 828–829, 846–847, 851
    sticky, 759
    target, 476–477
Price searchers, **263**–269
Price searching, 281–282
Price-setting policies, 65–68
Price stability, 472–473, 509–516, 520–522, 693–697, 877
Price supports, 66–68, 474–478, 481–483
Price takers, **236**–252, 263, 318–320
Price wars, 299
Pricing, 289–291, 297–299
  average-cost, 425
  marginal-cost, 424–425
  parity, 476
Primary exports, 881–883
Prison-building, 39
Prisoner of war camps, 100–101
Private benefits, 136

Private contracts for external benefits, 392–393
Private costs, 136
Private expenditures, 693
Private goods, **135**
Private investment, 778, 865, 885
Private property rights, 111
Private sector, **121**, 393–394, 541–551. *See also* Business firms; Households
Privatization of government enterprises, 394, 806
Producer choice, 174–195, 207–224
Producer surpluses, 249
Product demand, 320–321, 349
Product differentiation, 288–**289**, 295
Production:
  costs of, 174–195
  decision making in, 174–176
  large-scale, economies of, 122, 188–195, 261, 776
  in market economies, 107–110
  of public goods, 393–394
  in short run, 176–186
  in Soviet Union, 875
  team, 122
Production controls, 477
Production function, **177**, 178
Production possibilities curves, **29**–35
Production process, 90
Productivity, **181**–183
  and international trade, 824–828
  in less-developed countries, 776, 883
  types of:
    agricultural, 774, 776, 883
    labor, 367, **772**–774, 776, 778–780, 809, 825
    marginal, 367
Product markets, **101**–102, 326–327
  in circular-flow model, 314–315, 542, 600
Products. *See* Average product; Consumer products; Goods and services; Marginal product; Total product
Profit maximization, 174–175, 209–212, 293, 294, 316–317
  in cartels, 299–300
  in monopolies, 275
Profits, **103**, 109. *See also* Corporate income taxes; Retained earnings; Windfall profits taxes
  accounting, **175**–176, 244
  economic. *See* Economic profit

Profits *(cont.)*
  normal, **218**, 217–221, 244–245
  real, 672, 673
Program trading in stocks, 356–357
Progressive taxes, **400**–402, 405, 781
Progressivity of taxation, 405
Promotion of exports, 884
Property rights, 111
Property taxes, 404–405, 602
Proportional taxes, **401**–402, 405
Proprietorships, **124**, 125
Protectionism, 815. *See also* Trade restrictions
Public choice theory, **38**–41
Public enterprises. *See* Government enterprises
Public finance, **386**. *See also* Government expenditures; Tax *entries*
Public goods, **135**–136, 389, 391–395, 540
Public sector, **121**, 614. *See also* Government *entries*
Public sector goods, 393
Purchasing power of money, 511–514
Purchasing power parity, 851
Pure competition, **235**–236, 248, 250–252, 288, 297
Pure monopolies, **260**, 288, 297
Puth, Robert, 622*n*

Q

Quality:
  of labor, 777
  in Soviet Union, 877
Quantities (stocks), 547
Quantity bought, 831
Quantity demanded, **47.** *See also* Demand
  changes in, 50–51, 54, 78–80
  and general price levels, 663. *See also* Aggregate demand
  of money, 644–646
  and quantity produced, 579
Quantity produced, 579, 831
Quantity supplied, **55**, 59, 267–269. *See also* Supply
  changes in, 57–58
  of labor, 361–363
  in long run, 220–223
  of money, 644–646
  in short run, 208–209, 212–214
Quotas (import), 389, 814, 815, **836**–837

R

Race and employment, 454, 455, 466–467
Racial discrimination in South Africa, 466–467
Radford, R. A., 100–101
Raiders, corporate, 284–285
Railroad industry, 425–426
Rate bases, **425**
Rate of return, **338**, 349
Rate regulation, **423**–428
Rational choice, **35**–41, 148–162. *See also* Choice
  in drug regulation, 486–487
  and government policy analysis, 138, 389–390, 469–471, 791–793
  in income distribution, 442–443
  and labor markets, 359–360
  in market economies, 103–107
  and money demand, 641–644
  in monopolies, 273–274
  and production decisions, 174–176
  and profit maximization, 209–211, 316–317
  public, 38–41
  and resource buying, 314–318
  and supply decisions:
    long-run, 217–224
    short-run, 207–217
  in unemployment, 725–728
Rational expectations, 36, **702**–703, 756–758
Rational ignorance, 435
Rationing and competition, 26–27
Ratios. *See specific entries, for example:* Concentration ratios; Reserve ratios
Raw materials, 261. *See also* Resources
Reagan, Ronald, 119, 398, 461–462, 495, 735, 781, 807, 841
Real, defined, **511**
Real balances effect, 664
Real flows, 99
Real GNP, **513**, 517, 533, 740–742, 766–767, 769, 770. *See also* Aggregate output
  and contractionary gaps, 678
  in economic theories:
    classical quantity, 650, 651
    modern monetary, 650, 652–655
  and expansionary gaps, 676
  and investment expenditures, 576–577
  in long run, 767, 769, 771
  versus nominal GNP, 535–536, 766. *See also* GNP deflator
  per capita, **765**–771, 777, 778
    versus real GNP, 766–767
    and standard of living, 756, 767
  in short run, 767–770
  and standard of living, 541. *See also* per capita, and standard of living, *above*
  and unemployment, 518, 519
Real income, **512**–513, 665–666
Real interest rates, **344**–345, 572, 577, **578**, 648–650, 714
Real output, 653, 680–681. *See also* Real GNP
Real profits, 672, 673, 680
Real wages, 561–565, 671–672, 680
Real wealth, 664
Real-world multiplier effect, 675
Reasonable prices, 248
Recessions, **506**–507. *See also* Stagflation
  budget deficits during, 714
  and capital investment, 780
  versus depressions, 564*n. See also* Depressions
  and economic policies, 697
    accommodating, 799–801
    contractionary, 778, 802
    contractionary fiscal, 699
    monetary, 653
  in Keynesian economic theory, 584
  and labor productivity, 778–779
  national debt during, 693
  timing of, 705
    1950s, 607, 695, 709
    1960s, 607, 681, 695, 704, 759
    1970s, 681, 684, 704, 759, 778, 780, 802, 803
    1980s, 704, 743, 749, 759, 760, 778, 780, 803
  and unemployment, 724, 732, 759–760
  wages and prices during, 704–705
Recognition lags, **707**
Recoveries in business cycles, 506, **507**, 732, 778–779
Regional Ministries in Soviet Union, 873
Regressive taxes, **401**–402, 405
Regulation. *See* Government regulation
Relative efficiency of resources, 321–323

Relative poverty approach, **448**
Relative prices, **54**–55, 106–107, 157–158, 828–829, 846–847, 851
Relevant markets, 416, 421–422
Relocation assistance, 834, 839–840
Rent controls, 68
Rents, economic, 347–348, 350
Required reserve ratios, **627**–633, 796
Research and development, 784, 813
Reservation (nominal) wages, 671, 680–681, 726–727
Reserve ratios, 621
  required, **627**–633, 796
Reserves, **620**–622
  excess, 628–634
  legal, 627–633
Resource allocation, 104–114, 776–778, 836, 874–877
Resource demand, 317–318, 320–321, 326–327, 337–340
Resource immobilities, 329–330
Resource markets, **101**–102, 333–335
  in circular-flow model, 314–315, 542, 600
  efficiency of, 322, 325–331
    allocative, 329, 330, 335
  imperfect competition in, 327–329. *See also* types of, imperfectly competitive, *below*
  supply and demand in, 314–331
  types of:
    competitive, 318–325
    financial. *See* Financial markets
    imperfectly competitive, 334–335
    labor. *See* Labor markets
Resources, **9**. *See also* Raw materials
  availability of, 90
  buying, 314–318
  cost of, 90, 324
  efficiency of, 321–323
  elasticity of demand for, 323–324
  mix of, 202–203
    optimal, 186–188, 198–203, 315–317
  mobility of, 112–113
  owners of, income of, 539
  prices of, 58, 671
  scarcity of. *See* Scarcity
  supply of, 320, 349, 668, 771–772
  types of:
    capital. *See* Capital resources
    fixed, 177
    human, **9,** 367–368. *See also* Human capital

natural, **9**, 668, 771–773, 824
  variable, 177–179
Restaurant industry, 295
Retained earnings, **129**, 546
Retirement, travel during, 158–159
Retraining programs, 119, 834, 839–840. *See also* Job training *entries*
Return(s):
  diminishing. *See* Diminishing returns
  marginal. *See* Marginal returns
  rate of, 338
  to scale. *See* Constant returns to scale; Diseconomies of scale; Economies of scale
  yields as, 648
Revenue(s):
  government, 402–405, 690–691. *See also* Tax *entries*
  marginal, **209**–212, 264–265, 280. *See also* Marginal revenue product
  monopoly, 281
  total, **82**–87, 209
Revenue demand, 320–321
Rewards and economic profit, 348–350
Reynolds, Milton, 113, 261
Rights, property, 111
Right-to-work laws, **372**
Risks, 122–123, 347, 349, 621
Robinson–Patman Act of 1936, 414, 420
Rockefeller, John D., 413
Roosevelt, Franklin Delano, 699
Rosenweig, Jeffrey, 823
Rule of reason, **415**–417
Rule of 72, 767
Runs on banks, 625

S

Safety regulations, 484–488, 543
Salaries. *See* Wage *entries*
Sales taxes, 86–87, 404–405
Sanctions against South Africa, 467
Sanyo, 880
Sargent, Thomas, 757
Satisfaction. *See* Utility
Saudi Arabia and oil prices, 205
Saving, **543**–546. *See also* Consumption *entries*; Marginal propensity to save
  and aggregate demand, 565–575

and disposable income, 568–570
  in economic growth, 775, 782–783
  financial markets in, 545–547
  and flexible interest rates, 561, 562
  graphic view of, 568–570
  and inflation, 781
  and investment, 545–547, 582, 775. *See also* Investment
  in Keynesian economic theory, 564
  as leakage from circular flow, 553, 589–590
  in less-developed countries, 883–884
  multiplier effect of, 596–599
  negative (dissaving), 567–568, 570
  and paradox of thrift, 596–599, 775
  and wealth, 571
Savings, 545
Savings-and-loan associations, 623
Saving schedule, **568**
Savings deposits, 623, 624, 795
Say, Jean Baptiste, 561
Say's law, **561**, 564
Scale:
  constant returns to, 192, **193**
  diseconomies of, 192, **193**
  economies of, 122, **191**, 188–195, 261, **776**
Scarcity, **5**–7, 26–35, 40–41, 104–106
  versus shortages, 61
Scherer, F. M., 304*n*, 305*n*
Scholarships, 186
School lunch programs, 458
SEC (Securities and Exchange Commission), 356
Second accounting identity, 537–539, 554–555
"Second economy" in Soviet Union, 638–639, 875–876
Sectors. *See* Business firms; Foreign sector; Government; Households; Private sector
Securities. *See* Bonds; Government securities; Stocks (corporate)
Securities and Exchange Commission (SEC), 356
Securities markets, 356–357
Self-interest, 35, 102–107
Sellers, 59
Service industries, 118, 119
Services. *See* Goods and services
Sex:
  employment by, 454, 455
  labor markets by, 363–365
  unemployment by, 733, 735

Share draft accounts, 623
Shareholders, 125–126
Sheflin, Neil, 372, 373n
Sherman Antitrust Act of 1890, 413–415, 417
Shocks, 694
  demand, 694, 704, 746–747
  supply. *See* Supply shocks
Shoe industry, 836
Shortages, **61**. *See also* Scarcity
Short run, **177**
  quantity supplied in, 208–209, 212–214
Short-run allocative efficiency, 250–251
Short-run changes:
  in fixed costs, 268–269
  in real output, 653
Short-run consumption expenditures, 574–575
Short-run cost curves, 183–186
Short-run costs, 176–186, 195, 834
Short-run decisions, 177, 195, 207–217, 289–290
Short-run economic goals, 693–697. *See also* Full employment *entries*; Price stability
Short-run equilibrium, **674**, 673–675
  market, 240, 289–291
Short-run inflation–unemployment relationship, 750–755
Short-run loss minimization, 212–217
Short-run output, 177–179, 256, 281
  aggregate, 667, 671
Short-run Phillips curves, 753–755
Short-run price levels, 667, 670–675, 740–742, 749–750
Short-run pricing decisions, 289–291
Short-run production, 176–186
Short-run productivity, 181–183
Short-run profit maximization, 211–212
Short-run real GNP, 767–770
Short-run supply, 238–240
  aggregate, 670–675, 768–769
Short-run supply curves, aggregate, 671–673
Short-run supply decisions, 207–217
Short-run unemployment rates, 749–750
Short-sighted effect, 436
Shut-down option, 214–217, 222
Silver as commodity money, 619–620
Singapore economy, 880
Singatronics, 880

Slopes of lines, **22**–23
Smeeding, Timothy, 449n
Smith, Adam, 153–154, 417
  invisible hand of, 102, 110–114
Social benefits, **136**, 433, 435, 469–470
  marginal, 250
Social costs, **136**, 433, 435, 469–470
  marginal, 250
Social infrastructure of less-developed countries, 881–883, 886
Socialism, planned, **7**, 27–28, 867–871, 886
  in Soviet Union, 871–877
Social regulation, **428**–434
Social Security, 457–458, 806
Social Security benefits, 470
Social Security taxes, 403–405
Social value, 539–541
Soft drink industry, 296
Sony, 261
South African apartheid policy, 466–467
South Korean economy, 880
Soviet Union, 871–877
  economic growth of, 774, 775, 872, 876
  economic planning of, 872–875
  equity in, 876–877
  full employment and price stability in, 877
  income distribution in, 876–877
  innovation and quality in, 877
  nationalization of industry and agriculture in, 872
  resource allocation in, 874–877
  underground ("second") economy in, 638–639, 875–876
Special-interest effect, 435
Specialization in international trade, 824–828
Special orders, 214
Spending. *See specific entries, for example:* Aggregate expenditures; Defense spending
SSI (Supplemental Security Income), 458
Stability:
  of business firms, 109
  economic, 113–114, 138, 517, 705–706, 708, 709, 883–884. *See also* Automatic stabilizers
  political, 883–884
  price, 472–473, 509–516, 520–522, 693–697, 877

Stabilization policies, 577, 693–697, 709–710, 769, 771, 785
Stagflation, **521**, 684, 799. *See also* Inflation
Stalin, Joseph, 872
Standard of living, **514**, 541, 765, 767, 772
  in less-developed countries, 880–881
  in Soviet Union, 877
Standard Oil Company, 413, 494
Standard Oil of New Jersey, 415
State government, 691, 693
Statements:
  of fact, positive and normative, 14
  financial, 127–129, 620
Statistical discrepancies in balance of payments accounting, 855
Steel industry, 306, 780, 809, 837
Stein, Herbert, 761
Stewart, Potter, 420
Sticky-price view of inflation reduction, 759
Stiglitz, Joseph, 139n
Stock markets, 356–357
Stocks (corporate), **125**–126, 130, 131, 545, 571
  dividends on, **129**, 131
  new issues of, 794–795
  program trading in, 356–357
Stocks (quantities), **547**
Storage of goods, 90
Strategic Petroleum Reserve, 495
Strikes, 370–371, 377
Structural change in natural rate of unemployment, 734
Structural unemployment, **505**–506, 722, 724, 730–731, 734, 735
Subsidies, 392, 784, 839–840
  export, 815
  housing, 458
  in international trade, 815, 839–840
Substitutes, **52**–53, 85–86, 262, 323, 643–644
Substitution:
  import, 884
  marginal rate of, 166
  technical, marginal rate of, 198–199
Substitution effect, **161**–162, 362
Sullivan Code, 467
Summers, Lawrence H., 724–725
Sunk costs, **217**, 470
"Sunrise" industries, 813
"Sunset" industries, 813

Supplemental Security Income (SSI), 458

Supply, **55**–60. *See also* Quantity supplied
  changes in, 57–58, 64–65
  determinants of, 58–59
  elasticity of, **89**–90, 92–93
  equation for, 71
  law of, 55
  long-run, 245–248
  and marginal cost, 238–239
  in price-taker markets, 239–240
  profit-maximizing rule for, 209–211
  of resources, 320, 349, 668, 771–772
  short-run. *See* Short-run supply
  types of. *See* Aggregate supply; Labor supply; Market supply; Money supply

Supply and demand:
  and foreign exchange, 849–853
  in international trade, 829–832
  in labor markets, 360–365
  in resource markets, 314–331
    competitive, 319–325

Supply curves, **56**
  aggregate. *See* Aggregate supply curves
  long-run, **245**–248
  slopes of, 850

Supply decisions:
  long-run, 217–224
  short-run, 207–217

Supply function, **71**

Supply schedules, **55**–56

Supply shocks, **683**–684, 760, 778, 798–799, 802
  and contractionary gaps, 694
  counterbalancing, 710
  and economic policies, 760–761, 798–803
  and inflation, 746–747, 749
  oil, 683, 684, 704, 743, 747, 864. *See also* Oil prices, increases in

Supply-side economists, 785

Supply-side tax policies, 781, 782

Support prices, **66**–68, 474–478, 481–483

Surpluses, **62**
  agricultural, 476
  budget, **691**, 693
    full-employment, 700, 710*n*
  consumer, **160**, 159–161, 249
  money, 646–650. *See also* Money supply, growth in

producer, 249
trade, **821**, 855

Sweden, underground economy of, 639

T

TAA (Trade Adjustment Assistance) Program, 840

Tacit collusion, **417**–418

Taft–Hartley Act of 1947, 371–372

Taiwan economy, 880

Takeovers of corporations, 284–285

Target prices, 476–477

Tariffs, 814, 815, 834–836, 838, 840–841, 851

Tastes, 51–52, 106–107, 361–362, 824, 850

Taxable income, 402

Taxation:
  and economic goals, 395–406
  of economic profits, 350
  by government level, 691
  progressivity of, 405

Tax-based incomes policies (TIP), 808, 809

Tax credits, investment, 783

Tax cuts, 782
  1964, 575, 607, 683, 695, 740, 750–751
  1981, 398, 774
  1986, 774

Taxes:
  alternatives to, 395–396
  and disposable income, 602–605
  distribution of, 400–405
  and economic goals, 395–406
  effects of:
    efficiency and incentive, 396–398
    equity, 399–400
  and equilibrium output, 602–605
  and expenditures, 639
    private, 693
    research and development, 784
  and inflation, 781
  as leakage from circular flow, 553
  and multiplier effect, 602–605, 695
  in oil market, 494, 495
  supply-side policies on, 781, 782
  types of:
    consumption, 782–783
    corporate income, 404, 405, 783
    excise, 396–398
    "good," 398–399
    income. *See* Income taxes

indirect business, 554, 555
  lump-sum, **602**–604, 607, 614
  net, 602–605, 614
  pollution, 430–431
  progressive, **400**–402, 405, 781
  property, 404–405, 602
  proportional, **401**–402, 405
  regressive, **401**–402, 405
  sales, 86–87, 404–405
  Social Security payroll, 403–405
  windfall profits, 350, 495

Tax increases, 575, 699
  crowding-out effect of, 700–702
  in deficit reduction:
    budget, 715, 806, 807
    trade, 814

Tax policy, 577, 578, 781, 782

Tax rates, 788, 813
  average, 400
  indexation of, 781–783
  marginal, 400, 774

Tax reform of 1986, 40, 402, 462, 781, 783

Team production, 122

Teamsters Union, 369

Technical efficiency, **28**, 29
  and competition (pure), 248, 250
  of competitive resource markets, 322
  in market economies, 108–109
  in monopolistic competition, 294, 295
  of natural monopolies, 423
  of oligopolies, 306
  and optimal resource mix, 186–188
  and production possibilities curve, 31–32
  union impact on, 378–379

Technical substitution, marginal rate of, 198–199

Technological change. *See also* Innovation
  and demand for older workers, 363
  and economic growth, 772, 775–780, 783–784
  and investment expenditures, 577, 578
  in less-developed countries, 883
  in potential GNP, 668

Technology in supply, 58

Telephone monopoly, 426, 428

Telerate system, 356

"Telescoping" in stock markets, 356

Tennessee Valley Authority (TVA), 428

Terms of trade, **828**–829

Thalidomide, 484–485

Third accounting identity, 553, 582

Third-World countries. *See* Less-developed countries

Thrift, paradox of, 596–599, 775

Thrift institutions, 623

Time, leisure. *See* Leisure time

Time deposits, 624

Time lags in discretionary policy, 706–709

Time periods. *See also* Long run *entries*; Short run *entries*
in demand elasticity, 87–88, 324
in price elasticity, 90
for production, 535

Time value of money, **342**–344. *See also* Present value

TIP (tax-based incomes policies), 808, 809

Tobin, James, 781

Tokyo Round, 840–841

Total costs, **181**, 182, 209, 256, 324
average, **183**–186
fixed, **181**, 182
variable, **181**, 182

Total fixed costs, **181**, 182

Total product, **177**–179

Total revenue, **82**–87, 209

Total utility, **150**, 151

Total variable costs, **181**, 182

Trade, 6–7
international (foreign). *See* International trade
terms of, 828–829

Trade Adjustment Assistance (TAA) Program, 840

Trade balances (net exports), 551–554, 608–609, 666, 775, 812–816, **821**–822. *See also* Trade deficits; Trade surpluses

Trade barriers. *See* Trade restrictions

Trade deficits, 552, 553, 812–816, **821**, 823

Trade-offs in economic policies, 792

Trade policy, 812–816, 834, 839–841

Trade restrictions, 389, 814–816, 834–840, 851
alternatives to, 839–841
arguments for, 837–839
on less-developed countries, 885
on South African goods, 467

Trade surpluses, **821**, 855

Trading:
in POW camps, 100–101
in stock markets, 356–357

Trading practices, unfair, 814, 815

Training. *See* Job training *entries*

Transaction costs, **100**, 122, 392–393

Transactions motive (for holding money), **641**–642

Transfer payments, **129**, 137–139, 389, 457–462, 549, 553
types of:
cash, 449, 457–459, 478, 491, 806
in-kind, **449**–450, 458, 459

Transportation systems in less-developed countries, 883, 886

Treasury Department, 622, 626

"Triple witching hour" in stock markets, 356

Troughs in business cycles, 506, **507**. *See also* Recessions

Troy, Leo, 372, 373*n*

Trucking industry, 426, 427

Truman, Harry, 39

Tuition scholarships, 186

TVA (Tennessee Valley Authority), 428

U

Uaewoo, 880

Underemployed individuals, **504**–505

Underground economy, 540, 638–639, 875–876

Underwriting of new stock issues, 794–795

Undesired inventory disinvestment, 581

Undesired investment, 589–590
inventory, 579–583

Unemployed individuals, 503–505, 720–725

Unemployment, 503–505, 722–724, 750, 757
and accommodating policies, 799–801
and age, 733, 735
and business cycles, 517–519, 724, 732–733, 759–761
duration of, 723–729, 731
and efficiency, 507–508
and equity, 507–508
and inflation, 748–761
and international trade, 833–834, 839
and oil prices, 205
and real GNP, 518, 519
reasons for, 722–723
by sex, 733, 735
and tax cut of 1964, 607

theories of:
contracts, 729–731
job-search, 725–731
types of, 505–508
core, 722
cyclical, **506**–507, 583–584, 731
frictional, **505**, 722, 729, 731, 734
structural, **505**–506, 722, 724, 730–741, 734, 735
voluntary versus involuntary, 564
and underground economy, 638

Unemployment insurance, 507–508, 698, 733–735, 840

Unemployment policy, 731, 733–735, 750–758

Unemployment rates, **503**–504, 720–725. *See also* Full-employment *entries*
history of, 517–520, 722, 751, 752, 761
and inflation rates, 750–758
natural (full-employment), **508**, 722, 723, 731–735
versus actual, 732
official, 732–733
and price levels, 749–750

Unfair competition, 420

Unfair trading practices, 814–815

Union contracts, 681, 729, 730

Unions, **368**
and collective bargaining, 368–379
economic impact of, 375–379
history of, 369–370
legal status of, 370–373
membership trends of, 372–373
types of, 369

Union shops, **372**

Unitary price elasticity of demand, **81**

Unit costs, 183–186
variable, 183–185

United Mine Workers, 370

Unit variable cost, 183–185

Unplanned inventory disinvestment, 581

Unplanned investment, 589–590
inventory, 579–583

Urbanization of less-developed countries, 881, 882

U.S. Postal Service, 428

U.S. Steel Corporation, 306, 416

U.S. Treasury Department, 622, 626

Usury laws, 345–346

Utah Pie Company, 420

Utilities, 428
as monopolies, 262, 275–276

Utility, **150**, 869
　marginal, **150**–161
　　diminishing, law of, **150**–152, 166
　　total, **150**, 151

V

Value:
　economic, 535
　future (of present dollars), 352–353
　of the marginal product, **326**–327
　market, 533–534
　of money, 511
　present, 343, 344, 353
　　discounted, 352–354
　social, 539–541
Vanderbilt, William, 413
Variable costs, **181**, 182, 218–219, 267–268, 281
　average, **183**–185
　total, **181**, 182
Variable resources, **177**–179
Variables, dependent and independent, 18–19
Velocity (of money), **650**–653
Vertical axis, 19
Vertical equity, **400**
Vertical mergers, **419**
Vietnam War, 704, 740–741, 749
Voluntary quotas, 836–837
Voluntary unemployment, 564

W

Wage and price controls, 788, 808–810
Wage contracts, 681
Wage differentials, 365–368, 378
Wages. *See also* Income
　in aggregate supply, 669–671
　and contractionary gaps, 584
　and inflation, 749, 788
　during recessions, 704–705
　in Soviet Union, 877
　types of:
　　market, 362–363
　　minimum, 66, 489–492, 734
　　nominal (reservation), 671, 680–681, 726–727
　　real, 561–565, 671–672, 680
　union impact on, 375–378
Wagner Act of 1935, 370–371
Walker, Hershel, 348
Wallace, Neil, 757
Wants, satisfying. *See* Utility
War Labor Board, 371
War on Poverty, 679, 695, 740–741, 749
Wars, national debt during, 693. *See also* Korean War; Vietnam War; World War I; World War II
Wealth, 570, 571, 871. *See also* Income
　real, 664
　stored as money, 619

Wealth of Nations, The (Smith), 102, 153–154
Weighted averages, 528
Welfare programs, 458–462, 698
West German economic growth, 779
Whitt, Joseph A., Jr., 823
Windfall profits taxes, 350, 495
Winston, Clifford, 483n
Work and economic growth, 35. *See also* Employment *entries*; Right-to-work laws
Workers, discouraged, 504
Workfare programs, 461
Work incentives, 459–462
World Bank, 775
World War I, 858
World War II, 371, 571, 693, 777, 778, 809
Wriston, Walter, 357

X

Xerox, 261, 277

Y

Yellow-dog contracts, **370**
Yields (returns), **648**